Compendium
of Tourism Statistics

Data 2011–2015

2017 Edition

World Tourism Organization (UNWTO)
Calle Capitán Haya 42 · 28020 Madrid · Spain

Compendium of Tourism Statistics, Data 2011–2015, 2017 Edition
ISBN (printed version):   978-92-844-1843-5
ISBN (electronic version): 978-92-844-1844-2

Published by the World Tourism Organization (UNWTO), Madrid, Spain.
First printing: 2017
All rights reserved.

Printed in Spain.

The designations employed and the presentation of material in this publication do not imply the expression of any opinions whatsoever on the part of the Secretariat of the World Tourism Organization concerning the legal status of any country, territory, city or area, or of its authorities or concerning the delimitation of its frontiers or boundaries.

World Tourism Organization (UNWTO)   Tel.: (+34) 915 67 81 00
Calle Capitán Haya, 42   Fax: (+34) 915 71 37 33
28020 Madrid   Website: www.unwto.org
Spain   E-mail: omt@unwto.org

Citation:

English:

World Tourism Organization (2017), *Compendium of Tourism Statistics, Data 2011–2015, 2017 Edition*, UNWTO, Madrid.

Español:

Organización Mundial del Turismo (2017), *Compendio de estadísticas de turismo, 2011–2015, Edición 2017*, OMT, Madrid.

Français:

Organisation mondiale du tourisme (2017), *Compendium des statistiques du tourisme, 2011–2015, édition 2017*, OMT, Madrid.

Foreword

Decision-making requires reliable information to guide sound policies and development strategies. In order to support countries in monitoring and better understanding the impact and evolution of tourism across their economies, the World Tourism Organization (UNWTO) systematically gathers tourism statistics from countries and territories around the world into a vast database that is used to produce two key statistical publications every year: the *Compendium of Tourism Statistics* and the *Yearbook of Tourism Statistics*. Together, these two publications constitute the most comprehensive statistical information available on the tourism sector.

The UNWTO *Compendium of Tourism Statistics* provides data and indicators on inbound, outbound and domestic tourism, as well as on the number and types of tourism industries, the number of employees by tourism industry, and macroeconomic indicators related to international tourism. This is complemented by the *Yearbook of Tourism Statistics* which focuses specifically on data related to inbound tourism (total arrivals and overnight stays), broken down by country of origin.

The statistics presented in the 2017 editions of the *Compendium* and the *Yearbook* give an insight into tourism's multiple facets and its ever-growing importance and are an indispensable reference for all tourism stakeholders. Above all, they provide decision makers with the information needed for more evidence-based policymaking and, as a result, more sustainable tourism development.

Taleb Rifai
Secretary-General, World Tourism Organization (UNWTO)

Avant-propos

La prise de décision doit pouvoir s'appuyer sur des informations fiables permettant de définir des politiques et des stratégies de développement adéquates. Pour aider les pays à assurer le suivi de l'impact et de l'évolution du tourisme dans leurs économies et à en avoir une meilleure compréhension, l'Organisation mondiale du tourisme (OMT) procède à une collecte systématique de statistiques du tourisme auprès de pays et de territoires du monde entier. Ces statistiques sont rassemblées dans une vaste base de données qui permet, chaque année, de faire paraître deux publications statistiques clés : le *Compendium des statistiques du tourisme* et l'*Annuaire des statistiques du tourisme*. À elles deux, ces publications offrent les informations statistiques les plus complètes sur le secteur touristique.

Le *Compendium des statistiques du tourisme* préparé par l'OMT contient des données et des indicateurs sur le tourisme récepteur, émetteur et interne, sur le nombre et les types d'industries touristiques et le nombre de salariés par industrie touristique, ainsi que des indicateurs macroéconomiques liés au tourisme international. Ces données sont complétées par l'*Annuaire des statistiques du tourisme* qui se concentre spécifiquement sur les données liées au tourisme récepteur (nombre total d'arrivées et de nuitées), avec une ventilation par pays d'origine.

Les statistiques présentées dans les éditions 2017 du *Compendium* et de l'*Annuaire* apportent un éclairage sur les multiples facettes du tourisme et sur son importance croissante. Elles constituent un guide de référence incontournable pour toutes les parties prenantes du secteur touristique. Et par-dessus tout, elles fournissent aux décideurs les éléments d'appréciation dont ils ont besoin pour formuler des politiques en connaissance de cause et, partant, assurer un développement plus durable du tourisme.

Taleb Rifai
Secrétaire général, Organisation mondiale du tourisme

Prólogo

La adopción de decisiones requiere información fiable que permita orientar adecuadamente las políticas y las estrategias de desarrollo. Con el fin de ayudar a los países a supervisar y entender mejor la incidencia y la evolución del turismo en su economía, la Organización Mundial del Turismo (OMT) compila sistemáticamente estadísticas de turismo de países y territorios de todo el mundo en una extensa base de datos que cada año da lugar a dos publicaciones estadísticas clave: el *Compendio de estadísticas de turismo* y el *Anuario de estadísticas de turismo*. Juntas, estas dos publicaciones constituyen la más completa información estadística disponible sobre el sector turístico.

El *Compendio de estadísticas de turismo* de la OMT proporciona datos e indicadores sobre turismo receptor, emisor e interno, sobre el número y los tipos de industrias turísticas, sobre el número de asalariados por industria turística y sobre aspectos macroeconómicos relacionados con el turismo internacional. Estos datos se complementan con el *Anuario de estadísticas de turismo* que se centra específicamente en los datos relacionados con el turismo receptor (totales de llegadas y de pernoctaciones) desglosados por país de origen.

Las estadísticas presentadas en las ediciones de 2017 del *Compendio* y del *Anuario* permiten explorar las múltiples facetas del turismo y su creciente importancia y son una guía de referencia indispensable para todos los agentes del turismo. Sobre todo, proporcionan datos fehacientes a los responsables públicos para que sus políticas tengan mayor fundamento y, como resultado, promuevan el desarrollo de un turismo más sostenible.

Taleb Rifai
Secretario General, Organización Mundial del Turismo

Table of contents

TABLE OF CONTENTS

TABLE OF CONTENTS

Country tables by geographical order

AFRICA – AFRIQUE – ÁFRICA

East Africa – Afrique orientale – África Oriental

Central Africa – Afrique centrale – África Central

North Africa – Afrique du Nord – África del Norte

Southern Africa – Afrique australe – África Austral

West Africa – Afrique occidentale – África Occidental

AMERICAS – AMÉRIQUES – AMÉRICAS

Caribbean – Caraïbes – El Caribe

TABLE OF CONTENTS

TABLE OF CONTENTS

n.a. Not available

Introduction

The United Nations recognizes the World Tourism Organization (UNWTO) as the appropriate organization to collect, analyse, publish, standardize and improve statistics on tourism and to promote the integration of these statistics within the sphere of the United Nations system. Pursuant of this mandate, the UNWTO Statistics and Tourism Satellite Account Programme collects tourism statistics and disseminates them through two publications: the *Compendium of Tourism Statistics* and the *Yearbook of Tourism Statistics*.

The *Compendium of Tourism Statistics 2017* provides statistical information on tourism in 201 countries and territories for the period 2011–2015. This is a reference guide for the measurement and analysis of the tourism sector. Together with the *Yearbook of Tourism Statistics*, it constitutes the UNWTO's main dataset and publication of annual tourism statistics. Both publications are derived from UNWTO's tourism statistics database, which constitutes the most comprehensive statistical information available on the tourism sector.

The 2017 edition of the *Compendium* is the thirty-seventh in a series that began in 1975 as a biennial publication, and which has been produced annually since 1986. The structure of the Compendium is coherent with the internationally agreed system of definitions, concepts and classifications for tourism statistics, namely the *International Recommendations for Tourism Statistics 2008* (IRTS 2008), and therefore with the conceptual framework of the *Tourism Satellite Account* (TSA:RMF 2008).

The objective of the *Compendium* is to make readily available in one publication a comprehensive set of data on tourism. The *Compendium* contains 145 internationally-comparable basic data series and indicators on:

1. Inbound tourism
2. Domestic tourism
3. Outbound tourism
4. Tourism industries
5. Employment
6. Complementary (macroeconomic) indicators

The data included in the *Compendium* correspond to official statistics collected by governments or national tourism administrations and reported regularly to UNWTO through various questionnaires. The UNWTO Statistics and Tourism Satellite Account Programme disseminates the data after performing various data quality checks both in terms of data validation and data homogeneity with the historical series and related data as well as with the data set published in the *Yearbook of Tourism Statistics*. Not all countries and territories produce the complete data series requested in the questionnaires. For this reason you may not find data for all the 145 series for a specific country. The basic information framework underpinning the *Compendium* can be found in the Conceptual References and Technical Notes (Annex 1). The macroeconomic indicators are prepared by UNWTO.

The 2017 *Compendium* hardcover edition is available in English, with indicator names, conceptual references and country notes provided in English, French and Spanish. The figures included in this edition correspond to data entered in UNWTO's statistical database as of 31 December 2016. Therefore, any corrections or changes received after this date will only be included in the next edition.

Going beyond its print edition, the *Compendium* is principally a database of regularly updated annual information per country available in electronic format (PDF, Excel) from 1995 in the UNWTO Elibrary (www.e-unwto.org). Users seeking the latest available statistics for shorter reference periods or regional aggregates are invited to consult other UNWTO publications available in the UNWTO Elibrary. Of particular interest is the work by the UNWTO Tourism Market Trends Programme, notably the *UNWTO World Tourism Barometer*.

The UNWTO wishes to express its sincere gratitude to all those who contributed to the information published (national tourism administrations, national statistical offices, central banks, the International Monetary Fund and the World Bank) for their valuable support, recognizing especially the crucial role of all contributing countries and territories for their continued commitment to the development and improvement of tourism statistics.

Madrid, January 2017

Introduction

L'Organisation des Nations Unies reconnaît l'Organisation mondiale du tourisme (OMT) comme étant l'organisation compétente pour recueillir, analyser, publier, unifier et améliorer les statistiques du tourisme et promouvoir l'intégration de ces statistiques au sein du système des Nations Unies. Conformément à cette mission, le programme de l'OMT Statistiques et compte satellite du tourisme recueille les statistiques du tourisme et les diffuse au moyen de deux publications : le *Compendium des statistiques du tourisme* et l'*Annuaire des statistiques du tourisme*.

Le *Compendium des statistiques du tourisme 2017* fournit des informations statistiques sur le tourisme dans 201 pays et territoires pour la période 2011–2015. C'est un guide à usage de référence pour la mesure et l'analyse du secteur du tourisme. Avec l'*Annuaire des statistiques du tourisme*, il constitue le principal ensemble de données et la principale publication de l'OMT en matière de statistiques annuelles du tourisme. Ces deux publications sont préparées à partir de la base de données de l'OMT de statistiques du tourisme, laquelle représente le réservoir le plus complet d'informations statistiques disponibles sur le secteur du tourisme.

L'édition 2017 du *Compendium* est la trente-septième d'une série qui a commencé en 1975. L'ouvrage, d'abord publié tous les deux ans, paraît chaque année depuis 1986. La structure du *Compendium* suit le système adopté au niveau international de définitions, de concepts et de classifications pour les statistiques du tourisme, à savoir les *Recommandations internationales 2008 sur les statistiques du tourisme* (RIST 2008), et donc le cadre conceptuel du compte satellite du tourisme *(Compte satellite du tourisme : recommandations concernant le cadre conceptuel 2008)*.

Le *Compendium* répond à l'objectif de mettre facilement à disposition, dans une seule publication, un ensemble complet de données sur le tourisme. Il contient 145 séries de données et indicateurs de base, comparables à l'échelon international, sur :

1. Tourisme récepteur
2. Tourisme interne
3. Tourisme émetteur
4. Industries touristiques
5. Emploi
6. Indicateurs (macroéconomiques) complémentaires

Les données incluses dans le *Compendium* correspondent aux statistiques officielles recueillies par les gouvernements ou par les administrations nationales du tourisme et communiquées à l'OMT, à intervalles périodiques, à l'aide de divers questionnaires. Le programme de l'OMT Statistiques et compte satellite du tourisme diffuse les données après les avoir soumises à différents contrôles de qualité couvrant à la fois la validation des données et l'homogénéité des données avec les séries historiques et les données connexes ainsi qu'avec l'ensemble de données publié dans l'*Annuaire de statistiques du tourisme*. Tous les pays et territoires ne produisent pas les séries complètes de données qui sont demandées dans les questionnaires ; il se peut donc que vous ne trouviez pas, pour un pays en particulier, de données pour chacune des 145 séries. Le cadre d'informations de base sous-tendant le *Compendium* est fourni dans les Références conceptuelles et Notes techniques (Annexe 1). Les indicateurs macroéconomiques sont préparés par l'OMT.

INTRODUCTION

L'édition reliée du *Compendium* 2017 est disponible en anglais, les noms des indicateurs, les références conceptuelles et les notes sur les pays apparaissant en anglais, en espagnol et en français. Les chiffres inclus dans la présente édition correspondent aux données saisies dans la base de données statistiques de l'OMT en date du 31 décembre 2016. En conséquence, les éventuelles corrections ou modifications reçues après cette date n'apparaîtront que dans l'édition suivante.

Indépendamment de la publication papier, le *Compendium* est avant tout une base de données d'informations annuelles par pays, mise à jour régulièrement et disponible en version électronique (PDF, Excel), depuis 1995, dans la bibliothèque électronique de l'OMT (www.e-unwto.org). Les utilisateurs qui voudraient connaître les dernières statistiques disponibles pour des périodes de référence plus courtes ou des agrégats régionaux sont invités à consulter les autres publications de l'OMT dans la bibliothèque électronique de l'OMT. Les travaux du programme de l'OMT Tendances du marché du tourisme sont particulièrement intéressants, notamment le *Baromètre OMT du tourisme mondial*.

L'OMT exprime sa sincère gratitude, pour leur aide précieuse, à toutes celles et ceux qui ont permis de réunir ces informations (administrations nationales du tourisme, bureaux nationaux de statistique, banques centrales, Fonds monétaire international et Banque mondiale). L'Organisation tient à saluer plus spécialement tous les pays et territoires ayant apporté leur contribution pour leur rôle crucial et leur engagement constant en faveur du développement et de l'amélioration des statistiques du tourisme.

Madrid, janvier 2017

Introducción

Las Naciones Unidas reconocen que la Organización Mundial del Turismo (OMT) es la organización competente para recopilar, analizar, publicar, uniformar y mejorar las estadísticas de turismo y promover la integración de esas estadísticas en el marco del sistema de las Naciones Unidas. Siguiendo este mandato, el Programa de Estadísticas y Cuenta Satélite de Turismo de la OMT recopila estadísticas de turismo y las difunde a través de dos publicaciones: el *Compendio de estadísticas de turismo* y el *Anuario de estadísticas de turismo*.

El *Compendio de estadísticas de turismo 2017* ofrece información estadística sobre el turismo en 201 países y territorios para el periodo 2011–2015. Constituye una guía de referencia para la evaluación y el análisis del sector turístico. Junto con el *Anuario de estadísticas de turismo*, constituye el principal conjunto de datos de la OMT y la principal publicación de estadísticas anuales de turismo. Ambas publicaciones se alimentan de la base de datos de estadísticas de turismo de la OMT, que representa el más completo repositorio de información estadística disponible sobre el sector turístico.

La edición de 2017 del *Compendio* es la trigésima séptima de una serie que comenzó en 1975 como publicación bienal y que lleva preparándose anualmente desde 1986. La estructura del *Compendio* es coherente con el sistema de definiciones, conceptos y clasificaciones para estadísticas de turismo acordado a escala internacional, concretamente el de las *Recomendaciones internacionales para estadísticas de turismo 2008* (RIET 2008), y por lo tanto, también con las recomendaciones sobre el marco conceptual de la *Cuenta satélite de turismo* (CST: RMC 2008).

El objetivo del *Compendio* es poner a disposición del público interesado, en una sola publicación, un conjunto exhaustivo de datos sobre turismo. El *Compendio* contiene 145 series de datos básicos e indicadores comparables a escala internacional sobre:

1. Turismo receptor
2. Turismo interno
3. Turismo emisor
4. Industrias turísticas
5. Empleo
6. Indicadores complementarios (macroeconómicos)

Los datos incluidos en el *Compendio* corresponden a las estadísticas oficiales recopiladas por los gobiernos o las administraciones nacionales de turismo, y comunicadas con regularidad a la OMT a través de diversos cuestionarios. El Programa de Estadísticas y Cuenta Satélite de Turismo de la OMT difunde los datos, después de aplicar varios controles de calidad en términos de validación de los datos y homogeneidad en relación con las series históricas y otros datos afines, así como con el conjunto de datos publicado en el *Anuario de estadísticas de turismo*. No todos los países y territorios producen todas las series de datos que se solicitan en los cuestionarios, razón por la cual es posible que no encuentre los datos de las 145 series para un determinado país. El marco de información básica que sustenta el *Compendio* se explica en las referencias conceptuales y las notas técnicas (Anexo 1). Los indicadores macroeconómicos los prepara la OMT.

INTRODUCCIÓN

La edición impresa del *Compendio* de 2017 se publica en inglés, pero los enunciados de los indicadores, las referencias conceptuales y las notas de los países figuran en español, francés e inglés. Las cifras que figuran en esta edición corresponden a los datos introducidos en la base de datos estadística de la OMT a 31 de diciembre de 2016. Por lo tanto, cualquier corrección o cambio recibido después de esta fecha no aparecerá hasta la próxima edición.

Además de la edición impresa, el *Compendio* es principalmente una base de datos de información anual por países regularmente actualizada y puede consultarse también en formato electrónico (PDF, Excel) desde 1995 en la biblioteca virtual de la OMT (www.e-unwto.org). Los usuarios que busquen las últimas estadísticas disponibles para periodos de referencia más breves o agregados regionales pueden consultar otras publicaciones de la OMT disponibles también en biblioteca virtual. Cabe destacar como especialmente interesante el trabajo del Programa de la OMT de Tendencias de los Mercados Turísticos, y en particular el *Barómetro OMT del Turismo Mundial*.

La OMT desea expresar su sincero agradecimiento por su valioso apoyo a todos aquellos que han permitido, con sus aportaciones, reunir la información publicada (administraciones nacionales de turismo, oficinas nacionales de estadística, bancos centrales, el Fondo Monetario Internacional y el Banco Mundial) y reconocer especialmente el papel crucial de todos los países y territorios que mantienen su compromiso con el desarrollo y la mejora de las estadísticas del turismo.

Madrid, enero de 2017

Country tables
2011–2015

ALBANIA

Cod.	Basic data and indicators	Notes	Units	2011	2012	2013	2014	2015
1.	**INBOUND TOURISM**							
	Data							
	Arrivals	(1)						
1.1	Total	(2)	('000)	2,932	3,514	3,256	3,673	4,131
1.2	♦ Overnight visitors (tourists)		('000)	2,469	3,156	2,857	3,341	3,784
1.3	♦ Same-day visitors (excursionists)		('000)	67	71	220	127	162
1.4	* of which, cruise passengers		('000)	..	..	..	..	..
	Arrivals by region	(1)(2)						
1.5	Total		('000)	2,932	3,514	3,256	3,673	4,131
1.6	♦ Africa		('000)	0.5	1	1	1	5
1.7	♦ Americas		('000)	70	74	73	90	107
1.8	♦ East Asia and the Pacific		('000)	17	20	24	31	33
1.9	♦ Europe		('000)	2,739	3,214	2,964	3,424	3,748
1.10	♦ Middle East		('000)	1	2	4	3	4
1.11	♦ South Asia		('000)	1	1	1	1	2
1.12	♦ Other not classified		('000)	103	202	190	123	234
1.13	* of which, nationals residing abroad		('000)	..	..	..	..	..
	Arrivals by main purpose	(1)(2)						
1.14	Total		('000)	2,932	3,514	3,256	3,673	4,131
1.15	♦ Personal		('000)	2,889	3,472	3,206	3,624	4,089
1.16	* holidays, leisure and recreation		('000)	1,183	1,493	484	1,315	1,579
1.17	* other personal purposes		('000)	1,706	1,979	2,722	2,309	2,510
1.18	♦ Business and professional		('000)	43	42	50	48	42
	Arrivals by mode of transport	(1)(2)						
1.19	Total		('000)	2,932	3,514	3,256	3,673	4,131
1.20	♦ Air		('000)	267	273	314	337	401
1.21	♦ Water		('000)	191	180	182	198	211
1.22	♦ Land		('000)	2,474	3,061	2,760	3,138	3,519
1.23	* railway		('000)	..	..	..	..	..
1.24	* road		('000)	2,474	3,061	2,760	3,138	3,519
1.25	* others		('000)	..	..	..	..	..
	Accommodation							
	Hotels and similar establishments							
1.31	♦ Guests	(3)(4)	('000)	136	149	118	161	257
1.32	♦ Overnights	(3)(4)	('000)	356	352	215	259	484
	Expenditure							
1.33	Total		US$ Mn	1,833	1,623	1,670	1,849	1,614
1.34	♦ Travel		US$ Mn	1,632	1,464	1,473	1,700	1,500
1.35	♦ Passenger transport		US$ Mn	201	159	197	149	114
	Expenditure by main purpose of the trip							
1.36	Total		US$ Mn	1,632	1,463	1,473	1,700	1,500
1.37	♦ Personal		US$ Mn	1,239	1,155	1,165	1,370	1,160
1.38	♦ Business and professional		US$ Mn	393	308	308	330	340
	Indicators							
1.39	Average size of travel party		Persons	..	..	..	..	..
	Average length of stay							
1.40	Total		Days	..	..	..	..	..
1.41	♦ For all commercial accommodation services	(3)(4)	Nights	2.60	2.40	1.80	1.60	1.90
1.42	* of which, "hotels and similar establishments"		Nights	..	..	..	..	..
1.43	♦ For non commercial accommodation services		Days	..	..	..	..	..
1.44	Average expenditure per day		US$	..	..	..	..	..
2.	**DOMESTIC TOURISM**							
	Data							
	Accommodation							
	Hotels and similar establishments							
2.21	♦ Guests	(3)(4)	('000)	182	101	106	136	171
2.22	♦ Overnights	(3)(4)	('000)	445	238	179	199	307
	Indicators							
2.23	Average size of travel party		Persons	..	..	..	..	..
	Average length of stay							
2.24	Total		Days	..	..	..	..	..
2.25	♦ For all commercial accommodation services	(3)(4)	Nights	2.40	2.40	1.60	1.40	1.80
2.26	* of which, "hotels and similar establishments"		Nights	..	..	..	..	..
2.27	♦ For non commercial accommodation services		Days	..	..	..	..	..
2.28	Average expenditure per day		US$	..	..	..	..	..

ALBANIA

Cod.	Basic data and indicators	Notes	Units	2011	2012	2013	2014	2015
3.	**OUTBOUND TOURISM**							
	Data							
	Departures							
3.1	Total		('000)	4,120	3,959	3,928	4,146	4,504
3.2	♦ Overnight visitors (tourists)		('000)	..	..	..	..	
3.3	♦ Same-day visitors (excursionists)		('000)	..	..	..	..	
	Expenditure							
3.4	Total		US$ Mn	1,678	1,374	1,567	1,689	1,311
3.5	♦ Travel		US$ Mn	1,565	1,284	1,479	1,590	1,238
3.6	♦ Passenger transport		US$ Mn	113	90	88	99	73
	Expenditure by main purpose of the trip							
3.7	Total		US$ Mn	1,565	1,285	1,479	1,590	1,238
3.8	♦ Personal		US$ Mn	1,125	970	1,098	1,270	921
3.9	♦ Business and professional		US$ Mn	440	315	381	320	317
	Indicators							
3.10	Average length of stay		Days	7.00	7.00	7.00	7.00	..
3.11	Average expenditure per day		US$	96.0	80.0	63.0	64.0	..
4.	**TOURISM INDUSTRIES**	(4)						
	Data							
	Number of establishments							
4.1	Total		Units	20,475	20,351	20,760	20,976	..
4.2	♦ Accommodation for visitors		Units	12,773	13,677	13,784	14,637	..
4.3	* of which, "hotels and similar establishments"		Units	..	..	..	..	..
4.4	♦ Food and beverage serving activities		Units	..	..	..	5,719	..
4.5	♦ Passenger transportation		Units	6,851	6,116	6,294	..	..
4.6	♦ Travel agencies and other reservation services activities		Units	851	558	682	620	..
4.7	♦ Other tourism industries		Units	..	..	..	..	..
	Accommodation for visitors in hotels and similar establishments							
	Monetary data							
4.8	♦ Output		US$ Mn	286.9	264.1	285.6	290.4	..
4.9	♦ Intermediate consumption		US$ Mn	142.1	132.1	153.3	155.6	..
4.10	♦ Gross value added	(5)	US$ Mn	144.8	132.0	132.3	134.8	..
4.11	♦ Compensation of employees		US$ Mn	53.9	55.0	60.9	70.1	..
4.12	♦ Gross fixed capital formation	(6)	US$ Mn	17.7	22.8	18.2	12.1	..
	Non-monetary data							
4.13	♦ Number of establishments		Units	..	..	..	..	..
4.14	♦ Number of rooms	(7)	Units	12,428	14,652	14,146	15,081	..
4.15	♦ Number of bed-places	(7)	Units	24,301	32,004	29,737	32,879	..
	Indicators							
4.16	Occupancy rate / rooms		Percent	..	..	..	..	..
4.17	Occupancy rate / bed-places		Percent	..	..	..	..	..
4.18	Average length of stay		Nights	..	..	..	..	..
4.19	Available capacity (bed-places per 1000 inhabitants)		Units	8.42	11.11	10.31	11.38	..
	Travel agencies and other reservation service activities							
	Monetary data							
4.20	♦ Output		US$ Mn	212.3	44.3	65.5	78.2	..
4.21	♦ Intermediate consumption		US$ Mn	78.3	24.0	47.6	52.6	..
4.22	♦ Gross value added	(5)	US$ Mn	134.0	20.4	17.9	25.7	..
4.23	♦ Compensation of employees		US$ Mn	42.9	4.1	4.9	5.0	..
4.24	♦ Gross fixed capital formation	(6)	US$ Mn	118.6	47.2	3.7	3.4	..
5.	**EMPLOYMENT**	(4)						
	Data							
	Number of employees by tourism industries							
5.1	Total		('000)	22.7	21.4	25.3	26.7	..
5.2	♦ Accommodation services for visitors (hotels and similar establishments)	(8)	('000)	13.3	14.7	18.0	19.4	..
5.3	♦ Other accommodation services		('000)	..	..	..	..	..
5.4	♦ Food and beverage serving activities		('000)	..	..	..	..	..
5.5	♦ Passenger transportation	(9)	('000)	5.1	5.9	6.4	6.2	..
5.6	♦ Travel agencies and other reservation services activities	(10)	('000)	4.3	0.8	0.9	1.1	..
5.7	♦ Other tourism industries		('000)	..	..	..	..	..

ALBANIA

Cod.	Basic data and indicators	Notes	Units	2011	2012	2013	2014	2015
	Number of jobs by status in employment							
5.8	Total		('000)	45.6	44.5	47.7	49.4	..
5.9	♦ Employees		('000)	22.7	21.3	25.4	26.6	..
5.10	♦ Self employed		('000)	22.9	23.2	22.3	22.8	..
6.	**COMPLEMENTARY INDICATORS**							
	Demand							
6.1	Gross travel propensity		Units	..	..	..	..	..
6.2	(1.2 inbound tourists) / population		Units	0.86	1.10	0.99	1.16	1.31
	Macroeconomic indicators related to international tourism							
6.3	Inbound tourism expenditure over GDP		Percent	14.2	13.2	13.1	14.0	13.1
6.4	Outbound tourism expenditure over GDP		Percent	13.0	11.2	12.3	12.8	10.8
6.5	Tourism balance (inbound minus outbound tourism expenditure) over GDP		Percent	1.2	2.0	0.8	1.2	2.3
6.6	Tourism openness (inbound plus outbound tourism expenditure) over GDP		Percent	27.2	24.4	25.4	26.8	23.9
6.7	Tourism coverage (inbound over outbound tourism expenditure)		Percent	109.2	118.1	106.6	109.5	123.1
6.8	Inbound tourism expenditure over exports of goods		Percent	190.5	144.4	119.7	149.0	188.8
6.9	Inbound tourism expenditure over exports of services		Percent	65.1	66.7	73.2	74.2	71.7
6.10	Inbound tourism expenditure over exports of goods and services		Percent	48.5	45.6	45.4	49.5	52.0
6.11	Inbound tourism expenditure over current account credits		Percent	33.4	31.7	33.8	36.8	37.9
6.12	Outbound tourism expenditure over imports of goods		Percent	37.6	34.5	38.9	40.5	38.5
6.13	Outbound tourism expenditure over imports of services		Percent	74.6	73.4	79.1	81.6	78.6
6.14	Outbound tourism expenditure over imports of goods and		Percent	25.0	23.5	26.1	27.1	25.9
6.15	Outbound tourism expenditure over current account debits		Percent	23.4	21.9	24.6	25.7	24.4

ALGERIA

Cod.	Basic data and indicators	Notes	Units	2011	2012	2013	2014	2015
1.	**INBOUND TOURISM**							
	Data							
	Arrivals							
1.1	Total	(1)	('000)	2,395	2,634	2,733	2,301	1,710
1.2	♦ Overnight visitors (tourists)		('000)	..	..	..	..	..
1.3	♦ Same-day visitors (excursionists)		('000)	..	..	..	..	..
1.4	* of which, cruise passengers		('000)	..	..	..	..	..
	Arrivals by region							
1.5	Total		('000)	2,394	2,634	2,733	2,301	1,710
1.6	♦ Africa		('000)	554	635	591	542	659
1.7	♦ Americas		('000)	12	12	10	10	10
1.8	♦ East Asia and the Pacific		('000)	55	55	46	50	75
1.9	♦ Europe		('000)	219	240	245	258	289
1.10	♦ Middle East		('000)	61	40	73	81	50
1.11	♦ South Asia		('000)	..	..	..	..	..
1.12	♦ Other not classified		('000)	1,493	1,652	1,769	1,361	627
1.13	* of which, nationals residing abroad		('000)	1,493	1,652	1,769	1,361	627
	Arrivals by main purpose	(2)						
1.14	Total		('000)	902	982	964	940	1,083
1.15	♦ Personal		('000)	630	702	672	612	723
1.16	* holidays, leisure and recreation		('000)	630	702	672	612	723
1.17	* other personal purposes		('000)	..	..	..	..	
1.18	♦ Business and professional		('000)	272	280	292	329	360
	Accommodation							
	Hotels and similar establishments							
1.31	♦ Guests		('000)	..	..	..	..	..
1.32	♦ Overnights		('000)	845	937	994	838	839
	Expenditure							
1.33	Total		US$ Mn	300	295	326	348	357
1.34	♦ Travel		US$ Mn	209	217	250	258	308
1.35	♦ Passenger transport		US$ Mn	91	78	76	90	49
	Expenditure by main purpose of the trip							
1.36	Total		US$ Mn	209	217	250	258	308
1.37	♦ Personal		US$ Mn	208	213	250	258	307
1.38	♦ Business and professional		US$ Mn	1.8	4	0.1	0.1	1
2.	**DOMESTIC TOURISM**							
	Data							
	Accommodation							
	Hotels and similar establishments							
2.21	♦ Guests		('000)	..	..	..	..	..
2.22	♦ Overnights		('000)	5,484	5,704	5,927	6,216	6,307
3.	**OUTBOUND TOURISM**							
	Data							
	Departures							
3.1	Total		('000)	..	..	..	..	..
3.2	♦ Overnight visitors (tourists)		('000)	1,715	1,911	2,136	2,839	3,638
3.3	♦ Same-day visitors (excursionists)		('000)	..	..	..	..	..
	Expenditure							
3.4	Total		US$ Mn	595	598	532	684	765
3.5	♦ Travel		US$ Mn	527	529	471	612	687
3.6	♦ Passenger transport		US$ Mn	68	69	61	72	78
	Expenditure by main purpose of the trip							
3.7	Total		US$ Mn	528	530	471	611	687
3.8	♦ Personal		US$ Mn	454	451	371	504	607
3.9	♦ Business and professional		US$ Mn	74	79	100	107	80

ALGERIA

Cod.	Basic data and indicators	Notes	Units	2011	2012	2013	2014	2015
4.	**TOURISM INDUSTRIES**							
	Data							
	Accommodation for visitors in hotels and similar establishments							
	Non-monetary data							
4.13	♦ Number of establishments		Units	..	..	..	..	..
4.14	♦ Number of rooms		Units	..	..	..	..	..
4.15	♦ Number of bed-places		Units	94,021	96,898	98,804	99,605	102,244
	Indicators							
4.16	Occupancy rate / rooms		Percent	..	..	..	..	..
4.17	Occupancy rate / bed-places		Percent	..	..	..	..	..
4.18	Average length of stay		Nights	..	..	..	..	..
4.19	Available capacity (bed-places per 1000 inhabitants)		Units	2.56	2.59	2.59	2.56	2.58
6.	**COMPLEMENTARY INDICATORS**							
	Demand							
6.1	Gross travel propensity		Units	..	..	..	..	..
6.2	(1.1 inbound visitors) / population		Units	0.07	0.07	0.07	0.06	0.04
	Macroeconomic indicators related to international tourism							
6.3	Inbound tourism expenditure over GDP		Percent	0.1	0.1	0.2	0.2	..
6.4	Outbound tourism expenditure over GDP		Percent	0.3	0.3	0.3	0.3	..
6.5	Tourism balance (inbound minus outbound tourism expenditure) over GDP		Percent	-0.2	-0.2	-0.1	-0.1	..
6.6	Tourism openness (inbound plus outbound tourism expenditure) over GDP		Percent	0.4	0.4	0.5	0.5	..
6.7	Tourism coverage (inbound over outbound tourism expenditure)		Percent	50.4	49.3	61.3	50.9	46.7
6.8	Inbound tourism expenditure over exports of goods		Percent	0.4	0.4	0.5	0.6	..
6.9	Inbound tourism expenditure over exports of services		Percent	8.3	7.9	8.6	9.8	..
6.10	Inbound tourism expenditure over exports of goods and services		Percent	0.4	0.4	0.5	0.6	..
6.11	Inbound tourism expenditure over current account credits		Percent	0.4	0.4	0.4	0.5	..
6.12	Outbound tourism expenditure over imports of goods		Percent	1.3	1.2	1.0	1.2	..
6.13	Outbound tourism expenditure over imports of services		Percent	4.7	5.5	4.9	5.8	..
6.14	Outbound tourism expenditure over imports of goods and		Percent	1.0	1.0	0.8	1.0	..
6.15	Outbound tourism expenditure over current account debits		Percent	0.9	0.9	0.8	0.9	..

AMERICAN SAMOA

Cod.	Basic data and indicators	Notes	Units	2011	2012	2013	2014	2015
1.	**INBOUND TOURISM**							
	Data							
	Arrivals							
1.1	Total		('000)	41.3	50.2	49.3	51.6	47.1
1.2	♦ Overnight visitors (tourists)		('000)	22.6	22.6	20.8	21.6	20.3
1.3	♦ Same-day visitors (excursionists)		('000)	18.7	27.6	28.5	30.0	26.8
1.4	* of which, cruise passengers		('000)	18.7	27.6	28.5	30.0	26.8
	Arrivals by region							
1.5	Total		('000)	22.6	22.6	20.8	21.6	20.3
1.6	♦ Africa		('000)	..	..	..	..	..
1.7	♦ Americas		('000)	7.1	6.9	5.4	4.8	4.7
1.8	♦ East Asia and the Pacific		('000)	15.0	15.2	14.9	16.3	15.1
1.9	♦ Europe		('000)	0.4	0.4	0.4	0.4	0.4
1.10	♦ Middle East		('000)	..	..	..	..	..
1.11	♦ South Asia		('000)	..	..	..	..	..
1.12	♦ Other not classified		('000)	0.1	0.1	0.1	0.1	0.1
1.13	* of which, nationals residing abroad		('000)	..	..	..	..	..
	Arrivals by main purpose							
1.14	Total		('000)	22.6	22.6	20.8	21.6	20.3
1.15	♦ Personal		('000)	17.2	17.1	16.6	17.5	16.3
1.16	* holidays, leisure and recreation		('000)	5.7	5.5	5.1	4.8	4.6
1.17	* other personal purposes		('000)	11.5	11.6	11.5	12.7	11.7
1.18	♦ Business and professional		('000)	5.4	5.5	4.2	4.1	4.0
	Arrivals by mode of transport							
1.19	Total		('000)	22.6	22.6	20.8	21.6	20.3
1.20	♦ Air		('000)	19.3	19.3	17.6	16.6	16.4
1.21	♦ Water		('000)	3.3	3.3	3.2	5.0	3.9
1.22	♦ Land		('000)	..	..	..	..	..
1.23	* railway		('000)	..	..	..	..	..
1.24	* road		('000)	..	..	..	..	..
1.25	* others		('000)	..	..	..	..	..
4.	**TOURISM INDUSTRIES**							
	Data							
	Number of establishments							
4.1	Total		Units	..	..	..	..	..
4.2	♦ Accommodation for visitors		Units	..	..	..	..	..
4.3	* of which, "hotels and similar establishments"		Units	..	..	..	..	20
4.4	♦ Food and beverage serving activities		Units	..	..	..	..	..
4.5	♦ Passenger transportation		Units	..	..	..	..	..
4.6	♦ Travel agencies and other reservation services activities		Units	..	..	..	..	..
4.7	♦ Other tourism industries		Units	..	..	..	..	..
	Accommodation for visitors in hotels and similar establishments							
	Non-monetary data							
4.13	♦ Number of establishments		Units	..	..	..	..	20
4.14	♦ Number of rooms		Units	..	..	..	..	266
4.15	♦ Number of bed-places		Units	..	..	..	..	..
6.	**COMPLEMENTARY INDICATORS**							
	Demand							
6.1	Gross travel propensity		Units	..	..	..	..	..
6.2	(1.2 inbound tourists) / population		Units	0.41	0.41	0.38	0.39	0.36

ANDORRA

Cod.	Basic data and indicators	Notes	Units	2011	2012	2013	2014	2015
1.	**INBOUND TOURISM**							
	Data							
	Arrivals	(1)						
1.1	Total		('000)	7,983	7,900	7,676	7,797	7,851
1.2	♦ Overnight visitors (tourists)		('000)	2,242	2,238	2,328	2,363	2,670
1.3	♦ Same-day visitors (excursionists)		('000)	5,741	5,663	5,348	5,433	5,181
1.4	* of which, cruise passengers		('000)	..	..	..	..	..
	Arrivals by region							
1.5	Total		('000)	..	2,238	2,328	2,363	2,670
1.6	♦ Africa		('000)	..	..	..	..	..
1.7	♦ Americas		('000)	..	..	..	..	..
1.8	♦ East Asia and the Pacific		('000)	..	..	..	..	..
1.9	♦ Europe		('000)	..	2,202	2,283	2,330	2,604
1.10	♦ Middle East		('000)	..	..	..	..	..
1.11	♦ South Asia		('000)	..	..	..	..	..
1.12	♦ Other not classified		('000)	..	36	45	33	67
1.13	* of which, nationals residing abroad		('000)	..	..	..	..	..
	Arrivals by main purpose	(1)						
1.14	Total		('000)	7,983	7,900	7,676	7,797	7,851
1.15	♦ Personal		('000)	7,896	7,814	7,569	7,680	7,678
1.16	* holidays, leisure and recreation		('000)	7,322	7,246	7,200	7,228	7,090
1.17	* other personal purposes		('000)	574	568	369	452	589
1.18	♦ Business and professional		('000)	87	86	107	117	173
	Arrivals by mode of transport	(1)						
1.19	Total		('000)	7,983	7,900	7,676	7,797	7,851
1.20	♦ Air		('000)	..	..	..	..	..
1.21	♦ Water		('000)	..	..	..	..	..
1.22	♦ Land		('000)	7,983	7,900	7,676	7,797	7,851
1.23	* railway		('000)	..	..	..	..	..
1.24	* road		('000)	7,983	7,900	7,676	7,797	7,851
1.25	* others		('000)	..	..	..	..	..
	Accommodation	(1)						
	Total							
1.29	♦ Guests		('000)	..	..	..	..	..
1.30	♦ Overnights		('000)	6,515	6,636	6,976	6,780	8,125
	Hotels and similar establishments							
1.31	♦ Guests		('000)	..	..	..	..	..
1.32	♦ Overnights		('000)	4,579	4,705	4,882	4,654	5,217
	Indicators							
1.39	Average size of travel party		Persons	..	..	..	..	..
	Average length of stay							
1.40	Total		Days	..	..	..	..	..
1.41	♦ For all commercial accommodation services		Nights	2.91	2.97	2.99	2.87	3.04
1.42	* of which, "hotels and similar establishments"		Nights					
1.43	♦ For non commercial accommodation services		Days	..	..	..	..	..
1.44	Average expenditure per day		US$	..	..	..	..	..
4.	**TOURISM INDUSTRIES**							
	Data							
	Number of establishments							
4.1	Total		Units	..	..	..	..	..
4.2	♦ Accommodation for visitors		Units	..	..	..	..	..
4.3	* of which, "hotels and similar establishments"		Units	253	249	243	241	239
4.4	♦ Food and beverage serving activities		Units	..	..	..	..	..
4.5	♦ Passenger transportation		Units	..	..	..	..	..
4.6	♦ Travel agencies and other reservation services activities		Units	..	..	..	..	..
4.7	♦ Other tourism industries		Units	..	..	..	..	..
	Accommodation for visitors in hotels and similar establishments							
	Non-monetary data							
4.13	♦ Number of establishments		Units	253	249	243	241	239
4.14	♦ Number of rooms		Units	12,608	12,506	12,391	12,339	12,134
4.15	♦ Number of bed-places		Units	33,446	34,271	34,062	34,019	33,613

ANDORRA

Cod.	Basic data and indicators	Notes	Units	2011	2012	2013	2014	2015
	Indicators							
4.16	Occupancy rate / rooms		Percent	..	..	..	..	..
4.17	Occupancy rate / bed-places		Percent	..	..	..	..	..
4.18	Average length of stay		Nights	2.91	2.97	2.99	2.87	3.04
4.19	Available capacity (bed-places per 1000 inhabitants)		Units	429.54	437.35	429.98	424.43	480.19
6.	**COMPLEMENTARY INDICATORS**							
	Demand							
6.1	Gross travel propensity		Units	..	..	..	..	..
6.2	(1.2 inbound tourists) / population		Units	28.79	28.56	29.39	29.48	38.14

ANGOLA

Cod.	Basic data and indicators	Notes	Units	2011	2012	2013	2014	2015
1.	**INBOUND TOURISM**							
	Data							
	Arrivals							
1.1	Total		('000)	..	..	..	..	..
1.2	♦ Overnight visitors (tourists)		('000)	481	528	650	595	592
1.3	♦ Same-day visitors (excursionists)		('000)	..	..	..	..	..
1.4	* of which, cruise passengers		('000)	..	..	..	..	..
	Arrivals by region							
1.5	Total		('000)	481	528	650	595	592
1.6	♦ Africa		('000)	148	173	223	106	176
1.7	♦ Americas		('000)	58	68	74	84	105
1.8	♦ East Asia and the Pacific		('000)	88	94	106	66	98
1.9	♦ Europe		('000)	170	177	231	326	198
1.10	♦ Middle East		('000)	3	6	8	7	5
1.11	♦ South Asia		('000)	14	10	8	8	10
1.12	♦ Other not classified		('000)	..	..	..	..	..
1.13	* of which, nationals residing abroad		('000)	..	..	..	..	..
	Arrivals by main purpose							
1.14	Total		('000)	481	528	650	595	592
1.15	♦ Personal		('000)	246	289	386	360	320
1.16	* holidays, leisure and recreation		('000)	53	84	131	88	87
1.17	* other personal purposes		('000)	193	205	255	272	233
1.18	♦ Business and professional		('000)	235	239	264	235	272
	Arrivals by mode of transport							
1.19	Total		('000)	481	528	650	595	592
1.20	♦ Air		('000)	481	528	650	595	592
1.21	♦ Water		('000)	..	..	..	..	..
1.22	♦ Land		('000)	..	..	..	..	..
1.23	* railway		('000)	..	..	..	..	..
1.24	* road		('000)	..	..	..	..	..
1.25	* others		('000)	..	..	..	..	..
	Accommodation							
	Total							
1.29	♦ Guests		('000)	533	569	652	567	545
1.30	♦ Overnights		('000)	1,436	1,429	1,754	1,769	1,612
	Hotels and similar establishments							
1.31	♦ Guests	(1)	('000)	401	422	481	409	400
1.32	♦ Overnights	(1)	('000)	1,155	1,119	1,372	1,230	1,198
	Expenditure							
1.33	Total		US$ Mn	653	711	1,241	1,597	1,171
1.34	♦ Travel		US$ Mn	646	706	1,234	1,589	1,163
1.35	♦ Passenger transport		US$ Mn	7	5	7	8	8
	Expenditure by main purpose of the trip							
1.36	Total		US$ Mn	646	706	1,234	1,589	1,163
1.37	♦ Personal		US$ Mn	102	92	235	261	168
1.38	♦ Business and professional		US$ Mn	544	614	999	1,328	995
2.	**DOMESTIC TOURISM**							
	Data							
	Accommodation							
	Total							
2.19	♦ Guests		('000)	373	413	496	574	726
2.20	♦ Overnights		('000)	1,251	1,347	1,475	1,810	1,971
	Hotels and similar establishments							
2.21	♦ Guests	(1)	('000)	251	281	337	369	264
2.22	♦ Overnights	(1)	('000)	688	734	754	992	870
3.	**OUTBOUND TOURISM**							
	Data							
	Expenditure							
3.4	Total		US$ Mn	323	292	319	505	389
3.5	♦ Travel		US$ Mn	180	159	166	113	146
3.6	♦ Passenger transport		US$ Mn	143	133	153	392	243

ANGOLA

Cod.	Basic data and indicators	Notes	Units	2011	2012	2013	2014	2015
	Expenditure by main purpose of the trip							
3.7	Total		US$ Mn	180	159	166	113	146
3.8	♦ Personal		US$ Mn	78	68	79	6	70
3.9	♦ Business and professional		US$ Mn	102	91	87	107	77
4.	**TOURISM INDUSTRIES**							
	Data							
	Number of establishments							
4.1	Total		Units	4,911	5,482	5,766	6,277	6,378
4.2	♦ Accommodation for visitors		Units	1,192	1,224	1,323	1,360	1,482
4.3	* of which, "hotels and similar establishments"	(1)	Units	148	161	178	183	196
4.4	♦ Food and beverage serving activities		Units	3,632	4,132	4,294	4,785	4,736
4.5	♦ Passenger transportation		Units	..	..	..	..	..
4.6	♦ Travel agencies and other reservation services activities		Units	87	126	149	132	160
4.7	♦ Other tourism industries		Units	..	..	..	..	..
	Accommodation for visitors in hotels and similar establishments							
	Non-monetary data	(1)						
4.13	♦ Number of establishments		Units	148	161	178	183	196
4.14	♦ Number of rooms		Units	..	..	9,156	10,626	11,172
4.15	♦ Number of bed-places		Units	..	..	19,121	14,617	15,035
	Indicators							
4.16	Occupancy rate / rooms		Percent	73.00	83.00	86.00	85.80	88.30
4.17	Occupancy rate / bed-places		Percent	67.00	75.00	79.00	78.70	80.90
4.18	Average length of stay		Nights	..	..	..	..	..
4.19	Available capacity (bed-places per 1000 inhabitants)		Units	..	..	0.82	0.60	0.60
5.	**EMPLOYMENT**							
	Data							
	Number of employees by tourism industries							
5.1	Total		('000)	145.6	158.0	173.5	202.8	219.3
5.2	♦ Accommodation services for visitors (hotels and similar establishments)		('000)	72.1	78.7	84.1	89.0	92.3
5.3	♦ Other accommodation services		('000)	..	..	..	..	..
5.4	♦ Food and beverage serving activities		('000)	61.3	65.7	74.8	98.5	104.0
5.5	♦ Passenger transportation		('000)	..	..	..	..	..
5.6	♦ Travel agencies and other reservation services activities		('000)	12.2	13.5	14.5	15.3	23.0
5.7	♦ Other tourism industries		('000)	..	..	..	..	..
6.	**COMPLEMENTARY INDICATORS**							
	Demand							
6.1	Gross travel propensity		Units	..	..	..	..	..
6.2	(1.2 inbound tourists) / population		Units	0.02	0.02	0.03	0.02	0.02
	Macroeconomic indicators related to international tourism							
6.3	Inbound tourism expenditure over GDP		Percent	..	..	..	..	..
6.4	Outbound tourism expenditure over GDP		Percent	..	..	..	..	..
6.5	Tourism balance (inbound minus outbound tourism expenditure) over GDP		Percent	..	..	..	..	..
6.6	Tourism openness (inbound plus outbound tourism expenditure) over GDP		Percent	..	..	..	..	..
6.7	Tourism coverage (inbound over outbound tourism expenditure)		Percent	202.2	243.5	389.0	316.2	301.0
6.8	Inbound tourism expenditure over exports of goods		Percent	1.0	1.0	1.8	2.7	..
6.9	Inbound tourism expenditure over exports of services		Percent	89.2	91.2	94.3	95.0	..
6.10	Inbound tourism expenditure over exports of goods and services		Percent	1.0	1.0	1.8	2.6	..
6.11	Inbound tourism expenditure over current account credits		Percent	1.0	1.0	1.8	2.6	..
6.12	Outbound tourism expenditure over imports of goods		Percent	1.6	1.2	1.2	1.8	..
6.13	Outbound tourism expenditure over imports of services		Percent	1.4	1.3	1.4	2.0	..
6.14	Outbound tourism expenditure over imports of goods and		Percent	0.7	0.6	0.6	0.9	..
6.15	Outbound tourism expenditure over current account debits		Percent	0.7	0.6	0.6	0.9	..

ANGUILLA

Cod.	Basic data and indicators	Notes	Units	2011	2012	2013	2014	2015
1.	**INBOUND TOURISM**							
	Data							
	Arrivals	(1)						
1.1	Total		('000)	124	129	151	177	186
1.2	♦ Overnight visitors (tourists)		('000)	66	65	69	71	73
1.3	♦ Same-day visitors (excursionists)		('000)	58	64	82	106	113
1.4	* of which, cruise passengers		('000)	2	3	3	6	7
	Arrivals by region	(1)						
1.5	Total		('000)	66	65	69	71	73
1.6	♦ Africa		('000)	..	..	..	..	..
1.7	♦ Americas		('000)	57	55	60	61	63
1.8	♦ East Asia and the Pacific		('000)	..	..	..	..	..
1.9	♦ Europe		('000)	8	7	7	8	8
1.10	♦ Middle East		('000)	..	..	..	..	..
1.11	♦ South Asia		('000)	..	..	..	..	..
1.12	♦ Other not classified		('000)	1	2	2	2	2
1.13	* of which, nationals residing abroad		('000)	..	..	..	..	..
	Arrivals by main purpose							
1.14	Total		('000)	124	129	151	177	186
1.15	♦ Personal		('000)	121	127	148	174	182
1.16	* holidays, leisure and recreation	(2)	('000)	121	127	148	174	182
1.17	* other personal purposes		('000)	..	..	..	..	..
1.18	♦ Business and professional		('000)	3	3	3	3	4
	Arrivals by mode of transport							
1.19	Total		('000)	124	129	151	177	186
1.20	♦ Air		('000)	18	15	15	14	13
1.21	♦ Water		('000)	106	114	136	163	173
1.22	♦ Land		('000)	..	..	..	..	..
1.23	* railway		('000)	..	..	..	..	..
1.24	* road		('000)	..	..	..	..	..
1.25	* others		('000)	..	..	..	..	..
	Expenditure							
1.33	Total		US$ Mn	..	..	..	..	..
1.34	♦ Travel		US$ Mn	112	113	123	128	128
1.35	♦ Passenger transport		US$ Mn	..	..	..	..	..
	Indicators							
1.39	Average size of travel party	(3)	Persons	2.6	2.8	2.8	2.8	..
	Average length of stay							
1.40	Total		Days	..	..	..	..	..
1.41	♦ For all commercial accommodation services		Nights	7.80	7.71	7.53	7.50	7.30
1.42	* of which, "hotels and similar establishments"		Nights	..	..	..	..	..
1.43	♦ For non commercial accommodation services		Days	..	..	..	..	..
1.44	Average expenditure per day		US$	..	..	..	..	..
3.	**OUTBOUND TOURISM**							
	Data							
	Expenditure							
3.4	Total		US$ Mn	..	..	..	..	..
3.5	♦ Travel		US$ Mn	13	12	12	..	..
3.6	♦ Passenger transport		US$ Mn	..	..	..	..	..
6.	**COMPLEMENTARY INDICATORS**							
	Demand							
6.1	Gross travel propensity		Units	..	..	..	..	..
6.2	(1.2 inbound tourists) / population		Units	4.73	4.60	4.83	4.91	5.00
	Macroeconomic indicators related to international tourism							
6.3	Inbound tourism expenditure over GDP		Percent	37.9	39.7	42.5	41.8	..
6.4	Outbound tourism expenditure over GDP		Percent	4.4	4.2	4.1	..	..
6.5	Tourism balance (inbound minus outbound tourism expenditure) over GDP		Percent	33.5	35.5	38.4	41.8	..
6.6	Tourism openness (inbound plus outbound tourism expenditure) over GDP		Percent	42.3	43.9	46.6	41.8	..
6.7	Tourism coverage (inbound over outbound tourism expenditure)		Percent	861.5	941.7	1,025.0	..	..
6.8	Inbound tourism expenditure over exports of goods		Percent	1,547.0	1,514.7	2,853.8	..	..
6.9	Inbound tourism expenditure over exports of services		Percent	86.2	87.3	88.8	..	..
6.10	Inbound tourism expenditure over exports of goods and services		Percent	81.7	82.6	86.1	..	..
6.11	Inbound tourism expenditure over current account credits		Percent	66.7	75.0	78.5	..	..
6.12	Outbound tourism expenditure over imports of goods		Percent	10.1	9.3	9.4	..	..
6.13	Outbound tourism expenditure over imports of services		Percent	23.6	21.6	21.3	..	..
6.14	Outbound tourism expenditure over imports of goods and		Percent	7.1	6.5	6.5	..	..
6.15	Outbound tourism expenditure over current account debits		Percent	6.3	5.9	5.9	..	..

ANTIGUA AND BARBUDA

Cod.	Basic data and indicators	Notes	Units	2011	2012	2013	2014	2015
1.	**INBOUND TOURISM**							
	Data							
	Arrivals							
1.1	Total	(1)	('000)	848	819	777	771	894
1.2	♦ Overnight visitors (tourists)	(2)	('000)	241	247	243	249	250
1.3	♦ Same-day visitors (excursionists)		('000)	607	572	534	522	644
1.4	* of which, cruise passengers		('000)	607	572	534	522	644
	Arrivals by region	(2)						
1.5	Total		('000)	241	247	243	249	250
1.6	♦ Africa		('000)	..	..	..	..	..
1.7	♦ Americas		('000)	147	154	152	155	151
1.8	♦ East Asia and the Pacific		('000)	1	1	2	2	2
1.9	♦ Europe		('000)	92	90	88	91	96
1.10	♦ Middle East		('000)	..	..	..	..	..
1.11	♦ South Asia		('000)	..	..	..	..	..
1.12	♦ Other not classified		('000)	1	1	1	1	1
1.13	* of which, nationals residing abroad		('000)	..	..	..	..	..
	Arrivals by main purpose	(2)						
1.14	Total		('000)	241	..	..	249	250
1.15	♦ Personal		('000)	234	..	..	240	241
1.16	* holidays, leisure and recreation		('000)	194	..	..	199	197
1.17	* other personal purposes		('000)	40	..	..	42	44
1.18	♦ Business and professional		('000)	7	..	..	9	9
	Arrivals by mode of transport							
1.19	Total		('000)	848	819	777	771	894
1.20	♦ Air		('000)	241	247	243	249	250
1.21	♦ Water	(3)	('000)	607	572	534	522	644
1.22	♦ Land		('000)	..	..	..	..	..
1.23	* railway		('000)	..	..	..	..	..
1.24	* road		('000)	..	..	..	..	..
1.25	* others		('000)	..	..	..	..	..
	Accommodation							
	Total							
1.29	♦ Guests	(2)	('000)	241	247	243	249	250
1.30	♦ Overnights		('000)	..	..	..	..	..
	Hotels and similar establishments							
1.31	♦ Guests	(2)	('000)	189	..	199	..	..
1.32	♦ Overnights		('000)	..	..	..	..	..
	Expenditure							
1.33	Total		US$ Mn	..	..	..	..	..
1.34	♦ Travel		US$ Mn	312	319	299	..	..
1.35	♦ Passenger transport		US$ Mn	..	..	..	..	..
	Indicators							
1.39	Average size of travel party		Persons	..	..	..	..	..
	Average length of stay							
1.40	Total		Days	..	..	9.96	9.94	9.50
1.41	♦ For all commercial accommodation services		Nights	..	..	..	..	..
1.42	* of which, "hotels and similar establishments"		Nights	..	..	..	..	..
1.43	♦ For non commercial accommodation services		Days	..	..	..	..	..
1.44	Average expenditure per day		US$	..	..	..	..	..
3.	**OUTBOUND TOURISM**							
	Data							
	Expenditure							
3.4	Total		US$ Mn	..	..	..	..	..
3.5	♦ Travel		US$ Mn	49	49	50	..	..
3.6	♦ Passenger transport		US$ Mn	..	..	..	..	..
4.	**TOURISM INDUSTRIES**							
	Indicators							
4.16	Occupancy rate / rooms		Percent	57.50	58.30	62.10	..	..
4.17	Occupancy rate / bed-places		Percent	..	..	..	..	..
4.18	Average length of stay		Nights	..	..	..	..	..
4.19	Available capacity (bed-places per 1000 inhabitants)		Units	..	..	..	..	..

ANTIGUA AND BARBUDA

Cod.	Basic data and indicators	Notes	Units	2011	2012	2013	2014	2015
6.	**COMPLEMENTARY INDICATORS**							
	Demand							
6.1	Gross travel propensity		Units	..	..	..	..	..
6.2	(1.2 inbound tourists) / population		Units	2.73	2.77	2.70	2.74	2.72
	Macroeconomic indicators related to international tourism							
6.3	Inbound tourism expenditure over GDP		Percent	27.6	26.5	24.9	..	..
6.4	Outbound tourism expenditure over GDP		Percent	4.3	4.1	4.2	..	..
6.5	Tourism balance (inbound minus outbound tourism expenditure) over GDP		Percent	23.3	22.4	20.7	..	..
6.6	Tourism openness (inbound plus outbound tourism expenditure) over GDP		Percent	31.9	30.6	29.1	..	..
6.7	Tourism coverage (inbound over outbound tourism expenditure)		Percent	636.7	651.0	598.0	..	..
6.8	Inbound tourism expenditure over exports of goods		Percent	555.7	540.3	465.7	..	..
6.9	Inbound tourism expenditure over exports of services		Percent	64.8	66.1	64.3	..	..
6.10	Inbound tourism expenditure over exports of goods and services		Percent	58.0	58.9	56.5	..	..
6.11	Inbound tourism expenditure over current account credits		Percent	52.8	53.2	50.8	..	..
6.12	Outbound tourism expenditure over imports of goods		Percent	11.4	10.1	10.1	..	..
6.13	Outbound tourism expenditure over imports of services		Percent	23.2	24.0	22.8	..	..
6.14	Outbound tourism expenditure over imports of goods and		Percent	7.6	7.1	7.0	..	..
6.15	Outbound tourism expenditure over current account debits		Percent	7.3	6.8	6.7	..	..

ARGENTINA

Cod.	Basic data and indicators	Notes	Units	2011	2012	2013	2014	2015
1.	**INBOUND TOURISM**							
	Data							
	Arrivals	(1)						
1.1	Total		('000)	6,636	6,532	6,711	7,894	7,856
1.2	♦ Overnight visitors (tourists)		('000)	5,705	5,587	5,246	5,931	5,736
1.3	♦ Same-day visitors (excursionists)		('000)	931	945	1,465	1,963	2,120
1.4	* of which, cruise passengers		('000)	..	..	..	..	..
	Arrivals by region	(1)						
1.5	Total		('000)	5,704	5,587	5,246	5,931	5,736
1.6	♦ Africa		('000)	..	..	..	..	..
1.7	♦ Americas		('000)	4,760	4,671	4,353	5,029	4,829
1.8	♦ East Asia and the Pacific		('000)	..	..	..	..	..
1.9	♦ Europe		('000)	739	708	686	700	700
1.10	♦ Middle East		('000)	..	..	..	..	..
1.11	♦ South Asia		('000)	..	..	..	..	..
1.12	♦ Other not classified		('000)	205	208	207	202	208
1.13	* of which, nationals residing abroad		('000)	..	..	..	..	..
	Arrivals by main purpose	(1)						
1.14	Total		('000)	5,705	5,587	5,246	5,931	5,736
1.15	♦ Personal		('000)	4,900	4,791	4,494	5,076	4,869
1.16	* holidays, leisure and recreation		('000)	4,900	4,791	4,494	5,076	4,869
1.17	* other personal purposes		('000)	..	..	..	..	..
1.18	♦ Business and professional		('000)	805	796	752	855	867
	Arrivals by mode of transport	(1)						
1.19	Total		('000)	5,705	5,587	5,246	5,931	5,736
1.20	♦ Air		('000)	2,832	2,709	2,530	2,609	2,426
1.21	♦ Water		('000)	479	475	631	589	587
1.22	♦ Land		('000)	2,394	2,403	2,085	2,733	2,723
1.23	* railway		('000)	..	..	..	..	..
1.24	* road		('000)	2,394	2,403	2,085	2,733	2,723
1.25	* others		('000)	..	..	..	..	..
	Accommodation							
	Total							
1.29	♦ Guests		('000)	..	..	..	..	..
1.30	♦ Overnights		('000)	65,909	65,726	59,487	65,110	64,793
	Hotels and similar establishments							
1.31	♦ Guests	(2)	('000)	4,813	4,311	4,089	4,292	3,825
1.32	♦ Overnights	(2)	('000)	11,170	10,111	9,737	10,299	9,067
	Expenditure							
1.33	Total		US$ Mn	5,981	5,541	4,929	5,235	5,011
1.34	♦ Travel		US$ Mn	5,354	4,890	4,324	4,635	4,400
1.35	♦ Passenger transport		US$ Mn	627	651	605	600	611
	Expenditure by main purpose of the trip							
1.36	Total		US$ Mn	5,354	4,890	4,324	4,635	4,400
1.37	♦ Personal		US$ Mn	4,456	3,968	3,496	3,675	3,446
1.38	♦ Business and professional		US$ Mn	898	922	828	960	955
	Indicators							
1.39	Average size of travel party		Persons	..	..	..	..	..
	Average length of stay							
1.40	Total		Days	11.55	11.76	11.26	10.98	11.30
1.41	♦ For all commercial accommodation services		Nights	..	..	..	..	..
1.42	* of which, "hotels and similar establishments"		Nights	..	..	..	..	..
1.43	♦ For non commercial accommodation services		Days	..	..	..	..	..
1.44	Average expenditure per day		US$	79.1	72.1	70.1	68.5	65.1
2.	**DOMESTIC TOURISM**	(3)						
	Data							
	Trips							
2.1	Total		('000)	..	61,879	63,269	56,032	52,564
2.2	♦ Overnight visitors (tourists)		('000)	..	29,331	30,243	28,924	27,173
2.3	♦ Same-day visitors (excursionists)		('000)	..	32,548	33,026	27,108	25,391
	Trips by main purpose							
2.4	Total		('000)	..	29,331	30,243	28,923	27,172
2.5	♦ Personal		('000)	..	28,157	29,203	28,210	26,579
2.6	* holidays, leisure and recreation		('000)	..	17,789	16,273	15,329	14,594
2.7	* other personal purposes		('000)	..	10,368	12,930	12,881	11,985
2.8	♦ Business and professional		('000)	..	1,174	1,040	713	593

ARGENTINA

Cod.	Basic data and indicators	Notes	Units	2011	2012	2013	2014	2015
	Trips by mode of transport							
2.9	Total		('000)	..	29,331	30,243	28,924	27,200
2.10	♦ Air		('000)	..	958	1,032	1,172	1,386
2.11	♦ Water		('000)	..	..	..	..	..
2.12	♦ Land		('000)	..	28,373	29,211	27,752	25,814
2.13	* railway		('000)	..	..	..	..	..
2.14	* road		('000)	..	27,441	28,693	27,434	25,271
2.15	* others		('000)	..	932	518	318	543
	Trips by form of organization							
2.16	Total		('000)	..	29,331	30,242	28,924	27,200
2.17	♦ Package tour		('000)	..	990	1,040	915	1,061
2.18	♦ Other forms		('000)	..	28,341	29,202	28,009	26,139
	Accommodation							
	Total							
2.19	♦ Guests		('000)	..	..	..	..	..
2.20	♦ Overnights		('000)	..	163,136	170,895	157,278	169,190
	Hotels and similar establishments							
2.21	♦ Guests	(2)	('000)	15,248	15,384	14,993	15,078	15,708
2.22	♦ Overnights	(2)	('000)	35,992	36,611	35,368	36,096	37,569
	Indicators							
2.23	Average size of travel party		Persons	..	..	..	..	..
	Average length of stay							
2.24	Total		Days	..	..	..	..	..
2.25	♦ For all commercial accommodation services		Nights	..	5.60	5.65	5.44	6.23
2.26	* of which, "hotels and similar establishments"		Nights	..	..	..	..	..
2.27	♦ For non commercial accommodation services		Days	..	..	..	..	..
2.28	Average expenditure per day		US$	..	36.2	36.1	34.9	37.8
3.	**OUTBOUND TOURISM**							
	Data							
	Departures	(1)						
3.1	Total		('000)	7,676	8,295	9,844	10,022	13,159
3.2	♦ Overnight visitors (tourists)		('000)	6,686	7,266	6,746	6,517	7,807
3.3	♦ Same-day visitors (excursionists)		('000)	990	1,029	3,098	3,505	5,352
	Expenditure							
3.4	Total		US$ Mn	7,477	8,254	8,058	7,216	8,286
3.5	♦ Travel		US$ Mn	5,542	5,905	5,569	5,362	5,920
3.6	♦ Passenger transport		US$ Mn	1,935	2,349	2,489	1,854	2,366
	Expenditure by main purpose of the trip							
3.7	Total		US$ Mn	5,542	5,905	5,569	5,362	5,920
3.8	♦ Personal		US$ Mn	4,167	4,508	4,341	4,096	4,794
3.9	♦ Business and professional		US$ Mn	1,375	1,397	1,228	1,266	1,126
	Indicators							
3.10	Average length of stay		Days	10.44	10.32	10.36	10.43	10.11
3.11	Average expenditure per day		US$	76.6	76.4	76.3	75.1	71.2
4.	**TOURISM INDUSTRIES**							
	Data							
	Number of establishments							
4.1	Total		Units	19,158	19,374	20,813	21,631	21,661
4.2	♦ Accommodation for visitors		Units	13,398	13,526	14,906	15,591	15,725
4.3	* of which, "hotels and similar establishments"		Units	13,398	13,526	14,906	15,591	15,725
4.4	♦ Food and beverage serving activities		Units	..	..	..	..	..
4.5	♦ Passenger transportation		Units	..	..	..	..	..
4.6	♦ Travel agencies and other reservation services activities		Units	5,760	5,848	5,907	6,040	5,936
4.7	♦ Other tourism industries		Units	..	..	..	..	..
	Accommodation for visitors in hotels and similar establishments							
	Non-monetary data							
4.13	♦ Number of establishments		Units	13,398	13,526	14,906	15,591	15,725
4.14	♦ Number of rooms		Units	233,520	236,641	253,524	258,129	259,582
4.15	♦ Number of bed-places		Units	603,473	611,439	667,580	683,454	687,681
	Indicators							
4.16	Occupancy rate / rooms	(2)	Percent	43.37	41.04	41.55	42.64	42.77
4.17	Occupancy rate / bed-places	(2)	Percent	34.03	32.30	32.34	33.46	33.51
4.18	Average length of stay	(2)	Nights	2.35	2.37	2.36	2.40	2.39
4.19	Available capacity (bed-places per 1000 inhabitants)		Units	14.49	14.53	15.69	15.90	15.84

ARGENTINA

Cod.	Basic data and indicators	Notes	Units	2011	2012	2013	2014	2015
5.	**EMPLOYMENT**	**(4)**						
	Data							
	Number of employees by tourism industries							
5.1	Total		('000)	989.9	1,002.5	1,061.7	1,013.9	..
5.2	♦ Accommodation services for visitors (hotels and similar establishments)		('000)	90.3	95.5	82.5	79.6	..
5.3	♦ Other accommodation services		('000)	..	..	..	..	..
5.4	♦ Food and beverage serving activities		('000)	452.7	461.4	495.1	475.8	..
5.5	♦ Passenger transportation		('000)	210.9	217.6	233.0	217.7	..
5.6	♦ Travel agencies and other reservation services activities		('000)	..	..	..	..	..
5.7	♦ Other tourism industries		('000)	236.0	228.0	251.1	240.8	
	Number of jobs by status in employment							
5.8	Total		('000)	1,045.2	1,064.5	1,131.6	1,079.0	..
5.9	♦ Employees	(5)	('000)	819.2	855.1	862.3	821.5	..
5.10	♦ Self employed	(6)	('000)	226.0	209.4	269.3	257.5	..
6.	**COMPLEMENTARY INDICATORS**							
	Demand							
6.1	Gross travel propensity		Units	..	..	..	..	
6.2	(1.2 inbound tourists + 2.2 domestic tourists) / population		Units	..	0.83	0.83	0.81	0.76
	Macroeconomic indicators related to international tourism							
6.3	Inbound tourism expenditure over GDP		Percent	1.3	1.2	0.8	1.0	..
6.4	Outbound tourism expenditure over GDP		Percent	1.7	1.7	1.3	1.3	..
6.5	Tourism balance (inbound minus outbound tourism expenditure) over GDP		Percent	-0.4	-0.5	-0.5	-0.3	..
6.6	Tourism openness (inbound plus outbound tourism expenditure) over GDP		Percent	3.0	2.9	2.1	2.3	..
6.7	Tourism coverage (inbound over outbound tourism expenditure)		Percent	80.0	67.1	61.2	72.5	60.5
6.8	Inbound tourism expenditure over exports of goods		Percent	7.2	6.9	6.5	7.7	8.8
6.9	Inbound tourism expenditure over exports of services		Percent	39.1	36.9	33.8	38.1	35.9
6.10	Inbound tourism expenditure over exports of goods and services		Percent	6.1	5.8	5.4	6.4	7.1
6.11	Inbound tourism expenditure over current account credits		Percent	5.8	5.6	5.2	6.0	6.7
6.12	Outbound tourism expenditure over imports of goods		Percent	10.6	12.7	11.3	11.6	14.5
6.13	Outbound tourism expenditure over imports of services		Percent	42.8	45.9	44.1	42.9	46.4
6.14	Outbound tourism expenditure over imports of goods and		Percent	8.5	9.9	9.0	9.1	11.0
6.15	Outbound tourism expenditure over current account debits		Percent	7.9	9.4	8.5	8.6	10.4

ARMENIA

Cod.	Basic data and indicators	Notes	Units	2011	2012	2013	2014	2015
1.	**INBOUND TOURISM**							
	Data							
	Arrivals							
1.1	Total		('000)	..	..	..	..	..
1.2	♦ Overnight visitors (tourists)		('000)	758	963	1,084	1,204	1,192
1.3	♦ Same-day visitors (excursionists)		('000)	..	..	..	..	..
1.4	* of which, cruise passengers		('000)	..	..	..	..	..
	Arrivals by region							
1.5	Total		('000)	758	963	1,084	1,204	1,192
1.6	♦ Africa		('000)	1	1	1	1	1
1.7	♦ Americas		('000)	145	129	147	157	89
1.8	♦ East Asia and the Pacific		('000)	29	30	31	28	10
1.9	♦ Europe		('000)	375	606	702	812	922
1.10	♦ Middle East		('000)	49	50	52	56	21
1.11	♦ South Asia		('000)	159	148	151	150	148
1.12	♦ Other not classified		('000)	..	..	..	..	..
1.13	* of which, nationals residing abroad		('000)	..	..	..	..	..
	Arrivals by main purpose							
1.14	Total		('000)	758	963	1,084	1,204	1,192
1.15	♦ Personal		('000)	523	631	672	776	770
1.16	* holidays, leisure and recreation		('000)	437	532	564	577	581
1.17	* other personal purposes		('000)	86	99	108	199	189
1.18	♦ Business and professional		('000)	235	332	412	428	422
	Arrivals by mode of transport							
1.19	Total		('000)	758	963	1,084	1,204	1,192
1.20	♦ Air		('000)	503	564	618	701	693
1.21	♦ Water		('000)	..	..	..	..	..
1.22	♦ Land		('000)	255	399	466	503	499
1.23	* railway		('000)	77	86	92	95	92
1.24	* road		('000)	178	313	374	408	407
1.25	* others		('000)	..	..	..	..	..
	Arrivals by form of organization of the trip							
1.26	Total		('000)	758	963	1,084	1,204	1,192
1.27	♦ Package tour		('000)	261	369	423	441	337
1.28	♦ Other forms		('000)	497	594	661	763	855
	Accommodation							
	Total							
1.29	♦ Guests		('000)	..	..	..	..	..
1.30	♦ Overnights		('000)	7,580	9,632	10,842	11,500	10,073
	Expenditure							
1.33	Total		US$ Mn	762	853	905	994	956
1.34	♦ Travel		US$ Mn	722	817	880	966	936
1.35	♦ Passenger transport		US$ Mn	40	36	25	28	20
	Expenditure by main purpose of the trip							
1.36	Total		US$ Mn	723	817	880	966	936
1.37	♦ Personal		US$ Mn	596	683	756	832	814
1.38	♦ Business and professional		US$ Mn	127	134	124	134	122
	Indicators							
1.39	Average size of travel party		Persons	4.0	4.0	4.0	4.0	4.0
	Average length of stay							
1.40	Total		Days	..	..	..	..	..
1.41	♦ For all commercial accommodation services		Nights	10.00	17.40	17.40	17.40	17.40
1.42	* of which, "hotels and similar establishments"		Nights	..	..	..	..	..
1.43	♦ For non commercial accommodation services		Days	..	..	..	..	..
1.44	Average expenditure per day		US$	..	..	..	..	..
2.	**DOMESTIC TOURISM**							
	Data							
	Trips							
2.1	Total		('000)	..	..	..	..	..
2.2	♦ Overnight visitors (tourists)		('000)	489	515	670	860	871
2.3	♦ Same-day visitors (excursionists)		('000)	..	..	..	..	..
	Trips by main purpose							
2.4	Total		('000)	489	515	670	860	871
2.5	♦ Personal		('000)	375	356	513	670	671
2.6	* holidays, leisure and recreation		('000)	342	284	381	540	570
2.7	* other personal purposes		('000)	33	72	132	130	101
2.8	♦ Business and professional		('000)	114	159	157	190	200

ARMENIA

Cod.	Basic data and indicators	Notes	Units	2011	2012	2013	2014	2015
	Trips by mode of transport							
2.9	Total		('000)	489	515	670	860	871
2.10	♦ Air		('000)	..	..	..	..	..
2.11	♦ Water		('000)	..	..	..	..	..
2.12	♦ Land		('000)	489	515	670	860	871
2.13	* railway		('000)	288	293	263	257	263
2.14	* road		('000)	134	153	339	536	548
2.15	* others		('000)	67	69	68	67	60
	Trips by form of organization							
2.16	Total		('000)	489	515	670	860	871
2.17	♦ Package tour		('000)	183	204	345	461	585
2.18	♦ Other forms		('000)	306	311	325	399	286
	Accommodation							
	Total							
2.19	♦ Guests		('000)	..	..	..	..	..
2.20	♦ Overnights		('000)	5,868	6,180	8,034	10,320	10,462
	Indicators							
2.23	Average size of travel party		Persons	3.0	4.0	4.0	4.0	4.0
	Average length of stay							
2.24	Total		Days	..	..	..	..	..
2.25	♦ For all commercial accommodation services		Nights	12.00	12.00	12.00	12.00	12.00
2.26	* of which, "hotels and similar establishments"		Nights	..	..	..	..	..
2.27	♦ For non commercial accommodation services		Days	..	..	..	..	..
2.28	Average expenditure per day		US$	..	..	..	..	..
3.	**OUTBOUND TOURISM**							
	Data							
	Departures							
3.1	Total		('000)	..	..	..	..	..
3.2	♦ Overnight visitors (tourists)		('000)	715	965	1,083	1,198	1,187
3.3	♦ Same-day visitors (excursionists)		('000)	..	..	..	..	..
	Expenditure							
3.4	Total		US$ Mn	756	874	1,007	1,101	1,057
3.5	♦ Travel		US$ Mn	687	803	930	1,024	996
3.6	♦ Passenger transport		US$ Mn	69	71	77	77	61
	Expenditure by main purpose of the trip							
3.7	Total		US$ Mn	687	803	930	1,024	996
3.8	♦ Personal		US$ Mn	452	547	652	745	763
3.9	♦ Business and professional		US$ Mn	235	256	278	279	233
4.	**TOURISM INDUSTRIES**							
	Data							
	Number of establishments							
4.1	Total		Units	3,925	4,003	4,081	4,168	4,244
4.2	♦ Accommodation for visitors		Units	1,506	1,538	1,563	1,592	1,629
4.3	* of which, "hotels and similar establishments"		Units	1,375	1,405	1,430	1,459	1,496
4.4	♦ Food and beverage serving activities		Units	2,147	2,179	2,223	2,267	2,300
4.5	♦ Passenger transportation		Units	..	..	..	..	..
4.6	♦ Travel agencies and other reservation services activities		Units	272	286	295	309	315
4.7	♦ Other tourism industries		Units	..	..	..	..	..
	Accommodation for visitors in hotels and similar establishments							
	Non-monetary data							
4.13	♦ Number of establishments		Units	1,375	1,405	1,430	1,459	1,496
4.14	♦ Number of rooms		Units	..	13,438	13,902	14,377	14,500
4.15	♦ Number of bed-places		Units	28,869	30,379	31,780	33,274	33,385
	Indicators							
4.16	Occupancy rate / rooms		Percent	..	..	..	..	..
4.17	Occupancy rate / bed-places		Percent	81.00	83.00	87.00	88.00	89.00
4.18	Average length of stay		Nights	10.00	10.00	10.00	10.00	11.00
4.19	Available capacity (bed-places per 1000 inhabitants)		Units	9.73	10.20	10.62	11.07	11.06

ARMENIA

Cod.	Basic data and indicators	Notes	Units	2011	2012	2013	2014	2015
	Travel agencies and other reservation service activities							
	Non-monetary data							
	♦ Domestic trips							
4.25	* with package tour		Percent	..	..	51.6	53.6	..
4.26	* without package tour		Percent	..	..	48.4	46.4	..
	♦ Inbound trips							
4.27	* with package tour		Percent	..	..	39.0	36.6	..
4.28	* without package tour		Percent	..	..	61.0	63.4	..
	♦ Outbound trips							
4.29	* with package tour		Percent	..	..	0.9	0.9	..
4.30	* without package tour		Percent	..	..	99.1	99.1	..
6.	**COMPLEMENTARY INDICATORS**							
	Demand							
6.1	Gross travel propensity		Units	..	..	..	..	..
6.2	(1.2 inbound tourists + 2.2 domestic tourists) / population		Units	0.42	0.50	0.59	0.69	0.68
	Macroeconomic indicators related to international tourism							
6.3	Inbound tourism expenditure over GDP		Percent	7.5	8.6	8.1	8.6	9.1
6.4	Outbound tourism expenditure over GDP		Percent	7.5	8.8	9.1	9.5	10.0
6.5	Tourism balance (inbound minus outbound tourism expenditure) over GDP		Percent		-0.2	-1.0	-0.9	-0.9
6.6	Tourism openness (inbound plus outbound tourism expenditure) over GDP		Percent	15.0	17.4	17.2	18.1	19.1
6.7	Tourism coverage (inbound over outbound tourism expenditure)		Percent	100.8	97.6	89.9	90.3	90.4
6.8	Inbound tourism expenditure over exports of goods		Percent	53.2	56.3	55.3	58.5	58.9
6.9	Inbound tourism expenditure over exports of services		Percent	58.1	60.8	59.5	61.3	63.2
6.10	Inbound tourism expenditure over exports of goods and services		Percent	27.8	29.2	28.7	29.9	30.5
6.11	Inbound tourism expenditure over current account credits		Percent	15.9	17.0	16.4	17.8	19.4
6.12	Outbound tourism expenditure over imports of goods		Percent	21.3	24.1	26.3	29.3	37.6
6.13	Outbound tourism expenditure over imports of services		Percent	54.9	58.1	61.2	63.5	65.8
6.14	Outbound tourism expenditure over imports of goods and		Percent	15.4	17.0	18.4	20.1	23.9
6.15	Outbound tourism expenditure over current account debits		Percent	12.1	13.4	14.3	15.7	18.7

ARUBA

Cod. Basic data and indicators	Notes	Units	2011	2012	2013	2014	2015
1. INBOUND TOURISM							
Data							
Arrivals							
1.1 Total		('000)	1,469	1,481	1,667	1,739	1,832
1.2 ♦ Overnight visitors (tourists)	(1)	('000)	869	904	979	1,072	1,225
1.3 ♦ Same-day visitors (excursionists)		('000)	600	577	688	667	607
1.4 * of which, cruise passengers		('000)	600	577	688	667	607
Arrivals by region	(1)						
1.5 Total		('000)	869	904	979	1,072	1,225
1.6 ♦ Africa		('000)	..	..	..	..	..
1.7 ♦ Americas		('000)	785	820	898	988	1,133
1.8 ♦ East Asia and the Pacific		('000)	..	..	..	..	..
1.9 ♦ Europe		('000)	81	80	77	80	81
1.10 ♦ Middle East		('000)	..	..	..	..	..
1.11 ♦ South Asia		('000)	..	..	..	..	..
1.12 ♦ Other not classified		('000)	3	4	4	4	11
1.13 * of which, nationals residing abroad		('000)	..	..	..	..	..
Arrivals by main purpose	(1)						
1.14 Total		('000)	869	904	979	1,072	1,225
1.15 ♦ Personal		('000)	816	856	924	1,015	1,162
1.16 * holidays, leisure and recreation		('000)	638	643	775	816	944
1.17 * other personal purposes		('000)	178	213	149	199	218
1.18 ♦ Business and professional		('000)	53	48	55	57	63
Arrivals by mode of transport							
1.19 Total		('000)	1,469	1,481	1,667	1,739	1,832
1.20 ♦ Air		('000)	869	904	979	1,072	1,225
1.21 ♦ Water	(2)	('000)	600	577	688	667	607
1.22 ♦ Land		('000)	..	..	..	..	..
1.23 * railway		('000)	..	..	..	..	..
1.24 * road		('000)	..	..	..	..	..
1.25 * others		('000)	..	..	..	..	..
Accommodation							
Total							
1.29 ♦ Guests	(1)	('000)	869	904	979	1,072	1,225
1.30 ♦ Overnights		('000)	6,686	6,907	7,127	7,693	8,330
Hotels and similar establishments							
1.31 ♦ Guests	(1)	('000)	736	764	797	815	816
1.32 ♦ Overnights		('000)	5,255	5,433	5,504	5,614	5,670
Expenditure							
1.33 Total		US$ Mn	1,358	1,412	1,506	1,625	1,660
1.34 ♦ Travel		US$ Mn	1,351	1,402	1,495	1,605	1,652
1.35 ♦ Passenger transport		US$ Mn	7	10	11	20	8
Indicators							
1.39 Average size of travel party		Persons	..	..	..	..	..
Average length of stay							
1.40 Total		Days	7.69	7.64	7.28	7.18	6.80
1.41 ♦ For all commercial accommodation services		Nights	..	..	..	..	..
1.42 * of which, "hotels and similar establishments"		Nights	7.14	7.11	6.91	6.89	6.95
1.43 ♦ For non commercial accommodation services		Days	10.73	10.54	8.92	8.09	6.50
1.44 Average expenditure per day		US$	88.6	..	..	..	..
3. OUTBOUND TOURISM							
Data							
Expenditure							
3.4 Total		US$ Mn	287	294	342	349	358
3.5 ♦ Travel		US$ Mn	269	275	320	329	345
3.6 ♦ Passenger transport		US$ Mn	18	19	22	20	13
4. TOURISM INDUSTRIES							
Data							
Accommodation for visitors in hotels and similar establishments							
Non-monetary data							
4.13 ♦ Number of establishments		Units	..	..	..	..	..
4.14 ♦ Number of rooms		Units	9,984	9,984	9,402	11,075	11,075
4.15 ♦ Number of bed-places		Units	19,964	19,964	18,804	22,150	22,150

22

ARUBA

Cod.	Basic data and indicators	Notes	Units	2011	2012	2013	2014	2015
	Indicators							
4.16	Occupancy rate / rooms		Percent	77.70	78.80	73.20	..	..
4.17	Occupancy rate / bed-places		Percent	..	..	..	..	..
4.18	Average length of stay		Nights	..	..	..	..	..
4.19	Available capacity (bed-places per 1000 inhabitants)		Units	195.85	194.97	182.70	214.13	213.21
6.	**COMPLEMENTARY INDICATORS**							
	Demand							
6.1	Gross travel propensity		Units	..	..	..	..	..
6.2	(1.2 inbound tourists) / population		Units	8.52	8.83	9.51	10.36	11.79
	Macroeconomic indicators related to international tourism							
6.3	Inbound tourism expenditure over GDP		Percent	53.3	55.7	58.2	61.0	..
6.4	Outbound tourism expenditure over GDP		Percent	11.3	11.6	13.2	13.1	..
6.5	Tourism balance (inbound minus outbound tourism expenditure) over GDP		Percent	42.0	44.1	45.0	47.9	..
6.6	Tourism openness (inbound plus outbound tourism expenditure) over GDP		Percent	64.6	67.3	71.4	74.1	..
6.7	Tourism coverage (inbound over outbound tourism expenditure)		Percent	473.2	480.3	440.4	465.6	463.7
6.8	Inbound tourism expenditure over exports of goods		Percent	26.2	101.7	539.7	627.4	496.9
6.9	Inbound tourism expenditure over exports of services		Percent	80.8	80.1	80.0	79.7	79.5
6.10	Inbound tourism expenditure over exports of goods and services		Percent	19.8	44.8	69.7	70.7	68.6
6.11	Inbound tourism expenditure over current account credits		Percent	19.5	43.2	65.4	66.7	64.7
6.12	Outbound tourism expenditure over imports of goods		Percent	4.9	14.4	24.8	25.8	28.6
6.13	Outbound tourism expenditure over imports of services		Percent	34.0	35.7	38.3	38.3	40.7
6.14	Outbound tourism expenditure over imports of goods and		Percent	4.2	10.2	15.1	15.4	16.8
6.15	Outbound tourism expenditure over current account debits		Percent	4.1	9.6	13.9	14.1	15.3

AUSTRALIA

Cod.	Basic data and indicators	Notes	Units	2011	2012	2013	2014	2015
1.	**INBOUND TOURISM**							
	Data							
	Arrivals							
1.1	Total	(1)	('000)	5,771	6,032	6,382	6,868	7,444
1.2	♦ Overnight visitors (tourists)		('000)	..	..	..	..	..
1.3	♦ Same-day visitors (excursionists)		('000)	..	..	..	..	..
1.4	* of which, cruise passengers		('000)	..	..	..	..	..
	Arrivals by region	(1)						
1.5	Total		('000)	5,771	6,032	6,382	6,868	7,444
1.6	♦ Africa		('000)	89	82	80	82	85
1.7	♦ Americas		('000)	645	683	726	795	862
1.8	♦ East Asia and the Pacific		('000)	3,447	3,650	3,848	4,179	4,574
1.9	♦ Europe		('000)	1,336	1,346	1,434	1,476	1,519
1.10	♦ Middle East		('000)	62	63	71	77	81
1.11	♦ South Asia		('000)	192	209	223	259	309
1.12	♦ Other not classified		('000)	..	..	..	..	16
1.13	* of which, nationals residing abroad		('000)	..	..	..	..	..
	Arrivals by main purpose	(1)						
1.14	Total		('000)	5,771	6,032	6,383	6,868	7,444
1.15	♦ Personal		('000)	4,351	4,589	4,955	5,375	5,853
1.16	* holidays, leisure and recreation		('000)	2,576	2,709	2,930	3,171	3,484
1.17	* other personal purposes		('000)	1,775	1,880	2,025	2,204	2,369
1.18	♦ Business and professional		('000)	1,420	1,443	1,428	1,493	1,591
	Arrivals by mode of transport	(1)						
1.19	Total		('000)	5,771	6,033	6,382	6,868	7,444
1.20	♦ Air		('000)	5,760	6,017	6,352	6,813	7,391
1.21	♦ Water		('000)	11	16	30	55	53
1.22	♦ Land		('000)	..	..	..	..	..
1.23	* railway		('000)	..	..	..	..	..
1.24	* road		('000)	..	..	..	..	..
1.25	* others		('000)	..	..	..	..	..
	Expenditure							
1.33	Total		US$ Mn	34,315	34,537	33,576	34,115	31,409
1.34	♦ Travel		US$ Mn	31,582	31,962	31,310	31,948	29,430
1.35	♦ Passenger transport		US$ Mn	2,733	2,575	2,266	2,167	1,979
	Expenditure by main purpose of the trip							
1.36	Total		US$ Mn	31,582	31,962	31,310	31,948	29,430
1.37	♦ Personal		US$ Mn	27,699	27,649	27,238	28,158	26,113
1.38	♦ Business and professional		US$ Mn	3,883	4,313	4,072	3,790	3,317
2.	**DOMESTIC TOURISM**	(2)						
	Data							
	Trips							
2.1	Total		('000)	226,196	248,377	240,118	245,797	266,645
2.2	♦ Overnight visitors (tourists)		('000)	69,773	74,472	75,796	81,436	87,054
2.3	♦ Same-day visitors (excursionists)		('000)	156,423	173,905	164,322	164,361	179,591
	Trips by main purpose							
2.4	Total		('000)	69,773	74,472	75,796	81,436	88,866
2.5	♦ Personal		('000)	56,034	60,506	61,817	65,106	70,463
2.6	* holidays, leisure and recreation		('000)	30,000	31,284	32,986	32,750	34,899
2.7	* other personal purposes		('000)	26,034	29,222	28,831	32,356	35,564
2.8	♦ Business and professional		('000)	13,739	13,966	13,979	16,330	18,403
	Accommodation							
	Total							
2.19	♦ Guests		('000)	..	..	..	..	..
2.20	♦ Overnights		('000)	263,242	281,733	282,680	308,908	321,968
3.	**OUTBOUND TOURISM**							
	Data							
	Departures							
3.1	Total		('000)	..	..	..	..	..
3.2	♦ Overnight visitors (tourists)		('000)	7,788	8,212	8,768	9,114	9,459
3.3	♦ Same-day visitors (excursionists)		('000)	..	..	..	..	..
	Expenditure							
3.4	Total		US$ Mn	33,967	35,226	35,198	31,959	28,312
3.5	♦ Travel		US$ Mn	27,371	28,078	28,576	26,416	23,445
3.6	♦ Passenger transport		US$ Mn	6,596	7,148	6,622	5,543	4,867
	Expenditure by main purpose of the trip							
3.7	Total		US$ Mn	27,371	28,078	28,576	26,416	23,445
3.8	♦ Personal		US$ Mn	24,256	24,481	25,097	23,336	20,853
3.9	♦ Business and professional		US$ Mn	3,115	3,597	3,479	3,080	2,592

AUSTRALIA

Cod.	Basic data and indicators	Notes	Units	2011	2012	2013	2014	2015
4.	**TOURISM INDUSTRIES**							
	Data							
	Number of establishments							
4.1	Total		Units	..	..	..	..	..
4.2	♦ Accommodation for visitors		Units	..	..	..	..	..
4.3	* of which, "hotels and similar establishments"	(3)	Units	4,216	4,246	4,237	4,204	4,464
4.4	♦ Food and beverage serving activities		Units	..	..	..	..	..
4.5	♦ Passenger transportation		Units	..	..	..	..	..
4.6	♦ Travel agencies and other reservation services activities		Units	..	..	..	..	..
4.7	♦ Other tourism industries		Units	..	..	..	..	..
	Accommodation for visitors in hotels and similar establishments							
	Non-monetary data	(3)						
4.13	♦ Number of establishments		Units	4,216	4,246	4,237	4,204	4,464
4.14	♦ Number of rooms		Units	226,557	228,006	229,525	238,588	248,554
4.15	♦ Number of bed-places		Units	636,002	632,429	634,647	655,653	678,018
	Indicators	(3)						
4.16	Occupancy rate / rooms		Percent	67.30	67.00	62.00	61.50	62.40
4.17	Occupancy rate / bed-places		Percent	41.80	42.30	37.70	37.60	38.60
4.18	Average length of stay		Nights	2.30	2.30	2.20	..	..
4.19	Available capacity (bed-places per 1000 inhabitants)		Units	28.21	27.60	27.27	27.76	28.29
5.	**EMPLOYMENT**							
	Data							
	Number of employees by tourism industries	(4)						
5.1	Total		('000)	526.2	528.9	539.6	534.0	580.7
5.2	♦ Accommodation services for visitors (hotels and similar establishments)		('000)	72.2	69.0	70.9	69.7	87.5
5.3	♦ Other accommodation services		('000)	..	..	..	..	..
5.4	♦ Food and beverage serving activities		('000)	173.8	173.4	180.9	175.5	189.0
5.5	♦ Passenger transportation		('000)	56.4	60.0	58.3	..	61.7
5.6	♦ Travel agencies and other reservation services activities		('000)	31.2	32.9	31.9	32.2	42.9
5.7	♦ Other tourism industries		('000)	192.6	193.6	197.6	256.6	199.6
6.	**COMPLEMENTARY INDICATORS**							
	Demand							
6.1	Gross travel propensity		Units	..	..	..	..	..
6.2	(1.1 inbound visitors + 2.1 domestic visitors) / population		Units	10.29	11.10	10.59	10.70	11.44
	Macroeconomic indicators related to international tourism							
6.3	Inbound tourism expenditure over GDP		Percent	2.3	2.2	2.2	2.4	2.6
6.4	Outbound tourism expenditure over GDP		Percent	2.3	2.3	2.4	2.2	2.3
6.5	Tourism balance (inbound minus outbound tourism expenditure) over GDP		Percent		-0.1	-0.2	0.2	0.3
6.6	Tourism openness (inbound plus outbound tourism expenditure) over GDP		Percent	4.6	4.5	4.6	4.6	4.9
6.7	Tourism coverage (inbound over outbound tourism expenditure)		Percent	101.0	98.0	95.4	106.7	110.9
6.8	Inbound tourism expenditure over exports of goods		Percent	12.6	13.4	13.2	14.2	16.7
6.9	Inbound tourism expenditure over exports of services		Percent	65.7	64.0	62.7	62.9	63.2
6.10	Inbound tourism expenditure over exports of goods and services		Percent	10.6	11.1	10.9	11.6	13.2
6.11	Inbound tourism expenditure over current account credits		Percent	9.0	9.4	9.3	9.8	11.1
6.12	Outbound tourism expenditure over imports of goods		Percent	13.6	13.1	14.1	13.3	13.6
6.13	Outbound tourism expenditure over imports of services		Percent	54.4	52.8	51.8	50.3	49.4
6.14	Outbound tourism expenditure over imports of goods and		Percent	10.9	10.5	11.1	10.5	10.7
6.15	Outbound tourism expenditure over current account debits		Percent	9.2	9.0	9.4	8.9	9.1

AUSTRIA

Cod.	Basic data and indicators	Notes	Units	2011	2012	2013	2014	2015
1.	**INBOUND TOURISM**							
	Data							
	Arrivals							
1.1	Total		('000)	..	..	..	..	..
1.2	♦ Overnight visitors (tourists)	(1)(2)	('000)	23,012	24,151	24,813	25,291	26,719
1.3	♦ Same-day visitors (excursionists)		('000)	..	..	..	..	..
1.4	* of which, cruise passengers		('000)	..	..	..	..	..
	Arrivals by region	(1)(2)						
1.5	Total		('000)	23,012	24,151	24,813	25,291	26,719
1.6	♦ Africa		('000)	52	58	61	63	72
1.7	♦ Americas		('000)	743	806	860	919	1,020
1.8	♦ East Asia and the Pacific		('000)	915	1,105	1,227	1,381	1,740
1.9	♦ Europe		('000)	20,819	21,599	22,043	22,242	23,042
1.10	♦ Middle East		('000)	160	218	268	303	419
1.11	♦ South Asia		('000)	84	89	88	84	118
1.12	♦ Other not classified		('000)	239	276	265	300	307
1.13	* of which, nationals residing abroad		('000)	..	..	..	..	..
	Accommodation							
	Total							
1.29	♦ Guests	(2)	('000)	23,012	24,151	24,813	25,291	26,719
1.30	♦ Overnights	(2)	('000)	90,706	95,052	96,874	96,233	98,778
	Hotels and similar establishments							
1.31	♦ Guests	(3)	('000)	16,972	17,728	18,164	18,588	19,627
1.32	♦ Overnights	(3)	('000)	59,147	61,360	62,137	61,830	63,327
	Expenditure							
1.33	Total		US$ Mn	..	..	..	..	..
1.34	♦ Travel		US$ Mn	19,778	18,937	20,220	20,907	18,357
1.35	♦ Passenger transport		US$ Mn	..	..	..	..	..
	Expenditure by main purpose of the trip							
1.36	Total		US$ Mn	..	..	20,220	20,907	18,357
1.37	♦ Personal		US$ Mn	..	..	17,163	17,857	15,792
1.38	♦ Business and professional		US$ Mn	..	..	3,057	3,050	2,565
	Indicators							
1.39	Average size of travel party		Persons	..	..	..	..	..
	Average length of stay							
1.40	Total		Days	..	..	..	..	..
1.41	♦ For all commercial accommodation services		Nights	3.94	3.94	3.90	3.81	3.70
1.42	* of which, "hotels and similar establishments"		Nights	3.74	3.46	3.42	3.33	3.23
1.43	♦ For non commercial accommodation services		Days	..	..	..	..	..
1.44	Average expenditure per day		US$	..	..	..	..	..
2.	**DOMESTIC TOURISM**							
	Data							
	Trips							
2.1	Total		('000)	..	..	..	..	..
2.2	♦ Overnight visitors (tourists)	(4)	('000)	10,185	10,962	11,730	11,476	11,088
2.3	♦ Same-day visitors (excursionists)		('000)	..	..	..	..	..
	Trips by main purpose	(4)						
2.4	Total		('000)	10,185	10,962	11,730	11,476	11,088
2.5	♦ Personal		('000)	8,239	9,015	9,682	9,573	9,198
2.6	* holidays, leisure and recreation		('000)	..	..	..	..	..
2.7	* other personal purposes		('000)	..	..	..	..	..
2.8	♦ Business and professional		('000)	1,946	1,947	2,048	1,903	1,890
	Trips by mode of transport	(4)						
2.9	Total		('000)	10,186	10,962	11,730	11,476	11,088
2.10	♦ Air		('000)	28	68	39	50	12
2.11	♦ Water		('000)	2	..	2	11	..
2.12	♦ Land		('000)	10,156	10,894	11,689	11,415	11,076
2.13	* railway		('000)	1,494	1,738	1,889	1,828	1,683
2.14	* road		('000)	8,575	9,032	9,657	9,406	9,180
2.15	* others		('000)	87	124	143	181	213
	Trips by form of organization	(4)						
2.16	Total		('000)	10,185	10,962	11,730	11,476	11,088
2.17	♦ Package tour		('000)	1,296	1,568	2,070	1,087	2,111
2.18	♦ Other forms		('000)	8,889	9,394	9,660	10,389	8,977

AUSTRIA

Cod.	Basic data and indicators	Notes	Units	2011	2012	2013	2014	2015
	Accommodation							
	Total							
2.19	♦ Guests	(2)	('000)	11,617	12,013	12,034	12,265	12,696
2.20	♦ Overnights	(2)	('000)	35,297	35,964	35,755	35,668	36,423
	Hotels and similar establishments							
2.21	♦ Guests	(3)	('000)	8,966	9,310	9,366	9,574	9,861
2.22	♦ Overnights	(3)	('000)	23,180	23,762	23,635	23,482	23,939
	Indicators							
2.23	Average size of travel party		Persons	..	..	..	..	..
	Average length of stay							
2.24	Total		Days	..	..	..	..	..
2.25	♦ For all commercial accommodation services		Nights	3.04	2.99	2.97	2.91	2.89
2.26	* of which, "hotels and similar establishments"		Nights	2.64	2.55	2.52	2.46	2.43
2.27	♦ For non commercial accommodation services		Days	..	..	..	..	..
2.28	Average expenditure per day		US$	..	..	..	..	..
3.	**OUTBOUND TOURISM**							
	Data							
	Departures							
3.1	Total		('000)	..	..	..	..	..
3.2	♦ Overnight visitors (tourists)	(4)	('000)	9,874	10,960	10,671	10,994	10,628
3.3	♦ Same-day visitors (excursionists)		('000)	..	..	..	..	..
	Expenditure							
3.4	Total		US$ Mn	..	..	..	..	..
3.5	♦ Travel		US$ Mn	10,550	9,992	10,254	10,849	9,012
3.6	♦ Passenger transport		US$ Mn	..	..	..	..	..
	Expenditure by main purpose of the trip							
3.7	Total		US$ Mn	..	..	10,254	10,849	9,012
3.8	♦ Personal		US$ Mn	..	..	8,412	8,909	7,380
3.9	♦ Business and professional		US$ Mn	..	..	1,842	1,940	1,632
4.	**TOURISM INDUSTRIES**							
	Data							
	Number of establishments							
4.1	Total		Units	..	..	..	..	..
4.2	♦ Accommodation for visitors		Units	20,323	20,366	20,334	20,322	20,315
4.3	* of which, "hotels and similar establishments"	(3)	Units	13,359	13,203	13,073	12,839	12,625
4.4	♦ Food and beverage serving activities		Units	..	..	..	..	..
4.5	♦ Passenger transportation		Units	..	..	..	..	..
4.6	♦ Travel agencies and other reservation services activities		Units	..	..	..	..	..
4.7	♦ Other tourism industries		Units	..	..	..	..	..
	Accommodation for visitors in hotels and similar establishments							
	Monetary data							
4.8	♦ Output		US$ Mn	16,195.2	15,682.1	16,873.3	17,418.8	15,130.8
4.9	♦ Intermediate consumption		US$ Mn	5,065.1	5,023.8	5,507.5	5,670.1	4,831.6
4.10	♦ Gross value added		US$ Mn	11,130.1	10,658.3	11,366.0	11,748.6	10,299.1
4.11	♦ Compensation of employees		US$ Mn	..	..	..	..	..
4.12	♦ Gross fixed capital formation		US$ Mn	..	..	..	..	..
	Non-monetary data	(3)						
4.13	♦ Number of establishments		Units	13,359	13,203	13,073	12,839	12,625
4.14	♦ Number of rooms		Units	290,509	292,165	293,702	291,753	291,974
4.15	♦ Number of bed-places		Units	594,357	594,841	601,483	598,742	600,342
	Indicators							
4.16	Occupancy rate / rooms		Percent	..	..	..	..	..
4.17	Occupancy rate / bed-places	(5)	Percent	31.00	31.60	31.90	31.50	32.25
4.18	Average length of stay		Nights	3.64	3.62	3.60	3.52	3.43
4.19	Available capacity (bed-places per 1000 inhabitants)		Units	70.56	70.35	70.87	70.30	70.26
	Travel agencies and other reservation service activities							
	Monetary data	(6)						
4.20	♦ Output		US$ Mn	3,240.3	3,244.1	3,367.9	3,316.4	2,755.1
4.21	♦ Intermediate consumption		US$ Mn	2,451.2	2,503.6	2,628.9	2,578.2	2,134.4
4.22	♦ Gross value added		US$ Mn	789.0	740.5	739.2	738.2	620.7
4.23	♦ Compensation of employees		US$ Mn	..	..	..	..	..
4.24	♦ Gross fixed capital formation		US$ Mn	..	..	..	..	..

AUSTRIA

Cod.	Basic data and indicators	Notes	Units	2011	2012	2013	2014	2015
	Non-monetary data							
	♦ Domestic trips	(4)						
4.25	* with package tour		Percent	12.7	14.3	17.6	9.5	12.3
4.26	* without package tour		Percent	87.3	85.7	82.4	90.5	87.7
	♦ Inbound trips							
4.27	* with package tour		Percent	..	..	..	..	..
4.28	* without package tour		Percent	..	..	..	..	..
	♦ Outbound trips	(4)						
4.29	* with package tour		Percent	44.0	44.3	39.9	42.9	41.7
4.30	* without package tour		Percent	56.0	55.7	60.1	57.1	54.1
5.	**EMPLOYMENT**	(6)						
	Data							
	Number of employees by tourism industries	(7)						
5.1	Total		('000)	254.0	262.0	270.5	..	..
5.2	♦ Accommodation services for visitors (hotels and similar establishments)		('000)	58.4	61.6	63.8	..	..
5.3	♦ Other accommodation services		('000)	..	..	..	..	..
5.4	♦ Food and beverage serving activities		('000)	88.3	95.3	99.1	..	..
5.5	♦ Passenger transportation		('000)	54.7	53.4	54.1	..	..
5.6	♦ Travel agencies and other reservation services activities		('000)	30.6	31.6	32.8	..	..
5.7	♦ Other tourism industries		('000)	22.0	20.1	20.7	..	..
	Indicators							
	Number of full-time equivalent jobs by status in employment							
5.11	Total		('000)	254.0	262.0	..	..	..
5.12	♦ Employees		('000)	216.0	223.8	..	..	..
5.13	* male		('000)	113.0	115.9	..	..	..
5.14	* female		('000)	103.0	107.9	..	..	..
5.15	♦ Self employed		('000)	38.0	38.2	..	..	..
5.16	* male		('000)	21.0	21.0	..	..	..
5.17	* female		('000)	17.0	17.2	..	..	..
6.	**COMPLEMENTARY INDICATORS**							
	Demand							
6.1	Gross travel propensity	(4)	Units	2.8	3.1	3.1	3.1	3.0
6.2	(1.2 inbound tourists + 2.2 domestic tourists) / population		Units	3.94	4.15	4.31	4.32	4.42
	Macroeconomic indicators related to international tourism							
6.3	Inbound tourism expenditure over GDP		Percent	4.6	4.7	4.7	4.8	4.9
6.4	Outbound tourism expenditure over GDP		Percent	2.5	2.5	2.4	2.5	2.4
6.5	Tourism balance (inbound minus outbound tourism expenditure) over GDP		Percent	2.1	2.2	2.3	2.3	2.5
6.6	Tourism openness (inbound plus outbound tourism expenditure) over GDP		Percent	7.1	7.2	7.1	7.3	7.3
6.7	Tourism coverage (inbound over outbound tourism expenditure)		Percent	187.5	189.5	197.2	192.7	203.7
6.8	Inbound tourism expenditure over exports of goods		Percent	11.6	11.8	12.3	12.6	12.8
6.9	Inbound tourism expenditure over exports of services		Percent	33.4	32.7	31.3	31.1	31.4
6.10	Inbound tourism expenditure over exports of goods and services		Percent	8.6	8.7	8.8	9.0	9.1
6.11	Inbound tourism expenditure over current account credits		Percent	7.0	7.2	7.8	7.6	7.8
6.12	Outbound tourism expenditure over imports of goods		Percent	6.0	6.1	6.2	6.6	6.4
6.13	Outbound tourism expenditure over imports of services		Percent	23.7	22.6	20.1	20.3	19.8
6.14	Outbound tourism expenditure over imports of goods and		Percent	4.8	4.8	4.7	5.0	4.9
6.15	Outbound tourism expenditure over current account debits		Percent	3.8	3.9	4.0	4.1	4.0

AZERBAIJAN

Cod.	Basic data and indicators	Notes	Units	2011	2012	2013	2014	2015
1.	**INBOUND TOURISM**							
	Data							
	Arrivals							
1.1	Total		('000)	2,239	2,484	2,509	2,298	2,006
1.2	♦ Overnight visitors (tourists)		('000)	1,562	1,986	2,130	2,160	1,922
1.3	♦ Same-day visitors (excursionists)		('000)	677	498	379	138	84
1.4	* of which, cruise passengers		('000)	..	..	..	..	..
	Arrivals by region							
1.5	Total		('000)	2,239	2,484	2,509	2,298	2,006
1.6	♦ Africa		('000)	2	2	3	3	2
1.7	♦ Americas		('000)	16	19	21	20	18
1.8	♦ East Asia and the Pacific		('000)	15	16	20	20	20
1.9	♦ Europe		('000)	1,787	2,148	2,306	2,109	1,795
1.10	♦ Middle East		('000)	4	5	6	5	9
1.11	♦ South Asia		('000)	414	293	152	140	160
1.12	♦ Other not classified		('000)	1	2	2	2	2
1.13	* of which, nationals residing abroad		('000)	..	..	..	..	..
	Arrivals by main purpose							
1.14	Total		('000)	2,239	2,484	2,509	2,298	2,006
1.15	♦ Personal		('000)	1,647	1,889	1,860	1,627	1,374
1.16	* holidays, leisure and recreation		('000)	551	727	747	752	700
1.17	* other personal purposes		('000)	1,096	1,162	1,113	875	674
1.18	♦ Business and professional		('000)	592	595	649	670	632
	Arrivals by mode of transport							
1.19	Total		('000)	2,239	2,484	2,509	2,298	2,006
1.20	♦ Air		('000)	795	946	994	1,089	969
1.21	♦ Water		('000)	20	21	27	16	32
1.22	♦ Land		('000)	1,424	1,517	1,489	1,193	1,005
1.23	* railway		('000)	373	405	379	293	231
1.24	* road		('000)	1,051	1,112	1,110	899	775
1.25	* others		('000)	..	..	..	..	..
	Accommodation							
	Hotels and similar establishments							
1.31	♦ Guests		('000)	258	327	395	393	496
1.32	♦ Overnights		('000)	674	803	822	803	959
	Expenditure							
1.33	Total		US$ Mn	1,500	2,634	2,618	2,713	2,535
1.34	♦ Travel		US$ Mn	1,287	2,433	2,365	2,432	2,309
1.35	♦ Passenger transport		US$ Mn	213	201	253	281	226
	Expenditure by main purpose of the trip							
1.36	Total		US$ Mn	1,288	2,433	2,365	2,432	2,309
1.37	♦ Personal		US$ Mn	823	1,472	1,500	1,744	1,753
1.38	♦ Business and professional		US$ Mn	465	961	865	688	556
	Indicators							
1.39	Average size of travel party		Persons	..	..	..	..	..
	Average length of stay							
1.40	Total		Days	..	..	..	..	..
1.41	♦ For all commercial accommodation services		Nights	2.60	2.20	2.10	2.00	2.00
1.42	* of which, "hotels and similar establishments"		Nights	..	..	..	..	..
1.43	♦ For non commercial accommodation services		Days	..	..	..	..	..
1.44	Average expenditure per day		US$	..	..	..	..	..
2.	**DOMESTIC TOURISM**							
	Data							
	Accommodation							
	Hotels and similar establishments							
2.21	♦ Guests		('000)	252	253	271	280	342
2.22	♦ Overnights		('000)	831	838	853	885	685
	Indicators							
2.23	Average size of travel party		Persons	..	..	..	..	..
	Average length of stay							
2.24	Total		Days	..	..	..	..	..
2.25	♦ For all commercial accommodation services		Nights	3.50	3.30	3.20	3.20	2.00
2.26	* of which, "hotels and similar establishments"		Nights	..	..	..	..	..
2.27	♦ For non commercial accommodation services		Days	..	..	..	..	..
2.28	Average expenditure per day		US$	..	..	..	..	..

AZERBAIJAN

Cod.	Basic data and indicators	Notes	Units	2011	2012	2013	2014	2015
3.	**OUTBOUND TOURISM**							
	Data							
	Departures							
3.1	Total		('000)	3,550	3,874	4,285	4,244	4,096
3.2	♦ Overnight visitors (tourists)		('000)	2,308	2,829	3,307	3,319	..
3.3	♦ Same-day visitors (excursionists)		('000)	1,242	1,045	978	925	..
	Expenditure							
3.4	Total		US$ Mn	1,778	2,617	3,032	3,163	2,743
3.5	♦ Travel		US$ Mn	1,689	2,477	2,877	3,008	2,603
3.6	♦ Passenger transport		US$ Mn	89	140	155	155	140
	Expenditure by main purpose of the trip							
3.7	Total		US$ Mn	1,689	2,477	2,877	3,008	2,603
3.8	♦ Personal		US$ Mn	1,053	1,564	1,793	2,028	1,855
3.9	♦ Business and professional		US$ Mn	636	913	1,084	980	748
4.	**TOURISM INDUSTRIES**							
	Data							
	Number of establishments							
4.1	Total		Units	724	684	727	753	779
4.2	♦ Accommodation for visitors		Units	583	..	..	..	..
4.3	* of which, "hotels and similar establishments"		Units	508	514	530	535	536
4.4	♦ Food and beverage serving activities		Units	..	..	..	..	..
4.5	♦ Passenger transportation		Units	..	..	..	..	..
4.6	♦ Travel agencies and other reservation services activities		Units	141	170	197	218	243
4.7	♦ Other tourism industries		Units	..	..	..	..	..
	Accommodation for visitors in hotels and similar establishments							
	Monetary data							
4.8	♦ Output		US$ Mn	145.2	..	..	..	..
4.9	♦ Intermediate consumption		US$ Mn	31.4	..	..	..	..
4.10	♦ Gross value added		US$ Mn	111.2	..	..	..	..
4.11	♦ Compensation of employees		US$ Mn	23.0	..	..	..	..
4.12	♦ Gross fixed capital formation		US$ Mn	14.6	..	..	..	..
	Non-monetary data							
4.13	♦ Number of establishments		Units	508	514	530	535	536
4.14	♦ Number of rooms		Units	14,815	15,898	16,559	17,363	17,953
4.15	♦ Number of bed-places		Units	31,979	32,834	33,951	35,652	37,278
	Indicators							
4.16	Occupancy rate / rooms		Percent	..	..	..	..	..
4.17	Occupancy rate / bed-places		Percent	13.00	14.00	14.00	13.00	12.00
4.18	Average length of stay		Nights	2.90	2.63	2.52	2.51	1.96
4.19	Available capacity (bed-places per 1000 inhabitants)		Units	3.47	3.51	3.57	3.70	3.82
	Travel agencies and other reservation service activities							
	Monetary data							
4.20	♦ Output		US$ Mn	28.6	..	..	..	..
4.21	♦ Intermediate consumption		US$ Mn	2.3	..	..	..	..
4.22	♦ Gross value added		US$ Mn	22.5	..	..	..	..
4.23	♦ Compensation of employees		US$ Mn	7.1	..	..	..	..
4.24	♦ Gross fixed capital formation		US$ Mn	1.1	..	..	..	..
5.	**EMPLOYMENT**							
	Data							
	Number of employees by tourism industries							
5.1	Total		('000)	37.6	38.9	40.8	41.8	49.4
5.2	♦ Accommodation services for visitors (hotels and similar establishments)		('000)	6.2	7.3	8.3	9.0	8.4
5.3	♦ Other accommodation services		('000)	..	..	..	..	..
5.4	♦ Food and beverage serving activities		('000)	..	..	..	..	..
5.5	♦ Passenger transportation		('000)	..	..	..	..	..
5.6	♦ Travel agencies and other reservation services activities		('000)	1.5	1.7	1.7	1.8	1.6
5.7	♦ Other tourism industries		('000)	29.9	29.8	30.8	31.0	39.5
6.	**COMPLEMENTARY INDICATORS**							
	Demand							
6.1	Gross travel propensity		Units	..	..	..	..	..
6.2	(1.2 inbound tourists) / population		Units	0.17	0.21	0.22	0.22	0.20

AZERBAIJAN

Cod.	Basic data and indicators	Notes	Units	2011	2012	2013	2014	2015
	Macroeconomic indicators related to international tourism							
6.3	Inbound tourism expenditure over GDP		Percent	2.3	3.8	3.5	3.6	..
6.4	Outbound tourism expenditure over GDP		Percent	2.7	3.8	4.1	4.2	..
6.5	Tourism balance (inbound minus outbound tourism expenditure) over GDP		Percent	-0.4		-0.6	-0.6	..
6.6	Tourism openness (inbound plus outbound tourism expenditure) over GDP		Percent	5.0	7.6	7.6	7.8	..
6.7	Tourism coverage (inbound over outbound tourism expenditure)		Percent	84.4	100.6	86.3	85.8	92.4
6.8	Inbound tourism expenditure over exports of goods		Percent	4.4	8.3	8.2	9.6	16.3
6.9	Inbound tourism expenditure over exports of services		Percent	49.3	54.8	63.4	63.1	57.0
6.10	Inbound tourism expenditure over exports of goods and services		Percent	4.0	7.2	7.3	8.3	12.7
6.11	Inbound tourism expenditure over current account credits		Percent	3.8	6.6	6.8	7.5	11.3
6.12	Outbound tourism expenditure over imports of goods		Percent	18.0	26.3	27.1	33.9	28.1
6.13	Outbound tourism expenditure over imports of services		Percent	30.4	35.2	36.4	30.5	31.6
6.14	Outbound tourism expenditure over imports of goods and		Percent	11.3	15.0	15.6	16.0	14.9
6.15	Outbound tourism expenditure over current account debits		Percent	9.9	12.7	13.6	13.6	13.2

BAHAMAS

Cod.	Basic data and indicators	Notes	Units	2011	2012	2013	2014	2015
1.	**INBOUND TOURISM**							
	Data							
	Arrivals							
1.1	Total		('000)	5,588	5,940	6,151	6,320	6,114
1.2	♦ Overnight visitors (tourists)		('000)	1,346	1,422	1,366	1,427	1,484
1.3	♦ Same-day visitors (excursionists)		('000)	4,242	4,518	4,785	4,893	4,630
1.4	* of which, cruise passengers		('000)	4,161	4,434	4,709	4,805	4,513
	Arrivals by region							
1.5	Total		('000)	1,346	1,422	1,366	1,427	1,484
1.6	♦ Africa		('000)	2	2	2	2	3
1.7	♦ Americas		('000)	1,230	1,303	1,242	1,299	1,345
1.8	♦ East Asia and the Pacific		('000)	7	8	8	9	10
1.9	♦ Europe		('000)	79	80	81	84	89
1.10	♦ Middle East		('000)	1	1	1	1	1
1.11	♦ South Asia		('000)	1	1	1	1	1
1.12	♦ Other not classified		('000)	26	27	31	32	36
1.13	* of which, nationals residing abroad		('000)	..	..	..	..	..
	Arrivals by main purpose							
1.14	Total		('000)	1,346	1,422	1,366	1,427	1,484
1.15	♦ Personal		('000)	1,253	1,323	1,267	1,333	1,381
1.16	* holidays, leisure and recreation		('000)	1,098	1,221	1,144	1,234	1,257
1.17	* other personal purposes		('000)	155	102	123	99	124
1.18	♦ Business and professional		('000)	93	99	98	94	103
	Arrivals by mode of transport							
1.19	Total		('000)	5,588	5,940	6,151	6,320	6,114
1.20	♦ Air		('000)	1,268	1,357	1,281	1,343	1,392
1.21	♦ Water		('000)	4,320	4,583	4,870	4,977	4,722
1.22	♦ Land		('000)	..	..	..	..	..
1.23	* railway		('000)	..	..	..	..	..
1.24	* road		('000)	..	..	..	..	..
1.25	* others		('000)	..	..	..	..	..
	Accommodation							
	Total							
1.29	♦ Guests		('000)	1,346	1,422	1,366	1,427	1,484
1.30	♦ Overnights		('000)	9,123	9,629	9,358	9,567	9,942
	Hotels and similar establishments							
1.31	♦ Guests	(1)	('000)	980	1,043	982	1,034	1,057
1.32	♦ Overnights		('000)	5,082	5,443	5,133	5,299	5,455
	Expenditure							
1.33	Total		US$ Mn	2,157	2,333	2,305	2,328	2,396
1.34	♦ Travel		US$ Mn	2,142	2,311	2,285	2,308	2,379
1.35	♦ Passenger transport		US$ Mn	15	22	20	20	17
	Indicators							
1.39	Average size of travel party		Persons	..	..	..	..	..
	Average length of stay							
1.40	Total		Days	..	..	..	..	..
1.41	♦ For all commercial accommodation services		Nights	6.80	6.80	6.80	6.70	6.70
1.42	* of which, "hotels and similar establishments"		Nights	..	..	..	..	..
1.43	♦ For non commercial accommodation services		Days	..	..	..	..	..
1.44	Average expenditure per day		US$	..	..	..	..	..
3.	**OUTBOUND TOURISM**							
	Data							
	Expenditure							
3.4	Total		US$ Mn	347	384	362	328	348
3.5	♦ Travel		US$ Mn	246	286	262	212	238
3.6	♦ Passenger transport		US$ Mn	101	98	100	116	110
	Expenditure by main purpose of the trip							
3.7	Total		US$ Mn	246	286	262	212	238
3.8	♦ Personal		US$ Mn	213	255	230	185	207
3.9	♦ Business and professional		US$ Mn	33	31	32	26	31

BAHAMAS

Cod. Basic data and indicators	Notes	Units	2011	2012	2013	2014	2015
4. **TOURISM INDUSTRIES**							
Data							
Number of establishments							
4.1 Total		Units	..	..	..	..	..
4.2 ♦ Accommodation for visitors		Units	..	..	..	..	..
4.3 * of which, "hotels and similar establishments"	(2)	Units	286	277	312	316	304
4.4 ♦ Food and beverage serving activities		Units	..	..	..	..	..
4.5 ♦ Passenger transportation		Units	..	..	..	..	..
4.6 ♦ Travel agencies and other reservation services activities		Units	..	..	..	..	..
4.7 ♦ Other tourism industries		Units	..	..	..	..	..
Accommodation for visitors in hotels and similar establishments							
Non-monetary data	(2)						
4.13 ♦ Number of establishments		Units	286	277	312	316	304
4.14 ♦ Number of rooms		Units	15,153	14,693	14,836	15,300	14,727
4.15 ♦ Number of bed-places		Units	30,306	29,386	29,672	30,600	29,454
Indicators							
4.16 Occupancy rate / rooms		Percent	53.70	58.00	51.90	56.10	58.54
4.17 Occupancy rate / bed-places		Percent	..	..	..	..	..
4.18 Average length of stay		Nights	..	..	..	..	..
4.19 Available capacity (bed-places per 1000 inhabitants)		Units	82.64	78.91	78.53	79.88	75.91
6. **COMPLEMENTARY INDICATORS**							
Demand							
6.1 Gross travel propensity		Units	..	..	..	..	..
6.2 (1.2 inbound tourists) / population		Units	3.67	3.82	3.62	3.73	3.82
Macroeconomic indicators related to international tourism							
6.3 Inbound tourism expenditure over GDP		Percent	27.3	27.8	27.0	27.0	27.1
6.4 Outbound tourism expenditure over GDP		Percent	4.4	4.6	4.2	3.8	3.9
6.5 Tourism balance (inbound minus outbound tourism expenditure) over GDP		Percent	22.9	23.2	22.8	23.2	23.2
6.6 Tourism openness (inbound plus outbound tourism expenditure) over GDP		Percent	31.7	32.4	31.2	30.8	31.0
6.7 Tourism coverage (inbound over outbound tourism expenditure)		Percent	621.6	607.6	636.7	709.8	688.5
6.8 Inbound tourism expenditure over exports of goods		Percent	258.8	237.1	241.4	271.0	..
6.9 Inbound tourism expenditure over exports of services		Percent	86.5	86.7	86.3	85.7	..
6.10 Inbound tourism expenditure over exports of goods and services		Percent	64.8	63.5	63.6	65.1	..
6.11 Inbound tourism expenditure over current account credits		Percent	61.5	60.5	60.5	61.6	..
6.12 Outbound tourism expenditure over imports of goods		Percent	11.7	11.3	11.4	9.9	..
6.13 Outbound tourism expenditure over imports of services		Percent	26.8	25.0	22.2	19.0	..
6.14 Outbound tourism expenditure over imports of goods and		Percent	8.1	7.8	7.6	6.5	..
6.15 Outbound tourism expenditure over current account debits		Percent	7.8	7.5	7.3	6.3	..

BAHRAIN

Cod.	Basic data and indicators	Notes	Units	2011	2012	2013	2014	2015
1.	**INBOUND TOURISM**							
	Data							
	Arrivals	(1)						
1.1	Total		('000)	6,732	8,062	9,163	10,452	11,621
1.2	♦ Overnight visitors (tourists)		('000)	..	..	..	..	..
1.3	♦ Same-day visitors (excursionists)		('000)	..	..	..	..	..
1.4	* of which, cruise passengers		('000)	..	..	..	..	..
	Arrivals by region	(1)						
1.5	Total		('000)	6,732	8,062	9,163	10,452	11,621
1.6	♦ Africa		('000)	100	114	124	133	152
1.7	♦ Americas		('000)	291	326	335	345	367
1.8	♦ East Asia and the Pacific		('000)	339	367	335	378	390
1.9	♦ Europe		('000)	513	541	552	580	616
1.10	♦ Middle East		('000)	4,276	5,333	6,423	7,495	8,423
1.11	♦ South Asia		('000)	1,213	1,381	1,394	1,521	1,673
1.12	♦ Other not classified		('000)	..	..	..	..	..
1.13	* of which, nationals residing abroad		('000)	..	..	..	..	..
	Arrivals by main purpose	(1)						
1.14	Total		('000)	6,732	..	..	..	..
1.15	♦ Personal		('000)	6,082	..	..	..	..
1.16	* holidays, leisure and recreation		('000)	3,460	..	..	..	..
1.17	* other personal purposes		('000)	2,622	..	..	..	..
1.18	♦ Business and professional		('000)	650	..	..	..	..
	Arrivals by mode of transport	(1)						
1.19	Total		('000)	6,732	8,064	9,163	10,449	11,621
1.20	♦ Air	(2)	('000)	1,521	1,628	1,615	1,706	1,890
1.21	♦ Water	(3)	('000)	55	55	66	59	65
1.22	♦ Land	(4)	('000)	5,156	6,381	7,482	8,684	9,666
1.23	* railway		('000)	..	..	..	..	..
1.24	* road		('000)	5,156	6,381	7,482	8,684	9,666
1.25	* others		('000)	..	..	..	..	..
	Accommodation							
	Hotels and similar establishments							
1.31	♦ Guests		('000)	821	1,014	1,069	838	1,200
1.32	♦ Overnights	(5)	('000)	1,550	1,835	1,990	2,094	3,137
	Expenditure							
1.33	Total		US$ Mn	1,766	1,742	1,865	1,915	..
1.34	♦ Travel		US$ Mn	1,035	1,051	1,165	1,197	..
1.35	♦ Passenger transport		US$ Mn	731	691	700	718	..
	Indicators							
1.39	Average size of travel party		Persons	..	..	..	..	..
	Average length of stay							
1.40	Total		Days	..	..	..	..	..
1.41	♦ For all commercial accommodation services		Nights	1.89	1.81	1.86	2.50	2.61
1.42	* of which, "hotels and similar establishments"		Nights	..	..	..	..	..
1.43	♦ For non commercial accommodation services		Days	..	..	..	..	..
1.44	Average expenditure per day		US$	..	..	..	..	..
3.	**OUTBOUND TOURISM**							
	Data							
	Expenditure							
3.4	Total		US$ Mn	899	889	873	864	..
3.5	♦ Travel		US$ Mn	718	729	713	718	..
3.6	♦ Passenger transport		US$ Mn	181	160	160	146	..
4.	**TOURISM INDUSTRIES**							
	Data							
	Number of establishments							
4.1	Total		Units	..	..	..	..	..
4.2	♦ Accommodation for visitors		Units	..	..	..	..	..
4.3	* of which, "hotels and similar establishments"		Units	101	104	106	109	111
4.4	♦ Food and beverage serving activities		Units	..	..	..	..	..
4.5	♦ Passenger transportation		Units	..	..	..	..	..
4.6	♦ Travel agencies and other reservation services activities		Units	..	..	..	..	..
4.7	♦ Other tourism industries		Units	..	..	..	..	..

BAHRAIN

Cod.	Basic data and indicators	Notes	Units	2011	2012	2013	2014	2015
	Accommodation for visitors in hotels and similar establishments							
	Non-monetary data							
4.13	♦ Number of establishments		Units	101	104	106	109	111
4.14	♦ Number of rooms	(5)	Units	10,694	11,848	13,369	13,250	13,823
4.15	♦ Number of bed-places		Units	13,315	14,298	15,501	17,949	20,153
	Indicators							
4.16	Occupancy rate / rooms		Percent	33.40	33.04	43.00	45.00	48.00
4.17	Occupancy rate / bed-places		Percent	..	..	..	..	..
4.18	Average length of stay		Nights	1.89	1.81	1.86	2.50	2.61
4.19	Available capacity (bed-places per 1000 inhabitants)		Units	10.20	10.72	11.49	13.18	14.63
6.	**COMPLEMENTARY INDICATORS**							
	Demand							
6.1	Gross travel propensity		Units	..	..	..	..	..
6.2	(1.1 inbound visitors) / population		Units	5.15	6.05	6.79	7.67	8.44
	Macroeconomic indicators related to international tourism							
6.3	Inbound tourism expenditure over GDP		Percent	6.1	5.8	5.7	5.7	..
6.4	Outbound tourism expenditure over GDP		Percent	3.1	3.0	2.7	2.6	..
6.5	Tourism balance (inbound minus outbound tourism expenditure) over GDP		Percent	3.0	2.8	3.0	3.1	..
6.6	Tourism openness (inbound plus outbound tourism expenditure) over GDP		Percent	9.2	8.8	8.4	8.3	..
6.7	Tourism coverage (inbound over outbound tourism expenditure)		Percent	196.4	196.0	213.6	221.6	..
6.8	Inbound tourism expenditure over exports of goods		Percent	9.0	8.8	8.9	9.2	..
6.9	Inbound tourism expenditure over exports of services		Percent	53.6	56.5	56.5	57.4	..
6.10	Inbound tourism expenditure over exports of goods and services		Percent	7.7	7.6	7.7	7.9	..
6.11	Inbound tourism expenditure over current account credits		Percent	5.9	6.7	6.8	7.4	..
6.12	Outbound tourism expenditure over imports of goods		Percent	7.4	6.7	6.4	6.5	..
6.13	Outbound tourism expenditure over imports of services		Percent	50.5	60.1	55.9	53.4	..
6.14	Outbound tourism expenditure over imports of goods and		Percent	6.5	6.0	5.7	5.8	..
6.15	Outbound tourism expenditure over current account debits		Percent	4.0	4.5	4.2	4.5	..

BANGLADESH

Cod.	Basic data and indicators	Notes	Units	2011	2012	2013	2014	2015
1.	**INBOUND TOURISM**							
	Data							
	Arrivals							
1.1	Total		('000)	..	..	..	..	..
1.2	♦ Overnight visitors (tourists)		('000)	155	125	148	125	..
1.3	♦ Same-day visitors (excursionists)		('000)	..	..	..	..	..
1.4	* of which, cruise passengers		('000)	..	..	..	..	..
	Arrivals by region							
1.5	Total		('000)	155	125	148	125	..
1.6	♦ Africa		('000)	..	..	..	..	..
1.7	♦ Americas		('000)	7	1	5	6	..
1.8	♦ East Asia and the Pacific		('000)	8	9	6	9	..
1.9	♦ Europe		('000)	10	9	7	8	..
1.10	♦ Middle East		('000)	..	..	..	..	..
1.11	♦ South Asia		('000)	106	78	79	77	..
1.12	♦ Other not classified		('000)	24	29	51	26	..
1.13	* of which, nationals residing abroad		('000)	..	..	..	..	..
	Expenditure							
1.33	Total		US$ Mn	97	105	131	154	148
1.34	♦ Travel		US$ Mn	87	103	129	153	148
1.35	♦ Passenger transport		US$ Mn	10	2	2	1	0.4
	Expenditure by main purpose of the trip							
1.36	Total		US$ Mn	87	103	129	153	149
1.37	♦ Personal		US$ Mn	86	101	127	151	147
1.38	♦ Business and professional		US$ Mn	1	2	2	2	2
3.	**OUTBOUND TOURISM**							
	Data							
	Departures							
3.1	Total		('000)	..	..	..	..	..
3.2	♦ Overnight visitors (tourists)		('000)	2,127	2,273	1,460	..	..
3.3	♦ Same-day visitors (excursionists)		('000)	..	..	..	..	..
	Expenditure							
3.4	Total		US$ Mn	819	889	1,308	782	825
3.5	♦ Travel		US$ Mn	332	304	350	400	425
3.6	♦ Passenger transport		US$ Mn	487	585	958	382	400
	Expenditure by main purpose of the trip							
3.7	Total		US$ Mn	332	304	350	400	425
3.8	♦ Personal		US$ Mn	298	253	301	365	385
3.9	♦ Business and professional		US$ Mn	34	51	49	34	40
6.	**COMPLEMENTARY INDICATORS**							
	Demand							
6.1	Gross travel propensity		Units	..	..	..	..	..
6.2	(1.2 inbound tourists) / population		Units	0.001	0.001	0.001	0.001	..
	Macroeconomic indicators related to international tourism							
6.3	Inbound tourism expenditure over GDP		Percent	0.1	0.1	0.1	0.1	0.1
6.4	Outbound tourism expenditure over GDP		Percent	0.7	0.7	0.9	0.5	0.4
6.5	Tourism balance (inbound minus outbound tourism expenditure) over GDP		Percent	-0.6	-0.6	-0.8	-0.4	-0.3
6.6	Tourism openness (inbound plus outbound tourism expenditure) over GDP		Percent	0.8	0.8	1.0	0.6	0.5
6.7	Tourism coverage (inbound over outbound tourism expenditure)		Percent	11.8	11.8	10.0	19.7	18.0
6.8	Inbound tourism expenditure over exports of goods		Percent	0.4	0.4	0.5	0.5	0.5
6.9	Inbound tourism expenditure over exports of services		Percent	4.0	3.9	4.4	4.9	4.8
6.10	Inbound tourism expenditure over exports of goods and services		Percent	0.4	0.4	0.4	0.5	0.4
6.11	Inbound tourism expenditure over current account credits		Percent	0.2	0.2	0.3	0.3	0.3
6.12	Outbound tourism expenditure over imports of goods		Percent	2.5	2.8	3.7	2.1	2.2
6.13	Outbound tourism expenditure over imports of services		Percent	15.5	15.9	19.9	10.1	10.7
6.14	Outbound tourism expenditure over imports of goods and		Percent	2.2	2.4	3.1	1.7	1.8
6.15	Outbound tourism expenditure over current account debits		Percent	2.1	2.3	3.1	1.7	1.8

BARBADOS

Cod.	Basic data and indicators	Notes	Units	2011	2012	2013	2014	2015
1.	**INBOUND TOURISM**							
	Data							
	Arrivals							
1.1	Total		('000)	1,187	1,053	1,079	1,079	1,179
1.2	♦ Overnight visitors (tourists)		('000)	568	536	509	521	592
1.3	♦ Same-day visitors (excursionists)		('000)	619	517	570	558	587
1.4	* of which, cruise passengers		('000)	619	517	570	558	587
	Arrivals by region							
1.5	Total		('000)	568	536	509	521	592
1.6	♦ Africa		('000)	1	1	1	2	2
1.7	♦ Americas		('000)	337	318	292	281	328
1.8	♦ East Asia and the Pacific		('000)	4	4	4	4	5
1.9	♦ Europe		('000)	224	210	209	231	255
1.10	♦ Middle East		('000)	..	..	..	..	..
1.11	♦ South Asia		('000)	1	1	1	1	1
1.12	♦ Other not classified		('000)	1	2	2	3	2
1.13	* of which, nationals residing abroad		('000)	..	..	..	..	..
	Arrivals by main purpose							
1.14	Total		('000)	568	536	509	521	592
1.15	♦ Personal		('000)	514	485	451	462	533
1.16	* holidays, leisure and recreation		('000)	468	454	402	419	464
1.17	* other personal purposes		('000)	46	31	49	43	70
1.18	♦ Business and professional		('000)	54	51	58	59	59
	Arrivals by mode of transport							
1.19	Total		('000)	1,187	1,053	1,079	1,079	1,179
1.20	♦ Air		('000)	568	536	509	521	592
1.21	♦ Water		('000)	619	517	570	558	587
1.22	♦ Land		('000)	..	..	..	..	..
1.23	* railway		('000)	..	..	..	..	..
1.24	* road		('000)	..	..	..	..	..
1.25	* others		('000)	..	..	..	..	..
	Expenditure							
1.33	Total		US$ Mn	983	947	992	..	..
1.34	♦ Travel		US$ Mn	970	929	973	..	..
1.35	♦ Passenger transport		US$ Mn	13	18	19	..	..
	Expenditure by main purpose of the trip							
1.36	Total		US$ Mn	970	929	973	..	..
1.37	♦ Personal		US$ Mn	887	737	874	..	..
1.38	♦ Business and professional		US$ Mn	83	192	99	..	..
	Indicators							
1.39	Average size of travel party		Persons	..	..	..	..	..
	Average length of stay							
1.40	Total		Days	..	..	11.80	11.97	11.19
1.41	♦ For all commercial accommodation services		Nights	..	..	..	..	..
1.42	* of which, "hotels and similar establishments"		Nights	..	..	..	..	..
1.43	♦ For non commercial accommodation services		Days	..	..	..	..	..
1.44	Average expenditure per day		US$	..	..	..	..	..
3.	**OUTBOUND TOURISM**							
	Data							
	Expenditure							
3.4	Total		US$ Mn	124	84	78	..	..
3.5	♦ Travel		US$ Mn	65	47	43	..	..
3.6	♦ Passenger transport		US$ Mn	59	37	35	..	..
	Expenditure by main purpose of the trip							
3.7	Total		US$ Mn	65	47	43	..	..
3.8	♦ Personal		US$ Mn	50	31	29	..	..
3.9	♦ Business and professional		US$ Mn	15	16	14	..	..
4.	**TOURISM INDUSTRIES**							
	Data							
	Accommodation for visitors in hotels and similar establishments							
	Non-monetary data							
4.13	♦ Number of establishments		Units	..	..	..	..	..
4.14	♦ Number of rooms	(1)	Units	6,659	6,775	6,249	6,324	6,381
4.15	♦ Number of bed-places		Units	..	..	..	..	..

BARBADOS

Cod.	Basic data and indicators	Notes	Units	2011	2012	2013	2014	2015
6.	**COMPLEMENTARY INDICATORS**							
	Demand							
6.1	Gross travel propensity		Units	..	..	..	..	..
6.2	(1.2 inbound tourists) / population		Units	2.02	1.90	1.80	1.84	2.08
	Macroeconomic indicators related to international tourism							
6.3	Inbound tourism expenditure over GDP		Percent	22.5	22.4	..	..	..
6.4	Outbound tourism expenditure over GDP		Percent	2.8	2.0	..	..	..
6.5	Tourism balance (inbound minus outbound tourism expenditure) over GDP		Percent	19.7	20.4	..	..	..
6.6	Tourism openness (inbound plus outbound tourism expenditure) over GDP		Percent	25.3	24.4	..	..	..
6.7	Tourism coverage (inbound over outbound tourism expenditure)		Percent	792.7	1,127.4	1,271.8	..	..
6.8	Inbound tourism expenditure over exports of goods		Percent	114.0	111.3	112.0	..	..
6.9	Inbound tourism expenditure over exports of services		Percent	76.0	75.6	69.1	..	..
6.10	Inbound tourism expenditure over exports of goods and services		Percent	45.6	45.0	42.8	..	..
6.11	Inbound tourism expenditure over current account credits		Percent	36.0	39.3	37.1	..	..
6.12	Outbound tourism expenditure over imports of goods		Percent	7.1	4.9	4.6	..	..
6.13	Outbound tourism expenditure over imports of services		Percent	23.9	16.6	11.1	..	..
6.14	Outbound tourism expenditure over imports of goods and		Percent	5.5	3.8	3.3	..	..
6.15	Outbound tourism expenditure over current account debits		Percent	4.3	3.3	2.8	..	..

BELARUS

Cod.	Basic data and indicators	Notes	Units	2011	2012	2013	2014	2015
1.	**INBOUND TOURISM**							
	Data							
	Arrivals							
1.1	Total		('000)	5,877	6,127	6,240	5,374	4,385
1.2	♦ Overnight visitors (tourists)	(1)	('000)	783	955	966	973	860
1.3	♦ Same-day visitors (excursionists)		('000)	..	..	..	..	175
1.4	* of which, cruise passengers		('000)	..	..	..	..	..
	Arrivals by region	(2)						
1.5	Total		('000)	116	119	137	137	102
1.6	♦ Africa		('000)	..	..	..	..	..
1.7	♦ Americas		('000)	1	1	1	1	1
1.8	♦ East Asia and the Pacific		('000)	4	1	2	2	2
1.9	♦ Europe		('000)	110	116	132	133	97
1.10	♦ Middle East		('000)	..	..	..	1	1
1.11	♦ South Asia		('000)	..	..	..	..	..
1.12	♦ Other not classified		('000)	1	1	2	..	1
1.13	* of which, nationals residing abroad		('000)	..	..	..	..	..
	Arrivals by main purpose							
1.14	Total		('000)	5,877	6,127	6,240	5,374	4,385
1.15	♦ Personal		('000)	5,464	5,720	5,864	5,025	4,362
1.16	* holidays, leisure and recreation		('000)	3,624	3,892	4,069	3,479	3,019
1.17	* other personal purposes		('000)	1,840	1,828	1,795	1,546	1,343
1.18	♦ Business and professional		('000)	413	407	376	349	23
	Arrivals by mode of transport							
1.19	Total	(3)	('000)	5,682	5,910	5,953	5,092	4,179
1.20	♦ Air		('000)	256	253	268	294	324
1.21	♦ Water		('000)	..	..	..	..	..
1.22	♦ Land		('000)	5,426	5,657	5,685	4,798	3,855
1.23	* railway		('000)	1,413	1,341	1,266	954	786
1.24	* road		('000)	4,013	4,316	4,419	3,844	3,069
1.25	* others		('000)	..	..	..	..	..
	Arrivals by form of organization of the trip							
1.26	Total		('000)	5,877	6,127	6,240	5,374	4,385
1.27	♦ Package tour		('000)	116	119	137	137	102
1.28	♦ Other forms		('000)	5,761	6,008	6,103	5,237	4,283
	Accommodation							
	Total							
1.29	♦ Guests		('000)	783	955	966	973	860
1.30	♦ Overnights		('000)	3,523	4,152	4,112	4,289	3,470
	Hotels and similar establishments							
1.31	♦ Guests		('000)	594	728	740	741	688
1.32	♦ Overnights		('000)	1,310	1,610	1,612	1,704	1,585
	Expenditure							
1.33	Total		US$ Mn	747	986	1,156	1,230	1,018
1.34	♦ Travel		US$ Mn	487	685	791	868	734
1.35	♦ Passenger transport		US$ Mn	260	301	365	362	284
	Expenditure by main purpose of the trip							
1.36	Total		US$ Mn	487	684	791	868	734
1.37	♦ Personal		US$ Mn	273	380	517	672	640
1.38	♦ Business and professional		US$ Mn	214	304	274	196	94
2.	**DOMESTIC TOURISM**							
	Data							
	Trips							
2.1	Total		('000)	..	663	655	704	837
2.2	♦ Overnight visitors (tourists)		('000)	77	61	76	56	92
2.3	♦ Same-day visitors (excursionists)		('000)	..	602	579	647	745
	Trips by form of organization							
2.16	Total		('000)	77	61	76	56	92
2.17	♦ Package tour		('000)	77	61	76	56	92
2.18	♦ Other forms		('000)	..	..	..	..	..
	Accommodation							
	Total							
2.19	♦ Guests		('000)	1,768	1,714	1,672	1,614	1,506
2.20	♦ Overnights		('000)	10,067	9,646	9,547	9,186	8,675
	Hotels and similar establishments							
2.21	♦ Guests		('000)	1,144	1,097	1,065	998	918
2.22	♦ Overnights		('000)	3,071	2,902	2,906	2,707	2,291

BELARUS

Cod.	Basic data and indicators	Notes	Units	2011	2012	2013	2014	2015
3.	**OUTBOUND TOURISM**							
	Data							
	Departures							
3.1	Total		('000)	7,542	8,427	8,841	7,246	6,972
3.2	♦ Overnight visitors (tourists)		('000)	320	493	708	741	671
3.3	♦ Same-day visitors (excursionists)		('000)	7,222	7,934	8,133	6,505	6,301
	Expenditure							
3.4	Total		US$ Mn	729	948	1,333	1,308	1,011
3.5	♦ Travel		US$ Mn	588	789	1,153	1,159	912
3.6	♦ Passenger transport		US$ Mn	141	159	180	149	99
	Expenditure by main purpose of the trip							
3.7	Total		US$ Mn	589	788	1,153	1,158	912
3.8	♦ Personal		US$ Mn	415	596	919	891	735
3.9	♦ Business and professional		US$ Mn	174	192	235	267	178
4.	**TOURISM INDUSTRIES**							
	Data							
	Number of establishments							
4.1	Total		Units	1,656	1,877	2,030	2,250	2,378
4.2	♦ Accommodation for visitors		Units	865	919	945	996	1,014
4.3	* of which, "hotels and similar establishments"		Units	451	477	487	536	547
4.4	♦ Food and beverage serving activities		Units	..	..	..	..	..
4.5	♦ Passenger transportation		Units	..	..	..	..	..
4.6	♦ Travel agencies and other reservation services activities		Units	791	958	1,085	1,254	1,364
4.7	♦ Other tourism industries		Units	..	..	..	..	..
	Accommodation for visitors in hotels and similar establishments							
	Non-monetary data							
4.13	♦ Number of establishments		Units	451	477	487	536	547
4.14	♦ Number of rooms		Units	15,907	15,786	16,613	19,545	20,157
4.15	♦ Number of bed-places		Units	28,957	28,452	29,908	35,424	36,951
	Indicators							
4.16	Occupancy rate / rooms		Percent	75.45	78.10	74.51	61.82	52.68
4.17	Occupancy rate / bed-places		Percent	41.45	43.33	41.39	34.11	28.74
4.18	Average length of stay		Nights	2.52	2.47	2.50	2.54	2.41
4.19	Available capacity (bed-places per 1000 inhabitants)		Units	3.05	3.00	3.15	3.73	3.89
	Travel agencies and other reservation service activities							
	Non-monetary data							
	♦ Domestic trips							
4.25	* with package tour		Percent	..	..	..	..	..
4.26	* without package tour		Percent	..	..	..	..	..
	♦ Inbound trips							
4.27	* with package tour		Percent	2.0	1.9	2.1	2.6	2.3
4.28	* without package tour		Percent	98.0	98.1	97.9	97.4	97.7
	♦ Outbound trips							
4.29	* with package tour		Percent	4.2	5.8	7.4	10.2	9.6
4.30	* without package tour		Percent	95.8	94.2	92.6	89.8	90.4
5.	**EMPLOYMENT**							
	Data							
	Number of employees by tourism industries	(4)						
5.1	Total		('000)	30.1	30.9	31.4	33.0	32.0
5.2	♦ Accommodation services for visitors (hotels and similar establishments)		('000)	8.9	9.1	9.1	10.0	9.4
5.3	♦ Other accommodation services		('000)	17.6	17.8	17.9	18.1	17.8
5.4	♦ Food and beverage serving activities		('000)	..	..	..	..	..
5.5	♦ Passenger transportation		('000)	..	..	..	..	..
5.6	♦ Travel agencies and other reservation services activities		('000)	3.6	4.0	4.4	4.9	4.8
5.7	♦ Other tourism industries		('000)	..	..	..	..	..
6.	**COMPLEMENTARY INDICATORS**							
	Demand							
6.1	Gross travel propensity		Units	..	..	..	..	..
6.2	(1.2 inbound tourists + 2.2 domestic tourists) / population		Units	0.09	0.11	0.11	0.11	0.10

BELARUS

Cod.	Basic data and indicators	Notes	Units	2011	2012	2013	2014	2015
	Macroeconomic indicators related to international tourism							
6.3	Inbound tourism expenditure over GDP		Percent	1.3	1.5	1.6	1.6	1.9
6.4	Outbound tourism expenditure over GDP		Percent	1.2	1.5	1.8	1.7	1.9
6.5	Tourism balance (inbound minus outbound tourism expenditure) over GDP		Percent	0.1		-0.2	-0.1	
6.6	Tourism openness (inbound plus outbound tourism expenditure) over GDP		Percent	2.5	3.0	3.4	3.3	3.8
6.7	Tourism coverage (inbound over outbound tourism expenditure)		Percent	102.5	104.0	86.7	94.0	100.7
6.8	Inbound tourism expenditure over exports of goods		Percent	1.8	2.2	3.2	3.5	3.9
6.9	Inbound tourism expenditure over exports of services		Percent	13.3	15.6	15.4	15.6	15.3
6.10	Inbound tourism expenditure over exports of goods and services		Percent	1.6	1.9	2.6	2.8	3.1
6.11	Inbound tourism expenditure over current account credits		Percent	1.5	1.8	2.5	2.7	2.9
6.12	Outbound tourism expenditure over imports of goods		Percent	1.6	2.1	3.2	3.4	3.6
6.13	Outbound tourism expenditure over imports of services		Percent	21.8	23.4	25.4	22.8	23.3
6.14	Outbound tourism expenditure over imports of goods and		Percent	1.5	1.9	2.9	3.0	3.1
6.15	Outbound tourism expenditure over current account debits		Percent	1.4	1.7	2.6	2.7	3.0

BELGIUM

Cod.	Basic data and indicators	Notes	Units	2011	2012	2013	2014	2015
1.	**INBOUND TOURISM**							
	Data							
	Arrivals							
1.1	Total		('000)	..	..	..	..	..
1.2	♦ Overnight visitors (tourists)	(1)(2)	('000)	7,494	7,560	7,684	7,887	8,355
1.3	♦ Same-day visitors (excursionists)		('000)	..	..	..	..	..
1.4	* of which, cruise passengers		('000)	..	..	..	..	..
	Arrivals by region	(1)(2)						
1.5	Total		('000)	7,494	7,560	7,684	7,887	8,355
1.6	♦ Africa		('000)	62	61	64	66	65
1.7	♦ Americas		('000)	489	505	517	566	603
1.8	♦ East Asia and the Pacific		('000)	307	367	398	437	498
1.9	♦ Europe		('000)	6,523	6,508	6,560	6,658	7,018
1.10	♦ Middle East		('000)	31	36	40	48	59
1.11	♦ South Asia		('000)	55	53	56	67	78
1.12	♦ Other not classified		('000)	27	31	49	45	34
1.13	* of which, nationals residing abroad		('000)	..	..	..	..	..
	Arrivals by main purpose	(1)(2)						
1.14	Total		('000)	7,494	7,560	7,684	7,887	8,355
1.15	♦ Personal		('000)	4,886	4,772	4,846	5,045	5,450
1.16	* holidays, leisure and recreation		('000)	4,886	4,772	4,846	5,045	5,450
1.17	* other personal purposes		('000)	..	..	..	..	..
1.18	♦ Business and professional		('000)	2,608	2,788	2,838	2,842	2,905
	Accommodation							
	Total							
1.29	♦ Guests	(2)	('000)	7,494	7,560	7,684	7,887	8,355
1.30	♦ Overnights	(2)	('000)	16,724	16,433	16,512	17,069	18,852
	Hotels and similar establishments							
1.31	♦ Guests	(3)	('000)	6,077	6,146	6,228	6,389	6,440
1.32	♦ Overnights	(3)	('000)	11,436	11,546	11,624	12,082	12,035
	Expenditure							
1.33	Total		US$ Mn	..	13,711	14,429	15,218	12,849
1.34	♦ Travel		US$ Mn	12,742	12,504	13,278	13,905	11,727
1.35	♦ Passenger transport		US$ Mn	..	1,207	1,151	1,313	1,122
	Expenditure by main purpose of the trip							
1.36	Total		US$ Mn	..	12,504	13,279	13,905	11,727
1.37	♦ Personal		US$ Mn	..	9,714	10,343	10,811	9,049
1.38	♦ Business and professional		US$ Mn	..	2,790	2,936	3,093	2,678
	Indicators							
1.39	Average size of travel party		Persons	..	..	..	..	..
	Average length of stay							
1.40	Total		Days	..	..	..	..	..
1.41	♦ For all commercial accommodation services		Nights	2.23	2.17	2.15	2.16	2.26
1.42	* of which, "hotels and similar establishments"		Nights	1.88	1.88	1.87	1.89	1.87
1.43	♦ For non commercial accommodation services		Days	..	..	..	..	..
1.44	Average expenditure per day		US$	..	..	..	..	..
2.	**DOMESTIC TOURISM**							
	Data							
	Trips							
2.1	Total		('000)	..	..	..	..	..
2.2	♦ Overnight visitors (tourists)	(2)	('000)	6,124	6,313	6,468	6,754	7,492
2.3	♦ Same-day visitors (excursionists)		('000)	..	..	..	..	..
	Trips by main purpose	(2)						
2.4	Total		('000)	6,124	6,313	6,468	6,754	7,492
2.5	♦ Personal		('000)	4,656	4,811	4,951	5,100	5,811
2.6	* holidays, leisure and recreation		('000)	4,656	4,811	4,951	5,100	5,811
2.7	* other personal purposes		('000)	..	..	..	..	..
2.8	♦ Business and professional		('000)	1,468	1,502	1,517	1,654	1,681
	Accommodation							
	Total							
2.19	♦ Guests	(2)	('000)	6,124	6,313	6,468	6,754	7,492
2.20	♦ Overnights	(2)	('000)	14,656	14,835	14,936	15,537	19,528
	Hotels and similar establishments							
2.21	♦ Guests	(3)	('000)	3,883	3,806	3,947	4,175	4,304
2.22	♦ Overnights	(3)	('000)	6,529	6,328	6,525	6,926	7,048

BELGIUM

Cod.	Basic data and indicators	Notes	Units	2011	2012	2013	2014	2015
	Indicators							
2.23	Average size of travel party		Persons	..	..	..	..	..
	Average length of stay							
2.24	Total		Days	..	..	..	..	..
2.25	♦ For all commercial accommodation services		Nights	2.39	2.35	2.31	2.30	2.61
2.26	* of which, "hotels and similar establishments"		Nights	1.68	1.66	1.65	1.66	1.64
2.27	♦ For non commercial accommodation services		Days	..	..	..	..	..
2.28	Average expenditure per day		US$	..	..	..	..	..
3.	**OUTBOUND TOURISM**							
	Data							
	Departures							
3.1	Total		('000)	..	..	..	..	..
3.2	♦ Overnight visitors (tourists)		('000)	9,727	9,576	10,803	10,991	10,835
3.3	♦ Same-day visitors (excursionists)		('000)	..	..	..	..	..
	Expenditure							
3.4	Total		US$ Mn	..	22,367	24,201	26,404	20,964
3.5	♦ Travel		US$ Mn	20,658	20,174	21,850	23,811	18,739
3.6	♦ Passenger transport		US$ Mn	..	2,193	2,351	2,593	2,225
	Expenditure by main purpose of the trip							
3.7	Total		US$ Mn	..	20,174	21,850	23,811	18,739
3.8	♦ Personal		US$ Mn	..	17,201	18,736	20,525	15,961
3.9	♦ Business and professional		US$ Mn	..	2,973	3,114	3,286	2,778
4.	**TOURISM INDUSTRIES**							
	Data							
	Number of establishments							
4.1	Total		Units	83,030	84,924	86,164	..	..
4.2	♦ Accommodation for visitors	(2)	Units	3,506	4,548	4,691	5,139	7,990
4.3	* of which, "hotels and similar establishments"	(4)	Units	2,149	3,216	3,398	3,987	3,830
4.4	♦ Food and beverage serving activities		Units	52,916	52,918	52,597	..	..
4.5	♦ Passenger transportation		Units	3,791	3,858	4,717	..	..
4.6	♦ Travel agencies and other reservation services activities		Units	2,285	2,312	2,356	..	..
4.7	♦ Other tourism industries		Units	20,532	21,288	21,803	..	..
	Accommodation for visitors in hotels and similar establishments							
	Non-monetary data	(4)						
4.13	♦ Number of establishments		Units	2,149	3,216	3,398	3,987	3,830
4.14	♦ Number of rooms		Units	70,531	72,379	73,886	79,089	75,378
4.15	♦ Number of bed-places		Units	174,545	176,693	181,231	211,419	189,838
	Indicators							
4.16	Occupancy rate / rooms		Percent	..	..	..	..	..
4.17	Occupancy rate / bed-places		Percent	..	..	..	..	..
4.18	Average length of stay		Nights	..	..	..	..	..
4.19	Available capacity (bed-places per 1000 inhabitants)		Units	15.86	15.95	16.25	18.83	16.80
6.	**COMPLEMENTARY INDICATORS**							
	Demand							
6.1	Gross travel propensity		Units	..	..	..	..	..
6.2	(1.2 inbound tourists + 2.2 domestic tourists) / population		Units	1.24	1.25	1.27	1.30	1.40
	Macroeconomic indicators related to international tourism							
6.3	Inbound tourism expenditure over GDP		Percent	2.4	2.8	2.7	2.8	2.8
6.4	Outbound tourism expenditure over GDP		Percent	3.9	4.5	4.6	4.9	4.6
6.5	Tourism balance (inbound minus outbound tourism expenditure) over GDP		Percent	-1.5	-1.7	-1.9	-2.1	-1.8
6.6	Tourism openness (inbound plus outbound tourism expenditure) over GDP		Percent	6.3	7.3	7.3	7.7	7.4
6.7	Tourism coverage (inbound over outbound tourism expenditure)		Percent	61.7	61.3	59.6	57.6	61.3
6.8	Inbound tourism expenditure over exports of goods		Percent	3.9	4.6	4.6	4.8	4.9
6.9	Inbound tourism expenditure over exports of services		Percent	12.1	12.9	12.8	12.3	11.6
6.10	Inbound tourism expenditure over exports of goods and services		Percent	3.0	3.4	3.4	3.4	3.5
6.11	Inbound tourism expenditure over current account credits		Percent	2.5	2.8	2.9	2.9	3.0
6.12	Outbound tourism expenditure over imports of goods		Percent	6.1	7.1	7.5	8.1	8.1
6.13	Outbound tourism expenditure over imports of services		Percent	21.7	22.8	23.2	22.6	19.8
6.14	Outbound tourism expenditure over imports of goods and		Percent	4.8	5.4	5.6	6.0	5.7
6.15	Outbound tourism expenditure over current account debits		Percent	4.0	4.5	4.7	5.0	4.8

BELIZE

Cod.	Basic data and indicators	Notes	Units	2011	2012	2013	2014	2015
1.	**INBOUND TOURISM**							
	Data							
	Arrivals							
1.1	Total		('000)	1,106	1,028	1,022	1,289	1,299
1.2	♦ Overnight visitors (tourists)		('000)	250	277	294	321	341
1.3	♦ Same-day visitors (excursionists)		('000)	856	751	728	968	958
1.4	* of which, cruise passengers		('000)	735	641	677	968	958
	Arrivals by region							
1.5	Total		('000)	250	277	294	321	341
1.6	♦ Africa		('000)	0.5	0.5	0.4	0.5	0.6
1.7	♦ Americas		('000)	203	227	240	257	272
1.8	♦ East Asia and the Pacific		('000)	6	7	8	8	10
1.9	♦ Europe		('000)	30	29	32	39	41
1.10	♦ Middle East		('000)	0.6	1.3	1.9	2.5	2.4
1.11	♦ South Asia		('000)	..	..	..	..	..
1.12	♦ Other not classified		('000)	10	12	12	14	15
1.13	* of which, nationals residing abroad		('000)	10	12	12	14	15
	Arrivals by main purpose							
1.14	Total		('000)	250	277	294	321	341
1.15	♦ Personal		('000)	238	264	281	304	326
1.16	* holidays, leisure and recreation		('000)	238	264	281	304	326
1.17	* other personal purposes		('000)	..	..	..	..	..
1.18	♦ Business and professional		('000)	12	13	13	18	15
	Arrivals by mode of transport							
1.19	Total		('000)	1,106	1,028	1,023	1,289	1,299
1.20	♦ Air		('000)	182	212	224	239	256
1.21	♦ Water		('000)	747	651	688	979	968
1.22	♦ Land		('000)	177	165	111	71	76
1.23	* railway		('000)	..	..	..	..	..
1.24	* road		('000)	177	165	111	71	76
1.25	* others		('000)	..	..	..	..	..
	Expenditure							
1.33	Total		US$ Mn	..	..	..	..	..
1.34	♦ Travel		US$ Mn	248	298	351	380	372
1.35	♦ Passenger transport		US$ Mn	..	..	..	..	..
	Expenditure by main purpose of the trip							
1.36	Total		US$ Mn	248	298	351	380	372
1.37	♦ Personal		US$ Mn	234	283	333	356	353
1.38	♦ Business and professional		US$ Mn	14	15	18	23	19
	Indicators							
1.39	Average size of travel party		Persons	..	..	..	..	..
	Average length of stay							
1.40	Total		Days	..	..	..	..	..
1.41	♦ For all commercial accommodation services		Nights	7.23	7.03	7.36	6.69	6.58
1.42	* of which, "hotels and similar establishments"		Nights	..	..	..	..	..
1.43	♦ For non commercial accommodation services		Days	..	..	..	..	..
1.44	Average expenditure per day		US$	124.1	145.3	156.9	162.1	155.1
3.	**OUTBOUND TOURISM**							
	Data							
	Expenditure							
3.4	Total		US$ Mn	37	39	42	51	50
3.5	♦ Travel		US$ Mn	34	37	40	49	47
3.6	♦ Passenger transport		US$ Mn	3	2	2	2	3
	Expenditure by main purpose of the trip							
3.7	Total		US$ Mn	34	37	40	49	47
3.8	♦ Personal		US$ Mn	32	36	39	47	46
3.9	♦ Business and professional		US$ Mn	2	1	1	1	1
4.	**TOURISM INDUSTRIES**							
	Data							
	Number of establishments							
4.1	Total		Units	..	..	..	..	..
4.2	♦ Accommodation for visitors		Units	..	..	..	..	..
4.3	* of which, "hotels and similar establishments"		Units	716	723	757	805	850
4.4	♦ Food and beverage serving activities		Units	..	..	..	..	..
4.5	♦ Passenger transportation		Units	..	..	..	..	..
4.6	♦ Travel agencies and other reservation services activities		Units	18	18	18	18	18
4.7	♦ Other tourism industries		Units	..	..	..	..	..

BELIZE

Cod.	Basic data and indicators	Notes	Units	2011	2012	2013	2014	2015
	Accommodation for visitors in hotels and similar establishments							
	Non-monetary data							
4.13	♦ Number of establishments		Units	716	723	757	805	850
4.14	♦ Number of rooms		Units	7,111	6,932	7,377	7,364	7,619
4.15	♦ Number of bed-places		Units	12,113	12,058	13,015	12,804	13,211
	Indicators							
4.16	Occupancy rate / rooms		Percent	39.60	42.06	46.50	45.91	42.77
4.17	Occupancy rate / bed-places		Percent	..	..	..	..	..
4.18	Average length of stay		Nights	7.23	6.99	7.36	6.69	6.58
4.19	Available capacity (bed-places per 1000 inhabitants)		Units	36.80	35.81	37.81	36.41	36.77
5.	**EMPLOYMENT**							
	Data							
	Number of employees by tourism industries							
5.1	Total		('000)	13.2	15.5	18.9	19.2	18.1
5.2	♦ Accommodation services for visitors (hotels and similar establishments)		('000)	5.9	6.5	7.3	12.5	11.9
5.3	♦ Other accommodation services		('000)	..	..	..	..	..
5.4	♦ Food and beverage serving activities		('000)	..	..	..	..	..
5.5	♦ Passenger transportation		('000)	..	0.6	1.0	1.8	1.8
5.6	♦ Travel agencies and other reservation services activities		('000)	..	0.8	0.8	2.6	1.5
5.7	♦ Other tourism industries		('000)	..	7.6	9.8	2.3	2.9
	Number of jobs by status in employment							
5.8	Total		('000)	13.2	15.5	18.8	19.1	18.1
5.9	♦ Employees		('000)	13.2	15.5	18.8	19.1	18.1
5.10	♦ Self employed		('000)	..	..	..	..	..
6.	**COMPLEMENTARY INDICATORS**							
	Demand							
6.1	Gross travel propensity		Units	..	..	..	..	..
6.2	(1.2 inbound tourists) / population		Units	0.76	0.82	0.85	0.91	0.95
	Macroeconomic indicators related to international tourism							
6.3	Inbound tourism expenditure over GDP		Percent	16.7	18.9	21.6	22.1	..
6.4	Outbound tourism expenditure over GDP		Percent	2.5	2.5	2.6	3.0	..
6.5	Tourism balance (inbound minus outbound tourism expenditure) over GDP		Percent	14.2	16.4	19.0	19.1	..
6.6	Tourism openness (inbound plus outbound tourism expenditure) over GDP		Percent	19.2	21.4	24.2	25.1	..
6.7	Tourism coverage (inbound over outbound tourism expenditure)		Percent	670.3	764.1	835.7	745.1	744.0
6.8	Inbound tourism expenditure over exports of goods		Percent	41.1	47.5	57.7	64.6	69.2
6.9	Inbound tourism expenditure over exports of services		Percent	72.9	73.3	78.3	76.9	75.0
6.10	Inbound tourism expenditure over exports of goods and services		Percent	26.3	28.8	33.2	35.1	36.0
6.11	Inbound tourism expenditure over current account credits		Percent	23.5	26.1	30.1	31.7	32.3
6.12	Outbound tourism expenditure over imports of goods		Percent	4.8	4.7	4.8	5.5	5.2
6.13	Outbound tourism expenditure over imports of services		Percent	21.6	20.7	20.2	22.7	22.6
6.14	Outbound tourism expenditure over imports of goods and		Percent	3.9	3.8	3.9	4.4	4.2
6.15	Outbound tourism expenditure over current account debits		Percent	3.8	3.7	3.7	4.3	4.1

BENIN

Cod.	Basic data and indicators	Notes	Units	2011	2012	2013	2014	2015
1.	**INBOUND TOURISM**							
	Data							
	Arrivals							
1.1	Total		('000)	222	232	252	265	279
1.2	♦ Overnight visitors (tourists)		('000)	209	220	231	242	255
1.3	♦ Same-day visitors (excursionists)		('000)	11	12	21	23	24
1.4	* of which, cruise passengers		('000)	1	2	6	7	8
	Arrivals by region							
1.5	Total		('000)	210	220	231	242	255
1.6	♦ Africa		('000)	126	135	134	137	154
1.7	♦ Americas		('000)	3	5	8	9	10
1.8	♦ East Asia and the Pacific		('000)	1	3	6	12	10
1.9	♦ Europe		('000)	57	54	50	50	50
1.10	♦ Middle East		('000)	3	3	4	6	5
1.11	♦ South Asia		('000)	1	1	2	3	3
1.12	♦ Other not classified		('000)	19	19	27	27	22
1.13	* of which, nationals residing abroad		('000)	..	..	..	..	..
	Arrivals by main purpose							
1.14	Total		('000)	209	220	231	242	255
1.15	♦ Personal		('000)	115	121	117	118	118
1.16	* holidays, leisure and recreation		('000)	52	77	63	71	74
1.17	* other personal purposes		('000)	63	44	54	47	45
1.18	♦ Business and professional		('000)	94	99	114	124	136
	Arrivals by mode of transport							
1.19	Total		('000)	209	220	231	242	255
1.20	♦ Air		('000)	73	95	107	98	100
1.21	♦ Water		('000)	23	19	20	19	21
1.22	♦ Land		('000)	113	106	103	126	134
1.23	* railway		('000)	..	..	..	..	..
1.24	* road		('000)	113	106	103	126	134
1.25	* others		('000)	..	..	..	..	..
	Accommodation							
	Hotels and similar establishments							
1.31	♦ Guests		('000)	..	..	..	..	..
1.32	♦ Overnights		('000)	1,059	1,212	1,372	1,336	1,403
	Expenditure							
1.33	Total		US$ Mn	201	174	193	153	160
1.34	♦ Travel		US$ Mn	180	170	189	151	154
1.35	♦ Passenger transport		US$ Mn	21	4	4	2	6
	Expenditure by main purpose of the trip							
1.36	Total		US$ Mn	180	170	189	151	154
1.37	♦ Personal		US$ Mn	85	82	99	68	70
1.38	♦ Business and professional		US$ Mn	95	88	90	83	84
	Indicators							
1.39	Average size of travel party		Persons	..	..	..	..	..
	Average length of stay							
1.40	Total		Days	..	..	..	..	..
1.41	♦ For all commercial accommodation services		Nights	5.06	5.50	5.94	5.51	5.59
1.42	* of which, "hotels and similar establishments"		Nights	..	..	..	..	..
1.43	♦ For non commercial accommodation services		Days	..	..	..	..	..
1.44	Average expenditure per day		US$	..	..	..	..	..
3.	**OUTBOUND TOURISM**							
	Data							
	Expenditure							
3.4	Total		US$ Mn	81	96	40	54	68
3.5	♦ Travel		US$ Mn	53	43	39	54	56
3.6	♦ Passenger transport		US$ Mn	28	53	0.5	0.2	12
	Expenditure by main purpose of the trip							
3.7	Total		US$ Mn	53	43	39	54	56
3.8	♦ Personal		US$ Mn	26	29	35	32	34
3.9	♦ Business and professional		US$ Mn	27	14	4	22	22

BENIN

Cod.	Basic data and indicators	Notes	Units	2011	2012	2013	2014	2015
4.	**TOURISM INDUSTRIES**							
	Data							
	Number of establishments							
4.1	Total		Units	1,472	1,502	1,575	1,629	1,701
4.2	♦ Accommodation for visitors		Units	..	..	..	..	..
4.3	* of which, "hotels and similar establishments"		Units	861	891	935	982	1,031
4.4	♦ Food and beverage serving activities		Units	..	..	..	..	..
4.5	♦ Passenger transportation		Units	..	..	..	..	..
4.6	♦ Travel agencies and other reservation services activities		Units	91	91	120	127	150
4.7	♦ Other tourism industries		Units	520	520	520	520	520
	Accommodation for visitors in hotels and similar establishments							
	Non-monetary data							
4.13	♦ Number of establishments		Units	861	891	935	982	1,031
4.14	♦ Number of rooms		Units	11,576	12,155	12,763	13,401	14,071
4.15	♦ Number of bed-places		Units	27,231	28,593	30,022	31,524	33,100
	Indicators							
4.16	Occupancy rate / rooms		Percent	25.06	27.32	28.27	27.33	27.31
4.17	Occupancy rate / bed-places		Percent	10.66	11.61	12.52	11.61	11.77
4.18	Average length of stay		Nights	5.06	5.51	5.94	5.51	5.51
4.19	Available capacity (bed-places per 1000 inhabitants)		Units	2.78	2.85	2.91	2.97	3.04
6.	**COMPLEMENTARY INDICATORS**							
	Demand							
6.1	Gross travel propensity		Units	..	..	..	..	..
6.2	(1.2 inbound tourists) / population		Units	0.02	0.02	0.02	0.02	0.02
	Macroeconomic indicators related to international tourism							
6.3	Inbound tourism expenditure over GDP		Percent	2.8	2.3	2.3	1.7	..
6.4	Outbound tourism expenditure over GDP		Percent	1.1	1.3	0.5	0.6	..
6.5	Tourism balance (inbound minus outbound tourism expenditure) over GDP		Percent	1.7	1.0	1.8	1.1	..
6.6	Tourism openness (inbound plus outbound tourism expenditure) over GDP		Percent	3.9	3.6	2.8	2.3	..
6.7	Tourism coverage (inbound over outbound tourism expenditure)		Percent	248.1	181.3	488.6	282.3	235.3
6.8	Inbound tourism expenditure over exports of goods		Percent	16.1	12.1	9.7	6.0	..
6.9	Inbound tourism expenditure over exports of services		Percent	48.9	40.1	37.5	32.0	..
6.10	Inbound tourism expenditure over exports of goods and services		Percent	12.1	9.3	7.7	5.0	..
6.11	Inbound tourism expenditure over current account credits		Percent	10.2	7.7	6.4	4.2	..
6.12	Outbound tourism expenditure over imports of goods		Percent	4.5	4.8	1.5	1.7	..
6.13	Outbound tourism expenditure over imports of services		Percent	16.1	16.4	5.2	6.1	..
6.14	Outbound tourism expenditure over imports of goods and		Percent	3.5	3.7	1.2	1.3	..
6.15	Outbound tourism expenditure over current account debits		Percent	3.3	3.5	1.1	1.2	..

BERMUDA

Cod.	Basic data and indicators	Notes	Units	2011	2012	2013	2014	2015
1.	**INBOUND TOURISM**							
	Data							
	Arrivals	(1)						
1.1	Total		('000)	652	610	576	580	591
1.2	♦ Overnight visitors (tourists)		('000)	236	232	236	224	220
1.3	♦ Same-day visitors (excursionists)		('000)	416	378	340	356	371
1.4	* of which, cruise passengers		('000)	416	378	340	356	371
	Arrivals by region							
1.5	Total	(2)	('000)	236	232	236	224	220
1.6	♦ Africa		('000)	..	..	..	..	..
1.7	♦ Americas		('000)	202	199	199	189	182
1.8	♦ East Asia and the Pacific		('000)	1	1	..	1	..
1.9	♦ Europe		('000)	27	26	29	28	30
1.10	♦ Middle East		('000)	..	..	..	..	..
1.11	♦ South Asia		('000)	..	..	..	..	..
1.12	♦ Other not classified		('000)	6	6	8	7	8
1.13	* of which, nationals residing abroad		('000)	..	..	..	..	..
	Arrivals by main purpose							
1.14	Total	(2)	('000)	236	232	236	224	220
1.15	♦ Personal		('000)	184	187	187	178	175
1.16	* holidays, leisure and recreation		('000)	145	151	151	142	140
1.17	* other personal purposes		('000)	39	36	36	36	35
1.18	♦ Business and professional		('000)	52	45	49	47	45
	Arrivals by mode of transport							
1.19	Total		('000)	652	610	576	580	591
1.20	♦ Air		('000)	236	232	236	224	220
1.21	♦ Water	(3)	('000)	416	378	340	356	371
1.22	♦ Land		('000)	..	..	..	..	..
1.23	* railway		('000)	..	..	..	..	..
1.24	* road		('000)	..	..	..	..	..
1.25	* others		('000)	..	..	..	..	..
	Accommodation							
	Total							
1.29	♦ Guests		('000)	236	232	236	224	220
1.30	♦ Overnights	(4)	('000)	1,429	1,414	..	..	..
	Hotels and similar establishments							
1.31	♦ Guests		('000)	177	174	175	161	158
1.32	♦ Overnights		('000)	876	845	..	..	..
	Expenditure							
1.33	Total		US$ Mn	500	448	447	419	393
1.34	♦ Travel		US$ Mn	493	441	439	412	387
1.35	♦ Passenger transport		US$ Mn	7	7	8	7	6
	Expenditure by main purpose of the trip							
1.36	Total		US$ Mn	493	441	439	412	387
1.37	♦ Personal		US$ Mn	374	340	327	310	288
1.38	♦ Business and professional		US$ Mn	119	101	112	102	99
	Indicators							
1.39	Average size of travel party		Persons	..	..	..	..	..
	Average length of stay							
1.40	Total		Days	..	..	..	..	..
1.41	♦ For all commercial accommodation services		Nights	6.10	6.10	7.10	6.28	6.30
1.42	* of which, "hotels and similar establishments"		Nights	..	..	..	..	..
1.43	♦ For non commercial accommodation services		Days	..	..	..	..	..
1.44	Average expenditure per day		US$	..	..	..	..	..
3.	**OUTBOUND TOURISM**							
	Data							
	Expenditure							
3.4	Total		US$ Mn	326	327	322	360	381
3.5	♦ Travel		US$ Mn	216	221	222	253	262
3.6	♦ Passenger transport		US$ Mn	110	106	100	107	119
	Expenditure by main purpose of the trip							
3.7	Total		US$ Mn	216	221	222	253	262
3.8	♦ Personal		US$ Mn	205	210	211	241	251
3.9	♦ Business and professional		US$ Mn	11	11	11	12	11

BERMUDA

Cod.	Basic data and indicators	Notes	Units	2011	2012	2013	2014	2015
4.	**TOURISM INDUSTRIES**							
	Data							
	Number of establishments							
4.1	Total		Units	..	..	..	..	..
4.2	♦ Accommodation for visitors		Units	..	..	..	..	..
4.3	* of which, "hotels and similar establishments"		Units	48	48	47	45	43
4.4	♦ Food and beverage serving activities		Units	..	..	..	..	..
4.5	♦ Passenger transportation		Units	..	..	..	..	..
4.6	♦ Travel agencies and other reservation services activities		Units	..	..	..	..	..
4.7	♦ Other tourism industries		Units	..	..	..	..	..
	Accommodation for visitors in hotels and similar establishments							
	Non-monetary data							
4.13	♦ Number of establishments		Units	48	48	47	45	43
4.14	♦ Number of rooms		Units	2,591	2,531	2,538	2,415	2,372
4.15	♦ Number of bed-places		Units	5,401	5,243	5,265	5,018	4,934
	Indicators							
4.16	Occupancy rate / rooms		Percent	56.00	56.00	56.37	53.44	52.50
4.17	Occupancy rate / bed-places		Percent	..	..	..	..	..
4.18	Average length of stay		Nights	4.90	4.90	..	..	..
4.19	Available capacity (bed-places per 1000 inhabitants)		Units	84.95	82.99	83.87	80.45	79.58
6.	**COMPLEMENTARY INDICATORS**							
	Demand							
6.1	Gross travel propensity		Units	..	..	..	..	..
6.2	(1.2 inbound tourists) / population		Units	3.71	3.67	3.76	3.59	3.55
	Macroeconomic indicators related to international tourism							
6.3	Inbound tourism expenditure over GDP		Percent	..	..	..	..	..
6.4	Outbound tourism expenditure over GDP		Percent	..	..	..	..	..
6.5	Tourism balance (inbound minus outbound tourism expenditure) over GDP		Percent	..	..	..	..	..
6.6	Tourism openness (inbound plus outbound tourism expenditure) over GDP		Percent	..	..	..	..	..
6.7	Tourism coverage (inbound over outbound tourism expenditure)		Percent	153.4	137.0	138.8	116.4	103.1
6.8	Inbound tourism expenditure over exports of goods		Percent	3,958.8	4,021.5	3,522.5	3,949.1	2,021.6
6.9	Inbound tourism expenditure over exports of services		Percent	34.3	32.3	32.4	30.4	30.2
6.10	Inbound tourism expenditure over exports of goods and services		Percent	34.0	32.0	32.1	30.1	29.8
6.11	Inbound tourism expenditure over current account credits		Percent	15.4	13.9	11.7	12.5	11.9
6.12	Outbound tourism expenditure over imports of goods		Percent	36.2	36.3	31.8	37.2	40.8
6.13	Outbound tourism expenditure over imports of services		Percent	36.3	36.4	36.0	37.2	37.7
6.14	Outbound tourism expenditure over imports of goods and		Percent	18.1	18.2	16.9	18.6	19.6
6.15	Outbound tourism expenditure over current account debits		Percent	8.8	8.7	7.2	8.9	9.4

BHUTAN

Cod.	Basic data and indicators	Notes	Units	2011	2012	2013	2014	2015
1.	**INBOUND TOURISM**							
	Data							
	Arrivals							
1.1	Total		('000)	..	..	..	..	..
1.2	♦ Overnight visitors (tourists)	(1)	('000)	66	105	116	133	155
1.3	♦ Same-day visitors (excursionists)		('000)	..	..	..	..	..
1.4	* of which, cruise passengers		('000)	..	..	..	..	..
	Arrivals by region	(1)						
1.5	Total		('000)	38	44	44	58	49
1.6	♦ Africa		('000)	0.1	0.1	0.1	0.2	0.1
1.7	♦ Americas		('000)	8	8	9	10	9
1.8	♦ East Asia and the Pacific		('000)	15	21	21	32	25
1.9	♦ Europe		('000)	14	14	14	16	14
1.10	♦ Middle East		('000)	..	..	..	..	..
1.11	♦ South Asia		('000)	0.2	0.2	0.2	0.2	0.2
1.12	♦ Other not classified		('000)	..	..	..	..	..
1.13	* of which, nationals residing abroad		('000)	..	..	..	..	..
	Arrivals by main purpose	(1)						
1.14	Total		('000)	66	105	116	133	155
1.15	♦ Personal		('000)	43	85	98	118	140
1.16	* holidays, leisure and recreation		('000)	33	78	88	106	130
1.17	* other personal purposes		('000)	10	7	10	11	10
1.18	♦ Business and professional		('000)	23	20	18	16	15
	Arrivals by mode of transport	(1)						
1.19	Total		('000)	66	105	116	133	155
1.20	♦ Air		('000)	57	60	61	66	86
1.21	♦ Water		('000)	..	..	..	..	..
1.22	♦ Land		('000)	9	46	56	68	69
1.23	* railway		('000)	..	..	..	..	..
1.24	* road		('000)	9	46	56	68	69
1.25	* others		('000)	..	..	..	..	..
	Accommodation							
	Hotels and similar establishments							
1.31	♦ Guests		('000)	..	..	..	..	..
1.32	♦ Overnights	(2)	('000)	277	303	303	371	341
	Expenditure							
1.33	Total		US$ Mn	76	93	116	120	119
1.34	♦ Travel		US$ Mn	47	61	83	84	93
1.35	♦ Passenger transport		US$ Mn	29	32	33	36	26
	Expenditure by main purpose of the trip							
1.36	Total		US$ Mn	..	..	83	84	93
1.37	♦ Personal		US$ Mn	..	..	71	73	83
1.38	♦ Business and professional		US$ Mn	..	..	12	11	10
	Indicators							
1.39	Average size of travel party		Persons	4.0	3.9	3.8	..	..
	Average length of stay							
1.40	Total		Days	..	..	..	..	..
1.41	♦ For all commercial accommodation services		Nights	7.53	6.90	6.85	6.43	6.93
1.42	* of which, "hotels and similar establishments"		Nights	..	..	..	..	..
1.43	♦ For non commercial accommodation services		Days	..	..	..	..	..
1.44	Average expenditure per day		US$	..	..	..	..	..
3.	**OUTBOUND TOURISM**							
	Data							
	Expenditure							
3.4	Total		US$ Mn	58	70	67	45	44
3.5	♦ Travel		US$ Mn	56	68	64	42	40
3.6	♦ Passenger transport		US$ Mn	2	2	3	3	4
	Expenditure by main purpose of the trip							
3.7	Total		US$ Mn	56	68	64	42	40
3.8	♦ Personal		US$ Mn	48	55	53	30	26
3.9	♦ Business and professional		US$ Mn	8	13	11	12	14
	Indicators							
3.10	Average length of stay		Days	7.53	..	..	..	..
3.11	Average expenditure per day		US$	..	..	..	..	..

BHUTAN

Cod. Basic data and indicators	Notes	Units	2011	2012	2013	2014	2015
4. TOURISM INDUSTRIES							
Data							
Number of establishments							
4.1 Total		Units	..	..	..	..	..
4.2 ♦ Accommodation for visitors		Units	..	..	..	..	..
4.3 * of which, "hotels and similar establishments"		Units	128	123	123	139	..
4.4 ♦ Food and beverage serving activities		Units	..	..	..	..	..
4.5 ♦ Passenger transportation		Units	..	..	..	..	..
4.6 ♦ Travel agencies and other reservation services activities		Units	..	..	..	..	..
4.7 ♦ Other tourism industries		Units	..	..	..	..	..
Accommodation for visitors in hotels and similar establishments							
Non-monetary data							
4.13 ♦ Number of establishments		Units	128	123	123	139	..
4.14 ♦ Number of rooms		Units	2,805	2,749	2,805	3,204	..
4.15 ♦ Number of bed-places		Units	5,572	5,464	5,572	6,380	..
Indicators							
4.16 Occupancy rate / rooms		Percent	..	..	..	..	..
4.17 Occupancy rate / bed-places		Percent	..	..	..	..	..
4.18 Average length of stay		Nights	7.50	..	..	..	..
4.19 Available capacity (bed-places per 1000 inhabitants)		Units	7.61	7.35	7.38	8.34	..
6. COMPLEMENTARY INDICATORS							
Demand							
6.1 Gross travel propensity		Units	..	..	..	..	..
6.2 (1.2 inbound tourists) / population		Units	0.09	0.14	0.15	0.18	0.20
Macroeconomic indicators related to international tourism							
6.3 Inbound tourism expenditure over GDP		Percent	4.2	4.8	7.0	6.1	..
6.4 Outbound tourism expenditure over GDP		Percent	3.2	3.6	4.0	2.3	..
6.5 Tourism balance (inbound minus outbound tourism expenditure) over GDP		Percent	1.0	1.2	3.0	3.8	..
6.6 Tourism openness (inbound plus outbound tourism expenditure) over GDP		Percent	7.4	8.4	11.0	8.4	..
6.7 Tourism coverage (inbound over outbound tourism expenditure)		Percent	131.0	132.9	173.1	266.7	270.5
6.8 Inbound tourism expenditure over exports of goods		Percent	11.5	14.8	21.3	22.4	20.5
6.9 Inbound tourism expenditure over exports of services		Percent	92.8	91.0	94.1	96.4	96.1
6.10 Inbound tourism expenditure over exports of goods and services		Percent	10.2	12.8	17.4	18.2	16.9
6.11 Inbound tourism expenditure over current account credits		Percent	8.0	9.3	13.8	15.0	14.2
6.12 Outbound tourism expenditure over imports of goods		Percent	5.1	6.9	7.3	4.8	4.4
6.13 Outbound tourism expenditure over imports of services		Percent	32.8	35.6	37.7	23.7	23.9
6.14 Outbound tourism expenditure over imports of goods and		Percent	4.4	5.8	6.1	4.0	3.7
6.15 Outbound tourism expenditure over current account debits		Percent	4.2	5.5	5.8	3.9	3.6

BOLIVIA, PLURINATIONAL STATE OF

Cod. Basic data and indicators	Notes	Units	2011	2012	2013	2014	2015
1. INBOUND TOURISM							
Data							
Arrivals							
1.1 Total		('000)	..	..	..	..	..
1.2 ♦ Overnight visitors (tourists)	(1)	('000)	711	798	798	871	882
1.3 ♦ Same-day visitors (excursionists)		('000)	..	..	..	..	..
1.4 * of which, cruise passengers		('000)	..	..	..	..	..
Arrivals by region	(1)						
1.5 Total		('000)	711	798	798	871	882
1.6 ♦ Africa		('000)	1	3	1	2	1
1.7 ♦ Americas		('000)	500	580	584	633	642
1.8 ♦ East Asia and the Pacific		('000)	42	49	56	57	58
1.9 ♦ Europe		('000)	168	166	157	178	181
1.10 ♦ Middle East		('000)	..	..	..	..	..
1.11 ♦ South Asia		('000)	..	..	..	..	..
1.12 ♦ Other not classified		('000)	..	..	..	..	..
1.13 * of which, nationals residing abroad		('000)	..	..	..	..	..
Arrivals by main purpose	(2)						
1.14 Total		('000)	711	798	798	870	882
1.15 ♦ Personal		('000)	652	732	732	833	843
1.16 * holidays, leisure and recreation		('000)	344	386	386	520	529
1.17 * other personal purposes		('000)	308	346	346	313	314
1.18 ♦ Business and professional		('000)	59	66	66	37	39
Arrivals by mode of transport							
1.19 Total		('000)	711	798	798	870	882
1.20 ♦ Air		('000)	287	292	331	375	410
1.21 ♦ Water	(3)	('000)	1	1	1	1	2
1.22 ♦ Land		('000)	423	505	466	494	470
1.23 * railway		('000)	4	5	7	8	9
1.24 * road		('000)	419	500	459	486	461
1.25 * others		('000)	..	..	..	..	..
Arrivals by form of organization of the trip	(4)(5)						
1.26 Total		('000)	..	..	..	..	..
1.27 ♦ Package tour		('000)	..	..	..	..	..
1.28 ♦ Other forms		('000)	..	..	..	..	..
Accommodation							
Hotels and similar establishments	(6)						
1.31 ♦ Guests		('000)	560	564	572	588	582
1.32 ♦ Overnights		('000)	896	856	886	896	899
Expenditure							
1.33 Total		US$ Mn	499	631	639	736	804
1.34 ♦ Travel		US$ Mn	380	594	574	652	693
1.35 ♦ Passenger transport		US$ Mn	119	37	65	84	111
Expenditure by main purpose of the trip							
1.36 Total		US$ Mn	380	594	574	652	693
1.37 ♦ Personal		US$ Mn	270	416	402	489	520
1.38 ♦ Business and professional		US$ Mn	110	178	172	163	173
Indicators							
1.39 Average size of travel party	(7)	Persons	..	..	..	5.0	..
Average length of stay							
1.40 Total	(5)	Days	..	..	..	19.00	..
1.41 ♦ For all commercial accommodation services		Nights	..	..	..	..	..
1.42 * of which, "hotels and similar establishments"		Nights	..	..	..	..	..
1.43 ♦ For non commercial accommodation services		Days	..	..	..	..	..
1.44 Average expenditure per day	(5)	US$	..	..	..	61.5	..
2. DOMESTIC TOURISM							
Data							
Accommodation							
Hotels and similar establishments	(6)						
2.21 ♦ Guests		('000)	1,299	1,367	1,507	1,559	1,570
2.22 ♦ Overnights		('000)	1,010	1,000	1,037	1,060	1,057

BOLIVIA, PLURINATIONAL STATE OF

Cod. Basic data and indicators	Notes	Units	2011	2012	2013	2014	2015
3. OUTBOUND TOURISM							
Data							
Departures							
3.1 Total		('000)	..	..	..	..	..
3.2 ♦ Overnight visitors (tourists)		('000)	775	788	837	932	965
3.3 ♦ Same-day visitors (excursionists)		('000)	..	..	..	..	..
Expenditure							
3.4 Total		US$ Mn	410	502	660	977	846
3.5 ♦ Travel		US$ Mn	298	361	521	831	709
3.6 ♦ Passenger transport		US$ Mn	112	141	139	146	137
Expenditure by main purpose of the trip							
3.7 Total		US$ Mn	298	360	521	831	709
3.8 ♦ Personal		US$ Mn	209	252	120	563	532
3.9 ♦ Business and professional		US$ Mn	89	108	401	267	177
Indicators	(5)						
3.10 Average length of stay		Days	..	..	..	20.00	..
3.11 Average expenditure per day		US$	..	..	..	68.8	..
4. TOURISM INDUSTRIES							
Data							
Number of establishments							
4.1 Total		Units	..	..	..	..	..
4.2 ♦ Accommodation for visitors		Units	..	..	..	..	..
4.3 * of which, "hotels and similar establishments"	(6)	Units	1,072	1,148	1,177	1,293	1,381
4.4 ♦ Food and beverage serving activities		Units	..	..	..	..	..
4.5 ♦ Passenger transportation		Units	..	..	..	..	..
4.6 ♦ Travel agencies and other reservation services activities		Units	..	..	..	..	..
4.7 ♦ Other tourism industries		Units	..	..	..	..	..
Accommodation for visitors in hotels and similar establishments							
Non-monetary data	(6)						
4.13 ♦ Number of establishments		Units	1,072	1,148	1,177	1,293	1,381
4.14 ♦ Number of rooms		Units	22,772	25,399	26,190	28,256	29,809
4.15 ♦ Number of bed-places		Units	36,801	41,701	42,923	46,216	48,719
Indicators							
4.16 Occupancy rate / rooms		Percent	..	..	..	..	..
4.17 Occupancy rate / bed-places		Percent	..	..	..	..	..
4.18 Average length of stay		Nights	..	..	..	..	..
4.19 Available capacity (bed-places per 1000 inhabitants)		Units	3.65	4.07	4.13	4.38	4.54
6. COMPLEMENTARY INDICATORS							
Demand							
6.1 Gross travel propensity		Units	..	..	..	..	..
6.2 (1.2 inbound tourists) / population		Units	0.07	0.08	0.08	0.08	0.08
Macroeconomic indicators related to international tourism							
6.3 Inbound tourism expenditure over GDP		Percent	2.1	2.3	2.1	2.2	2.4
6.4 Outbound tourism expenditure over GDP		Percent	1.7	1.9	2.2	3.0	2.6
6.5 Tourism balance (inbound minus outbound tourism expenditure) over GDP		Percent	0.4	0.4	-0.1	-0.8	-0.2
6.6 Tourism openness (inbound plus outbound tourism expenditure) over GDP		Percent	3.8	4.2	4.3	5.2	5.0
6.7 Tourism coverage (inbound over outbound tourism expenditure)		Percent	121.7	125.7	96.8	75.3	95.0
6.8 Inbound tourism expenditure over exports of goods		Percent	6.1	5.7	5.5	6.1	..
6.9 Inbound tourism expenditure over exports of services		Percent	52.6	56.1	52.6	54.6	..
6.10 Inbound tourism expenditure over exports of goods and services		Percent	5.5	5.1	5.0	5.5	..
6.11 Inbound tourism expenditure over current account credits		Percent	4.7	4.6	4.4	4.9	..
6.12 Outbound tourism expenditure over imports of goods		Percent	5.8	6.3	7.6	9.8	..
6.13 Outbound tourism expenditure over imports of services		Percent	24.8	26.1	28.3	32.0	..
6.14 Outbound tourism expenditure over imports of goods and		Percent	4.7	5.1	6.0	7.5	..
6.15 Outbound tourism expenditure over current account debits		Percent	4.5	4.9	5.8	7.3	..

BOSNIA AND HERZEGOVINA

Cod. Basic data and indicators	Notes	Units	2011	2012	2013	2014	2015
1. INBOUND TOURISM							
Data							
Arrivals							
1.1 Total		('000)	..	..	..	..	..
1.2 ♦ Overnight visitors (tourists)	(1)	('000)	392	439	529	536	678
1.3 ♦ Same-day visitors (excursionists)		('000)	..	..	..	..	..
1.4 * of which, cruise passengers		('000)	..	..	..	..	..
Arrivals by region	(1)						
1.5 Total		('000)	392	439	529	536	678
1.6 ♦ Africa	(2)	('000)	..	..	1	1	2
1.7 ♦ Americas		('000)	10	12	19	22	29
1.8 ♦ East Asia and the Pacific		('000)	9	12	35	58	89
1.9 ♦ Europe		('000)	356	384	462	441	536
1.10 ♦ Middle East		('000)	1	2	12	13	21
1.11 ♦ South Asia	(2)	('000)	..	..	1	1	1
1.12 ♦ Other not classified		('000)	16	29	..	..	..
1.13 * of which, nationals residing abroad		('000)	..	..	..	..	..
Arrivals by mode of transport	(3)						
1.19 Total		('000)	..	13,432	12,972	12,731	13,120
1.20 ♦ Air		('000)	..	262	290	334	395
1.21 ♦ Water		('000)	..	18	14	3	3
1.22 ♦ Land		('000)	..	13,152	12,668	12,394	12,722
1.23 * railway		('000)	..	41	15	12	12
1.24 * road		('000)	..	13,111	12,653	12,382	12,710
1.25 * others		('000)	..	..	..	..	..
Accommodation							
Total							
1.29 ♦ Guests		('000)	392	439	529	536	678
1.30 ♦ Overnights		('000)	836	931	1,109	1,088	1,426
Hotels and similar establishments							
1.31 ♦ Guests		('000)	380	418	509	511	640
1.32 ♦ Overnights		('000)	807	884	1,063	1,031	1,341
Expenditure							
1.33 Total		US$ Mn	722	686	752	771	713
1.34 ♦ Travel		US$ Mn	635	615	685	707	656
1.35 ♦ Passenger transport		US$ Mn	87	71	67	64	57
Expenditure by main purpose of the trip							
1.36 Total		US$ Mn	635	615	685	707	656
1.37 ♦ Personal		US$ Mn	594	487	542	566	554
1.38 ♦ Business and professional		US$ Mn	41	128	143	141	102
Indicators							
1.39 Average size of travel party		Persons	..	..	..	..	..
Average length of stay							
1.40 Total		Days	..	..	..	..	..
1.41 ♦ For all commercial accommodation services		Nights	2.13	2.10	2.20	2.00	2.10
1.42 * of which, "hotels and similar establishments"		Nights	2.12	2.11	2.10	2.00	2.00
1.43 ♦ For non commercial accommodation services		Days	..	..	..	..	..
1.44 Average expenditure per day		US$	..	..	..	..	..
2. DOMESTIC TOURISM							
Data							
Accommodation							
Total							
2.19 ♦ Guests		('000)	294	309	316	310	351
2.20 ♦ Overnights		('000)	668	714	714	623	717
Hotels and similar establishments							
2.21 ♦ Guests		('000)	262	274	297	293	329
2.22 ♦ Overnights		('000)	509	540	614	567	657
Indicators							
2.23 Average size of travel party		Persons	..	..	..	..	..
Average length of stay							
2.24 Total		Days	..	..	..	..	..
2.25 ♦ For all commercial accommodation services		Nights	2.27	2.30	2.30	2.00	2.00
2.26 * of which, "hotels and similar establishments"		Nights	1.94	1.97	2.10	1.90	2.00
2.27 ♦ For non commercial accommodation services		Days	..	..	..	..	..
2.28 Average expenditure per day		US$	..	..	..	..	..

BOSNIA AND HERZEGOVINA

Cod.	Basic data and indicators	Notes	Units	2011	2012	2013	2014	2015
3.	**OUTBOUND TOURISM**							
	Data							
	Expenditure							
3.4	Total		US$ Mn	214	196	198	211	201
3.5	♦ Travel		US$ Mn	160	139	133	135	130
3.6	♦ Passenger transport		US$ Mn	54	57	65	76	71
	Expenditure by main purpose of the trip							
3.7	Total		US$ Mn	160	139	133	135	130
3.8	♦ Personal		US$ Mn	134	121	118	121	110
3.9	♦ Business and professional		US$ Mn	26	19	15	14	20
4.	**TOURISM INDUSTRIES**							
	Data							
	Number of establishments							
4.1	Total		Units	..	..	..	..	..
4.2	♦ Accommodation for visitors		Units	434	432	462	503	554
4.3	* of which, "hotels and similar establishments"		Units	379	369	445	487	530
4.4	♦ Food and beverage serving activities		Units	..	..	..	..	..
4.5	♦ Passenger transportation		Units	..	..	..	..	..
4.6	♦ Travel agencies and other reservation services activities		Units	..	..	..	..	..
4.7	♦ Other tourism industries		Units	..	..	..	..	..
	Accommodation for visitors in hotels and similar establishments							
	Non-monetary data							
4.13	♦ Number of establishments		Units	379	369	445	487	530
4.14	♦ Number of rooms		Units	11,317	10,146	12,624	13,197	14,315
4.15	♦ Number of bed-places		Units	23,840	21,127	24,232	27,096	29,585
	Indicators							
4.16	Occupancy rate / rooms		Percent	..	..	..	..	..
4.17	Occupancy rate / bed-places		Percent	..	..	..	..	..
4.18	Average length of stay		Nights	..	..	..	..	..
4.19	Available capacity (bed-places per 1000 inhabitants)		Units	6.22	5.52	6.34	7.10	7.76
5.	**EMPLOYMENT**							
	Data							
	Number of employees by tourism industries	(4)						
5.1	Total		('000)	27.6	26.6	27.3	29.7	30.1
5.2	♦ Accommodation services for visitors (hotels and similar establishments)		('000)	5.3	5.3	5.2	5.4	5.3
5.3	♦ Other accommodation services		('000)	..	..	..	..	..
5.4	♦ Food and beverage serving activities		('000)	15.3	14.3	15.1	17.3	17.8
5.5	♦ Passenger transportation		('000)	..	..	..	..	..
5.6	♦ Travel agencies and other reservation services activities		('000)	7.0	7.0	7.0	7.0	7.0
5.7	♦ Other tourism industries		('000)	..	..	..	..	..
6.	**COMPLEMENTARY INDICATORS**							
	Demand							
6.1	Gross travel propensity		Units	..	..	..	..	..
6.2	(1.2 inbound tourists) / population		Units	0.10	0.11	0.14	0.14	0.18
	Macroeconomic indicators related to international tourism							
6.3	Inbound tourism expenditure over GDP		Percent	3.8	3.8	3.9	4.0	..
6.4	Outbound tourism expenditure over GDP		Percent	1.1	1.1	1.0	1.1	..
6.5	Tourism balance (inbound minus outbound tourism expenditure) over GDP		Percent	2.7	2.7	2.9	2.9	..
6.6	Tourism openness (inbound plus outbound tourism expenditure) over GDP		Percent	4.9	4.9	4.9	5.1	..
6.7	Tourism coverage (inbound over outbound tourism expenditure)		Percent	337.4	350.0	379.8	365.4	354.7
6.8	Inbound tourism expenditure over exports of goods		Percent	17.6	17.9	17.2	17.2	18.1
6.9	Inbound tourism expenditure over exports of services		Percent	38.6	39.7	42.5	42.0	43.4
6.10	Inbound tourism expenditure over exports of goods and services		Percent	12.1	12.3	12.3	12.2	12.8
6.11	Inbound tourism expenditure over current account credits		Percent	7.7	7.9	8.0	7.8	8.6
6.12	Outbound tourism expenditure over imports of goods		Percent	2.2	2.2	2.1	2.1	2.5
6.13	Outbound tourism expenditure over imports of services		Percent	38.4	38.2	39.1	39.6	41.1
6.14	Outbound tourism expenditure over imports of goods and		Percent	2.1	2.0	2.0	2.0	2.3
6.15	Outbound tourism expenditure over current account debits		Percent	1.9	1.9	1.9	1.9	2.1

BOTSWANA

Cod.	Basic data and indicators	Notes	Units	2011	2012	2013	2014	2015
1.	**INBOUND TOURISM**							
	Data							
	Arrivals							
1.1	Total		('000)	..	..	..	..	..
1.2	♦ Overnight visitors (tourists)		('000)	..	1,614	1,544	1,966	..
1.3	♦ Same-day visitors (excursionists)		('000)	..	..	..	..	..
1.4	* of which, cruise passengers		('000)	..	..	..	..	..
	Arrivals by region							
1.5	Total		('000)	..	1,614	1,544	1,966	..
1.6	♦ Africa		('000)	..	1,364	1,182	1,723	..
1.7	♦ Americas		('000)	..	40	150	60	..
1.8	♦ East Asia and the Pacific		('000)	..	46	53	37	..
1.9	♦ Europe		('000)	..	140	151	131	..
1.10	♦ Middle East		('000)	..	..	..	1	..
1.11	♦ South Asia		('000)	..	9	3	9	..
1.12	♦ Other not classified		('000)	..	16	6	4	..
1.13	* of which, nationals residing abroad		('000)	..	..	..	..	..
	Arrivals by main purpose							
1.14	Total		('000)	..	1,614	1,544	1,966	..
1.15	♦ Personal		('000)	..	1,465	1,187	1,357	..
1.16	* holidays, leisure and recreation		('000)	..	367	474	275	..
1.17	* other personal purposes		('000)	..	1,098	713	1,082	..
1.18	♦ Business and professional		('000)	..	149	357	609	..
	Arrivals by mode of transport	(1)						
1.19	Total		('000)	..	..	..	2,083	..
1.20	♦ Air		('000)	..	..	..	130	..
1.21	♦ Water		('000)	..	..	..	..	..
1.22	♦ Land		('000)	..	..	..	1,953	..
1.23	* railway		('000)	..	..	..	..	..
1.24	* road		('000)	..	..	..	1,953	..
1.25	* others		('000)	..	..	..	..	..
	Accommodation							
	Hotels and similar establishments							
1.31	♦ Guests		('000)	446	..	494	..	..
1.32	♦ Overnights		('000)	..	..	..	..	..
	Expenditure							
1.33	Total		US$ Mn	865	858	888	978	950
1.34	♦ Travel		US$ Mn	862	856	885	977	948
1.35	♦ Passenger transport		US$ Mn	3	2	3	1	2
	Expenditure by main purpose of the trip							
1.36	Total		US$ Mn	862	856	885	977	948
1.37	♦ Personal		US$ Mn	861	855	884	975	947
1.38	♦ Business and professional		US$ Mn	1	1	1	2	1
2.	**DOMESTIC TOURISM**							
	Data							
	Accommodation							
	Hotels and similar establishments							
2.21	♦ Guests		('000)	481	..	503	..	..
2.22	♦ Overnights		('000)	..	..	..	..	..
3.	**OUTBOUND TOURISM**							
	Data							
	Departures							
3.1	Total		('000)	..	..	..	..	..
3.2	♦ Overnight visitors (tourists)		('000)	..	..	..	178	..
3.3	♦ Same-day visitors (excursionists)		('000)	..	..	..	..	..
	Expenditure							
3.4	Total		US$ Mn	316	298	262	277	242
3.5	♦ Travel		US$ Mn	316	297	262	276	241
3.6	♦ Passenger transport		US$ Mn	0.5	0.9	0.2	1.0	0.5
	Expenditure by main purpose of the trip							
3.7	Total		US$ Mn	316	297	262	276	241
3.8	♦ Personal		US$ Mn	300	262	258	272	238
3.9	♦ Business and professional		US$ Mn	16	35	4	4	3

BOTSWANA

Cod.	Basic data and indicators	Notes	Units	2011	2012	2013	2014	2015
4.	**TOURISM INDUSTRIES**							
	Data							
	Number of establishments							
4.1	Total		Units	..	..	..	..	..
4.2	♦ Accommodation for visitors		Units	..	..	..	..	..
4.3	* of which, "hotels and similar establishments"		Units	428	..	528	..	..
4.4	♦ Food and beverage serving activities		Units	..	..	..	..	..
4.5	♦ Passenger transportation		Units	..	..	..	..	..
4.6	♦ Travel agencies and other reservation services activities		Units	..	..	..	..	..
4.7	♦ Other tourism industries		Units	..	..	..	..	..
	Accommodation for visitors in hotels and similar establishments							
	Non-monetary data							
4.13	♦ Number of establishments		Units	428	..	528	..	..
4.14	♦ Number of rooms		Units	7,131	..	8,362	..	..
4.15	♦ Number of bed-places		Units	14,386	..	15,804	..	..
	Indicators							
4.16	Occupancy rate / rooms		Percent	51.50	..	47.10	..	..
4.17	Occupancy rate / bed-places		Percent	43.30	..	38.60	..	..
4.18	Average length of stay		Nights	2.50	..	2.20	..	..
4.19	Available capacity (bed-places per 1000 inhabitants)		Units	6.88	..	7.26	..	..
6.	**COMPLEMENTARY INDICATORS**							
	Demand							
6.1	Gross travel propensity		Units	..	..	..	..	
6.2	(1.2 inbound tourists) / population		Units	..	0.76	0.71	0.89	..
	Macroeconomic indicators related to international tourism							
6.3	Inbound tourism expenditure over GDP		Percent	5.7	5.9	6.0	6.2	..
6.4	Outbound tourism expenditure over GDP		Percent	2.1	2.0	1.8	1.8	..
6.5	Tourism balance (inbound minus outbound tourism expenditure) over GDP		Percent	3.6	3.9	4.2	4.4	..
6.6	Tourism openness (inbound plus outbound tourism expenditure) over GDP		Percent	7.8	7.9	7.8	8.0	..
6.7	Tourism coverage (inbound over outbound tourism expenditure)		Percent	273.4	288.2	338.8	353.1	393.4
6.8	Inbound tourism expenditure over exports of goods		Percent	13.4	14.7	11.2	11.5	15.1
6.9	Inbound tourism expenditure over exports of services		Percent	70.5	79.5	71.5	72.3	75.8
6.10	Inbound tourism expenditure over exports of goods and services		Percent	11.3	12.4	9.7	9.9	12.6
6.11	Inbound tourism expenditure over current account credits		Percent	9.3	9.5	7.9	8.2	10.0
6.12	Outbound tourism expenditure over imports of goods		Percent	4.4	3.7	3.2	3.5	3.4
6.13	Outbound tourism expenditure over imports of services		Percent	29.1	35.5	29.5	35.8	38.4
6.14	Outbound tourism expenditure over imports of goods and		Percent	3.8	3.4	2.9	3.2	3.1
6.15	Outbound tourism expenditure over current account debits		Percent	3.6	3.2	2.8	3.0	3.0

BRAZIL

Cod.	Basic data and indicators	Notes	Units	2011	2012	2013	2014	2015
1.	**INBOUND TOURISM**							
	Data							
	Arrivals							
1.1	Total		('000)	..	..	..	..	..
1.2	♦ Overnight visitors (tourists)	(1)	('000)	5,433	5,677	5,813	6,430	6,306
1.3	♦ Same-day visitors (excursionists)		('000)	..	..	..	..	..
1.4	* of which, cruise passengers		('000)	..	..	..	..	..
	Arrivals by region	(1)						
1.5	Total		('000)	5,433	5,676	5,813	6,430	6,306
1.6	♦ Africa		('000)	86	92	95	128	111
1.7	♦ Americas		('000)	3,402	3,582	3,726	4,041	4,209
1.8	♦ East Asia and the Pacific		('000)	261	294	299	344	296
1.9	♦ Europe		('000)	1,663	1,686	1,670	1,891	1,667
1.10	♦ Middle East		('000)	..	..	..	..	..
1.11	♦ South Asia		('000)	21	22	23	26	23
1.12	♦ Other not classified		('000)	..	..	..	..	..
1.13	* of which, nationals residing abroad		('000)	..	..	..	..	..
	Arrivals by main purpose	(1)						
1.14	Total		('000)	5,433	5,677	5,813	6,430	6,306
1.15	♦ Personal		('000)	4,042	4,246	4,290	5,022	5,032
1.16	* holidays, leisure and recreation		('000)	2,711	2,861	2,767	3,517	3,235
1.17	* other personal purposes		('000)	1,331	1,385	1,523	1,505	1,797
1.18	♦ Business and professional		('000)	1,391	1,431	1,523	1,408	1,274
	Arrivals by mode of transport	(1)						
1.19	Total		('000)	5,433	5,678	5,813	6,430	6,306
1.20	♦ Air		('000)	3,808	3,987	4,066	4,540	4,318
1.21	♦ Water	(2)	('000)	182	150	135	130	117
1.22	♦ Land		('000)	1,443	1,541	1,612	1,760	1,871
1.23	* railway		('000)	..	..	..	..	..
1.24	* road		('000)	1,443	1,541	1,612	1,760	1,871
1.25	* others		('000)	..	..	..	..	..
	Expenditure							
1.33	Total		US$ Mn	6,370	6,623	6,784	7,405	6,254
1.34	♦ Travel		US$ Mn	6,095	6,378	6,474	6,843	5,844
1.35	♦ Passenger transport		US$ Mn	275	245	310	562	410
	Expenditure by main purpose of the trip							
1.36	Total		US$ Mn	6,095	6,378	6,474	6,843	5,844
1.37	♦ Personal		US$ Mn	3,924	4,169	4,233	4,692	3,815
1.38	♦ Business and professional		US$ Mn	2,171	2,209	2,241	2,151	2,029
2.	**DOMESTIC TOURISM**							
	Data							
	Trips							
2.1	Total		('000)	..	..	..	..	..
2.2	♦ Overnight visitors (tourists)		('000)	190,884	..	..	..	..
2.3	♦ Same-day visitors (excursionists)		('000)	..	..	..	..	..
	Trips by main purpose							
2.4	Total		('000)	190,884	..	..	..	..
2.5	♦ Personal		('000)	173,505	..	..	..	..
2.6	* holidays, leisure and recreation		('000)	67,443	..	..	..	..
2.7	* other personal purposes		('000)	106,062	..	..	..	..
2.8	♦ Business and professional		('000)	17,379	..	..	..	..
	Trips by mode of transport							
2.9	Total		('000)	190,884	..	..	..	..
2.10	♦ Air		('000)	33,030	..	..	..	..
2.11	♦ Water		('000)	3,021	..	..	..	..
2.12	♦ Land		('000)	154,833	..	..	..	..
2.13	* railway		('000)	..	..	..	..	..
2.14	* road		('000)	154,833	..	..	..	..
2.15	* others		('000)	..	..	..	..	..
	Trips by form of organization							
2.16	Total		('000)	190,884	..	..	..	..
2.17	♦ Package tour		('000)	8,307	..	..	..	..
2.18	♦ Other forms		('000)	182,577	..	..	..	..

BRAZIL

Cod.	Basic data and indicators	Notes	Units	2011	2012	2013	2014	2015
	Indicators							
2.23	Average size of travel party		Persons	2.2	..	..	..	..
	Average length of stay							
2.24	Total		Days	10.00	..	..	..	..
2.25	♦ For all commercial accommodation services		Nights	7.10	..	..	..	..
2.26	* of which, "hotels and similar establishments"		Nights	7.10	..	..	..	..
2.27	♦ For non commercial accommodation services		Days	10.80	..	..	..	..
2.28	Average expenditure per day		US$	335.9	..	..	..	..
3.	**OUTBOUND TOURISM**							
	Data							
	Departures							
3.1	Total		('000)	..	..	..	..	..
3.2	♦ Overnight visitors (tourists)		('000)	7,807	8,512	8,870	9,622	9,469
3.3	♦ Same-day visitors (excursionists)		('000)	..	..		..	..
	Expenditure							
3.4	Total		US$ Mn	24,608	26,008	29,286	29,998	20,356
3.5	♦ Travel		US$ Mn	20,802	22,039	25,028	25,567	17,357
3.6	♦ Passenger transport		US$ Mn	3,806	3,969	4,258	4,431	2,999
	Expenditure by main purpose of the trip							
3.7	Total		US$ Mn	20,802	20,039	25,028	25,567	17,357
3.8	♦ Personal		US$ Mn	15,742	16,913	19,761	19,715	13,737
3.9	♦ Business and professional		US$ Mn	5,060	3,126	5,267	5,852	3,620
4.	**TOURISM INDUSTRIES**							
	Data							
	Number of establishments	(3)						
4.1	Total		Units	210,975	224,062	237,217	250,043	254,566
4.2	♦ Accommodation for visitors		Units	26,254	27,262	28,331	29,280	29,616
4.3	* of which, "hotels and similar establishments"		Units	..	..	..	..	..
4.4	♦ Food and beverage serving activities		Units	146,142	156,664	167,382	178,471	183,428
4.5	♦ Passenger transportation		Units	13,128	13,794	14,457	14,688	14,539
4.6	♦ Travel agencies and other reservation services activities		Units	11,229	11,820	12,130	12,327	12,077
4.7	♦ Other tourism industries		Units	14,222	14,522	14,917	15,277	14,906
	Accommodation for visitors in hotels and similar establishments							
	Monetary data							
4.8	♦ Output		US$ Mn	9,513.8	8,826.9	9,593.7	..	..
4.9	♦ Intermediate consumption		US$ Mn	4,025.3	3,619.4	3,737.3	..	..
4.10	♦ Gross value added		US$ Mn	5,488.5	5,207.5	5,856.4	..	..
4.11	♦ Compensation of employees		US$ Mn	2,026.4	2,038.5	2,198.7	..	..
4.12	♦ Gross fixed capital formation		US$ Mn	..	..	..	..	..
	Non-monetary data	(4)						
4.13	♦ Number of establishments		Units	9,963	..	7,602	8,138	7,117
4.14	♦ Number of rooms		Units	396,804	..	383,466	448,087	393,970
4.15	♦ Number of bed-places		Units	925,598	..	835,747	955,557	837,169
	Indicators							
4.16	Occupancy rate / rooms		Percent	..	..	..	..	..
4.17	Occupancy rate / bed-places		Percent	..	..	..	..	..
4.18	Average length of stay		Nights	..	..	..	..	..
4.19	Available capacity (bed-places per 1000 inhabitants)		Units	4.62	..	4.09	4.64	4.03
	Travel agencies and other reservation service activities							
	Monetary data							
4.20	♦ Output		US$ Mn	3,544.9	3,665.9	3,994.5	..	..
4.21	♦ Intermediate consumption		US$ Mn	1,442.7	1,632.2	1,634.8	..	..
4.22	♦ Gross value added		US$ Mn	2,102.2	2,033.7	2,359.7	..	..
4.23	♦ Compensation of employees		US$ Mn	832.4	816.7	888.6	..	..
4.24	♦ Gross fixed capital formation		US$ Mn	..	..	..	..	..

59

BRAZIL

Cod.	Basic data and indicators	Notes	Units	2011	2012	2013	2014	2015
5.	**EMPLOYMENT**							
	Data							
	Number of employees by tourism industries	**(5)**						
5.1	Total		('000)	2,052.6	2,059.7	1,938.9	2,045.1	2,074.9
5.2	♦ Accommodation services for visitors (hotels and similar establishments)		('000)	298.1	301.9	318.8	340.2	340.4
5.3	♦ Other accommodation services		('000)	..	..	..	..	..
5.4	♦ Food and beverage serving activities		('000)	1,111.0	1,119.0	1,009.7	1,085.9	1,132.5
5.5	♦ Passenger transportation		('000)	470.2	468.9	443.4	447.3	433.7
5.6	♦ Travel agencies and other reservation services activities		('000)	102.6	102.0	98.3	96.3	90.6
5.7	♦ Other tourism industries		('000)	70.7	67.9	68.7	75.4	77.7
	Number of jobs by status in employment	**(5)**						
5.8	Total		('000)	2,052.6	2,059.7	1,938.9	2,045.1	2,075.0
5.9	♦ Employees		('000)	946.8	990.7	985.3	1,033.0	1,038.6
5.10	♦ Self employed		('000)	1,105.8	1,069.0	953.6	1,012.1	1,036.4
	Indicators							
	Number of full-time equivalent jobs by status in employment							
5.11	Total		('000)	1,296.9	1,320.3	1,260.6	1,265.5	1,310.2
5.12	♦ Employees		('000)	845.8	885.8	881.2	886.1	930.8
5.13	* male		('000)	471.8	486.7	477.6	477.1	499.6
5.14	* female		('000)	374.0	399.1	403.6	409.0	431.2
5.15	♦ Self employed		('000)	451.1	434.5	379.4	379.4	379.4
5.16	* male		('000)	285.8	276.5	240.7	240.7	240.7
5.17	* female		('000)	165.3	158.0	138.7	138.7	138.7
6.	**COMPLEMENTARY INDICATORS**							
	Demand							
6.1	Gross travel propensity		Units	..	..	..	..	..
6.2	(1.2 inbound tourists + 2.2 domestic tourists) / population		Units	0.98	..	..	..	..
	Macroeconomic indicators related to international tourism							
6.3	Inbound tourism expenditure over GDP		Percent	0.3	0.3	0.3	0.3	0.4
6.4	Outbound tourism expenditure over GDP		Percent	1.0	1.2	1.3	1.3	1.1
6.5	Tourism balance (inbound minus outbound tourism expenditure) over GDP		Percent	-0.7	-0.9	-1.0	-1.0	-0.7
6.6	Tourism openness (inbound plus outbound tourism expenditure) over GDP		Percent	1.3	1.5	1.6	1.6	1.5
6.7	Tourism coverage (inbound over outbound tourism expenditure)		Percent	25.9	25.5	23.2	24.7	30.7
6.8	Inbound tourism expenditure over exports of goods		Percent	2.5	2.7	2.8	3.3	3.3
6.9	Inbound tourism expenditure over exports of services		Percent	17.2	16.9	17.8	18.5	18.5
6.10	Inbound tourism expenditure over exports of goods and services		Percent	2.2	2.4	2.4	2.8	2.8
6.11	Inbound tourism expenditure over current account credits		Percent	2.0	2.2	2.3	2.6	2.6
6.12	Outbound tourism expenditure over imports of goods		Percent	10.8	11.6	12.1	13.0	11.8
6.13	Outbound tourism expenditure over imports of services		Percent	33.2	32.9	34.7	34.1	28.8
6.14	Outbound tourism expenditure over imports of goods and		Percent	8.1	8.6	9.0	9.4	8.4
6.15	Outbound tourism expenditure over current account debits		Percent	7.5	8.3	8.6	9.0	7.9

BRITISH VIRGIN ISLANDS

Cod.	Basic data and indicators	Notes	Units	2011	2012	2013	2014	2015
1.	**INBOUND TOURISM**							
	Data							
	Arrivals							
1.1	Total		('000)	831	753	742	773	922
1.2	♦ Overnight visitors (tourists)		('000)	338	351	366	386	393
1.3	♦ Same-day visitors (excursionists)		('000)	493	402	376	387	529
1.4	* of which, cruise passengers		('000)	485	391	367	361	516
	Arrivals by region							
1.5	Total		('000)	338	351	366	..	..
1.6	♦ Africa		('000)	1	1	1	..	..
1.7	♦ Americas		('000)	301	316	321	..	..
1.8	♦ East Asia and the Pacific		('000)	4	3	4	..	..
1.9	♦ Europe		('000)	32	32	39	..	..
1.10	♦ Middle East		('000)	..	..	..	..	..
1.11	♦ South Asia		('000)	..	..	..	..	..
1.12	♦ Other not classified		('000)	1	..	..	..	..
1.13	* of which, nationals residing abroad		('000)	..	..	..	..	..
	Arrivals by main purpose							
1.14	Total		('000)	338	351	366	..	..
1.15	♦ Personal		('000)	317	330	343	..	..
1.16	* holidays, leisure and recreation		('000)	305	317	328	..	..
1.17	* other personal purposes		('000)	12	13	15	..	..
1.18	♦ Business and professional		('000)	21	21	23	..	..
	Arrivals by mode of transport							
1.19	Total		('000)	831	753	742	773	..
1.20	♦ Air		('000)	93	86	88	84	..
1.21	♦ Water	(1)	('000)	738	667	654	688	..
1.22	♦ Land		('000)	..	..	..	..	..
1.23	* railway		('000)	..	..	..	..	..
1.24	* road		('000)	..	..	..	..	..
1.25	* others		('000)	..	..	..	..	..
	Accommodation							
	Total							
1.29	♦ Guests		('000)	338	351	366	386	393
1.30	♦ Overnights		('000)	..	..	..	..	..
	Hotels and similar establishments							
1.31	♦ Guests		('000)	137	142	148	156	159
1.32	♦ Overnights		('000)	..	..	..	..	..
	Expenditure							
1.33	Total	(2)	US$ Mn	388	398	421	459	484
1.34	♦ Travel		US$ Mn	..	..	..	..	..
1.35	♦ Passenger transport		US$ Mn	..	..	..	..	..
3.	**OUTBOUND TOURISM**							
	Data							
	Departures							
3.1	Total		('000)	145	139	..	..	..
3.2	♦ Overnight visitors (tourists)		('000)	..	..	..	..	..
3.3	♦ Same-day visitors (excursionists)		('000)	..	..	..	..	..
4.	**TOURISM INDUSTRIES**							
	Data							
	Number of establishments							
4.1	Total		Units	..	..	..	..	..
4.2	♦ Accommodation for visitors		Units	223	223	223	..	..
4.3	* of which, "hotels and similar establishments"		Units	52	52	52	..	..
4.4	♦ Food and beverage serving activities		Units	..	..	..	..	..
4.5	♦ Passenger transportation		Units	..	..	..	..	..
4.6	♦ Travel agencies and other reservation services activities		Units	..	..	..	..	..
4.7	♦ Other tourism industries		Units	..	..	..	..	..
	Accommodation for visitors in hotels and similar establishments							
	Non-monetary data							
4.13	♦ Number of establishments		Units	52	52	52	..	..
4.14	♦ Number of rooms		Units	2,191	2,196	2,195	2,195	2,240
4.15	♦ Number of bed-places		Units	..	..	..	..	..

BRITISH VIRGIN ISLANDS

Cod.	Basic data and indicators	Notes	Units	2011	2012	2013	2014	2015
	Indicators							
4.16	Occupancy rate / rooms		Percent	63.30	61.60	53.70	51.60	78.60
4.17	Occupancy rate / bed-places		Percent	54.16	54.16	53.45	..	..
4.18	Average length of stay		Nights	6.70	6.80	6.50	6.80	6.70
4.19	Available capacity (bed-places per 1000 inhabitants)		Units	..	..	..	..	..
6.	**COMPLEMENTARY INDICATORS**							
	Demand							
6.1	Gross travel propensity		Units	..	..	..	..	..
6.2	(1.2 inbound tourists) / population		Units	12.11	12.31	12.60	13.05	13.05

BRUNEI DARUSSALAM

Cod. Basic data and indicators	Notes	Units	2011	2012	2013	2014	2015
1. INBOUND TOURISM							
Data							
Arrivals							
1.1 Total		('000)	..	..	..	..	..
1.2 ♦ Overnight visitors (tourists)	(1)	('000)	242	209	225	201	218
1.3 ♦ Same-day visitors (excursionists)		('000)	..	..	..	..	..
1.4 * of which, cruise passengers		('000)	..	..	..	..	..
Arrivals by region							
1.5 Total	(1)	('000)	242	209	225	201	218
1.6 ♦ Africa		('000)	..	..	..	..	..
1.7 ♦ Americas		('000)	7	6	8	6	6
1.8 ♦ East Asia and the Pacific		('000)	195	170	181	161	178
1.9 ♦ Europe		('000)	28	21	23	20	20
1.10 ♦ Middle East		('000)	2	1	1	1	1
1.11 ♦ South Asia		('000)	7	8	10	9	10
1.12 ♦ Other not classified		('000)	3	4	4	4	3
1.13 * of which, nationals residing abroad		('000)	..	..	..	..	..
Arrivals by main purpose	(1)						
1.14 Total		('000)	242	209	225	201	218
1.15 ♦ Personal		('000)	195	157	163	149	169
1.16 * holidays, leisure and recreation		('000)	89	83	87	78	89
1.17 * other personal purposes		('000)	106	74	76	70	80
1.18 ♦ Business and professional		('000)	47	52	62	52	49
Arrivals by mode of transport							
1.19 Total		('000)	242	209	225	201	218
1.20 ♦ Air		('000)	242	209	225	201	218
1.21 ♦ Water		('000)	..	..	..	..	..
1.22 ♦ Land		('000)	..	..	..	..	..
1.23 * railway		('000)	..	..	..	..	..
1.24 * road		('000)	..	..	..	..	..
1.25 * others		('000)	..	..	..	..	..
Expenditure							
1.33 Total		US$ Mn	..	..	..	..	..
1.34 ♦ Travel		US$ Mn	..	92	96	79	140
1.35 ♦ Passenger transport		US$ Mn	..	..	..	..	..
Indicators							
1.39 Average size of travel party		Persons	..	..	..	..	..
Average length of stay							
1.40 Total		Days	..	..	..	6.00	5.90
1.41 ♦ For all commercial accommodation services		Nights	..	..	..	..	..
1.42 * of which, "hotels and similar establishments"		Nights	..	..	..	..	..
1.43 ♦ For non commercial accommodation services		Days	..	..	..	..	..
1.44 Average expenditure per day		US$	..	..	..	..	..
3. OUTBOUND TOURISM							
Data							
Expenditure							
3.4 Total		US$ Mn	..	..	..	..	..
3.5 ♦ Travel		US$ Mn	..	591	624	616	459
3.6 ♦ Passenger transport		US$ Mn	..	..	..	..	..
4. TOURISM INDUSTRIES							
Data							
Number of establishments							
4.1 Total		Units	..	..	..	..	..
4.2 ♦ Accommodation for visitors		Units	..	..	..	..	..
4.3 * of which, "hotels and similar establishments"		Units	..	47	54	69	74
4.4 ♦ Food and beverage serving activities		Units	..	..	..	..	..
4.5 ♦ Passenger transportation		Units	..	..	..	..	..
4.6 ♦ Travel agencies and other reservation services activities		Units	..	..	..	..	..
4.7 ♦ Other tourism industries		Units	..	..	..	..	..
Accommodation for visitors in hotels and similar establishments							
Non-monetary data							
4.13 ♦ Number of establishments		Units	..	47	54	69	74
4.14 ♦ Number of rooms		Units	2,845	3,143	3,364	3,678	3,680
4.15 ♦ Number of bed-places		Units	..	4,207	4,648	5,107	5,297

BRUNEI DARUSSALAM

Cod.	Basic data and indicators	Notes	Units	2011	2012	2013	2014	2015
	Indicators							
4.16	Occupancy rate / rooms		Percent	..	..	..	..	..
4.17	Occupancy rate / bed-places		Percent	..	..	..	..	..
4.18	Average length of stay		Nights	..	..	..		
4.19	Available capacity (bed-places per 1000 inhabitants)		Units	..	10.37	11.30	12.24	12.52
5.	**EMPLOYMENT**							
	Data							
	Number of employees by tourism industries							
5.1	Total		('000)	..	..	2.5	2.7	2.8
5.2	♦ Accommodation services for visitors (hotels and similar establishments)		('000)	..	..	1.9	2.0	2.1
5.3	♦ Other accommodation services		('000)	..	..	..	..	..
5.4	♦ Food and beverage serving activities		('000)	..	..	..	..	..
5.5	♦ Passenger transportation		('000)	..	..	..	..	..
5.6	♦ Travel agencies and other reservation services activities		('000)	..	..	0.6	0.7	0.7
5.7	♦ Other tourism industries		('000)	..	..	..	..	..
6.	**COMPLEMENTARY INDICATORS**							
	Demand							
6.1	Gross travel propensity		Units	..	..	..	..	..
6.2	(1.2 inbound tourists) / population		Units	0.61	0.52	0.55	0.48	0.52
	Macroeconomic indicators related to international tourism							
6.3	Inbound tourism expenditure over GDP		Percent	..	0.5	0.6	0.5	..
6.4	Outbound tourism expenditure over GDP		Percent	..	3.5	3.9	3.6	..
6.5	Tourism balance (inbound minus outbound tourism expenditure) over GDP		Percent	..	-3.0	-3.3	-3.1	..
6.6	Tourism openness (inbound plus outbound tourism expenditure) over GDP		Percent	..	4.0	4.5	4.1	..
6.7	Tourism coverage (inbound over outbound tourism expenditure)		Percent	..	15.6	15.4	12.8	30.5
6.8	Inbound tourism expenditure over exports of goods		Percent	..	0.7	0.8	0.7	..
6.9	Inbound tourism expenditure over exports of services		Percent	..	19.1	19.5	14.2	..
6.10	Inbound tourism expenditure over exports of goods and services		Percent	..	0.7	0.8	0.7	..
6.11	Inbound tourism expenditure over current account credits		Percent	..	0.6	0.7	0.6	..
6.12	Outbound tourism expenditure over imports of goods		Percent	..	14.4	12.7	16.8	..
6.13	Outbound tourism expenditure over imports of services		Percent	..	22.4	21.8	28.2	..
6.14	Outbound tourism expenditure over imports of goods and		Percent	..	8.7	8.0	10.5	..
6.15	Outbound tourism expenditure over current account debits		Percent	..	7.2	6.7	7.7	..

BULGARIA

Cod.	Basic data and indicators	Notes	Units	2011	2012	2013	2014	2015
1.	**INBOUND TOURISM**							
	Data							
	Arrivals							
1.1	Total		('000)	8,713	8,867	9,192	9,409	9,317
1.2	♦ Overnight visitors (tourists)		('000)	6,328	6,541	6,898	7,311	7,099
1.3	♦ Same-day visitors (excursionists)	(1)	('000)	2,385	2,326	2,294	2,098	2,218
1.4	* of which, cruise passengers		('000)	..	..	..	..	..
	Arrivals by region							
1.5	Total		('000)	8,712	8,867	9,192	9,409	9,317
1.6	♦ Africa		('000)	2	3	6	6	7
1.7	♦ Americas		('000)	88	94	102	113	114
1.8	♦ East Asia and the Pacific		('000)	51	56	78	92	93
1.9	♦ Europe		('000)	8,389	8,525	8,889	9,078	8,978
1.10	♦ Middle East		('000)	24	30	44	36	34
1.11	♦ South Asia		('000)	27	26	24	33	36
1.12	♦ Other not classified		('000)	131	133	50	51	55
1.13	* of which, nationals residing abroad		('000)	..	..	..	..	..
	Arrivals by main purpose							
1.14	Total		('000)	8,713	8,867	9,192	9,409	9,317
1.15	♦ Personal		('000)	7,741	7,826	8,166	8,191	8,126
1.16	* holidays, leisure and recreation		('000)	4,484	4,623	4,914	4,532	4,269
1.17	* other personal purposes		('000)	3,257	3,203	3,252	3,660	3,857
1.18	♦ Business and professional		('000)	972	1,041	1,026	1,217	1,191
	Arrivals by form of organization of the trip							
1.26	Total		('000)	..	..	..	..	9,317
1.27	♦ Package tour		('000)	..	..	..	..	1,820
1.28	♦ Other forms		('000)	..	..	..	..	7,497
	Accommodation							
	Total							
1.29	♦ Guests		('000)	2,423	2,632	2,821	2,792	2,864
1.30	♦ Overnights		('000)	12,461	13,451	14,370	14,078	13,352
	Hotels and similar establishments							
1.31	♦ Guests	(2)	('000)	2,387	2,579	2,754	2,733	2,806
1.32	♦ Overnights	(2)	('000)	12,287	13,152	13,988	13,764	13,096
	Expenditure							
1.33	Total		US$ Mn	4,297	3,975	4,410	4,518	3,583
1.34	♦ Travel		US$ Mn	3,764	3,462	3,829	3,927	3,154
1.35	♦ Passenger transport		US$ Mn	533	513	581	591	429
	Expenditure by main purpose of the trip							
1.36	Total		US$ Mn	3,764	3,161	3,829	3,927	3,153
1.37	♦ Personal		US$ Mn	2,865	2,620	2,906	2,970	2,346
1.38	♦ Business and professional		US$ Mn	899	541	923	957	807
	Indicators							
1.39	Average size of travel party		Persons	..	..	..	..	..
	Average length of stay							
1.40	Total		Days	..	..	..	..	..
1.41	♦ For all commercial accommodation services		Nights	5.14	5.11	5.09	5.04	4.66
1.42	* of which, "hotels and similar establishments"		Nights	5.14	5.11	5.09	5.04	4.66
1.43	♦ For non commercial accommodation services		Days	..	..	..	..	..
1.44	Average expenditure per day		US$	..	..	..	..	..
2.	**DOMESTIC TOURISM**							
	Data							
	Trips							
2.1	Total		('000)	..	..	..	..	..
2.2	♦ Overnight visitors (tourists)	(2)	('000)	..	3,107	3,413	3,170	..
2.3	♦ Same-day visitors (excursionists)		('000)	..	..	..	..	..
	Accommodation							
	Total							
2.19	♦ Guests		('000)	2,528	2,862	3,027	3,154	3,415
2.20	♦ Overnights		('000)	6,229	6,801	7,247	7,621	8,046
	Hotels and similar establishments							
2.21	♦ Guests	(2)	('000)	2,242	2,450	2,611	2,727	2,938
2.22	♦ Overnights	(2)	('000)	5,167	5,531	5,927	6,219	6,559

BULGARIA

Cod.	Basic data and indicators	Notes	Units	2011	2012	2013	2014	2015
	Indicators							
2.23	Average size of travel party		Persons	..	..	..	..	..
	Average length of stay							
2.24	Total		Days	..	..	..	..	..
2.25	♦ For all commercial accommodation services		Nights	2.43	2.38	2.39	2.40	2.36
2.26	* of which, "hotels and similar establishments"		Nights	2.43	2.26	2.27	2.28	2.23
2.27	♦ For non commercial accommodation services		Days	..	..	..	..	..
2.28	Average expenditure per day		US$	..	..	..	..	..
3.	**OUTBOUND TOURISM**							
	Data							
	Departures							
3.1	Total		('000)	..	..	..	..	..
3.2	♦ Overnight visitors (tourists)		('000)	3,803	3,758	3,930	4,158	4,632
3.3	♦ Same-day visitors (excursionists)		('000)	..	..	..	..	..
	Expenditure							
3.4	Total		US$ Mn	1,063	1,096	1,342	1,459	1,346
3.5	♦ Travel		US$ Mn	904	923	1,113	1,202	1,116
3.6	♦ Passenger transport		US$ Mn	159	173	229	257	230
	Expenditure by main purpose of the trip							
3.7	Total		US$ Mn	904	923	1,113	1,202	1,116
3.8	♦ Personal		US$ Mn	546	539	622	663	609
3.9	♦ Business and professional		US$ Mn	358	384	491	539	507
4.	**TOURISM INDUSTRIES**							
	Data							
	Number of establishments							
4.1	Total		Units	6,294	5,322	5,715	5,963	..
4.2	♦ Accommodation for visitors		Units	3,776	2,758	2,953	3,163	3,202
4.3	* of which, "hotels and similar establishments"		Units	1,862	1,936	2,055	2,166	2,180
4.4	♦ Food and beverage serving activities		Units	..	..	..	..	..
4.5	♦ Passenger transportation		Units	..	..	..	..	..
4.6	♦ Travel agencies and other reservation services activities		Units	2,518	2,564	2,762	2,800	..
4.7	♦ Other tourism industries		Units	..	..	..	..	..
	Accommodation for visitors in hotels and similar establishments							
	Non-monetary data							
4.13	♦ Number of establishments		Units	1,862	1,936	2,055	2,166	2,180
4.14	♦ Number of rooms		Units	110,564	118,752	118,107	123,274	124,568
4.15	♦ Number of bed-places		Units	241,665	261,159	262,196	271,526	279,100
	Indicators							
4.16	Occupancy rate / rooms		Percent	..	..	..	..	48.70
4.17	Occupancy rate / bed-places	(3)	Percent	20.70	38.70	39.55	35.31	37.00
4.18	Average length of stay		Nights	3.73	3.71	3.71	3.70	3.40
4.19	Available capacity (bed-places per 1000 inhabitants)		Units	32.86	35.76	36.15	37.71	39.04
6.	**COMPLEMENTARY INDICATORS**							
	Demand							
6.1	Gross travel propensity		Units	..	..	..	..	..
6.2	(1.2 inbound tourists + 2.2 domestic tourists) / population		Units	..	1.32	1.42	1.46	..
	Macroeconomic indicators related to international tourism							
6.3	Inbound tourism expenditure over GDP		Percent	6.8	6.6	6.9	8.0	..
6.4	Outbound tourism expenditure over GDP		Percent	1.6	1.7	2.0	2.6	..
6.5	Tourism balance (inbound minus outbound tourism expenditure) over GDP		Percent	5.2	4.9	4.9	5.4	..
6.6	Tourism openness (inbound plus outbound tourism expenditure) over GDP		Percent	8.4	8.3	8.9	10.6	..
6.7	Tourism coverage (inbound over outbound tourism expenditure)		Percent	424.3	381.7	348.1	312.3	..
6.8	Inbound tourism expenditure over exports of goods		Percent	14.5	14.0	13.8	16.3	..
6.9	Inbound tourism expenditure over exports of services		Percent	42.3	40.4	42.6	50.8	..
6.10	Inbound tourism expenditure over exports of goods and services		Percent	10.8	10.4	10.4	12.4	..
6.11	Inbound tourism expenditure over current account credits		Percent	9.7	9.2	9.1	11.1	..
6.12	Outbound tourism expenditure over imports of goods		Percent	3.0	3.0	3.5	4.6	..
6.13	Outbound tourism expenditure over imports of services		Percent	18.2	17.5	20.3	26.1	..
6.14	Outbound tourism expenditure over imports of goods and		Percent	2.6	2.6	3.0	3.9	..
6.15	Outbound tourism expenditure over current account debits		Percent	2.5	2.5	2.8	3.7	..

BURKINA FASO

Cod. Basic data and indicators	Notes	Units	2011	2012	2013	2014	2015
1. INBOUND TOURISM							
Data							
Arrivals							
1.1 Total		('000)	..	..	..	..	..
1.2 ♦ Overnight visitors (tourists)	(1)	('000)	238	237	218	191	163
1.3 ♦ Same-day visitors (excursionists)		('000)	..	..	..	..	..
1.4 * of which, cruise passengers		('000)	..	..	..	..	..
Arrivals by region	(1)						
1.5 Total		('000)	238	237	218	191	163
1.6 ♦ Africa		('000)	117	118	108	84	85
1.7 ♦ Americas		('000)	17	19	20	12	13
1.8 ♦ East Asia and the Pacific		('000)	8	9	9	25	9
1.9 ♦ Europe		('000)	86	79	68	59	47
1.10 ♦ Middle East		('000)	2	2	2	1	1
1.11 ♦ South Asia		('000)	..	..	..	..	..
1.12 ♦ Other not classified		('000)	8	11	11	10	8
1.13 * of which, nationals residing abroad		('000)	8	11	11	10	8
Arrivals by main purpose	(2)						
1.14 Total		('000)	434	483	506	486	475
1.15 ♦ Personal		('000)	178	192	187	208	199
1.16 * holidays, leisure and recreation		('000)	88	97	81	92	88
1.17 * other personal purposes		('000)	90	95	106	116	112
1.18 ♦ Business and professional		('000)	256	291	319	278	275
Accommodation							
Hotels and similar establishments							
1.31 ♦ Guests		('000)	238	237	218	191	163
1.32 ♦ Overnights		('000)	708	710	697	544	481
Expenditure							
1.33 Total		US$ Mn	116	128	200	183	..
1.34 ♦ Travel		US$ Mn	75	84	153	135	..
1.35 ♦ Passenger transport		US$ Mn	41	44	47	48	..
Expenditure by main purpose of the trip							
1.36 Total		US$ Mn	75	84	153	135	..
1.37 ♦ Personal		US$ Mn	34	41	104	92	..
1.38 ♦ Business and professional		US$ Mn	41	43	49	43	..
Indicators							
1.39 Average size of travel party		Persons	..	..	..	..	..
Average length of stay							
1.40 Total		Days	..	..	..	..	..
1.41 ♦ For all commercial accommodation services		Nights	3.00	3.00	3.19	2.85	2.90
1.42 * of which, "hotels and similar establishments"		Nights	..	..	..	..	..
1.43 ♦ For non commercial accommodation services		Days	..	..	..	..	..
1.44 Average expenditure per day		US$	109.1	110.0	101.9	102.3	..
2. DOMESTIC TOURISM							
Data							
Accommodation							
Hotels and similar establishments							
2.21 ♦ Guests		('000)	196	246	289	295	311
2.22 ♦ Overnights		('000)	311	376	434	470	452
Indicators							
2.23 Average size of travel party		Persons	..	..	..	..	..
Average length of stay							
2.24 Total		Days	..	..	..	..	..
2.25 ♦ For all commercial accommodation services		Nights	1.60	1.50	1.50	1.50	1.50
2.26 * of which, "hotels and similar establishments"		Nights	..	..	..	..	..
2.27 ♦ For non commercial accommodation services		Days	..	..	..	..	..
2.28 Average expenditure per day		US$	..	..	..	..	..
3. OUTBOUND TOURISM							
Data							
Expenditure							
3.4 Total		US$ Mn	129	146	215	176	..
3.5 ♦ Travel		US$ Mn	72	77	144	132	..
3.6 ♦ Passenger transport		US$ Mn	57	69	71	44	..
Expenditure by main purpose of the trip							
3.7 Total		US$ Mn	72	77	144	132	..
3.8 ♦ Personal		US$ Mn	33	26	88	85	..
3.9 ♦ Business and professional		US$ Mn	38	51	56	47	..

BURKINA FASO

Cod.	Basic data and indicators	Notes	Units	2011	2012	2013	2014	2015
4.	**TOURISM INDUSTRIES**							
	Data							
	Number of establishments							
4.1	Total		Units	..	..	..	..	..
4.2	♦ Accommodation for visitors		Units	..	..	..	..	..
4.3	* of which, "hotels and similar establishments"		Units	329	441	321	321	407
4.4	♦ Food and beverage serving activities		Units	..	..	..	..	..
4.5	♦ Passenger transportation		Units	..	..	..	..	..
4.6	♦ Travel agencies and other reservation services activities		Units	69	76	88	96	144
4.7	♦ Other tourism industries		Units	..	..	..	..	..
	Accommodation for visitors in hotels and similar establishments							
	Non-monetary data							
4.13	♦ Number of establishments		Units	329	441	321	321	407
4.14	♦ Number of rooms		Units	7,187	7,443	8,397	8,397	10,646
4.15	♦ Number of bed-places		Units	14,120	14,565	16,784	16,784	21,280
	Indicators							
4.16	Occupancy rate / rooms		Percent	39.10	43.83	46.72	32.65	33.02
4.17	Occupancy rate / bed-places		Percent	21.70	23.11	26.17	18.78	19.09
4.18	Average length of stay		Nights	2.50	2.25	2.23	2.08	1.97
4.19	Available capacity (bed-places per 1000 inhabitants)		Units	0.88	0.88	0.98	0.95	1.18
6.	**COMPLEMENTARY INDICATORS**							
	Demand							
6.1	Gross travel propensity		Units	..	..	..	..	..
6.2	(1.2 inbound tourists) / population		Units	0.01	0.01	0.01	0.01	0.01
	Macroeconomic indicators related to international tourism							
6.3	Inbound tourism expenditure over GDP		Percent	1.1	1.1	1.7	1.5	..
6.4	Outbound tourism expenditure over GDP		Percent	1.2	1.3	1.8	1.4	..
6.5	Tourism balance (inbound minus outbound tourism expenditure) over GDP		Percent	-0.1	-0.2	-0.1	0.1	..
6.6	Tourism openness (inbound plus outbound tourism expenditure) over GDP		Percent	2.3	2.4	3.5	2.9	..
6.7	Tourism coverage (inbound over outbound tourism expenditure)		Percent	89.9	87.7	93.0	104.0	..
6.8	Inbound tourism expenditure over exports of goods		Percent	4.8	4.5	7.5	6.6	..
6.9	Inbound tourism expenditure over exports of services		Percent	27.9	30.4	40.3	40.4	..
6.10	Inbound tourism expenditure over exports of goods and services		Percent	4.1	3.9	6.3	5.7	..
6.11	Inbound tourism expenditure over current account credits		Percent	3.2	3.2	5.1	4.5	..
6.12	Outbound tourism expenditure over imports of goods		Percent	5.4	5.5	6.5	5.8	..
6.13	Outbound tourism expenditure over imports of services		Percent	11.3	12.0	15.1	13.5	..
6.14	Outbound tourism expenditure over imports of goods and		Percent	3.7	3.8	4.5	4.1	..
6.15	Outbound tourism expenditure over current account debits		Percent	3.4	3.6	4.2	3.8	..

BURUNDI

Cod. Basic data and indicators	Notes	Units	2011	2012	2013	2014	2015
1. INBOUND TOURISM							
Data							
Arrivals							
1.1 Total		('000)	..	..	..	..	..
1.2 ♦ Overnight visitors (tourists)	(1)	('000)	144	147	234	235	131
1.3 ♦ Same-day visitors (excursionists)		('000)	..	..	..	..	..
1.4 * of which, cruise passengers		('000)	..	..	..	..	..
Arrivals by region	(1)						
1.5 Total		('000)	144	147	234	235	131
1.6 ♦ Africa		('000)	123	125	148	152	58
1.7 ♦ Americas		('000)	2	3	10	5	26
1.8 ♦ East Asia and the Pacific		('000)	4	4	11	12	7
1.9 ♦ Europe		('000)	8	9	38	37	1
1.10 ♦ Middle East		('000)	2	1	14	13	22
1.11 ♦ South Asia		('000)	2	3	7	8	11
1.12 ♦ Other not classified		('000)	3	2	6	8	6
1.13 * of which, nationals residing abroad		('000)	..	..	..	..	..
Arrivals by main purpose	(1)						
1.14 Total		('000)	144	147	234	235	131
1.15 ♦ Personal		('000)	111	134	217	193	121
1.16 * holidays, leisure and recreation		('000)	102	121	183	172	103
1.17 * other personal purposes		('000)	9	13	34	21	18
1.18 ♦ Business and professional		('000)	33	13	17	42	10
Arrivals by mode of transport	(1)						
1.19 Total		('000)	144	147	234	235	131
1.20 ♦ Air		('000)	31	41	92	86	46
1.21 ♦ Water	(2)	('000)	26	14	21	26	13
1.22 ♦ Land		('000)	87	92	121	123	72
1.23 * railway		('000)	..	..	..	..	..
1.24 * road		('000)	87	92	121	123	72
1.25 * others		('000)	..	..	..	..	..
Expenditure							
1.33 Total		US$ Mn	3.7	2.7	3.1	5.5	3.1
1.34 ♦ Travel		US$ Mn	2.5	1.5	2.3	4.1	2.2
1.35 ♦ Passenger transport		US$ Mn	1.2	1.2	0.8	1.4	0.9
3. OUTBOUND TOURISM							
Data							
Expenditure							
3.4 Total		US$ Mn	49	41	54	55	46
3.5 ♦ Travel		US$ Mn	31	25	34	38	29
3.6 ♦ Passenger transport		US$ Mn	18	16	20	17	17
Expenditure by main purpose of the trip							
3.7 Total		US$ Mn	31	25	34	38	29
3.8 ♦ Personal		US$ Mn	15	13	13	30	22
3.9 ♦ Business and professional		US$ Mn	16	12	22	9	8
6. COMPLEMENTARY INDICATORS							
Demand							
6.1 Gross travel propensity		Units	..	..	..	..	..
6.2 (1.2 inbound tourists) / population		Units	0.01	0.01	0.02	0.02	0.01
Macroeconomic indicators related to international tourism							
6.3 Inbound tourism expenditure over GDP		Percent	0.2	0.1	0.1	0.2	0.1
6.4 Outbound tourism expenditure over GDP		Percent	2.2	1.8	2.2	1.9	1.6
6.5 Tourism balance (inbound minus outbound tourism expenditure) over GDP		Percent	-2.0	-1.7	-2.1	-1.7	-1.5
6.6 Tourism openness (inbound plus outbound tourism expenditure) over GDP		Percent	2.4	1.9	2.3	2.1	1.7
6.7 Tourism coverage (inbound over outbound tourism expenditure)		Percent	7.6	6.6	5.7	10.0	6.7
6.8 Inbound tourism expenditure over exports of goods		Percent	3.0	2.0	3.4	..	..
6.9 Inbound tourism expenditure over exports of services		Percent	3.3	2.9	2.4	..	..
6.10 Inbound tourism expenditure over exports of goods and services		Percent	1.6	1.2	1.4	..	..
6.11 Inbound tourism expenditure over current account credits		Percent	0.7	0.4	0.5	..	..
6.12 Outbound tourism expenditure over imports of goods		Percent	8.9	5.8	8.0	..	..
6.13 Outbound tourism expenditure over imports of services		Percent	23.0	19.4	23.1	..	..
6.14 Outbound tourism expenditure over imports of goods and		Percent	6.4	4.4	5.9	..	..
6.15 Outbound tourism expenditure over current account debits		Percent	6.2	4.3	5.7	..	..

CABO VERDE

Cod.	Basic data and indicators	Notes	Units	2011	2012	2013	2014	2015
1.	**INBOUND TOURISM**							
	Data							
	Arrivals							
1.1	Total		('000)	..	..	..	..	..
1.2	♦ Overnight visitors (tourists)	(1)	('000)	428	482	503	494	520
1.3	♦ Same-day visitors (excursionists)		('000)	..	..	..	..	..
1.4	* of which, cruise passengers		('000)	..	..	..	..	..
	Arrivals by region	(1)						
1.5	Total		('000)	428	482	503	494	520
1.6	♦ Africa		('000)	3	0.3	1.3	0.4	0.2
1.7	♦ Americas		('000)	4	5	4	3	4
1.8	♦ East Asia and the Pacific		('000)	..	..	..	..	..
1.9	♦ Europe		('000)	385	403	394	382	426
1.10	♦ Middle East		('000)	..	..	..	..	..
1.11	♦ South Asia		('000)	..	..	..	..	..
1.12	♦ Other not classified		('000)	36	74	103	108	89
1.13	* of which, nationals residing abroad		('000)	..	..	..	..	..
	Accommodation							
	Hotels and similar establishments							
1.31	♦ Guests		('000)	428	482	503	494	520
1.32	♦ Overnights		('000)	2,704	3,185	3,280	3,284	3,573
	Expenditure							
1.33	Total		US$ Mn	438	454	483	453	396
1.34	♦ Travel		US$ Mn	368	396	422	405	352
1.35	♦ Passenger transport		US$ Mn	70	58	61	48	44
	Expenditure by main purpose of the trip							
1.36	Total		US$ Mn	368	396	422	405	352
1.37	♦ Personal		US$ Mn	351	376	402	387	334
1.38	♦ Business and professional		US$ Mn	17	20	20	18	18
2.	**DOMESTIC TOURISM**							
	Data							
	Accommodation							
	Hotels and similar establishments							
2.21	♦ Guests		('000)	47	52	49	46	50
2.22	♦ Overnights		('000)	124	150	156	131	137
3.	**OUTBOUND TOURISM**							
	Data							
	Expenditure							
3.4	Total		US$ Mn	142	136	127	115	109
3.5	♦ Travel		US$ Mn	132	128	120	110	101
3.6	♦ Passenger transport		US$ Mn	10	8	7	5	8
	Expenditure by main purpose of the trip							
3.7	Total		US$ Mn	132	128	120	110	101
3.8	♦ Personal		US$ Mn	72	66	59	46	34
3.9	♦ Business and professional		US$ Mn	60	62	61	64	67
4.	**TOURISM INDUSTRIES**							
	Data							
	Number of establishments							
4.1	Total		Units	..	..	..	..	..
4.2	♦ Accommodation for visitors		Units	..	..	..	..	..
4.3	* of which, "hotels and similar establishments"		Units	195	207	222	229	226
4.4	♦ Food and beverage serving activities		Units	..	..	..	..	..
4.5	♦ Passenger transportation		Units	..	..	..	..	..
4.6	♦ Travel agencies and other reservation services activities		Units	..	..	..	..	..
4.7	♦ Other tourism industries		Units	..	..	..	..	..
	Accommodation for visitors in hotels and similar establishments							
	Non-monetary data							
4.13	♦ Number of establishments		Units	195	207	222	229	226
4.14	♦ Number of rooms		Units	7,901	8,522	9,058	10,839	10,626
4.15	♦ Number of bed-places		Units	14,076	14,999	15,995	18,188	18,055
	Indicators							
4.16	Occupancy rate / rooms		Percent	..	..	..	..	..
4.17	Occupancy rate / bed-places		Percent	58.19	57.00	56.00	53.00	49.00
4.18	Average length of stay		Nights	5.70	6.00	6.00	6.00	6.30
4.19	Available capacity (bed-places per 1000 inhabitants)		Units	28.43	29.95	31.53	35.39	34.69

CABO VERDE

Cod.	Basic data and indicators	Notes	Units	2011	2012	2013	2014	2015
6.	**COMPLEMENTARY INDICATORS**							
	Demand							
6.1	Gross travel propensity		Units	..	..	..	..	..
6.2	(1.2 inbound tourists) / population		Units	0.86	0.96	0.99	0.96	1.00
	Macroeconomic indicators related to international tourism							
6.3	Inbound tourism expenditure over GDP		Percent	23.5	..	..	..	..
6.4	Outbound tourism expenditure over GDP		Percent	7.6	..	..	..	..
6.5	Tourism balance (inbound minus outbound tourism expenditure) over GDP		Percent	15.9	..	..	..	..
6.6	Tourism openness (inbound plus outbound tourism expenditure) over GDP		Percent	31.1	..	..	..	..
6.7	Tourism coverage (inbound over outbound tourism expenditure)		Percent	308.5	333.8	380.3	393.9	363.3
6.8	Inbound tourism expenditure over exports of goods		Percent	222.9	262.3	262.3	178.8	265.3
6.9	Inbound tourism expenditure over exports of services		Percent	74.8	75.9	74.2	71.6	76.5
6.10	Inbound tourism expenditure over exports of goods and services		Percent	56.0	58.8	57.8	51.1	59.4
6.11	Inbound tourism expenditure over current account credits		Percent	35.1	41.6	41.2	37.8	41.1
6.12	Outbound tourism expenditure over imports of goods		Percent	13.7	16.4	15.8	13.4	17.3
6.13	Outbound tourism expenditure over imports of services		Percent	42.6	36.7	36.6	31.2	35.6
6.14	Outbound tourism expenditure over imports of goods and		Percent	10.3	11.3	11.0	9.4	11.6
6.15	Outbound tourism expenditure over current account debits		Percent	9.6	10.8	10.4	9.0	11.2

CAMBODIA

Cod.	Basic data and indicators	Notes	Units	2011	2012	2013	2014	2015
1.	**INBOUND TOURISM**							
	Data							
	Arrivals							
1.1	Total		('000)	..	..	..	..	..
1.2	♦ Overnight visitors (tourists)	(1)	('000)	2,882	3,584	4,210	4,503	4,775
1.3	♦ Same-day visitors (excursionists)		('000)	..	..	..	..	..
1.4	* of which, cruise passengers		('000)	..	..	..	..	..
	Arrivals by region							
1.5	Total		('000)	2,882	3,584	4,210	4,503	4,775
1.6	♦ Africa		('000)	6	6	6	6	9
1.7	♦ Americas		('000)	218	244	263	277	316
1.8	♦ East Asia and the Pacific		('000)	2,085	2,685	3,199	3,460	3,672
1.9	♦ Europe		('000)	551	622	709	721	729
1.10	♦ Middle East		('000)	1	2	3	2	5
1.11	♦ South Asia		('000)	21	25	30	36	45
1.12	♦ Other not classified		('000)	..	..	..	..	..
1.13	* of which, nationals residing abroad		('000)	..	..	..	..	..
	Arrivals by main purpose							
1.14	Total		('000)	2,882	3,584	4,210	4,503	4,775
1.15	♦ Personal		('000)	2,739	3,416	4,025	4,297	4,476
1.16	* holidays, leisure and recreation		('000)	2,707	3,287	3,992	4,255	4,299
1.17	* other personal purposes		('000)	32	129	33	42	176
1.18	♦ Business and professional		('000)	143	168	185	206	300
	Arrivals by mode of transport							
1.19	Total		('000)	2,882	3,584	4,210	4,503	4,775
1.20	♦ Air		('000)	1,481	1,722	2,018	2,274	2,476
1.21	♦ Water	(2)	('000)	81	76	75	97	148
1.22	♦ Land		('000)	1,320	1,786	2,117	2,132	2,151
1.23	* railway		('000)	..	..	..	..	..
1.24	* road		('000)	1,320	1,786	2,117	2,132	2,151
1.25	* others		('000)	..	..	..	..	..
	Expenditure							
1.33	Total		US$ Mn	2,258	2,663	2,895	3,220	3,411
1.34	♦ Travel		US$ Mn	2,084	2,463	2,660	2,953	3,130
1.35	♦ Passenger transport		US$ Mn	174	200	235	267	281
	Expenditure by main purpose of the trip							
1.36	Total		US$ Mn	2,084	2,463	2,660	2,953	..
1.37	♦ Personal		US$ Mn	1,961	2,314	2,481	2,751	..
1.38	♦ Business and professional		US$ Mn	123	149	179	202	..
	Indicators							
1.39	Average size of travel party		Persons	..	..	..	..	..
	Average length of stay							
1.40	Total		Days	..	..	..	..	..
1.41	♦ For all commercial accommodation services	(3)	Nights	6.50	6.30	6.75	6.50	6.80
1.42	* of which, "hotels and similar establishments"		Nights	..	..	..	..	..
1.43	♦ For non commercial accommodation services		Days	..	..	..	..	..
1.44	Average expenditure per day		US$	115.8	117.6	120.8	93.5	92.8
2.	**DOMESTIC TOURISM**							
	Data							
	Trips							
2.1	Total		('000)	7,811	8,254	8,519	9,004	9,679
2.2	♦ Overnight visitors (tourists)		('000)	..	..	..	..	..
2.3	♦ Same-day visitors (excursionists)		('000)	..	..	..	..	..
3.	**OUTBOUND TOURISM**							
	Data							
	Departures							
3.1	Total		('000)	..	..	..	..	..
3.2	♦ Overnight visitors (tourists)		('000)	710	792	872	956	1,194
3.3	♦ Same-day visitors (excursionists)		('000)	..	..	..	..	..
	Expenditure							
3.4	Total		US$ Mn	344	406	469	527	621
3.5	♦ Travel		US$ Mn	264	314	355	401	491
3.6	♦ Passenger transport		US$ Mn	80	92	114	126	130
	Expenditure by main purpose of the trip							
3.7	Total		US$ Mn	..	..	..	401	..
3.8	♦ Personal		US$ Mn	..	..	..	41	..
3.9	♦ Business and professional		US$ Mn	..	..	..	361	..

CAMBODIA

Cod. Basic data and indicators	Notes	Units	2011	2012	2013	2014	2015
4. TOURISM INDUSTRIES							
Data							
Number of establishments							
4.1 Total		Units	..	..	..	..	..
4.2 ♦ Accommodation for visitors		Units	..	..	..	..	..
4.3 * of which, "hotels and similar establishments"		Units	1,618	1,863	2,007	2,117	2,897
4.4 ♦ Food and beverage serving activities		Units	..	..	..	..	..
4.5 ♦ Passenger transportation		Units	..	..	..	..	..
4.6 ♦ Travel agencies and other reservation services activities		Units	..	..	..	..	..
4.7 ♦ Other tourism industries		Units	..	..	..	..	..
Accommodation for visitors in hotels and similar establishments							
Non-monetary data							
4.13 ♦ Number of establishments		Units	1,618	1,863	2,007	2,117	2,897
4.14 ♦ Number of rooms		Units	43,236	49,913	51,223	51,985	63,279
4.15 ♦ Number of bed-places		Units	73,501	84,852	87,079	88,375	107,574
Indicators							
4.16 Occupancy rate / rooms		Percent	..	..	..	..	..
4.17 Occupancy rate / bed-places		Percent	66.15	68.49	69.53	67.55	70.20
4.18 Average length of stay		Nights	..	..	..	..	..
4.19 Available capacity (bed-places per 1000 inhabitants)		Units	5.04	5.72	5.78	5.77	6.91
6. COMPLEMENTARY INDICATORS							
Demand							
6.1 Gross travel propensity		Units	..	..	..	..	..
6.2 (1.2 inbound tourists + 2.1 domestic visitors) / population		Units	0.73	0.80	0.84	0.88	0.93
Macroeconomic indicators related to international tourism							
6.3 Inbound tourism expenditure over GDP		Percent	17.6	18.9	19.0	19.2	..
6.4 Outbound tourism expenditure over GDP		Percent	2.7	2.9	3.1	3.1	..
6.5 Tourism balance (inbound minus outbound tourism expenditure) over GDP		Percent	14.9	16.0	15.9	16.1	..
6.6 Tourism openness (inbound plus outbound tourism expenditure) over GDP		Percent	20.3	21.8	22.1	22.3	..
6.7 Tourism coverage (inbound over outbound tourism expenditure)		Percent	656.4	655.9	617.3	611.0	549.3
6.8 Inbound tourism expenditure over exports of goods		Percent	44.8	47.3	44.3	43.2	..
6.9 Inbound tourism expenditure over exports of services		Percent	82.7	83.4	83.0	84.5	..
6.10 Inbound tourism expenditure over exports of goods and services		Percent	29.1	30.2	28.9	28.6	..
6.11 Inbound tourism expenditure over current account credits		Percent	26.8	28.4	27.3	26.6	..
6.12 Outbound tourism expenditure over imports of goods		Percent	5.0	5.0	4.9	4.9	..
6.13 Outbound tourism expenditure over imports of services		Percent	26.2	26.4	26.7	28.0	..
6.14 Outbound tourism expenditure over imports of goods and		Percent	4.2	4.2	4.2	4.2	..
6.15 Outbound tourism expenditure over current account debits		Percent	4.1	4.2	4.1	4.1	..

CAMEROON

Cod.	Basic data and indicators	Notes	Units	2011	2012	2013	2014	2015
1.	**INBOUND TOURISM**							
	Data							
	Arrivals							
1.1	Total		('000)	604	817	783	822	..
1.2	♦ Overnight visitors (tourists)		('000)	600	812	..	..	..
1.3	♦ Same-day visitors (excursionists)		('000)	4	5	..	..	..
1.4	* of which, cruise passengers		('000)	1	1	..	..	..
	Arrivals by region							
1.5	Total	(1)	('000)	..	..	462	434	..
1.6	♦ Africa		('000)	..	..	215	211	..
1.7	♦ Americas		('000)	..	..	23	21	..
1.8	♦ East Asia and the Pacific		('000)	..	..	24	21	..
1.9	♦ Europe		('000)	..	..	182	151	..
1.10	♦ Middle East		('000)	..	..	9	8	..
1.11	♦ South Asia		('000)	..	..	..	..	..
1.12	♦ Other not classified		('000)	..	..	9	22	..
1.13	* of which, nationals residing abroad		('000)	..	..	..	..	..
	Arrivals by mode of transport							
1.19	Total		('000)	604	817	783	822	..
1.20	♦ Air		('000)	279	351	269	244	..
1.21	♦ Water		('000)	11	32	21	24	..
1.22	♦ Land		('000)	314	434	493	554	..
1.23	* railway		('000)	..	..	..	..	..
1.24	* road		('000)	314	434	493	554	..
1.25	* others		('000)	..	..	..	..	..
	Accommodation							
	Hotels and similar establishments							
1.31	♦ Guests		('000)	412	437	462	434	..
1.32	♦ Overnights		('000)	795	811	839	833	..
	Expenditure							
1.33	Total		US$ Mn	423	377	607	..	..
1.34	♦ Travel		US$ Mn	409	349	576	..	..
1.35	♦ Passenger transport		US$ Mn	14	28	31	..	..
	Expenditure by main purpose of the trip							
1.36	Total		US$ Mn	409	349	576	..	..
1.37	♦ Personal		US$ Mn	385	288	439	..	..
1.38	♦ Business and professional		US$ Mn	24	61	137	..	..
	Indicators							
1.39	Average size of travel party		Persons	..	..	..	..	..
	Average length of stay							
1.40	Total		Days	7.60	8.20	..	..	..
1.41	♦ For all commercial accommodation services		Nights	7.80	7.90	..	..	..
1.42	* of which, "hotels and similar establishments"		Nights	1.53	1.48	..	..	..
1.43	♦ For non commercial accommodation services		Days	1.60	1.75	..	..	..
1.44	Average expenditure per day		US$	62.4	58.9	..	..	..
2.	**DOMESTIC TOURISM**							
	Data							
	Accommodation							
	Hotels and similar establishments							
2.21	♦ Guests		('000)	1,980	2,115	1,546	1,590	..
2.22	♦ Overnights		('000)	2,210	2,850	2,321	2,441	..
	Indicators							
2.23	Average size of travel party		Persons	..	..	..	..	..
	Average length of stay							
2.24	Total		Days	..	..	..	..	..
2.25	♦ For all commercial accommodation services		Nights	1.38	1.50	..	..	..
2.26	* of which, "hotels and similar establishments"		Nights	1.60	1.58	..	..	..
2.27	♦ For non commercial accommodation services		Days	1.48	1.52	..	..	..
2.28	Average expenditure per day		US$	55.4	50.5	..	..	..
3.	**OUTBOUND TOURISM**							
	Data							
	Expenditure							
3.4	Total		US$ Mn	622	668	795	..	..
3.5	♦ Travel		US$ Mn	529	518	612	..	..
3.6	♦ Passenger transport		US$ Mn	93	150	183	..	..

CAMEROON

Cod.	Basic data and indicators	Notes	Units	2011	2012	2013	2014	2015
	Expenditure by main purpose of the trip							
3.7	Total		US$ Mn	528	517	612	..	..
3.8	♦ Personal		US$ Mn	308	345	406	..	..
3.9	♦ Business and professional		US$ Mn	220	172	206	..	..
4.	**TOURISM INDUSTRIES**							
	Data							
	Number of establishments							
4.1	Total		Units	3,913	4,299	..	..	..
4.2	♦ Accommodation for visitors		Units	2,885	3,210	2,020	2,000	2,092
4.3	* of which, "hotels and similar establishments"		Units	2,885	3,210	2,020	2,000	2,092
4.4	♦ Food and beverage serving activities		Units	565	610	..	..	..
4.5	♦ Passenger transportation		Units	132	138	..	..	..
4.6	♦ Travel agencies and other reservation services activities		Units	121	123	224	230	242
4.7	♦ Other tourism industries		Units	210	218	..	..	..
	Accommodation for visitors in hotels and similar establishments							
	Non-monetary data							
4.13	♦ Number of establishments		Units	2,885	3,210	2,020	2,000	2,092
4.14	♦ Number of rooms		Units	37,050	38,200	30,383	31,485	32,710
4.15	♦ Number of bed-places		Units	41,800	42,170	32,067	33,096	34,414
	Indicators							
4.16	Occupancy rate / rooms		Percent	22.14	24.00	28.49	28.49	24.90
4.17	Occupancy rate / bed-places		Percent	18.92	19.20	27.00	27.11	..
4.18	Average length of stay		Nights	1.38	1.52	1.57	1.62	1.48
4.19	Available capacity (bed-places per 1000 inhabitants)		Units	1.98	1.95	1.44	1.45	1.47
5.	**EMPLOYMENT**							
	Data							
	Number of employees by tourism industries							
5.1	Total		('000)	27.0	28.4	..	..	..
5.2	♦ Accommodation services for visitors (hotels and similar establishments)		('000)	8.2	8.5	..	..	..
5.3	♦ Other accommodation services		('000)	1.2	1.2	..	..	..
5.4	♦ Food and beverage serving activities		('000)	16.0	17.0	..	..	..
5.5	♦ Passenger transportation		('000)	..	..	..	..	..
5.6	♦ Travel agencies and other reservation services activities		('000)	1.6	1.7	..	..	..
5.7	♦ Other tourism industries		('000)	..	..	..	..	..
	Indicators							
	Number of full-time equivalent jobs by status in employment							
5.11	Total		('000)	24.8	26.0	..	..	..
5.12	♦ Employees		('000)	22.0	22.9	..	..	..
5.13	* male		('000)	12.0	12.9	..	..	..
5.14	* female		('000)	10.0	10.0	..	..	..
5.15	♦ Self employed		('000)	2.8	3.1	..	..	..
5.16	* male		('000)	1.6	1.8	..	..	..
5.17	* female		('000)	1.2	1.3	..	..	..
6.	**COMPLEMENTARY INDICATORS**							
	Demand							
6.1	Gross travel propensity		Units	..	..	..	..	..
6.2	(1.2 inbound tourists) / population		Units	0.03	0.04	..	..	..
	Macroeconomic indicators related to international tourism							
6.3	Inbound tourism expenditure over GDP		Percent	1.6	1.4	2.1	..	..
6.4	Outbound tourism expenditure over GDP		Percent	2.3	2.5	2.7	..	..
6.5	Tourism balance (inbound minus outbound tourism expenditure) over GDP		Percent	-0.7	-1.1	-0.6	..	..
6.6	Tourism openness (inbound plus outbound tourism expenditure) over GDP		Percent	3.9	3.9	4.8	..	..
6.7	Tourism coverage (inbound over outbound tourism expenditure)		Percent	68.0	56.4	76.4	..	..
6.8	Inbound tourism expenditure over exports of goods		Percent	7.5	6.5	10.0	..	..
6.9	Inbound tourism expenditure over exports of services		Percent	22.8	23.2	30.7	..	..
6.10	Inbound tourism expenditure over exports of goods and services		Percent	5.6	5.1	7.5	..	..
6.11	Inbound tourism expenditure over current account credits		Percent	5.1	4.7	6.9	..	..
6.12	Outbound tourism expenditure over imports of goods		Percent	10.0	11.1	12.9	..	..
6.13	Outbound tourism expenditure over imports of services		Percent	31.4	31.4	29.4	..	..
6.14	Outbound tourism expenditure over imports of goods and		Percent	7.6	8.2	9.0	..	..
6.15	Outbound tourism expenditure over current account debits		Percent	7.2	7.8	8.6	..	..

CANADA

Cod.	Basic data and indicators	Notes	Units	2011	2012	2013	2014	2015
1.	**INBOUND TOURISM**							
	Data							
	Arrivals							
1.1	Total	(1)	('000)	25,066	25,318	25,144	25,557	27,555
1.2	♦ Overnight visitors (tourists)		('000)	16,014	16,344	16,059	16,537	17,971
1.3	♦ Same-day visitors (excursionists)	(1)	('000)	9,052	8,974	9,085	9,020	9,584
1.4	* of which, cruise passengers		('000)	..	..	..	..	..
	Arrivals by region							
1.5	Total		('000)	16,015	16,344	16,059	16,537	17,971
1.6	♦ Africa		('000)	86	92	98	104	111
1.7	♦ Americas		('000)	12,080	12,395	12,002	12,082	13,283
1.8	♦ East Asia and the Pacific		('000)	1,223	1,286	1,389	1,590	1,691
1.9	♦ Europe		('000)	2,356	2,299	2,286	2,437	2,541
1.10	♦ Middle East		('000)	85	85	91	103	107
1.11	♦ South Asia		('000)	185	187	192	221	239
1.12	♦ Other not classified		('000)	..	..	..	..	..
1.13	* of which, nationals residing abroad		('000)	..	..	..	..	..
	Arrivals by main purpose							
1.14	Total		('000)	16,014	16,344	16,059	16,537	17,971
1.15	♦ Personal		('000)	13,552	13,855	13,506	13,849	14,847
1.16	* holidays, leisure and recreation		('000)	7,647	7,690	7,096	7,314	7,677
1.17	* other personal purposes		('000)	5,905	6,166	6,410	6,536	7,170
1.18	♦ Business and professional		('000)	2,463	2,489	2,553	2,688	3,124
	Arrivals by mode of transport							
1.19	Total		('000)	16,014	16,344	16,059	16,537	17,971
1.20	♦ Air		('000)	7,255	7,418	7,171	7,732	8,423
1.21	♦ Water		('000)	764	725	722	692	706
1.22	♦ Land		('000)	7,996	8,201	8,167	8,113	8,842
1.23	* railway		('000)	114	111	113	102	122
1.24	* road		('000)	7,882	8,090	8,053	8,012	8,721
1.25	* others		('000)	..	..	..	..	..
	Accommodation							
	Total							
1.29	♦ Guests		('000)	..	..	..	..	..
1.30	♦ Overnights		('000)	124,396	129,165	151,078	144,881	147,349
	Expenditure							
1.33	Total		US$ Mn	19,989	20,696	20,941	20,509	..
1.34	♦ Travel		US$ Mn	16,834	17,407	17,656	17,476	16,203
1.35	♦ Passenger transport		US$ Mn	3,155	3,289	3,285	3,033	..
	Expenditure by main purpose of the trip							
1.36	Total		US$ Mn	16,833	17,407	17,656	17,476	16,203
1.37	♦ Personal		US$ Mn	13,933	14,507	14,766	14,699	13,800
1.38	♦ Business and professional		US$ Mn	2,900	2,900	2,890	2,776	2,403
2.	**DOMESTIC TOURISM**							
	Data							
	Trips	(2)						
2.1	Total		('000)	317,021	316,254	320,266	318,209	315,746
2.2	♦ Overnight visitors (tourists)		('000)	105,743	108,393	108,925	108,647	109,805
2.3	♦ Same-day visitors (excursionists)		('000)	211,278	207,861	211,342	209,562	205,941
	Trips by main purpose	(2)						
2.4	Total		('000)	317,022	316,254	320,267	318,209	315,746
2.5	♦ Personal		('000)	279,660	282,410	287,132	286,986	288,369
2.6	* holidays, leisure and recreation		('000)	97,593	104,921	105,164	107,075	108,226
2.7	* other personal purposes		('000)	182,067	177,489	181,968	179,911	180,143
2.8	♦ Business and professional		('000)	37,362	33,844	33,135	31,223	27,377
	Trips by mode of transport	(2)						
2.9	Total		('000)	317,022	316,254	320,268	318,209	315,745
2.10	♦ Air		('000)	7,291	6,912	6,357	7,317	7,673
2.11	♦ Water		('000)	1,299	1,202	1,074	1,076	1,251
2.12	♦ Land		('000)	308,432	308,140	312,837	309,816	306,821
2.13	* railway		('000)	3,595	2,703	3,785	3,705	2,994
2.14	* road		('000)	298,392	297,887	301,269	300,387	298,915
2.15	* others		('000)	6,445	7,550	7,783	5,724	4,912
	Accommodation							
	Total							
2.19	♦ Guests		('000)	..	..	..	..	..
2.20	♦ Overnights		('000)	288,945	297,302	287,115	292,569	306,212
	Hotels and similar establishments							
2.21	♦ Guests		('000)	..	..	..	..	..
2.22	♦ Overnights		('000)	51,681	53,257	51,235	51,805	53,650

CANADA

Cod.	Basic data and indicators	Notes	Units	2011	2012	2013	2014	2015
	Indicators							
2.23	Average size of travel party		Persons	1.8	1.8	1.8	1.8	1.8
	Average length of stay							
2.24	Total		Days	..	..	..	..	..
2.25	♦ For all commercial accommodation services		Nights	..	..	..	..	..
2.26	* of which, "hotels and similar establishments"		Nights	..	..	..	..	..
2.27	♦ For non commercial accommodation services		Days	..	..	..	..	..
2.28	Average expenditure per day		US$	..	..	..	..	..
3.	**OUTBOUND TOURISM**							
	Data	(3)						
	Departures							
3.1	Total		('000)	61,909	65,175	65,780	63,737	55,971
3.2	♦ Overnight visitors (tourists)		('000)	30,450	32,276	32,971	33,518	32,267
3.3	♦ Same-day visitors (excursionists)		('000)	31,459	32,900	32,809	30,219	23,704
	Expenditure							
3.4	Total		US$ Mn	41,234	43,010	43,092	41,084	..
3.5	♦ Travel		US$ Mn	33,388	35,038	35,170	33,817	29,514
3.6	♦ Passenger transport		US$ Mn	7,846	7,972	7,922	7,267	
	Expenditure by main purpose of the trip							
3.7	Total		US$ Mn	33,388	35,038	35,170	33,817	29,514
3.8	♦ Personal		US$ Mn	29,225	30,761	30,908	29,706	25,994
3.9	♦ Business and professional		US$ Mn	4,163	4,277	4,262	4,111	3,520
	Indicators							
3.10	Average length of stay		Days	10.56	10.67	12.41	12.77	13.68
3.11	Average expenditure per day		US$	..	..	..	..	..
4.	**TOURISM INDUSTRIES**							
	Data							
	Number of establishments							
4.1	Total		Units	156,482	159,347	170,550	192,328	198,378
4.2	♦ Accommodation for visitors		Units	16,933	16,835	17,790	19,411	19,575
4.3	* of which, "hotels and similar establishments"		Units	..	..	..	..	..
4.4	♦ Food and beverage serving activities		Units	74,073	75,417	80,749	80,666	82,873
4.5	♦ Passenger transportation		Units	28,188	28,441	30,934	39,324	40,552
4.6	♦ Travel agencies and other reservation services activities		Units	6,733	6,729	7,010	7,962	8,314
4.7	♦ Other tourism industries		Units	30,555	31,925	34,067	44,965	47,064
	Accommodation for visitors in hotels and similar establishments							
	Monetary data							
4.8	♦ Output		US$ Mn	17,470.9	17,838.5	..	..	..
4.9	♦ Intermediate consumption		US$ Mn	7,097.3	7,028.7	..	..	..
4.10	♦ Gross value added		US$ Mn	10,373.6	10,809.8	..	..	..
4.11	♦ Compensation of employees		US$ Mn	6,530.4	6,770.5	..	..	..
4.12	♦ Gross fixed capital formation		US$ Mn			..	..	..
	Travel agencies and other reservation service activities							
	Monetary data							
4.20	♦ Output		US$ Mn	4,427.4	4,554.7	..	..	..
4.21	♦ Intermediate consumption		US$ Mn	1,728.1	1,811.5	..	..	..
4.22	♦ Gross value added		US$ Mn	2,699.3	2,743.2	..	..	..
4.23	♦ Compensation of employees		US$ Mn	2,046.4	2,073.7	..	..	..
4.24	♦ Gross fixed capital formation		US$ Mn			..	..	..
5.	**EMPLOYMENT**							
	Number of jobs by status in employment							
5.8	Total		('000)	1,668.9	1,684.1	1,700.6	1,692.8	..
5.9	♦ Employees		('000)	1,553.6	1,572.8	1,574.7	1,571.0	..
5.10	♦ Self employed		('000)	115.3	111.3	125.9	121.8	..
	Indicators							
	Number of full-time equivalent jobs by status in employment							
5.11	Total		('000)	1,270.1	1,289.3	1,287.7	1,286.5	..
5.12	♦ Employees	(4)	('000)	1,270.1	1,289.3	1,287.7	1,286.5	..
5.13	* male		('000)	608.9	627.4	628.7	628.8	..
5.14	* female		('000)	661.2	661.9	659.0	657.7	..
5.15	♦ Self employed		('000)	..	..	..	..	..
5.16	* male		('000)	..	..	..	..	..
5.17	* female		('000)	..	..	..	..	..

CANADA

Cod.	Basic data and indicators	Notes	Units	2011	2012	2013	2014	2015
6.	**COMPLEMENTARY INDICATORS**							
	Demand							
6.1	Gross travel propensity		Units	..	..	..	..	..
6.2	(1.2 inbound tourists + 2.2 domestic tourists) / population		Units	3.53	3.58	3.55	3.52	3.56
	Macroeconomic indicators related to international tourism							
6.3	Inbound tourism expenditure over GDP		Percent	1.2	1.1	1.1	1.2	1.0
6.4	Outbound tourism expenditure over GDP		Percent	2.4	2.4	2.4	2.3	1.9
6.5	Tourism balance (inbound minus outbound tourism expenditure) over GDP		Percent	-1.2	-1.3	-1.3	-1.1	-0.9
6.6	Tourism openness (inbound plus outbound tourism expenditure) over GDP		Percent	3.6	3.5	3.5	3.5	2.9
6.7	Tourism coverage (inbound over outbound tourism expenditure)		Percent	48.5	48.1	48.6	49.9	54.9
6.8	Inbound tourism expenditure over exports of goods		Percent	4.3	4.5	4.5	4.3	3.9
6.9	Inbound tourism expenditure over exports of services		Percent	23.4	23.2	23.2	23.7	20.7
6.10	Inbound tourism expenditure over exports of goods and services		Percent	3.7	3.8	3.8	3.6	3.3
6.11	Inbound tourism expenditure over current account credits		Percent	3.2	3.3	3.3	3.1	2.8
6.12	Outbound tourism expenditure over imports of goods		Percent	8.9	9.1	9.1	8.7	6.9
6.13	Outbound tourism expenditure over imports of services		Percent	38.4	38.4	38.2	38.1	30.5
6.14	Outbound tourism expenditure over imports of goods and		Percent	7.3	7.3	7.4	7.1	5.6
6.15	Outbound tourism expenditure over current account debits		Percent	6.3	6.4	6.4	6.1	4.9

CAYMAN ISLANDS

Cod.	Basic data and indicators	Notes	Units	2011	2012	2013	2014	2015
1.	**INBOUND TOURISM**							
	Data							
	Arrivals							
1.1	Total		('000)	1,710	1,829	1,721	1,993	2,102
1.2	♦ Overnight visitors (tourists)	(1)	('000)	309	322	345	383	385
1.3	♦ Same-day visitors (excursionists)		('000)	1,401	1,507	1,376	1,610	1,717
1.4	* of which, cruise passengers		('000)	1,401	1,507	1,376	1,610	1,717
	Arrivals by region	(1)						
1.5	Total		('000)	309	322	345	383	385
1.6	♦ Africa		('000)	1	1	1	1	1
1.7	♦ Americas		('000)	285	297	313	342	346
1.8	♦ East Asia and the Pacific		('000)	2	2	3	3	3
1.9	♦ Europe		('000)	21	22	28	37	35
1.10	♦ Middle East		('000)	..	..	..	..	..
1.11	♦ South Asia		('000)	..	..	..	..	..
1.12	♦ Other not classified		('000)	..	..	..	..	..
1.13	* of which, nationals residing abroad		('000)	..	..	..	..	..
	Arrivals by main purpose	(1)						
1.14	Total		('000)	309	322	345	383	385
1.15	♦ Personal		('000)	291	302	325	364	367
1.16	* holidays, leisure and recreation		('000)	245	255	263	283	287
1.17	* other personal purposes		('000)	46	47	62	81	80
1.18	♦ Business and professional		('000)	18	20	20	19	19
	Arrivals by mode of transport							
1.19	Total		('000)	1,710	1,829	1,721	1,993	2,102
1.20	♦ Air		('000)	309	322	345	383	385
1.21	♦ Water	(2)	('000)	1,401	1,507	1,376	1,610	1,717
1.22	♦ Land		('000)	..	..	..	..	..
1.23	* railway		('000)	..	..	..	..	..
1.24	* road		('000)	..	..	..	..	..
1.25	* others		('000)	..	..	..	..	..
	Accommodation							
	Total							
1.29	♦ Guests	(1)	('000)	309	322	345	383	385
1.30	♦ Overnights		('000)	..	..	..	..	..
	Expenditure							
1.33	Total	(3)(4)	US$ Mn	472	470	480	..	..
1.34	♦ Travel		US$ Mn	..	..	..	..	..
1.35	♦ Passenger transport		US$ Mn	..	..	..	..	..
	Indicators							
1.39	Average size of travel party		Persons	..	..	..	..	..
	Average length of stay							
1.40	Total		Days	6.25	6.27	6.17	6.11	6.26
1.41	♦ For all commercial accommodation services		Nights	..	..	..	..	..
1.42	* of which, "hotels and similar establishments"		Nights	..	..	..	..	..
1.43	♦ For non commercial accommodation services		Days	..	..	..	..	..
1.44	Average expenditure per day		US$	..	..	..	..	..
3.	**OUTBOUND TOURISM**							
	Data							
	Expenditure							
3.4	Total	(3)	US$ Mn	145	161	170	..	..
3.5	♦ Travel		US$ Mn	..	..	..	..	..
3.6	♦ Passenger transport		US$ Mn	..	..	..	..	..
4.	**TOURISM INDUSTRIES**							
	Data							
	Number of establishments							
4.1	Total		Units	..	..	..	..	..
4.2	♦ Accommodation for visitors		Units	..	..	..	..	..
4.3	* of which, "hotels and similar establishments"		Units	..	..	400	420	501
4.4	♦ Food and beverage serving activities		Units	..	..	..	..	..
4.5	♦ Passenger transportation		Units	..	..	..	..	..
4.6	♦ Travel agencies and other reservation services activities		Units	..	..	..	..	..
4.7	♦ Other tourism industries		Units	..	..	..	..	..

CAYMAN ISLANDS

Cod.	Basic data and indicators	Notes	Units	2011	2012	2013	2014	2015
	Accommodation for visitors in hotels and similar establishments							
	Non-monetary data							
4.13	♦ Number of establishments		Units	..	..	400	420	501
4.14	♦ Number of rooms	(5)	Units	4,974	4,923	5,248	5,264	5,515
4.15	♦ Number of bed-places		Units	..	..	7,989	7,966	8,088
	Indicators							
4.16	Occupancy rate / rooms		Percent	..	..	..	..	..
4.17	Occupancy rate / bed-places		Percent	..	..	..	..	..
4.18	Average length of stay	(6)	Nights	6.25	6.27	6.17	6.11	6.26
4.19	Available capacity (bed-places per 1000 inhabitants)		Units	..	..	136.72	134.50	134.80
5.	**EMPLOYMENT**							
	Data							
	Number of employees by tourism industries							
5.1	Total		('000)	8.0	11.0	..	..	..
5.2	♦ Accommodation services for visitors (hotels and similar establishments)		('000)	..	..	..	..	..
5.3	♦ Other accommodation services		('000)	..	..	..	..	..
5.4	♦ Food and beverage serving activities		('000)	..	..	..	..	..
5.5	♦ Passenger transportation		('000)	..	..	..	..	..
5.6	♦ Travel agencies and other reservation services activities		('000)	..	..	..	..	..
5.7	♦ Other tourism industries		('000)	..	..	..	..	..
6.	**COMPLEMENTARY INDICATORS**							
	Demand							
6.1	Gross travel propensity		Units	..	..	..	..	..
6.2	(1.2 inbound tourists) / population		Units	5.46	5.59	5.90	6.47	6.42
	Macroeconomic indicators related to international tourism							
6.3	Inbound tourism expenditure over GDP		Percent	..	..	..	..	..
6.4	Outbound tourism expenditure over GDP		Percent	..	..	..	..	..
6.5	Tourism balance (inbound minus outbound tourism expenditure) over GDP		Percent	..	..	..	..	..
6.6	Tourism openness (inbound plus outbound tourism expenditure) over GDP		Percent	..	..	..	..	..
6.7	Tourism coverage (inbound over outbound tourism expenditure)		Percent	325.5	291.9	282.4	..	..
6.8	Inbound tourism expenditure over exports of goods		Percent	..	..	..	..	..
6.9	Inbound tourism expenditure over exports of services		Percent	..	..	..	..	..
6.10	Inbound tourism expenditure over exports of goods and services		Percent	..	..	..	..	..
6.11	Inbound tourism expenditure over current account credits		Percent	..	..	..	..	..
6.12	Outbound tourism expenditure over imports of goods		Percent	..	..	..	..	..
6.13	Outbound tourism expenditure over imports of services		Percent	..	..	..	..	..
6.14	Outbound tourism expenditure over imports of goods and		Percent	..	..	..	..	..
6.15	Outbound tourism expenditure over current account debits		Percent	..	..	..	..	..

CENTRAL AFRICAN REPUBLIC

Cod.	Basic data and indicators	Notes	Units	2011	2012	2013	2014	2015
1.	**INBOUND TOURISM**							
	Data							
	Arrivals							
1.1	Total		('000)	..	..	..	..	..
1.2	♦ Overnight visitors (tourists)	(1)	('000)	65	71	84	96	121
1.3	♦ Same-day visitors (excursionists)		('000)	..	..	..	..	..
1.4	* of which, cruise passengers		('000)	..	..	..	..	..
	Arrivals by region	(1)						
1.5	Total		('000)	66	71	84	96	121
1.6	♦ Africa		('000)	33	36	44	51	63
1.7	♦ Americas		('000)	5	5	6	7	8
1.8	♦ East Asia and the Pacific		('000)	6	6	6	7	10
1.9	♦ Europe		('000)	17	18	20	23	28
1.10	♦ Middle East		('000)	4	5	5	6	8
1.11	♦ South Asia		('000)	..	..	..	..	..
1.12	♦ Other not classified		('000)	2	2	2	2	4
1.13	* of which, nationals residing abroad		('000)	..	..	..	..	..
	Arrivals by main purpose	(1)						
1.14	Total		('000)	65	71	84	96	121
1.15	♦ Personal		('000)	28	32	49	56	77
1.16	* holidays, leisure and recreation		('000)	9	11	14	15	19
1.17	* other personal purposes		('000)	19	21	35	41	58
1.18	♦ Business and professional		('000)	37	39	35	40	44
	Arrivals by mode of transport							
1.19	Total		('000)	65	71	84	96	121
1.20	♦ Air		('000)	65	71	84	96	121
1.21	♦ Water		('000)	..	..	..	..	..
1.22	♦ Land		('000)	..	..	..	..	..
1.23	* railway		('000)	..	..	..	..	..
1.24	* road		('000)	..	..	..	..	..
1.25	* others		('000)	..	..	..	..	..
	Accommodation							
	Hotels and similar establishments							
1.31	♦ Guests		('000)	24	24	28	..	..
1.32	♦ Overnights		('000)	52	55	37	..	..
	Expenditure							
1.33	Total		US$ Mn	15	15	16	..	..
1.34	♦ Travel		US$ Mn	11	11	12	..	..
1.35	♦ Passenger transport		US$ Mn	4	4	4	..	..
	Indicators							
1.39	Average size of travel party		Persons	..	..	..	..	..
	Average length of stay							
1.40	Total		Days	..	..	..	..	..
1.41	♦ For all commercial accommodation services		Nights	..	..	..	..	..
1.42	* of which, "hotels and similar establishments"		Nights	3.16	2.28	2.00	..	..
1.43	♦ For non commercial accommodation services		Days	..	..	..	..	..
1.44	Average expenditure per day		US$	..	..	..	..	..
2.	**DOMESTIC TOURISM**							
	Data							
	Accommodation							
	Hotels and similar establishments							
2.21	♦ Guests		('000)	3.3	3.8	11.2	12.2	14.7
2.22	♦ Overnights		('000)	7.2	7.8	16.4	17.8	22.0
	Indicators							
2.23	Average size of travel party		Persons	..	..	..	..	..
	Average length of stay							
2.24	Total		Days	..	..	..	..	..
2.25	♦ For all commercial accommodation services		Nights	3.16	..	..	..	..
2.26	* of which, "hotels and similar establishments"		Nights	2.53	2.05	1.45	1.47	1.49
2.27	♦ For non commercial accommodation services		Days	..	..	..	..	..
2.28	Average expenditure per day		US$	..	..	..	..	..
3.	**OUTBOUND TOURISM**							
	Data							
	Expenditure							
3.4	Total		US$ Mn	68	69	70	..	..
3.5	♦ Travel		US$ Mn	50	50	50	..	..
3.6	♦ Passenger transport		US$ Mn	18	19	19	..	..

CENTRAL AFRICAN REPUBLIC

Cod.	Basic data and indicators	Notes	Units	2011	2012	2013	2014	2015
4.	**TOURISM INDUSTRIES**							
	Data							
	Number of establishments							
4.1	Total		Units	..	..	..	..	..
4.2	♦ Accommodation for visitors		Units	..	..	..	..	..
4.3	* of which, "hotels and similar establishments"		Units	62	69	51	59	68
4.4	♦ Food and beverage serving activities		Units	..	..	..	..	..
4.5	♦ Passenger transportation		Units	..	..	..	..	..
4.6	♦ Travel agencies and other reservation services activities		Units	..	..	..	..	..
4.7	♦ Other tourism industries		Units	..	..	..	..	..
	Accommodation for visitors in hotels and similar establishments							
	Non-monetary data							
4.13	♦ Number of establishments		Units	62	69	51	59	68
4.14	♦ Number of rooms		Units	992	1,151	845	972	1,138
4.15	♦ Number of bed-places		Units	1,153	1,403	1,097	1,224	1,390
	Indicators							
4.16	Occupancy rate / rooms		Percent	60.37	50.93	45.89	50.64	52.15
4.17	Occupancy rate / bed-places		Percent	..	..	..	..	..
4.18	Average length of stay		Nights	2.13	2.25	2.36	2.95	2.79
4.19	Available capacity (bed-places per 1000 inhabitants)		Units	0.25	0.30	0.23	0.25	0.28
6.	**COMPLEMENTARY INDICATORS**							
	Demand							
6.1	Gross travel propensity		Units	..	..	..	..	..
6.2	(1.2 inbound tourists) / population		Units	0.01	0.02	0.02	0.02	0.02
	Macroeconomic indicators related to international tourism	(2)						
6.3	Inbound tourism expenditure over GDP		Percent	..	..	..	..	..
6.4	Outbound tourism expenditure over GDP		Percent	..	..	..	..	..
6.5	Tourism balance (inbound minus outbound tourism expenditure) over GDP		Percent	..	..	..	..	..
6.6	Tourism openness (inbound plus outbound tourism expenditure) over GDP		Percent	..	..	..	..	..
6.7	Tourism coverage (inbound over outbound tourism expenditure)		Percent	22.1	21.7	22.3	..	..
6.8	Inbound tourism expenditure over exports of goods		Percent	7.5	7.6	14.7	..	..
6.9	Inbound tourism expenditure over exports of services		Percent	18.4	18.3	14.1	..	..
6.10	Inbound tourism expenditure over exports of goods and services		Percent	5.3	5.4	7.2	..	..
6.11	Inbound tourism expenditure over current account credits		Percent	..	..	..	..	..
6.12	Outbound tourism expenditure over imports of goods		Percent	21.5	20.8	31.9	..	..
6.13	Outbound tourism expenditure over imports of services		Percent	35.8	34.9	43.8	..	..
6.14	Outbound tourism expenditure over imports of goods and		Percent	13.4	13.0	18.5	..	..
6.15	Outbound tourism expenditure over current account debits		Percent	..	..	..	..	..

CHAD

Cod.	Basic data and indicators	Notes	Units	2011	2012	2013	2014	2015
1.	**INBOUND TOURISM**							
	**Data**							
	Arrivals							
1.1	Total		('000)	..	..	..	..	..
1.2	♦ Overnight visitors (tourists)		('000)	77	86	100	122	120
1.3	♦ Same-day visitors (excursionists)		('000)	..	..	..	..	..
1.4	* of which, cruise passengers		('000)	..	..	..	..	..
	Arrivals by region							
1.5	Total		('000)	77	86	100	122	120
1.6	♦ Africa		('000)	51	60	68	70	84
1.7	♦ Americas		('000)	4	3	4	6	5
1.8	♦ East Asia and the Pacific		('000)	10	9	10	10	10
1.9	♦ Europe		('000)	11	13	14	33	20
1.10	♦ Middle East		('000)	1	1	3	3	1
1.11	♦ South Asia		('000)	..	..	1	..	..
1.12	♦ Other not classified		('000)	..	..	..	..	..
1.13	* of which, nationals residing abroad		('000)	..	..	..	..	..
	Arrivals by main purpose							
1.14	Total		('000)	77	86	100	122	120
1.15	♦ Personal		('000)	65	57	68	79	87
1.16	* holidays, leisure and recreation		('000)	7	19	18	25	38
1.17	* other personal purposes		('000)	58	38	50	54	49
1.18	♦ Business and professional		('000)	12	29	32	43	32
	Arrivals by mode of transport							
1.19	Total		('000)	77	86	100	122	120
1.20	♦ Air		('000)	74	84	97	119	115
1.21	♦ Water		('000)	..	..	..	..	..
1.22	♦ Land		('000)	3	2	3	4	4
1.23	* railway		('000)	..	..	..	..	..
1.24	* road		('000)	3	2	3	4	4
1.25	* others		('000)	..	..	..	..	..
	Accommodation							
	Hotels and similar establishments							
1.31	♦ Guests		('000)	25	30	32	43	65
1.32	♦ Overnights		('000)	59	70	86	84	89
	**Indicators**							
1.39	Average size of travel party		Persons	..	..	..	..	..
	Average length of stay							
1.40	Total		Days	2.30	2.30	2.60	1.90	1.30
1.41	♦ For all commercial accommodation services		Nights	..	..	..	..	..
1.42	* of which, "hotels and similar establishments"		Nights	..	..	..	..	..
1.43	♦ For non commercial accommodation services		Days	..	..	..	..	..
1.44	Average expenditure per day		US$	..	..	..	..	..
2.	**DOMESTIC TOURISM**							
	**Data**							
	Accommodation							
	Hotels and similar establishments							
2.21	♦ Guests		('000)	2	5	6	7	..
2.22	♦ Overnights		('000)	5	9	10	7	..
	**Indicators**							
2.23	Average size of travel party		Persons	..	..	..	..	..
	Average length of stay							
2.24	Total		Days	2.40	1.86	1.86	1.07	..
2.25	♦ For all commercial accommodation services		Nights	..	..	..	..	..
2.26	* of which, "hotels and similar establishments"		Nights	..	..	..	..	..
2.27	♦ For non commercial accommodation services		Days	..	..	..	..	..
2.28	Average expenditure per day		US$	..	..	..	..	..
3.	**OUTBOUND TOURISM**							
	**Data**							
	Departures							
3.1	Total		('000)	76	79	86	98	94
3.2	♦ Overnight visitors (tourists)		('000)	..	..	..	..	..
3.3	♦ Same-day visitors (excursionists)		('000)	..	..	..	..	..

CHAD

Cod.	Basic data and indicators	Notes	Units	2011	2012	2013	2014	2015
4.	**TOURISM INDUSTRIES**							
	Data							
	Accommodation for visitors in hotels and similar establishments							
	Non-monetary data							
4.13	♦ Number of establishments		Units	..	..	..	..	..
4.14	♦ Number of rooms		Units	1,330	1,424	1,424	1,684	1,799
4.15	♦ Number of bed-places		Units	2,380	2,380	2,380	3,020	3,220
	Indicators							
4.16	Occupancy rate / rooms		Percent	..	..	..	..	..
4.17	Occupancy rate / bed-places		Percent	..	..	..	..	..
4.18	Average length of stay		Nights	..	..	..	..	..
4.19	Available capacity (bed-places per 1000 inhabitants)		Units	0.19	0.19	0.18	0.22	0.23
6.	**COMPLEMENTARY INDICATORS**							
	Demand							
6.1	Gross travel propensity		Units	..	..	..	..	..
6.2	(1.2 inbound tourists) / population		Units	0.01	0.01	0.01	0.01	0.01

CHILE

Cod.	Basic data and indicators	Notes	Units	2011	2012	2013	2014	2015
1.	**INBOUND TOURISM**							
	Data							
	Arrivals							
1.1	Total		('000)	3,963	4,397	4,457	4,601	5,487
1.2	♦ Overnight visitors (tourists)	(1)	('000)	3,137	3,554	3,576	3,674	4,478
1.3	♦ Same-day visitors (excursionists)	(2)	('000)	826	843	881	926	1,009
1.4	* of which, cruise passengers		('000)	..	..	..	..	..
	Arrivals by region	(1)						
1.5	Total		('000)	3,137	3,554	3,576	3,674	4,478
1.6	♦ Africa		('000)	4	4	4	4	4
1.7	♦ Americas		('000)	2,533	2,899	2,901	2,952	3,735
1.8	♦ East Asia and the Pacific		('000)	78	98	100	104	111
1.9	♦ Europe		('000)	376	388	396	426	432
1.10	♦ Middle East		('000)	1	1	1	1	1
1.11	♦ South Asia		('000)	3	3	3	3	4
1.12	♦ Other not classified		('000)	143	161	172	185	191
1.13	* of which, nationals residing abroad		('000)	143	160	171	185	191
	Arrivals by main purpose							
1.14	Total	(1)	('000)	3,137	3,554	3,576	3,674	4,478
1.15	♦ Personal		('000)	2,435	2,904	2,952	3,009	3,786
1.16	* holidays, leisure and recreation		('000)	1,467	1,834	1,863	1,910	2,409
1.17	* other personal purposes		('000)	967	1,070	1,089	1,099	1,377
1.18	♦ Business and professional		('000)	702	651	624	666	692
	Arrivals by mode of transport							
1.19	Total		('000)	3,137	3,554	3,576	3,674	4,478
1.20	♦ Air		('000)	1,265	1,445	1,475	1,535	1,710
1.21	♦ Water		('000)	..	..	..	..	..
1.22	♦ Land		('000)	1,872	2,109	2,101	2,140	2,768
1.23	* railway		('000)	..	..	..	..	..
1.24	* road		('000)	1,872	2,109	2,101	2,140	2,768
1.25	* others		('000)	..	..	..	..	..
	Accommodation							
	Hotels and similar establishments							
1.31	♦ Guests	(3)	('000)	1,691	2,042	2,161	3,151	3,262
1.32	♦ Overnights	(3)	('000)	3,775	4,342	4,553	6,181	6,501
	Expenditure							
1.33	Total		US$ Mn	2,751	3,114	3,144	3,143	3,229
1.34	♦ Travel		US$ Mn	1,889	2,150	2,181	2,259	2,408
1.35	♦ Passenger transport		US$ Mn	862	964	963	884	821
	Expenditure by main purpose of the trip							
1.36	Total		US$ Mn	1,889	2,151	2,181	2,259	2,408
1.37	♦ Personal		US$ Mn	1,323	1,509	1,547	1,614	1,707
1.38	♦ Business and professional		US$ Mn	566	642	634	645	702
	Indicators							
1.39	Average size of travel party		Persons	..	..	..	..	..
	Average length of stay							
1.40	Total		Days	..	..	..	..	..
1.41	♦ For all commercial accommodation services		Nights	8.50	8.70	8.90	8.80	8.50
1.42	* of which, "hotels and similar establishments"		Nights	..	..	..	..	..
1.43	♦ For non commercial accommodation services		Days	..	..	..	..	..
1.44	Average expenditure per day		US$	66.6	68.6	66.9	68.2	64.0
2.	**DOMESTIC TOURISM**							
	Data							
	Trips							
2.1	Total		('000)	40,178	41,423	42,867	44,585	46,927
2.2	♦ Overnight visitors (tourists)		('000)	20,740	20,506	21,531	22,823	24,512
2.3	♦ Same-day visitors (excursionists)		('000)	19,438	20,917	21,335	21,762	22,415
	Trips by main purpose							
2.4	Total		('000)	20,740	20,506	21,532	22,824	24,512
2.5	♦ Personal		('000)	20,190	20,068	21,016	22,277	23,925
2.6	* holidays, leisure and recreation		('000)	13,405	12,886	13,725	14,548	15,624
2.7	* other personal purposes		('000)	6,785	7,182	7,291	7,729	8,301
2.8	♦ Business and professional		('000)	550	438	516	547	587
	Trips by mode of transport							
2.9	Total		('000)	20,739	20,506	21,532	22,723	24,512
2.10	♦ Air		('000)	1,029	1,489	1,315	1,294	1,396
2.11	♦ Water		('000)	..	..	..	..	..
2.12	♦ Land		('000)	19,710	19,017	20,217	21,429	23,116
2.13	* railway		('000)	120	119	125	132	142
2.14	* road		('000)	19,273	18,740	19,844	21,034	22,690
2.15	* others		('000)	317	158	248	263	284

CHILE

Cod.	Basic data and indicators	Notes	Units	2011	2012	2013	2014	2015
	Trips by form of organization							
2.16	Total		('000)	..	20,506	21,531	22,823	24,512
2.17	♦ Package tour		('000)	..	187	196	208	223
2.18	♦ Other forms		('000)	..	20,319	21,335	22,615	24,289
	Accommodation							
	Hotels and similar establishments							
2.21	♦ Guests	(3)	('000)	3,978	4,438	4,614	6,116	5,977
2.22	♦ Overnights	(3)	('000)	7,725	8,381	8,687	11,351	11,119
	Indicators							
2.23	Average size of travel party		Persons	3.9	4.7	..	..	..
	Average length of stay							
2.24	Total		Days	6.40	6.20	..	..	..
2.25	♦ For all commercial accommodation services		Nights	..	..	..	..	..
2.26	* of which, "hotels and similar establishments"		Nights	..	..	..	..	..
2.27	♦ For non commercial accommodation services		Days	..	..	..	..	..
2.28	Average expenditure per day		US$	17.5	17.4	..	..	..
3.	**OUTBOUND TOURISM**							
	Data							
	Departures							
3.1	Total		('000)	3,220	3,448	3,674	3,842	4,103
3.2	♦ Overnight visitors (tourists)		('000)	2,638	2,837	2,999	3,169	3,359
3.3	♦ Same-day visitors (excursionists)		('000)	582	611	675	673	744
	Expenditure							
3.4	Total		US$ Mn	2,047	2,400	2,499	2,706	2,563
3.5	♦ Travel		US$ Mn	1,624	1,833	1,867	2,089	1,986
3.6	♦ Passenger transport		US$ Mn	423	567	632	617	577
	Expenditure by main purpose of the trip							
3.7	Total		US$ Mn	1,624	1,833	1,867	2,089	1,986
3.8	♦ Personal		US$ Mn	1,018	1,286	1,278	1,473	1,520
3.9	♦ Business and professional		US$ Mn	606	547	589	616	466
	Indicators							
3.10	Average length of stay		Days	6.80	7.90	7.90	7.80	7.80
3.11	Average expenditure per day		US$	89.8	80.2	77.0	83.0	72.7
4.	**TOURISM INDUSTRIES**							
	Data							
	Number of establishments							
4.1	Total		Units	10,353	10,782	11,843	12,770	13,679
4.2	♦ Accommodation for visitors		Units	5,360	5,453	6,102	6,584	7,078
4.3	* of which, "hotels and similar establishments"	(4)	Units	4,778	4,890	5,576	6,027	6,497
4.4	♦ Food and beverage serving activities		Units	3,584	3,789	4,045	4,318	4,606
4.5	♦ Passenger transportation		Units	..	..	..	..	..
4.6	♦ Travel agencies and other reservation services activities		Units	1,409	1,540	1,696	1,868	1,995
4.7	♦ Other tourism industries		Units	..	..	..	..	..
	Accommodation for visitors in hotels and similar establishments							
	Non-monetary data							
4.13	♦ Number of establishments		Units	4,778	4,890	5,576	6,027	6,497
4.14	♦ Number of rooms		Units	76,560	82,088	88,150	95,280	100,203
4.15	♦ Number of bed-places		Units	156,605	175,613	186,455	201,536	208,450
	Indicators							
4.16	Occupancy rate / rooms		Percent	42.80	42.60	42.20	41.88	41.01
4.17	Occupancy rate / bed-places		Percent	27.20	28.30	27.90	27.96	23.88
4.18	Average length of stay		Nights	2.00	1.90	2.00	1.95	1.91
4.19	Available capacity (bed-places per 1000 inhabitants)		Units	9.10	10.10	10.61	11.35	11.61
	Travel agencies and other reservation service activities							
	Non-monetary data							
	♦ Domestic trips							
4.25	* with package tour		Percent	..	0.9	..	..	..
4.26	* without package tour		Percent	..	99.1	..	..	..
	♦ Inbound trips	(5)						
4.27	* with package tour		Percent	6.8	11.0	10.3	11.7	12.0
4.28	* without package tour		Percent	93.2	89.0	89.7	88.3	88.0
	♦ Outbound trips	(5)						
4.29	* with package tour		Percent	6.9	14.6	13.1	18.5	15.0
4.30	* without package tour		Percent	93.1	85.4	86.9	81.5	85.0

CHILE

Cod.	Basic data and indicators	Notes	Units	2011	2012	2013	2014	2015
5.	**EMPLOYMENT**	**(6)(7)**						
	Data							
	Number of employees by tourism industries							
5.1	Total		('000)	314.1	348.1	355.2	361.6	368.5
5.2	♦ Accommodation services for visitors (hotels and similar establishments)		('000)	67.8	75.2	74.0	74.8	78.0
5.3	♦ Other accommodation services		('000)	..	..	..	..	..
5.4	♦ Food and beverage serving activities		('000)	146.2	153.2	161.4	163.4	166.9
5.5	♦ Passenger transportation		('000)	40.8	50.8	49.0	51.2	51.2
5.6	♦ Travel agencies and other reservation services activities		('000)	8.2	7.9	7.8	8.2	8.6
5.7	♦ Other tourism industries		('000)	51.1	61.0	63.0	64.0	63.8
	Number of jobs by status in employment							
5.8	Total		('000)	314.1	348.1	355.2	361.6	368.5
5.9	♦ Employees		('000)	314.1	348.1	355.2	361.6	368.5
5.10	♦ Self employed		('000)	..	..	..	..	..
6.	**COMPLEMENTARY INDICATORS**							
	Demand							
6.1	Gross travel propensity		Units	..	..	..	..	..
6.2	(1.2 inbound tourists + 2.2 domestic tourists) / population		Units	1.39	1.38	1.43	1.49	1.62
	Macroeconomic indicators related to international tourism							
6.3	Inbound tourism expenditure over GDP		Percent	1.1	1.2	1.1	1.2	1.3
6.4	Outbound tourism expenditure over GDP		Percent	0.8	0.9	0.9	1.0	1.1
6.5	Tourism balance (inbound minus outbound tourism expenditure) over GDP		Percent	0.3	0.3	0.2	0.2	0.2
6.6	Tourism openness (inbound plus outbound tourism expenditure) over GDP		Percent	1.9	2.1	2.0	2.2	2.4
6.7	Tourism coverage (inbound over outbound tourism expenditure)		Percent	134.4	129.8	125.8	116.1	126.0
6.8	Inbound tourism expenditure over exports of goods		Percent	3.4	4.0	4.1	4.2	5.2
6.9	Inbound tourism expenditure over exports of services		Percent	21.0	25.1	25.4	28.5	33.0
6.10	Inbound tourism expenditure over exports of goods and services		Percent	2.9	3.5	3.5	3.7	4.5
6.11	Inbound tourism expenditure over current account credits		Percent	2.6	3.0	3.1	3.2	3.9
6.12	Outbound tourism expenditure over imports of goods		Percent	2.9	3.2	3.3	3.9	4.4
6.13	Outbound tourism expenditure over imports of services		Percent	12.7	15.9	15.5	18.2	18.9
6.14	Outbound tourism expenditure over imports of goods and		Percent	2.4	2.6	2.8	3.2	3.5
6.15	Outbound tourism expenditure over current account debits		Percent	2.2	2.4	2.5	2.9	3.1

CHINA

Cod.	Basic data and indicators	Notes	Units	2011	2012	2013	2014	2015
1.	**INBOUND TOURISM**							
	Data							
	Arrivals							
1.1	Total	(1)	('000)	135,423	132,405	129,078	128,499	133,820
1.2	♦ Overnight visitors (tourists)		('000)	57,581	57,725	55,686	55,622	56,886
1.3	♦ Same-day visitors (excursionists)		('000)	..	..	..	..	..
1.4	* of which, cruise passengers		('000)	..	..	..	..	..
	Arrivals by region	(1)						
1.5	Total		('000)	135,423	132,405	129,078	128,498	133,820
1.6	♦ Africa		('000)	424	440	461	497	580
1.7	♦ Americas		('000)	3,201	3,179	3,124	3,107	3,115
1.8	♦ East Asia and the Pacific		('000)	123,828	120,802	117,744	117,276	123,995
1.9	♦ Europe		('000)	6,772	6,770	6,422	6,209	5,177
1.10	♦ Middle East		('000)	239	264	269	278	..
1.11	♦ South Asia		('000)	957	948	1,055	1,125	952
1.12	♦ Other not classified		('000)	2	2	2	7	2
1.13	* of which, nationals residing abroad		('000)	..	..	..	..	..
	Arrivals by main purpose	(2)						
1.14	Total		('000)	27,111	27,191	26,290	26,361	25,985
1.15	♦ Personal		('000)	20,785	20,911	20,096	20,965	20,608
1.16	* holidays, leisure and recreation		('000)	12,218	11,629	10,123	8,930	8,249
1.17	* other personal purposes		('000)	8,567	9,282	9,973	12,035	12,359
1.18	♦ Business and professional		('000)	6,326	6,280	6,194	5,396	5,377
	Arrivals by mode of transport	(1)						
1.19	Total		('000)	135,423	132,405	129,078	128,498	133,820
1.20	♦ Air		('000)	20,911	21,421	20,744	21,086	21,012
1.21	♦ Water		('000)	5,082	4,793	4,644	4,594	4,540
1.22	♦ Land		('000)	109,430	106,191	103,690	102,818	108,268
1.23	* railway		('000)	1,442	1,357	1,339	1,256	1,220
1.24	* road		('000)	30,899	29,844	29,467	29,275	29,225
1.25	* others	(3)	('000)	77,089	74,990	72,885	72,287	77,823
	Accommodation							
	Hotels and similar establishments							
1.31	♦ Guests		('000)	106,552	116,266	89,924	..	..
1.32	♦ Overnights		('000)	294,757	330,080	243,761	..	..
	Expenditure							
1.33	Total		US$ Mn	..	..	..	..	..
1.34	♦ Travel		US$ Mn	48,464	50,028	51,664	105,380	114,109
1.35	♦ Passenger transport		US$ Mn	..	..	..	..	..
	Indicators							
1.39	Average size of travel party		Persons	..	..	..	..	..
	Average length of stay							
1.40	Total		Days	..	..	..	..	..
1.41	♦ For all commercial accommodation services		Nights	2.77	2.84	2.71	..	..
1.42	* of which, "hotels and similar establishments"		Nights	..	..	..	..	..
1.43	♦ For non commercial accommodation services		Days	..	..	..	..	..
1.44	Average expenditure per day		US$	..	..	..	..	..
2.	**DOMESTIC TOURISM**							
	Data							
	Trips							
2.1	Total		('000)	2,641,000	2,957,000	3,262,000	3,611,000	..
2.2	♦ Overnight visitors (tourists)		('000)	..	..	..	..	..
2.3	♦ Same-day visitors (excursionists)		('000)	..	..	..	..	..
3.	**OUTBOUND TOURISM**							
	Data							
	Departures							
3.1	Total		('000)	..	..	..	..	..
3.2	♦ Overnight visitors (tourists)	(4)	('000)	70,250	83,183	98,185	107,276	116,886
3.3	♦ Same-day visitors (excursionists)		('000)	..	..	..	..	..
	Expenditure							
3.4	Total		US$ Mn	..	..	..	..	..
3.5	♦ Travel		US$ Mn	72,585	101,977	128,576	234,662	292,200
3.6	♦ Passenger transport		US$ Mn	..	..	..	..	..

CHINA

Cod.	Basic data and indicators	Notes	Units	2011	2012	2013	2014	2015
4.	**TOURISM INDUSTRIES**							
	Data							
	Number of establishments							
4.1	Total		Units	..	..	..	..	..
4.2	♦ Accommodation for visitors		Units	..	..	..	..	..
4.3	* of which, "hotels and similar establishments"	(5)	Units	11,676	11,367	11,687	11,180	10,956
4.4	♦ Food and beverage serving activities		Units	..	..	..	..	..
4.5	♦ Passenger transportation		Units	..	..	..	..	..
4.6	♦ Travel agencies and other reservation services activities		Units	..	..	..	..	..
4.7	♦ Other tourism industries		Units	..	..	..	..	..
	Accommodation for visitors in hotels and similar establishments							
	Non-monetary data	(5)						
4.13	♦ Number of establishments		Units	11,676	11,367	11,687	11,180	10,956
4.14	♦ Number of rooms		Units	1,474,900	1,497,200	1,539,141	1,497,899	1,462,454
4.15	♦ Number of bed-places		Units	2,586,400	2,677,400	2,705,013	2,624,815	2,593,585
	Indicators							
4.16	Occupancy rate / rooms		Percent	61.00	59.46	55.97	54.00	55.59
4.17	Occupancy rate / bed-places		Percent	..	..	..	..	..
4.18	Average length of stay	(6)	Nights	2.77	2.84	2.71	..	..
4.19	Available capacity (bed-places per 1000 inhabitants)		Units	1.92	1.98	1.99	1.92	1.88
6.	**COMPLEMENTARY INDICATORS**							
	Demand							
6.1	Gross travel propensity		Units	..	..	..	..	..
6.2	(1.2 inbound tourists + 2.1 domestic visitors) / population		Units	2.00	2.22	2.43	2.68	..
	Macroeconomic indicators related to international tourism							
6.3	Inbound tourism expenditure over GDP		Percent	0.7	0.6	0.5	1.0	..
6.4	Outbound tourism expenditure over GDP		Percent	1.0	1.2	1.4	2.2	..
6.5	Tourism balance (inbound minus outbound tourism expenditure) over GDP		Percent	-0.3	-0.6	-0.9	-1.2	..
6.6	Tourism openness (inbound plus outbound tourism expenditure) over GDP		Percent	1.7	1.8	1.9	3.2	..
6.7	Tourism coverage (inbound over outbound tourism expenditure)		Percent	66.8	49.1	40.2	44.9	39.1
6.8	Inbound tourism expenditure over exports of goods		Percent	2.7	2.5	2.4	4.7	5.3
6.9	Inbound tourism expenditure over exports of services		Percent	24.1	24.8	25.0	37.6	39.8
6.10	Inbound tourism expenditure over exports of goods and services		Percent	2.4	2.3	2.2	4.2	4.7
6.11	Inbound tourism expenditure over current account credits		Percent	2.2	2.1	2.0	3.8	4.2
6.12	Outbound tourism expenditure over imports of goods		Percent	4.6	6.1	7.2	13.0	18.5
6.13	Outbound tourism expenditure over imports of services		Percent	29.3	36.3	38.9	51.8	62.3
6.14	Outbound tourism expenditure over imports of goods and		Percent	4.0	5.2	6.1	10.4	14.3
6.15	Outbound tourism expenditure over current account debits		Percent	3.6	4.7	5.4	9.2	12.6

COLOMBIA

Cod.	Basic data and indicators	Notes	Units	2011	2012	2013	2014	2015
1.	**INBOUND TOURISM**							
	Data							
	Arrivals							
1.1	Total	(1)(2)(3)	('000)	3,324	3,492	3,748	4,193	4,447
1.2	♦ Overnight visitors (tourists)		('000)	2,042	2,175	2,288	2,565	2,978
1.3	♦ Same-day visitors (excursionists)		('000)	282	254	307	314	272
1.4	* of which, cruise passengers		('000)	282	254	307	314	272
	Arrivals by region	(1)(3)(4)						
1.5	Total		('000)	2,042	2,175	2,288	2,565	2,978
1.6	♦ Africa		('000)	3	3	3	4	4
1.7	♦ Americas		('000)	1,193	1,278	1,389	1,562	1,825
1.8	♦ East Asia and the Pacific		('000)	29	34	36	44	50
1.9	♦ Europe		('000)	267	272	294	352	400
1.10	♦ Middle East		('000)	1	1	1	2	2
1.11	♦ South Asia		('000)	3	3	3	4	6
1.12	♦ Other not classified		('000)	546	584	562	599	692
1.13	* of which, nationals residing abroad		('000)	546	584	562	598	690
	Arrivals by main purpose	(1)(4)(5)						
1.14	Total		('000)	1,496	1,591	1,726	1,968	2,288
1.15	♦ Personal		('000)	1,153	1,210	1,301	1,518	1,832
1.16	* holidays, leisure and recreation		('000)	971	1,029	1,136	1,369	1,633
1.17	* other personal purposes		('000)	182	182	165	150	199
1.18	♦ Business and professional		('000)	343	381	425	450	456
	Arrivals by mode of transport	(1)(4)(5)						
1.19	Total		('000)	1,496	1,591	1,726	1,968	2,288
1.20	♦ Air		('000)	1,321	1,416	1,542	1,714	2,027
1.21	♦ Water		('000)	15	15	22	65	232
1.22	♦ Land		('000)	160	160	162	189	29
1.23	* railway		('000)	..	..	..	..	..
1.24	* road		('000)	160	160	162	189	29
1.25	* others		('000)	..	..	..	..	..
	Expenditure							
1.33	Total		US$ Mn	3,801	4,363	4,759	4,887	5,251
1.34	♦ Travel		US$ Mn	3,010	3,460	3,611	3,825	4,245
1.35	♦ Passenger transport		US$ Mn	791	903	1,148	1,062	1,006
2.	**DOMESTIC TOURISM**							
	Data							
	Trips							
2.1	Total		('000)	114,406	120,996	127,544	127,914	130,297
2.2	♦ Overnight visitors (tourists)		('000)	..	..	..	..	..
2.3	♦ Same-day visitors (excursionists)		('000)	..	..	..	..	..
	Trips by mode of transport							
2.9	Total		('000)	114,405	120,996	127,544	127,914	130,297
2.10	♦ Air		('000)	10,482	16,104	18,924	20,103	22,238
2.11	♦ Water		('000)	..	..	..	..	..
2.12	♦ Land		('000)	103,923	104,892	108,620	107,811	108,059
2.13	* railway		('000)	..	..	..	..	..
2.14	* road		('000)	103,923	104,892	108,620	107,811	108,059
2.15	* others		('000)	..	..	..	..	..
3.	**OUTBOUND TOURISM**							
	Data							
	Departures							
3.1	Total		('000)	..	..	..	..	..
3.2	♦ Overnight visitors (tourists)		('000)	2,522	3,165	3,605	3,911	3,860
3.3	♦ Same-day visitors (excursionists)		('000)	..	..	..	..	..
	Expenditure							
3.4	Total		US$ Mn	3,631	4,363	4,485	5,170	4,668
3.5	♦ Travel		US$ Mn	3,032	3,626	3,941	4,678	4,324
3.6	♦ Passenger transport		US$ Mn	599	737	544	492	344

COLOMBIA

Cod.	Basic data and indicators	Notes	Units	2011	2012	2013	2014	2015
4.	**TOURISM INDUSTRIES**							
	Data							
	Number of establishments							
4.1	Total		Units	15,665	19,282	17,961	20,333	22,000
4.2	♦ Accommodation for visitors		Units	7,416	8,884	9,090	10,810	12,342
4.3	* of which, "hotels and similar establishments"		Units	5,662	6,633	6,239	7,180	7,885
4.4	♦ Food and beverage serving activities		Units	839	1,175	921	945	1,027
4.5	♦ Passenger transportation		Units	231	251	280	294	361
4.6	♦ Travel agencies and other reservation services activities		Units	4,840	6,377	5,070	5,577	6,347
4.7	♦ Other tourism industries		Units	2,339	2,595	2,600	2,707	1,923
	Accommodation for visitors in hotels and similar establishments							
	Non-monetary data							
4.13	♦ Number of establishments		Units	5,662	6,633	6,239	7,180	7,885
4.14	♦ Number of rooms		Units	139,670	155,401	159,094	177,724	198,450
4.15	♦ Number of bed-places		Units	225,064	250,079	254,955	280,790	308,299
	Indicators							
4.16	Occupancy rate / rooms		Percent	51.97	53.78	52.64	52.39	53.55
4.17	Occupancy rate / bed-places		Percent	..	..	..	..	..
4.18	Average length of stay		Nights	..	..	..	..	..
4.19	Available capacity (bed-places per 1000 inhabitants)		Units	4.85	5.33	5.39	5.88	6.39
6.	**COMPLEMENTARY INDICATORS**							
	Demand							
6.1	Gross travel propensity		Units	..	..	..	..	..
6.2	(1.2 inbound tourists + 2.1 domestic visitors) / population		Units	2.51	2.63	2.74	2.73	2.76
	Macroeconomic indicators related to international tourism							
6.3	Inbound tourism expenditure over GDP		Percent	1.1	1.2	1.3	1.3	1.8
6.4	Outbound tourism expenditure over GDP		Percent	1.1	1.2	1.2	1.4	1.6
6.5	Tourism balance (inbound minus outbound tourism expenditure) over GDP		Percent			0.1	-0.1	0.2
6.6	Tourism openness (inbound plus outbound tourism expenditure) over GDP		Percent	2.2	2.4	2.5	2.7	3.4
6.7	Tourism coverage (inbound over outbound tourism expenditure)		Percent	104.7	100.0	106.1	94.5	112.5
6.8	Inbound tourism expenditure over exports of goods		Percent	6.5	7.1	7.9	8.6	13.8
6.9	Inbound tourism expenditure over exports of services		Percent	67.4	67.9	69.3	70.9	73.4
6.10	Inbound tourism expenditure over exports of goods and services		Percent	5.9	6.4	7.1	7.7	11.6
6.11	Inbound tourism expenditure over current account credits		Percent	5.3	5.6	6.2	6.7	9.4
6.12	Outbound tourism expenditure over imports of goods		Percent	7.0	7.7	7.9	8.4	9.0
6.13	Outbound tourism expenditure over imports of services		Percent	33.5	35.6	35.0	38.1	41.3
6.14	Outbound tourism expenditure over imports of goods and		Percent	5.8	6.3	6.4	6.9	7.4
6.15	Outbound tourism expenditure over current account debits		Percent	5.5	5.9	6.0	6.5	6.8

CONGO

Cod.	Basic data and indicators	Notes	Units	2011	2012	2013	2014	2015
1.	**INBOUND TOURISM**							
	Data							
	Arrivals							
1.1	Total	(1)(2)	('000)	224	259	345	375	..
1.2	♦ Overnight visitors (tourists)	(1)	('000)	218	256	343	373	..
1.3	♦ Same-day visitors (excursionists)	(1)	('000)	6	3	2	2	..
1.4	* of which, cruise passengers		('000)	..	..	..	..	..
	Arrivals by region	(3)						
1.5	Total		('000)	224	260	345	375	..
1.6	♦ Africa		('000)	153	148	262	273	..
1.7	♦ Americas		('000)	4	10	10	13	..
1.8	♦ East Asia and the Pacific		('000)	9	20	25	28	..
1.9	♦ Europe		('000)	51	76	46	58	..
1.10	♦ Middle East		('000)	5	3	1	2	..
1.11	♦ South Asia		('000)	2	3	2	2	..
1.12	♦ Other not classified		('000)	..	..	..	..	..
1.13	* of which, nationals residing abroad		('000)	..	..	..	..	..
	Arrivals by main purpose	(3)						
1.14	Total		('000)	224	259	345	375	..
1.15	♦ Personal		('000)	148	159	221	239	..
1.16	* holidays, leisure and recreation		('000)	103	100	141	156	..
1.17	* other personal purposes		('000)	45	59	80	84	..
1.18	♦ Business and professional		('000)	76	100	124	136	..
	Arrivals by mode of transport	(1)						
1.19	Total		('000)	224	259	345	375	..
1.20	♦ Air		('000)	115	136	150	162	..
1.21	♦ Water		('000)	109	123	195	214	..
1.22	♦ Land		('000)	..	..	..	..	..
1.23	* railway		('000)	..	..	..	..	..
1.24	* road		('000)	..	..	..	..	..
1.25	* others		('000)	..	..	..	..	..
	Accommodation							
	Hotels and similar establishments	(1)						
1.31	♦ Guests		('000)	168	204	231	273	263
1.32	♦ Overnights		('000)	365	553	594	799	769
	Expenditure							
1.33	Total		US$ Mn	..	..	..	..	..
1.34	♦ Travel	(4)	US$ Mn	72	73	38	..	..
1.35	♦ Passenger transport		US$ Mn	..	..	..	..	..
	Indicators							
1.39	Average size of travel party		Persons	..	..	4.0	..	..
	Average length of stay							
1.40	Total		Days	..	..	7.00	..	..
1.41	♦ For all commercial accommodation services		Nights	..	..	..	..	..
1.42	* of which, "hotels and similar establishments"	(1)	Nights	2.20	2.70	2.60	..	..
1.43	♦ For non commercial accommodation services		Days	..	..	3.00	..	..
1.44	Average expenditure per day		US$	..	..	215.0	..	..
2.	**DOMESTIC TOURISM**							
	Data							
	Accommodation							
	Hotels and similar establishments	(1)						
2.21	♦ Guests		('000)	76	80	152	188	208
2.22	♦ Overnights		('000)	161	222	371	536	593
	Indicators							
2.23	Average size of travel party		Persons	..	..	..	..	..
	Average length of stay							
2.24	Total		Days	..	..	7.00	..	..
2.25	♦ For all commercial accommodation services		Nights	..	..	..	..	..
2.26	* of which, "hotels and similar establishments"	(1)	Nights	2.10	2.80	2.40	..	..
2.27	♦ For non commercial accommodation services		Days	..	..	..	..	..
2.28	Average expenditure per day		US$	..	..	..	..	..

CONGO

Cod.	Basic data and indicators	Notes	Units	2011	2012	2013	2014	2015
3.	**OUTBOUND TOURISM**							
	Data							
	Departures							
3.1	Total		('000)	..	161	180	..	..
3.2	♦ Overnight visitors (tourists)		('000)	..	..	..	..	..
3.3	♦ Same-day visitors (excursionists)		('000)	..	..	..	..	..
	Expenditure							
3.4	Total		US$ Mn	..	..	..	..	..
3.5	♦ Travel	(4)	US$ Mn	246	258	236	..	..
3.6	♦ Passenger transport		US$ Mn	..	..	..	..	..
	Indicators							
3.10	Average length of stay		Days	..	..	10.00	..	..
3.11	Average expenditure per day		US$	..	..	100.0	..	..
4.	**TOURISM INDUSTRIES**	(1)						
	Data							
	Number of establishments							
4.1	Total		Units	1,278	1,573	2,008	..	..
4.2	♦ Accommodation for visitors		Units	..	..	..	..	..
4.3	* of which, "hotels and similar establishments"		Units	889	987	1,270	..	..
4.4	♦ Food and beverage serving activities		Units	338	534	680	..	..
4.5	♦ Passenger transportation		Units	..	..	..	..	..
4.6	♦ Travel agencies and other reservation services activities		Units	51	52	58	66	..
4.7	♦ Other tourism industries		Units	..	..	..	..	..
	Accommodation for visitors in hotels and similar establishments							
	Non-monetary data							
4.13	♦ Number of establishments		Units	889	987	1,270	..	..
4.14	♦ Number of rooms		Units	10,084	12,427	14,583	..	..
4.15	♦ Number of bed-places		Units	20,168	24,854	29,166	..	..
	Indicators							
4.16	Occupancy rate / rooms		Percent	48.00	30.60	24.00	..	..
4.17	Occupancy rate / bed-places		Percent	..	..	..	..	..
4.18	Average length of stay		Nights	2.20	2.70	2.50	..	..
4.19	Available capacity (bed-places per 1000 inhabitants)		Units	4.83	5.80	6.64	..	..
	Travel agencies and other reservation service activities							
	Monetary data							
4.20	♦ Output		US$ Mn	..	..	3.1	..	..
4.21	♦ Intermediate consumption		US$ Mn	..	..	2.1	..	..
4.22	♦ Gross value added		US$ Mn	..	..	1.0	..	..
4.23	♦ Compensation of employees		US$ Mn	..	..	0.8	..	..
4.24	♦ Gross fixed capital formation		US$ Mn	..	..	0.2	..	..
	Non-monetary data							
	♦ Domestic trips							
4.25	* with package tour		Percent	..	..	30.0	..	..
4.26	* without package tour		Percent	..	..	70.0	..	..
	♦ Inbound trips							
4.27	* with package tour		Percent	..	..	40.0	..	..
4.28	* without package tour		Percent	..	..	60.0	..	..
	♦ Outbound trips							
4.29	* with package tour		Percent	..	..	30.0	..	..
4.30	* without package tour		Percent	..	..	70.0	..	..
5.	**EMPLOYMENT**							
	Data							
	Number of employees by tourism industries							
5.1	Total		('000)	..	..	22.1	..	..
5.2	♦ Accommodation services for visitors (hotels and similar establishments)		('000)	..	..	6.5	..	..
5.3	♦ Other accommodation services		('000)	..	..	..	..	..
5.4	♦ Food and beverage serving activities		('000)	..	..	15.3	..	..
5.5	♦ Passenger transportation		('000)	..	..	..	..	..
5.6	♦ Travel agencies and other reservation services activities		('000)	..	..	0.3	..	..
5.7	♦ Other tourism industries		('000)	..	..	..	..	..

CONGO

Cod.	Basic data and indicators	Notes	Units	2011	2012	2013	2014	2015
	Number of jobs by status in employment							
5.8	Total		('000)	..	..	22.1	..	..
5.9	♦ Employees		('000)	..	..	17.7	..	..
5.10	♦ Self employed		('000)	..	..	4.4	..	..
	Indicators							
	Number of full-time equivalent jobs by status in employment							
5.11	Total		('000)	..	..	14.2	..	..
5.12	♦ Employees		('000)	..	..	10.6	..	..
5.13	* male		('000)	..	..	7.1	..	..
5.14	* female		('000)	..	..	3.5	..	..
5.15	♦ Self employed		('000)	..	..	3.5	..	..
5.16	* male		('000)	..	..	2.4	..	..
5.17	* female		('000)	..	..	1.2	..	..
6.	**COMPLEMENTARY INDICATORS**							
	Demand							
6.1	Gross travel propensity		Units	..	..	..	..	..
6.2	(1.2 inbound tourists) / population		Units	0.05	0.06	0.08	0.08	..
	Macroeconomic indicators related to international tourism							
6.3	Inbound tourism expenditure over GDP		Percent	..	..	..	..	..
6.4	Outbound tourism expenditure over GDP		Percent	..	..	..	..	..
6.5	Tourism balance (inbound minus outbound tourism expenditure) over GDP		Percent	..	..	..	..	..
6.6	Tourism openness (inbound plus outbound tourism expenditure) over GDP		Percent	..	..	..	..	..
6.7	Tourism coverage (inbound over outbound tourism expenditure)		Percent	29.3	28.3	16.1	..	..
6.8	Inbound tourism expenditure over exports of goods		Percent	..	..	..	..	..
6.9	Inbound tourism expenditure over exports of services		Percent	..	..	..	..	..
6.10	Inbound tourism expenditure over exports of goods and services		Percent	..	..	..	..	..
6.11	Inbound tourism expenditure over current account credits		Percent	..	..	..	..	..
6.12	Outbound tourism expenditure over imports of goods		Percent	..	..	..	..	..
6.13	Outbound tourism expenditure over imports of services		Percent	..	..	..	..	..
6.14	Outbound tourism expenditure over imports of goods and		Percent	..	..	..	..	..
6.15	Outbound tourism expenditure over current account debits		Percent	..	..	..	..	..

CONGO, DEMOCRATIC REPUBLIC OF THE

Cod.	Basic data and indicators	Notes	Units	2011	2012	2013	2014	2015
1.	**INBOUND TOURISM**							
	Data							
	Arrivals	(1)						
1.1	Total		('000)	197	..	..	..	..
1.2	♦ Overnight visitors (tourists)		('000)	186	167	191	..	..
1.3	♦ Same-day visitors (excursionists)		('000)	11	..	..	..	..
1.4	* of which, cruise passengers		('000)	..	..	..	..	..
	Arrivals by region	(1)						
1.5	Total		('000)	186	167	191	..	..
1.6	♦ Africa		('000)	44	66	72	..	..
1.7	♦ Americas		('000)	21	18	20	..	..
1.8	♦ East Asia and the Pacific		('000)	14	22	14	..	..
1.9	♦ Europe		('000)	68	51	49	..	..
1.10	♦ Middle East		('000)	6	11	3	..	..
1.11	♦ South Asia		('000)	6	..	5	..	..
1.12	♦ Other not classified		('000)	27	..	28	..	..
1.13	* of which, nationals residing abroad		('000)	..	..	4	..	..
	Arrivals by main purpose	(1)						
1.14	Total		('000)	186	167	191	..	..
1.15	♦ Personal		('000)	67	91	107	..	..
1.16	* holidays, leisure and recreation		('000)	20	35	28	..	..
1.17	* other personal purposes		('000)	47	56	80	..	..
1.18	♦ Business and professional		('000)	119	76	84	..	..
	Arrivals by mode of transport	(1)						
1.19	Total		('000)	186	167	191	..	..
1.20	♦ Air		('000)	160	156	180	..	..
1.21	♦ Water		('000)	..	1	3	..	..
1.22	♦ Land		('000)	26	10	8	..	..
1.23	* railway		('000)	..	..	..	..	..
1.24	* road		('000)	26	8	6	..	..
1.25	* others		('000)	..	2	2	..	..
	Accommodation							
	Total							
1.29	♦ Guests		('000)	..	..	..	..	..
1.30	♦ Overnights		('000)	103	..	..	..	..
	Hotels and similar establishments							
1.31	♦ Guests		('000)	30	..	..	..	..
1.32	♦ Overnights		('000)	..	..	..	..	..
	Expenditure							
1.33	Total		US$ Mn	..	..	..	..	..
1.34	♦ Travel		US$ Mn	11.4	6.9	8.4	45.4	0.1
1.35	♦ Passenger transport		US$ Mn	..	..	..	..	..
	Indicators							
1.39	Average size of travel party		Persons	..	..	..	..	..
	Average length of stay							
1.40	Total		Days	..	..	..	..	..
1.41	♦ For all commercial accommodation services		Nights	4.00	..	..	..	..
1.42	* of which, "hotels and similar establishments"		Nights	..	..	..	..	..
1.43	♦ For non commercial accommodation services		Days	..	..	..	..	..
1.44	Average expenditure per day		US$	..	..	..	..	..
3.	**OUTBOUND TOURISM**							
	Data							
	Expenditure							
3.4	Total		US$ Mn	..	..	..	..	..
3.5	♦ Travel		US$ Mn	298	108	170	283	65
3.6	♦ Passenger transport		US$ Mn	..	..	..	..	..
4.	**TOURISM INDUSTRIES**							
	Indicators							
4.16	Occupancy rate / rooms		Percent	..	..	..	..	..
4.17	Occupancy rate / bed-places		Percent	..	..	..	..	..
4.18	Average length of stay		Nights	4.00	..	..	..	..
4.19	Available capacity (bed-places per 1000 inhabitants)		Units	..	..	..	..	..

CONGO, DEMOCRATIC REPUBLIC OF THE

Cod.	Basic data and indicators	Notes	Units	2011	2012	2013	2014	2015
6.	**COMPLEMENTARY INDICATORS**							
	Demand							
6.1	Gross travel propensity		Units	..	..	..	..	..
6.2	(1.2 inbound tourists) / population		Units	0.003	0.002	0.003	..	..
	Macroeconomic indicators related to international tourism							
6.3	Inbound tourism expenditure over GDP		Percent	0.0	0.0	0.0	..	..
6.4	Outbound tourism expenditure over GDP		Percent	1.0	0.3	0.4	..	..
6.5	Tourism balance (inbound minus outbound tourism expenditure) over GDP		Percent	-1.0	-0.3	-0.4	..	..
6.6	Tourism openness (inbound plus outbound tourism expenditure) over GDP		Percent	1.0	0.3	0.4	..	..
6.7	Tourism coverage (inbound over outbound tourism expenditure)		Percent	3.8	6.4	4.9	16.0	0.2
6.8	Inbound tourism expenditure over exports of goods		Percent	0.1	0.1	0.1	0.4	0.0
6.9	Inbound tourism expenditure over exports of services		Percent	1.5	2.4	2.8	14.4	0.1
6.10	Inbound tourism expenditure over exports of goods and services		Percent	0.1	0.1	0.1	0.4	0.0
6.11	Inbound tourism expenditure over current account credits		Percent	0.1	0.1	0.1	0.3	0.0
6.12	Outbound tourism expenditure over imports of goods		Percent	3.3	1.2	1.6	2.2	0.6
6.13	Outbound tourism expenditure over imports of services		Percent	10.3	4.6	6.6	9.2	3.2
6.14	Outbound tourism expenditure over imports of goods and		Percent	2.5	1.0	1.3	1.8	0.5
6.15	Outbound tourism expenditure over current account debits		Percent	2.3	0.9	1.2	1.7	0.5

COOK ISLANDS

Cod.	Basic data and indicators	Notes	Units	2011	2012	2013	2014	2015
1.	**INBOUND TOURISM**							
	Data							
	Arrivals							
1.1	Total		('000)	..	..	..	..	..
1.2	♦ Overnight visitors (tourists)	(1)	('000)	113	122	121	121	125
1.3	♦ Same-day visitors (excursionists)		('000)	..	..	..	..	..
1.4	* of which, cruise passengers		('000)	..	..	..	..	..
	Arrivals by region	(1)						
1.5	Total		('000)	113	122	121	121	125
1.6	♦ Africa		('000)	..	..	..	..	..
1.7	♦ Americas		('000)	7	7	7	7	7
1.8	♦ East Asia and the Pacific		('000)	96	105	103	104	107
1.9	♦ Europe		('000)	10	9	9	9	9
1.10	♦ Middle East		('000)	..	..	..	..	..
1.11	♦ South Asia		('000)	..	..	..	..	..
1.12	♦ Other not classified		('000)	..	1	2	1	1
1.13	* of which, nationals residing abroad		('000)	..	..	..	..	..
	Arrivals by main purpose	(1)						
1.14	Total		('000)	113	122	121	121	125
1.15	♦ Personal		('000)	110	118	117	117	121
1.16	* holidays, leisure and recreation		('000)	97	105	104	105	108
1.17	* other personal purposes		('000)	13	13	13	13	13
1.18	♦ Business and professional		('000)	3	4	4	4	4
	Accommodation							
	Hotels and similar establishments							
1.31	♦ Guests		('000)	..	..	..	..	..
1.32	♦ Overnights		('000)	250	..	..	..	..
	Expenditure							
1.33	Total	(2)	US$ Mn	150	168	168	175	..
1.34	♦ Travel		US$ Mn	..	..	..	..	..
1.35	♦ Passenger transport		US$ Mn	..	..	..	..	..
	Expenditure by main purpose of the trip							
1.36	Total		US$ Mn	150	168	168	175	..
1.37	♦ Personal		US$ Mn	142	160	158	164	..
1.38	♦ Business and professional		US$ Mn	7	8	10	11	..
	Indicators							
1.39	Average size of travel party		Persons	..	..	..	..	..
	Average length of stay							
1.40	Total		Days	..	..	..	..	..
1.41	♦ For all commercial accommodation services		Nights	10.06	10.15	10.65	8.06	10.35
1.42	* of which, "hotels and similar establishments"		Nights	..	..	..	..	..
1.43	♦ For non commercial accommodation services		Days	..	..	..	..	..
1.44	Average expenditure per day		US$	..	..	..	..	..
3.	**OUTBOUND TOURISM**							
	Data							
	Departures							
3.1	Total		('000)	..	..	..	..	..
3.2	♦ Overnight visitors (tourists)		('000)	13	12	12	12	13
3.3	♦ Same-day visitors (excursionists)		('000)	..	..	..	..	..
4.	**TOURISM INDUSTRIES**							
	Data							
	Number of establishments							
4.1	Total		Units	..	..	..	249	..
4.2	♦ Accommodation for visitors		Units	..	..	..	147	..
4.3	* of which, "hotels and similar establishments"		Units	..	..	..	..	..
4.4	♦ Food and beverage serving activities		Units	..	..	..	53	..
4.5	♦ Passenger transportation		Units	..	..	..	20	..
4.6	♦ Travel agencies and other reservation services activities		Units	..	..	..	5	..
4.7	♦ Other tourism industries		Units	..	..	..	24	..

97

COOK ISLANDS

Cod.	Basic data and indicators	Notes	Units	2011	2012	2013	2014	2015
	Accommodation for visitors in hotels and similar establishments							
	Monetary data							
4.8	♦ Output		US$ Mn	..	23.5	17.2	23.6	..
4.9	♦ Intermediate consumption		US$ Mn	..	12.1	8.9	12.1	..
4.10	♦ Gross value added		US$ Mn	..	11.4	8.4	11.5	..
4.11	♦ Compensation of employees		US$ Mn	..	..	..	..	..
4.12	♦ Gross fixed capital formation		US$ Mn	..	..	..	..	..
	Non-monetary data							
4.13	♦ Number of establishments		Units	..	..	..	147	..
4.14	♦ Number of rooms		Units	..	..	..	..	..
4.15	♦ Number of bed-places		Units	..	..	..	..	..
	Indicators							
4.16	Occupancy rate / rooms		Percent	51.60	..	..	..	..
4.17	Occupancy rate / bed-places		Percent	47.40	..	..	..	..
4.18	Average length of stay		Nights	..	..	..	..	..
4.19	Available capacity (bed-places per 1000 inhabitants)		Units	..	..	..	..	..
6.	**COMPLEMENTARY INDICATORS**							
	Demand							
6.1	Gross travel propensity		Units	..	..	..	..	..
6.2	(1.2 inbound tourists) / population		Units	5.54	5.95	5.87	5.84	6.00

COSTA RICA

Cod.	Basic data and indicators	Notes	Units	2011	2012	2013	2014	2015
1.	**INBOUND TOURISM**							
	Data							
	Arrivals							
1.1	Total		('000)	2,526	2,590	2,641	2,760	2,883
1.2	♦ Overnight visitors (tourists)		('000)	2,192	2,343	2,428	2,527	2,660
1.3	♦ Same-day visitors (excursionists)		('000)	334	247	213	233	223
1.4	* of which, cruise passengers		('000)	334	247	213	233	223
	Arrivals by region							
1.5	Total		('000)	2,192	2,343	2,428	2,527	2,660
1.6	♦ Africa		('000)	2	2	2	3	3
1.7	♦ Americas		('000)	1,857	2,009	2,075	2,111	2,218
1.8	♦ East Asia and the Pacific		('000)	27	31	33	35	38
1.9	♦ Europe		('000)	302	296	312	371	393
1.10	♦ Middle East		('000)	0.5	0.6	0.7	0.8	0.9
1.11	♦ South Asia		('000)	4	5	5	6	7
1.12	♦ Other not classified		('000)	..	..	..	..	..
1.13	* of which, nationals residing abroad		('000)	..	..	..	..	..
	Arrivals by main purpose							
1.14	Total		('000)	2,192	2,343	2,428	2,527	2,660
1.15	♦ Personal		('000)	1,890	2,037	2,141	2,180	2,241
1.16	* holidays, leisure and recreation		('000)	1,672	1,689	1,820	1,904	1,939
1.17	* other personal purposes		('000)	218	348	321	276	302
1.18	♦ Business and professional		('000)	302	306	287	347	419
	Arrivals by mode of transport							
1.19	Total		('000)	2,192	2,343	2,428	2,527	2,660
1.20	♦ Air		('000)	1,464	1,552	1,617	1,721	1,859
1.21	♦ Water		('000)	7	10	8	10	8
1.22	♦ Land		('000)	721	781	802	796	793
1.23	* railway		('000)	..	..	..	..	..
1.24	* road		('000)	721	781	802	796	793
1.25	* others		('000)	..	..	..	..	..
	Expenditure							
1.33	Total		US$ Mn	2,646	2,773	3,171	3,150	3,402
1.34	♦ Travel		US$ Mn	2,423	2,529	2,928	3,061	3,326
1.35	♦ Passenger transport		US$ Mn	223	244	243	89	76
	Expenditure by main purpose of the trip							
1.36	Total		US$ Mn	2,423	2,529	2,928	3,061	3,326
1.37	♦ Personal		US$ Mn	1,940	1,966	2,562	2,675	2,906
1.38	♦ Business and professional		US$ Mn	483	563	366	386	420
	Indicators							
1.39	Average size of travel party		Persons	..	..	..	..	..
	Average length of stay							
1.40	Total		Days	..	..	..	..	..
1.41	♦ For all commercial accommodation services	(1)	Nights	11.00	11.60	11.60	12.40	12.20
1.42	* of which, "hotels and similar establishments"		Nights	..	..	..	..	..
1.43	♦ For non commercial accommodation services		Days	..	..	..	..	..
1.44	Average expenditure per day		US$	..	..	..	..	..
3.	**OUTBOUND TOURISM**							
	Data							
	Departures							
3.1	Total		('000)	..	..	..	..	..
3.2	♦ Overnight visitors (tourists)		('000)	717	773	790	798	919
3.3	♦ Same-day visitors (excursionists)		('000)	..	..	..	..	..
	Expenditure							
3.4	Total		US$ Mn	620	647	649	694	778
3.5	♦ Travel		US$ Mn	400	422	425	461	545
3.6	♦ Passenger transport		US$ Mn	220	225	224	233	233
	Expenditure by main purpose of the trip							
3.7	Total		US$ Mn	400	422	425	461	545
3.8	♦ Personal		US$ Mn	217	232	247	269	318
3.9	♦ Business and professional		US$ Mn	183	190	178	192	227
4.	**TOURISM INDUSTRIES**							
	Data							
	Number of establishments							
4.1	Total		Units	3,383	3,342	3,337	3,145	3,123
4.2	♦ Accommodation for visitors		Units	2,476	2,497	2,515	2,405	2,402
4.3	* of which, "hotels and similar establishments"		Units	2,476	2,497	2,515	2,405	2,402
4.4	♦ Food and beverage serving activities		Units	428	366	356	329	329
4.5	♦ Passenger transportation		Units	51	52	48	42	38

COSTA RICA

Cod.	Basic data and indicators	Notes	Units	2011	2012	2013	2014	2015
4.6	♦ Travel agencies and other reservation services activities		Units	383	379	358	306	292
4.7	♦ Other tourism industries		Units	45	48	60	63	62
	Accommodation for visitors in hotels and similar establishments							
	Monetary data							
4.8	♦ Output		US$ Mn	1,329.3	1,425.3	1,434.3	..	..
4.9	♦ Intermediate consumption		US$ Mn	539.2	578.2	581.8	..	..
4.10	♦ Gross value added		US$ Mn	790.0	847.2	852.5	..	..
4.11	♦ Compensation of employees		US$ Mn	331.0	317.7	319.7	..	..
4.12	♦ Gross fixed capital formation		US$ Mn	..	..	..	..	..
	Non-monetary data							
4.13	♦ Number of establishments		Units	2,476	2,497	2,515	2,405	2,402
4.14	♦ Number of rooms		Units	44,307	45,531	46,633	46,375	46,819
4.15	♦ Number of bed-places		Units	..	..	..	..	..
	Indicators							
4.16	Occupancy rate / rooms	(2)	Percent	63.40	54.30	48.70	54.70	54.70
4.17	Occupancy rate / bed-places		Percent	..	..	..	..	..
4.18	Average length of stay		Nights	11.00	11.60	11.60	12.40	12.20
4.19	Available capacity (bed-places per 1000 inhabitants)		Units	..	..	..	..	..
	Travel agencies and other reservation service activities							
	Monetary data							
4.20	♦ Output		US$ Mn	215.6	241.4	302.2	..	..
4.21	♦ Intermediate consumption		US$ Mn	95.1	106.4	133.3	..	..
4.22	♦ Gross value added		US$ Mn	120.5	135.0	169.0	..	..
4.23	♦ Compensation of employees		US$ Mn	27.3	23.6	29.9	..	..
4.24	♦ Gross fixed capital formation		US$ Mn	..	..	..	..	..
5.	**EMPLOYMENT**	(3)						
	Data							
	Number of employees by tourism industries							
5.1	Total		('000)	..	..	150.5	147.9	153.2
5.2	♦ Accommodation services for visitors (hotels and similar establishments)		('000)	..	..	25.8	26.4	30.1
5.3	♦ Other accommodation services		('000)	..	..	..	..	..
5.4	♦ Food and beverage serving activities		('000)	..	..	89.3	87.4	92.7
5.5	♦ Passenger transportation		('000)	..	..	3.1	2.9	1.5
5.6	♦ Travel agencies and other reservation services activities		('000)	..	..	6.5	7.9	6.3
5.7	♦ Other tourism industries		('000)	..	..	25.8	23.3	22.6
	Number of jobs by status in employment							
5.8	Total		('000)	..	..	150.6	147.9	153.2
5.9	♦ Employees		('000)	..	..	112.6	109.9	113.6
5.10	♦ Self employed		('000)	..	..	38.0	38.0	39.6
6.	**COMPLEMENTARY INDICATORS**							
	Demand							
6.1	Gross travel propensity		Units	..	..	..	..	..
6.2	(1.2 inbound tourists) / population		Units	0.48	0.50	0.52	0.53	0.55
	Macroeconomic indicators related to international tourism							
6.3	Inbound tourism expenditure over GDP		Percent	6.4	6.1	6.4	6.4	..
6.4	Outbound tourism expenditure over GDP		Percent	1.5	1.4	1.3	1.4	..
6.5	Tourism balance (inbound minus outbound tourism expenditure) over GDP		Percent	4.9	4.7	5.1	5.0	..
6.6	Tourism openness (inbound plus outbound tourism expenditure) over GDP		Percent	7.9	7.5	7.7	7.8	..
6.7	Tourism coverage (inbound over outbound tourism expenditure)		Percent	426.8	428.6	488.6	453.9	437.3
6.8	Inbound tourism expenditure over exports of goods		Percent	31.9	31.1	35.8	34.0	35.8
6.9	Inbound tourism expenditure over exports of services		Percent	45.8	44.7	46.5	44.2	44.8
6.10	Inbound tourism expenditure over exports of goods and services		Percent	18.8	18.3	20.2	19.2	19.9
6.11	Inbound tourism expenditure over current account credits		Percent	17.6	17.2	19.1	18.1	18.9
6.12	Outbound tourism expenditure over imports of goods		Percent	4.7	4.5	4.5	4.7	5.4
6.13	Outbound tourism expenditure over imports of services		Percent	31.8	29.1	27.2	29.1	27.2
6.14	Outbound tourism expenditure over imports of goods and		Percent	4.1	3.9	3.9	4.0	4.5
6.15	Outbound tourism expenditure over current account debits		Percent	3.9	3.8	3.7	3.9	4.3

COTE D´IVOIRE

Cod.	Basic data and indicators	Notes	Units	2011	2012	2013	2014	2015
1.	**INBOUND TOURISM**							
	Data							
	Arrivals							
1.1	Total	(1)	('000)	270	289	380	471	1,441
1.2	♦ Overnight visitors (tourists)		('000)	..	..	..	..	..
1.3	♦ Same-day visitors (excursionists)		('000)	..	..	..	..	..
1.4	* of which, cruise passengers		('000)	..	..	..	..	..
	Arrivals by region	(1)						
1.5	Total		('000)	270	289	380	471	1,441
1.6	♦ Africa		('000)	185	199	258	316	966
1.7	♦ Americas		('000)	11	12	13	14	72
1.8	♦ East Asia and the Pacific		('000)	11	12	17	28	72
1.9	♦ Europe		('000)	62	67	91	113	332
1.10	♦ Middle East		('000)	..	..	..	..	..
1.11	♦ South Asia		('000)	..	..	..	..	..
1.12	♦ Other not classified		('000)	..	..	..	..	..
1.13	* of which, nationals residing abroad		('000)	..	..	..	..	..
	Arrivals by main purpose	(1)						
1.14	Total		('000)	270	289	380	471	1,441
1.15	♦ Personal		('000)	163	174	228	273	836
1.16	* holidays, leisure and recreation		('000)	54	58	76	104	318
1.17	* other personal purposes		('000)	109	116	152	170	518
1.18	♦ Business and professional		('000)	107	116	152	198	605
	Arrivals by mode of transport							
1.19	Total		('000)	270	289	380	471	1,441
1.20	♦ Air		('000)	270	289	380	471	537
1.21	♦ Water		('000)	..	..	..	..	..
1.22	♦ Land		('000)	..	..	..	..	904
1.23	* railway		('000)	..	..	..	..	38
1.24	* road		('000)	..	..	..	..	866
1.25	* others		('000)	..	..	..	..	..
	Expenditure							
1.33	Total		US$ Mn	186	173	191	..	..
1.34	♦ Travel		US$ Mn	180	172	181	184	..
1.35	♦ Passenger transport		US$ Mn	6	1	10	..	..
	Expenditure by main purpose of the trip							
1.36	Total		US$ Mn	180	172	181	..	..
1.37	♦ Personal		US$ Mn	117	112	118	..	..
1.38	♦ Business and professional		US$ Mn	63	60	63	..	..
	Indicators							
1.39	Average size of travel party		Persons	..	..	..	..	..
	Average length of stay							
1.40	Total		Days	3.00	3.00	3.00	3.00	4.00
1.41	♦ For all commercial accommodation services		Nights	..	..	..	..	..
1.42	* of which, "hotels and similar establishments"		Nights	..	..	..	..	..
1.43	♦ For non commercial accommodation services		Days	..	..	..	..	..
1.44	Average expenditure per day		US$	..	..	..	..	..
3.	**OUTBOUND TOURISM**							
	Data							
	Expenditure							
3.4	Total		US$ Mn	580	560	583	..	..
3.5	♦ Travel		US$ Mn	380	364	381	402	..
3.6	♦ Passenger transport		US$ Mn	200	196	202	..	..
	Expenditure by main purpose of the trip							
3.7	Total		US$ Mn	379	364	381	..	..
3.8	♦ Personal		US$ Mn	351	325	340	..	..
3.9	♦ Business and professional		US$ Mn	28	39	41	..	..
4.	**TOURISM INDUSTRIES**							
	Data							
	Number of establishments							
4.1	Total		Units	..	..		..	..
4.2	♦ Accommodation for visitors		Units	1,788	1,788	1,890	2,000	2,041
4.3	* of which, "hotels and similar establishments"		Units	..	..	..	..	..
4.4	♦ Food and beverage serving activities		Units	..	..	..	..	..
4.5	♦ Passenger transportation		Units	..	..	..	..	..
4.6	♦ Travel agencies and other reservation services activities		Units	..	..	..	..	..
4.7	♦ Other tourism industries		Units	..	..	..	..	..

COTE D´IVOIRE

Cod.	Basic data and indicators	Notes	Units	2011	2012	2013	2014	2015
	Accommodation for visitors in hotels and similar establishments							
	Non-monetary data							
4.13	♦ Number of establishments		Units	1,788	1,788	1,890	2,000	2,041
4.14	♦ Number of rooms		Units	23,141	23,141	27,431	28,000	34,000
4.15	♦ Number of bed-places		Units	46,510	46,510	54,862	56,000	68,000
	Indicators							
4.16	Occupancy rate / rooms		Percent	53.33	57.50	65.00	69.40	70.00
4.17	Occupancy rate / bed-places		Percent	..	..	..	..	..
4.18	Average length of stay		Nights	3.00	3.00	3.00	3.00	4.00
4.19	Available capacity (bed-places per 1000 inhabitants)		Units	2.26	2.20	2.54	2.53	3.00
6.	**COMPLEMENTARY INDICATORS**							
	Demand							
6.1	Gross travel propensity		Units	..	..	..	..	..
6.2	(1.1 inbound visitors) / population		Units	0.01	0.01	0.02	0.02	0.06
	Macroeconomic indicators related to international tourism							
6.3	Inbound tourism expenditure over GDP		Percent	0.7	0.6	0.6	..	..
6.4	Outbound tourism expenditure over GDP		Percent	2.2	2.1	1.9	..	..
6.5	Tourism balance (inbound minus outbound tourism expenditure) over GDP		Percent	-1.5	-1.5	-1.3	..	..
6.6	Tourism openness (inbound plus outbound tourism expenditure) over GDP		Percent	2.9	2.7	2.5	..	..
6.7	Tourism coverage (inbound over outbound tourism expenditure)		Percent	32.1	30.8	32.8	..	..
6.8	Inbound tourism expenditure over exports of goods		Percent	1.5	1.4	1.6	..	..
6.9	Inbound tourism expenditure over exports of services		Percent	18.3	17.5	20.4	..	..
6.10	Inbound tourism expenditure over exports of goods and services		Percent	1.4	1.3	1.5	..	..
6.11	Inbound tourism expenditure over current account credits		Percent	1.3	1.3	1.4	..	..
6.12	Outbound tourism expenditure over imports of goods		Percent	8.7	6.2	6.4	..	..
6.13	Outbound tourism expenditure over imports of services		Percent	20.7	19.1	18.1	..	..
6.14	Outbound tourism expenditure over imports of goods and		Percent	6.1	4.7	4.7	..	..
6.15	Outbound tourism expenditure over current account debits		Percent	5.5	4.3	4.4	..	..

CROATIA

Cod.	Basic data and indicators	Notes	Units	2011	2012	2013	2014	2015
.	**INBOUND TOURISM**							
	Data							
	Arrivals							
.1	Total		('000)	49,969	47,185	48,345	51,168	55,858
.2	♦ Overnight visitors (tourists)	(1)(2)	('000)	9,927	10,369	10,948	11,623	12,683
.3	♦ Same-day visitors (excursionists)		('000)	..	..	..	..	..
.4	* of which, cruise passengers		('000)	..	..	..	..	..
	Arrivals by region	(1)(2)						
.5	Total		('000)	9,927	10,369	10,948	11,623	12,683
.6	♦ Africa		('000)	13	17	20	23	25
.7	♦ Americas		('000)	251	292	381	435	531
.8	♦ East Asia and the Pacific		('000)	360	469	545	823	979
.9	♦ Europe		('000)	9,303	9,591	10,003	10,342	11,149
.10	♦ Middle East		('000)	..	..	..	..	..
.11	♦ South Asia		('000)	..	..	..	..	..
.12	♦ Other not classified		('000)	..	..	..	..	..
.13	* of which, nationals residing abroad		('000)	..	..	..	..	..
	Arrivals by mode of transport							
.19	Total	(3)	('000)	49,969	47,185	48,345	51,168	55,858
.20	♦ Air	(4)	('000)	2,299	2,505	2,689	2,879	3,119
.21	♦ Water	(5)	('000)	1,638	1,619	1,602	1,451	1,439
.22	♦ Land		('000)	46,032	43,061	44,054	46,838	51,300
.23	* railway	(6)	('000)	261	256	212	188	179
.24	* road	(7)	('000)	45,771	42,805	43,842	46,650	51,121
.25	* others		('000)	..	..	..	..	..
	Accommodation							
	Total							
.29	♦ Guests	(2)	('000)	9,927	10,369	10,948	11,623	12,683
.30	♦ Overnights	(2)	('000)	54,751	57,522	59,680	61,324	65,863
	Hotels and similar establishments							
.31	♦ Guests	(8)	('000)	4,308	4,522	4,666	4,911	5,251
.32	♦ Overnights	(8)	('000)	18,054	18,879	18,892	18,892	19,851
	Expenditure							
.33	Total		US$ Mn	9,598	8,912	9,715	10,079	9,018
.34	♦ Travel		US$ Mn	9,348	8,683	9,512	9,863	8,833
.35	♦ Passenger transport		US$ Mn	250	229	203	216	185
	Expenditure by main purpose of the trip							
.36	Total		US$ Mn	9,348	8,683	9,512	9,864	8,833
.37	♦ Personal		US$ Mn	9,033	8,384	9,214	9,605	8,590
.38	♦ Business and professional		US$ Mn	315	299	298	259	243
	Indicators							
.39	Average size of travel party		Persons	..	..	..	..	..
	Average length of stay							
.40	Total		Days	..	..	..	..	..
.41	♦ For all commercial accommodation services		Nights	5.52	5.55	5.45	5.28	5.19
.42	* of which, "hotels and similar establishments"		Nights	4.19	4.18	4.04	3.85	3.78
.43	♦ For non commercial accommodation services		Days	..	..	..	..	..
.44	Average expenditure per day		US$	..	..	..	..	..
.	**DOMESTIC TOURISM**							
	Data							
	Trips	(9)(10)						
.1	Total		('000)	14,852	15,088	15,843	16,514	12,162
.2	♦ Overnight visitors (tourists)		('000)	6,010	6,056	6,225	5,410	4,040
.3	♦ Same-day visitors (excursionists)		('000)	8,842	9,032	9,618	11,104	8,122
	Trips by main purpose	(9)(10)						
.4	Total		('000)	14,852	15,088	15,843	16,514	12,162
.5	♦ Personal		('000)	12,030	12,645	13,195	14,292	10,557
.6	* holidays, leisure and recreation		('000)	6,667	5,958	6,394	9,669	4,867
.7	* other personal purposes		('000)	5,363	6,687	6,801	4,623	5,690
.8	♦ Business and professional		('000)	2,822	2,443	2,648	2,222	1,605
	Trips by mode of transport	(9)						
.9	Total		('000)	14,852	15,088	15,843	16,513	12,160
.10	♦ Air		('000)	88	91	70	129	41
.11	♦ Water		('000)	360	300	365	251	139
.12	♦ Land		('000)	14,404	14,697	15,408	16,133	11,980
.13	* railway		('000)	513	585	554	449	304
.14	* road		('000)	13,718	13,886	14,620	15,542	11,194
.15	* others		('000)	173	226	234	142	482

CROATIA

Cod.	Basic data and indicators	Notes	Units	2011	2012	2013	2014	201
	Trips by form of organization	**(9)**						
2.16	Total		('000)	14,852	15,088	15,843	..	
2.17	♦ Package tour		('000)	378	294	290	..	
2.18	♦ Other forms		('000)	14,474	14,794	15,553	..	
	Accommodation							
	Total							
2.19	♦ Guests	**(2)**	('000)	1,529	1,466	1,485	1,505	1,66
2.20	♦ Overnights	**(2)**	('000)	5,602	5,221	5,138	5,160	5,74
	Hotels and similar establishments							
2.21	♦ Guests	**(8)**	('000)	942	889	888	874	94
2.22	♦ Overnights	**(8)**	('000)	2,412	2,259	2,192	2,112	2,30
	Indicators							
2.23	Average size of travel party		Persons	..	..	..	..	
	Average length of stay							
2.24	Total		Days	..	..	..	..	
2.25	♦ For all commercial accommodation services		Nights	3.66	3.56	3.46	3.43	3.4
2.26	* of which, "hotels and similar establishments"		Nights	2.57	2.55	2.47	2.42	2.4
2.27	♦ For non commercial accommodation services		Days	..	..	..	..	
2.28	Average expenditure per day		US$	..	..	..	..	
3.	**OUTBOUND TOURISM**							
	Data							
	Departures	**(9)**						
3.1	Total		('000)	5,526	5,159	5,444	4,638	4,21
3.2	♦ Overnight visitors (tourists)		('000)	2,880	2,680	2,927	2,763	2,57
3.3	♦ Same-day visitors (excursionists)		('000)	2,646	2,479	2,517	1,875	1,64
	Expenditure							
3.4	Total		US$ Mn	918	962	923	865	77
3.5	♦ Travel		US$ Mn	881	926	903	846	75
3.6	♦ Passenger transport		US$ Mn	37	36	20	19	1
	Expenditure by main purpose of the trip							
3.7	Total		US$ Mn	881	926	902	846	75
3.8	♦ Personal		US$ Mn	626	638	621	606	53.
3.9	♦ Business and professional		US$ Mn	255	288	281	240	22
4.	**TOURISM INDUSTRIES**							
	Data							
	Number of establishments							
4.1	Total		Units	..	..	..	..	
4.2	♦ Accommodation for visitors	**(2)(11)**	Units	2,189	2,326	4,247	4,651	4,81
4.3	* of which, "hotels and similar establishments"	**(12)**	Units	926	950	970	985	1,01
4.4	♦ Food and beverage serving activities		Units	..	..	..	..	
4.5	♦ Passenger transportation		Units	..	..	..	..	
4.6	♦ Travel agencies and other reservation services activities		Units	..	..	..	..	
4.7	♦ Other tourism industries		Units	..	..	..	..	
	Accommodation for visitors in hotels and similar establishments							
	Non-monetary data	**(8)(13)(14)**						
4.13	♦ Number of establishments		Units	857	878	898	909	93
4.14	♦ Number of rooms		Units	74,616	75,363	77,157	77,312	78,43
4.15	♦ Number of bed-places		Units	154,733	156,792	161,957	161,875	164,67
	Indicators							
4.16	Occupancy rate / rooms	**(15)**	Percent	..	..	35.30	36.10	37.5
4.17	Occupancy rate / bed-places	**(15)**	Percent	35.87	37.28	35.70	35.50	36.9
4.18	Average length of stay		Nights	3.89	3.91	3.79	3.63	3.5
4.19	Available capacity (bed-places per 1000 inhabitants)		Units	35.97	36.57	37.92	38.04	38.8
5.	**EMPLOYMENT**							
	Data							
	Number of employees by tourism industries	**(16)**						
5.1	Total		('000)	52.7	54.9	55.9	62.5	61.
5.2	♦ Accommodation services for visitors (hotels and similar establishments)		('000)	30.3	31.0	30.9	32.2	31.
5.3	♦ Other accommodation services		('000)	..	..	..	..	
5.4	♦ Food and beverage serving activities		('000)	17.2	18.5	19.8	24.5	23.
5.5	♦ Passenger transportation		('000)	..	..	..	..	
5.6	♦ Travel agencies and other reservation services activities		('000)	5.2	5.4	5.2	5.8	5.
5.7	♦ Other tourism industries		('000)	..	..	..	..	

CROATIA

Cod.	Basic data and indicators	Notes	Units	2011	2012	2013	2014	2015
6.	**COMPLEMENTARY INDICATORS**							
	Demand							
6.1	Gross travel propensity		Units	..	..	..	..	..
6.2	(1.2 inbound tourists + 2.2 domestic tourists) / population		Units	3.70	3.83	4.02	4.00	3.94
	Macroeconomic indicators related to international tourism							
6.3	Inbound tourism expenditure over GDP		Percent	15.4	15.8	16.8	17.6	18.5
6.4	Outbound tourism expenditure over GDP		Percent	1.5	1.7	1.6	1.5	1.6
6.5	Tourism balance (inbound minus outbound tourism expenditure) over GDP		Percent	13.9	14.1	15.2	16.1	16.9
6.6	Tourism openness (inbound plus outbound tourism expenditure) over GDP		Percent	16.9	17.5	18.4	19.1	20.1
6.7	Tourism coverage (inbound over outbound tourism		Percent	1,045.5	926.4	1,052.5	1,165.2	1,171.2
6.8	Inbound tourism expenditure over exports of goods		Percent	78.8	80.0	82.0	77.8	75.7
6.9	Inbound tourism expenditure over exports of services		Percent	72.8	72.7	74.6	74.1	72.3
6.10	Inbound tourism expenditure over exports of goods and		Percent	37.8	38.1	39.1	38.0	37.0
6.11	Inbound tourism expenditure over current account credits		Percent	33.0	33.1	34.0	33.4	32.3
6.12	Outbound tourism expenditure over imports of goods		Percent	4.4	5.0	4.5	4.0	4.0
6.13	Outbound tourism expenditure over imports of services		Percent	20.8	23.9	22.7	21.8	20.7
6.14	Outbound tourism expenditure over imports of goods and		Percent	3.6	4.1	3.7	3.4	3.3
6.15	Outbound tourism expenditure over current account debits		Percent	3.3	3.8	3.4	3.1	3.1

CUBA

Cod.	Basic data and indicators	Notes	Units	2011	2012	2013	2014	2015
1.	**INBOUND TOURISM**							
	Data							
	Arrivals							
1.1	Total		('000)	2,716	2,839	2,853	3,003	3,525
1.2	♦ Overnight visitors (tourists)	(1)	('000)	2,688	2,815	2,829	2,970	3,491
1.3	♦ Same-day visitors (excursionists)		('000)	28	24	24	33	34
1.4	* of which, cruise passengers		('000)	1	3	2	8	10
	Arrivals by region							
1.5	Total		('000)	2,716	2,839	2,853	3,003	3,525
1.6	♦ Africa		('000)	8	11	13	15	14
1.7	♦ Americas		('000)	1,401	1,542	1,591	1,681	1,960
1.8	♦ East Asia and the Pacific		('000)	49	53	56	68	90
1.9	♦ Europe		('000)	852	839	810	867	1,058
1.10	♦ Middle East		('000)	2	2	2	3	3
1.11	♦ South Asia		('000)	6	6	7	9	9
1.12	♦ Other not classified		('000)	399	385	374	361	391
1.13	* of which, nationals residing abroad		('000)	398	384	373	361	391
	Arrivals by main purpose	(1)						
1.14	Total		('000)	2,688	2,815	2,829	2,970	3,491
1.15	♦ Personal		('000)	2,672	2,798	2,814	2,955	3,472
1.16	* holidays, leisure and recreation		('000)	2,578	2,701	2,722	2,861	3,363
1.17	* other personal purposes		('000)	94	97	92	94	109
1.18	♦ Business and professional		('000)	16	17	15	14	19
	Arrivals by mode of transport							
1.19	Total		('000)	2,688	2,815	2,829	2,970	3,491
1.20	♦ Air		('000)	2,688	2,815	2,829	2,970	3,491
1.21	♦ Water		('000)	..	..	..	..	..
1.22	♦ Land		('000)	..	..	..	..	..
1.23	* railway		('000)	..	..	..	..	..
1.24	* road		('000)	..	..	..	..	..
1.25	* others		('000)	..	..	..	..	..
	Accommodation							
	Total							
1.29	♦ Guests	(2)	('000)	3,427	3,428	3,397	3,547	3,601
1.30	♦ Overnights	(2)	('000)	23,165	24,753	25,612	25,740	29,917
	Hotels and similar establishments							
1.31	♦ Guests	(3)	('000)	3,289	3,290	3,261	3,412	3,471
1.32	♦ Overnights	(3)	('000)	16,830	17,776	18,342	18,899	21,247
	Expenditure	(4)						
1.33	Total		US$ Mn	2,503	2,613	2,608	2,546	2,819
1.34	♦ Travel		US$ Mn	2,283	2,326	2,325	2,367	2,601
1.35	♦ Passenger transport		US$ Mn	220	287	283	179	218
	Indicators							
1.39	Average size of travel party		Persons	..	..	..	..	..
	Average length of stay							
1.40	Total		Days	..	..	..	..	..
1.41	♦ For all commercial accommodation services		Nights	11.00	11.00	11.00	10.40	10.00
1.42	* of which, "hotels and similar establishments"		Nights	..	..	..	..	..
1.43	♦ For non commercial accommodation services		Days	..	..	..	..	..
1.44	Average expenditure per day		US$	..	..	..	..	..
2.	**DOMESTIC TOURISM**							
	Data							
	Accommodation							
	Total							
2.19	♦ Guests		('000)	..	..	..	..	..
2.20	♦ Overnights	(2)	('000)	7,724	7,611	7,415	7,318	7,395
	Hotels and similar establishments							
2.21	♦ Guests		('000)	..	..	..	..	..
2.22	♦ Overnights	(3)	('000)	3,296	3,275	3,539	3,502	3,645
3.	**OUTBOUND TOURISM**							
	Data							
	Departures							
3.1	Total		('000)	..	..	..	..	..
3.2	♦ Overnight visitors (tourists)	(5)	('000)	253	213	286	355	580
3.3	♦ Same-day visitors (excursionists)		('000)	..	..	..	..	..

CUBA

Cod.	Basic data and indicators	Notes	Units	2011	2012	2013	2014	2015
4.	**TOURISM INDUSTRIES**							
	Data							
	Number of establishments							
4.1	Total		Units	..	..	..	..	..
4.2	♦ Accommodation for visitors		Units	562	473	450	430	434
4.3	* of which, "hotels and similar establishments"	(3)	Units	450	370	356	349	358
4.4	♦ Food and beverage serving activities		Units	..	..	..	..	..
4.5	♦ Passenger transportation		Units	..	..	..	..	..
4.6	♦ Travel agencies and other reservation services activities		Units	..	..	..	..	..
4.7	♦ Other tourism industries		Units	..	..	..	..	..
	Accommodation for visitors in hotels and similar establishments							
	Non-monetary data	(3)						
4.13	♦ Number of establishments		Units	450	370	356	349	358
4.14	♦ Number of rooms		Units	58,959	55,439	55,752	55,535	55,640
4.15	♦ Number of bed-places		Units	103,224	106,118	111,043	111,712	111,419
	Indicators							
4.16	Occupancy rate / rooms		Percent	53.20	54.40	54.60	57.10	58.40
4.17	Occupancy rate / bed-places		Percent	..	..	..	..	..
4.18	Average length of stay		Nights	..	..	..	..	..
4.19	Available capacity (bed-places per 1000 inhabitants)		Units	9.15	9.42	9.86	9.92	9.78
6.	**COMPLEMENTARY INDICATORS**							
	Demand							
6.1	Gross travel propensity		Units	..	..	..	..	..
6.2	(1.2 inbound tourists) / population		Units	0.24	0.25	0.25	0.26	0.31

CURAÇAO

Cod.	Basic data and indicators	Notes	Units	2011	2012	2013	2014	2015
1.	**INBOUND TOURISM**							
	Data							
	Arrivals							
1.1	Total		('000)	837	908	1,071	1,129	1,072
1.2	♦ Overnight visitors (tourists)	(1)	('000)	390	421	441	452	468
1.3	♦ Same-day visitors (excursionists)		('000)	447	487	630	677	604
1.4	* of which, cruise passengers		('000)	401	436	584	629	566
	Arrivals by region	(1)						
1.5	Total		('000)	390	421	441	452	468
1.6	♦ Africa		('000)	..	..	..	..	..
1.7	♦ Americas		('000)	210	235	245	242	257
1.8	♦ East Asia and the Pacific		('000)	..	..	..	..	..
1.9	♦ Europe		('000)	169	175	176	187	200
1.10	♦ Middle East		('000)	..	..	..	..	..
1.11	♦ South Asia		('000)	..	..	..	..	..
1.12	♦ Other not classified		('000)	11	11	20	23	11
1.13	* of which, nationals residing abroad		('000)	..	..	..	..	..
	Arrivals by main purpose	(1)(2)						
1.14	Total		('000)	390	420	441	452	468
1.15	♦ Personal		('000)	360	394	409	418	437
1.16	* holidays, leisure and recreation		('000)	320	350	367	378	387
1.17	* other personal purposes		('000)	40	44	43	40	49
1.18	♦ Business and professional		('000)	30	26	31	34	31
	Arrivals by mode of transport							
1.19	Total		('000)	837	907	1,071	1,129	1,072
1.20	♦ Air		('000)	436	471	487	500	507
1.21	♦ Water	(3)	('000)	401	436	584	629	566
1.22	♦ Land		('000)	..	..	..	..	..
1.23	* railway		('000)	..	..	..	..	..
1.24	* road		('000)	..	..	..	..	..
1.25	* others		('000)	..	..	..	..	..
	Accommodation							
	Total							
1.29	♦ Guests		('000)	336	350	370	390	390
1.30	♦ Overnights		('000)	3,200	3,687	3,754	4,009	3,839
	Hotels and similar establishments							
1.31	♦ Guests	(4)	('000)	249	230	291	308	302
1.32	♦ Overnights		('000)	1,712	1,749	2,249	2,507	2,398
	Expenditure							
1.33	Total		US$ Mn	540	676	778	820	714
1.34	♦ Travel		US$ Mn	453	543	583	635	609
1.35	♦ Passenger transport		US$ Mn	87	133	195	185	105
	Indicators							
1.39	Average size of travel party		Persons	..	..	2.6	2.6	2.6
	Average length of stay							
1.40	Total		Days	..	..	..	..	..
1.41	♦ For all commercial accommodation services		Nights	8.20	8.80	8.52	8.81	8.20
1.42	* of which, "hotels and similar establishments"		Nights	..	..	..	..	..
1.43	♦ For non commercial accommodation services		Days	..	..	..	..	..
1.44	Average expenditure per day		US$	..	..	..	..	..
3.	**OUTBOUND TOURISM**							
	Data							
	Expenditure							
3.4	Total		US$ Mn	321	357	377	383	412
3.5	♦ Travel		US$ Mn	267	278	299	310	339
3.6	♦ Passenger transport		US$ Mn	54	79	78	73	73
4.	**TOURISM INDUSTRIES**							
	Data							
	Accommodation for visitors in hotels and similar establishments							
	Non-monetary data							
4.13	♦ Number of establishments		Units	..	..	..	..	..
4.14	♦ Number of rooms	(5)	Units	5,562	5,562	6,070	6,300	6,300
4.15	♦ Number of bed-places		Units	..	..	..	..	..

CURAÇAO

Cod.	Basic data and indicators	Notes	Units	2011	2012	2013	2014	2015
	Indicators							
4.16	Occupancy rate / rooms		Percent	76.18	72.30	68.00	70.00	71.00
4.17	Occupancy rate / bed-places		Percent	..	..	..	..	..
4.18	Average length of stay		Nights	8.20	8.80	8.52	8.81	8.14
4.19	Available capacity (bed-places per 1000 inhabitants)		Units	..	..	..	..	..
6.	**COMPLEMENTARY INDICATORS**							
	Demand							
6.1	Gross travel propensity		Units	..	..	..	..	..
6.2	(1.2 inbound tourists) / population		Units	2.59	2.76	2.86	2.90	2.98
	Macroeconomic indicators related to international tourism							
6.3	Inbound tourism expenditure over GDP		Percent	..	..	..	..	..
6.4	Outbound tourism expenditure over GDP		Percent	..	..	..	..	..
6.5	Tourism balance (inbound minus outbound tourism expenditure) over GDP		Percent	..	..	..	..	..
6.6	Tourism openness (inbound plus outbound tourism expenditure) over GDP		Percent	..	..	..	..	..
6.7	Tourism coverage (inbound over outbound tourism expenditure)		Percent	168.2	189.4	206.4	214.1	173.3
6.8	Inbound tourism expenditure over exports of goods		Percent	67.7	79.1	125.8	128.6	170.9
6.9	Inbound tourism expenditure over exports of services		Percent	39.9	44.8	47.2	46.4	45.9
6.10	Inbound tourism expenditure over exports of goods and services		Percent	25.1	28.6	34.3	34.1	36.2
6.11	Inbound tourism expenditure over current account credits		Percent	21.3	25.1	30.2	29.8	30.9
6.12	Outbound tourism expenditure over imports of goods		Percent	15.3	16.0	20.0	21.2	27.5
6.13	Outbound tourism expenditure over imports of services		Percent	39.0	40.1	41.4	43.1	45.2
6.14	Outbound tourism expenditure over imports of goods and		Percent	11.0	11.4	13.5	14.2	17.1
6.15	Outbound tourism expenditure over current account debits		Percent	9.6	10.1	11.8	12.4	14.8

CYPRUS

Cod.	Basic data and indicators	Notes	Units	2011	2012	2013	2014	2015
1.	**INBOUND TOURISM**							
	Data							
	Arrivals							
1.1	Total		('000)	2,626	2,635	2,626	2,558	2,780
1.2	♦ Overnight visitors (tourists)	(1)	('000)	2,392	2,465	2,405	2,441	2,659
1.3	♦ Same-day visitors (excursionists)	(2)	('000)	234	170	221	147	121
1.4	* of which, cruise passengers		('000)	216	163	207	135	108
	Arrivals by region							
1.5	Total		('000)	2,392	2,465	2,405	2,441	2,659
1.6	♦ Africa		('000)	7	6	6	5	4
1.7	♦ Americas		('000)	32	25	28	20	23
1.8	♦ East Asia and the Pacific		('000)	16	16	16	17	17
1.9	♦ Europe		('000)	2,279	2,356	2,291	2,321	2,511
1.10	♦ Middle East		('000)	51	56	59	72	81
1.11	♦ South Asia		('000)	7	6	5	6	7
1.12	♦ Other not classified		('000)	..	..	..	..	17
1.13	* of which, nationals residing abroad		('000)	..	..	..	..	..
	Arrivals by main purpose	(3)						
1.14	Total		('000)	2,392	2,370	2,363	2,441	2,659
1.15	♦ Personal		('000)	2,231	2,245	2,263	2,326	2,522
1.16	* holidays, leisure and recreation		('000)	1,908	1,955	1,979	2,054	2,161
1.17	* other personal purposes		('000)	323	290	284	272	361
1.18	♦ Business and professional		('000)	161	125	100	115	137
	Arrivals by mode of transport							
1.19	Total		('000)	2,626	2,634	2,626	2,588	2,659
1.20	♦ Air		('000)	2,410	2,471	2,419	2,453	2,551
1.21	♦ Water	(4)	('000)	216	163	207	135	108
1.22	♦ Land		('000)	..	..	..	..	..
1.23	* railway		('000)	..	..	..	..	..
1.24	* road		('000)	..	..	..	..	..
1.25	* others		('000)	..	..	..	..	..
	Arrivals by form of organization of the trip							
1.26	Total		('000)	2,392	2,465	2,405	2,441	2,659
1.27	♦ Package tour		('000)	1,459	1,578	1,534	1,338	1,646
1.28	♦ Other forms		('000)	933	887	871	1,103	1,013
	Accommodation	(5)						
	Total							
1.29	♦ Guests		('000)	1,947	2,021	1,948	1,936	1,874
1.30	♦ Overnights		('000)	13,113	13,488	13,153	12,884	12,550
	Hotels and similar establishments							
1.31	♦ Guests	(6)	('000)	1,946	2,020	1,947	1,935	1,862
1.32	♦ Overnights	(6)	('000)	13,100	13,476	13,141	12,873	12,485
	Expenditure							
1.33	Total		US$ Mn	2,707	2,732	3,020	2,920	2,489
1.34	♦ Travel		US$ Mn	2,554	2,599	2,893	2,844	2,487
1.35	♦ Passenger transport		US$ Mn	153	133	127	76	2
	Expenditure by main purpose of the trip							
1.36	Total		US$ Mn	2,554	2,599	2,893	2,844	2,487
1.37	♦ Personal		US$ Mn	2,397	2,460	2,756	2,700	2,365
1.38	♦ Business and professional		US$ Mn	157	139	137	144	122
	Indicators							
1.39	Average size of travel party	(3)	Persons	1.9	1.9	1.9	1.7	1.7
	Average length of stay							
1.40	Total		Days	9.79	9.44	10.25	10.69	9.94
1.41	♦ For all commercial accommodation services	(3)	Nights	8.77	8.30	8.77	8.61	8.36
1.42	* of which, "hotels and similar establishments"	(3)	Nights	8.30	8.02	8.29	7.99	8.04
1.43	♦ For non commercial accommodation services	(3)	Days	15.76	15.43	18.71	18.65	15.15
1.44	Average expenditure per day	(7)	US$	116.3	116.6	121.5	111.4	93.5
2.	**DOMESTIC TOURISM**							
	Data							
	Trips							
2.1	Total		('000)	..	..	..	..	..
2.2	♦ Overnight visitors (tourists)		('000)	..	1,370	1,304	1,297	..
2.3	♦ Same-day visitors (excursionists)		('000)	..	..	..	..	..
	Accommodation							
	Total							
2.19	♦ Guests		('000)	547	509	441	434	442
2.20	♦ Overnights		('000)	1,172	1,088	896	831	825

CYPRUS

od.	Basic data and indicators	Notes	Units	2011	2012	2013	2014	2015
	Hotels and similar establishments							
.21	♦ Guests	(6)	('000)	546	505	438	432	440
.22	♦ Overnights	(6)	('000)	1,162	1,070	881	817	821
	Indicators							
.23	Average size of travel party		Persons	..	..	..	..	..
	Average length of stay							
.24	Total		Days	..	..	..	..	..
.25	♦ For all commercial accommodation services	(8)	Nights	2.14	2.14	2.03	1.91	1.87
.26	* of which, "hotels and similar establishments"	(8)	Nights	2.13	2.12	2.01	1.89	1.87
.27	♦ For non commercial accommodation services		Days	..	..	..	..	..
.28	Average expenditure per day		US$	..	..	..	..	..
.	**OUTBOUND TOURISM**							
	Data							
	Departures							
1	Total	(1)	('000)	1,209	1,194	1,115	1,209	1,119
.2	♦ Overnight visitors (tourists)		('000)	..	..	..	..	..
.3	♦ Same-day visitors (excursionists)		('000)	..	..	..	..	..
	Expenditure							
4	Total		US$ Mn	1,730	1,687	1,633	1,771	1,439
.5	♦ Travel		US$ Mn	1,310	1,290	1,236	1,326	1,065
6	♦ Passenger transport		US$ Mn	420	397	397	445	374
	Expenditure by main purpose of the trip							
7	Total		US$ Mn	1,310	1,290	1,236	1,326	1,065
.8	♦ Personal		US$ Mn	1,102	1,097	1,041	1,130	902
.9	♦ Business and professional		US$ Mn	208	193	195	196	163
	Indicators							
10	Average length of stay		Days	9.40	..	..	9.90	9.50
.11	Average expenditure per day	(9)	US$	152.2	..	..	138.2	135.2
.	**TOURISM INDUSTRIES**							
	Data							
	Number of establishments							
.1	Total		Units	5,621	5,686	5,687	5,764	..
.2	♦ Accommodation for visitors	(10)	Units	512	516	518	532	..
.3	* of which, "hotels and similar establishments"	(11)	Units	360	371	387	395	..
.4	♦ Food and beverage serving activities	(12)	Units	4,642	4,712	4,732	4,807	..
.5	♦ Passenger transportation		Units	..	..	..	..	..
.6	♦ Travel agencies and other reservation services activities	(13)	Units	467	458	437	425	..
.7	♦ Other tourism industries		Units	..	..	..	..	..
	Accommodation for visitors in hotels and similar establishments							
	Monetary data	(14)						
.8	♦ Output		US$ Mn	1,204.5	1,148.4	1,171.6	1,182.4	..
.9	♦ Intermediate consumption		US$ Mn	520.8	485.0	479.2	488.3	..
.10	♦ Gross value added		US$ Mn	683.8	663.4	692.4	694.1	..
.11	♦ Compensation of employees		US$ Mn	424.9	386.5	376.9	366.5	..
.12	♦ Gross fixed capital formation		US$ Mn	98.5	118.8	138.6	104.2	..
	Non-monetary data	(15)						
.13	♦ Number of establishments		Units	821	806	797	799	786
.14	♦ Number of rooms		Units	41,756	41,568	41,747	41,894	41,218
.15	♦ Number of bed-places		Units	84,654	84,316	84,674	85,017	83,541
	Indicators							
.16	Occupancy rate / rooms	(6)(15)	Percent	62.43	64.00	61.50	62.70	63.02
.17	Occupancy rate / bed-places	(6)(15)	Percent	62.60	64.50	63.00	61.60	63.20
.18	Average length of stay	(6)(15)(16)	Nights	5.72	5.76	5.88	5.78	5.78
.19	Available capacity (bed-places per 1000 inhabitants)		Units	75.81	74.66	74.17	73.69	71.69
	Travel agencies and other reservation service activities							
	Monetary data	(13)						
.20	♦ Output		US$ Mn	125.6	117.2	92.5	93.6	..
.21	♦ Intermediate consumption		US$ Mn	43.0	45.8	33.8	30.9	..
.22	♦ Gross value added		US$ Mn	82.6	71.4	58.7	62.7	..
.23	♦ Compensation of employees		US$ Mn	60.0	51.8	43.9	40.9	..
.24	♦ Gross fixed capital formation		US$ Mn	3.2	2.2	-1.9	0.4	..

CYPRUS

Cod.	Basic data and indicators	Notes	Units	2011	2012	2013	2014	201
	Non-monetary data							
	♦ Domestic trips							
4.25	* with package tour		Percent	..	..	..	..	
4.26	* without package tour		Percent	..	..	..	..	
	♦ Inbound trips							
4.27	* with package tour	(3)	Percent	61.0	65.1	63.8	54.8	61.
4.28	* without package tour	(3)	Percent	39.0	34.9	36.2	45.2	38.
	♦ Outbound trips							
4.29	* with package tour		Percent	12.5	..	..	..	
4.30	* without package tour		Percent	87.5	..	..	..	

5. EMPLOYMENT

Data

Number of employees by tourism industries

Cod.		Notes	Units	2011	2012	2013	2014	201
5.1	Total		('000)	38.8	37.7	35.1	37.9	
5.2	♦ Accommodation services for visitors (hotels and similar establishments)	(11)	('000)	16.8	16.8	16.3	17.0	
5.3	♦ Other accommodation services	(17)	('000)	0.5	0.5	0.4	0.5	
5.4	♦ Food and beverage serving activities	(12)	('000)	19.4	18.5	16.9	18.9	
5.5	♦ Passenger transportation		('000)	..	..	..	..	
5.6	♦ Travel agencies and other reservation services activities	(13)	('000)	2.1	1.9	1.5	1.5	
5.7	♦ Other tourism industries		('000)	..	..	..	..	

6. COMPLEMENTARY INDICATORS

Demand

Cod.		Notes	Units	2011	2012	2013	2014	201
6.1	Gross travel propensity		Units	..	..	..	..	
6.2	(1.2 inbound tourists + 2.2 domestic tourists) / population		Units	..	3.40	3.25	3.24	

Macroeconomic indicators related to international tourism

Cod.		Notes	Units	2011	2012	2013	2014	201
6.3	Inbound tourism expenditure over GDP		Percent	9.9	10.9	12.6	12.5	12.
6.4	Outbound tourism expenditure over GDP		Percent	6.3	6.7	6.8	7.6	7.
6.5	Tourism balance (inbound minus outbound tourism expenditure) over GDP		Percent	3.6	4.2	5.8	4.9	5.
6.6	Tourism openness (inbound plus outbound tourism expenditure) over GDP		Percent	16.2	17.7	19.3	20.1	20.
6.7	Tourism coverage (inbound over outbound tourism		Percent	156.5	161.9	185.0	164.9	173.
6.8	Inbound tourism expenditure over exports of goods		Percent	64.3	70.0	83.8	78.3	90.
6.9	Inbound tourism expenditure over exports of services		Percent	26.2	28.8	28.7	27.1	27.
6.10	Inbound tourism expenditure over exports of goods and		Percent	18.6	20.4	21.4	20.1	20.
6.11	Inbound tourism expenditure over current account credits		Percent	9.8	12.8	15.1	14.2	14.
6.12	Outbound tourism expenditure over imports of goods		Percent	17.7	20.0	21.7	23.7	23.
6.13	Outbound tourism expenditure over imports of services		Percent	31.0	31.6	26.4	27.0	25.
6.14	Outbound tourism expenditure over imports of goods and		Percent	11.3	12.3	11.9	12.6	12.
6.15	Outbound tourism expenditure over current account debits		Percent	6.0	7.4	7.7	8.2	8.

CZECH REPUBLIC

Cod.	Basic data and indicators	Notes	Units	2011	2012	2013	2014	2015
1.	**INBOUND TOURISM**							
	Data							
	Arrivals	(1)(2)						
.1	Total		('000)	22,810	25,750	26,332	27,166	2,810
.2	♦ Overnight visitors (tourists)		('000)	9,019	10,123	10,300	10,649	11,148
.3	♦ Same-day visitors (excursionists)	(3)	('000)	13,792	15,627	16,032	16,518	16,993
.4	* of which, cruise passengers		('000)	..	..	..	..	..
	Arrivals by region	(4)						
.5	Total		('000)	6,715	7,646	7,852	8,096	8,707
.6	♦ Africa		('000)	30	37	39	44	44
.7	♦ Americas		('000)	480	613	650	690	770
.8	♦ East Asia and the Pacific		('000)	674	781	837	934	1,150
.9	♦ Europe		('000)	5,531	6,190	6,297	6,391	6,687
.10	♦ Middle East		('000)	..	..	..	..	..
.11	♦ South Asia		('000)	..	25	29	38	56
.12	♦ Other not classified		('000)	..	..	..	..	..
.13	* of which, nationals residing abroad		('000)	..	..	..	..	..
	Accommodation							
	Total							
.29	♦ Guests		('000)	6,715	7,647	7,852	8,096	8,707
.30	♦ Overnights		('000)	19,425	21,794	22,145	22,110	23,287
	Hotels and similar establishments							
.31	♦ Guests		('000)	6,377	7,167	7,327	7,513	8,024
.32	♦ Overnights		('000)	18,027	19,936	20,072	19,971	20,970
	Expenditure							
.33	Total		US$ Mn	8,930	8,174	7,792	7,614	6,758
.34	♦ Travel		US$ Mn	8,096	7,456	7,042	6,822	6,048
.35	♦ Passenger transport		US$ Mn	834	718	750	792	710
	Expenditure by main purpose of the trip							
.36	Total		US$ Mn	8,096	7,456	7,042	6,822	6,048
.37	♦ Personal		US$ Mn	5,799	5,237	5,167	5,095	4,657
.38	♦ Business and professional		US$ Mn	2,297	2,219	1,875	1,727	1,391
	Indicators							
.39	Average size of travel party		Persons	..	..	..	..	..
	Average length of stay							
.40	Total		Days	..	..	..	..	..
.41	♦ For all commercial accommodation services		Nights	2.89	2.85	2.90	2.73	2.67
.42	* of which, "hotels and similar establishments"		Nights	2.90	2.61	2.62	2.66	2.61
.43	♦ For non commercial accommodation services		Days	..	..	..	..	..
.44	Average expenditure per day		US$	..	..	..	..	..
2.	**DOMESTIC TOURISM**							
	Data							
	Trips							
2.1	Total		('000)	..	..	..	..	..
2.2	♦ Overnight visitors (tourists)	(5)	('000)	29,847	26,881	25,499	27,042	23,964
2.3	♦ Same-day visitors (excursionists)		('000)	..	..	..	..	..
	Trips by main purpose							
2.4	Total		('000)	29,846	26,881	25,499	27,042	23,963
2.5	♦ Personal		('000)	28,705	25,987	24,304	26,197	23,287
2.6	* holidays, leisure and recreation	(6)	('000)	28,705	25,987	24,304	26,197	23,287
2.7	* other personal purposes		('000)	..	..	..	..	..
2.8	♦ Business and professional	(7)	('000)	1,141	894	1,195	845	676
	Accommodation							
	Total							
2.19	♦ Guests		('000)	6,184	7,452	7,556	7,491	8,489
2.20	♦ Overnights		('000)	18,810	21,484	21,163	20,837	23,807
	Hotels and similar establishments							
2.21	♦ Guests		('000)	4,102	5,048	5,046	5,053	5,736
2.22	♦ Overnights		('000)	9,853	11,910	11,825	11,716	13,290
	Indicators							
2.23	Average size of travel party		Persons	..	..	..	..	..
	Average length of stay							
2.24	Total		Days	..	..	..	..	..
2.25	♦ For all commercial accommodation services		Nights	3.04	2.88	2.84	2.78	2.80
2.26	* of which, "hotels and similar establishments"		Nights	2.40	2.36	2.34	2.32	2.32
2.27	♦ For non commercial accommodation services		Days	..	..	..	..	..
2.28	Average expenditure per day		US$	..	..	..	..	..

CZECH REPUBLIC

Cod.	Basic data and indicators	Notes	Units	2011	2012	2013	2014	201
3.	**OUTBOUND TOURISM**							
	Data							
	Departures	(5)(8)						
3.1	Total		('000)	..	..	..	..	
3.2	◆ Overnight visitors (tourists)		('000)	5,279	5,419	5,781	5,651	5,85
3.3	◆ Same-day visitors (excursionists)		('000)	..	..	..	..	
	Expenditure							
3.4	Total		US$ Mn	4,876	4,556	4,698	5,173	4,91
3.5	◆ Travel		US$ Mn	4,789	4,472	4,637	5,133	4,86
3.6	◆ Passenger transport		US$ Mn	87	84	61	40	4
	Expenditure by main purpose of the trip							
3.7	Total		US$ Mn	4,789	4,472	4,637	5,133	4,86
3.8	◆ Personal		US$ Mn	3,688	3,399	3,564	3,947	3,99
3.9	◆ Business and professional		US$ Mn	1,101	1,072	1,073	1,186	87
4.	**TOURISM INDUSTRIES**							
	Data							
	Number of establishments	(9)						
4.1	Total		Units	146,681	151,762	148,456	150,423	151,64
4.2	◆ Accommodation for visitors		Units	7,657	10,057	9,970	9,013	9,16
4.3	* of which, "hotels and similar establishments"		Units	4,612	6,350	6,301	5,833	5,99
4.4	◆ Food and beverage serving activities		Units	122,166	125,166	123,082	125,872	126,75
4.5	◆ Passenger transportation		Units	4,879	4,721	4,027	3,982	4,00
4.6	◆ Travel agencies and other reservation services activities		Units	11,979	11,818	11,377	11,556	11,72
4.7	◆ Other tourism industries		Units	..	..	..	..	
	Accommodation for visitors in hotels and similar establishments							
	Monetary data	(10)						
4.8	◆ Output	(1)(2)	US$ Mn	2,518.8	2,261.2	2,298.5	2,247.8	2,013.
4.9	◆ Intermediate consumption	(1)(2)	US$ Mn	1,253.0	1,075.7	1,167.6	1,216.0	1,132.
4.10	◆ Gross value added	(1)(2)	US$ Mn	1,109.1	980.3	1,013.2	1,048.4	918.
4.11	◆ Compensation of employees	(11)	US$ Mn	571.6	525.1	528.8	502.3	439.
4.12	◆ Gross fixed capital formation	(11)(12)	US$ Mn	224.4	206.1	198.2	192.3	169.
	Non-monetary data							
4.13	◆ Number of establishments		Units	4,612	6,350	6,301	5,833	15,992
4.14	◆ Number of rooms		Units	115,795	137,701	137,257	132,520	136,02
4.15	◆ Number of bed-places		Units	261,858	319,692	317,875	306,430	314,21
	Indicators							
4.16	Occupancy rate / rooms		Percent	42.32	38.58	41.30	44.69	42.9
4.17	Occupancy rate / bed-places	(13)	Percent	35.89	34.80	34.76	35.17	36.1
4.18	Average length of stay		Nights	2.96	2.53	2.54	2.52	2.4
4.19	Available capacity (bed-places per 1000 inhabitants)		Units	24.86	30.32	30.14	29.07	29.8
	Travel agencies and other reservation service activities							
	Monetary data	(14)						
4.20	◆ Output	(1)(2)	US$ Mn	2,557.8	2,395.9	2,630.9	2,457.2	2,126.
4.21	◆ Intermediate consumption	(1)(2)	US$ Mn	2,247.8	1,952.7	1,944.9	2,283.0	1,964.
4.22	◆ Gross value added	(1)(2)	US$ Mn	294.6	273.9	283.6	256.5	275.
4.23	◆ Compensation of employees	(11)	US$ Mn	171.6	153.6	152.2	144.4	130.
4.24	◆ Gross fixed capital formation	(11)(12)	US$ Mn	35.1	33.0	40.0	39.3	34.
	Non-monetary data							
	◆ Domestic trips	(15)						
4.25	* with package tour		Percent	0.8	2.5	3.5	0.9	1.
4.26	* without package tour		Percent	99.2	97.5	96.5	99.1	98.7
	◆ Inbound trips							
4.27	* with package tour		Percent	..	..	..	..	
4.28	* without package tour		Percent	..	..	..	..	
	◆ Outbound trips	(15)						
4.29	* with package tour		Percent	34.4	45.8	46.2	40.7	39.
4.30	* without package tour		Percent	65.6	54.2	53.8	59.3	60.9

CZECH REPUBLIC

Cod.	Basic data and indicators	Notes	Units	2011	2012	2013	2014	2015
5.	**EMPLOYMENT**							
	Data							
	Number of employees by tourism industries							
5.1	Total		('000)	232.6	229.6	231.3	225.3	..
5.2	♦ Accommodation services for visitors (hotels and similar establishments)		('000)	41.9	39.9	39.6	38.8	..
5.3	♦ Other accommodation services		('000)	..	..	..	..	..
5.4	♦ Food and beverage serving activities		('000)	69.7	69.8	70.4	67.0	..
5.5	♦ Passenger transportation		('000)	28.8	27.5	27.6	27.3	..
5.6	♦ Travel agencies and other reservation services activities		('000)	12.1	12.2	12.9	12.1	..
5.7	♦ Other tourism industries		('000)	80.1	80.2	80.8	80.1	..
	Number of jobs by status in employment							
5.8	Total		('000)	232.5	229.6	231.2	225.5	..
5.9	♦ Employees		('000)	186.2	185.9	186.9	183.8	..
5.10	♦ Self employed		('000)	46.3	43.7	44.3	41.7	..
	Indicators							
	Number of full-time equivalent jobs by status in employment							
5.11	Total		('000)	232.4	229.6	231.2	225.3	..
5.12	♦ Employees		('000)	186.1	185.9	186.9	182.9	..
5.13	* male		('000)	84.3	83.8	84.2	82.5	..
5.14	* female		('000)	101.8	102.1	102.7	100.4	..
5.15	♦ Self employed		('000)	46.3	43.7	44.3	42.4	..
5.16	* male		('000)	24.8	24.0	24.3	23.3	..
5.17	* female		('000)	21.5	19.7	20.0	19.1	..
6.	**COMPLEMENTARY INDICATORS**							
	Demand							
6.1	Gross travel propensity		Units	..	..	..	..	..
6.2	(1.2 inbound tourists + 2.2 domestic tourists) / population		Units	3.69	3.51	3.39	3.58	3.33
	Macroeconomic indicators related to international tourism							
6.3	Inbound tourism expenditure over GDP		Percent	3.9	4.0	3.7	3.7	3.7
6.4	Outbound tourism expenditure over GDP		Percent	2.1	2.2	2.3	2.5	2.7
6.5	Tourism balance (inbound minus outbound tourism expenditure) over GDP		Percent	1.8	1.8	1.4	1.2	1.0
6.6	Tourism openness (inbound plus outbound tourism expenditure) over GDP		Percent	6.0	6.2	6.0	6.2	6.4
6.7	Tourism coverage (inbound over outbound tourism expenditure)		Percent	183.1	179.4	165.9	147.2	137.6
6.8	Inbound tourism expenditure over exports of goods		Percent	6.5	6.1	5.7	5.2	5.2
6.9	Inbound tourism expenditure over exports of services		Percent	35.8	33.7	32.5	30.4	29.8
6.10	Inbound tourism expenditure over exports of goods and services		Percent	5.5	5.2	4.8	4.4	4.4
6.11	Inbound tourism expenditure over current account credits		Percent	5.2	4.8	4.5	4.2	4.1
6.12	Outbound tourism expenditure over imports of goods		Percent	3.6	3.6	3.7	3.8	4.0
6.13	Outbound tourism expenditure over imports of services		Percent	24.0	22.5	23.0	23.1	25.0
6.14	Outbound tourism expenditure over imports of goods and		Percent	3.2	3.1	3.2	3.3	3.5
6.15	Outbound tourism expenditure over current account debits		Percent	2.9	2.8	2.9	3.0	3.2

DENMARK

Cod.	Basic data and indicators	Notes	Units	2011	2012	2013	2014	2015
1.	**INBOUND TOURISM**	(1)						
	Data							
	Arrivals							
1.1	Total		('000)	25,811	26,402	26,516	28,070	28,209
1.2	♦ Overnight visitors (tourists)		('000)	7,864	8,443	8,557	10,267	10,424
1.3	♦ Same-day visitors (excursionists)		('000)	17,947	17,959	17,959	17,803	17,785
1.4	* of which, cruise passengers		('000)	607	619	619	470	445
	Arrivals by region	(2)(3)						
1.5	Total		('000)	8,471	8,443	8,557	10,267	10,424
1.6	♦ Africa		('000)	..	..	..	..	..
1.7	♦ Americas		('000)	684	589	599	672	689
1.8	♦ East Asia and the Pacific		('000)	166	231	249	278	292
1.9	♦ Europe		('000)	7,174	7,250	7,292	8,834	9,023
1.10	♦ Middle East		('000)	..	..	..	..	..
1.11	♦ South Asia		('000)	..	..	..	..	..
1.12	♦ Other not classified		('000)	447	373	418	483	420
1.13	* of which, nationals residing abroad		('000)	..	..	..	..	..
	Arrivals by main purpose							
1.14	Total		('000)	25,812	26,403	26,516	28,070	28,209
1.15	♦ Personal		('000)	25,078	25,632	25,727	26,966	27,038
1.16	* holidays, leisure and recreation		('000)	25,078	25,632	25,727	26,966	27,038
1.17	* other personal purposes		('000)	..	..	..	..	..
1.18	♦ Business and professional		('000)	734	771	789	1,104	1,171
	Accommodation							
	Total	(3)						
1.29	♦ Guests		('000)	8,471	8,443	8,557	10,267	10,424
1.30	♦ Overnights		('000)	45,921	46,039	45,746	48,734	50,187
	Hotels and similar establishments	(4)						
1.31	♦ Guests		('000)	1,499	1,588	1,653	2,627	2,646
1.32	♦ Overnights		('000)	5,590	5,946	6,241	6,677	6,804
	Expenditure							
1.33	Total		US$ Mn	..	..	..	..	..
1.34	♦ Travel	(5)	US$ Mn	6,366	6,135	6,490	7,617	6,685
1.35	♦ Passenger transport		US$ Mn	..	..	..	..	..
	Expenditure by main purpose of the trip	(5)						
1.36	Total		US$ Mn	6,366	6,135	6,490	7,617	6,686
1.37	♦ Personal		US$ Mn	5,407	5,173	5,503	6,285	5,488
1.38	♦ Business and professional		US$ Mn	959	962	987	1,332	1,198
	Indicators							
1.39	Average size of travel party		Persons	..	..	..	..	..
	Average length of stay							
1.40	Total		Days	..	..	..	..	..
1.41	♦ For all commercial accommodation services		Nights	8.33	8.26	8.12	4.77	5.03
1.42	* of which, "hotels and similar establishments"		Nights	..	..	..	..	..
1.43	♦ For non commercial accommodation services		Days	..	..	..	..	..
1.44	Average expenditure per day		US$	..	..	..	..	..
2.	**DOMESTIC TOURISM**							
	Data							
	Trips							
2.1	Total		('000)	..	..	..	..	..
2.2	♦ Overnight visitors (tourists)	(6)	('000)	..	21,407	23,590	23,995	..
2.3	♦ Same-day visitors (excursionists)		('000)	..	..	..	..	..
	Accommodation							
	Total	(1)(3)						
2.19	♦ Guests		('000)	11,685	11,743	11,783	14,620	14,954
2.20	♦ Overnights		('000)	62,120	62,139	62,305	63,727	64,664
	Hotels and similar establishments	(1)(4)						
2.21	♦ Guests		('000)	1,666	1,713	1,767	3,631	3,917
2.22	♦ Overnights		('000)	7,048	7,242	7,454	7,844	8,465
	Indicators							
2.23	Average size of travel party		Persons	..	..	..	..	..
	Average length of stay							
2.24	Total		Days	..	..	..	..	..
2.25	♦ For all commercial accommodation services	(1)	Nights	8.07	8.13	8.10	3.58	3.63
2.26	* of which, "hotels and similar establishments"		Nights	..	..	..	..	..
2.27	♦ For non commercial accommodation services		Days	..	..	..	..	..
2.28	Average expenditure per day		US$	..	..	..	..	..

DENMARK

Cod.	Basic data and indicators	Notes	Units	2011	2012	2013	2014	2015
3.	**OUTBOUND TOURISM**							
	Data							
	Departures							
3.1	Total		('000)	..	..	..	..	..
3.2	♦ Overnight visitors (tourists)		('000)	7,846	7,843	6,977	8,528	8,991
3.3	♦ Same-day visitors (excursionists)		('000)	..	..	..	..	..
	Expenditure							
3.4	Total		US$ Mn	..	..	..	..	..
3.5	♦ Travel	(5)	US$ Mn	9,840	9,600	10,072	10,443	8,918
3.6	♦ Passenger transport		US$ Mn	..	..	..	..	..
	Expenditure by main purpose of the trip	(5)						
3.7	Total		US$ Mn	9,840	9,600	10,073	10,443	8,917
3.8	♦ Personal		US$ Mn	7,473	7,255	7,500	7,793	6,617
3.9	♦ Business and professional		US$ Mn	2,367	2,345	2,573	2,650	2,300
4.	**TOURISM INDUSTRIES**							
	Data							
	Number of establishments							
4.1	Total		Units	17,539	17,928	17,750	18,139	..
4.2	♦ Accommodation for visitors		Units	1,524	1,533	1,524	1,550	..
4.3	* of which, "hotels and similar establishments"	(7)	Units	515	511	511	523	519
4.4	♦ Food and beverage serving activities		Units	12,040	12,423	12,385	12,748	..
4.5	♦ Passenger transportation		Units	3,419	3,424	3,277	3,285	..
4.6	♦ Travel agencies and other reservation services activities		Units	556	548	564	556	..
4.7	♦ Other tourism industries		Units	..	..	..	..	..
	Accommodation for visitors in hotels and similar establishments							
	Non-monetary data	(7)						
4.13	♦ Number of establishments		Units	515	511	511	523	519
4.14	♦ Number of rooms		Units	42,351	42,808	43,032	43,715	44,078
4.15	♦ Number of bed-places		Units	85,315	86,619	76,458	87,870	88,397
	Indicators							
4.16	Occupancy rate / rooms		Percent	53.00	54.00	55.00	57.00	61.00
4.17	Occupancy rate / bed-places	(7)	Percent	40.00	40.00	42.00	44.00	47.00
4.18	Average length of stay		Nights	..	..	..	..	..
4.19	Available capacity (bed-places per 1000 inhabitants)		Units	15.30	15.46	13.59	15.56	15.59
5.	**EMPLOYMENT**							
	Data							
	Number of employees by tourism industries							
5.1	Total		('000)	151.0	158.5	158.9	165.1	..
5.2	♦ Accommodation services for visitors (hotels and similar establishments)		('000)	14.0	14.5	14.7	15.2	..
5.3	♦ Other accommodation services		('000)	6.1	6.1	6.1	6.5	..
5.4	♦ Food and beverage serving activities		('000)	83.5	88.7	91.4	96.6	..
5.5	♦ Passenger transportation		('000)	42.2	43.9	41.4	41.5	..
5.6	♦ Travel agencies and other reservation services activities		('000)	5.2	5.3	5.3	5.3	..
5.7	♦ Other tourism industries		('000)	..	..	..	..	..
6.	**COMPLEMENTARY INDICATORS**							
	Demand							
6.1	Gross travel propensity		Units	..	..	..	..	..
6.2	(1.2 inbound tourists + 2.2 domestic tourists) / population		Units	..	5.33	5.72	6.07	..
	Macroeconomic indicators related to international tourism							
6.3	Inbound tourism expenditure over GDP		Percent	1.9	1.9	1.9	2.2	2.3
6.4	Outbound tourism expenditure over GDP		Percent	2.9	3.0	3.0	3.1	3.0
6.5	Tourism balance (inbound minus outbound tourism expenditure) over GDP		Percent	-1.0	-1.1	-1.1	-0.9	-0.7
6.6	Tourism openness (inbound plus outbound tourism expenditure) over GDP		Percent	4.8	4.9	4.9	5.3	5.3
6.7	Tourism coverage (inbound over outbound tourism		Percent	64.7	63.9	64.4	72.9	75.0
6.8	Inbound tourism expenditure over exports of goods		Percent	5.7	5.8	5.8	6.8	7.0
6.9	Inbound tourism expenditure over exports of services		Percent	9.6	9.3	9.2	10.5	10.9
6.10	Inbound tourism expenditure over exports of goods and services		Percent	3.6	3.6	3.6	4.1	4.2
6.11	Inbound tourism expenditure over current account credits		Percent	3.0	3.0	3.0	3.5	3.5
6.12	Outbound tourism expenditure over imports of goods		Percent	9.7	9.9	10.1	10.3	10.5
6.13	Outbound tourism expenditure over imports of services		Percent	16.8	16.5	15.9	16.3	16.6
6.14	Outbound tourism expenditure over imports of goods and		Percent	6.2	6.2	6.2	6.3	6.4
6.15	Outbound tourism expenditure over current account debits		Percent	4.9	5.0	4.9	5.0	5.1

DJIBOUTI

Cod. Basic data and indicators	Notes	Units	2011	2012	2013	2014	2015
1. INBOUND TOURISM							
Data							
Arrivals							
1.1 Total		('000)	..	..	..	..	..
1.2 ♦ Overnight visitors (tourists)	(1)	('000)	56	60	63	..	..
1.3 ♦ Same-day visitors (excursionists)		('000)	..	..	..	..	..
1.4 * of which, cruise passengers		('000)	..	..	..	..	..
Accommodation							
Hotels and similar establishments							
1.31 ♦ Guests		('000)	56	60	63	..	..
1.32 ♦ Overnights		('000)	146	178	162	..	..
Expenditure							
1.33 Total		US$ Mn	..	..	..	..	..
1.34 ♦ Travel		US$ Mn	19	21	22	25	31
1.35 ♦ Passenger transport		US$ Mn	..	..	..	..	..
3. OUTBOUND TOURISM							
Data							
Expenditure							
3.4 Total		US$ Mn	34	30	31	..	..
3.5 ♦ Travel		US$ Mn	21	18	19	22	23
3.6 ♦ Passenger transport		US$ Mn	13	11	12	..	..
4. TOURISM INDUSTRIES							
Data							
Accommodation for visitors in hotels and similar establishments							
Non-monetary data							
4.13 ♦ Number of establishments		Units	..	..	..	..	..
4.14 ♦ Number of rooms		Units	726	878	955	..	..
4.15 ♦ Number of bed-places		Units	974	1,031	1,076	..	..
Indicators							
4.16 Occupancy rate / rooms		Percent	..	..	..	..	..
4.17 Occupancy rate / bed-places		Percent	38.06	47.53	41.37	..	..
4.18 Average length of stay		Nights	..	..	..	..	..
4.19 Available capacity (bed-places per 1000 inhabitants)		Units	1.16	1.21	1.24	..	..
6. COMPLEMENTARY INDICATORS							
Demand							
6.1 Gross travel propensity		Units	..	..	..	..	..
6.2 (1.2 inbound tourists) / population		Units	0.07	0.07	0.07	..	..
Macroeconomic indicators related to international tourism							
6.3 Inbound tourism expenditure over GDP		Percent	..	..	..	..	..
6.4 Outbound tourism expenditure over GDP		Percent	..	..	..	..	..
6.5 Tourism balance (inbound minus outbound tourism expenditure) over GDP		Percent	..	..	..	..	..
6.6 Tourism openness (inbound plus outbound tourism expenditure) over GDP		Percent	..	..	..	..	..
6.7 Tourism coverage (inbound over outbound tourism expenditure)		Percent	57.3	69.3	69.9	114.9	132.1
6.8 Inbound tourism expenditure over exports of goods		Percent	22.6	18.4	19.2	..	..
6.9 Inbound tourism expenditure over exports of services		Percent	6.0	6.2	6.1	..	..
6.10 Inbound tourism expenditure over exports of goods and services		Percent	4.8	4.6	4.6	..	..
6.11 Inbound tourism expenditure over current account credits		Percent	3.6	3.5	3.5	..	..
6.12 Outbound tourism expenditure over imports of goods		Percent	6.6	5.2	4.3	..	..
6.13 Outbound tourism expenditure over imports of services		Percent	22.7	20.5	17.4	..	..
6.14 Outbound tourism expenditure over imports of goods and		Percent	5.1	4.2	3.4	..	..
6.15 Outbound tourism expenditure over current account debits		Percent	4.7	3.9	3.2	..	..

118

DOMINICA

Cod.	Basic data and indicators	Notes	Units	2011	2012	2013	2014	2015
1.	**INBOUND TOURISM**							
	Data							
	Arrivals							
1.1	Total		('000)	418	348	311	370	358
1.2	♦ Overnight visitors (tourists)		('000)	76	79	78	82	75
1.3	♦ Same-day visitors (excursionists)		('000)	342	269	233	289	283
1.4	* of which, cruise passengers		('000)	341	267	231	287	281
	Arrivals by region							
1.5	Total		('000)	76	79	78	81	75
1.6	♦ Africa		('000)	0.2	0.3	0.4	0.5	0.6
1.7	♦ Americas		('000)	63	65	63	65	59
1.8	♦ East Asia and the Pacific		('000)	0.7	0.9	0.7	0.7	1.1
1.9	♦ Europe		('000)	12	13	14	15	14
1.10	♦ Middle East		('000)	..	..	..	..	0.1
1.11	♦ South Asia		('000)	0.1	0.2	0.1	0.1	0.1
1.12	♦ Other not classified		('000)	..	..	..	0.1	..
1.13	* of which, nationals residing abroad		('000)	..	..	..	..	..
	Arrivals by main purpose							
1.14	Total		('000)	76	79	78	82	75
1.15	♦ Personal		('000)	62	66	66	68	62
1.16	* holidays, leisure and recreation		('000)	62	57	57	58	51
1.17	* other personal purposes		('000)	0.2	8	9	10	11
1.18	♦ Business and professional		('000)	14	13	13	14	13
	Arrivals by mode of transport							
1.19	Total		('000)	76	79	78	82	75
1.20	♦ Air		('000)	48	47	47	51	44
1.21	♦ Water		('000)	28	32	31	31	31
1.22	♦ Land		('000)	..	..	..	..	..
1.23	* railway		('000)	..	..	..	..	..
1.24	* road		('000)	..	..	..	..	..
1.25	* others		('000)	..	..	..	..	..
	Accommodation							
	Total							
1.29	♦ Guests		('000)	76	79	78	82	75
1.30	♦ Overnights		('000)	..	..	..	..	..
	Hotels and similar establishments							
1.31	♦ Guests		('000)	31	33	34	36	32
1.32	♦ Overnights		('000)	..	..	..	..	..
	Expenditure							
1.33	Total		US$ Mn	..	..	..	..	..
1.34	♦ Travel		US$ Mn	106	76	103	127	128
1.35	♦ Passenger transport		US$ Mn	..	..	..	..	..
	Indicators							
1.39	Average size of travel party		Persons	..	..	..	..	..
	Average length of stay							
1.40	Total		Days	..	..	..	..	..
1.41	♦ For all commercial accommodation services	(1)	Nights	9.58	7.84	7.01	7.00	7.59
1.42	* of which, "hotels and similar establishments"		Nights	6.48	6.78	6.55	5.66	6.35
1.43	♦ For non commercial accommodation services		Days	11.50	10.41	9.71	10.33	9.82
1.44	Average expenditure per day		US$	146.3	..	..	..	..
3.	**OUTBOUND TOURISM**							
	Data							
	Expenditure							
3.4	Total		US$ Mn	..	..	..	..	..
3.5	♦ Travel		US$ Mn	12	12	12	12	13
3.6	♦ Passenger transport		US$ Mn	..	..	..	..	..
4.	**TOURISM INDUSTRIES**							
	Data							
	Number of establishments							
4.1	Total		Units	..	..	..	..	..
4.2	♦ Accommodation for visitors		Units	..	..	..	..	..
4.3	* of which, "hotels and similar establishments"		Units	114	117	119	120	117
4.4	♦ Food and beverage serving activities		Units	..	..	..	..	..
4.5	♦ Passenger transportation		Units	..	..	..	..	..
4.6	♦ Travel agencies and other reservation services activities		Units	..	..	..	..	..
4.7	♦ Other tourism industries		Units	..	..	..	..	..

DOMINICA

Cod.	Basic data and indicators	Notes	Units	2011	2012	2013	2014	2015
	Accommodation for visitors in hotels and similar establishments							
	Non-monetary data							
4.13	♦ Number of establishments		Units	114	117	119	120	117
4.14	♦ Number of rooms		Units	1,062	1,080	1,129	1,141	1,097
4.15	♦ Number of bed-places		Units	..	..	..	..	..
	Indicators							
4.16	Occupancy rate / rooms		Percent	..	43.90	48.50	51.80	50.60
4.17	Occupancy rate / bed-places		Percent	..	..	..	..	..
4.18	Average length of stay		Nights	9.60	8.51	9.09	8.87	8.52
4.19	Available capacity (bed-places per 1000 inhabitants)		Units	..	..	..	..	..
6.	**COMPLEMENTARY INDICATORS**							
	Demand							
6.1	Gross travel propensity		Units	..	..	..	..	..
6.2	(1.2 inbound tourists) / population		Units	1.06	1.10	1.08	1.13	1.03
	Macroeconomic indicators related to international tourism							
6.3	Inbound tourism expenditure over GDP		Percent	20.8	14.8	19.9	23.6	..
6.4	Outbound tourism expenditure over GDP		Percent	2.4	2.3	2.3	2.2	..
6.5	Tourism balance (inbound minus outbound tourism expenditure) over GDP		Percent	18.4	12.5	17.6	21.4	..
6.6	Tourism openness (inbound plus outbound tourism expenditure) over GDP		Percent	23.2	17.1	22.2	25.8	..
6.7	Tourism coverage (inbound over outbound tourism expenditure)		Percent	883.3	633.3	858.3	1,058.3	984.6
6.8	Inbound tourism expenditure over exports of goods		Percent	293.1	196.9	251.0	..	..
6.9	Inbound tourism expenditure over exports of services		Percent	68.5	62.5	80.1	..	..
6.10	Inbound tourism expenditure over exports of goods and services		Percent	55.5	47.4	60.7	..	..
6.11	Inbound tourism expenditure over current account credits		Percent	47.9	39.5	50.0	..	..
6.12	Outbound tourism expenditure over imports of goods		Percent	6.0	6.5	6.7	..	..
6.13	Outbound tourism expenditure over imports of services		Percent	18.2	17.7	17.0	..	..
6.14	Outbound tourism expenditure over imports of goods and		Percent	4.5	4.8	4.8	..	..
6.15	Outbound tourism expenditure over current account debits		Percent	4.3	4.5	4.5	..	..

DOMINICAN REPUBLIC

Cod.	Basic data and indicators	Notes	Units	2011	2012	2013	2014	2015
1.	**INBOUND TOURISM**							
	Data							
	Arrivals	(1)						
1.1	Total		('000)	4,654	4,901	5,114	5,629	6,150
1.2	♦ Overnight visitors (tourists)	(2)	('000)	4,306	4,563	4,690	5,141	5,600
1.3	♦ Same-day visitors (excursionists)		('000)	348	338	424	488	550
1.4	* of which, cruise passengers	(3)	('000)	348	338	424	488	550
	Arrivals by region	(2)						
1.5	Total		('000)	4,306	4,563	4,690	5,141	5,600
1.6	♦ Africa		('000)	..	..	..	..	..
1.7	♦ Americas		('000)	2,559	2,818	2,973	3,316	3,722
1.8	♦ East Asia and the Pacific		('000)	10	9	9	8	9
1.9	♦ Europe		('000)	1,132	1,095	1,082	1,138	1,101
1.10	♦ Middle East		('000)	..	..	..	..	..
1.11	♦ South Asia		('000)	1	1	1	1	1
1.12	♦ Other not classified		('000)	604	640	626	678	768
1.13	* of which, nationals residing abroad		('000)	603	639	625	677	767
	Arrivals by main purpose	(2)						
1.14	Total		('000)	4,306	4,563	4,690	5,141	5,600
1.15	♦ Personal		('000)	4,147	4,413	4,535	5,007	5,485
1.16	* holidays, leisure and recreation		('000)	3,958	4,218	4,321	4,704	5,103
1.17	* other personal purposes		('000)	189	195	214	303	382
1.18	♦ Business and professional		('000)	159	150	155	134	115
	Arrivals by mode of transport							
1.19	Total		('000)	4,654	4,901	5,114	5,629	6,150
1.20	♦ Air		('000)	4,306	4,563	4,690	5,141	5,600
1.21	♦ Water		('000)	348	338	424	488	550
1.22	♦ Land		('000)	..	..	..	..	..
1.23	* railway		('000)	..	..	..	..	..
1.24	* road		('000)	..	..	..	..	..
1.25	* others		('000)	..	..	..	..	..
	Accommodation							
	Hotels and similar establishments							
1.31	♦ Guests		('000)	..	..	..	..	..
1.32	♦ Overnights		('000)	29,420	29,657	30,970	33,710	37,144
	Expenditure							
1.33	Total		US$ Mn	..	..	..	..	..
1.34	♦ Travel		US$ Mn	4,391	4,687	5,064	5,630	6,118
1.35	♦ Passenger transport		US$ Mn	..	..	..	..	..
	Expenditure by main purpose of the trip							
1.36	Total		US$ Mn	4,391	4,687	5,064	5,630	6,118
1.37	♦ Personal		US$ Mn	4,332	4,626	5,002	5,575	6,062
1.38	♦ Business and professional		US$ Mn	59	61	62	55	56
	Indicators							
1.39	Average size of travel party		Persons	..	..	..	..	..
	Average length of stay							
1.40	Total		Days	..	..	..	..	..
1.41	♦ For all commercial accommodation services		Nights	8.91	8.48	8.46	8.37	8.32
1.42	* of which, "hotels and similar establishments"		Nights	..	..	..	..	..
1.43	♦ For non commercial accommodation services		Days	..	..	..	..	..
1.44	Average expenditure per day		US$	109.1	118.5	124.9	128.5	129.6
3.	**OUTBOUND TOURISM**							
	Data							
	Departures							
3.1	Total		('000)	..	..	..	..	..
3.2	♦ Overnight visitors (tourists)		('000)	408	418	392	427	478
3.3	♦ Same-day visitors (excursionists)		('000)	..	..	..	..	..
	Expenditure							
3.4	Total		US$ Mn	689	690	712	727	803
3.5	♦ Travel		US$ Mn	396	399	378	417	463
3.6	♦ Passenger transport		US$ Mn	293	291	334	310	340
	Indicators							
3.10	Average length of stay		Days	13.31	13.56	11.94	10.95	11.68
3.11	Average expenditure per day		US$	64.6	65.4	69.3	76.9	75.3

DOMINICAN REPUBLIC

Cod. Basic data and indicators	Notes	Units	2011	2012	2013	2014	2015
4. TOURISM INDUSTRIES							
Data							
Number of establishments							
4.1 Total		Units	..	..	..	..	..
4.2 ♦ Accommodation for visitors		Units	..	..	..	..	..
4.3 * of which, "hotels and similar establishments"		Units	690	690	697	697	724
4.4 ♦ Food and beverage serving activities		Units	..	..	..	..	..
4.5 ♦ Passenger transportation		Units	..	..	..	..	..
4.6 ♦ Travel agencies and other reservation services activities		Units	123	172	194	217	231
4.7 ♦ Other tourism industries		Units	..	..	..	..	..
Accommodation for visitors in hotels and similar establishments							
Monetary data							
4.8 ♦ Output		US$ Mn	..	..	..	..	..
4.9 ♦ Intermediate consumption		US$ Mn	..	..	..	..	..
4.10 ♦ Gross value added		US$ Mn	4,203.2	4,400.3	4,480.0	4,768.1	5,210.0
4.11 ♦ Compensation of employees		US$ Mn	..	..	..	..	..
4.12 ♦ Gross fixed capital formation		US$ Mn	..	..	..	..	..
Non-monetary data							
4.13 ♦ Number of establishments		Units	690	690	697	697	724
4.14 ♦ Number of rooms	(4)	Units	66,790	66,054	68,542	69,607	70,030
4.15 ♦ Number of bed-places	(4)	Units	200,370	198,162	205,626	208,821	210,090
Indicators							
4.16 Occupancy rate / rooms		Percent	69.30	70.30	71.70	74.80	75.50
4.17 Occupancy rate / bed-places		Percent	..	..	..	..	..
4.18 Average length of stay		Nights	8.91	8.52	8.46	8.37	8.32
4.19 Available capacity (bed-places per 1000 inhabitants)		Units	19.98	19.51	20.00	20.07	19.95
5. EMPLOYMENT							
Data							
Number of employees by tourism industries							
5.1 Total		('000)	194.8	201.2	216.5	219.9	254.2
5.2 ♦ Accommodation services for visitors (hotels and similar establishments)		('000)	55.7	57.5	61.8	62.2	71.7
5.3 ♦ Other accommodation services		('000)	..	..	..	..	..
5.4 ♦ Food and beverage serving activities		('000)	..	..	..	..	..
5.5 ♦ Passenger transportation		('000)	..	..	..	..	..
5.6 ♦ Travel agencies and other reservation services activities		('000)	..	..	..	..	..
5.7 ♦ Other tourism industries		('000)	139.1	143.7	154.7	157.7	182.5
6. COMPLEMENTARY INDICATORS							
Demand							
6.1 Gross travel propensity		Units	4.5	4.2	4.2	4.6	4.8
6.2 (1.2 inbound tourists) / population		Units	0.43	0.45	0.46	0.49	0.53
Macroeconomic indicators related to international tourism							
6.3 Inbound tourism expenditure over GDP		Percent	7.6	7.8	8.3	8.8	9.1
6.4 Outbound tourism expenditure over GDP		Percent	1.2	1.1	1.2	1.1	1.2
6.5 Tourism balance (inbound minus outbound tourism expenditure) over GDP		Percent	6.4	6.7	7.1	7.7	7.9
6.6 Tourism openness (inbound plus outbound tourism expenditure) over GDP		Percent	8.8	8.9	9.5	9.9	10.3
6.7 Tourism coverage (inbound over outbound tourism expenditure)		Percent	637.3	679.3	711.2	774.4	761.9
6.8 Inbound tourism expenditure over exports of goods		Percent	52.5	52.5	53.7	56.9	64.2
6.9 Inbound tourism expenditure over exports of services		Percent	75.4	76.3	78.5	80.1	81.2
6.10 Inbound tourism expenditure over exports of goods and services		Percent	31.0	31.1	31.9	33.3	35.9
6.11 Inbound tourism expenditure over current account credits		Percent	22.5	22.9	23.6	24.8	26.4
6.12 Outbound tourism expenditure over imports of goods		Percent	4.0	3.9	4.2	4.2	4.8
6.13 Outbound tourism expenditure over imports of services		Percent	23.8	23.5	25.8	25.6	25.6
6.14 Outbound tourism expenditure over imports of goods and		Percent	3.4	3.3	3.6	3.6	4.0
6.15 Outbound tourism expenditure over current account debits		Percent	3.2	3.1	3.4	3.4	3.7

ECUADOR

Cod. Basic data and indicators	Notes	Units	2011	2012	2013	2014	2015
1. INBOUND TOURISM							
Data							
Arrivals							
1.1 Total	(1)(2)	('000)	1,141	1,272	1,364	1,557	1,543
1.2 ♦ Overnight visitors (tourists)		('000)	..	..	..	..	..
1.3 ♦ Same-day visitors (excursionists)		('000)	..	..	..	..	..
1.4 * of which, cruise passengers		('000)	..	..	..	..	..
Arrivals by region	(1)(2)						
1.5 Total		('000)	1,141	1,272	1,364	1,557	1,543
1.6 ♦ Africa		('000)	2	3	5	4	6
1.7 ♦ Americas		('000)	885	996	1,086	1,215	1,201
1.8 ♦ East Asia and the Pacific		('000)	41	49	44	71	76
1.9 ♦ Europe		('000)	207	218	218	248	249
1.10 ♦ Middle East		('000)	1	1	1	1	1
1.11 ♦ South Asia		('000)	4	5	4	9	11
1.12 ♦ Other not classified		('000)	..	..	7	8	..
1.13 * of which, nationals residing abroad		('000)	..	..	..	..	..
Arrivals by main purpose	(1)(2)						
1.14 Total		('000)	1,141	1,272	1,364	1,557	1,543
1.15 ♦ Personal		('000)	858	1,016	1,195	1,364	1,279
1.16 * holidays, leisure and recreation		('000)	858	1,016	1,195	1,364	1,279
1.17 * other personal purposes		('000)	..	..	..	..	..
1.18 ♦ Business and professional		('000)	283	256	169	193	264
Arrivals by mode of transport	(1)(2)						
1.19 Total		('000)	1,141	1,272	1,364	1,557	1,543
1.20 ♦ Air		('000)	783	848	959	1,041	1,019
1.21 ♦ Water		('000)	21	27	12	64	66
1.22 ♦ Land		('000)	337	396	393	452	459
1.23 * railway		('000)	..	..	..	..	..
1.24 * road		('000)	337	396	393	452	459
1.25 * others		('000)	..	..	..	..	..
Arrivals by form of organization of the trip							
1.26 Total		('000)	1,141	1,252	1,364	1,557	1,543
1.27 ♦ Package tour		('000)	46	57	68	254	260
1.28 ♦ Other forms		('000)	1,095	1,195	1,296	1,303	1,283
Accommodation							
Total							
1.29 ♦ Guests		('000)	1,100	1,249	1,310	1,496	1,542
1.30 ♦ Overnights		('000)	9,898	9,989	10,483	11,967	12,337
Hotels and similar establishments							
1.31 ♦ Guests		('000)	693	929	861	983	1,154
1.32 ♦ Overnights		('000)	5,543	5,573	5,165	5,896	8,079
Expenditure							
1.33 Total		US$ Mn	849	1,039	1,251	1,487	1,557
1.34 ♦ Travel		US$ Mn	843	1,033	1,246	1,482	1,551
1.35 ♦ Passenger transport		US$ Mn	6	6	5	5	6
Expenditure by main purpose of the trip							
1.36 Total		US$ Mn	843	1,033	1,246	1,483	1,552
1.37 ♦ Personal		US$ Mn	626	766	925	1,100	1,151
1.38 ♦ Business and professional		US$ Mn	217	267	321	383	401
Indicators							
1.39 Average size of travel party		Persons	3.0	3.0	3.0	3.0	3.0
Average length of stay							
1.40 Total		Days	..	..	..	..	..
1.41 ♦ For all commercial accommodation services		Nights	8.00	7.00	7.00	7.00	7.00
1.42 * of which, "hotels and similar establishments"		Nights	..	..	..	..	..
1.43 ♦ For non commercial accommodation services		Days	9.00	9.00	9.00	9.00	8.00
1.44 Average expenditure per day		US$	82.7	90.7	101.9	106.1	126.2
2. DOMESTIC TOURISM							
Data							
Trips							
2.1 Total		('000)	11,337	11,598	11,786	11,974	12,162
2.2 ♦ Overnight visitors (tourists)		('000)	7,389	7,906	7,652	7,982	8,629
2.3 ♦ Same-day visitors (excursionists)		('000)	3,948	3,692	4,134	3,992	3,533
Trips by main purpose							
2.4 Total		('000)	11,337	11,598	11,786	11,974	12,162
2.5 ♦ Personal		('000)	10,882	11,156	11,336	11,509	11,698
2.6 * holidays, leisure and recreation		('000)	3,663	4,519	4,592	4,400	4,558
2.7 * other personal purposes		('000)	7,219	6,637	6,744	7,109	7,140
2.8 ♦ Business and professional		('000)	455	442	450	465	464

ECUADOR

Cod.	Basic data and indicators	Notes	Units	2011	2012	2013	2014	2015
	Trips by mode of transport							
2.9	Total		('000)	11,337	11,598	11,786	11,974	12,163
2.10	♦ Air		('000)	119	145	148	142	140
2.11	♦ Water		('000)	3	7	7	6	12
2.12	♦ Land		('000)	11,215	11,446	11,631	11,826	12,011
2.13	* railway		('000)	1	2	2	2	1
2.14	* road		('000)	10,685	10,841	11,017	11,224	11,344
2.15	* others		('000)	529	603	612	600	666
	Trips by form of organization							
2.16	Total		('000)	11,337	11,598	11,786	11,974	12,163
2.17	♦ Package tour		('000)	69	74	75	74	84
2.18	♦ Other forms		('000)	11,268	11,524	11,711	11,900	12,079
	Accommodation							
	Total							
2.19	♦ Guests		('000)	7,389	7,906	7,652	7,982	8,629
2.20	♦ Overnights		('000)	21,586	22,955	22,216	23,223	25,064
	Hotels and similar establishments							
2.21	♦ Guests		('000)	1,718	1,708	1,652	1,768	1,856
2.22	♦ Overnights		('000)	4,133	3,939	3,812	4,084	4,283
	Indicators							
2.23	Average size of travel party		Persons	3.0	3.0	3.0	3.0	3.0
	Average length of stay							
2.24	Total		Days	3.00	3.00	3.00	3.00	3.00
2.25	♦ For all commercial accommodation services		Nights	..	..	..	..	..
2.26	* of which, "hotels and similar establishments"		Nights	..	..	..	..	..
2.27	♦ For non commercial accommodation services		Days	..	..	..	..	..
2.28	Average expenditure per day		US$	..	..	..	..	..
3.	**OUTBOUND TOURISM**							
	Data							
	Departures							
3.1	Total		('000)	..	..	..	..	..
3.2	♦ Overnight visitors (tourists)		('000)	1,022	1,022	1,138	1,278	1,398
3.3	♦ Same-day visitors (excursionists)		('000)	..	..	..	..	..
	Expenditure							
3.4	Total		US$ Mn	917	944	987	1,021	994
3.5	♦ Travel		US$ Mn	594	611	621	635	639
3.6	♦ Passenger transport		US$ Mn	323	333	366	386	355
	Expenditure by main purpose of the trip							
3.7	Total		US$ Mn	594	611	621	634	638
3.8	♦ Personal		US$ Mn	433	445	453	462	465
3.9	♦ Business and professional		US$ Mn	161	166	168	172	173
4.	**TOURISM INDUSTRIES**							
	Data							
	Number of establishments							
4.1	Total	(2)	Units	18,678	19,729	21,069	23,484	25,672
4.2	♦ Accommodation for visitors		Units	4,032	4,334	4,672	5,175	5,488
4.3	* of which, "hotels and similar establishments"		Units	2,925	3,166	3,423	3,750	4,066
4.4	♦ Food and beverage serving activities		Units	12,496	13,261	14,057	15,783	17,325
4.5	♦ Passenger transportation		Units	353	362	378	401	444
4.6	♦ Travel agencies and other reservation services activities		Units	1,462	1,440	1,564	1,656	2,135
4.7	♦ Other tourism industries		Units	335	332	398	469	280
	Accommodation for visitors in hotels and similar establishments							
	Monetary data							
4.8	♦ Output		US$ Mn	266.3	310.1	..	..	..
4.9	♦ Intermediate consumption		US$ Mn	127.4	147.8	..	..	..
4.10	♦ Gross value added		US$ Mn	138.9	162.3	..	..	..
4.11	♦ Compensation of employees		US$ Mn	..	..	..	..	..
4.12	♦ Gross fixed capital formation		US$ Mn	..	..	..	..	..
	Non-monetary data							
4.13	♦ Number of establishments		Units	2,925	3,166	3,423	3,750	4,066
4.14	♦ Number of rooms		Units	61,524	64,653	69,628	72,958	77,418
4.15	♦ Number of bed-places		Units	137,780	146,480	157,591	163,469	175,236
	Indicators							
4.16	Occupancy rate / rooms		Percent	..	..	..	..	..
4.17	Occupancy rate / bed-places		Percent	..	..	..	..	..
4.18	Average length of stay		Nights	..	..	..	..	..
4.19	Available capacity (bed-places per 1000 inhabitants)		Units	9.08	9.50	10.06	10.28	10.85

124

ECUADOR

Cod.	Basic data and indicators	Notes	Units	2011	2012	2013	2014	2015
	Travel agencies and other reservation service activities							
	Monetary data							
4.20	♦ Output		US$ Mn	455.0	495.9	..	..	..
4.21	♦ Intermediate consumption		US$ Mn	121.0	135.6	..	..	..
4.22	♦ Gross value added		US$ Mn	333.9	360.3	..	..	..
4.23	♦ Compensation of employees		US$ Mn	..	..	..	..	..
4.24	♦ Gross fixed capital formation		US$ Mn	..	..	..	..	..
	Non-monetary data							
	♦ Domestic trips							
4.25	* with package tour		Percent	0.6	0.6	0.6	0.6	0.6
4.26	* without package tour		Percent	99.4	99.4	99.4	99.4	99.4
	♦ Inbound trips							
4.27	* with package tour		Percent	20.8	20.3	16.3	16.3	16.9
4.28	* without package tour		Percent	79.2	79.7	83.7	83.7	83.1
	♦ Outbound trips							
4.29	* with package tour		Percent	5.1	8.6	8.6	8.6	10.5
4.30	* without package tour		Percent	94.9	91.4	91.4	91.4	89.5
5.	**EMPLOYMENT**							
	Data							
	Number of employees by tourism industries							
5.1	Total	(2)	('000)	102.4	106.3	114.1	122.1	135.0
5.2	♦ Accommodation services for visitors (hotels and similar establishments)		('000)	28.1	29.6	31.9	33.5	35.5
5.3	♦ Other accommodation services		('000)	..	..	..	..	..
5.4	♦ Food and beverage serving activities		('000)	61.6	65.1	69.8	75.6	85.4
5.5	♦ Passenger transportation		('000)	2.7	2.7	3.0	2.9	3.0
5.6	♦ Travel agencies and other reservation services activities		('000)	7.6	7.8	8.2	8.7	9.5
5.7	♦ Other tourism industries		('000)	2.4	1.1	1.2	1.4	1.6
6.	**COMPLEMENTARY INDICATORS**							
	Demand							
6.1	Gross travel propensity		Units	..	..	..	..	..
6.2	(1.1 inbound visitors + 2.1 domestic visitors) / population		Units	0.82	0.83	0.84	0.85	0.85
	Macroeconomic indicators related to international tourism							
6.3	Inbound tourism expenditure over GDP		Percent	1.1	1.2	1.3	1.5	1.5
6.4	Outbound tourism expenditure over GDP		Percent	1.2	1.1	1.0	1.0	1.0
6.5	Tourism balance (inbound minus outbound tourism expenditure) over GDP		Percent	-0.1	0.1	0.3	0.5	0.5
6.6	Tourism openness (inbound plus outbound tourism expenditure) over GDP		Percent	2.3	2.3	2.3	2.5	2.5
6.7	Tourism coverage (inbound over outbound tourism expenditure)		Percent	92.6	110.1	126.7	145.6	156.6
6.8	Inbound tourism expenditure over exports of goods		Percent	3.7	4.2	4.9	5.6	8.2
6.9	Inbound tourism expenditure over exports of services		Percent	53.3	57.3	61.2	63.4	66.1
6.10	Inbound tourism expenditure over exports of goods and services		Percent	3.4	3.9	4.5	5.1	7.3
6.11	Inbound tourism expenditure over current account credits		Percent	3.1	3.6	4.1	4.7	6.4
6.12	Outbound tourism expenditure over imports of goods		Percent	3.9	3.9	3.8	3.8	4.8
6.13	Outbound tourism expenditure over imports of services		Percent	29.1	29.5	28.5	28.7	30.7
6.14	Outbound tourism expenditure over imports of goods and		Percent	3.5	3.4	3.3	3.4	4.2
6.15	Outbound tourism expenditure over current account debits		Percent	3.4	3.4	3.3	3.3	4.0

EGYPT

Cod.	Basic data and indicators	Notes	Units	2011	2012	2013	2014	2015
1.	**INBOUND TOURISM**							
	Data							
	Arrivals							
1.1	Total		('000)	9,845	11,532	9,464	9,878	9,328
1.2	♦ Overnight visitors (tourists)		('000)	9,497	11,196	9,174	9,628	9,139
1.3	♦ Same-day visitors (excursionists)		('000)	348	336	290	249	189
1.4	* of which, cruise passengers		('000)	..	..	..	..	..
	Arrivals by region							
1.5	Total		('000)	9,845	11,532	9,464	9,878	9,328
1.6	♦ Africa		('000)	435	428	399	399	418
1.7	♦ Americas		('000)	287	285	240	244	294
1.8	♦ East Asia and the Pacific		('000)	278	305	248	213	280
1.9	♦ Europe		('000)	7,211	8,416	6,976	7,578	6,794
1.10	♦ Middle East		('000)	1,511	1,966	1,494	1,343	1,422
1.11	♦ South Asia		('000)	102	108	84	76	94
1.12	♦ Other not classified		('000)	21	25	23	25	25
1.13	* of which, nationals residing abroad		('000)	..	..	..	..	..
	Arrivals by main purpose							
1.14	Total		('000)	9,497	11,196	9,174	9,628	9,139
1.15	♦ Personal		('000)	9,411	11,095	9,025	9,484	9,057
1.16	* holidays, leisure and recreation		('000)	9,335	11,005	8,943	9,407	8,984
1.17	* other personal purposes		('000)	76	90	82	77	73
1.18	♦ Business and professional		('000)	86	101	149	144	82
	Arrivals by mode of transport							
1.19	Total		('000)	9,845	11,532	9,464	9,878	9,328
1.20	♦ Air		('000)	8,159	9,845	8,237	9,010	8,521
1.21	♦ Water		('000)	185	235	233	126	100
1.22	♦ Land		('000)	1,501	1,452	994	742	706
1.23	* railway		('000)	..	..	..	..	..
1.24	* road		('000)	1,501	1,452	994	742	706
1.25	* others		('000)	..	..	..	..	..
	Arrivals by form of organization of the trip							
1.26	Total		('000)	9,845	11,532	9,464	9,878	9,327
1.27	♦ Package tour		('000)	7,709	7,999	7,002	7,486	7,798
1.28	♦ Other forms		('000)	2,136	3,533	2,462	2,392	1,529
	Accommodation							
	Hotels and similar establishments							
1.31	♦ Guests		('000)	..	..	..	..	..
1.32	♦ Overnights		('000)	114,214	137,819	94,410	97,256	84,128
	Expenditure							
1.33	Total		US$ Mn	9,333	10,823	6,747	7,979	6,897
1.34	♦ Travel		US$ Mn	8,707	9,940	6,047	7,208	6,065
1.35	♦ Passenger transport		US$ Mn	626	883	700	771	832
	Indicators							
1.39	Average size of travel party		Persons	..	..	..	..	..
	Average length of stay							
1.40	Total		Days	..	..	..	..	..
1.41	♦ For all commercial accommodation services		Nights	11.60	12.00	10.00	9.50	9.00
1.42	* of which, "hotels and similar establishments"		Nights	..	..	..	..	..
1.43	♦ For non commercial accommodation services		Days	..	..	..	..	..
1.44	Average expenditure per day		US$	76.2	72.2	64.0	74.4	72.1
2.	**DOMESTIC TOURISM**							
	Data							
	Trips							
2.1	Total		('000)	20,630	20,935	24,468	25,077	25,697
2.2	♦ Overnight visitors (tourists)		('000)	8,180	8,300	9,698	9,931	10,176
2.3	♦ Same-day visitors (excursionists)		('000)	12,450	12,635	14,770	15,147	15,521
	Trips by main purpose							
2.4	Total		('000)	22,630	20,935	24,468	25,077	25,697
2.5	♦ Personal		('000)	22,291	20,621	24,101	24,700	25,312
2.6	* holidays, leisure and recreation		('000)	5,328	4,928	5,750	5,893	6,039
2.7	* other personal purposes		('000)	16,963	15,693	18,351	18,807	19,273
2.8	♦ Business and professional		('000)	339	314	367	377	385

EGYPT

Cod.	Basic data and indicators	Notes	Units	2011	2012	2013	2014	2015
	Trips by mode of transport							
2.9	Total		('000)	20,630	20,935	24,468	25,077	25,697
2.10	♦ Air		('000)	20	21	25	26	26
2.11	♦ Water		('000)	42	42	49	50	51
2.12	♦ Land		('000)	20,568	20,872	24,394	25,001	25,620
2.13	* railway		('000)	1,173	1,190	1,395	1,430	1,465
2.14	* road		('000)	19,128	19,411	22,681	23,245	23,821
2.15	* others		('000)	267	271	318	326	334
	Trips by form of organization							
2.16	Total		('000)	20,630	20,935	24,468	25,077	25,697
2.17	♦ Package tour		('000)	1,052	1,068	1,248	1,279	1,311
2.18	♦ Other forms		('000)	19,578	19,867	23,220	23,798	24,386
	Indicators							
2.23	Average size of travel party		Persons	..	..	..	..	..
	Average length of stay							
2.24	Total		Days	..	..	..	..	..
2.25	♦ For all commercial accommodation services		Nights	..	..	..	..	..
2.26	* of which, "hotels and similar establishments"		Nights	2.40	2.40	2.40	2.40	2.40
2.27	♦ For non commercial accommodation services		Days	..	..	..	..	..
2.28	Average expenditure per day		US$	72.1	70.6	64.0	74.4	..

3. OUTBOUND TOURISM

	Data							
	Departures							
3.1	Total		('000)	4,863	5,678	5,782	6,180	..
3.2	♦ Overnight visitors (tourists)		('000)	..	..	..	..	..
3.3	♦ Same-day visitors (excursionists)		('000)	..	..	..	..	..
	Expenditure							
3.4	Total		US$ Mn	2,575	3,037	3,261	3,486	3,636
3.5	♦ Travel		US$ Mn	2,203	2,618	3,014	3,140	3,442
3.6	♦ Passenger transport		US$ Mn	372	419	247	346	194
	Expenditure by main purpose of the trip							
3.7	Total		US$ Mn	2,202	2,618	3,014	3,140	3,442
3.8	♦ Personal		US$ Mn	2,100	2,529	2,920	3,045	3,315
3.9	♦ Business and professional		US$ Mn	102	89	93	95	127

4. TOURISM INDUSTRIES

	Data							
	Number of establishments							
4.1	Total		Units	..	..	..	..	..
4.2	♦ Accommodation for visitors		Units	..	..	..	..	..
4.3	* of which, "hotels and similar establishments"		Units	1,319	1,267	1,219	1,261	1,267
4.4	♦ Food and beverage serving activities		Units	..	..	..	..	..
4.5	♦ Passenger transportation		Units	..	..	..	..	..
4.6	♦ Travel agencies and other reservation services activities		Units	..	..	..	..	..
4.7	♦ Other tourism industries		Units	..	..	..	..	..
	Accommodation for visitors in hotels and similar establishments							
	Non-monetary data							
4.13	♦ Number of establishments		Units	1,319	1,267	1,219	1,261	1,267
4.14	♦ Number of rooms		Units	209,111	206,054	199,739	199,753	206,054
4.15	♦ Number of bed-places		Units	418,222	412,108	399,478	399,506	412,108
	Indicators							
4.16	Occupancy rate / rooms		Percent	45.00	40.00	30.60	30.90	31.00
4.17	Occupancy rate / bed-places		Percent	..	..	..	..	..
4.18	Average length of stay		Nights	11.60	12.00	10.00	10.00	9.00
4.19	Available capacity (bed-places per 1000 inhabitants)		Units	4.99	4.81	4.56	4.46	4.50
	Travel agencies and other reservation service activities							
	Non-monetary data							
	♦ Domestic trips							
4.25	* with package tour		Percent	5.1	5.1	5.1	5.1	5.1
4.26	* without package tour		Percent	94.1	94.9	94.9	94.9	94.9
	♦ Inbound trips							
4.27	* with package tour		Percent	78.3	69.4	74.0	82.9	83.6
4.28	* without package tour		Percent	21.7	30.6	26.0	17.1	16.4
	♦ Outbound trips							
4.29	* with package tour		Percent	82.0	82.0	82.0	82.0	82.0
4.30	* without package tour		Percent	18.0	18.0	18.0	18.0	18.0

EGYPT

Cod.	Basic data and indicators	Notes	Units	2011	2012	2013	2014	2015
5.	**EMPLOYMENT**							
	Data							
	Number of employees by tourism industries							
5.1	Total		('000)	1,655.0	1,706.7	1,698.8	1,752.0	..
5.2	♦ Accommodation services for visitors (hotels and similar establishments)		('000)	137.7	153.0	133.4	128.0	..
5.3	♦ Other accommodation services		('000)	9.5	13.9	23.5	28.0	..
5.4	♦ Food and beverage serving activities		('000)	326.4	366.0	382.4	408.0	..
5.5	♦ Passenger transportation		('000)	1,017.6	1,028.8	1,022.7	1,069.0	..
5.6	♦ Travel agencies and other reservation services activities		('000)	84.4	70.1	58.2	48.0	..
5.7	♦ Other tourism industries		('000)	79.4	74.9	78.6	71.0	..
	Number of jobs by status in employment							
5.8	Total		('000)	1,655.0	1,706.7	1,698.8	1,752.0	..
5.9	♦ Employees		('000)	1,179.5	1,206.0	1,143.3	1,117.0	..
5.10	♦ Self employed		('000)	475.5	500.7	555.5	635.0	..
	Indicators							
	Number of full-time equivalent jobs by status in employment							
5.11	Total		('000)	1,755.7	1,858.7	1,857.6	1,929.0	..
5.12	♦ Employees		('000)	1,241.7	1,302.7	1,247.6	1,226.0	..
5.13	* male		('000)	1,210.2	1,271.0	1,210.2	1,201.0	..
5.14	* female		('000)	31.5	31.7	37.4	25.0	..
5.15	♦ Self employed		('000)	514.0	556.1	610.0	703.0	..
5.16	* male		('000)	506.4	550.7	602.9	687.0	..
5.17	* female		('000)	7.6	5.4	7.1	16.0	..
6.	**COMPLEMENTARY INDICATORS**							
	Demand							
6.1	Gross travel propensity		Units	..	..	..	..	..
6.2	(1.2 inbound tourists + 2.2 domestic tourists) / population		Units	0.21	0.23	0.22	0.22	0.21
	Macroeconomic indicators related to international tourism							
6.3	Inbound tourism expenditure over GDP		Percent	4.0	4.3	2.5	..	..
6.4	Outbound tourism expenditure over GDP		Percent	1.1	1.2	1.2	..	..
6.5	Tourism balance (inbound minus outbound tourism expenditure) over GDP		Percent	2.9	3.1	1.3	..	..
6.6	Tourism openness (inbound plus outbound tourism expenditure) over GDP		Percent	5.1	5.5	3.7	..	..
6.7	Tourism coverage (inbound over outbound tourism expenditure)		Percent	362.4	356.4	206.9	228.9	189.7
6.8	Inbound tourism expenditure over exports of goods		Percent	33.4	40.3	25.4	31.7	..
6.9	Inbound tourism expenditure over exports of services		Percent	48.8	49.7	36.9	36.4	..
6.10	Inbound tourism expenditure over exports of goods and services		Percent	19.8	22.3	15.1	16.9	..
6.11	Inbound tourism expenditure over current account credits		Percent	14.8	15.7	9.7	10.6	..
6.12	Outbound tourism expenditure over imports of goods		Percent	5.4	5.8	6.7	6.2	..
6.13	Outbound tourism expenditure over imports of services		Percent	18.3	18.5	19.9	19.9	..
6.14	Outbound tourism expenditure over imports of goods and		Percent	4.2	4.4	5.0	4.7	..
6.15	Outbound tourism expenditure over current account debits		Percent	4.2	4.4	4.9	4.7	..

EL SALVADOR

Cod.	Basic data and indicators	Notes	Units	2011	2012	2013	2014	2015
1.	**INBOUND TOURISM**							
	Data							
	Arrivals							
1.1	Total		('000)	1,634	1,738	1,822	1,886	1,973
1.2	♦ Overnight visitors (tourists)		('000)	1,184	1,255	1,283	1,345	1,402
1.3	♦ Same-day visitors (excursionists)		('000)	450	483	539	541	571
1.4	* of which, cruise passengers		('000)	1	2	2	2	..
	Arrivals by region							
1.5	Total		('000)	1,184	1,255	1,283	1,345	1,402
1.6	♦ Africa		('000)	..	1	1	0.5	0.4
1.7	♦ Americas		('000)	1,140	1,220	1,242	1,305	1,361
1.8	♦ East Asia and the Pacific		('000)	10	8	8	9	9
1.9	♦ Europe		('000)	34	26	32	30	31
1.10	♦ Middle East		('000)	..	..	..	..	..
1.11	♦ South Asia		('000)	..	..	..	..	0.9
1.12	♦ Other not classified		('000)	..	..	..	..	..
1.13	* of which, nationals residing abroad		('000)	..	..	..	..	..
	Arrivals by main purpose							
1.14	Total		('000)	1,184	1,255	1,283	1,345	1,402
1.15	♦ Personal		('000)	1,041	1,100	1,136	1,188	1,236
1.16	* holidays, leisure and recreation		('000)	566	501	493	513	605
1.17	* other personal purposes		('000)	475	599	643	674	631
1.18	♦ Business and professional		('000)	143	155	146	158	165
	Arrivals by mode of transport							
1.19	Total		('000)	1,184	1,255	1,283	1,345	1,402
1.20	♦ Air		('000)	470	541	589	591	599
1.21	♦ Water		('000)	..	..	..	..	..
1.22	♦ Land		('000)	714	714	694	754	803
1.23	* railway		('000)	..	..	..	..	..
1.24	* road		('000)	714	714	694	754	803
1.25	* others		('000)	..	..	..	..	..
	Accommodation							
	Total							
1.29	♦ Guests		('000)	..	..	..	..	..
1.30	♦ Overnights	(1)	('000)	6,405	7,517	7,593	9,564	9,559
	Hotels and similar establishments							
1.31	♦ Guests		('000)	642	600	616	687	712
1.32	♦ Overnights		('000)	2,694	2,368	2,864	3,844	3,586
	Expenditure							
1.33	Total		US$ Mn	729	900	1,054	1,285	1,203
1.34	♦ Travel		US$ Mn	415	558	621	821	817
1.35	♦ Passenger transport		US$ Mn	314	342	433	464	386
	Expenditure by main purpose of the trip							
1.36	Total		US$ Mn	414	558	621	822	817
1.37	♦ Personal		US$ Mn	375	511	577	800	774
1.38	♦ Business and professional		US$ Mn	39	47	44	22	43
	Indicators							
1.39	Average size of travel party		Persons	..	..	..	..	..
	Average length of stay							
1.40	Total		Days	..	..	..	..	..
1.41	♦ For all commercial accommodation services		Nights	5.40	6.00	6.50	7.10	6.80
1.42	* of which, "hotels and similar establishments"		Nights	..	..	..	..	..
1.43	♦ For non commercial accommodation services		Days	..	..	..	..	..
1.44	Average expenditure per day		US$	94.1	98.5	103.2	105.7	112.9
3.	**OUTBOUND TOURISM**							
	Data							
	Departures							
3.1	Total		('000)	1,469	1,462	1,515	1,515	1,618
3.2	♦ Overnight visitors (tourists)		('000)	1,160	1,163	1,166	1,163	1,250
3.3	♦ Same-day visitors (excursionists)		('000)	309	299	348	352	367
	Expenditure							
3.4	Total		US$ Mn	244	287	270	277	332
3.5	♦ Travel		US$ Mn	203	261	242	248	294
3.6	♦ Passenger transport		US$ Mn	41	26	28	29	38
	Expenditure by main purpose of the trip							
3.7	Total		US$ Mn	203	261	242	248	294
3.8	♦ Personal		US$ Mn	191	252	236	244	289
3.9	♦ Business and professional		US$ Mn	12	9	6	4	5

EL SALVADOR

Cod.	Basic data and indicators	Notes	Units	2011	2012	2013	2014	2015
4.	**TOURISM INDUSTRIES**							
	Data							
	Number of establishments							
4.1	Total		Units	..	..	..	..	..
4.2	♦ Accommodation for visitors		Units	..	..	..	..	..
4.3	* of which, "hotels and similar establishments"		Units	402	408	408	465	465
4.4	♦ Food and beverage serving activities		Units	..	..	..	..	..
4.5	♦ Passenger transportation		Units	..	..	..	..	..
4.6	♦ Travel agencies and other reservation services activities		Units	10	10	29	29	..
4.7	♦ Other tourism industries		Units	..	..	..	..	..
	Accommodation for visitors in hotels and similar establishments							
	Non-monetary data							
4.13	♦ Number of establishments		Units	402	408	408	465	465
4.14	♦ Number of rooms		Units	8,373	8,805	8,805	9,261	9,261
4.15	♦ Number of bed-places		Units	14,286	15,862	15,862	16,660	16,660
	Indicators							
4.16	Occupancy rate / rooms		Percent	..	..	..	..	..
4.17	Occupancy rate / bed-places		Percent	65.33	66.30	69.73	65.06	65.67
4.18	Average length of stay		Nights	5.40	6.00	6.50	7.10	6.80
4.19	Available capacity (bed-places per 1000 inhabitants)		Units	2.36	2.61	2.60	2.73	2.72
5.	**EMPLOYMENT**							
	Data							
	Number of employees by tourism industries							
5.1	Total		('000)	42.7	44.6	45.6	48.4	48.7
5.2	♦ Accommodation services for visitors (hotels and similar establishments)		('000)	5.5	4.6	4.6	4.7	5.4
5.3	♦ Other accommodation services		('000)	..	..	..	..	..
5.4	♦ Food and beverage serving activities		('000)	17.3	19.0	19.8	20.8	21.5
5.5	♦ Passenger transportation		('000)	7.7	8.3	13.5	13.7	13.6
5.6	♦ Travel agencies and other reservation services activities		('000)	..	..	..	..	..
5.7	♦ Other tourism industries		('000)	12.2	12.7	7.7	9.2	8.2
6.	**COMPLEMENTARY INDICATORS**							
	Demand							
6.1	Gross travel propensity		Units	..	..	..	..	..
6.2	(1.2 inbound tourists) / population		Units	0.20	0.21	0.21	0.22	0.23
	Macroeconomic indicators related to international tourism							
6.3	Inbound tourism expenditure over GDP		Percent	3.2	3.8	4.3	5.1	4.7
6.4	Outbound tourism expenditure over GDP		Percent	1.1	1.2	1.1	1.1	1.3
6.5	Tourism balance (inbound minus outbound tourism expenditure) over GDP		Percent	2.1	2.6	3.2	4.0	3.4
6.6	Tourism openness (inbound plus outbound tourism expenditure) over GDP		Percent	4.3	5.0	5.4	6.2	6.0
6.7	Tourism coverage (inbound over outbound tourism expenditure)		Percent	298.8	313.6	390.4	463.9	362.3
6.8	Inbound tourism expenditure over exports of goods		Percent	17.2	21.3	24.3	30.2	27.5
6.9	Inbound tourism expenditure over exports of services		Percent	44.6	48.2	50.5	57.7	51.6
6.10	Inbound tourism expenditure over exports of goods and services		Percent	12.4	14.8	16.4	19.8	17.9
6.11	Inbound tourism expenditure over current account credits		Percent	7.4	8.7	9.9	11.8	10.6
6.12	Outbound tourism expenditure over imports of goods		Percent	2.7	3.1	2.8	2.9	3.6
6.13	Outbound tourism expenditure over imports of services		Percent	20.6	21.5	18.4	18.6	21.5
6.14	Outbound tourism expenditure over imports of goods and		Percent	2.4	2.7	2.4	2.5	3.1
6.15	Outbound tourism expenditure over current account debits		Percent	2.4	2.7	2.4	2.5	3.0

ESTONIA

Cod.	Basic data and indicators	Notes	Units	2011	2012	2013	2014	2015
1.	**INBOUND TOURISM**							
	Data							
	Arrivals							
1.1	Total	(1)(2)	('000)	5,280	5,306	6,113	6,193	5,729
1.2	♦ Overnight visitors (tourists)	(1)(2)	('000)	2,665	2,744	2,873	2,918	2,989
1.3	♦ Same-day visitors (excursionists)	(1)(2)	('000)	2,615	2,562	3,240	3,276	2,740
1.4	* of which, cruise passengers		('000)	436	425	509	470	506
	Arrivals by region	(3)						
1.5	Total		('000)	1,808	1,874	1,940	1,983	1,929
1.6	♦ Africa		('000)	2	2	2	2	2
1.7	♦ Americas		('000)	32	40	37	44	56
1.8	♦ East Asia and the Pacific		('000)	29	36	44	59	70
1.9	♦ Europe		('000)	1,731	1,782	1,850	1,872	1,780
1.10	♦ Middle East		('000)	..	..	..	..	..
1.11	♦ South Asia		('000)	..	..	..	..	..
1.12	♦ Other not classified		('000)	14	14	8	6	21
1.13	* of which, nationals residing abroad		('000)	..	..	..	..	..
	Accommodation							
	Total							
1.29	♦ Guests		('000)	1,808	1,874	1,940	1,983	1,929
1.30	♦ Overnights		('000)	3,749	3,823	3,909	3,919	3,770
	Hotels and similar establishments							
1.31	♦ Guests		('000)	1,703	1,747	1,798	1,816	1,766
1.32	♦ Overnights		('000)	3,478	3,499	3,537	3,516	3,368
	Expenditure							
1.33	Total		US$ Mn	..	..	2,022	2,231	1,891
1.34	♦ Travel		US$ Mn	1,256	1,221	1,626	1,817	1,499
1.35	♦ Passenger transport		US$ Mn	..	..	396	414	392
	Expenditure by main purpose of the trip							
1.36	Total		US$ Mn	..	..	1,626	1,817	1,498
1.37	♦ Personal		US$ Mn	..	..	1,285	1,440	1,183
1.38	♦ Business and professional		US$ Mn	..	..	341	377	315
	Indicators							
1.39	Average size of travel party		Persons	..	..	..	..	..
	Average length of stay							
1.40	Total		Days	..	..	..	..	..
1.41	♦ For all commercial accommodation services		Nights	2.07	2.04	2.01	1.98	1.95
1.42	* of which, "hotels and similar establishments"		Nights	2.04	2.00	1.97	1.94	1.91
1.43	♦ For non commercial accommodation services		Days	..	..	..	..	..
1.44	Average expenditure per day		US$	..	..	..	..	..
2.	**DOMESTIC TOURISM**							
	Data							
	Trips							
2.1	Total		('000)	..	..	..	..	..
2.2	♦ Overnight visitors (tourists)	(4)	('000)	1,561	1,761	1,734	2,572	2,704
2.3	♦ Same-day visitors (excursionists)		('000)	..	..	..	..	..
	Trips by main purpose	(4)						
2.4	Total		('000)	1,561	1,761	1,733	2,573	2,705
2.5	♦ Personal		('000)	1,414	1,604	1,556	2,257	2,383
2.6	* holidays, leisure and recreation		('000)	519	685	676	832	1,030
2.7	* other personal purposes		('000)	895	919	880	1,425	1,353
2.8	♦ Business and professional		('000)	147	157	177	316	322
	Accommodation							
	Total							
2.19	♦ Guests		('000)	918	966	1,041	1,104	1,183
2.20	♦ Overnights		('000)	1,651	1,721	1,825	1,890	2,012
	Hotels and similar establishments							
2.21	♦ Guests		('000)	668	705	756	818	880
2.22	♦ Overnights		('000)	1,117	1,151	1,220	1,290	1,379
	Indicators							
2.23	Average size of travel party		Persons	..	..	..	..	..
	Average length of stay							
2.24	Total		Days	..	..	..	..	..
2.25	♦ For all commercial accommodation services		Nights	1.80	1.78	1.80	1.71	1.70
2.26	* of which, "hotels and similar establishments"		Nights	1.67	1.63	1.70	1.58	1.57
2.27	♦ For non commercial accommodation services		Days	..	..	..	..	..
2.28	Average expenditure per day		US$	..	..	..	..	..

ESTONIA

Cod. Basic data and indicators	Notes	Units	2011	2012	2013	2014	2015
3. **OUTBOUND TOURISM**							
Data							
Departures							
3.1 Total	(5)	('000)	..	..	..	..	..
3.2 ♦ Overnight visitors (tourists)		('000)	1,054	1,147	1,166	1,426	1,250
3.3 ♦ Same-day visitors (excursionists)		('000)	..	..	..	..	..
Expenditure							
3.4 Total		US$ Mn	..	..	1,233	1,328	1,193
3.5 ♦ Travel		US$ Mn	806	796	1,056	1,163	1,052
3.6 ♦ Passenger transport		US$ Mn	..	..	177	165	141
Expenditure by main purpose of the trip							
3.7 Total		US$ Mn	..	..	1,057	1,163	1,052
3.8 ♦ Personal		US$ Mn	..	..	708	774	719
3.9 ♦ Business and professional		US$ Mn	..	..	349	389	333
Indicators							
3.10 Average length of stay		Days	5.88	6.03	6.80	6.10	7.60
3.11 Average expenditure per day		US$	..	..	..	..	..
4. **TOURISM INDUSTRIES**							
Data							
Number of establishments							
4.1 Total		Units	3,429	3,599	3,766	3,932	4,094
4.2 ♦ Accommodation for visitors		Units	1,158	1,238	1,320	1,419	1,417
4.3 * of which, "hotels and similar establishments"		Units	374	390	404	410	414
4.4 ♦ Food and beverage serving activities		Units	1,746	1,831	1,919	1,982	2,118
4.5 ♦ Passenger transportation		Units	..	..	..	..	..
4.6 ♦ Travel agencies and other reservation services activities		Units	525	530	527	531	559
4.7 ♦ Other tourism industries		Units	..	..	..	..	..
Accommodation for visitors in hotels and similar establishments							
Non-monetary data							
4.13 ♦ Number of establishments		Units	374	390	404	410	414
4.14 ♦ Number of rooms		Units	15,132	15,088	15,321	15,624	15,474
4.15 ♦ Number of bed-places		Units	31,349	31,590	31,989	32,437	32,620
Indicators							
4.16 Occupancy rate / rooms		Percent	46.91	51.88	51.76	51.18	52.48
4.17 Occupancy rate / bed-places		Percent	40.16	45.12	44.86	43.94	44.49
4.18 Average length of stay		Nights	1.94	1.90	1.86	1.82	1.79
4.19 Available capacity (bed-places per 1000 inhabitants)		Units	23.60	23.86	24.23	24.64	24.85
5. **EMPLOYMENT**							
Data							
Number of employees by tourism industries							
5.1 Total		('000)	20.2	21.0	21.9	23.6	..
5.2 ♦ Accommodation services for visitors (hotels and similar establishments)		('000)	5.8	5.8	5.9	6.2	..
5.3 ♦ Other accommodation services		('000)	..	..	..	..	..
5.4 ♦ Food and beverage serving activities		('000)	12.9	13.7	14.4	15.9	..
5.5 ♦ Passenger transportation		('000)	..	..	..	..	..
5.6 ♦ Travel agencies and other reservation services activities		('000)	1.5	1.5	1.6	1.5	..
5.7 ♦ Other tourism industries		('000)	..	..	..	..	..
6. **COMPLEMENTARY INDICATORS**							
Demand							
6.1 Gross travel propensity		Units	..	..	..	..	..
6.2 (1.2 inbound tourists + 2.2 domestic tourists) / population		Units	3.18	3.40	3.49	4.17	4.34
Macroeconomic indicators related to international tourism							
6.3 Inbound tourism expenditure over GDP		Percent	5.5	5.4	8.1	8.6	8.3
6.4 Outbound tourism expenditure over GDP		Percent	3.5	3.5	4.9	5.1	5.2
6.5 Tourism balance (inbound minus outbound tourism expenditure) over GDP		Percent	2.0	1.9	3.2	3.5	3.1
6.6 Tourism openness (inbound plus outbound tourism expenditure) over GDP		Percent	9.0	8.9	13.0	13.7	13.5

ESTONIA

Cod.	Basic data and indicators	Notes	Units	2011	2012	2013	2014	2015
6.7	Tourism coverage (inbound over outbound tourism expenditure)		Percent	155.8	153.4	164.0	168.0	158.5
6.8	Inbound tourism expenditure over exports of goods		Percent	8.7	8.6	13.1	14.7	15.4
6.9	Inbound tourism expenditure over exports of services		Percent	22.3	21.2	31.2	31.6	32.3
6.10	Inbound tourism expenditure over exports of goods and services		Percent	6.3	6.1	9.2	10.0	10.4
6.11	Inbound tourism expenditure over current account credits		Percent	5.7	5.6	8.4	9.2	9.6
6.12	Outbound tourism expenditure over imports of goods		Percent	5.4	5.0	7.4	8.0	9.0
6.13	Outbound tourism expenditure over imports of services		Percent	21.2	19.8	26.1	27.5	30.0
6.14	Outbound tourism expenditure over imports of goods and		Percent	4.3	4.0	5.8	6.2	6.9
6.15	Outbound tourism expenditure over current account debits		Percent	3.9	3.7	5.3	5.7	6.4

ETHIOPIA

Cod.	Basic data and indicators	Notes	Units	2011	2012	2013	2014	2015
1.	**INBOUND TOURISM**							
	Data							
	Arrivals							
1.1	Total		('000)	..	..	..	..	..
1.2	♦ Overnight visitors (tourists)	(1)	('000)	523	597	681	770	864
1.3	♦ Same-day visitors (excursionists)		('000)	..	..	..	..	..
1.4	* of which, cruise passengers		('000)	..	..	..	..	..
	Arrivals by region	(1)						
1.5	Total		('000)	523	597	681	770	864
1.6	♦ Africa		('000)	160	169	217	232	261
1.7	♦ Americas		('000)	96	121	130	150	169
1.8	♦ East Asia and the Pacific		('000)	36	52	52	61	68
1.9	♦ Europe		('000)	163	181	201	231	259
1.10	♦ Middle East		('000)	47	51	59	68	76
1.11	♦ South Asia		('000)	21	22	23	28	31
1.12	♦ Other not classified		('000)	..	..	..	..	..
1.13	* of which, nationals residing abroad		('000)	..	..	..	..	..
	Arrivals by main purpose	(1)						
1.14	Total		('000)	523	596	681	770	864
1.15	♦ Personal		('000)	382	408	493	557	623
1.16	* holidays, leisure and recreation		('000)	183	191	232	269	298
1.17	* other personal purposes		('000)	199	217	261	288	324
1.18	♦ Business and professional		('000)	141	188	189	214	241
	Arrivals by mode of transport	(1)						
1.19	Total		('000)	523	596	681	770	864
1.20	♦ Air		('000)	450	513	661	749	839
1.21	♦ Water		('000)	..	..	..	..	..
1.22	♦ Land		('000)	73	83	20	22	25
1.23	* railway		('000)	..	..	..	..	..
1.24	* road		('000)	73	83	20	22	25
1.25	* others		('000)	..	..	..	..	..
	Expenditure							
1.33	Total		US$ Mn	1,998	1,980	..	..	..
1.34	♦ Travel		US$ Mn	758	607	..	..	..
1.35	♦ Passenger transport		US$ Mn	1,240	1,373	..	..	..
	Expenditure by main purpose of the trip							
1.36	Total		US$ Mn	758	607	..	..	..
1.37	♦ Personal		US$ Mn	758	607	..	..	..
1.38	♦ Business and professional		US$ Mn	0	1	..	..	..
	Indicators							
1.39	Average size of travel party		Persons	..	..	..	..	..
	Average length of stay							
1.40	Total		Days	6.50	..	16.00	..	..
1.41	♦ For all commercial accommodation services		Nights	..	..	..	..	..
1.42	* of which, "hotels and similar establishments"		Nights	..	..	..	..	..
1.43	♦ For non commercial accommodation services		Days	..	..	..	..	..
1.44	Average expenditure per day		US$	121.0	..	234.0	..	..
3.	**OUTBOUND TOURISM**							
	Data							
	Expenditure							
3.4	Total		US$ Mn	..	..	..	..	..
3.5	♦ Travel		US$ Mn	170	181	..	..	..
3.6	♦ Passenger transport		US$ Mn	..	..	..	..	..
	Expenditure by main purpose of the trip							
3.7	Total		US$ Mn	170	181	..	..	..
3.8	♦ Personal		US$ Mn	56	63	..	..	..
3.9	♦ Business and professional		US$ Mn	114	118	..	..	..
4.	**TOURISM INDUSTRIES**							
	Data							
	Number of establishments							
4.1	Total		Units	..	..	..	..	..
4.2	♦ Accommodation for visitors		Units	..	..	..	..	..
4.3	* of which, "hotels and similar establishments"		Units	574	595	607	666	700
4.4	♦ Food and beverage serving activities		Units	..	..	..	..	..
4.5	♦ Passenger transportation		Units	..	..	..	..	..
4.6	♦ Travel agencies and other reservation services activities		Units	..	..	..	..	..
4.7	♦ Other tourism industries		Units	..	..	..	..	..

ETHIOPIA

Cod.	Basic data and indicators	Notes	Units	2011	2012	2013	2014	2015
	Accommodation for visitors in hotels and similar establishments							
	Non-monetary data							
4.13	♦ Number of establishments		Units	574	595	607	666	700
4.14	♦ Number of rooms		Units	19,025	19,998	20,234	22,285	23,506
4.15	♦ Number of bed-places		Units	24,083	24,978	25,294	26,345	27,147
	Indicators							
4.16	Occupancy rate / rooms		Percent	..	..	..	..	..
4.17	Occupancy rate / bed-places		Percent	..	..	..	..	..
4.18	Average length of stay		Nights	..	..	..	..	..
4.19	Available capacity (bed-places per 1000 inhabitants)		Units	0.27	0.27	0.27	0.27	0.27
6.	**COMPLEMENTARY INDICATORS**							
	Demand							
6.1	Gross travel propensity		Units	..	..	..	..	..
6.2	(1.2 inbound tourists) / population		Units	0.01	0.01	0.01	0.01	0.01
	Macroeconomic indicators related to international tourism							
6.3	Inbound tourism expenditure over GDP		Percent	6.6	4.7	..	..	..
6.4	Outbound tourism expenditure over GDP		Percent	0.6	0.4	..	..	..
6.5	Tourism balance (inbound minus outbound tourism expenditure) over GDP		Percent	6.0	4.3	..	..	..
6.6	Tourism openness (inbound plus outbound tourism expenditure) over GDP		Percent	7.2	5.1	..	..	..
6.7	Tourism coverage (inbound over outbound tourism expenditure)		Percent	1,175.3	1,093.9	..	..	..
6.8	Inbound tourism expenditure over exports of goods		Percent	66.0	60.8	..	..	..
6.9	Inbound tourism expenditure over exports of services		Percent	71.7	72.4	..	..	..
6.10	Inbound tourism expenditure over exports of goods and services		Percent	34.4	33.0	..	..	..
6.11	Inbound tourism expenditure over current account credits		Percent	18.2	17.5	..	..	..
6.12	Outbound tourism expenditure over imports of goods		Percent	2.0	1.7	..	..	..
6.13	Outbound tourism expenditure over imports of services		Percent	5.1	5.1	..	..	..
6.14	Outbound tourism expenditure over imports of goods and		Percent	1.5	1.3	..	..	..
6.15	Outbound tourism expenditure over current account debits		Percent	1.5	1.3	..	..	..

FIJI

Cod.	Basic data and indicators	Notes	Units	2011	2012	2013	2014	2015
1.	**INBOUND TOURISM**							
	Data							
	Arrivals	(1)						
1.1	Total		('000)	734	741	768	781	869
1.2	♦ Overnight visitors (tourists)		('000)	675	661	658	693	755
1.3	♦ Same-day visitors (excursionists)		('000)	59	80	110	88	114
1.4	* of which, cruise passengers		('000)	59	80	110	88	114
	Arrivals by region	(1)						
1.5	Total		('000)	675	661	658	693	755
1.6	♦ Africa		('000)	..	..	..	..	..
1.7	♦ Americas		('000)	69	70	68	74	80
1.8	♦ East Asia and the Pacific		('000)	542	535	533	562	618
1.9	♦ Europe		('000)	56	46	46	47	48
1.10	♦ Middle East		('000)	..	..	..	..	..
1.11	♦ South Asia		('000)	2	3	3	3	3
1.12	♦ Other not classified		('000)	6	7	8	6	6
1.13	* of which, nationals residing abroad		('000)	..	..	..	..	..
	Arrivals by main purpose	(1)						
1.14	Total		('000)	675	660	658	693	755
1.15	♦ Personal		('000)	627	619	623	656	711
1.16	* holidays, leisure and recreation		('000)	503	492	484	537	595
1.17	* other personal purposes		('000)	124	127	139	119	116
1.18	♦ Business and professional		('000)	48	41	35	37	44
	Arrivals by mode of transport	(1)						
1.19	Total		('000)	675	661	..	..	..
1.20	♦ Air		('000)	654	642	..	..	..
1.21	♦ Water		('000)	21	19	..	..	..
1.22	♦ Land		('000)	..	..	..	..	..
1.23	* railway		('000)	..	..	..	..	..
1.24	* road		('000)	..	..	..	..	..
1.25	* others		('000)	..	..	..	..	..
	Accommodation							
	Hotels and similar establishments							
1.31	♦ Guests		('000)	..	..	..	..	..
1.32	♦ Overnights		('000)	3,102	3,121	3,172	3,301	3,515
	Expenditure							
1.33	Total		US$ Mn	955	989	966	1,034	1,037
1.34	♦ Travel		US$ Mn	724	730	717	752	760
1.35	♦ Passenger transport		US$ Mn	231	259	249	282	277
	Expenditure by main purpose of the trip							
1.36	Total		US$ Mn	724	730	717	752	760
1.37	♦ Personal		US$ Mn	681	693	677	711	720
1.38	♦ Business and professional		US$ Mn	43	36	40	41	40
	Indicators							
1.39	Average size of travel party		Persons	..	..	..	..	..
	Average length of stay							
1.40	Total		Days	..	..	..	..	..
1.41	♦ For all commercial accommodation services	(2)	Nights	9.40	9.60	9.50	9.50	9.50
1.42	* of which, "hotels and similar establishments"		Nights	..	..	..	..	..
1.43	♦ For non commercial accommodation services		Days	..	..	..	..	..
1.44	Average expenditure per day		US$	..	..	..	..	..
2.	**DOMESTIC TOURISM**							
	Data							
	Accommodation							
	Hotels and similar establishments							
2.21	♦ Guests		('000)	..	..	..	..	..
2.22	♦ Overnights		('000)	650	649	712	760	782
3.	**OUTBOUND TOURISM**							
	Data							
	Departures							
3.1	Total		('000)	..	..	..	..	..
3.2	♦ Overnight visitors (tourists)		('000)	132	132	..	..	..
3.3	♦ Same-day visitors (excursionists)		('000)	..	..	..	..	..
	Expenditure							
3.4	Total		US$ Mn	116	110	105	99	115
3.5	♦ Travel		US$ Mn	98	91	91	89	104
3.6	♦ Passenger transport		US$ Mn	18	19	14	10	11

FIJI

Cod.	Basic data and indicators	Notes	Units	2011	2012	2013	2014	2015
	Expenditure by main purpose of the trip							
3.7	Total		US$ Mn	98	91	91	89	104
3.8	♦ Personal		US$ Mn	93	87	86	84	99
3.9	♦ Business and professional		US$ Mn	5	4	5	5	5
4.	**TOURISM INDUSTRIES**							
	Data							
	Accommodation for visitors in hotels and similar establishments							
	Non-monetary data							
4.13	♦ Number of establishments		Units	..	..	..	..	..
4.14	♦ Number of rooms		Units	10,211	10,138	10,197	10,393	10,447
4.15	♦ Number of bed-places		Units	23,851	23,539	23,845	24,700	24,388
	Indicators							
4.16	Occupancy rate / rooms		Percent	47.40	47.20	48.80	50.20	52.70
4.17	Occupancy rate / bed-places		Percent	43.60	43.40	44.60	45.70	47.30
4.18	Average length of stay		Nights	..	..	..	..	..
4.19	Available capacity (bed-places per 1000 inhabitants)		Units	27.50	26.93	27.08	27.86	27.34
6.	**COMPLEMENTARY INDICATORS**							
	Demand							
6.1	Gross travel propensity		Units	..	..	..	..	..
6.2	(1.2 inbound tourists) / population		Units	0.78	0.76	0.75	0.78	0.85
	Macroeconomic indicators related to international tourism							
6.3	Inbound tourism expenditure over GDP		Percent	25.3	24.9	23.0	22.8	..
6.4	Outbound tourism expenditure over GDP		Percent	3.1	2.8	2.5	2.2	..
6.5	Tourism balance (inbound minus outbound tourism expenditure) over GDP		Percent	22.2	22.1	20.5	20.6	..
6.6	Tourism openness (inbound plus outbound tourism expenditure) over GDP		Percent	28.4	27.7	25.5	25.0	..
6.7	Tourism coverage (inbound over outbound tourism expenditure)		Percent	823.3	899.1	920.0	1,044.4	901.7
6.8	Inbound tourism expenditure over exports of goods		Percent	89.9	81.5	92.2	..	..
6.9	Inbound tourism expenditure over exports of services		Percent	81.7	81.0	78.9	..	..
6.10	Inbound tourism expenditure over exports of goods and services		Percent	42.8	40.6	42.5	..	..
6.11	Inbound tourism expenditure over current account credits		Percent	37.7	35.5	37.0	..	..
6.12	Outbound tourism expenditure over imports of goods		Percent	6.1	5.6	4.4	..	..
6.13	Outbound tourism expenditure over imports of services		Percent	21.5	19.1	18.6	..	..
6.14	Outbound tourism expenditure over imports of goods and		Percent	4.7	4.3	3.6	..	..
6.15	Outbound tourism expenditure over current account debits		Percent	4.4	4.1	3.4	..	..

FINLAND

Cod.	Basic data and indicators	Notes	Units	2011	2012	2013	2014	2015
1.	**INBOUND TOURISM**							
	Data							
	Arrivals							
1.1	Total	(1)	('000)	7,260	7,636	..	..	..
1.2	♦ Overnight visitors (tourists)		('000)	4,192	4,226	..	..	..
1.3	♦ Same-day visitors (excursionists)		('000)	3,068	3,410	..	..	..
1.4	* of which, cruise passengers		('000)	..	..			
	Arrivals by region	(1)						
1.5	Total		('000)	7,260	7,636	..	..	..
1.6	♦ Africa		('000)	11	16	..	..	..
1.7	♦ Americas		('000)	181	223	..	..	..
1.8	♦ East Asia and the Pacific		('000)	427	474	..	..	..
1.9	♦ Europe		('000)	6,641	6,923	..	..	..
1.10	♦ Middle East		('000)	..	..	..	..	..
1.11	♦ South Asia		('000)	..	..	..	..	..
1.12	♦ Other not classified		('000)	..	..	..	..	..
1.13	* of which, nationals residing abroad		('000)	..	..	..	..	..
	Arrivals by main purpose	(1)						
1.14	Total		('000)	7,260	7,636	..	..	..
1.15	♦ Personal		('000)	5,604	5,860	..	..	..
1.16	* holidays, leisure and recreation		('000)	3,818	4,201	..	..	..
1.17	* other personal purposes		('000)	1,786	1,659	..	..	..
1.18	♦ Business and professional		('000)	1,656	1,776	..	..	..
	Arrivals by mode of transport	(1)						
1.19	Total		('000)	7,260	7,636	..	..	..
1.20	♦ Air		('000)	2,533	2,434	..	..	..
1.21	♦ Water		('000)	1,722	1,865	..	..	..
1.22	♦ Land		('000)	3,005	3,337	..	..	..
1.23	* railway		('000)	..	..	..	..	..
1.24	* road		('000)	3,005	3,337	..	..	..
1.25	* others		('000)	..	..	..	..	..
	Arrivals by form of organization of the trip	(1)						
1.26	Total		('000)	7,260	7,636	..	..	..
1.27	♦ Package tour		('000)	799	916	..	..	..
1.28	♦ Other forms		('000)	6,461	6,720	..	..	..
	Accommodation	(2)						
	Total							
1.29	♦ Guests		('000)	2,623	2,778	2,797	2,731	2,622
1.30	♦ Overnights		('000)	5,507	5,803	5,860	5,711	5,510
	Hotels and similar establishments							
1.31	♦ Guests		('000)	2,294	2,461	2,458	2,397	2,333
1.32	♦ Overnights		('000)	4,711	4,948	4,906	4,795	4,677
	Expenditure	(3)						
1.33	Total		US$ Mn	5,591	5,415	..	..	..
1.34	♦ Travel		US$ Mn	3,823	3,874	4,048	3,599	2,751
1.35	♦ Passenger transport		US$ Mn	1,768	1,541	..	..	..
	Expenditure by main purpose of the trip	(3)						
1.36	Total		US$ Mn	3,822	3,874	4,048	3,599	2,751
1.37	♦ Personal		US$ Mn	2,620	2,757	2,914	2,446	1,724
1.38	♦ Business and professional		US$ Mn	1,202	1,117	1,134	1,153	1,027
	Indicators							
1.39	Average size of travel party		Persons	..	..	..	..	..
	Average length of stay							
1.40	Total		Days	..	..	..	..	..
1.41	♦ For all commercial accommodation services	(2)	Nights	2.10	2.09	2.10	2.09	2.10
1.42	* of which, "hotels and similar establishments"	(2)	Nights	2.02	2.00	1.99	2.00	2.01
1.43	♦ For non commercial accommodation services	(1)	Days	12.20	13.80	..	..	..
1.44	Average expenditure per day	(1)	US$	77.6	77.4	..	..	..
2.	**DOMESTIC TOURISM**							
	Data							
	Trips	(4)						
2.1	Total		('000)	..	..	..	..	..
2.2	♦ Overnight visitors (tourists)		('000)	35,561	30,915	30,480	28,850	29,156
2.3	♦ Same-day visitors (excursionists)		('000)	..	..	..	..	..
	Trips by main purpose	(4)						
2.4	Total		('000)	35,562	30,915	30,479	28,851	29,156
2.5	♦ Personal		('000)	31,200	26,771	26,527	25,214	25,721
2.6	* holidays, leisure and recreation		('000)	11,756	10,819	11,284	10,668	10,900
2.7	* other personal purposes		('000)	19,444	15,952	15,243	14,546	14,821
2.8	♦ Business and professional		('000)	4,362	4,144	3,952	3,637	3,435

FINLAND

Cod.	Basic data and indicators	Notes	Units	2011	2012	2013	2014	2015
	Trips by mode of transport	(4)						
2.9	Total		('000)	35,560	30,915	30,479	28,851	29,156
2.10	♦ Air		('000)	867	948	715	666	689
2.11	♦ Water		('000)	272	240	313	222	247
2.12	♦ Land		('000)	34,421	29,727	29,451	27,963	28,220
2.13	* railway		('000)	3,768	3,970	3,881	3,560	3,156
2.14	* road		('000)	30,265	25,479	25,370	24,221	24,924
2.15	* others		('000)	388	278	200	182	140
	Trips by form of organization	(4)(5)						
2.16	Total		('000)	5,816	6,381	6,553	5,892	6,372
2.17	♦ Package tour		('000)	173	263	217	221	202
2.18	♦ Other forms		('000)	5,643	6,118	6,336	5,671	6,170
	Accommodation	(2)						
	Total							
2.19	♦ Guests		('000)	8,104	8,109	8,044	7,929	8,113
2.20	♦ Overnights		('000)	14,480	14,515	14,381	14,075	14,228
	Hotels and similar establishments							
2.21	♦ Guests		('000)	6,945	6,967	6,857	6,743	6,960
2.22	♦ Overnights		('000)	11,655	11,718	11,455	11,171	11,464
	Indicators							
2.23	Average size of travel party		Persons	..	..	..	..	..
	Average length of stay							
2.24	Total		Days	..	..	..	..	..
2.25	♦ For all commercial accommodation services	(2)	Nights	1.79	1.79	1.79	1.78	1.75
2.26	* of which, "hotels and similar establishments"	(2)	Nights	1.67	1.67	1.66	1.65	1.65
2.27	♦ For non commercial accommodation services	(4)	Days	2.65	2.77	2.90	2.79	2.96
2.28	Average expenditure per day		US$	..	..	..	..	..
3.	**OUTBOUND TOURISM**							
	Data							
	Departures	(4)						
3.1	Total		('000)	8,238	9,978	9,526	9,783	10,022
3.2	♦ Overnight visitors (tourists)	(6)	('000)	7,274	9,055	8,562	8,731	8,904
3.3	♦ Same-day visitors (excursionists)		('000)	964	923	964	1,052	1,118
	Expenditure	(3)						
3.4	Total		US$ Mn	6,009	5,839	..	..	..
3.5	♦ Travel		US$ Mn	4,878	4,885	5,292	5,286	4,563
3.6	♦ Passenger transport		US$ Mn	1,131	954	..	..	..
	Expenditure by main purpose of the trip	(3)						
3.7	Total		US$ Mn	4,878	4,885	5,292	5,286	4,563
3.8	♦ Personal		US$ Mn	3,807	3,743	4,128	4,164	3,554
3.9	♦ Business and professional		US$ Mn	1,071	1,142	1,164	1,122	1,009
	Indicators							
3.10	Average length of stay	(4)	Days	5.20	5.31	5.13	5.06	4.87
3.11	Average expenditure per day	(4)	US$	138.0	156.7	161.7	145.5	154.2
4.	**TOURISM INDUSTRIES**							
	Data							
	Number of establishments	(7)						
4.1	Total		Units	31,566	31,690	31,770	31,547	..
4.2	♦ Accommodation for visitors		Units	1,894	1,881	2,095	2,075	..
4.3	* of which, "hotels and similar establishments"		Units	899	889	939	929	..
4.4	♦ Food and beverage serving activities		Units	12,557	12,589	11,936	11,850	..
4.5	♦ Passenger transportation		Units	9,792	9,682	9,753	9,573	..
4.6	♦ Travel agencies and other reservation services activities		Units	1,549	1,556	1,613	1,591	..
4.7	♦ Other tourism industries		Units	5,774	5,982	6,373	6,458	..
	Accommodation for visitors in hotels and similar establishments							
	Non-monetary data	(2)						
4.13	♦ Number of establishments		Units	830	839	828	785	777
4.14	♦ Number of rooms		Units	55,892	57,009	56,566	56,688	56,723
4.15	♦ Number of bed-places		Units	122,182	123,979	123,655	123,305	122,855
	Indicators	(2)						
4.16	Occupancy rate / rooms		Percent	51.40	51.29	50.03	50.28	51.13
4.17	Occupancy rate / bed-places		Percent	39.80	40.03	38.97	38.25	38.92
4.18	Average length of stay		Nights	1.77	1.77	1.76	1.75	1.74
4.19	Available capacity (bed-places per 1000 inhabitants)		Units	22.64	22.85	22.68	22.50	22.32

FINLAND

Cod.	Basic data and indicators	Notes	Units	2011	2012	2013	2014	2015
	Travel agencies and other reservation service activities							
	Non-monetary data							
	♦ Domestic trips	(4)						
4.25	* with package tour	(5)	Percent	3.0	4.0	2.8	3.1	3.2
4.26	* without package tour		Percent	97.0	96.0	97.2	96.9	96.8
	♦ Inbound trips	(1)						
4.27	* with package tour		Percent	11.0	12.0	..	..	..
4.28	* without package tour		Percent	89.0	88.0	..	..	..
	♦ Outbound trips	(4)						
4.29	* with package tour		Percent	41.1	36.0	33.3	33.2	30.3
4.30	* without package tour		Percent	58.9	63.0	66.7	66.8	69.7
5.	**EMPLOYMENT**	(7)						
	Data							
	Number of employees by tourism industries							
5.1	Total		('000)	130.4	136.5	136.7	139.2	..
5.2	♦ Accommodation services for visitors (hotels and similar establishments)		('000)	14.5	14.8	14.5	14.6	..
5.3	♦ Other accommodation services		('000)	..	..	..	..	..
5.4	♦ Food and beverage serving activities		('000)	61.6	63.5	63.8	65.7	..
5.5	♦ Passenger transportation		('000)	33.9	37.7	37.5	37.8	..
5.6	♦ Travel agencies and other reservation services activities		('000)	2.2	2.0	2.0	2.1	..
5.7	♦ Other tourism industries		('000)	18.2	18.5	18.9	19.0	..
	Number of jobs by status in employment							
5.8	Total		('000)	130.4	136.5	136.7	139.2	..
5.9	♦ Employees		('000)	111.7	116.9	117.1	118.5	..
5.10	♦ Self employed		('000)	18.7	19.6	19.6	20.7	..
	Indicators							
	Number of full-time equivalent jobs by status in employment							
5.11	Total		('000)	115.4	120.4	119.4	122.6	..
5.12	♦ Employees		('000)	95.9	100.1	100.0	101.4	..
5.13	* male		('000)	..	..	..	..	..
5.14	* female		('000)	..	..	..	..	..
5.15	♦ Self employed		('000)	19.5	20.3	19.4	21.2	..
5.16	* male		('000)	..	..	..	..	..
5.17	* female		('000)	..	..	..	..	..
6.	**COMPLEMENTARY INDICATORS**							
	Demand							
6.1	Gross travel propensity	(8)	Units	7.9	7.4	7.2	6.9	6.9
6.2	(1.2 inbound tourists + 2.2 domestic tourists) / population		Units	7.37	6.48	..	..	..
	Macroeconomic indicators related to international tourism							
6.3	Inbound tourism expenditure over GDP		Percent	2.0	2.1	1.5	1.3	1.2
6.4	Outbound tourism expenditure over GDP		Percent	2.2	2.3	2.0	1.9	2.0
6.5	Tourism balance (inbound minus outbound tourism expenditure) over GDP		Percent	-0.2	-0.2	-0.5	-0.6	-0.8
6.6	Tourism openness (inbound plus outbound tourism expenditure) over GDP		Percent	4.2	4.4	3.5	3.2	3.2
6.7	Tourism coverage (inbound over outbound tourism expenditure)		Percent	93.0	92.7	76.5	68.1	60.3
6.8	Inbound tourism expenditure over exports of goods		Percent	7.2	7.4	5.4	4.8	4.5
6.9	Inbound tourism expenditure over exports of services		Percent	19.0	18.8	13.6	12.8	11.3
6.10	Inbound tourism expenditure over exports of goods and services		Percent	5.2	5.3	3.8	3.5	3.2
6.11	Inbound tourism expenditure over current account credits		Percent	4.3	4.4	3.2	2.8	2.6
6.12	Outbound tourism expenditure over imports of goods		Percent	7.5	7.9	7.0	7.1	7.8
6.13	Outbound tourism expenditure over imports of services		Percent	20.3	18.8	16.8	17.3	17.7
6.14	Outbound tourism expenditure over imports of goods and		Percent	5.5	5.6	5.0	5.0	5.4
6.15	Outbound tourism expenditure over current account debits		Percent	4.5	4.6	4.1	4.0	4.3

FRANCE

Cod.	Basic data and indicators	Notes	Units	2011	2012	2013	2014	2015
1.	**INBOUND TOURISM**							
	Data							
	Arrivals	(1)						
1.1	Total		('000)	196,595	197,522	204,410	206,599	203,302
1.2	♦ Overnight visitors (tourists)		('000)	80,499	81,980	83,634	83,701	84,452
1.3	♦ Same-day visitors (excursionists)		('000)	116,096	115,543	120,776	122,898	118,851
1.4	* of which, cruise passengers		('000)	..	..	..	..	..
	Arrivals by region	(1)						
1.5	Total		('000)	80,499	81,980	83,634	83,701	84,452
1.6	♦ Africa		('000)	2,311	2,276	2,350	2,483	2,774
1.7	♦ Americas		('000)	6,339	6,133	6,225	6,620	7,091
1.8	♦ East Asia and the Pacific		('000)	3,905	4,159	4,661	5,175	6,198
1.9	♦ Europe		('000)	67,123	68,554	69,388	68,323	67,037
1.10	♦ Middle East		('000)	821	859	1,011	1,099	1,352
1.11	♦ South Asia		('000)	..	..	..	..	..
1.12	♦ Other not classified		('000)	..	..	..	..	..
1.13	* of which, nationals residing abroad		('000)	..	..	..	..	..
	Arrivals by main purpose	(1)						
1.14	Total		('000)	80,499	81,980	83,634	83,701	84,452
1.15	♦ Personal	(2)	('000)	69,378	71,801	73,455	71,929	72,605
1.16	* holidays, leisure and recreation		('000)	58,530	60,738	62,954	62,253	62,838
1.17	* other personal purposes	(3)	('000)	10,848	11,063	10,502	9,676	9,767
1.18	♦ Business and professional		('000)	11,120	10,179	10,179	11,773	11,847
	Arrivals by mode of transport	(1)						
1.19	Total		('000)	80,499	81,980	83,634	83,701	84,452
1.20	♦ Air		('000)	21,190	22,233	23,581	23,670	26,327
1.21	♦ Water		('000)	6,652	6,095	6,677	5,256	5,607
1.22	♦ Land		('000)	52,656	53,652	53,376	54,775	52,518
1.23	* railway		('000)	4,931	4,896	5,121	5,515	5,452
1.24	* road		('000)	47,725	48,756	48,255	49,260	47,065
1.25	* others		('000)	..	..	..	..	..
	Accommodation							
	Total							
1.29	♦ Guests	(4)	('000)	41,605	42,378	46,001	46,074	46,639
1.30	♦ Overnights	(4)	('000)	123,228	125,038	131,723	130,215	129,785
	Hotels and similar establishments							
1.31	♦ Guests	(5)	('000)	30,487	30,966	33,348	34,241	34,936
1.32	♦ Overnights	(5)	('000)	67,176	68,426	71,992	72,941	73,782
	Expenditure							
1.33	Total		US$ Mn	66,087	64,001	66,049	66,803	54,003
1.34	♦ Travel		US$ Mn	55,115	53,349	56,463	57,668	45,888
1.35	♦ Passenger transport		US$ Mn	10,972	10,652	9,586	9,135	8,115
	Expenditure by main purpose of the trip							
1.36	Total		US$ Mn	55,116	53,349	56,463	57,668	45,888
1.37	♦ Personal		US$ Mn	48,325	46,769	50,345	50,973	40,312
1.38	♦ Business and professional		US$ Mn	6,791	6,580	6,118	6,695	5,576
	Indicators							
1.39	Average size of travel party		Persons	..	..	..	..	..
	Average length of stay							
1.40	Total	(1)(6)	Days	6.86	6.84	6.69	6.83	6.83
1.41	♦ For all commercial accommodation services	(4)	Nights	2.96	2.95	2.87	2.84	2.60
1.42	* of which, "hotels and similar establishments"	(5)	Nights	2.20	2.21	2.16	2.13	2.11
1.43	♦ For non commercial accommodation services		Days	..	..	..	..	..
1.44	Average expenditure per day		US$	..	..	..	..	..
2.	**DOMESTIC TOURISM**							
	Data							
	Trips	(7)						
2.1	Total		('000)	276,752	268,673	265,182	266,027	256,078
2.2	♦ Overnight visitors (tourists)		('000)	198,784	198,466	197,242	196,232	191,644
2.3	♦ Same-day visitors (excursionists)		('000)	77,968	70,207	67,940	69,795	64,434
	Trips by main purpose	(7)						
2.4	Total		('000)	198,784	198,466	197,241	196,232	191,644
2.5	♦ Personal		('000)	180,481	179,661	179,130	179,145	175,034
2.6	* holidays, leisure and recreation		('000)	57,922	64,493	62,154	56,049	58,252
2.7	* other personal purposes		('000)	122,559	115,168	116,976	123,096	116,782
2.8	♦ Business and professional		('000)	18,303	18,805	18,111	17,087	16,610

FRANCE

Cod.	Basic data and indicators	Notes	Units	2011	2012	2013	2014	2015
	Trips by mode of transport	**(7)(8)**						
2.9	Total		('000)	180,481	179,661	179,131	179,145	175,034
2.10	♦ Air		('000)	2,593	2,765	3,037	2,662	3,015
2.11	♦ Water		('000)	500	527	489	501	448
2.12	♦ Land		('000)	177,388	176,369	175,605	175,982	171,571
2.13	* railway		('000)	24,782	25,816	25,831	26,304	24,078
2.14	* road		('000)	151,646	149,935	149,222	148,958	146,779
2.15	* others		('000)	960	618	552	720	714
	Accommodation							
	Total							
2.19	♦ Guests	**(4)**	('000)	107,196	106,539	106,571	105,883	109,639
2.20	♦ Overnights	**(4)**	('000)	277,802	275,405	272,370	268,436	276,583
	Hotels and similar establishments							
2.21	♦ Guests	**(5)**	('000)	78,793	77,835	77,580	76,003	77,756
2.22	♦ Overnights	**(5)**	('000)	131,859	129,951	128,275	125,568	128,300
	Indicators							
2.23	Average size of travel party		Persons	..	..	..	..	..
	Average length of stay							
2.24	Total	**(6)(7)(8)**	Days	5.37	5.23	5.27	5.23	5.20
2.25	♦ For all commercial accommodation services	**(4)**	Nights	2.59	2.59	2.56	2.54	2.52
2.26	* of which, "hotels and similar establishments"	**(5)**	Nights	1.67	1.67	1.65	1.65	1.65
2.27	♦ For non commercial accommodation services		Days	..	..	..	..	..
2.28	Average expenditure per day		US$	..	..	..	..	..

3. OUTBOUND TOURISM

Cod.		Notes	Units	2011	2012	2013	2014	2015
	Data							
	Departures	**(7)**						
3.1	Total		('000)	31,153	29,642	30,457	31,941	30,608
3.2	♦ Overnight visitors (tourists)		('000)	26,155	25,317	26,062	27,919	26,648
3.3	♦ Same-day visitors (excursionists)		('000)	4,998	4,325	4,395	4,023	3,960
	Expenditure							
3.4	Total		US$ Mn	55,472	50,087	53,420	59,377	46,838
3.5	♦ Travel		US$ Mn	44,695	39,851	42,944	48,733	38,406
3.6	♦ Passenger transport		US$ Mn	10,777	10,236	10,476	10,644	8,429
	Expenditure by main purpose of the trip							
3.7	Total		US$ Mn	44,694	39,851	42,944	48,733	38,405
3.8	♦ Personal		US$ Mn	31,304	26,216	28,852	31,544	24,631
3.9	♦ Business and professional		US$ Mn	13,390	13,635	14,092	17,189	13,774
	Indicators							
3.10	Average length of stay	**(7)(8)**	Days	9.37	9.19	9.33	9.26	9.03
3.11	Average expenditure per day		US$	..	..	..	..	..

4. TOURISM INDUSTRIES

Cod.		Notes	Units	2011	2012	2013	2014	2015
	Data							
	Number of establishments							
4.1	Total		Units	167,595	170,150	172,573	181,514	178,751
4.2	♦ Accommodation for visitors	**(9)**	Units	28,283	28,338	28,218	30,865	30,134
4.3	* of which, "hotels and similar establishments"	**(10)**	Units	17,000	16,981	17,370	18,358	18,454
4.4	♦ Food and beverage serving activities	**(11)**	Units	117,540	119,842	122,320	125,677	123,766
4.5	♦ Passenger transportation	**(11)**	Units	3,016	3,109	3,180	6,072	6,075
4.6	♦ Travel agencies and other reservation services activities	**(11)**	Units	8,005	7,914	7,776	7,492	7,602
4.7	♦ Other tourism industries	**(11)(12)**	Units	10,751	10,947	11,079	11,408	11,174
	Accommodation for visitors in hotels and similar establishments							
	Non-monetary data	**(10)**						
4.13	♦ Number of establishments		Units	17,000	16,981	17,370	18,358	18,454
4.14	♦ Number of rooms		Units	614,684	619,322	638,887	653,878	657,728
4.15	♦ Number of bed-places		Units	1,229,368	1,238,644	1,277,774	1,307,756	1,315,456
	Indicators							
4.16	Occupancy rate / rooms	**(5)(13)**	Percent	60.99	60.26	59.63	59.17	59.23
4.17	Occupancy rate / bed-places		Percent	..	..	..	..	..
4.18	Average length of stay	**(5)**	Nights	1.82	1.82	1.81	1.80	1.79
4.19	Available capacity (bed-places per 1000 inhabitants)	**(14)**	Units	19.43	19.49	20.01	20.40	20.43

FRANCE

Cod.	Basic data and indicators	Notes	Units	2011	2012	2013	2014	2015
5.	**EMPLOYMENT**							
	Data							
	Number of employees by tourism industries							
5.1	Total	(11)	('000)	1,245.0	1,256.2	1,232.2	1,215.4	1,219.5
5.2	♦ Accommodation services for visitors (hotels and similar establishments)		('000)	176.4	174.4	171.5	172.3	172.2
5.3	♦ Other accommodation services		('000)	40.1	40.9	40.4	39.8	40.0
5.4	♦ Food and beverage serving activities		('000)	588.6	597.5	597.5	602.9	618.2
5.5	♦ Passenger transportation		('000)	275.4	276.5	256.1	244.4	231.9
5.6	♦ Travel agencies and other reservation services activities		('000)	47.8	46.7	46.0	45.2	44.6
5.7	♦ Other tourism industries	(12)	('000)	116.7	120.2	120.7	110.8	112.6
6.	**COMPLEMENTARY INDICATORS**							
	Demand							
6.1	Gross travel propensity		Units	..	..	..	..	..
6.2	(1.2 inbound tourists + 2.2 domestic tourists) / population		Units	4.41	4.41	4.40	4.37	4.29
	Macroeconomic indicators related to international tourism							
6.3	Inbound tourism expenditure over GDP		Percent	2.3	2.4	2.3	2.3	2.2
6.4	Outbound tourism expenditure over GDP		Percent	1.9	1.9	1.9	2.1	1.9
6.5	Tourism balance (inbound minus outbound tourism expenditure) over GDP		Percent	0.4	0.5	0.4	0.2	0.3
6.6	Tourism openness (inbound plus outbound tourism expenditure) over GDP		Percent	4.2	4.3	4.2	4.4	4.1
6.7	Tourism coverage (inbound over outbound tourism expenditure)		Percent	119.1	127.8	123.6	112.5	115.3
6.8	Inbound tourism expenditure over exports of goods		Percent	11.3	11.4	11.3	11.4	10.6
6.9	Inbound tourism expenditure over exports of services		Percent	27.9	27.3	25.7	24.2	22.4
6.10	Inbound tourism expenditure over exports of goods and services		Percent	8.0	8.0	7.9	7.8	7.2
6.11	Inbound tourism expenditure over current account credits		Percent	6.1	6.2	6.2	6.1	5.7
6.12	Outbound tourism expenditure over imports of goods		Percent	8.2	7.9	8.4	9.4	8.7
6.13	Outbound tourism expenditure over imports of services		Percent	27.3	24.7	23.6	23.5	20.3
6.14	Outbound tourism expenditure over imports of goods and		Percent	6.3	6.0	6.2	6.7	6.1
6.15	Outbound tourism expenditure over current account debits		Percent	4.7	4.5	4.6	5.1	4.6

FRENCH GUIANA

Cod.	Basic data and indicators	Notes	Units	2011	2012	2013	2014	2015
1.	**INBOUND TOURISM**							
	Data							
	Arrivals							
1.1	Total		('000)	..	..	..	188	208
1.2	♦ Overnight visitors (tourists)	(1)	('000)	192	187	180	185	199
1.3	♦ Same-day visitors (excursionists)		('000)	..	..	..	3	9
1.4	* of which, cruise passengers		('000)	..	..	..	3	9
	Arrivals by region							
1.5	Total		('000)	192	187	180	185	199
1.6	♦ Africa		('000)	..	..	..	..	..
1.7	♦ Americas		('000)	67	63	55	55	68
1.8	♦ East Asia and the Pacific		('000)	..	..	..	..	..
1.9	♦ Europe	(2)	('000)	125	124	125	130	131
1.10	♦ Middle East		('000)	..	..	..	..	..
1.11	♦ South Asia		('000)	..	..	..	..	..
1.12	♦ Other not classified		('000)	..	..	..	..	..
1.13	* of which, nationals residing abroad		('000)	..	..	..	..	..
	Arrivals by mode of transport							
1.19	Total		('000)	192	187	180	185	199
1.20	♦ Air		('000)	192	187	180	185	199
1.21	♦ Water		('000)	..	..	..	..	..
1.22	♦ Land		('000)	..	..	..	..	..
1.23	* railway		('000)	..	..	..	..	..
1.24	* road		('000)	..	..	..	..	..
1.25	* others		('000)	..	..	..	..	..
	Accommodation							
	Hotels and similar establishments							
1.31	♦ Guests		('000)	111	120	126	117	140
1.32	♦ Overnights	(3)	('000)	346	349	328	322	354
	Indicators							
1.39	Average size of travel party		Persons	..	..	..	..	
	Average length of stay							
1.40	Total		Days	..	..	..	..	
1.41	♦ For all commercial accommodation services		Nights	..	..	..	..	
1.42	* of which, "hotels and similar establishments"		Nights	3.10	2.90	2.60	2.80	2.52
1.43	♦ For non commercial accommodation services		Days	..	..	..	..	
1.44	Average expenditure per day		US$	..	..	..	..	
4.	**TOURISM INDUSTRIES**							
	Data							
	Number of establishments							
4.1	Total		Units	..	..	..	740	..
4.2	♦ Accommodation for visitors		Units	..	..	..	270	348
4.3	* of which, "hotels and similar establishments"		Units	..	31	..	39	37
4.4	♦ Food and beverage serving activities		Units	..	..	..	470	..
4.5	♦ Passenger transportation		Units	..	..	..	..	..
4.6	♦ Travel agencies and other reservation services activities		Units	..	..	..	..	..
4.7	♦ Other tourism industries		Units	..	..	..	..	..
	Accommodation for visitors in hotels and similar establishments							
	Non-monetary data							
4.13	♦ Number of establishments		Units	..	31	..	39	37
4.14	♦ Number of rooms		Units	..	1,259	..	1,690	1,692
4.15	♦ Number of bed-places		Units	..	2,148	..	3,761	3,780
	Indicators							
4.16	Occupancy rate / rooms		Percent	..	..	..	52.27	47.62
4.17	Occupancy rate / bed-places		Percent	..	..	..	..	
4.18	Average length of stay		Nights	3.10	2.90	2.60	2.80	2.52
4.19	Available capacity (bed-places per 1000 inhabitants)		Units	..	8.69	..	14.38	14.07
6.	**COMPLEMENTARY INDICATORS**							
	Demand							
6.1	Gross travel propensity		Units	..	..	..	..	..
6.2	(1.2 inbound tourists) / population		Units	0.80	0.76	0.71	0.71	0.74

FRENCH POLYNESIA

Cod.	Basic data and indicators	Notes	Units	2011	2012	2013	2014	2015
1.	**INBOUND TOURISM**							
	Data							
	Arrivals							
1.1	Total		('000)	196	210	214	228	239
1.2	♦ Overnight visitors (tourists)	(1)	('000)	163	169	164	181	184
1.3	♦ Same-day visitors (excursionists)		('000)	33	41	50	48	55
1.4	* of which, cruise passengers		('000)	..	..	..	..	..
	Arrivals by region	(1)						
1.5	Total		('000)	163	169	164	181	184
1.6	♦ Africa		('000)	..	..	..	..	..
1.7	♦ Americas		('000)	64	67	68	78	79
1.8	♦ East Asia and the Pacific		('000)	34	38	37	39	41
1.9	♦ Europe		('000)	64	63	58	62	63
1.10	♦ Middle East		('000)	..	..	..	..	..
1.11	♦ South Asia		('000)	..	..	..	..	..
1.12	♦ Other not classified		('000)	1	1	1	1	1
1.13	* of which, nationals residing abroad		('000)	..	..	..	..	..
	Arrivals by main purpose	(1)						
1.14	Total		('000)	163	169	164	181	184
1.15	♦ Personal		('000)	151	157	153	167	171
1.16	* holidays, leisure and recreation		('000)	133	138	135	150	156
1.17	* other personal purposes		('000)	18	19	18	17	15
1.18	♦ Business and professional		('000)	12	12	11	14	13
	Arrivals by mode of transport							
1.19	Total		('000)	163	169	164	181	184
1.20	♦ Air		('000)	163	169	164	181	184
1.21	♦ Water		('000)	..	..	..	..	..
1.22	♦ Land		('000)	..	..	..	..	..
1.23	* railway		('000)	..	..	..	..	..
1.24	* road		('000)	..	..	..	..	..
1.25	* others		('000)	..	..	..	..	..
	Arrivals by form of organization of the trip							
1.26	Total		('000)	163	..	164	..	183
1.27	♦ Package tour		('000)	103	..	108	..	125
1.28	♦ Other forms		('000)	60	..	56	..	58
	Accommodation							
	Total							
1.29	♦ Guests		('000)	163	169	164	181	184
1.30	♦ Overnights		('000)	2,282	2,380	2,311	2,633	2,618
	Hotels and similar establishments							
1.31	♦ Guests		('000)	142	148	146	162	166
1.32	♦ Overnights		('000)	1,657	1,733	1,754	2,068	2,047
	Expenditure							
1.33	Total		US$ Mn	..	..	..	..	..
1.34	♦ Travel		US$ Mn	457	435	458	510	..
1.35	♦ Passenger transport		US$ Mn	..	..	..	..	..
	Indicators							
1.39	Average size of travel party		Persons	..	..	..	..	..
	Average length of stay							
1.40	Total		Days	..	..	..	..	..
1.41	♦ For all commercial accommodation services	(2)	Nights	14.00	14.07	14.06	14.58	14.20
1.42	* of which, "hotels and similar establishments"		Nights	11.66	11.67	11.99	12.73	12.30
1.43	♦ For non commercial accommodation services		Days	30.09	31.35	30.82	31.13	31.90
1.44	Average expenditure per day		US$	..	..	..	..	..
3.	**OUTBOUND TOURISM**							
	Data							
	Departures							
3.1	Total		('000)	..	..	..	..	..
3.2	♦ Overnight visitors (tourists)		('000)	84	83	80	79	78
3.3	♦ Same-day visitors (excursionists)		('000)	..	..	..	..	..
	Expenditure							
3.4	Total		US$ Mn	..	..	..	..	..
3.5	♦ Travel		US$ Mn	168	158	156	169	..
3.6	♦ Passenger transport		US$ Mn	..	..	..	..	..

FRENCH POLYNESIA

Cod.	Basic data and indicators	Notes	Units	2011	2012	2013	2014	2015
4.	**TOURISM INDUSTRIES**							
	Data							
	Number of establishments							
4.1	Total		Units	..	..	..	..	..
4.2	♦ Accommodation for visitors		Units	..	..	..	..	..
4.3	* of which, "hotels and similar establishments"	(3)	Units	331	339	339	341	337
4.4	♦ Food and beverage serving activities		Units	..	..	..	..	..
4.5	♦ Passenger transportation		Units	..	..	..	..	..
4.6	♦ Travel agencies and other reservation services activities		Units	..	..	..	..	..
4.7	♦ Other tourism industries		Units	..	..	..	..	..
	Accommodation for visitors in hotels and similar establishments							
	Non-monetary data	(3)						
4.13	♦ Number of establishments		Units	331	339	339	341	337
4.14	♦ Number of rooms		Units	4,469	4,206	4,141	4,146	4,146
4.15	♦ Number of bed-places		Units	12,211	11,501	11,139	11,122	11,198
	Indicators							
4.16	Occupancy rate / rooms	(4)	Percent	53.70	56.80	60.50	63.10	64.60
4.17	Occupancy rate / bed-places		Percent	..	..	..	..	..
4.18	Average length of stay	(2)	Nights	11.70	11.70	12.00	12.73	12.30
4.19	Available capacity (bed-places per 1000 inhabitants)		Units	45.08	42.00	40.24	39.74	39.57
5.	**EMPLOYMENT**							
	Data							
	Number of employees by tourism industries							
5.1	Total		('000)	9.9	9.8	9.8	10.1	10.2
5.2	♦ Accommodation services for visitors (hotels and similar establishments)		('000)	4.1	4.1	4.1	4.3	4.5
5.3	♦ Other accommodation services		('000)	..	..	..	..	..
5.4	♦ Food and beverage serving activities		('000)	2.0	1.9	2.0	1.9	2.0
5.5	♦ Passenger transportation		('000)	3.3	3.2	3.2	3.3	3.3
5.6	♦ Travel agencies and other reservation services activities		('000)	0.2	0.2	0.2	0.2	0.2
5.7	♦ Other tourism industries		('000)	0.3	0.3	0.3	0.3	0.3
6.	**COMPLEMENTARY INDICATORS**							
	Demand							
6.1	Gross travel propensity		Units	..	..	..	..	..
6.2	(1.2 inbound tourists) / population		Units	0.60	0.62	0.59	0.65	0.65
	Macroeconomic indicators related to international tourism							
6.3	Inbound tourism expenditure over GDP		Percent	..	..	..	..	..
6.4	Outbound tourism expenditure over GDP		Percent	..	..	..	..	..
6.5	Tourism balance (inbound minus outbound tourism expenditure) over GDP		Percent	..	..	..	..	..
6.6	Tourism openness (inbound plus outbound tourism expenditure) over GDP		Percent	..	..	..	..	..
6.7	Tourism coverage (inbound over outbound tourism expenditure)		Percent	272.0	275.3	293.6	301.8	..
6.8	Inbound tourism expenditure over exports of goods		Percent	300.9	340.6	305.7	306.3	..
6.9	Inbound tourism expenditure over exports of services		Percent	40.6	43.2	45.0	47.3	..
6.10	Inbound tourism expenditure over exports of goods and services		Percent	35.8	38.3	39.2	41.0	..
6.11	Inbound tourism expenditure over current account credits		Percent	14.6	15.6	16.1	18.5	..
6.12	Outbound tourism expenditure over imports of goods		Percent	9.4	9.3	8.8	9.7	..
6.13	Outbound tourism expenditure over imports of services		Percent	30.1	31.2	31.9	34.6	..
6.14	Outbound tourism expenditure over imports of goods and		Percent	7.2	7.2	6.9	7.6	..
6.15	Outbound tourism expenditure over current account debits		Percent	4.7	4.8	4.7	5.3	..

GAMBIA

Cod.	Basic data and indicators	Notes	Units	2011	2012	2013	2014	2015
1.	**INBOUND TOURISM**							
	Data							
	Arrivals	(1)						
1.1	Total		('000)	..	..	..	..	..
1.2	♦ Overnight visitors (tourists)	(2)	('000)	106	157	171	156	135
1.3	♦ Same-day visitors (excursionists)		('000)	..	..	..	..	..
1.4	* of which, cruise passengers		('000)	..	..	..	..	..
	Arrivals by region	(1)(2)						
1.5	Total		('000)	106	157	171	156	135
1.6	♦ Africa		('000)	15	16	23	15	15
1.7	♦ Americas		('000)	2	3	3	4	4
1.8	♦ East Asia and the Pacific		('000)	..	..	..	..	..
1.9	♦ Europe		('000)	87	109	109	102	81
1.10	♦ Middle East		('000)	..	..	..	..	..
1.11	♦ South Asia		('000)	..	..	..	..	..
1.12	♦ Other not classified		('000)	2	29	36	35	35
1.13	* of which, nationals residing abroad		('000)	..	23	29	30	29
	Arrivals by main purpose	(1)(2)						
1.14	Total		('000)	106	..	..	..	135
1.15	♦ Personal		('000)	85	..	..	..	133
1.16	* holidays, leisure and recreation		('000)	70	..	..	..	127
1.17	* other personal purposes		('000)	15	..	..	..	7
1.18	♦ Business and professional		('000)	21	..	..	..	1
	Arrivals by mode of transport	(1)						
1.19	Total		('000)	106	157	171	156	449
1.20	♦ Air	(2)	('000)	106	157	171	156	135
1.21	♦ Water		('000)	..	..	..	..	17
1.22	♦ Land		('000)	..	..	..	..	297
1.23	* railway		('000)	..	..	..	..	..
1.24	* road		('000)	..	..	..	..	297
1.25	* others		('000)	..	..	..	..	..
	Expenditure							
1.33	Total		US$ Mn	109	127	103	127	138
1.34	♦ Travel		US$ Mn	78	94	72	107	120
1.35	♦ Passenger transport		US$ Mn	31	33	31	20	18
3.	**OUTBOUND TOURISM**							
	Data							
	Expenditure							
3.4	Total		US$ Mn	..	..	11	56	60
3.5	♦ Travel		US$ Mn	12	8	10	54	58
3.6	♦ Passenger transport		US$ Mn	..	..	1	2	2
	Expenditure by main purpose of the trip							
3.7	Total		US$ Mn	12	8	10	54	58
3.8	♦ Personal		US$ Mn	7	3	4	33	41
3.9	♦ Business and professional		US$ Mn	5	5	6	21	17
6.	**COMPLEMENTARY INDICATORS**							
	Demand							
6.1	Gross travel propensity		Units	..	..	..	..	..
6.2	(1.2 inbound tourists) / population		Units	0.06	0.09	0.09	0.08	0.07
	Macroeconomic indicators related to international tourism							
6.3	Inbound tourism expenditure over GDP		Percent	12.1	13.9	11.6	..	..
6.4	Outbound tourism expenditure over GDP		Percent	1.3	0.9	1.2	..	..
6.5	Tourism balance (inbound minus outbound tourism expenditure) over GDP		Percent	10.8	13.0	10.4	..	..
6.6	Tourism openness (inbound plus outbound tourism expenditure) over GDP		Percent	13.4	14.8	12.8	..	..
6.7	Tourism coverage (inbound over outbound tourism expenditure)		Percent	908.3	1,587.5	936.4	226.8	230.0
6.8	Inbound tourism expenditure over exports of goods		Percent	67.2	69.6	..	..	..
6.9	Inbound tourism expenditure over exports of services		Percent	75.8	83.8	..	..	..
6.10	Inbound tourism expenditure over exports of goods and services		Percent	35.6	38.0	..	..	..
6.11	Inbound tourism expenditure over current account credits		Percent	19.4	21.9	..	..	..
6.12	Outbound tourism expenditure over imports of goods		Percent	4.1	2.2	..	..	..
6.13	Outbound tourism expenditure over imports of services		Percent	17.5	10.0	..	..	..
6.14	Outbound tourism expenditure over imports of goods and		Percent	3.3	1.8	..	..	..
6.15	Outbound tourism expenditure over current account debits		Percent	2.7	1.6	..	..	..

GEORGIA

Cod.	Basic data and indicators	Notes	Units	2011	2012	2013	2014	2015
1.	**INBOUND TOURISM**							
	Data							
	Arrivals							
1.1	Total		('000)	2,822	4,428	5,392	5,516	5,901
1.2	♦ Overnight visitors (tourists)		('000)	1,319	1,790	2,065	2,229	2,282
1.3	♦ Same-day visitors (excursionists)		('000)	1,503	2,638	3,327	3,286	3,619
1.4	* of which, cruise passengers		('000)	..	..	..	..	..
	Arrivals by region							
1.5	Total		('000)	2,822	4,428	5,392	5,516	5,901
1.6	♦ Africa		('000)	4	7	5	4	4
1.7	♦ Americas		('000)	29	34	33	35	39
1.8	♦ East Asia and the Pacific		('000)	20	26	29	28	33
1.9	♦ Europe		('000)	2,695	4,226	5,168	5,355	5,723
1.10	♦ Middle East		('000)	6	17	63	39	56
1.11	♦ South Asia		('000)	66	98	93	54	41
1.12	♦ Other not classified		('000)	2	20	2	2	4
1.13	* of which, nationals residing abroad		('000)	..	..	..	..	..
	Arrivals by main purpose	(1)						
1.14	Total		('000)	439	626	774	866	1,170
1.15	♦ Personal		('000)	280	414	583	600	913
1.16	* holidays, leisure and recreation		('000)	219	315	417	442	750
1.17	* other personal purposes		('000)	61	99	166	158	164
1.18	♦ Business and professional		('000)	159	212	191	266	257
	Arrivals by mode of transport							
1.19	Total		('000)	2,822	4,428	5,392	5,516	5,901
1.20	♦ Air		('000)	336	429	586	643	765
1.21	♦ Water		('000)	50	62	44	44	40
1.22	♦ Land		('000)	2,436	3,937	4,762	4,829	5,097
1.23	* railway		('000)	55	64	63	72	63
1.24	* road		('000)	2,381	3,873	4,699	4,757	5,034
1.25	* others		('000)	..	..	..	..	..
	Arrivals by form of organization of the trip							
1.26	Total		('000)	2,822	4,428	5,392	..	..
1.27	♦ Package tour		('000)	40	44	113	..	..
1.28	♦ Other forms		('000)	2,782	4,384	5,279	..	..
	Accommodation							
	Hotels and similar establishments							
1.31	♦ Guests		('000)	438	626	774	866	1,170
1.32	♦ Overnights		('000)	..	..	..	..	..
	Expenditure							
1.33	Total		US$ Mn	1,069	1,565	1,916	1,972	2,117
1.34	♦ Travel		US$ Mn	955	1,411	1,720	1,787	1,936
1.35	♦ Passenger transport		US$ Mn	114	154	196	185	181
	Expenditure by main purpose of the trip							
1.36	Total		US$ Mn	955	1,411	1,719	1,787	1,936
1.37	♦ Personal		US$ Mn	567	860	1,094	1,144	1,182
1.38	♦ Business and professional		US$ Mn	388	551	625	643	754
	Indicators							
1.39	Average size of travel party		Persons	..	..	..	..	..
	Average length of stay							
1.40	Total		Days	9.00	..	4.80	5.60	5.10
1.41	♦ For all commercial accommodation services		Nights	..	..	5.00	..	..
1.42	* of which, "hotels and similar establishments"		Nights	..	..	..	..	..
1.43	♦ For non commercial accommodation services		Days	..	..	..	..	..
1.44	Average expenditure per day		US$	37.6	..	..	..	..
2.	**DOMESTIC TOURISM**							
	Data							
	Trips							
2.1	Total		('000)	..	..	..	..	12,361
2.2	♦ Overnight visitors (tourists)		('000)	..	..	..	..	5,823
2.3	♦ Same-day visitors (excursionists)		('000)	..	..	..	..	6,538
	Trips by main purpose							
2.4	Total		('000)	..	..	..	..	12,361
2.5	♦ Personal		('000)	..	..	..	..	11,618
2.6	* holidays, leisure and recreation		('000)	..	..	..	..	940
2.7	* other personal purposes		('000)	..	..	..	..	10,678
2.8	♦ Business and professional		('000)	..	..	..	..	743

GEORGIA

Cod.	Basic data and indicators	Notes	Units	2011	2012	2013	2014	2015
	Trips by mode of transport							
2.9	Total		('000)	..	..	..	..	12,361
2.10	♦ Air		('000)	..	..	..	..	..
2.11	♦ Water		('000)	..	..	..	..	..
2.12	♦ Land		('000)	..	..	..	..	12,361
2.13	* railway		('000)	..	..	..	..	471
2.14	* road		('000)	..	..	..	..	11,871
2.15	* others		('000)	..	..	..	..	19
	Trips by form of organization							
2.16	Total		('000)	..	..	..	..	12,361
2.17	♦ Package tour		('000)	..	..	..	..	14
2.18	♦ Other forms		('000)	..	..	..	..	12,347
	Accommodation							
	Total							
2.19	♦ Guests		('000)	..	..	..	5,187	5,051
2.20	♦ Overnights		('000)	..	..	..	26,512	26,935
	Hotels and similar establishments							
2.21	♦ Guests		('000)	415	560	482	525	685
2.22	♦ Overnights		('000)	..	..	..	3,187	2,342
	Indicators							
2.23	Average size of travel party		Persons	..	..	..	..	..
	Average length of stay							
2.24	Total		Days	..	..	..	3.40	..
2.25	♦ For all commercial accommodation services		Nights	..	..	3.00	4.95	4.50
2.26	* of which, "hotels and similar establishments"		Nights	..	..	..	5.09	3.20
2.27	♦ For non commercial accommodation services		Days	..	..	..	..	..
2.28	Average expenditure per day		US$	..	..	..	24.3	..
3.	**OUTBOUND TOURISM**							
	Data							
	Departures							
3.1	Total		('000)	..	..	..	..	..
3.2	♦ Overnight visitors (tourists)		('000)	2,237	2,734	3,220	3,106	3,135
3.3	♦ Same-day visitors (excursionists)		('000)	..	..	..	..	..
	Expenditure							
3.4	Total		US$ Mn	384	471	537	563	609
3.5	♦ Travel		US$ Mn	213	256	294	299	330
3.6	♦ Passenger transport		US$ Mn	171	215	243	264	279
	Expenditure by main purpose of the trip							
3.7	Total		US$ Mn	213	256	294	299	330
3.8	♦ Personal		US$ Mn	71	77	94	89	131
3.9	♦ Business and professional		US$ Mn	142	179	200	209	199
4.	**TOURISM INDUSTRIES**							
	Data							
	Number of establishments							
4.1	Total		Units	3,129	..	1,920	..	..
4.2	♦ Accommodation for visitors		Units	616	777	836	986	1,225
4.3	* of which, "hotels and similar establishments"	(2)	Units	616	777	836	986	1,225
4.4	♦ Food and beverage serving activities		Units	1,626	..	861	..	..
4.5	♦ Passenger transportation	(3)	Units	497	..	..	..	..
4.6	♦ Travel agencies and other reservation services activities		Units	390	..	223	..	..
4.7	♦ Other tourism industries		Units	..	..	..	..	..
	Accommodation for visitors in hotels and similar establishments							
	Monetary data							
4.8	♦ Output		US$ Mn	122.0	144.4	195.2	221.2	219.9
4.9	♦ Intermediate consumption		US$ Mn	54.3	64.2	84.0	95.2	94.7
4.10	♦ Gross value added		US$ Mn	67.7	80.2	111.2	126.0	125.3
4.11	♦ Compensation of employees		US$ Mn	23.6	..	..	..	..
4.12	♦ Gross fixed capital formation	(4)	US$ Mn	23.9	..	..	..	..
	Non-monetary data	(2)						
4.13	♦ Number of establishments		Units	616	777	836	986	1,225
4.14	♦ Number of rooms		Units	12,901	14,463	15,351	18,248	23,097
4.15	♦ Number of bed-places		Units	25,833	33,029	32,165	38,425	48,457
	Indicators							
4.16	Occupancy rate / rooms		Percent	..	..	..	..	..
4.17	Occupancy rate / bed-places		Percent	23.12	29.21	24.50	23.51	..
4.18	Average length of stay	(2)	Nights	4.00	4.00	5.00	4.00	..
4.19	Available capacity (bed-places per 1000 inhabitants)	(2)	Units	6.16	7.98	7.88	9.52	12.11

149

GEORGIA

Cod.	Basic data and indicators	Notes	Units	2011	2012	2013	2014	2015
	Travel agencies and other reservation service activities							
	Monetary data							
4.20	♦ Output		US$ Mn	277.2	333.0	391.3	408.4	410.2
4.21	♦ Intermediate consumption		US$ Mn	67.6	81.2	95.4	99.6	100.0
4.22	♦ Gross value added		US$ Mn	209.6	251.8	295.9	308.8	310.2
4.23	♦ Compensation of employees		US$ Mn	30.9	..	..	..	..
4.24	♦ Gross fixed capital formation	(4)	US$ Mn	2.4	..	..	..	..
	Non-monetary data							
	♦ Domestic trips							
4.25	* with package tour		Percent	..	..	..	0.2	0.1
4.26	* without package tour		Percent	..	..	..	98.8	99.9
	♦ Inbound trips							
4.27	* with package tour		Percent	..	..	..	..	..
4.28	* without package tour		Percent	..	..	..	..	..
	♦ Outbound trips							
4.29	* with package tour		Percent	..	..	..	..	..
4.30	* without package tour		Percent	..	..	..	..	..
5.	**EMPLOYMENT**							
	Data							
	Number of employees by tourism industries							
5.1	Total		('000)	53.6	59.2	53.8	62.0	..
5.2	♦ Accommodation services for visitors (hotels and similar establishments)		('000)	6.3	7.9	8.7	8.5	..
5.3	♦ Other accommodation services		('000)	..	..	..	..	..
5.4	♦ Food and beverage serving activities		('000)	18.0	19.9	19.2	21.5	..
5.5	♦ Passenger transportation	(3)	('000)	24.1	25.7	25.9	26.1	..
5.6	♦ Travel agencies and other reservation services activities		('000)	5.2	5.6	..	5.9	..
5.7	♦ Other tourism industries		('000)	..	..	..	..	..
	Number of jobs by status in employment							
5.8	Total		('000)	53.6	59.2	53.8	62.0	..
5.9	♦ Employees		('000)	53.6	59.2	53.8	62.0	..
5.10	♦ Self employed		('000)	..	..	..	..	..
	Indicators							
	Number of full-time equivalent jobs by status in employment							
5.11	Total		('000)	45.2	59.2	..	..	..
5.12	♦ Employees		('000)	45.2	59.2	..	..	..
5.13	* male		('000)	26.5	35.0	..	..	..
5.14	* female		('000)	18.7	24.2	..	..	..
5.15	♦ Self employed		('000)	..	..	..	..	..
5.16	* male		('000)	..	..	..	..	..
5.17	* female		('000)	..	..	..	..	..
6.	**COMPLEMENTARY INDICATORS**							
	Demand							
6.1	Gross travel propensity		Units	..	..	..	..	..
6.2	(1.2 inbound tourists + 2.2 domestic tourists) / population		Units	..	..	..	..	2.03
	Macroeconomic indicators related to international tourism							
6.3	Inbound tourism expenditure over GDP		Percent	7.4	9.9	11.8	12.0	..
6.4	Outbound tourism expenditure over GDP		Percent	2.7	3.0	3.3	3.4	..
6.5	Tourism balance (inbound minus outbound tourism expenditure) over GDP		Percent	4.7	6.9	8.5	8.6	..
6.6	Tourism openness (inbound plus outbound tourism expenditure) over GDP		Percent	10.1	12.9	15.1	15.4	..
6.7	Tourism coverage (inbound over outbound tourism expenditure)		Percent	278.4	332.3	356.8	350.3	347.6
6.8	Inbound tourism expenditure over exports of goods		Percent	33.2	45.2	45.7	49.4	69.6
6.9	Inbound tourism expenditure over exports of services		Percent	52.9	61.1	64.2	64.8	67.1
6.10	Inbound tourism expenditure over exports of goods and services		Percent	20.4	26.0	26.7	28.0	34.2
6.11	Inbound tourism expenditure over current account credits		Percent	14.3	18.2	19.8	20.5	24.3
6.12	Outbound tourism expenditure over imports of goods		Percent	5.7	6.1	7.0	6.8	8.3
6.13	Outbound tourism expenditure over imports of services		Percent	30.4	32.5	34.4	32.6	36.1
6.14	Outbound tourism expenditure over imports of goods and		Percent	4.8	5.2	5.8	5.6	6.7
6.15	Outbound tourism expenditure over current account debits		Percent	4.3	4.6	5.2	5.0	6.1

GERMANY

Cod.	Basic data and indicators	Notes	Units	2011	2012	2013	2014	2015
1.	**INBOUND TOURISM**							
	Data							
	Arrivals							
1.1	Total		('000)	..	..	..	..	..
1.2	♦ Overnight visitors (tourists)	(1)	('000)	28,374	30,411	31,545	32,999	34,970
1.3	♦ Same-day visitors (excursionists)		('000)	..	..	..	..	..
1.4	* of which, cruise passengers		('000)	..	..	..	..	..
	Arrivals by region	(1)						
1.5	Total		('000)	28,374	30,411	31,545	32,999	34,970
1.6	♦ Africa		('000)	193	227	246	254	274
1.7	♦ Americas		('000)	2,914	3,155	3,192	3,272	3,487
1.8	♦ East Asia and the Pacific		('000)	2,297	2,666	2,805	3,024	3,556
1.9	♦ Europe		('000)	21,861	23,121	23,899	24,915	25,951
1.10	♦ Middle East		('000)	343	449	517	587	698
1.11	♦ South Asia		('000)	161	172	190	194	213
1.12	♦ Other not classified		('000)	605	621	696	753	791
1.13	* of which, nationals residing abroad		('000)	..	..	..	..	..
	Arrivals by mode of transport							
1.19	Total		('000)	75,672	77,771	79,298	82,072	85,658
1.20	♦ Air		('000)	75,672	77,771	79,298	82,072	85,658
1.21	♦ Water		('000)	..	..	..	..	..
1.22	♦ Land		('000)	..	..	..	..	..
1.23	* railway		('000)	..	..	..	..	..
1.24	* road		('000)	..	..	..	..	..
1.25	* others		('000)	..	..	..	..	..
	Accommodation							
	Total							
1.29	♦ Guests		('000)	28,374	30,411	31,545	32,999	34,970
1.30	♦ Overnights		('000)	63,746	68,828	71,919	75,577	79,672
	Hotels and similar establishments							
1.31	♦ Guests		('000)	25,311	27,076	28,123	29,433	31,227
1.32	♦ Overnights		('000)	53,793	58,096	60,804	63,843	67,433
	Expenditure							
1.33	Total		US$ Mn	53,431	51,645	55,318	55,939	47,393
1.34	♦ Travel		US$ Mn	38,903	38,068	41,285	43,263	36,842
1.35	♦ Passenger transport		US$ Mn	14,528	13,577	14,033	12,676	10,551
	Indicators							
1.39	Average size of travel party		Persons	..	..	..	..	..
	Average length of stay							
1.40	Total		Days	..	..	..	..	..
1.41	♦ For all commercial accommodation services		Nights	2.20	2.30	2.30	2.30	2.30
1.42	* of which, "hotels and similar establishments"		Nights	2.10	2.10	2.20	2.20	2.20
1.43	♦ For non commercial accommodation services		Days	..	..	..	..	..
1.44	Average expenditure per day		US$	..	..	..	..	..
2.	**DOMESTIC TOURISM**							
	Data							
	Trips							
2.1	Total		('000)	..	..	..	..	..
2.2	♦ Overnight visitors (tourists)	(2)	('000)	..	164,795	161,123	153,902	..
2.3	♦ Same-day visitors (excursionists)		('000)	..	..	..	..	..
	Trips by mode of transport							
2.9	Total		('000)	24,394	23,479	22,599	22,762	23,089
2.10	♦ Air		('000)	24,394	23,479	22,599	22,762	23,089
2.11	♦ Water		('000)	..	..	..	..	..
2.12	♦ Land		('000)	..	..	..	..	..
2.13	* railway		('000)	..	..	..	..	..
2.14	* road		('000)	..	..	..	..	..
2.15	* others		('000)	..	..	..	..	..
	Accommodation							
	Total							
2.19	♦ Guests		('000)	118,962	122,328	123,646	127,791	131,817
2.20	♦ Overnights		('000)	330,290	338,432	339,860	348,484	356,560
	Hotels and similar establishments							
2.21	♦ Guests		('000)	92,473	95,238	96,475	99,760	103,021
2.22	♦ Overnights		('000)	196,112	201,844	203,794	209,484	215,061

GERMANY

Cod.	Basic data and indicators	Notes	Units	2011	2012	2013	2014	2015
	Indicators							
2.23	Average size of travel party		Persons	..	..	..	..	
	Average length of stay							
2.24	Total		Days	..	..	..	..	
2.25	♦ For all commercial accommodation services		Nights	2.80	2.80	2.70	2.70	2.70
2.26	* of which, "hotels and similar establishments"		Nights	2.10	2.10	2.10	2.10	2.10
2.27	♦ For non commercial accommodation services		Days	..	..	..	..	
2.28	Average expenditure per day		US$	..	..	..	..	
3.	**OUTBOUND TOURISM**							
	Data							
	Departures							
3.1	Total		('000)	..	..	..	..	
3.2	♦ Overnight visitors (tourists)	(2)	('000)	84,692	82,729	87,459	83,008	..
3.3	♦ Same-day visitors (excursionists)		('000)	..	..	..	..	
	Expenditure							
3.4	Total		US$ Mn	99,840	96,235	105,495	106,663	88,843
3.5	♦ Travel		US$ Mn	86,166	83,235	91,320	93,253	76,278
3.6	♦ Passenger transport		US$ Mn	13,674	13,000	14,175	13,410	12,565
4.	**TOURISM INDUSTRIES**							
	Data							
	Number of establishments							
4.1	Total		Units	257,028	250,568	241,022	258,018	..
4.2	♦ Accommodation for visitors		Units	54,949	53,246	52,473	51,865	51,419
4.3	* of which, "hotels and similar establishments"		Units	35,766	34,696	34,116	33,512	33,084
4.4	♦ Food and beverage serving activities		Units	162,456	158,270	147,164	165,327	..
4.5	♦ Passenger transportation		Units	26,256	25,694	27,020	25,324	..
4.6	♦ Travel agencies and other reservation services activities		Units	13,367	13,358	14,365	15,502	..
4.7	♦ Other tourism industries		Units	..	..	..	..	
	Accommodation for visitors in hotels and similar establishments							
	Monetary data							
4.8	♦ Output		US$ Mn	30,303.5	32,133.4	29,096.1	32,055.2	..
4.9	♦ Intermediate consumption		US$ Mn	16,834.5	17,827.5	16,288.7	17,564.6	..
4.10	♦ Gross value added		US$ Mn	14,529.7	15,552.0	13,955.9	15,701.9	..
4.11	♦ Compensation of employees		US$ Mn	7,237.0	8,010.1	7,378.3	8,090.4	..
4.12	♦ Gross fixed capital formation		US$ Mn	2,274.3	2,596.4	2,157.6	2,308.5	..
	Non-monetary data							
4.13	♦ Number of establishments		Units	35,766	34,696	34,116	33,512	33,084
4.14	♦ Number of rooms		Units	952,330	948,825	950,216	949,900	953,889
4.15	♦ Number of bed-places		Units	1,813,153	1,817,567	1,827,060	1,832,167	1,908,880
	Indicators							
4.16	Occupancy rate / rooms		Percent	..	57.10	57.90	59.10	60.20
4.17	Occupancy rate / bed-places		Percent	38.60	39.90	40.67	41.94	43.11
4.18	Average length of stay	(3)	Nights	2.12	2.13	2.12	2.12	2.10
4.19	Available capacity (bed-places per 1000 inhabitants)		Units	22.54	22.58	22.68	22.72	23.66
	Travel agencies and other reservation service activities							
	Monetary data							
4.20	♦ Output		US$ Mn	15,509.7	14,430.8	16,699.4	15,677.9	..
4.21	♦ Intermediate consumption		US$ Mn	6,781.2	6,370.0	7,856.9	6,455.9	..
4.22	♦ Gross value added		US$ Mn	8,634.0	7,948.5	8,657.9	9,043.0	..
4.23	♦ Compensation of employees		US$ Mn	3,265.6	3,226.8	3,532.3	3,530.2	..
4.24	♦ Gross fixed capital formation		US$ Mn	361.4	387.6	338.6	360.7	..
5.	**EMPLOYMENT**							
	Data							
	Number of employees by tourism industries							
5.1	Total		('000)	2,299.0	2,305.5	2,244.7	2,398.3	..
5.2	♦ Accommodation services for visitors (hotels and similar establishments)		('000)	456.8	479.4	453.9	485.8	..
5.3	♦ Other accommodation services		('000)	57.8	52.5	52.8	56.8	..
5.4	♦ Food and beverage serving activities		('000)	1,255.0	1,236.5	1,176.8	1,306.6	..
5.5	♦ Passenger transportation		('000)	442.9	447.4	463.6	456.1	..
5.6	♦ Travel agencies and other reservation services activities		('000)	86.5	89.7	97.6	93.0	..
5.7	♦ Other tourism industries		('000)	..	..	..	..	

GERMANY

Cod.	Basic data and indicators	Notes	Units	2011	2012	2013	2014	2015
	Number of jobs by status in employment							
5.8	Total		('000)	2,459.2	2,483.4	2,423.5	2,590.4	..
5.9	♦ Employees		('000)	2,210.4	2,239.4	2,191.6	2,339.4	..
5.10	♦ Self employed		('000)	248.8	244.0	231.9	251.0	..
6.	**COMPLEMENTARY INDICATORS**							
	Demand							
6.1	Gross travel propensity		Units	..	..	..	..	..
6.2	(1.2 inbound tourists + 2.2 domestic tourists) / population		Units	..	2.43	2.39	2.32	..
	Macroeconomic indicators related to international tourism							
6.3	Inbound tourism expenditure over GDP		Percent	1.4	1.5	1.5	1.4	1.4
6.4	Outbound tourism expenditure over GDP		Percent	2.7	2.7	2.8	2.8	2.6
6.5	Tourism balance (inbound minus outbound tourism expenditure) over GDP		Percent	-1.3	-1.2	-1.3	-1.4	-1.2
6.6	Tourism openness (inbound plus outbound tourism expenditure) over GDP		Percent	4.1	4.2	4.3	4.2	4.0
6.7	Tourism coverage (inbound over outbound tourism expenditure)		Percent	53.5	53.7	52.4	52.4	53.3
6.8	Inbound tourism expenditure over exports of goods		Percent	3.7	3.8	3.9	3.8	3.6
6.9	Inbound tourism expenditure over exports of services		Percent	21.3	20.5	20.3	19.2	17.9
6.10	Inbound tourism expenditure over exports of goods and services		Percent	3.2	3.2	3.2	3.2	3.0
6.11	Inbound tourism expenditure over current account credits		Percent	2.6	2.6	2.7	2.7	2.5
6.12	Outbound tourism expenditure over imports of goods		Percent	8.3	8.6	9.1	9.0	8.7
6.13	Outbound tourism expenditure over imports of services		Percent	33.7	32.7	32.1	31.5	29.8
6.14	Outbound tourism expenditure over imports of goods and		Percent	6.6	6.8	7.1	7.0	6.8
6.15	Outbound tourism expenditure over current account debits		Percent	5.2	5.4	5.6	5.6	5.4

GHANA

Cod.	Basic data and indicators	Notes	Units	2011	2012	2013	2014	2015
1.	**INBOUND TOURISM**							
	Data							
	Arrivals							
1.1	Total	(1)	('000)	..	..	..	..	..
1.2	♦ Overnight visitors (tourists)		('000)	821	903	994	825	897
1.3	♦ Same-day visitors (excursionists)		('000)	..	..	..	..	..
1.4	* of which, cruise passengers		('000)	..	..	..	..	..
	Expenditure							
1.33	Total		US$ Mn	797	1,154	1,010	1,027	911
1.34	♦ Travel		US$ Mn	694	914	853	897	819
1.35	♦ Passenger transport		US$ Mn	103	240	157	130	92
	Expenditure by main purpose of the trip							
1.36	Total		US$ Mn	694	914	853	897	819
1.37	♦ Personal		US$ Mn	208	274	256	269	246
1.38	♦ Business and professional		US$ Mn	486	640	597	628	573
3.	**OUTBOUND TOURISM**							
	Data							
	Expenditure							
3.4	Total		US$ Mn	1,026	976	982	947	1,405
3.5	♦ Travel		US$ Mn	464	464	473	458	737
3.6	♦ Passenger transport		US$ Mn	562	512	509	489	668
	Expenditure by main purpose of the trip							
3.7	Total		US$ Mn	464	464	473	459	737
3.8	♦ Personal		US$ Mn	139	139	142	138	221
3.9	♦ Business and professional		US$ Mn	325	325	331	321	516
4.	**TOURISM INDUSTRIES**							
	Data							
	Number of establishments							
4.1	Total		Units	..	..	..	..	..
4.2	♦ Accommodation for visitors		Units	2,135	..	2,228	2,578	..
4.3	* of which, "hotels and similar establishments"		Units	..	..	..	..	..
4.4	♦ Food and beverage serving activities		Units	..	..	..	..	..
4.5	♦ Passenger transportation		Units	..	..	..	..	..
4.6	♦ Travel agencies and other reservation services activities		Units	..	..	..	..	..
4.7	♦ Other tourism industries		Units	..	..	..	..	..
	Accommodation for visitors in hotels and similar establishments							
	Non-monetary data							
4.13	♦ Number of establishments		Units	2,135	..	2,228	2,578	..
4.14	♦ Number of rooms		Units	..	..	..	..	..
4.15	♦ Number of bed-places		Units	..	..	..	..	..
5.	**EMPLOYMENT**							
	Data							
	Number of employees by tourism industries							
5.1	Total	(2)	('000)	259.0	287.0	319.0	354.0	..
5.2	♦ Accommodation services for visitors (hotels and similar establishments)		('000)	..	..	..	..	..
5.3	♦ Other accommodation services		('000)	..	..	..	..	..
5.4	♦ Food and beverage serving activities		('000)	..	..	..	..	..
5.5	♦ Passenger transportation		('000)	..	..	..	..	..
5.6	♦ Travel agencies and other reservation services activities		('000)	..	..	..	..	..
5.7	♦ Other tourism industries		('000)	..	..	..	..	..
6.	**COMPLEMENTARY INDICATORS**							
	Demand							
6.1	Gross travel propensity		Units	..	..	..	..	..
6.2	(1.2 inbound tourists) / population		Units	0.03	0.04	0.04	0.03	0.03
	Macroeconomic indicators related to international tourism							
6.3	Inbound tourism expenditure over GDP		Percent	2.0	2.8	2.1	..	..
6.4	Outbound tourism expenditure over GDP		Percent	2.6	2.3	2.0	..	..
6.5	Tourism balance (inbound minus outbound tourism expenditure) over GDP		Percent	-0.6	0.5	0.1	..	..
6.6	Tourism openness (inbound plus outbound tourism expenditure) over GDP		Percent	4.6	5.1	4.1	..	..

GHANA

Cod.	Basic data and indicators	Notes	Units	2011	2012	2013	2014	2015
6.7	Tourism coverage (inbound over outbound tourism expenditure)		Percent	77.7	118.2	102.9	108.4	64.8
6.8	Inbound tourism expenditure over exports of goods		Percent	6.2	8.5	7.3	7.8	8.8
6.9	Inbound tourism expenditure over exports of services		Percent	44.0	35.4	41.2	50.2	14.8
6.10	Inbound tourism expenditure over exports of goods and services		Percent	5.5	6.9	6.2	6.7	5.5
6.11	Inbound tourism expenditure over current account credits		Percent	4.6	6.0	5.5	5.9	4.1
6.12	Outbound tourism expenditure over imports of goods		Percent	6.5	5.5	5.6	6.5	10.4
6.13	Outbound tourism expenditure over imports of services		Percent	28.0	23.0	20.0	20.4	19.2
6.14	Outbound tourism expenditure over imports of goods and		Percent	5.3	4.4	4.4	4.9	6.8
6.15	Outbound tourism expenditure over current account debits		Percent	5.2	4.4	4.3	4.9	5.9

GREECE

Cod.	Basic data and indicators	Notes	Units	2011	2012	2013	2014	2015
1.	**INBOUND TOURISM**							
	Data							
	Arrivals	(1)						
1.1	Total		('000)	..	..	20,112	24,272	26,114
1.2	♦ Overnight visitors (tourists)		('000)	16,427	15,518	17,920	22,033	23,599
1.3	♦ Same-day visitors (excursionists)		('000)	..	..	2,192	2,239	2,515
1.4	* of which, cruise passengers		('000)	..	..	2,192	2,239	2,515
	Arrivals by region	(1)						
1.5	Total		('000)	16,427	15,518	17,920	22,033	23,599
1.6	♦ Africa		('000)	34	33	27	40	36
1.7	♦ Americas		('000)	719	559	754	890	1,095
1.8	♦ East Asia and the Pacific		('000)	207	216	238	365	362
1.9	♦ Europe		('000)	15,430	14,661	16,822	20,651	21,985
1.10	♦ Middle East		('000)	28	36	73	86	112
1.11	♦ South Asia		('000)	9	13	5	1	11
1.12	♦ Other not classified		('000)	..	..	..	..	..
1.13	* of which, nationals residing abroad		('000)	..	..	..	..	..
	Arrivals by mode of transport	(1)						
1.19	Total		('000)	16,427	15,517	17,920	22,033	23,599
1.20	♦ Air		('000)	11,671	10,993	12,302	14,057	14,981
1.21	♦ Water		('000)	948	790	807	701	632
1.22	♦ Land		('000)	3,808	3,734	4,810	7,275	7,986
1.23	* railway		('000)	4	..	..	7	5
1.24	* road		('000)	3,804	3,734	4,810	7,268	7,981
1.25	* others		('000)	..	..	..	..	..
	Arrivals by form of organization of the trip	(1)						
1.26	Total		('000)	16,427	15,518	17,920	22,033	23,599
1.27	♦ Package tour		('000)	4,479	4,122	4,781	4,576	3,090
1.28	♦ Other forms		('000)	11,948	11,396	13,139	17,457	20,509
	Accommodation							
	Total							
1.29	♦ Guests		('000)	10,266	9,396	10,667	12,082	12,949
1.30	♦ Overnights		('000)	54,518	51,095	57,746	61,659	64,365
	Hotels and similar establishments							
1.31	♦ Guests		('000)	10,042	9,244	10,490	11,882	12,735
1.32	♦ Overnights		('000)	53,768	50,540	57,058	60,902	63,571
	Expenditure							
1.33	Total		US$ Mn	16,256	14,671	17,436	19,481	17,260
1.34	♦ Travel		US$ Mn	14,801	13,216	16,087	17,813	15,662
1.35	♦ Passenger transport		US$ Mn	1,455	1,455	1,349	1,668	1,598
	Expenditure by main purpose of the trip							
1.36	Total		US$ Mn	14,801	13,217	16,087	17,813	15,662
1.37	♦ Personal		US$ Mn	13,805	12,470	15,245	16,782	14,796
1.38	♦ Business and professional		US$ Mn	996	747	842	1,031	866
	Indicators							
1.39	Average size of travel party		Persons	..	..	..	..	..
	Average length of stay							
1.40	Total		Days	..	..	..	..	..
1.41	♦ For all commercial accommodation services		Nights	5.31	5.44	5.41	5.10	4.97
1.42	* of which, "hotels and similar establishments"		Nights	5.35	5.47	5.44	5.13	4.99
1.43	♦ For non commercial accommodation services		Days	..	..	..	..	..
1.44	Average expenditure per day		US$	..	..	..	..	..
2.	**DOMESTIC TOURISM**							
	Data							
	Trips							
2.1	Total		('000)	..	..	..	..	..
2.2	♦ Overnight visitors (tourists)	(2)	('000)	4,909	3,598	3,258	3,744	3,369
2.3	♦ Same-day visitors (excursionists)		('000)	..	..	..	..	..
	Trips by mode of transport	(2)						
2.9	Total		('000)	4,909	3,598	3,258	3,744	3,370
2.10	♦ Air		('000)	251	180	128	228	216
2.11	♦ Water		('000)	1,073	729	764	844	820
2.12	♦ Land		('000)	3,585	2,689	2,366	2,672	2,334
2.13	* railway		('000)	89	40	49	47	42
2.14	* road		('000)	3,479	2,621	2,314	2,623	2,291
2.15	* others		('000)	18	28	4	2	1
	Trips by form of organization	(2)						
2.16	Total		('000)	4,909	3,598	3,258	3,744	3,369
2.17	♦ Package tour		('000)	61	72	51	107	69
2.18	♦ Other forms		('000)	4,849	3,526	3,207	3,637	3,300

GREECE

Cod.	Basic data and indicators	Notes	Units	2011	2012	2013	2014	2015
	Accommodation							
	Total							
2.19	♦ Guests		('000)	6,479	5,395	5,659	5,662	5,873
2.20	♦ Overnights		('000)	16,330	13,290	13,723	13,732	13,967
	Hotels and similar establishments							
2.21	♦ Guests		('000)	6,313	5,257	5,519	5,537	5,744
2.22	♦ Overnights		('000)	15,370	12,515	13,007	13,050	13,201
	Indicators							
2.23	Average size of travel party		Persons	..	..	..	..	..
	Average length of stay							
2.24	Total		Days	..	..	..	..	..
2.25	♦ For all commercial accommodation services		Nights	2.52	2.46	2.42	2.43	2.38
2.26	* of which, "hotels and similar establishments"		Nights	2.43	2.38	2.36	2.36	2.30
2.27	♦ For non commercial accommodation services		Days	..	..	..	..	..
2.28	Average expenditure per day		US$	..	..	..	..	..
3.	**OUTBOUND TOURISM**							
	Data							
	Departures							
3.1	Total		('000)	..	..	..	..	..
3.2	♦ Overnight visitors (tourists)	(1)	('000)	4,941	4,681	4,594	5,802	6,291
3.3	♦ Same-day visitors (excursionists)		('000)	..	..	..	..	..
	Expenditure							
3.4	Total		US$ Mn	3,807	3,006	3,768	4,001	3,537
3.5	♦ Travel		US$ Mn	3,159	2,365	2,435	2,754	2,259
3.6	♦ Passenger transport		US$ Mn	648	641	1,333	1,247	1,278
	Expenditure by main purpose of the trip							
3.7	Total		US$ Mn	3,159	2,365	2,435	2,754	2,259
3.8	♦ Personal		US$ Mn	1,617	1,278	1,283	1,374	1,156
3.9	♦ Business and professional		US$ Mn	1,542	1,087	1,152	1,380	1,103
	Indicators							
3.10	Average length of stay	(1)	Days	6.76	7.70	7.73	7.20	6.43
3.11	Average expenditure per day		US$	..	..	..	..	..
4.	**TOURISM INDUSTRIES**							
	Data							
	Number of establishments							
4.1	Total		Units	..	..	..	..	..
4.2	♦ Accommodation for visitors		Units	..	..	..	..	..
4.3	* of which, "hotels and similar establishments"	(3)	Units	9,648	9,670	9,677	9,745	9,757
4.4	♦ Food and beverage serving activities		Units	..	..	..	..	..
4.5	♦ Passenger transportation		Units	..	..	..	..	..
4.6	♦ Travel agencies and other reservation services activities		Units	..	..	..	..	..
4.7	♦ Other tourism industries		Units	..	..	..	..	..
	Accommodation for visitors in hotels and similar establishments							
	Non-monetary data	(3)						
4.13	♦ Number of establishments		Units	9,648	9,670	9,677	9,745	9,757
4.14	♦ Number of rooms		Units	397,322	400,433	401,196	404,779	406,200
4.15	♦ Number of bed-places		Units	763,668	771,271	773,445	780,721	784,315
	Indicators							
4.16	Occupancy rate / rooms		Percent	..	..	..	..	..
4.17	Occupancy rate / bed-places		Percent	48.30	43.20	45.20	47.30	49.10
4.18	Average length of stay		Nights	4.23	4.35	4.38	4.25	4.15
4.19	Available capacity (bed-places per 1000 inhabitants)		Units	68.47	69.42	69.96	70.97	71.60
6.	**COMPLEMENTARY INDICATORS**							
	Demand							
6.1	Gross travel propensity		Units	..	..	..	..	..
6.2	(1.2 inbound tourists + 2.2 domestic tourists) / population		Units	1.91	1.72	1.92	2.34	2.46
	Macroeconomic indicators related to international tourism							
6.3	Inbound tourism expenditure over GDP		Percent	5.7	6.0	7.2	8.2	8.8
6.4	Outbound tourism expenditure over GDP		Percent	1.3	1.2	1.6	1.7	1.8
6.5	Tourism balance (inbound minus outbound tourism expenditure) over GDP		Percent	4.4	4.8	5.6	6.5	7.0
6.6	Tourism openness (inbound plus outbound tourism expenditure) over GDP		Percent	7.0	7.2	8.8	9.9	10.6

GREECE

Cod.	Basic data and indicators	Notes	Units	2011	2012	2013	2014	2015
6.7	Tourism coverage (inbound over outbound tourism expenditure)		Percent	427.0	488.1	462.7	486.9	488.0
6.8	Inbound tourism expenditure over exports of goods		Percent	59.2	52.6	48.8	54.8	62.8
6.9	Inbound tourism expenditure over exports of services		Percent	40.5	41.5	46.9	47.2	55.7
6.10	Inbound tourism expenditure over exports of goods and services		Percent	24.0	23.2	23.9	25.4	29.5
6.11	Inbound tourism expenditure over current account credits		Percent	20.7	19.6	19.9	21.8	25.7
6.12	Outbound tourism expenditure over imports of goods		Percent	5.8	5.7	6.0	6.1	7.6
6.13	Outbound tourism expenditure over imports of services		Percent	19.4	18.7	23.1	23.6	29.0
6.14	Outbound tourism expenditure over imports of goods and		Percent	4.5	4.3	4.7	4.9	6.0
6.15	Outbound tourism expenditure over current account debits		Percent	3.9	3.7	4.1	4.2	5.2

GRENADA

Cod.	Basic data and indicators	Notes	Units	2011	2012	2013	2014	2015
1.	**INBOUND TOURISM**							
	**Data**							
	Arrivals							
1.1	Total		('000)	447	379	332	393	443
1.2	♦ Overnight visitors (tourists)	(1)	('000)	118	116	113	134	141
1.3	♦ Same-day visitors (excursionists)	(2)	('000)	328	263	219	260	303
1.4	* of which, cruise passengers		('000)	310	243	197	235	281
	Arrivals by region	(1)						
1.5	Total		('000)	118	117	113	134	141
1.6	♦ Africa		('000)	1	1	1	1	1
1.7	♦ Americas		('000)	65	67	71	83	86
1.8	♦ East Asia and the Pacific		('000)	1	1	1	1	2
1.9	♦ Europe		('000)	36	33	24	31	33
1.10	♦ Middle East		('000)	..	..	..	..	..
1.11	♦ South Asia		('000)	..	..	..	..	..
1.12	♦ Other not classified		('000)	15	15	17	18	20
1.13	* of which, nationals residing abroad		('000)	15	15	15	16	18
	Arrivals by main purpose	(1)						
1.14	Total		('000)	118	116	113	134	141
1.15	♦ Personal		('000)	98	99	99	113	121
1.16	* holidays, leisure and recreation		('000)	71	70	71	74	80
1.17	* other personal purposes		('000)	27	29	28	39	41
1.18	♦ Business and professional		('000)	20	17	14	20	20
	Arrivals by mode of transport							
1.19	Total		('000)	133	132	135	159	163
1.20	♦ Air		('000)	114	112	113	134	141
1.21	♦ Water		('000)	19	20	22	25	22
1.22	♦ Land		('000)	..	..	..	..	..
1.23	* railway		('000)	..	..	..	..	..
1.24	* road		('000)	..	..	..	..	..
1.25	* others		('000)	..	..	..	..	..
	Accommodation							
	Total							
1.29	♦ Guests	(1)	('000)	118	116	113	134	141
1.30	♦ Overnights		('000)	..	..	..	..	..
	Hotels and similar establishments							
1.31	♦ Guests		('000)	58	60	78	85	90
1.32	♦ Overnights		('000)	..	..	..	..	..
	Expenditure							
1.33	Total		US$ Mn	..	..	..	..	..
1.34	♦ Travel		US$ Mn	117	122	121	139	147
1.35	♦ Passenger transport		US$ Mn	..	..	..	..	..
	**Indicators**							
1.39	Average size of travel party		Persons	..	..	..	..	2.0
	Average length of stay							
1.40	Total		Days	..	..	..	..	8.71
1.41	♦ For all commercial accommodation services		Nights	8.21	8.93	..	..	8.81
1.42	* of which, "hotels and similar establishments"		Nights	7.36	8.24	..	..	8.62
1.43	♦ For non commercial accommodation services		Days	9.26	10.63	..	..	11.06
1.44	Average expenditure per day		US$	..	..	..	..	..
3.	**OUTBOUND TOURISM**							
	**Data**							
	Expenditure							
3.4	Total		US$ Mn	..	..	..	..	..
3.5	♦ Travel		US$ Mn	10	11	11	..	..
3.6	♦ Passenger transport		US$ Mn	..	..	..	..	..
4.	**TOURISM INDUSTRIES**							
	**Data**							
	Number of establishments							
4.1	Total		Units	..	..	..	..	..
4.2	♦ Accommodation for visitors		Units	..	..	..	..	..
4.3	* of which, "hotels and similar establishments"		Units	79	79	83	82	85
4.4	♦ Food and beverage serving activities		Units	..	..	..	..	..
4.5	♦ Passenger transportation		Units	..	..	..	..	..
4.6	♦ Travel agencies and other reservation services activities		Units	..	..	..	..	..
4.7	♦ Other tourism industries		Units	..	..	..	..	..

GRENADA

Cod.	Basic data and indicators	Notes	Units	2011	2012	2013	2014	2015
	Accommodation for visitors in hotels and similar establishments							
	Non-monetary data							
4.13	♦ Number of establishments		Units	79	79	83	82	85
4.14	♦ Number of rooms	(3)	Units	1,889	1,889	1,967	1,968	2,017
4.15	♦ Number of bed-places	(3)	Units	2,879	2,879	2,967	2,992	3,061
	Indicators							
4.16	Occupancy rate / rooms		Percent	..	..	..	..	..
4.17	Occupancy rate / bed-places		Percent	..	..	..	..	..
4.18	Average length of stay		Nights	8.21	9.08	9.12	8.71	8.81
4.19	Available capacity (bed-places per 1000 inhabitants)		Units	27.40	27.30	28.02	28.13	28.65
6.	**COMPLEMENTARY INDICATORS**							
	Demand							
6.1	Gross travel propensity		Units	..	..	..	..	..
6.2	(1.2 inbound tourists) / population		Units	1.12	1.10	1.07	1.26	1.32
	Macroeconomic indicators related to international tourism							
6.3	Inbound tourism expenditure over GDP		Percent	15.0	15.3	14.5	15.8	..
6.4	Outbound tourism expenditure over GDP		Percent	1.3	1.4	1.3	..	..
6.5	Tourism balance (inbound minus outbound tourism expenditure) over GDP		Percent	13.7	13.9	13.2	15.8	..
6.6	Tourism openness (inbound plus outbound tourism expenditure) over GDP		Percent	16.3	16.7	15.8	15.8	..
6.7	Tourism coverage (inbound over outbound tourism expenditure)		Percent	1,170.0	1,109.1	1,100.0	..	..
6.8	Inbound tourism expenditure over exports of goods		Percent	314.9	285.0	260.1	..	..
6.9	Inbound tourism expenditure over exports of services		Percent	73.6	74.5	74.1	..	..
6.10	Inbound tourism expenditure over exports of goods and services		Percent	59.6	59.1	57.7	..	..
6.11	Inbound tourism expenditure over current account credits		Percent	48.7	47.6	47.3	..	..
6.12	Outbound tourism expenditure over imports of goods		Percent	3.4	3.7	3.4	..	..
6.13	Outbound tourism expenditure over imports of services		Percent	10.0	11.5	11.1	..	..
6.14	Outbound tourism expenditure over imports of goods and		Percent	2.5	2.8	2.6	..	..
6.15	Outbound tourism expenditure over current account debits		Percent	2.4	2.7	2.5	..	..

GUADELOUPE

Cod.	Basic data and indicators	Notes	Units	2011	2012	2013	2014	2015
1.	**INBOUND TOURISM**							
	Data							
	Arrivals							
1.1	Total		('000)	419	487	645	720	822
1.2	♦ Overnight visitors (tourists)	(1)	('000)	317	325	487	486	512
1.3	♦ Same-day visitors (excursionists)		('000)	102	162	158	234	310
1.4	* of which, cruise passengers		('000)	102	162	158	234	310
	Arrivals by region	(1)						
1.5	Total		('000)	..	..	487	..	512
1.6	♦ Africa		('000)	..	..	..	..	..
1.7	♦ Americas		('000)	..	..	57	..	24
1.8	♦ East Asia and the Pacific		('000)	..	..	..	..	..
1.9	♦ Europe		('000)	..	..	374	..	453
1.10	♦ Middle East		('000)	..	..	..	..	..
1.11	♦ South Asia		('000)	..	..	..	..	..
1.12	♦ Other not classified		('000)	..	..	56	..	35
1.13	* of which, nationals residing abroad		('000)	..	..	..	..	..
	Arrivals by main purpose	(2)						
1.14	Total		('000)	418	..	646	486	512
1.15	♦ Personal		('000)	393	..	622	408	435
1.16	* holidays, leisure and recreation		('000)	251	..	490	316	333
1.17	* other personal purposes		('000)	142	..	132	92	102
1.18	♦ Business and professional		('000)	25	..	24	78	77
	Arrivals by mode of transport							
1.19	Total		('000)	419	487	645	720	822
1.20	♦ Air		('000)	317	325	487	486	512
1.21	♦ Water		('000)	102	162	158	234	310
1.22	♦ Land		('000)	..	..	..	..	..
1.23	* railway		('000)	..	..	..	..	..
1.24	* road		('000)	..	..	..	..	..
1.25	* others		('000)	..	..	..	..	..
	Arrivals by form of organization of the trip							
1.26	Total		('000)	..	..	487	..	..
1.27	♦ Package tour		('000)	..	..	126	..	..
1.28	♦ Other forms		('000)	..	..	361	..	..
	Accommodation							
	Total							
1.29	♦ Guests		('000)	..	..	..	..	..
1.30	♦ Overnights		('000)	5,374	..	5,129	..	..
	Hotels and similar establishments							
1.31	♦ Guests		('000)	424	..	..	..	..
1.32	♦ Overnights		('000)	1,421	..	1,487	..	..
	Expenditure							
1.33	Total	(3)	US$ Mn	582	..	671	..	614
1.34	♦ Travel		US$ Mn	..	..	..	..	..
1.35	♦ Passenger transport		US$ Mn	..	..	..	..	..
	Expenditure by main purpose of the trip							
1.36	Total		US$ Mn	..	..	669	..	..
1.37	♦ Personal		US$ Mn	..	..	636	..	..
1.38	♦ Business and professional		US$ Mn	..	..	33	..	..
	Indicators							
1.39	Average size of travel party		Persons	..	..	2.0	..	3.6
	Average length of stay							
1.40	Total		Days	13.00	..	14.00	16.20	16.40
1.41	♦ For all commercial accommodation services		Nights	..	..	..	..	..
1.42	* of which, "hotels and similar establishments"		Nights	..	..	..	..	14.50
1.43	♦ For non commercial accommodation services		Days	..	..	..	..	21.00
1.44	Average expenditure per day		US$	78.0	..	76.0	72.8	73.2
3.	**OUTBOUND TOURISM**							
	Data							
	Departures							
3.1	Total		('000)	..	..	113	..	..
3.2	♦ Overnight visitors (tourists)		('000)	..	..	..	..	..
3.3	♦ Same-day visitors (excursionists)		('000)	..	..	..	..	..
	Indicators							
3.10	Average length of stay		Days	..	..	..	..	15.80
3.11	Average expenditure per day		US$	..	..	..	..	..

GUADELOUPE

Cod.	Basic data and indicators	Notes	Units	2011	2012	2013	2014	2015
4.	**TOURISM INDUSTRIES**							
	Data							
	Number of establishments							
4.1	Total		Units	..	..	..	..	..
4.2	♦ Accommodation for visitors		Units	..	..	241	..	..
4.3	* of which, "hotels and similar establishments"	(4)	Units	75	..	41	40	40
4.4	♦ Food and beverage serving activities		Units	..	..	..	..	..
4.5	♦ Passenger transportation		Units	..	..	..	..	..
4.6	♦ Travel agencies and other reservation services activities		Units	..	..	..	..	..
4.7	♦ Other tourism industries		Units	..	..	..	..	..
	Accommodation for visitors in hotels and similar establishments							
	Non-monetary data	(4)						
4.13	♦ Number of establishments		Units	75	..	41	40	40
4.14	♦ Number of rooms		Units	..	..	2,826	..	2,549
4.15	♦ Number of bed-places		Units	8,870	..	7,050	..	..
	Indicators							
4.16	Occupancy rate / rooms		Percent	58.00	56.60	57.60	..	..
4.17	Occupancy rate / bed-places		Percent	..	..	..	..	..
4.18	Average length of stay		Nights	3.40	3.40	3.00	..	..
4.19	Available capacity (bed-places per 1000 inhabitants)		Units	19.34	..	15.21	..	..
6.	**COMPLEMENTARY INDICATORS**							
	Demand							
6.1	Gross travel propensity		Units	..	..	..	..	..
6.2	(1.2 inbound tourists) / population		Units	0.69	0.71	1.05	1.04	1.09

GUAM

Cod.	Basic data and indicators	Notes	Units	2011	2012	2013	2014	2015
1.	**INBOUND TOURISM**							
	Data							
	Arrivals							
1.1	Total	(1)	('000)	..	..	..	..	..
1.2	♦ Overnight visitors (tourists)	(1)	('000)	1,160	1,308	1,334	1,343	1,409
1.3	♦ Same-day visitors (excursionists)		('000)	..	..	..	..	..
1.4	* of which, cruise passengers		('000)	..	..	..	..	..
	Arrivals by region							
1.5	Total		('000)	1,160	1,308	1,334	1,343	1,409
1.6	♦ Africa		('000)	..	..	..	..	..
1.7	♦ Americas		('000)	62	63	60	70	71
1.8	♦ East Asia and the Pacific		('000)	1,082	1,225	1,252	1,237	1,320
1.9	♦ Europe		('000)	2	6	10	18	5
1.10	♦ Middle East		('000)	..	..	..	..	..
1.11	♦ South Asia		('000)	..	..	..	..	..
1.12	♦ Other not classified		('000)	14	14	12	18	13
1.13	* of which, nationals residing abroad		('000)	..	..	..	..	..
	Arrivals by main purpose	(2)						
1.14	Total		('000)	1,150	1,299	1,329	1,331	..
1.15	♦ Personal		('000)	1,111	1,255	1,287	1,286	..
1.16	* holidays, leisure and recreation		('000)	762	852	882	904	..
1.17	* other personal purposes		('000)	349	403	405	382	..
1.18	♦ Business and professional		('000)	39	44	42	45	..
	Arrivals by mode of transport							
1.19	Total		('000)	1,160	1,308	1,334	1,343	1,409
1.20	♦ Air		('000)	1,150	1,299	1,329	1,331	1,400
1.21	♦ Water		('000)	10	9	6	12	9
1.22	♦ Land		('000)	..	..	..	..	..
1.23	* railway		('000)	..	..	..	..	..
1.24	* road		('000)	..	..	..	..	..
1.25	* others		('000)	..	..	..	..	..
	Accommodation							
	Hotels and similar establishments							
1.31	♦ Guests		('000)	859	959	977	994	..
1.32	♦ Overnights		('000)	..	..	..	..	..
	Indicators							
1.39	Average size of travel party		Persons	..	..	..	..	..
	Average length of stay							
1.40	Total		Days	..	..	..	..	..
1.41	♦ For all commercial accommodation services		Nights	3.42	3.40	3.40	3.50	..
1.42	* of which, "hotels and similar establishments"		Nights	..	..	..	..	..
1.43	♦ For non commercial accommodation services		Days	..	..	..	..	..
1.44	Average expenditure per day		US$	..	..	..	..	..
4.	**TOURISM INDUSTRIES**							
	Data							
	Accommodation for visitors in hotels and similar establishments							
	Non-monetary data							
4.13	♦ Number of establishments		Units	..	..	..	..	..
4.14	♦ Number of rooms		Units	8,844	8,285	8,443	8,051	..
4.15	♦ Number of bed-places		Units	..	..	..	..	..
	Indicators							
4.16	Occupancy rate / rooms	(3)	Percent	70.00	..	..	75.00	76.00
4.17	Occupancy rate / bed-places		Percent	..	..	..	..	..
4.18	Average length of stay		Nights	..	..	..	..	..
4.19	Available capacity (bed-places per 1000 inhabitants)		Units	..	..	..	..	..
6.	**COMPLEMENTARY INDICATORS**							
	Demand							
6.1	Gross travel propensity		Units	..	..	..	..	..
6.2	(1.2 inbound tourists) / population		Units	7.21	8.03	8.08	8.02	8.29

GUATEMALA

Cod.	Basic data and indicators	Notes	Units	2011	2012	2013	2014	2015
1.	**INBOUND TOURISM**							
	Data							
	Arrivals	(1)						
1.1	Total		('000)	1,434	1,491	1,516	1,739	1,865
1.2	♦ Overnight visitors (tourists)		('000)	1,160	1,200	1,224	1,371	1,473
1.3	♦ Same-day visitors (excursionists)		('000)	274	291	292	368	392
1.4	* of which, cruise passengers		('000)	72	73	72	71	71
	Arrivals by region	(1)						
1.5	Total		('000)	1,434	1,491	1,516	1,739	1,865
1.6	♦ Africa		('000)	..	..	..	..	
1.7	♦ Americas		('000)	1,275	1,332	1,349	1,548	1,671
1.8	♦ East Asia and the Pacific		('000)	..	..	..	..	
1.9	♦ Europe		('000)	116	115	119	137	138
1.10	♦ Middle East		('000)	..	..	..	..	
1.11	♦ South Asia		('000)	..	..	..	..	
1.12	♦ Other not classified		('000)	43	44	48	54	56
1.13	* of which, nationals residing abroad		('000)	..	..	..	..	
	Arrivals by main purpose	(1)						
1.14	Total		('000)	1,434	1,492	1,515	1,739	1,865
1.15	♦ Personal		('000)	1,161	1,208	1,228	1,412	1,483
1.16	* holidays, leisure and recreation		('000)	704	730	748	867	926
1.17	* other personal purposes		('000)	457	478	480	545	557
1.18	♦ Business and professional		('000)	273	284	287	327	382
	Arrivals by mode of transport	(1)						
1.19	Total		('000)	1,434	1,492	1,516	1,739	1,865
1.20	♦ Air		('000)	508	537	553	598	640
1.21	♦ Water		('000)	83	84	83	82	87
1.22	♦ Land		('000)	843	871	880	1,059	1,138
1.23	* railway		('000)	..	..	..	..	
1.24	* road		('000)	843	871	880	1,059	1,138
1.25	* others		('000)	..	..	..	..	
	Expenditure							
1.33	Total		US$ Mn	..	..	..	..	
1.34	♦ Travel		US$ Mn	1,350	1,419	1,479	1,564	1,580
1.35	♦ Passenger transport		US$ Mn	..	..	..	..	
	Expenditure by main purpose of the trip							
1.36	Total		US$ Mn	1,350	1,419	1,479	1,564	1,580
1.37	♦ Personal		US$ Mn	1,094	1,149	1,198	1,267	1,280
1.38	♦ Business and professional		US$ Mn	256	270	281	297	300
	Indicators							
1.39	Average size of travel party		Persons	..	..	..	..	
	Average length of stay							
1.40	Total		Days	..	..	..	..	
1.41	♦ For all commercial accommodation services		Nights	7.75	7.75	7.70	6.10	8.90
1.42	* of which, "hotels and similar establishments"		Nights	..	..	..	..	
1.43	♦ For non commercial accommodation services		Days	..	..	..	..	
1.44	Average expenditure per day		US$	110.0	103.0	96.0	85.0	86.5
3.	**OUTBOUND TOURISM**							
	Data							
	Departures							
3.1	Total		('000)	718	721	846	992	1,130
3.2	♦ Overnight visitors (tourists)		('000)	596	580	686	840	939
3.3	♦ Same-day visitors (excursionists)		('000)	122	141	159	152	191
	Expenditure							
3.4	Total		US$ Mn	935	920	952	1,033	1,005
3.5	♦ Travel		US$ Mn	708	706	725	788	756
3.6	♦ Passenger transport		US$ Mn	227	214	227	245	249
	Expenditure by main purpose of the trip							
3.7	Total		US$ Mn	707	706	725	788	756
3.8	♦ Personal		US$ Mn	500	500	514	561	538
3.9	♦ Business and professional		US$ Mn	207	206	210	227	218

GUATEMALA

Cod.	Basic data and indicators	Notes	Units	2011	2012	2013	2014	2015
4.	**TOURISM INDUSTRIES**							
	Data							
	Number of establishments							
4.1	Total		Units	3,390	3,395	3,506	3,423	3,513
4.2	♦ Accommodation for visitors		Units	..	..	..	..	..
4.3	* of which, "hotels and similar establishments"		Units	2,689	2,690	2,778	2,625	2,718
4.4	♦ Food and beverage serving activities		Units	..	..	..	..	..
4.5	♦ Passenger transportation		Units	..	..	..	..	..
4.6	♦ Travel agencies and other reservation services activities		Units	701	705	728	798	795
4.7	♦ Other tourism industries		Units	..	..	..	..	..
	Accommodation for visitors in hotels and similar establishments							
	Non-monetary data							
4.13	♦ Number of establishments		Units	2,689	2,690	2,778	2,625	2,718
4.14	♦ Number of rooms	(2)	Units	44,821	45,185	46,797	44,056	45,228
4.15	♦ Number of bed-places	(2)	Units	114,691	115,663	119,778	115,447	120,020
	Indicators							
4.16	Occupancy rate / rooms		Percent	48.32	52.20	55.06	57.04	58.63
4.17	Occupancy rate / bed-places		Percent	..	..	..	..	..
4.18	Average length of stay		Nights	..	..	..	..	..
4.19	Available capacity (bed-places per 1000 inhabitants)		Units	7.62	7.53	7.63	7.21	7.34
6.	**COMPLEMENTARY INDICATORS**							
	Demand							
6.1	Gross travel propensity		Units	..	..	..	..	..
6.2	(1.2 inbound tourists) / population		Units	0.08	0.08	0.08	0.09	0.09
	Macroeconomic indicators related to international tourism							
6.3	Inbound tourism expenditure over GDP		Percent	2.8	2.8	2.7	2.7	2.5
6.4	Outbound tourism expenditure over GDP		Percent	2.0	1.8	1.8	1.8	1.6
6.5	Tourism balance (inbound minus outbound tourism expenditure) over GDP		Percent	0.8	1.0	0.9	0.9	0.9
6.6	Tourism openness (inbound plus outbound tourism expenditure) over GDP		Percent	4.8	4.6	4.5	4.5	4.1
6.7	Tourism coverage (inbound over outbound tourism expenditure)		Percent	144.4	154.2	155.4	151.4	157.2
6.8	Inbound tourism expenditure over exports of goods		Percent	12.8	14.0	14.5	14.2	14.6
6.9	Inbound tourism expenditure over exports of services		Percent	60.3	58.3	58.4	55.3	57.2
6.10	Inbound tourism expenditure over exports of goods and services		Percent	10.6	11.3	11.6	11.3	11.6
6.11	Inbound tourism expenditure over current account credits		Percent	7.4	7.6	7.7	7.5	7.4
6.12	Outbound tourism expenditure over imports of goods		Percent	6.0	5.8	5.8	6.1	6.1
6.13	Outbound tourism expenditure over imports of services		Percent	37.1	36.2	34.5	34.1	32.7
6.14	Outbound tourism expenditure over imports of goods and		Percent	5.2	5.0	5.0	5.1	5.2
6.15	Outbound tourism expenditure over current account debits		Percent	5.1	4.9	4.9	5.0	5.0

GUINEA

Cod.	Basic data and indicators	Notes	Units	2011	2012	2013	2014	2015
1.	**INBOUND TOURISM**							
	Data							
	Arrivals							
1.1	Total		('000)	..	..	..	..	
1.2	◆ Overnight visitors (tourists)	(1)	('000)	131	96	56	33	35
1.3	◆ Same-day visitors (excursionists)		('000)	..	..	..	..	
1.4	* of which, cruise passengers		('000)	..	..	..	..	
	Arrivals by region							
1.5	Total	(1)	('000)	131	96	56	33	35
1.6	◆ Africa		('000)	44	40	20	11	12
1.7	◆ Americas		('000)	18	9	6	3	4
1.8	◆ East Asia and the Pacific		('000)	10	5	6	4	3
1.9	◆ Europe		('000)	55	37	22	13	15
1.10	◆ Middle East		('000)	2	2	1	0.7	0.7
1.11	◆ South Asia		('000)	3	3	2	1	
1.12	◆ Other not classified		('000)	..	..	..	..	
1.13	* of which, nationals residing abroad		('000)	..	..	..	..	
	Arrivals by main purpose							
1.14	Total	(1)	('000)	131	96	56	33	35
1.15	◆ Personal		('000)	76	58	28	17	17
1.16	* holidays, leisure and recreation		('000)	49	50	19	10	9
1.17	* other personal purposes		('000)	27	8	9	7	8
1.18	◆ Business and professional		('000)	55	38	29	16	18
	Arrivals by mode of transport							
1.19	Total		('000)	131	96	56	33	35
1.20	◆ Air	(1)	('000)	131	96	56	33	35
1.21	◆ Water		('000)	..	..	..	..	
1.22	◆ Land		('000)	..	..	..	..	
1.23	* railway		('000)	..	..	..	..	
1.24	* road		('000)	..	..	..	..	
1.25	* others		('000)	..	..	..	..	
	Accommodation							
	Total							
1.29	◆ Guests		('000)	..	..	..	..	
1.30	◆ Overnights	(2)(3)	('000)	5,581	3,306	8,523	4,318	2,681
	Hotels and similar establishments							
1.31	◆ Guests	(1)(4)	('000)	63	35	16	15	20
1.32	◆ Overnights	(2)	('000)	1,302	1,145	1,829	333	1,840
	Expenditure							
1.33	Total		US$ Mn	2.1	1.7	..	..	
1.34	◆ Travel		US$ Mn	2.1	1.4	..	..	
1.35	◆ Passenger transport		US$ Mn	0.0	0.3	..	..	
	Expenditure by main purpose of the trip							
1.36	Total		US$ Mn	2.1	1.4	..	..	
1.37	◆ Personal		US$ Mn	1.9	1.1	..	..	
1.38	◆ Business and professional		US$ Mn	0.2	0.3	..	..	
3.	**OUTBOUND TOURISM**							
	Data							
	Expenditure							
3.4	Total		US$ Mn	49	41	61	..	
3.5	◆ Travel		US$ Mn	33	23	50	..	
3.6	◆ Passenger transport		US$ Mn	16	18	11	..	
	Expenditure by main purpose of the trip							
3.7	Total		US$ Mn	33	23	50	..	
3.8	◆ Personal		US$ Mn	29	18	39	..	
3.9	◆ Business and professional		US$ Mn	4	5	11	..	
4.	**TOURISM INDUSTRIES**							
	Data							
	Number of establishments							
4.1	Total		Units	..	..	..	..	
4.2	◆ Accommodation for visitors		Units	376	376	378	380	410
4.3	* of which, "hotels and similar establishments"		Units	..	..	..	..	
4.4	◆ Food and beverage serving activities		Units	..	..	..	..	
4.5	◆ Passenger transportation		Units	..	..	..	..	
4.6	◆ Travel agencies and other reservation services activities		Units	..	..	..	..	
4.7	◆ Other tourism industries		Units	..	..	..	..	

GUINEA

Cod.	Basic data and indicators	Notes	Units	2011	2012	2013	2014	2015
	Accommodation for visitors in hotels and similar establishments							
	Non-monetary data							
4.13	♦ Number of establishments		Units	376	376	378	380	410
4.14	♦ Number of rooms		Units	..	..	5,382	5,384	..
4.15	♦ Number of bed-places		Units	..	..	..	..	..
6.	**COMPLEMENTARY INDICATORS**							
	Demand							
6.1	Gross travel propensity		Units	..	..	..		..
6.2	(1.2 inbound tourists) / population		Units	0.01	0.01	0.005	0.003	0.003
	Macroeconomic indicators related to international tourism							
6.3	Inbound tourism expenditure over GDP		Percent	..	..	..	..	..
6.4	Outbound tourism expenditure over GDP		Percent	..	..	..	..	..
6.5	Tourism balance (inbound minus outbound tourism expenditure) over GDP		Percent	..	..	..	..	..
6.6	Tourism openness (inbound plus outbound tourism expenditure) over GDP		Percent	..	..	..	..	..
6.7	Tourism coverage (inbound over outbound tourism expenditure)		Percent	4.3	4.1	..	..	..
6.8	Inbound tourism expenditure over exports of goods		Percent	0.1	0.1	..	..	..
6.9	Inbound tourism expenditure over exports of services		Percent	2.7	1.1	..	..	..
6.10	Inbound tourism expenditure over exports of goods and services		Percent	0.1	0.1	..	..	..
6.11	Inbound tourism expenditure over current account credits		Percent	0.1	0.1	..	..	..
6.12	Outbound tourism expenditure over imports of goods		Percent	2.3	1.8	2.9	..	..
6.13	Outbound tourism expenditure over imports of services		Percent	8.5	4.6	8.8	..	..
6.14	Outbound tourism expenditure over imports of goods and		Percent	1.8	1.3	2.2	..	..
6.15	Outbound tourism expenditure over current account debits		Percent	1.7	1.2	2.0	..	..

GUINEA-BISSAU

Cod.	Basic data and indicators	Notes	Units	2011	2012	2013	2014	2015
1.	**INBOUND TOURISM**							
	Data							
	Arrivals							
1.1	Total		('000)	..	..	..	..	..
1.2	♦ Overnight visitors (tourists)	(1)	('000)	37	35	36	36	44
1.3	♦ Same-day visitors (excursionists)		('000)	..	..	..	..	..
1.4	* of which, cruise passengers		('000)	..	..	..	..	..
	Arrivals by mode of transport							
1.19	Total		('000)	37	35	36	36	44
1.20	♦ Air	(1)	('000)	37	35	36	36	44
1.21	♦ Water		('000)	..	..	..	..	..
1.22	♦ Land		('000)	..	..	..	..	..
1.23	* railway		('000)	..	..	..	..	..
1.24	* road		('000)	..	..	..	..	..
1.25	* others		('000)	..	..	..	..	..
	Expenditure							
1.33	Total		US$ Mn	14.5	6.8	..	..	..
1.34	♦ Travel		US$ Mn	14.1	6.6	17.4	..	..
1.35	♦ Passenger transport		US$ Mn	0.4	0.2	..	..	..
	Expenditure by main purpose of the trip							
1.36	Total		US$ Mn	14.1	6.7	17.4	..	..
1.37	♦ Personal		US$ Mn	14.1	0.1	12.8	..	..
1.38	♦ Business and professional		US$ Mn	..	6.5	4.6	..	..
3.	**OUTBOUND TOURISM**							
	Data							
	Expenditure							
3.4	Total		US$ Mn	39	25	..	..	..
3.5	♦ Travel		US$ Mn	32	20	27	..	..
3.6	♦ Passenger transport		US$ Mn	7	5	..	..	..
	Expenditure by main purpose of the trip							
3.7	Total		US$ Mn	32	20	27	..	..
3.8	♦ Personal		US$ Mn	26	16	16	..	..
3.9	♦ Business and professional		US$ Mn	6	4	12	..	..
6.	**COMPLEMENTARY INDICATORS**							
	Demand							
6.1	Gross travel propensity		Units	..	..	..	..	..
6.2	(1.2 inbound tourists) / population		Units	0.02	0.02	0.02	0.02	0.02
	Macroeconomic indicators related to international tourism							
6.3	Inbound tourism expenditure over GDP		Percent	1.3	0.6	1.5	..	..
6.4	Outbound tourism expenditure over GDP		Percent	3.5	2.3	2.3	..	..
6.5	Tourism balance (inbound minus outbound tourism expenditure) over GDP		Percent	-2.2	-1.7	-0.8	..	..
6.6	Tourism openness (inbound plus outbound tourism expenditure) over GDP		Percent	4.8	2.9	3.8	..	..
6.7	Tourism coverage (inbound over outbound tourism expenditure)		Percent	37.6	28.2	64.0	..	..
6.8	Inbound tourism expenditure over exports of goods		Percent	6.1	5.3	11.4	..	..
6.9	Inbound tourism expenditure over exports of services		Percent	32.5	31.8	45.6	..	..
6.10	Inbound tourism expenditure over exports of goods and services		Percent	5.1	4.5	9.1	..	..
6.11	Inbound tourism expenditure over current account credits		Percent	3.7	3.0	6.6	..	..
6.12	Outbound tourism expenditure over imports of goods		Percent	16.1	13.5	14.9	..	..
6.13	Outbound tourism expenditure over imports of services		Percent	38.7	33.8	31.2	..	..
6.14	Outbound tourism expenditure over imports of goods and		Percent	11.4	9.6	10.1	..	..
6.15	Outbound tourism expenditure over current account debits		Percent	10.1	8.8	8.8	..	..

GUYANA

Cod.	Basic data and indicators	Notes	Units	2011	2012	2013	2014	2015
1.	**INBOUND TOURISM**							
	Data							
	Arrivals							
1.1	Total		('000)	..	..	..	..	..
1.2	♦ Overnight visitors (tourists)	(1)	('000)	157	177	158	206	207
1.3	♦ Same-day visitors (excursionists)		('000)	..	..	..	..	..
1.4	* of which, cruise passengers		('000)	..	..	..	..	..
	Arrivals by region	(1)						
1.5	Total		('000)	157	177	..	206	207
1.6	♦ Africa		('000)	..	..	..	..	..
1.7	♦ Americas	(2)	('000)	107	125	..	111	109
1.8	♦ East Asia and the Pacific		('000)	..	..	..	..	..
1.9	♦ Europe		('000)	8	9	..	11	11
1.10	♦ Middle East		('000)	..	..	..	..	..
1.11	♦ South Asia		('000)	..	..	..	..	..
1.12	♦ Other not classified		('000)	42	43	..	84	86
1.13	* of which, nationals residing abroad		('000)	..	..	..	..	..
	Arrivals by mode of transport	(1)						
1.19	Total		('000)	157	177	158	206	207
1.20	♦ Air		('000)	157	177	158	206	207
1.21	♦ Water		('000)	..	..	..	..	..
1.22	♦ Land		('000)	..	..	..	..	..
1.23	* railway		('000)	..	..	..	..	..
1.24	* road		('000)	..	..	..	..	..
1.25	* others		('000)	..	..	..	..	..
	Expenditure							
1.33	Total		US$ Mn	..	..	..	..	..
1.34	♦ Travel		US$ Mn	95	64	77	79	65
1.35	♦ Passenger transport		US$ Mn	..	..	..	..	..
3.	**OUTBOUND TOURISM**							
	Data							
	Expenditure							
3.4	Total		US$ Mn	..	..	..	..	..
3.5	♦ Travel		US$ Mn	79	82	81	77	93
3.6	♦ Passenger transport		US$ Mn	..	..	..	..	..
6.	**COMPLEMENTARY INDICATORS**							
	Demand							
6.1	Gross travel propensity		Units	..	..	..	..	..
6.2	(1.2 inbound tourists) / population		Units	0.21	0.23	0.21	0.27	0.27
	Macroeconomic indicators related to international tourism							
6.3	Inbound tourism expenditure over GDP		Percent	3.7	2.2	..	..	..
6.4	Outbound tourism expenditure over GDP		Percent	3.1	2.9	..	..	..
6.5	Tourism balance (inbound minus outbound tourism expenditure) over GDP		Percent	0.6	-0.7	..	..	..
6.6	Tourism openness (inbound plus outbound tourism expenditure) over GDP		Percent	6.8	5.1	..	..	..
6.7	Tourism coverage (inbound over outbound tourism expenditure)		Percent	120.3	78.0	95.1	102.6	69.9
6.8	Inbound tourism expenditure over exports of goods		Percent	8.4	4.5	5.6	6.8	5.6
6.9	Inbound tourism expenditure over exports of services		Percent	31.9	21.5	46.8	43.7	45.5
6.10	Inbound tourism expenditure over exports of goods and services		Percent	6.7	3.7	5.0	5.9	5.0
6.11	Inbound tourism expenditure over current account credits		Percent	4.5	2.5	3.5	3.8	3.3
6.12	Outbound tourism expenditure over imports of goods		Percent	4.5	4.1	4.3	4.3	6.3
6.13	Outbound tourism expenditure over imports of services		Percent	18.2	15.6	16.1	18.1	22.0
6.14	Outbound tourism expenditure over imports of goods and		Percent	3.6	3.2	3.4	3.5	4.9
6.15	Outbound tourism expenditure over current account debits		Percent	3.2	2.8	3.0	3.1	4.3

HAITI

Cod.	Basic data and indicators	Notes	Units	2011	2012	2013	2014	2015
1.	**INBOUND TOURISM**							
	Data							
	Arrivals							
1.1	Total		('000)	946	959	1,064	1,128	1,190
1.2	♦ Overnight visitors (tourists)	(1)(2)	('000)	349	349	420	465	516
1.3	♦ Same-day visitors (excursionists)		('000)	597	610	644	662	674
1.4	* of which, cruise passengers		('000)	597	610	644	662	674
	Arrivals by region	(1)(2)						
1.5	Total		('000)	349	349	420	465	..
1.6	♦ Africa		('000)	..	..	..	..	..
1.7	♦ Americas		('000)	309	297	359	420	..
1.8	♦ East Asia and the Pacific		('000)	..	..	..	..	..
1.9	♦ Europe		('000)	32	28	48	40	..
1.10	♦ Middle East		('000)	..	..	..	..	..
1.11	♦ South Asia		('000)	..	..	..	..	..
1.12	♦ Other not classified		('000)	8	24	14	5	..
1.13	* of which, nationals residing abroad		('000)	..	..	..	..	..
	Arrivals by main purpose	(1)(2)						
1.14	Total		('000)	348	..	420	465	..
1.15	♦ Personal		('000)	303	..	367	414	..
1.16	* holidays, leisure and recreation		('000)	147	..	207	227	..
1.17	* other personal purposes		('000)	156	..	160	187	..
1.18	♦ Business and professional		('000)	45	..	53	51	..
	Arrivals by mode of transport							
1.19	Total		('000)	946	959	1,064	1,128	1,190
1.20	♦ Air	(2)	('000)	349	349	420	465	516
1.21	♦ Water		('000)	597	610	644	662	674
1.22	♦ Land		('000)	..	..	..	..	..
1.23	* railway		('000)	..	..	..	..	..
1.24	* road		('000)	..	..	..	..	..
1.25	* others		('000)	..	..	..	..	..
	Expenditure							
1.33	Total		US$ Mn	..	..	..	..	..
1.34	♦ Travel		US$ Mn	456	447	546	578	609
1.35	♦ Passenger transport		US$ Mn	..	..	..	..	..
3.	**OUTBOUND TOURISM**							
	Data							
	Expenditure							
3.4	Total		US$ Mn	458	473	418	475	447
3.5	♦ Travel		US$ Mn	62	64	62	71	70
3.6	♦ Passenger transport		US$ Mn	396	409	356	404	377
6.	**COMPLEMENTARY INDICATORS**							
	Demand							
6.1	Gross travel propensity		Units	..	..	..	..	..
6.2	(1.2 inbound tourists) / population		Units	0.03	0.03	0.04	0.04	0.05
	Macroeconomic indicators related to international tourism							
6.3	Inbound tourism expenditure over GDP		Percent	6.1	5.7	6.5	..	..
6.4	Outbound tourism expenditure over GDP		Percent	6.1	6.0	5.0	..	..
6.5	Tourism balance (inbound minus outbound tourism expenditure) over GDP		Percent		-0.3	1.5	..	..
6.6	Tourism openness (inbound plus outbound tourism expenditure) over GDP		Percent	12.2	11.7	11.5	..	..
6.7	Tourism coverage (inbound over outbound tourism expenditure)		Percent	99.6	94.5	130.6	121.7	136.2
6.8	Inbound tourism expenditure over exports of goods		Percent	59.4	57.4	59.7	60.2	59.2
6.9	Inbound tourism expenditure over exports of services		Percent	83.9	81.4	83.7	82.4	84.2
6.10	Inbound tourism expenditure over exports of goods and services		Percent	34.8	33.7	34.8	34.8	34.8
6.11	Inbound tourism expenditure over current account credits		Percent	10.5	11.2	13.2	13.7	13.6
6.12	Outbound tourism expenditure over imports of goods		Percent	13.8	15.4	12.6	13.0	13.0
6.13	Outbound tourism expenditure over imports of services		Percent	40.9	42.4	38.3	43.3	45.3
6.14	Outbound tourism expenditure over imports of goods and		Percent	10.3	11.3	9.5	10.0	10.1
6.15	Outbound tourism expenditure over current account debits		Percent	9.7	10.5	8.9	9.4	9.5

HONDURAS

Cod.	Basic data and indicators	Notes	Units	2011	2012	2013	2014	2015
1.	**INBOUND TOURISM**							
	Data							
	Arrivals							
1.1	Total		('000)	1,852	1,903	1,857	2,082	2,093
1.2	♦ Overnight visitors (tourists)		('000)	871	895	863	868	880
1.3	♦ Same-day visitors (excursionists)		('000)	980	1,009	994	1,214	1,212
1.4	* of which, cruise passengers		('000)	787	655	708	943	918
	Arrivals by region							
1.5	Total		('000)	871	895	863	868	880
1.6	♦ Africa		('000)	0.4	0.7	0.7	0.2	0.3
1.7	♦ Americas		('000)	759	734	714	790	782
1.8	♦ East Asia and the Pacific		('000)	16	30	27	10	16
1.9	♦ Europe		('000)	94	126	119	68	81
1.10	♦ Middle East		('000)	0.2	0.5	0.3	0.4	0.2
1.11	♦ South Asia		('000)	0.6	1.1	0.7	0.3	0.8
1.12	♦ Other not classified		('000)	1.0	1.8	1.6	0.2	..
1.13	* of which, nationals residing abroad		('000)	..	..	..	..	..
	Arrivals by main purpose							
1.14	Total		('000)	871	895	862	868	880
1.15	♦ Personal		('000)	661	647	683	657	697
1.16	* holidays, leisure and recreation		('000)	334	397	369	332	342
1.17	* other personal purposes		('000)	327	250	314	325	355
1.18	♦ Business and professional		('000)	210	248	179	211	183
	Arrivals by mode of transport							
1.19	Total		('000)	871	895	863	868	880
1.20	♦ Air		('000)	426	378	394	413	427
1.21	♦ Water		('000)	..	..	..	..	..
1.22	♦ Land		('000)	445	516	469	455	453
1.23	* railway		('000)	..	..	..	..	..
1.24	* road		('000)	445	516	469	455	453
1.25	* others		('000)	..	..	..	..	..
	Arrivals by form of organization of the trip							
1.26	Total		('000)	871	895	863	868	880
1.27	♦ Package tour		('000)	69	77	70	110	68
1.28	♦ Other forms		('000)	802	818	793	758	812
	Expenditure							
1.33	Total		US$ Mn	642	684	618	642	653
1.34	♦ Travel		US$ Mn	637	679	608	630	651
1.35	♦ Passenger transport		US$ Mn	5	5	10	12	2
	Expenditure by main purpose of the trip							
1.36	Total		US$ Mn	637	680	609	630	651
1.37	♦ Personal		US$ Mn	488	503	493	510	527
1.38	♦ Business and professional		US$ Mn	149	177	116	120	124
	Indicators							
1.39	Average size of travel party		Persons	..	..	..	..	..
	Average length of stay							
1.40	Total	(1)	Days	10.40	10.50	9.90	10.10	11.60
1.41	♦ For all commercial accommodation services		Nights	..	..	..	..	..
1.42	* of which, "hotels and similar establishments"		Nights	..	..	..	..	..
1.43	♦ For non commercial accommodation services		Days	..	..	..	..	..
1.44	Average expenditure per day		US$	62.1	65.3	64.8	71.9	65.4
3.	**OUTBOUND TOURISM**							
	Data							
	Departures							
3.1	Total		('000)	1,092	1,072	1,055	1,065	1,150
3.2	♦ Overnight visitors (tourists)		('000)	449	464	471	557	692
3.3	♦ Same-day visitors (excursionists)		('000)	643	608	584	508	458
	Expenditure							
3.4	Total		US$ Mn	446	549	506	509	507
3.5	♦ Travel		US$ Mn	354	454	404	412	405
3.6	♦ Passenger transport		US$ Mn	92	95	102	97	102
	Expenditure by main purpose of the trip							
3.7	Total		US$ Mn	354	454	404	412	405
3.8	♦ Personal		US$ Mn	254	312	277	337	330
3.9	♦ Business and professional		US$ Mn	100	142	127	75	75
	Indicators							
3.10	Average length of stay		Days	12.20	13.20	14.20	9.10	14.20
3.11	Average expenditure per day		US$	58.6	58.8	50.2	60.2	48.2

HONDURAS

Cod.	Basic data and indicators	Notes	Units	2011	2012	2013	2014	2015
4.	**TOURISM INDUSTRIES**							
	Data							
	Number of establishments							
4.1	Total		Units	..	..	..	3,440	3,785
4.2	♦ Accommodation for visitors		Units	..	..	..	1,071	1,059
4.3	* of which, "hotels and similar establishments"		Units	..	..	..	1,071	1,059
4.4	♦ Food and beverage serving activities		Units	..	..	..	1,797	1,993
4.5	♦ Passenger transportation		Units	..	..	..	121	145
4.6	♦ Travel agencies and other reservation services activities		Units	..	..	..	76	106
4.7	♦ Other tourism industries		Units	..	..	..	375	482
	Accommodation for visitors in hotels and similar establishments							
	Monetary data							
4.8	♦ Output		US$ Mn	168.6	176.9	179.9	189.1	..
4.9	♦ Intermediate consumption		US$ Mn	58.8	61.7	61.5	79.9	..
4.10	♦ Gross value added		US$ Mn	109.8	115.2	118.4	109.2	..
4.11	♦ Compensation of employees		US$ Mn	..	..	..	..	..
4.12	♦ Gross fixed capital formation		US$ Mn	..	..	..	..	..
	Non-monetary data							
4.13	♦ Number of establishments		Units	..	..	..	1,071	1,059
4.14	♦ Number of rooms		Units	..	..	..	20,490	22,761
4.15	♦ Number of bed-places		Units	..	..	..	..	..
	Travel agencies and other reservation service activities							
	Monetary data							
4.20	♦ Output		US$ Mn	33.1	36.2	47.8	50.4	..
4.21	♦ Intermediate consumption		US$ Mn	10.7	11.4	16.6	13.3	..
4.22	♦ Gross value added		US$ Mn	22.4	24.8	31.2	37.1	..
4.23	♦ Compensation of employees		US$ Mn	..	..	..	..	..
4.24	♦ Gross fixed capital formation		US$ Mn	..	..	..	..	..
5.	**EMPLOYMENT**							
	Data							
	Number of employees by tourism industries	(2)						
5.1	Total		('000)	183.6	179.5	208.4	210.4	233.7
5.2	♦ Accommodation services for visitors (hotels and similar establishments)		('000)	11.5	9.7	9.3	12.0	9.5
5.3	♦ Other accommodation services		('000)	..	..	..	..	..
5.4	♦ Food and beverage serving activities		('000)	104.3	98.2	120.8	122.8	145.3
5.5	♦ Passenger transportation		('000)	53.1	57.7	65.9	62.2	68.3
5.6	♦ Travel agencies and other reservation services activities		('000)	0.8	1.5	1.3	1.1	0.8
5.7	♦ Other tourism industries		('000)	13.9	12.4	11.1	12.3	9.8
	Number of jobs by status in employment							
5.8	Total		('000)	..	..	..	210.3	233.7
5.9	♦ Employees		('000)	..	..	..	93.4	91.1
5.10	♦ Self employed		('000)	..	..	..	116.9	142.6
6.	**COMPLEMENTARY INDICATORS**							
	Demand							
6.1	Gross travel propensity		Units	..	..	..	..	..
6.2	(1.2 inbound tourists) / population		Units	0.11	0.12	0.11	0.11	0.11
	Macroeconomic indicators related to international tourism							
6.3	Inbound tourism expenditure over GDP		Percent	3.6	3.7	..	..	..
6.4	Outbound tourism expenditure over GDP		Percent	2.5	3.0	..	..	..
6.5	Tourism balance (inbound minus outbound tourism expenditure) over GDP		Percent	1.1	0.7	..	..	..
6.6	Tourism openness (inbound plus outbound tourism expenditure) over GDP		Percent	6.1	6.7	..	..	..
6.7	Tourism coverage (inbound over outbound tourism expenditure)		Percent	143.8	124.5	122.1	126.1	128.8
6.8	Inbound tourism expenditure over exports of goods		Percent	16.1	15.5	15.8	15.7	16.5
6.9	Inbound tourism expenditure over exports of services		Percent	28.5	30.4	26.4	25.6	24.4
6.10	Inbound tourism expenditure over exports of goods and services		Percent	10.3	10.3	9.9	9.7	9.8
6.11	Inbound tourism expenditure over current account credits		Percent	6.7	6.8	6.3	6.2	6.1
6.12	Outbound tourism expenditure over imports of goods		Percent	5.3	6.4	6.0	6.0	5.9
6.13	Outbound tourism expenditure over imports of services		Percent	30.8	31.9	30.1	28.5	28.3
6.14	Outbound tourism expenditure over imports of goods and		Percent	4.5	5.3	5.0	4.9	4.9
6.15	Outbound tourism expenditure over current account debits		Percent	4.5	5.3	4.9	4.8	4.8

HONG KONG, CHINA

Cod.	Basic data and indicators	Notes	Units	2011	2012	2013	2014	2015
1.	**INBOUND TOURISM**							
	**Data**							
	Arrivals							
1.1	Total		('000)	41,921	48,615	54,299	60,839	59,308
1.2	♦ Overnight visitors (tourists)		('000)	22,316	23,770	25,661	27,770	26,686
1.3	♦ Same-day visitors (excursionists)		('000)	19,605	24,845	28,638	33,068	32,622
1.4	* of which, cruise passengers		('000)	40	39	23	34	37
	Arrivals by region							
1.5	Total		('000)	41,921	48,615	54,299	60,839	59,308
1.6	♦ Africa		('000)	193	173	168	166	156
1.7	♦ Americas		('000)	1,821	1,778	1,666	1,679	1,728
1.8	♦ East Asia and the Pacific		('000)	37,378	44,166	49,915	56,393	54,847
1.9	♦ Europe		('000)	1,913	1,973	1,999	1,965	1,927
1.10	♦ Middle East		('000)	85	78	84	83	80
1.11	♦ South Asia		('000)	531	447	468	553	570
1.12	♦ Other not classified		('000)	..	..	..	..	..
1.13	* of which, nationals residing abroad		('000)	..	..	..	..	..
	Arrivals by main purpose							
1.14	Total		('000)	22,316	23,770	25,661	27,770	26,686
1.15	♦ Personal		('000)	18,753	20,185	22,094	23,940	22,690
1.16	* holidays, leisure and recreation		('000)	13,399	14,350	15,798	17,280	16,033
1.17	* other personal purposes		('000)	5,354	5,835	6,296	6,660	6,657
1.18	♦ Business and professional		('000)	3,563	3,585	3,567	3,830	3,996
	Arrivals by mode of transport							
1.19	Total		('000)	41,921	48,615	54,299	60,839	59,308
1.20	♦ Air		('000)	11,026	11,559	12,332	12,849	13,173
1.21	♦ Water		('000)	4,469	4,694	5,056	5,181	4,757
1.22	♦ Land		('000)	26,426	32,362	36,911	42,809	41,378
1.23	* railway		('000)	..	..	..	..	..
1.24	* road		('000)	26,426	32,362	36,911	42,809	41,378
1.25	* others		('000)	..	..	..	..	..
	Expenditure	(1)						
1.33	Total		US$ Mn	33,169	37,098	42,426	46,079	42,601
1.34	♦ Travel		US$ Mn	27,038	31,205	36,108	39,243	35,574
1.35	♦ Passenger transport	(2)	US$ Mn	6,131	5,893	6,318	6,836	7,027
	**Indicators**							
1.39	Average size of travel party		Persons	..	..	..	..	..
	Average length of stay							
1.40	Total	(3)	Days	3.60	3.50	3.40	3.30	3.30
1.41	♦ For all commercial accommodation services		Nights	..	..	..	..	..
1.42	* of which, "hotels and similar establishments"		Nights	..	..	..	..	..
1.43	♦ For non commercial accommodation services		Days	..	..	..	..	..
1.44	Average expenditure per day		US$	..	..	..	..	..
3.	**OUTBOUND TOURISM**							
	**Data**							
	Departures							
3.1	Total		('000)	84,816	85,276	84,414	84,519	89,082
3.2	♦ Overnight visitors (tourists)		('000)	..	..	..	..	..
3.3	♦ Same-day visitors (excursionists)		('000)	..	..	..	..	..
	Expenditure							
3.4	Total		US$ Mn	..	..	..	..	..
3.5	♦ Travel	(2)	US$ Mn	19,022	20,077	21,215	22,011	23,059
3.6	♦ Passenger transport		US$ Mn	..	..	..	..	..
4.	**TOURISM INDUSTRIES**							
	**Data**							
	Number of establishments							
4.1	Total		Units	..	..	..	..	..
4.2	♦ Accommodation for visitors		Units	..	..	..	..	..
4.3	* of which, "hotels and similar establishments"	(4)	Units	1,079	1,179	1,299	1,449	1,609
4.4	♦ Food and beverage serving activities		Units	..	..	..	..	..
4.5	♦ Passenger transportation		Units	..	..	..	..	..
4.6	♦ Travel agencies and other reservation services activities		Units	..	..	..	..	..
4.7	♦ Other tourism industries		Units	..	..	..	..	..

HONG KONG, CHINA

Cod. Basic data and indicators	Notes	Units	2011	2012	2013	2014	2015
Accommodation for visitors in hotels and similar establishments							
Monetary data							
4.8 ♦ Output		US$ Mn	..	..	..	..	..
4.9 ♦ Intermediate consumption		US$ Mn	..	..	..	..	..
4.10 ♦ Gross value added	(2)(5)	US$ Mn	2,982.0	3,230.0	3,296.0	3,384.0	..
4.11 ♦ Compensation of employees		US$ Mn	..	..	..	..	..
4.12 ♦ Gross fixed capital formation		US$ Mn	..	..	..	..	..
Non-monetary data							
4.13 ♦ Number of establishments	(4)	Units	1,079	1,179	1,299	1,449	1,609
4.14 ♦ Number of rooms	(4)	Units	70,925	76,125	79,599	83,435	85,558
4.15 ♦ Number of bed-places		Units	..	..	..	..	..
Indicators							
4.16 Occupancy rate / rooms		Percent	89.00	89.00	89.00	90.00	86.00
4.17 Occupancy rate / bed-places		Percent	..	..	..	..	..
4.18 Average length of stay		Nights	..	..	..	..	..
4.19 Available capacity (bed-places per 1000 inhabitants)		Units	..	..	..	..	..
Travel agencies and other reservation service activities							
Monetary data							
4.20 ♦ Output		US$ Mn	..	..	..	..	..
4.21 ♦ Intermediate consumption		US$ Mn	..	..	..	..	..
4.22 ♦ Gross value added	(2)(6)	US$ Mn	721.0	772.0	783.0	817.0	..
4.23 ♦ Compensation of employees		US$ Mn	..	..	..	..	..
4.24 ♦ Gross fixed capital formation		US$ Mn	..	..	..	..	..
5. EMPLOYMENT							
Data							
Number of employees by tourism industries	(2)						
5.1 Total		('000)	235.9	250.8	269.7	271.9	..
5.2 ♦ Accommodation services for visitors (hotels and similar establishments)	(5)	('000)	39.0	39.4	39.8	40.5	..
5.3 ♦ Other accommodation services		('000)	..	..	..	..	..
5.4 ♦ Food and beverage serving activities	(5)	('000)	42.8	45.9	48.8	51.6	..
5.5 ♦ Passenger transportation		('000)	..	..	..	..	..
5.6 ♦ Travel agencies and other reservation services activities	(6)	('000)	19.4	19.8	19.9	19.7	..
5.7 ♦ Other tourism industries	(7)	('000)	134.7	145.7	161.2	160.1	..
6. COMPLEMENTARY INDICATORS							
Demand							
6.1 Gross travel propensity		Units	..	..	..	..	..
6.2 (1.2 inbound tourists) / population		Units	3.17	3.35	3.58	3.84	3.66
Macroeconomic indicators related to international tourism							
6.3 Inbound tourism expenditure over GDP		Percent	13.3	14.1	15.4	15.8	13.8
6.4 Outbound tourism expenditure over GDP		Percent	7.7	7.6	7.7	7.6	7.5
6.5 Tourism balance (inbound minus outbound tourism expenditure) over GDP		Percent	5.6	6.5	7.7	8.2	6.3
6.6 Tourism openness (inbound plus outbound tourism expenditure) over GDP		Percent	21.0	21.7	23.1	23.4	21.3
6.7 Tourism coverage (inbound over outbound tourism expenditure)		Percent	174.4	184.8	200.0	209.3	184.7
6.8 Inbound tourism expenditure over exports of goods		Percent	7.6	7.9	8.4	8.9	8.4
6.9 Inbound tourism expenditure over exports of services		Percent	36.3	37.7	40.5	43.2	40.9
6.10 Inbound tourism expenditure over exports of goods and services		Percent	6.3	6.5	6.9	7.4	7.0
6.11 Inbound tourism expenditure over current account credits		Percent	5.0	5.2	5.5	5.9	5.5
6.12 Outbound tourism expenditure over imports of goods		Percent	4.3	4.1	4.0	4.0	4.4
6.13 Outbound tourism expenditure over imports of services		Percent	25.6	26.2	28.2	29.8	31.1
6.14 Outbound tourism expenditure over imports of goods and		Percent	3.7	3.6	3.5	3.5	3.8
6.15 Outbound tourism expenditure over current account debits		Percent	2.9	2.8	2.8	2.8	3.0

HUNGARY

Cod.	Basic data and indicators	Notes	Units	2011	2012	2013	2014	2015
1.	**INBOUND TOURISM**							
	Data							
	Arrivals							
1.1	Total		('000)	41,304	43,565	43,611	45,984	48,345
1.2	♦ Overnight visitors (tourists)		('000)	10,250	10,353	10,624	12,140	14,316
1.3	♦ Same-day visitors (excursionists)		('000)	31,054	33,212	32,987	33,844	34,029
1.4	* of which, cruise passengers		('000)	..	..	..	..	..
	Arrivals by region							
1.5	Total		('000)	41,304	43,565	43,611	45,984	48,345
1.6	♦ Africa		('000)	26	26	28	29	32
1.7	♦ Americas		('000)	615	577	635	723	811
1.8	♦ East Asia and the Pacific		('000)	515	459	591	650	730
1.9	♦ Europe		('000)	40,148	42,503	42,357	44,582	46,772
1.10	♦ Middle East		('000)	..	..	..	..	..
1.11	♦ South Asia		('000)	..	..	..	..	..
1.12	♦ Other not classified		('000)	..	..	..	..	..
1.13	* of which, nationals residing abroad		('000)	..	..	..	..	..
	Arrivals by main purpose							
1.14	Total		('000)	41,304	43,565	43,610	45,984	48,345
1.15	♦ Personal		('000)	39,882	42,175	42,283	44,780	47,016
1.16	* holidays, leisure and recreation		('000)	12,197	13,489	13,509	16,049	18,860
1.17	* other personal purposes		('000)	27,685	28,686	28,774	28,731	28,156
1.18	♦ Business and professional		('000)	1,422	1,390	1,327	1,204	1,329
	Arrivals by mode of transport	(1)(2)						
1.19	Total		('000)	41,304	43,565	43,611	45,984	48,345
1.20	♦ Air		('000)	3,531	3,305	3,518	3,724	4,408
1.21	♦ Water	(3)	('000)	..	..	..	..	..
1.22	♦ Land		('000)	37,773	40,260	40,093	42,260	43,937
1.23	* railway		('000)	..	..	..	..	..
1.24	* road	(4)	('000)	37,773	40,260	40,093	42,260	43,937
1.25	* others		('000)	..	..	..	..	..
	Accommodation							
	Total							
1.29	♦ Guests		('000)	3,822	4,164	4,388	4,618	4,929
1.30	♦ Overnights		('000)	10,411	11,392	11,983	12,351	12,962
	Hotels and similar establishments							
1.31	♦ Guests		('000)	3,518	3,825	4,007	4,187	4,438
1.32	♦ Overnights		('000)	9,049	9,938	10,367	10,653	11,093
	Expenditure							
1.33	Total		US$ Mn	7,239	6,149	6,671	7,487	6,944
1.34	♦ Travel		US$ Mn	5,929	5,057	5,362	5,868	5,338
1.35	♦ Passenger transport		US$ Mn	1,310	1,092	1,309	1,619	1,606
	Expenditure by main purpose of the trip							
1.36	Total		US$ Mn	5,929	5,057	5,362	5,868	5,338
1.37	♦ Personal		US$ Mn	5,221	4,471	4,698	5,298	4,789
1.38	♦ Business and professional		US$ Mn	708	586	664	570	549
	Indicators							
1.39	Average size of travel party		Persons	..	..	..	..	..
	Average length of stay							
1.40	Total		Days	2.40	2.30	2.33	2.39	2.47
1.41	♦ For all commercial accommodation services		Nights	2.72	2.74	2.73	2.67	2.63
1.42	* of which, "hotels and similar establishments"		Nights	2.57	2.60	2.59	2.54	2.50
1.43	♦ For non commercial accommodation services	(5)	Days	6.10	5.80	6.43	5.96	4.93
1.44	Average expenditure per day		US$	144.6	119.7	129.6	136.5	119.0
2.	**DOMESTIC TOURISM**							
	Data							
	Trips							
2.1	Total		('000)	..	..	..	..	..
2.2	♦ Overnight visitors (tourists)		('000)	18,801	17,119	14,378	14,854	15,255
2.3	♦ Same-day visitors (excursionists)		('000)	..	..	..	..	..
	Trips by main purpose							
2.4	Total		('000)	18,801	17,119	14,378	14,854	15,254
2.5	♦ Personal		('000)	18,600	16,908	14,055	14,526	14,925
2.6	* holidays, leisure and recreation		('000)	8,514	7,920	6,838	7,033	7,491
2.7	* other personal purposes		('000)	10,086	8,988	7,217	7,494	7,434
2.8	♦ Business and professional		('000)	201	211	324	328	329

175

HUNGARY

Cod.	Basic data and indicators	Notes	Units	2011	2012	2013	2014	2015
	Trips by mode of transport							
2.9	Total		('000)	18,801	17,119	14,378	14,854	15,254
2.10	♦ Air		('000)	11	4	5	1	3
2.11	♦ Water		('000)	1	7	1	3	.
2.12	♦ Land		('000)	18,790	17,108	14,372	14,850	15,251
2.13	* railway		('000)	2,688	2,078	1,712	1,670	1,604
2.14	* road		('000)	16,052	14,984	12,624	13,136	13,581
2.15	* others		('000)	50	45	36	44	66
	Trips by form of organization							
2.16	Total		('000)	18,701	17,119	14,378	14,854	15,255
2.17	♦ Package tour		('000)	279	272	239	146	217
2.18	♦ Other forms		('000)	18,422	16,847	14,139	14,708	15,038
	Accommodation							
	Total							
2.19	♦ Guests		('000)	4,199	4,222	4,497	5,022	5,474
2.20	♦ Overnights		('000)	10,205	10,413	10,986	12,082	12,925
	Hotels and similar establishments							
2.21	♦ Guests		('000)	3,337	3,371	3,626	4,054	4,450
2.22	♦ Overnights		('000)	7,866	8,060	8,597	9,419	10,126
	Indicators							
2.23	Average size of travel party		Persons	..	..	..	..	..
	Average length of stay							
2.24	Total	(6)	Days	2.77	2.86	2.85	2.76	2.74
2.25	♦ For all commercial accommodation services		Nights	2.43	2.47	2.44	2.41	2.36
2.26	* of which, "hotels and similar establishments"		Nights	2.36	2.39	2.41	2.32	2.28
2.27	♦ For non commercial accommodation services	(5)(6)	Days	2.86	2.99	3.03	2.93	2.95
2.28	Average expenditure per day		US$	17.4	16.7	19.3	20.6	17.7
3.	**OUTBOUND TOURISM**							
	Data							
	Departures							
3.1	Total		('000)	16,634	16,143	16,038	16,340	17,276
3.2	♦ Overnight visitors (tourists)		('000)	5,335	4,881	4,912	5,587	6,382
3.3	♦ Same-day visitors (excursionists)		('000)	11,299	11,262	11,126	10,753	10,893
	Expenditure							
3.4	Total		US$ Mn	3,048	2,457	2,526	2,712	2,468
3.5	♦ Travel		US$ Mn	2,485	1,886	1,906	2,036	1,830
3.6	♦ Passenger transport		US$ Mn	563	571	620	676	638
	Expenditure by main purpose of the trip							
3.7	Total		US$ Mn	2,485	1,885	1,906	2,036	1,830
3.8	♦ Personal		US$ Mn	1,925	1,508	1,509	1,691	1,504
3.9	♦ Business and professional		US$ Mn	560	377	397	345	326
	Indicators							
3.10	Average length of stay		Days	3.10	2.72	2.78	2.92	2.95
3.11	Average expenditure per day		US$	51.7	52.2	50.7	52.2	44.5
4.	**TOURISM INDUSTRIES**							
	Data							
	Number of establishments							
4.1	Total	(7)	Units	167,878	169,739	172,648	175,010	175,125
4.2	♦ Accommodation for visitors	(8)	Units	33,387	33,115	33,013	32,781	32,993
4.3	* of which, "hotels and similar establishments"		Units	2,155	2,094	2,064	2,123	2,185
4.4	♦ Food and beverage serving activities		Units	41,910	42,024	41,606	40,824	38,159
4.5	♦ Passenger transportation		Units	11,053	10,763	10,584	10,516	10,263
4.6	♦ Travel agencies and other reservation services activities		Units	2,980	3,043	3,091	3,122	3,118
4.7	♦ Other tourism industries	(9)	Units	78,548	80,794	84,354	87,767	90,592
	Accommodation for visitors in hotels and similar establishments							
	Monetary data	(8)						
4.8	♦ Output		US$ Mn	1,004.8	907.8	969.9	1,078.6	..
4.9	♦ Intermediate consumption		US$ Mn	593.6	543.5	567.8	620.1	..
4.10	♦ Gross value added		US$ Mn	411.2	364.3	402.0	458.5	..
4.11	♦ Compensation of employees		US$ Mn	..	..	..	..	..
4.12	♦ Gross fixed capital formation		US$ Mn	..	..	..	..	..
	Non-monetary data							
4.13	♦ Number of establishments		Units	2,155	2,094	2,064	2,123	2,185
4.14	♦ Number of rooms		Units	70,670	70,252	71,041	71,486	72,319
4.15	♦ Number of bed-places		Units	170,439	170,592	173,156	173,914	177,182

176

HUNGARY

Cod.	Basic data and indicators	Notes	Units	2011	2012	2013	2014	2015
	Indicators							
4.16	Occupancy rate / rooms	(10)	Percent	41.70	39.40	42.00	47.80	49.80
4.17	Occupancy rate / bed-places		Percent	30.80	24.70	26.60	35.00	36.30
4.18	Average length of stay		Nights	2.47	2.60	2.59	2.53	2.39
4.19	Available capacity (bed-places per 1000 inhabitants)		Units	17.06	17.13	17.45	17.59	17.98
	Travel agencies and other reservation service activities							
	Monetary data							
4.20	♦ Output		US$ Mn	560.4	461.9	477.6	501.7	..
4.21	♦ Intermediate consumption		US$ Mn	416.8	343.0	346.2	362.9	..
4.22	♦ Gross value added		US$ Mn	143.6	118.9	131.4	138.8	..
4.23	♦ Compensation of employees		US$ Mn	76.8	76.7	72.3	72.2	..
4.24	♦ Gross fixed capital formation		US$ Mn	16.5	19.4	21.8	14.0	..
5.	**EMPLOYMENT**	(11)						
	Data							
	Number of employees by tourism industries	(12)						
5.1	Total		('000)	331.3	338.0	300.1	320.6	338.0
5.2	♦ Accommodation services for visitors (hotels and similar establishments)	(8)	('000)	37.3	38.4	29.5	33.9	34.9
5.3	♦ Other accommodation services		('000)	..	..	8.4	8.1	6.3
5.4	♦ Food and beverage serving activities		('000)	112.1	113.4	105.1	126.1	112.8
5.5	♦ Passenger transportation		('000)	81.0	72.6	73.7	77.3	93.6
5.6	♦ Travel agencies and other reservation services activities		('000)	7.8	5.0	6.4	3.2	7.9
5.7	♦ Other tourism industries	(9)	('000)	93.0	108.6	77.0	72.0	82.5
	Number of jobs by status in employment	(12)						
5.8	Total		('000)	331.3	338.0	..	..	..
5.9	♦ Employees		('000)	284.8	292.0	..	..	..
5.10	♦ Self employed		('000)	46.5	46.0	..	..	..
	Indicators							
	Number of full-time equivalent jobs by status in employment	(12)						
5.11	Total		('000)	331.3	338.0	..	..	..
5.12	♦ Employees		('000)	284.8	292.0	..	..	..
5.13	* male		('000)	147.8	153.3	..	..	..
5.14	* female		('000)	137.0	138.7	..	..	..
5.15	♦ Self employed		('000)	46.5	46.0	..	..	..
5.16	* male		('000)	28.8	28.3	..	..	..
5.17	* female		('000)	17.7	17.7	..	..	..
6.	**COMPLEMENTARY INDICATORS**							
	Demand							
6.1	Gross travel propensity		Units	..	..	..	..	..
6.2	(1.2 inbound tourists + 2.2 domestic tourists) / population		Units	2.91	2.76	2.52	2.73	3.00
	Macroeconomic indicators related to international tourism							
6.3	Inbound tourism expenditure over GDP		Percent	5.2	4.8	5.0	5.4	5.8
6.4	Outbound tourism expenditure over GDP		Percent	2.2	1.9	1.9	2.0	2.0
6.5	Tourism balance (inbound minus outbound tourism expenditure) over GDP		Percent	3.0	2.9	3.1	3.4	3.8
6.6	Tourism openness (inbound plus outbound tourism expenditure) over GDP		Percent	7.4	6.7	6.9	7.4	7.8
6.7	Tourism coverage (inbound over outbound tourism expenditure)		Percent	237.5	250.3	264.1	276.1	281.4
6.8	Inbound tourism expenditure over exports of goods		Percent	7.2	6.8	7.0	7.5	7.8
6.9	Inbound tourism expenditure over exports of services		Percent	32.4	29.8	29.5	30.3	32.0
6.10	Inbound tourism expenditure over exports of goods and services		Percent	5.9	5.6	5.6	6.0	6.2
6.11	Inbound tourism expenditure over current account credits		Percent	5.1	4.8	4.8	5.3	5.5
6.12	Outbound tourism expenditure over imports of goods		Percent	3.2	2.9	2.8	2.8	2.9
6.13	Outbound tourism expenditure over imports of services		Percent	17.2	15.6	14.6	15.0	15.4
6.14	Outbound tourism expenditure over imports of goods and		Percent	2.7	2.4	2.3	2.4	2.4
6.15	Outbound tourism expenditure over current account debits		Percent	2.3	2.0	2.0	2.1	2.1

ICELAND

Cod.	Basic data and indicators	Notes	Units	2011	2012	2013	2014	2015
1.	**INBOUND TOURISM**							
	Data							
	Arrivals	(1)						
1.1	Total		('000)	628	765	900	1,102	1,389
1.2	♦ Overnight visitors (tourists)		('000)	566	673	807	998	1,289
1.3	♦ Same-day visitors (excursionists)		('000)	63	92	92	105	100
1.4	* of which, cruise passengers		('000)	63	92	92	105	100
	Arrivals by region	(1)(2)						
1.5	Total		('000)	565	647	781	969	1,262
1.6	♦ Africa		('000)	..	..	..	..	..
1.7	♦ Americas		('000)	95	114	144	191	290
1.8	♦ East Asia and the Pacific		('000)	16	24	30	39	64
1.9	♦ Europe		('000)	355	426	499	597	708
1.10	♦ Middle East		('000)	..	..	..	..	..
1.11	♦ South Asia		('000)	..	..	..	..	..
1.12	♦ Other not classified		('000)	99	83	108	142	200
1.13	* of which, nationals residing abroad		('000)	..	..	..	..	..
	Arrivals by mode of transport	(1)						
1.19	Total		('000)	628	765	900	1,102	1,389
1.20	♦ Air		('000)	553	660	781	969	1,262
1.21	♦ Water	(3)	('000)	75	105	119	133	127
1.22	♦ Land		('000)	..	..	..	..	..
1.23	* railway		('000)	..	..	..	..	..
1.24	* road		('000)	..	..	..	..	..
1.25	* others		('000)	..	..	..	..	..
	Accommodation							
	Total							
1.29	♦ Guests		('000)	1,419	1,642	2,019	2,597	3,380
1.30	♦ Overnights		('000)	2,444	2,898	3,522	4,405	5,606
	Hotels and similar establishments							
1.31	♦ Guests		('000)	963	1,117	1,321	1,573	2,083
1.32	♦ Overnights		('000)	1,723	2,037	2,374	2,787	3,613
	Expenditure							
1.33	Total		US$ Mn	..	..	..	..	..
1.34	♦ Travel		US$ Mn	751	865	1,076	1,367	1,580
1.35	♦ Passenger transport		US$ Mn	..	..	..	..	..
	Indicators							
1.39	Average size of travel party		Persons	..	..	..	..	..
	Average length of stay							
1.40	Total		Days	..	..	..	..	..
1.41	♦ For all commercial accommodation services		Nights	1.72	1.77	1.74	1.70	1.66
1.42	* of which, "hotels and similar establishments"		Nights	1.79	1.82	1.80	1.77	1.73
1.43	♦ For non commercial accommodation services		Days	..	..	..	..	..
1.44	Average expenditure per day		US$	..	..	..	..	..
2.	**DOMESTIC TOURISM**							
	Data							
	Accommodation							
	Total							
2.19	♦ Guests		('000)	508	525	638	700	603
2.20	♦ Overnights		('000)	805	854	1,025	1,085	931
	Hotels and similar establishments							
2.21	♦ Guests		('000)	258	273	298	315	..
2.22	♦ Overnights		('000)	416	441	493	500	496
	Indicators							
2.23	Average size of travel party		Persons	..	..	..	..	..
	Average length of stay							
2.24	Total		Days	..	..	..	..	..
2.25	♦ For all commercial accommodation services		Nights	1.58	1.63	1.61	1.55	1.55
2.26	* of which, "hotels and similar establishments"		Nights	1.56	1.61	1.63	1.59	1.54
2.27	♦ For non commercial accommodation services		Days	..	..	..	..	..
2.28	Average expenditure per day		US$	..	..	..	..	..
3.	**OUTBOUND TOURISM**							
	Data							
	Departures							
3.1	Total		('000)	..	..	..	..	..
3.2	♦ Overnight visitors (tourists)		('000)	341	358	365	400	450
3.3	♦ Same-day visitors (excursionists)		('000)	..	..	..	..	..

ICELAND

Cod.	Basic data and indicators	Notes	Units	2011	2012	2013	2014	2015
	Expenditure							
3.4	Total		US$ Mn	..	..	..	..	..
3.5	♦ Travel		US$ Mn	740	780	850	972	997
3.6	♦ Passenger transport		US$ Mn	..	..	..	..	..
4.	**TOURISM INDUSTRIES**							
	Data							
	Number of establishments							
4.1	Total		Units	1,904	..	..	..	..
4.2	♦ Accommodation for visitors		Units	831	871	964	1,149	1,189
4.3	* of which, "hotels and similar establishments"		Units	343	368	422	379	402
4.4	♦ Food and beverage serving activities		Units	753	..	..	..	..
4.5	♦ Passenger transportation	(4)	Units	9	..	..	..	..
4.6	♦ Travel agencies and other reservation services activities		Units	311	..	..	..	..
4.7	♦ Other tourism industries		Units	..	..	..	..	..
	Accommodation for visitors in hotels and similar establishments							
	Monetary data							
4.8	♦ Output		US$ Mn	205.6	..	..	..	..
4.9	♦ Intermediate consumption		US$ Mn	121.2	..	..	..	..
4.10	♦ Gross value added		US$ Mn	84.4	..	..	..	..
4.11	♦ Compensation of employees		US$ Mn	65.5	..	..	..	..
4.12	♦ Gross fixed capital formation		US$ Mn	..	..	..	..	..
	Non-monetary data							
4.13	♦ Number of establishments		Units	343	368	422	379	402
4.14	♦ Number of rooms		Units	9,996	10,382	12,206	12,018	13,490
4.15	♦ Number of bed-places		Units	20,956	21,825	23,431	24,933	28,055
	Indicators							
4.16	Occupancy rate / rooms		Percent	45.90	49.90	54.30	52.40	57.60
4.17	Occupancy rate / bed-places		Percent	36.80	39.60	43.60	44.60	48.80
4.18	Average length of stay		Nights	1.74	1.78	1.77	1.74	1.71
4.19	Available capacity (bed-places per 1000 inhabitants)		Units	65.28	67.48	72.01	76.17	85.16
5.	**EMPLOYMENT**							
	Data							
	Number of employees by tourism industries							
5.1	Total		('000)	15.4	16.7	18.4	20.3	22.7
5.2	♦ Accommodation services for visitors (hotels and similar establishments)		('000)	2.8	3.2	3.9	4.2	5.0
5.3	♦ Other accommodation services		('000)	0.2	0.3	0.4	0.5	0.5
5.4	♦ Food and beverage serving activities		('000)	7.6	7.9	8.2	9.0	9.5
5.5	♦ Passenger transportation		('000)	3.4	3.6	3.9	4.3	5.0
5.6	♦ Travel agencies and other reservation services activities		('000)	1.4	1.7	2.0	2.3	2.7
5.7	♦ Other tourism industries		('000)	..	..	..	..	..
6.	**COMPLEMENTARY INDICATORS**							
	Demand							
6.1	Gross travel propensity		Units	..	..	..	..	..
6.2	(1.2 inbound tourists) / population		Units	1.76	2.08	2.48	3.05	3.91
	Macroeconomic indicators related to international tourism							
6.3	Inbound tourism expenditure over GDP		Percent	5.1	6.1	7.0	8.0	9.5
6.4	Outbound tourism expenditure over GDP		Percent	5.0	5.5	5.5	5.7	6.0
6.5	Tourism balance (inbound minus outbound tourism expenditure) over GDP		Percent	0.1	0.6	1.5	2.3	3.5
6.6	Tourism openness (inbound plus outbound tourism expenditure) over GDP		Percent	10.1	11.6	12.5	13.7	15.5
6.7	Tourism coverage (inbound over outbound tourism expenditure)		Percent	101.5	110.9	126.6	140.6	158.5
6.8	Inbound tourism expenditure over exports of goods		Percent	15.5	18.8	23.4	28.1	34.0
6.9	Inbound tourism expenditure over exports of services		Percent	115.2	151.0	26.9	32.0	37.0
6.10	Inbound tourism expenditure over exports of goods and services		Percent	13.6	16.7	12.5	15.0	17.7
6.11	Inbound tourism expenditure over current account credits		Percent	11.4	14.1	11.1	13.5	16.1
6.12	Outbound tourism expenditure over imports of goods		Percent	16.3	17.3	18.8	19.6	20.2
6.13	Outbound tourism expenditure over imports of services		Percent	386.2	463.0	30.1	31.2	35.3
6.14	Outbound tourism expenditure over imports of goods and		Percent	15.6	16.7	11.6	12.0	12.9
6.15	Outbound tourism expenditure over current account debits		Percent	12.5	13.6	9.9	10.5	11.1

INDIA

Cod.	Basic data and indicators	Notes	Units	2011	2012	2013	2014	2015
1.	**INBOUND TOURISM**							
	Data							
	Arrivals	**(1)**						
1.1	Total		('000)	..	..	..	..	..
1.2	♦ Overnight visitors (tourists)		('000)	6,309	6,578	6,968	7,679	8,027
1.3	♦ Same-day visitors (excursionists)		('000)	..	..	..	..	
1.4	* of which, cruise passengers		('000)	..	..	..	..	
	Arrivals by region	**(1)**						
1.5	Total		('000)	6,309	6,578	6,968	7,679	8,027
1.6	♦ Africa		('000)	224	251	262	268	274
1.7	♦ Americas		('000)	1,301	1,360	1,411	1,459	1,566
1.8	♦ East Asia and the Pacific		('000)	1,230	1,322	1,441	1,519	1,568
1.9	♦ Europe		('000)	2,173	2,237	2,335	2,362	2,287
1.10	♦ Middle East		('000)	221	231	285	357	361
1.11	♦ South Asia		('000)	1,140	1,171	1,215	1,695	1,946
1.12	♦ Other not classified		('000)	20	6	19	19	25
1.13	* of which, nationals residing abroad		('000)	..	..	..	..	
	Arrivals by main purpose	**(1)**						
1.14	Total		('000)	6,309	6,578	6,968	7,679	
1.15	♦ Personal		('000)	4,890	5,098	5,275	6,535	
1.16	* holidays, leisure and recreation	**(2)**	('000)	4,890	3,572	3,916	4,976	
1.17	* other personal purposes		('000)	..	1,526	1,359	1,559	
1.18	♦ Business and professional		('000)	1,419	1,480	1,693	1,144	
	Arrivals by mode of transport	**(1)**						
1.19	Total		('000)	6,308	6,578	6,968	7,679	
1.20	♦ Air		('000)	5,804	6,032	6,341	6,612	
1.21	♦ Water		('000)	50	46	35	31	
1.22	♦ Land		('000)	454	500	592	1,037	
1.23	* railway		('000)	..	..	..	..	
1.24	* road		('000)	454	500	592	1,037	
1.25	* others		('000)	..	..	..	..	
	Expenditure							
1.33	Total		US$ Mn	..	18,340	19,042	20,756	21,472
1.34	♦ Travel		US$ Mn	17,708	17,972	18,397	19,700	21,013
1.35	♦ Passenger transport		US$ Mn	..	368	645	1,056	459
	Expenditure by main purpose of the trip							
1.36	Total		US$ Mn	..	17,972	18,397	19,700	21,013
1.37	♦ Personal		US$ Mn	..	17,013	16,530	17,301	18,662
1.38	♦ Business and professional		US$ Mn	..	959	1,867	2,399	2,351
2.	**DOMESTIC TOURISM**							
	Data							
	Trips							
2.1	Total		('000)	..	..	..	..	..
2.2	♦ Overnight visitors (tourists)		('000)	864,533	1,045,050	1,142,529	1,282,802	1,431,974
2.3	♦ Same-day visitors (excursionists)		('000)	..	..	..	..	
3.	**OUTBOUND TOURISM**							
	Data							
	Departures							
3.1	Total		('000)	..	..	..	..	
3.2	♦ Overnight visitors (tourists)	**(3)**	('000)	13,994	14,920	16,626	18,330	
3.3	♦ Same-day visitors (excursionists)		('000)	..	..	..	..	
	Expenditure							
3.4	Total		US$ Mn	..	14,107	13,884	17,492	17,686
3.5	♦ Travel		US$ Mn	13,699	12,342	11,615	14,595	14,838
3.6	♦ Passenger transport		US$ Mn	..	1,765	2,269	2,897	2,848
	Expenditure by main purpose of the trip							
3.7	Total		US$ Mn	13,699	12,342	11,614	14,595	14,838
3.8	♦ Personal		US$ Mn	6,646	6,002	6,356	8,776	8,992
3.9	♦ Business and professional		US$ Mn	7,053	6,340	5,258	5,819	5,846
4.	**TOURISM INDUSTRIES**							
	Data							
	Number of establishments							
4.1	Total		Units	..	..	..	..	..
4.2	♦ Accommodation for visitors		Units	..	..	..	..	..
4.3	* of which, "hotels and similar establishments"	**(4)**	Units	..	1,376	1,257	1,233	
4.4	♦ Food and beverage serving activities		Units	..	..	..	..	..

INDIA

Cod.	Basic data and indicators	Notes	Units	2011	2012	2013	2014	2015
4.5	♦ Passenger transportation		Units	..	..	..	..	..
4.6	♦ Travel agencies and other reservation services activities		Units	..	..	..	..	..
4.7	♦ Other tourism industries		Units	..	..	..	..	..
	Accommodation for visitors in hotels and similar establishments							
	Non-monetary data	(4)						
4.13	♦ Number of establishments		Units	..	1,376	1,257	1,233	..
4.14	♦ Number of rooms		Units	..	76,567	75,353	79,567	..
4.15	♦ Number of bed-places		Units	..	153,134	150,706	159,134	..
	Indicators							
4.16	Occupancy rate / rooms		Percent	..	..	..	..	..
4.17	Occupancy rate / bed-places		Percent	..	..	..	..	..
4.18	Average length of stay		Nights	..	..	..	..	..
4.19	Available capacity (bed-places per 1000 inhabitants)		Units	..	0.12	0.12	0.12	..
6.	**COMPLEMENTARY INDICATORS**							
	Demand							
6.1	Gross travel propensity		Units	..	..	..	..	..
6.2	(1.2 inbound tourists + 2.2 domestic tourists) / population		Units	0.70	0.83	0.90	1.00	1.10
	Macroeconomic indicators related to international tourism							
6.3	Inbound tourism expenditure over GDP		Percent	0.9	1.0	1.0	1.0	1.0
6.4	Outbound tourism expenditure over GDP		Percent	0.7	0.8	0.7	0.9	0.8
6.5	Tourism balance (inbound minus outbound tourism expenditure) over GDP		Percent	0.2	0.2	0.3	0.1	0.2
6.6	Tourism openness (inbound plus outbound tourism expenditure) over GDP		Percent	1.6	1.8	1.7	1.9	1.8
6.7	Tourism coverage (inbound over outbound tourism expenditure)		Percent	129.3	130.0	137.2	118.7	121.4
6.8	Inbound tourism expenditure over exports of goods		Percent	5.8	6.1	6.0	6.3	..
6.9	Inbound tourism expenditure over exports of services		Percent	12.8	12.6	12.8	13.3	..
6.10	Inbound tourism expenditure over exports of goods and services		Percent	4.0	4.1	4.1	4.3	..
6.11	Inbound tourism expenditure over current account credits		Percent	3.4	3.5	3.5	3.7	..
6.12	Outbound tourism expenditure over imports of goods		Percent	3.2	3.1	3.2	4.2	..
6.13	Outbound tourism expenditure over imports of services		Percent	11.0	10.9	11.0	12.7	..
6.14	Outbound tourism expenditure over imports of goods and		Percent	2.5	2.4	2.5	3.2	..
6.15	Outbound tourism expenditure over current account debits		Percent	2.4	2.4	2.4	3.1	..

INDONESIA

Cod.	Basic data and indicators	Notes	Units	2011	2012	2013	2014	2015
1.	**INBOUND TOURISM**							
	Data							
	Arrivals							
1.1	Total		('000)	7,650	8,044	8,802	9,435	10,407
1.2	♦ Overnight visitors (tourists)		('000)	..	..	..	..	9,963
1.3	♦ Same-day visitors (excursionists)		('000)	..	..	..	..	444
1.4	* of which, cruise passengers		('000)	..	..	..	..	..
	Arrivals by region							
1.5	Total	(1)	('000)	7,650	8,044	8,802	9,435	10,407
1.6	♦ Africa		('000)	32	41	51	56	57
1.7	♦ Americas		('000)	297	312	333	359	412
1.8	♦ East Asia and the Pacific		('000)	5,924	6,237	6,757	7,227	7,882
1.9	♦ Europe		('000)	1,046	1,108	1,243	1,358	1,462
1.10	♦ Middle East		('000)	176	149	189	194	238
1.11	♦ South Asia		('000)	175	197	229	242	355
1.12	♦ Other not classified		('000)	..	..	..	..	..
1.13	* of which, nationals residing abroad		('000)	..	..	..	..	..
	Arrivals by main purpose							
1.14	Total		('000)	7,650	8,044	8,802	9,435	10,407
1.15	♦ Personal		('000)	4,904	5,260	5,721	6,273	7,903
1.16	* holidays, leisure and recreation		('000)	4,601	4,744	4,973	5,445	6,889
1.17	* other personal purposes		('000)	303	516	748	827	1,014
1.18	♦ Business and professional		('000)	2,746	2,784	3,081	3,163	2,504
	Arrivals by mode of transport							
1.19	Total		('000)	7,650	8,044	8,802	9,435	10,407
1.20	♦ Air		('000)	5,446	5,755	6,429	6,978	7,331
1.21	♦ Water		('000)	2,148	2,241	2,325	2,399	2,745
1.22	♦ Land		('000)	56	48	48	59	331
1.23	* railway		('000)	..	..	..	..	..
1.24	* road		('000)	56	48	48	59	331
1.25	* others		('000)	..	..	..	..	..
	Accommodation							
	Hotels and similar establishments							
1.31	♦ Guests	(2)	('000)	6,045	6,351	6,924	7,473	7,875
1.32	♦ Overnights		('000)	..	..	..	..	..
	Expenditure							
1.33	Total		US$ Mn	9,038	9,463	10,302	11,567	12,054
1.34	♦ Travel		US$ Mn	7,997	8,324	9,119	10,261	10,761
1.35	♦ Passenger transport		US$ Mn	1,041	1,139	1,183	1,306	1,293
	Expenditure by main purpose of the trip							
1.36	Total		US$ Mn	7,997	8,324	9,119	10,261	10,761
1.37	♦ Personal		US$ Mn	5,433	5,583	6,097	6,845	7,147
1.38	♦ Business and professional		US$ Mn	2,564	2,741	3,022	3,416	3,614
	Indicators							
1.39	Average size of travel party		Persons	..	..	..	..	..
	Average length of stay							
1.40	Total		Days	7.84	7.70	7.65	7.66	8.53
1.41	♦ For all commercial accommodation services		Nights	..	..	..	..	..
1.42	* of which, "hotels and similar establishments"	(2)	Nights	2.82	2.67	2.81	3.10	2.83
1.43	♦ For non commercial accommodation services		Days	..	..	..	..	..
1.44	Average expenditure per day		US$	142.7	147.2	149.3	154.4	141.7
2.	**DOMESTIC TOURISM**							
	Data							
	Trips							
2.1	Total	(3)	('000)	236,751	245,290	250,036	251,237	255,000
2.2	♦ Overnight visitors (tourists)		('000)	..	..	..	..	..
2.3	♦ Same-day visitors (excursionists)		('000)	..	..	..	..	..
	Trips by main purpose							
2.4	Total		('000)	236,751	245,290	250,037	251,237	255,000
2.5	♦ Personal		('000)	219,256	220,638	230,509	229,706	227,256
2.6	* holidays, leisure and recreation		('000)	198,019	193,656	197,554	208,703	209,279
2.7	* other personal purposes		('000)	21,237	26,982	32,955	21,003	17,977
2.8	♦ Business and professional		('000)	17,495	24,652	19,528	21,531	27,744

INDONESIA

Cod.	Basic data and indicators	Notes	Units	2011	2012	2013	2014	2015
	Trips by mode of transport							
2.9	Total		('000)	236,751	245,290	250,038	251,212	255,001
2.10	♦ Air		('000)	19,011	22,762	24,804	25,350	57,885
2.11	♦ Water		('000)	11,767	8,807	10,627	9,296	2,550
2.12	♦ Land		('000)	205,973	213,721	214,607	216,566	194,566
2.13	* railway		('000)	5,539	5,936	6,451	7,185	22,874
2.14	* road		('000)	152,397	156,446	155,098	201,040	171,309
2.15	* others		('000)	48,037	51,339	53,058	8,341	383
	Accommodation							
	Total							
2.19	♦ Guests		('000)	59,111	63,637	79,342	87,718	68,908
2.20	♦ Overnights		('000)	..	..	..	..	..
	Hotels and similar establishments							
2.21	♦ Guests	(2)	('000)	22,083	24,763	38,168	41,396	46,224
2.22	♦ Overnights		('000)	..	..	..	..	..
	Indicators							
2.23	Average size of travel party		Persons	..	..	..	..	..
	Average length of stay							
2.24	Total		Days	..	..	..	..	..
2.25	♦ For all commercial accommodation services		Nights	..	..	..	..	..
2.26	* of which, "hotels and similar establishments"	(2)	Nights	1.79	1.76	1.77	1.89	1.63
2.27	♦ For non commercial accommodation services		Days	..	..	..	..	..
2.28	Average expenditure per day		US$	..	..	..	..	..
3.	**OUTBOUND TOURISM**							
	Data							
	Departures							
3.1	Total		('000)	..	..	..	..	..
3.2	♦ Overnight visitors (tourists)		('000)	6,750	7,454	8,025	8,074	8,176
3.3	♦ Same-day visitors (excursionists)		('000)	..	..	..	..	..
	Expenditure							
3.4	Total		US$ Mn	8,653	9,055	10,280	10,263	9,800
3.5	♦ Travel		US$ Mn	6,255	6,771	7,675	7,682	7,292
3.6	♦ Passenger transport		US$ Mn	2,398	2,284	2,605	2,581	2,508
	Expenditure by main purpose of the trip							
3.7	Total		US$ Mn	6,256	6,770	7,675	7,682	7,292
3.8	♦ Personal		US$ Mn	4,474	4,820	5,421	5,429	5,153
3.9	♦ Business and professional		US$ Mn	1,782	1,950	2,254	2,253	2,139
	Indicators							
3.10	Average length of stay		Days	7.67	7.67	6.49	6.49	6.49
3.11	Average expenditure per day		US$	121.5	127.0	140.4	134.1	136.1
4.	**TOURISM INDUSTRIES**							
	Data							
	Number of establishments							
4.1	Total		Units	22,189	..	..	..	..
4.2	♦ Accommodation for visitors	(4)	Units	15,283	15,998	16,685	17,484	18,353
4.3	* of which, "hotels and similar establishments"	(2)	Units	1,489	1,623	1,778	1,996	2,197
4.4	♦ Food and beverage serving activities		Units	3,570	..	..	..	..
4.5	♦ Passenger transportation		Units	..	..	..	..	..
4.6	♦ Travel agencies and other reservation services activities		Units	3,336	..	..	..	..
4.7	♦ Other tourism industries		Units	..	..	..	..	..
	Accommodation for visitors in hotels and similar establishments							
	Monetary data							
4.8	♦ Output		US$ Mn	..	..	..	..	..
4.9	♦ Intermediate consumption		US$ Mn	..	..	..	..	..
4.10	♦ Gross value added	(5)	US$ Mn	4,532.7	5,301.4	5,688.0	6,251.3	6,066.2
4.11	♦ Compensation of employees		US$ Mn	..	..	..	..	..
4.12	♦ Gross fixed capital formation		US$ Mn	..	..	..	..	..
	Non-monetary data	(4)						
4.13	♦ Number of establishments		Units	15,283	15,998	16,685	17,484	18,353
4.14	♦ Number of rooms		Units	381,457	405,778	430,793	469,277	507,201
4.15	♦ Number of bed-places		Units	584,207	627,754	664,843	706,436	744,233
	Indicators							
4.16	Occupancy rate / rooms	(2)	Percent	51.25	51.55	52.50	53.04	51.84
4.17	Occupancy rate / bed-places		Percent	64.40	62.72	65.59	65.67	61.20
4.18	Average length of stay	(2)	Nights	1.99	1.93	1.98	2.15	1.94
4.19	Available capacity (bed-places per 1000 inhabitants)		Units	2.39	2.53	2.65	2.78	2.89

INDONESIA

Cod.	Basic data and indicators	Notes	Units	2011	2012	2013	2014	2015
5.	**EMPLOYMENT**							
	Data							
	Number of employees by tourism industries							
5.1	Total		('000)	280.4	293.2	307.5	326.1	333.1
5.2	♦ Accommodation services for visitors (hotels and similar establishments)		('000)	164.1	172.8	183.7	198.5	202.7
5.3	♦ Other accommodation services		('000)	116.3	120.4	123.7	127.6	130.4
5.4	♦ Food and beverage serving activities		('000)	..	..	..	..	..
5.5	♦ Passenger transportation		('000)	..	..	..	..	..
5.6	♦ Travel agencies and other reservation services activities		('000)	..	..	..	..	..
5.7	♦ Other tourism industries		('000)	..	..	..	..	..
6.	**COMPLEMENTARY INDICATORS**							
	Demand							
6.1	Gross travel propensity		Units	..	..	..	..	..
6.2	(1.2 inbound tourists + 2.1 domestic visitors) / population		Units	1.00	1.02	1.03	1.02	1.03
	Macroeconomic indicators related to international tourism							
6.3	Inbound tourism expenditure over GDP		Percent	1.0	1.0	1.1	1.3	1.4
6.4	Outbound tourism expenditure over GDP		Percent	1.0	1.0	1.1	1.2	1.1
6.5	Tourism balance (inbound minus outbound tourism expenditure) over GDP		Percent				0.1	0.3
6.6	Tourism openness (inbound plus outbound tourism expenditure) over GDP		Percent	2.0	2.0	2.2	2.5	2.5
6.7	Tourism coverage (inbound over outbound tourism expenditure)		Percent	104.4	104.5	100.2	112.7	123.0
6.8	Inbound tourism expenditure over exports of goods		Percent	4.7	5.1	5.7	6.6	..
6.9	Inbound tourism expenditure over exports of services		Percent	41.3	40.0	44.9	49.2	..
6.10	Inbound tourism expenditure over exports of goods and services		Percent	4.2	4.5	5.0	5.8	..
6.11	Inbound tourism expenditure over current account credits		Percent	4.0	4.3	4.8	5.5	..
6.12	Outbound tourism expenditure over imports of goods		Percent	5.5	5.1	5.8	6.1	..
6.13	Outbound tourism expenditure over imports of services		Percent	27.3	26.5	29.4	30.6	..
6.14	Outbound tourism expenditure over imports of goods and		Percent	4.6	4.3	4.9	5.1	..
6.15	Outbound tourism expenditure over current account debits		Percent	4.4	4.1	4.7	4.9	..

IRAN, ISLAMIC REPUBLIC OF

Cod.	Basic data and indicators	Notes	Units	2011	2012	2013	2014	2015
1.	**INBOUND TOURISM**							
	Data							
	Arrivals							
1.1	Total		('000)	3,354	3,834	4,769	4,967	5,237
1.2	♦ Overnight visitors (tourists)		('000)	..	..	..	..	..
1.3	♦ Same-day visitors (excursionists)		('000)	..	..	..	..	..
1.4	* of which, cruise passengers		('000)	..	..	..	..	..
	Arrivals by region							
1.5	Total		('000)	3,354	3,834	4,769	4,967	5,237
1.6	♦ Africa		('000)	7	12	17	19	22
1.7	♦ Americas		('000)	6	6	7	9	11
1.8	♦ East Asia and the Pacific		('000)	53	92	125	147	194
1.9	♦ Europe		('000)	1,474	1,328	1,780	1,918	1,964
1.10	♦ Middle East		('000)	782	1,333	1,977	1,983	2,073
1.11	♦ South Asia		('000)	427	538	621	708	837
1.12	♦ Other not classified		('000)	605	525	242	184	136
1.13	* of which, nationals residing abroad		('000)	..	147	166	184	136
	Arrivals by mode of transport							
1.19	Total		('000)	3,353	3,833	4,769	4,967	5,237
1.20	♦ Air		('000)	637	862	1,253	1,518	1,664
1.21	♦ Water		('000)	27	19	28	29	26
1.22	♦ Land		('000)	2,689	2,952	3,488	3,420	3,547
1.23	* railway		('000)	1	5	1	..	..
1.24	* road		('000)	2,688	2,947	3,487	3,330	3,361
1.25	* others		('000)	..	..	..	90	186
	Expenditure	(1)						
1.33	Total		US$ Mn	2,489	2,483	3,212	3,676	..
1.34	♦ Travel		US$ Mn	2,348	2,345	3,076	3,483	..
1.35	♦ Passenger transport		US$ Mn	141	138	136	193	..
	Expenditure by main purpose of the trip	(1)						
1.36	Total		US$ Mn	2,348	2,345	3,075	3,483	..
1.37	♦ Personal		US$ Mn	1,822	1,852	2,495	2,812	..
1.38	♦ Business and professional		US$ Mn	526	493	580	671	..
2.	**DOMESTIC TOURISM**							
	Data							
	Trips							
2.1	Total		('000)	..	..	..	..	..
2.2	♦ Overnight visitors (tourists)		('000)	57,121	..	..	..	..
2.3	♦ Same-day visitors (excursionists)		('000)	..	..	..	..	..
	Trips by mode of transport							
2.9	Total		('000)	57,120	..	..	..	..
2.10	♦ Air		('000)	12,566	..	..	..	..
2.11	♦ Water		('000)	571	..	..	..	..
2.12	♦ Land		('000)	43,983	..	..	..	..
2.13	* railway		('000)	5,712	..	..	..	..
2.14	* road		('000)	38,271	..	..	..	..
2.15	* others		('000)	..	..	..	..	..
	Trips by form of organization							
2.16	Total		('000)	63,121	..	..	..	..
2.17	♦ Package tour		('000)	5,712	..	..	..	..
2.18	♦ Other forms		('000)	57,409	..	..	..	..
	Accommodation							
	Total							
2.19	♦ Guests		('000)	57,121	..	..	..	..
2.20	♦ Overnights		('000)	..	..	..	..	..
	Hotels and similar establishments							
2.21	♦ Guests		('000)	25,704	..	..	..	..
2.22	♦ Overnights		('000)	77,113	..	..	..	..
3.	**OUTBOUND TOURISM**							
	Data							
	Departures							
3.1	Total		('000)	..	..	..	7,698	6,620
3.2	♦ Overnight visitors (tourists)		('000)	..	..	..	..	..
3.3	♦ Same-day visitors (excursionists)		('000)	..	..	..	..	..
	Expenditure	(1)						
3.4	Total		US$ Mn	10,555	8,435	9,380	8,989	..
3.5	♦ Travel		US$ Mn	9,775	7,825	8,974	8,533	..
3.6	♦ Passenger transport		US$ Mn	780	610	406	456	..

IRAN, ISLAMIC REPUBLIC OF

Cod.	Basic data and indicators	Notes	Units	2011	2012	2013	2014	2015
	Expenditure by main purpose of the trip	(1)						
3.7	Total		US$ Mn	9,775	7,825	8,974	8,933	..
3.8	♦ Personal		US$ Mn	8,158	6,439	7,478	7,432	..
3.9	♦ Business and professional		US$ Mn	1,617	1,386	1,496	1,501	..
4.	**TOURISM INDUSTRIES**							
	Data							
	Number of establishments							
4.1	Total		Units	8,725	8,958	9,215	..	..
4.2	♦ Accommodation for visitors		Units	3,274	3,280	3,280	3,342	3,346
4.3	* of which, "hotels and similar establishments"		Units	..	..	..	..	..
4.4	♦ Food and beverage serving activities		Units	2,295	2,157	2,191	..	..
4.5	♦ Passenger transportation		Units	..	..	..	..	..
4.6	♦ Travel agencies and other reservation services activities		Units	3,156	3,521	3,744	3,924	4,005
4.7	♦ Other tourism industries		Units	..	..	..	..	..
	Accommodation for visitors in hotels and similar establishments							
	Non-monetary data							
4.13	♦ Number of establishments		Units	3,274	3,280	3,280	3,342	3,346
4.14	♦ Number of rooms		Units	81,842	83,656	82,738	83,952	89,077
4.15	♦ Number of bed-places		Units	221,003	223,266	219,505	229,845	239,228
	Indicators							
4.16	Occupancy rate / rooms		Percent	..	..	..	..	..
4.17	Occupancy rate / bed-places		Percent	..	..	..	..	..
4.18	Average length of stay		Nights	..	..	..	..	..
4.19	Available capacity (bed-places per 1000 inhabitants)		Units	2.94	2.93	2.85	2.94	3.02
6.	**COMPLEMENTARY INDICATORS**							
	Demand							
6.1	Gross travel propensity		Units	..	..	..	..	..
6.2	(1.1 inbound visitors + 2.1 domestic visitors) / population		Units	0.80	..	..	..	..
	Macroeconomic indicators related to international tourism							
6.3	Inbound tourism expenditure over GDP		Percent	0.4	0.4	0.6	0.9	..
6.4	Outbound tourism expenditure over GDP		Percent	1.8	1.4	1.8	2.1	..
6.5	Tourism balance (inbound minus outbound tourism expenditure) over GDP		Percent	-1.4	-1.0	-1.2	-1.2	..
6.6	Tourism openness (inbound plus outbound tourism expenditure) over GDP		Percent	2.2	1.8	2.4	3.0	..
6.7	Tourism coverage (inbound over outbound tourism expenditure)		Percent	23.6	29.4	34.2	40.9	..
6.8	Inbound tourism expenditure over exports of goods		Percent	..	..	..	..	..
6.9	Inbound tourism expenditure over exports of services		Percent	..	..	..	..	..
6.10	Inbound tourism expenditure over exports of goods and services		Percent	..	..	..	..	..
6.11	Inbound tourism expenditure over current account credits		Percent	..	..	..	..	..
6.12	Outbound tourism expenditure over imports of goods		Percent	..	..	..	..	..
6.13	Outbound tourism expenditure over imports of services		Percent	..	..	..	..	..
6.14	Outbound tourism expenditure over imports of goods and		Percent	..	..	..	..	..
6.15	Outbound tourism expenditure over current account debits		Percent	..	..	..	..	..

IRAQ

Cod.	Basic data and indicators	Notes	Units	2011	2012	2013	2014	2015
1.	**INBOUND TOURISM**							
	Data							
	Arrivals							
1.1	Total		('000)	1,510	1,111	892	..	..
1.2	♦ Overnight visitors (tourists)		('000)	..	..	..	..	..
1.3	♦ Same-day visitors (excursionists)		('000)	..	..	..	..	..
1.4	* of which, cruise passengers		('000)	..	..	..	..	..
	Arrivals by region							
1.5	Total		('000)	1,510	1,111	892	..	..
1.6	♦ Africa		('000)	..	1	..	..	..
1.7	♦ Americas		('000)	..	1	1	..	..
1.8	♦ East Asia and the Pacific		('000)	..	..	..	..	..
1.9	♦ Europe		('000)	7	19	17	..	..
1.10	♦ Middle East		('000)	10	..	..	..	..
1.11	♦ South Asia		('000)	1,480	1,065	860	..	..
1.12	♦ Other not classified		('000)	13	25	14	..	..
1.13	* of which, nationals residing abroad		('000)	..	..	..	..	..
	Expenditure							
1.33	Total		US$ Mn	1,557	1,640	..	..	..
1.34	♦ Travel		US$ Mn	1,543	1,634	..	..	..
1.35	♦ Passenger transport		US$ Mn	14	6	..	..	..
3.	**OUTBOUND TOURISM**							
	Data							
	Expenditure							
3.4	Total		US$ Mn	1,879	2,363	..	..	..
3.5	♦ Travel		US$ Mn	1,836	2,281	..	..	..
3.6	♦ Passenger transport		US$ Mn	43	82	..	..	..
	Expenditure by main purpose of the trip							
3.7	Total		US$ Mn	1,836	2,281	..	..	..
3.8	♦ Personal		US$ Mn	1,825	2,259	..	..	..
3.9	♦ Business and professional		US$ Mn	11	22	..	..	..
4.	**TOURISM INDUSTRIES**							
	Data							
	Accommodation for visitors in hotels and similar establishments							
	Non-monetary data							
4.13	♦ Number of establishments		Units	..	..	..	..	..
4.14	♦ Number of rooms		Units	803	821	909	..	..
4.15	♦ Number of bed-places		Units	..	..	..	..	..
6.	**COMPLEMENTARY INDICATORS**							
	Demand							
6.1	Gross travel propensity		Units	..	..	..	..	..
6.2	(1.1 inbound visitors) / population		Units	0.05	0.03	0.03	..	..
	Macroeconomic indicators related to international tourism							
6.3	Inbound tourism expenditure over GDP		Percent	0.9	0.9	..	..	..
6.4	Outbound tourism expenditure over GDP		Percent	1.0	1.3	..	..	..
6.5	Tourism balance (inbound minus outbound tourism expenditure) over GDP		Percent	-0.1	-0.4	..	..	..
6.6	Tourism openness (inbound plus outbound tourism expenditure) over GDP		Percent	1.9	2.2	..	..	..
6.7	Tourism coverage (inbound over outbound tourism expenditure)		Percent	82.9	69.4	..	..	..
6.8	Inbound tourism expenditure over exports of goods		Percent	2.0	1.7	..	..	..
6.9	Inbound tourism expenditure over exports of services		Percent	55.2	57.9	..	..	..
6.10	Inbound tourism expenditure over exports of goods and services		Percent	1.9	1.7	..	..	..
6.11	Inbound tourism expenditure over current account credits		Percent	1.9	1.6	..	..	..
6.12	Outbound tourism expenditure over imports of goods		Percent	4.6	4.7	..	..	..
6.13	Outbound tourism expenditure over imports of services		Percent	16.9	17.8	..	..	..
6.14	Outbound tourism expenditure over imports of goods and		Percent	3.6	3.7	..	..	..
6.15	Outbound tourism expenditure over current account debits		Percent	3.3	3.3	..	..	..

IRELAND

Cod.	Basic data and indicators	Notes	Units	2011	2012	2013	2014	2015
1.	**INBOUND TOURISM**							
	Data							
	Arrivals							
1.1	Total		('000)	..	..	..	..	..
1.2	♦ Overnight visitors (tourists)	(1)	('000)	7,630	7,550	8,260	8,813	9,528
1.3	♦ Same-day visitors (excursionists)		('000)	489	478	595	776	894
1.4	* of which, cruise passengers		('000)	..	..	..	..	..
	Arrivals by region	(1)						
1.5	Total		('000)	7,630	7,549	8,261	8,813	9,530
1.6	♦ Africa		('000)	..	40	38	42	40
1.7	♦ Americas		('000)	917	988	1,092	1,208	1,357
1.8	♦ East Asia and the Pacific		('000)	..	289	341	358	414
1.9	♦ Europe		('000)	6,361	6,232	6,790	7,205	7,719
1.10	♦ Middle East		('000)	..	..	..	..	..
1.11	♦ South Asia		('000)	..	..	..	..	..
1.12	♦ Other not classified		('000)	352	..	..	..	..
1.13	* of which, nationals residing abroad		('000)	..	..	..	..	..
	Arrivals by main purpose	(1)						
1.14	Total		('000)	7,630	7,551	8,259	8,814	9,527
1.15	♦ Personal		('000)	6,548	6,411	7,039	7,513	8,149
1.16	* holidays, leisure and recreation		('000)	3,599	3,690	4,026	4,492	5,118
1.17	* other personal purposes		('000)	2,949	2,721	3,013	3,021	3,031
1.18	♦ Business and professional		('000)	1,082	1,140	1,220	1,301	1,378
	Arrivals by mode of transport							
1.19	Total		('000)	7,630	7,550	8,260	8,813	9,528
1.20	♦ Air		('000)	5,339	5,314	5,626	6,010	6,931
1.21	♦ Water		('000)	791	730	781	814	816
1.22	♦ Land		('000)	1,500	1,506	1,853	1,989	1,781
1.23	* railway		('000)	..	..	..	..	..
1.24	* road	(1)(2)	('000)	1,500	1,506	1,853	1,989	1,781
1.25	* others		('000)	..	..	..	..	..
	Accommodation							
	Total							
1.29	♦ Guests		('000)	..	..	..	..	..
1.30	♦ Overnights		('000)	55,248	52,075	55,935	60,655	66,494
	Hotels and similar establishments							
1.31	♦ Guests		('000)	..	..	..	..	..
1.32	♦ Overnights		('000)	17,342	19,949	20,805	21,746	26,839
	Expenditure							
1.33	Total		US$ Mn	9,526	9,064	9,538	11,093	10,802
1.34	♦ Travel		US$ Mn	4,212	3,867	4,426	4,862	4,785
1.35	♦ Passenger transport		US$ Mn	5,314	5,197	5,112	6,231	6,017
	Expenditure by main purpose of the trip							
1.36	Total		US$ Mn	4,212	3,867	4,425	4,862	4,785
1.37	♦ Personal		US$ Mn	3,493	3,134	3,605	4,028	3,981
1.38	♦ Business and professional		US$ Mn	720	733	820	834	804
2.	**DOMESTIC TOURISM**	(3)(4)						
	Data							
	Trips							
2.1	Total		('000)	..	..	..	..	..
2.2	♦ Overnight visitors (tourists)		('000)	7,169	8,291	8,413	8,991	9,125
2.3	♦ Same-day visitors (excursionists)		('000)	..	..	..	..	..
	Trips by main purpose							
2.4	Total		('000)	7,168	8,291	8,413	8,991	9,123
2.5	♦ Personal		('000)	6,818	7,941	8,049	8,538	8,716
2.6	* holidays, leisure and recreation		('000)	3,696	4,036	4,073	4,436	4,658
2.7	* other personal purposes		('000)	3,122	3,905	3,976	4,102	4,058
2.8	♦ Business and professional		('000)	350	350	364	453	407
	Accommodation							
	Total							
2.19	♦ Guests		('000)	7,169	8,291	8,413	8,991	9,125
2.20	♦ Overnights		('000)	21,628	23,703	24,195	26,086	25,267
	Hotels and similar establishments							
2.21	♦ Guests		('000)	3,162	3,680	3,712	4,055	4,179
2.22	♦ Overnights		('000)	6,677	7,911	7,626	9,307	8,140

IRELAND

Cod.	Basic data and indicators	Notes	Units	2011	2012	2013	2014	2015
	Indicators							
2.23	Average size of travel party		Persons	..	..	..	..	..
	Average length of stay							
2.24	Total		Days	..	..	..	..	..
2.25	♦ For all commercial accommodation services		Nights	2.78	2.84	2.82	2.87	2.59
2.26	* of which, "hotels and similar establishments"		Nights	2.11	2.15	2.05	2.05	1.95
2.27	♦ For non commercial accommodation services		Days	..	..	..	..	..
2.28	Average expenditure per day		US$	..	..	..	..	..
3.	**OUTBOUND TOURISM**							
	Data							
	Departures							
3.1	Total		('000)	6,514	6,600	6,579	6,676	7,094
3.2	♦ Overnight visitors (tourists)		('000)	..	..	..	..	..
3.3	♦ Same-day visitors (excursionists)		('000)	..	..	..	..	..
	Expenditure							
3.4	Total		US$ Mn	6,837	6,001	6,222	6,173	5,774
3.5	♦ Travel		US$ Mn	6,723	5,897	6,112	6,059	5,679
3.6	♦ Passenger transport		US$ Mn	114	104	110	114	95
	Expenditure by main purpose of the trip							
3.7	Total		US$ Mn	6,723	5,897	6,112	6,059	5,679
3.8	♦ Personal		US$ Mn	5,778	4,987	5,186	5,105	4,829
3.9	♦ Business and professional		US$ Mn	945	910	926	954	850
4.	**TOURISM INDUSTRIES**							
	Data							
	Accommodation for visitors in hotels and similar establishments							
	Non-monetary data							
4.13	♦ Number of establishments		Units	..	..	..	..	..
4.14	♦ Number of rooms	(5)	Units	70,833	68,869	67,377	65,519	64,635
4.15	♦ Number of bed-places		Units	166,961	161,165	157,284	151,273	150,083
	Indicators							
4.16	Occupancy rate / rooms	(6)	Percent	57.00	60.00	61.00	63.00	70.00
4.17	Occupancy rate / bed-places		Percent	42.00	44.00	45.00	47.00	53.00
4.18	Average length of stay		Nights	..	..	..	..	..
4.19	Available capacity (bed-places per 1000 inhabitants)		Units	35.88	34.53	33.67	32.36	32.01
6.	**COMPLEMENTARY INDICATORS**							
	Demand							
6.1	Gross travel propensity		Units	..	..	..	..	..
6.2	(1.2 inbound tourists + 2.2 domestic tourists) / population		Units	3.18	3.39	3.57	3.81	3.98
	Macroeconomic indicators related to international tourism							
6.3	Inbound tourism expenditure over GDP		Percent	3.9	4.0	4.0	4.4	4.5
6.4	Outbound tourism expenditure over GDP		Percent	2.8	2.7	2.6	2.4	2.3
6.5	Tourism balance (inbound minus outbound tourism expenditure) over GDP		Percent	1.1	1.3	1.4	2.0	2.2
6.6	Tourism openness (inbound plus outbound tourism expenditure) over GDP		Percent	6.7	6.7	6.6	6.8	6.8
6.7	Tourism coverage (inbound over outbound tourism expenditure)		Percent	139.3	151.0	153.3	179.7	195.9
6.8	Inbound tourism expenditure over exports of goods		Percent	7.5	7.6	8.2	7.3	6.7
6.9	Inbound tourism expenditure over exports of services		Percent	9.1	8.5	8.1	8.3	8.4
6.10	Inbound tourism expenditure over exports of goods and services		Percent	4.1	4.0	4.1	3.9	3.7
6.11	Inbound tourism expenditure over current account credits		Percent	3.0	3.0	3.0	3.0	2.9
6.12	Outbound tourism expenditure over imports of goods		Percent	10.2	9.4	9.4	6.6	6.3
6.13	Outbound tourism expenditure over imports of services		Percent	5.9	5.4	5.3	4.3	3.6
6.14	Outbound tourism expenditure over imports of goods and		Percent	3.7	3.4	3.4	2.6	2.3
6.15	Outbound tourism expenditure over current account debits		Percent	2.5	2.3	2.3	1.9	1.7

ISRAEL

Cod.	Basic data and indicators	Notes	Units	2011	2012	2013	2014	2015
1.	**INBOUND TOURISM**							
	Data							
	Arrivals	(1)						
1.1	Total		('000)	3,362	3,520	3,540	3,251	3,109
1.2	♦ Overnight visitors (tourists)		('000)	2,820	2,886	2,962	2,927	2,799
1.3	♦ Same-day visitors (excursionists)		('000)	542	635	578	324	309
1.4	* of which, cruise passengers		('000)	237	251	257	88	95
	Arrivals by region	(1)						
1.5	Total		('000)	2,820	2,886	2,962	2,927	2,799
1.6	♦ Africa		('000)	85	71	69	63	62
1.7	♦ Americas		('000)	776	791	803	794	809
1.8	♦ East Asia and the Pacific		('000)	147	172	182	176	177
1.9	♦ Europe		('000)	1,730	1,761	1,826	1,821	1,671
1.10	♦ Middle East		('000)	23	28	23	23	28
1.11	♦ South Asia		('000)	41	47	43	39	44
1.12	♦ Other not classified		('000)	18	16	16	11	8
1.13	* of which, nationals residing abroad		('000)	..	..	..	..	..
	Arrivals by main purpose	(1)						
1.14	Total		('000)	2,820	2,886	2,961	2,927	2,799
1.15	♦ Personal		('000)	2,425	2,453	2,606	2,549	2,435
1.16	* holidays, leisure and recreation		('000)	1,156	981	1,066	989	896
1.17	* other personal purposes	(2)	('000)	1,269	1,472	1,540	1,560	1,539
1.18	♦ Business and professional		('000)	395	433	355	378	364
	Arrivals by mode of transport	(1)						
1.19	Total		('000)	2,820	2,886	2,962	2,927	2,799
1.20	♦ Air		('000)	2,438	2,482	2,580	2,528	2,509
1.21	♦ Water		('000)	..	..	..	..	..
1.22	♦ Land		('000)	382	404	381	399	290
1.23	* railway		('000)	..	..	..	..	..
1.24	* road	(3)	('000)	382	404	381	399	290
1.25	* others		('000)	..	..	..	..	..
	Arrivals by form of organization of the trip							
1.26	Total		('000)	2,820	2,885	2,962	2,927	2,799
1.27	♦ Package tour		('000)	874	923	830	263	224
1.28	♦ Other forms		('000)	1,946	1,962	2,132	2,664	2,575
	Accommodation							
	Total							
1.29	♦ Guests		('000)	3,700	3,658	3,635	3,603	3,265
1.30	♦ Overnights		('000)	11,390	11,249	11,298	10,967	9,974
	Hotels and similar establishments							
1.31	♦ Guests		('000)	3,232	3,171	3,135	3,020	2,692
1.32	♦ Overnights	(4)	('000)	9,949	9,750	9,746	9,190	8,223
	Expenditure							
1.33	Total		US$ Mn	6,041	6,177	6,411	6,348	6,061
1.34	♦ Travel	(5)	US$ Mn	5,316	5,443	5,642	5,619	5,365
1.35	♦ Passenger transport		US$ Mn	725	734	769	729	696
	Indicators							
1.39	Average size of travel party		Persons	1.9	1.9	1.8	1.8	1.8
	Average length of stay							
1.40	Total		Days	14.50	14.40	14.50	14.90	15.70
1.41	♦ For all commercial accommodation services		Nights	..	..	..	..	..
1.42	* of which, "hotels and similar establishments"		Nights	3.08	3.07	3.11	3.04	3.05
1.43	♦ For non commercial accommodation services		Days	..	..	..	..	..
1.44	Average expenditure per day		US$	..	169.0	164.0	174.0	158.0
2.	**DOMESTIC TOURISM**							
	Data							
	Accommodation							
	Total							
2.19	♦ Guests		('000)	6,070	6,997	7,113	7,233	7,629
2.20	♦ Overnights		('000)	15,865	16,260	16,452	16,453	17,065
	Hotels and similar establishments							
2.21	♦ Guests		('000)	5,038	5,331	5,506	5,699	6,018
2.22	♦ Overnights		('000)	11,911	12,387	12,736	12,963	13,463
	Indicators							
2.23	Average size of travel party		Persons	..	..	..	..	..
	Average length of stay							
2.24	Total		Days	..	..	..	..	..
2.25	♦ For all commercial accommodation services		Nights	2.61	2.32	2.31	2.27	2.24
2.26	* of which, "hotels and similar establishments"		Nights	2.36	2.32	2.31	2.27	2.24
2.27	♦ For non commercial accommodation services		Days	..	..	..	..	..
2.28	Average expenditure per day		US$	..	..	..	..	..

ISRAEL

Cod.	Basic data and indicators	Notes	Units	2011	2012	2013	2014	2015
3.	**OUTBOUND TOURISM**							
	Data							
	Departures							
3.1	Total		('000)	..	..	..	..	..
3.2	♦ Overnight visitors (tourists)		('000)	4,387	4,349	4,757	5,181	5,891
3.3	♦ Same-day visitors (excursionists)		('000)	..	..	..	..	..
	Expenditure							
3.4	Total		US$ Mn	4,937	4,851	5,176	5,583	6,244
3.5	♦ Travel		US$ Mn	3,838	3,752	3,961	4,238	4,750
3.6	♦ Passenger transport		US$ Mn	1,099	1,099	1,215	1,345	1,494
	Indicators							
3.10	Average length of stay		Days	20.80	21.00	20.20	20.30	18.50
3.11	Average expenditure per day		US$	40.0	49.7	53.9	45.4	45.3
4.	**TOURISM INDUSTRIES**							
	Data							
	Number of establishments							
4.1	Total		Units	18,490	15,232	17,406	13,152	13,128
4.2	♦ Accommodation for visitors		Units	1,704	1,665	1,676	1,602	1,577
4.3	* of which, "hotels and similar establishments"		Units	338	342	357	366	374
4.4	♦ Food and beverage serving activities		Units	9,109	9,351	9,840	10,060	10,127
4.5	♦ Passenger transportation		Units	..	..	1,200	..	..
4.6	♦ Travel agencies and other reservation services activities		Units	1,217	1,216	1,403	1,490	1,424
4.7	♦ Other tourism industries		Units	6,460	3,000	3,287	..	..
	Accommodation for visitors in hotels and similar establishments							
	Monetary data							
4.8	♦ Output		US$ Mn	2,314.9	2,231.5	2,359.5	2,378.2	2,397.0
4.9	♦ Intermediate consumption		US$ Mn	1,049.0	1,019.6	1,060.0	1,046.9	1,030.7
4.10	♦ Gross value added		US$ Mn	1,265.8	1,211.9	1,299.5	1,331.3	1,285.0
4.11	♦ Compensation of employees		US$ Mn	803.6	759.4	841.7	883.6	836.3
4.12	♦ Gross fixed capital formation		US$ Mn	..	..	..	..	..
	Non-monetary data							
4.13	♦ Number of establishments		Units	338	342	357	366	374
4.14	♦ Number of rooms		Units	47,443	47,796	48,454	49,654	50,358
4.15	♦ Number of bed-places		Units	113,411	114,162	115,909	120,440	123,793
	Indicators							
4.16	Occupancy rate / rooms		Percent	65.80	65.70	65.70	62.60	61.40
4.17	Occupancy rate / bed-places	(6)	Percent	56.10	56.40	56.60	53.50	51.70
4.18	Average length of stay	(7)	Nights	2.72	2.72	2.60	2.54	2.51
4.19	Available capacity (bed-places per 1000 inhabitants)		Units	14.99	14.84	14.83	15.17	15.35
	Travel agencies and other reservation service activities							
	Non-monetary data							
	♦ Domestic trips							
4.25	* with package tour		Percent	..	..	..	..	..
4.26	* without package tour		Percent	..	..	..	..	..
	♦ Inbound trips							
4.27	* with package tour		Percent	..	54.0	41.0	..	..
4.28	* without package tour		Percent	..	46.0	59.0	..	..
	♦ Outbound trips							
4.29	* with package tour		Percent	..	..	..	..	..
4.30	* without package tour		Percent	..	..	..	..	..
5.	**EMPLOYMENT**							
	Data							
	Number of employees by tourism industries							
5.1	Total		('000)	234.6	197.4	213.1	221.9	226.7
5.2	♦ Accommodation services for visitors (hotels and similar establishments)		('000)	34.1	33.9	34.2	35.2	36.9
5.3	♦ Other accommodation services		('000)	4.2	5.0	4.8	4.9	4.5
5.4	♦ Food and beverage serving activities		('000)	135.5	84.4	90.1	95.7	97.4
5.5	♦ Passenger transportation		('000)	60.8	59.3	65.9	65.9	66.6
5.6	♦ Travel agencies and other reservation services activities		('000)	..	14.8	18.1	20.2	21.3
5.7	♦ Other tourism industries		('000)	..	..	..	..	..

ISRAEL

Cod.	Basic data and indicators	Notes	Units	2011	2012	2013	2014	2015
6.	**COMPLEMENTARY INDICATORS**							
	Demand							
6.1	Gross travel propensity		Units	..	..	..	..	..
6.2	(1.2 inbound tourists) / population		Units	0.37	0.38	0.38	0.37	0.35
	Macroeconomic indicators related to international tourism							
6.3	Inbound tourism expenditure over GDP		Percent	2.3	2.4	2.2	2.1	2.0
6.4	Outbound tourism expenditure over GDP		Percent	1.9	1.9	1.8	1.8	2.1
6.5	Tourism balance (inbound minus outbound tourism expenditure) over GDP		Percent	0.4	0.5	0.4	0.3	-0.1
6.6	Tourism openness (inbound plus outbound tourism expenditure) over GDP		Percent	4.2	4.3	4.0	3.9	4.1
6.7	Tourism coverage (inbound over outbound tourism expenditure)		Percent	122.4	127.3	123.9	113.7	97.1
6.8	Inbound tourism expenditure over exports of goods		Percent	9.3	10.1	10.2	10.0	10.8
6.9	Inbound tourism expenditure over exports of services		Percent	20.5	19.4	18.4	17.8	17.0
6.10	Inbound tourism expenditure over exports of goods and services		Percent	6.4	6.6	6.5	6.4	6.6
6.11	Inbound tourism expenditure over current account credits		Percent	5.3	5.6	5.5	5.2	5.4
6.12	Outbound tourism expenditure over imports of goods		Percent	6.8	6.9	7.4	7.9	10.5
6.13	Outbound tourism expenditure over imports of services		Percent	24.3	21.9	24.4	24.2	27.7
6.14	Outbound tourism expenditure over imports of goods and		Percent	5.3	5.2	5.7	6.0	7.6
6.15	Outbound tourism expenditure over current account debits		Percent	4.8	4.7	5.1	5.3	6.6

ITALY

Cod.	Basic data and indicators	Notes	Units	2011	2012	2013	2014	2015
1.	**INBOUND TOURISM**							
	Data							
	Arrivals	(1)(2)						
.1	Total		('000)	75,866	76,293	76,762	77,694	81,068
.2	♦ Overnight visitors (tourists)		('000)	46,119	46,360	47,704	48,576	50,732
.3	♦ Same-day visitors (excursionists)	(3)	('000)	29,747	29,933	29,058	29,118	30,336
.4	* of which, cruise passengers		('000)	..	..	..	..	..
	Arrivals by region	(1)(2)						
.5	Total		('000)	46,119	46,359	47,704	48,576	50,732
.6	♦ Africa		('000)	280	225	185	206	229
.7	♦ Americas		('000)	4,067	3,910	4,477	4,831	5,203
.8	♦ East Asia and the Pacific		('000)	1,512	1,528	1,795	1,762	1,806
.9	♦ Europe		('000)	39,743	40,063	40,644	41,148	42,723
.10	♦ Middle East		('000)	247	276	304	345	391
.11	♦ South Asia		('000)	269	357	298	283	380
.12	♦ Other not classified		('000)	1	..	1	1	1
.13	* of which, nationals residing abroad		('000)	..	..	..	..	..
	Arrivals by main purpose	(1)(2)						
.14	Total		('000)	75,866	76,292	76,762	77,694	81,068
.15	♦ Personal		('000)	61,958	61,770	62,576	64,058	67,747
.16	* holidays, leisure and recreation		('000)	30,041	29,832	31,112	32,427	35,368
.17	* other personal purposes		('000)	31,917	31,938	31,464	31,631	32,379
.18	♦ Business and professional		('000)	13,908	14,522	14,186	13,636	13,321
	Arrivals by mode of transport	(1)(2)						
.19	Total		('000)	75,866	76,294	76,762	77,694	81,068
.20	♦ Air		('000)	23,079	23,276	24,883	25,737	28,114
.21	♦ Water		('000)	2,062	1,820	1,562	1,511	1,609
.22	♦ Land		('000)	50,725	51,198	50,318	50,446	51,345
.23	* railway		('000)	1,432	1,212	1,209	1,245	1,276
.24	* road		('000)	49,293	49,986	49,109	49,202	50,069
.25	* others		('000)	..	..	..	..	..
	Accommodation							
	Total							
.29	♦ Guests		('000)	47,461	48,739	50,263	51,636	55,034
.30	♦ Overnights		('000)	176,474	180,595	184,793	186,793	192,608
	Hotels and similar establishments	(4)						
.31	♦ Guests		('000)	37,984	38,868	39,989	40,770	43,093
.32	♦ Overnights		('000)	120,014	122,700	126,330	127,374	129,681
	Expenditure							
.33	Total		US$ Mn	..	..	..	..	..
.34	♦ Travel		US$ Mn	43,241	40,960	43,829	45,547	39,805
.35	♦ Passenger transport		US$ Mn	..	..	..	..	..
	Indicators							
.39	Average size of travel party		Persons	..	..	..	..	..
	Average length of stay							
.40	Total		Days	4.23	4.22	4.14	4.15	4.10
.41	♦ For all commercial accommodation services		Nights	5.71	5.79	5.69	5.62	5.53
.42	* of which, "hotels and similar establishments"		Nights	5.03	5.15	5.11	5.14	5.15
.43	♦ For non commercial accommodation services		Days	9.36	9.01	8.45	8.52	8.50
.44	Average expenditure per day		US$	133.2	127.1	137.4	140.2	118.3
2.	**DOMESTIC TOURISM**							
	Data							
	Trips	(5)						
.1	Total		('000)	..	..	..	..	..
.2	♦ Overnight visitors (tourists)		('000)	67,059	61,594	49,809	50,156	47,093
.3	♦ Same-day visitors (excursionists)		('000)	..	..	..	76,359	65,767
	Trips by main purpose	(5)						
.4	Total		('000)	67,059	61,594	49,809	50,156	47,093
.5	♦ Personal		('000)	58,805	54,110	45,471	43,862	41,737
.6	* holidays, leisure and recreation		('000)	39,894	37,389	28,226	28,017	29,250
.7	* other personal purposes		('000)	18,911	16,721	17,245	15,845	12,487
.8	♦ Business and professional		('000)	8,254	7,484	4,338	6,294	5,356
	Trips by mode of transport	(5)						
.9	Total		('000)	67,059	61,594	49,809	50,156	47,093
.10	♦ Air		('000)	6,114	5,487	3,629	2,504	3,174
.11	♦ Water		('000)	1,822	1,579	1,604	1,014	529
.12	♦ Land		('000)	59,123	54,528	44,576	46,638	43,390
.13	* railway		('000)	6,457	6,244	5,703	6,597	7,137
.14	* road		('000)	52,403	47,972	38,791	38,961	35,482
.15	* others		('000)	263	312	82	1,080	771

ITALY

Cod.	Basic data and indicators	Notes	Units	2011	2012	2013	2014	201
	Trips by form of organization	**(5)**						
2.16	Total		('000)	67,059	61,594	49,809	50,156	47,09
2.17	♦ Package tour		('000)	1,449	1,426	809	804	1,24
2.18	♦ Other forms		('000)	65,610	60,168	49,000	49,352	45,84
	Accommodation							
	Total							
2.19	♦ Guests		('000)	56,263	54,995	53,599	54,917	57,19
2.20	♦ Overnights		('000)	210,421	200,116	191,992	190,978	200,15
	Hotels and similar establishments							
2.21	♦ Guests		('000)	45,072	43,777	42,650	43,471	45,89
2.22	♦ Overnights		('000)	139,897	132,910	128,429	127,568	122,63
	Indicators							
2.23	Average size of travel party	(5)	Persons	2.5	2.4	2.5	2.2	2.
	Average length of stay							
2.24	Total	(5)(6)	Days	6.00	6.00	6.20	5.20	5.2
2.25	♦ For all commercial accommodation services		Nights	..	..	..	..	
2.26	* of which, "hotels and similar establishments"		Nights	..	..	..	..	
2.27	♦ For non commercial accommodation services	(5)(6)(7)	Days	7.10	7.50	7.30	5.70	5.3
2.28	Average expenditure per day		US$	..	..	..	..	
3.	**OUTBOUND TOURISM**							
	Data							
	Departures							
3.1	Total		('000)	54,155	54,838	54,152	56,806	59,03
3.2	♦ Overnight visitors (tourists)	(2)(8)	('000)	29,295	28,810	27,798	28,460	29,04
3.3	♦ Same-day visitors (excursionists)		('000)	24,860	26,028	26,354	28,346	29,99
	Expenditure							
3.4	Total		US$ Mn	..	..	..	..	
3.5	♦ Travel		US$ Mn	28,727	26,249	26,950	28,857	24,72
3.6	♦ Passenger transport		US$ Mn	..	..	..	..	
4.	**TOURISM INDUSTRIES**							
	Data							
	Number of establishments							
4.1	Total		Units	..	..	..	..	
4.2	♦ Accommodation for visitors	(9)	Units	81,748	83,424	85,007	87,342	94,64
4.3	* of which, "hotels and similar establishments"		Units	33,918	33,728	33,316	33,290	33,19
4.4	♦ Food and beverage serving activities		Units	..	..	..	..	
4.5	♦ Passenger transportation		Units	..	..	..	..	
4.6	♦ Travel agencies and other reservation services activities		Units	..	..	..	..	
4.7	♦ Other tourism industries		Units	..	..	..	..	
	Accommodation for visitors in hotels and similar establishments							
	Non-monetary data							
4.13	♦ Number of establishments		Units	33,918	33,728	33,316	33,290	33,19
4.14	♦ Number of rooms		Units	1,096,540	1,093,286	1,089,770	1,090,300	1,091,56
4.15	♦ Number of bed-places		Units	2,253,003	2,250,704	2,233,823	2,241,239	2,250,71
	Indicators							
4.16	Occupancy rate / rooms		Percent	..	42.80	39.70	41.90	44.9
4.17	Occupancy rate / bed-places		Percent	40.20	40.90	37.60	40.60	42.5
4.18	Average length of stay		Nights	3.13	3.09	3.08	3.03	2.9
4.19	Available capacity (bed-places per 1000 inhabitants)		Units	37.75	37.68	37.37	37.49	37.6
6.	**COMPLEMENTARY INDICATORS**							
	Demand							
6.1	Gross travel propensity		Units	..	..	..	..	
6.2	(1.2 inbound tourists + 2.2 domestic tourists) / population		Units	1.90	1.81	1.63	1.65	1.6
	Macroeconomic indicators related to international tourism							
6.3	Inbound tourism expenditure over GDP		Percent	1.9	2.0	2.0	2.1	2.
6.4	Outbound tourism expenditure over GDP		Percent	1.3	1.3	1.3	1.3	1.
6.5	Tourism balance (inbound minus outbound tourism expenditure) over GDP		Percent	0.6	0.7	0.7	0.8	0.
6.6	Tourism openness (inbound plus outbound tourism expenditure) over GDP		Percent	3.2	3.3	3.3	3.4	3.

TALY

od. Basic data and indicators	Notes	Units	2011	2012	2013	2014	2015
7 Tourism coverage (inbound over outbound tourism expenditure)		Percent	150.5	156.0	162.6	157.8	161.0
8 Inbound tourism expenditure over exports of goods		Percent	8.5	8.4	8.7	8.8	8.8
9 Inbound tourism expenditure over exports of services		Percent	39.1	37.8	39.2	39.9	40.3
10 Inbound tourism expenditure over exports of goods and services		Percent	7.0	6.9	7.1	7.2	7.3
11 Inbound tourism expenditure over current account credits		Percent	6.0	6.0	6.2	6.2	6.3
12 Outbound tourism expenditure over imports of goods		Percent	5.4	5.7	5.9	6.3	6.3
13 Outbound tourism expenditure over imports of services		Percent	24.1	24.2	24.2	25.1	24.6
14 Outbound tourism expenditure over imports of goods and		Percent	4.4	4.6	4.8	5.1	5.0
15 Outbound tourism expenditure over current account debits		Percent	3.7	3.8	3.9	4.2	4.2

195

JAMAICA

Cod.	Basic data and indicators	Notes	Units	2011	2012	2013	2014	2015
1.	**INBOUND TOURISM**							
	Data							
	Arrivals							
1.1	Total		('000)	3,077	3,306	3,274	3,504	3,692
1.2	♦ Overnight visitors (tourists)	(1)	('000)	1,952	1,986	2,008	2,080	2,123
1.3	♦ Same-day visitors (excursionists)		('000)	1,125	1,320	1,265	1,424	1,569
1.4	* of which, cruise passengers		('000)	1,125	1,320	1,265	1,424	1,569
	Arrivals by region	(1)						
1.5	Total		('000)	1,951	1,986	2,008	2,080	2,123
1.6	♦ Africa		('000)	1	2	1	1	2
1.7	♦ Americas		('000)	1,687	1,751	1,759	1,805	1,828
1.8	♦ East Asia and the Pacific		('000)	7	8	9	9	11
1.9	♦ Europe		('000)	254	223	237	262	281
1.10	♦ Middle East		('000)	1	1	1	1	1
1.11	♦ South Asia		('000)	1	1	2	2	2
1.12	♦ Other not classified		('000)	..	..	..	..	..
1.13	* of which, nationals residing abroad		('000)	..	..	..	..	..
	Arrivals by main purpose	(1)						
1.14	Total		('000)	1,952	1,986	2,008	2,080	2,123
1.15	♦ Personal		('000)	1,846	1,886	1,912	1,983	2,022
1.16	* holidays, leisure and recreation		('000)	1,524	1,574	1,609	1,668	1,604
1.17	* other personal purposes		('000)	322	312	303	315	418
1.18	♦ Business and professional		('000)	106	100	96	97	101
	Arrivals by mode of transport							
1.19	Total		('000)	3,077	3,306	3,273	3,504	3,692
1.20	♦ Air	(1)	('000)	1,952	1,986	2,008	2,080	2,123
1.21	♦ Water	(2)	('000)	1,125	1,320	1,265	1,424	1,569
1.22	♦ Land		('000)	..	..	..	..	..
1.23	* railway		('000)	..	..	..	..	..
1.24	* road		('000)	..	..	..	..	..
1.25	* others		('000)	..	..	..	..	..
	Arrivals by form of organization of the trip							
1.26	Total		('000)	1,951	1,986	2,009	2,080	..
1.27	♦ Package tour		('000)	831	844	894	961	..
1.28	♦ Other forms	(3)	('000)	1,120	1,142	1,115	1,119	..
	Accommodation							
	Total							
1.29	♦ Guests		('000)	1,952	1,986	2,008	2,080	2,123
1.30	♦ Overnights	(4)	('000)	18,436	18,764	18,582	19,199	19,749
	Hotels and similar establishments							
1.31	♦ Guests		('000)	1,324	1,354	1,400	1,437	1,446
1.32	♦ Overnights		('000)	9,155	9,256	9,585	9,872	9,932
	Expenditure							
1.33	Total		US$ Mn	2,060	..	..	..	..
1.34	♦ Travel		US$ Mn	2,013	2,069	2,074	2,255	2,379
1.35	♦ Passenger transport		US$ Mn	47	..	..	..	..
	Indicators							
1.39	Average size of travel party		Persons	..	..	..	..	..
	Average length of stay							
1.40	Total	(5)	Days	9.45	9.45	9.25	9.23	9.30
1.41	♦ For all commercial accommodation services	(6)	Nights	7.06	6.98	7.00	7.03	7.04
1.42	* of which, "hotels and similar establishments"		Nights	6.90	6.80	6.85	6.87	6.87
1.43	♦ For non commercial accommodation services	(5)	Days	15.63	15.95	15.64	15.41	15.47
1.44	Average expenditure per day	(7)	US$	115.7	117.2	120.3	122.2	125.5
3.	**OUTBOUND TOURISM**							
	Data							
	Expenditure							
3.4	Total		US$ Mn	213	418	392	457	412
3.5	♦ Travel		US$ Mn	159	184	178	198	235
3.6	♦ Passenger transport		US$ Mn	54	234	214	259	177
	Expenditure by main purpose of the trip							
3.7	Total		US$ Mn	..	184	178	198	235
3.8	♦ Personal		US$ Mn	..	141	140	158	186
3.9	♦ Business and professional		US$ Mn	..	43	38	40	49

JAMAICA

Cod.	Basic data and indicators	Notes	Units	2011	2012	2013	2014	2015
4.	**TOURISM INDUSTRIES**							
	Data							
	Number of establishments							
4.1	Total		Units	..	..	..	..	..
4.2	♦ Accommodation for visitors	(8)	Units	2,060	2,040	1,753	1,761	1,773
4.3	* of which, "hotels and similar establishments"	(8)	Units	886	887	920	921	933
4.4	♦ Food and beverage serving activities		Units	..	..	..	..	..
4.5	♦ Passenger transportation		Units	..	..	..	..	..
4.6	♦ Travel agencies and other reservation services activities		Units	..	..	..	..	..
4.7	♦ Other tourism industries		Units	..	..	..	..	..
	Accommodation for visitors in hotels and similar establishments							
	Non-monetary data	(8)						
4.13	♦ Number of establishments		Units	886	887	920	921	933
4.14	♦ Number of rooms		Units	24,430	24,735	24,067	24,140	25,227
4.15	♦ Number of bed-places		Units	50,743	51,332	49,705	49,783	51,786
	Indicators							
4.16	Occupancy rate / rooms		Percent	60.50	62.30	67.90	68.10	69.00
4.17	Occupancy rate / bed-places		Percent	59.50	61.70	66.10	68.30	68.50
4.18	Average length of stay	(9)	Nights	6.90	6.80	6.85	6.88	6.87
4.19	Available capacity (bed-places per 1000 inhabitants)		Units	18.44	18.58	17.92	17.89	18.54
5.	**EMPLOYMENT**							
	Data							
	Number of employees by tourism industries							
5.1	Total		('000)	..	..	..	..	..
5.2	♦ Accommodation services for visitors (hotels and similar establishments)		('000)	34.9	35.2	33.9	35.2	36.8
5.3	♦ Other accommodation services		('000)	..	..	..	..	..
5.4	♦ Food and beverage serving activities		('000)	..	..	..	..	..
5.5	♦ Passenger transportation		('000)	..	..	..	..	..
5.6	♦ Travel agencies and other reservation services activities		('000)	..	..	..	..	..
5.7	♦ Other tourism industries		('000)	..	..	..	..	..
6.	**COMPLEMENTARY INDICATORS**							
	Demand							
6.1	Gross travel propensity		Units	..	..	..	..	..
6.2	(1.2 inbound tourists) / population		Units	0.71	0.72	0.72	0.75	0.76
	Macroeconomic indicators related to international tourism							
6.3	Inbound tourism expenditure over GDP		Percent	14.3	14.0	14.5	16.2	17.0
6.4	Outbound tourism expenditure over GDP		Percent	1.5	2.8	2.7	3.3	2.9
6.5	Tourism balance (inbound minus outbound tourism expenditure) over GDP		Percent	12.8	11.2	11.8	12.9	14.1
6.6	Tourism openness (inbound plus outbound tourism expenditure) over GDP		Percent	15.8	16.8	17.2	19.5	19.9
6.7	Tourism coverage (inbound over outbound tourism expenditure)		Percent	967.1	495.0	529.1	493.4	577.4
6.8	Inbound tourism expenditure over exports of goods		Percent	123.6	119.7	131.2	155.7	188.6
6.9	Inbound tourism expenditure over exports of services		Percent	78.6	76.8	77.6	78.9	80.8
6.10	Inbound tourism expenditure over exports of goods and services		Percent	48.1	46.8	48.7	52.3	56.6
6.11	Inbound tourism expenditure over current account credits		Percent	30.3	28.4	29.1	31.6	33.7
6.12	Outbound tourism expenditure over imports of goods		Percent	3.6	7.4	7.2	8.8	9.3
6.13	Outbound tourism expenditure over imports of services		Percent	10.9	19.3	19.2	20.5	19.3
6.14	Outbound tourism expenditure over imports of goods and		Percent	2.7	5.4	5.2	6.1	6.3
6.15	Outbound tourism expenditure over current account debits		Percent	2.6	4.9	4.8	5.7	5.8

JAPAN

Cod.	Basic data and indicators	Notes	Units	2011	2012	2013	2014	2015
1.	**INBOUND TOURISM**							
	Data							
	Arrivals							
1.1	Total	(1)	('000)	6,219	8,358	10,364	13,413	19,737
1.2	♦ Overnight visitors (tourists)		('000)	..	..	..	..	
1.3	♦ Same-day visitors (excursionists)		('000)	..	..	..	..	
1.4	* of which, cruise passengers		('000)	..	..	..	..	
	Arrivals by region	(1)						
1.5	Total		('000)	6,219	8,358	10,364	13,413	19,737
1.6	♦ Africa		('000)	17	21	23	24	27
1.7	♦ Americas		('000)	717	927	1,032	1,169	1,385
1.8	♦ East Asia and the Pacific		('000)	4,796	6,489	8,240	10,974	16,848
1.9	♦ Europe		('000)	583	797	931	1,082	1,285
1.10	♦ Middle East		('000)	7	11	13	16	18
1.11	♦ South Asia		('000)	98	113	125	148	174
1.12	♦ Other not classified		('000)	1	..	..	1	
1.13	* of which, nationals residing abroad		('000)	..	..	..	..	
	Arrivals by main purpose	(1)						
1.14	Total		('000)	6,219	8,358	10,364	13,413	19,737
1.15	♦ Personal		('000)	4,975	6,915	8,899	11,876	18,096
1.16	* holidays, leisure and recreation		('000)	4,057	6,041	7,963	10,881	16,969
1.17	* other personal purposes		('000)	918	874	936	996	1,127
1.18	♦ Business and professional		('000)	1,244	1,443	1,465	1,537	1,641
	Arrivals by mode of transport	(2)						
1.19	Total		('000)	7,135	9,172	11,255	14,150	19,688
1.20	♦ Air		('000)	6,681	8,567	10,635	13,511	19,117
1.21	♦ Water		('000)	454	605	620	639	571
1.22	♦ Land		('000)	..	..	..	..	
1.23	* railway		('000)	..	..	..	..	
1.24	* road		('000)	..	..	..	..	
1.25	* others		('000)	..	..	..	..	
	Arrivals by form of organization of the trip							
1.26	Total		('000)	6,219	8,358	10,364	13,414	19,738
1.27	♦ Package tour		('000)	1,400	1,816	2,456	3,052	5,055
1.28	♦ Other forms		('000)	4,819	6,542	7,908	10,362	14,683
	Accommodation							
	Total							
1.29	♦ Guests	(3)(4)	('000)	11,362	16,642	21,046	28,487	42,229
1.30	♦ Overnights	(3)(4)	('000)	18,416	26,314	33,496	44,825	65,615
	Hotels and similar establishments							
1.31	♦ Guests	(3)(4)	('000)	11,000	15,924	20,380	27,635	41,138
1.32	♦ Overnights	(4)	('000)	17,632	24,886	32,136	43,247	63,493
	Expenditure							
1.33	Total		US$ Mn	12,533	16,197	16,865	20,790	27,288
1.34	♦ Travel		US$ Mn	11,000	14,581	15,093	18,812	24,968
1.35	♦ Passenger transport		US$ Mn	1,533	1,616	1,772	1,978	2,317
	Expenditure by main purpose of the trip							
1.36	Total		US$ Mn	11,000	14,581	15,093	18,812	24,968
1.37	♦ Personal		US$ Mn	8,501	11,533	12,347	16,204	22,443
1.38	♦ Business and professional		US$ Mn	2,499	3,048	2,746	2,608	2,525
	Indicators							
1.39	Average size of travel party		Persons	..	..	..	..	
	Average length of stay							
1.40	Total		Days	14.65	13.33	12.94	12.66	11.24
1.41	♦ For all commercial accommodation services		Nights	5.96	6.06	5.70	5.88	5.75
1.42	* of which, "hotels and similar establishments"		Nights	5.96	6.06	5.70	5.88	5.75
1.43	♦ For non commercial accommodation services		Days	33.45	31.55	31.02	40.13	39.50
1.44	Average expenditure per day		US$	137.6	145.4	125.8	122.4	123.1
2.	**DOMESTIC TOURISM**							
	Data							
	Trips							
2.1	Total		('000)	612,525	612,750	630,950	595,221	604,715
2.2	♦ Overnight visitors (tourists)		('000)	313,561	315,549	320,416	297,343	312,985
2.3	♦ Same-day visitors (excursionists)		('000)	298,964	297,201	310,534	297,878	291,730

JAPAN

Cod.	Basic data and indicators	Notes	Units	2011	2012	2013	2014	2015
	Trips by main purpose							
2.4	Total		('000)	612,524	612,749	630,950	595,221	604,714
2.5	♦ Personal		('000)	504,163	505,586	523,711	482,732	495,472
2.6	* holidays, leisure and recreation		('000)	359,501	367,662	382,693	348,655	365,391
2.7	* other personal purposes		('000)	144,662	137,924	141,018	134,077	130,081
2.8	♦ Business and professional		('000)	108,361	107,163	107,239	112,489	109,242
	Trips by mode of transport	(5)						
2.9	Total		('000)	970,302	963,079	992,863	963,206	945,063
2.10	♦ Air		('000)	50,207	50,054	53,989	51,646	55,064
2.11	♦ Water		('000)	18,222	18,718	17,904	15,685	16,802
2.12	♦ Land		('000)	901,873	894,307	920,970	895,875	873,197
2.13	* railway		('000)	282,834	284,917	299,442	295,299	313,993
2.14	* road		('000)	612,038	602,865	615,433	594,683	552,146
2.15	* others		('000)	7,001	6,525	6,095	5,893	7,058
	Trips by form of organization							
2.16	Total		('000)	612,525	612,750	630,950	595,220	604,715
2.17	♦ Package tour		('000)	107,051	106,273	109,317	92,494	96,279
2.18	♦ Other forms		('000)	505,474	506,477	521,633	502,726	508,436
	Accommodation	(3)						
	Total							
2.19	♦ Guests		('000)	300,818	315,056	329,534	326,258	336,544
2.20	♦ Overnights		('000)	398,819	413,181	433,697	428,677	438,464
	Hotels and similar establishments							
2.21	♦ Guests		('000)	282,478	294,667	307,224	304,680	312,900
2.22	♦ Overnights		('000)	370,896	383,163	400,365	397,701	405,129
	Indicators							
2.23	Average size of travel party		Persons	..	..	..	..	..
	Average length of stay							
2.24	Total		Days	5.46	5.57	5.84	5.72	5.75
2.25	♦ For all commercial accommodation services		Nights	1.33	1.31	1.32	1.31	1.30
2.26	* of which, "hotels and similar establishments"		Nights	1.32	1.31	1.31	1.31	1.23
2.27	♦ For non commercial accommodation services		Days	2.34	2.33	2.44	2.34	2.30
2.28	Average expenditure per day		US$	353.0	341.7	277.4	239.4	..
3.	**OUTBOUND TOURISM**							
	Data							
	Departures							
3.1	Total		('000)	16,994	18,491	17,473	16,903	16,214
3.2	♦ Overnight visitors (tourists)		('000)	..	..	..	..	..
3.3	♦ Same-day visitors (excursionists)		('000)	..	..	..	..	..
	Expenditure							
3.4	Total		US$ Mn	39,760	40,967	32,244	28,609	23,165
3.5	♦ Travel		US$ Mn	27,262	27,906	21,861	19,314	15,971
3.6	♦ Passenger transport		US$ Mn	12,498	13,061	10,383	9,295	7,194
	Expenditure by main purpose of the trip							
3.7	Total		US$ Mn	27,262	27,906	21,861	19,313	15,971
3.8	♦ Personal		US$ Mn	23,280	24,502	18,866	16,304	13,491
3.9	♦ Business and professional		US$ Mn	3,982	3,404	2,995	3,009	2,480
	Indicators							
3.10	Average length of stay		Days	9.00	9.07	9.66	9.95	10.20
3.11	Average expenditure per day		US$	178.3	166.4	129.5	121.4	116.9
4.	**TOURISM INDUSTRIES**							
	Data							
	Number of establishments							
4.1	Total		Units	62,961	61,063	61,300	60,103	..
4.2	♦ Accommodation for visitors	(3)(6)	Units	52,721	50,917	51,155	50,125	49,979
4.3	* of which, "hotels and similar establishments"	(3)(6)	Units	38,780	36,690	35,470	33,530	32,720
4.4	♦ Food and beverage serving activities		Units	..	..	..	..	..
4.5	♦ Passenger transportation		Units	..	..	..	..	..
4.6	♦ Travel agencies and other reservation services activities		Units	10,240	10,146	10,145	9,978	..
4.7	♦ Other tourism industries		Units	..	..	..	..	..
	Accommodation for visitors in hotels and similar establishments							
	Monetary data							
4.8	♦ Output		US$ Mn	75,070.0	79,466.7	67,766.4	69,682.4	..
4.9	♦ Intermediate consumption		US$ Mn	34,733.0	33,380.0	28,575.8	28,063.5	..
4.10	♦ Gross value added		US$ Mn	40,337.0	46,086.7	39,190.6	41,618.9	..
4.11	♦ Compensation of employees		US$ Mn	16,121.7	15,050.9	12,243.9	13,606.6	..
4.12	♦ Gross fixed capital formation		US$ Mn	9,688.0	10,134.1	8,360.7	8,729.5	..

JAPAN

Cod.	Basic data and indicators	Notes	Units	2011	2012	2013	2014	2015
	Non-monetary data	(3)						
4.13	♦ Number of establishments		Units	52,721	50,917	51,155	50,125	49,979
4.14	♦ Number of rooms		Units	1,388,479	1,366,566	1,427,107	1,404,954	1,419,996
4.15	♦ Number of bed-places	(7)	Units	3,332,677	3,307,957	3,516,309	3,450,175	3,474,963
	Indicators							
4.16	Occupancy rate / rooms		Percent	51.80	54.80	55.20	57.40	60.33
4.17	Occupancy rate / bed-places		Percent	34.30	36.40	36.30	37.60	39.74
4.18	Average length of stay		Nights	1.34	1.32	1.33	1.33	1.33
4.19	Available capacity (bed-places per 1000 inhabitants)		Units	26.19	26.02	27.69	27.21	27.45
	Travel agencies and other reservation service activities							
	Non-monetary data							
	♦ Domestic trips							
4.25	* with package tour		Percent	17.5	17.3	17.3	15.5	15.9
4.26	* without package tour		Percent	82.5	82.7	82.7	84.5	84.1
	♦ Inbound trips							
4.27	* with package tour		Percent	25.1	24.2	25.8	22.8	25.6
4.28	* without package tour		Percent	74.9	75.8	74.2	77.2	74.4
	♦ Outbound trips							
4.29	* with package tour		Percent	52.1	52.3	50.0	45.3	53.3
4.30	* without package tour		Percent	47.9	47.7	50.0	54.7	46.7
5.	**EMPLOYMENT**							
	Data							
	Number of employees by tourism industries							
5.1	Total		('000)	3,951.4	3,949.0	4,010.0	4,140.0	..
5.2	♦ Accommodation services for visitors (hotels and similar establishments)		('000)	391.7	366.5	360.0	400.0	..
5.3	♦ Other accommodation services		('000)	..	..	..	..	..
5.4	♦ Food and beverage serving activities		('000)	943.0	936.5	920.0	920.0	..
5.5	♦ Passenger transportation		('000)	1,326.5	1,314.5	1,350.0	1,440.0	..
5.6	♦ Travel agencies and other reservation services activities	(8)	('000)	594.6	601.3	630.0	630.0	..
5.7	♦ Other tourism industries		('000)	695.7	730.3	750.0	750.0	..
	Number of jobs by status in employment							
5.8	Total		('000)	4,445.0	4,424.7	4,480.0	4,610.0	..
5.9	♦ Employees		('000)	3,951.4	3,949.0	4,010.0	4,140.0	..
5.10	♦ Self employed		('000)	493.6	475.7	470.0	470.0	..
6.	**COMPLEMENTARY INDICATORS**							
	Demand							
6.1	Gross travel propensity		Units	4.9	5.0	5.1	4.8	4.9
6.2	(1.1 inbound visitors + 2.1 domestic visitors) / population		Units	4.86	4.89	5.05	4.80	4.93
	Macroeconomic indicators related to international tourism							
6.3	Inbound tourism expenditure over GDP		Percent	0.2	0.3	0.3	0.4	..
6.4	Outbound tourism expenditure over GDP		Percent	0.7	0.7	0.7	0.6	..
6.5	Tourism balance (inbound minus outbound tourism expenditure) over GDP		Percent	-0.5	-0.4	-0.4	-0.2	..
6.6	Tourism openness (inbound plus outbound tourism expenditure) over GDP		Percent	0.9	1.0	1.0	1.0	..
6.7	Tourism coverage (inbound over outbound tourism expenditure)		Percent	31.5	39.5	52.3	72.7	117.8
6.8	Inbound tourism expenditure over exports of goods		Percent	1.6	2.1	2.4	3.0	4.4
6.9	Inbound tourism expenditure over exports of services		Percent	8.9	11.8	12.5	12.7	16.8
6.10	Inbound tourism expenditure over exports of goods and services		Percent	1.3	1.8	2.0	2.4	3.5
6.11	Inbound tourism expenditure over current account credits		Percent	1.1	1.4	1.6	1.8	2.6
6.12	Outbound tourism expenditure over imports of goods		Percent	5.0	4.9	4.1	3.6	3.7
6.13	Outbound tourism expenditure over imports of services		Percent	22.6	22.2	18.9	14.9	13.1
6.14	Outbound tourism expenditure over imports of goods and		Percent	4.1	4.0	3.4	2.9	2.9
6.15	Outbound tourism expenditure over current account debits		Percent	3.2	3.2	2.6	2.2	2.1

JORDAN

Cod.	Basic data and indicators	Notes	Units	2011	2012	2013	2014	2015
1.	**INBOUND TOURISM**							
	Data							
	Arrivals	(1)						
1.1	Total		('000)	6,813	6,314	5,389	5,327	4,809
1.2	♦ Overnight visitors (tourists)		('000)	3,960	4,162	3,945	3,990	3,761
1.3	♦ Same-day visitors (excursionists)		('000)	2,853	2,152	1,444	1,337	1,048
1.4	* of which, cruise passengers		('000)	72	85	96	36	34
	Arrivals by region	(1)						
1.5	Total		('000)	3,959	4,162	3,945	3,990	3,761
1.6	♦ Africa		('000)	50	55	55	58	52
1.7	♦ Americas		('000)	189	199	188	196	192
1.8	♦ East Asia and the Pacific		('000)	154	175	177	170	137
1.9	♦ Europe		('000)	627	590	537	533	427
1.10	♦ Middle East		('000)	1,893	2,007	1,828	1,755	1,607
1.11	♦ South Asia		('000)	77	78	75	75	71
1.12	♦ Other not classified		('000)	969	1,058	1,085	1,203	1,276
1.13	* of which, nationals residing abroad		('000)	969	1,058	1,085	1,203	1,276
	Arrivals by main purpose							
1.14	Total		('000)	3,960	4,162	3,945	3,990	3,761
1.15	♦ Personal		('000)	3,679	3,866	3,647	3,735	3,494
1.16	* holidays, leisure and recreation		('000)	1,126	1,183	1,023	1,013	1,069
1.17	* other personal purposes		('000)	2,553	2,683	2,624	2,722	2,425
1.18	♦ Business and professional		('000)	281	296	298	255	267
	Arrivals by mode of transport	(2)						
1.19	Total		('000)	8,713	8,065	6,979	6,941	4,809
1.20	♦ Air		('000)	2,270	2,604	2,686	2,910	2,095
1.21	♦ Water		('000)	366	408	330	269	192
1.22	♦ Land		('000)	6,077	5,053	3,963	3,762	2,522
1.23	* railway		('000)	..	..	..	..	..
1.24	* road		('000)	6,077	5,053	3,963	3,762	2,522
1.25	* others		('000)	..	..	..	..	..
	Arrivals by form of organization of the trip							
1.26	Total		('000)	..	..	3,945	3,990	3,761
1.27	♦ Package tour		('000)	..	..	433	443	301
1.28	♦ Other forms		('000)	..	..	3,512	3,547	3,460
	Accommodation							
	Total							
1.29	♦ Guests		('000)	1,707	1,840	1,761	1,771	1,268
1.30	♦ Overnights		('000)	3,765	4,854	3,766	3,770	2,819
	Hotels and similar establishments							
1.31	♦ Guests		('000)	1,691	1,822	..	..	..
1.32	♦ Overnights		('000)	3,741	4,827	3,739	3,749	2,806
	Expenditure							
1.33	Total		US$ Mn	4,351	5,123	5,145	5,518	4,997
1.34	♦ Travel		US$ Mn	3,425	4,061	4,117	4,375	4,065
1.35	♦ Passenger transport		US$ Mn	926	1,062	1,028	1,143	932
	Expenditure by main purpose of the trip							
1.36	Total		US$ Mn	..	..	..	4,376	4,065
1.37	♦ Personal		US$ Mn	..	..	..	4,036	3,763
1.38	♦ Business and professional		US$ Mn	..	..	..	340	302
	Indicators							
1.39	Average size of travel party		Persons	..	..	..	..	..
	Average length of stay							
1.40	Total		Days	..	..	..	..	..
1.41	♦ For all commercial accommodation services	(3)	Nights	4.30	4.20	4.30	4.60	3.70
1.42	* of which, "hotels and similar establishments"		Nights	..	..	..	..	..
1.43	♦ For non commercial accommodation services		Days	..	..	..	..	..
1.44	Average expenditure per day		US$	..	..	..	..	..
2.	**DOMESTIC TOURISM**							
	Data							
	Accommodation							
	Total							
2.19	♦ Guests		('000)	551	583	674	649	626
2.20	♦ Overnights		('000)	1,012	1,082	1,205	1,287	1,189
	Hotels and similar establishments							
2.21	♦ Guests		('000)	550	582	..	..	..
2.22	♦ Overnights		('000)	1,011	1,080	1,203	1,286	1,188

JORDAN

Cod.	Basic data and indicators	Notes	Units	2011	2012	2013	2014	2015
	Indicators							
2.23	Average size of travel party		Persons	..	..	..	..	..
	Average length of stay							
2.24	Total		Days	..	..	..	..	..
2.25	♦ For all commercial accommodation services		Nights	2.00	2.40	2.00	2.00	..
2.26	* of which, "hotels and similar establishments"		Nights	..	..	..	..	..
2.27	♦ For non commercial accommodation services		Days	..	..	..	..	..
2.28	Average expenditure per day		US$	..	..	..	..	..
3.	**OUTBOUND TOURISM**							
	Data							
	Departures							
3.1	Total		('000)	2,194	1,780	1,744	1,407	1,633
3.2	♦ Overnight visitors (tourists)		('000)	1,931	1,567	1,498	1,230	..
3.3	♦ Same-day visitors (excursionists)		('000)	263	214	246	177	..
	Expenditure							
3.4	Total		US$ Mn	1,280	1,257	1,206	1,251	1,267
3.5	♦ Travel		US$ Mn	1,161	1,144	1,096	1,142	1,160
3.6	♦ Passenger transport		US$ Mn	119	113	110	109	107
	Expenditure by main purpose of the trip							
3.7	Total		US$ Mn	..	..	..	1,142	1,159
3.8	♦ Personal		US$ Mn	..	..	..	907	918
3.9	♦ Business and professional		US$ Mn	..	..	..	235	241
4.	**TOURISM INDUSTRIES**							
	Data							
	Number of establishments							
4.1	Total		Units	2,415	2,502	2,717	2,758	3,089
4.2	♦ Accommodation for visitors		Units	492	496	525	536	558
4.3	* of which, "hotels and similar establishments"		Units	474	478	506	517	539
4.4	♦ Food and beverage serving activities		Units	833	868	991	983	1,006
4.5	♦ Passenger transportation		Units	8	8	8	8	8
4.6	♦ Travel agencies and other reservation services activities		Units	763	779	822	856	868
4.7	♦ Other tourism industries		Units	319	351	371	375	649
	Accommodation for visitors in hotels and similar establishments							
	Non-monetary data							
4.13	♦ Number of establishments		Units	474	478	506	517	539
4.14	♦ Number of rooms		Units	23,578	23,881	25,785	26,221	26,812
4.15	♦ Number of bed-places		Units	45,059	45,533	49,157	50,031	51,092
	Indicators							
4.16	Occupancy rate / rooms		Percent	41.00	50.30	44.00	43.90	38.40
4.17	Occupancy rate / bed-places		Percent	34.50	44.70	36.00	38.00	31.30
4.18	Average length of stay		Nights	2.00	2.40	2.00	2.00	..
4.19	Available capacity (bed-places per 1000 inhabitants)		Units	6.67	6.51	6.81	6.75	6.73
	Travel agencies and other reservation service activities							
	Non-monetary data							
	♦ Domestic trips							
4.25	* with package tour		Percent	..	..	..	..	..
4.26	* without package tour		Percent	..	..	..	..	..
	♦ Inbound trips							
4.27	* with package tour		Percent	11.0	11.0	11.0	11.0	19.0
4.28	* without package tour		Percent	89.0	89.0	89.0	89.0	81.0
	♦ Outbound trips							
4.29	* with package tour		Percent	10.0	10.0	10.0	10.0	..
4.30	* without package tour		Percent	90.0	90.0	90.0	90.0	..
5.	**EMPLOYMENT**							
	Data							
	Number of employees by tourism industries							
5.1	Total		('000)	42.8	43.9	48.4	48.6	49.1
5.2	♦ Accommodation services for visitors (hotels and similar establishments)		('000)	15.2	15.4	18.4	18.6	19.1
5.3	♦ Other accommodation services		('000)	..	..	..	..	..
5.4	♦ Food and beverage serving activities		('000)	17.6	18.4	19.6	19.5	19.5
5.5	♦ Passenger transportation		('000)	0.9	0.9	1.0	1.0	1.0
5.6	♦ Travel agencies and other reservation services activities		('000)	4.6	4.7	4.8	4.9	5.0
5.7	♦ Other tourism industries		('000)	4.5	4.4	4.6	4.6	4.5

JORDAN

Cod.	Basic data and indicators	Notes	Units	2011	2012	2013	2014	2015
	Indicators							
	Number of full-time equivalent jobs by status in employment							
5.11	Total		('000)	42.7	43.9	48.4	48.6	..
5.12	♦ Employees		('000)	42.7	43.9	48.4	48.6	..
5.13	* male		('000)	38.3	39.5	43.7	44.0	..
5.14	* female		('000)	4.4	4.5	4.7	4.6	..
5.15	♦ Self employed		('000)	..	..	..	..	..
5.16	* male		('000)	..	..	..	..	..
5.17	* female		('000)	..	..	..	..	..
6.	**COMPLEMENTARY INDICATORS**							
	Demand							
6.1	Gross travel propensity		Units	..	..	..	..	..
6.2	(1.2 inbound tourists) / population		Units	0.59	0.60	0.55	0.54	0.50
	Macroeconomic indicators related to international tourism							
6.3	Inbound tourism expenditure over GDP		Percent	15.1	16.6	15.3	15.4	..
6.4	Outbound tourism expenditure over GDP		Percent	4.4	4.1	3.6	3.5	..
6.5	Tourism balance (inbound minus outbound tourism expenditure) over GDP		Percent	10.7	12.5	11.7	11.9	..
6.6	Tourism openness (inbound plus outbound tourism expenditure) over GDP		Percent	19.5	20.7	18.9	18.9	..
6.7	Tourism coverage (inbound over outbound tourism expenditure)		Percent	339.9	407.6	426.6	441.1	394.4
6.8	Inbound tourism expenditure over exports of goods		Percent	54.3	65.0	65.0	65.8	63.8
6.9	Inbound tourism expenditure over exports of services		Percent	75.8	79.8	81.5	77.3	79.2
6.10	Inbound tourism expenditure over exports of goods and services		Percent	31.7	35.8	36.2	35.5	35.3
6.11	Inbound tourism expenditure over current account credits		Percent	22.0	25.6	23.1	22.7	23.8
6.12	Outbound tourism expenditure over imports of goods		Percent	7.6	6.8	6.2	6.1	7.0
6.13	Outbound tourism expenditure over imports of services		Percent	28.6	27.7	26.2	27.0	28.2
6.14	Outbound tourism expenditure over imports of goods and		Percent	6.0	5.5	5.0	5.0	5.6
6.15	Outbound tourism expenditure over current account debits		Percent	5.7	5.2	4.7	4.7	5.3

KAZAKHSTAN

Cod.	Basic data and indicators	Notes	Units	2011	2012	2013	2014	2015
1.	**INBOUND TOURISM**							
	Data							
	Arrivals							
1.1	Total		('000)	5,685	6,163	6,841	6,333	6,430
1.2	♦ Overnight visitors (tourists)		('000)	4,093	4,437	4,926	4,560	..
1.3	♦ Same-day visitors (excursionists)		('000)	1,592	1,726	1,915	1,773	..
1.4	* of which, cruise passengers		('000)	..	..	..	..	..
	Arrivals by region							
1.5	Total		('000)	5,685	6,163	6,841	6,333	6,430
1.6	♦ Africa		('000)	2	12	2	2	3
1.7	♦ Americas		('000)	29	34	30	33	37
1.8	♦ East Asia and the Pacific		('000)	178	200	249	278	171
1.9	♦ Europe		('000)	5,436	5,874	6,523	5,980	6,178
1.10	♦ Middle East		('000)	5	5	4	5	6
1.11	♦ South Asia		('000)	23	25	22	24	26
1.12	♦ Other not classified		('000)	12	13	11	11	11
1.13	* of which, nationals residing abroad		('000)	..	..	..	..	..
	Arrivals by main purpose							
1.14	Total		('000)	5,685	6,164	6,841	6,333	6,430
1.15	♦ Personal		('000)	5,446	5,887	5,745	5,154	5,385
1.16	* holidays, leisure and recreation		('000)	238	92	57	56	47
1.17	* other personal purposes		('000)	5,207	5,796	5,689	5,098	5,339
1.18	♦ Business and professional		('000)	239	277	1,096	1,179	1,045
	Arrivals by mode of transport							
1.19	Total		('000)	5,685	6,163	6,841	6,333	..
1.20	♦ Air		('000)	785	850	944	874	..
1.21	♦ Water		('000)	6	6	7	6	..
1.22	♦ Land		('000)	4,894	5,307	5,890	5,453	..
1.23	* railway		('000)	1,170	1,268	1,408	1,303	..
1.24	* road		('000)	3,724	4,039	4,482	4,150	..
1.25	* others		('000)	..	..	..	..	..
	Arrivals by form of organization of the trip							
1.26	Total		('000)	5,685	6,163	6,841	..	..
1.27	♦ Package tour		('000)	36	30	23	..	..
1.28	♦ Other forms		('000)	5,649	6,133	6,818	..	..
	Accommodation							
	Hotels and similar establishments							
1.31	♦ Guests		('000)	..	..	..		..
1.32	♦ Overnights		('000)	584	519	586	679	692
	Expenditure							
1.33	Total		US$ Mn	1,524	1,572	1,779	1,701	1,825
1.34	♦ Travel		US$ Mn	1,209	1,347	1,522	1,467	1,625
1.35	♦ Passenger transport		US$ Mn	315	225	257	234	200
	Expenditure by main purpose of the trip							
1.36	Total		US$ Mn	1,209	1,347	1,522	1,467	1,625
1.37	♦ Personal		US$ Mn	1,077	1,220	1,381	1,323	1,472
1.38	♦ Business and professional		US$ Mn	132	127	141	144	153
2.	**DOMESTIC TOURISM**							
	Data							
	Trips							
2.1	Total		('000)	5,328	6,222	6,504	6,022	7,293
2.2	♦ Overnight visitors (tourists)		('000)	..	..	5,610	5,194	6,166
2.3	♦ Same-day visitors (excursionists)		('000)	..	..	894	828	1,127
	Trips by main purpose							
2.4	Total		('000)	5,328	6,222	6,504	6,022	7,293
2.5	♦ Personal		('000)	4,950	5,780	5,562	5,594	6,512
2.6	* holidays, leisure and recreation		('000)	4,485	5,237	5,359	5,070	6,459
2.7	* other personal purposes		('000)	465	543	203	524	53
2.8	♦ Business and professional		('000)	378	442	942	428	781
	Trips by mode of transport							
2.9	Total		('000)	5,328	6,222	6,504	6,022	7,293
2.10	♦ Air		('000)	421	492	361	475	385
2.11	♦ Water		('000)	..	..	..	..	1
2.12	♦ Land		('000)	4,907	5,730	6,143	5,547	6,907
2.13	* railway		('000)	937	1,094	1,729	1,059	2,411
2.14	* road		('000)	3,970	4,636	4,414	4,488	4,496
2.15	* others		('000)	..	..	..	..	..
	Trips by form of organization							
2.16	Total		('000)	5,328	6,222	6,504	6,022	7,293
2.17	♦ Package tour		('000)	203	202	463	428	360
2.18	♦ Other forms		('000)	5,125	6,020	6,041	5,594	6,933

KAZAKHSTAN

Cod.	Basic data and indicators	Notes	Units	2011	2012	2013	2014	2015
	Accommodation							
	Hotels and similar establishments							
2.21	♦ Guests		('000)	..	..	..	..	..
2.22	♦ Overnights		('000)	2,209	2,448	2,718	1,815	2,141
3.	**OUTBOUND TOURISM**							
	Data							
	Departures							
3.1	Total		('000)	8,020	9,066	10,144	10,450	11,303
3.2	♦ Overnight visitors (tourists)		('000)	7,852	8,875	9,931	10,230	..
3.3	♦ Same-day visitors (excursionists)		('000)	168	190	213	220	..
	Expenditure							
3.4	Total		US$ Mn	1,831	2,023	2,147	2,164	2,185
3.5	♦ Travel		US$ Mn	1,611	1,686	1,843	1,932	2,009
3.6	♦ Passenger transport		US$ Mn	220	337	304	232	176
	Expenditure by main purpose of the trip							
3.7	Total		US$ Mn	1,611	1,686	1,843	1,932	2,009
3.8	♦ Personal		US$ Mn	1,531	1,592	1,794	1,882	1,959
3.9	♦ Business and professional		US$ Mn	80	94	49	50	50
4.	**TOURISM INDUSTRIES**							
	Data							
	Number of establishments							
4.1	Total		Units	22,552	23,728	24,605	28,771	25,207
4.2	♦ Accommodation for visitors		Units	..	..	..	..	..
4.3	* of which, "hotels and similar establishments"		Units	1,494	1,526	1,678	2,056	2,338
4.4	♦ Food and beverage serving activities		Units	19,343	20,208	20,738	26,715	22,869
4.5	♦ Passenger transportation		Units	..	..	..	..	..
4.6	♦ Travel agencies and other reservation services activities		Units	1,715	1,994	2,189	..	..
4.7	♦ Other tourism industries		Units	..	..	..	..	..
	Accommodation for visitors in hotels and similar establishments							
	Non-monetary data							
4.13	♦ Number of establishments		Units	1,494	1,526	1,678	2,056	2,338
4.14	♦ Number of rooms		Units	37,368	37,786	41,197	49,128	53,126
4.15	♦ Number of bed-places		Units	81,015	83,103	92,053	109,094	118,355
	Indicators							
4.16	Occupancy rate / rooms		Percent	..	..	..	..	..
4.17	Occupancy rate / bed-places		Percent	24.00	24.90	21.40	22.00	23.50
4.18	Average length of stay		Nights	..	..	..	..	..
4.19	Available capacity (bed-places per 1000 inhabitants)		Units	4.89	4.94	5.38	6.28	6.72
5.	**EMPLOYMENT**							
	Data							
	Number of employees by tourism industries							
5.1	Total		('000)	125.1	119.2	129.3	136.5	103.6
5.2	♦ Accommodation services for visitors (hotels and similar establishments)		('000)	47.7	42.6	50.4	53.9	17.6
5.3	♦ Other accommodation services		('000)	10.9	11.1	10.8	10.3	10.5
5.4	♦ Food and beverage serving activities		('000)	..	..	..	..	..
5.5	♦ Passenger transportation		('000)	..	..	..	..	..
5.6	♦ Travel agencies and other reservation services activities		('000)	4.9	5.0	6.6	6.5	7.3
5.7	♦ Other tourism industries		('000)	61.6	60.5	61.5	65.8	68.2
6.	**COMPLEMENTARY INDICATORS**							
	Demand							
6.1	Gross travel propensity		Units	..	..	..	..	..
6.2	(1.2 inbound tourists + 2.2 domestic tourists) / population		Units	..	..	0.62	0.56	..
	Macroeconomic indicators related to international tourism							
6.3	Inbound tourism expenditure over GDP		Percent	0.8	0.8	0.8	0.8	1.1
6.4	Outbound tourism expenditure over GDP		Percent	1.0	1.0	1.0	1.0	1.3
6.5	Tourism balance (inbound minus outbound tourism expenditure) over GDP		Percent	-0.2	-0.2	-0.2	-0.2	-0.2
6.6	Tourism openness (inbound plus outbound tourism expenditure) over GDP		Percent	1.8	1.8	1.8	1.8	2.4

KAZAKHSTAN

Cod.	Basic data and indicators	Notes	Units	2011	2012	2013	2014	2015
6.7	Tourism coverage (inbound over outbound tourism expenditure)		Percent	83.2	77.7	82.9	78.6	83.5
6.8	Inbound tourism expenditure over exports of goods		Percent	1.8	1.8	2.1	2.2	..
6.9	Inbound tourism expenditure over exports of services		Percent	35.1	32.6	34.7	26.8	..
6.10	Inbound tourism expenditure over exports of goods and services		Percent	1.7	1.7	2.0	2.0	..
6.11	Inbound tourism expenditure over current account credits		Percent	1.6	1.6	1.9	1.9	..
6.12	Outbound tourism expenditure over imports of goods		Percent	4.5	4.1	4.2	5.0	..
6.13	Outbound tourism expenditure over imports of services		Percent	16.7	15.8	17.6	16.9	..
6.14	Outbound tourism expenditure over imports of goods and		Percent	3.6	3.3	3.4	3.8	..
6.15	Outbound tourism expenditure over current account debits		Percent	3.2	3.0	3.1	3.5	..

KENYA

Cod.	Basic data and indicators	Notes	Units	2011	2012	2013	2014	2015
1.	**INBOUND TOURISM**							
	Data							
	Arrivals	(1)						
1.1	Total		('000)	1,823	1,711	1,520	1,350	1,181
1.2	♦ Overnight visitors (tourists)		('000)	1,750	1,619	1,434	1,261	1,114
1.3	♦ Same-day visitors (excursionists)		('000)	73	92	86	89	66
1.4	* of which, cruise passengers		('000)	..	..	..	..	..
	Arrivals by region	(1)						
1.5	Total		('000)	1,823	1,711	1,520	1,350	1,181
1.6	♦ Africa		('000)	355	310	286	320	316
1.7	♦ Americas		('000)	186	190	166	183	167
1.8	♦ East Asia and the Pacific		('000)	218	206	125	110	106
1.9	♦ Europe		('000)	931	865	826	609	473
1.10	♦ Middle East		('000)	..	..	..	..	..
1.11	♦ South Asia		('000)	..	..	..	..	..
1.12	♦ Other not classified		('000)	134	140	117	129	118
1.13	* of which, nationals residing abroad		('000)	..	..	..	..	..
	Arrivals by main purpose	(1)						
1.14	Total		('000)	1,823	1,711	1,520	1,350	1,181
1.15	♦ Personal		('000)	1,513	1,420	1,261	1,122	1,022
1.16	* holidays, leisure and recreation		('000)	1,242	1,164	1,035	915	845
1.17	* other personal purposes		('000)	271	256	226	207	177
1.18	♦ Business and professional		('000)	310	291	259	229	159
	Arrivals by mode of transport	(1)						
1.19	Total		('000)	1,823	1,711	1,520	1,350	1,181
1.20	♦ Air		('000)	1,301	1,292	1,133	888	771
1.21	♦ Water		('000)	35	6	6	23	7
1.22	♦ Land		('000)	487	413	381	439	403
1.23	* railway		('000)	..	..	..	..	..
1.24	* road		('000)	487	413	381	439	403
1.25	* others		('000)	..	..	..	..	..
	Accommodation							
	Hotels and similar establishments							
1.31	♦ Guests		('000)	..	..	..	..	..
1.32	♦ Overnights		('000)	4,353	4,027	3,840	3,234	2,622
	Expenditure							
1.33	Total		US$ Mn	1,844	2,004	1,829	1,833	..
1.34	♦ Travel		US$ Mn	926	935	881	811	..
1.35	♦ Passenger transport		US$ Mn	918	1,069	948	1,022	..
	Expenditure by main purpose of the trip							
1.36	Total		US$ Mn	926	935	881	811	..
1.37	♦ Personal		US$ Mn	823	839	846	780	..
1.38	♦ Business and professional		US$ Mn	103	95	34	31	..
	Indicators							
1.39	Average size of travel party		Persons	..	..	..	..	..
	Average length of stay							
1.40	Total		Days	..	..	..	..	..
1.41	♦ For all commercial accommodation services		Nights	13.40	13.20	13.20	12.93	12.30
1.42	* of which, "hotels and similar establishments"		Nights	..	..	..	..	..
1.43	♦ For non commercial accommodation services		Days	..	..	..	..	..
1.44	Average expenditure per day		US$	..	..	..	..	..
2.	**DOMESTIC TOURISM**							
	Data							
	Accommodation							
	Hotels and similar establishments							
2.21	♦ Guests		('000)	..	..	..	..	..
2.22	♦ Overnights		('000)	2,603	2,788	2,699	2,948	3,154
3.	**OUTBOUND TOURISM**							
	Data							
	Expenditure							
3.4	Total		US$ Mn	..	..	..	..	..
3.5	♦ Travel		US$ Mn	197	174	233	206	..
3.6	♦ Passenger transport		US$ Mn	..	..	..	..	..
	Expenditure by main purpose of the trip							
3.7	Total		US$ Mn	197	174	233	206	..
3.8	♦ Personal		US$ Mn	111	94	132	108	..
3.9	♦ Business and professional		US$ Mn	86	80	101	98	..

KENYA

Cod. Basic data and indicators	Notes	Units	2011	2012	2013	2014	2015
4. TOURISM INDUSTRIES							
Indicators							
4.16 Occupancy rate / rooms		Percent	45.40	42.30	42.00	38.10	37.20
4.17 Occupancy rate / bed-places		Percent	40.30	36.40	36.10	31.60	29.10
4.18 Average length of stay	(2)	Nights	13.42	13.22	13.23	12.93	13.20
4.19 Available capacity (bed-places per 1000 inhabitants)		Units	..	..	..	..	.
6. COMPLEMENTARY INDICATORS							
Demand							
6.1 Gross travel propensity		Units	..	..	..	..	
6.2 (1.2 inbound tourists) / population		Units	0.04	0.04	0.03	0.03	0.02
Macroeconomic indicators related to international tourism							
6.3 Inbound tourism expenditure over GDP		Percent	5.4	4.9	3.3	3.0	.
6.4 Outbound tourism expenditure over GDP		Percent	0.6	0.4	0.4	0.3	.
6.5 Tourism balance (inbound minus outbound tourism expenditure) over GDP		Percent	4.8	4.5	2.9	2.7	.
6.6 Tourism openness (inbound plus outbound tourism expenditure) over GDP		Percent	6.0	5.3	3.7	3.3	.
6.7 Tourism coverage (inbound over outbound tourism expenditure)		Percent	936.0	1,151.7	785.0	889.8	.
6.8 Inbound tourism expenditure over exports of goods		Percent	31.8	32.5	31.5	29.7	.
6.9 Inbound tourism expenditure over exports of services		Percent	44.8	41.2	36.8	37.1	.
6.10 Inbound tourism expenditure over exports of goods and services		Percent	18.6	18.2	17.0	16.5	.
6.11 Inbound tourism expenditure over current account credits		Percent	14.4	14.3	12.9	12.0	.
6.12 Outbound tourism expenditure over imports of goods		Percent	1.4	1.1	1.5	1.2	.
6.13 Outbound tourism expenditure over imports of services		Percent	9.0	7.1	9.6	7.0	.
6.14 Outbound tourism expenditure over imports of goods and		Percent	1.2	1.0	1.3	1.0	.
6.15 Outbound tourism expenditure over current account debits		Percent	1.2	1.0	1.2	1.0	.

KIRIBATI

Cod.	Basic data and indicators	Notes	Units	2011	2012	2013	2014	2015
1.	**INBOUND TOURISM**							
	Data							
	Arrivals							
1.1	Total		('000)	..	..	..	9.6	9.6
1.2	♦ Overnight visitors (tourists)	(1)	('000)	5.3	4.9	5.9	5.1	4.4
1.3	♦ Same-day visitors (excursionists)		('000)	..	..	..	4.5	4.4
1.4	* of which, cruise passengers		('000)	..	..	..	4.5	5.2
	Arrivals by region	(1)						
1.5	Total		('000)	5.3	4.9	5.9	5.1	4.4
1.6	♦ Africa		('000)	..	..	..	..	..
1.7	♦ Americas		('000)	1.1	0.7	1.4	1.0	1.0
1.8	♦ East Asia and the Pacific		('000)	2.9	2.5	3.5	1.5	1.2
1.9	♦ Europe		('000)	0.4	0.3	0.6	0.1	0.2
1.10	♦ Middle East		('000)	..	..	..	..	..
1.11	♦ South Asia		('000)	..	..	..	..	..
1.12	♦ Other not classified		('000)	0.9	1.4	0.4	2.5	2.0
1.13	* of which, nationals residing abroad		('000)	..	..	..	..	..
	Arrivals by main purpose	(1)						
1.14	Total		('000)	5.3	4.9	5.9	5.1	4.4
1.15	♦ Personal		('000)	3.3	3.2	3.7	3.1	2.9
1.16	* holidays, leisure and recreation		('000)	1.3	1.0	1.4	1.4	1.4
1.17	* other personal purposes		('000)	2.0	2.2	2.3	1.7	1.5
1.18	♦ Business and professional		('000)	2.0	1.7	2.2	2.0	1.5
	Arrivals by mode of transport							
1.19	Total		('000)	5.3	4.9	5.9	9.6	9.6
1.20	♦ Air	(1)	('000)	5.3	4.9	5.9	5.1	4.4
1.21	♦ Water		('000)	..	..	..	4.5	5.2
1.22	♦ Land		('000)	..	..	..	..	..
1.23	* railway		('000)	..	..	..	..	..
1.24	* road		('000)	..	..	..	..	..
1.25	* others		('000)	..	..	..	..	..
	Expenditure							
1.33	Total		US$ Mn	6.4	4.5	4.4	3.9	..
1.34	♦ Travel		US$ Mn	4.9	3.2	3.3	2.9	..
1.35	♦ Passenger transport		US$ Mn	1.5	1.3	1.1	1.0	..
	Expenditure by main purpose of the trip							
1.36	Total		US$ Mn	4.9	3.2	3.2	2.9	..
1.37	♦ Personal		US$ Mn	1.3	1.0	0.9	0.6	..
1.38	♦ Business and professional		US$ Mn	3.7	2.2	2.3	2.3	..
	Indicators							
1.39	Average size of travel party		Persons	..	..	..	..	..
	Average length of stay							
1.40	Total		Days	..	..	..	..	..
1.41	♦ For all commercial accommodation services		Nights	..	..	..	13.40	..
1.42	* of which, "hotels and similar establishments"		Nights	..	..	..	..	..
1.43	♦ For non commercial accommodation services		Days	..	..	..	..	..
1.44	Average expenditure per day		US$	..	..	..	..	..
3.	**OUTBOUND TOURISM**							
	Data							
	Expenditure							
3.4	Total		US$ Mn	26.3	23.6	23.9	16.9	..
3.5	♦ Travel		US$ Mn	10.1	9.8	11.4	6.0	..
3.6	♦ Passenger transport		US$ Mn	16.2	13.8	12.5	10.9	..
	Expenditure by main purpose of the trip							
3.7	Total		US$ Mn	10.1	9.8	11.4	6.0	..
3.8	♦ Personal		US$ Mn	8.4	8.3	9.3	5.0	..
3.9	♦ Business and professional		US$ Mn	1.7	1.5	2.1	1.0	..
4.	**TOURISM INDUSTRIES**							
	Data							
	Number of establishments							
4.1	Total		Units	..	..	..	..	60
4.2	♦ Accommodation for visitors		Units	..	..	..	..	30
4.3	* of which, "hotels and similar establishments"		Units	..	..	..	..	26
4.4	♦ Food and beverage serving activities		Units	..	..	..	..	24
4.5	♦ Passenger transportation		Units	..	..	..	..	..
4.6	♦ Travel agencies and other reservation services activities		Units	..	..	..	..	3
4.7	♦ Other tourism industries		Units	..	..	..	..	3

209

KIRIBATI

Cod.	Basic data and indicators	Notes	Units	2011	2012	2013	2014	2015
	Accommodation for visitors in hotels and similar establishments							
	Non-monetary data							
4.13	♦ Number of establishments		Units	..	..	..	..	26
4.14	♦ Number of rooms		Units	..	..	..	..	320
4.15	♦ Number of bed-places		Units	..	..	..	..	640
	Indicators							
4.16	Occupancy rate / rooms		Percent	..	..	..	..	..
4.17	Occupancy rate / bed-places		Percent	..	..	..	..	..
4.18	Average length of stay		Nights	..	..	..	..	..
4.19	Available capacity (bed-places per 1000 inhabitants)		Units	..	..	..	..	5.71
5.	**EMPLOYMENT**							
	Data							
	Number of employees by tourism industries							
5.1	Total		('000)	..	..	..	..	..
5.2	♦ Accommodation services for visitors (hotels and similar establishments)		('000)	..	..	..	..	0.4
5.3	♦ Other accommodation services		('000)	..	..	..	..	..
5.4	♦ Food and beverage serving activities		('000)	..	..	..	..	..
5.5	♦ Passenger transportation		('000)	..	..	..	..	..
5.6	♦ Travel agencies and other reservation services activities		('000)	..	..	..	..	..
5.7	♦ Other tourism industries		('000)	..	..	..	..	..
6.	**COMPLEMENTARY INDICATORS**							
	Demand							
6.1	Gross travel propensity		Units	..	..		..	
6.2	(1.2 inbound tourists) / population		Units	0.05	0.05	0.06	0.05	0.04
	Macroeconomic indicators related to international tourism							
6.3	Inbound tourism expenditure over GDP		Percent	..	..	..	..	..
6.4	Outbound tourism expenditure over GDP		Percent	..	..	..	..	..
6.5	Tourism balance (inbound minus outbound tourism expenditure) over GDP		Percent	..	..	..	..	..
6.6	Tourism openness (inbound plus outbound tourism expenditure) over GDP		Percent	..	..	..	..	..
6.7	Tourism coverage (inbound over outbound tourism expenditure)		Percent	24.3	19.1	18.4	23.1	..
6.8	Inbound tourism expenditure over exports of goods		Percent	55.7	44.2	44.3	35.2	..
6.9	Inbound tourism expenditure over exports of services		Percent	42.1	31.6	32.0	32.4	..
6.10	Inbound tourism expenditure over exports of goods and services		Percent	24.0	18.4	18.6	16.9	..
6.11	Inbound tourism expenditure over current account credits		Percent	4.8	2.6	2.3	1.8	..
6.12	Outbound tourism expenditure over imports of goods		Percent	29.7	22.7	22.9	14.6	..
6.13	Outbound tourism expenditure over imports of services		Percent	41.2	33.3	34.2	31.5	..
6.14	Outbound tourism expenditure over imports of goods and		Percent	17.2	13.5	13.7	10.0	..
6.15	Outbound tourism expenditure over current account debits		Percent	11.5	8.5	7.9	5.1	..

KOREA, REPUBLIC OF

Cod.	Basic data and indicators	Notes	Units	2011	2012	2013	2014	2015
1.	**INBOUND TOURISM**							
	Data							
	Arrivals							
1.1	Total	(1)	('000)	9,795	11,140	12,176	14,202	13,232
1.2	♦ Overnight visitors (tourists)		('000)	..	..	..	..	..
1.3	♦ Same-day visitors (excursionists)		('000)	..	..	..	..	..
1.4	* of which, cruise passengers		('000)	..	..	..	..	..
	Arrivals by region	(1)						
1.5	Total		('000)	9,795	11,140	12,176	14,202	13,232
1.6	♦ Africa		('000)	30	32	34	35	36
1.7	♦ Americas		('000)	827	876	916	974	974
1.8	♦ East Asia and the Pacific		('000)	7,679	8,913	9,826	11,682	10,754
1.9	♦ Europe		('000)	753	807	864	961	936
1.10	♦ Middle East		('000)	29	35	40	46	42
1.11	♦ South Asia		('000)	148	147	188	211	219
1.12	♦ Other not classified		('000)	329	330	310	293	271
1.13	* of which, nationals residing abroad		('000)	327	329	310	293	270
	Arrivals by main purpose	(1)						
1.14	Total		('000)	9,795	11,140	12,176	14,202	13,232
1.15	♦ Personal		('000)	9,524	10,895	11,848	13,886	12,988
1.16	* holidays, leisure and recreation		('000)	7,203	8,657	9,076	10,928	10,136
1.17	* other personal purposes		('000)	2,321	2,238	2,772	2,959	2,853
1.18	♦ Business and professional		('000)	271	245	328	315	244
	Arrivals by mode of transport	(2)						
1.19	Total		('000)	9,795	11,140	12,176	14,202	13,232
1.20	♦ Air		('000)	8,375	9,759	9,892	11,557	10,733
1.21	♦ Water		('000)	1,420	1,381	2,284	2,644	2,499
1.22	♦ Land		('000)	..	..	..	..	..
1.23	* railway		('000)	..	..	..	..	..
1.24	* road		('000)	..	..	..	..	..
1.25	* others		('000)	..	..	..	..	..
	Arrivals by form of organization of the trip							
1.26	Total		('000)	9,596	11,140	12,176	14,201	13,232
1.27	♦ Package tour		('000)	2,596	2,818	3,373	3,536	3,467
1.28	♦ Other forms		('000)	7,000	8,322	8,803	10,665	9,765
	Accommodation							
	Hotels and similar establishments							
1.31	♦ Guests		('000)	8,857	9,808	8,616	8,853	..
1.32	♦ Overnights		('000)	19,248	18,487	15,062	15,001	..
	Expenditure							
1.33	Total		US$ Mn	17,418	18,851	19,644	22,704	19,126
1.34	♦ Travel		US$ Mn	12,476	13,429	14,629	17,836	15,285
1.35	♦ Passenger transport		US$ Mn	4,942	5,422	5,015	4,868	3,841
	Expenditure by main purpose of the trip							
1.36	Total		US$ Mn	12,475	13,429	14,629	17,836	15,285
1.37	♦ Personal		US$ Mn	8,554	10,068	11,230	14,320	11,825
1.38	♦ Business and professional		US$ Mn	3,921	3,361	3,399	3,516	3,460
	Indicators							
1.39	Average size of travel party		Persons	4.8	4.4	4.0	3.6	3.4
	Average length of stay							
1.40	Total		Days	7.50	6.70	6.80	6.10	6.60
1.41	♦ For all commercial accommodation services		Nights	..	..	..	..	..
1.42	* of which, "hotels and similar establishments"		Nights	..	..	..	..	..
1.43	♦ For non commercial accommodation services		Days	..	..	..	..	..
1.44	Average expenditure per day		US$	169.8	179.9	176.7	205.9	175.0
2.	**DOMESTIC TOURISM**							
	Data							
	Trips							
2.1	Total		('000)	156,594	213,468	231,035	227,100	238,297
2.2	♦ Overnight visitors (tourists)		('000)	71,622	92,289	99,667	98,521	99,776
2.3	♦ Same-day visitors (excursionists)		('000)	84,972	121,180	131,368	128,579	138,522
	Trips by main purpose							
2.4	Total		('000)	156,594	213,468	231,035	227,101	238,297
2.5	♦ Personal		('000)	152,679	207,491	224,566	220,969	232,101
2.6	* holidays, leisure and recreation		('000)	72,346	94,566	108,124	103,558	108,663
2.7	* other personal purposes		('000)	80,333	112,925	116,442	117,411	123,438
2.8	♦ Business and professional		('000)	3,915	5,977	6,469	6,132	6,196

KOREA, REPUBLIC OF

Cod.	Basic data and indicators	Notes	Units	2011	2012	2013	2014	2015
	Trips by mode of transport							
2.9	Total		('000)	156,593	213,468	231,035	227,100	238,297
2.10	♦ Air		('000)	4,071	4,483	4,852	3,861	5,243
2.11	♦ Water		('000)	1,253	1,067	1,155	908	715
2.12	♦ Land		('000)	151,269	207,918	225,028	222,331	232,339
2.13	* railway		('000)	7,203	9,606	10,859	10,220	9,770
2.14	* road		('000)	141,874	195,750	212,321	209,386	219,948
2.15	* others		('000)	2,192	2,562	1,848	2,725	2,621
	Trips by form of organization							
2.16	Total		('000)	156,594	213,468	231,035	227,100	238,297
2.17	♦ Package tour		('000)	20,514	24,122	24,952	26,344	22,162
2.18	♦ Other forms		('000)	136,080	189,346	206,083	200,756	216,135
	Accommodation							
	Hotels and similar establishments							
2.21	♦ Guests		('000)	12,023	12,080	12,029	10,939	..
2.22	♦ Overnights		('000)	22,273	19,494	17,497	16,828	
	Indicators							
2.23	Average size of travel party		Persons	8.4	8.1	7.7	6.6	5.1
	Average length of stay							
2.24	Total		Days	6.69	8.43	8.90	9.03	9.34
2.25	♦ For all commercial accommodation services		Nights	..	..	..	..	..
2.26	* of which, "hotels and similar establishments"		Nights	..	..	..	..	..
2.27	♦ For non commercial accommodation services		Days	..	..	..	..	..
2.28	Average expenditure per day		US$	63.5	58.0	54.5	59.3	55.2
3.	**OUTBOUND TOURISM**							
	Data							
	Departures							
3.1	Total		('000)	12,694	13,737	14,846	16,081	19,310
3.2	♦ Overnight visitors (tourists)		('000)	..	..	..	..	..
3.3	♦ Same-day visitors (excursionists)		('000)	..	..	..	..	..
	Expenditure							
3.4	Total		US$ Mn	22,195	22,934	24,459	26,136	27,559
3.5	♦ Travel	(3)	US$ Mn	19,920	20,645	21,648	23,192	24,958
3.6	♦ Passenger transport		US$ Mn	2,275	2,289	2,811	2,944	2,601
	Expenditure by main purpose of the trip							
3.7	Total		US$ Mn	19,920	20,645	21,648	23,192	24,958
3.8	♦ Personal		US$ Mn	16,764	18,000	19,203	21,511	22,160
3.9	♦ Business and professional		US$ Mn	3,156	2,645	2,445	1,681	2,798
	Indicators							
3.10	Average length of stay		Days	11.36	9.65	9.95	10.27	9.32
3.11	Average expenditure per day		US$	138.1	155.7	146.5	140.4	138.7
4.	**TOURISM INDUSTRIES**							
	Data							
	Number of establishments							
4.1	Total		Units	714,124	759,578	773,314	788,000	..
4.2	♦ Accommodation for visitors		Units	41,918	42,599	44,320	46,210	..
4.3	* of which, "hotels and similar establishments"	(4)	Units	644	683	734	837	..
4.4	♦ Food and beverage serving activities		Units	327,093	334,917	339,988	343,415	..
4.5	♦ Passenger transportation		Units	329,889	364,209	371,639	378,884	..
4.6	♦ Travel agencies and other reservation services activities		Units	10,725	12,438	11,722	12,854	..
4.7	♦ Other tourism industries		Units	4,499	5,415	5,645	6,637	..
	Accommodation for visitors in hotels and similar establishments							
	Monetary data							
4.8	♦ Output		US$ Mn	9,055.0	9,186.0	9,620.0	10,550.0	..
4.9	♦ Intermediate consumption		US$ Mn	..	..	..	..	..
4.10	♦ Gross value added		US$ Mn	..	..	..	..	..
4.11	♦ Compensation of employees		US$ Mn	..	..	..	..	..
4.12	♦ Gross fixed capital formation		US$ Mn	..	..	..	..	..
	Non-monetary data							
4.13	♦ Number of establishments	(4)	Units	644	683	734	837	..
4.14	♦ Number of rooms	(4)	Units	70,763	74,737	79,393	92,150	..
4.15	♦ Number of bed-places		Units	..	..	..	..	..

KOREA, REPUBLIC OF

Cod.	Basic data and indicators	Notes	Units	2011	2012	2013	2014	2015
	Indicators							
4.16	Occupancy rate / rooms		Percent	65.15	64.65	62.85	63.52	..
4.17	Occupancy rate / bed-places		Percent	..	..	..	..	..
4.18	Average length of stay		Nights	..	..	..	..	..
4.19	Available capacity (bed-places per 1000 inhabitants)		Units	..	..	..	..	..
	Travel agencies and other reservation service activities							
	Monetary data							
4.20	♦ Output		US$ Mn	466.2	643.3	602.8	504.4	..
4.21	♦ Intermediate consumption		US$ Mn	..	..	..	..	..
4.22	♦ Gross value added		US$ Mn	..	..	..	..	..
4.23	♦ Compensation of employees		US$ Mn	..	..	..	..	..
4.24	♦ Gross fixed capital formation		US$ Mn	..	..	..	..	..
	Non-monetary data							
	♦ Domestic trips							
4.25	* with package tour		Percent	13.1	11.3	10.8	11.6	9.3
4.26	* without package tour		Percent	86.9	88.7	89.2	88.4	90.7
	♦ Inbound trips							
4.27	* with package tour		Percent	26.5	25.3	27.7	24.9	26.2
4.28	* without package tour		Percent	73.5	74.7	72.3	75.1	73.8
	♦ Outbound trips							
4.29	* with package tour		Percent	66.9	79.7	72.8	65.1	63.4
4.30	* without package tour		Percent	33.1	20.3	27.2	34.9	36.6
5.	**EMPLOYMENT**							
	Data							
	Number of employees by tourism industries							
5.1	Total		('000)	2,020.0	2,088.0	2,130.0	2,177.0	..
5.2	♦ Accommodation services for visitors (hotels and similar establishments)		('000)	63.0	71.0	64.0	67.0	..
5.3	♦ Other accommodation services		('000)	81.0	79.0	91.0	97.0	..
5.4	♦ Food and beverage serving activities		('000)	964.0	993.0	1,027.0	1,047.0	..
5.5	♦ Passenger transportation		('000)	770.0	786.0	784.0	804.0	..
5.6	♦ Travel agencies and other reservation services activities		('000)	59.0	70.0	71.0	69.0	..
5.7	♦ Other tourism industries		('000)	83.0	89.0	93.0	93.0	..
6.	**COMPLEMENTARY INDICATORS**							
	Demand							
6.1	Gross travel propensity		Units	..	..	..	..	..
6.2	(1.1 inbound visitors + 2.1 domestic visitors) / population		Units	3.37	4.53	4.88	4.82	5.00
	Macroeconomic indicators related to international tourism							
6.3	Inbound tourism expenditure over GDP		Percent	1.4	1.5	1.5	1.6	1.4
6.4	Outbound tourism expenditure over GDP		Percent	1.8	1.9	1.9	1.9	2.0
6.5	Tourism balance (inbound minus outbound tourism expenditure) over GDP		Percent	-0.4	-0.4	-0.4	-0.3	-0.6
6.6	Tourism openness (inbound plus outbound tourism expenditure) over GDP		Percent	3.2	3.4	3.4	3.5	3.4
6.7	Tourism coverage (inbound over outbound tourism expenditure)		Percent	78.5	82.2	80.3	86.9	69.4
6.8	Inbound tourism expenditure over exports of goods		Percent	3.0	3.1	3.2	3.7	3.5
6.9	Inbound tourism expenditure over exports of services		Percent	19.2	18.2	18.9	20.3	19.5
6.10	Inbound tourism expenditure over exports of goods and services		Percent	2.6	2.7	2.7	3.1	3.0
6.11	Inbound tourism expenditure over current account credits		Percent	2.4	2.5	2.6	3.0	2.8
6.12	Outbound tourism expenditure over imports of goods		Percent	4.0	4.1	4.6	5.0	6.4
6.13	Outbound tourism expenditure over imports of services		Percent	21.5	21.1	22.2	22.6	24.3
6.14	Outbound tourism expenditure over imports of goods and		Percent	3.4	3.5	3.8	4.1	5.1
6.15	Outbound tourism expenditure over current account debits		Percent	3.2	3.2	3.6	3.8	4.7

KUWAIT

Cod.	Basic data and indicators	Notes	Units	2011	2012	2013	2014	201⁵
1.	**INBOUND TOURISM**							
	Data							
	Arrivals							
1.1	Total		('000)	5,574	5,729	6,217	6,528	6,94⁴
1.2	♦ Overnight visitors (tourists)	(1)	('000)	269	300	307	198	18²
1.3	♦ Same-day visitors (excursionists)		('000)	..	..	..	..	
1.4	* of which, cruise passengers		('000)	..	..	..	..	
	Arrivals by region							
1.5	Total		('000)	5,574	5,729	6,217	6,528	6,94¹
1.6	♦ Africa		('000)	113	114	132	103	10⁴
1.7	♦ Americas		('000)	223	185	175	162	16⁷
1.8	♦ East Asia and the Pacific		('000)	227	231	232	260	29⁵
1.9	♦ Europe		('000)	188	185	201	212	22³
1.10	♦ Middle East		('000)	3,434	3,609	3,951	4,161	4,46³
1.11	♦ South Asia		('000)	1,352	1,355	1,475	1,585	1,65¹
1.12	♦ Other not classified		('000)	37	50	52	44	3⁸
1.13	* of which, nationals residing abroad		('000)	..	..	..	..	
	Arrivals by main purpose	(1)						
1.14	Total		('000)	269	300	307	198	18²
1.15	♦ Personal		('000)	259	289	263	188	13⁰
1.16	* holidays, leisure and recreation		('000)	21	23	29	50	4⁶
1.17	* other personal purposes		('000)	238	266	235	138	8⁴
1.18	♦ Business and professional		('000)	10	11	43	10	5²
	Arrivals by mode of transport							
1.19	Total		('000)	5,574	5,729	6,217	6,528	6,94¹
1.20	♦ Air		('000)	2,571	2,670	2,914	3,114	3,39⁰
1.21	♦ Water		('000)	24	21	30	28	2²
1.22	♦ Land		('000)	2,979	3,038	3,273	3,385	3,52⁹
1.23	* railway		('000)	..	..	..	..	
1.24	* road		('000)	2,979	3,038	3,273	3,385	3,52⁹
1.25	* others		('000)	..	..	..	..	
	Accommodation							
	Hotels and similar establishments							
1.31	♦ Guests		('000)	269	300	307	198	18²
1.32	♦ Overnights		('000)	309	317	329	412	45²
	Expenditure							
1.33	Total		US$ Mn	644	780	619	615	93¹
1.34	♦ Travel		US$ Mn	320	426	297	369	50⁰
1.35	♦ Passenger transport		US$ Mn	324	354	322	246	43¹
3.	**OUTBOUND TOURISM**							
	Data							
	Expenditure							
3.4	Total		US$ Mn	8,879	10,073	10,567	12,280	13,14⁸
3.5	♦ Travel		US$ Mn	8,064	9,249	9,653	11,268	12,38¹
3.6	♦ Passenger transport		US$ Mn	815	824	914	1,012	76⁷
4.	**TOURISM INDUSTRIES**							
	Data							
	Number of establishments							
4.1	Total		Units	..	..	..	..	
4.2	♦ Accommodation for visitors		Units	..	..	..	..	
4.3	* of which, "hotels and similar establishments"		Units	88	92	93	86	8⁴
4.4	♦ Food and beverage serving activities		Units	..	..	..	..	
4.5	♦ Passenger transportation		Units	..	..	..	..	
4.6	♦ Travel agencies and other reservation services activities		Units	..	..	..	..	
4.7	♦ Other tourism industries		Units	..	..	..	..	
	Accommodation for visitors in hotels and similar establishments							
	Non-monetary data							
4.13	♦ Number of establishments		Units	88	92	93	86	8⁴
4.14	♦ Number of rooms		Units	8,311	8,814	8,573	8,338	6,55⁴
4.15	♦ Number of bed-places		Units	14,576	15,001	15,365	14,293	12,81⁰
	Indicators							
4.16	Occupancy rate / rooms		Percent	..	..	..	..	
4.17	Occupancy rate / bed-places		Percent	..	..	..	..	
4.18	Average length of stay		Nights	..	..	..	..	
4.19	Available capacity (bed-places per 1000 inhabitants)		Units	4.50	4.39	4.28	3.81	3.29

KUWAIT

Cod.	Basic data and indicators	Notes	Units	2011	2012	2013	2014	2015
6.	**COMPLEMENTARY INDICATORS**							
	Demand							
6.1	Gross travel propensity		Units	..	..	..	..	..
6.2	(1.2 inbound tourists) / population		Units	0.08	0.09	0.09	0.05	0.05
	Macroeconomic indicators related to international tourism							
6.3	Inbound tourism expenditure over GDP		Percent	0.4	0.4	0.4	0.4	..
6.4	Outbound tourism expenditure over GDP		Percent	5.8	5.8	6.0	7.4	..
6.5	Tourism balance (inbound minus outbound tourism expenditure) over GDP		Percent	-5.4	-5.4	-5.6	-7.0	..
6.6	Tourism openness (inbound plus outbound tourism expenditure) over GDP		Percent	6.2	6.2	6.4	7.8	..
6.7	Tourism coverage (inbound over outbound tourism expenditure)		Percent	7.3	7.7	5.9	5.0	7.1
6.8	Inbound tourism expenditure over exports of goods		Percent	0.6	0.7	0.5	0.6	1.7
6.9	Inbound tourism expenditure over exports of services		Percent	6.4	8.8	10.0	9.8	15.4
6.10	Inbound tourism expenditure over exports of goods and services		Percent	0.6	0.6	0.5	0.6	1.5
6.11	Inbound tourism expenditure over current account credits		Percent	0.5	0.5	0.5	0.5	1.2
6.12	Outbound tourism expenditure over imports of goods		Percent	39.3	41.6	41.3	44.8	48.1
6.13	Outbound tourism expenditure over imports of services		Percent	46.7	47.7	50.3	51.6	55.3
6.14	Outbound tourism expenditure over imports of goods and		Percent	21.3	22.2	22.7	24.0	25.7
6.15	Outbound tourism expenditure over current account debits		Percent	13.3	13.2	13.2	14.0	15.5

215

KYRGYZSTAN

Cod.	Basic data and indicators	Notes	Units	2011	2012	2013	2014	2015
1.	**INBOUND TOURISM**							
	Data							
	Arrivals							
1.1	Total		('000)	2,278	2,406	3,076	2,849	3,051
1.2	♦ Overnight visitors (tourists)		('000)	..	..	..	..	..
1.3	♦ Same-day visitors (excursionists)		('000)	..	..	..	..	..
1.4	* of which, cruise passengers		('000)	..	..	..	..	..
	Arrivals by region							
1.5	Total		('000)	2,278	2,406	3,076	2,849	3,051
1.6	♦ Africa		('000)	..	..	..	..	..
1.7	♦ Americas		('000)	18	19	22	17	22
1.8	♦ East Asia and the Pacific		('000)	33	34	39	46	49
1.9	♦ Europe		('000)	2,208	2,333	2,983	2,755	2,943
1.10	♦ Middle East		('000)	..	..	1	1	1
1.11	♦ South Asia		('000)	7	7	7	8	11
1.12	♦ Other not classified		('000)	11	12	24	22	24
1.13	* of which, nationals residing abroad		('000)	..	..	..	..	..
	Accommodation							
	Total							
1.29	♦ Guests		('000)	..	..	..	..	..
1.30	♦ Overnights		('000)	247	364	332	425	..
	Hotels and similar establishments							
1.31	♦ Guests		('000)	41	47	46	43	..
1.32	♦ Overnights		('000)	95	109	98	70	..
	Expenditure							
1.33	Total		US$ Mn	405	486	585	468	481
1.34	♦ Travel		US$ Mn	356	434	530	423	426
1.35	♦ Passenger transport		US$ Mn	49	52	55	45	55
	Expenditure by main purpose of the trip							
1.36	Total		US$ Mn	356	434	530	423	426
1.37	♦ Personal		US$ Mn	203	248	302	241	243
1.38	♦ Business and professional		US$ Mn	153	187	228	182	183
2.	**DOMESTIC TOURISM**							
	Data							
	Accommodation							
	Total							
2.19	♦ Guests		('000)	..	..	..	..	..
2.20	♦ Overnights		('000)	1,027	1,448	1,366	1,328	..
	Hotels and similar establishments							
2.21	♦ Guests		('000)	118	148	160	155	..
2.22	♦ Overnights		('000)	161	214	257	208	..
3.	**OUTBOUND TOURISM**							
	Data							
	Departures							
3.1	Total		('000)	931	1,326	1,401	1,442	1,720
3.2	♦ Overnight visitors (tourists)		('000)	..	..	..	..	..
3.3	♦ Same-day visitors (excursionists)		('000)	..	..	..	..	..
	Expenditure							
3.4	Total		US$ Mn	392	529	505	568	445
3.5	♦ Travel		US$ Mn	247	350	350	390	306
3.6	♦ Passenger transport		US$ Mn	145	179	155	178	139
	Expenditure by main purpose of the trip							
3.7	Total		US$ Mn	247	350	350	390	306
3.8	♦ Personal		US$ Mn	116	164	165	183	144
3.9	♦ Business and professional		US$ Mn	131	185	186	207	162
4.	**TOURISM INDUSTRIES**							
	Data							
	Number of establishments							
4.1	Total		Units	..	..	..	..	..
4.2	♦ Accommodation for visitors		Units	405	406	416	418	464
4.3	* of which, "hotels and similar establishments"		Units	149	147	146	139	184
4.4	♦ Food and beverage serving activities		Units	..	..	..	..	..
4.5	♦ Passenger transportation		Units	..	..	..	..	..
4.6	♦ Travel agencies and other reservation services activities		Units	..	..	..	..	..
4.7	♦ Other tourism industries		Units	..	..	..	..	..

KYRGYZSTAN

Cod.	Basic data and indicators	Notes	Units	2011	2012	2013	2014	2015
	Accommodation for visitors in hotels and similar establishments							
	Non-monetary data							
4.13	♦ Number of establishments		Units	149	147	146	139	184
4.14	♦ Number of rooms		Units	2,875	2,824	2,851	2,684	3,951
4.15	♦ Number of bed-places		Units	4,911	4,544	4,615	4,889	6,420
	Indicators							
4.16	Occupancy rate / rooms		Percent	..	..	..	..	..
4.17	Occupancy rate / bed-places		Percent	14.00	19.00	21.00	16.00	..
4.18	Average length of stay		Nights	..	..	..	..	..
4.19	Available capacity (bed-places per 1000 inhabitants)		Units	0.88	0.80	0.80	0.84	1.08
5.	**EMPLOYMENT**							
	Data							
	Number of employees by tourism industries							
5.1	Total		('000)	7.8	7.8	7.8	8.1	..
5.2	♦ Accommodation services for visitors (hotels and similar establishments)		('000)	1.6	1.5	1.6	1.7	..
5.3	♦ Other accommodation services		('000)	..	..	..	..	..
5.4	♦ Food and beverage serving activities		('000)	0.7	0.9	0.7	1.1	..
5.5	♦ Passenger transportation		('000)	..	..	..	..	..
5.6	♦ Travel agencies and other reservation services activities		('000)	1.3	1.2	1.4	1.2	..
5.7	♦ Other tourism industries		('000)	4.1	4.3	4.1	4.1	..
6.	**COMPLEMENTARY INDICATORS**							
	Demand							
6.1	Gross travel propensity		Units	..	..	..	..	..
6.2	(1.1 inbound visitors) / population		Units	0.41	0.43	0.54	0.49	0.51
	Macroeconomic indicators related to international tourism							
6.3	Inbound tourism expenditure over GDP		Percent	6.5	7.4	8.0	6.3	7.3
6.4	Outbound tourism expenditure over GDP		Percent	6.3	8.0	6.9	7.6	6.8
6.5	Tourism balance (inbound minus outbound tourism expenditure) over GDP		Percent	0.2	-0.6	1.1	-1.3	0.5
6.6	Tourism openness (inbound plus outbound tourism expenditure) over GDP		Percent	12.8	15.4	14.9	13.9	14.1
6.7	Tourism coverage (inbound over outbound tourism expenditure)		Percent	103.3	91.9	115.8	82.4	108.1
6.8	Inbound tourism expenditure over exports of goods		Percent	17.9	24.9	28.4	26.1	29.9
6.9	Inbound tourism expenditure over exports of services		Percent	47.1	50.3	56.1	52.2	57.0
6.10	Inbound tourism expenditure over exports of goods and services		Percent	13.0	16.6	18.9	17.4	19.6
6.11	Inbound tourism expenditure over current account credits		Percent	7.8	9.2	10.2	8.8	10.8
6.12	Outbound tourism expenditure over imports of goods		Percent	10.0	10.2	9.0	10.9	12.2
6.13	Outbound tourism expenditure over imports of services		Percent	40.7	40.0	45.5	45.6	45.8
6.14	Outbound tourism expenditure over imports of goods and		Percent	8.0	8.2	7.5	8.8	9.6
6.15	Outbound tourism expenditure over current account debits		Percent	7.6	7.8	7.1	8.2	8.9

LAO PEOPLE´S DEMOCRATIC REPUBLIC

Cod.	Basic data and indicators	Notes	Units	2011	2012	2013	2014	2015
1.	**INBOUND TOURISM**							
	Data							
	Arrivals							
1.1	Total		('000)	2,724	3,330	3,779	4,159	4,684
1.2	♦ Overnight visitors (tourists)		('000)	1,894	2,291	2,700	3,164	3,543
1.3	♦ Same-day visitors (excursionists)		('000)	830	1,039	1,079	995	1,141
1.4	* of which, cruise passengers		('000)	..	..	..	..	
	Arrivals by region							
1.5	Total		('000)	2,723	3,330	3,779	4,159	4,684
1.6	♦ Africa		('000)	..	..	..	..	.
1.7	♦ Americas		('000)	70	76	86	86	89
1.8	♦ East Asia and the Pacific		('000)	2,461	3,058	3,469	3,850	4,362
1.9	♦ Europe		('000)	186	189	216	213	222
1.10	♦ Middle East		('000)	..	..	..	..	.
1.11	♦ South Asia		('000)	3	3	4	5	6
1.12	♦ Other not classified		('000)	3	4	5	5	6
1.13	* of which, nationals residing abroad		('000)	..	..	..	..	
	Arrivals by main purpose							
1.14	Total		('000)	2,724	3,330	3,779	4,159	4,684
1.15	♦ Personal		('000)	2,591	3,081	3,450	3,901	4,408
1.16	* holidays, leisure and recreation		('000)	2,271	2,494	3,160	3,726	4,268
1.17	* other personal purposes		('000)	320	587	290	175	140
1.18	♦ Business and professional		('000)	133	249	329	258	276
	Arrivals by mode of transport							
1.19	Total		('000)	2,724	3,330	3,779	4,159	4,684
1.20	♦ Air		('000)	1,329	340	421	500	520
1.21	♦ Water		('000)	..	..	..	..	
1.22	♦ Land		('000)	1,395	2,990	3,358	3,659	4,164
1.23	* railway		('000)	..	..	..	..	
1.24	* road		('000)	1,395	2,990	3,358	3,659	4,164
1.25	* others		('000)	..	..	..	..	
	Expenditure							
1.33	Total		US$ Mn	413	461	613	642	680
1.34	♦ Travel		US$ Mn	406	451	596	642	679
1.35	♦ Passenger transport		US$ Mn	7	10	17	0.4	1
	Indicators							
1.39	Average size of travel party		Persons	..	..	..	..	
	Average length of stay							
1.40	Total		Days	4.50	4.60	5.20	4.90	4.75
1.41	♦ For all commercial accommodation services		Nights	..	..	..	..	
1.42	* of which, "hotels and similar establishments"		Nights	..	..	..	..	
1.43	♦ For non commercial accommodation services		Days	..	..	..	..	
1.44	Average expenditure per day		US$	72.0	81.0	69.5	73.3	76.5
2.	**DOMESTIC TOURISM**							
	Data							
	Trips							
2.1	Total		('000)	..	..	2,028	2,078	2,313
2.2	♦ Overnight visitors (tourists)		('000)	..	..	..	..	
2.3	♦ Same-day visitors (excursionists)		('000)	..	..	..	..	
3.	**OUTBOUND TOURISM**							
	Data							
	Departures							
3.1	Total		('000)	1,788	2,052	2,857	3,320	3,067
3.2	♦ Overnight visitors (tourists)		('000)	..	..	..	..	..
3.3	♦ Same-day visitors (excursionists)		('000)	..	..	..	..	..
	Expenditure							
3.4	Total		US$ Mn	248	241	401	416	528
3.5	♦ Travel		US$ Mn	237	232	398	413	524
3.6	♦ Passenger transport		US$ Mn	11	9	3	3	4

LAO PEOPLE´S DEMOCRATIC REPUBLIC

Cod.	Basic data and indicators	Notes	Units	2011	2012	2013	2014	2015
4.	**TOURISM INDUSTRIES**							
	Data							
	Number of establishments							
4.1	Total		Units	2,162	3,801	4,393	4,037	4,481
4.2	♦ Accommodation for visitors		Units	..	..	..	..	..
4.3	* of which, "hotels and similar establishments"		Units	1,926	2,030	2,359	2,426	2,449
4.4	♦ Food and beverage serving activities		Units	..	1,496	1,744	1,269	1,664
4.5	♦ Passenger transportation		Units	..	..	..	..	..
4.6	♦ Travel agencies and other reservation services activities		Units	236	275	290	342	368
4.7	♦ Other tourism industries		Units	..	..	..	..	..
	Accommodation for visitors in hotels and similar establishments							
	Non-monetary data							
4.13	♦ Number of establishments		Units	1,926	2,030	2,359	2,426	2,449
4.14	♦ Number of rooms		Units	32,960	35,857	39,782	44,714	48,386
4.15	♦ Number of bed-places		Units	43,274	47,412	52,301	55,754	57,642
	Indicators							
4.16	Occupancy rate / rooms		Percent	..	..	..	..	..
4.17	Occupancy rate / bed-places		Percent	56.00	57.00	55.00	54.00	57.00
4.18	Average length of stay		Nights	..	..	..	..	..
4.19	Available capacity (bed-places per 1000 inhabitants)		Units	6.80	7.32	7.95	8.33	8.47
6.	**COMPLEMENTARY INDICATORS**							
	Demand							
6.1	Gross travel propensity		Units	..	..	..	..	..
6.2	(1.2 inbound tourists + 2.1 domestic visitors) / population		Units	..	..	0.72	0.78	0.86
	Macroeconomic indicators related to international tourism							
6.3	Inbound tourism expenditure over GDP		Percent	5.1	5.1	5.8	..	..
6.4	Outbound tourism expenditure over GDP		Percent	3.1	2.7	3.8	..	..
6.5	Tourism balance (inbound minus outbound tourism expenditure) over GDP		Percent	2.0	2.4	2.0	..	..
6.6	Tourism openness (inbound plus outbound tourism expenditure) over GDP		Percent	8.2	7.8	9.6	..	..
6.7	Tourism coverage (inbound over outbound tourism expenditure)		Percent	166.5	191.3	152.9	154.4	128.8
6.8	Inbound tourism expenditure over exports of goods		Percent	22.3	20.3	27.1	24.1	24.6
6.9	Inbound tourism expenditure over exports of services		Percent	75.1	79.9	78.5	84.0	85.1
6.10	Inbound tourism expenditure over exports of goods and services		Percent	17.2	16.2	20.1	18.7	19.1
6.11	Inbound tourism expenditure over current account credits		Percent	14.8	14.3	17.9	16.9	17.1
6.12	Outbound tourism expenditure over imports of goods		Percent	10.2	7.9	13.3	9.7	10.1
6.13	Outbound tourism expenditure over imports of services		Percent	75.0	71.0	75.1	83.7	90.2
6.14	Outbound tourism expenditure over imports of goods and		Percent	9.0	7.1	11.3	8.7	9.1
6.15	Outbound tourism expenditure over current account debits		Percent	8.5	6.8	10.9	8.6	8.7

LATVIA

Cod.	Basic data and indicators	Notes	Units	2011	2012	2013	2014	2015
1.	**INBOUND TOURISM**							
	Data							
	Arrivals							
1.1	Total	(1)	('000)	5,538	5,569	5,822	6,246	6,842
1.2	♦ Overnight visitors (tourists)	(2)	('000)	1,493	1,435	1,536	1,843	2,024
1.3	♦ Same-day visitors (excursionists)	(2)	('000)	4,045	4,134	4,286	4,403	4,818
1.4	* of which, cruise passengers	(2)	('000)	268	..	..	..	254
	Arrivals by region	(2)						
1.5	Total		('000)	5,538	5,569	5,822	6,246	6,842
1.6	♦ Africa		('000)	4	..	..	..	..
1.7	♦ Americas		('000)	77	41	32	30	28
1.8	♦ East Asia and the Pacific		('000)	49	..	..	..	..
1.9	♦ Europe		('000)	5,386	5,349	5,622	6,057	6,603
1.10	♦ Middle East		('000)	2	..	..	..	..
1.11	♦ South Asia		('000)	11	..	..	..	..
1.12	♦ Other not classified		('000)	9	179	169	159	211
1.13	* of which, nationals residing abroad		('000)	..	..	..	..	..
	Arrivals by main purpose	(2)						
1.14	Total		('000)	5,538	5,569	5,822	6,246	6,842
1.15	♦ Personal		('000)	4,741	4,819	5,106	5,503	6,023
1.16	* holidays, leisure and recreation		('000)	1,527	1,548	1,670	2,472	2,938
1.17	* other personal purposes	(3)	('000)	3,214	3,270	3,436	3,032	3,085
1.18	♦ Business and professional		('000)	797	750	715	743	819
	Arrivals by mode of transport	(1)						
1.19	Total		('000)	5,538	5,569	5,822	6,246	6,842
1.20	♦ Air		('000)	1,698	1,597	1,628	1,652	1,789
1.21	♦ Water		('000)	399	429	433	418	347
1.22	♦ Land		('000)	3,441	3,543	3,761	4,176	4,706
1.23	* railway		('000)	139	147	155	131	87
1.24	* road		('000)	3,302	3,396	3,606	4,045	4,619
1.25	* others		('000)	..	..	..	..	
	Accommodation							
	Total							
1.29	♦ Guests		('000)	1,063	1,096	1,250	1,431	1,475
1.30	♦ Overnights		('000)	2,257	2,429	2,639	2,876	2,874
	Hotels and similar establishments							
1.31	♦ Guests	(4)	('000)	985	1,027	1,168	1,342	1,373
1.32	♦ Overnights	(4)	('000)	2,069	2,223	2,383	2,620	2,553
	Expenditure							
1.33	Total		US$ Mn	..	..	1,190	1,244	1,133
1.34	♦ Travel		US$ Mn	771	745	865	954	893
1.35	♦ Passenger transport		US$ Mn	..	..	325	290	240
	Expenditure by main purpose of the trip							
1.36	Total		US$ Mn	..	..	865	954	893
1.37	♦ Personal		US$ Mn	..	..	661	755	707
1.38	♦ Business and professional		US$ Mn	..	..	204	199	186
	Indicators							
1.39	Average size of travel party		Persons	..	..	..	..	..
	Average length of stay							
1.40	Total		Days	..	..	..	..	..
1.41	♦ For all commercial accommodation services	(5)	Nights	2.12	2.20	2.10	2.01	1.95
1.42	* of which, "hotels and similar establishments"	(5)	Nights	2.10	2.10	2.00	1.95	1.86
1.43	♦ For non commercial accommodation services	(6)	Days	6.60	7.00	7.30	6.70	6.15
1.44	Average expenditure per day	(6)	US$	94.0	101.3	94.2	73.1	73.4
2.	**DOMESTIC TOURISM**							
	Data							
	Trips	(7)						
2.1	Total		('000)	13,589	11,717	12,151	11,413	10,690
2.2	♦ Overnight visitors (tourists)		('000)	3,472	3,796	3,156	3,258	2,972
2.3	♦ Same-day visitors (excursionists)		('000)	10,117	7,921	8,995	8,155	7,718
	Trips by main purpose	(7)						
2.4	Total		('000)	13,589	11,717	12,150	11,413	10,690
2.5	♦ Personal		('000)	13,368	10,780	11,419	10,810	10,108
2.6	* holidays, leisure and recreation		('000)	13,368	10,780	11,419	10,810	10,108
2.7	* other personal purposes		('000)	..	..	..	..	..
2.8	♦ Business and professional		('000)	221	937	731	603	582

LATVIA

Cod.	Basic data and indicators	Notes	Units	2011	2012	2013	2014	2015
	Trips by mode of transport	(7)						
2.9	Total		('000)	3,471	3,796	3,156	3,258	2,972
2.10	♦ Air		('000)	13	..	..	..	..
2.11	♦ Water		('000)	..	..	..	..	1
2.12	♦ Land		('000)	3,458	3,796	3,156	3,258	2,971
2.13	* railway		('000)	257	182	237	143	140
2.14	* road		('000)	3,167	3,595	2,901	3,089	2,828
2.15	* others		('000)	34	19	18	26	3
	Accommodation							
	Total							
2.19	♦ Guests		('000)	522	548	589	667	665
2.20	♦ Overnights		('000)	1,037	1,118	1,136	1,282	1,236
	Hotels and similar establishments							
2.21	♦ Guests	(4)	('000)	427	..	474	545	493
2.22	♦ Overnights	(4)	('000)	757	..	803	947	821
	Indicators							
2.23	Average size of travel party		Persons	..	..	..	..	..
	Average length of stay							
2.24	Total		Days	..	..	..	..	..
2.25	♦ For all commercial accommodation services	(5)	Nights	1.99	..	1.93	1.92	1.86
2.26	* of which, "hotels and similar establishments"	(5)	Nights	1.77	..	1.69	1.74	1.67
2.27	♦ For non commercial accommodation services	(7)	Days	2.18	2.15	2.31	2.53	2.10
2.28	Average expenditure per day	(7)	US$	17.3	18.4	20.3	16.7	20.4
3.	**OUTBOUND TOURISM**							
	Data							
	Departures	(8)						
3.1	Total		('000)	3,257	183	1,776	1,846	1,720
3.2	♦ Overnight visitors (tourists)		('000)	1,530	1,398	1,246	1,362	1,242
3.3	♦ Same-day visitors (excursionists)		('000)	1,727	432	530	484	478
	Expenditure							
3.4	Total		US$ Mn	..	..	900	908	801
3.5	♦ Travel		US$ Mn	765	680	715	714	615
3.6	♦ Passenger transport		US$ Mn	..	..	185	194	186
	Expenditure by main purpose of the trip							
3.7	Total		US$ Mn	..	..	715	714	615
3.8	♦ Personal		US$ Mn	..	..	558	560	490
3.9	♦ Business and professional		US$ Mn	..	..	157	154	125
	Indicators							
3.10	Average length of stay	(8)	Days	7.83	5.89	6.38	6.36	5.40
3.11	Average expenditure per day	(8)	US$	45.9	64.6	67.1	60.4	73.9
4.	**TOURISM INDUSTRIES**							
	Data							
	Number of establishments							
4.1	Total		Units	..	..	..	..	..
4.2	♦ Accommodation for visitors		Units	641	632	546	544	563
4.3	* of which, "hotels and similar establishments"	(4)	Units	497	489	441	444	306
4.4	♦ Food and beverage serving activities		Units	..	..	..	..	..
4.5	♦ Passenger transportation		Units	..	..	..	..	..
4.6	♦ Travel agencies and other reservation services activities		Units	..	..	..	..	..
4.7	♦ Other tourism industries		Units	..	..	..	..	..
	Accommodation for visitors in hotels and similar establishments							
	Non-monetary data	(4)						
4.13	♦ Number of establishments		Units	497	489	441	444	306
4.14	♦ Number of rooms		Units	13,176	13,404	12,637	13,025	11,970
4.15	♦ Number of bed-places		Units	27,067	27,474	26,004	26,943	24,109
	Indicators							
4.16	Occupancy rate / rooms		Percent	..	..	..	..	..
4.17	Occupancy rate / bed-places		Percent	..	..	..	..	..
4.18	Average length of stay		Nights	2.00	2.20	2.10	1.89	1.81
4.19	Available capacity (bed-places per 1000 inhabitants)		Units	13.12	13.49	12.93	13.54	12.23

LATVIA

Cod.	Basic data and indicators	Notes	Units	2011	2012	2013	2014	2015
5.	**EMPLOYMENT**							
	Data							
	Number of employees by tourism industries							
5.1	Total		('000)	62.3	72.0	69.5	74.8	
5.2	♦ Accommodation services for visitors (hotels and similar establishments)		('000)	3.7	2.5	3.2	4.6	..
5.3	♦ Other accommodation services		('000)	0.7	0.9	1.1	1.1	..
5.4	♦ Food and beverage serving activities		('000)	20.8	24.9	22.2	23.6	..
5.5	♦ Passenger transportation		('000)	18.9	18.0	18.8	20.2	..
5.6	♦ Travel agencies and other reservation services activities		('000)	2.0	2.7	2.6	2.8	
5.7	♦ Other tourism industries		('000)	16.2	23.0	21.6	22.5	
6.	**COMPLEMENTARY INDICATORS**							
	Demand							
6.1	Gross travel propensity		Units	..	..	..	..	
6.2	(1.2 inbound tourists + 2.2 domestic tourists) / population		Units	2.41	2.57	2.33	2.56	2.54
	Macroeconomic indicators related to international tourism							
6.3	Inbound tourism expenditure over GDP		Percent	2.7	2.6	3.9	..	..
6.4	Outbound tourism expenditure over GDP		Percent	2.7	2.4	2.9	..	..
6.5	Tourism balance (inbound minus outbound tourism expenditure) over GDP		Percent		0.2	1.0	..	
6.6	Tourism openness (inbound plus outbound tourism expenditure) over GDP		Percent	5.4	5.0	6.8	..	..
6.7	Tourism coverage (inbound over outbound tourism expenditure)		Percent	100.8	109.6	132.2	137.0	141.4
6.8	Inbound tourism expenditure over exports of goods		Percent	6.7	6.0	9.1	9.2	9.9
6.9	Inbound tourism expenditure over exports of services		Percent	16.0	15.4	23.0	24.3	25.3
6.10	Inbound tourism expenditure over exports of goods and services		Percent	4.7	4.3	6.5	6.7	7.1
6.11	Inbound tourism expenditure over current account credits		Percent	4.0	3.7	5.6	5.8	6.1
6.12	Outbound tourism expenditure over imports of goods		Percent	5.1	4.3	5.5	5.5	5.8
6.13	Outbound tourism expenditure over imports of services		Percent	27.6	24.7	31.8	32.5	31.7
6.14	Outbound tourism expenditure over imports of goods and		Percent	4.3	3.7	4.7	4.7	4.9
6.15	Outbound tourism expenditure over current account debits		Percent	3.8	3.2	4.1	4.1	4.3

LEBANON

Cod.	Basic data and indicators	Notes	Units	2011	2012	2013	2014	2015
1.	**INBOUND TOURISM**							
	Data							
	Arrivals							
1.1	Total		('000)	..	..	..	..	..
1.2	♦ Overnight visitors (tourists)	(1)	('000)	1,655	1,366	1,274	1,355	1,518
1.3	♦ Same-day visitors (excursionists)		('000)	..	..	..	..	..
1.4	* of which, cruise passengers		('000)	..	..	..	..	..
	Arrivals by region	(1)						
1.5	Total		('000)	1,655	1,366	1,274	1,355	1,518
1.6	♦ Africa		('000)	83	82	85	76	108
1.7	♦ Americas		('000)	223	221	210	225	264
1.8	♦ East Asia and the Pacific		('000)	112	102	98	100	109
1.9	♦ Europe		('000)	487	446	435	449	507
1.10	♦ Middle East		('000)	560	437	381	441	458
1.11	♦ South Asia		('000)	188	76	63	63	71
1.12	♦ Other not classified		('000)	2	2	1	1	1
1.13	* of which, nationals residing abroad		('000)	..	..	..	..	..
	Arrivals by mode of transport							
1.19	Total		('000)	1,678	1,415	1,274	1,355	1,518
1.20	♦ Air		('000)	1,368	1,287	1,203	1,282	1,422
1.21	♦ Water		('000)	26	56	7	7	19
1.22	♦ Land		('000)	284	72	64	65	77
1.23	* railway		('000)	..	..	..	..	..
1.24	* road		('000)	284	72	64	65	77
1.25	* others		('000)	..	..	..	..	..
	Accommodation							
	Hotels and similar establishments	(2)						
1.31	♦ Guests		('000)	739	572	567	626	701
1.32	♦ Overnights		('000)	1,741	1,611	2,167	1,993	2,479
	Expenditure							
1.33	Total		US$ Mn	6,797	7,361	7,032	6,835	7,087
1.34	♦ Travel		US$ Mn	6,545	6,836	6,492	6,523	6,857
1.35	♦ Passenger transport		US$ Mn	252	525	540	312	230
	Expenditure by main purpose of the trip							
1.36	Total		US$ Mn	6,545	6,836	6,491	6,523	6,857
1.37	♦ Personal		US$ Mn	6,146	6,411	6,387	6,407	6,547
1.38	♦ Business and professional		US$ Mn	399	425	104	116	310
	Indicators							
1.39	Average size of travel party		Persons	..	..	..	..	..
	Average length of stay							
1.40	Total		Days	..	..	..	..	..
1.41	♦ For all commercial accommodation services		Nights	2.36	2.81	3.82	3.00	3.53
1.42	* of which, "hotels and similar establishments"		Nights	..	..	..	..	..
1.43	♦ For non commercial accommodation services		Days	..	..	..	..	..
1.44	Average expenditure per day		US$	..	..	..	..	..
3.	**OUTBOUND TOURISM**							
	Data							
	Expenditure							
3.4	Total		US$ Mn	4,440	4,511	4,692	5,198	5,187
3.5	♦ Travel		US$ Mn	4,004	4,199	4,388	4,995	4,741
3.6	♦ Passenger transport		US$ Mn	436	312	304	203	446
	Expenditure by main purpose of the trip							
3.7	Total		US$ Mn	4,004	4,200	4,388	4,994	4,741
3.8	♦ Personal		US$ Mn	3,803	3,638	3,936	4,671	4,498
3.9	♦ Business and professional		US$ Mn	201	562	452	323	243
4.	**TOURISM INDUSTRIES**							
	Data							
	Number of establishments							
4.1	Total		Units	7,704	6,004	6,014	5,712	5,708
4.2	♦ Accommodation for visitors		Units	..	..	..	..	..
4.3	* of which, "hotels and similar establishments"	(3)	Units	544	544	549	557	566
4.4	♦ Food and beverage serving activities		Units	6,500	4,800	4,800	4,555	4,592
4.5	♦ Passenger transportation		Units	..	..	..	..	..
4.6	♦ Travel agencies and other reservation services activities		Units	660	660	665	600	550
4.7	♦ Other tourism industries		Units	..	..	..	..	..

LEBANON

Cod.	Basic data and indicators	Notes	Units	2011	2012	2013	2014	2015
	Accommodation for visitors in hotels and similar establishments							
	Non-monetary data	(3)						
4.13	♦ Number of establishments		Units	544	544	549	557	566
4.14	♦ Number of rooms		Units	32,000	32,000	32,307	32,741	33,408
4.15	♦ Number of bed-places		Units	123,331	123,331	123,694	124,311	125,364
	Indicators							
4.16	Occupancy rate / rooms	(2)	Percent	26.10	22.31	22.70	32.07	25.76
4.17	Occupancy rate / bed-places		Percent	27.34	22.16	23.37	36.03	27.37
4.18	Average length of stay		Nights	2.36	2.81	3.82	3.18	3.53
4.19	Available capacity (bed-places per 1000 inhabitants)		Units	26.86	25.05	23.40	22.15	21.43
5.	**EMPLOYMENT**							
	Data							
	Number of employees by tourism industries	(4)						
5.1	Total		('000)	325.7	..	..	..	..
5.2	♦ Accommodation services for visitors (hotels and similar establishments)		('000)	71.7	40.5	35.5	..	..
5.3	♦ Other accommodation services		('000)	..	..	..	..	..
5.4	♦ Food and beverage serving activities		('000)	250.0	..	..	..	..
5.5	♦ Passenger transportation		('000)	..	..	..	..	..
5.6	♦ Travel agencies and other reservation services activities		('000)	4.0	4.0	3.0	2.5	2.0
5.7	♦ Other tourism industries		('000)	..	..	..	..	..
6.	**COMPLEMENTARY INDICATORS**							
	Demand							
6.1	Gross travel propensity		Units	..	..	..	..	..
6.2	(1.2 inbound tourists) / population		Units	0.36	0.28	0.24	0.24	0.26
	Macroeconomic indicators related to international tourism							
6.3	Inbound tourism expenditure over GDP		Percent	17.0	16.7	14.9	..	..
6.4	Outbound tourism expenditure over GDP		Percent	11.1	10.2	9.9	..	..
6.5	Tourism balance (inbound minus outbound tourism expenditure) over GDP		Percent	5.9	6.5	5.0	..	..
6.6	Tourism openness (inbound plus outbound tourism expenditure) over GDP		Percent	28.1	26.9	24.8	..	..
6.7	Tourism coverage (inbound over outbound tourism expenditure)		Percent	153.1	163.2	149.9	131.5	136.6
6.8	Inbound tourism expenditure over exports of goods		Percent	126.2	147.0	156.3	166.7	199.6
6.9	Inbound tourism expenditure over exports of services		Percent	34.6	48.7	45.4	46.3	44.8
6.10	Inbound tourism expenditure over exports of goods and services		Percent	27.1	36.6	35.2	36.3	36.6
6.11	Inbound tourism expenditure over current account credits		Percent	19.7	24.6	23.3	22.0	23.1
6.12	Outbound tourism expenditure over imports of goods		Percent	23.0	22.7	23.9	* 27.1	31.0
6.13	Outbound tourism expenditure over imports of services		Percent	34.3	39.4	36.5	39.6	38.2
6.14	Outbound tourism expenditure over imports of goods and		Percent	13.8	14.4	14.4	16.1	17.1
6.15	Outbound tourism expenditure over current account debits		Percent	11.3	11.5	11.3	12.3	13.6

LESOTHO

Cod.	Basic data and indicators	Notes	Units	2011	2012	2013	2014	2015
.	**INBOUND TOURISM**							
	Data							
	Arrivals							
.1	Total	(1)	('000)	398	423	433	1,079	1,082
.2	♦ Overnight visitors (tourists)		('000)	397	317	320	..	..
.3	♦ Same-day visitors (excursionists)		('000)	0.5	106	113	..	..
.4	* of which, cruise passengers		('000)	..	..	..	..	..
	Arrivals by region	(1)						
.5	Total		('000)	398	423	433	1,079	1,082
.6	♦ Africa		('000)	380	404	408	1,018	1,019
.7	♦ Americas		('000)	3	3	3	11	11
.8	♦ East Asia and the Pacific		('000)	2	3	4	21	20
.9	♦ Europe		('000)	13	13	17	24	28
.10	♦ Middle East		('000)	..	..	..	..	..
.11	♦ South Asia		('000)	..	..	..	5	4
.12	♦ Other not classified		('000)	..	..	..	0.5	0.5
.13	* of which, nationals residing abroad		('000)	..	..	..	..	..
	Arrivals by main purpose							
.14	Total		('000)	398	423	433	..	..
.15	♦ Personal		('000)	347	373	387	..	..
.16	* holidays, leisure and recreation		('000)	117	130	119	..	..
.17	* other personal purposes		('000)	230	243	268	..	..
.18	♦ Business and professional		('000)	51	50	46	..	..
	Arrivals by mode of transport	(1)						
.19	Total		('000)	398	423	433	1,079	1,082
.20	♦ Air		('000)	12	11	14	..	..
.21	♦ Water		('000)	..	..	..	..	..
.22	♦ Land		('000)	386	412	419	1,079	1,082
.23	* railway		('000)	..	..	..	..	..
.24	* road		('000)	386	412	419	1,079	1,082
.25	* others		('000)	..	..	..	..	..
	Expenditure							
.33	Total		US$ Mn	..	..	..	..	..
.34	♦ Travel		US$ Mn	24	22	17	16	13
.35	♦ Passenger transport		US$ Mn	..	..	..	..	..
B.	**OUTBOUND TOURISM**							
	Data							
	Expenditure							
.4	Total		US$ Mn	300	255	217	180	176
.5	♦ Travel		US$ Mn	290	248	211	173	170
.6	♦ Passenger transport		US$ Mn	10	7	6	7	6
	Expenditure by main purpose of the trip							
.7	Total		US$ Mn	290	248	211	173	169
.8	♦ Personal		US$ Mn	21	15	11	10	8
.9	♦ Business and professional		US$ Mn	269	233	200	163	161
C.	**TOURISM INDUSTRIES**							
	Data							
	Number of establishments							
.1	Total		Units	..	..	..	..	..
.2	♦ Accommodation for visitors		Units	..	..	..	..	..
.3	* of which, "hotels and similar establishments"		Units	135	145	..	153	155
.4	♦ Food and beverage serving activities		Units	..	..	..	..	..
.5	♦ Passenger transportation		Units	..	..	..	..	..
.6	♦ Travel agencies and other reservation services activities		Units	..	..	..	..	..
.7	♦ Other tourism industries		Units	..	..	..	..	..
	Accommodation for visitors in hotels and similar establishments							
	Non-monetary data							
.13	♦ Number of establishments		Units	135	145	..	153	155
.14	♦ Number of rooms		Units	2,756	3,018	..	2,746	2,917
.15	♦ Number of bed-places		Units	5,025	4,846	..	5,225	5,649
	Indicators							
.16	Occupancy rate / rooms		Percent	..	..	..	..	..
.17	Occupancy rate / bed-places		Percent	19.10	20.05	21.00	19.00	18.00
.18	Average length of stay		Nights	9.00	10.00	12.00	5.00	..
.19	Available capacity (bed-places per 1000 inhabitants)		Units	2.47	2.36	..	2.48	2.65

LESOTHO

Cod.	Basic data and indicators	Notes	Units	2011	2012	2013	2014	2015
5.	**EMPLOYMENT**							
	Data							
	Number of employees by tourism industries							
5.1	Total		('000)	..	..	..	..	
5.2	♦ Accommodation services for visitors (hotels and similar establishments)		('000)	2.3	2.7	..	2.6	.
5.3	♦ Other accommodation services		('000)	..	..	..	..	
5.4	♦ Food and beverage serving activities		('000)	..	..	..	..	..
5.5	♦ Passenger transportation		('000)	..	..	..	..	
5.6	♦ Travel agencies and other reservation services activities		('000)	..	..	..	..	
5.7	♦ Other tourism industries		('000)	..	..	..	..	
6.	**COMPLEMENTARY INDICATORS**							
	Demand							
6.1	Gross travel propensity		Units	..	..	..	..	
6.2	(1.2 inbound tourists) / population		Units	0.20	0.15	0.15	..	.
	Macroeconomic indicators related to international tourism							
6.3	Inbound tourism expenditure over GDP		Percent	1.0	0.9	0.8	0.7	..
6.4	Outbound tourism expenditure over GDP		Percent	11.9	10.7	9.8	8.2	..
6.5	Tourism balance (inbound minus outbound tourism expenditure) over GDP		Percent	-10.9	-9.8	-9.0	-7.5	
6.6	Tourism openness (inbound plus outbound tourism expenditure) over GDP		Percent	12.9	11.6	10.6	8.9	..
6.7	Tourism coverage (inbound over outbound tourism expenditure)		Percent	8.0	8.6	7.8	8.9	7.4
6.8	Inbound tourism expenditure over exports of goods		Percent	2.0	2.3	2.0	1.9	1.5
6.9	Inbound tourism expenditure over exports of services		Percent	52.2	53.2	51.8	53.6	50.7
6.10	Inbound tourism expenditure over exports of goods and services		Percent	2.0	2.2	1.9	1.9	1.5
6.11	Inbound tourism expenditure over current account credits		Percent	0.9	0.9	0.7	0.7	0.6
6.12	Outbound tourism expenditure over imports of goods		Percent	13.9	11.3	11.5	9.7	10.1
6.13	Outbound tourism expenditure over imports of services		Percent	61.5	56.1	58.2	54.0	55.8
6.14	Outbound tourism expenditure over imports of goods and		Percent	11.3	9.4	9.6	8.2	8.6
6.15	Outbound tourism expenditure over current account debits		Percent	9.0	7.6	7.7	6.7	7.0

LIECHTENSTEIN

od.	Basic data and indicators	Notes	Units	2011	2012	2013	2014	2015
	INBOUND TOURISM							
	Data							
	Arrivals							
1	Total		('000)	..	..	..	..	..
2	♦ Overnight visitors (tourists)	(1)(2)	('000)	67.0	62.4	59.6	61.3	56.7
3	♦ Same-day visitors (excursionists)		('000)	..	..	..	..	..
4	* of which, cruise passengers		('000)	..	..	..	..	..
	Arrivals by region	(2)(3)(4)						
5	Total		('000)	53.3	62.4	59.7	61.3	56.7
6	♦ Africa		('000)	0.1	0.4	0.2	0.2	0.2
7	♦ Americas		('000)	2.7	3.5	3.4	3.6	3.9
8	♦ East Asia and the Pacific		('000)	1.9	2.5	2.8	3.6	4.1
9	♦ Europe		('000)	48.3	54.4	53.0	53.8	48.4
10	♦ Middle East		('000)	..	..	..	..	..
11	♦ South Asia		('000)	0.1	0.1	0.1	0.1	0.1
12	♦ Other not classified		('000)	0.2	1.5	0.2	..	..
13	* of which, nationals residing abroad		('000)	..	..	..	..	..
	Accommodation							
	Total							
29	♦ Guests	(2)	('000)	67.0	62.4	59.6	61.3	56.7
30	♦ Overnights	(2)	('000)	149.0	136.3	132.5	130.2	110.5
	Hotels and similar establishments							
31	♦ Guests		('000)	53.3	53.6	52.4	53.7	48.6
32	♦ Overnights		('000)	112.5	111.3	111.5	109.0	90.4
	Indicators							
39	Average size of travel party		Persons	..	..	..	..	..
	Average length of stay							
40	Total		Days	..	..	..	..	..
41	♦ For all commercial accommodation services	(2)	Nights	2.22	2.18	2.22	2.13	1.95
42	* of which, "hotels and similar establishments"		Nights	2.11	2.08	2.13	2.03	1.86
43	♦ For non commercial accommodation services		Days	..	..	..	..	..
44	Average expenditure per day		US$	..	..	..	..	..
	DOMESTIC TOURISM							
	Data							
	Accommodation							
	Total							
19	♦ Guests	(2)	('000)	5.9	2.2	1.1	1.1	1.0
20	♦ Overnights	(2)	('000)	18.2	4.8	2.8	2.1	2.0
	Hotels and similar establishments							
21	♦ Guests		('000)	2.5	1.6	0.7	0.4	0.5
22	♦ Overnights		('000)	4.9	3.5	1.7	1.0	1.1
	Indicators							
23	Average size of travel party		Persons	..	..	..	..	..
	Average length of stay							
24	Total		Days	..	..	..	..	..
25	♦ For all commercial accommodation services	(2)	Nights	3.10	2.12	2.50	1.96	2.05
26	* of which, "hotels and similar establishments"		Nights	1.94	2.15	2.50	2.23	2.09
27	♦ For non commercial accommodation services		Days	..	..	..	..	..
28	Average expenditure per day		US$	..	..	..	..	..
	TOURISM INDUSTRIES							
	Data							
	Number of establishments							
1	Total		Units	..	..	..	..	..
2	♦ Accommodation for visitors	(5)	Units	145	90	89	86	87
3	* of which, "hotels and similar establishments"	(6)	Units	40	38	36	40	35
4	♦ Food and beverage serving activities		Units	..	..	..	..	..
5	♦ Passenger transportation		Units	..	..	..	..	..
6	♦ Travel agencies and other reservation services activities		Units	..	..	..	..	..
7	♦ Other tourism industries		Units	..	..	..	..	..
	Accommodation for visitors in hotels and similar establishments							
	Non-monetary data							
13	♦ Number of establishments	(6)	Units	40	38	36	40	35
14	♦ Number of rooms	(7)	Units	589	515	476	500	459
15	♦ Number of bed-places	(8)	Units	1,121	1,029	978	1,025	912

LIECHTENSTEIN

Cod.	Basic data and indicators	Notes	Units	2011	2012	2013	2014	201
	Indicators							
4.16	Occupancy rate / rooms		Percent	..	..	..	..	36.9
4.17	Occupancy rate / bed-places		Percent	28.74	30.50	31.75	29.44	27.5
4.18	Average length of stay		Nights	2.10	2.08	2.13	2.03	1.8
4.19	Available capacity (bed-places per 1000 inhabitants)		Units	30.81	28.07	26.49	27.56	24.0
5.	**EMPLOYMENT**							
	Data							
	Number of employees by tourism industries							
5.1	Total		('000)	..	..	..	..	
5.2	♦ Accommodation services for visitors (hotels and similar establishments)	(6)	('000)	0.3	0.3	0.3	0.3	0
5.3	♦ Other accommodation services		('000)	..	..	..	..	
5.4	♦ Food and beverage serving activities		('000)	..	..	..	..	
5.5	♦ Passenger transportation		('000)	..	..	..	..	
5.6	♦ Travel agencies and other reservation services activities		('000)	..	..	..	..	
5.7	♦ Other tourism industries		('000)	..	..	..	..	
6.	**COMPLEMENTARY INDICATORS**							
	Demand							
6.1	Gross travel propensity		Units	..	..	..	..	
6.2	(1.2 inbound tourists) / population		Units	1.84	1.70	1.61	1.65	1.4

LITHUANIA

Cod.	Basic data and indicators	Notes	Units	2011	2012	2013	2014	2015
1.	**INBOUND TOURISM**							
	Data							
	Arrivals							
.1	Total		('000)	4,504	4,979	5,264	5,217	5,048
.2	♦ Overnight visitors (tourists)		('000)	1,775	1,900	2,012	2,063	2,071
.3	♦ Same-day visitors (excursionists)		('000)	2,729	3,079	3,252	3,155	2,977
.4	* of which, cruise passengers		('000)	22	27	33	58	60
	Arrivals by region							
.5	Total		('000)	1,775	1,900	2,012	2,063	2,072
.6	♦ Africa		('000)	3	5	6	6	7
.7	♦ Americas		('000)	33	41	40	48	49
.8	♦ East Asia and the Pacific		('000)	..	..	..	..	..
.9	♦ Europe		('000)	1,690	1,788	1,864	1,895	1,797
.10	♦ Middle East		('000)	..	..	..	..	..
.11	♦ South Asia		('000)	..	..	..	..	96
.12	♦ Other not classified		('000)	49	66	102	114	123
.13	* of which, nationals residing abroad		('000)	..	..	..	..	..
	Arrivals by main purpose							
.14	Total		('000)	1,775	1,899	2,012	2,063	2,071
.15	♦ Personal		('000)	1,248	1,352	1,435	1,453	1,455
.16	* holidays, leisure and recreation		('000)	592	676	734	764	693
.17	* other personal purposes		('000)	656	676	701	689	762
.18	♦ Business and professional		('000)	527	547	577	610	616
	Arrivals by mode of transport							
.19	Total		('000)	1,775	1,900	2,012	2,062	2,072
.20	♦ Air		('000)	605	655	704	736	785
.21	♦ Water		('000)	26	33	31	29	31
.22	♦ Land		('000)	1,144	1,212	1,277	1,297	1,256
.23	* railway		('000)	102	91	108	103	73
.24	* road		('000)	992	1,063	1,104	1,135	1,140
.25	* others		('000)	50	58	65	59	43
	Arrivals by form of organization of the trip							
.26	Total		('000)	1,775	1,900	2,012	2,063	2,071
.27	♦ Package tour		('000)	104	128	139	100	113
.28	♦ Other forms		('000)	1,671	1,772	1,873	1,963	1,958
	Accommodation							
	Total							
.29	♦ Guests		('000)	1,004	1,125	1,235	1,330	1,361
.30	♦ Overnights		('000)	2,377	2,622	2,839	2,966	2,943
	Hotels and similar establishments							
.31	♦ Guests	(1)	('000)	909	1,008	1,098	1,166	1,182
.32	♦ Overnights	(1)	('000)	1,818	2,002	2,169	2,251	2,247
	Expenditure							
.33	Total		US$ Mn	..	..	..	..	1,303
.34	♦ Travel		US$ Mn	1,321	1,317	1,374	1,383	1,146
.35	♦ Passenger transport		US$ Mn	..	..	..	..	157
	Indicators							
.39	Average size of travel party		Persons	..	..	..	..	..
	Average length of stay							
.40	Total		Days	4.40	4.39	4.40	4.39	4.40
.41	♦ For all commercial accommodation services		Nights	2.37	2.33	2.30	2.20	2.20
.42	* of which, "hotels and similar establishments"		Nights	2.00	1.99	1.95	1.93	1.90
.43	♦ For non commercial accommodation services		Days	7.04	7.39	..	..	..
.44	Average expenditure per day		US$	113.9	107.7	110.5	112.6	93.2
2.	**DOMESTIC TOURISM**							
	Data							
	Trips							
2.1	Total		('000)	14,188	13,855	13,575	13,894	14,147
2.2	♦ Overnight visitors (tourists)		('000)	2,479	2,516	2,589	2,649	2,663
2.3	♦ Same-day visitors (excursionists)		('000)	11,709	11,339	10,986	11,245	11,484
	Trips by main purpose							
2.4	Total		('000)	2,480	2,515	2,589	2,649	2,663
2.5	♦ Personal		('000)	2,168	2,204	2,272	2,316	2,321
2.6	* holidays, leisure and recreation		('000)	710	737	797	821	864
2.7	* other personal purposes		('000)	1,458	1,467	1,475	1,495	1,457
2.8	♦ Business and professional		('000)	312	311	317	333	342

LITHUANIA

Cod.	Basic data and indicators	Notes	Units	2011	2012	2013	2014	2015
	Trips by mode of transport							
2.9	Total		('000)	2,480	2,516	2,589	2,649	2,664
2.10	♦ Air		('000)	..	..	..	..	.
2.11	♦ Water		('000)	..	..	..	..	
2.12	♦ Land		('000)	2,480	2,516	2,589	2,649	2,664
2.13	* railway		('000)	51	36	105	57	47
2.14	* road		('000)	2,421	2,473	2,469	2,556	2,574
2.15	* others		('000)	8	7	15	36	43
	Accommodation							
	Total							
2.19	♦ Guests		('000)	789	852	950	1,034	1,140
2.20	♦ Overnights		('000)	2,546	2,643	2,725	2,908	3,058
	Hotels and similar establishments							
2.21	♦ Guests	(1)	('000)	519	586	647	708	777
2.22	♦ Overnights	(1)	('000)	1,019	1,168	1,230	1,292	1,367
	Indicators							
2.23	Average size of travel party		Persons	..	..	..	..	
	Average length of stay							
2.24	Total		Days	2.73	2.72	2.50	..	
2.25	♦ For all commercial accommodation services		Nights	3.23	3.10	2.90	2.81	2.66
2.26	* of which, "hotels and similar establishments"		Nights	1.96	2.00	1.90	1.82	1.76
2.27	♦ For non commercial accommodation services		Days	2.50	2.52	..	..	..
2.28	Average expenditure per day		US$	23.4	22.0	24.0	26.1	24.0
3.	**OUTBOUND TOURISM**							
	Data							
	Departures							
3.1	Total		('000)	4,020	4,108	4,228	4,292	3,981
3.2	♦ Overnight visitors (tourists)		('000)	1,526	1,708	1,764	1,789	1,860
3.3	♦ Same-day visitors (excursionists)		('000)	2,493	2,401	2,464	2,503	2,121
	Expenditure							
3.4	Total		US$ Mn	..	..	..	..	1,075
3.5	♦ Travel		US$ Mn	859	925	1,069	1,058	894
3.6	♦ Passenger transport		US$ Mn	..	..	..	..	181
	Indicators							
3.10	Average length of stay		Days	7.03	7.58	7.73	6.80	6.80
3.11	Average expenditure per day		US$	85.4	73.4	77.7	86.1	71.3
4.	**TOURISM INDUSTRIES**							
	Data							
	Number of establishments	(2)						
4.1	Total		Units	6,135	6,185	..	..	.
4.2	♦ Accommodation for visitors		Units	1,425	1,413	1,305	1,400	1,664
4.3	* of which, "hotels and similar establishments"		Units	234	227	224	421	418
4.4	♦ Food and beverage serving activities		Units	2,793	2,851	..	..	..
4.5	♦ Passenger transportation		Units	1,059	1,064	..	..	..
4.6	♦ Travel agencies and other reservation services activities		Units	858	857	..	..	..
4.7	♦ Other tourism industries		Units	..	..	..	..	..
	Accommodation for visitors in hotels and similar establishments							
	Monetary data	(3)						
4.8	♦ Output		US$ Mn	210.4	201.6	292.8	272.0	..
4.9	♦ Intermediate consumption		US$ Mn	78.4	73.6	106.6	89.3	..
4.10	♦ Gross value added		US$ Mn	132.1	128.0	186.1	182.7	..
4.11	♦ Compensation of employees		US$ Mn	..	..	..	..	..
4.12	♦ Gross fixed capital formation		US$ Mn	..	..	..	..	..
	Non-monetary data	(1)						
4.13	♦ Number of establishments		Units	379	397	414	421	418
4.14	♦ Number of rooms		Units	12,622	13,248	13,468	13,788	13,839
4.15	♦ Number of bed-places		Units	26,114	27,453	27,793	28,459	28,585
	Indicators							
4.16	Occupancy rate / rooms	(1)	Percent	44.50	45.50	47.90	48.70	49.30
4.17	Occupancy rate / bed-places	(1)	Percent	33.90	35.40	36.80	37.10	36.80
4.18	Average length of stay		Nights	1.99	1.99	2.04	1.89	1.84
4.19	Available capacity (bed-places per 1000 inhabitants)		Units	8.50	9.10	9.38	9.76	9.93

ITHUANIA

Cod.	Basic data and indicators	Notes	Units	2011	2012	2013	2014	2015
	Travel agencies and other reservation service activities							
	Monetary data	(3)						
.20	♦ Output		US$ Mn	119.7	143.3	151.5	215.6	..
.21	♦ Intermediate consumption		US$ Mn	73.8	80.3	81.3	101.4	..
.22	♦ Gross value added		US$ Mn	45.9	63.1	70.2	114.2	..
.23	♦ Compensation of employees		US$ Mn	..	..	..	..	..
.24	♦ Gross fixed capital formation		US$ Mn	..	..	..	..	..
	Non-monetary data							
	♦ Domestic trips							
.25	* with package tour		Percent	..	..	..	..	..
.26	* without package tour		Percent	..	..	..	..	..
	♦ Inbound trips							
.27	* with package tour		Percent	5.9	6.8	5.5	4.9	5.5
.28	* without package tour		Percent	94.1	93.2	94.6	95.1	94.6
	♦ Outbound trips							
.29	* with package tour		Percent	12.1	10.7	11.6	13.3	14.3
.30	* without package tour		Percent	87.9	89.3	88.4	86.7	85.7
.	**EMPLOYMENT**							
	Data							
	Number of employees by tourism industries	(4)						
.1	Total		('000)	40.4	40.4	42.1	46.1	..
.2	♦ Accommodation services for visitors (hotels and similar establishments)		('000)	10.5	11.0	11.3	11.8	..
.3	♦ Other accommodation services		('000)	..	..	..	..	..
.4	♦ Food and beverage serving activities		('000)	12.7	12.0	12.6	13.1	..
.5	♦ Passenger transportation		('000)	9.3	9.1	9.2	10.1	..
.6	♦ Travel agencies and other reservation services activities		('000)	2.6	2.8	3.0	3.1	..
.7	♦ Other tourism industries		('000)	5.3	5.5	6.0	8.0	..
.	**COMPLEMENTARY INDICATORS**							
	Demand							
.1	Gross travel propensity		Units	6.0	6.0	6.1	6.3	6.3
.2	(1.2 inbound tourists + 2.2 domestic tourists) / population		Units	1.39	1.46	1.55	1.62	1.64
	Macroeconomic indicators related to international tourism							
.3	Inbound tourism expenditure over GDP		Percent	3.0	3.1	3.0	2.9	2.3
.4	Outbound tourism expenditure over GDP		Percent	2.0	2.2	2.3	2.2	1.8
.5	Tourism balance (inbound minus outbound tourism expenditure) over GDP		Percent	1.0	0.9	0.7	0.7	0.5
.6	Tourism openness (inbound plus outbound tourism expenditure) over GDP		Percent	5.0	5.3	5.3	5.1	4.1
.7	Tourism coverage (inbound over outbound tourism expenditure)		Percent	153.8	142.4	128.5	130.7	128.2
.8	Inbound tourism expenditure over exports of goods		Percent	4.9	4.6	4.3	4.4	4.6
.9	Inbound tourism expenditure over exports of services		Percent	23.5	21.4	19.2	17.8	17.2
.10	Inbound tourism expenditure over exports of goods and services		Percent	4.0	3.8	3.5	3.5	3.6
.11	Inbound tourism expenditure over current account credits		Percent	3.6	3.5	3.2	3.2	3.4
.12	Outbound tourism expenditure over imports of goods		Percent	2.9	3.1	3.2	3.2	3.3
.13	Outbound tourism expenditure over imports of services		Percent	22.3	21.2	19.9	18.9	19.1
.14	Outbound tourism expenditure over imports of goods and		Percent	2.5	2.7	2.8	2.8	2.8
.15	Outbound tourism expenditure over current account debits		Percent	2.3	2.5	2.6	2.6	2.7

231

LUXEMBOURG

Cod.	Basic data and indicators	Notes	Units	2011	2012	2013	2014	2015
1.	**INBOUND TOURISM**							
	Data							
	Arrivals							
1.1	Total		('000)	..	..	..	..	..
1.2	♦ Overnight visitors (tourists)	(1)	('000)	874	950	945	1,038	1,090
1.3	♦ Same-day visitors (excursionists)		('000)	..	..	..	..	..
1.4	* of which, cruise passengers		('000)	..	..	..	..	..
	Arrivals by region	(1)						
1.5	Total		('000)	874	950	945	1,038	1,090
1.6	♦ Africa		('000)	10	14	5	7	6
1.7	♦ Americas		('000)	38	39	39	45	52
1.8	♦ East Asia and the Pacific		('000)	56	75	60	71	79
1.9	♦ Europe		('000)	771	822	840	915	953
1.10	♦ Middle East		('000)	..	..	..	..	..
1.11	♦ South Asia		('000)	..	..	..	..	..
1.12	♦ Other not classified		('000)	..	..	..	..	..
1.13	* of which, nationals residing abroad		('000)	..	..	..	..	..
	Arrivals by main purpose	(2)						
1.14	Total		('000)	870	950	945	1,038	1,090
1.15	♦ Personal		('000)	713	760	744	799	844
1.16	* holidays, leisure and recreation		('000)	617	636	631	666	633
1.17	* other personal purposes		('000)	96	124	113	133	211
1.18	♦ Business and professional		('000)	157	190	200	239	246
	Accommodation							
	Total							
1.29	♦ Guests	(1)	('000)	874	950	945	1,038	1,090
1.30	♦ Overnights	(1)	('000)	2,058	2,298	2,317	2,514	2,656
	Hotels and similar establishments							
1.31	♦ Guests	(3)	('000)	682	770	763	834	870
1.32	♦ Overnights	(3)	('000)	1,282	1,424	1,415	1,538	1,586
	Expenditure	(4)						
1.33	Total		US$ Mn	5,358	5,476	5,744	6,153	4,875
1.34	♦ Travel		US$ Mn	4,861	4,982	5,151	5,484	4,295
1.35	♦ Passenger transport		US$ Mn	497	494	593	669	580
	Expenditure by main purpose of the trip	(4)						
1.36	Total		US$ Mn	4,861	4,982	5,150	5,484	4,295
1.37	♦ Personal		US$ Mn	2,392	2,600	2,662	2,953	2,196
1.38	♦ Business and professional		US$ Mn	2,469	2,382	2,488	2,531	2,099
	Indicators							
1.39	Average size of travel party	(2)	Persons	11.6	12.8	13.9	12.4	13.5
	Average length of stay							
1.40	Total		Days	..	..	..	..	..
1.41	♦ For all commercial accommodation services	(1)	Nights	2.37	2.42	2.45	2.42	2.71
1.42	* of which, "hotels and similar establishments"	(3)	Nights	1.88	1.85	1.85	1.84	1.82
1.43	♦ For non commercial accommodation services		Days	..	..	..	..	..
1.44	Average expenditure per day		US$	..	..	..	..	..
2.	**DOMESTIC TOURISM**							
	Data							
	Trips							
2.1	Total		('000)	..	..	..	..	..
2.2	♦ Overnight visitors (tourists)	(5)	('000)	61	71	100	104	107
2.3	♦ Same-day visitors (excursionists)		('000)	..	..	..	..	..
	Trips by main purpose	(2)(5)						
2.4	Total		('000)	61	71	100	104	107
2.5	♦ Personal		('000)	53	61	83	83	94
2.6	* holidays, leisure and recreation		('000)	40	45	63	63	65
2.7	* other personal purposes		('000)	13	16	20	20	29
2.8	♦ Business and professional		('000)	8	10	17	21	13
	Accommodation							
	Total							
2.19	♦ Guests	(5)	('000)	61	71	100	104	107
2.20	♦ Overnights	(5)	('000)	180	246	324	354	324
	Hotels and similar establishments							
2.21	♦ Guests	(3)	('000)	34	43	68	70	69
2.22	♦ Overnights	(3)	('000)	96	118	156	161	152

LUXEMBOURG

Cod.	Basic data and indicators	Notes	Units	2011	2012	2013	2014	2015
	Indicators							
2.23	Average size of travel party		Persons	..	..	..	..	..
	Average length of stay							
2.24	Total		Days	..	..	..	..	..
2.25	♦ For all commercial accommodation services	(5)	Nights	3.11	3.46	3.24	3.40	3.00
2.26	* of which, "hotels and similar establishments"	(3)	Nights	2.82	2.74	2.29	2.30	2.20
2.27	♦ For non commercial accommodation services		Days	..	..	..	..	..
2.28	Average expenditure per day		US$	..	..	..	..	..
3.	**OUTBOUND TOURISM**							
	Data							
	Departures							
3.1	Total		('000)	..	..	..	3,543	2,960
3.2	♦ Overnight visitors (tourists)		('000)	1,643	1,580	1,624	1,815	1,702
3.3	♦ Same-day visitors (excursionists)		('000)	..	..	..	1,728	1,258
	Expenditure	(4)						
3.4	Total		US$ Mn	3,873	3,685	3,877	3,948	3,369
3.5	♦ Travel		US$ Mn	3,774	3,589	3,801	3,870	3,313
3.6	♦ Passenger transport		US$ Mn	99	96	76	78	56
	Expenditure by main purpose of the trip	(4)						
3.7	Total		US$ Mn	3,774	3,589	3,801	3,870	3,313
3.8	♦ Personal		US$ Mn	3,524	3,359	3,566	3,634	3,110
3.9	♦ Business and professional		US$ Mn	250	230	235	236	203
4.	**TOURISM INDUSTRIES**							
	Data							
	Number of establishments							
4.1	Total		Units	..	..	..	..	..
4.2	♦ Accommodation for visitors		Units	550	532	498	474	466
4.3	* of which, "hotels and similar establishments"		Units	260	252	244	237	235
4.4	♦ Food and beverage serving activities		Units	..	..	..	..	..
4.5	♦ Passenger transportation		Units	..	..	..	..	..
4.6	♦ Travel agencies and other reservation services activities		Units	..	..	..	..	..
4.7	♦ Other tourism industries		Units	..	..	..	..	..
	Accommodation for visitors in hotels and similar establishments							
	Non-monetary data							
4.13	♦ Number of establishments		Units	260	252	244	237	235
4.14	♦ Number of rooms		Units	8,393	8,206	7,837	7,778	7,635
4.15	♦ Number of bed-places		Units	15,388	15,345	15,012	14,718	14,493
	Indicators							
4.16	Occupancy rate / rooms	(6)	Percent	36.62	41.13	43.25	46.89	47.12
4.17	Occupancy rate / bed-places	(6)	Percent	27.08	30.60	31.82	35.31	36.33
4.18	Average length of stay		Nights	1.93	1.89	1.89	1.88	1.54
4.19	Available capacity (bed-places per 1000 inhabitants)		Units	29.59	28.82	27.55	26.44	25.56
6.	**COMPLEMENTARY INDICATORS**							
	Demand							
6.1	Gross travel propensity		Units	..	..	..	..	..
6.2	(1.2 inbound tourists + 2.2 domestic tourists) / population		Units	1.80	1.92	1.92	2.05	2.11
	Macroeconomic indicators related to international tourism							
6.3	Inbound tourism expenditure over GDP		Percent	9.1	9.7	9.5	9.6	8.4
6.4	Outbound tourism expenditure over GDP		Percent	6.6	6.6	6.4	6.2	5.8
6.5	Tourism balance (inbound minus outbound tourism expenditure) over GDP		Percent	2.5	3.1	3.1	3.4	2.6
6.6	Tourism openness (inbound plus outbound tourism expenditure) over GDP		Percent	15.7	16.3	15.9	15.8	14.2
6.7	Tourism coverage (inbound over outbound tourism expenditure)		Percent	138.3	148.6	148.2	155.9	144.7
6.8	Inbound tourism expenditure over exports of goods		Percent	22.7	24.4	23.7	25.0	27.4
6.9	Inbound tourism expenditure over exports of services		Percent	7.4	7.2	6.4	6.2	5.2
6.10	Inbound tourism expenditure over exports of goods and services		Percent	5.6	5.6	5.1	5.0	4.4
6.11	Inbound tourism expenditure over current account credits		Percent	1.7	1.6	1.4	1.8	1.5
6.12	Outbound tourism expenditure over imports of goods		Percent	14.6	15.1	15.2	15.9	16.7
6.13	Outbound tourism expenditure over imports of services		Percent	7.2	6.5	5.7	5.1	4.7
6.14	Outbound tourism expenditure over imports of goods and		Percent	4.8	4.5	4.2	3.9	3.7
6.15	Outbound tourism expenditure over current account debits		Percent	1.3	1.1	1.0	1.2	1.1

MACAO, CHINA

Cod.	Basic data and indicators	Notes	Units	2011	2012	2013	2014	2015
1.	**INBOUND TOURISM**							
	Data							
	Arrivals							
1.1	Total		('000)	28,002	28,082	29,325	31,526	30,715
1.2	♦ Overnight visitors (tourists)		('000)	12,925	13,577	14,268	14,566	14,308
1.3	♦ Same-day visitors (excursionists)		('000)	15,077	14,505	15,056	16,960	16,407
1.4	* of which, cruise passengers		('000)	..	..	..	..	..
	Arrivals by region							
1.5	Total		('000)	28,002	28,082	29,325	31,526	30,715
1.6	♦ Africa		('000)	25	27	29	35	31
1.7	♦ Americas		('000)	311	307	289	286	286
1.8	♦ East Asia and the Pacific		('000)	27,207	27,295	28,533	30,726	29,930
1.9	♦ Europe		('000)	271	281	290	287	273
1.10	♦ Middle East		('000)	12	14	15	14	15
1.11	♦ South Asia		('000)	177	159	169	178	179
1.12	♦ Other not classified		('000)	..	..	..	..	..
1.13	* of which, nationals residing abroad		('000)	..	..	..	..	..
	Arrivals by mode of transport							
1.19	Total		('000)	28,002	28,082	29,325	31,526	30,715
1.20	♦ Air		('000)	1,682	1,768	1,950	2,055	2,090
1.21	♦ Water		('000)	11,021	11,485	11,558	12,081	11,414
1.22	♦ Land		('000)	15,299	14,830	15,818	17,390	17,211
1.23	* railway		('000)	..	..	..	..	..
1.24	* road		('000)	15,299	14,830	15,818	17,390	17,211
1.25	* others		('000)	..	..	..	..	..
	Arrivals by form of organization of the trip							
1.26	Total		('000)	28,002	28,082	29,325	31,526	30,715
1.27	♦ Package tour	(1)	('000)	7,537	9,122	9,776	9,220	8,589
1.28	♦ Other forms		('000)	20,465	18,960	19,549	22,306	22,126
	Accommodation							
	Hotels and similar establishments							
1.31	♦ Guests		('000)	8,052	8,885	10,016	10,018	9,851
1.32	♦ Overnights		('000)	11,684	11,614	13,080	13,427	13,404
	Expenditure							
1.33	Total		US$ Mn	31,118	36,521	43,665	43,289	31,997
1.34	♦ Travel		US$ Mn	30,595	36,013	43,133	42,724	31,476
1.35	♦ Passenger transport		US$ Mn	523	508	532	565	521
	Expenditure by main purpose of the trip							
1.36	Total		US$ Mn	30,595	36,013	43,133	42,724	31,476
1.37	♦ Personal		US$ Mn	29,069	34,576	41,067	40,506	29,843
1.38	♦ Business and professional		US$ Mn	1,526	1,437	2,066	2,218	1,633
	Indicators							
1.39	Average size of travel party		Persons	..	..	..	..	..
	Average length of stay							
1.40	Total	(2)	Days	1.00	1.00	1.00	1.00	1.10
1.41	♦ For all commercial accommodation services		Nights	1.51	1.36	1.36	1.40	1.42
1.42	* of which, "hotels and similar establishments"		Nights	1.51	1.36	1.36	1.40	1.42
1.43	♦ For non commercial accommodation services		Days	..	..	..	..	..
1.44	Average expenditure per day		US$	..	..	253.8	244.9	208.1
3.	**OUTBOUND TOURISM**							
	Data							
	Departures							
3.1	Total		('000)	908	1,291	1,446	1,537	1,466
3.2	♦ Overnight visitors (tourists)		('000)	..	..	..	..	..
3.3	♦ Same-day visitors (excursionists)		('000)	..	..	..	..	..
	Expenditure							
3.4	Total		US$ Mn	1,064	1,155	1,236	1,314	1,364
3.5	♦ Travel		US$ Mn	964	1,083	1,132	1,210	1,265
3.6	♦ Passenger transport		US$ Mn	100	72	104	104	99
	Expenditure by main purpose of the trip							
3.7	Total		US$ Mn	964	1,083	1,133	1,210	1,265
3.8	♦ Personal		US$ Mn	942	1,058	1,106	1,176	1,236
3.9	♦ Business and professional		US$ Mn	22	25	27	34	29

MACAO, CHINA

Cod.	Basic data and indicators	Notes	Units	2011	2012	2013	2014	2015
4.	**TOURISM INDUSTRIES**							
	Data							
	Number of establishments							
4.1	Total		Units	2,904	2,946	3,336	3,644	..
4.2	♦ Accommodation for visitors	(3)	Units	95	100	100	99	107
4.3	* of which, "hotels and similar establishments"	(3)	Units	95	100	100	99	107
4.4	♦ Food and beverage serving activities	(4)	Units	1,714	1,678	1,918	2,112	..
4.5	♦ Passenger transportation	(5)	Units	899	961	1,097	1,186	..
4.6	♦ Travel agencies and other reservation services activities	(6)	Units	186	197	211	237	224
4.7	♦ Other tourism industries	(7)	Units	10	10	10	10	10
	Accommodation for visitors in hotels and similar establishments							
	Monetary data							
4.8	♦ Output		US$ Mn	2,352.5	2,744.9	3,166.5	3,489.5	..
4.9	♦ Intermediate consumption		US$ Mn	1,185.4	1,450.2	1,625.3	1,668.3	..
4.10	♦ Gross value added		US$ Mn	1,167.1	1,294.7	1,541.2	1,821.2	..
4.11	♦ Compensation of employees		US$ Mn	714.0	977.6	1,024.2	1,200.6	..
4.12	♦ Gross fixed capital formation		US$ Mn	2,068.7	1,031.7	283.5	346.0	..
	Non-monetary data	(3)						
4.13	♦ Number of establishments		Units	95	100	100	99	107
4.14	♦ Number of rooms		Units	22,356	26,069	27,764	27,904	32,249
4.15	♦ Number of bed-places		Units	54,666	66,577	72,199	72,492	84,620
	Indicators							
4.16	Occupancy rate / rooms		Percent	84.12	83.60	83.12	86.46	80.77
4.17	Occupancy rate / bed-places		Percent	65.85	57.22	54.65	56.06	52.60
4.18	Average length of stay		Nights	1.53	1.40	1.40	1.44	1.48
4.19	Available capacity (bed-places per 1000 inhabitants)		Units	100.00	119.36	127.10	125.44	144.01
	Travel agencies and other reservation service activities							
	Monetary data							
4.20	♦ Output		US$ Mn	690.5	747.7	792.4	896.0	..
4.21	♦ Intermediate consumption		US$ Mn	613.4	689.4	689.7	769.3	..
4.22	♦ Gross value added		US$ Mn	77.2	98.2	102.7	126.8	..
4.23	♦ Compensation of employees		US$ Mn	55.6	64.9	71.7	79.1	..
4.24	♦ Gross fixed capital formation		US$ Mn	24.9	20.7	30.0	29.7	..
	Non-monetary data							
	♦ Domestic trips							
4.25	* with package tour		Percent	..	..	..	..	..
4.26	* without package tour		Percent	..	..	..	..	..
	♦ Inbound trips							
4.27	* with package tour	(1)	Percent	26.9	32.5	33.3	29.2	28.0
4.28	* without package tour		Percent	73.1	67.5	66.7	70.8	72.0
	♦ Outbound trips							
4.29	* with package tour		Percent	27.7	33.3	38.0	38.1	41.7
4.30	* without package tour		Percent	72.3	66.7	62.0	61.9	58.3
5.	**EMPLOYMENT**	(8)						
	Data							
	Number of employees by tourism industries							
5.1	Total		('000)	113.5	125.9	132.7	139.9	..
5.2	♦ Accommodation services for visitors (hotels and similar establishments)	(3)	('000)	33.1	39.5	39.9	39.4	..
5.3	♦ Other accommodation services		('000)	..	..	..	..	..
5.4	♦ Food and beverage serving activities	(4)	('000)	21.2	22.0	26.1	30.4	..
5.5	♦ Passenger transportation	(5)	('000)	6.7	6.9	7.0	8.1	..
5.6	♦ Travel agencies and other reservation services activities	(6)	('000)	3.4	3.7	3.9	4.2	..
5.7	♦ Other tourism industries	(7)	('000)	49.1	53.8	55.8	57.8	56.2
6.	**COMPLEMENTARY INDICATORS**							
	Demand							
6.1	Gross travel propensity		Units	..	..	..	..	..
6.2	(1.2 inbound tourists) / population		Units	23.64	24.34	25.12	25.20	24.35
	Macroeconomic indicators related to international tourism							
6.3	Inbound tourism expenditure over GDP		Percent	106.2	103.1	101.6	92.9	..
6.4	Outbound tourism expenditure over GDP		Percent	4.0	3.9	3.5	3.5	..
6.5	Tourism balance (inbound minus outbound tourism expenditure) over GDP		Percent	102.2	99.2	98.1	89.4	..

MACAO, CHINA

Cod.	Basic data and indicators	Notes	Units	2011	2012	2013	2014	2015
6.6	Tourism openness (inbound plus outbound tourism expenditure) over GDP		Percent	110.2	107.0	105.1	96.4	..
6.7	Tourism coverage (inbound over outbound tourism expenditure)		Percent	2,644.8	2,658.4	2,899.2	2,650.7	..
6.8	Inbound tourism expenditure over exports of goods		Percent	3,463.6	2,994.3	3,297.1	2,709.6	..
6.9	Inbound tourism expenditure over exports of services		Percent	97.8	97.8	97.7	97.0	..
6.10	Inbound tourism expenditure over exports of goods and services		Percent	95.2	94.7	94.9	93.7	..
6.11	Inbound tourism expenditure over current account credits		Percent	91.3	90.1	90.1	86.6	..
6.12	Outbound tourism expenditure over imports of goods		Percent	16.5	16.2	14.7	13.7	..
6.13	Outbound tourism expenditure over imports of services		Percent	13.8	14.6	15.2	18.3	..
6.14	Outbound tourism expenditure over imports of goods and		Percent	7.5	7.7	7.5	7.8	..
6.15	Outbound tourism expenditure over current account debits		Percent	6.7	6.7	6.4	6.4	..

MADAGASCAR

Cod.	Basic data and indicators	Notes	Units	2011	2012	2013	2014	2015
1.	**INBOUND TOURISM**							
	Data							
	Arrivals							
1.1	Total		('000)	..	..	..	..	..
1.2	♦ Overnight visitors (tourists)		('000)	225	256	196	222	244
1.3	♦ Same-day visitors (excursionists)		('000)	..	..	..	..	..
1.4	* of which, cruise passengers		('000)	..	..	..	..	..
	Arrivals by region	(1)						
1.5	Total		('000)	225	256	196	222	244
1.6	♦ Africa		('000)	39	45	35	37	12
1.7	♦ Americas		('000)	10	10	6	9	6
1.8	♦ East Asia and the Pacific		('000)	23	23	12	13	7
1.9	♦ Europe		('000)	153	177	142	162	100
1.10	♦ Middle East		('000)	..	..	..	..	..
1.11	♦ South Asia		('000)	..	..	..	..	4
1.12	♦ Other not classified		('000)	..	..	1	2	116
1.13	* of which, nationals residing abroad		('000)	..	..	..	..	..
	Arrivals by main purpose	(1)						
1.14	Total		('000)	225	256	196	222	244
1.15	♦ Personal		('000)	185	210	159	182	192
1.16	* holidays, leisure and recreation		('000)	151	172	104	141	171
1.17	* other personal purposes		('000)	34	38	55	40	21
1.18	♦ Business and professional		('000)	40	46	37	41	53
	Arrivals by mode of transport							
1.19	Total		('000)	225	256	196	222	244
1.20	♦ Air		('000)	225	256	196	222	244
1.21	♦ Water		('000)	..	..	..	..	..
1.22	♦ Land		('000)	..	..	..	..	..
1.23	* railway		('000)	..	..	..	..	..
1.24	* road		('000)	..	..	..	..	..
1.25	* others		('000)	..	..	..	..	..
	Accommodation							
	Hotels and similar establishments							
1.31	♦ Guests		('000)	..	..	..	..	..
1.32	♦ Overnights		('000)	3,764	..	..	..	..
	Expenditure							
1.33	Total		US$ Mn	479	563	578	..	..
1.34	♦ Travel		US$ Mn	476	559	574	..	..
1.35	♦ Passenger transport		US$ Mn	3	4	4	..	..
	Expenditure by main purpose of the trip							
1.36	Total		US$ Mn	476	558	574	..	..
1.37	♦ Personal		US$ Mn	469	553	570	..	..
1.38	♦ Business and professional		US$ Mn	7	5	4	..	..
	Indicators							
1.39	Average size of travel party		Persons	..	..	..	..	
	Average length of stay							
1.40	Total		Days	..	..	..	..	
1.41	♦ For all commercial accommodation services		Nights	21.00	21.00	23.00	20.00	..
1.42	* of which, "hotels and similar establishments"		Nights	..	..	..	..	..
1.43	♦ For non commercial accommodation services		Days	..	..	..	..	..
1.44	Average expenditure per day		US$	..	..	..	..	..
3.	**OUTBOUND TOURISM**							
	Data							
	Expenditure							
3.4	Total		US$ Mn	180	136	161	..	..
3.5	♦ Travel		US$ Mn	150	108	134	..	..
3.6	♦ Passenger transport		US$ Mn	30	28	27	..	..
	Expenditure by main purpose of the trip							
3.7	Total		US$ Mn	150	108	134	..	..
3.8	♦ Personal		US$ Mn	127	96	122	..	..
3.9	♦ Business and professional		US$ Mn	23	12	12	..	..

MADAGASCAR

Cod.	Basic data and indicators	Notes	Units	2011	2012	2013	2014	2015
4.	**TOURISM INDUSTRIES**							
	Data							
	Number of establishments							
4.1	Total		Units	2,712	3,290	3,607	3,757	3,981
4.2	♦ Accommodation for visitors		Units	..	..	..	..	..
4.3	* of which, "hotels and similar establishments"		Units	1,693	2,010	2,251	2,377	2,558
4.4	♦ Food and beverage serving activities		Units	..	..	..	..	..
4.5	♦ Passenger transportation		Units	..	..	..	..	..
4.6	♦ Travel agencies and other reservation services activities		Units	1,019	1,280	1,356	1,380	1,423
4.7	♦ Other tourism industries		Units	..	..	..	..	..
	Accommodation for visitors in hotels and similar establishments							
	Non-monetary data							
4.13	♦ Number of establishments		Units	1,693	2,010	2,251	2,377	2,558
4.14	♦ Number of rooms		Units	19,112	20,520	22,263	23,382	24,046
4.15	♦ Number of bed-places		Units	30,388	32,627	35,398	37,154	..
	Indicators							
4.16	Occupancy rate / rooms		Percent	49.00	..	..	..	..
4.17	Occupancy rate / bed-places		Percent	..	..	..	..	..
4.18	Average length of stay		Nights	..	..	..	..	..
4.19	Available capacity (bed-places per 1000 inhabitants)		Units	1.40	1.46	1.54	1.58	..
5.	**EMPLOYMENT**							
	Data							
	Number of employees by tourism industries							
5.1	Total		('000)	31.2	34.3	36.7	38.0	39.4
5.2	♦ Accommodation services for visitors (hotels and similar establishments)		('000)	25.4	28.3	30.4	31.5	32.7
5.3	♦ Other accommodation services		('000)	..	..	..	..	..
5.4	♦ Food and beverage serving activities		('000)	..	..	..	..	..
5.5	♦ Passenger transportation		('000)	..	..	..	..	..
5.6	♦ Travel agencies and other reservation services activities		('000)	5.8	6.0	6.3	6.5	6.7
5.7	♦ Other tourism industries		('000)	..	..	..	..	..
6.	**COMPLEMENTARY INDICATORS**							
	Demand							
6.1	Gross travel propensity		Units	..	..	..	..	..
6.2	(1.2 inbound tourists) / population		Units	0.01	0.01	0.01	0.01	0.01
	Macroeconomic indicators related to international tourism							
6.3	Inbound tourism expenditure over GDP		Percent	4.8	5.7	5.5	..	..
6.4	Outbound tourism expenditure over GDP		Percent	1.8	1.4	1.5	..	..
6.5	Tourism balance (inbound minus outbound tourism expenditure) over GDP		Percent	3.0	4.3	4.0	..	..
6.6	Tourism openness (inbound plus outbound tourism expenditure) over GDP		Percent	6.6	7.1	7.0	..	..
6.7	Tourism coverage (inbound over outbound tourism expenditure)		Percent	266.1	414.0	359.0	..	..
6.8	Inbound tourism expenditure over exports of goods		Percent	32.5	37.1	30.1	..	..
6.9	Inbound tourism expenditure over exports of services		Percent	40.8	42.8	45.7	..	..
6.10	Inbound tourism expenditure over exports of goods and services		Percent	18.1	19.9	18.1	..	..
6.11	Inbound tourism expenditure over current account credits		Percent	14.3	15.9	14.7	..	..
6.12	Outbound tourism expenditure over imports of goods		Percent	7.3	5.2	5.8	..	..
6.13	Outbound tourism expenditure over imports of services		Percent	13.8	10.9	12.1	..	..
6.14	Outbound tourism expenditure over imports of goods and		Percent	4.8	3.5	3.9	..	..
6.15	Outbound tourism expenditure over current account debits		Percent	4.6	3.4	3.8	..	..

MALAWI

Cod.	Basic data and indicators	Notes	Units	2011	2012	2013	2014	2015
1.	**INBOUND TOURISM**							
	Data							
	Arrivals							
1.1	Total		('000)	..	..	..	..	..
1.2	♦ Overnight visitors (tourists)	(1)	('000)	767	770	795	819	805
1.3	♦ Same-day visitors (excursionists)		('000)	..	..	..	..	..
1.4	* of which, cruise passengers		('000)	..	..	..	..	..
	Arrivals by region	(1)						
1.5	Total		('000)	766	770	795	819	805
1.6	♦ Africa		('000)	588	631	642	637	636
1.7	♦ Americas		('000)	45	28	50	48	48
1.8	♦ East Asia and the Pacific		('000)	10	7	19	8	9
1.9	♦ Europe		('000)	102	92	72	107	97
1.10	♦ Middle East		('000)	3	2	..	1	1
1.11	♦ South Asia		('000)	16	4	..	10	6
1.12	♦ Other not classified		('000)	2	5	13	8	8
1.13	* of which, nationals residing abroad		('000)	..	..	..	..	..
	Arrivals by main purpose	(1)						
1.14	Total		('000)	767	770	795	819	805
1.15	♦ Personal		('000)	307	284	320	240	216
1.16	* holidays, leisure and recreation		('000)	206	203	253	165	146
1.17	* other personal purposes		('000)	101	81	68	75	70
1.18	♦ Business and professional		('000)	460	487	475	579	589
	Arrivals by mode of transport	(1)						
1.19	Total		('000)	767	770	795	819	805
1.20	♦ Air		('000)	227	199	220	230	221
1.21	♦ Water		('000)	4	3	9	5	2
1.22	♦ Land		('000)	536	569	566	584	582
1.23	* railway		('000)	8	5	7	9	9
1.24	* road		('000)	528	564	559	575	574
1.25	* others		('000)	..	..	..	..	..
	Arrivals by form of organization of the trip							
1.26	Total		('000)	767	770	..	..	..
1.27	♦ Package tour		('000)	80	139	..	..	..
1.28	♦ Other forms		('000)	687	631	..	..	..
	Accommodation							
	Total							
1.29	♦ Guests		('000)	767	770	795	819	805
1.30	♦ Overnights		('000)	5,821	6,702	..	8,274	7,244
	Hotels and similar establishments							
1.31	♦ Guests		('000)	496	491	..	511	516
1.32	♦ Overnights		('000)	3,966	4,269	..	5,164	4,640
	Expenditure							
1.33	Total		US$ Mn	36	35	33	36	39
1.34	♦ Travel		US$ Mn	31	31	29	32	35
1.35	♦ Passenger transport		US$ Mn	5	4	4	4	4
	Expenditure by main purpose of the trip							
1.36	Total		US$ Mn	31	31	29	32	35
1.37	♦ Personal		US$ Mn	13	13	12	13	14
1.38	♦ Business and professional		US$ Mn	18	18	17	19	21
	Indicators							
1.39	Average size of travel party		Persons	..	..	..	..	..
	Average length of stay							
1.40	Total		Days	8.00	8.70	..	10.10	8.80
1.41	♦ For all commercial accommodation services		Nights	7.60	8.75	..	..	..
1.42	* of which, "hotels and similar establishments"		Nights	..	..	..	..	..
1.43	♦ For non commercial accommodation services		Days	11.00	8.77	..	..	..
1.44	Average expenditure per day		US$	78.1	28.0	..	..	..
3.	**OUTBOUND TOURISM**							
	Data							
	Expenditure							
3.4	Total		US$ Mn	92	96	90	106	120
3.5	♦ Travel		US$ Mn	61	65	62	74	86
3.6	♦ Passenger transport		US$ Mn	31	31	28	32	34
	Expenditure by main purpose of the trip							
3.7	Total		US$ Mn	61	65	61	74	86
3.8	♦ Personal		US$ Mn	23	27	26	34	43
3.9	♦ Business and professional		US$ Mn	38	38	35	40	43

MALAWI

Cod.	Basic data and indicators	Notes	Units	2011	2012	2013	2014	2015
4.	**TOURISM INDUSTRIES**							
	Indicators							
4.16	Occupancy rate / rooms		Percent	51.70	54.00	..	..	..
4.17	Occupancy rate / bed-places		Percent	42.30	44.80	..	..	..
4.18	Average length of stay		Nights	8.00	8.70	..	10.10	8.80
4.19	Available capacity (bed-places per 1000 inhabitants)		Units	..	..	..	..	
6.	**COMPLEMENTARY INDICATORS**							
	Demand							
6.1	Gross travel propensity		Units	..	..	..	..	
6.2	(1.2 inbound tourists) / population		Units	0.05	0.05	0.05	0.05	0.05
	Macroeconomic indicators related to international tourism							
6.3	Inbound tourism expenditure over GDP		Percent	0.5	0.6	0.6	0.6	..
6.4	Outbound tourism expenditure over GDP		Percent	1.3	1.7	1.7	1.8	..
6.5	Tourism balance (inbound minus outbound tourism expenditure) over GDP		Percent	-0.8	-1.1	-1.1	-1.2	..
6.6	Tourism openness (inbound plus outbound tourism expenditure) over GDP		Percent	1.8	2.3	2.3	2.4	..
6.7	Tourism coverage (inbound over outbound tourism expenditure)		Percent	39.1	36.5	36.7	34.0	32.5
6.8	Inbound tourism expenditure over exports of goods		Percent	2.4	2.7	2.5	2.4	..
6.9	Inbound tourism expenditure over exports of services		Percent	41.7	33.2	29.7	35.8	..
6.10	Inbound tourism expenditure over exports of goods and services		Percent	2.2	2.5	2.3	2.2	..
6.11	Inbound tourism expenditure over current account credits		Percent	1.7	1.9	1.6	1.6	..
6.12	Outbound tourism expenditure over imports of goods		Percent	3.5	4.1	3.3	3.9	..
6.13	Outbound tourism expenditure over imports of services		Percent	36.8	42.2	36.7	39.4	..
6.14	Outbound tourism expenditure over imports of goods and		Percent	3.2	3.8	3.0	3.5	..
6.15	Outbound tourism expenditure over current account debits		Percent	3.2	3.7	3.0	3.5	..

MALAYSIA

Cod.	Basic data and indicators	Notes	Units	2011	2012	2013	2014	2015
1.	**INBOUND TOURISM**							
	Data							
	Arrivals							
.1	Total		('000)	..	..	..	..	..
.2	♦ Overnight visitors (tourists)	(1)	('000)	24,714	25,033	25,715	27,437	25,721
.3	♦ Same-day visitors (excursionists)		('000)	..	..	..	..	..
.4	* of which, cruise passengers		('000)	..	..	..	..	..
	Arrivals by region	(1)						
.5	Total		('000)	24,714	25,033	25,715	27,437	25,721
.6	♦ Africa		('000)	111	99	101	108	96
.7	♦ Americas		('000)	340	362	377	400	360
.8	♦ East Asia and the Pacific		('000)	21,667	21,946	22,568	23,846	22,567
.9	♦ Europe		('000)	1,136	1,161	1,227	1,372	1,242
.10	♦ Middle East		('000)	237	266	274	313	279
.11	♦ South Asia		('000)	1,125	1,185	1,156	1,383	1,163
.12	♦ Other not classified		('000)	98	14	12	15	14
.13	* of which, nationals residing abroad		('000)	..	..	..	..	..
	Arrivals by mode of transport							
.19	Total		('000)	..	..	25,715	27,437	25,721
.20	♦ Air		('000)	..	..	7,096	7,789	7,450
.21	♦ Water		('000)	..	..	738	837	971
.22	♦ Land		('000)	..	..	17,882	18,812	17,299
.23	* railway		('000)	..	..	40	43	68
.24	* road		('000)	..	..	17,842	18,769	17,231
.25	* others		('000)	..	..	..	..	..
	Accommodation							
	Hotels and similar establishments							
.31	♦ Guests	(2)	('000)	26,019	26,171	22,860	26,284	25,571
.32	♦ Overnights		('000)	..	..	..	..	..
	Expenditure							
.33	Total		US$ Mn	..	..	..	..	..
.34	♦ Travel		US$ Mn	19,649	20,251	21,500	22,600	17,614
.35	♦ Passenger transport		US$ Mn	..	..	..	..	..
	Indicators							
.39	Average size of travel party		Persons	..	..	..	..	..
	Average length of stay							
.40	Total		Days	..	..	..	..	..
.41	♦ For all commercial accommodation services		Nights	7.00	7.00	6.80	6.60	5.50
.42	* of which, "hotels and similar establishments"		Nights	..	..	..	..	..
.43	♦ For non commercial accommodation services		Days	..	..	..	..	..
.44	Average expenditure per day		US$	..	..	..	..	..
2.	**DOMESTIC TOURISM**							
	Data							
	Trips	(3)						
.1	Total		('000)	162,835	174,448	193,274	217,452	235,191
.2	♦ Overnight visitors (tourists)		('000)	51,543	55,364	63,115	71,735	80,563
.3	♦ Same-day visitors (excursionists)		('000)	111,292	119,084	130,119	145,717	154,628
	Trips by main purpose	(3)						
.4	Total		('000)	162,835	174,448	193,274	217,452	235,191
.5	♦ Personal		('000)	158,927	170,014	188,829	213,103	228,371
.6	* holidays, leisure and recreation		('000)	22,797	21,283	27,252	36,967	30,575
.7	* other personal purposes		('000)	136,130	148,731	161,577	176,136	197,796
.8	♦ Business and professional		('000)	3,908	4,434	4,445	4,349	6,820
	Trips by mode of transport	(3)						
.9	Total		('000)	162,835	174,448	193,274	217,452	235,191
.10	♦ Air		('000)	1,954	2,000	2,512	4,395	3,763
.11	♦ Water		('000)	2,117	2,420	3,286	3,600	4,469
.12	♦ Land		('000)	158,764	170,028	187,476	209,457	226,959
.13	* railway		('000)	953	1,278	3,187	2,505	3,404
.14	* road		('000)	153,842	167,688	182,602	205,384	220,733
.15	* others		('000)	3,969	1,062	1,687	1,568	2,822
	Accommodation							
	Hotels and similar establishments							
.21	♦ Guests	(2)	('000)	27,737	29,901	34,270	45,377	45,941
.22	♦ Overnights		('000)	..	..	..	..	..

MALAYSIA

Cod.	Basic data and indicators	Notes	Units	2011	2012	2013	2014	2015
	Indicators							
2.23	Average size of travel party		Persons	..	..	..	..	..
	Average length of stay							
2.24	Total	(3)	Days	2.45	2.53	2.56	2.60	2.30
2.25	♦ For all commercial accommodation services		Nights	..	..	..	..	
2.26	* of which, "hotels and similar establishments"		Nights	..	..	..	..	
2.27	♦ For non commercial accommodation services		Days	..	..	..	..	
2.28	Average expenditure per day		US$	45.1	45.3	44.7	43.7	..
3.	**OUTBOUND TOURISM**							
	Data							
	Expenditure							
3.4	Total		US$ Mn	..	..	..	..	
3.5	♦ Travel		US$ Mn	10,180	12,217	12,236	12,442	10,589
3.6	♦ Passenger transport		US$ Mn	..	..	..	..	
4.	**TOURISM INDUSTRIES**							
	Data							
	Number of establishments							
4.1	Total		Units	..	..	..	..	
4.2	♦ Accommodation for visitors		Units	..	..	..	..	
4.3	* of which, "hotels and similar establishments"	(4)(5)	Units	2,707	2,724	3,094	4,072	4,799
4.4	♦ Food and beverage serving activities		Units	..	..	..	..	
4.5	♦ Passenger transportation		Units	..	..	..	..	
4.6	♦ Travel agencies and other reservation services activities		Units	..	..	..	..	
4.7	♦ Other tourism industries		Units	..	..	..	..	
	Accommodation for visitors in hotels and similar establishments							
	Non-monetary data							
4.13	♦ Number of establishments	(4)(5)	Units	2,707	2,724	3,094	4,072	4,799
4.14	♦ Number of rooms	(4)(5)	Units	193,340	195,445	209,527	262,021	304,721
4.15	♦ Number of bed-places		Units	..	..	..	..	
	Indicators							
4.16	Occupancy rate / rooms	(5)	Percent	60.60	62.40	62.60	63.60	61.90
4.17	Occupancy rate / bed-places		Percent	..	..	..	..	..
4.18	Average length of stay		Nights	..	..	..	..	
4.19	Available capacity (bed-places per 1000 inhabitants)		Units	..	..	..	..	
6.	**COMPLEMENTARY INDICATORS**							
	Demand							
6.1	Gross travel propensity		Units	..	..	..	..	
6.2	(1.2 inbound tourists + 2.2 domestic tourists) / population		Units	2.67	2.77	3.01	3.32	3.50
	Macroeconomic indicators related to international tourism							
6.3	Inbound tourism expenditure over GDP		Percent	6.6	6.4	6.6	6.7	6.0
6.4	Outbound tourism expenditure over GDP		Percent	3.4	3.9	3.8	3.7	3.6
6.5	Tourism balance (inbound minus outbound tourism expenditure) over GDP		Percent	3.2	2.5	2.8	3.0	2.4
6.6	Tourism openness (inbound plus outbound tourism expenditure) over GDP		Percent	10.0	10.3	10.4	10.4	9.6
6.7	Tourism coverage (inbound over outbound tourism expenditure)		Percent	193.0	165.8	175.7	181.6	166.3
6.8	Inbound tourism expenditure over exports of goods		Percent	9.1	9.7	10.6	10.9	10.0
6.9	Inbound tourism expenditure over exports of services		Percent	50.6	49.9	51.1	53.7	50.8
6.10	Inbound tourism expenditure over exports of goods and services		Percent	7.7	8.1	8.8	9.1	8.4
6.11	Inbound tourism expenditure over current account credits		Percent	7.2	7.6	8.2	8.4	7.8
6.12	Outbound tourism expenditure over imports of goods		Percent	6.0	7.1	7.1	7.2	7.2
6.13	Outbound tourism expenditure over imports of services		Percent	26.5	28.2	27.1	27.5	26.5
6.14	Outbound tourism expenditure over imports of goods and		Percent	4.9	5.7	5.6	5.7	5.6
6.15	Outbound tourism expenditure over current account debits		Percent	4.4	5.1	5.1	5.1	5.1

MALDIVES

Cod.	Basic data and indicators	Notes	Units	2011	2012	2013	2014	2015
I.	**INBOUND TOURISM**							
	Data							
	Arrivals							
.1	Total		('000)	..	..	..	..	..
.2	♦ Overnight visitors (tourists)		('000)	931	958	1,125	1,205	1,234
.3	♦ Same-day visitors (excursionists)		('000)	0.2	9	2	..	..
.4	* of which, cruise passengers		('000)	0.2	9	2	..	..
	Arrivals by region	(1)						
.5	Total		('000)	931	958	1,125	1,205	1,234
.6	♦ Africa		('000)	6	7	8	8	9
.7	♦ Americas		('000)	24	27	33	41	47
.8	♦ East Asia and the Pacific		('000)	303	339	468	522	522
.9	♦ Europe		('000)	538	518	527	529	536
.10	♦ Middle East		('000)	14	22	32	37	42
.11	♦ South Asia		('000)	46	45	57	67	78
.12	♦ Other not classified		('000)	..	..	..	..	..
.13	* of which, nationals residing abroad		('000)	..	..	..	..	..
	Arrivals by main purpose	(1)						
.14	Total		('000)	931	958	1,125	1,205	1,234
.15	♦ Personal		('000)	931	958	1,125	1,205	1,234
.16	* holidays, leisure and recreation		('000)	931	958	1,125	1,205	1,234
.17	* other personal purposes		('000)	..	..	..	..	..
.18	♦ Business and professional		('000)	..	..	..	..	..
	Arrivals by mode of transport							
.19	Total		('000)	931	958	1,125	1,205	1,234
.20	♦ Air		('000)	931	958	1,125	1,205	1,234
.21	♦ Water		('000)	..	..	..	..	..
.22	♦ Land		('000)	..	..	..	..	..
.23	* railway		('000)	..	..	..	..	..
.24	* road		('000)	..	..	..	..	..
.25	* others		('000)	..	..	..	..	..
	Accommodation							
	Hotels and similar establishments							
.31	♦ Guests		('000)	..	..	..	..	..
.32	♦ Overnights		('000)	6,529	6,451	7,058	7,290	6,976
	Expenditure							
.33	Total		US$ Mn	1,966	2,032	2,422	2,811	2,664
.34	♦ Travel		US$ Mn	1,940	1,958	2,335	2,696	2,567
.35	♦ Passenger transport		US$ Mn	26	74	87	115	97
II.	**OUTBOUND TOURISM**							
	Data							
	Expenditure							
.4	Total		US$ Mn	231	207	252	271	296
.5	♦ Travel		US$ Mn	184	164	204	208	238
.6	♦ Passenger transport		US$ Mn	47	43	48	63	58
	Expenditure by main purpose of the trip							
.7	Total		US$ Mn	184	164	205	208	239
.8	♦ Personal		US$ Mn	172	158	195	200	231
.9	♦ Business and professional		US$ Mn	12	6	10	8	8
III.	**TOURISM INDUSTRIES**							
	Data							
	Number of establishments							
.1	Total		Units	..	..	..	..	..
.2	♦ Accommodation for visitors		Units	..	..	..	..	..
.3	* of which, "hotels and similar establishments"		Units	315	353	429	511	616
.4	♦ Food and beverage serving activities		Units	..	..	..	..	..
.5	♦ Passenger transportation		Units	..	..	..	..	..
.6	♦ Travel agencies and other reservation services activities		Units	..	..	..	..	..
.7	♦ Other tourism industries		Units	..	..	..	..	..
	Accommodation for visitors in hotels and similar establishments							
	Non-monetary data							
.13	♦ Number of establishments		Units	315	353	429	511	616
.14	♦ Number of rooms		Units	13,448	14,060	15,066	15,837	17,052
.15	♦ Number of bed-places		Units	26,896	28,120	30,133	31,673	34,105

MALDIVES

Cod. Basic data and indicators	Notes	Units	2011	2012	2013	2014	2015
Indicators							
4.16 Occupancy rate / rooms		Percent	..	..	..	..	.
4.17 Occupancy rate / bed-places		Percent	73.10	70.60	74.00	74.50	69.00
4.18 Average length of stay	(2)	Nights	7.00	6.70	6.30	6.10	5.70
4.19 Available capacity (bed-places per 1000 inhabitants)		Units	79.43	81.55	85.82	88.62	93.78
6. COMPLEMENTARY INDICATORS							
Demand							
6.1 Gross travel propensity		Units	..	..	..	..	.
6.2 (1.2 inbound tourists) / population		Units	2.75	2.78	3.20	3.37	3.39
Macroeconomic indicators related to international tourism							
6.3 Inbound tourism expenditure over GDP		Percent	80.2	80.7	..	91.7	..
6.4 Outbound tourism expenditure over GDP		Percent	9.4	8.2	..	8.8	..
6.5 Tourism balance (inbound minus outbound tourism expenditure) over GDP		Percent	70.8	72.5	..	82.9	
6.6 Tourism openness (inbound plus outbound tourism expenditure) over GDP		Percent	89.6	88.9	..	100.5	
6.7 Tourism coverage (inbound over outbound tourism expenditure)		Percent	851.1	981.6	961.1	1,037.3	900.0
6.8 Inbound tourism expenditure over exports of goods		Percent	567.6	646.3	731.8	934.3	1,111.3
6.9 Inbound tourism expenditure over exports of services		Percent	93.4	93.3	93.4	93.2	91.8
6.10 Inbound tourism expenditure over exports of goods and services		Percent	80.2	81.5	82.9	84.8	84.8
6.11 Inbound tourism expenditure over current account credits		Percent	79.5	80.7	82.7	84.5	83.9
6.12 Outbound tourism expenditure over imports of goods		Percent	13.5	13.1	14.8	13.8	15.6
6.13 Outbound tourism expenditure over imports of services		Percent	39.8	36.3	36.2	34.2	35.7
6.14 Outbound tourism expenditure over imports of goods and		Percent	10.1	9.6	10.5	9.8	10.9
6.15 Outbound tourism expenditure over current account debits		Percent	9.0	8.5	9.4	8.8	9.5

MALI

Cod.	Basic data and indicators	Notes	Units	2011	2012	2013	2014	2015
1.	**INBOUND TOURISM**							
	Data							
	Arrivals							
.1	Total		('000)	..	..	..	..	..
.2	♦ Overnight visitors (tourists)		('000)	160	134	142	168	159
.3	♦ Same-day visitors (excursionists)		('000)	..	..	..	..	..
.4	* of which, cruise passengers		('000)	..	..	..	..	..
	Arrivals by region	(1)						
.5	Total		('000)	160	101	121	152	159
.6	♦ Africa		('000)	52	41	53	62	74
.7	♦ Americas		('000)	21	6	6	8	9
.8	♦ East Asia and the Pacific		('000)	3	5	4	5	5
.9	♦ Europe		('000)	69	45	55	71	67
.10	♦ Middle East		('000)	4	2	1	2	3
.11	♦ South Asia		('000)	..	2	2	3	2
.12	♦ Other not classified		('000)	11	..	..	..	..
.13	* of which, nationals residing abroad		('000)	..	..	..	..	..
	Arrivals by main purpose							
.14	Total		('000)	160	134	142	168	159
.15	♦ Personal		('000)	90	92	93	119	114
.16	* holidays, leisure and recreation		('000)	27	52	35	36	29
.17	* other personal purposes		('000)	63	40	58	83	86
.18	♦ Business and professional		('000)	70	42	49	50	45
	Arrivals by mode of transport							
.19	Total		('000)	160	134	142	168	159
.20	♦ Air	(2)	('000)	130	101	121	152	159
.21	♦ Water		('000)	..	..	..	..	..
.22	♦ Land		('000)	30	33	21	16	0.1
.23	* railway		('000)	..	..	..	..	..
.24	* road	(3)	('000)	30	33	21	16	0.1
.25	* others		('000)	..	..	..	..	..
	Accommodation							
	Hotels and similar establishments							
.31	♦ Guests		('000)	..	32	57	53	15
.32	♦ Overnights		('000)	284	61	103	72	33
	Expenditure							
.33	Total		US$ Mn	218	144	178	214	..
.34	♦ Travel		US$ Mn	210	142	178	212	..
.35	♦ Passenger transport		US$ Mn	8	2	0.2	2	..
	Expenditure by main purpose of the trip							
.36	Total		US$ Mn	210	142	178	212	..
.37	♦ Personal		US$ Mn	100	58	86	100	..
.38	♦ Business and professional		US$ Mn	110	84	93	112	..
	Indicators							
.39	Average size of travel party		Persons	..	..	..	..	..
	Average length of stay							
.40	Total		Days	..	..	..	..	..
.41	♦ For all commercial accommodation services		Nights	2.10	0.80	..	..	..
.42	* of which, "hotels and similar establishments"		Nights	..	..	..	..	..
.43	♦ For non commercial accommodation services		Days	..	..	..	..	..
.44	Average expenditure per day		US$	..	..	..	..	101.4
2.	**DOMESTIC TOURISM**							
	Data							
	Trips							
2.1	Total		('000)	..	..	..	..	..
2.2	♦ Overnight visitors (tourists)		('000)	38	30	34	23	21
2.3	♦ Same-day visitors (excursionists)		('000)	..	..	..	..	..
	Trips by mode of transport							
2.9	Total		('000)	38	..	..	..	..
2.10	♦ Air		('000)	..	..	..	..	..
2.11	♦ Water		('000)	..	..	..	..	..
2.12	♦ Land		('000)	38	..	..	..	..
2.13	* railway		('000)	3	..	..	..	..
2.14	* road		('000)	35	..	..	..	..
2.15	* others		('000)	..	..	..	..	..
	Accommodation							
	Hotels and similar establishments							
2.21	♦ Guests		('000)	38	30	34	23	31
2.22	♦ Overnights		('000)	80	42	62	38	30

MALI

Cod.	Basic data and indicators	Notes	Units	2011	2012	2013	2014	201
	Indicators							
2.23	Average size of travel party		Persons	..	..	..	..	
	Average length of stay							
2.24	Total		Days	..	..	..	..	
2.25	♦ For all commercial accommodation services		Nights	2.10	..	..	..	
2.26	* of which, "hotels and similar establishments"		Nights	..	..	..	..	
2.27	♦ For non commercial accommodation services		Days	..	..	..	..	
2.28	Average expenditure per day		US$	..	..	..	..	59.

3. OUTBOUND TOURISM

Data

Expenditure

Cod.	Basic data and indicators	Notes	Units	2011	2012	2013	2014	201
3.4	Total		US$ Mn	171	164	189	231	
3.5	♦ Travel		US$ Mn	119	102	118	144	
3.6	♦ Passenger transport		US$ Mn	52	62	71	87	
	Expenditure by main purpose of the trip							
3.7	Total		US$ Mn	119	102	118	144	
3.8	♦ Personal		US$ Mn	47	33	47	64	
3.9	♦ Business and professional		US$ Mn	72	69	71	80	

4. TOURISM INDUSTRIES

Data

Number of establishments

Cod.	Basic data and indicators	Notes	Units	2011	2012	2013	2014	201
4.1	Total		Units	950	974	997	1,069	1,23
4.2	♦ Accommodation for visitors		Units	..	..	..	..	
4.3	* of which, "hotels and similar establishments"		Units	644	675	659	707	72
4.4	♦ Food and beverage serving activities		Units	70	41	52	43	14
4.5	♦ Passenger transportation		Units	..	..	..	..	
4.6	♦ Travel agencies and other reservation services activities		Units	236	258	286	319	36
4.7	♦ Other tourism industries		Units	..	..	..	..	

Accommodation for visitors in hotels and similar establishments

Non-monetary data

Cod.	Basic data and indicators	Notes	Units	2011	2012	2013	2014	201
4.13	♦ Number of establishments		Units	644	675	659	707	72
4.14	♦ Number of rooms		Units	9,504	9,905	9,543	10,214	10,77
4.15	♦ Number of bed-places		Units	11,892	12,319	12,666	14,119	14,81
	Indicators							
4.16	Occupancy rate / rooms		Percent	10.00	2.27	..	..	
4.17	Occupancy rate / bed-places		Percent	8.00	1.83	..	..	
4.18	Average length of stay		Nights	2.10	0.60	..	..	
4.19	Available capacity (bed-places per 1000 inhabitants)		Units	0.76	0.76	0.76	0.83	0.8

5. EMPLOYMENT

Data

Number of employees by tourism industries

Cod.	Basic data and indicators	Notes	Units	2011	2012	2013	2014	201
5.1	Total		('000)	..	28.8	31.1	31.6	
5.2	♦ Accommodation services for visitors (hotels and similar establishments)		('000)	..	8.6	8.9	10.5	13.
5.3	♦ Other accommodation services		('000)	..	..	..	..	
5.4	♦ Food and beverage serving activities		('000)	..	..	..	..	
5.5	♦ Passenger transportation		('000)	..	..	..	..	
5.6	♦ Travel agencies and other reservation services activities		('000)	..	..	..	..	
5.7	♦ Other tourism industries		('000)	..	20.2	22.2	21.1	
	Number of jobs by status in employment							
5.8	Total		('000)	26.4	28.8	31.1	31.6	
5.9	♦ Employees		('000)	26.4	28.8	31.1	31.6	
5.10	♦ Self employed		('000)	..	..	..	..	

6. COMPLEMENTARY INDICATORS

Demand

Cod.	Basic data and indicators	Notes	Units	2011	2012	2013	2014	201
6.1	Gross travel propensity		Units	..	..	..	..	
6.2	(1.2 inbound tourists + 2.2 domestic tourists) / population		Units	0.01	0.01	0.01	0.01	0.01

MALI

Cod.	Basic data and indicators	Notes	Units	2011	2012	2013	2014	2015
	Macroeconomic indicators related to international tourism							
6.3	Inbound tourism expenditure over GDP		Percent	2.0	1.4	1.6	1.8	..
6.4	Outbound tourism expenditure over GDP		Percent	1.6	1.6	1.7	1.9	..
6.5	Tourism balance (inbound minus outbound tourism expenditure) over GDP		Percent	0.4	-0.2	-0.1	-0.1	..
6.6	Tourism openness (inbound plus outbound tourism expenditure) over GDP		Percent	3.6	3.0	3.3	3.7	..
6.7	Tourism coverage (inbound over outbound tourism expenditure)		Percent	127.5	87.8	94.3	92.6	..
6.8	Inbound tourism expenditure over exports of goods		Percent	9.1	4.8	6.2	..	..
6.9	Inbound tourism expenditure over exports of services		Percent	53.1	41.7	41.6	..	..
6.10	Inbound tourism expenditure over exports of goods and services		Percent	7.8	4.3	5.4	..	..
6.11	Inbound tourism expenditure over current account credits		Percent	5.7	3.3	3.2	..	..
6.12	Outbound tourism expenditure over imports of goods		Percent	6.3	5.7	6.1	..	..
6.13	Outbound tourism expenditure over imports of services		Percent	15.2	15.4	8.8	..	..
6.14	Outbound tourism expenditure over imports of goods and		Percent	4.4	4.1	3.6	..	..
6.15	Outbound tourism expenditure over current account debits		Percent	4.2	4.0	3.4	..	..

MALTA

Cod.	Basic data and indicators	Notes	Units	2011	2012	2013	2014	2015
1.	**INBOUND TOURISM**	(1)						
	Data							
	Arrivals							
1.1	Total		('000)	1,916	2,007	2,013	2,162	2,391
1.2	♦ Overnight visitors (tourists)		('000)	1,415	1,443	1,582	1,690	1,791
1.3	♦ Same-day visitors (excursionists)		('000)	501	563	431	472	600
1.4	* of which, cruise passengers		('000)	501	563	431	472	600
	Arrivals by region							
1.5	Total		('000)	1,415	1,443	1,582	1,690	1,791
1.6	♦ Africa		('000)	..	..	..	..	..
1.7	♦ Americas		('000)	16	18	20	22	26
1.8	♦ East Asia and the Pacific		('000)	..	..	..	..	..
1.9	♦ Europe		('000)	1,304	1,325	1,432	1,527	1,630
1.10	♦ Middle East		('000)	6	17	35	31	7
1.11	♦ South Asia		('000)	..	..	..	..	..
1.12	♦ Other not classified		('000)	88	83	96	110	129
1.13	* of which, nationals residing abroad		('000)	..	..	..	..	..
	Arrivals by main purpose							
1.14	Total		('000)	1,415	1,443	1,582	1,690	1,791
1.15	♦ Personal		('000)	1,297	1,328	1,464	1,560	1,664
1.16	* holidays, leisure and recreation		('000)	1,087	1,120	1,222	1,300	1,349
1.17	* other personal purposes		('000)	210	208	242	260	314
1.18	♦ Business and professional		('000)	118	115	118	130	128
	Arrivals by mode of transport							
1.19	Total		('000)	1,415	1,443	1,582	1,690	1,791
1.20	♦ Air		('000)	1,375	1,401	1,539	1,641	1,738
1.21	♦ Water		('000)	40	42	43	49	54
1.22	♦ Land		('000)	..	..	..	..	..
1.23	* railway		('000)	..	..	..	..	..
1.24	* road		('000)	..	..	..	..	..
1.25	* others		('000)	..	..	..	..	..
	Arrivals by form of organization of the trip							
1.26	Total		('000)	1,415	1,444	1,582	1,690	1,791
1.27	♦ Package tour		('000)	671	683	737	776	784
1.28	♦ Other forms		('000)	744	761	845	914	1,008
	Accommodation							
	Total							
1.29	♦ Guests		('000)	1,415	1,443	1,582	1,690	1,791
1.30	♦ Overnights		('000)	11,241	11,860	12,890	13,522	14,217
	Hotels and similar establishments							
1.31	♦ Guests		('000)	1,094	1,099	1,190	1,262	1,285
1.32	♦ Overnights		('000)	7,830	8,049	8,627	8,867	8,827
	Expenditure							
1.33	Total		US$ Mn	..	..	..	..	..
1.34	♦ Travel		US$ Mn	1,276	1,260	1,402	1,521	1,367
1.35	♦ Passenger transport		US$ Mn	..	..	..	..	..
	Indicators							
1.39	Average size of travel party		Persons	2.2	2.2	2.3	2.5	2.3
	Average length of stay							
1.40	Total		Days	..	..	..	..	..
1.41	♦ For all commercial accommodation services		Nights	..	..	..	..	..
1.42	* of which, "hotels and similar establishments"		Nights	7.20	7.30	7.30	7.00	6.90
1.43	♦ For non commercial accommodation services		Days	..	..	..	..	..
1.44	Average expenditure per day		US$	..	..	..	..	..
2.	**DOMESTIC TOURISM**							
	Data							
	Trips							
2.1	Total		('000)	..	..	..	..	
2.2	♦ Overnight visitors (tourists)	(2)	('000)	..	205	190	158	
2.3	♦ Same-day visitors (excursionists)		('000)	..	..	..	..	
	Accommodation							
	Hotels and similar establishments							
2.21	♦ Guests		('000)	144	154	149	156	157
2.22	♦ Overnights		('000)	319	332	329	354	373

MALTA

Cod.	Basic data and indicators	Notes	Units	2011	2012	2013	2014	2015
3.	**OUTBOUND TOURISM**							
	Data							
	Departures							
3.1	Total		('000)	348	368	404	430	456
3.2	♦ Overnight visitors (tourists)		('000)	309	331	363	391	428
3.3	♦ Same-day visitors (excursionists)		('000)	39	37	41	39	48
	Expenditure							
3.4	Total		US$ Mn	..	..	..	..	..
3.5	♦ Travel		US$ Mn	333	339	384	397	359
3.6	♦ Passenger transport		US$ Mn	..	..	..	..	..
	Indicators							
3.10	Average length of stay		Days	7.50	7.70	7.90	8.10	7.60
3.11	Average expenditure per day		US$	..	..	..	..	..
4.	**TOURISM INDUSTRIES**							
	Data							
	Number of establishments							
4.1	Total		Units	..	..	..	..	..
4.2	♦ Accommodation for visitors		Units	..	..	..	..	..
4.3	* of which, "hotels and similar establishments"	(3)	Units	191	193	196	197	203
4.4	♦ Food and beverage serving activities		Units	..	..	..	..	..
4.5	♦ Passenger transportation		Units	..	..	..	..	..
4.6	♦ Travel agencies and other reservation services activities		Units	..	..	..	..	..
4.7	♦ Other tourism industries		Units	..	..	..	..	..
	Accommodation for visitors in hotels and similar establishments							
	Non-monetary data							
4.13	♦ Number of establishments	(3)	Units	191	193	196	197	203
4.14	♦ Number of rooms	(2)	Units	17,723	17,791	18,420	17,875	18,412
4.15	♦ Number of bed-places	(3)	Units	38,286	37,946	37,814	38,779	39,204
	Indicators							
4.16	Occupancy rate / rooms		Percent	..	..	..	..	..
4.17	Occupancy rate / bed-places		Percent	56.03	58.11	62.50	62.60	63.50
4.18	Average length of stay	(1)	Nights	7.20	7.30	7.30	7.00	7.90
4.19	Available capacity (bed-places per 1000 inhabitants)		Units	92.46	91.31	90.74	92.83	93.64
6.	**COMPLEMENTARY INDICATORS**							
	Demand							
6.1	Gross travel propensity		Units	..	..	..	..	..
6.2	(1.2 inbound tourists + 2.2 domestic tourists) / population		Units	..	3.97	4.25	4.42	..
	Macroeconomic indicators related to international tourism							
6.3	Inbound tourism expenditure over GDP		Percent	13.3	13.6	14.0	14.4	14.1
6.4	Outbound tourism expenditure over GDP		Percent	3.5	3.7	3.8	3.8	3.7
6.5	Tourism balance (inbound minus outbound tourism expenditure) over GDP		Percent	9.8	9.9	10.2	10.6	10.4
6.6	Tourism openness (inbound plus outbound tourism expenditure) over GDP		Percent	16.8	17.3	17.8	18.2	17.8
6.7	Tourism coverage (inbound over outbound tourism expenditure)		Percent	383.2	371.7	365.1	383.1	380.8
6.8	Inbound tourism expenditure over exports of goods		Percent	32.3	30.6	36.7	43.7	45.7
6.9	Inbound tourism expenditure over exports of services		Percent	11.3	11.3	11.6	12.2	12.7
6.10	Inbound tourism expenditure over exports of goods and services		Percent	8.3	8.3	8.8	9.5	9.9
6.11	Inbound tourism expenditure over current account credits		Percent	4.2	4.3	4.6	4.9	5.2
6.12	Outbound tourism expenditure over imports of goods		Percent	5.9	6.1	7.3	8.0	7.3
6.13	Outbound tourism expenditure over imports of services		Percent	3.6	3.7	3.9	3.9	4.2
6.14	Outbound tourism expenditure over imports of goods and		Percent	2.2	2.3	2.5	2.6	2.7
6.15	Outbound tourism expenditure over current account debits		Percent	1.1	1.2	1.3	1.3	1.4

MARSHALL ISLANDS

Cod.	Basic data and indicators	Notes	Units	2011	2012	2013	2014	2015
1.	**INBOUND TOURISM**							
	Data							
	Arrivals							
1.1	Total		('000)	..	..	..	..	..
1.2	♦ Overnight visitors (tourists)	(1)	('000)	4.6	4.6	..	4.9	6.3
1.3	♦ Same-day visitors (excursionists)		('000)	..	..	..	..	..
1.4	* of which, cruise passengers		('000)	..	..	..	..	..
	Arrivals by region	(1)						
1.5	Total		('000)	4.6	4.6	..	4.9	6.3
1.6	♦ Africa		('000)	..	..	..	..	..
1.7	♦ Americas		('000)	1.3	1.1	..	1.1	1.8
1.8	♦ East Asia and the Pacific		('000)	2.9	3.2	..	3.4	4.0
1.9	♦ Europe		('000)	0.1	0.1	..	0.2	0.3
1.10	♦ Middle East		('000)	..	..	..	..	..
1.11	♦ South Asia		('000)	..	..	..	..	..
1.12	♦ Other not classified		('000)	0.3	0.2	..	0.2	0.2
1.13	* of which, nationals residing abroad		('000)	..	..	..	..	..
	Arrivals by main purpose	(1)						
1.14	Total		('000)	4.6	..	..	4.9	6.3
1.15	♦ Personal		('000)	2.5	..	..	3.6	4.0
1.16	* holidays, leisure and recreation		('000)	1.1	..	..	2.0	1.9
1.17	* other personal purposes		('000)	1.4	..	..	1.6	2.1
1.18	♦ Business and professional		('000)	2.1	..	..	1.3	2.3
	Arrivals by mode of transport	(1)						
1.19	Total		('000)	4.6	4.6	..	4.9	6.3
1.20	♦ Air		('000)	4.6	4.6	..	4.9	6.3
1.21	♦ Water		('000)	..	..	..	..	..
1.22	♦ Land		('000)	..	..	..	..	..
1.23	* railway		('000)	..	..	..	..	..
1.24	* road		('000)	..	..	..	..	..
1.25	* others		('000)	..	..	..	..	..
	Accommodation							
	Total							
1.29	♦ Guests		('000)	..	..	..	..	..
1.30	♦ Overnights		('000)	35	..	..	..	..
	Expenditure							
1.33	Total		US$ Mn	4.8	4.1	4.3	5.4	..
1.34	♦ Travel		US$ Mn	4.5	3.9	4.1	5.2	..
1.35	♦ Passenger transport		US$ Mn	0.3	0.2	0.2	0.2	..
	Expenditure by main purpose of the trip							
1.36	Total		US$ Mn	4.5	3.9	4.1	5.3	..
1.37	♦ Personal		US$ Mn	2.2	2.0	1.0	2.5	..
1.38	♦ Business and professional		US$ Mn	2.3	1.9	3.1	2.8	..
	Indicators							
1.39	Average size of travel party		Persons	..	..	..	..	..
	Average length of stay							
1.40	Total		Days	..	..	..	..	..
1.41	♦ For all commercial accommodation services		Nights	4.94	..	..	..	..
1.42	* of which, "hotels and similar establishments"		Nights	..	..	..	..	..
1.43	♦ For non commercial accommodation services		Days	..	..	..	..	..
1.44	Average expenditure per day		US$	..	..	..	..	..
3.	**OUTBOUND TOURISM**							
	Data							
	Expenditure							
3.4	Total		US$ Mn	23.8	25.5	24.7	23.8	..
3.5	♦ Travel		US$ Mn	12.7	12.9	12.7	12.3	..
3.6	♦ Passenger transport		US$ Mn	11.1	12.6	12.0	11.5	..
	Expenditure by main purpose of the trip							
3.7	Total		US$ Mn	12.7	12.9	12.7	12.4	..
3.8	♦ Personal		US$ Mn	11.2	11.0	11.6	10.9	..
3.9	♦ Business and professional		US$ Mn	1.5	1.9	1.1	1.5	..

MARSHALL ISLANDS

Cod.	Basic data and indicators	Notes	Units	2011	2012	2013	2014	2015
6.	**COMPLEMENTARY INDICATORS**							
	Demand							
6.1	Gross travel propensity		Units	..	..	..	..	..
6.2	(1.2 inbound tourists) / population		Units	0.09	0.09	..	0.09	0.12
	Macroeconomic indicators related to international tourism							
6.3	Inbound tourism expenditure over GDP		Percent	..	..	..	..	..
6.4	Outbound tourism expenditure over GDP		Percent	..	..	..	..	..
6.5	Tourism balance (inbound minus outbound tourism expenditure) over GDP		Percent	..	..	..	..	..
6.6	Tourism openness (inbound plus outbound tourism expenditure) over GDP		Percent	..	..	..	..	..
6.7	Tourism coverage (inbound over outbound tourism expenditure)		Percent	20.1	16.0	17.4	22.7	..
6.8	Inbound tourism expenditure over exports of goods		Percent	7.2	3.8	4.2	7.1	..
6.9	Inbound tourism expenditure over exports of services		Percent	44.5	41.3	39.0	41.9	..
6.10	Inbound tourism expenditure over exports of goods and services		Percent	6.2	3.5	3.8	6.1	..
6.11	Inbound tourism expenditure over current account credits		Percent	2.4	1.7	1.8	2.4	..
6.12	Outbound tourism expenditure over imports of goods		Percent	20.1	20.3	18.2	19.6	..
6.13	Outbound tourism expenditure over imports of services		Percent	40.8	41.9	36.9	39.4	..
6.14	Outbound tourism expenditure over imports of goods and		Percent	13.4	13.7	12.2	13.1	..
6.15	Outbound tourism expenditure over current account debits		Percent	9.9	10.0	8.9	9.1	..

MARTINIQUE

Cod.	Basic data and indicators	Notes	Units	2011	2012	2013	2014	2015
1.	**INBOUND TOURISM**							
	Data							
	Arrivals							
1.1	Total		('000)	538	582	594	685	747
1.2	♦ Overnight visitors (tourists)		('000)	497	488	490	490	487
1.3	♦ Same-day visitors (excursionists)		('000)	41	94	104	195	260
1.4	* of which, cruise passengers		('000)	41	94	104	178	242
	Arrivals by region							
1.5	Total		('000)	497	488	490	490	..
1.6	♦ Africa		('000)	..	..	..	..	..
1.7	♦ Americas		('000)	86	78	68	75	..
1.8	♦ East Asia and the Pacific		('000)	..	..	..	..	..
1.9	♦ Europe		('000)	405	408	419	413	..
1.10	♦ Middle East		('000)	..	..	..	..	..
1.11	♦ South Asia		('000)	..	..	..	..	..
1.12	♦ Other not classified		('000)	6	2	3	2	..
1.13	* of which, nationals residing abroad		('000)	..	..	..	..	..
	Arrivals by main purpose							
1.14	Total		('000)	496	488	490	490	..
1.15	♦ Personal		('000)	456	432	451	433	..
1.16	* holidays, leisure and recreation		('000)	441	411	438	412	..
1.17	* other personal purposes		('000)	15	21	13	21	..
1.18	♦ Business and professional		('000)	40	56	39	56	..
	Arrivals by mode of transport							
1.19	Total		('000)	496	488	490	490	..
1.20	♦ Air		('000)	475	462	476	476	..
1.21	♦ Water		('000)	21	26	14	14	..
1.22	♦ Land		('000)	..	..	..	..	..
1.23	* railway		('000)	..	..	..	..	..
1.24	* road		('000)	..	..	..	..	..
1.25	* others		('000)	..	..	..	..	..
	Arrivals by form of organization of the trip							
1.26	Total		('000)	496	488	490	490	..
1.27	♦ Package tour		('000)	193	199	201	108	..
1.28	♦ Other forms		('000)	303	289	289	382	..
	Accommodation							
	Total							
1.29	♦ Guests		('000)	497	488	490	490	487
1.30	♦ Overnights		('000)	6,196	6,901	7,301	6,797	
	Hotels and similar establishments							
1.31	♦ Guests		('000)	193	177	159	143	
1.32	♦ Overnights		('000)	1,652	1,379	1,362	1,259	
	Expenditure							
1.33	Total	(1)	US$ Mn	516	462	484	483	340
1.34	♦ Travel		US$ Mn	..	..	..	..	..
1.35	♦ Passenger transport		US$ Mn	..	..	..	..	..
	Expenditure by main purpose of the trip							
1.36	Total		US$ Mn	..	..	466	464	..
1.37	♦ Personal		US$ Mn	..	..	447	420	..
1.38	♦ Business and professional		US$ Mn	..	..	19	44	..
	Indicators							
1.39	Average size of travel party		Persons	2.5	2.7	2.8	2.7	..
	Average length of stay							
1.40	Total		Days	12.50	14.00	13.80	13.90	..
1.41	♦ For all commercial accommodation services		Nights	..	..	12.20	12.20	..
1.42	* of which, "hotels and similar establishments"		Nights	8.52	7.68	8.60	8.80	..
1.43	♦ For non commercial accommodation services		Days	..	..	19.50	18.70	..
1.44	Average expenditure per day		US$	83.1	66.9	71.6	68.1	..
4.	**TOURISM INDUSTRIES**							
	Data							
	Number of establishments							
4.1	Total		Units	2,510	2,510	2,510	2,507	..
4.2	♦ Accommodation for visitors		Units	795	795	795	795	..
4.3	* of which, "hotels and similar establishments"		Units	151	151	148	148	..
4.4	♦ Food and beverage serving activities		Units	735	735	735	735	..
4.5	♦ Passenger transportation		Units	502	502	502	502	..
4.6	♦ Travel agencies and other reservation services activities		Units	28	28	28	25	..
4.7	♦ Other tourism industries		Units	450	450	450	450	..

MARTINIQUE

Cod.	Basic data and indicators	Notes	Units	2011	2012	2013	2014	2015
	Accommodation for visitors in hotels and similar establishments							
	Non-monetary data							
4.13	♦ Number of establishments		Units	151	151	148	148	..
4.14	♦ Number of rooms		Units	5,461	5,461	5,189	5,189	..
4.15	♦ Number of bed-places		Units	12,701	12,701	12,102	12,102	..
	Indicators							
4.16	Occupancy rate / rooms		Percent	57.25	56.20	59.10	..	..
4.17	Occupancy rate / bed-places		Percent	..	..	..	..	..
4.18	Average length of stay		Nights	8.52	8.68	8.60	8.80	..
4.19	Available capacity (bed-places per 1000 inhabitants)		Units	32.18	321.48	30.59	30.55	..
5.	**EMPLOYMENT**							
	Data							
	Number of employees by tourism industries							
5.1	Total		('000)	10.5	10.5	10.5	10.5	..
5.2	♦ Accommodation services for visitors (hotels and similar establishments)		('000)	1.6	1.6	1.6	1.6	..
5.3	♦ Other accommodation services		('000)	0.8	0.8	0.8	0.8	..
5.4	♦ Food and beverage serving activities		('000)	3.9	3.9	3.9	3.9	..
5.5	♦ Passenger transportation		('000)	1.4	1.4	1.4	1.4	..
5.6	♦ Travel agencies and other reservation services activities		('000)	0.2	0.2	0.2	0.2	..
5.7	♦ Other tourism industries		('000)	2.7	2.7	2.7	2.7	..
	Number of jobs by status in employment							
5.8	Total		('000)	10.5	10.5	10.5	10.5	..
5.9	♦ Employees		('000)	9.4	9.4	9.4	9.4	..
5.10	♦ Self employed		('000)	1.2	1.2	1.2	1.2	..
	Indicators							
	Number of full-time equivalent jobs by status in employment							
5.11	Total		('000)	10.5	10.5	10.5	10.5	..
5.12	♦ Employees		('000)	9.4	9.4	9.4	9.4	..
5.13	* male		('000)	4.7	4.7	4.7	4.7	..
5.14	* female		('000)	4.6	4.6	4.6	4.6	..
5.15	♦ Self employed		('000)	1.2	1.2	1.2	1.2	..
5.16	* male		('000)	0.6	0.6	0.6	0.6	..
5.17	* female		('000)	0.6	0.6	0.6	0.6	..
6.	**COMPLEMENTARY INDICATORS**							
	Demand							
6.1	Gross travel propensity		Units	0.9	0.9	0.9	..	..
6.2	(1.2 inbound tourists) / population		Units	1.26	12.35	1.24	1.24	1.23

MAURITIUS

Cod.	Basic data and indicators	Notes	Units	2011	2012	2013	2014	2015
1.	**INBOUND TOURISM**							
	Data							
	Arrivals							
1.1	Total		('000)	983	984	1,015	1,066	1,175
1.2	♦ Overnight visitors (tourists)		('000)	965	965	993	1,039	1,152
1.3	♦ Same-day visitors (excursionists)		('000)	18	19	22	27	23
1.4	* of which, cruise passengers		('000)	12	12	9	13	7
	Arrivals by region							
1.5	Total		('000)	965	965	993	1,039	1,152
1.6	♦ Africa		('000)	231	265	277	274	284
1.7	♦ Americas		('000)	14	16	15	17	18
1.8	♦ East Asia and the Pacific		('000)	46	55	79	99	126
1.9	♦ Europe		('000)	610	561	548	571	633
1.10	♦ Middle East		('000)	6	9	13	13	14
1.11	♦ South Asia		('000)	56	58	60	65	76
1.12	♦ Other not classified		('000)	2	1	1	1	1
1.13	* of which, nationals residing abroad		('000)	..	..	..	..	..
	Arrivals by main purpose							
1.14	Total		('000)	983	984	993	1,039	1,152
1.15	♦ Personal		('000)	942	941	950	994	1,104
1.16	* holidays, leisure and recreation		('000)	898	897	923	970	1,078
1.17	* other personal purposes		('000)	44	44	27	24	26
1.18	♦ Business and professional		('000)	41	43	43	45	48
	Arrivals by mode of transport							
1.19	Total		('000)	965	965	993	1,039	1,152
1.20	♦ Air		('000)	940	948	980	1,035	1,132
1.21	♦ Water		('000)	25	17	13	4	20
1.22	♦ Land		('000)	..	..	..	..	..
1.23	* railway		('000)	..	..	..	..	..
1.24	* road		('000)	..	..	..	..	..
1.25	* others		('000)	..	..	..	..	..
	Arrivals by form of organization of the trip	(1)						
1.26	Total		('000)	..	..	1,015	1,066	1,152
1.27	♦ Package tour		('000)	..	..	653	699	737
1.28	♦ Other forms		('000)	..	..	362	367	415
	Accommodation							
	Total							
1.29	♦ Guests		('000)	940	951	987	1,030	1,137
1.30	♦ Overnights		('000)	9,494	10,044	10,667	11,266	12,043
	Hotels and similar establishments							
1.31	♦ Guests	(1)	('000)	870	858	910	950	1,060
1.32	♦ Overnights	(1)	('000)	7,793	7,838	8,044	9,394	10,729
	Expenditure							
1.33	Total		US$ Mn	1,808	1,778	1,593	1,719	1,679
1.34	♦ Travel		US$ Mn	1,484	1,480	1,322	1,447	1,432
1.35	♦ Passenger transport		US$ Mn	324	298	271	272	247
	Expenditure by main purpose of the trip							
1.36	Total		US$ Mn	1,484	1,480	1,322	1,447	1,432
1.37	♦ Personal		US$ Mn	947	960	818	944	983
1.38	♦ Business and professional		US$ Mn	537	520	505	503	449
	Indicators							
1.39	Average size of travel party		Persons	..	..	2.2	2.2	2.2
	Average length of stay							
1.40	Total		Days	..	..	..	..	..
1.41	♦ For all commercial accommodation services	(2)	Nights	10.10	10.60	10.80	10.90	10.60
1.42	* of which, "hotels and similar establishments"		Nights	..	..	..	..	..
1.43	♦ For non commercial accommodation services		Days	..	..	..	..	..
1.44	Average expenditure per day		US$	..	..	..	..	..
3.	**OUTBOUND TOURISM**							
	Data							
	Departures							
3.1	Total		('000)	..	..	..	..	..
3.2	♦ Overnight visitors (tourists)		('000)	219	237	250	257	254
3.3	♦ Same-day visitors (excursionists)		('000)	..	..	..	..	..
	Expenditure							
3.4	Total		US$ Mn	427	394	458	503	622
3.5	♦ Travel		US$ Mn	400	366	438	481	553
3.6	♦ Passenger transport		US$ Mn	27	28	20	22	69

MAURITIUS

Cod.	Basic data and indicators	Notes	Units	2011	2012	2013	2014	2015
	Expenditure by main purpose of the trip							
3.7	Total		US$ Mn	400	366	438	481	553
3.8	♦ Personal		US$ Mn	373	344	402	435	509
3.9	♦ Business and professional		US$ Mn	27	22	36	46	45
4.	**TOURISM INDUSTRIES**							
	Data							
	Number of establishments							
4.1	Total		Units	..	..	..	..	..
4.2	♦ Accommodation for visitors		Units	..	..	..	..	..
4.3	* of which, "hotels and similar establishments"	(3)	Units	109	117	107	112	115
4.4	♦ Food and beverage serving activities		Units	..	..	..	..	..
4.5	♦ Passenger transportation		Units	..	..	..	..	..
4.6	♦ Travel agencies and other reservation services activities		Units	..	..	..	..	..
4.7	♦ Other tourism industries		Units	..	..	..	..	..
	Accommodation for visitors in hotels and similar establishments							
	Non-monetary data	(3)						
4.13	♦ Number of establishments		Units	109	117	107	112	115
4.14	♦ Number of rooms		Units	11,925	12,527	12,376	12,799	13,617
4.15	♦ Number of bed-places		Units	24,242	25,496	25,105	26,174	28,732
	Indicators							
4.16	Occupancy rate / rooms		Percent	65.00	62.00	63.00	65.00	70.00
4.17	Occupancy rate / bed-places		Percent	57.00	55.00	55.00	58.00	63.00
4.18	Average length of stay		Nights	..	..	..	..	..
4.19	Available capacity (bed-places per 1000 inhabitants)		Units	19.35	20.26	19.87	20.63	22.57
5.	**EMPLOYMENT**							
	Data							
	Number of employees by tourism industries	(4)						
5.1	Total		('000)	28.2	28.4	28.5	28.8	29.1
5.2	♦ Accommodation services for visitors (hotels and similar establishments)		('000)	21.8	22.2	22.3	22.5	22.7
5.3	♦ Other accommodation services		('000)	..	..	..	..	..
5.4	♦ Food and beverage serving activities		('000)	2.3	2.3	2.4	2.5	2.7
5.5	♦ Passenger transportation		('000)	..	..	..	..	..
5.6	♦ Travel agencies and other reservation services activities		('000)	4.1	3.9	3.8	3.7	3.7
5.7	♦ Other tourism industries		('000)	..	..	..	..	..
6.	**COMPLEMENTARY INDICATORS**							
	Demand							
6.1	Gross travel propensity		Units	..	..	..	..	..
6.2	(1.2 inbound tourists) / population		Units	0.77	0.77	0.79	0.82	0.90
	Macroeconomic indicators related to international tourism							
6.3	Inbound tourism expenditure over GDP		Percent	16.1	15.5	13.4	13.6	14.6
6.4	Outbound tourism expenditure over GDP		Percent	3.8	3.4	3.8	4.0	5.4
6.5	Tourism balance (inbound minus outbound tourism expenditure) over GDP		Percent	12.3	12.1	9.6	9.6	9.2
6.6	Tourism openness (inbound plus outbound tourism expenditure) over GDP		Percent	19.9	18.9	17.2	17.6	20.0
6.7	Tourism coverage (inbound over outbound tourism expenditure)		Percent	423.4	451.3	347.8	341.7	269.9
6.8	Inbound tourism expenditure over exports of goods		Percent	70.5	67.1	55.5	55.6	62.5
6.9	Inbound tourism expenditure over exports of services		Percent	55.4	52.2	57.4	53.9	59.1
6.10	Inbound tourism expenditure over exports of goods and services		Percent	31.0	29.4	28.2	27.4	30.4
6.11	Inbound tourism expenditure over current account credits		Percent	24.5	21.1	12.7	12.8	13.9
6.12	Outbound tourism expenditure over imports of goods		Percent	8.7	7.7	8.9	9.4	13.7
6.13	Outbound tourism expenditure over imports of services		Percent	17.3	16.1	20.7	20.1	27.7
6.14	Outbound tourism expenditure over imports of goods and		Percent	5.8	5.2	6.2	6.4	9.2
6.15	Outbound tourism expenditure over current account debits		Percent	4.8	4.0	3.2	3.3	4.6

MEXICO

Cod.	Basic data and indicators	Notes	Units	2011	2012	2013	2014	2015
1.	**INBOUND TOURISM**							
	Data							
	Arrivals							
1.1	Total		('000)	75,732	76,749	78,100	81,042	87,129
1.2	♦ Overnight visitors (tourists)	(1)	('000)	23,403	23,403	24,151	29,346	32,093
1.3	♦ Same-day visitors (excursionists)	(2)	('000)	52,329	53,346	53,950	51,696	55,035
1.4	* of which, cruise passengers		('000)	5,289	5,199	4,555	5,785	6,115
	Arrivals by region	(1)						
1.5	Total		('000)	23,403	23,403	24,151	29,346	32,093
1.6	♦ Africa	(3)	('000)	15	13	15	20	25
1.7	♦ Americas	(4)	('000)	21,152	21,419	22,062	27,003	29,671
1.8	♦ East Asia and the Pacific	(3)	('000)	112	97	115	134	154
1.9	♦ Europe	(3)	('000)	1,510	1,439	1,525	1,617	1,660
1.10	♦ Middle East		('000)	..	..	..	..	..
1.11	♦ South Asia		('000)	..	..	..	..	..
1.12	♦ Other not classified		('000)	614	435	435	572	584
1.13	* of which, nationals residing abroad		('000)	..	..	..	..	..
	Arrivals by main purpose	(1)						
1.14	Total		('000)	23,403	23,403	24,151	29,346	32,093
1.15	♦ Personal		('000)	22,568	22,472	23,087	28,092	30,702
1.16	* holidays, leisure and recreation		('000)	7,888	7,356	8,299	9,554	11,515
1.17	* other personal purposes	(4)	('000)	14,680	15,116	14,788	18,538	19,188
1.18	♦ Business and professional		('000)	835	931	1,064	1,254	1,391
	Arrivals by mode of transport	(1)						
1.19	Total		('000)	23,403	23,403	24,151	29,346	32,093
1.20	♦ Air		('000)	10,844	11,361	12,221	13,463	15,248
1.21	♦ Water		('000)	..	..	..	..	..
1.22	♦ Land		('000)	12,559	12,042	11,929	15,883	16,845
1.23	* railway		('000)	..	..	..	..	..
1.24	* road	(5)	('000)	12,559	12,042	11,929	15,883	16,845
1.25	* others		('000)	..	..	..	..	..
	Accommodation							
	Hotels and similar establishments							
1.31	♦ Guests	(6)	('000)	12,655	13,552	14,413	15,889	16,700
1.32	♦ Overnights	(7)	('000)	49,064	52,936	58,221	61,075	65,729
	Expenditure							
1.33	Total		US$ Mn	12,458	13,320	14,311	16,607	18,451
1.34	♦ Travel		US$ Mn	11,869	12,739	13,949	16,208	17,457
1.35	♦ Passenger transport		US$ Mn	589	581	362	399	994
	Expenditure by main purpose of the trip							
1.36	Total		US$ Mn	11,869	12,739	13,949	16,208	17,457
1.37	♦ Personal		US$ Mn	10,997	11,812	12,842	14,916	16,082
1.38	♦ Business and professional		US$ Mn	872	927	1,107	1,292	1,375
	Indicators							
1.39	Average size of travel party		Persons	..	..	..	..	..
	Average length of stay							
1.40	Total		Days	..	..	..	..	..
1.41	♦ For all commercial accommodation services	(8)	Nights	10.33	10.42	10.58	10.55	10.26
1.42	* of which, "hotels and similar establishments"		Nights	..	..	..	..	..
1.43	♦ For non commercial accommodation services		Days	..	..	..	..	..
1.44	Average expenditure per day		US$	..	..	..	..	..
2.	**DOMESTIC TOURISM**							
	Data							
	Accommodation							
	Hotels and similar establishments	(6)(7)						
2.21	♦ Guests		('000)	46,582	50,776	52,745	54,161	57,361
2.22	♦ Overnights		('000)	84,296	93,531	94,163	94,279	101,270
3.	**OUTBOUND TOURISM**							
	Data							
	Departures							
3.1	Total		('000)	88,113	87,332	90,787	90,982	94,988
3.2	♦ Overnight visitors (tourists)		('000)	14,799	15,581	15,911	18,261	19,603
3.3	♦ Same-day visitors (excursionists)		('000)	73,314	71,913	74,876	72,721	75,385

MEXICO

Cod.	Basic data and indicators	Notes	Units	2011	2012	2013	2014	2015
	Expenditure							
.4	Total		US$ Mn	9,704	10,735	11,970	12,556	12,669
.5	♦ Travel		US$ Mn	7,832	8,449	9,122	9,606	10,100
.6	♦ Passenger transport		US$ Mn	1,872	2,286	2,848	2,950	2,569
	Expenditure by main purpose of the trip							
.7	Total		US$ Mn	7,832	8,449	9,122	9,606	10,100
.8	♦ Personal		US$ Mn	6,484	7,077	7,553	8,060	8,433
.9	♦ Business and professional		US$ Mn	1,348	1,372	1,570	1,546	1,667
4.	**TOURISM INDUSTRIES**							
	Data							
	Number of establishments							
4.1	Total		Units	63,508	65,881	64,803	79,228	99,984
4.2	♦ Accommodation for visitors		Units	..	..	..	..	..
4.3	* of which, "hotels and similar establishments"		Units	17,294	17,669	18,199	18,711	20,038
4.4	♦ Food and beverage serving activities		Units	37,658	39,302	37,784	50,244	70,144
4.5	♦ Passenger transportation		Units	..	..	..	..	..
4.6	♦ Travel agencies and other reservation services activities		Units	8,556	8,910	8,820	10,273	9,802
4.7	♦ Other tourism industries		Units	..	..	..	..	..
	Accommodation for visitors in hotels and similar establishments							
	Monetary data							
4.8	♦ Output		US$ Mn	10,852.4	11,218.0	12,538.6	13,091.6	..
4.9	♦ Intermediate consumption		US$ Mn	3,279.9	3,381.5	3,794.1	3,920.8	..
4.10	♦ Gross value added		US$ Mn	7,572.5	7,836.5	8,744.5	9,170.7	..
4.11	♦ Compensation of employees		US$ Mn	818.8	786.2	871.6	912.2	..
4.12	♦ Gross fixed capital formation		US$ Mn	..	..	..	..	..
	Non-monetary data							
4.13	♦ Number of establishments		Units	17,294	17,669	18,199	18,711	20,038
4.14	♦ Number of rooms		Units	651,160	660,546	672,296	692,351	736,512
4.15	♦ Number of bed-places		Units	1,302,320	1,321,092	1,344,592	1,384,702	1,473,024
	Indicators							
4.16	Occupancy rate / rooms		Percent	50.03	53.23	59.22	56.12	58.56
4.17	Occupancy rate / bed-places		Percent	..	..	..	..	..
4.18	Average length of stay	(9)	Nights	3.88	3.91	2.27	2.22	2.25
4.19	Available capacity (bed-places per 1000 inhabitants)		Units	10.82	10.82	10.87	11.04	11.60
	Travel agencies and other reservation service activities							
	Monetary data							
4.20	♦ Output		US$ Mn	1,326.6	1,408.3	1,565.3	1,633.4	..
4.21	♦ Intermediate consumption		US$ Mn	534.2	569.3	631.5	660.3	..
4.22	♦ Gross value added		US$ Mn	792.4	839.0	933.8	973.1	..
4.23	♦ Compensation of employees		US$ Mn	138.9	143.2	155.8	163.4	..
4.24	♦ Gross fixed capital formation		US$ Mn	..	..	..	..	..
5.	**EMPLOYMENT**							
	Data							
	Number of employees by tourism industries	(10)						
5.1	Total		('000)	2,215.4	2,265.9	2,298.5	2,300.6	..
5.2	♦ Accommodation services for visitors (hotels and similar establishments)		('000)	136.1	134.5	138.7	142.5	..
5.3	♦ Other accommodation services		('000)	13.3	13.7	13.5	14.4	..
5.4	♦ Food and beverage serving activities		('000)	778.0	814.2	839.4	828.0	..
5.5	♦ Passenger transportation		('000)	184.0	185.0	186.4	190.9	..
5.6	♦ Travel agencies and other reservation services activities		('000)	18.1	19.0	19.2	20.1	..
5.7	♦ Other tourism industries		('000)	1,085.9	1,099.5	1,101.3	1,104.7	..
6.	**COMPLEMENTARY INDICATORS**							
	Demand							
6.1	Gross travel propensity		Units	..	..	..	..	..
6.2	(1.2 inbound tourists) / population		Units	0.19	0.19	0.20	0.23	0.25

257

MEXICO

Cod.	Basic data and indicators	Notes	Units	2011	2012	2013	2014	2015
	Macroeconomic indicators related to international tourism							
6.3	Inbound tourism expenditure over GDP		Percent	1.1	1.1	1.1	1.3	1.6
6.4	Outbound tourism expenditure over GDP		Percent	0.8	0.9	1.0	1.0	1.1
6.5	Tourism balance (inbound minus outbound tourism expenditure) over GDP		Percent	0.3	0.2	0.1	0.3	0.5
6.6	Tourism openness (inbound plus outbound tourism expenditure) over GDP		Percent	1.9	2.0	2.1	2.3	2.7
6.7	Tourism coverage (inbound over outbound tourism expenditure)		Percent	128.4	124.1	119.6	132.3	145.6
6.8	Inbound tourism expenditure over exports of goods		Percent	3.6	3.6	3.8	4.2	4.8
6.9	Inbound tourism expenditure over exports of services		Percent	80.0	82.5	70.9	78.8	81.6
6.10	Inbound tourism expenditure over exports of goods and services		Percent	3.4	3.4	3.6	4.0	4.6
6.11	Inbound tourism expenditure over current account credits		Percent	3.1	3.1	3.3	3.7	4.2
6.12	Outbound tourism expenditure over imports of goods		Percent	2.8	2.9	3.1	3.1	3.2
6.13	Outbound tourism expenditure over imports of services		Percent	31.9	35.6	38.4	37.4	39.5
6.14	Outbound tourism expenditure over imports of goods and		Percent	2.5	2.7	2.9	2.9	3.0
6.15	Outbound tourism expenditure over current account debits		Percent	2.5	2.6	2.8	2.8	2.9

MICRONESIA, FEDERATED STATES OF

Cod.	Basic data and indicators	Notes	Units	2011	2012	2013	2014	2015
1.	**INBOUND TOURISM**							
	Data							
	Arrivals							
1.1	Total		('000)	..	..	..	..	..
1.2	♦ Overnight visitors (tourists)	(1)	('000)	35.4	38.3	42.1	35.4	30.2
1.3	♦ Same-day visitors (excursionists)		('000)	..	..	..	..	..
1.4	* of which, cruise passengers		('000)	..	..	..	..	..
	Arrivals by region	(1)						
1.5	Total		('000)	35.4	38.3	42.1	35.4	30.2
1.6	♦ Africa		('000)	..	..	..	..	..
1.7	♦ Americas		('000)	8.0	7.6	8.4	8.2	6.9
1.8	♦ East Asia and the Pacific		('000)	24.8	27.9	30.4	24.3	20.9
1.9	♦ Europe		('000)	2.4	2.5	3.0	2.5	2.2
1.10	♦ Middle East		('000)	..	..	..	..	..
1.11	♦ South Asia		('000)	..	..	..	..	..
1.12	♦ Other not classified		('000)	0.2	0.3	0.3	0.4	0.2
1.13	* of which, nationals residing abroad		('000)	..	..	..	..	..
	Arrivals by main purpose	(1)						
1.14	Total		('000)	35.4	38.3	42.1	35.4	30.2
1.15	♦ Personal		('000)	29.2	32.5	36.4	30.0	24.3
1.16	* holidays, leisure and recreation		('000)	12.1	12.9	13.7	13.8	11.2
1.17	* other personal purposes		('000)	17.1	19.6	22.7	16.2	13.1
1.18	♦ Business and professional		('000)	6.2	5.8	5.7	5.4	5.9
	Expenditure	(2)						
1.33	Total		US$ Mn	..	..	..	..	..
1.34	♦ Travel		US$ Mn	22	22	24	25	..
1.35	♦ Passenger transport		US$ Mn	..	..	..	..	..
3.	**OUTBOUND TOURISM**							
	Data							
	Expenditure	(2)						
3.4	Total		US$ Mn	27	30	29	29	..
3.5	♦ Travel		US$ Mn	12	13	12	12	..
3.6	♦ Passenger transport		US$ Mn	15	17	17	17	..
	Expenditure by main purpose of the trip							
3.7	Total		US$ Mn	11.9	12.5	11.6	11.9	..
3.8	♦ Personal		US$ Mn	10.6	11.3	10.3	10.3	..
3.9	♦ Business and professional		US$ Mn	1.3	1.2	1.3	1.6	..
6.	**COMPLEMENTARY INDICATORS**							
	Demand							
6.1	Gross travel propensity		Units	..	..	..	..	..
6.2	(1.2 inbound tourists) / population		Units	0.34	0.37	0.41	0.34	0.29
	Macroeconomic indicators related to international tourism							
6.3	Inbound tourism expenditure over GDP		Percent	..	..	..	..	..
6.4	Outbound tourism expenditure over GDP		Percent	..	..	..	..	..
6.5	Tourism balance (inbound minus outbound tourism expenditure) over GDP		Percent	..	..	..	..	..
6.6	Tourism openness (inbound plus outbound tourism expenditure) over GDP		Percent	..	..	..	..	..
6.7	Tourism coverage (inbound over outbound tourism expenditure)		Percent	81.5	73.3	82.8	86.2	..
6.8	Inbound tourism expenditure over exports of goods		Percent	37.5	26.2	25.9	28.4	..
6.9	Inbound tourism expenditure over exports of services		Percent	68.0	64.8	70.4	65.6	..
6.10	Inbound tourism expenditure over exports of goods and services		Percent	24.2	18.7	19.0	19.8	..
6.11	Inbound tourism expenditure over current account credits		Percent	9.3	8.1	8.4	8.4	..
6.12	Outbound tourism expenditure over imports of goods		Percent	15.5	16.4	16.2	18.8	..
6.13	Outbound tourism expenditure over imports of services		Percent	34.3	37.1	36.1	37.8	..
6.14	Outbound tourism expenditure over imports of goods and		Percent	10.7	11.4	11.2	12.5	..
6.15	Outbound tourism expenditure over current account debits		Percent	9.3	9.7	9.2	9.6	..

MOLDOVA, REPUBLIC OF

Cod.	Basic data and indicators	Notes	Units	2011	2012	2013	2014	2015
1.	**INBOUND TOURISM**							
	Data							
	Arrivals							
1.1	Total		('000)	..	..	..	..	..
1.2	♦ Overnight visitors (tourists)	(1)	('000)	75	89	96	94	94
1.3	♦ Same-day visitors (excursionists)		('000)	..	..	..	..	..
1.4	* of which, cruise passengers		('000)	..	..	..	..	..
	Arrivals by region	(1)						
1.5	Total		('000)	75	89	96	94	94
1.6	♦ Africa		('000)	0.3	0.3	0.5	0.5	0.3
1.7	♦ Americas		('000)	5	7	6	7	5
1.8	♦ East Asia and the Pacific		('000)	2	2	2	2	2
1.9	♦ Europe		('000)	68	79	87	84	88
1.10	♦ Middle East		('000)	..	..	..	..	..
1.11	♦ South Asia		('000)	..	..	..	..	..
1.12	♦ Other not classified		('000)	..	..	..	..	..
1.13	* of which, nationals residing abroad		('000)	..	..	..	..	..
	Accommodation							
	Total							
1.29	♦ Guests		('000)	75	89	96	94	94
1.30	♦ Overnights		('000)	174	191	216	218	253
	Hotels and similar establishments							
1.31	♦ Guests		('000)	71	85	90	89	89
1.32	♦ Overnights		('000)	158	175	193	200	233
	Expenditure							
1.33	Total		US$ Mn	253	279	318	313	291
1.34	♦ Travel		US$ Mn	186	198	226	229	210
1.35	♦ Passenger transport		US$ Mn	67	81	92	84	81
	Expenditure by main purpose of the trip							
1.36	Total		US$ Mn	186	198	226	229	210
1.37	♦ Personal		US$ Mn	136	142	158	163	138
1.38	♦ Business and professional		US$ Mn	50	56	68	66	72
	Indicators							
1.39	Average size of travel party		Persons	..	..	..	..	..
	Average length of stay							
1.40	Total		Days	..	..	..	..	..
1.41	♦ For all commercial accommodation services		Nights	2.32	2.14	2.26	2.32	2.68
1.42	* of which, "hotels and similar establishments"		Nights	..	..	..	..	..
1.43	♦ For non commercial accommodation services		Days	..	..	..	..	..
1.44	Average expenditure per day		US$	..	..	..	..	..
2.	**DOMESTIC TOURISM**							
	Data							
	Trips							
2.1	Total		('000)	38	34	34	43	37
2.2	♦ Overnight visitors (tourists)		('000)	28	28	26	27	25
2.3	♦ Same-day visitors (excursionists)		('000)	10	6	9	16	13
	Accommodation							
	Total							
2.19	♦ Guests		('000)	173	179	176	189	185
2.20	♦ Overnights		('000)	1,251	1,272	1,263	1,296	1,252
	Hotels and similar establishments							
2.21	♦ Guests		('000)	59	60	63	65	58
2.22	♦ Overnights		('000)	211	207	216	215	203
	Indicators							
2.23	Average size of travel party		Persons	..	..	..	..	..
	Average length of stay							
2.24	Total		Days	..	..	..	..	..
2.25	♦ For all commercial accommodation services		Nights	7.22	7.09	7.18	6.86	6.79
2.26	* of which, "hotels and similar establishments"		Nights	..	..	..	..	..
2.27	♦ For non commercial accommodation services		Days	..	..	..	..	..
2.28	Average expenditure per day		US$	..	..	..	..	..
3.	**OUTBOUND TOURISM**							
	Data							
	Departures	(2)						
3.1	Total		('000)	136	147	158	181	190
3.2	♦ Overnight visitors (tourists)		('000)	136	146	157	180	186
3.3	♦ Same-day visitors (excursionists)		('000)	0.2	0.4	0.3	1.1	4

MOLDOVA, REPUBLIC OF

Cod.	Basic data and indicators	Notes	Units	2011	2012	2013	2014	2015
	Expenditure							
3.4	Total		US$ Mn	349	396	434	453	364
3.5	♦ Travel		US$ Mn	277	308	334	351	279
3.6	♦ Passenger transport		US$ Mn	72	88	100	102	85
	Expenditure by main purpose of the trip							
3.7	Total		US$ Mn	277	308	334	351	279
3.8	♦ Personal		US$ Mn	128	144	157	172	154
3.9	♦ Business and professional		US$ Mn	149	164	177	179	125
4.	**TOURISM INDUSTRIES**							
	Data							
	Number of establishments							
4.1	Total		Units	..	..	..	..	..
4.2	♦ Accommodation for visitors		Units	247	257	264	275	249
4.3	* of which, "hotels and similar establishments"		Units	106	112	119	129	126
4.4	♦ Food and beverage serving activities		Units	..	..	..	..	..
4.5	♦ Passenger transportation		Units	..	..	..	..	..
4.6	♦ Travel agencies and other reservation services activities		Units	..	..	..	..	..
4.7	♦ Other tourism industries		Units	..	..	..	..	..
	Accommodation for visitors in hotels and similar establishments							
	Non-monetary data							
4.13	♦ Number of establishments		Units	106	112	119	129	126
4.14	♦ Number of rooms		Units	2,864	2,996	3,053	3,205	3,146
4.15	♦ Number of bed-places		Units	5,454	5,667	5,811	6,152	6,072
	Indicators							
4.16	Occupancy rate / rooms		Percent	..	..	..	..	..
4.17	Occupancy rate / bed-places		Percent	20.00	20.30	21.20	21.70	21.40
4.18	Average length of stay		Nights	2.82	2.64	2.69	2.68	2.96
4.19	Available capacity (bed-places per 1000 inhabitants)		Units	1.34	1.39	1.43	1.51	1.49
5.	**EMPLOYMENT**							
	Data							
	Number of employees by tourism industries							
5.1	Total		('000)	2.9	3.1	3.0	3.1	3.1
5.2	♦ Accommodation services for visitors (hotels and similar establishments)		('000)	1.6	1.6	1.6	1.6	1.6
5.3	♦ Other accommodation services		('000)	..	..	..	..	..
5.4	♦ Food and beverage serving activities		('000)	..	..	..	..	..
5.5	♦ Passenger transportation		('000)	..	..	..	..	..
5.6	♦ Travel agencies and other reservation services activities		('000)	1.3	1.5	1.4	1.5	1.5
5.7	♦ Other tourism industries		('000)	..	..	..	..	..
6.	**COMPLEMENTARY INDICATORS**							
	Demand							
6.1	Gross travel propensity		Units	..	..	..	..	..
6.2	(1.2 inbound tourists + 2.2 domestic tourists) / population		Units	0.03	0.03	0.03	0.03	0.03
	Macroeconomic indicators related to international tourism							
6.3	Inbound tourism expenditure over GDP		Percent	3.6	3.8	4.0	3.9	4.5
6.4	Outbound tourism expenditure over GDP		Percent	5.0	5.4	5.4	5.7	5.6
6.5	Tourism balance (inbound minus outbound tourism expenditure) over GDP		Percent	-1.4	-1.6	-1.4	-1.8	-1.1
6.6	Tourism openness (inbound plus outbound tourism expenditure) over GDP		Percent	8.6	9.2	9.4	9.6	10.1
6.7	Tourism coverage (inbound over outbound tourism expenditure)		Percent	72.5	70.5	73.3	69.1	79.9
6.8	Inbound tourism expenditure over exports of goods		Percent	14.5	16.5	16.8	17.3	19.3
6.9	Inbound tourism expenditure over exports of services		Percent	25.3	27.3	27.9	27.8	29.9
6.10	Inbound tourism expenditure over exports of goods and services		Percent	9.2	10.3	10.5	10.7	11.7
6.11	Inbound tourism expenditure over current account credits		Percent	4.9	5.2	5.4	5.5	6.4
6.12	Outbound tourism expenditure over imports of goods		Percent	7.4	8.3	8.6	9.3	10.1
6.13	Outbound tourism expenditure over imports of services		Percent	41.6	43.4	43.8	45.0	43.8
6.14	Outbound tourism expenditure over imports of goods and		Percent	6.3	7.0	7.2	7.7	8.2
6.15	Outbound tourism expenditure over current account debits		Percent	5.3	5.8	5.9	6.4	6.8

MONACO

Cod.	Basic data and indicators	Notes	Units	2011	2012	2013	2014	2015
1.	**INBOUND TOURISM**							
	Data							
	Arrivals							
1.1	Total		('000)	..	..	..	..	..
1.2	♦ Overnight visitors (tourists)	(1)	('000)	295	292	328	329	331
1.3	♦ Same-day visitors (excursionists)		('000)	285	233	245	194	255
1.4	* of which, cruise passengers		('000)	285	233	245	194	255
	Arrivals by region	(1)						
1.5	Total		('000)	295	292	328	329	331
1.6	♦ Africa		('000)	3	4	4	4	3
1.7	♦ Americas		('000)	33	38	46	46	40
1.8	♦ East Asia and the Pacific		('000)	15	16	17	16	16
1.9	♦ Europe		('000)	233	222	226	230	237
1.10	♦ Middle East		('000)	5	5	9	7	6
1.11	♦ South Asia		('000)	..	..	..	..	..
1.12	♦ Other not classified		('000)	6	7	26	26	29
1.13	* of which, nationals residing abroad		('000)	..	..	..	..	..
	Arrivals by main purpose	(1)						
1.14	Total		('000)	295	292	328	329	331
1.15	♦ Personal		('000)	235	235	268	272	258
1.16	* holidays, leisure and recreation		('000)	235	235	268	272	258
1.17	* other personal purposes		('000)	..	..	..	..	..
1.18	♦ Business and professional		('000)	60	57	60	57	73
	Accommodation							
	Hotels and similar establishments							
1.31	♦ Guests		('000)	295	292	328	329	331
1.32	♦ Overnights		('000)	853	802	893	902	861
2.	**DOMESTIC TOURISM**							
	Data							
	Accommodation							
	Hotels and similar establishments							
2.21	♦ Guests		('000)	..	..	..	..	10
2.22	♦ Overnights		('000)	..	..	..	..	26
4.	**TOURISM INDUSTRIES**							
	Data							
	Number of establishments							
4.1	Total		Units	..	..	..	..	..
4.2	♦ Accommodation for visitors		Units	..	..	..	..	..
4.3	* of which, "hotels and similar establishments"		Units	15	15	14	14	13
4.4	♦ Food and beverage serving activities		Units	..	..	178	176	..
4.5	♦ Passenger transportation		Units	..	..	..	..	..
4.6	♦ Travel agencies and other reservation services activities		Units	..	..	..	..	..
4.7	♦ Other tourism industries		Units	..	..	..	..	..
	Accommodation for visitors in hotels and similar establishments							
	Non-monetary data							
4.13	♦ Number of establishments		Units	15	15	14	14	13
4.14	♦ Number of rooms		Units	2,535	2,527	2,508	2,508	2,319
4.15	♦ Number of bed-places		Units	5,526	5,510	4,642	4,642	4,717
	Indicators							
4.16	Occupancy rate / rooms		Percent	59.79	62.41	64.50	65.48	66.20
4.17	Occupancy rate / bed-places		Percent	..	..	..	..	..
4.18	Average length of stay		Nights	2.89	2.74	2.71	2.74	2.58
4.19	Available capacity (bed-places per 1000 inhabitants)		Units	148.31	146.62	122.70	121.95	124.13

MONACO

Cod.	Basic data and indicators	Notes	Units	2011	2012	2013	2014	2015
5.	**EMPLOYMENT**							
	Data							
	Number of employees by tourism industries							
5.1	Total		('000)	..	..	5.9	5.8	..
5.2	♦ Accommodation services for visitors (hotels and similar establishments)		('000)	..	..	4.1	4.0	..
5.3	♦ Other accommodation services		('000)	..	..	..	..	..
5.4	♦ Food and beverage serving activities		('000)	..	..	1.8	1.8	..
5.5	♦ Passenger transportation		('000)	..	..	..	..	..
5.6	♦ Travel agencies and other reservation services activities		('000)	..	..	..	..	..
5.7	♦ Other tourism industries		('000)	..	..	..	..	..
6.	**COMPLEMENTARY INDICATORS**							
	Demand							
6.1	Gross travel propensity		Units	..	..	..	..	..
6.2	(1.2 inbound tourists) / population		Units	7.92	7.77	8.67	8.64	8.71

263

MONGOLIA

Cod.	Basic data and indicators	Notes	Units	2011	2012	2013	2014	2015
1.	**INBOUND TOURISM**							
	Data							
	Arrivals							
1.1	Total	(1)	('000)	627	624	515	506	467
1.2	♦ Overnight visitors (tourists)	(1)	('000)	460	476	418	393	386
1.3	♦ Same-day visitors (excursionists)		('000)	..	..	..	..	..
1.4	* of which, cruise passengers		('000)	..	..	..	..	..
	Arrivals by region	(1)						
1.5	Total		('000)	460	476	418	393	386
1.6	♦ Africa		('000)	..	..	..	..	..
1.7	♦ Americas		('000)	19	18	17	16	17
1.8	♦ East Asia and the Pacific		('000)	274	306	257	235	226
1.9	♦ Europe		('000)	148	132	125	124	123
1.10	♦ Middle East		('000)	..	..	..	..	..
1.11	♦ South Asia		('000)	1	1	2	1	1
1.12	♦ Other not classified		('000)	18	18	17	17	19
1.13	* of which, nationals residing abroad		('000)	..	..	..	..	..
	Expenditure							
1.33	Total		US$ Mn	258	480	228	215	265
1.34	♦ Travel		US$ Mn	218	442	189	173	232
1.35	♦ Passenger transport		US$ Mn	40	38	39	42	33
	Expenditure by main purpose of the trip							
1.36	Total		US$ Mn	218	442	189	173	232
1.37	♦ Personal		US$ Mn	206	436	185	167	226
1.38	♦ Business and professional		US$ Mn	12	6	4	6	6
3.	**OUTBOUND TOURISM**							
	Data							
	Expenditure							
3.4	Total		US$ Mn	404	420	458	557	469
3.5	♦ Travel		US$ Mn	344	357	399	501	418
3.6	♦ Passenger transport		US$ Mn	60	63	59	56	51
	Expenditure by main purpose of the trip							
3.7	Total		US$ Mn	344	358	399	501	418
3.8	♦ Personal		US$ Mn	333	349	390	493	407
3.9	♦ Business and professional		US$ Mn	11	9	9	8	11
6.	**COMPLEMENTARY INDICATORS**							
	Demand							
6.1	Gross travel propensity		Units	..	..	..	..	..
6.2	(1.2 inbound tourists) / population		Units	0.17	0.17	0.15	0.14	0.13
	Macroeconomic indicators related to international tourism							
6.3	Inbound tourism expenditure over GDP		Percent	2.9	4.5	1.8	..	..
6.4	Outbound tourism expenditure over GDP		Percent	4.6	3.9	3.6	..	..
6.5	Tourism balance (inbound minus outbound tourism expenditure) over GDP		Percent	-1.7	0.6	-1.8	..	..
6.6	Tourism openness (inbound plus outbound tourism expenditure) over GDP		Percent	7.5	8.4	5.4	..	..
6.7	Tourism coverage (inbound over outbound tourism expenditure)		Percent	63.9	114.3	49.8	38.6	56.5
6.8	Inbound tourism expenditure over exports of goods		Percent	5.4	11.0	5.3	3.7	5.7
6.9	Inbound tourism expenditure over exports of services		Percent	41.5	49.8	32.1	37.4	39.2
6.10	Inbound tourism expenditure over exports of goods and services		Percent	4.7	9.0	4.6	3.4	5.0
6.11	Inbound tourism expenditure over current account credits		Percent	4.3	8.1	4.2	3.2	4.7
6.12	Outbound tourism expenditure over imports of goods		Percent	7.0	7.1	8.2	11.7	13.7
6.13	Outbound tourism expenditure over imports of services		Percent	22.6	20.3	22.5	25.8	30.4
6.14	Outbound tourism expenditure over imports of goods and		Percent	5.3	5.3	6.0	8.1	9.4
6.15	Outbound tourism expenditure over current account debits		Percent	5.1	5.0	5.8	7.8	9.0

264

MONTENEGRO

Cod.	Basic data and indicators	Notes	Units	2011	2012	2013	2014	2015
1.	**INBOUND TOURISM**							
	Data							
	Arrivals							
1.1	Total		('000)	..	..	..	..	..
1.2	♦ Overnight visitors (tourists)	(1)	('000)	1,201	1,264	1,324	1,350	1,560
1.3	♦ Same-day visitors (excursionists)		('000)	..	..	..	..	..
1.4	* of which, cruise passengers		('000)	..	..	..	..	..
	Arrivals by region	(1)						
1.5	Total		('000)	1,201	1,264	1,324	1,350	1,560
1.6	♦ Africa		('000)	..	..	..	1	2
1.7	♦ Americas		('000)	13	13	13	20	26
1.8	♦ East Asia and the Pacific		('000)	5	6	7	25	26
1.9	♦ Europe		('000)	1,172	1,227	1,282	1,302	1,496
1.10	♦ Middle East		('000)	..	..	..	..	..
1.11	♦ South Asia		('000)	..	..	..	1	1
1.12	♦ Other not classified		('000)	11	18	22	1	8
1.13	* of which, nationals residing abroad		('000)	..	..	..	..	..
	Accommodation							
	Total							
1.29	♦ Guests		('000)	1,201	1,264	1,324	1,350	1,560
1.30	♦ Overnights		('000)	7,819	8,143	8,414	8,597	10,307
	Hotels and similar establishments							
1.31	♦ Guests		('000)	524	557	604	587	629
1.32	♦ Overnights		('000)	2,648	2,703	2,921	2,627	2,764
	Expenditure							
1.33	Total		US$ Mn	926	860	929	959	947
1.34	♦ Travel		US$ Mn	875	809	880	908	903
1.35	♦ Passenger transport		US$ Mn	51	51	49	51	44
	Indicators							
1.39	Average size of travel party		Persons	..	..	..	..	..
	Average length of stay							
1.40	Total		Days	..	..	..	..	..
1.41	♦ For all commercial accommodation services		Nights	6.51	6.43	6.35	6.37	6.60
1.42	* of which, "hotels and similar establishments"		Nights	4.95	4.85	4.78	4.28	4.39
1.43	♦ For non commercial accommodation services		Days	..	..	..	..	..
1.44	Average expenditure per day		US$	..	..	..	..	..
2.	**DOMESTIC TOURISM**							
	Data							
	Accommodation							
	Total							
2.19	♦ Guests		('000)	172	175	168	167	153
2.20	♦ Overnights		('000)	956	1,008	998	957	748
	Hotels and similar establishments							
2.21	♦ Guests		('000)	83	80	69	63	76
2.22	♦ Overnights		('000)	292	286	241	205	229
	Indicators							
2.23	Average size of travel party		Persons	..	..	..	..	..
	Average length of stay							
2.24	Total		Days	..	..	..	..	..
2.25	♦ For all commercial accommodation services		Nights	5.55	5.76	5.95	5.73	4.88
2.26	* of which, "hotels and similar establishments"		Nights	3.54	3.57	3.49	3.25	3.01
2.27	♦ For non commercial accommodation services		Days	..	..	..	..	..
2.28	Average expenditure per day		US$	..	..	..	..	..
3.	**OUTBOUND TOURISM**							
	Data							
	Expenditure							
3.4	Total		US$ Mn	70	67	81	79	68
3.5	♦ Travel		US$ Mn	39	39	48	47	44
3.6	♦ Passenger transport		US$ Mn	31	28	33	32	24
	Expenditure by main purpose of the trip							
3.7	Total		US$ Mn	39	39	48	47	45
3.8	♦ Personal		US$ Mn	38	38	47	46	44
3.9	♦ Business and professional		US$ Mn	1	1	1	1	1

MONTENEGRO

Cod.	Basic data and indicators	Notes	Units	2011	2012	2013	2014	2015
4.	**TOURISM INDUSTRIES**							
	Data							
	Number of establishments							
4.1	Total		Units	..	..	..	..	..
4.2	♦ Accommodation for visitors		Units	310	332	333	320	320
4.3	* of which, "hotels and similar establishments"		Units	275	293	293	287	287
4.4	♦ Food and beverage serving activities		Units	..	..	..	..	..
4.5	♦ Passenger transportation		Units	..	..	..	..	..
4.6	♦ Travel agencies and other reservation services activities		Units	..	..	..	..	..
4.7	♦ Other tourism industries		Units	..	..	..	..	..
	Accommodation for visitors in hotels and similar establishments							
	Non-monetary data							
4.13	♦ Number of establishments		Units	275	293	293	287	287
4.14	♦ Number of rooms		Units	15,470	15,508	15,548	15,137	15,137
4.15	♦ Number of bed-places		Units	35,319	35,557	34,935	34,560	34,560
	Indicators							
4.16	Occupancy rate / rooms		Percent	..	..	..	..	..
4.17	Occupancy rate / bed-places		Percent	16.86	16.91	17.21	16.43	16.43
4.18	Average length of stay		Nights	..	..	..	..	..
4.19	Available capacity (bed-places per 1000 inhabitants)		Units	56.70	56.99	55.93	55.27	55.23
5.	**EMPLOYMENT**							
	Data							
	Number of employees by tourism industries							
5.1	Total		('000)	12.0	13.0	14.0	14.0	17.5
5.2	♦ Accommodation services for visitors (hotels and similar establishments)		('000)	..	..	..	..	..
5.3	♦ Other accommodation services		('000)	..	..	..	..	..
5.4	♦ Food and beverage serving activities		('000)	..	..	..	..	..
5.5	♦ Passenger transportation		('000)	..	..	..	..	..
5.6	♦ Travel agencies and other reservation services activities		('000)	..	..	..	..	..
5.7	♦ Other tourism industries		('000)	..	..	..	..	..
6.	**COMPLEMENTARY INDICATORS**							
	Demand							
6.1	Gross travel propensity		Units	..	..	..	..	..
6.2	(1.2 inbound tourists) / population		Units	1.93	2.03	2.12	2.16	2.49
	Macroeconomic indicators related to international tourism							
6.3	Inbound tourism expenditure over GDP		Percent	20.4	21.1	20.7	20.8	..
6.4	Outbound tourism expenditure over GDP		Percent	1.5	1.6	1.8	1.7	..
6.5	Tourism balance (inbound minus outbound tourism expenditure) over GDP		Percent	18.9	19.5	18.9	19.1	
6.6	Tourism openness (inbound plus outbound tourism expenditure) over GDP		Percent	21.9	22.7	22.5	22.5	..
6.7	Tourism coverage (inbound over outbound tourism expenditure)		Percent	1,322.9	1,283.6	1,146.9	1,213.9	1,392.6
6.8	Inbound tourism expenditure over exports of goods		Percent	141.6	172.5	176.9	202.7	262.7
6.9	Inbound tourism expenditure over exports of services		Percent	72.6	71.0	70.5	70.1	70.3
6.10	Inbound tourism expenditure over exports of goods and services		Percent	48.0	50.3	50.4	52.1	55.5
6.11	Inbound tourism expenditure over current account credits		Percent	38.4	39.0	39.1	40.2	43.6
6.12	Outbound tourism expenditure over imports of goods		Percent	2.8	2.9	3.5	3.4	3.4
6.13	Outbound tourism expenditure over imports of services		Percent	15.6	14.9	17.9	17.5	14.5
6.14	Outbound tourism expenditure over imports of goods and		Percent	2.4	2.5	3.0	2.9	2.8
6.15	Outbound tourism expenditure over current account debits		Percent	2.2	2.2	2.6	2.5	2.4

MONTSERRAT

Cod. Basic data and indicators	Notes	Units	2011	2012	2013	2014	2015
1. INBOUND TOURISM							
Data							
Arrivals							
1.1 Total		('000)	7.4	9.9	8.7	10.6	13.2
1.2 ♦ Overnight visitors (tourists)		('000)	5.4	7.3	7.2	8.8	8.9
1.3 ♦ Same-day visitors (excursionists)		('000)	2.0	2.6	1.5	1.8	4.3
1.4 * of which, cruise passengers		('000)	1.1	0.8	0.4	0.2	2.6
Arrivals by region							
1.5 Total		('000)	5.4	7.3	7.2	8.8	8.9
1.6 ♦ Africa		('000)	..	..	..	..	..
1.7 ♦ Americas		('000)	3.8	4.9	4.9	6.3	6.2
1.8 ♦ East Asia and the Pacific		('000)	..	..	..	..	..
1.9 ♦ Europe		('000)	1.5	2.3	2.2	2.4	2.6
1.10 ♦ Middle East		('000)	..	..	..	..	..
1.11 ♦ South Asia		('000)	..	..	..	..	..
1.12 ♦ Other not classified		('000)	0.1	0.1	0.1	0.1	0.1
1.13 * of which, nationals residing abroad		('000)	..	..	..	..	..
Arrivals by main purpose							
1.14 Total		('000)	5.4	7.3	7.2	8.8	8.9
1.15 ♦ Personal		('000)	4.0	6.2	6.0	7.7	7.8
1.16 * holidays, leisure and recreation		('000)	3.2	4.5	3.5	5.3	4.6
1.17 * other personal purposes		('000)	0.8	1.7	2.5	2.4	3.2
1.18 ♦ Business and professional		('000)	1.4	1.1	1.2	1.1	1.1
Arrivals by mode of transport							
1.19 Total		('000)	5.4	7.3	7.2	8.8	8.9
1.20 ♦ Air		('000)	4.1	4.1	4.5	4.1	4.1
1.21 ♦ Water		('000)	1.3	3.2	2.7	4.7	4.8
1.22 ♦ Land		('000)	..	..	..	..	..
1.23 * railway		('000)	..	..	..	..	..
1.24 * road		('000)	..	..	..	..	..
1.25 * others		('000)	..	..	..	..	..
Accommodation							
Hotels and similar establishments							
1.31 ♦ Guests		('000)	1.2	2.4	2.7	3.5	3.7
1.32 ♦ Overnights		('000)	..	..	..	..	..
Expenditure							
1.33 Total		US$ Mn	..	..	..	..	..
1.34 ♦ Travel		US$ Mn	5.2	7.0	7.6	8.2	..
1.35 ♦ Passenger transport		US$ Mn	..	..	..	..	..
3. OUTBOUND TOURISM							
Data							
Expenditure							
3.4 Total		US$ Mn	..	..	..	..	..
3.5 ♦ Travel		US$ Mn	3.2	3.0	3.1	..	..
3.6 ♦ Passenger transport		US$ Mn	..	..	..	..	..
6. COMPLEMENTARY INDICATORS							
Demand							
6.1 Gross travel propensity		Units	..	..	..	..	..
6.2 (1.2 inbound tourists) / population		Units	1.08	1.45	1.42	1.73	1.74
Macroeconomic indicators related to international tourism							
6.3 Inbound tourism expenditure over GDP		Percent	8.2	11.1	12.6	13.0	..
6.4 Outbound tourism expenditure over GDP		Percent	5.0	4.7	5.1	..	..
6.5 Tourism balance (inbound minus outbound tourism expenditure) over GDP		Percent	3.2	6.4	7.5	13.0	..
6.6 Tourism openness (inbound plus outbound tourism expenditure) over GDP		Percent	13.2	15.8	17.7	13.0	..
6.7 Tourism coverage (inbound over outbound tourism expenditure)		Percent	162.5	233.3	245.2	..	..
6.8 Inbound tourism expenditure over exports of goods		Percent	209.7	378.4	123.8	..	..
6.9 Inbound tourism expenditure over exports of services		Percent	43.5	52.6	54.5	..	..
6.10 Inbound tourism expenditure over exports of goods and services		Percent	36.0	46.2	37.8	..	..
6.11 Inbound tourism expenditure over current account credits		Percent	11.4	15.2	21.5	..	..
6.12 Outbound tourism expenditure over imports of goods		Percent	10.8	9.1	8.7	..	..
6.13 Outbound tourism expenditure over imports of services		Percent	17.8	16.5	16.6	..	..
6.14 Outbound tourism expenditure over imports of goods and		Percent	6.7	5.9	5.7	..	..
6.15 Outbound tourism expenditure over current account debits		Percent	6.1	5.3	5.2	..	..

MOROCCO

Cod.	Basic data and indicators	Notes	Units	2011	2012	2013	2014	2015
1.	**INBOUND TOURISM**							
	Data							
	Arrivals	(1)						
1.1	Total		('000)	9,784	9,830	10,349	10,642	10,542
1.2	♦ Overnight visitors (tourists)		('000)	9,342	9,375	10,046	10,283	10,177
1.3	♦ Same-day visitors (excursionists)		('000)	442	455	303	359	365
1.4	* of which, cruise passengers		('000)	442	455	303	359	365
	Arrivals by region	(1)						
1.5	Total		('000)	9,342	9,375	10,046	10,283	10,177
1.6	♦ Africa		('000)	291	317	331	344	355
1.7	♦ Americas		('000)	240	258	295	304	333
1.8	♦ East Asia and the Pacific		('000)	97	113	125	127	118
1.9	♦ Europe		('000)	4,138	4,107	4,308	4,441	4,124
1.10	♦ Middle East		('000)	152	198	249	203	202
1.11	♦ South Asia		('000)	12	14	14	16	18
1.12	♦ Other not classified		('000)	4,412	4,368	4,726	4,848	5,028
1.13	* of which, nationals residing abroad		('000)	4,408	4,363	4,723	4,846	5,025
	Arrivals by main purpose	(1)						
1.14	Total		('000)	9,342	..	10,046	10,283	10,177
1.15	♦ Personal		('000)	9,083	..	9,547	9,766	9,426
1.16	* holidays, leisure and recreation		('000)	4,823	..	3,983	4,602	4,065
1.17	* other personal purposes		('000)	4,260	..	5,564	5,164	5,362
1.18	♦ Business and professional		('000)	259	..	499	517	750
	Arrivals by mode of transport	(1)						
1.19	Total		('000)	9,342	9,375	10,046	10,283	10,177
1.20	♦ Air		('000)	6,254	6,019	6,691	6,950	6,772
1.21	♦ Water		('000)	1,902	1,941	1,993	2,036	2,113
1.22	♦ Land		('000)	1,186	1,415	1,362	1,297	1,291
1.23	* railway		('000)	..	..	..	..	..
1.24	* road		('000)	1,186	1,415	1,362	1,297	1,291
1.25	* others		('000)	..	..	..	..	..
	Arrivals by form of organization of the trip	(1)						
1.26	Total		('000)	9,342	..	10,046	10,283	10,177
1.27	♦ Package tour		('000)	1,962	..	933	1,412	1,298
1.28	♦ Other forms		('000)	7,380	..	9,113	8,871	8,879
	Accommodation							
	Total							
1.29	♦ Guests		('000)	..	..	15,546	18,349	19,193
1.30	♦ Overnights		('000)	..	..	132,076	132,459	125,470
	Hotels and similar establishments							
1.31	♦ Guests	(2)	('000)	3,456	3,570	4,010	4,204	3,668
1.32	♦ Overnights	(2)	('000)	12,419	12,548	13,931	14,326	12,525
	Expenditure							
1.33	Total		US$ Mn	9,101	8,491	8,201	8,747	7,534
1.34	♦ Travel		US$ Mn	7,321	6,697	6,851	7,060	5,999
1.35	♦ Passenger transport		US$ Mn	1,780	1,794	1,350	1,687	1,535
	Expenditure by main purpose of the trip							
1.36	Total		US$ Mn	9,101	..	..	7,060	5,999
1.37	♦ Personal		US$ Mn	8,771	..	..	6,742	5,729
1.38	♦ Business and professional		US$ Mn	330	..	..	318	270
	Indicators							
1.39	Average size of travel party		Persons	..	..	1.9	2.0	2.3
	Average length of stay							
1.40	Total		Days	..	..	8.50	7.27	6.39
1.41	♦ For all commercial accommodation services		Nights	..	..	4.90	3.98	3.76
1.42	* of which, "hotels and similar establishments"		Nights	3.49	..	3.50	3.78	3.59
1.43	♦ For non commercial accommodation services		Days	..	..	11.60	10.78	9.42
1.44	Average expenditure per day		US$	..	..	..	..	..
2.	**DOMESTIC TOURISM**							
	Data							
	Trips							
2.1	Total		('000)	..	..	..	..	..
2.2	♦ Overnight visitors (tourists)		('000)	..	..	..	23,600	..
2.3	♦ Same-day visitors (excursionists)		('000)	..	..	..	..	..

MOROCCO

Cod.	Basic data and indicators	Notes	Units	2011	2012	2013	2014	2015
	Trips by main purpose							
2.4	Total		('000)	..	..	..	23,600	..
2.5	♦ Personal		('000)	..	..	..	19,981	..
2.6	* holidays, leisure and recreation		('000)	..	..	..	10,567	..
2.7	* other personal purposes		('000)	..	..	..	9,414	..
2.8	♦ Business and professional		('000)	..	..	..	3,619	..
	Trips by mode of transport							
2.9	Total		('000)	..	..	..	23,600	..
2.10	♦ Air		('000)	..	..	..	608	..
2.11	♦ Water		('000)	..	..	..	..	..
2.12	♦ Land		('000)	..	..	..	22,992	..
2.13	* railway		('000)	..	..	..	2,372	..
2.14	* road		('000)	..	..	..	20,620	..
2.15	* others		('000)	..	..	..	..	..
	Accommodation							
	Total							
2.19	♦ Guests		('000)	..	..	..	23,600	..
2.20	♦ Overnights		('000)	..	..	..	198,000	..
	Hotels and similar establishments							
2.21	♦ Guests	(2)	('000)	2,061	2,265	2,399	2,403	2,645
2.22	♦ Overnights	(2)	('000)	4,449	4,936	5,183	5,307	5,899
	Indicators							
2.23	Average size of travel party		Persons	..	..	..	2.2	..
	Average length of stay							
2.24	Total		Days	..	..	..	8.40	..
2.25	♦ For all commercial accommodation services		Nights	..	..	..	5.60	..
2.26	* of which, "hotels and similar establishments"		Nights	2.16	2.18	2.16	2.21	2.23
2.27	♦ For non commercial accommodation services		Days	..	..	..	10.20	..
2.28	Average expenditure per day		US$	..	..	..	11.5	..
3.	**OUTBOUND TOURISM**							
	Data							
	Departures							
3.1	Total		('000)	..	..	..	..	..
3.2	♦ Overnight visitors (tourists)		('000)	2,378	2,323	2,195	1,850	1,910
3.3	♦ Same-day visitors (excursionists)		('000)	..	..	..	..	..
	Expenditure							
3.4	Total		US$ Mn	2,260	2,095	2,002	2,218	2,153
3.5	♦ Travel		US$ Mn	1,363	1,253	1,318	1,401	1,400
3.6	♦ Passenger transport		US$ Mn	897	842	684	817	753
	Expenditure by main purpose of the trip							
3.7	Total		US$ Mn	1,363	1,253	1,318	1,401	1,400
3.8	♦ Personal		US$ Mn	1,197	1,115	1,194	1,264	1,282
3.9	♦ Business and professional		US$ Mn	166	138	124	137	118
	Indicators							
3.10	Average length of stay		Days	..	..	..	..	..
3.11	Average expenditure per day		US$	..	..	..	40.0	..
4.	**TOURISM INDUSTRIES**							
	Data							
	Number of establishments							
4.1	Total		Units	3,227	3,697	4,030	4,362	4,708
4.2	♦ Accommodation for visitors		Units	..	..	..	..	..
4.3	* of which, "hotels and similar establishments"	(2)	Units	2,253	2,675	2,961	3,198	3,509
4.4	♦ Food and beverage serving activities		Units	..	..	..	..	..
4.5	♦ Passenger transportation		Units	..	..	..	..	..
4.6	♦ Travel agencies and other reservation services activities		Units	974	1,022	1,069	1,164	1,199
4.7	♦ Other tourism industries		Units	..	..	..	..	..
	Accommodation for visitors in hotels and similar establishments							
	Non-monetary data	(2)						
4.13	♦ Number of establishments		Units	2,253	2,675	2,961	3,198	3,509
4.14	♦ Number of rooms		Units	87,801	93,727	98,882	102,746	107,140
4.15	♦ Number of bed-places		Units	187,874	200,091	211,974	221,611	231,334
	Indicators							
4.16	Occupancy rate / rooms	(2)	Percent	40.00	40.00	43.00	44.00	40.00
4.17	Occupancy rate / bed-places		Percent	31.00	31.00	34.00	35.00	32.00
4.18	Average length of stay	(3)	Nights	6.40	..	8.50	7.27	6.52
4.19	Available capacity (bed-places per 1000 inhabitants)		Units	5.78	6.07	6.34	6.53	6.73

MOROCCO

Cod.	Basic data and indicators	Notes	Units	2011	2012	2013	2014	2015
5.	**EMPLOYMENT**							
	Data							
	Number of employees by tourism industries							
5.1	Total		('000)	460.0	485.0	500.0	505.1	515.0
5.2	♦ Accommodation services for visitors (hotels and similar establishments)		('000)	135.5	142.8	147.3	151.5	155.0
5.3	♦ Other accommodation services		('000)	..	..	..	..	..
5.4	♦ Food and beverage serving activities		('000)	110.1	116.1	119.7	111.6	113.6
5.5	♦ Passenger transportation		('000)	41.9	44.2	45.5	47.5	48.4
5.6	♦ Travel agencies and other reservation services activities		('000)	23.5	24.7	25.5	27.8	28.0
5.7	♦ Other tourism industries		('000)	149.0	157.1	162.0	166.7	170.0
6.	**COMPLEMENTARY INDICATORS**							
	Demand							
6.1	Gross travel propensity		Units	..	..	..	..	..
6.2	(1.2 inbound tourists + 2.2 domestic tourists) / population		Units	..	..	..	1.00	..
	Macroeconomic indicators related to international tourism							
6.3	Inbound tourism expenditure over GDP		Percent	9.0	8.6	7.7	8.0	..
6.4	Outbound tourism expenditure over GDP		Percent	2.2	2.1	1.9	2.0	..
6.5	Tourism balance (inbound minus outbound tourism expenditure) over GDP		Percent	6.8	6.5	5.8	6.0	..
6.6	Tourism openness (inbound plus outbound tourism expenditure) over GDP		Percent	11.2	10.7	9.6	10.0	..
6.7	Tourism coverage (inbound over outbound tourism expenditure)		Percent	402.7	405.3	409.6	394.4	349.9
6.8	Inbound tourism expenditure over exports of goods		Percent	57.1	50.0	44.9	43.7	40.8
6.9	Inbound tourism expenditure over exports of services		Percent	57.2	55.3	57.1	55.3	52.8
6.10	Inbound tourism expenditure over exports of goods and services		Percent	28.6	26.3	25.1	24.4	23.0
6.11	Inbound tourism expenditure over current account credits		Percent	22.2	20.9	19.4	18.6	18.1
6.12	Outbound tourism expenditure over imports of goods		Percent	6.1	5.4	5.0	5.5	6.6
6.13	Outbound tourism expenditure over imports of services		Percent	26.4	25.7	26.4	25.2	27.2
6.14	Outbound tourism expenditure over imports of goods and		Percent	4.9	4.5	4.2	4.5	5.3
6.15	Outbound tourism expenditure over current account debits		Percent	4.8	4.4	4.1	4.4	5.2

MOZAMBIQUE

Cod.	Basic data and indicators	Notes	Units	2011	2012	2013	2014	2015
1.	**INBOUND TOURISM**							
	Data							
	Arrivals	(1)						
1.1	Total		('000)	2,013	2,206	1,970	1,751	1,634
1.2	♦ Overnight visitors (tourists)		('000)	1,902	2,113	1,886	1,661	1,552
1.3	♦ Same-day visitors (excursionists)		('000)	111	93	83	90	82
1.4	* of which, cruise passengers		('000)	..	..	..	..	..
	Arrivals by region	(1)						
1.5	Total		('000)	2,013	2,206	1,970	1,751	1,634
1.6	♦ Africa		('000)	1,584	1,581	1,411	1,255	1,275
1.7	♦ Americas		('000)	107	135	121	108	76
1.8	♦ East Asia and the Pacific		('000)	33	29	26	23	42
1.9	♦ Europe		('000)	273	444	397	353	213
1.10	♦ Middle East		('000)	..	..	..	..	..
1.11	♦ South Asia		('000)	..	..	..	..	..
1.12	♦ Other not classified		('000)	16	17	15	12	28
1.13	* of which, nationals residing abroad		('000)	..	..	..	..	..
	Arrivals by main purpose	(1)						
1.14	Total		('000)	1,901	2,112	1,886	1,751	1,634
1.15	♦ Personal		('000)	1,283	1,675	1,575	1,487	1,443
1.16	* holidays, leisure and recreation		('000)	1,010	1,450	1,295	1,145	1,158
1.17	* other personal purposes		('000)	273	225	280	341	285
1.18	♦ Business and professional		('000)	618	437	312	264	191
	Arrivals by mode of transport	(1)						
1.19	Total		('000)	2,013	2,206	1,970	1,751	1,634
1.20	♦ Air		('000)	604	730	675	739	616
1.21	♦ Water		('000)	..	..	..	..	..
1.22	♦ Land		('000)	1,409	1,476	1,295	1,012	1,018
1.23	* railway		('000)	15	29	26	29	..
1.24	* road		('000)	1,276	1,420	1,266	960	1,006
1.25	* others		('000)	118	27	3	23	12
	Arrivals by form of organization of the trip							
1.26	Total		('000)	2,013	2,205	1,969	1,750	1,634
1.27	♦ Package tour		('000)	217	251	217	87	113
1.28	♦ Other forms		('000)	1,796	1,954	1,752	1,663	1,521
	Accommodation							
	Hotels and similar establishments							
1.31	♦ Guests		('000)	278	248	260	273	256
1.32	♦ Overnights		('000)	579	425	434	551	410
	Expenditure							
1.33	Total		US$ Mn	171	224	228	225	202
1.34	♦ Travel		US$ Mn	138	189	199	207	193
1.35	♦ Passenger transport		US$ Mn	33	35	29	18	9
	Expenditure by main purpose of the trip							
1.36	Total		US$ Mn	138	189	199	207	193
1.37	♦ Personal		US$ Mn	138	188	196	207	193
1.38	♦ Business and professional		US$ Mn	0	1	3	..	..
	Indicators							
1.39	Average size of travel party		Persons	..	..	..	..	..
	Average length of stay							
1.40	Total		Days	..	..	..	..	..
1.41	♦ For all commercial accommodation services		Nights	2.10	1.70	1.70	2.00	1.60
1.42	* of which, "hotels and similar establishments"		Nights	..	..	..	..	..
1.43	♦ For non commercial accommodation services		Days	..	9.00	..	7.00	..
1.44	Average expenditure per day		US$	..	135.4	..	141.0	..
2.	**DOMESTIC TOURISM**	(2)						
	Data							
	Trips							
2.1	Total		('000)	..	..	6,283	..	1,089
2.2	♦ Overnight visitors (tourists)		('000)	..	..	..	..	..
2.3	♦ Same-day visitors (excursionists)		('000)	..	..	..	..	..
	Trips by main purpose							
2.4	Total		('000)	..	..	6,283	..	1,089
2.5	♦ Personal		('000)	..	..	5,732	..	841
2.6	* holidays, leisure and recreation		('000)	..	..	403	..	94
2.7	* other personal purposes		('000)	..	..	5,329	..	747
2.8	♦ Business and professional		('000)	..	..	551	..	248

MOZAMBIQUE

Cod.	Basic data and indicators	Notes	Units	2011	2012	2013	2014	2015
	Trips by mode of transport							
2.9	Total		('000)	..	..	6,283	..	1,089
2.10	♦ Air		('000)	..	..	25	..	15
2.11	♦ Water		('000)	..	..	145	..	10
2.12	♦ Land		('000)	..	..	6,113	..	1,064
2.13	* railway		('000)	..	..	343	..	21
2.14	* road		('000)	..	..	5,645	..	945
2.15	* others		('000)	..	..	125	..	98
	Accommodation							
	Hotels and similar establishments							
2.21	♦ Guests		('000)	278	248	251	264	257
2.22	♦ Overnights		('000)	616	425	434	443	431
	Indicators							
2.23	Average size of travel party		Persons	..	..	..	..	..
	Average length of stay							
2.24	Total		Days	..	..	..	..	..
2.25	♦ For all commercial accommodation services		Nights	2.00	3.00	4.00	..	1.70
2.26	* of which, "hotels and similar establishments"		Nights	..	..	..	..	..
2.27	♦ For non commercial accommodation services		Days	..	..	..	..	..
2.28	Average expenditure per day		US$	115.0	130.0	120.0	..	..
3.	**OUTBOUND TOURISM**							
	Data							
	Expenditure							
3.4	Total		US$ Mn	264	247	313	331	322
3.5	♦ Travel		US$ Mn	230	186	241	253	223
3.6	♦ Passenger transport		US$ Mn	34	61	72	78	99
	Expenditure by main purpose of the trip							
3.7	Total		US$ Mn	230	186	241	253	224
3.8	♦ Personal		US$ Mn	176	167	162	174	157
3.9	♦ Business and professional		US$ Mn	54	19	79	79	67
4.	**TOURISM INDUSTRIES**							
	Data							
	Number of establishments							
4.1	Total		Units	..	..	..	..	..
4.2	♦ Accommodation for visitors		Units	1,221	1,307	1,435	1,527	1,686
4.3	* of which, "hotels and similar establishments"		Units	1,208	1,294	1,422	1,514	1,663
4.4	♦ Food and beverage serving activities		Units	..	..	..	..	..
4.5	♦ Passenger transportation		Units	65	..	..	..	..
4.6	♦ Travel agencies and other reservation services activities		Units	120	145	188	232	232
4.7	♦ Other tourism industries		Units	..	..	..	..	..
	Accommodation for visitors in hotels and similar establishments							
	Monetary data							
4.8	♦ Output		US$ Mn	525.5	497.6	489.5	501.0	498.3
4.9	♦ Intermediate consumption		US$ Mn	247.0	233.9	230.1	235.4	234.2
4.10	♦ Gross value added		US$ Mn	278.5	263.7	259.5	265.5	264.1
4.11	♦ Compensation of employees		US$ Mn	45.2	42.8	42.1	43.1	42.8
4.12	♦ Gross fixed capital formation		US$ Mn	..	..	..	..	..
	Non-monetary data							
4.13	♦ Number of establishments		Units	1,208	1,294	1,422	1,514	1,663
4.14	♦ Number of rooms		Units	21,061	22,145	22,339	22,339	29,952
4.15	♦ Number of bed-places		Units	38,461	40,883	45,403	45,403	56,426
	Indicators							
4.16	Occupancy rate / rooms		Percent	..	..	..	..	..
4.17	Occupancy rate / bed-places		Percent	35.10	28.80	25.60	28.20	24.00
4.18	Average length of stay		Nights	2.10	1.70	1.70	1.70	1.60
4.19	Available capacity (bed-places per 1000 inhabitants)		Units	1.54	1.59	1.72	1.67	2.02
	Travel agencies and other reservation service activities							
	Monetary data							
4.20	♦ Output		US$ Mn	37.4	56.8	56.3	66.0	49.2
4.21	♦ Intermediate consumption		US$ Mn	18.9	28.8	28.5	34.7	24.9
4.22	♦ Gross value added		US$ Mn	18.5	28.0	27.8	31.3	24.3
4.23	♦ Compensation of employees		US$ Mn	1.3	1.9	1.9	2.2	1.7
4.24	♦ Gross fixed capital formation		US$ Mn	..	..	..	..	..

MOZAMBIQUE

Cod.	Basic data and indicators	Notes	Units	2011	2012	2013	2014	2015
5.	**EMPLOYMENT**							
	Data							
	Number of employees by tourism industries							
5.1	Total		('000)	42.0	45.3	..	..	..
5.2	♦ Accommodation services for visitors (hotels and similar establishments)		('000)	12.6	15.1	..	..	..
5.3	♦ Other accommodation services		('000)	..	..	..	..	..
5.4	♦ Food and beverage serving activities		('000)	17.1	17.4	..	..	..
5.5	♦ Passenger transportation		('000)	10.0	10.0	..	..	..
5.6	♦ Travel agencies and other reservation services activities		('000)	0.2	0.7	..	..	..
5.7	♦ Other tourism industries		('000)	2.1	2.1	..	..	..
	Number of jobs by status in employment							
5.8	Total		('000)	42.0	45.3	..	..	..
5.9	♦ Employees		('000)	42.0	45.3	..	..	..
5.10	♦ Self employed		('000)	..	..	..	..	..
	Indicators							
	Number of full-time equivalent jobs by status in employment							
5.11	Total		('000)	42.0	45.3	52.0	53.8	58.0
5.12	♦ Employees		('000)	42.0	45.3	52.0	53.8	58.0
5.13	* male		('000)	23.6	24.8	28.2	29.2	31.2
5.14	* female		('000)	18.4	20.5	23.8	24.6	26.8
5.15	♦ Self employed		('000)	..	..	..	..	..
5.16	* male		('000)	..	..	..	..	..
5.17	* female		('000)	..	..	..	..	..
6.	**COMPLEMENTARY INDICATORS**							
	Demand							
6.1	Gross travel propensity		Units	..	..	..	..	..
6.2	(1.2 inbound tourists + 2.1 domestic visitors) / population		Units	..	..	0.31	..	0.09
	Macroeconomic indicators related to international tourism							
6.3	Inbound tourism expenditure over GDP		Percent	1.3	1.5	1.4	1.3	..
6.4	Outbound tourism expenditure over GDP		Percent	2.0	1.6	2.0	2.0	..
6.5	Tourism balance (inbound minus outbound tourism expenditure) over GDP		Percent	-0.7	-0.1	-0.6	-0.7	..
6.6	Tourism openness (inbound plus outbound tourism expenditure) over GDP		Percent	3.3	3.1	3.4	3.3	..
6.7	Tourism coverage (inbound over outbound tourism expenditure)		Percent	64.8	90.7	72.8	68.0	62.7
6.8	Inbound tourism expenditure over exports of goods		Percent	5.5	5.8	5.5	5.7	5.9
6.9	Inbound tourism expenditure over exports of services		Percent	46.7	28.3	35.3	31.0	28.0
6.10	Inbound tourism expenditure over exports of goods and services		Percent	4.9	4.8	4.8	4.8	4.9
6.11	Inbound tourism expenditure over current account credits		Percent	3.6	3.8	3.6	3.6	3.9
6.12	Outbound tourism expenditure over imports of goods		Percent	4.9	3.1	3.7	4.2	4.2
6.13	Outbound tourism expenditure over imports of services		Percent	11.7	5.5	8.0	9.1	9.6
6.14	Outbound tourism expenditure over imports of goods and		Percent	3.5	2.0	2.5	2.9	2.9
6.15	Outbound tourism expenditure over current account debits		Percent	3.4	2.0	2.5	2.8	2.9

MYANMAR

Cod.	Basic data and indicators	Notes	Units	2011	2012	2013	2014	2015
1.	**INBOUND TOURISM**							
	Data							
	Arrivals							
1.1	Total		('000)	..	..	..	..	
1.2	♦ Overnight visitors (tourists)		('000)	816	1,059	2,044	3,081	4,681
1.3	♦ Same-day visitors (excursionists)		('000)	..	..	..	..	
1.4	* of which, cruise passengers		('000)	..	..	..	..	
	Arrivals by region							
1.5	Total		('000)	817	1,059	2,044	3,081	4,681
1.6	♦ Africa		('000)	1	1	3	3	4
1.7	♦ Americas		('000)	28	48	67	82	93
1.8	♦ East Asia and the Pacific		('000)	680	848	1,747	2,719	4,283
1.9	♦ Europe		('000)	88	139	168	200	225
1.10	♦ Middle East		('000)	3	4	3	5	6
1.11	♦ South Asia		('000)	17	19	55	72	70
1.12	♦ Other not classified		('000)	..	..	..	..	
1.13	* of which, nationals residing abroad		('000)	..	..	..	..	
	Arrivals by main purpose							
1.14	Total		('000)	816	1,059	2,044	3,081	4,681
1.15	♦ Personal		('000)	733	928	1,873	2,867	4,468
1.16	* holidays, leisure and recreation		('000)	251	380	493	585	547
1.17	* other personal purposes		('000)	482	548	1,380	2,282	3,921
1.18	♦ Business and professional		('000)	83	131	171	215	213
	Arrivals by mode of transport							
1.19	Total		('000)	816	1,059	2,044	3,081	4,681
1.20	♦ Air		('000)	385	586	796	1,082	1,221
1.21	♦ Water		('000)	3	3	6	19	27
1.22	♦ Land		('000)	428	470	1,242	1,981	3,433
1.23	* railway		('000)	..	..	..	..	
1.24	* road		('000)	428	470	1,242	1,981	3,433
1.25	* others		('000)	..	..	..	..	
	Accommodation							
	Hotels and similar establishments							
1.31	♦ Guests		('000)	..	..	..	..	
1.32	♦ Overnights	(1)	('000)	3,129	4,014	6,301	27,733	42,129
	Expenditure							
1.33	Total		US$ Mn	334	550	964	1,613	2,092
1.34	♦ Travel		US$ Mn	325	539	959	1,612	2,092
1.35	♦ Passenger transport		US$ Mn	9	11	5	1	0.4
	Indicators							
1.39	Average size of travel party		Persons	..	..	..	..	
	Average length of stay							
1.40	Total		Days	..	..	..	..	
1.41	♦ For all commercial accommodation services		Nights	8.00	7.00	7.00	9.00	9.00
1.42	* of which, "hotels and similar establishments"		Nights	..	..	..	..	
1.43	♦ For non commercial accommodation services		Days	..	..	..	..	
1.44	Average expenditure per day		US$	120.0	135.0	145.0	170.0	171.0
3.	**OUTBOUND TOURISM**							
	Data							
	Expenditure							
3.4	Total		US$ Mn	132	265	131	137	124
3.5	♦ Travel		US$ Mn	123	257	115	121	91
3.6	♦ Passenger transport		US$ Mn	9	8	16	16	33
4.	**TOURISM INDUSTRIES**							
	Data							
	Number of establishments							
4.1	Total		Units	..	..	..	..	
4.2	♦ Accommodation for visitors		Units	..	..	..	..	
4.3	* of which, "hotels and similar establishments"	(2)	Units	729	787	923	1,106	1,279
4.4	♦ Food and beverage serving activities		Units	..	..	..	..	
4.5	♦ Passenger transportation		Units	..	..	..	..	
4.6	♦ Travel agencies and other reservation services activities		Units	..	..	..	..	
4.7	♦ Other tourism industries		Units	..	..	..	..	

MYANMAR

Cod.	Basic data and indicators	Notes	Units	2011	2012	2013	2014	2015
	Accommodation for visitors in hotels and similar establishments							
	Non-monetary data	(2)						
.13	♦ Number of establishments		Units	729	787	923	1,106	1,279
.14	♦ Number of rooms		Units	25,002	28,291	34,834	43,243	49,946
.15	♦ Number of bed-places		Units	50,004	56,582	69,668	86,486	99,892
	Indicators							
.16	Occupancy rate / rooms		Percent	..	..	..	..	..
.17	Occupancy rate / bed-places		Percent	..	..	..	..	..
.18	Average length of stay		Nights	..	..	..	..	..
.19	Available capacity (bed-places per 1000 inhabitants)		Units	0.96	1.08	1.31	1.62	1.85
6.	**COMPLEMENTARY INDICATORS**							
	Demand							
6.1	Gross travel propensity		Units	..	..	..	..	..
6.2	(1.2 inbound tourists) / population		Units	0.02	0.02	0.04	0.06	0.09
	Macroeconomic indicators related to international tourism							
6.3	Inbound tourism expenditure over GDP		Percent	..	..	..	..	..
6.4	Outbound tourism expenditure over GDP		Percent	..	..	..	..	..
6.5	Tourism balance (inbound minus outbound tourism expenditure) over GDP		Percent	..	..	..	..	..
6.6	Tourism openness (inbound plus outbound tourism expenditure) over GDP		Percent	..	..	..	..	..
6.7	Tourism coverage (inbound over outbound tourism expenditure)		Percent	253.0	207.5	735.9	1,177.4	1,687.4
6.8	Inbound tourism expenditure over exports of goods		Percent	4.3	6.7	10.3	17.8	22.9
6.9	Inbound tourism expenditure over exports of services		Percent	44.0	44.7	35.1	38.3	53.2
6.10	Inbound tourism expenditure over exports of goods and services		Percent	3.9	5.8	7.9	12.1	16.0
6.11	Inbound tourism expenditure over current account credits		Percent	3.6	5.3	6.9	9.6	12.5
6.12	Outbound tourism expenditure over imports of goods		Percent	1.8	3.5	1.4	1.1	0.9
6.13	Outbound tourism expenditure over imports of services		Percent	12.1	18.2	6.0	5.3	5.4
6.14	Outbound tourism expenditure over imports of goods and		Percent	1.5	2.9	1.1	0.9	0.7
6.15	Outbound tourism expenditure over current account debits		Percent	1.5	2.8	1.1	0.9	0.7

NAMIBIA

Cod.	Basic data and indicators	Notes	Units	2011	2012	2013	2014	2015
1.	**INBOUND TOURISM**							
	Data							
	Arrivals							
1.1	Total		('000)	1,163	1,245	1,327	1,429	1,488
1.2	♦ Overnight visitors (tourists)		('000)	1,027	1,079	1,176	1,320	1,388
1.3	♦ Same-day visitors (excursionists)		('000)	136	166	151	109	100
1.4	* of which, cruise passengers		('000)	..	..	..	..	..
	Arrivals by region							
1.5	Total		('000)	1,027	1,079	1,176	1,320	1,388
1.6	♦ Africa		('000)	784	827	913	1,029	1,083
1.7	♦ Americas		('000)	25	27	29	31	34
1.8	♦ East Asia and the Pacific		('000)	12	14	17	20	19
1.9	♦ Europe		('000)	194	198	200	222	234
1.10	♦ Middle East		('000)	..	..	..	..	..
1.11	♦ South Asia		('000)	..	..	..	..	..
1.12	♦ Other not classified		('000)	12	14	18	17	18
1.13	* of which, nationals residing abroad		('000)	..	..	..	..	..
	Arrivals by main purpose							
1.14	Total		('000)	1,027	1,079	1,176	1,320	1,388
1.15	♦ Personal		('000)	904	931	1,029	1,153	1,209
1.16	* holidays, leisure and recreation		('000)	423	429	422	511	539
1.17	* other personal purposes		('000)	481	501	607	642	670
1.18	♦ Business and professional		('000)	123	148	147	167	179
	Arrivals by mode of transport							
1.19	Total		('000)	1,027	1,079	1,176	1,320	1,388
1.20	♦ Air		('000)	282	291	321	341	377
1.21	♦ Water		('000)	15	10	12	9	10
1.22	♦ Land		('000)	730	778	844	970	1,001
1.23	* railway		('000)	..	..	..	..	..
1.24	* road		('000)	730	778	844	958	983
1.25	* others		('000)	..	..	..	13	18
	Accommodation							
	Total							
1.29	♦ Guests		('000)	739	914	873	..	..
1.30	♦ Overnights		('000)	..	..	..	..	..
	Expenditure							
1.33	Total		US$ Mn	645	598	524	522	472
1.34	♦ Travel		US$ Mn	518	485	411	413	378
1.35	♦ Passenger transport		US$ Mn	127	113	113	109	94
	Expenditure by main purpose of the trip							
1.36	Total		US$ Mn	518	485	411	413	378
1.37	♦ Personal		US$ Mn	461	435	374	404	371
1.38	♦ Business and professional		US$ Mn	57	50	38	9	7
	Indicators							
1.39	Average size of travel party		Persons	..	..	..	..	..
	Average length of stay							
1.40	Total		Days	..	..	..	..	..
1.41	♦ For all commercial accommodation services		Nights	17.00	17.00	19.00	..	18.00
1.42	* of which, "hotels and similar establishments"		Nights	..	..	..	..	..
1.43	♦ For non commercial accommodation services		Days	..	..	..	..	..
1.44	Average expenditure per day		US$	..	..	..	..	..
2.	**DOMESTIC TOURISM**							
	Data							
	Trips							
2.1	Total		('000)	..	..	..	..	5,790
2.2	♦ Overnight visitors (tourists)		('000)	..	..	..	..	3,740
2.3	♦ Same-day visitors (excursionists)		('000)	..	..	..	..	2,050
	Trips by main purpose							
2.4	Total		('000)	..	..	..	..	5,790
2.5	♦ Personal		('000)	..	..	..	..	5,184
2.6	* holidays, leisure and recreation		('000)	..	..	..	..	1,461
2.7	* other personal purposes		('000)	..	..	..	..	3,723
2.8	♦ Business and professional		('000)	..	..	..	..	606
	Trips by mode of transport							
2.9	Total		('000)	..	..	..	..	5,790
2.10	♦ Air		('000)	..	..	..	..	..
2.11	♦ Water		('000)	..	..	..	..	..
2.12	♦ Land		('000)	..	..	..	..	5,790
2.13	* railway		('000)	..	..	..	..	..
2.14	* road		('000)	..	..	..	..	5,790
2.15	* others		('000)	..	..	..	..	

NAMIBIA

Cod.	Basic data and indicators	Notes	Units	2011	2012	2013	2014	2015
	Accommodation							
	Total							
2.19	♦ Guests		('000)	420	528	581	..	..
2.20	♦ Overnights		('000)	..	..	..	..	..
3.	**OUTBOUND TOURISM**							
	Data							
	Expenditure							
3.4	Total		US$ Mn	..	..	..	..	..
3.5	♦ Travel		US$ Mn	207	154	124	150	136
3.6	♦ Passenger transport		US$ Mn	..	..	..	..	..
	Expenditure by main purpose of the trip							
3.7	Total		US$ Mn	207	154	124	150	136
3.8	♦ Personal		US$ Mn	199	147	116	142	133
3.9	♦ Business and professional		US$ Mn	8	7	8	8	3
4.	**TOURISM INDUSTRIES**							
	Data							
	Number of establishments							
4.1	Total		Units	..	..	..	..	..
4.2	♦ Accommodation for visitors		Units	620	513	535	..	..
4.3	* of which, "hotels and similar establishments"		Units	278	251	276	..	..
4.4	♦ Food and beverage serving activities		Units	..	..	..	..	..
4.5	♦ Passenger transportation		Units	..	..	..	..	..
4.6	♦ Travel agencies and other reservation services activities		Units	..	..	..	..	..
4.7	♦ Other tourism industries		Units	..	..	..	..	..
	Accommodation for visitors in hotels and similar establishments							
	Non-monetary data							
4.13	♦ Number of establishments		Units	278	251	276	..	..
4.14	♦ Number of rooms		Units	4,734	3,525	4,438	..	..
4.15	♦ Number of bed-places		Units	9,399	7,186	8,570	..	..
	Indicators							
4.16	Occupancy rate / rooms		Percent	..	..	..	..	..
4.17	Occupancy rate / bed-places		Percent	30.00	29.00	37.00	38.00	28.00
4.18	Average length of stay		Nights	..	..	..	..	..
4.19	Available capacity (bed-places per 1000 inhabitants)		Units	4.20	3.14	3.65	..	..
5.	**EMPLOYMENT**							
	Data							
	Number of employees by tourism industries							
5.1	Total		('000)	21.9	22.9	23.1	24.0	25.0
5.2	♦ Accommodation services for visitors (hotels and similar establishments)		('000)	..	..	..	..	..
5.3	♦ Other accommodation services		('000)	..	..	..	..	..
5.4	♦ Food and beverage serving activities		('000)	..	..	..	..	..
5.5	♦ Passenger transportation		('000)	..	..	..	..	..
5.6	♦ Travel agencies and other reservation services activities		('000)	..	..	..	..	..
5.7	♦ Other tourism industries		('000)	..	..	..	..	..
6.	**COMPLEMENTARY INDICATORS**							
	Demand							
6.1	Gross travel propensity		Units	..	..	..	..	..
6.2	(1.2 inbound tourists + 2.2 domestic tourists) / population		Units	..	..	..	..	2.09
	Macroeconomic indicators related to international tourism							
6.3	Inbound tourism expenditure over GDP		Percent	5.2	4.6	4.1	3.9	..
6.4	Outbound tourism expenditure over GDP		Percent	1.7	1.2	1.0	1.1	..
6.5	Tourism balance (inbound minus outbound tourism expenditure) over GDP		Percent	3.5	3.4	3.1	2.8	..
6.6	Tourism openness (inbound plus outbound tourism expenditure) over GDP		Percent	6.9	5.8	5.1	5.0	..
6.7	Tourism coverage (inbound over outbound tourism		Percent	311.6	388.3	422.6	348.0	347.1
6.8	Inbound tourism expenditure over exports of goods		Percent	14.6	13.6	11.3	11.3	11.8
6.9	Inbound tourism expenditure over exports of services		Percent	86.9	55.6	56.5	50.0	49.6
6.10	Inbound tourism expenditure over exports of goods and services		Percent	12.5	10.9	9.4	9.2	9.5
6.11	Inbound tourism expenditure over current account credits		Percent	9.6	8.0	6.9	6.7	6.9
6.12	Outbound tourism expenditure over imports of goods		Percent	3.8	2.4	1.9	2.1	2.0
6.13	Outbound tourism expenditure over imports of services		Percent	26.4	21.2	13.3	13.3	13.9
6.14	Outbound tourism expenditure over imports of goods and		Percent	3.3	2.1	1.6	1.8	1.7
6.15	Outbound tourism expenditure over current account debits		Percent	3.1	2.0	1.6	1.7	1.6

NEPAL

Cod.	Basic data and indicators	Notes	Units	2011	2012	2013	2014	2015
1.	**INBOUND TOURISM**							
	Data							
	Arrivals							
1.1	Total		('000)	..	..	..	..	
1.2	♦ Overnight visitors (tourists)	(1)	('000)	736	803	798	790	539
1.3	♦ Same-day visitors (excursionists)		('000)	..	..	..	..	
1.4	* of which, cruise passengers		('000)	..	..	..	..	
	Arrivals by region							
1.5	Total		('000)	736	803	798	790	539
1.6	♦ Africa		('000)	2	1	..	..	
1.7	♦ Americas		('000)	63	67	60	61	51
1.8	♦ East Asia and the Pacific		('000)	196	231	260	269	174
1.9	♦ Europe		('000)	207	217	154	147	101
1.10	♦ Middle East		('000)	4	1	..	..	
1.11	♦ South Asia		('000)	236	262	241	199	137
1.12	♦ Other not classified		('000)	28	24	84	114	76
1.13	* of which, nationals residing abroad		('000)	..	..	..	..	
	Arrivals by main purpose							
1.14	Total		('000)	736	803	798	790	539
1.15	♦ Personal		('000)	683	734	712	720	488
1.16	* holidays, leisure and recreation		('000)	512	485	535	493	395
1.17	* other personal purposes		('000)	171	249	177	227	92
1.18	♦ Business and professional		('000)	53	69	86	70	51
	Arrivals by mode of transport							
1.19	Total		('000)	736	803	798	790	539
1.20	♦ Air		('000)	545	598	595	586	407
1.21	♦ Water		('000)	..	..	..	..	
1.22	♦ Land		('000)	191	205	203	204	132
1.23	* railway		('000)	..	..	..	..	
1.24	* road		('000)	191	205	203	204	132
1.25	* others		('000)	..	..	..	..	
	Expenditure							
1.33	Total		US$ Mn	415	379	460	511	509
1.34	♦ Travel		US$ Mn	383	351	436	487	483
1.35	♦ Passenger transport		US$ Mn	32	28	24	24	26
	Indicators							
1.39	Average size of travel party		Persons	..	..	..	..	
	Average length of stay							
1.40	Total		Days	..	..	..	..	
1.41	♦ For all commercial accommodation services	(2)	Nights	13.12	12.16	12.60	12.44	13.16
1.42	* of which, "hotels and similar establishments"		Nights	..	..	..	..	
1.43	♦ For non commercial accommodation services		Days	..	..	..	..	
1.44	Average expenditure per day		US$	39.9	36.2	42.8	48.0	68.6
3.	**OUTBOUND TOURISM**							
	Data							
	Departures							
3.1	Total		('000)	..	..	..	..	
3.2	♦ Overnight visitors (tourists)		('000)	774	862	983	..	
3.3	♦ Same-day visitors (excursionists)		('000)	..	..	..	..	
	Expenditure							
3.4	Total		US$ Mn	420	562	598	680	669
3.5	♦ Travel		US$ Mn	320	413	422	504	527
3.6	♦ Passenger transport		US$ Mn	100	149	176	176	142
4.	**TOURISM INDUSTRIES**							
	Data							
	Number of establishments							
4.1	Total		Units	3,817	4,162	4,558	4,959	5,317
4.2	♦ Accommodation for visitors		Units	..	..	..	..	
4.3	* of which, "hotels and similar establishments"	(3)	Units	503	522	557	532	533
4.4	♦ Food and beverage serving activities		Units	..	..	..	..	
4.5	♦ Passenger transportation		Units	..	..	..	..	
4.6	♦ Travel agencies and other reservation services activities	(4)	Units	3,314	3,640	4,001	4,427	4,784
4.7	♦ Other tourism industries		Units	..	..	..	..	

NEPAL

Cod.	Basic data and indicators	Notes	Units	2011	2012	2013	2014	2015
	Accommodation for visitors in hotels and similar establishments							
	Non-monetary data	(3)						
4.13	♦ Number of establishments		Units	503	522	557	532	533
4.14	♦ Number of rooms		Units	10,752	11,087	11,835	11,519	11,531
4.15	♦ Number of bed-places		Units	20,941	21,498	22,871	19,589	20,360
	Indicators							
4.16	Occupancy rate / rooms		Percent	..	..	..	..	..
4.17	Occupancy rate / bed-places		Percent	..	..	..	..	..
4.18	Average length of stay		Nights	13.12	12.16	12.60	12.44	13.16
4.19	Available capacity (bed-places per 1000 inhabitants)		Units	0.77	0.78	0.82	0.70	0.71
6.	**COMPLEMENTARY INDICATORS**							
	Demand							
6.1	Gross travel propensity		Units	..	..	..	..	..
6.2	(1.2 inbound tourists) / population		Units	0.03	0.03	0.03	0.03	0.02
	Macroeconomic indicators related to international tourism							
6.3	Inbound tourism expenditure over GDP		Percent	2.2	2.1	2.5	2.6	..
6.4	Outbound tourism expenditure over GDP		Percent	2.3	3.1	3.3	3.4	..
6.5	Tourism balance (inbound minus outbound tourism expenditure) over GDP		Percent	-0.1	-1.0	-0.8	-0.8	..
6.6	Tourism openness (inbound plus outbound tourism expenditure) over GDP		Percent	4.5	5.2	5.8	6.0	..
6.7	Tourism coverage (inbound over outbound tourism expenditure)		Percent	98.8	67.4	76.9	75.1	76.1
6.8	Inbound tourism expenditure over exports of goods		Percent	41.5	37.7	46.1	50.0	62.6
6.9	Inbound tourism expenditure over exports of services		Percent	48.1	41.0	38.7	36.8	35.6
6.10	Inbound tourism expenditure over exports of goods and services		Percent	22.3	19.6	21.0	21.2	22.7
6.11	Inbound tourism expenditure over current account credits		Percent	6.0	5.0	5.2	5.5	5.0
6.12	Outbound tourism expenditure over imports of goods		Percent	7.4	9.4	9.1	9.0	10.3
6.13	Outbound tourism expenditure over imports of services		Percent	53.7	62.7	60.7	56.8	55.7
6.14	Outbound tourism expenditure over imports of goods and		Percent	6.5	8.2	7.9	7.7	8.7
6.15	Outbound tourism expenditure over current account debits		Percent	6.2	7.8	7.6	7.4	8.2

NETHERLANDS

Cod.	Basic data and indicators	Notes	Units	2011	2012	2013	2014	2015
1.	**INBOUND TOURISM**							
	Data							
	Arrivals							
1.1	Total		('000)	..	..	..	..	..
1.2	♦ Overnight visitors (tourists)	(1)(2)	('000)	11,300	11,680	12,783	13,925	15,007
1.3	♦ Same-day visitors (excursionists)		('000)	..	..	..	..	..
1.4	* of which, cruise passengers		('000)	..	..	..	..	..
	Arrivals by region	(1)(2)						
1.5	Total		('000)	11,300	11,680	12,784	13,925	15,007
1.6	♦ Africa		('000)	114	112	121	135	130
1.7	♦ Americas		('000)	1,320	1,323	1,337	1,431	1,508
1.8	♦ East Asia and the Pacific		('000)	850	949	1,040	1,164	1,319
1.9	♦ Europe		('000)	9,016	9,296	10,286	11,195	12,050
1.10	♦ Middle East		('000)	..	..	..	..	..
1.11	♦ South Asia		('000)	..	..	..	..	..
1.12	♦ Other not classified		('000)	..	..	..	..	..
1.13	* of which, nationals residing abroad		('000)	..	..	..	..	..
	Accommodation	(2)						
	Total							
1.29	♦ Guests		('000)	11,300	11,680	12,783	13,925	15,007
1.30	♦ Overnights		('000)	27,739	27,898	31,771	34,424	37,298
	Hotels and similar establishments							
1.31	♦ Guests	(3)	('000)	9,027	9,357	10,017	10,978	11,766
1.32	♦ Overnights	(3)	('000)	16,685	17,066	18,351	20,184	21,708
	Expenditure	(4)						
1.33	Total		US$ Mn	..	..	20,910	18,632	19,320
1.34	♦ Travel		US$ Mn	12,897	12,261	15,581	12,951	13,560
1.35	♦ Passenger transport		US$ Mn	..	..	5,329	5,681	5,760
	Expenditure by main purpose of the trip	(4)						
1.36	Total		US$ Mn	..	..	15,581	12,951	13,560
1.37	♦ Personal		US$ Mn	..	..	10,642	9,112	9,289
1.38	♦ Business and professional		US$ Mn	..	..	4,939	3,839	4,271
	Indicators							
1.39	Average size of travel party		Persons	..	..	..	..	..
	Average length of stay							
1.40	Total		Days	..	..	..	..	..
1.41	♦ For all commercial accommodation services		Nights	2.45	2.39	2.49	2.47	2.48
1.42	* of which, "hotels and similar establishments"		Nights	..	..	..	..	..
1.43	♦ For non commercial accommodation services		Days	..	..	..	..	..
1.44	Average expenditure per day		US$	..	..	..	..	..
2.	**DOMESTIC TOURISM**							
	Data							
	Trips							
2.1	Total		('000)	..	..	..	..	..
2.2	♦ Overnight visitors (tourists)	(5)	('000)	..	28,640	25,840	24,778	..
2.3	♦ Same-day visitors (excursionists)		('000)	..	..	..	..	..
	Accommodation	(2)						
	Total							
2.19	♦ Guests		('000)	19,367	19,633	21,267	21,931	22,311
2.20	♦ Overnights		('000)	57,629	56,265	64,304	65,328	66,237
	Hotels and similar establishments							
2.21	♦ Guests	(3)	('000)	10,849	11,113	11,504	12,143	12,410
2.22	♦ Overnights	(3)	('000)	17,891	18,352	19,039	19,680	19,910
	Indicators							
2.23	Average size of travel party		Persons	..	..	..	..	..
	Average length of stay							
2.24	Total		Days	..	..	..	..	..
2.25	♦ For all commercial accommodation services		Nights	2.98	2.87	3.02	2.98	2.97
2.26	* of which, "hotels and similar establishments"		Nights	..	..	..	..	..
2.27	♦ For non commercial accommodation services		Days	..	..	..	..	..
2.28	Average expenditure per day		US$	..	..	..	..	..
3.	**OUTBOUND TOURISM**							
	Data							
	Departures							
3.1	Total		('000)	..	..	..	..	..
3.2	♦ Overnight visitors (tourists)	(6)	('000)	18,560	18,628	18,094	17,928	18,070
3.3	♦ Same-day visitors (excursionists)		('000)	..	..	..	..	..

NETHERLANDS

Cod.	Basic data and indicators	Notes	Units	2011	2012	2013	2014	2015
	Expenditure	(4)						
3.4	Total		US$ Mn	..	..	20,706	22,417	21,110
3.5	♦ Travel		US$ Mn	20,741	19,678	20,490	20,435	19,385
3.6	♦ Passenger transport		US$ Mn	..	..	216	1,982	1,725
	Expenditure by main purpose of the trip	(4)						
3.7	Total		US$ Mn	..	..	20,490	20,434	19,387
3.8	♦ Personal		US$ Mn	..	..	15,544	16,767	15,611
3.9	♦ Business and professional		US$ Mn	..	..	4,946	3,667	3,776
4.	**TOURISM INDUSTRIES**							
	Data							
	Number of establishments							
4.1	Total		Units	..	..	..	..	..
4.2	♦ Accommodation for visitors		Units	..	..	..	..	..
4.3	* of which, "hotels and similar establishments"	(2)	Units	3,194	3,155	3,510	3,561	3,525
4.4	♦ Food and beverage serving activities		Units	..	..	..	..	..
4.5	♦ Passenger transportation		Units	..	..	..	..	..
4.6	♦ Travel agencies and other reservation services activities		Units	..	..	..	..	..
4.7	♦ Other tourism industries		Units	..	..	..	..	..
	Accommodation for visitors in hotels and similar establishments							
	Non-monetary data	(2)						
4.13	♦ Number of establishments		Units	3,194	3,155	3,510	3,561	3,525
4.14	♦ Number of rooms	(7)	Units	104,704	105,940	113,813	117,917	118,121
4.15	♦ Number of bed-places	(7)	Units	213,932	216,824	244,145	252,115	254,589
	Indicators							
4.16	Occupancy rate / rooms		Percent	..	..	..	..	..
4.17	Occupancy rate / bed-places	(2)	Percent	45.18	45.49	41.96	44.00	45.46
4.18	Average length of stay	(8)	Nights	1.74	1.73	1.74	1.72	1.72
4.19	Available capacity (bed-places per 1000 inhabitants)		Units	12.82	12.95	14.52	14.95	15.04
6.	**COMPLEMENTARY INDICATORS**							
	Demand							
6.1	Gross travel propensity		Units	..	..	..	..	..
6.2	(1.2 inbound tourists + 2.2 domestic tourists) / population		Units	..	2.41	2.30	2.29	..
	Macroeconomic indicators related to international tourism							
6.3	Inbound tourism expenditure over GDP		Percent	1.4	1.5	2.4	2.1	2.6
6.4	Outbound tourism expenditure over GDP		Percent	2.3	2.4	2.4	2.5	2.8
6.5	Tourism balance (inbound minus outbound tourism expenditure) over GDP		Percent	-0.9	-0.9		-0.4	-0.2
6.6	Tourism openness (inbound plus outbound tourism expenditure) over GDP		Percent	3.7	3.9	4.8	4.6	5.4
6.7	Tourism coverage (inbound over outbound tourism expenditure)		Percent	62.2	62.3	101.0	83.1	91.5
6.8	Inbound tourism expenditure over exports of goods		Percent	2.3	2.2	3.7	3.3	4.1
6.9	Inbound tourism expenditure over exports of services		Percent	9.4	9.2	14.6	11.9	13.4
6.10	Inbound tourism expenditure over exports of goods and services		Percent	1.9	1.8	2.9	2.6	3.1
6.11	Inbound tourism expenditure over current account credits		Percent	1.2	1.2	2.0	1.7	2.2
6.12	Outbound tourism expenditure over imports of goods		Percent	4.5	4.3	4.4	4.8	5.4
6.13	Outbound tourism expenditure over imports of services		Percent	13.7	13.6	13.7	13.9	14.2
6.14	Outbound tourism expenditure over imports of goods and		Percent	3.4	3.3	3.3	3.5	3.9
6.15	Outbound tourism expenditure over current account debits		Percent	2.1	2.1	2.2	2.3	2.6

NEW CALEDONIA

Cod. Basic data and indicators	Notes	Units	2011	2012	2013	2014	2015
1. INBOUND TOURISM							
Data							
Arrivals							
1.1 Total		('000)	348	390	494	529	558
1.2 ♦ Overnight visitors (tourists)	(1)	('000)	112	112	108	107	114
1.3 ♦ Same-day visitors (excursionists)		('000)	236	278	386	422	444
1.4 * of which, cruise passengers		('000)	236	278	386	422	444
Arrivals by region	(1)						
1.5 Total		('000)	112	112	108	107	114
1.6 ♦ Africa		('000)	2	1	1	1	1
1.7 ♦ Americas		('000)	3	3	3	3	3
1.8 ♦ East Asia and the Pacific		('000)	68	65	60	62	67
1.9 ♦ Europe		('000)	39	43	44	41	43
1.10 ♦ Middle East		('000)	..	..	..	..	
1.11 ♦ South Asia		('000)	..	..	..	..	
1.12 ♦ Other not classified		('000)	..	..	..	..	1
1.13 * of which, nationals residing abroad		('000)	..	..	..	..	
Arrivals by main purpose	(1)						
1.14 Total		('000)	112	112	108	107	114
1.15 ♦ Personal		('000)	92	94	90	92	99
1.16 * holidays, leisure and recreation		('000)	51	53	49	54	60
1.17 * other personal purposes		('000)	41	41	41	39	39
1.18 ♦ Business and professional		('000)	20	18	18	15	15
Arrivals by mode of transport	(1)						
1.19 Total		('000)	112	112	108	107	114
1.20 ♦ Air		('000)	112	112	108	107	114
1.21 ♦ Water		('000)	..	..	..	..	
1.22 ♦ Land		('000)	..	..	..	..	
1.23 * railway		('000)	..	..	..	..	
1.24 * road		('000)	..	..	..	..	
1.25 * others		('000)	..	..	..	..	
Accommodation							
Hotels and similar establishments							
1.31 ♦ Guests	(2)	('000)	142	121	117	123	
1.32 ♦ Overnights	(2)	('000)	316	288	286	282	
Expenditure							
1.33 Total		US$ Mn	..	..	..	..	
1.34 ♦ Travel		US$ Mn	166	165	168	184	
1.35 ♦ Passenger transport		US$ Mn	..	..	..	..	
Indicators							
1.39 Average size of travel party		Persons	..	..	..	..	
Average length of stay							
1.40 Total		Days	..	..	..	..	
1.41 ♦ For all commercial accommodation services		Nights	20.10	21.00	20.30	20.20	19.30
1.42 * of which, "hotels and similar establishments"		Nights	..	..	..	..	
1.43 ♦ For non commercial accommodation services		Days	..	..	..	..	
1.44 Average expenditure per day		US$	..	..	..	..	
2. DOMESTIC TOURISM							
Data							
Accommodation							
Hotels and similar establishments							
2.21 ♦ Guests	(2)	('000)	173	166	158	147	
2.22 ♦ Overnights	(2)	('000)	348	344	321	286	
3. OUTBOUND TOURISM							
Data							
Departures							
3.1 Total		('000)	..	..	..	..	
3.2 ♦ Overnight visitors (tourists)	(3)	('000)	124	121	121	124	127
3.3 ♦ Same-day visitors (excursionists)		('000)	..	..	..	..	
Expenditure							
3.4 Total		US$ Mn	..	..	..	..	
3.5 ♦ Travel		US$ Mn	176	159	164	169	
3.6 ♦ Passenger transport		US$ Mn	..	..	..	..	

NEW CALEDONIA

Cod.	Basic data and indicators	Notes	Units	2011	2012	2013	2014	2015
4.	**TOURISM INDUSTRIES**							
	Data							
	Number of establishments							
4.1	Total		Units	..	..	..	..	..
4.2	♦ Accommodation for visitors		Units	..	..	..	..	..
4.3	* of which, "hotels and similar establishments"	(2)	Units	23	22	20	20	21
4.4	♦ Food and beverage serving activities		Units	..	..	..	..	..
4.5	♦ Passenger transportation		Units	..	..	..	..	..
4.6	♦ Travel agencies and other reservation services activities		Units	..	..	..	..	..
4.7	♦ Other tourism industries		Units	..	..	..	..	..
	Accommodation for visitors in hotels and similar establishments							
	Non-monetary data							
4.13	♦ Number of establishments	(2)	Units	23	22	20	20	21
4.14	♦ Number of rooms	(4)	Units	1,785	1,849	1,764	1,764	1,594
4.15	♦ Number of bed-places		Units	..	..	..	..	..
	Indicators							
4.16	Occupancy rate / rooms	(4)	Percent	61.10	58.50	56.60	58.60	62.90
4.17	Occupancy rate / bed-places		Percent	..	..	..	..	..
4.18	Average length of stay	(5)	Nights	2.10	2.34	2.55	2.80	..
4.19	Available capacity (bed-places per 1000 inhabitants)		Units	..	..	..	..	..
6.	**COMPLEMENTARY INDICATORS**							
	Demand							
6.1	Gross travel propensity		Units	..	..	..	..	..
6.2	(1.2 inbound tourists) / population		Units	0.44	0.43	0.41	0.40	0.42
	Macroeconomic indicators related to international tourism							
6.3	Inbound tourism expenditure over GDP		Percent	..	..	..	..	..
6.4	Outbound tourism expenditure over GDP		Percent	..	..	..	..	..
6.5	Tourism balance (inbound minus outbound tourism expenditure) over GDP		Percent	..	..	..	..	..
6.6	Tourism openness (inbound plus outbound tourism expenditure) over GDP		Percent	..	..	..	..	..
6.7	Tourism coverage (inbound over outbound tourism expenditure)		Percent	94.3	103.8	102.4	108.9	..
6.8	Inbound tourism expenditure over exports of goods		Percent	9.9	12.4	13.6	11.6	..
6.9	Inbound tourism expenditure over exports of services		Percent	27.1	26.9	25.0	29.6	..
6.10	Inbound tourism expenditure over exports of goods and services		Percent	7.2	8.5	8.8	8.3	..
6.11	Inbound tourism expenditure over current account credits		Percent	4.1	4.7	4.8	4.9	..
6.12	Outbound tourism expenditure over imports of goods		Percent	5.2	5.1	5.3	5.5	..
6.13	Outbound tourism expenditure over imports of services		Percent	12.8	11.2	11.8	12.9	..
6.14	Outbound tourism expenditure over imports of goods and		Percent	3.7	3.5	3.7	3.8	..
6.15	Outbound tourism expenditure over current account debits		Percent	3.0	2.8	2.9	3.0	..

NEW ZEALAND

Cod.	Basic data and indicators	Notes	Units	2011	2012	2013	2014	201
1.	**INBOUND TOURISM**							
	Data							
	Arrivals							
1.1	Total	(1)(2)	('000)	2,617	2,574	2,745	2,854	3,12
1.2	♦ Overnight visitors (tourists)		('000)	2,511	2,473	2,629	2,772	3,03
1.3	♦ Same-day visitors (excursionists)		('000)	105	101	116	82	9
1.4	* of which, cruise passengers		('000)	22	19	35	33	2
	Arrivals by region	(1)						
1.5	Total		('000)	2,594	2,555	2,710	2,854	3,12
1.6	♦ Africa		('000)	30	19	18	19	2
1.7	♦ Americas		('000)	269	253	279	300	33
1.8	♦ East Asia and the Pacific		('000)	1,695	1,742	1,857	1,956	2,17
1.9	♦ Europe		('000)	476	411	424	447	47
1.10	♦ Middle East		('000)	16	13	14	14	1
1.11	♦ South Asia		('000)	32	33	35	42	5
1.12	♦ Other not classified		('000)	76	83	83	76	6
1.13	* of which, nationals residing abroad		('000)	30	33	27	24	2
	Arrivals by main purpose	(1)						
1.14	Total		('000)	2,594	2,555	2,710	2,854	3,13
1.15	♦ Personal		('000)	2,236	2,202	2,342	2,476	2,73
1.16	* holidays, leisure and recreation		('000)	1,217	1,167	1,281	1,369	1,56
1.17	* other personal purposes		('000)	1,019	1,035	1,061	1,107	1,16
1.18	♦ Business and professional		('000)	358	353	368	378	39
	Arrivals by mode of transport	(1)						
1.19	Total		('000)	2,594	2,555	2,710	2,854	3,12
1.20	♦ Air		('000)	2,568	2,532	2,672	2,817	3,09
1.21	♦ Water		('000)	26	23	38	36	3
1.22	♦ Land		('000)	..	..	..	..	
1.23	* railway		('000)	..	..	..	..	
1.24	* road		('000)	..	..	..	..	
1.25	* others		('000)	..	..	..	..	
	Accommodation							
	Total							
1.29	♦ Guests		('000)	..	..	..	..	
1.30	♦ Overnights	(3)	('000)	12,985	12,188	13,081	13,854	14,71
	Hotels and similar establishments							
1.31	♦ Guests		('000)	..	..	..	..	
1.32	♦ Overnights	(3)(4)	('000)	10,711	10,179	11,084	11,668	12,42
	Expenditure							
1.33	Total		US$ Mn	..	..	..	..	
1.34	♦ Travel		US$ Mn	7,295	7,142	7,419	8,402	9,00
1.35	♦ Passenger transport		US$ Mn	..	..	..	..	
	Expenditure by main purpose of the trip							
1.36	Total		US$ Mn	7,295	7,142	7,420	8,403	9,00
1.37	♦ Personal		US$ Mn	6,710	6,613	6,774	7,760	8,16
1.38	♦ Business and professional		US$ Mn	584	529	646	643	83
	Indicators							
1.39	Average size of travel party		Persons	..	..	..	..	
	Average length of stay							
1.40	Total	(1)	Days	20.00	19.00	19.00	20.00	20.0
1.41	♦ For all commercial accommodation services		Nights	..	..	..	..	
1.42	* of which, "hotels and similar establishments"		Nights	..	..	..	..	
1.43	♦ For non commercial accommodation services		Days	..	..	..	..	
1.44	Average expenditure per day	(1)(5)	US$	141.7	146.9	145.2	149.0	146.
2.	**DOMESTIC TOURISM**							
	Data							
	Trips	(6)						
2.1	Total		('000)	50,068	47,643	..	..	
2.2	♦ Overnight visitors (tourists)		('000)	17,681	16,559	..	..	
2.3	♦ Same-day visitors (excursionists)		('000)	32,387	31,083	..	..	
	Trips by main purpose	(6)						
2.4	Total		('000)	50,068	47,643	..	..	
2.5	♦ Personal		('000)	35,817	34,335	..	..	
2.6	* holidays, leisure and recreation		('000)	33,552	32,398	..	..	
2.7	* other personal purposes		('000)	2,264	1,937	..	..	
2.8	♦ Business and professional		('000)	14,251	13,308	..	..	

NEW ZEALAND

od.	Basic data and indicators	Notes	Units	2011	2012	2013	2014	2015
	Trips by mode of transport	(6)(7)						
9	Total		('000)	57,026	54,322	..	..	..
10	♦ Air		('000)	4,034	4,005	..	..	..
11	♦ Water		('000)	1,856	1,587	..	..	..
12	♦ Land		('000)	51,136	48,729	..	..	..
13	* railway		('000)	704	535	..	..	..
14	* road		('000)	50,231	48,006	..	..	..
15	* others		('000)	201	188	..	..	..
	Accommodation							
	Total							
19	♦ Guests		('000)	..	..	..	..	..
20	♦ Overnights	(3)	('000)	19,033	19,250	19,630	20,758	21,537
	Hotels and similar establishments							
21	♦ Guests		('000)	..	..	..	..	..
22	♦ Overnights	(3)(4)	('000)	14,814	15,022	15,347	16,340	16,804
	Indicators							
23	Average size of travel party	(6)	Persons	3.7	3.8	..	..	..
	Average length of stay							
24	Total	(6)	Days	2.90	3.00	..	..	..
25	♦ For all commercial accommodation services		Nights	..	..	..	..	..
26	* of which, "hotels and similar establishments"		Nights	..	..	..	..	..
27	♦ For non commercial accommodation services		Days	..	..	..	..	..
28	Average expenditure per day	(6)(8)(9)	US$	93.6	100.3	..	..	..
	OUTBOUND TOURISM							
	Data							
	Departures							
1	Total		('000)	..	..	..	..	..
2	♦ Overnight visitors (tourists)	(1)	('000)	2,096	2,172	2,197	2,276	2,412
3	♦ Same-day visitors (excursionists)		('000)	..	..	..	..	..
	Expenditure							
4	Total		US$ Mn	..	..	..	..	..
5	♦ Travel		US$ Mn	3,461	3,715	3,861	4,108	3,727
6	♦ Passenger transport		US$ Mn	..	..	..	..	..
	Expenditure by main purpose of the trip							
7	Total		US$ Mn	3,461	3,715	3,861	4,108	3,727
8	♦ Personal		US$ Mn	2,770	2,983	3,134	3,348	3,055
9	♦ Business and professional		US$ Mn	691	732	727	760	671
	Indicators							
10	Average length of stay	(1)	Days	19.00	20.00	19.00	18.00	18.00
11	Average expenditure per day		US$	..	..	..	..	..
	TOURISM INDUSTRIES							
	Data							
	Number of establishments	(10)(11)						
1	Total		Units	24,564	24,559	24,776	25,395	26,232
2	♦ Accommodation for visitors		Units	4,684	4,653	4,633	4,687	4,731
3	* of which, "hotels and similar establishments"		Units	..	..	..	..	..
4	♦ Food and beverage serving activities		Units	13,530	13,592	13,785	14,155	14,619
5	♦ Passenger transportation		Units	4,172	4,176	4,174	4,309	4,536
6	♦ Travel agencies and other reservation services activities		Units	1,596	1,570	1,607	1,678	1,761
7	♦ Other tourism industries		Units	582	568	577	566	585
	Accommodation for visitors in hotels and similar establishments							
	Non-monetary data	(3)(4)						
13	♦ Number of establishments		Units	2,826	2,797	2,806	2,771	2,756
14	♦ Number of rooms		Units	86,835	87,695	88,791	88,914	89,057
15	♦ Number of bed-places		Units	..	..	..	..	..
	Indicators	(3)(4)						
16	Occupancy rate / rooms		Percent	50.40	48.90	50.90	53.20	60.30
17	Occupancy rate / bed-places		Percent	..	..	..	..	..
18	Average length of stay		Nights	1.90	1.90	1.90	2.00	1.90
19	Available capacity (bed-places per 1000 inhabitants)		Units	..	..	..	..	..

NEW ZEALAND

Cod. Basic data and indicators	Notes	Units	2011	2012	2013	2014	2015
5. EMPLOYMENT							
Data							
Number of employees by tourism industries	(10)						
5.1 Total		('000)	160.5	161.4	162.8	167.4	173.6
5.2 ♦ Accommodation services for visitors (hotels and similar establishments)		('000)	30.1	28.9	28.6	29.1	29.7
5.3 ♦ Other accommodation services		('000)	..	..	..	..	
5.4 ♦ Food and beverage serving activities		('000)	99.1	101.2	103.1	106.1	110.8
5.5 ♦ Passenger transportation		('000)	23.1	23.2	22.9	23.5	24.
5.6 ♦ Travel agencies and other reservation services activities		('000)	6.3	6.2	6.3	6.5	6.8
5.7 ♦ Other tourism industries		('000)	1.9	1.9	1.9	2.2	2.
6. COMPLEMENTARY INDICATORS							
Demand							
6.1 Gross travel propensity		Units	..	..	..	..	
6.2 (1.2 inbound tourists + 2.2 domestic tourists) / population		Units	4.58	4.29	..	..	
Macroeconomic indicators related to international tourism							
6.3 Inbound tourism expenditure over GDP		Percent	4.3	4.0	3.9	4.2	5.2
6.4 Outbound tourism expenditure over GDP		Percent	2.1	2.1	2.0	2.1	2.
6.5 Tourism balance (inbound minus outbound tourism expenditure) over GDP		Percent	2.2	1.9	1.9	2.1	3.
6.6 Tourism openness (inbound plus outbound tourism expenditure) over GDP		Percent	6.4	6.1	5.9	6.3	7.
6.7 Tourism coverage (inbound over outbound tourism expenditure)		Percent	210.8	192.2	192.2	204.5	241.6
6.8 Inbound tourism expenditure over exports of goods		Percent	19.1	19.0	18.7	20.0	26.2
6.9 Inbound tourism expenditure over exports of services		Percent	55.1	54.4	55.0	58.4	62.9
6.10 Inbound tourism expenditure over exports of goods and services		Percent	14.2	14.1	13.9	14.9	18.5
6.11 Inbound tourism expenditure over current account credits		Percent	12.7	12.5	12.4	13.1	16.2
6.12 Outbound tourism expenditure over imports of goods		Percent	9.6	9.9	10.0	10.0	10.4
6.13 Outbound tourism expenditure over imports of services		Percent	28.5	29.9	30.5	31.1	31.9
6.14 Outbound tourism expenditure over imports of goods and		Percent	7.2	7.4	7.5	7.6	7.8
6.15 Outbound tourism expenditure over current account debits		Percent	6.4	6.5	6.6	6.6	6.8

NICARAGUA

Cod.	Basic data and indicators	Notes	Units	2011	2012	2013	2014	2015
1.	**INBOUND TOURISM**							
	Data							
	Arrivals							
1.1	Total		('000)	1,122	1,233	1,273	1,390	1,456
1.2	♦ Overnight visitors (tourists)	(1)	('000)	1,060	1,180	1,229	1,330	1,386
1.3	♦ Same-day visitors (excursionists)		('000)	61	53	44	61	70
1.4	* of which, cruise passengers		('000)	39	41	32	51	46
	Arrivals by region	(1)						
1.5	Total		('000)	1,060	1,180	1,229	1,330	1,386
1.6	♦ Africa		('000)	..	1	1	1	1
1.7	♦ Americas		('000)	894	1,000	1,032	1,024	1,092
1.8	♦ East Asia and the Pacific		('000)	10	11	12	22	25
1.9	♦ Europe		('000)	76	79	83	98	102
1.10	♦ Middle East		('000)	..	..	..	..	..
1.11	♦ South Asia		('000)	2	1	4	2	2
1.12	♦ Other not classified		('000)	78	88	98	182	164
1.13	* of which, nationals residing abroad		('000)	78	88	98	182	164
	Arrivals by main purpose	(1)						
1.14	Total		('000)	1,060	1,180	1,229	1,330	1,386
1.15	♦ Personal		('000)	936	955	960	1,044	1,102
1.16	* holidays, leisure and recreation		('000)	851	852	850	931	973
1.17	* other personal purposes		('000)	85	103	111	113	129
1.18	♦ Business and professional		('000)	124	225	269	286	284
	Arrivals by mode of transport	(1)						
1.19	Total		('000)	1,060	1,180	1,229	1,330	1,386
1.20	♦ Air		('000)	360	392	400	433	466
1.21	♦ Water		('000)	15	17	19	22	19
1.22	♦ Land		('000)	685	771	810	875	901
1.23	* railway		('000)	..	..	..	..	..
1.24	* road		('000)	685	771	810	875	901
1.25	* others		('000)	..	..	..	..	..
	Accommodation							
	Total							
1.29	♦ Guests	(2)	('000)	357	389	410	426	..
1.30	♦ Overnights	(2)	('000)	822	880	973	1,040	..
	Hotels and similar establishments							
1.31	♦ Guests	(3)	('000)	320	344	343	357	..
1.32	♦ Overnights	(3)	('000)	746	801	872	948	..
	Expenditure							
1.33	Total		US$ Mn	..	..	..	..	..
1.34	♦ Travel		US$ Mn	390	421	417	445	529
1.35	♦ Passenger transport		US$ Mn	..	..	..	..	..
	Expenditure by main purpose of the trip							
1.36	Total		US$ Mn	390	421	417	446	529
1.37	♦ Personal		US$ Mn	381	411	407	435	515
1.38	♦ Business and professional		US$ Mn	9	10	10	11	13
	Indicators							
1.39	Average size of travel party		Persons	..	..	..	..	..
	Average length of stay							
1.40	Total		Days	8.10	7.75	7.80	7.67	..
1.41	♦ For all commercial accommodation services		Nights	2.30	2.30	2.20	2.40	..
1.42	* of which, "hotels and similar establishments"		Nights	..	..	..	..	..
1.43	♦ For non commercial accommodation services		Days	..	..	..	..	..
1.44	Average expenditure per day		US$	42.1	42.5	40.3	41.8	41.5
2.	**DOMESTIC TOURISM**							
	Data							
	Accommodation							
	Total							
2.19	♦ Guests	(2)	('000)	191	230	277	287	..
2.20	♦ Overnights	(2)	('000)	267	319	370	387	..
	Hotels and similar establishments							
2.21	♦ Guests	(3)	('000)	145	171	176	197	..
2.22	♦ Overnights	(3)	('000)	200	241	239	264	..
	Indicators							
2.23	Average size of travel party		Persons	..	..	..	..	..
	Average length of stay							
2.24	Total		Days	..	..	..	..	..
2.25	♦ For all commercial accommodation services		Nights	1.40	1.40	1.30	1.30	..
2.26	* of which, "hotels and similar establishments"		Nights	..	..	..	..	..
2.27	♦ For non commercial accommodation services		Days	..	..	..	..	..
2.28	Average expenditure per day		US$	..	..	..	..	..

NICARAGUA

Cod. Basic data and indicators	Notes	Units	2011	2012	2013	2014	2015
3. OUTBOUND TOURISM							
Data							
Departures							
3.1 Total		('000)	..	..	..	..	..
3.2 ♦ Overnight visitors (tourists)		('000)	912	979	994	959	925
3.3 ♦ Same-day visitors (excursionists)		('000)	..	..	..	..	..
Expenditure							
3.4 Total		US$ Mn	240	241	277	361	273
3.5 ♦ Travel		US$ Mn	135	136	143	237	154
3.6 ♦ Passenger transport		US$ Mn	105	105	134	124	119
Expenditure by main purpose of the trip							
3.7 Total		US$ Mn	135	136	143	237	154
3.8 ♦ Personal		US$ Mn	134	133	140	232	150
3.9 ♦ Business and professional		US$ Mn	1	3	3	5	4
Indicators							
3.10 Average length of stay		Days	13.80	14.30	13.40	17.30	..
3.11 Average expenditure per day		US$	23.1	20.3	24.9	23.3	20.6
4. TOURISM INDUSTRIES							
Data							
Number of establishments							
4.1 Total		Units	..	..	..	..	..
4.2 ♦ Accommodation for visitors		Units	..	..	..	..	..
4.3 * of which, "hotels and similar establishments"	(4)	Units	732	821	873	992	1,057
4.4 ♦ Food and beverage serving activities		Units	..	..	..	..	..
4.5 ♦ Passenger transportation		Units	..	..	..	..	..
4.6 ♦ Travel agencies and other reservation services activities		Units	22	21	24	22	27
4.7 ♦ Other tourism industries		Units	..	..	..	..	..
Accommodation for visitors in hotels and similar establishments							
Non-monetary data	(4)						
4.13 ♦ Number of establishments		Units	732	821	873	992	1,057
4.14 ♦ Number of rooms		Units	10,235	11,273	11,817	13,242	13,891
4.15 ♦ Number of bed-places		Units	16,526	18,621	19,850	22,295	23,562
Indicators							
4.16 Occupancy rate / rooms		Percent	63.00	66.00	65.00	64.00	..
4.17 Occupancy rate / bed-places		Percent	..	..	..	..	..
4.18 Average length of stay	(5)	Nights	2.00	1.90	1.90	1.90	..
4.19 Available capacity (bed-places per 1000 inhabitants)		Units	2.85	3.17	3.34	3.71	3.87
5. EMPLOYMENT							
Data							
Number of employees by tourism industries							
5.1 Total		('000)	37.0	43.0	48.0	48.0	..
5.2 ♦ Accommodation services for visitors (hotels and similar establishments)		('000)	..	..	..	..	..
5.3 ♦ Other accommodation services		('000)	..	..	..	..	..
5.4 ♦ Food and beverage serving activities		('000)	..	..	..	..	..
5.5 ♦ Passenger transportation		('000)	..	..	..	..	..
5.6 ♦ Travel agencies and other reservation services activities		('000)	..	..	..	..	..
5.7 ♦ Other tourism industries		('000)	..	..	..	..	..
6. COMPLEMENTARY INDICATORS							
Demand							
6.1 Gross travel propensity		Units	..	..	..	..	..
6.2 (1.2 inbound tourists) / population		Units	0.18	0.20	0.21	0.22	0.23
Macroeconomic indicators related to international tourism							
6.3 Inbound tourism expenditure over GDP		Percent	4.0	4.0	3.8	3.8	..
6.4 Outbound tourism expenditure over GDP		Percent	2.5	2.3	2.6	3.1	..
6.5 Tourism balance (inbound minus outbound tourism expenditure) over GDP		Percent	1.5	1.7	1.2	0.7	..
6.6 Tourism openness (inbound plus outbound tourism expenditure) over GDP		Percent	6.5	6.3	6.4	6.9	..

NICARAGUA

Cod.	Basic data and indicators	Notes	Units	2011	2012	2013	2014	2015
6.7	Tourism coverage (inbound over outbound tourism expenditure)		Percent	162.5	174.7	150.5	123.3	193.8
6.8	Inbound tourism expenditure over exports of goods		Percent	12.8	12.1	12.5	12.3	15.8
6.9	Inbound tourism expenditure over exports of services		Percent	34.4	33.8	31.5	32.1	36.8
6.10	Inbound tourism expenditure over exports of goods and services		Percent	9.4	8.9	9.0	8.9	11.1
6.11	Inbound tourism expenditure over current account credits		Percent	7.2	6.9	6.9	6.9	8.3
6.12	Outbound tourism expenditure over imports of goods		Percent	4.4	4.1	4.8	6.0	4.5
6.13	Outbound tourism expenditure over imports of services		Percent	28.5	26.8	25.9	34.8	28.8
6.14	Outbound tourism expenditure over imports of goods and		Percent	3.8	3.5	4.0	5.1	3.9
6.15	Outbound tourism expenditure over current account debits		Percent	3.8	3.5	4.0	5.1	3.9

NIGER

Cod.	Basic data and indicators	Notes	Units	2011	2012	2013	2014	2015
1.	**INBOUND TOURISM**							
	Data							
	Arrivals							
1.1	Total		('000)	..	..	..	..	..
1.2	♦ Overnight visitors (tourists)		('000)	82	94	123	135	135
1.3	♦ Same-day visitors (excursionists)		('000)	..	..	..	..	..
1.4	* of which, cruise passengers		('000)	..	..	..	..	..
	Arrivals by region							
1.5	Total		('000)	82	94	123	135	135
1.6	♦ Africa		('000)	53	57	70	76	76
1.7	♦ Americas		('000)	5	7	11	12	12
1.8	♦ East Asia and the Pacific		('000)	4	6	10	11	11
1.9	♦ Europe		('000)	20	24	33	36	36
1.10	♦ Middle East		('000)	..	..	..	..	..
1.11	♦ South Asia		('000)	..	..	..	..	..
1.12	♦ Other not classified		('000)	..	..	..	..	..
1.13	* of which, nationals residing abroad		('000)	..	..	..	..	..
	Arrivals by main purpose							
1.14	Total		('000)	82	94	123	135	135
1.15	♦ Personal		('000)	40	46	61	67	67
1.16	* holidays, leisure and recreation		('000)	10	12	16	18	18
1.17	* other personal purposes		('000)	30	34	45	50	50
1.18	♦ Business and professional		('000)	42	48	63	67	67
	Arrivals by mode of transport							
1.19	Total		('000)	82	94	123	135	135
1.20	♦ Air		('000)	82	94	123	135	135
1.21	♦ Water		('000)	..	..	..	..	..
1.22	♦ Land		('000)	..	..	..	..	..
1.23	* railway		('000)	..	..	..	..	..
1.24	* road		('000)	..	..	..	..	..
1.25	* others		('000)	..	..	..	..	..
	Accommodation							
	Total							
1.29	♦ Guests		('000)	75	103	108	79	95
1.30	♦ Overnights		('000)	210	238	226	160	161
	Expenditure							
1.33	Total		US$ Mn	54	51	59	..	..
1.34	♦ Travel		US$ Mn	51	50	58	..	..
1.35	♦ Passenger transport		US$ Mn	3	1	1	..	..
	Expenditure by main purpose of the trip							
1.36	Total		US$ Mn	51	50	58	..	..
1.37	♦ Personal		US$ Mn	17	1	1	..	..
1.38	♦ Business and professional		US$ Mn	34	49	57	..	..
	Indicators							
1.39	Average size of travel party		Persons	..	..	..	..	..
	Average length of stay							
1.40	Total		Days	..	..	..	..	..
1.41	♦ For all commercial accommodation services	(1)	Nights	8.00	8.00	8.00	8.00	8.00
1.42	* of which, "hotels and similar establishments"		Nights	..	..	..	..	..
1.43	♦ For non commercial accommodation services		Days	..	..	..	..	..
1.44	Average expenditure per day		US$	..	..	..	..	..
3.	**OUTBOUND TOURISM**							
	Data							
	Expenditure							
3.4	Total		US$ Mn	57	132	81	..	..
3.5	♦ Travel		US$ Mn	40	36	47	..	..
3.6	♦ Passenger transport		US$ Mn	17	96	34	..	..
	Expenditure by main purpose of the trip							
3.7	Total		US$ Mn	40	36	47	..	..
3.8	♦ Personal		US$ Mn	16	..	0.1	..	..
3.9	♦ Business and professional		US$ Mn	23	36	47	..	..
4.	**TOURISM INDUSTRIES**							
	Data							
	Number of establishments							
4.1	Total		Units	..	..	..	..	..
4.2	♦ Accommodation for visitors		Units	..	..	..	..	..
4.3	* of which, "hotels and similar establishments"		Units	94	92	99	103	125
4.4	♦ Food and beverage serving activities		Units	..	..	..	..	..
4.5	♦ Passenger transportation		Units	..	..	..	..	..

NIGER

Cod.	Basic data and indicators	Notes	Units	2011	2012	2013	2014	2015
4.6	♦ Travel agencies and other reservation services activities		Units	..	..	..	..	..
4.7	♦ Other tourism industries		Units	..	..	..	..	..
	Accommodation for visitors in hotels and similar establishments							
	Non-monetary data							
4.13	♦ Number of establishments		Units	94	92	99	103	125
4.14	♦ Number of rooms		Units	2,123	2,226	2,583	2,284	3,052
4.15	♦ Number of bed-places		Units	3,056	2,892	3,414	2,961	3,812
	Indicators							
4.16	Occupancy rate / rooms		Percent	..	..	..	..	..
4.17	Occupancy rate / bed-places		Percent	..	..	..	..	..
4.18	Average length of stay		Nights	..	..	..	..	..
4.19	Available capacity (bed-places per 1000 inhabitants)		Units	0.18	0.16	0.19	0.15	0.19
6.	**COMPLEMENTARY INDICATORS**							
	Demand							
6.1	Gross travel propensity		Units	..	..	..	..	..
6.2	(1.2 inbound tourists) / population		Units	0.00	0.01	0.01	0.01	0.01
	Macroeconomic indicators related to international tourism							
6.3	Inbound tourism expenditure over GDP		Percent	0.8	0.7	0.8	..	..
6.4	Outbound tourism expenditure over GDP		Percent	0.9	1.9	1.1	..	..
6.5	Tourism balance (inbound minus outbound tourism expenditure) over GDP		Percent	-0.1	-1.2	-0.3	..	..
6.6	Tourism openness (inbound plus outbound tourism expenditure) over GDP		Percent	1.7	2.6	1.9	..	..
6.7	Tourism coverage (inbound over outbound tourism expenditure)		Percent	94.7	38.6	72.8	..	..
6.8	Inbound tourism expenditure over exports of goods		Percent	4.3	3.5	3.7	..	..
6.9	Inbound tourism expenditure over exports of services		Percent	77.9	67.6	40.0	..	..
6.10	Inbound tourism expenditure over exports of goods and services		Percent	4.0	3.4	3.4	..	..
6.11	Inbound tourism expenditure over current account credits		Percent	2.8	2.5	2.7	..	..
6.12	Outbound tourism expenditure over imports of goods		Percent	2.6	6.9	4.0	..	..
6.13	Outbound tourism expenditure over imports of services		Percent	6.5	15.9	8.3	..	..
6.14	Outbound tourism expenditure over imports of goods and		Percent	1.9	4.8	2.7	..	..
6.15	Outbound tourism expenditure over current account debits		Percent	1.7	4.5	2.6	..	..

NIGERIA

Cod.	Basic data and indicators	Notes	Units	2011	2012	2013	2014	2015
1.	**INBOUND TOURISM**							
	Data							
	Arrivals							
1.1	Total		('000)	3,765	4,673	4,038	4,803	6,017
1.2	♦ Overnight visitors (tourists)		('000)	715	486	600	..	1,255
1.3	♦ Same-day visitors (excursionists)		('000)	..	..	..	..	..
1.4	* of which, cruise passengers		('000)	..	..	..	..	..
	Arrivals by region							
1.5	Total		('000)	3,765	4,673	4,038	4,803	6,017
1.6	♦ Africa		('000)	872	1,092	1,281	1,267	1,584
1.7	♦ Americas		('000)	177	478	241	258	405
1.8	♦ East Asia and the Pacific		('000)	340	415	181	168	277
1.9	♦ Europe		('000)	449	699	319	357	594
1.10	♦ Middle East		('000)	38	113	62	66	99
1.11	♦ South Asia		('000)	213	221	98	105	171
1.12	♦ Other not classified		('000)	1,676	1,655	1,856	2,582	2,887
1.13	* of which, nationals residing abroad		('000)	1,676	1,653	1,856	2,582	2,886
	Arrivals by main purpose							
1.14	Total		('000)	3,765	4,673	4,038	4,803	6,017
1.15	♦ Personal		('000)	1,977	2,341	3,224	3,238	4,311
1.16	* holidays, leisure and recreation		('000)	599	300	910	1,234	3,273
1.17	* other personal purposes		('000)	1,378	2,041	2,314	2,004	1,038
1.18	♦ Business and professional		('000)	1,788	2,333	813	1,565	1,706
	Arrivals by mode of transport							
1.19	Total		('000)	3,765	4,673	4,038	4,803	6,017
1.20	♦ Air		('000)	2,503	2,313	2,439	2,699	3,310
1.21	♦ Water		('000)	67	257	319	624	786
1.22	♦ Land		('000)	1,195	2,103	1,280	1,480	1,922
1.23	* railway		('000)	..	..	..	..	..
1.24	* road		('000)	1,195	2,103	1,280	1,480	1,922
1.25	* others		('000)	..	..	..	..	..
	Arrivals by form of organization of the trip							
1.26	Total		('000)	3,765	4,673	4,038	4,803	6,017
1.27	♦ Package tour		('000)	230	348	772	1,205	1,233
1.28	♦ Other forms		('000)	3,535	4,325	3,266	3,598	4,784
	Expenditure							
1.33	Total		US$ Mn	688	639	616	601	470
1.34	♦ Travel		US$ Mn	623	555	538	539	412
1.35	♦ Passenger transport		US$ Mn	65	84	78	62	58
	Indicators							
1.39	Average size of travel party		Persons	..	..	..	6.0	6.0
	Average length of stay							
1.40	Total		Days	..	..	..	7.00	8.00
1.41	♦ For all commercial accommodation services		Nights	..	..	..	..	..
1.42	* of which, "hotels and similar establishments"		Nights	..	..	..	..	..
1.43	♦ For non commercial accommodation services		Days	..	..	..	..	..
1.44	Average expenditure per day		US$	..	..	..	..	..
2.	**DOMESTIC TOURISM**							
	Data							
	Trips							
2.1	Total		('000)	..	..	9,246	12,888	17,536
2.2	♦ Overnight visitors (tourists)		('000)	..	..	3,606	2,320	7,622
2.3	♦ Same-day visitors (excursionists)		('000)	..	..	5,640	10,568	9,914
	Trips by main purpose							
2.4	Total		('000)	..	..	9,246	12,888	17,536
2.5	♦ Personal		('000)	..	..	7,392	8,165	11,662
2.6	* holidays, leisure and recreation		('000)	..	..	2,110	3,858	6,927
2.7	* other personal purposes		('000)	..	..	5,282	4,308	4,735
2.8	♦ Business and professional		('000)	..	..	1,854	4,723	5,874
	Trips by mode of transport							
2.9	Total		('000)	..	..	9,246	12,888	17,536
2.10	♦ Air		('000)	..	..	2,589	6,251	7,007
2.11	♦ Water		('000)	..	..	1,073	982	900
2.12	♦ Land		('000)	..	..	5,584	5,656	9,629
2.13	* railway		('000)	..	..	..	..	..
2.14	* road		('000)	..	..	5,584	5,656	9,629
2.15	* others		('000)	..	..	..	..	..

NIGERIA

Cod.	Basic data and indicators	Notes	Units	2011	2012	2013	2014	2015
	Trips by form of organization							
2.16	Total		('000)	..	..	9,246	12,888	17,536
2.17	♦ Package tour		('000)	..	..	3,504	2,475	3,578
2.18	♦ Other forms		('000)	..	..	5,742	10,414	13,958
	Indicators							
2.23	Average size of travel party		Persons	..	..	..	6.0	7.0
	Average length of stay							
2.24	Total		Days	..	..	7.00	9.00	9.00
2.25	♦ For all commercial accommodation services		Nights	..	..	..	..	..
2.26	* of which, "hotels and similar establishments"		Nights	..	..	..	..	..
2.27	♦ For non commercial accommodation services		Days	..	..	..	..	..
2.28	Average expenditure per day		US$	..	..	..	..	..
3.	**OUTBOUND TOURISM**							
	Data							
	Expenditure							
3.4	Total		US$ Mn	9,533	9,240	9,150	9,068	9,200
3.5	♦ Travel		US$ Mn	6,598	6,141	5,864	5,764	5,723
3.6	♦ Passenger transport		US$ Mn	2,935	3,099	3,286	3,304	3,477
	Expenditure by main purpose of the trip							
3.7	Total		US$ Mn	6,599	6,141	5,864	5,764	5,723
3.8	♦ Personal		US$ Mn	5,497	5,318	5,179	4,618	4,385
3.9	♦ Business and professional		US$ Mn	1,102	823	685	1,146	1,338
4.	**TOURISM INDUSTRIES**							
	Data							
	Number of establishments	(1)						
4.1	Total		Units	24,605	31,128	35,187	41,491	126,559
4.2	♦ Accommodation for visitors		Units	..	..	..	..	..
4.3	* of which, "hotels and similar establishments"		Units	9,250	14,008	17,110	21,036	27,403
4.4	♦ Food and beverage serving activities		Units	..	..	..	..	62,200
4.5	♦ Passenger transportation		Units	..	..	..	..	5,242
4.6	♦ Travel agencies and other reservation services activities		Units	..	..	..	..	5,084
4.7	♦ Other tourism industries		Units	15,355	17,120	18,077	20,455	26,630
	Accommodation for visitors in hotels and similar establishments							
	Non-monetary data	(1)						
4.13	♦ Number of establishments		Units	9,250	14,008	17,110	21,036	27,403
4.14	♦ Number of rooms		Units	..	..	..	..	..
4.15	♦ Number of bed-places		Units	277,522	345,514	367,972	417,368	568,556
	Indicators							
4.16	Occupancy rate / rooms		Percent	..	..	..	..	..
4.17	Occupancy rate / bed-places		Percent	..	..	..	..	..
4.18	Average length of stay		Nights	..	5.00	7.00	7.00	8.00
4.19	Available capacity (bed-places per 1000 inhabitants)		Units	1.69	2.05	2.13	2.35	3.12
5.	**EMPLOYMENT**							
	Data							
	Number of employees by tourism industries							
5.1	Total		('000)	..	..	..	881.5	1,082.9
5.2	♦ Accommodation services for visitors (hotels and similar establishments)		('000)	..	..	..	194.2	240.7
5.3	♦ Other accommodation services		('000)	..	..	..	86.0	72.5
5.4	♦ Food and beverage serving activities		('000)	..	..	..	416.0	562.0
5.5	♦ Passenger transportation		('000)	..	..	..	47.4	51.8
5.6	♦ Travel agencies and other reservation services activities		('000)	..	..	..	42.0	27.1
5.7	♦ Other tourism industries		('000)	..	..	..	95.9	128.8
6.	**COMPLEMENTARY INDICATORS**							
	Demand							
6.1	Gross travel propensity		Units	..	..	..	..	..
6.2	(1.2 inbound tourists + 2.2 domestic tourists) / population		Units	..	..	0.02	..	0.05

NIGERIA

Cod.	Basic data and indicators	Notes	Units	2011	2012	2013	2014	2015
	Macroeconomic indicators related to international tourism							
6.3	Inbound tourism expenditure over GDP		Percent	0.2	0.1	0.1	0.1	..
6.4	Outbound tourism expenditure over GDP		Percent	2.3	2.0	1.8	1.6	..
6.5	Tourism balance (inbound minus outbound tourism expenditure) over GDP		Percent	-2.1	-1.9	-1.7	-1.5	..
6.6	Tourism openness (inbound plus outbound tourism expenditure) over GDP		Percent	2.5	2.1	1.9	1.7	..
6.7	Tourism coverage (inbound over outbound tourism expenditure)		Percent	7.2	6.9	6.7	6.6	5.1
6.8	Inbound tourism expenditure over exports of goods		Percent	0.7	0.7	0.6	0.7	..
6.9	Inbound tourism expenditure over exports of services		Percent	20.3	26.6	25.7	30.4	..
6.10	Inbound tourism expenditure over exports of goods and services		Percent	0.7	0.6	0.6	0.7	..
6.11	Inbound tourism expenditure over current account credits		Percent	0.5	0.5	0.5	0.6	..
6.12	Outbound tourism expenditure over imports of goods		Percent	14.4	16.2	16.7	14.8	..
6.13	Outbound tourism expenditure over imports of services		Percent	38.8	38.6	42.0	37.4	..
6.14	Outbound tourism expenditure over imports of goods and		Percent	10.5	11.4	11.9	10.6	..
6.15	Outbound tourism expenditure over current account debits		Percent	10.3	11.2	11.7	10.3	..

NIUE

Cod.	Basic data and indicators	Notes	Units	2011	2012	2013	2014	2015
1.	**INBOUND TOURISM**							
	**Data**							
	Arrivals							
1.1	Total		('000)	..	..	..	..	..
1.2	♦ Overnight visitors (tourists)	(1)	('000)	6.1	5.0	7.0	7.4	7.7
1.3	♦ Same-day visitors (excursionists)		('000)	..	..	..	..	..
1.4	* of which, cruise passengers		('000)	..	..	..	..	..
	Arrivals by region							
1.5	Total		('000)	6.1	5.0	7.0	7.4	7.7
1.6	♦ Africa		('000)	..	..	..	..	..
1.7	♦ Americas		('000)	1.2	0.1	0.2	0.2	0.1
1.8	♦ East Asia and the Pacific		('000)	4.4	4.6	6.4	6.9	7.3
1.9	♦ Europe		('000)	0.4	0.3	0.4	0.3	0.3
1.10	♦ Middle East		('000)	..	..	..	..	..
1.11	♦ South Asia		('000)	..	..	..	..	..
1.12	♦ Other not classified		('000)	0.1	..	..	..	..
1.13	* of which, nationals residing abroad		('000)	..	..	..	..	..
	Arrivals by main purpose							
1.14	Total		('000)	..	..	..	..	7.7
1.15	♦ Personal		('000)	..	..	..	..	6.6
1.16	* holidays, leisure and recreation		('000)	..	..	..	..	4.7
1.17	* other personal purposes		('000)	..	..	..	..	1.9
1.18	♦ Business and professional		('000)	..	..	..	..	1.1
6.	**COMPLEMENTARY INDICATORS**							
	Demand							
6.1	Gross travel propensity		Units	..	..	..	..	..
6.2	(1.2 inbound tourists) / population		Units	3.77	3.10	4.35	4.60	4.78

NORTHERN MARIANA ISLANDS

Cod.	Basic data and indicators	Notes	Units	2011	2012	2013	2014	2015
1.	**INBOUND TOURISM**							
	Data							
	Arrivals							
1.1	Total	(1)	('000)	341	401	439	460	479
1.2	♦ Overnight visitors (tourists)		('000)	336	..	..	..	..
1.3	♦ Same-day visitors (excursionists)		('000)	5	..	..	..	..
1.4	* of which, cruise passengers		('000)	5	..	..	..	..
	Arrivals by region							
1.5	Total		('000)	341	401	439	460	479
1.6	♦ Africa		('000)	..	..	..	..	..
1.7	♦ Americas		('000)	24	22	21	20	20
1.8	♦ East Asia and the Pacific	(2)	('000)	310	370	400	424	452
1.9	♦ Europe		('000)	6	6	12	11	2
1.10	♦ Middle East		('000)	..	..	..	..	..
1.11	♦ South Asia		('000)	..	..	..	..	..
1.12	♦ Other not classified		('000)	1	3	5	4	4
1.13	* of which, nationals residing abroad		('000)	..	..	..	..	..
	Arrivals by main purpose							
1.14	Total		('000)	341	..	..	..	..
1.15	♦ Personal		('000)	341	..	..	..	..
1.16	* holidays, leisure and recreation		('000)	341	..	..	..	..
1.17	* other personal purposes		('000)	..	..	..	..	..
1.18	♦ Business and professional		('000)	..	..	..	..	..
	Arrivals by mode of transport							
1.19	Total		('000)	341	..	..	..	..
1.20	♦ Air		('000)	336	..	..	..	..
1.21	♦ Water		('000)	5	..	..	..	..
1.22	♦ Land		('000)	..	..	..	..	..
1.23	* railway		('000)	..	..	..	..	..
1.24	* road		('000)	..	..	..	..	..
1.25	* others		('000)	..	..	..	..	..
4.	**TOURISM INDUSTRIES**							
	Data							
	Number of establishments							
4.1	Total		Units	..	..	..	..	..
4.2	♦ Accommodation for visitors		Units	..	..	..	..	..
4.3	* of which, "hotels and similar establishments"	(3)	Units	33	..	..	..	..
4.4	♦ Food and beverage serving activities		Units	..	..	..	..	..
4.5	♦ Passenger transportation		Units	..	..	..	..	..
4.6	♦ Travel agencies and other reservation services activities		Units	..	..	..	..	..
4.7	♦ Other tourism industries		Units	..	..	..	..	..
	Accommodation for visitors in hotels and similar establishments							
	Non-monetary data							
4.13	♦ Number of establishments	(3)	Units	33	..	..	..	..
4.14	♦ Number of rooms	(3)	Units	3,484	..	..	..	..
4.15	♦ Number of bed-places		Units	..	..	..	..	..
	Indicators							
4.16	Occupancy rate / rooms		Percent	63.70	..	..	..	..
4.17	Occupancy rate / bed-places		Percent	..	..	..	..	..
4.18	Average length of stay		Nights	..	..	..	..	..
4.19	Available capacity (bed-places per 1000 inhabitants)		Units	..	..	..	..	..
6.	**COMPLEMENTARY INDICATORS**							
	Demand							
6.1	Gross travel propensity		Units	..	..	..	..	..
6.2	(1.2 inbound tourists) / population		Units	6.31	..	..	..	..

NORWAY

Cod.	Basic data and indicators	Notes	Units	2011	2012	2013	2014	2015
1.	**INBOUND TOURISM**							
	Data							
	Arrivals	(1)						
1.1	Total		('000)	6,693	..	..	..	..
1.2	♦ Overnight visitors (tourists)	(2)	('000)	4,963	4,538	4,778	4,855	5,361
1.3	♦ Same-day visitors (excursionists)		('000)	1,730	..	..	..	..
1.4	* of which, cruise passengers		('000)	457	588	620	574	511
	Arrivals by region	(1)(2)						
1.5	Total		('000)	4,963	4,538	4,778	4,855	5,361
1.6	♦ Africa		('000)	..	22	25	26	29
1.7	♦ Americas	(3)	('000)	164	245	262	326	332
1.8	♦ East Asia and the Pacific	(4)	('000)	27	378	492	489	654
1.9	♦ Europe		('000)	4,471	3,894	4,000	4,013	4,346
1.10	♦ Middle East		('000)	..	..	..	..	..
1.11	♦ South Asia		('000)	..	..	..	..	..
1.12	♦ Other not classified		('000)	301	..	..	..	..
1.13	* of which, nationals residing abroad		('000)	..	..	..	..	..
	Arrivals by main purpose	(1)						
1.14	Total		('000)	4,963	..	..	..	..
1.15	♦ Personal		('000)	3,867	..	..	..	..
1.16	* holidays, leisure and recreation		('000)	3,867	..	..	..	..
1.17	* other personal purposes		('000)	..	..	..	..	..
1.18	♦ Business and professional		('000)	1,096	..	..	..	..
	Arrivals by mode of transport	(1)						
1.19	Total		('000)	4,964	..	..	..	..
1.20	♦ Air		('000)	2,137	..	..	..	..
1.21	♦ Water		('000)	827	..	..	..	..
1.22	♦ Land		('000)	2,000	..	..	..	..
1.23	* railway		('000)	121	..	..	..	..
1.24	* road		('000)	1,879	..	..	..	..
1.25	* others		('000)	..	..	..	..	..
	Accommodation							
	Total							
1.29	♦ Guests		('000)	..	4,538	4,778	4,855	5,361
1.30	♦ Overnights		('000)	7,844	7,940	7,693	8,154	8,829
	Hotels and similar establishments							
1.31	♦ Guests		('000)	2,973	2,928	3,173	3,252	3,634
1.32	♦ Overnights	(5)(6)	('000)	4,899	5,051	5,069	5,428	6,032
	Expenditure							
1.33	Total		US$ Mn	6,565	6,784	7,175	6,682	5,749
1.34	♦ Travel		US$ Mn	5,329	5,436	5,627	5,650	4,942
1.35	♦ Passenger transport		US$ Mn	1,236	1,348	1,548	1,032	807
2.	**DOMESTIC TOURISM**							
	Data							
	Trips							
2.1	Total		('000)	22,300	22,530	24,340	24,650	22,520
2.2	♦ Overnight visitors (tourists)		('000)	..	..	..	..	..
2.3	♦ Same-day visitors (excursionists)		('000)	..	..	..	..	..
	Accommodation							
	Total							
2.19	♦ Guests		('000)	..	14,124	13,826	18,679	17,095
2.20	♦ Overnights		('000)	29,074	29,915	29,243	30,307	31,654
	Hotels and similar establishments							
2.21	♦ Guests		('000)	9,016	9,483	9,511	9,472	9,724
2.22	♦ Overnights		('000)	14,304	14,753	14,706	15,007	15,634
3.	**OUTBOUND TOURISM**							
	Data							
	Expenditure							
3.4	Total		US$ Mn	16,958	18,131	20,116	19,504	16,329
3.5	♦ Travel		US$ Mn	15,823	16,603	18,465	18,853	15,821
3.6	♦ Passenger transport		US$ Mn	1,135	1,528	1,651	651	508
	Expenditure by main purpose of the trip							
3.7	Total		US$ Mn	15,823	16,603	18,465	18,853	15,821
3.8	♦ Personal		US$ Mn	12,544	13,211	15,091	15,596	13,278
3.9	♦ Business and professional		US$ Mn	3,279	3,392	3,374	3,257	2,543

NORWAY

Cod.	Basic data and indicators	Notes	Units	2011	2012	2013	2014	2015
4.	**TOURISM INDUSTRIES**							
	Data							
	Number of establishments							
4.1	Total		Units	..	..	..	..	..
4.2	♦ Accommodation for visitors		Units	2,250	2,249	2,798	2,690	2,547
4.3	* of which, "hotels and similar establishments"	(6)	Units	1,115	1,102	1,201	1,145	1,086
4.4	♦ Food and beverage serving activities		Units	..	..	..	..	..
4.5	♦ Passenger transportation		Units	..	..	..	..	..
4.6	♦ Travel agencies and other reservation services activities		Units	..	..	..	..	..
4.7	♦ Other tourism industries		Units	..	..	..	..	..
	Accommodation for visitors in hotels and similar establishments							
	Monetary data							
4.8	♦ Output	(7)	US$ Mn	4,234.9	4,317.3	4,419.1	4,363.0	..
4.9	♦ Intermediate consumption		US$ Mn	..	..	..	..	..
4.10	♦ Gross value added	(7)(8)	US$ Mn	1,870.6	1,864.5	1,894.6	1,860.4	..
4.11	♦ Compensation of employees		US$ Mn	..	..	..	..	..
4.12	♦ Gross fixed capital formation	(8)	US$ Mn	164.2	243.6	196.0	..	..
	Non-monetary data	(6)						
4.13	♦ Number of establishments		Units	1,115	1,102	1,201	1,145	1,086
4.14	♦ Number of rooms		Units	80,150	81,923	84,341	84,810	85,063
4.15	♦ Number of bed-places		Units	178,203	186,675	186,338	185,437	184,720
	Indicators							
4.16	Occupancy rate / rooms		Percent	52.40	52.60	52.40	52.90	53.70
4.17	Occupancy rate / bed-places		Percent	35.60	35.40	35.10	35.70	37.40
4.18	Average length of stay		Nights	1.60	1.60	1.56	1.61	1.62
4.19	Available capacity (bed-places per 1000 inhabitants)		Units	35.97	37.20	36.66	36.02	35.45
	Travel agencies and other reservation service activities							
	Monetary data							
4.20	♦ Output	(7)	US$ Mn	3,051.2	3,225.7	3,333.3	2,995.9	..
4.21	♦ Intermediate consumption		US$ Mn	..	..	..	..	..
4.22	♦ Gross value added	(7)(8)	US$ Mn	581.6	580.7	551.7	510.5	..
4.23	♦ Compensation of employees		US$ Mn	..	..	..	..	..
4.24	♦ Gross fixed capital formation	(8)	US$ Mn	30.5	20.8	31.5	..	..
5.	**EMPLOYMENT**							
	Data							
	Number of employees by tourism industries							
5.1	Total	(7)(8)	('000)	151.5	153.0	153.9	157.3	..
5.2	♦ Accommodation services for visitors (hotels and similar establishments)		('000)	22.8	23.3	23.4	24.4	..
5.3	♦ Other accommodation services		('000)	..	..	..	..	..
5.4	♦ Food and beverage serving activities		('000)	41.8	42.1	43.8	45.6	..
5.5	♦ Passenger transportation		('000)	49.3	49.8	50.1	50.2	..
5.6	♦ Travel agencies and other reservation services activities		('000)	5.1	5.3	5.3	5.3	..
5.7	♦ Other tourism industries		('000)	32.5	32.5	31.3	31.8	..
6.	**COMPLEMENTARY INDICATORS**							
	Demand							
6.1	Gross travel propensity		Units	..	..	..	..	..
6.2	(1.2 inbound tourists + 2.1 domestic visitors) / population		Units	5.50	5.39	5.73	5.73	5.26
	Macroeconomic indicators related to international tourism							
6.3	Inbound tourism expenditure over GDP		Percent	1.3	1.4	1.4	1.3	1.5
6.4	Outbound tourism expenditure over GDP		Percent	3.5	3.6	3.9	3.9	4.2
6.5	Tourism balance (inbound minus outbound tourism expenditure) over GDP		Percent	-2.2	-2.2	-2.5	-2.6	-2.7
6.6	Tourism openness (inbound plus outbound tourism expenditure) over GDP		Percent	4.8	5.0	5.3	5.2	5.7
6.7	Tourism coverage (inbound over outbound tourism expenditure)		Percent	38.7	37.4	35.7	34.3	35.2
6.8	Inbound tourism expenditure over exports of goods		Percent	4.0	4.2	4.6	4.6	5.6
6.9	Inbound tourism expenditure over exports of services		Percent	16.0	14.6	14.8	13.5	14.2
6.10	Inbound tourism expenditure over exports of goods and services		Percent	3.2	3.3	3.5	3.5	4.0
6.11	Inbound tourism expenditure over current account credits		Percent	2.6	2.7	2.9	2.7	3.0
6.12	Outbound tourism expenditure over imports of goods		Percent	18.6	20.7	22.0	21.5	21.5
6.13	Outbound tourism expenditure over imports of services		Percent	35.5	34.6	35.7	34.7	35.5
6.14	Outbound tourism expenditure over imports of goods and		Percent	12.2	12.9	13.6	13.3	13.4
6.15	Outbound tourism expenditure over current account debits		Percent	9.0	9.4	9.9	9.3	9.4

OMAN

Cod.	Basic data and indicators	Notes	Units	2011	2012	2013	2014	2015
1.	**INBOUND TOURISM**							
	Data							
	Arrivals	(1)						
1.1	Total		('000)	1,393	1,714	1,923	2,225	2,619
1.2	♦ Overnight visitors (tourists)		('000)	1,018	1,241	1,392	1,611	1,897
1.3	♦ Same-day visitors (excursionists)		('000)	375	473	531	614	721
1.4	* of which, cruise passengers		('000)	..	257	202	125	147
	Arrivals by region	(1)						
1.5	Total		('000)	1,393	1,713	1,923	2,225	2,619
1.6	♦ Africa		('000)	..	..	..	..	31
1.7	♦ Americas		('000)	..	..	..	..	117
1.8	♦ East Asia and the Pacific		('000)	..	..	..	..	171
1.9	♦ Europe		('000)	250	321	372	508	515
1.10	♦ Middle East		('000)	730	799	995	1,091	1,222
1.11	♦ South Asia		('000)	258	389	435	478	429
1.12	♦ Other not classified		('000)	155	204	121	148	132
1.13	* of which, nationals residing abroad		('000)	..	..	..	..	130
	Arrivals by main purpose	(1)						
1.14	Total		('000)	1,392	1,713	1,923	2,225	2,619
1.15	♦ Personal		('000)	1,162	1,392	1,563	1,821	2,136
1.16	* holidays, leisure and recreation		('000)	479	587	648	804	892
1.17	* other personal purposes		('000)	683	805	915	1,017	1,244
1.18	♦ Business and professional		('000)	230	321	360	404	483
	Accommodation							
	Hotels and similar establishments							
1.31	♦ Guests	(2)	('000)	1,678	1,890	2,048	2,409	2,736
1.32	♦ Overnights	(2)	('000)	1,808	2,207	2,518	2,678	2,975
	Expenditure							
1.33	Total		US$ Mn	1,515	1,723	1,888	1,972	2,247
1.34	♦ Travel		US$ Mn	995	1,096	1,295	1,375	1,540
1.35	♦ Passenger transport		US$ Mn	520	627	593	597	707
	Expenditure by main purpose of the trip							
1.36	Total		US$ Mn	995	1,096	1,295	1,375	1,540
1.37	♦ Personal		US$ Mn	692	762	900	969	1,117
1.38	♦ Business and professional		US$ Mn	303	334	395	406	423
	Indicators							
1.39	Average size of travel party		Persons	..	..	..	..	..
	Average length of stay							
1.40	Total		Days	6.38	6.91	6.88	7.43	6.90
1.41	♦ For all commercial accommodation services		Nights	..	..	..	..	..
1.42	* of which, "hotels and similar establishments"		Nights	..	..	..	..	..
1.43	♦ For non commercial accommodation services		Days	..	..	..	..	..
1.44	Average expenditure per day		US$	..	..	..	..	..
3.	**OUTBOUND TOURISM**							
	Data							
	Departures							
3.1	Total		('000)	3,341	3,972	4,301	4,727	5,424
3.2	♦ Overnight visitors (tourists)		('000)	2,446	2,888	3,103	3,358	3,838
3.3	♦ Same-day visitors (excursionists)		('000)	895	1,084	1,198	1,369	1,586
	Expenditure							
3.4	Total		US$ Mn	1,493	1,644	1,824	2,080	2,178
3.5	♦ Travel		US$ Mn	1,168	1,282	1,426	1,654	1,739
3.6	♦ Passenger transport		US$ Mn	325	362	398	426	439
	Expenditure by main purpose of the trip							
3.7	Total		US$ Mn	1,168	1,282	1,426	1,654	1,739
3.8	♦ Personal		US$ Mn	978	1,072	1,182	1,361	1,425
3.9	♦ Business and professional		US$ Mn	190	210	244	293	314
	Indicators							
3.10	Average length of stay		Days	20.67	19.65	22.59	21.60	21.30
3.11	Average expenditure per day		US$	..	..	..	..	..

OMAN

Cod.	Basic data and indicators	Notes	Units	2011	2012	2013	2014	2015
4.	**TOURISM INDUSTRIES**							
	Data							
	Number of establishments							
4.1	Total		Units	..	..	..	..	..
4.2	♦ Accommodation for visitors		Units	..	..	..	..	..
4.3	* of which, "hotels and similar establishments"		Units	235	248	266	286	318
4.4	♦ Food and beverage serving activities		Units	..	..	..	..	..
4.5	♦ Passenger transportation		Units	..	..	..	..	..
4.6	♦ Travel agencies and other reservation services activities		Units	..	..	..	..	..
4.7	♦ Other tourism industries		Units	..	..	..	..	..
	Accommodation for visitors in hotels and similar establishments							
	Monetary data							
4.8	♦ Output		US$ Mn	398.4	468.7	506.5	537.7	540.3
4.9	♦ Intermediate consumption		US$ Mn	..	..	..	..	..
4.10	♦ Gross value added		US$ Mn	..	..	..	..	..
4.11	♦ Compensation of employees		US$ Mn	..	..	..	..	..
4.12	♦ Gross fixed capital formation		US$ Mn	..	..	..	..	..
	Non-monetary data							
4.13	♦ Number of establishments		Units	235	248	266	286	318
4.14	♦ Number of rooms		Units	11,753	12,352	13,603	14,815	15,568
4.15	♦ Number of bed-places		Units	19,264	20,061	22,521	23,997	25,966
	Indicators							
4.16	Occupancy rate / rooms		Percent	43.38	45.79	47.72	49.24	50.00
4.17	Occupancy rate / bed-places		Percent	..	..	..	..	..
4.18	Average length of stay		Nights	1.08	1.17	1.23	1.11	..
4.19	Available capacity (bed-places per 1000 inhabitants)		Units	6.00	5.66	5.76	5.66	5.78
5.	**EMPLOYMENT**							
	Data							
	Number of employees by tourism industries							
5.1	Total		('000)	..	..	..	..	..
5.2	♦ Accommodation services for visitors (hotels and similar establishments)		('000)	9.5	9.6	9.9	10.7	11.1
5.3	♦ Other accommodation services		('000)	..	..	..	..	..
5.4	♦ Food and beverage serving activities		('000)	..	..	..	..	..
5.5	♦ Passenger transportation		('000)	..	..	..	..	..
5.6	♦ Travel agencies and other reservation services activities		('000)	..	..	..	..	..
5.7	♦ Other tourism industries		('000)	..	..	..	..	..
6.	**COMPLEMENTARY INDICATORS**							
	Demand							
6.1	Gross travel propensity		Units	..	..	..	..	..
6.2	(1.2 inbound tourists) / population		Units	0.32	0.35	0.36	0.38	0.42
	Macroeconomic indicators related to international tourism							
6.3	Inbound tourism expenditure over GDP		Percent	2.2	2.2	2.4	2.4	..
6.4	Outbound tourism expenditure over GDP		Percent	2.2	2.1	2.3	2.5	..
6.5	Tourism balance (inbound minus outbound tourism expenditure) over GDP		Percent		0.1	0.1	-0.1	..
6.6	Tourism openness (inbound plus outbound tourism expenditure) over GDP		Percent	4.4	4.3	4.7	4.9	..
6.7	Tourism coverage (inbound over outbound tourism expenditure)		Percent	101.5	104.8	103.5	94.8	103.2
6.8	Inbound tourism expenditure over exports of goods		Percent	3.2	3.3	3.3	3.7	..
6.9	Inbound tourism expenditure over exports of services		Percent	65.0	64.1	64.4	64.3	..
6.10	Inbound tourism expenditure over exports of goods and services		Percent	3.1	3.1	3.2	3.5	..
6.11	Inbound tourism expenditure over current account credits		Percent	3.0	3.1	3.1	3.4	..
6.12	Outbound tourism expenditure over imports of goods		Percent	6.9	6.4	5.7	7.5	..
6.13	Outbound tourism expenditure over imports of services		Percent	19.3	18.8	18.6	20.3	..
6.14	Outbound tourism expenditure over imports of goods and		Percent	5.1	4.8	4.4	5.5	..
6.15	Outbound tourism expenditure over current account debits		Percent	4.0	3.8	3.4	4.2	..

PALAU

Cod.	Basic data and indicators	Notes	Units	2011	2012	2013	2014	2015
1.	**INBOUND TOURISM**							
	Data							
	Arrivals							
1.1	Total		('000)	..	..	..	..	..
1.2	♦ Overnight visitors (tourists)	(1)	('000)	111	120	108	140	162
1.3	♦ Same-day visitors (excursionists)		('000)	..	..	..	..	..
1.4	* of which, cruise passengers		('000)	..	..	..	..	..
	Arrivals by region	(1)						
1.5	Total		('000)	111	120	108	140	162
1.6	♦ Africa		('000)	..	..	..	..	..
1.7	♦ Americas		('000)	9	8	9	9	9
1.8	♦ East Asia and the Pacific		('000)	98	107	93	126	149
1.9	♦ Europe		('000)	5	5	6	5	4
1.10	♦ Middle East		('000)	..	..	..	..	..
1.11	♦ South Asia		('000)	..	..	..	..	..
1.12	♦ Other not classified		('000)	..	..	..	..	..
1.13	* of which, nationals residing abroad		('000)	..	..	..	..	..
	Arrivals by main purpose	(1)						
1.14	Total		('000)	109	119	105	141	162
1.15	♦ Personal		('000)	106	116	102	139	160
1.16	* holidays, leisure and recreation		('000)	106	116	102	139	160
1.17	* other personal purposes		('000)	..	..	..	..	..
1.18	♦ Business and professional		('000)	3	3	3	2	2
	Arrivals by mode of transport							
1.19	Total		('000)	111	120	108	140	162
1.20	♦ Air		('000)	111	120	108	140	162
1.21	♦ Water		('000)	..	..	..	..	..
1.22	♦ Land		('000)	..	..	..	..	..
1.23	* railway		('000)	..	..	..	..	..
1.24	* road		('000)	..	..	..	..	..
1.25	* others		('000)	..	..	..	..	..
	Accommodation							
	Hotels and similar establishments							
1.31	♦ Guests		('000)	..	..	..	..	..
1.32	♦ Overnights		('000)	512	555	520	663	749
	Expenditure							
1.33	Total		US$ Mn	94	109	117	131	156
1.34	♦ Travel	(2)	US$ Mn	91	105	113	127	149
1.35	♦ Passenger transport		US$ Mn	3	4	4	4	7
	Indicators							
1.39	Average size of travel party		Persons	..	..	..	..	..
	Average length of stay							
1.40	Total		Days	..	..	..	..	..
1.41	♦ For all commercial accommodation services		Nights	..	..	..	..	..
1.42	* of which, "hotels and similar establishments"		Nights	4.61	4.61	4.80	4.72	4.57
1.43	♦ For non commercial accommodation services		Days	..	..	..	..	..
1.44	Average expenditure per day		US$	..	..	..	..	..
3.	**OUTBOUND TOURISM**							
	Data							
	Expenditure	(2)						
3.4	Total		US$ Mn	17	19	19	17	22
3.5	♦ Travel		US$ Mn	8	10	10	9	13
3.6	♦ Passenger transport		US$ Mn	9	9	8	8	9
4.	**TOURISM INDUSTRIES**							
	Data							
	Accommodation for visitors in hotels and similar establishments							
	Non-monetary data							
4.13	♦ Number of establishments		Units	..	..	..	..	..
4.14	♦ Number of rooms		Units	1,394	1,419	1,426	1,548	1,741
4.15	♦ Number of bed-places		Units	..	..	..	..	..

301

PALAU

Cod.	Basic data and indicators	Notes	Units	2011	2012	2013	2014	2015
6.	**COMPLEMENTARY INDICATORS**							
	Demand							
6.1	Gross travel propensity		Units	..	..	..	..	..
6.2	(1.2 inbound tourists) / population		Units	5.39	5.78	5.16	6.64	7.81
	Macroeconomic indicators related to international tourism							
6.3	Inbound tourism expenditure over GDP		Percent	..	..	..	..	..
6.4	Outbound tourism expenditure over GDP		Percent	..	..	..	..	..
6.5	Tourism balance (inbound minus outbound tourism expenditure) over GDP		Percent	..	..	..	..	..
6.6	Tourism openness (inbound plus outbound tourism expenditure) over GDP		Percent	..	..	..	..	..
6.7	Tourism coverage (inbound over outbound tourism expenditure)		Percent	552.9	561.9	632.4	761.6	712.3
6.8	Inbound tourism expenditure over exports of goods		Percent	732.1	725.7	813.6	686.6	..
6.9	Inbound tourism expenditure over exports of services		Percent	92.2	93.5	93.7	94.1	..
6.10	Inbound tourism expenditure over exports of goods and services		Percent	81.9	82.8	84.0	82.7	..
6.11	Inbound tourism expenditure over current account credits		Percent	56.0	59.4	59.7	61.4	..
6.12	Outbound tourism expenditure over imports of goods		Percent	13.6	14.0	12.6	9.7	..
6.13	Outbound tourism expenditure over imports of services		Percent	43.6	43.0	43.0	39.1	..
6.14	Outbound tourism expenditure over imports of goods and		Percent	10.4	10.5	9.8	7.8	..
6.15	Outbound tourism expenditure over current account debits		Percent	8.9	9.3	8.4	6.9	..

PANAMA

Cod.	Basic data and indicators	Notes	Units	2011	2012	2013	2014	2015
1.	**INBOUND TOURISM**							
	Data							
	Arrivals							
1.1	Total	(1)	('000)	2,004	2,086	2,202	2,305	2,553
1.2	♦ Overnight visitors (tourists)		('000)	1,473	1,606	1,658	1,745	2,110
1.3	♦ Same-day visitors (excursionists)		('000)	531	480	544	560	443
1.4	* of which, cruise passengers		('000)	429	334	374	366	238
	Arrivals by region	(2)						
1.5	Total		('000)	1,311	1,479	1,527	1,610	1,941
1.6	♦ Africa		('000)	2	2	3	3	4
1.7	♦ Americas		('000)	1,134	1,285	1,311	1,355	1,608
1.8	♦ East Asia and the Pacific		('000)	27	31	29	32	45
1.9	♦ Europe		('000)	142	155	179	214	276
1.10	♦ Middle East		('000)	1	1	1	1	1
1.11	♦ South Asia		('000)	5	5	5	5	7
1.12	♦ Other not classified		('000)	..	..	..	..	..
1.13	* of which, nationals residing abroad		('000)	..	..	..	..	..
	Arrivals by main purpose	(3)						
1.14	Total		('000)	1,209	1,349	1,527	1,610	1,941
1.15	♦ Personal		('000)	744	830	1,367	1,431	1,857
1.16	* holidays, leisure and recreation		('000)	652	730	1,151	1,217	1,438
1.17	* other personal purposes		('000)	92	100	216	214	419
1.18	♦ Business and professional		('000)	465	519	160	179	84
	Arrivals by mode of transport							
1.19	Total		('000)	1,473	1,606	1,658	1,745	2,110
1.20	♦ Air		('000)	1,209	1,349	1,392	1,450	1,764
1.21	♦ Water		('000)	..	..	..	..	..
1.22	♦ Land		('000)	264	257	266	295	346
1.23	* railway		('000)	..	..	..	..	..
1.24	* road		('000)	174	156	155	148	151
1.25	* others		('000)	90	101	111	147	195
	Accommodation							
	Hotels and similar establishments							
1.31	♦ Guests	(4)	('000)	946	1,235	1,442	1,473	1,397
1.32	♦ Overnights	(4)	('000)	2,305	3,164	3,854	3,655	3,602
	Expenditure							
1.33	Total		US$ Mn	3,630	4,534	5,379	5,750	6,007
1.34	♦ Travel		US$ Mn	2,519	3,013	3,493	3,730	4,201
1.35	♦ Passenger transport		US$ Mn	1,111	1,521	1,886	2,020	1,806
	Expenditure by main purpose of the trip							
1.36	Total		US$ Mn	2,519	3,013	3,493	3,730	4,201
1.37	♦ Personal		US$ Mn	2,288	2,751	3,206	3,481	3,987
1.38	♦ Business and professional		US$ Mn	231	262	287	249	214
	Indicators							
1.39	Average size of travel party		Persons	..	..	..	..	..
	Average length of stay							
1.40	Total		Days	8.00	8.00	9.30	8.50	8.50
1.41	♦ For all commercial accommodation services		Nights	2.40	2.60	2.70	2.50	2.60
1.42	* of which, "hotels and similar establishments"		Nights	..	..	..	..	..
1.43	♦ For non commercial accommodation services		Days	..	..	..	..	..
1.44	Average expenditure per day		US$	225.0	274.0	248.0	280.0	276.0
2.	**OUTBOUND TOURISM**							
	Data							
	Departures							
2.1	Total		('000)	..	..	..	..	..
2.2	♦ Overnight visitors (tourists)		('000)	414	447	619	853	740
2.3	♦ Same-day visitors (excursionists)		('000)	..	..	..	..	..
	Expenditure							
2.4	Total		US$ Mn	679	591	1,046	1,107	1,023
2.5	♦ Travel		US$ Mn	505	415	869	939	806
2.6	♦ Passenger transport		US$ Mn	174	176	177	168	217
	Expenditure by main purpose of the trip							
2.7	Total		US$ Mn	505	415	869	939	806
2.8	♦ Personal		US$ Mn	398	350	703	723	613
2.9	♦ Business and professional		US$ Mn	107	65	166	215	193

PANAMA

Cod.	Basic data and indicators	Notes	Units	2011	2012	2013	2014	2015
4.	**TOURISM INDUSTRIES**							
	Data							
	Number of establishments							
4.1	Total		Units	1,325	1,386	1,415	1,444	1,518
4.2	♦ Accommodation for visitors		Units	600	655	673	705	747
4.3	* of which, "hotels and similar establishments"		Units	533	580	593	618	651
4.4	♦ Food and beverage serving activities		Units	146	146	148	155	161
4.5	♦ Passenger transportation		Units	20	16	17	19	19
4.6	♦ Travel agencies and other reservation services activities		Units	270	279	283	272	299
4.7	♦ Other tourism industries		Units	289	290	294	293	292
	Accommodation for visitors in hotels and similar establishments							
	Non-monetary data							
4.13	♦ Number of establishments		Units	533	580	593	618	651
4.14	♦ Number of rooms	(5)	Units	20,539	22,768	23,572	24,330	27,992
4.15	♦ Number of bed-places	(5)	Units	40,538	45,538	47,144	48,660	55,984
	Indicators							
4.16	Occupancy rate / rooms		Percent	64.71	58.88	56.70	56.00	52.30
4.17	Occupancy rate / bed-places		Percent	..	..	..	..	..
4.18	Average length of stay		Nights	2.40	2.60	2.70	2.50	2.60
4.19	Available capacity (bed-places per 1000 inhabitants)		Units	11.01	12.16	12.39	12.58	14.25
6.	**COMPLEMENTARY INDICATORS**							
	Demand							
6.1	Gross travel propensity		Units	..	..	..	..	..
6.2	(1.2 inbound tourists) / population		Units	0.40	0.43	0.44	0.45	0.54
	Macroeconomic indicators related to international tourism							
6.3	Inbound tourism expenditure over GDP		Percent	10.6	11.3	12.0	11.7	11.5
6.4	Outbound tourism expenditure over GDP		Percent	2.0	1.5	2.3	2.3	1.9
6.5	Tourism balance (inbound minus outbound tourism expenditure) over GDP		Percent	8.6	9.8	9.7	9.4	9.6
6.6	Tourism openness (inbound plus outbound tourism expenditure) over GDP		Percent	12.6	12.8	14.3	14.0	13.4
6.7	Tourism coverage (inbound over outbound tourism expenditure)		Percent	534.6	767.2	514.2	519.4	587.2
6.8	Inbound tourism expenditure over exports of goods		Percent	19.0	21.5	27.4	33.4	37.7
6.9	Inbound tourism expenditure over exports of services		Percent	44.8	48.5	52.9	53.1	53.2
6.10	Inbound tourism expenditure over exports of goods and services		Percent	13.4	14.9	18.1	20.5	22.1
6.11	Inbound tourism expenditure over current account credits		Percent	12.2	13.7	16.4	18.4	19.9
6.12	Outbound tourism expenditure over imports of goods		Percent	2.6	2.1	3.9	4.3	4.5
6.13	Outbound tourism expenditure over imports of services		Percent	15.8	13.8	21.2	23.9	23.0
6.14	Outbound tourism expenditure over imports of goods and		Percent	2.3	1.8	3.3	3.7	3.8
6.15	Outbound tourism expenditure over current account debits		Percent	2.1	1.7	3.0	3.3	3.4

PAPUA NEW GUINEA

Cod.	Basic data and indicators	Notes	Units	2011	2012	2013	2014	2015
1.	**INBOUND TOURISM**							
	Data							
	Arrivals							
.1	Total		('000)	165	175	182	191	199
.2	♦ Overnight visitors (tourists)		('000)	158	168	174	182	184
.3	♦ Same-day visitors (excursionists)		('000)	7	7	8	9	14
.4	* of which, cruise passengers		('000)	7	7	8	9	14
	Arrivals by region							
.5	Total		('000)	165	175	182	191	199
.6	♦ Africa		('000)	2	2	1	1	1
.7	♦ Americas		('000)	12	12	13	15	16
.8	♦ East Asia and the Pacific		('000)	131	143	149	156	160
.9	♦ Europe		('000)	15	13	13	17	17
.10	♦ Middle East		('000)	..	..	..	..	..
.11	♦ South Asia		('000)	5	5	5	3	4
.12	♦ Other not classified		('000)	..	..	..	..	..
.13	* of which, nationals residing abroad		('000)	..	..	..	..	..
	Arrivals by main purpose							
.14	Total		('000)	165	175	182	191	199
.15	♦ Personal		('000)	45	47	50	62	67
.16	* holidays, leisure and recreation		('000)	36	38	41	51	54
.17	* other personal purposes		('000)	9	9	9	11	13
.18	♦ Business and professional		('000)	120	128	132	130	132
	Arrivals by mode of transport							
.19	Total		('000)	165	175	182	191	198
.20	♦ Air		('000)	158	168	174	182	184
.21	♦ Water		('000)	7	7	8	9	14
.22	♦ Land		('000)	..	..	..	..	..
.23	* railway		('000)	..	..	..	..	..
.24	* road		('000)	..	..	..	..	..
.25	* others		('000)	..	..	..	..	..
	Arrivals by form of organization of the trip							
.26	Total		('000)	165	175	182	191	198
.27	♦ Package tour		('000)	36	38	41	45	50
.28	♦ Other forms		('000)	129	137	141	146	148
	Expenditure							
.33	Total		US$ Mn	5.1	..	3.7	2.8	..
.34	♦ Travel		US$ Mn	4.9	2.4	3.6	2.7	1.7
.35	♦ Passenger transport		US$ Mn	0.2	..	0.1	0.1	..
	Expenditure by main purpose of the trip							
.36	Total		US$ Mn	4.9	2.4	3.7	2.7	1.7
.37	♦ Personal		US$ Mn	2.7	1.4	0.4	0.2	..
.38	♦ Business and professional		US$ Mn	2.2	1.0	3.3	2.5	1.7
	Indicators							
.39	Average size of travel party		Persons	..	..	..	..	..
	Average length of stay							
.40	Total		Days	15.41	18.20	20.40	19.70	23.00
.41	♦ For all commercial accommodation services		Nights	..	..	..	..	..
.42	* of which, "hotels and similar establishments"		Nights	..	..	..	..	..
.43	♦ For non commercial accommodation services		Days	..	..	..	..	..
.44	Average expenditure per day		US$	227.0	198.0	174.0	183.0	125.0
2.	**OUTBOUND TOURISM**							
	Data							
	Expenditure							
.4	Total		US$ Mn	186	203	214	168	135
.5	♦ Travel		US$ Mn	161	155	153	125	125
.6	♦ Passenger transport		US$ Mn	25	48	61	43	10
	Expenditure by main purpose of the trip							
.7	Total		US$ Mn	161	155	152	125	125
.8	♦ Personal		US$ Mn	113	109	105	89	96
.9	♦ Business and professional		US$ Mn	48	46	47	36	29

PAPUA NEW GUINEA

Cod.	Basic data and indicators	Notes	Units	2011	2012	2013	2014	2015
4.	**TOURISM INDUSTRIES**							
	Data							
	Number of establishments							
4.1	Total		Units	..	..	..	..	..
4.2	♦ Accommodation for visitors		Units	..	..	..	..	..
4.3	* of which, "hotels and similar establishments"	(1)	Units	..	..	483	497	509
4.4	♦ Food and beverage serving activities		Units	..	..	..	..	..
4.5	♦ Passenger transportation		Units	..	..	..	..	..
4.6	♦ Travel agencies and other reservation services activities		Units	..	..	..	..	..
4.7	♦ Other tourism industries		Units	..	..	..	..	..
	Accommodation for visitors in hotels and similar establishments							
	Non-monetary data	(1)						
4.13	♦ Number of establishments		Units	..	..	483	497	509
4.14	♦ Number of rooms		Units	..	..	5,823	5,963	6,195
4.15	♦ Number of bed-places		Units	..	..	7,355	7,861	8,942
	Indicators							
4.16	Occupancy rate / rooms		Percent	..	..	..	..	..
4.17	Occupancy rate / bed-places		Percent	..	..	..	..	..
4.18	Average length of stay	(2)	Nights	15.40	..	18.00	18.40	21.30
4.19	Available capacity (bed-places per 1000 inhabitants)		Units	..	..	1.01	1.05	1.17
6.	**COMPLEMENTARY INDICATORS**							
	Demand							
6.1	Gross travel propensity		Units	..	..	..	..	..
6.2	(1.2 inbound tourists) / population		Units	0.02	0.02	0.02	0.02	0.02
	Macroeconomic indicators related to international tourism							
6.3	Inbound tourism expenditure over GDP		Percent	..	..	..	..	..
6.4	Outbound tourism expenditure over GDP		Percent	..	..	..	..	..
6.5	Tourism balance (inbound minus outbound tourism expenditure) over GDP		Percent	..	..	..	..	..
6.6	Tourism openness (inbound plus outbound tourism expenditure) over GDP		Percent	..	..	..	..	..
6.7	Tourism coverage (inbound over outbound tourism expenditure)		Percent	2.7	1.2	1.7	1.7	1.3
6.8	Inbound tourism expenditure over exports of goods		Percent	0.1	0.0	0.1	0.0	..
6.9	Inbound tourism expenditure over exports of services		Percent	1.2	0.5	0.9	1.3	..
6.10	Inbound tourism expenditure over exports of goods and services		Percent	0.1	0.0	0.1	0.0	..
6.11	Inbound tourism expenditure over current account credits		Percent	0.1	0.0	0.1	0.0	..
6.12	Outbound tourism expenditure over imports of goods		Percent	4.4	4.3	3.9	4.2	..
6.13	Outbound tourism expenditure over imports of services		Percent	6.3	5.4	5.5	7.3	..
6.14	Outbound tourism expenditure over imports of goods and		Percent	2.6	2.4	2.3	2.7	..
6.15	Outbound tourism expenditure over current account debits		Percent	2.5	2.3	2.2	2.5	..

PARAGUAY

Cod.	Basic data and indicators	Notes	Units	2011	2012	2013	2014	2015
1.	**INBOUND TOURISM**							
	Data							
	Arrivals							
.1	Total	(1)	('000)	3,365	3,655	3,538	3,455	4,101
.2	♦ Overnight visitors (tourists)	(1)(2)	('000)	524	579	610	649	1,214
.3	♦ Same-day visitors (excursionists)	(1)	('000)	2,841	3,076	2,928	2,806	2,887
.4	* of which, cruise passengers		('000)	..	..	..	..	
	Arrivals by region	(1)(2)						
.5	Total		('000)	524	579	610	649	1,214
.6	♦ Africa		('000)	0.4	0.6	0.7	1	1
.7	♦ Americas		('000)	481	519	553	587	1,149
.8	♦ East Asia and the Pacific		('000)	8	12	12	13	12
.9	♦ Europe		('000)	34	46	43	46	50
.10	♦ Middle East		('000)	0.5	0.7	0.7	0.7	0.4
.11	♦ South Asia		('000)	0.3	0.5	0.6	0.5	0.5
.12	♦ Other not classified		('000)	..	..	..	0.5	0.6
.13	* of which, nationals residing abroad		('000)	..	..	..	..	..
	Arrivals by main purpose	(1)(2)						
.14	Total		('000)	524	579	610	649	1,214
.15	♦ Personal		('000)	414	457	482	513	959
.16	* holidays, leisure and recreation		('000)	94	104	110	117	219
.17	* other personal purposes		('000)	320	353	372	396	741
.18	♦ Business and professional		('000)	110	122	128	136	255
	Arrivals by mode of transport	(1)(2)						
.19	Total		('000)	524	579	610	649	1,214
.20	♦ Air		('000)	173	213	210	246	233
.21	♦ Water	(3)	('000)	24	29	31	18	51
.22	♦ Land		('000)	327	337	369	385	930
.23	* railway		('000)	..	..	..	..	..
.24	* road		('000)	327	337	369	385	930
.25	* others		('000)	..	..	..	..	..
	Expenditure							
.33	Total		US$ Mn	261	291	299	314	347
.34	♦ Travel		US$ Mn	241	265	273	288	317
.35	♦ Passenger transport		US$ Mn	20	26	26	26	30
	Indicators							
.39	Average size of travel party		Persons	..	..	..	..	..
	Average length of stay							
.40	Total		Days	..	..	..	..	..
.41	♦ For all commercial accommodation services		Nights	3.00	3.00	3.00	3.00	3.00
.42	* of which, "hotels and similar establishments"		Nights	..	..	..	..	..
.43	♦ For non commercial accommodation services		Days	..	..	..	..	..
.44	Average expenditure per day		US$	..	..	..	..	..
3.	**OUTBOUND TOURISM**							
	Data							
	Departures							
3.1	Total		('000)	2,475	3,059	4,037	4,300	5,269
3.2	♦ Overnight visitors (tourists)	(1)	('000)	347	400	440	426	1,008
3.3	♦ Same-day visitors (excursionists)		('000)	2,128	2,660	3,597	3,874	4,261
	Expenditure							
3.4	Total		US$ Mn	308	363	425	449	494
3.5	♦ Travel		US$ Mn	174	207	243	256	281
3.6	♦ Passenger transport		US$ Mn	134	156	182	193	213
4.	**TOURISM INDUSTRIES**							
	Data							
	Number of establishments							
4.1	Total		Units	700	799	875	947	322
4.2	♦ Accommodation for visitors		Units	..	..	..	..	..
4.3	* of which, "hotels and similar establishments"		Units	470	563	616	721	818
4.4	♦ Food and beverage serving activities		Units	..	..	..	..	..
4.5	♦ Passenger transportation		Units	..	..	..	..	..
4.6	♦ Travel agencies and other reservation services activities		Units	230	236	259	226	322
4.7	♦ Other tourism industries		Units	..	..	..	..	..

PARAGUAY

Cod.	Basic data and indicators	Notes	Units	2011	2012	2013	2014	2015
	Accommodation for visitors in hotels and similar establishments							
	Non-monetary data							
4.13	♦ Number of establishments		Units	470	563	616	721	818
4.14	♦ Number of rooms		Units	11,085	12,120	12,764	13,820	15,003
4.15	♦ Number of bed-places		Units	22,144	23,896	25,281	28,283	31,669
	Indicators							
4.16	Occupancy rate / rooms		Percent	..	..	..	..	.
4.17	Occupancy rate / bed-places		Percent	55.00	60.00	60.00	60.00	60.00
4.18	Average length of stay		Nights	3.00	3.50	3.50	3.50	3.50
4.19	Available capacity (bed-places per 1000 inhabitants)		Units	3.52	3.75	3.91	4.32	4.77
5.	**EMPLOYMENT**							
	Data							
	Number of employees by tourism industries							
5.1	Total		('000)	7.5	7.9	9.0	9.7	10.6
5.2	♦ Accommodation services for visitors (hotels and similar establishments)		('000)	5.3	6.1	6.9	6.8	7.4
5.3	♦ Other accommodation services		('000)	..	..	..	..	.
5.4	♦ Food and beverage serving activities		('000)	..	..	..	..	.
5.5	♦ Passenger transportation		('000)	0.2	0.2	0.4	1.3	1.3
5.6	♦ Travel agencies and other reservation services activities		('000)	2.0	1.6	1.7	1.6	1.9
5.7	♦ Other tourism industries		('000)	..	..	..	..	.
6.	**COMPLEMENTARY INDICATORS**							
	Demand							
6.1	Gross travel propensity		Units	..	..	..	..	.
6.2	(1.2 inbound tourists) / population		Units	0.08	0.09	0.09	0.10	0.18
	Macroeconomic indicators related to international tourism							
6.3	Inbound tourism expenditure over GDP		Percent	1.0	1.1	0.1	0.1	1.7
6.4	Outbound tourism expenditure over GDP		Percent	0.7	0.8	0.8	0.8	1.0
6.5	Tourism balance (inbound minus outbound tourism expenditure) over GDP		Percent	0.3	0.2	0.1	0.1	0.7
6.6	Tourism openness (inbound plus outbound tourism expenditure) over GDP		Percent	1.6	1.9	1.8	1.8	2.7
6.7	Tourism coverage (inbound over outbound tourism expenditure)		Percent	138.6	127.9	112.2	112.2	171.9
6.8	Inbound tourism expenditure over exports of goods		Percent	4.5	5.4	3.9	4.0	8.0
6.9	Inbound tourism expenditure over exports of services		Percent	33.0	35.0	32.0	32.0	56.0
6.10	Inbound tourism expenditure over exports of goods and services		Percent	1.8	2.1	1.9	2.1	4.1
6.11	Inbound tourism expenditure over current account credits		Percent	1.7	2.0	1.8	2.0	3.9
6.12	Outbound tourism expenditure over imports of goods		Percent	1.5	1.9	2.2	2.3	2.9
6.13	Outbound tourism expenditure over imports of services		Percent	19.2	22.3	22.8	22.9	25.5
6.14	Outbound tourism expenditure over imports of goods and		Percent	1.4	1.7	1.9	1.9	2.5
6.15	Outbound tourism expenditure over current account debits		Percent	1.2	1.5	1.6	-1.7	-2.2

PERU

Cod.	Basic data and indicators	Notes	Units	2011	2012	2013	2014	2015
1.	**INBOUND TOURISM**							
	Data							
	Arrivals							
.1	Total		('000)	3,299	3,642	4,010	4,062	4,381
.2	♦ Overnight visitors (tourists)	(1)	('000)	2,598	2,846	3,164	3,215	3,456
.3	♦ Same-day visitors (excursionists)		('000)	701	796	847	847	925
.4	* of which, cruise passengers	(2)	('000)	41	80	63	61	62
	Arrivals by region	(1)						
.5	Total		('000)	2,598	2,846	3,164	3,215	3,456
.6	♦ Africa		('000)	4	5	4	5	5
.7	♦ Americas		('000)	1,997	2,191	2,473	2,479	2,680
.8	♦ East Asia and the Pacific		('000)	117	139	154	163	168
.9	♦ Europe		('000)	475	506	527	562	596
.10	♦ Middle East		('000)	..	..	..	..	..
.11	♦ South Asia		('000)	4	4	4	5	6
.12	♦ Other not classified		('000)	1	1	1	1	1
.13	* of which, nationals residing abroad		('000)	..	..	..	..	..
	Arrivals by main purpose	(1)						
.14	Total		('000)	2,598	2,846	3,164	3,215	3,456
.15	♦ Personal		('000)	2,531	2,772	3,082	3,132	3,366
.16	* holidays, leisure and recreation		('000)	2,445	2,678	2,978	3,026	3,253
.17	* other personal purposes		('000)	86	94	104	106	114
.18	♦ Business and professional		('000)	67	74	82	83	89
	Arrivals by mode of transport	(1)						
.19	Total		('000)	2,598	2,846	3,164	3,215	3,456
.20	♦ Air		('000)	1,563	1,717	1,935	1,925	2,034
.21	♦ Water	(3)	('000)	24	22	19	32	31
.22	♦ Land		('000)	1,011	1,107	1,210	1,257	1,391
.23	* railway		('000)	6	3	1	..	..
.24	* road		('000)	1,005	1,104	1,209	1,257	1,391
.25	* others		('000)	..	..	..	..	..
	Accommodation							
	Hotels and similar establishments							
.31	♦ Guests		('000)	5,707	7,135	8,033	7,182	7,571
.32	♦ Overnights		('000)	10,213	13,256	15,159	13,453	13,521
	Expenditure							
.33	Total		US$ Mn	2,814	3,074	3,925	3,831	4,151
.34	♦ Travel		US$ Mn	2,262	2,443	3,009	3,001	3,320
.35	♦ Passenger transport		US$ Mn	552	631	916	830	831
	Indicators							
.39	Average size of travel party		Persons	..	..	..	..	..
	Average length of stay							
.40	Total		Days	..	..	..	..	..
.41	♦ For all commercial accommodation services		Nights	1.79	1.86	1.89	1.87	1.79
.42	* of which, "hotels and similar establishments"		Nights	..	..	..	..	..
.43	♦ For non commercial accommodation services		Days	..	..	..	..	..
.44	Average expenditure per day		US$	..	..	..	..	..
2.	**DOMESTIC TOURISM**							
	Data							
	Accommodation							
	Hotels and similar establishments							
2.21	♦ Guests		('000)	31,052	35,175	37,660	38,298	39,066
2.22	♦ Overnights		('000)	38,880	44,138	48,431	49,983	50,950
	Indicators							
2.23	Average size of travel party		Persons	..	..	..	..	..
	Average length of stay							
2.24	Total		Days	..	..	..	..	..
2.25	♦ For all commercial accommodation services		Nights	1.25	1.25	1.29	1.31	1.30
2.26	* of which, "hotels and similar establishments"		Nights	..	..	..	..	..
2.27	♦ For non commercial accommodation services		Days	..	..	..	..	..
2.28	Average expenditure per day		US$	..	..	..	..	..

PERU

Cod.	Basic data and indicators	Notes	Units	2011	2012	2013	2014	2015
3.	**OUTBOUND TOURISM**							
	Data							
	Departures							
3.1	Total		('000)	..	..	..	..	..
3.2	♦ Overnight visitors (tourists)		('000)	2,132	2,296	2,364	2,442	2,595
3.3	♦ Same-day visitors (excursionists)		('000)	..	..	..	..	..
	Expenditure							
3.4	Total		US$ Mn	1,768	1,900	2,114	2,113	2,351
3.5	♦ Travel		US$ Mn	1,356	1,439	1,601	1,584	1,691
3.6	♦ Passenger transport		US$ Mn	412	461	513	529	660
4.	**TOURISM INDUSTRIES**							
	Data							
	Number of establishments							
4.1	Total		Units	..	..	..	..	..
4.2	♦ Accommodation for visitors		Units	..	..	..	..	..
4.3	* of which, "hotels and similar establishments"		Units	1,473	15,509	16,721	18,166	19,273
4.4	♦ Food and beverage serving activities		Units	..	..	..	..	..
4.5	♦ Passenger transportation		Units	..	..	..	..	..
4.6	♦ Travel agencies and other reservation services activities		Units	..	..	..	..	..
4.7	♦ Other tourism industries		Units	..	..	..	..	..
	Accommodation for visitors in hotels and similar establishments							
	Non-monetary data							
4.13	♦ Number of establishments		Units	1,473	15,509	16,721	18,166	19,273
4.14	♦ Number of rooms		Units	306,795	215,591	225,669	237,245	248,667
4.15	♦ Number of bed-places		Units	361,015	375,255	392,531	411,512	431,049
	Indicators							
4.16	Occupancy rate / rooms		Percent	..	..	..	..	..
4.17	Occupancy rate / bed-places		Percent	..	..	..	..	..
4.18	Average length of stay		Nights	1.34	1.36	1.39	1.39	1.38
4.19	Available capacity (bed-places per 1000 inhabitants)		Units	12.13	12.44	12.84	13.29	13.74
6.	**COMPLEMENTARY INDICATORS**							
	Demand							
6.1	Gross travel propensity		Units	..	..	..	..	..
6.2	(1.2 inbound tourists) / population		Units	0.09	0.09	0.10	0.10	0.11
	Macroeconomic indicators related to international tourism							
6.3	Inbound tourism expenditure over GDP		Percent	1.6	1.6	1.9	1.9	.
6.4	Outbound tourism expenditure over GDP		Percent	1.0	1.0	1.0	1.0	.
6.5	Tourism balance (inbound minus outbound tourism expenditure) over GDP		Percent	0.6	0.6	0.9	0.9	.
6.6	Tourism openness (inbound plus outbound tourism expenditure) over GDP		Percent	2.6	2.6	2.9	2.9	.
6.7	Tourism coverage (inbound over outbound tourism expenditure)		Percent	159.2	161.8	185.7	181.3	176.6
6.8	Inbound tourism expenditure over exports of goods		Percent	6.1	6.5	9.2	9.7	12.2
6.9	Inbound tourism expenditure over exports of services		Percent	78.9	73.5	76.0	69.1	70.8
6.10	Inbound tourism expenditure over exports of goods and services		Percent	5.6	6.0	8.2	8.5	10.4
6.11	Inbound tourism expenditure over current account credits		Percent	5.2	5.5	7.5	7.6	9.4
6.12	Outbound tourism expenditure over imports of goods		Percent	4.9	4.7	5.1	5.2	6.4
6.13	Outbound tourism expenditure over imports of services		Percent	27.1	25.9	27.7	27.5	29.5
6.14	Outbound tourism expenditure over imports of goods and		Percent	4.1	4.0	4.3	4.4	5.2
6.15	Outbound tourism expenditure over current account debits		Percent	4.0	3.9	4.2	4.3	5.1

PHILIPPINES

Cod.	Basic data and indicators	Notes	Units	2011	2012	2013	2014	2015
1.	**INBOUND TOURISM**							
	Data							
	Arrivals							
1.1	Total		('000)	..	..	..	..	..
1.2	♦ Overnight visitors (tourists)	(1)	('000)	3,917	4,273	4,681	4,833	5,361
1.3	♦ Same-day visitors (excursionists)		('000)	8	11	16	60	70
1.4	* of which, cruise passengers		('000)	8	11	16	60	70
	Arrivals by region	(1)						
1.5	Total		('000)	3,917	4,273	4,681	4,833	5,361
1.6	♦ Africa		('000)	4	5	6	5	6
1.7	♦ Americas		('000)	748	783	815	875	946
1.8	♦ East Asia and the Pacific		('000)	2,405	2,667	2,997	3,048	3,421
1.9	♦ Europe		('000)	402	443	480	499	549
1.10	♦ Middle East		('000)	56	57	69	76	84
1.11	♦ South Asia		('000)	61	64	69	79	95
1.12	♦ Other not classified		('000)	241	254	246	251	261
1.13	* of which, nationals residing abroad		('000)	207	216	204	208	212
	Arrivals by main purpose	(1)(2)						
1.14	Total		('000)	3,884	4,238	4,637	4,773	5,291
1.15	♦ Personal		('000)	3,481	3,757	4,131	4,275	4,805
1.16	* holidays, leisure and recreation		('000)	1,578	2,364	2,763	2,675	2,982
1.17	* other personal purposes		('000)	1,903	1,393	1,368	1,600	1,822
1.18	♦ Business and professional		('000)	403	481	506	498	486
	Arrivals by mode of transport	(1)						
1.19	Total		('000)	3,917	4,273	4,681	4,833	5,361
1.20	♦ Air		('000)	3,884	4,238	4,637	4,773	5,291
1.21	♦ Water		('000)	33	35	44	60	70
1.22	♦ Land		('000)	..	..	..	..	..
1.23	* railway		('000)	..	..	..	..	..
1.24	* road		('000)	..	..	..	..	..
1.25	* others		('000)	..	..	..	..	..
	Arrivals by form of organization of the trip							
1.26	Total	(2)	('000)	3,884	4,238	4,637	..	..
1.27	♦ Package tour		('000)	181	60	33	..	..
1.28	♦ Other forms		('000)	3,703	4,178	4,604	..	..
	Expenditure							
1.33	Total		US$ Mn	4,053	4,963	5,599	6,059	6,418
1.34	♦ Travel		US$ Mn	3,198	4,061	4,690	5,030	5,276
1.35	♦ Passenger transport		US$ Mn	855	902	909	1,029	1,142
	Expenditure by main purpose of the trip							
1.36	Total		US$ Mn	3,198	4,060	4,690	5,030	5,276
1.37	♦ Personal		US$ Mn	3,187	4,038	4,643	5,005	5,257
1.38	♦ Business and professional		US$ Mn	11	22	46	25	19
	Indicators							
1.39	Average size of travel party		Persons	..	..	..	..	..
	Average length of stay							
1.40	Total	(3)	Days	8.04	9.61	9.56	10.63	9.89
1.41	♦ For all commercial accommodation services		Nights	..	..	..	..	..
1.42	* of which, "hotels and similar establishments"	(4)	Nights	2.48	2.48	2.49	2.46	2.39
1.43	♦ For non commercial accommodation services		Days	..	..	..	..	..
1.44	Average expenditure per day		US$	91.9	93.0	101.1	103.6	107.9
2.	**DOMESTIC TOURISM**							
	Data							
	Trips							
2.1	Total		('000)	150,253	165,278	182,392	218,307	271,237
2.2	♦ Overnight visitors (tourists)		('000)	73,874	81,261	89,675	107,333	133,357
2.3	♦ Same-day visitors (excursionists)		('000)	76,379	84,017	92,717	110,974	137,880
	Indicators							
2.23	Average size of travel party		Persons	..	..	..	..	..
	Average length of stay							
2.24	Total	(3)	Days	5.00	5.00	5.00	5.00	5.00
2.25	♦ For all commercial accommodation services		Nights	..	..	..	..	..
2.26	* of which, "hotels and similar establishments"		Nights	..	..	..	..	..
2.27	♦ For non commercial accommodation services		Days	..	..	..	..	..
2.28	Average expenditure per day		US$	..	..	..	..	..

311

PHILIPPINES

Cod.	Basic data and indicators	Notes	Units	2011	2012	2013	2014	2015
3.	**OUTBOUND TOURISM**							
	Data							
	Expenditure							
3.4	Total		US$ Mn	6,055	7,140	8,400	11,130	12,191
3.5	♦ Travel		US$ Mn	5,616	6,548	7,833	10,598	11,660
3.6	♦ Passenger transport		US$ Mn	439	592	567	532	531
	Expenditure by main purpose of the trip							
3.7	Total		US$ Mn	5,616	6,548	7,833	10,598	11,660
3.8	♦ Personal		US$ Mn	5,528	6,441	7,705	10,460	11,521
3.9	♦ Business and professional		US$ Mn	88	107	128	138	139
4.	**TOURISM INDUSTRIES**							
	Data							
	Number of establishments							
4.1	Total		Units	..	..	..	..	
4.2	♦ Accommodation for visitors		Units	..	..	..	..	
4.3	* of which, "hotels and similar establishments"	(5)	Units	387	305	422	1,149	1,121
4.4	♦ Food and beverage serving activities		Units	..	..	..	..	
4.5	♦ Passenger transportation		Units	..	..	..	..	
4.6	♦ Travel agencies and other reservation services activities		Units	..	..	..	..	
4.7	♦ Other tourism industries		Units	..	..	..	..	
	Accommodation for visitors in hotels and similar establishments							
	Monetary data							
4.8	♦ Output		US$ Mn	..	..	..	..	
4.9	♦ Intermediate consumption		US$ Mn	..	..	..	..	
4.10	♦ Gross value added		US$ Mn	2,591.6	3,181.2	3,793.3	4,573.8	5,602.4
4.11	♦ Compensation of employees		US$ Mn	..	..	..	..	
4.12	♦ Gross fixed capital formation		US$ Mn	..	..	..	..	
	Non-monetary data	(5)						
4.13	♦ Number of establishments		Units	387	305	422	1,149	1,121
4.14	♦ Number of rooms		Units	26,705	18,713	40,045	56,023	60,232
4.15	♦ Number of bed-places		Units	53,410	37,426	80,090	112,046	120,464
	Indicators							
4.16	Occupancy rate / rooms		Percent	..	..	..	..	
4.17	Occupancy rate / bed-places	(6)	Percent	69.26	67.25	67.20	67.21	66.95
4.18	Average length of stay	(6)	Nights	2.48	2.48	2.49	2.46	2.39
4.19	Available capacity (bed-places per 1000 inhabitants)		Units	0.57	0.39	0.82	1.13	1.20
	Travel agencies and other reservation service activities							
	Monetary data							
4.20	♦ Output		US$ Mn	..	..	..	..	
4.21	♦ Intermediate consumption		US$ Mn	..	..	..	..	
4.22	♦ Gross value added		US$ Mn	976.6	1,116.7	1,145.9	1,350.9	1,662.6
4.23	♦ Compensation of employees		US$ Mn	..	..	..	..	
4.24	♦ Gross fixed capital formation		US$ Mn	..	..	..	..	
5.	**EMPLOYMENT**							
	Data							
	Number of employees by tourism industries	(7)						
5.1	Total		('000)	4,266.0	4,561.0	4,709.0	4,820.0	4,982.0
5.2	♦ Accommodation services for visitors (hotels and similar establishments)		('000)	1,116.0	1,579.0	1,601.0	1,694.0	1,734.0
5.3	♦ Other accommodation services		('000)	..	..	..	..	
5.4	♦ Food and beverage serving activities		('000)	..	..	..	..	
5.5	♦ Passenger transportation		('000)	1,870.0	1,675.0	1,746.0	1,713.0	1,792.0
5.6	♦ Travel agencies and other reservation services activities		('000)	30.0	26.0	29.0	30.0	32.0
5.7	♦ Other tourism industries		('000)	1,250.0	1,281.0	1,333.0	1,383.0	1,424.0
6.	**COMPLEMENTARY INDICATORS**							
	Demand							
6.1	Gross travel propensity		Units	..	..	..	..	
6.2	(1.2 inbound tourists + 2.2 domestic tourists) / population		Units	0.82	0.89	0.97	1.13	1.38

PHILIPPINES

Cod.	Basic data and indicators	Notes	Units	2011	2012	2013	2014	2015
	Macroeconomic indicators related to international tourism							
6.3	Inbound tourism expenditure over GDP		Percent	1.8	2.0	2.1	2.1	2.2
6.4	Outbound tourism expenditure over GDP		Percent	2.7	2.9	3.1	3.9	4.2
6.5	Tourism balance (inbound minus outbound tourism expenditure) over GDP		Percent	-0.9	-0.9	-1.0	-1.8	-2.0
6.6	Tourism openness (inbound plus outbound tourism expenditure) over GDP		Percent	4.5	4.9	5.2	6.0	6.4
6.7	Tourism coverage (inbound over outbound tourism expenditure)		Percent	66.9	69.5	66.7	54.4	52.6
6.8	Inbound tourism expenditure over exports of goods		Percent	10.6	10.7	12.6	12.2	14.8
6.9	Inbound tourism expenditure over exports of services		Percent	21.5	24.3	24.0	23.8	22.8
6.10	Inbound tourism expenditure over exports of goods and services		Percent	7.1	7.4	8.3	8.0	9.0
6.11	Inbound tourism expenditure over current account credits		Percent	4.8	5.2	5.7	5.6	6.1
6.12	Outbound tourism expenditure over imports of goods		Percent	10.3	10.9	13.5	16.6	18.8
6.13	Outbound tourism expenditure over imports of services		Percent	49.2	50.1	51.5	53.2	51.0
6.14	Outbound tourism expenditure over imports of goods and		Percent	8.5	9.0	10.7	12.6	13.7
6.15	Outbound tourism expenditure over current account debits		Percent	7.7	8.1	9.6	11.4	12.3

POLAND

Cod.	Basic data and indicators	Notes	Units	2011	2012	2013	2014	2015
1.	**INBOUND TOURISM**							
	Data							
	Arrivals							
1.1	Total	(1)(2)	('000)	60,745	67,390	72,310	73,750	77,744
1.2	♦ Overnight visitors (tourists)	(2)	('000)	13,350	14,840	15,800	16,000	16,722
1.3	♦ Same-day visitors (excursionists)		('000)	47,395	52,550	56,510	57,750	61,022
1.4	* of which, cruise passengers		('000)	..	..	..	..	..
	Arrivals by region	(1)(2)						
1.5	Total		('000)	60,745	67,390	72,310	73,750	77,744
1.6	♦ Africa		('000)	15	15	15	10	10
1.7	♦ Americas		('000)	400	425	425	648	703
1.8	♦ East Asia and the Pacific		('000)	300	320	355	344	368
1.9	♦ Europe		('000)	59,950	66,545	71,430	72,661	76,579
1.10	♦ Middle East		('000)	15	15	15	15	15
1.11	♦ South Asia		('000)	20	20	20	32	39
1.12	♦ Other not classified		('000)	45	50	50	40	30
1.13	* of which, nationals residing abroad		('000)	..	..	..	..	..
	Arrivals by main purpose	(2)						
1.14	Total		('000)	13,350	14,840	15,800	16,000	16,722
1.15	♦ Personal		('000)	9,590	10,680	11,850	12,724	12,658
1.16	* holidays, leisure and recreation		('000)	4,570	5,070	5,692	5,826	5,002
1.17	* other personal purposes		('000)	5,020	5,610	6,158	6,898	7,656
1.18	♦ Business and professional		('000)	3,760	4,160	3,950	3,276	4,064
	Arrivals by mode of transport	(1)(2)						
1.19	Total		('000)	60,745	67,390	72,310	73,750	77,734
1.20	♦ Air		('000)	3,650	4,040	4,338	4,425	4,655
1.21	♦ Water		('000)	310	370	361	368	389
1.22	♦ Land		('000)	56,785	62,980	67,611	68,957	72,690
1.23	* railway		('000)	1,600	2,020	2,164	2,212	2,326
1.24	* road		('000)	55,185	60,960	65,447	66,745	70,364
1.25	* others		('000)	..	..	..	..	..
	Arrivals by form of organization of the trip	(2)						
1.26	Total		('000)	13,350	14,840	15,800	16,000	16,722
1.27	♦ Package tour		('000)	2,300	1,632	1,738	1,920	2,007
1.28	♦ Other forms		('000)	11,050	13,208	14,062	14,080	14,715
	Accommodation	(3)						
	Total							
1.29	♦ Guests		('000)	4,410	4,940	5,205	5,427	5,690
1.30	♦ Overnights		('000)	10,620	11,755	12,362	12,860	13,758
	Hotels and similar establishments							
1.31	♦ Guests		('000)	3,907	4,370	4,687	4,886	5,074
1.32	♦ Overnights		('000)	8,397	9,425	10,129	10,667	11,302
	Expenditure							
1.33	Total		US$ Mn	11,649	11,888	12,432	12,311	10,600
1.34	♦ Travel		US$ Mn	10,732	10,985	11,344	11,234	9,728
1.35	♦ Passenger transport		US$ Mn	917	903	1,088	1,077	872
	Expenditure by main purpose of the trip							
1.36	Total		US$ Mn	10,732	10,985	11,344	11,234	9,728
1.37	♦ Personal		US$ Mn	8,702	8,796	9,238	9,632	8,163
1.38	♦ Business and professional		US$ Mn	2,030	2,189	2,106	1,602	1,565
	Indicators							
1.39	Average size of travel party		Persons	1.5	1.5	1.5	1.5	1.5
	Average length of stay							
1.40	Total		Days	..	..	..	..	..
1.41	♦ For all commercial accommodation services	(4)(2)	Nights	3.96	3.80	4.50	6.20	5.50
1.42	* of which, "hotels and similar establishments"		Nights	..	..	..	..	..
1.43	♦ For non commercial accommodation services		Days	..	..	..	..	..
1.44	Average expenditure per day		US$	..	..	..	..	..
2.	**DOMESTIC TOURISM**							
	Data							
	Trips							
2.1	Total		('000)	..	..	..	..	..
2.2	♦ Overnight visitors (tourists)	(2)	('000)	29,600	40,700	42,450	38,300	39,900
2.3	♦ Same-day visitors (excursionists)		('000)	..	..	..	..	..

POLAND

Cod.	Basic data and indicators	Notes	Units	2011	2012	2013	2014	2015
	Trips by main purpose	(2)(5)						
2.4	Total		('000)	12,500	14,900	16,600	15,000	15,700
2.5	♦ Personal		('000)	11,250	12,367	14,110	14,400	15,370
2.6	* holidays, leisure and recreation		('000)	6,500	7,301	9,296	8,550	9,059
2.7	* other personal purposes		('000)	4,750	5,066	4,814	5,850	6,311
2.8	♦ Business and professional		('000)	1,250	2,533	2,490	600	330
	Trips by form of organization	(2)(5)						
2.16	Total		('000)	12,500	14,900	16,600	15,000	15,700
2.17	♦ Package tour		('000)	1,125	1,937	1,992	1,125	1,146
2.18	♦ Other forms		('000)	11,375	12,963	14,608	13,875	14,554
	Accommodation	(3)						
	Total							
2.19	♦ Guests		('000)	17,067	17,116	17,614	19,044	21,253
2.20	♦ Overnights		('000)	46,528	48,241	48,533	51,527	5,747
	Hotels and similar establishments							
2.21	♦ Guests		('000)	11,765	11,968	12,696	14,110	15,445
2.22	♦ Overnights		('000)	21,114	22,119	23,244	25,772	28,329
	Indicators							
2.23	Average size of travel party		Persons	..	..	..	..	..
	Average length of stay							
2.24	Total		Days	..	..	..	..	..
2.25	♦ For all commercial accommodation services		Nights	2.73	2.82	2.76	2.71	2.70
2.26	* of which, "hotels and similar establishments"		Nights	..	..	..	..	..
2.27	♦ For non commercial accommodation services		Days	..	..	..	..	..
2.28	Average expenditure per day		US$	..	..	..	..	..
3.	**OUTBOUND TOURISM**							
	Data							
	Departures							
3.1	Total		('000)	43,270	48,290	52,580	35,400	44,300
3.2	♦ Overnight visitors (tourists)		('000)	6,300	9,300	10,050	10,300	10,900
3.3	♦ Same-day visitors (excursionists)		('000)	36,970	38,990	42,530	25,100	33,400
	Expenditure							
3.4	Total		US$ Mn	8,882	9,129	9,132	9,540	8,492
3.5	♦ Travel		US$ Mn	8,461	8,758	8,821	8,868	7,939
3.6	♦ Passenger transport		US$ Mn	421	371	311	672	553
	Expenditure by main purpose of the trip							
3.7	Total		US$ Mn	8,461	8,758	8,821	8,868	7,939
3.8	♦ Personal		US$ Mn	6,201	6,510	6,395	6,980	6,311
3.9	♦ Business and professional		US$ Mn	2,260	2,248	2,426	1,888	1,628
	Indicators							
3.10	Average length of stay		Days	10.20	8.80	10.10	10.05	9.00
3.11	Average expenditure per day		US$	..	..	..	..	..
4.	**TOURISM INDUSTRIES**							
	Data							
	Number of establishments							
4.1	Total	(6)	Units	..	..	..	..	..
4.2	♦ Accommodation for visitors		Units	7,039	7,177	7,152	7,251	10,024
4.3	* of which, "hotels and similar establishments"		Units	3,369	3,522	3,595	3,760	3,844
4.4	♦ Food and beverage serving activities		Units	..	..	..	..	..
4.5	♦ Passenger transportation		Units	..	..	..	..	..
4.6	♦ Travel agencies and other reservation services activities		Units	..	..	..	..	..
4.7	♦ Other tourism industries		Units	..	..	..	..	..
	Accommodation for visitors in hotels and similar establishments							
	Non-monetary data	(6)						
4.13	♦ Number of establishments		Units	3,369	3,522	3,595	3,760	3,844
4.14	♦ Number of rooms		Units	123,733	129,095	134,417	142,364	146,114
4.15	♦ Number of bed-places		Units	256,869	271,069	281,774	300,349	309,697
	Indicators							
4.16	Occupancy rate / rooms		Percent	41.10	41.10	41.60	42.70	45.30
4.17	Occupancy rate / bed-places		Percent	33.60	33.60	33.80	34.80	36.70
4.18	Average length of stay		Nights	1.82	1.91	1.92	1.91	1.93
4.19	Available capacity (bed-places per 1000 inhabitants)		Units	6.66	7.02	7.30	7.78	8.02

POLAND

Cod.	Basic data and indicators	Notes	Units	2011	2012	2013	2014	2015
6.	**COMPLEMENTARY INDICATORS**							
	Demand							
6.1	Gross travel propensity		Units	..	..	..	..	..
6.2	(1.2 inbound tourists + 2.2 domestic tourists) / population		Units	1.11	1.44	1.51	1.41	1.47
	Macroeconomic indicators related to international tourism							
6.3	Inbound tourism expenditure over GDP		Percent	2.3	2.4	2.4	2.2	2.2
6.4	Outbound tourism expenditure over GDP		Percent	1.7	1.9	1.8	1.7	1.8
6.5	Tourism balance (inbound minus outbound tourism expenditure) over GDP		Percent	0.6	0.5	0.6	0.5	0.4
6.6	Tourism openness (inbound plus outbound tourism expenditure) over GDP		Percent	4.0	4.3	4.2	3.9	4.0
6.7	Tourism coverage (inbound over outbound tourism expenditure)		Percent	131.2	130.2	136.1	129.0	124.8
6.8	Inbound tourism expenditure over exports of goods		Percent	6.3	6.6	6.3	5.8	5.6
6.9	Inbound tourism expenditure over exports of services		Percent	28.5	29.0	27.9	25.6	24.4
6.10	Inbound tourism expenditure over exports of goods and services		Percent	5.2	5.3	5.1	4.8	4.5
6.11	Inbound tourism expenditure over current account credits		Percent	4.7	4.9	4.7	4.4	4.2
6.12	Outbound tourism expenditure over imports of goods		Percent	4.4	4.8	4.6	4.4	4.5
6.13	Outbound tourism expenditure over imports of services		Percent	26.4	27.4	26.5	26.0	26.0
6.14	Outbound tourism expenditure over imports of goods and		Percent	3.8	4.1	3.9	3.8	3.8
6.15	Outbound tourism expenditure over current account debits		Percent	3.4	3.7	3.6	3.5	3.5

PORTUGAL

Cod.	Basic data and indicators	Notes	Units	2011	2012	2013	2014	2015
1.	**INBOUND TOURISM**							
	Data							
	Arrivals							
1.1	Total		('000)	..	..	..	..	..
1.2	♦ Overnight visitors (tourists)	(1)	('000)	7,264	7,503	8,097	9,092	9,957
1.3	♦ Same-day visitors (excursionists)		('000)	..	..	..	..	..
1.4	* of which, cruise passengers		('000)	..	..	..	..	..
	Arrivals by region	(1)						
1.5	Total		('000)	7,263	7,503	8,097	9,092	9,957
1.6	♦ Africa		('000)	84	96	121	146	141
1.7	♦ Americas		('000)	874	947	1,029	1,138	1,192
1.8	♦ East Asia and the Pacific		('000)	261	301	412	521	611
1.9	♦ Europe		('000)	6,044	6,159	6,534	7,287	8,014
1.10	♦ Middle East		('000)	..	..	..	..	..
1.11	♦ South Asia		('000)	..	..	..	..	..
1.12	♦ Other not classified		('000)	..	..	..	..	..
1.13	* of which, nationals residing abroad		('000)	..	..	..	..	..
	Accommodation							
	Total							
1.29	♦ Guests		('000)	7,264	7,503	8,097	9,092	9,957
1.30	♦ Overnights		('000)	27,860	29,034	31,094	33,992	36,417
	Hotels and similar establishments							
1.31	♦ Guests		('000)	6,792	7,043	7,630	8,576	9,390
1.32	♦ Overnights		('000)	26,004	27,257	29,360	32,095	34,368
	Expenditure							
1.33	Total		US$ Mn	14,901	14,582	16,210	17,723	15,721
1.34	♦ Travel		US$ Mn	11,376	11,001	12,282	13,777	12,594
1.35	♦ Passenger transport		US$ Mn	3,525	3,581	3,928	3,946	3,127
	Indicators							
1.39	Average size of travel party		Persons	..	..	..	..	..
	Average length of stay							
1.40	Total		Days	..	..	..	..	..
1.41	♦ For all commercial accommodation services		Nights	3.83	3.86	3.18	2.91	3.66
1.42	* of which, "hotels and similar establishments"		Nights	3.82	3.50	3.08	2.86	3.66
1.43	♦ For non commercial accommodation services		Days	..	..	..	..	..
1.44	Average expenditure per day		US$	..	..	..	..	..
2.	**DOMESTIC TOURISM**							
	Data							
	Trips							
2.1	Total		('000)	..	..	..	..	..
2.2	♦ Overnight visitors (tourists)	(2)	('000)	..	12,670	13,611	..	..
2.3	♦ Same-day visitors (excursionists)		('000)	..	..	..	..	..
	Accommodation							
	Total							
2.19	♦ Guests		('000)	7,586	7,142	7,013	7,623	8,111
2.20	♦ Overnights		('000)	19,012	17,747	16,903	18,223	18,913
	Hotels and similar establishments							
2.21	♦ Guests		('000)	6,322	5,937	5,863	6,545	6,961
2.22	♦ Overnights		('000)	13,437	12,424	12,210	13,777	14,483
3.	**OUTBOUND TOURISM**							
	Data							
	Departures							
3.1	Total		('000)	..	..	..	..	..
3.2	♦ Overnight visitors (tourists)	(2)	('000)	..	1,361	1,329	..	..
3.3	♦ Same-day visitors (excursionists)		('000)	..	..	..	..	..
	Expenditure							
3.4	Total		US$ Mn	4,948	4,485	4,976	5,379	4,782
3.5	♦ Travel		US$ Mn	4,144	3,784	4,142	4,407	4,005
3.6	♦ Passenger transport		US$ Mn	804	701	834	972	777

317

PORTUGAL

Cod.	Basic data and indicators	Notes	Units	2011	2012	2013	2014	2015
4.	**TOURISM INDUSTRIES**							
	Data							
	Number of establishments	(3)						
4.1	Total		Units	99,153	97,224	96,281	98,109	..
4.2	♦ Accommodation for visitors		Units	7,106	7,324	7,837	9,660	
4.3	* of which, "hotels and similar establishments"		Units	..	..	..	..	..
4.4	♦ Food and beverage serving activities		Units	78,077	75,779	74,374	74,462	..
4.5	♦ Passenger transportation		Units	11,714	11,486	11,295	11,076	..
4.6	♦ Travel agencies and other reservation services activities		Units	2,256	2,635	2,775	2,911	
4.7	♦ Other tourism industries		Units	..	..	..	..	..
	Accommodation for visitors in hotels and similar establishments							
	Non-monetary data							
4.13	♦ Number of establishments		Units	2,019	2,028	2,008	2,041	2,028
4.14	♦ Number of rooms		Units	128,336	131,357	132,331	136,761	137,359
4.15	♦ Number of bed-places		Units	289,107	296,321	297,962	308,385	312,028
	Indicators							
4.16	Occupancy rate / rooms	(4)	Percent	51.84	..	..	..	..
4.17	Occupancy rate / bed-places	(4)	Percent	40.00	39.50	42.60	45.20	46.27
4.18	Average length of stay	(5)	Nights	3.83	3.86	3.18	2.91	3.66
4.19	Available capacity (bed-places per 1000 inhabitants)		Units	27.38	28.18	28.49	29.65	30.15
5.	**EMPLOYMENT**							
	Data							
	Number of employees by tourism industries	(3)						
5.1	Total		('000)	342.3	327.3	319.2	327.1	..
5.2	♦ Accommodation services for visitors (hotels and similar establishments)		('000)	56.4	54.8	54.5	58.7	..
5.3	♦ Other accommodation services		('000)	..	..	..	..	..
5.4	♦ Food and beverage serving activities		('000)	230.4	218.1	211.2	214.6	..
5.5	♦ Passenger transportation		('000)	45.7	44.5	43.8	43.6	..
5.6	♦ Travel agencies and other reservation services activities		('000)	9.8	9.9	9.7	10.2	..
5.7	♦ Other tourism industries		('000)	..	..	..	..	..
6.	**COMPLEMENTARY INDICATORS**							
	Demand							
6.1	Gross travel propensity		Units	..	..	..	..	..
6.2	(1.2 inbound tourists + 2.2 domestic tourists) / population		Units	..	1.92	2.08	..	..
	Macroeconomic indicators related to international tourism							
6.3	Inbound tourism expenditure over GDP		Percent	6.1	6.8	7.1	7.7	7.9
6.4	Outbound tourism expenditure over GDP		Percent	2.0	2.1	2.2	2.3	2.4
6.5	Tourism balance (inbound minus outbound tourism expenditure) over GDP		Percent	4.1	4.7	4.9	5.4	5.5
6.6	Tourism openness (inbound plus outbound tourism expenditure) over GDP		Percent	8.1	8.9	9.3	10.0	10.3
6.7	Tourism coverage (inbound over outbound tourism expenditure)		Percent	301.2	325.1	325.8	329.5	328.8
6.8	Inbound tourism expenditure over exports of goods		Percent	25.3	25.6	26.3	28.3	28.9
6.9	Inbound tourism expenditure over exports of services		Percent	55.4	56.7	55.2	56.8	56.6
6.10	Inbound tourism expenditure over exports of goods and services		Percent	17.4	17.6	17.8	18.9	19.1
6.11	Inbound tourism expenditure over current account credits		Percent	13.6	14.4	14.6	15.7	16.2
6.12	Outbound tourism expenditure over imports of goods		Percent	6.3	6.5	6.9	7.1	7.4
6.13	Outbound tourism expenditure over imports of services		Percent	31.5	33.0	34.3	33.6	33.7
6.14	Outbound tourism expenditure over imports of goods and		Percent	5.2	5.4	5.7	5.9	6.1
6.15	Outbound tourism expenditure over current account debits		Percent	4.2	4.5	4.7	4.9	5.2

PUERTO RICO

Cod.	Basic data and indicators	Notes	Units	2011	2012	2013	2014	2015
1.	**INBOUND TOURISM**							
	Data							
	Arrivals							
1.1	Total		('000)	4,214	4,197	4,210	4,456	5,051
1.2	♦ Overnight visitors (tourists)	(1)	('000)	3,048	3,069	3,172	3,246	3,542
1.3	♦ Same-day visitors (excursionists)		('000)	1,166	1,128	1,038	1,210	1,509
1.4	* of which, cruise passengers		('000)	1,166	1,128	1,038	1,210	1,509
	Arrivals by region	(1)						
1.5	Total		('000)	3,048	3,069	3,172	3,246	3,542
1.6	♦ Africa		('000)	..	..	..	..	..
1.7	♦ Americas	(2)	('000)	2,594	2,588	2,711	2,784	3,069
1.8	♦ East Asia and the Pacific		('000)	..	..	..	..	..
1.9	♦ Europe		('000)	..	..	..	..	..
1.10	♦ Middle East		('000)	..	..	..	..	..
1.11	♦ South Asia		('000)	..	..	..	..	..
1.12	♦ Other not classified		('000)	454	481	461	463	473
1.13	* of which, nationals residing abroad		('000)	..	..	..	..	..
	Arrivals by mode of transport							
1.19	Total		('000)	4,214	4,197	4,210	4,456	5,051
1.20	♦ Air		('000)	3,048	3,069	3,172	3,246	3,542
1.21	♦ Water		('000)	1,166	1,128	1,038	1,210	1,509
1.22	♦ Land		('000)	..	..	..	..	..
1.23	* railway		('000)	..	..	..	..	..
1.24	* road		('000)	..	..	..	..	..
1.25	* others		('000)	..	..	..	..	..
	Accommodation							
	Hotels and similar establishments							
1.31	♦ Guests		('000)	1,415	1,505	1,588	1,635	1,745
1.32	♦ Overnights		('000)	..	..	..	..	..
	Expenditure							
1.33	Total	(3)	US$ Mn	3,143	3,193	3,311	3,439	3,825
1.34	♦ Travel		US$ Mn	..	..	..	..	..
1.35	♦ Passenger transport		US$ Mn	..	..	..	..	..
	Indicators							
1.39	Average size of travel party		Persons	..	..	..	..	..
	Average length of stay							
1.40	Total		Days	..	..	..	..	..
1.41	♦ For all commercial accommodation services	(4)	Nights	2.65	2.62	2.63	2.62	2.62
1.42	* of which, "hotels and similar establishments"		Nights	..	..	..	..	..
1.43	♦ For non commercial accommodation services		Days	..	..	..	..	..
1.44	Average expenditure per day		US$	..	..	..	..	..
2.	**DOMESTIC TOURISM**							
	Data							
	Accommodation							
	Hotels and similar establishments							
2.21	♦ Guests		('000)	716	817	852	844	851
2.22	♦ Overnights		('000)	..	..	..	..	..
3.	**OUTBOUND TOURISM**							
	Data							
	Departures							
3.1	Total		('000)	..	..	..	..	..
3.2	♦ Overnight visitors (tourists)		('000)	924	876	839	793	746
3.3	♦ Same-day visitors (excursionists)		('000)	..	..	..	..	..
	Expenditure	(3)						
3.4	Total		US$ Mn	1,196	1,156	1,139	1,088	1,055
3.5	♦ Travel		US$ Mn	816	787	782	763	744
3.6	♦ Passenger transport		US$ Mn	380	369	357	325	311

PUERTO RICO

Cod.	Basic data and indicators	Notes	Units	2011	2012	2013	2014	2015
4.	**TOURISM INDUSTRIES**							
	Data							
	Number of establishments							
4.1	Total		Units	..	..	..	..	..
4.2	♦ Accommodation for visitors		Units	..	..	..	..	..
4.3	* of which, "hotels and similar establishments"		Units	151	151	151	150	149
4.4	♦ Food and beverage serving activities		Units	..	..	..	..	..
4.5	♦ Passenger transportation		Units	..	..	..	..	..
4.6	♦ Travel agencies and other reservation services activities		Units	..	..	..	..	..
4.7	♦ Other tourism industries		Units	..	..	..	..	..
	Accommodation for visitors in hotels and similar establishments							
	Non-monetary data							
4.13	♦ Number of establishments		Units	151	151	151	150	149
4.14	♦ Number of rooms	(5)	Units	14,283	14,191	14,164	14,781	14,844
4.15	♦ Number of bed-places		Units	..	..	..	..	..
	Indicators							
4.16	Occupancy rate / rooms	(6)	Percent	66.18	67.94	69.85	69.82	710.00
4.17	Occupancy rate / bed-places		Percent	..	..	..	..	..
4.18	Average length of stay		Nights	2.65	2.62	2.63	2.64	2.57
4.19	Available capacity (bed-places per 1000 inhabitants)		Units	..	..	..	..	..
5.	**EMPLOYMENT**							
	Data							
	Number of employees by tourism industries							
5.1	Total		('000)	..	..	..	..	..
5.2	♦ Accommodation services for visitors (hotels and similar establishments)		('000)	13.0	13.8	14.8	15.5	15.5
5.3	♦ Other accommodation services		('000)	..	..	..	..	..
5.4	♦ Food and beverage serving activities		('000)	..	..	..	..	..
5.5	♦ Passenger transportation		('000)	..	..	..	..	..
5.6	♦ Travel agencies and other reservation services activities		('000)	..	..	..	..	..
5.7	♦ Other tourism industries		('000)	..	..	..	..	..
6.	**COMPLEMENTARY INDICATORS**							
	Demand							
6.1	Gross travel propensity		Units	..	..	..	..	..
6.2	(1.2 inbound tourists) / population		Units	0.83	0.84	0.88	0.91	1.00
	Macroeconomic indicators related to international tourism							
6.3	Inbound tourism expenditure over GDP		Percent	..	..	..	..	..
6.4	Outbound tourism expenditure over GDP		Percent	..	..	..	..	..
6.5	Tourism balance (inbound minus outbound tourism expenditure) over GDP		Percent	..	..	..	..	..
6.6	Tourism openness (inbound plus outbound tourism expenditure) over GDP		Percent	..	..	..	..	..
6.7	Tourism coverage (inbound over outbound tourism expenditure)		Percent	262.8	276.2	290.7	316.1	362.6
6.8	Inbound tourism expenditure over exports of goods		Percent	..	..	..	..	..
6.9	Inbound tourism expenditure over exports of services		Percent	..	..	..	..	..
6.10	Inbound tourism expenditure over exports of goods and services		Percent	..	..	..	..	..
6.11	Inbound tourism expenditure over current account credits		Percent	..	..	..	..	..
6.12	Outbound tourism expenditure over imports of goods		Percent	..	..	..	..	..
6.13	Outbound tourism expenditure over imports of services		Percent	..	..	..	..	..
6.14	Outbound tourism expenditure over imports of goods and		Percent	..	..	..	..	..
6.15	Outbound tourism expenditure over current account debits		Percent	..	..	..	..	..

QATAR

Cod.	Basic data and indicators	Notes	Units	2011	2012	2013	2014	2015
1.	**INBOUND TOURISM**							
	Data							
	Arrivals							
1.1	Total		('000)	..	..	..	..	..
1.2	♦ Overnight visitors (tourists)		('000)	2,057	2,346	2,611	2,826	2,930
1.3	♦ Same-day visitors (excursionists)		('000)	..	..	..	..	..
1.4	* of which, cruise passengers		('000)	..	..	..	..	..
	Arrivals by region							
1.5	Total		('000)	2,057	2,346	2,611	2,826	2,930
1.6	♦ Africa		('000)	84	93	95	105	104
1.7	♦ Americas		('000)	102	117	130	144	146
1.8	♦ East Asia and the Pacific		('000)	130	153	165	192	205
1.9	♦ Europe		('000)	302	366	409	421	437
1.10	♦ Middle East		('000)	1,058	1,179	1,323	1,374	1,508
1.11	♦ South Asia		('000)	381	439	489	591	531
1.12	♦ Other not classified		('000)	..	..	..	..	..
1.13	* of which, nationals residing abroad		('000)	..	..	..	..	..
	Arrivals by mode of transport							
1.19	Total		('000)	2,057	2,346	2,611	2,826	2,930
1.20	♦ Air		('000)	1,182	1,372	1,515	1,670	1,760
1.21	♦ Water		('000)	12	16	19	19	19
1.22	♦ Land		('000)	863	959	1,078	1,137	1,151
1.23	* railway		('000)	..	..	..	..	..
1.24	* road		('000)	863	959	1,078	1,137	1,151
1.25	* others		('000)	..	..	..	..	..
	Accommodation							
	Hotels and similar establishments							
1.31	♦ Guests		('000)	..	..	..	..	..
1.32	♦ Overnights	(1)	('000)	2,684	2,815	3,224	3,624	5,159
	Expenditure							
1.33	Total		US$ Mn	4,463	7,220	8,452	10,576	12,131
1.34	♦ Travel		US$ Mn	1,170	2,857	3,456	4,591	5,035
1.35	♦ Passenger transport		US$ Mn	3,293	4,363	4,996	5,985	7,096
3.	**OUTBOUND TOURISM**							
	Data							
	Expenditure							
3.4	Total		US$ Mn	7,813	10,702	11,729	12,871	11,641
3.5	♦ Travel		US$ Mn	1,807	5,648	6,616	8,682	8,171
3.6	♦ Passenger transport		US$ Mn	6,006	5,054	5,113	4,189	3,470
4.	**TOURISM INDUSTRIES**							
	Data							
	Number of establishments							
4.1	Total		Units	..	..	..	..	..
4.2	♦ Accommodation for visitors		Units	..	..	..	..	..
4.3	* of which, "hotels and similar establishments"	(1)	Units	74	81	83	85	119
4.4	♦ Food and beverage serving activities		Units	..	..	..	..	..
4.5	♦ Passenger transportation		Units	..	..	..	..	..
4.6	♦ Travel agencies and other reservation services activities		Units	..	..	..	..	..
4.7	♦ Other tourism industries		Units	..	..	..	..	..
	Accommodation for visitors in hotels and similar establishments							
	Non-monetary data	(1)						
4.13	♦ Number of establishments		Units	74	81	83	85	119
4.14	♦ Number of rooms		Units	9,976	13,407	13,577	13,937	20,713
4.15	♦ Number of bed-places		Units	..	..	..	..	..
	Indicators							
4.16	Occupancy rate / rooms		Percent	..	60.00	65.00	73.00	71.00
4.17	Occupancy rate / bed-places		Percent	..	..	..	..	..
4.18	Average length of stay		Nights	..	..	..	..	..
4.19	Available capacity (bed-places per 1000 inhabitants)		Units	..	..	..	..	..

QATAR

Cod.	Basic data and indicators	Notes	Units	2011	2012	2013	2014	2015
6.	**COMPLEMENTARY INDICATORS**							
	Demand							
6.1	Gross travel propensity		Units	..	..	..	..	..
6.2	(1.2 inbound tourists) / population		Units	1.08	1.16	1.24	1.30	1.31
	Macroeconomic indicators related to international tourism							
6.3	Inbound tourism expenditure over GDP		Percent	2.6	3.8	4.2	5.0	..
6.4	Outbound tourism expenditure over GDP		Percent	4.6	5.6	5.8	6.1	..
6.5	Tourism balance (inbound minus outbound tourism expenditure) over GDP		Percent	-2.0	-1.8	-1.6	-1.1	..
6.6	Tourism openness (inbound plus outbound tourism expenditure) over GDP		Percent	7.2	9.4	10.0	11.1	..
6.7	Tourism coverage (inbound over outbound tourism expenditure)		Percent	57.1	67.5	72.1	82.2	104.2
6.8	Inbound tourism expenditure over exports of goods		Percent	3.9	5.4	6.3	8.3	15.7
6.9	Inbound tourism expenditure over exports of services		Percent	60.4	72.8	75.6	78.2	80.9
6.10	Inbound tourism expenditure over exports of goods and services		Percent	3.7	5.1	5.8	7.5	13.1
6.11	Inbound tourism expenditure over current account credits		Percent	3.4	4.8	5.6	7.1	12.0
6.12	Outbound tourism expenditure over imports of goods		Percent	29.0	34.8	37.3	41.3	40.9
6.13	Outbound tourism expenditure over imports of services		Percent	46.3	44.8	42.7	39.2	37.8
6.14	Outbound tourism expenditure over imports of goods and		Percent	17.8	19.6	19.9	20.1	19.6
6.15	Outbound tourism expenditure over current account debits		Percent	12.1	13.9	14.4	14.4	14.0

REUNION

Cod.	Basic data and indicators	Notes	Units	2011	2012	2013	2014	2015
1.	**INBOUND TOURISM**							
	Data							
	Arrivals							
1.1	Total		('000)	..	..	..	..	..
1.2	♦ Overnight visitors (tourists)	(1)(2)	('000)	471	447	416	406	426
1.3	♦ Same-day visitors (excursionists)		('000)	..	..	..	..	..
1.4	* of which, cruise passengers		('000)	..	..	..	..	..
	Arrivals by region	(1)(2)						
1.5	Total		('000)	471	447	416	406	426
1.6	♦ Africa		('000)	42	46	46	48	61
1.7	♦ Americas		('000)	..	..	..	..	..
1.8	♦ East Asia and the Pacific		('000)	..	..	..	..	..
1.9	♦ Europe		('000)	406	379	359	348	356
1.10	♦ Middle East		('000)	..	..	..	..	..
1.11	♦ South Asia		('000)	..	..	..	..	..
1.12	♦ Other not classified		('000)	23	22	11	10	10
1.13	* of which, nationals residing abroad		('000)	..	..	..	..	..
	Arrivals by main purpose	(1)(2)						
1.14	Total		('000)	471	447	416	406	426
1.15	♦ Personal		('000)	428	404	380	361	377
1.16	* holidays, leisure and recreation		('000)	197	180	168	151	159
1.17	* other personal purposes		('000)	231	224	212	210	218
1.18	♦ Business and professional		('000)	43	43	36	45	50
	Arrivals by mode of transport	(1)(2)						
1.19	Total		('000)	471	447	416	406	426
1.20	♦ Air		('000)	471	447	416	406	426
1.21	♦ Water		('000)	..	..	..	..	..
1.22	♦ Land		('000)	..	..	..	..	..
1.23	* railway		('000)	..	..	..	..	..
1.24	* road		('000)	..	..	..	..	..
1.25	* others		('000)	..	..	..	..	..
	Arrivals by form of organization of the trip	(1)(2)						
1.26	Total		('000)	471	447	416	406	426
1.27	♦ Package tour		('000)	61	61	63	62	61
1.28	♦ Other forms		('000)	410	386	353	344	365
	Accommodation							
	Hotels and similar establishments	(3)						
1.31	♦ Guests		('000)	186	149	143	144	143
1.32	♦ Overnights	(4)	('000)	864	842	814	749	1,025
	Expenditure							
1.33	Total	(5)	US$ Mn	479	404	403	387	339
1.34	♦ Travel		US$ Mn	..	..	..	..	..
1.35	♦ Passenger transport		US$ Mn	..	..	..	..	..
	Indicators							
1.39	Average size of travel party		Persons	..	..	..	..	..
	Average length of stay							
1.40	Total		Days	17.00	17.10	16.70	17.40	16.80
1.41	♦ For all commercial accommodation services		Nights	..	..	..	..	..
1.42	* of which, "hotels and similar establishments"		Nights	7.00	6.60	6.20	6.30	6.30
1.43	♦ For non commercial accommodation services		Days	..	..	..	..	..
1.44	Average expenditure per day		US$	59.8	52.7	58.4	54.9	52.6
4.	**TOURISM INDUSTRIES**							
	Data							
	Number of establishments	(6)						
4.1	Total		Units	4,313	4,557	4,174	..	..
4.2	♦ Accommodation for visitors		Units	426	472	435	..	..
4.3	* of which, "hotels and similar establishments"		Units	153	162	148	..	..
4.4	♦ Food and beverage serving activities		Units	3,067	3,230	2,947	..	..
4.5	♦ Passenger transportation		Units	661	675	638	..	..
4.6	♦ Travel agencies and other reservation services activities		Units	159	180	154	..	..
4.7	♦ Other tourism industries		Units	..	..	..	..	..

REUNION

Cod.	Basic data and indicators	Notes	Units	2011	2012	2013	2014	2015
	Accommodation for visitors in hotels and similar establishments							
	Non-monetary data	(3)(7)						
4.13	♦ Number of establishments		Units	53	53	53	46	78
4.14	♦ Number of rooms		Units	2,077	2,120	2,117	2,070	3,100
4.15	♦ Number of bed-places		Units	4,154	4,240	4,234	4,140	6,200
	Indicators							
4.16	Occupancy rate / rooms		Percent	67.00	62.60	62.30	59.10	61.10
4.17	Occupancy rate / bed-places		Percent	..	..	..	..	..
4.18	Average length of stay		Nights	7.00	6.60	6.20	6.30	6.30
4.19	Available capacity (bed-places per 1000 inhabitants)		Units	4.96	5.03	4.99	4.84	7.20
5.	**EMPLOYMENT**							
	Data							
	Number of employees by tourism industries	(8)						
5.1	Total		('000)	11.3	11.3	11.8	..	..
5.2	♦ Accommodation services for visitors (hotels and similar establishments)		('000)	1.6	1.6	1.7	..	..
5.3	♦ Other accommodation services		('000)	0.2	0.2	0.2	..	..
5.4	♦ Food and beverage serving activities		('000)	4.9	5.1	5.2	..	..
5.5	♦ Passenger transportation		('000)	3.9	3.8	4.0	..	..
5.6	♦ Travel agencies and other reservation services activities		('000)	0.7	0.6	0.7	..	..
5.7	♦ Other tourism industries		('000)	..	..	..	..	..
6.	**COMPLEMENTARY INDICATORS**							
	Demand							
6.1	Gross travel propensity		Units	..	..	..	..	..
6.2	(1.2 inbound tourists) / population		Units	0.56	0.53	0.49	0.47	0.49

ROMANIA

Cod.	Basic data and indicators	Notes	Units	2011	2012	2013	2014	2015
1.	**INBOUND TOURISM**							
	Data							
	Arrivals							
1.1	Total		('000)	7,611	7,937	8,019	8,442	9,331
1.2	♦ Overnight visitors (tourists)		('000)	..	..	..	..	..
1.3	♦ Same-day visitors (excursionists)		('000)	..	..	..	..	..
1.4	* of which, cruise passengers		('000)	..	..	..	..	..
	Arrivals by region							
1.5	Total		('000)	7,611	7,937	8,019	8,442	9,331
1.6	♦ Africa		('000)	16	16	17	20	23
1.7	♦ Americas		('000)	182	208	209	294	247
1.8	♦ East Asia and the Pacific		('000)	92	98	103	107	120
1.9	♦ Europe		('000)	7,267	7,556	7,625	7,955	8,869
1.10	♦ Middle East		('000)	33	37	42	43	45
1.11	♦ South Asia		('000)	21	22	22	23	27
1.12	♦ Other not classified		('000)	..	..	..	1	1
1.13	* of which, nationals residing abroad		('000)	..	..	..	..	..
	Arrivals by mode of transport							
1.19	Total		('000)	7,611	7,937	8,019	8,442	9,331
1.20	♦ Air		('000)	1,509	1,469	1,347	1,690	1,535
1.21	♦ Water		('000)	168	187	196	189	178
1.22	♦ Land		('000)	5,934	6,281	6,476	6,563	7,618
1.23	* railway		('000)	258	255	232	173	143
1.24	* road		('000)	5,676	6,027	6,244	6,390	7,475
1.25	* others		('000)	..	..	..	..	..
	Accommodation							
	Total							
1.29	♦ Guests		('000)	1,517	1,653	1,716	1,912	2,234
1.30	♦ Overnights		('000)	3,067	3,292	3,471	3,762	4,460
	Hotels and similar establishments							
1.31	♦ Guests		('000)	1,496	1,543	1,596	1,798	2,085
1.32	♦ Overnights		('000)	2,982	3,001	3,168	3,515	4,115
	Expenditure							
1.33	Total		US$ Mn	2,016	1,904	2,048	2,225	2,089
1.34	♦ Travel		US$ Mn	1,419	1,466	1,591	1,826	1,703
1.35	♦ Passenger transport		US$ Mn	597	438	457	399	386
	Expenditure by main purpose of the trip							
1.36	Total		US$ Mn	1,421	1,463	1,591	1,826	1,703
1.37	♦ Personal		US$ Mn	311	325	524	727	331
1.38	♦ Business and professional		US$ Mn	1,110	1,138	1,067	1,099	1,372
	Indicators							
1.39	Average size of travel party		Persons	..	..	..	..	..
	Average length of stay							
1.40	Total		Days	..	..	..	..	..
1.41	♦ For all commercial accommodation services		Nights	2.02	1.99	2.02	..	..
1.42	* of which, "hotels and similar establishments"		Nights	1.99	1.97	1.98	..	..
1.43	♦ For non commercial accommodation services		Days	..	..	..	..	..
1.44	Average expenditure per day		US$	..	..	..	..	..
2.	**DOMESTIC TOURISM**							
	Data							
	Trips							
2.1	Total		('000)	41,004	53,513	52,410	50,084	52,762
2.2	♦ Overnight visitors (tourists)	(1)	('000)	11,986	15,833	16,357	15,840	16,194
2.3	♦ Same-day visitors (excursionists)		('000)	29,018	37,680	36,053	34,244	36,568
	Trips by main purpose							
2.4	Total		('000)	11,986	15,833	16,357	15,840	16,193
2.5	♦ Personal		('000)	11,625	15,374	15,856	15,435	15,846
2.6	* holidays, leisure and recreation		('000)	4,140	5,518	6,154	5,904	6,263
2.7	* other personal purposes	(2)	('000)	7,485	9,856	9,702	9,531	9,583
2.8	♦ Business and professional		('000)	361	459	501	405	347
	Trips by mode of transport							
2.9	Total		('000)	11,986	15,834	16,357	15,840	16,193
2.10	♦ Air		('000)	..	..	..	..	..
2.11	♦ Water		('000)	..	..	..	..	..
2.12	♦ Land		('000)	11,986	15,834	16,357	15,840	16,193
2.13	* railway		('000)	1,832	2,744	2,384	2,107	2,159
2.14	* road		('000)	9,444	12,184	13,722	13,372	13,732
2.15	* others	(3)	('000)	710	906	251	361	302

325

ROMANIA

Cod.	Basic data and indicators	Notes	Units	2011	2012	2013	2014	2015
	Accommodation							
	Total							
2.19	♦ Guests		('000)	5,515	6,030	6,226	6,551	7,691
2.20	♦ Overnights		('000)	14,913	15,869	15,885	16,512	19,048
	Hotels and similar establishments							
2.21	♦ Guests		('000)	5,356	5,893	6,105	6,422	7,539
2.22	♦ Overnights		('000)	14,385	15,429	15,491	16,092	18,531
	Indicators							
2.23	Average size of travel party		Persons	..	..	..	..	..
	Average length of stay							
2.24	Total	(4)	Days	5.24	3.77	..	..	..
2.25	♦ For all commercial accommodation services		Nights	2.71	2.63	..	..	..
2.26	* of which, "hotels and similar establishments"		Nights	2.69	2.62	..	..	..
2.27	♦ For non commercial accommodation services		Days	..	..	..	..	..
2.28	Average expenditure per day	(5)	US$	29.3	29.6	..	..	..
3.	**OUTBOUND TOURISM**							
	Data							
	Departures							
3.1	Total		('000)	11,228	11,548	..	..	..
3.2	♦ Overnight visitors (tourists)	(6)	('000)	10,936	11,149	11,364	12,299	13,118
3.3	♦ Same-day visitors (excursionists)		('000)	292	399	..	..	..
	Expenditure							
3.4	Total		US$ Mn	2,294	2,108	2,176	2,636	2,330
3.5	♦ Travel		US$ Mn	1,965	1,832	2,059	2,412	2,059
3.6	♦ Passenger transport		US$ Mn	329	276	117	224	271
	Expenditure by main purpose of the trip							
3.7	Total		US$ Mn	1,966	1,833	2,059	2,412	2,059
3.8	♦ Personal		US$ Mn	720	645	779	1,252	1,307
3.9	♦ Business and professional		US$ Mn	1,246	1,188	1,280	1,160	752
	Indicators							
3.10	Average length of stay		Days	..	..	..	..	..
3.11	Average expenditure per day	(5)	US$	40.4	49.6	..	..	..
4.	**TOURISM INDUSTRIES**							
	Data							
	Number of establishments							
4.1	Total		Units	..	..	..	..	..
4.2	♦ Accommodation for visitors		Units	5,003	5,821	6,009	6,130	6,821
4.3	* of which, "hotels and similar establishments"		Units	4,612	5,376	5,560	5,677	6,308
4.4	♦ Food and beverage serving activities		Units	..	..	..	..	..
4.5	♦ Passenger transportation		Units	..	..	..	..	..
4.6	♦ Travel agencies and other reservation services activities		Units	..	..	..	..	..
4.7	♦ Other tourism industries		Units	..	..	..	..	..
	Accommodation for visitors in hotels and similar establishments							
	Non-monetary data	(7)						
4.13	♦ Number of establishments		Units	4,612	5,376	5,560	5,677	6,308
4.14	♦ Number of rooms		Units	119,349	128,713	131,756	133,530	140,434
4.15	♦ Number of bed-places		Units	248,592	270,172	276,095	280,810	298,571
	Indicators							
4.16	Occupancy rate / rooms		Percent	..	..	..	..	..
4.17	Occupancy rate / bed-places		Percent	26.30	25.90	25.10	..	23.90
4.18	Average length of stay		Nights	2.54	2.50	2.43	..	2.12
4.19	Available capacity (bed-places per 1000 inhabitants)		Units	12.36	13.55	13.95	14.29	15.30
	Travel agencies and other reservation service activities							
	Non-monetary data	(8)						
	♦ Domestic trips							
4.25	* with package tour		Percent	61.4	38.4	51.3	54.2	56.2
4.26	* without package tour		Percent	38.6	61.6	48.7	45.8	43.8
	♦ Inbound trips							
4.27	* with package tour		Percent	70.6	75.0	55.0	88.9	84.8
4.28	* without package tour		Percent	29.4	25.0	45.0	11.1	15.2
	♦ Outbound trips							
4.29	* with package tour		Percent	61.3	38.1	46.3	66.4	68.4
4.30	* without package tour		Percent	38.7	61.9	53.7	33.6	31.6

ROMANIA

Cod.	Basic data and indicators	Notes	Units	2011	2012	2013	2014	2015
5.	**EMPLOYMENT**							
	Data							
	Number of employees by tourism industries	**(9)**						
5.1	Total		('000)	397.6	..	..	..	..
5.2	♦ Accommodation services for visitors (hotels and similar establishments)		('000)	35.4	..	..	..	..
5.3	♦ Other accommodation services		('000)	8.1	..	..	..	..
5.4	♦ Food and beverage serving activities		('000)	102.0	..	..	..	..
5.5	♦ Passenger transportation	**(10)**	('000)	210.6	..	..	..	..
5.6	♦ Travel agencies and other reservation services activities		('000)	9.2	..	..	..	..
5.7	♦ Other tourism industries	**(11)**	('000)	32.3	..	..	..	..
6.	**COMPLEMENTARY INDICATORS**							
	Demand							
6.1	Gross travel propensity		Units	..	..	..	..	..
6.2	(1.1 inbound visitors + 2.1 domestic visitors) / population		Units	2.42	3.08	3.05	2.98	3.18
	Macroeconomic indicators related to international tourism							
6.3	Inbound tourism expenditure over GDP		Percent	1.1	1.1	1.1	1.1	1.2
6.4	Outbound tourism expenditure over GDP		Percent	1.3	1.2	1.2	1.3	1.3
6.5	Tourism balance (inbound minus outbound tourism expenditure) over GDP		Percent	-0.2	-0.1	-0.1	-0.2	-0.1
6.6	Tourism openness (inbound plus outbound tourism expenditure) over GDP		Percent	2.4	2.3	2.3	2.4	2.5
6.7	Tourism coverage (inbound over outbound tourism expenditure)		Percent	87.9	90.3	94.1	84.4	89.7
6.8	Inbound tourism expenditure over exports of goods		Percent	3.6	3.7	3.5	3.6	3.8
6.9	Inbound tourism expenditure over exports of services		Percent	16.7	15.0	11.5	11.1	11.2
6.10	Inbound tourism expenditure over exports of goods and services		Percent	3.0	3.0	2.7	2.7	2.9
6.11	Inbound tourism expenditure over current account credits		Percent	2.6	2.6	2.4	2.4	2.5
6.12	Outbound tourism expenditure over imports of goods		Percent	3.3	3.3	3.3	3.7	3.7
6.13	Outbound tourism expenditure over imports of services		Percent	23.4	22.2	18.7	21.5	21.3
6.14	Outbound tourism expenditure over imports of goods and		Percent	2.9	2.9	2.8	3.2	3.1
6.15	Outbound tourism expenditure over current account debits		Percent	2.7	2.7	2.6	2.9	2.9

RUSSIAN FEDERATION

Cod.	Basic data and indicators	Notes	Units	2011	2012	2013	2014	2015
1.	**INBOUND TOURISM**							
	Data							
	Arrivals							
1.1	Total		('000)	24,932	28,177	30,792	32,421	33,729
1.2	♦ Overnight visitors (tourists)		('000)	..	..	..	..	..
1.3	♦ Same-day visitors (excursionists)		('000)	1,269	1,351	1,486	..	1,670
1.4	* of which, cruise passengers		('000)	1,269	1,351	1,486	..	1,670
	Arrivals by region							
1.5	Total		('000)	24,933	28,177	30,792	32,421	33,729
1.6	♦ Africa		('000)	40	40	56	54	42
1.7	♦ Americas		('000)	439	444	494	426	407
1.8	♦ East Asia and the Pacific		('000)	1,548	1,904	1,938	2,017	2,005
1.9	♦ Europe		('000)	21,896	24,741	27,257	28,890	27,110
1.10	♦ Middle East		('000)	42	51	59	58	56
1.11	♦ South Asia		('000)	99	123	138	147	125
1.12	♦ Other not classified		('000)	869	874	851	829	3,985
1.13	* of which, nationals residing abroad		('000)	..	..	..	..	..
	Arrivals by main purpose							
1.14	Total		('000)	24,932	28,177	30,792	32,421	33,729
1.15	♦ Personal		('000)	19,457	21,976	24,975	26,158	26,212
1.16	* holidays, leisure and recreation		('000)	2,336	2,571	2,665	2,583	2,937
1.17	* other personal purposes		('000)	17,121	19,405	22,311	23,575	23,275
1.18	♦ Business and professional		('000)	5,475	6,201	5,817	6,263	7,517
	Arrivals by mode of transport							
1.19	Total		('000)	24,932	28,176	30,792	32,421	33,729
1.20	♦ Air		('000)	6,383	7,537	8,045	8,198	7,646
1.21	♦ Water		('000)	1,269	1,351	1,487	1,333	1,290
1.22	♦ Land		('000)	17,280	19,288	21,260	22,890	24,793
1.23	* railway		('000)	5,534	5,283	5,168	5,276	2,453
1.24	* road		('000)	10,336	12,399	14,482	15,738	18,897
1.25	* others	(1)	('000)	1,410	1,606	1,610	1,876	3,443
	Accommodation							
	Total							
1.29	♦ Guests		('000)	3,866	4,214	4,444	4,608	5,627
1.30	♦ Overnights		('000)	..	..	..	..	..
	Hotels and similar establishments							
1.31	♦ Guests		('000)	3,789	4,127	4,351	4,481	5,440
1.32	♦ Overnights		('000)	..	..	..	..	..
	Expenditure							
1.33	Total		US$ Mn	16,961	17,876	20,198	19,451	13,249
1.34	♦ Travel		US$ Mn	11,328	10,759	11,988	11,759	8,465
1.35	♦ Passenger transport		US$ Mn	5,633	7,117	8,210	7,692	4,784
	Expenditure by main purpose of the trip							
1.36	Total		US$ Mn	11,328	10,759	11,988	11,759	8,465
1.37	♦ Personal		US$ Mn	5,085	4,002	5,084	5,778	4,551
1.38	♦ Business and professional		US$ Mn	6,243	6,757	6,904	5,981	3,914
2.	**DOMESTIC TOURISM**							
	Data							
	Accommodation							
	Total							
2.19	♦ Guests		('000)	29,310	31,798	32,561	33,799	43,657
2.20	♦ Overnights		('000)	..	..	..	..	..
	Hotels and similar establishments							
2.21	♦ Guests		('000)	20,336	22,477	23,351	24,475	31,378
2.22	♦ Overnights		('000)	..	..	..	..	..
3.	**OUTBOUND TOURISM**							
	Data							
	Departures							
3.1	Total		('000)	..	..	..	..	..
3.2	♦ Overnight visitors (tourists)		('000)	43,726	47,813	54,069	45,889	34,550
3.3	♦ Same-day visitors (excursionists)		('000)	..	..	..	..	..
	Expenditure							
3.4	Total		US$ Mn	37,343	48,096	59,504	55,383	38,436
3.5	♦ Travel		US$ Mn	32,902	42,798	53,453	50,428	34,934
3.6	♦ Passenger transport		US$ Mn	4,441	5,298	6,051	4,955	3,502

RUSSIAN FEDERATION

Cod.	Basic data and indicators	Notes	Units	2011	2012	2013	2014	2015
	Expenditure by main purpose of the trip							
3.7	Total		US$ Mn	32,902	42,797	53,452	50,428	34,934
3.8	♦ Personal		US$ Mn	30,793	40,767	51,579	48,785	33,633
3.9	♦ Business and professional		US$ Mn	2,109	2,030	1,873	1,643	1,301
4.	**TOURISM INDUSTRIES**							
	Data							
	Number of establishments							
4.1	Total		Units	88,989	93,326	97,992	105,345	110,690
4.2	♦ Accommodation for visitors		Units	13,062	14,019	14,583	15,590	20,136
4.3	* of which, "hotels and similar establishments"		Units	8,416	9,316	9,869	10,714	13,958
4.4	♦ Food and beverage serving activities		Units	63,505	66,462	70,275	76,367	78,661
4.5	♦ Passenger transportation		Units	2,156	2,072	1,810	1,774	..
4.6	♦ Travel agencies and other reservation services activities		Units	10,266	10,773	11,324	11,614	11,893
4.7	♦ Other tourism industries		Units	..	..	..	..	..
	Accommodation for visitors in hotels and similar establishments							
	Non-monetary data							
4.13	♦ Number of establishments		Units	8,416	9,316	9,869	10,714	13,958
4.14	♦ Number of rooms	(2)	Units	277,916	300,629	319,143	371,796	433,000
4.15	♦ Number of bed-places	(2)	Units	571,226	617,849	675,515	814,913	923,000
	Indicators							
4.16	Occupancy rate / rooms		Percent	..	..	..	..	..
4.17	Occupancy rate / bed-places		Percent	32.00	33.00	31.00	28.00	30.00
4.18	Average length of stay		Nights	..	..	..	..	..
4.19	Available capacity (bed-places per 1000 inhabitants)		Units	3.99	4.31	4.71	5.68	6.43
5.	**EMPLOYMENT**							
	Data							
	Number of employees by tourism industries							
5.1	Total		('000)	499.2	491.8	478.8	501.0	1,338.0
5.2	♦ Accommodation services for visitors (hotels and similar establishments)		('000)	150.5	153.7	154.9	166.1	478.5
5.3	♦ Other accommodation services		('000)	301.2	289.5	273.8	289.4	811.5
5.4	♦ Food and beverage serving activities		('000)	..	..	..	..	..
5.5	♦ Passenger transportation		('000)	..	..	..	..	..
5.6	♦ Travel agencies and other reservation services activities		('000)	47.5	48.7	50.1	45.5	48.0
5.7	♦ Other tourism industries		('000)	..	..	..	..	..
6.	**COMPLEMENTARY INDICATORS**							
	Demand							
6.1	Gross travel propensity		Units	..	..	..	..	..
6.2	(1.1 inbound visitors) / population		Units	0.17	0.20	0.21	0.23	0.24
	Macroeconomic indicators related to international tourism							
6.3	Inbound tourism expenditure over GDP		Percent	0.9	0.9	1.0	1.0	1.0
6.4	Outbound tourism expenditure over GDP		Percent	1.9	2.4	2.8	3.0	2.8
6.5	Tourism balance (inbound minus outbound tourism expenditure) over GDP		Percent	-1.0	-1.5	-1.8	-2.0	-1.8
6.6	Tourism openness (inbound plus outbound tourism expenditure) over GDP		Percent	2.8	3.3	3.8	4.0	3.8
6.7	Tourism coverage (inbound over outbound tourism expenditure)		Percent	45.4	37.2	33.9	35.1	34.5
6.8	Inbound tourism expenditure over exports of goods		Percent	3.3	3.4	3.9	3.9	3.9
6.9	Inbound tourism expenditure over exports of services		Percent	29.2	28.7	28.8	29.6	25.6
6.10	Inbound tourism expenditure over exports of goods and services		Percent	3.0	3.0	3.4	3.5	3.4
6.11	Inbound tourism expenditure over current account credits		Percent	2.7	2.7	3.1	3.1	3.0
6.12	Outbound tourism expenditure over imports of goods		Percent	11.7	14.3	17.4	18.0	19.9
6.13	Outbound tourism expenditure over imports of services		Percent	40.8	44.2	46.3	45.8	43.4
6.14	Outbound tourism expenditure over imports of goods and		Percent	9.1	10.8	12.7	12.9	13.7
6.15	Outbound tourism expenditure over current account debits		Percent	7.9	9.3	11.1	11.0	11.5

RWANDA

Cod.	Basic data and indicators	Notes	Units	2011	2012	2013	2014	2015
1.	**INBOUND TOURISM**							
	Data							
	Arrivals							
1.1	Total		('000)	908	1,061	1,122	1,220	1,298
1.2	♦ Overnight visitors (tourists)		('000)	688	815	864	926	987
1.3	♦ Same-day visitors (excursionists)		('000)	220	246	258	294	311
1.4	* of which, cruise passengers		('000)	..	..	..	..	..
	Arrivals by region							
1.5	Total		('000)	908	1,061	1,122	1,220	1,298
1.6	♦ Africa		('000)	774	936	988	1,088	1,154
1.7	♦ Americas		('000)	38	33	38	35	39
1.8	♦ East Asia and the Pacific		('000)	13	12	15	12	14
1.9	♦ Europe		('000)	67	62	61	61	72
1.10	♦ Middle East		('000)	2	2	3	3	3
1.11	♦ South Asia		('000)	14	16	16	15	15
1.12	♦ Other not classified		('000)	..	1	2	6	1
1.13	* of which, nationals residing abroad		('000)	..	..	..	..	..
	Arrivals by main purpose							
1.14	Total		('000)	908	1,061	1,122	1,220	1,298
1.15	♦ Personal		('000)	513	647	703	824	889
1.16	* holidays, leisure and recreation		('000)	82	95	104	105	116
1.17	* other personal purposes		('000)	431	551	599	719	772
1.18	♦ Business and professional		('000)	395	415	419	395	410
	Arrivals by mode of transport							
1.19	Total		('000)	908	1,061	1,122	1,220	1,298
1.20	♦ Air		('000)	134	124	133	126	171
1.21	♦ Water		('000)	..	..	..	..	..
1.22	♦ Land		('000)	774	938	989	1,094	1,128
1.23	* railway		('000)	..	..	..	..	..
1.24	* road		('000)	774	938	989	1,094	1,128
1.25	* others		('000)	..	..	..	..	..
	Expenditure							
1.33	Total		US$ Mn	298	337	351	..	407
1.34	♦ Travel		US$ Mn	252	282	294	304	318
1.35	♦ Passenger transport		US$ Mn	46	55	57	..	89
	Expenditure by main purpose of the trip							
1.36	Total		US$ Mn	..	..	294	304	317
1.37	♦ Personal		US$ Mn	..	..	195	210	219
1.38	♦ Business and professional		US$ Mn	..	..	98	94	98
3.	**OUTBOUND TOURISM**							
	Data							
	Expenditure							
3.4	Total		US$ Mn	147	133	144	..	210
3.5	♦ Travel		US$ Mn	89	79	101	..	96
3.6	♦ Passenger transport		US$ Mn	58	54	43	..	114
	Expenditure by main purpose of the trip							
3.7	Total		US$ Mn	..	..	101	..	96
3.8	♦ Personal		US$ Mn	..	..	49	..	46
3.9	♦ Business and professional		US$ Mn	..	..	52	..	50
4.	**TOURISM INDUSTRIES**							
	Data							
	Number of establishments							
4.1	Total		Units	420	453	..	..	..
4.2	♦ Accommodation for visitors		Units	363	396	436	453	489
4.3	* of which, "hotels and similar establishments"		Units	329	357	395	412	444
4.4	♦ Food and beverage serving activities		Units	..	..	..	..	..
4.5	♦ Passenger transportation		Units	..	..	..	..	..
4.6	♦ Travel agencies and other reservation services activities		Units	57	57	..	..	..
4.7	♦ Other tourism industries		Units	..	..	..	..	..
	Accommodation for visitors in hotels and similar establishments							
	Non-monetary data							
4.13	♦ Number of establishments		Units	329	357	395	412	444
4.14	♦ Number of rooms		Units	5,856	6,470	7,316	7,678	8,270
4.15	♦ Number of bed-places		Units	11,784	12,974	14,658	15,430	16,597

RWANDA

Cod.	Basic data and indicators	Notes	Units	2011	2012	2013	2014	2015
	Indicators							
4.16	Occupancy rate / rooms		Percent	..	..	..	..	..
4.17	Occupancy rate / bed-places		Percent	..	..	..	..	..
4.18	Average length of stay		Nights	..	..	..	..	..
4.19	Available capacity (bed-places per 1000 inhabitants)		Units	1.12	1.20	1.32	1.36	1.43
6.	**COMPLEMENTARY INDICATORS**							
	Demand							
6.1	Gross travel propensity		Units	..	..	..	..	..
6.2	(1.2 inbound tourists) / population		Units	0.07	0.08	0.08	0.08	0.09
	Macroeconomic indicators related to international tourism							
6.3	Inbound tourism expenditure over GDP		Percent	4.3	4.4	4.4	3.7	5.3
6.4	Outbound tourism expenditure over GDP		Percent	2.1	1.7	1.8	..	2.6
6.5	Tourism balance (inbound minus outbound tourism expenditure) over GDP		Percent	2.2	2.7	2.6	3.7	2.7
6.6	Tourism openness (inbound plus outbound tourism expenditure) over GDP		Percent	6.4	6.1	6.2	3.7	8.0
6.7	Tourism coverage (inbound over outbound tourism expenditure)		Percent	202.7	253.4	243.8	..	193.8
6.8	Inbound tourism expenditure over exports of goods		Percent	63.5	57.0	49.9	42.0	59.5
6.9	Inbound tourism expenditure over exports of services		Percent	67.2	79.2	60.4	58.8	56.5
6.10	Inbound tourism expenditure over exports of goods and services		Percent	32.6	33.2	27.3	24.5	29.0
6.11	Inbound tourism expenditure over current account credits		Percent	15.8	18.4	16.1	16.3	20.2
6.12	Outbound tourism expenditure over imports of goods		Percent	9.4	6.8	7.6	..	11.0
6.13	Outbound tourism expenditure over imports of services		Percent	23.1	25.6	16.3	..	22.9
6.14	Outbound tourism expenditure over imports of goods and		Percent	6.7	5.4	5.2	..	7.4
6.15	Outbound tourism expenditure over current account debits		Percent	6.4	5.2	5.0	..	7.2

SAINT KITTS AND NEVIS

Cod.	Basic data and indicators	Notes	Units	2011	2012	2013	2014	2015
1.	**INBOUND TOURISM**							
	Data							
	Arrivals							
1.1	Total		('000)	723	666	695	818	1,036
1.2	♦ Overnight visitors (tourists)	(1)	('000)	104	104	107	113	122
1.3	♦ Same-day visitors (excursionists)		('000)	619	562	588	705	914
1.4	* of which, cruise passengers	(2)	('000)	604	553	575	695	910
	Arrivals by region	(1)						
1.5	Total		('000)	104	104	107	113	122
1.6	♦ Africa		('000)	..	..	..	..	..
1.7	♦ Americas		('000)	92	92	94	98	106
1.8	♦ East Asia and the Pacific		('000)	0.3	0.5	0.8	1.1	1.3
1.9	♦ Europe		('000)	10	10	11	12	13
1.10	♦ Middle East		('000)	0.3	0.4	0.6	0.5	0.5
1.11	♦ South Asia		('000)	0.5	0.3	0.3	0.4	0.4
1.12	♦ Other not classified		('000)	1.0	0.8	0.7	1.1	0.9
1.13	* of which, nationals residing abroad		('000)	..	..	..	..	
	Arrivals by main purpose	(1)						
1.14	Total		('000)	104	104	107	113	122
1.15	♦ Personal		('000)	89	89	91	95	102
1.16	* holidays, leisure and recreation		('000)	71	72	75	76	79
1.17	* other personal purposes		('000)	18	17	16	19	23
1.18	♦ Business and professional		('000)	15	15	16	18	20
	Arrivals by mode of transport							
1.19	Total		('000)	723	666	695	818	1,036
1.20	♦ Air		('000)	113	109	113	117	122
1.21	♦ Water	(2)	('000)	610	557	582	701	914
1.22	♦ Land		('000)	..	..	..	..	..
1.23	* railway		('000)	..	..	..	..	..
1.24	* road		('000)	..	..	..	..	..
1.25	* others		('000)	..	..	..	..	..
	Expenditure							
1.33	Total		US$ Mn	..	..	..	..	
1.34	♦ Travel		US$ Mn	108	109	117	126	134
1.35	♦ Passenger transport		US$ Mn	..	..	..	..	
	Indicators							
1.39	Average size of travel party		Persons	..	..	..	..	..
	Average length of stay							
1.40	Total		Days	..	..	..	..	..
1.41	♦ For all commercial accommodation services		Nights	..	..	10.00	..	..
1.42	* of which, "hotels and similar establishments"		Nights	..	..	..	..	..
1.43	♦ For non commercial accommodation services		Days	..	..	..	..	..
1.44	Average expenditure per day		US$	..	..	242.1	..	..
3.	**OUTBOUND TOURISM**							
	Data							
	Expenditure							
3.4	Total		US$ Mn	..	..	..	..	
3.5	♦ Travel		US$ Mn	14	15	16	16	
3.6	♦ Passenger transport		US$ Mn	..	..	..	..	
6.	**COMPLEMENTARY INDICATORS**							
	Demand							
6.1	Gross travel propensity		Units	..	..	..	..	..
6.2	(1.2 inbound tourists) / population		Units	1.96	1.94	1.97	2.06	2.20
	Macroeconomic indicators related to international tourism							
6.3	Inbound tourism expenditure over GDP		Percent	14.8	14.9	15.1	15.1	..
6.4	Outbound tourism expenditure over GDP		Percent	1.9	2.0	2.1	1.9	
6.5	Tourism balance (inbound minus outbound tourism expenditure) over GDP		Percent	12.9	12.9	13.0	13.2	
6.6	Tourism openness (inbound plus outbound tourism expenditure) over GDP		Percent	16.7	16.9	17.2	17.0	..
6.7	Tourism coverage (inbound over outbound tourism expenditure)		Percent	771.4	726.7	731.3	787.5	..
6.8	Inbound tourism expenditure over exports of goods		Percent	159.5	173.5	201.6	..	..
6.9	Inbound tourism expenditure over exports of services		Percent	61.8	56.1	49.5	..	..
6.10	Inbound tourism expenditure over exports of goods and services		Percent	44.5	42.4	39.8	..	..
6.11	Inbound tourism expenditure over current account credits		Percent	34.1	33.8	31.9	..	..
6.12	Outbound tourism expenditure over imports of goods		Percent	5.7	6.6	6.4	..	..
6.13	Outbound tourism expenditure over imports of services		Percent	12.1	12.5	12.7	..	..
6.14	Outbound tourism expenditure over imports of goods and		Percent	3.9	4.3	4.2	..	..
6.15	Outbound tourism expenditure over current account debits		Percent	3.6	3.9	3.9	..	..

SAINT LUCIA

Cod.	Basic data and indicators	Notes	Units	2011	2012	2013	2014	2015
1.	**INBOUND TOURISM**							
	Data							
	Arrivals	(1)						
1.1	Total	(2)	('000)	950	889	921	987	1,031
1.2	♦ Overnight visitors (tourists)		('000)	312	307	319	338	345
1.3	♦ Same-day visitors (excursionists)		('000)	638	582	602	649	686
1.4	* of which, cruise passengers		('000)	630	572	594	641	677
	Arrivals by region	(1)						
1.5	Total		('000)	312	307	319	338	345
1.6	♦ Africa		('000)	..	..	..	..	..
1.7	♦ Americas		('000)	216	212	229	241	256
1.8	♦ East Asia and the Pacific		('000)	..	..	..	..	..
1.9	♦ Europe		('000)	92	93	89	94	86
1.10	♦ Middle East		('000)	..	..	..	..	..
1.11	♦ South Asia		('000)	..	..	..	..	..
1.12	♦ Other not classified		('000)	4	1	1	3	3
1.13	* of which, nationals residing abroad		('000)	..	..	..	..	..
	Arrivals by main purpose	(1)						
1.14	Total		('000)	312	307	319	338	345
1.15	♦ Personal		('000)	292	291	303	324	333
1.16	* holidays, leisure and recreation		('000)	219	222	239	254	264
1.17	* other personal purposes		('000)	73	69	64	70	69
1.18	♦ Business and professional		('000)	20	16	15	14	12
	Arrivals by mode of transport	(1)						
1.19	Total		('000)	312	307	319	338	345
1.20	♦ Air		('000)	289	291	303	323	321
1.21	♦ Water		('000)	23	16	15	15	24
1.22	♦ Land		('000)	..	..	..	..	..
1.23	* railway		('000)	..	..	..	..	..
1.24	* road		('000)	..	..	..	..	..
1.25	* others		('000)	..	..	..	..	..
	Accommodation							
	Hotels and similar establishments							
1.31	♦ Guests		('000)	281	253	264	280	276
1.32	♦ Overnights		('000)	..	..	..	..	..
	Expenditure							
1.33	Total		US$ Mn	..	..	..	..	..
1.34	♦ Travel		US$ Mn	321	337	354	390	397
1.35	♦ Passenger transport		US$ Mn	..	..	..	..	..
	Indicators							
1.39	Average size of travel party		Persons	3.0	2.2	2.2	2.0	2.2
	Average length of stay							
1.40	Total		Days	..	..	..	..	..
1.41	♦ For all commercial accommodation services		Nights	8.90	8.70	8.89	8.81	8.69
1.42	* of which, "hotels and similar establishments"		Nights	..	..	..	..	..
1.43	♦ For non commercial accommodation services		Days	..	..	..	..	..
1.44	Average expenditure per day		US$	215.1	234.3	226.6	256.2	259.2
3.	**OUTBOUND TOURISM**							
	Data							
	Expenditure							
3.4	Total		US$ Mn	..	..	..	..	..
3.5	♦ Travel		US$ Mn	48	45	46	..	..
3.6	♦ Passenger transport		US$ Mn	..	..	..	..	..
4.	**TOURISM INDUSTRIES**							
	Data							
	Number of establishments							
4.1	Total		Units	..	..	..	..	..
4.2	♦ Accommodation for visitors		Units	..	..	..	..	..
4.3	* of which, "hotels and similar establishments"		Units	..	..	..	..	105
4.4	♦ Food and beverage serving activities		Units	..	..	..	..	..
4.5	♦ Passenger transportation		Units	..	..	..	..	..
4.6	♦ Travel agencies and other reservation services activities		Units	..	..	..	..	..
4.7	♦ Other tourism industries		Units	..	..	..	..	..

SAINT LUCIA

Cod.	Basic data and indicators	Notes	Units	2011	2012	2013	2014	2015
	Accommodation for visitors in hotels and similar establishments							
	Non-monetary data							
4.13	♦ Number of establishments		Units	..	..	..	..	105
4.14	♦ Number of rooms		Units	4,845	4,845	4,847	4,847	4,273
4.15	♦ Number of bed-places		Units	..	..	..	..	..
	Indicators							
4.16	Occupancy rate / rooms		Percent	58.00	62.00	62.00	62.00	68.00
4.17	Occupancy rate / bed-places		Percent	..	..	..	..	..
4.18	Average length of stay		Nights	8.80	8.70	8.89	8.81	8.69
4.19	Available capacity (bed-places per 1000 inhabitants)		Units	..	..	..	..	..
6.	**COMPLEMENTARY INDICATORS**							
	Demand							
6.1	Gross travel propensity		Units	..	..	..	..	..
6.2	(1.2 inbound tourists) / population		Units	1.74	1.70	1.75	1.84	1.86
	Macroeconomic indicators related to international tourism							
6.3	Inbound tourism expenditure over GDP		Percent	24.9	25.9	26.5	28.6	..
6.4	Outbound tourism expenditure over GDP		Percent	3.7	3.5	3.4	..	..
6.5	Tourism balance (inbound minus outbound tourism expenditure) over GDP		Percent	21.2	22.4	23.1	28.6	..
6.6	Tourism openness (inbound plus outbound tourism expenditure) over GDP		Percent	28.6	29.4	29.9	28.6	..
6.7	Tourism coverage (inbound over outbound tourism expenditure)		Percent	668.8	748.9	769.6	..	..
6.8	Inbound tourism expenditure over exports of goods		Percent	167.0	158.6	172.4	..	..
6.9	Inbound tourism expenditure over exports of services		Percent	84.3	86.0	86.6	..	..
6.10	Inbound tourism expenditure over exports of goods and services		Percent	56.0	55.8	57.6	..	..
6.11	Inbound tourism expenditure over current account credits		Percent	51.5	51.5	53.3	..	..
6.12	Outbound tourism expenditure over imports of goods		Percent	7.8	7.9	9.3	..	..
6.13	Outbound tourism expenditure over imports of services		Percent	23.6	23.7	24.5	..	..
6.14	Outbound tourism expenditure over imports of goods and		Percent	5.9	5.9	6.7	..	..
6.15	Outbound tourism expenditure over current account debits		Percent	5.7	5.6	6.3	..	..

SAINT VINCENT AND THE GRENADINES

Cod.	Basic data and indicators	Notes	Units	2011	2012	2013	2014	2015
1.	**INBOUND TOURISM**							
	Data							
	Arrivals							
1.1	Total		('000)	208	200	200	205	207
1.2	♦ Overnight visitors (tourists)	(1)	('000)	74	74	72	71	75
1.3	♦ Same-day visitors (excursionists)		('000)	134	126	128	134	131
1.4	* of which, cruise passengers	(2)	('000)	130	122	126	132	130
	Arrivals by region	(1)						
1.5	Total		('000)	74	74	72	71	75
1.6	♦ Africa		('000)	..	..	..	..	..
1.7	♦ Americas		('000)	52	53	50	49	53
1.8	♦ East Asia and the Pacific		('000)	..	..	..	..	..
1.9	♦ Europe		('000)	21	20	20	21	22
1.10	♦ Middle East		('000)	..	..	..	..	..
1.11	♦ South Asia		('000)	..	..	..	..	..
1.12	♦ Other not classified		('000)	1	1	1	1	1
1.13	* of which, nationals residing abroad		('000)	..	..	..	..	..
	Arrivals by main purpose	(1)						
1.14	Total		('000)	74	74	72	71	75
1.15	♦ Personal		('000)	60	61	59	58	62
1.16	* holidays, leisure and recreation		('000)	39	42	37	37	43
1.17	* other personal purposes		('000)	21	19	22	21	19
1.18	♦ Business and professional		('000)	14	13	13	13	13
	Arrivals by mode of transport							
1.19	Total		('000)	208	200	200	205	207
1.20	♦ Air		('000)	78	77	74	73	77
1.21	♦ Water	(2)	('000)	130	122	126	132	130
1.22	♦ Land		('000)	..	..	..	..	..
1.23	* railway		('000)	..	..	..	..	..
1.24	* road		('000)	..	..	..	..	..
1.25	* others		('000)	..	..	..	..	..
	Accommodation							
	Hotels and similar establishments							
1.31	♦ Guests		('000)	29	29	29	30	31
1.32	♦ Overnights		('000)	..	..	..	..	..
	Expenditure							
1.33	Total		US$ Mn	..	..	..	..	..
1.34	♦ Travel		US$ Mn	92	94	92	93	96
1.35	♦ Passenger transport		US$ Mn	..	..	..	..	..
	Indicators							
1.39	Average size of travel party		Persons	..	..	..	..	..
	Average length of stay							
1.40	Total		Days	..	..	..	..	..
1.41	♦ For all commercial accommodation services		Nights	11.10	11.90	12.80	13.30	13.50
1.42	* of which, "hotels and similar establishments"		Nights	..	..	..	..	..
1.43	♦ For non commercial accommodation services		Days	..	..	..	..	..
1.44	Average expenditure per day		US$	..	..	..	..	..
2.	**OUTBOUND TOURISM**							
	Data							
	Expenditure							
2.4	Total		US$ Mn	..	..	..	..	..
2.5	♦ Travel		US$ Mn	13	14	14	13	13
2.6	♦ Passenger transport		US$ Mn	..	..	..	..	..
4.	**TOURISM INDUSTRIES**							
	Data							
	Accommodation for visitors in hotels and similar establishments							
	Non-monetary data							
4.13	♦ Number of establishments		Units	..	..	..	..	..
4.14	♦ Number of rooms		Units	..	..	2,076	2,133	2,231
4.15	♦ Number of bed-places		Units	..	..	..	..	..

SAINT VINCENT AND THE GRENADINES

Cod. Basic data and indicators	Notes	Units	2011	2012	2013	2014	2015
6. COMPLEMENTARY INDICATORS							
Demand							
6.1 Gross travel propensity		Units	..	..	..	..	..
6.2 (1.2 inbound tourists) / population		Units	0.68	0.68	0.66	0.65	0.69
Macroeconomic indicators related to international tourism							
6.3 Inbound tourism expenditure over GDP		Percent	13.6	13.5	12.8	12.8	..
6.4 Outbound tourism expenditure over GDP		Percent	1.9	2.0	1.9	..	..
6.5 Tourism balance (inbound minus outbound tourism expenditure) over GDP		Percent	11.7	11.5	10.9	12.8	..
6.6 Tourism openness (inbound plus outbound tourism expenditure) over GDP		Percent	15.5	15.5	14.7	12.8	..
6.7 Tourism coverage (inbound over outbound tourism expenditure)		Percent	707.7	671.4	657.1	..	..
6.8 Inbound tourism expenditure over exports of goods		Percent	211.9	196.7	172.4	..	..
6.9 Inbound tourism expenditure over exports of services		Percent	66.0	66.9	65.4	..	..
6.10 Inbound tourism expenditure over exports of goods and services		Percent	50.3	49.9	47.4	..	..
6.11 Inbound tourism expenditure over current account credits		Percent	42.1	39.1	37.3	..	..
6.12 Outbound tourism expenditure over imports of goods		Percent	4.4	4.4	4.2	..	..
6.13 Outbound tourism expenditure over imports of services		Percent	15.4	16.1	15.3	..	..
6.14 Outbound tourism expenditure over imports of goods and		Percent	3.5	3.5	3.3	..	..
6.15 Outbound tourism expenditure over current account debits		Percent	3.2	3.3	3.1	..	..

SAMOA

Cod.	Basic data and indicators	Notes	Units	2011	2012	2013	2014	2015
1.	**INBOUND TOURISM**							
	Data							
	Arrivals							
1.1	Total		('000)	128	135	125	132	139
1.2	♦ Overnight visitors (tourists)		('000)	121	126	116	120	128
1.3	♦ Same-day visitors (excursionists)		('000)	7	9	9	11	11
1.4	* of which, cruise passengers		('000)	..	..	..	..	..
	Arrivals by region							
1.5	Total		('000)	128	135	125	132	139
1.6	♦ Africa		('000)	..	..	..	..	..
1.7	♦ Americas		('000)	8	8	8	9	11
1.8	♦ East Asia and the Pacific		('000)	115	123	112	117	119
1.9	♦ Europe		('000)	4	3	3	4	4
1.10	♦ Middle East		('000)	..	..	..	..	..
1.11	♦ South Asia		('000)	..	..	..	..	..
1.12	♦ Other not classified		('000)	0.9	0.7	2	3	5
1.13	* of which, nationals residing abroad		('000)	..	..	..	..	..
	Arrivals by main purpose							
1.14	Total		('000)	128	135	125	132	139
1.15	♦ Personal		('000)	117	102	113	118	127
1.16	* holidays, leisure and recreation		('000)	46	55	47	47	55
1.17	* other personal purposes		('000)	71	47	66	71	73
1.18	♦ Business and professional		('000)	11	33	12	13	12
	Arrivals by mode of transport							
1.19	Total		('000)	128	135	125	132	139
1.20	♦ Air		('000)	125	132	122	129	135
1.21	♦ Water		('000)	3	3	3	3	4
1.22	♦ Land		('000)	..	..	..	..	..
1.23	* railway		('000)	..	..	..	..	..
1.24	* road		('000)	..	..	..	..	..
1.25	* others		('000)	..	..	..	..	..
	Accommodation							
	Total							
1.29	♦ Guests		('000)	121	126	116	120	128
1.30	♦ Overnights		('000)	..	..	..	..	..
	Hotels and similar establishments							
1.31	♦ Guests		('000)	41	43	37	40	41
1.32	♦ Overnights		('000)	..	..	..	..	..
	Expenditure							
1.33	Total		US$ Mn	135	148	137	147	165
1.34	♦ Travel		US$ Mn	134	148	136	146	165
1.35	♦ Passenger transport		US$ Mn	0.9	0.2	1.2	0.7	0.4
B.	**OUTBOUND TOURISM**							
	Data							
	Departures							
3.1	Total		('000)	..	..	..	..	..
3.2	♦ Overnight visitors (tourists)		('000)	57	56	51	57	54
3.3	♦ Same-day visitors (excursionists)		('000)	..	..	..	..	..
	Expenditure							
3.4	Total		US$ Mn	22.2	22.3	13.9	4.1	2.8
3.5	♦ Travel		US$ Mn	12.9	10.0	2.4	1.5	1.7
3.6	♦ Passenger transport		US$ Mn	9.3	12.3	11.5	2.6	1.1
5.	**COMPLEMENTARY INDICATORS**							
	Demand							
5.1	Gross travel propensity		Units	..	..	..	..	..
5.2	(1.2 inbound tourists) / population		Units	0.65	0.67	0.61	0.63	0.66
	Macroeconomic indicators related to international tourism							
5.3	Inbound tourism expenditure over GDP		Percent	..	..	..	..	..
5.4	Outbound tourism expenditure over GDP		Percent	..	..	..	..	..
5.5	Tourism balance (inbound minus outbound tourism expenditure) over GDP		Percent	..	..	..	..	..
5.6	Tourism openness (inbound plus outbound tourism expenditure) over GDP		Percent	..	..	..	..	..

SAMOA

Cod.	Basic data and indicators	Notes	Units	2011	2012	2013	2014	2015
6.7	Tourism coverage (inbound over outbound tourism expenditure)		Percent	607.7	664.6	987.1	3,578.0	5,907.1
6.8	Inbound tourism expenditure over exports of goods		Percent	547.5	475.3	573.1	533.5	.
6.9	Inbound tourism expenditure over exports of services		Percent	74.4	74.2	66.5	74.7	..
6.10	Inbound tourism expenditure over exports of goods and services		Percent	65.5	64.1	59.6	65.6	..
6.11	Inbound tourism expenditure over current account credits		Percent	34.2	34.0	31.2	35.2	..
6.12	Outbound tourism expenditure over imports of goods		Percent	6.4	7.2	4.3	1.2	
6.13	Outbound tourism expenditure over imports of services		Percent	28.2	24.9	15.6	5.5	..
6.14	Outbound tourism expenditure over imports of goods and		Percent	5.2	5.6	3.4	1.0	..
6.15	Outbound tourism expenditure over current account debits		Percent	5.0	5.3	3.1	0.9	..

SAN MARINO

Cod.	Basic data and indicators	Notes	Units	2011	2012	2013	2014	2015
1.	**INBOUND TOURISM**							
	Data							
	Arrivals							
1.1	Total	(1)	('000)	2,038	1,869	1,905	2,004	1,888
1.2	♦ Overnight visitors (tourists)	(2)	('000)	156	139	71	75	54
1.3	♦ Same-day visitors (excursionists)		('000)	1,882	1,730	1,834	1,929	1,834
1.4	* of which, cruise passengers		('000)	4	4	3	1	1
	Arrivals by region							
1.5	Total		('000)	2,038	1,869	1,905	2,004	1,888
1.6	♦ Africa		('000)	..	..	..	1	..
1.7	♦ Americas		('000)	19	18	17	26	16
1.8	♦ East Asia and the Pacific		('000)	20	22	22	22	26
1.9	♦ Europe		('000)	1,997	1,828	1,865	1,954	1,845
1.10	♦ Middle East		('000)	..	..	..	..	1
1.11	♦ South Asia		('000)	..	..	..	1	..
1.12	♦ Other not classified		('000)	2	1	1	1	1
1.13	* of which, nationals residing abroad		('000)	..	..	..	..	..
	Arrivals by main purpose							
1.14	Total		('000)	2,038	1,869	1,905	2,004	1,888
1.15	♦ Personal		('000)	1,780	1,271	1,294	1,392	1,416
1.16	* holidays, leisure and recreation		('000)	1,780	729	729	801	699
1.17	* other personal purposes		('000)	..	542	564	591	718
1.18	♦ Business and professional		('000)	258	598	612	612	472
	Arrivals by mode of transport							
1.19	Total		('000)	2,038	1,869	1,905	2,004	1,888
1.20	♦ Air		('000)	..	..	..	..	..
1.21	♦ Water		('000)	..	..	..	..	..
1.22	♦ Land		('000)	2,038	1,869	1,905	2,004	1,888
1.23	* railway		('000)	..	..	..	..	..
1.24	* road		('000)	2,038	1,869	1,905	2,004	1,888
1.25	* others		('000)	..	..	..	..	..
	Accommodation							
	Total							
1.29	♦ Guests		('000)	156	139	71	75	54
1.30	♦ Overnights		('000)	316	237	117	134	107
	Hotels and similar establishments							
1.31	♦ Guests		('000)	126	115	57	58	40
1.32	♦ Overnights		('000)	220	151	77	86	63
	Indicators							
1.39	Average size of travel party		Persons	..	..	..	..	..
	Average length of stay							
1.40	Total		Days	..	..	..	..	..
1.41	♦ For all commercial accommodation services		Nights	1.92	1.62	1.57	1.69	1.81
1.42	* of which, "hotels and similar establishments"		Nights	1.69	1.33	1.34	1.45	1.48
1.43	♦ For non commercial accommodation services		Days	..	..	..	..	..
1.44	Average expenditure per day		US$	..	..	..	..	..
4.	**TOURISM INDUSTRIES**							
	Data							
	Number of establishments							
4.1	Total		Units	294	292	292	269	276
4.2	♦ Accommodation for visitors		Units	43	41	41	40	35
4.3	* of which, "hotels and similar establishments"	(3)	Units	28	24	24	24	21
4.4	♦ Food and beverage serving activities		Units	190	190	190	166	178
4.5	♦ Passenger transportation		Units	11	11	11	20	19
4.6	♦ Travel agencies and other reservation services activities		Units	50	50	50	43	44
4.7	♦ Other tourism industries		Units	..	..	..	..	..
	Accommodation for visitors in hotels and similar establishments							
	Non-monetary data	(3)						
4.13	♦ Number of establishments		Units	28	24	24	24	21
4.14	♦ Number of rooms		Units	837	757	757	677	577
4.15	♦ Number of bed-places		Units	1,858	1,680	1,680	1,538	1,282
	Indicators							
4.16	Occupancy rate / rooms		Percent	..	..	62.06	..	77.38
4.17	Occupancy rate / bed-places		Percent	55.50	54.20	54.60	54.80	56.10
4.18	Average length of stay		Nights	1.92	1.62	1.57	1.69	1.81
4.19	Available capacity (bed-places per 1000 inhabitants)		Units	60.06	53.89	53.52	48.68	40.34

SAN MARINO

Cod.	Basic data and indicators	Notes	Units	2011	2012	2013	2014	2015
5.	**EMPLOYMENT**							
	Data							
	Number of employees by tourism industries							
5.1	Total		('000)	3.3	3.3	3.3	3.5	3.5
5.2	♦ Accommodation services for visitors (hotels and similar establishments)		('000)	0.2	0.2	0.2	0.7	0.7
5.3	♦ Other accommodation services		('000)	..	..	..	..	..
5.4	♦ Food and beverage serving activities		('000)	..	..	..	..	..
5.5	♦ Passenger transportation		('000)	..	..	..	0.2	0.2
5.6	♦ Travel agencies and other reservation services activities		('000)	..	..	..	0.1	0.1
5.7	♦ Other tourism industries		('000)	3.1	3.1	3.1	2.5	2.5
	Number of jobs by status in employment							
5.8	Total		('000)	3.9	3.9	3.9	3.9	3.9
5.9	♦ Employees		('000)	3.3	3.3	3.3	3.3	3.3
5.10	♦ Self employed		('000)	0.6	0.6	0.6	0.6	0.6
	Indicators							
	Number of full-time equivalent jobs by status in employment							
5.11	Total		('000)	3.9	4.0	4.0	4.0	4.0
5.12	♦ Employees		('000)	3.3	3.3	3.3	3.3	3.3
5.13	* male		('000)	1.6	1.6	1.6	1.6	1.6
5.14	* female		('000)	1.7	1.7	1.7	1.7	1.7
5.15	♦ Self employed		('000)	0.6	0.7	0.7	0.7	0.7
5.16	* male		('000)	0.4	0.4	0.4	0.4	0.4
5.17	* female		('000)	0.3	0.3	0.3	0.3	0.3
6.	**COMPLEMENTARY INDICATORS**							
	Demand							
6.1	Gross travel propensity		Units	..	..	..	..	..
6.2	(1.2 inbound tourists) / population		Units	5.04	4.46	2.26	2.37	1.70

SAUDI ARABIA

Cod.	Basic data and indicators	Notes	Units	2011	2012	2013	2014	2015
1.	**INBOUND TOURISM**							
	Data							
	Arrivals							
1.1	Total		('000)	15,776	19,847	19,934	23,010	21,834
1.2	♦ Overnight visitors (tourists)		('000)	14,179	16,332	15,772	18,260	17,994
1.3	♦ Same-day visitors (excursionists)		('000)	1,597	3,515	4,162	4,750	3,840
1.4	* of which, cruise passengers		('000)	..	..	..	..	..
	Arrivals by region							
1.5	Total		('000)	14,179	16,332	15,772	18,260	17,994
1.6	♦ Africa		('000)	667	895	769	848	1,139
1.7	♦ Americas		('000)	54	157	179	209	284
1.8	♦ East Asia and the Pacific		('000)	696	771	1,197	1,177	1,608
1.9	♦ Europe		('000)	644	839	1,126	1,148	1,381
1.10	♦ Middle East		('000)	9,545	10,637	9,608	11,144	9,935
1.11	♦ South Asia		('000)	2,566	3,024	2,892	3,685	3,616
1.12	♦ Other not classified		('000)	7	9	2	50	31
1.13	* of which, nationals residing abroad		('000)	..	..	..	..	..
	Arrivals by main purpose							
1.14	Total		('000)	14,178	16,332	15,772	18,260	17,994
1.15	♦ Personal		('000)	12,266	13,508	14,296	15,576	16,113
1.16	* holidays, leisure and recreation		('000)	551	487	516	772	1,511
1.17	* other personal purposes		('000)	11,715	13,021	13,780	14,804	14,602
1.18	♦ Business and professional		('000)	1,912	2,824	1,476	2,684	1,881
	Arrivals by mode of transport							
1.19	Total		('000)	14,179	16,332	15,772	18,260	17,994
1.20	♦ Air		('000)	8,778	10,756	10,860	12,395	11,967
1.21	♦ Water		('000)	5	1	19	69	48
1.22	♦ Land		('000)	5,396	5,575	4,893	5,797	5,979
1.23	* railway		('000)	..	..	..	..	..
1.24	* road		('000)	5,396	5,575	4,893	5,797	5,979
1.25	* others		('000)	..	..	..	..	..
	Arrivals by form of organization of the trip							
1.26	Total		('000)	14,179	16,332	15,772	18,260	17,994
1.27	♦ Package tour		('000)	2,916	7,408	7,055	5,486	7,760
1.28	♦ Other forms		('000)	11,263	8,924	8,717	12,774	10,234
	Accommodation							
	Total							
1.29	♦ Guests		('000)	14,179	16,332	15,772	18,260	17,994
1.30	♦ Overnights		('000)	272,428	318,652	304,417	355,059	193,084
	Hotels and similar establishments							
1.31	♦ Guests		('000)	8,437	10,670	9,604	12,209	13,797
1.32	♦ Overnights		('000)	118,608	115,707	117,402	131,795	120,405
	Expenditure							
1.33	Total		US$ Mn	9,317	8,400	8,690	9,263	11,183
1.34	♦ Travel		US$ Mn	8,459	7,432	7,651	8,238	10,130
1.35	♦ Passenger transport		US$ Mn	858	968	1,039	1,025	1,053
	Expenditure by main purpose of the trip	(1)						
1.36	Total		US$ Mn	8,459	7,432	7,651	..	..
1.37	♦ Personal		US$ Mn	7,128	5,777	7,121	..	..
1.38	♦ Business and professional		US$ Mn	1,331	1,655	530	..	..
	Indicators							
1.39	Average size of travel party		Persons	2.3	2.3	2.1	2.2	2.0
	Average length of stay							
1.40	Total	(2)	Days	19.21	19.51	19.30	19.45	10.37
1.41	♦ For all commercial accommodation services		Nights	14.06	10.84	12.22	10.79	8.73
1.42	* of which, "hotels and similar establishments"		Nights	14.06	10.84	12.22	10.79	8.73
1.43	♦ For non commercial accommodation services	(2)	Days	26.79	35.85	30.32	35.23	13.43
1.44	Average expenditure per day		US$	39.0	46.2	44.9	40.8	113.9
2.	**DOMESTIC TOURISM**							
	Data							
	Trips							
2.1	Total		('000)	29,329	23,280	26,433	43,771	54,117
2.2	♦ Overnight visitors (tourists)		('000)	26,155	21,006	23,783	37,101	46,450
2.3	♦ Same-day visitors (excursionists)		('000)	3,174	2,274	2,650	6,670	7,666
	Trips by main purpose							
2.4	Total		('000)	26,155	21,006	23,783	37,101	46,451
2.5	♦ Personal		('000)	23,680	19,920	21,987	34,210	44,591
2.6	* holidays, leisure and recreation		('000)	10,235	4,124	3,265	6,329	19,019
2.7	* other personal purposes		('000)	13,445	15,796	18,722	27,881	25,572
2.8	♦ Business and professional		('000)	2,475	1,086	1,796	2,891	1,860

SAUDI ARABIA

Cod.	Basic data and indicators	Notes	Units	2011	2012	2013	2014	2015
	Trips by mode of transport							
2.9	Total		('000)	26,155	21,006	23,783	37,101	46,450
2.10	♦ Air		('000)	1,914	2,841	1,919	3,226	3,757
2.11	♦ Water		('000)	..	..	..	..	22
2.12	♦ Land		('000)	24,241	18,165	21,864	33,875	42,671
2.13	* railway		('000)	..	..	..	..	..
2.14	* road		('000)	24,241	18,165	21,864	33,875	42,671
2.15	* others		('000)	..	..	..	..	
	Trips by form of organization							
2.16	Total		('000)	26,155	21,006	23,783	37,101	46,450
2.17	♦ Package tour		('000)	..	..	..	..	
2.18	♦ Other forms		('000)	26,155	21,006	23,783	37,101	46,450
	Accommodation							
	Total							
2.19	♦ Guests		('000)	26,155	19,039	23,783	37,101	46,450
2.20	♦ Overnights		('000)	121,989	103,392	98,573	165,274	240,623
	Hotels and similar establishments							
2.21	♦ Guests		('000)	16,471	11,792	13,842	22,954	34,475
2.22	♦ Overnights		('000)	69,011	53,333	53,565	86,941	163,674
	Indicators							
2.23	Average size of travel party		Persons	2.3	2.4	2.5	2.4	3.0
	Average length of stay							
2.24	Total	(2)	Days	4.66	4.92	4.14	4.50	5.13
2.25	♦ For all commercial accommodation services		Nights	4.19	4.52	3.87	3.79	5.13
2.26	* of which, "hotels and similar establishments"		Nights	4.19	4.52	3.87	3.38	4.75
2.27	♦ For non commercial accommodation services	(2)	Days	4.42	4.89	4.53	5.13	6.14
2.28	Average expenditure per day		US$	83.9	97.6	63.2	72.1	53.2
3.	**OUTBOUND TOURISM**							
	Data							
	Departures							
3.1	Total		('000)	15,865	20,084	22,535	22,323	25,054
3.2	♦ Overnight visitors (tourists)		('000)	15,281	18,671	19,154	19,824	20,819
3.3	♦ Same-day visitors (excursionists)		('000)	584	1,414	3,381	2,498	4,235
	Expenditure							
3.4	Total		US$ Mn	18,202	17,986	18,648	25,137	21,745
3.5	♦ Travel		US$ Mn	17,271	17,023	17,660	24,118	20,725
3.6	♦ Passenger transport		US$ Mn	931	963	988	1,019	1,020
	Expenditure by main purpose of the trip	(1)						
3.7	Total		US$ Mn	17,271	17,023	17,660	..	
3.8	♦ Personal		US$ Mn	16,196	16,697	15,528	..	..
3.9	♦ Business and professional		US$ Mn	1,075	326	2,132	..	..
	Indicators							
3.10	Average length of stay		Days	13.09	7.24	9.25	11.56	13.22
3.11	Average expenditure per day		US$	80.8	124.0	111.7	80.7	81.5
4.	**TOURISM INDUSTRIES**							
	Data							
	Number of establishments							
4.1	Total		Units	43,263	46,297	48,973	53,894	51,729
4.2	♦ Accommodation for visitors		Units	..	..	..	..	..
4.3	* of which, "hotels and similar establishments"		Units	3,019	3,111	3,551	3,697	4,394
4.4	♦ Food and beverage serving activities		Units	29,546	30,092	31,524	32,785	32,785
4.5	♦ Passenger transportation		Units	1,651	4,757	3,702	3,702	3,702
4.6	♦ Travel agencies and other reservation services activities		Units	1,166	1,268	2,846	2,858	2,900
4.7	♦ Other tourism industries	(3)	Units	7,881	7,069	7,350	10,852	7,948
	Accommodation for visitors in hotels and similar establishments							
	Monetary data	(4)						
4.8	♦ Output		US$ Mn	5,672.0	5,469.0	5,862.6	5,979.8	6,099.4
4.9	♦ Intermediate consumption		US$ Mn	2,079.0	2,354.0	2,560.9	2,539.8	2,763.2
4.10	♦ Gross value added		US$ Mn	3,593.0	3,115.0	3,301.7	3,448.3	3,682.8
4.11	♦ Compensation of employees		US$ Mn	687.0	856.0	1,033.0	1,098.6	1,168.3
4.12	♦ Gross fixed capital formation		US$ Mn	8,161.3	13,354.0	9,474.7	10,725.3	12,141.1
	Non-monetary data							
4.13	♦ Number of establishments		Units	3,019	3,111	3,551	3,697	4,394
4.14	♦ Number of rooms		Units	244,184	275,583	276,441	303,716	349,098
4.15	♦ Number of bed-places		Units	627,917	696,661	708,556	743,109	860,209

SAUDI ARABIA

Cod.	Basic data and indicators	Notes	Units	2011	2012	2013	2014	2015
	Indicators							
4.16	Occupancy rate / rooms		Percent	63.00	64.00	65.20	66.00	67.00
4.17	Occupancy rate / bed-places		Percent	62.10	63.60	61.20	65.00	66.20
4.18	Average length of stay		Nights	4.00	4.00	4.00	..	..
4.19	Available capacity (bed-places per 1000 inhabitants)		Units	21.81	23.62	23.46	24.06	27.27
	Travel agencies and other reservation service activities							
	Monetary data	(4)						
4.20	♦ Output		US$ Mn	440.3	619.1	1,450.3	1,479.4	1,508.9
4.21	♦ Intermediate consumption		US$ Mn	112.1	67.8	481.1	519.1	560.1
4.22	♦ Gross value added		US$ Mn	328.2	551.3	969.3	960.3	948.8
4.23	♦ Compensation of employees		US$ Mn	105.3	125.3	411.7	437.9	465.7
4.24	♦ Gross fixed capital formation		US$ Mn	365.0	432.2	834.3	944.4	1,069.0
	Non-monetary data							
	♦ Domestic trips							
4.25	* with package tour		Percent	..	..	..	..	..
4.26	* without package tour		Percent	100.0	100.0	100.0	100.0	100.0
	♦ Inbound trips							
4.27	* with package tour		Percent	21.2	42.0	44.1	36.9	40.0
4.28	* without package tour		Percent	78.8	58.0	55.9	63.1	60.0
	♦ Outbound trips							
4.29	* with package tour		Percent	2.0	1.5	4.0	1.9	15.0
4.30	* without package tour		Percent	98.0	98.5	96.0	98.1	85.0
5.	**EMPLOYMENT**							
	Data							
	Number of employees by tourism industries	(4)						
5.1	Total		('000)	629.3	698.1	797.1	832.1	882.9
5.2	♦ Accommodation services for visitors (hotels and similar establishments)		('000)	97.7	103.8	110.2	115.1	122.1
5.3	♦ Other accommodation services		('000)	..	..	..	..	..
5.4	♦ Food and beverage serving activities		('000)	314.7	348.7	376.2	392.8	416.7
5.5	♦ Passenger transportation		('000)	133.9	145.4	146.4	152.8	162.2
5.6	♦ Travel agencies and other reservation services activities		('000)	12.5	13.8	35.3	36.8	39.1
5.7	♦ Other tourism industries		('000)	70.6	86.4	128.9	134.6	142.8
	Number of jobs by status in employment	(4)						
5.8	Total		('000)	629.3	698.1	797.1	832.1	882.9
5.9	♦ Employees		('000)	579.8	641.8	735.3	767.1	814.0
5.10	♦ Self employed		('000)	49.5	56.4	61.7	65.0	68.9
	Indicators							
	Number of full-time equivalent jobs by status in employment							
5.11	Total		('000)	629.3	698.1	797.1	832.1	882.9
5.12	♦ Employees		('000)	579.8	641.8	735.3	767.1	814.0
5.13	* male		('000)	579.8	641.8	735.3	767.1	814.0
5.14	* female		('000)	..	..	..	..	..
5.15	♦ Self employed		('000)	49.5	56.4	61.7	65.0	68.9
5.16	* male		('000)	49.5	56.4	61.7	65.0	68.9
5.17	* female		('000)	..	..	..	..	..
6.	**COMPLEMENTARY INDICATORS**							
	Demand							
6.1	Gross travel propensity		Units	..	..	..	..	..
6.2	(1.2 inbound tourists + 2.2 domestic tourists) / population		Units	1.40	1.27	1.31	1.79	2.04
	Macroeconomic indicators related to international tourism							
6.3	Inbound tourism expenditure over GDP		Percent	1.4	1.1	1.2	1.2	1.7
6.4	Outbound tourism expenditure over GDP		Percent	2.7	2.5	2.5	3.3	3.4
6.5	Tourism balance (inbound minus outbound tourism expenditure) over GDP		Percent	-1.3	-1.4	-1.3	-2.1	-1.7
6.6	Tourism openness (inbound plus outbound tourism expenditure) over GDP		Percent	4.1	3.6	3.7	4.5	5.1
6.7	Tourism coverage (inbound over outbound tourism expenditure)		Percent	51.2	46.7	46.6	36.9	51.4
6.8	Inbound tourism expenditure over exports of goods		Percent	2.6	2.2	2.3	2.7	5.5
6.9	Inbound tourism expenditure over exports of services		Percent	81.1	76.0	73.4	74.0	77.3
6.10	Inbound tourism expenditure over exports of goods and services		Percent	2.5	2.1	2.2	2.6	5.2
6.11	Inbound tourism expenditure over current account credits		Percent	2.4	2.0	2.1	2.4	4.6
6.12	Outbound tourism expenditure over imports of goods		Percent	15.2	12.7	12.2	15.9	14.0
6.13	Outbound tourism expenditure over imports of services		Percent	23.3	24.5	24.3	25.0	24.1
6.14	Outbound tourism expenditure over imports of goods and		Percent	9.2	8.4	8.1	9.7	8.9
6.15	Outbound tourism expenditure over current account debits		Percent	7.4	6.7	6.4	7.7	7.0

SENEGAL

Cod.	Basic data and indicators	Notes	Units	2011	2012	2013	2014	2015
1.	**INBOUND TOURISM**							
	Data							
	Arrivals	(1)						
1.1	Total		('000)	977	967	1,069	976	1,014
1.2	♦ Overnight visitors (tourists)		('000)	968	962	1,063	963	1,007
1.3	♦ Same-day visitors (excursionists)		('000)	9	5	6	13	8
1.4	* of which, cruise passengers		('000)	9	5	6	13	8
	Arrivals by main purpose	(2)						
1.14	Total		('000)	450	436	..	..	..
1.15	♦ Personal		('000)	361	357	..	..	..
1.16	* holidays, leisure and recreation		('000)	232	226	..	..	..
1.17	* other personal purposes		('000)	129	131	..	..	..
1.18	♦ Business and professional		('000)	89	79	..	..	..
	Arrivals by mode of transport	(1)						
1.19	Total		('000)	977	967	1,069	976	1,014
1.20	♦ Air		('000)	488	466	499	731	767
1.21	♦ Water		('000)	9	5	7	13	8
1.22	♦ Land		('000)	480	496	564	232	240
1.23	* railway		('000)	..	..	..	..	
1.24	* road		('000)	480	496	564	232	240
1.25	* others		('000)	..	..	..	..	
	Accommodation							
	Hotels and similar establishments							
1.31	♦ Guests		('000)	..	..	..	908	680
1.32	♦ Overnights		('000)	..	..	..	1,813	1,532
	Expenditure							
1.33	Total		US$ Mn	524	469	495	481	..
1.34	♦ Travel		US$ Mn	468	407	439	423	..
1.35	♦ Passenger transport		US$ Mn	56	62	56	58	..
	Expenditure by main purpose of the trip							
1.36	Total		US$ Mn	468	407	439	423	..
1.37	♦ Personal		US$ Mn	372	323	347	335	..
1.38	♦ Business and professional		US$ Mn	96	84	92	88	..
2.	**DOMESTIC TOURISM**							
	Data							
	Accommodation							
	Hotels and similar establishments							
2.21	♦ Guests		('000)	..	..	..	308	396
2.22	♦ Overnights		('000)	..	..	..	563	774
	Indicators							
2.23	Average size of travel party		Persons	..	..	..	..	..
	Average length of stay							
2.24	Total		Days	..	..	..	..	..
2.25	♦ For all commercial accommodation services		Nights	3.40	..	..	..	..
2.26	* of which, "hotels and similar establishments"		Nights	..	..	..	..	..
2.27	♦ For non commercial accommodation services		Days	..	..	..	..	..
2.28	Average expenditure per day	(1)	US$	70.7	..	..	..	..
3.	**OUTBOUND TOURISM**							
	Data							
	Expenditure							
3.4	Total		US$ Mn	250	248	265	279	..
3.5	♦ Travel		US$ Mn	151	144	150	148	..
3.6	♦ Passenger transport		US$ Mn	99	104	115	131	..
	Expenditure by main purpose of the trip							
3.7	Total		US$ Mn	151	144	150	148	..
3.8	♦ Personal		US$ Mn	84	73	73	71	..
3.9	♦ Business and professional		US$ Mn	67	71	77	77	..
4.	**TOURISM INDUSTRIES**							
	Data							
	Number of establishments							
4.1	Total		Units	..	..	..	..	..
4.2	♦ Accommodation for visitors		Units	..	..	..	..	..
4.3	* of which, "hotels and similar establishments"	(1)(3)	Units	815	744	744	744	744
4.4	♦ Food and beverage serving activities		Units	..	..	..	..	..
4.5	♦ Passenger transportation		Units	..	..	..	..	..
4.6	♦ Travel agencies and other reservation services activities		Units	300	..	..	..	357
4.7	♦ Other tourism industries		Units	..	..	..	..	..

SENEGAL

Cod.	Basic data and indicators	Notes	Units	2011	2012	2013	2014	2015
	Accommodation for visitors in hotels and similar establishments							
	Non-monetary data	(1)(3)						
4.13	♦ Number of establishments		Units	815	744	744	744	744
4.14	♦ Number of rooms		Units	20,000	17,098	17,098	17,098	18,266
4.15	♦ Number of bed-places		Units	40,000	34,196	34,196	34,296	28,035
	Indicators							
4.16	Occupancy rate / rooms		Percent	..	..	..	..	..
4.17	Occupancy rate / bed-places		Percent	..	..	..	..	..
4.18	Average length of stay		Nights	..	..	..	..	..
4.19	Available capacity (bed-places per 1000 inhabitants)		Units	2.99	2.48	2.40	2.34	1.85
5.	**EMPLOYMENT**							
	Data							
	Number of employees by tourism industries							
5.1	Total		('000)	100.0	100.0	100.0	100.0	100.0
5.2	♦ Accommodation services for visitors (hotels and similar establishments)		('000)	..	..	..	..	..
5.3	♦ Other accommodation services		('000)	..	..	..	..	..
5.4	♦ Food and beverage serving activities		('000)	..	..	..	..	..
5.5	♦ Passenger transportation		('000)	..	..	..	..	..
5.6	♦ Travel agencies and other reservation services activities		('000)	..	..	..	..	..
5.7	♦ Other tourism industries		('000)	..	..	..	..	..
6.	**COMPLEMENTARY INDICATORS**							
	Demand							
6.1	Gross travel propensity		Units	..	..	..		
6.2	(1.2 inbound tourists) / population		Units	0.07	0.07	0.07	0.07	0.07
	Macroeconomic indicators related to international tourism							
6.3	Inbound tourism expenditure over GDP		Percent	3.6	3.3	3.3	3.1	..
6.4	Outbound tourism expenditure over GDP		Percent	1.7	1.7	1.8	1.8	..
6.5	Tourism balance (inbound minus outbound tourism expenditure) over GDP		Percent	1.9	1.6	1.5	1.3	..
6.6	Tourism openness (inbound plus outbound tourism expenditure) over GDP		Percent	5.3	5.0	5.1	4.9	..
6.7	Tourism coverage (inbound over outbound tourism expenditure)		Percent	209.6	189.1	186.8	172.4	..
6.8	Inbound tourism expenditure over exports of goods		Percent	20.0	..	..	..	..
6.9	Inbound tourism expenditure over exports of services		Percent	44.9	..	..	..	..
6.10	Inbound tourism expenditure over exports of goods and services		Percent	13.8	..	..	..	..
6.11	Inbound tourism expenditure over current account credits		Percent	8.6	..	..	..	..
6.12	Outbound tourism expenditure over imports of goods		Percent	4.9	..	..	..	..
6.13	Outbound tourism expenditure over imports of services		Percent	19.4	..	..	..	..
6.14	Outbound tourism expenditure over imports of goods and		Percent	3.9	..	..	..	..
6.15	Outbound tourism expenditure over current account debits		Percent	3.6	..	..	..	..

345

SERBIA

Cod.	Basic data and indicators	Notes	Units	2011	2012	2013	2014	2015
1.	**INBOUND TOURISM**							
	Data							
	Arrivals							
1.1	Total		('000)	..	..	..	..	..
1.2	♦ Overnight visitors (tourists)	(1)	('000)	764	810	922	1,029	1,132
1.3	♦ Same-day visitors (excursionists)		('000)	..	..	..	..	..
1.4	* of which, cruise passengers		('000)	..	..	..	..	..
	Arrivals by region	(1)						
1.5	Total		('000)	764	810	922	1,029	1,132
1.6	♦ Africa		('000)	..	..	..	11	11
1.7	♦ Americas		('000)	19	22	24	31	37
1.8	♦ East Asia and the Pacific		('000)	12	15	23	53	73
1.9	♦ Europe		('000)	711	746	837	932	1,011
1.10	♦ Middle East		('000)	..	..	..	..	..
1.11	♦ South Asia		('000)	..	..	..	..	..
1.12	♦ Other not classified		('000)	22	27	38	2	..
1.13	* of which, nationals residing abroad		('000)	..	..	..	..	..
	Arrivals by form of organization of the trip	(1)						
1.26	Total		('000)	764	810	922	1,029	1,132
1.27	♦ Package tour		('000)	126	134	105	179	177
1.28	♦ Other forms		('000)	638	676	817	850	955
	Accommodation							
	Total							
1.29	♦ Guests		('000)	764	810	922	1,029	1,132
1.30	♦ Overnights		('000)	1,643	1,796	1,988	2,161	2,410
	Hotels and similar establishments							
1.31	♦ Guests		('000)	680	707	767	880	1,013
1.32	♦ Overnights		('000)	1,387	1,519	1,617	1,785	2,066
	Expenditure							
1.33	Total		US$ Mn	1,149	1,080	1,221	1,352	1,322
1.34	♦ Travel		US$ Mn	990	921	1,053	1,142	1,048
1.35	♦ Passenger transport		US$ Mn	159	159	168	210	274
	Expenditure by main purpose of the trip							
1.36	Total		US$ Mn	990	921	1,054	1,142	1,048
1.37	♦ Personal		US$ Mn	979	909	1,040	1,126	1,034
1.38	♦ Business and professional		US$ Mn	11	12	14	16	14
	Indicators							
1.39	Average size of travel party		Persons	..	..	..	..	..
	Average length of stay							
1.40	Total		Days	..	..	..	..	..
1.41	♦ For all commercial accommodation services		Nights	2.15	2.22	2.16	2.10	2.13
1.42	* of which, "hotels and similar establishments"		Nights	2.04	2.15	2.11	2.03	2.04
1.43	♦ For non commercial accommodation services		Days	..	..	..	..	..
1.44	Average expenditure per day		US$	..	..	..	..	..
2.	**DOMESTIC TOURISM**							
	Data							
	Accommodation							
	Total							
2.19	♦ Guests		('000)	1,304	1,270	1,271	1,164	1,305
2.20	♦ Overnights		('000)	5,002	4,689	4,579	3,925	4,242
	Hotels and similar establishments							
2.21	♦ Guests		('000)	864	855	857	801	904
2.22	♦ Overnights		('000)	2,396	2,427	2,369	2,073	2,307
	Indicators							
2.23	Average size of travel party		Persons	..	..	..	..	..
	Average length of stay							
2.24	Total		Days	..	..	..	..	..
2.25	♦ For all commercial accommodation services		Nights	3.84	3.70	3.60	3.37	3.25
2.26	* of which, "hotels and similar establishments"		Nights	2.77	2.84	2.76	2.59	2.55
2.27	♦ For non commercial accommodation services		Days	..	..	..	..	..
2.28	Average expenditure per day		US$	..	..	..	..	..
3.	**OUTBOUND TOURISM**							
	Data							
	Expenditure							
3.4	Total		US$ Mn	1,263	1,188	1,290	1,360	1,254
3.5	♦ Travel		US$ Mn	1,105	1,031	1,117	1,179	1,102
3.6	♦ Passenger transport		US$ Mn	158	157	173	181	152
	Expenditure by main purpose of the trip							
3.7	Total		US$ Mn	1,105	1,032	1,117	1,179	1,102
3.8	♦ Personal		US$ Mn	882	818	880	932	891
3.9	♦ Business and professional		US$ Mn	223	214	237	247	211

SERBIA

Cod.	Basic data and indicators	Notes	Units	2011	2012	2013	2014	2015
4.	**TOURISM INDUSTRIES**							
	Data							
	Number of establishments							
4.1	Total		Units	22,527	22,588	23,318	24,068	26,507
4.2	♦ Accommodation for visitors		Units	975	964	911	891	991
4.3	* of which, "hotels and similar establishments"		Units	731	716	657	676	664
4.4	♦ Food and beverage serving activities		Units	20,609	20,810	21,538	22,360	24,751
4.5	♦ Passenger transportation		Units	..	..	..	..	..
4.6	♦ Travel agencies and other reservation services activities		Units	943	814	869	817	765
4.7	♦ Other tourism industries		Units	..	..	..	..	..
	Accommodation for visitors in hotels and similar establishments							
	Non-monetary data							
4.13	♦ Number of establishments		Units	731	716	657	676	664
4.14	♦ Number of rooms		Units	26,052	25,130	24,759	25,634	24,402
4.15	♦ Number of bed-places	(2)	Units	55,389	53,217	55,729	54,075	52,112
	Indicators							
4.16	Occupancy rate / rooms		Percent	..	..	29.10	27.40	29.50
4.17	Occupancy rate / bed-places	(3)	Percent	18.71	26.80	27.80	26.30	28.60
4.18	Average length of stay		Nights	2.45	2.53	2.45	2.78	2.28
4.19	Available capacity (bed-places per 1000 inhabitants)		Units	6.14	5.92	6.24	6.08	5.89
	Travel agencies and other reservation service activities							
	Non-monetary data							
	♦ Domestic trips	(1)						
4.25	* with package tour		Percent	14.6	14.3	14.9	22.7	23.9
4.26	* without package tour		Percent	85.4	85.7	85.1	77.3	76.1
	♦ Inbound trips	(1)						
4.27	* with package tour		Percent	16.8	17.9	11.4	17.4	15.6
4.28	* without package tour		Percent	83.2	82.1	88.6	82.6	84.4
	♦ Outbound trips							
4.29	* with package tour		Percent	..	..	..	..	..
4.30	* without package tour		Percent	..	..	..	..	..
5.	**EMPLOYMENT**							
	Data							
	Number of employees by tourism industries	(4)						
5.1	Total		('000)	134.0	127.5	127.6	135.4	155.0
5.2	♦ Accommodation services for visitors (hotels and similar establishments)		('000)	14.0	11.8	8.0	9.6	12.9
5.3	♦ Other accommodation services		('000)	3.3	4.0	1.5	2.7	4.6
5.4	♦ Food and beverage serving activities		('000)	44.8	45.8	49.4	54.9	70.3
5.5	♦ Passenger transportation		('000)	65.8	61.0	66.0	66.0	61.2
5.6	♦ Travel agencies and other reservation services activities		('000)	6.1	4.9	2.7	2.2	6.0
5.7	♦ Other tourism industries		('000)	..	..	..	..	..
6.	**COMPLEMENTARY INDICATORS**							
	Demand							
6.1	Gross travel propensity		Units	..	..	..	..	..
6.2	(1.2 inbound tourists) / population		Units	0.08	0.09	0.10	0.12	0.13
	Macroeconomic indicators related to international tourism							
6.3	Inbound tourism expenditure over GDP		Percent	2.5	2.7	2.7	3.1	3.6
6.4	Outbound tourism expenditure over GDP		Percent	2.7	2.9	2.8	3.1	3.4
6.5	Tourism balance (inbound minus outbound tourism expenditure) over GDP		Percent	-0.2	-0.2	-0.1		0.2
6.6	Tourism openness (inbound plus outbound tourism expenditure) over GDP		Percent	5.2	5.6	5.5	6.2	7.0
6.7	Tourism coverage (inbound over outbound tourism		Percent	91.0	90.9	94.7	99.4	105.4
6.8	Inbound tourism expenditure over exports of goods		Percent	10.2	10.0	8.7	9.6	10.5
6.9	Inbound tourism expenditure over exports of services		Percent	27.3	27.2	26.8	26.8	27.9
6.10	Inbound tourism expenditure over exports of goods and services		Percent	7.4	7.3	6.6	7.0	7.6
6.11	Inbound tourism expenditure over current account credits		Percent	5.5	5.5	5.1	5.5	5.9
6.12	Outbound tourism expenditure over imports of goods		Percent	6.7	6.6	6.6	6.9	7.4
6.13	Outbound tourism expenditure over imports of services		Percent	31.6	31.0	31.2	30.7	31.9
6.14	Outbound tourism expenditure over imports of goods and		Percent	5.5	5.4	5.5	5.7	6.0
6.15	Outbound tourism expenditure over current account debits		Percent	5.2	5.1	5.2	5.4	5.6

SEYCHELLES

Cod.	Basic data and indicators	Notes	Units	2011	2012	2013	2014	2015
1.	**INBOUND TOURISM**							
	Data							
	Arrivals							
1.1	Total		('000)	210	216	237	239	296
1.2	♦ Overnight visitors (tourists)		('000)	194	208	230	233	276
1.3	♦ Same-day visitors (excursionists)		('000)	16	8	7	6	20
1.4	* of which, cruise passengers		('000)	16	8	7	6	20
	Arrivals by region							
1.5	Total		('000)	194	207	230	233	276
1.6	♦ Africa		('000)	24	25	27	28	36
1.7	♦ Americas		('000)	5	6	6	7	9
1.8	♦ East Asia and the Pacific		('000)	6	9	13	19	20
1.9	♦ Europe		('000)	144	146	161	156	175
1.10	♦ Middle East		('000)	12	18	20	19	27
1.11	♦ South Asia		('000)	3	3	4	5	10
1.12	♦ Other not classified		('000)	..	..	..	..	..
1.13	* of which, nationals residing abroad		('000)	..	..	..	..	..
	Arrivals by main purpose							
1.14	Total		('000)	194	208	230	233	276
1.15	♦ Personal		('000)	187	202	222	224	266
1.16	* holidays, leisure and recreation		('000)	176	192	213	215	250
1.17	* other personal purposes		('000)	11	10	9	9	16
1.18	♦ Business and professional		('000)	7	6	8	9	10
	Arrivals by mode of transport							
1.19	Total		('000)	194	208	230	233	276
1.20	♦ Air		('000)	193	207	230	232	275
1.21	♦ Water		('000)	1	1	0.7	1	1
1.22	♦ Land		('000)	..	..	..	..	..
1.23	* railway		('000)	..	..	..	..	..
1.24	* road		('000)	..	..	..	..	..
1.25	* others		('000)	..	..	..	..	..
	Accommodation							
	Total							
1.29	♦ Guests		('000)	..	..	..	..	..
1.30	♦ Overnights		('000)	1,945	2,060	2,349	2,373	2,735
	Hotels and similar establishments							
1.31	♦ Guests		('000)	167	181	201	204	245
1.32	♦ Overnights		('000)	1,338	1,375	1,512	1,934	2,217
	Expenditure							
1.33	Total		US$ Mn	380	429	484	480	483
1.34	♦ Travel		US$ Mn	291	388	430	397	392
1.35	♦ Passenger transport		US$ Mn	89	41	54	83	91
	Expenditure by main purpose of the trip							
1.36	Total		US$ Mn	291	388	430	397	393
1.37	♦ Personal		US$ Mn	236	315	348	322	318
1.38	♦ Business and professional		US$ Mn	55	74	82	75	75
	Indicators							
1.39	Average size of travel party		Persons	..	..	..	..	..
	Average length of stay							
1.40	Total		Days	..	..	..	..	..
1.41	♦ For all commercial accommodation services	(1)(2)	Nights	10.00	9.90	10.20	10.20	9.90
1.42	* of which, "hotels and similar establishments"		Nights	..	..	..	..	..
1.43	♦ For non commercial accommodation services		Days	..	..	..	..	..
1.44	Average expenditure per day		US$	..	..	..	..	..
2.	**DOMESTIC TOURISM**							
	Data							
	Accommodation							
	Hotels and similar establishments							
2.21	♦ Guests		('000)	..	..	..	..	..
2.22	♦ Overnights		('000)	21	28	25	30	21
3.	**OUTBOUND TOURISM**							
	Data							
	Departures							
3.1	Total		('000)	..	..	..	..	..
3.2	♦ Overnight visitors (tourists)		('000)	48	45	47	50	56
3.3	♦ Same-day visitors (excursionists)		('000)	..	..	..	..	..

SEYCHELLES

Cod.	Basic data and indicators	Notes	Units	2011	2012	2013	2014	2015
	Expenditure							
3.4	Total		US$ Mn	65	58	62	65	54
3.5	♦ Travel		US$ Mn	40	35	37	37	30
3.6	♦ Passenger transport		US$ Mn	25	23	25	28	24
	Expenditure by main purpose of the trip							
3.7	Total		US$ Mn	39	35	37	37	30
3.8	♦ Personal		US$ Mn	36	34	36	37	29
3.9	♦ Business and professional		US$ Mn	3	1	2	1	1
4.	**TOURISM INDUSTRIES**							
	Data							
	Number of establishments							
4.1	Total		Units	..	..	..	..	..
4.2	♦ Accommodation for visitors		Units	..	..	..	..	..
4.3	* of which, "hotels and similar establishments"		Units	391	417	438	435	487
4.4	♦ Food and beverage serving activities		Units	..	..	..	..	..
4.5	♦ Passenger transportation		Units	..	..	..	..	..
4.6	♦ Travel agencies and other reservation services activities		Units	..	..	..	..	..
4.7	♦ Other tourism industries		Units	..	..	..	..	..
	Accommodation for visitors in hotels and similar establishments							
	Non-monetary data							
4.13	♦ Number of establishments		Units	391	417	438	435	487
4.14	♦ Number of rooms	(3)	Units	2,874	3,105	3,169	4,519	5,150
4.15	♦ Number of bed-places	(3)	Units	6,040	6,550	6,490	9,080	10,280
	Indicators							
4.16	Occupancy rate / rooms		Percent	64.00	60.00	65.00	57.00	62.00
4.17	Occupancy rate / bed-places		Percent	61.00	57.00	64.00	58.00	59.00
4.18	Average length of stay		Nights	..	..	..	..	..
4.19	Available capacity (bed-places per 1000 inhabitants)		Units	64.39	69.29	68.16	94.71	106.56
6.	**COMPLEMENTARY INDICATORS**							
	Demand							
6.1	Gross travel propensity		Units	..	..	..	..	..
6.2	(1.2 inbound tourists) / population		Units	2.07	2.20	2.42	2.43	2.86
	Macroeconomic indicators related to international tourism							
6.3	Inbound tourism expenditure over GDP		Percent	35.7	37.8	34.3	31.8	..
6.4	Outbound tourism expenditure over GDP		Percent	6.1	5.1	4.4	4.3	..
6.5	Tourism balance (inbound minus outbound tourism expenditure) over GDP		Percent	29.6	32.7	29.9	27.5	..
6.6	Tourism openness (inbound plus outbound tourism expenditure) over GDP		Percent	41.8	42.9	38.7	36.1	..
6.7	Tourism coverage (inbound over outbound tourism expenditure)		Percent	584.6	739.7	780.6	738.5	894.4
6.8	Inbound tourism expenditure over exports of goods		Percent	79.7	76.7	76.9	89.1	107.5
6.9	Inbound tourism expenditure over exports of services		Percent	81.6	63.7	58.5	57.6	57.0
6.10	Inbound tourism expenditure over exports of goods and services		Percent	40.3	34.8	33.2	35.0	37.2
6.11	Inbound tourism expenditure over current account credits		Percent	37.8	30.1	31.1	33.4	35.8
6.12	Outbound tourism expenditure over imports of goods		Percent	7.1	5.6	5.8	6.0	5.9
6.13	Outbound tourism expenditure over imports of services		Percent	24.4	15.0	13.1	12.9	10.8
6.14	Outbound tourism expenditure over imports of goods and		Percent	5.5	4.1	4.0	4.1	3.8
6.15	Outbound tourism expenditure over current account debits		Percent	5.3	3.7	3.8	3.9	3.6

SIERRA LEONE

Cod.	Basic data and indicators	Notes	Units	2011	2012	2013	2014	2015
1.	**INBOUND TOURISM**							
	Data							
	Arrivals							
1.1	Total		('000)	..	75	95	53	31
1.2	♦ Overnight visitors (tourists)	(1)	('000)	52	60	81	44	24
1.3	♦ Same-day visitors (excursionists)		('000)	..	15	14	9	7
1.4	* of which, cruise passengers		('000)	..	1	2	1	2
	Arrivals by region	(1)						
1.5	Total		('000)	52	60	81	44	24
1.6	♦ Africa		('000)	16	16	22	12	7
1.7	♦ Americas		('000)	11	11	20	9	6
1.8	♦ East Asia and the Pacific		('000)	9	8	7	4	2
1.9	♦ Europe		('000)	14	16	26	15	7
1.10	♦ Middle East		('000)	1	6	4	2	1
1.11	♦ South Asia		('000)	1	3	3	1	1
1.12	♦ Other not classified		('000)	..	..	..	..	..
1.13	* of which, nationals residing abroad		('000)	..	..	..	..	..
	Arrivals by main purpose	(1)						
1.14	Total		('000)	52	60	81	44	24
1.15	♦ Personal		('000)	28	30	39	21	13
1.16	* holidays, leisure and recreation		('000)	11	9	13	8	5
1.17	* other personal purposes		('000)	17	21	26	14	7
1.18	♦ Business and professional		('000)	24	30	42	22	11
	Arrivals by mode of transport							
1.19	Total		('000)	52	60	81	44	24
1.20	♦ Air		('000)	52	60	81	44	24
1.21	♦ Water		('000)	..	..	..	..	..
1.22	♦ Land		('000)	..	..	..	..	..
1.23	* railway		('000)	..	..	..	..	..
1.24	* road		('000)	..	..	..	..	..
1.25	* others		('000)	..	..	..	..	..
	Accommodation							
	Hotels and similar establishments							
1.31	♦ Guests		('000)	..	..	..	..	..
1.32	♦ Overnights		('000)	367	418	569	306	167
	Expenditure							
1.33	Total		US$ Mn	..	..	..	..	..
1.34	♦ Travel		US$ Mn	44	47	66	35	23
1.35	♦ Passenger transport		US$ Mn	..	..	..	..	..
	Expenditure by main purpose of the trip							
1.36	Total		US$ Mn	44	47	66	35	23
1.37	♦ Personal		US$ Mn	20	22	30	16	14
1.38	♦ Business and professional		US$ Mn	24	25	36	19	9
	Indicators							
1.39	Average size of travel party		Persons	..	..	..	..	..
	Average length of stay							
1.40	Total		Days	..	..	..	..	..
1.41	♦ For all commercial accommodation services		Nights	..	..	..	..	..
1.42	* of which, "hotels and similar establishments"		Nights	7.00	7.00	7.00	7.00	7.00
1.43	♦ For non commercial accommodation services		Days	..	..	..	..	..
1.44	Average expenditure per day		US$	..	..	..	80.0	90.0
3.	**OUTBOUND TOURISM**							
	Data							
	Departures							
3.1	Total		('000)	..	..	..	..	..
3.2	♦ Overnight visitors (tourists)		('000)	99	104	111	93	61
3.3	♦ Same-day visitors (excursionists)		('000)	..	..	..	..	..
	Expenditure							
3.4	Total		US$ Mn	26	32	55	24	..
3.5	♦ Travel		US$ Mn	14	15	20	19	..
3.6	♦ Passenger transport		US$ Mn	12	17	35	5	..
	Expenditure by main purpose of the trip							
3.7	Total		US$ Mn	14	15	20	20	..
3.8	♦ Personal		US$ Mn	6	8	12	7	..
3.9	♦ Business and professional		US$ Mn	8	7	8	13	..
	Indicators							
3.10	Average length of stay		Days	7.00	7.00	7.00	7.00	7.00
3.11	Average expenditure per day		US$	80.0	40.0	40.0	50.0	60.0

SIERRA LEONE

Cod.	Basic data and indicators	Notes	Units	2011	2012	2013	2014	2015
4.	**TOURISM INDUSTRIES**							
	Data							
	Number of establishments							
4.1	Total		Units	192	193	203	190	189
4.2	♦ Accommodation for visitors		Units	108	108	112	115	111
4.3	* of which, "hotels and similar establishments"		Units	108	108	112	115	111
4.4	♦ Food and beverage serving activities		Units	62	62	67	48	52
4.5	♦ Passenger transportation		Units	..	..	..	..	..
4.6	♦ Travel agencies and other reservation services activities		Units	18	18	17	17	19
4.7	♦ Other tourism industries		Units	4	5	7	10	7
	Accommodation for visitors in hotels and similar establishments							
	Non-monetary data							
4.13	♦ Number of establishments		Units	108	108	112	115	111
4.14	♦ Number of rooms		Units	..	1,758	..	..	2,137
4.15	♦ Number of bed-places		Units	3,901	4,041	4,720	4,014	3,432
	Indicators							
4.16	Occupancy rate / rooms		Percent	..	42.00	46.00	50.00	60.00
4.17	Occupancy rate / bed-places		Percent	52.00	53.00	57.00	36.00	30.00
4.18	Average length of stay		Nights	7.00	7.00	7.00	7.00	7.00
4.19	Available capacity (bed-places per 1000 inhabitants)		Units	0.66	0.67	0.76	0.64	0.53
5.	**EMPLOYMENT**							
	Data							
	Number of employees by tourism industries							
5.1	Total		('000)	4.7	6.0	10.4	6.1	4.4
5.2	♦ Accommodation services for visitors (hotels and similar establishments)		('000)	2.6	3.1	6.0	3.6	1.7
5.3	♦ Other accommodation services		('000)	..	..	..	..	1.0
5.4	♦ Food and beverage serving activities		('000)	1.7	2.0	3.0	1.6	0.6
5.5	♦ Passenger transportation		('000)	..	0.1	0.2	..	..
5.6	♦ Travel agencies and other reservation services activities		('000)	0.3	0.5	0.7	0.4	0.5
5.7	♦ Other tourism industries		('000)	0.2	0.3	0.5	0.5	0.6
	Number of jobs by status in employment							
5.8	Total		('000)	..	..	..	..	15.0
5.9	♦ Employees		('000)	..	..	..	..	3.0
5.10	♦ Self employed		('000)	..	..	..	..	12.0
	Indicators							
	Number of full-time equivalent jobs by status in employment							
5.11	Total		('000)	..	5.5	..	9.3	12.7
5.12	♦ Employees		('000)	..	5.5	..	6.1	2.7
5.13	* male		('000)	..	3.6	..	3.6	1.5
5.14	* female		('000)	..	1.9	..	2.5	1.2
5.15	♦ Self employed		('000)	..	..	..	3.3	10.0
5.16	* male		('000)	..	..	..	2.0	4.0
5.17	* female		('000)	..	..	..	1.2	6.0
6.	**COMPLEMENTARY INDICATORS**							
	Demand							
6.1	Gross travel propensity		Units	..	..	..	..	..
6.2	(1.2 inbound tourists) / population		Units	0.01	0.01	0.01	0.01	0.00
	Macroeconomic indicators related to international tourism							
6.3	Inbound tourism expenditure over GDP		Percent	1.5	1.2	1.3	0.7	..
6.4	Outbound tourism expenditure over GDP		Percent	0.9	0.8	1.1	0.5	..
6.5	Tourism balance (inbound minus outbound tourism expenditure) over GDP		Percent	0.6	0.4	0.2	0.2	..
6.6	Tourism openness (inbound plus outbound tourism expenditure) over GDP		Percent	2.4	2.0	2.4	1.2	..
6.7	Tourism coverage (inbound over outbound tourism expenditure)		Percent	169.2	146.9	120.0	145.8	..
6.8	Inbound tourism expenditure over exports of goods		Percent	11.5	4.5	4.3	2.7	..
6.9	Inbound tourism expenditure over exports of services		Percent	28.1	26.4	29.8	17.1	..
6.10	Inbound tourism expenditure over exports of goods and services		Percent	8.2	3.8	3.8	2.4	..
6.11	Inbound tourism expenditure over current account credits		Percent	5.4	3.1	3.3	1.5	..
6.12	Outbound tourism expenditure over imports of goods		Percent	1.3	1.6	3.5	1.5	..
6.13	Outbound tourism expenditure over imports of services		Percent	6.1	6.1	8.0	2.0	..
6.14	Outbound tourism expenditure over imports of goods and		Percent	1.0	1.3	2.4	0.8	..
6.15	Outbound tourism expenditure over current account debits		Percent	1.0	1.3	2.4	0.8	..

SINGAPORE

Cod.	Basic data and indicators	Notes	Units	2011	2012	2013	2014	2015
1.	**INBOUND TOURISM**							
	Data							
	Arrivals							
1.1	Total	(1)	('000)	13,171	14,496	15,568	15,095	15,231
1.2	♦ Overnight visitors (tourists)		('000)	10,390	11,098	11,899	11,864	12,051
1.3	♦ Same-day visitors (excursionists)		('000)	2,781	3,398	3,669	3,231	3,180
1.4	* of which, cruise passengers		('000)	..	..	..	..	..
	Arrivals by region	(1)						
1.5	Total		('000)	13,171	14,496	15,568	15,095	15,231
1.6	♦ Africa		('000)	69	64	63	62	63
1.7	♦ Americas		('000)	564	616	641	635	657
1.8	♦ East Asia and the Pacific		('000)	9,887	10,988	11,920	11,406	11,427
1.9	♦ Europe		('000)	1,414	1,551	1,606	1,633	1,652
1.10	♦ Middle East		('000)	113	118	135	147	142
1.11	♦ South Asia		('000)	1,124	1,151	1,202	1,213	1,291
1.12	♦ Other not classified		('000)	..	8	1	..	..
1.13	* of which, nationals residing abroad		('000)	..	..	..	..	..
	Arrivals by main purpose	(1)						
1.14	Total		('000)	13,171	14,496	15,568	15,095	15,231
1.15	♦ Personal		('000)	9,905	11,090	12,011	11,940	12,185
1.16	* holidays, leisure and recreation		('000)	4,887	5,295	5,549	5,887	5,940
1.17	* other personal purposes		('000)	5,018	5,795	6,461	6,053	6,245
1.18	♦ Business and professional		('000)	3,267	3,406	3,558	3,155	3,046
	Arrivals by mode of transport	(1)						
1.19	Total		('000)	13,171	14,496	15,568	15,095	15,231
1.20	♦ Air		('000)	10,142	11,109	11,852	11,693	11,831
1.21	♦ Water		('000)	1,328	1,464	1,518	1,543	1,603
1.22	♦ Land		('000)	1,701	1,923	2,198	1,858	1,798
1.23	* railway		('000)	..	..	..	..	..
1.24	* road		('000)	1,701	1,923	2,198	1,858	1,798
1.25	* others		('000)	..	..	..	..	..
	Accommodation							
	Hotels and similar establishments							
1.31	♦ Guests		('000)	8,298	9,422	10,091	9,480	8,870
1.32	♦ Overnights		('000)	..	..	..	..	..
	Expenditure							
1.33	Total		US$ Mn	..	..	..	..	..
1.34	♦ Travel		US$ Mn	17,930	18,796	19,209	19,134	16,743
1.35	♦ Passenger transport		US$ Mn	..	..	..	..	..
	Indicators							
1.39	Average size of travel party		Persons	..	..	..	..	..
	Average length of stay							
1.40	Total		Days	..	..	..	..	..
1.41	♦ For all commercial accommodation services	(2)	Nights	3.73	3.54	3.48	3.71	3.61
1.42	* of which, "hotels and similar establishments"		Nights	..	..	..	..	..
1.43	♦ For non commercial accommodation services		Days	..	..	..	..	..
1.44	Average expenditure per day		US$	..	..	..	..	..
3.	**OUTBOUND TOURISM**							
	Data							
	Departures							
3.1	Total		('000)	..	..	..	..	..
3.2	♦ Overnight visitors (tourists)		('000)	7,753	8,048	8,647	8,903	9,125
3.3	♦ Same-day visitors (excursionists)		('000)	..	..	..	..	..
	Expenditure							
3.4	Total		US$ Mn	..	..	..	..	..
3.5	♦ Travel		US$ Mn	21,505	23,147	24,506	24,360	22,056
3.6	♦ Passenger transport		US$ Mn	..	..	..	..	..
4.	**TOURISM INDUSTRIES**							
	Data							
	Number of establishments							
4.1	Total		Units	..	..	..	..	..
4.2	♦ Accommodation for visitors		Units	..	..	..	..	..
4.3	* of which, "hotels and similar establishments"	(3)	Units	304	338	373	391	398
4.4	♦ Food and beverage serving activities		Units	..	..	..	..	..
4.5	♦ Passenger transportation		Units	..	..	..	..	..
4.6	♦ Travel agencies and other reservation services activities		Units	..	..	..	..	..
4.7	♦ Other tourism industries		Units	..	..	..	..	..

SINGAPORE

Cod.	Basic data and indicators	Notes	Units	2011	2012	2013	2014	2015
	Accommodation for visitors in hotels and similar establishments							
	Non-monetary data							
4.13	♦ Number of establishments	(3)	Units	304	338	373	391	398
4.14	♦ Number of rooms	(3)	Units	49,719	51,579	55,018	57,050	60,841
4.15	♦ Number of bed-places		Units	..	..	..	..	..
	Indicators							
4.16	Occupancy rate / rooms	(4)	Percent	86.00	86.00	86.30	85.50	84.90
4.17	Occupancy rate / bed-places		Percent	..	..	..	..	..
4.18	Average length of stay		Nights	..	..	..	..	..
4.19	Available capacity (bed-places per 1000 inhabitants)		Units	..	..	..	..	..
6.	**COMPLEMENTARY INDICATORS**							
	Demand							
6.1	Gross travel propensity		Units	..	..	..	..	..
6.2	(1.2 inbound tourists) / population		Units	2.00	2.09	2.20	2.15	2.15
	Macroeconomic indicators related to international tourism							
6.3	Inbound tourism expenditure over GDP		Percent	6.5	6.5	6.3	6.2	..
6.4	Outbound tourism expenditure over GDP		Percent	7.8	8.0	8.1	7.9	..
6.5	Tourism balance (inbound minus outbound tourism expenditure) over GDP		Percent	-1.3	-1.5	-1.8	-1.7	..
6.6	Tourism openness (inbound plus outbound tourism expenditure) over GDP		Percent	14.3	14.5	14.4	14.1	..
6.7	Tourism coverage (inbound over outbound tourism expenditure)		Percent	83.4	81.2	78.4	78.5	75.9
6.8	Inbound tourism expenditure over exports of goods		Percent	4.1	4.3	4.4	4.4	4.4
6.9	Inbound tourism expenditure over exports of services		Percent	15.1	14.7	13.7	12.7	12.0
6.10	Inbound tourism expenditure over exports of goods and services		Percent	3.2	3.3	3.3	3.3	3.2
6.11	Inbound tourism expenditure over current account credits		Percent	2.9	2.9	2.9	2.9	2.9
6.12	Outbound tourism expenditure over imports of goods		Percent	6.0	6.3	6.8	6.8	7.5
6.13	Outbound tourism expenditure over imports of services		Percent	18.2	17.8	16.7	15.7	15.4
6.14	Outbound tourism expenditure over imports of goods and		Percent	4.5	4.7	4.8	4.7	5.0
6.15	Outbound tourism expenditure over current account debits		Percent	3.9	4.0	4.2	4.1	4.3

353

SINT MAARTEN (DUTCH PART)

Cod.	Basic data and indicators	Notes	Units	2011	2012	2013	2014	2015
1.	**INBOUND TOURISM**							
	Data							
	Arrivals							
1.1	Total		('000)	2,080	2,210	2,253	2,502	2,407
1.2	♦ Overnight visitors (tourists)	(1)	('000)	424	457	467	500	505
1.3	♦ Same-day visitors (excursionists)		('000)	1,656	1,753	1,786	2,002	1,902
1.4	* of which, cruise passengers		('000)	1,656	1,753	1,786	2,002	1,902
	Arrivals by region	(1)						
1.5	Total		('000)	424	457	467	500	505
1.6	♦ Africa		('000)	..	..	..	..	..
1.7	♦ Americas		('000)	292	319	333	361	355
1.8	♦ East Asia and the Pacific		('000)	..	..	..	..	..
1.9	♦ Europe		('000)	102	105	104	107	115
1.10	♦ Middle East		('000)	..	..	..	..	..
1.11	♦ South Asia		('000)	..	..	..	..	..
1.12	♦ Other not classified		('000)	30	33	30	32	36
1.13	* of which, nationals residing abroad		('000)	..	..	..	..	..
	Arrivals by mode of transport							
1.19	Total		('000)	2,080	2,210	2,253	2,502	2,407
1.20	♦ Air	(2)	('000)	424	457	467	500	505
1.21	♦ Water		('000)	1,656	1,753	1,786	2,002	1,902
1.22	♦ Land		('000)	..	..	..	..	..
1.23	* railway		('000)	..	..	..	..	..
1.24	* road		('000)	..	..	..	..	..
1.25	* others		('000)	..	..	..	..	..
	Expenditure							
1.33	Total		US$ Mn	729	854	871	922	951
1.34	♦ Travel		US$ Mn	719	842	857	906	936
1.35	♦ Passenger transport		US$ Mn	10	12	14	16	15
3.	**OUTBOUND TOURISM**							
	Data							
	Expenditure							
3.4	Total		US$ Mn	112	120	114	117	118
3.5	♦ Travel		US$ Mn	88	92	89	88	92
3.6	♦ Passenger transport		US$ Mn	24	28	25	29	26
4.	**TOURISM INDUSTRIES**							
	Indicators							
4.16	Occupancy rate / rooms		Percent	..	..	..	..	..
4.17	Occupancy rate / bed-places		Percent	57.40	62.90	67.50	67.90	67.50
4.18	Average length of stay		Nights	..	..	..	..	..
4.19	Available capacity (bed-places per 1000 inhabitants)		Units	..	..	..	..	..
6.	**COMPLEMENTARY INDICATORS**							
	Demand							
6.1	Gross travel propensity		Units	..	..	..	..	..
6.2	(1.2 inbound tourists) / population		Units	12.48	13.01	12.81	13.26	13.03
	Macroeconomic indicators related to international tourism							
6.3	Inbound tourism expenditure over GDP		Percent	..	..	..	..	..
6.4	Outbound tourism expenditure over GDP		Percent	..	..	..	..	..
6.5	Tourism balance (inbound minus outbound tourism expenditure) over GDP		Percent	..	..	..	..	..
6.6	Tourism openness (inbound plus outbound tourism expenditure) over GDP		Percent	..	..	..	..	..
6.7	Tourism coverage (inbound over outbound tourism expenditure)		Percent	650.9	711.7	764.0	788.0	805.9
6.8	Inbound tourism expenditure over exports of goods		Percent	575.1	654.3	530.3	697.5	737.8
6.9	Inbound tourism expenditure over exports of services		Percent	81.0	82.1	81.9	82.6	84.5
6.10	Inbound tourism expenditure over exports of goods and services		Percent	71.0	73.0	71.0	73.9	75.8
6.11	Inbound tourism expenditure over current account credits		Percent	64.7	66.3	63.5	66.8	68.7
6.12	Outbound tourism expenditure over imports of goods		Percent	15.3	15.6	12.3	11.6	13.3
6.13	Outbound tourism expenditure over imports of services		Percent	47.0	45.9	43.2	40.1	42.3
6.14	Outbound tourism expenditure over imports of goods and		Percent	11.5	11.7	9.6	9.0	10.1
6.15	Outbound tourism expenditure over current account debits		Percent	10.1	10.1	8.3	7.9	8.7

SLOVAKIA

Cod.	Basic data and indicators	Notes	Units	2011	2012	2013	2014	2015
1.	**INBOUND TOURISM**							
	**Data**							
	Arrivals	(1)						
1.1	Total		('000)	18,228	20,375	19,989	..	..
1.2	♦ Overnight visitors (tourists)		('000)	5,961	6,235	6,816	..	..
1.3	♦ Same-day visitors (excursionists)		('000)	12,268	14,140	13,173	..	..
1.4	* of which, cruise passengers		('000)	..	..	..	..	..
	Arrivals by region	(2)						
1.5	Total		('000)	1,460	1,527	1,670	1,475	1,721
1.6	♦ Africa		('000)	3	5	5	4	5
1.7	♦ Americas		('000)	43	46	52	45	61
1.8	♦ East Asia and the Pacific		('000)	72	80	85	62	89
1.9	♦ Europe		('000)	1,337	1,389	1,521	1,358	1,558
1.10	♦ Middle East		('000)	1	1	1	1	2
1.11	♦ South Asia		('000)	2	3	4	4	5
1.12	♦ Other not classified		('000)	2	3	1	1	1
1.13	* of which, nationals residing abroad		('000)	..	..	..	..	..
	Accommodation							
	Total							
1.29	♦ Guests		('000)	1,460	1,528	1,670	1,475	1,721
1.30	♦ Overnights		('000)	4,039	4,101	4,340	3,904	4,456
	Hotels and similar establishments							
1.31	♦ Guests		('000)	1,235	1,293	1,423	1,252	1,469
1.32	♦ Overnights		('000)	3,276	3,330	3,529	3,171	3,642
	Expenditure							
1.33	Total		US$ Mn	2,514	2,366	2,633	2,619	2,411
1.34	♦ Travel		US$ Mn	2,431	2,296	2,556	2,577	2,361
1.35	♦ Passenger transport		US$ Mn	83	70	77	42	50
	**Indicators**							
1.39	Average size of travel party		Persons	..	..	..	..	..
	Average length of stay							
1.40	Total		Days	..	..	..	..	..
1.41	♦ For all commercial accommodation services		Nights	2.80	2.70	2.60	2.60	2.48
1.42	* of which, "hotels and similar establishments"		Nights	2.70	2.60	2.50	2.50	2.59
1.43	♦ For non commercial accommodation services		Days	..	..	..	..	..
1.44	Average expenditure per day		US$	..	..	..	..	..
2.	**DOMESTIC TOURISM**							
	**Data**							
	Trips							
2.1	Total		('000)	5,324	4,477	4,766	4,932	5,595
2.2	♦ Overnight visitors (tourists)		('000)	..	..	..	..	..
2.3	♦ Same-day visitors (excursionists)		('000)	..	..	..	..	..
	Trips by main purpose							
2.4	Total		('000)	5,324	4,477	4,766	4,932	5,595
2.5	♦ Personal		('000)	4,130	3,215	3,839	4,090	4,737
2.6	* holidays, leisure and recreation		('000)	1,857	1,856	2,167	1,850	2,418
2.7	* other personal purposes		('000)	2,273	1,359	1,672	2,240	2,319
2.8	♦ Business and professional		('000)	1,194	1,262	927	842	858
	Trips by mode of transport							
2.9	Total		('000)	5,324	4,477	4,766	4,932	4,737
2.10	♦ Air		('000)	8	12	7	..	..
2.11	♦ Water		('000)	4	..	..	..	..
2.12	♦ Land		('000)	5,312	4,465	4,759	4,932	4,737
2.13	* railway		('000)	789	617	493	561	805
2.14	* road		('000)	4,435	3,836	4,248	4,356	3,928
2.15	* others		('000)	88	12	18	15	4
	Trips by form of organization							
2.16	Total		('000)	5,324	..	..	4,932	4,737
2.17	♦ Package tour		('000)	121	..	..	237	218
2.18	♦ Other forms		('000)	5,203	..	..	4,695	4,519
	Accommodation							
	Total							
2.19	♦ Guests		('000)	2,111	2,247	2,379	2,253	2,609
2.20	♦ Overnights		('000)	6,486	6,807	7,147	6,996	7,894
	Hotels and similar establishments							
2.21	♦ Guests		('000)	1,479	1,593	1,704	1,629	1,910
2.22	♦ Overnights		('000)	3,744	3,925	4,151	4,138	4,784

SLOVAKIA

Cod.	Basic data and indicators	Notes	Units	2011	2012	2013	2014	2015
	Indicators							
2.23	Average size of travel party		Persons	..	..	..	..	..
	Average length of stay							
2.24	Total		Days	4.56	5.07	4.33	4.47	4.57
2.25	♦ For all commercial accommodation services		Nights	3.10	3.00	3.00	3.10	3.03
2.26	* of which, "hotels and similar establishments"		Nights	2.50	2.50	2.40	2.50	2.50
2.27	♦ For non commercial accommodation services		Days	4.40	5.04	4.12	4.49	4.13
2.28	Average expenditure per day		US$	43.0	51.7	36.8	36.7	31.4
3.	**OUTBOUND TOURISM**							
	Data							
	Departures							
3.1	Total		('000)	3,285	2,689	2,129	2,406	2,777
3.2	♦ Overnight visitors (tourists)		('000)	..	..	..	..	..
3.3	♦ Same-day visitors (excursionists)		('000)	..	..	..	..	..
	Expenditure							
3.4	Total		US$ Mn	2,449	2,310	2,569	2,622	2,260
3.5	♦ Travel		US$ Mn	2,186	2,141	2,367	2,468	2,125
3.6	♦ Passenger transport		US$ Mn	263	169	202	154	135
	Indicators							
3.10	Average length of stay		Days	7.80	8.45	8.86	6.92	7.89
3.11	Average expenditure per day		US$	84.0	94.7	86.2	86.0	75.7
4.	**TOURISM INDUSTRIES**							
	Data							
	Number of establishments	(3)						
4.1	Total		Units	26,078	26,016	23,293	..	..
4.2	♦ Accommodation for visitors		Units	3,011	3,643	3,485	3,318	3,724
4.3	* of which, "hotels and similar establishments"		Units	1,645	1,883	1,439	1,397	1,509
4.4	♦ Food and beverage serving activities		Units	13,277	12,537	11,554	..	..
4.5	♦ Passenger transportation		Units	3,941	4,029	3,549	..	..
4.6	♦ Travel agencies and other reservation services activities		Units	1,435	1,302	1,146	..	..
4.7	♦ Other tourism industries	(4)	Units	4,414	4,505	3,559	..	..
	Accommodation for visitors in hotels and similar establishments							
	Non-monetary data							
4.13	♦ Number of establishments		Units	1,297	1,473	1,439	1,397	1,509
4.14	♦ Number of rooms		Units	36,208	38,921	38,690	38,498	40,667
4.15	♦ Number of bed-places		Units	85,832	92,790	92,261	91,663	96,997
	Indicators							
4.16	Occupancy rate / rooms		Percent	..	..	..	..	..
4.17	Occupancy rate / bed-places		Percent	27.50	26.80	22.30	24.80	26.10
4.18	Average length of stay		Nights	2.60	2.50	2.80	2.90	2.90
4.19	Available capacity (bed-places per 1000 inhabitants)		Units	15.86	17.13	17.02	16.90	17.88
5.	**EMPLOYMENT**							
	Data							
	Number of employees by tourism industries	(5)						
5.1	Total		('000)	106.9	115.1	118.7	..	..
5.2	♦ Accommodation services for visitors (hotels and similar establishments)		('000)	13.1	12.2	12.8	..	..
5.3	♦ Other accommodation services		('000)	..	..	..	..	..
5.4	♦ Food and beverage serving activities		('000)	47.5	56.3	58.8	..	..
5.5	♦ Passenger transportation		('000)	22.4	22.6	23.1	..	..
5.6	♦ Travel agencies and other reservation services activities		('000)	2.2	2.3	2.3	..	..
5.7	♦ Other tourism industries	(4)	('000)	21.7	21.7	21.7	..	..
	Number of jobs by status in employment							
5.8	Total		('000)	131.2	136.4	142.2	..	..
5.9	♦ Employees		('000)	108.5	117.2	123.1	..	..
5.10	♦ Self employed		('000)	22.7	19.2	19.1	..	..

SLOVAKIA

Cod.	Basic data and indicators	Notes	Units	2011	2012	2013	2014	2015
	Indicators							
	Number of full-time equivalent jobs by status in employment							
5.11	Total		('000)	125.4	131.9	136.2	..	..
5.12	♦ Employees		('000)	105.3	113.7	118.3	..	..
5.13	* male		('000)	52.4	51.6	56.0	..	..
5.14	* female		('000)	52.9	62.1	62.3	..	..
5.15	♦ Self employed		('000)	20.1	18.2	17.9	..	..
5.16	* male		('000)	13.7	13.1	12.3	..	..
5.17	* female		('000)	6.4	5.1	5.6	..	..
6.	**COMPLEMENTARY INDICATORS**							
	Demand							
6.1	Gross travel propensity	(6)	Units	1.9	1.6	1.5	1.6	1.8
6.2	(1.2 inbound tourists + 2.1 domestic visitors) / population		Units	2.09	1.98	2.14	..	..
	Macroeconomic indicators related to international tourism							
6.3	Inbound tourism expenditure over GDP		Percent	2.6	2.5	2.7	2.6	2.8
6.4	Outbound tourism expenditure over GDP		Percent	2.5	2.5	2.6	2.6	2.6
6.5	Tourism balance (inbound minus outbound tourism expenditure) over GDP		Percent	0.1		0.1		0.2
6.6	Tourism openness (inbound plus outbound tourism expenditure) over GDP		Percent	5.1	5.0	5.3	5.2	5.4
6.7	Tourism coverage (inbound over outbound tourism expenditure)		Percent	102.7	102.4	102.5	99.9	106.7
6.8	Inbound tourism expenditure over exports of goods		Percent	3.3	3.1	3.2	3.2	3.3
6.9	Inbound tourism expenditure over exports of services		Percent	34.6	30.4	28.8	28.9	30.0
6.10	Inbound tourism expenditure over exports of goods and services		Percent	3.0	2.8	2.9	2.8	3.0
6.11	Inbound tourism expenditure over current account credits		Percent	2.8	2.6	2.7	2.7	2.8
6.12	Outbound tourism expenditure over imports of goods		Percent	3.2	3.1	3.3	3.3	3.2
6.13	Outbound tourism expenditure over imports of services		Percent	32.0	31.9	29.8	29.3	28.5
6.14	Outbound tourism expenditure over imports of goods and		Percent	2.9	2.8	2.9	3.0	2.9
6.15	Outbound tourism expenditure over current account debits		Percent	2.7	2.6	2.7	2.8	2.7

357

SLOVENIA

Cod.	Basic data and indicators	Notes	Units	2011	2012	2013	2014	201
1.	**INBOUND TOURISM**							
	Data							
	Arrivals							
1.1	Total		('000)	..	..	..	..	
1.2	♦ Overnight visitors (tourists)	(1)	('000)	2,037	2,156	2,259	2,411	2,70
1.3	♦ Same-day visitors (excursionists)		('000)	..	..	..	..	
1.4	* of which, cruise passengers		('000)	..	..	..	..	
	Arrivals by region	(1)						
1.5	Total		('000)	2,037	2,156	2,259	2,411	2,70
1.6	♦ Africa		('000)	4	5	6	5	
1.7	♦ Americas		('000)	68	76	88	96	11
1.8	♦ East Asia and the Pacific	(2)	('000)	106	133	148	218	27
1.9	♦ Europe		('000)	1,859	1,942	2,017	2,091	2,31
1.10	♦ Middle East		('000)	..	..	..	..	
1.11	♦ South Asia		('000)	..	..	..	..	
1.12	♦ Other not classified		('000)	..	..	..	..	
1.13	* of which, nationals residing abroad		('000)	..	..	..	..	
	Arrivals by main purpose	(3)						
1.14	Total		('000)	2,037	2,156	2,259	2,411	2,70
1.15	♦ Personal		('000)	1,764	1,968	2,062	2,201	2,33
1.16	* holidays, leisure and recreation		('000)	1,446	1,543	1,617	1,726	1,96
1.17	* other personal purposes		('000)	318	425	445	475	37
1.18	♦ Business and professional		('000)	273	188	197	210	37
	Arrivals by mode of transport	(3)						
1.19	Total		('000)	2,037	2,156	2,259	2,411	2,70
1.20	♦ Air		('000)	436	446	467	498	80
1.21	♦ Water		('000)	..	2	2	2	
1.22	♦ Land		('000)	1,601	1,708	1,790	1,911	1,89
1.23	* railway		('000)	61	39	41	44	5
1.24	* road		('000)	1,540	1,668	1,748	1,866	1,84
1.25	* others		('000)	..	1	1	1	
	Arrivals by form of organization of the trip	(3)						
1.26	Total		('000)	2,037	2,156	2,259	2,411	2,70
1.27	♦ Package tour		('000)	271	220	230	246	39
1.28	♦ Other forms		('000)	1,766	1,936	2,029	2,165	2,31
	Accommodation	(1)						
	Total							
1.29	♦ Guests		('000)	2,037	2,156	2,259	2,411	2,70
1.30	♦ Overnights		('000)	5,464	5,777	5,962	6,090	6,61
	Hotels and similar establishments							
1.31	♦ Guests		('000)	1,528	1,593	1,640	1,762	1,93
1.32	♦ Overnights		('000)	4,006	4,150	4,202	4,294	4,54
	Expenditure							
1.33	Total		US$ Mn	2,953	2,737	2,900	2,944	2,69
1.34	♦ Travel		US$ Mn	2,755	2,570	2,712	2,735	2,50
1.35	♦ Passenger transport		US$ Mn	198	167	188	209	19
	Expenditure by main purpose of the trip							
1.36	Total		US$ Mn	2,755	2,570	2,712	2,735	2,50
1.37	♦ Personal		US$ Mn	2,636	2,449	2,585	2,604	2,38
1.38	♦ Business and professional		US$ Mn	119	121	127	131	11
	Indicators							
1.39	Average size of travel party	(4)	Persons	..	2.3	..	..	2.
	Average length of stay	(1)						
1.40	Total		Days	..	..	..	..	
1.41	♦ For all commercial accommodation services		Nights	2.68	2.68	2.64	2.53	2.4
1.42	* of which, "hotels and similar establishments"		Nights	2.62	2.61	2.56	2.44	2.3
1.43	♦ For non commercial accommodation services		Days	..	..	..	..	
1.44	Average expenditure per day	(4)	US$	..	142.8	..	..	127.
2.	**DOMESTIC TOURISM**							
	Data							
	Trips	(5)						
2.1	Total		('000)	..	10,890	..	..	10,01
2.2	♦ Overnight visitors (tourists)		('000)	2,044	2,065	2,025	1,888	1,53
2.3	♦ Same-day visitors (excursionists)		('000)	..	8,825	..	..	8,48

358

SLOVENIA

od.	Basic data and indicators	Notes	Units	2011	2012	2013	2014	2015
	Trips by main purpose	**(5)**						
.4	Total		('000)	2,044	2,065	2,025	1,888	1,535
.5	♦ Personal		('000)	1,889	1,975	1,923	1,795	1,454
.6	* holidays, leisure and recreation		('000)	1,613	1,417	1,231	1,317	1,022
.7	* other personal purposes		('000)	276	558	692	478	432
.8	♦ Business and professional		('000)	155	90	102	93	81
	Trips by mode of transport	**(5)**						
.9	Total		('000)	2,045	2,065	2,025	1,888	1,535
.10	♦ Air		('000)	1	..	..	..	..
.11	♦ Water		('000)	..	..	..	..	..
.12	♦ Land		('000)	2,044	2,065	2,025	1,888	1,535
.13	* railway		('000)	57	51	60	48	19
.14	* road		('000)	1,986	2,013	1,964	1,839	1,516
.15	* others		('000)	1	1	1	1	..
	Trips by form of organization	**(5)**						
.16	Total		('000)	2,044	2,064	2,025	1,888	1,535
.17	♦ Package tour		('000)	4	5	16	22	15
.18	♦ Other forms		('000)	2,040	2,059	2,009	1,866	1,520
	Accommodation	**(1)**						
	Total							
.19	♦ Guests		('000)	1,181	1,142	1,126	1,113	1,221
.20	♦ Overnights		('000)	3,924	3,733	3,617	3,500	3,727
	Hotels and similar establishments							
.21	♦ Guests		('000)	656	626	613	626	675
.22	♦ Overnights		('000)	2,179	2,046	1,973	1,945	2,052
	Indicators							
.23	Average size of travel party	**(6)**	Persons	2.3	2.4	2.4	2.4	2.4
	Average length of stay							
.24	Total	**(5)(7)**	Days	2.84	2.69	2.65	2.59	2.94
.25	♦ For all commercial accommodation services	**(5)**	Nights	3.34	3.39	3.37	3.13	3.32
.26	* of which, "hotels and similar establishments"	**(6)**	Nights	3.23	3.42	3.26	3.00	3.33
.27	♦ For non commercial accommodation services	**(5)(7)**	Days	2.39	2.21	2.16	2.18	2.48
.28	Average expenditure per day		US$	53.0	45.8	48.7	52.6	41.7
.	**OUTBOUND TOURISM**							
	Data							
	Departures							
.1	Total		('000)	5,073	4,465	4,440	4,672	4,909
.2	♦ Overnight visitors (tourists)		('000)	2,722	2,474	2,612	2,642	2,867
.3	♦ Same-day visitors (excursionists)		('000)	2,351	1,991	1,828	2,030	2,042
	Expenditure							
.4	Total		US$ Mn	1,315	1,081	1,081	1,149	1,051
.5	♦ Travel		US$ Mn	1,143	932	939	991	912
.6	♦ Passenger transport		US$ Mn	172	149	142	158	139
	Expenditure by main purpose of the trip							
.7	Total		US$ Mn	1,143	931	939	991	912
.8	♦ Personal		US$ Mn	917	679	717	732	675
.9	♦ Business and professional		US$ Mn	226	252	222	259	237
	Indicators							
.10	Average length of stay	**(7)**	Days	5.50	5.48	5.29	5.18	5.64
.11	Average expenditure per day		US$	83.3	79.9	77.7	82.0	65.3
.	**TOURISM INDUSTRIES**							
	Data							
	Number of establishments	**(8)**						
.1	Total		Units	10,147	10,300	11,899	11,947	..
.2	♦ Accommodation for visitors	**(9)**	Units	1,057	1,106	2,216	2,138	..
.3	* of which, "hotels and similar establishments"		Units	376	395	405	415	..
.4	♦ Food and beverage serving activities		Units	7,118	7,163	7,626	7,706	..
.5	♦ Passenger transportation		Units	1,300	1,316	1,290	1,300	..
.6	♦ Travel agencies and other reservation services activities		Units	672	715	767	803	..
.7	♦ Other tourism industries		Units	..	..	..	..	..
	Accommodation for visitors in hotels and similar establishments							
	Monetary data	**(8)**						
.8	♦ Output		US$ Mn	660.4	604.8	603.3	587.9	..
.9	♦ Intermediate consumption		US$ Mn	331.1	310.3	316.3	309.2	..
.10	♦ Gross value added		US$ Mn	329.3	294.5	287.0	278.7	..
.11	♦ Compensation of employees		US$ Mn	232.1	208.4	204.8	202.6	..
.12	♦ Gross fixed capital formation		US$ Mn	112.2	51.8	60.4	61.7	..

SLOVENIA

Cod.	Basic data and indicators	Notes	Units	2011	2012	2013	2014	201
	Non-monetary data	(1)						
4.13	♦ Number of establishments		Units	648	642	639	647	68
4.14	♦ Number of rooms		Units	22,082	22,015	22,102	22,072	22,34
4.15	♦ Number of bed-places		Units	49,293	49,291	49,351	49,507	50,26
	Indicators	(1)						
4.16	Occupancy rate / rooms		Percent	..	47.70	46.90	47.30	49.5
4.17	Occupancy rate / bed-places	(10)	Percent	42.40	42.60	42.30	42.80	44.7
4.18	Average length of stay		Nights	2.83	2.79	2.74	2.61	2.5
4.19	Available capacity (bed-places per 1000 inhabitants)		Units	23.94	23.89	23.90	23.96	24.3
	Travel agencies and other reservation service activities							
	Monetary data	(8)						
4.20	♦ Output		US$ Mn	533.9	485.4	504.0	510.7	
4.21	♦ Intermediate consumption		US$ Mn	476.4	432.0	447.5	455.5	
4.22	♦ Gross value added		US$ Mn	57.6	53.4	56.5	55.2	
4.23	♦ Compensation of employees		US$ Mn	44.7	40.8	40.1	39.9	
4.24	♦ Gross fixed capital formation		US$ Mn	8.8	5.9	8.1	5.1	
5.	**EMPLOYMENT**							
	Data							
	Number of employees by tourism industries	(11)						
5.1	Total		('000)	50.4	49.4	48.5	50.1	51.
5.2	♦ Accommodation services for visitors (hotels and similar establishments)		('000)	9.1	8.9	8.4	8.3	8.
5.3	♦ Other accommodation services		('000)	1.2	1.2	1.2	1.2	1
5.4	♦ Food and beverage serving activities		('000)	21.8	21.0	20.7	21.7	22.
5.5	♦ Passenger transportation		('000)	6.1	6.2	6.1	6.4	6.
5.6	♦ Travel agencies and other reservation services activities		('000)	1.7	1.8	1.8	1.8	1.
5.7	♦ Other tourism industries		('000)	10.5	10.3	10.3	10.7	11.
	Number of jobs by status in employment	(11)						
5.8	Total		('000)	50.4	49.4	48.5	50.1	51.
5.9	♦ Employees		('000)	41.9	41.0	39.9	41.1	42.
5.10	♦ Self employed		('000)	8.5	8.4	8.6	9.0	9.
	Indicators							
	Number of full-time equivalent jobs by status in employment	(11)(12)						
5.11	Total		('000)	50.4	49.4	48.6	50.1	51.
5.12	♦ Employees		('000)	41.9	41.0	39.9	41.1	42.
5.13	* male		('000)	19.8	19.4	18.8	19.2	19.
5.14	* female		('000)	22.1	21.6	21.1	21.9	22.
5.15	♦ Self employed		('000)	8.5	8.4	8.7	9.0	9.
5.16	* male		('000)	5.0	4.9	5.0	5.1	5.
5.17	* female		('000)	3.5	3.5	3.7	3.9	4.
6.	**COMPLEMENTARY INDICATORS**							
	Demand							
6.1	Gross travel propensity	(5)	Units	2.7	2.6	2.6	2.6	2.
6.2	(1.2 inbound tourists + 2.2 domestic tourists) / population		Units	1.98	2.05	2.07	2.08	2.0
	Macroeconomic indicators related to international tourism							
6.3	Inbound tourism expenditure over GDP		Percent	5.8	5.9	6.1	5.9	6.
6.4	Outbound tourism expenditure over GDP		Percent	2.6	2.3	2.3	2.3	2.
6.5	Tourism balance (inbound minus outbound tourism expenditure) over GDP		Percent	3.2	3.6	3.8	3.6	3
6.6	Tourism openness (inbound plus outbound tourism expenditure) over GDP		Percent	8.4	8.2	8.4	8.2	8.
6.7	Tourism coverage (inbound over outbound tourism expenditure)		Percent	224.6	253.2	268.3	256.2	256
6.8	Inbound tourism expenditure over exports of goods		Percent	10.1	10.0	10.1	9.7	10.
6.9	Inbound tourism expenditure over exports of services		Percent	43.2	41.8	41.1	39.9	40.
6.10	Inbound tourism expenditure over exports of goods and services		Percent	8.2	8.1	8.1	7.8	8.
6.11	Inbound tourism expenditure over current account credits		Percent	7.5	7.5	7.6	7.2	7.
6.12	Outbound tourism expenditure over imports of goods		Percent	4.3	3.9	3.9	4.0	4.
6.13	Outbound tourism expenditure over imports of services		Percent	27.0	23.4	22.7	22.4	23.
6.14	Outbound tourism expenditure over imports of goods and		Percent	3.7	3.4	3.3	3.4	3
6.15	Outbound tourism expenditure over current account debits		Percent	3.4	3.1	3.0	3.1	3

SOLOMON ISLANDS

Cod.	Basic data and indicators	Notes	Units	2011	2012	2013	2014	2015
1.	**INBOUND TOURISM**							
	Data							
	Arrivals							
1.1	Total		('000)	..	..	..	..	..
1.2	♦ Overnight visitors (tourists)		('000)	22.9	23.9	24.4	20.1	21.6
1.3	♦ Same-day visitors (excursionists)		('000)	..	..	..	..	..
1.4	* of which, cruise passengers		('000)	..	..	..	..	..
	Arrivals by region							
1.5	Total		('000)	22.9	23.9	24.4	20.1	21.6
1.6	♦ Africa		('000)	..	..	..	..	..
1.7	♦ Americas		('000)	1.2	1.4	1.3	1.3	1.6
1.8	♦ East Asia and the Pacific		('000)	20.5	21.2	21.8	17.6	18.7
1.9	♦ Europe		('000)	0.9	1.1	1.1	1.1	1.2
1.10	♦ Middle East		('000)	..	..	..	..	..
1.11	♦ South Asia		('000)	..	..	..	..	..
1.12	♦ Other not classified		('000)	0.3	0.2	0.2	0.1	0.1
1.13	* of which, nationals residing abroad		('000)	..	..	..	..	..
	Arrivals by main purpose							
1.14	Total		('000)	22.9	23.9	24.4	20.1	21.6
1.15	♦ Personal		('000)	14.1	16.1	16.4	12.7	14.8
1.16	* holidays, leisure and recreation		('000)	5.8	6.1	6.2	5.5	5.7
1.17	* other personal purposes		('000)	8.3	10.0	10.2	7.2	9.1
1.18	♦ Business and professional		('000)	8.8	7.8	8.0	7.4	6.8
	Arrivals by mode of transport							
1.19	Total		('000)	22.9	23.9	24.4	20.1	21.6
1.20	♦ Air		('000)	22.9	23.9	24.4	20.1	21.6
1.21	♦ Water		('000)	..	..	..	..	..
1.22	♦ Land		('000)	..	..	..	..	..
1.23	* railway		('000)	..	..	..	..	..
1.24	* road		('000)	..	..	..	..	..
1.25	* others		('000)	..	..	..	..	..
	Expenditure							
1.33	Total		US$ Mn	66	65	71	64	56
1.34	♦ Travel		US$ Mn	57	54	61	55	47
1.35	♦ Passenger transport		US$ Mn	9	11	10	9	8
	Expenditure by main purpose of the trip							
1.36	Total		US$ Mn	58	54	60	55	47
1.37	♦ Personal		US$ Mn	32	33	37	32	29
1.38	♦ Business and professional		US$ Mn	26	21	23	23	18
	Indicators							
1.39	Average size of travel party		Persons	..	..	..	..	..
	Average length of stay							
1.40	Total		Days	16.00	15.00	15.00	..	..
1.41	♦ For all commercial accommodation services		Nights	..	..	..	..	..
1.42	* of which, "hotels and similar establishments"		Nights	..	..	..	..	..
1.43	♦ For non commercial accommodation services		Days	..	..	..	..	..
1.44	Average expenditure per day		US$	..	..	..	..	..
3.	**OUTBOUND TOURISM**							
	Data							
	Expenditure							
3.4	Total		US$ Mn	66	68	68	66	57
3.5	♦ Travel		US$ Mn	65	68	68	64	57
3.6	♦ Passenger transport		US$ Mn	1.1	0.2	0.7	1.2	0.3
	Expenditure by main purpose of the trip							
3.7	Total		US$ Mn	65	68	68	64	57
3.8	♦ Personal		US$ Mn	38	39	37	35	30
3.9	♦ Business and professional		US$ Mn	27	29	31	29	27
4.	**TOURISM INDUSTRIES**							
	Data							
	Number of establishments							
4.1	Total		Units	..	..	..	..	..
4.2	♦ Accommodation for visitors		Units	..	..	..	..	..
4.3	* of which, "hotels and similar establishments"		Units	141	..	..	..	..
4.4	♦ Food and beverage serving activities		Units	..	..	..	..	..
4.5	♦ Passenger transportation		Units	..	..	..	..	..
4.6	♦ Travel agencies and other reservation services activities		Units	..	..	..	..	..
4.7	♦ Other tourism industries		Units	..	..	..	..	..

361

SOLOMON ISLANDS

Cod.	Basic data and indicators	Notes	Units	2011	2012	2013	2014	2015
	Accommodation for visitors in hotels and similar establishments							
	Non-monetary data							
4.13	♦ Number of establishments		Units	141	..	..	..	..
4.14	♦ Number of rooms		Units	1,556	..	..	..	..
4.15	♦ Number of bed-places		Units	..	..	..	..	..
6.	**COMPLEMENTARY INDICATORS**							
	Demand							
6.1	Gross travel propensity		Units	..	..	..	..	
6.2	(1.2 inbound tourists) / population		Units	0.04	0.04	0.04	0.04	0.04
	Macroeconomic indicators related to international tourism							
6.3	Inbound tourism expenditure over GDP		Percent	8.0	7.2	7.0	6.2	..
6.4	Outbound tourism expenditure over GDP		Percent	8.0	7.5	6.8	6.3	..
6.5	Tourism balance (inbound minus outbound tourism expenditure) over GDP		Percent		-0.3	0.2	-0.1	..
6.6	Tourism openness (inbound plus outbound tourism expenditure) over GDP		Percent	16.0	14.7	13.8	12.5	..
6.7	Tourism coverage (inbound over outbound tourism expenditure)		Percent	99.8	96.0	103.1	97.7	97.9
6.8	Inbound tourism expenditure over exports of goods		Percent	15.7	13.1	15.7	14.1	13.3
6.9	Inbound tourism expenditure over exports of services		Percent	56.1	54.9	56.1	57.3	55.1
6.10	Inbound tourism expenditure over exports of goods and services		Percent	12.3	10.6	12.3	11.3	10.7
6.11	Inbound tourism expenditure over current account credits		Percent	8.7	8.2	9.5	8.7	7.8
6.12	Outbound tourism expenditure over imports of goods		Percent	15.6	15.7	14.7	14.3	13.4
6.13	Outbound tourism expenditure over imports of services		Percent	35.3	33.5	27.6	29.3	32.1
6.14	Outbound tourism expenditure over imports of goods and		Percent	10.8	10.7	9.6	9.6	9.4
6.15	Outbound tourism expenditure over current account debits		Percent	9.4	9.5	8.7	8.4	8.0

SOUTH AFRICA

Cod.	Basic data and indicators	Notes	Units	2011	2012	2013	2014	2015
1.	**INBOUND TOURISM**							
	Data							
	Arrivals	(1)						
1.1	Total		('000)	12,097	13,069	14,318	14,530	13,952
1.2	♦ Overnight visitors (tourists)		('000)	8,339	9,188	9,537	9,549	8,904
1.3	♦ Same-day visitors (excursionists)		('000)	3,758	3,881	4,781	4,980	5,048
1.4	* of which, cruise passengers		('000)	..	..	..	..	..
	Arrivals by region	(1)						
1.5	Total		('000)	8,339	9,188	9,537	9,549	8,904
1.6	♦ Africa		('000)	6,130	6,648	6,847	7,272	6,738
1.7	♦ Americas		('000)	433	514	546	435	404
1.8	♦ East Asia and the Pacific		('000)	305	401	437	293	270
1.9	♦ Europe		('000)	1,307	1,434	1,517	1,400	1,351
1.10	♦ Middle East		('000)	20	23	26	24	25
1.11	♦ South Asia		('000)	119	142	145	110	102
1.12	♦ Other not classified		('000)	25	26	20	15	14
1.13	* of which, nationals residing abroad		('000)	..	..	..	..	..
	Arrivals by main purpose	(1)						
1.14	Total		('000)	8,339	9,188	9,537	9,549	8,904
1.15	♦ Personal		('000)	8,072	8,895	9,265	9,142	8,503
1.16	* holidays, leisure and recreation		('000)	7,868	8,310	8,610	9,142	8,503
1.17	* other personal purposes		('000)	204	585	655	..	..
1.18	♦ Business and professional		('000)	267	293	272	407	400
	Arrivals by mode of transport	(1)						
1.19	Total		('000)	8,339	9,188	9,537	9,549	8,904
1.20	♦ Air		('000)	2,503	2,937	3,164	2,573	2,536
1.21	♦ Water		('000)	9	11	7	4	7
1.22	♦ Land		('000)	5,827	6,240	6,366	6,972	6,362
1.23	* railway		('000)	..	..	..	..	..
1.24	* road		('000)	5,827	6,240	6,366	6,972	6,362
1.25	* others		('000)	..	..	..	..	..
	Expenditure							
1.33	Total		US$ Mn	10,706	11,202	10,468	10,484	9,140
1.34	♦ Travel		US$ Mn	9,515	9,996	9,245	9,338	8,259
1.35	♦ Passenger transport		US$ Mn	1,191	1,206	1,223	1,146	881
	Expenditure by main purpose of the trip							
1.36	Total		US$ Mn	9,515	9,996	9,245	9,338	8,259
1.37	♦ Personal		US$ Mn	7,879	8,334	7,759	7,910	6,993
1.38	♦ Business and professional		US$ Mn	1,636	1,662	1,486	1,428	1,266
2.	**DOMESTIC TOURISM**	(2)						
	Data							
	Trips							
2.1	Total		('000)	26,448	25,438	25,175	28,014	24,451
2.2	♦ Overnight visitors (tourists)		('000)	13,900	12,500	12,000	12,000	12,400
2.3	♦ Same-day visitors (excursionists)		('000)	12,300	18,500	13,600	13,100	12,500
	Trips by main purpose							
2.4	Total		('000)	24,227	23,017	22,991	25,113	22,498
2.5	♦ Personal		('000)	23,034	21,322	20,942	23,466	20,133
2.6	* holidays, leisure and recreation		('000)	3,966	2,946	3,055	2,777	2,706
2.7	* other personal purposes		('000)	19,068	18,376	17,887	20,689	17,427
2.8	♦ Business and professional		('000)	1,193	1,695	2,049	1,647	2,365
	Trips by mode of transport							
2.9	Total		('000)	26,283	23,267	23,652	27,754	24,245
2.10	♦ Air		('000)	573	599	548	464	424
2.11	♦ Water		('000)	..	..	..	..	..
2.12	♦ Land		('000)	25,710	22,668	23,104	27,290	23,821
2.13	* railway		('000)	206	59	402	344	230
2.14	* road		('000)	25,432	22,587	22,702	26,916	23,519
2.15	* others		('000)	72	22	..	30	72
	Trips by form of organization							
2.16	Total		('000)	26,270	23,958	24,447	27,642	24,231
2.17	♦ Package tour		('000)	300	702	640	408	653
2.18	♦ Other forms		('000)	25,970	23,256	23,807	27,234	23,578
	Accommodation							
	Total							
2.19	♦ Guests		('000)	..	..	..	..	..
2.20	♦ Overnights		('000)	115,173	121,154	111,312	113,115	102,486

SOUTH AFRICA

Cod.	Basic data and indicators	Notes	Units	2011	2012	2013	2014	2015
	Hotels and similar establishments							
2.21	♦ Guests		('000)	..	..	..	..	..
2.22	♦ Overnights	(3)	('000)	17,667	16,491	45,766	17,730	16,243
	Indicators							
2.23	Average size of travel party	(4)	Persons	3.3	5.1	3.7	3.2	2.8
	Average length of stay							
2.24	Total		Days	4.40	4.80	4.40	4.00	4.20
2.25	♦ For all commercial accommodation services	(5)	Nights	4.00	3.90	4.30	3.80	3.30
2.26	* of which, "hotels and similar establishments"		Nights	..	..			
2.27	♦ For non commercial accommodation services	(6)	Days	3.30	3.60	3.40	3.30	3.10
2.28	Average expenditure per day		US$	170.0	180.0	210.0	230.0	230.0

3. OUTBOUND TOURISM

Data

Expenditure

Cod.		Notes	Units	2011	2012	2013	2014	2015
3.4	Total		US$ Mn	8,397	7,145	6,491	6,314	5,735
3.5	♦ Travel		US$ Mn	5,283	4,069	3,429	3,169	2,998
3.6	♦ Passenger transport		US$ Mn	3,114	3,076	3,062	3,145	2,737
	Expenditure by main purpose of the trip							
3.7	Total		US$ Mn	5,283	4,069	3,429	3,169	2,998
3.8	♦ Personal		US$ Mn	3,732	2,909	2,454	2,271	2,145
3.9	♦ Business and professional		US$ Mn	1,551	1,160	975	897	853

4. TOURISM INDUSTRIES

Data

Number of establishments

Cod.		Notes	Units	2011	2012	2013	2014	2015
4.1	Total		Units	45,729	44,778	40,251	44,056	44,820
4.2	♦ Accommodation for visitors		Units	9,831	9,760	9,683	9,748	10,109
4.3	* of which, "hotels and similar establishments"		Units	2,670	2,657	2,651	2,689	2,725
4.4	♦ Food and beverage serving activities		Units	18,444	17,787	16,823	17,256	17,535
4.5	♦ Passenger transportation		Units	6,889	6,787	6,700	6,755	6,722
4.6	♦ Travel agencies and other reservation services activities		Units	2,324	2,219	2,093	2,095	2,091
4.7	♦ Other tourism industries		Units	8,241	8,225	4,952	8,202	8,363

Accommodation for visitors in hotels and similar establishments

Monetary data

Cod.		Notes	Units	2011	2012	2013	2014	2015
4.8	♦ Output		US$ Mn	5,763.6	5,640.5	5,225.9	4,986.5	..
4.9	♦ Intermediate consumption		US$ Mn	3,180.5	3,312.4	3,050.3	2,910.5	..
4.10	♦ Gross value added		US$ Mn	2,583.1	2,328.1	2,175.6	2,076.0	..
4.11	♦ Compensation of employees		US$ Mn	997.2	940.5	890.4	848.2	..
4.12	♦ Gross fixed capital formation		US$ Mn	..	..	..	..	..

Non-monetary data

Cod.		Notes	Units	2011	2012	2013	2014	2015
4.13	♦ Number of establishments		Units	2,670	2,657	2,651	2,689	2,725
4.14	♦ Number of rooms		Units	72,900	73,200	73,700	74,000	75,100
4.15	♦ Number of bed-places		Units	..	..	..	..	..

Indicators

Cod.		Notes	Units	2011	2012	2013	2014	2015
4.16	Occupancy rate / rooms	(7)	Percent	51.80	54.40	56.50	57.30	56.60
4.17	Occupancy rate / bed-places		Percent	..	..	..	..	..
4.18	Average length of stay		Nights	8.30	7.70	8.70	..	..
4.19	Available capacity (bed-places per 1000 inhabitants)		Units	..	..	..	..	..

Travel agencies and other reservation service activities

Monetary data

Cod.		Notes	Units	2011	2012	2013	2014	2015
4.20	♦ Output		US$ Mn	922.4	958.7	914.7	870.0	..
4.21	♦ Intermediate consumption		US$ Mn	512.1	542.8	526.8	510.0	..
4.22	♦ Gross value added		US$ Mn	410.3	415.9	387.9	369.0	..
4.23	♦ Compensation of employees		US$ Mn	328.4	335.9	310.4	297.3	..
4.24	♦ Gross fixed capital formation		US$ Mn	..	..	..	..	..

5. EMPLOYMENT

Data

Number of employees by tourism industries (8)

Cod.		Notes	Units	2011	2012	2013	2014	2015
5.1	Total		('000)	622.9	646.4	655.9	680.8	
5.2	♦ Accommodation services for visitors (hotels and similar establishments)		('000)	125.3	119.4	103.3	115.3	..
5.3	♦ Other accommodation services		('000)	..	..	..	..	..

SOUTH AFRICA

Cod.	Basic data and indicators	Notes	Units	2011	2012	2013	2014	2015
5.4	♦ Food and beverage serving activities		('000)	123.7	121.2	127.4	137.2	..
5.5	♦ Passenger transportation		('000)	222.4	244.0	249.7	244.3	..
5.6	♦ Travel agencies and other reservation services activities		('000)	19.2	17.8	24.7	30.1	..
5.7	♦ Other tourism industries		('000)	132.3	144.0	150.8	153.9	..
6.	**COMPLEMENTARY INDICATORS**							
	Demand							
6.1	Gross travel propensity		Units	..	..	..	..	..
6.2	(1.2 inbound tourists + 2.2 domestic tourists) / population		Units	0.43	0.41	0.40	0.40	0.39
	Macroeconomic indicators related to international tourism							
6.3	Inbound tourism expenditure over GDP		Percent	2.6	2.9	3.0	3.0	2.9
6.4	Outbound tourism expenditure over GDP		Percent	2.1	1.9	1.9	1.8	1.8
6.5	Tourism balance (inbound minus outbound tourism expenditure) over GDP		Percent	0.5	1.0	1.1	1.2	1.1
6.6	Tourism openness (inbound plus outbound tourism expenditure) over GDP		Percent	4.7	4.8	4.9	4.8	4.7
6.7	Tourism coverage (inbound over outbound tourism expenditure)		Percent	127.5	156.8	161.3	166.0	159.4
6.8	Inbound tourism expenditure over exports of goods		Percent	9.8	11.2	10.9	11.3	11.2
6.9	Inbound tourism expenditure over exports of services		Percent	61.7	63.5	62.3	62.3	60.7
6.10	Inbound tourism expenditure over exports of goods and services		Percent	8.4	9.5	9.3	9.6	9.4
6.11	Inbound tourism expenditure over current account credits		Percent	8.0	8.9	8.6	8.8	8.6
6.12	Outbound tourism expenditure over imports of goods		Percent	8.2	6.8	6.2	6.4	6.8
6.13	Outbound tourism expenditure over imports of services		Percent	40.2	37.8	36.0	37.0	36.9
6.14	Outbound tourism expenditure over imports of goods and		Percent	6.8	5.8	5.3	5.5	5.7
6.15	Outbound tourism expenditure over current account debits		Percent	6.3	5.3	4.9	4.9	5.1

SPAIN

Cod.	Basic data and indicators	Notes	Units	2011	2012	2013	2014	2015
1.	**INBOUND TOURISM**							
	Data							
	Arrivals	(1)						
1.1	Total		('000)	99,187	98,128	103,231	107,144	109,764
1.2	♦ Overnight visitors (tourists)		('000)	56,177	57,464	60,675	64,939	68,215
1.3	♦ Same-day visitors (excursionists)		('000)	43,010	40,664	42,555	42,206	41,549
1.4	* of which, cruise passengers		('000)	..	..	..	..	..
	Arrivals by region	(1)						
1.5	Total		('000)	56,177	57,464	60,675	64,939	68,215
1.6	♦ Africa		('000)	509	492	487	552	727
1.7	♦ Americas		('000)	2,887	3,123	3,065	3,132	3,501
1.8	♦ East Asia and the Pacific		('000)	1,176	1,345	1,531	1,850	2,305
1.9	♦ Europe		('000)	51,420	52,243	55,273	59,035	61,374
1.10	♦ Middle East		('000)	110	170	217	251	186
1.11	♦ South Asia		('000)	74	91	102	119	122
1.12	♦ Other not classified		('000)	1	..	..	..	..
1.13	* of which, nationals residing abroad		('000)	..	..	..	..	..
	Arrivals by main purpose	(1)						
1.14	Total		('000)	56,177	57,464	60,675	64,938	68,215
1.15	♦ Personal		('000)	52,062	53,490	56,604	60,625	63,236
1.16	* holidays, leisure and recreation		('000)	47,391	49,205	52,581	56,191	58,097
1.17	* other personal purposes		('000)	4,670	4,286	4,023	4,434	5,139
1.18	♦ Business and professional		('000)	4,115	3,974	4,071	4,313	4,979
	Arrivals by mode of transport	(1)						
1.19	Total		('000)	56,177	57,464	60,676	64,939	68,215
1.20	♦ Air		('000)	44,614	46,159	48,763	51,823	54,425
1.21	♦ Water		('000)	1,416	1,079	908	859	974
1.22	♦ Land		('000)	10,147	10,226	11,005	12,257	12,816
1.23	* railway		('000)	140	128	116	304	342
1.24	* road		('000)	10,007	10,099	10,889	11,953	12,474
1.25	* others		('000)	..	..	..	..	..
	Arrivals by form of organization of the trip							
1.26	Total		('000)	56,177	57,464	60,676	64,939	68,215
1.27	♦ Package tour		('000)	17,273	17,729	18,225	19,357	19,648
1.28	♦ Other forms		('000)	38,904	39,736	42,451	45,582	48,567
	Accommodation							
	Total							
1.29	♦ Guests	(2)	('000)	47,653	48,101	49,799	52,359	55,427
1.30	♦ Overnights	(2)	('000)	239,387	243,389	252,448	259,636	269,418
	Hotels and similar establishments							
1.31	♦ Guests	(3)	('000)	39,542	39,937	41,252	43,132	45,693
1.32	♦ Overnights	(3)	('000)	175,237	178,558	185,396	190,531	197,981
	Expenditure							
1.33	Total		US$ Mn	..	..	..	..	..
1.34	♦ Travel		US$ Mn	62,447	57,877	62,584	65,100	56,484
1.35	♦ Passenger transport		US$ Mn	..	..	..	..	..
	Indicators							
1.39	Average size of travel party		Persons	..	..	..	..	2.8
	Average length of stay							
1.40	Total		Days	9.22	8.92	8.94	8.87	8.78
1.41	♦ For all commercial accommodation services		Nights	8.26	8.11	8.10	8.05	7.95
1.42	* of which, "hotels and similar establishments"	(3)	Nights	6.86	6.77	6.84	6.81	6.74
1.43	♦ For non commercial accommodation services		Days	12.81	12.51	12.65	12.48	12.31
1.44	Average expenditure per day		US$	140.0	135.6	145.0	145.3	136.1
2.	**DOMESTIC TOURISM**							
	Data							
	Trips							
2.1	Total		('000)	347,695	372,811	398,423	462,761	372,265
2.2	♦ Overnight visitors (tourists)		('000)	147,408	148,369	144,527	139,615	150,589
2.3	♦ Same-day visitors (excursionists)		('000)	200,287	224,442	253,896	323,146	221,676
	Trips by main purpose							
2.4	Total		('000)	147,408	148,369	144,527	139,615	150,588
2.5	♦ Personal		('000)	133,648	137,080	135,382	132,206	144,837
2.6	* holidays, leisure and recreation		('000)	79,849	78,495	74,999	75,754	71,272
2.7	* other personal purposes		('000)	53,799	58,585	60,383	56,452	73,565
2.8	♦ Business and professional		('000)	13,760	11,289	9,146	7,409	5,751

SPAIN

Cod.	Basic data and indicators	Notes	Units	2011	2012	2013	2014	2015
	Trips by mode of transport							
2.9	Total		('000)	147,408	148,368	144,527	139,615	150,588
2.10	♦ Air		('000)	9,535	8,325	7,130	6,821	6,662
2.11	♦ Water		('000)	978	951	1,101	1,222	1,251
2.12	♦ Land		('000)	136,895	139,092	136,296	131,572	142,675
2.13	* railway		('000)	7,124	6,692	7,256	6,770	8,030
2.14	* road		('000)	128,955	132,085	128,647	124,437	134,224
2.15	* others		('000)	816	315	392	365	421
	Trips by form of organization							
2.16	Total		('000)	147,408	148,369	144,527	139,615	150,588
2.17	♦ Package tour		('000)	2,757	2,293	2,570	2,911	4,926
2.18	♦ Other forms		('000)	144,650	146,076	141,958	136,704	145,662
	Accommodation							
	Total							
2.19	♦ Guests	(2)	('000)	55,431	52,309	51,874	55,186	59,022
2.20	♦ Overnights	(2)	('000)	150,489	139,282	136,764	144,327	152,808
	Hotels and similar establishments							
2.21	♦ Guests	(3)	('000)	45,825	43,026	42,569	44,683	47,524
2.22	♦ Overnights	(3)	('000)	111,524	102,101	100,634	104,730	110,255
	Indicators							
2.23	Average size of travel party		Persons	..	..	..	..	2.3
	Average length of stay							
2.24	Total		Days	4.41	4.37	4.55	4.45	3.85
2.25	♦ For all commercial accommodation services	(3)	Nights	4.77	4.73	4.77	4.59	3.91
2.26	* of which, "hotels and similar establishments"		Nights	3.90	3.75	3.83	3.68	3.28
2.27	♦ For non commercial accommodation services		Days	4.22	4.20	4.46	4.39	3.83
2.28	Average expenditure per day		US$	47.0	41.1	41.3	42.2	49.7
3.	**OUTBOUND TOURISM**							
	Data							
	Departures							
3.1	Total		('000)	15,944	14,916	13,434	13,952	17,625
3.2	♦ Overnight visitors (tourists)		('000)	13,347	12,422	11,246	11,783	14,407
3.3	♦ Same-day visitors (excursionists)		('000)	2,597	2,494	2,188	2,169	3,218
	Expenditure							
3.4	Total		US$ Mn	..	..	..	..	..
3.5	♦ Travel		US$ Mn	17,373	15,401	16,435	17,969	17,759
3.6	♦ Passenger transport		US$ Mn	..	..	..	..	..
	Indicators							
3.10	Average length of stay		Days	8.88	8.90	9.38	9.25	8.60
3.11	Average expenditure per day		US$	109.0	95.6	97.2	95.7	107.8
4.	**TOURISM INDUSTRIES**							
	Data							
	Number of establishments							
4.1	Total		Units	547,404	554,860	557,403	559,472	571,873
4.2	♦ Accommodation for visitors		Units	113,292	121,121	127,863	135,366	144,491
4.3	* of which, "hotels and similar establishments"		Units	14,674	14,669	14,716	26,479	27,078
4.4	♦ Food and beverage serving activities		Units	276,586	274,826	271,267	265,366	264,636
4.5	♦ Passenger transportation		Units	65,905	65,726	64,919	63,838	62,912
4.6	♦ Travel agencies and other reservation services activities		Units	16,540	16,794	16,385	15,812	16,239
4.7	♦ Other tourism industries		Units	75,081	76,393	76,969	79,090	83,595
	Accommodation for visitors in hotels and similar establishments							
	Monetary data	(4)						
4.8	♦ Output		US$ Mn	16,882.3	14,768.6	15,036.1	15,740.1	..
4.9	♦ Intermediate consumption		US$ Mn	8,180.0	7,283.5	7,338.5	7,521.9	..
4.10	♦ Gross value added		US$ Mn	8,702.3	7,485.0	7,697.6	8,218.2	..
4.11	♦ Compensation of employees		US$ Mn	6,511.4	5,651.2	5,599.9	5,662.8	..
4.12	♦ Gross fixed capital formation		US$ Mn	1,300.6	1,088.5	1,030.6	1,133.6	..
	Non-monetary data	(3)						
4.13	♦ Number of establishments		Units	19,210	19,149	19,318	19,207	19,352
4.14	♦ Number of rooms		Units	903,441	902,624	906,289	904,946	910,091
4.15	♦ Number of bed-places		Units	1,833,726	1,838,958	1,874,896	1,862,329	1,879,369
	Indicators							
4.16	Occupancy rate / rooms		Percent	57.87	55.96	57.21	59.11	61.96
4.17	Occupancy rate / bed-places	(3)	Percent	53.55	52.05	53.02	54.71	56.92
4.18	Average length of stay	(3)	Nights	3.36	3.38	3.41	3.36	3.31
4.19	Available capacity (bed-places per 1000 inhabitants)		Units	39.26	39.43	40.36	40.26	40.75

SPAIN

Cod.	Basic data and indicators	Notes	Units	2011	2012	2013	2014	2015
	Travel agencies and other reservation service activities							
	Monetary data	(4)						
4.20	♦ Output		US$ Mn	3,458.2	3,248.7	3,205.0	3,427.1	..
4.21	♦ Intermediate consumption		US$ Mn	1,505.5	1,427.6	1,388.2	1,521.4	..
4.22	♦ Gross value added		US$ Mn	1,952.7	1,821.1	1,816.8	1,905.8	..
4.23	♦ Compensation of employees		US$ Mn	1,451.1	1,435.2	1,323.6	1,336.1	..
4.24	♦ Gross fixed capital formation		US$ Mn	86.5	63.1	45.0	46.5	..
	Non-monetary data							
	♦ Domestic trips							
4.25	* with package tour		Percent	1.9	1.5	1.8	2.1	3.3
4.26	* without package tour		Percent	98.1	98.5	98.2	97.9	96.7
	♦ Inbound trips							
4.27	* with package tour		Percent	30.7	30.9	30.0	29.8	28.8
4.28	* without package tour		Percent	69.2	69.1	70.0	70.2	71.2
	♦ Outbound trips							
4.29	* with package tour		Percent	12.9	11.4	11.7	11.6	16.1
4.30	* without package tour		Percent	87.1	88.6	88.3	88.4	83.9
5.	**EMPLOYMENT**							
	Data							
	Number of employees by tourism industries							
5.1	Total		('000)	2,160.9	2,077.0	2,083.5	2,203.0	2,322.3
5.2	♦ Accommodation services for visitors (hotels and similar establishments)		('000)	320.0	282.1	276.2	281.4	303.2
5.3	♦ Other accommodation services		('000)	40.7	38.3	37.0	40.4	41.1
5.4	♦ Food and beverage serving activities		('000)	1,040.3	1,016.5	1,019.4	1,082.0	1,160.8
5.5	♦ Passenger transportation		('000)	273.2	257.9	257.3	267.6	264.9
5.6	♦ Travel agencies and other reservation services activities		('000)	53.7	54.4	55.7	62.1	74.7
5.7	♦ Other tourism industries		('000)	433.0	427.8	437.9	469.6	477.6
	Number of jobs by status in employment							
5.8	Total		('000)	2,538.1	2,523.2	2,547.8	2,622.3	2,715.7
5.9	♦ Employees		('000)	2,069.5	2,059.3	2,069.3	2,113.8	2,197.8
5.10	♦ Self employed		('000)	468.6	463.9	478.5	508.5	517.9
	Indicators							
	Number of full-time equivalent jobs by status in employment							
5.11	Total		('000)	1,712.3	1,617.1	1,588.3	1,670.4	1,771.5
5.12	♦ Employees		('000)	1,301.8	1,219.0	1,177.6	1,228.0	1,317.5
5.13	* male		('000)	737.3	709.8	681.6	734.9	774.8
5.14	* female		('000)	564.5	509.2	496.0	493.0	542.7
5.15	♦ Self employed		('000)	410.5	398.1	410.8	442.4	454.0
5.16	* male		('000)	273.5	256.1	266.1	292.8	298.1
5.17	* female		('000)	136.9	142.0	144.7	149.6	155.9
6.	**COMPLEMENTARY INDICATORS**							
	Demand							
6.1	Gross travel propensity		Units	..	..	..	..	3.6
6.2	(1.2 inbound tourists + 2.2 domestic tourists) / population		Units	4.36	4.41	4.42	4.42	4.74
	Macroeconomic indicators related to international tourism							
6.3	Inbound tourism expenditure over GDP		Percent	4.2	4.3	4.5	4.6	4.7
6.4	Outbound tourism expenditure over GDP		Percent	1.2	1.1	1.2	1.3	1.5
6.5	Tourism balance (inbound minus outbound tourism expenditure) over GDP		Percent	3.0	3.2	3.3	3.3	3.2
6.6	Tourism openness (inbound plus outbound tourism expenditure) over GDP		Percent	5.4	5.4	5.7	5.9	6.2
6.7	Tourism coverage (inbound over outbound tourism expenditure)		Percent	359.4	375.8	380.8	362.3	318.1
6.8	Inbound tourism expenditure over exports of goods		Percent	20.8	20.1	20.1	20.5	20.3
6.9	Inbound tourism expenditure over exports of services		Percent	47.7	47.4	49.5	49.1	47.9
6.10	Inbound tourism expenditure over exports of goods and services		Percent	14.5	14.1	14.3	14.5	14.3
6.11	Inbound tourism expenditure over current account credits		Percent	12.0	11.8	12.1	12.2	12.0
6.12	Outbound tourism expenditure over imports of goods		Percent	4.8	4.7	5.0	5.2	5.9
6.13	Outbound tourism expenditure over imports of services		Percent	24.3	23.9	26.0	26.3	27.4
6.14	Outbound tourism expenditure over imports of goods and		Percent	4.0	3.9	4.2	4.3	4.8
6.15	Outbound tourism expenditure over current account debits		Percent	3.2	3.2	3.3	3.5	3.9

SRI LANKA

Cod.	Basic data and indicators	Notes	Units	2011	2012	2013	2014	2015
1.	**INBOUND TOURISM**							
	Data							
	Arrivals							
1.1	Total		('000)	976	1,133	1,415	1,665	1,993
1.2	♦ Overnight visitors (tourists)	(1)	('000)	856	1,006	1,275	1,527	1,798
1.3	♦ Same-day visitors (excursionists)		('000)	120	127	140	138	195
1.4	* of which, cruise passengers		('000)	..	..	..	..	..
	Arrivals by region	(1)						
1.5	Total		('000)	856	1,006	1,275	1,527	1,799
1.6	♦ Africa		('000)	3	5	8	12	13
1.7	♦ Americas		('000)	50	61	69	77	90
1.8	♦ East Asia and the Pacific		('000)	143	191	244	346	435
1.9	♦ Europe		('000)	372	453	556	641	711
1.10	♦ Middle East		('000)	48	47	69	78	88
1.11	♦ South Asia		('000)	240	249	329	373	463
1.12	♦ Other not classified		('000)	..	..	..	..	..
1.13	* of which, nationals residing abroad		('000)	..	..	..	..	..
	Arrivals by main purpose	(1)						
1.14	Total		('000)	856	1,006	1,274	1,527	1,798
1.15	♦ Personal		('000)	773	893	1,180	1,496	1,760
1.16	* holidays, leisure and recreation		('000)	688	748	915	1,046	1,210
1.17	* other personal purposes		('000)	85	145	265	450	550
1.18	♦ Business and professional		('000)	83	112	94	31	38
	Arrivals by mode of transport	(1)						
1.19	Total		('000)	856	1,006	1,274	1,527	1,798
1.20	♦ Air		('000)	854	1,002	1,248	1,501	1,773
1.21	♦ Water		('000)	2	3	26	27	25
1.22	♦ Land		('000)	..	..	..	..	..
1.23	* railway		('000)	..	..	..	..	..
1.24	* road		('000)	..	..	..	..	..
1.25	* others		('000)	..	..	..	..	..
	Accommodation							
	Total							
1.29	♦ Guests		('000)	..	..	..	..	..
1.30	♦ Overnights		('000)	8,560	10,056	10,909	15,119	18,164
	Hotels and similar establishments							
1.31	♦ Guests		('000)	..	..	..	..	..
1.32	♦ Overnights		('000)	7,259	7,410	9,698	11,579	13,294
	Expenditure							
1.33	Total		US$ Mn	1,421	1,756	2,506	3,278	3,978
1.34	♦ Travel		US$ Mn	830	1,039	1,715	2,431	2,981
1.35	♦ Passenger transport		US$ Mn	591	717	791	847	997
	Indicators							
1.39	Average size of travel party		Persons	..	..	..	..	..
	Average length of stay							
1.40	Total		Days	..	..	..	..	..
1.41	♦ For all commercial accommodation services		Nights	10.00	10.00	8.60	9.90	10.10
1.42	* of which, "hotels and similar establishments"		Nights	..	..	..	..	..
1.43	♦ For non commercial accommodation services		Days	..	..	..	..	..
1.44	Average expenditure per day		US$	98.0	103.0	156.5	160.8	164.1
2.	**DOMESTIC TOURISM**							
	Data							
	Accommodation							
	Hotels and similar establishments							
2.21	♦ Guests		('000)	..	..	..	..	..
2.22	♦ Overnights		('000)	2,182	2,139	2,079	2,585	2,225
3.	**OUTBOUND TOURISM**							
	Data							
	Departures							
3.1	Total		('000)	..	..	..	..	..
3.2	♦ Overnight visitors (tourists)		('000)	1,239	1,269	1,262	1,311	1,356
3.3	♦ Same-day visitors (excursionists)		('000)	..	..	..	..	..
	Expenditure							
3.4	Total		US$ Mn	926	1,219	1,808	1,922	2,152
3.5	♦ Travel		US$ Mn	501	710	1,188	1,263	1,420
3.6	♦ Passenger transport		US$ Mn	425	509	620	659	732

SRI LANKA

Cod.	Basic data and indicators	Notes	Units	2011	2012	2013	2014	2015
4.	**TOURISM INDUSTRIES**							
	Data							
	Number of establishments							
4.1	Total		Units	..	..	..	..	..
4.2	♦ Accommodation for visitors		Units	..	..	..	..	..
4.3	* of which, "hotels and similar establishments"	(2)	Units	906	1,194	1,325	1,599	1,763
4.4	♦ Food and beverage serving activities		Units	..	..	..	..	..
4.5	♦ Passenger transportation		Units	..	..	..	..	..
4.6	♦ Travel agencies and other reservation services activities		Units	..	..	..	..	..
4.7	♦ Other tourism industries		Units	..	..	..	..	..
	Accommodation for visitors in hotels and similar establishments							
	Non-monetary data	(2)						
4.13	♦ Number of establishments		Units	906	1,194	1,325	1,599	1,763
4.14	♦ Number of rooms		Units	20,794	23,415	25,168	28,426	30,078
4.15	♦ Number of bed-places		Units	40,445	43,746	50,945	55,223	58,581
	Indicators							
4.16	Occupancy rate / rooms		Percent	77.10	71.20	71.70	74.30	74.50
4.17	Occupancy rate / bed-places		Percent	..	..	..	..	..
4.18	Average length of stay		Nights	10.00	10.00	8.60	9.90	10.10
4.19	Available capacity (bed-places per 1000 inhabitants)		Units	1.93	2.07	2.39	2.58	2.81
5.	**EMPLOYMENT**							
	Data							
	Number of employees by tourism industries							
5.1	Total		('000)	57.8	67.8	112.5	129.8	135.9
5.2	♦ Accommodation services for visitors (hotels and similar establishments)	(3)	('000)	39.9	47.7	90.4	105.0	109.6
5.3	♦ Other accommodation services		('000)	..	..	..	..	..
5.4	♦ Food and beverage serving activities		('000)	..	..	..	..	..
5.5	♦ Passenger transportation		('000)	5.7	5.7	5.9	5.9	6.4
5.6	♦ Travel agencies and other reservation services activities		('000)	4.2	6.4	7.0	9.1	9.5
5.7	♦ Other tourism industries		('000)	8.0	8.0	9.2	9.8	10.5
6.	**COMPLEMENTARY INDICATORS**							
	Demand							
6.1	Gross travel propensity		Units	..	..	..	..	..
6.2	(1.2 inbound tourists) / population		Units	0.04	0.05	0.06	0.07	0.09
	Macroeconomic indicators related to international tourism							
6.3	Inbound tourism expenditure over GDP		Percent	2.4	3.0	3.7	4.4	..
6.4	Outbound tourism expenditure over GDP		Percent	1.6	2.1	2.7	2.6	..
6.5	Tourism balance (inbound minus outbound tourism expenditure) over GDP		Percent	0.8	0.9	1.0	1.8	
6.6	Tourism openness (inbound plus outbound tourism expenditure) over GDP		Percent	4.0	5.1	6.4	7.0	
6.7	Tourism coverage (inbound over outbound tourism expenditure)		Percent	153.5	144.1	138.6	170.6	184.9
6.8	Inbound tourism expenditure over exports of goods		Percent	13.5	18.0	24.1	29.5	37.9
6.9	Inbound tourism expenditure over exports of services		Percent	46.1	46.2	53.5	58.5	62.2
6.10	Inbound tourism expenditure over exports of goods and services		Percent	10.4	12.9	16.6	19.6	23.5
6.11	Inbound tourism expenditure over current account credits		Percent	7.4	8.9	11.6	13.7	16.6
6.12	Outbound tourism expenditure over imports of goods		Percent	5.1	6.4	10.0	9.9	11.4
6.13	Outbound tourism expenditure over imports of services		Percent	23.1	48.0	51.6	51.6	52.9
6.14	Outbound tourism expenditure over imports of goods and		Percent	4.2	5.6	8.4	8.3	9.4
6.15	Outbound tourism expenditure over current account debits		Percent	4.0	5.4	8.1	8.0	9.0

STATE OF PALESTINE

Cod.	Basic data and indicators	Notes	Units	2011	2012	2013	2014	2015
1.	**INBOUND TOURISM**							
	Data							
	Arrivals							
1.1	Total		('000)	2,730	3,051	3,206	3,083	2,339
1.2	♦ Overnight visitors (tourists)	(1)	('000)	449	490	545	556	432
1.3	♦ Same-day visitors (excursionists)		('000)	2,281	2,561	2,661	2,527	1,907
1.4	* of which, cruise passengers		('000)	..	..	..	..	..
	Arrivals by region	(1)						
1.5	Total		('000)	449	490	545	556	432
1.6	♦ Africa		('000)	28	24	33	27	18
1.7	♦ Americas		('000)	57	54	68	74	54
1.8	♦ East Asia and the Pacific		('000)	58	52	64	64	71
1.9	♦ Europe		('000)	301	353	373	385	279
1.10	♦ Middle East		('000)	5	7	7	6	10
1.11	♦ South Asia		('000)	..	..	..	..	..
1.12	♦ Other not classified		('000)	..	..	..	..	..
1.13	* of which, nationals residing abroad		('000)	..	..	..	..	..
	Accommodation							
	Hotels and similar establishments							
1.31	♦ Guests		('000)	449	490	545	556	432
1.32	♦ Overnights		('000)	1,113	1,163	1,326	1,389	1,255
	Expenditure							
1.33	Total		US$ Mn	..	..	..	..	..
1.34	♦ Travel	(2)	US$ Mn	615	469	524	543	478
1.35	♦ Passenger transport		US$ Mn	..	..	..	..	..
	Indicators							
1.39	Average size of travel party		Persons	..	..	..	..	..
	Average length of stay							
1.40	Total		Days	..	..	..	..	..
1.41	♦ For all commercial accommodation services		Nights	2.30	2.50	2.43	2.52	2.93
1.42	* of which, "hotels and similar establishments"		Nights	..	..	..	..	..
1.43	♦ For non commercial accommodation services		Days	..	..	..	..	..
1.44	Average expenditure per day		US$	..	..	..	..	..
2.	**DOMESTIC TOURISM**							
	Data							
	Accommodation							
	Hotels and similar establishments							
2.21	♦ Guests		('000)	62	85	55	54	52
2.22	♦ Overnights		('000)	142	174	142	148	166
	Indicators							
2.23	Average size of travel party		Persons	..	..	..	..	..
	Average length of stay							
2.24	Total		Days	..	..	..	..	..
2.25	♦ For all commercial accommodation services		Nights	2.30	2.04	2.58	2.72	3.16
2.26	* of which, "hotels and similar establishments"		Nights	..	..	..	..	..
2.27	♦ For non commercial accommodation services		Days	..	..	..	..	..
2.28	Average expenditure per day		US$	..	..	..	..	..
3.	**OUTBOUND TOURISM**							
	Data							
	Expenditure	(2)						
3.4	Total		US$ Mn	603	647	643	586	438
3.5	♦ Travel		US$ Mn	595	643	638	578	431
3.6	♦ Passenger transport		US$ Mn	8	4	5	8	7
	Expenditure by main purpose of the trip	(2)						
3.7	Total		US$ Mn	595	643	637	578	431
3.8	♦ Personal		US$ Mn	510	524	479	345	201
3.9	♦ Business and professional		US$ Mn	85	119	158	233	229
4.	**TOURISM INDUSTRIES**							
	Data							
	Number of establishments							
4.1	Total		Units	5,524	6,692	7,752	7,057	..
4.2	♦ Accommodation for visitors		Units	..	..	..	..	..
4.3	* of which, "hotels and similar establishments"		Units	103	98	113	109	112

371

STATE OF PALESTINE

Cod.	Basic data and indicators	Notes	Units	2011	2012	2013	2014	2015
4.4	♦ Food and beverage serving activities		Units	3,241	4,455	4,827	4,301	..
4.5	♦ Passenger transportation		Units	21	54	23	24	..
4.6	♦ Travel agencies and other reservation services activities		Units	369	277	380	251	..
4.7	♦ Other tourism industries		Units	1,790	1,808	2,409	2,372	..
	Accommodation for visitors in hotels and similar establishments							
	Monetary data							
4.8	♦ Output		US$ Mn	90.1	130.6	96.9	132.0	..
4.9	♦ Intermediate consumption		US$ Mn	37.6	24.3	30.9	39.0	..
4.10	♦ Gross value added		US$ Mn	52.5	106.2	65.9	93.0	..
4.11	♦ Compensation of employees		US$ Mn	26.7	30.3	29.5	35.9	..
4.12	♦ Gross fixed capital formation		US$ Mn	..	..	..	..	..
	Non-monetary data							
4.13	♦ Number of establishments		Units	103	98	113	109	112
4.14	♦ Number of rooms		Units	5,833	5,377	6,072	6,691	6,792
4.15	♦ Number of bed-places		Units	12,759	12,286	13,902	14,857	14,965
	Indicators							
4.16	Occupancy rate / rooms		Percent	26.10	29.10	24.76	25.23	22.54
4.17	Occupancy rate / bed-places		Percent	29.40	30.70	29.88	28.52	25.84
4.18	Average length of stay		Nights	2.50	2.30	2.44	2.52	2.93
4.19	Available capacity (bed-places per 1000 inhabitants)		Units	3.05	2.86	3.15	3.27	3.21
	Travel agencies and other reservation service activities							
	Monetary data							
4.20	♦ Output		US$ Mn	92.2	19.2	27.6	47.0	..
4.21	♦ Intermediate consumption		US$ Mn	5.9	3.1	6.1	3.7	..
4.22	♦ Gross value added		US$ Mn	86.4	16.1	21.5	43.3	..
4.23	♦ Compensation of employees		US$ Mn	5.8	8.2	4.8	4.3	..
4.24	♦ Gross fixed capital formation		US$ Mn	..	..	..	..	..
5.	**EMPLOYMENT**							
	Data							
	Number of employees by tourism industries							
5.1	Total		('000)	16.0	23.1	21.2	26.5	..
5.2	♦ Accommodation services for visitors (hotels and similar establishments)		('000)	2.7	3.1	2.9	3.3	..
5.3	♦ Other accommodation services		('000)	..	..	..	..	..
5.4	♦ Food and beverage serving activities		('000)	8.8	13.5	13.6	16.3	..
5.5	♦ Passenger transportation		('000)	0.9	0.6	0.3	0.4	..
5.6	♦ Travel agencies and other reservation services activities		('000)	0.8	0.8	0.9	0.8	..
5.7	♦ Other tourism industries		('000)	2.8	5.1	3.5	5.7	..
	Number of jobs by status in employment							
5.8	Total		('000)	16.0	23.0	21.2	26.5	..
5.9	♦ Employees		('000)	13.0	14.4	13.5	18.3	..
5.10	♦ Self employed		('000)	3.0	8.6	7.7	8.2	..
	Indicators							
	Number of full-time equivalent jobs by status in employment							
5.11	Total		('000)	16.0	23.0	..	..	..
5.12	♦ Employees		('000)	13.0	14.4	..	..	..
5.13	* male		('000)	12.1	13.1	..	..	..
5.14	* female		('000)	0.9	1.3	..	..	..
5.15	♦ Self employed		('000)	3.0	8.6	..	..	..
5.16	* male		('000)	3.0	8.4	..	..	..
5.17	* female		('000)	0.0	0.2	..	..	..
6.	**COMPLEMENTARY INDICATORS**							
	Demand							
6.1	Gross travel propensity		Units	..	..	..	..	..
6.2	(1.2 inbound tourists) / population		Units	0.11	0.11	0.12	0.12	0.09
	Macroeconomic indicators related to international tourism							
6.3	Inbound tourism expenditure over GDP		Percent	..	..	..	..	..
6.4	Outbound tourism expenditure over GDP		Percent	..	..	..	..	..
6.5	Tourism balance (inbound minus outbound tourism expenditure) over GDP		Percent	..	..	..	..	
6.6	Tourism openness (inbound plus outbound tourism expenditure) over GDP		Percent	..	..	..	..	

STATE OF PALESTINE

Cod.	Basic data and indicators	Notes	Units	2011	2012	2013	2014	2015
6.7	Tourism coverage (inbound over outbound tourism expenditure)		Percent	102.0	72.5	81.5	92.7	109.1
6.8	Inbound tourism expenditure over exports of goods		Percent	58.5	41.4	46.2	43.2	..
6.9	Inbound tourism expenditure over exports of services		Percent	82.2	63.6	55.8	52.1	..
6.10	Inbound tourism expenditure over exports of goods and services		Percent	34.2	25.1	25.3	23.6	..
6.11	Inbound tourism expenditure over current account credits		Percent	14.3	9.1	10.1	7.8	..
6.12	Outbound tourism expenditure over imports of goods		Percent	12.5	12.3	11.1	8.8	..
6.13	Outbound tourism expenditure over imports of services		Percent	67.7	62.9	65.1	51.9	..
6.14	Outbound tourism expenditure over imports of goods and		Percent	10.5	10.3	9.4	7.5	..
6.15	Outbound tourism expenditure over current account debits		Percent	8.5	8.3	7.4	6.0	..

SUDAN

Cod.	Basic data and indicators	Notes	Units	2011	2012	2013	2014	2015
1.	**INBOUND TOURISM**							
	Data							
	Arrivals							
1.1	Total		('000)	..	..	..	..	..
1.2	♦ Overnight visitors (tourists)	(1)	('000)	536	575	591	684	741
1.3	♦ Same-day visitors (excursionists)		('000)	..	..	..	..	
1.4	* of which, cruise passengers		('000)	..	..	..	..	
	Arrivals by region	(1)						
1.5	Total		('000)	536	575	591	684	741
1.6	♦ Africa		('000)	54	104	108	120	142
1.7	♦ Americas		('000)	21	24	26	38	43
1.8	♦ East Asia and the Pacific		('000)	32	36	39	45	48
1.9	♦ Europe		('000)	80	51	51	80	82
1.10	♦ Middle East		('000)	295	297	302	326	347
1.11	♦ South Asia		('000)	43	47	49	54	59
1.12	♦ Other not classified		('000)	11	16	16	20	21
1.13	* of which, nationals residing abroad		('000)	..	..	..	..	
	Arrivals by main purpose	(1)						
1.14	Total		('000)	536	575	591	684	
1.15	♦ Personal		('000)	429	443	455	506	
1.16	* holidays, leisure and recreation		('000)	429	379	390	431	
1.17	* other personal purposes		('000)	..	63	65	75	
1.18	♦ Business and professional		('000)	107	132	136	178	
	Arrivals by mode of transport	(1)						
1.19	Total		('000)	536	575	591	684	
1.20	♦ Air		('000)	311	402	414	479	
1.21	♦ Water		('000)	214	115	118	191	
1.22	♦ Land		('000)	11	58	59	14	
1.23	* railway		('000)	..	..	..	..	
1.24	* road		('000)	11	58	59	14	
1.25	* others		('000)	..	..	..	..	
	Expenditure							
1.33	Total		US$ Mn	..	..	..	..	
1.34	♦ Travel		US$ Mn	179	772	773	967	949
1.35	♦ Passenger transport		US$ Mn	..	..	..	..	
	Expenditure by main purpose of the trip							
1.36	Total		US$ Mn	..	..	..	..	949
1.37	♦ Personal		US$ Mn	..	..	..	..	9
1.38	♦ Business and professional		US$ Mn	..	..	..	..	940
	Indicators							
1.39	Average size of travel party		Persons	..	..	..	..	
	Average length of stay							
1.40	Total		Days	..	..	..	..	
1.41	♦ For all commercial accommodation services		Nights	8.00	..	..	..	
1.42	* of which, "hotels and similar establishments"		Nights	..	..	..	..	
1.43	♦ For non commercial accommodation services		Days	..	..	..	..	
1.44	Average expenditure per day		US$	..	..	..	..	
3.	**OUTBOUND TOURISM**							
	Data							
	Expenditure							
3.4	Total		US$ Mn	..	..	..	..	
3.5	♦ Travel		US$ Mn	937	699	460	439	195
3.6	♦ Passenger transport		US$ Mn	..	..	..	..	
	Expenditure by main purpose of the trip							
3.7	Total		US$ Mn	..	..	..	..	195
3.8	♦ Personal		US$ Mn	..	..	..	..	41
3.9	♦ Business and professional		US$ Mn	..	..	..	..	154
4.	**TOURISM INDUSTRIES**							
	Data							
	Number of establishments							
4.1	Total		Units	..	..	..	..	
4.2	♦ Accommodation for visitors		Units	..	..	..	..	
4.3	* of which, "hotels and similar establishments"		Units	216	216	234	256	289
4.4	♦ Food and beverage serving activities		Units	..	..	..	..	
4.5	♦ Passenger transportation		Units	..	..	..	..	
4.6	♦ Travel agencies and other reservation services activities		Units	..	..	..	..	
4.7	♦ Other tourism industries		Units	..	..	..	..	

SUDAN

Cod.	Basic data and indicators	Notes	Units	2011	2012	2013	2014	2015
	Accommodation for visitors in hotels and similar establishments							
	Non-monetary data							
4.13	♦ Number of establishments		Units	216	216	234	256	289
4.14	♦ Number of rooms		Units	..	..	..	..	..
4.15	♦ Number of bed-places		Units	10,985	11,314	16,705	17,705	..
	Indicators							
4.16	Occupancy rate / rooms		Percent	..	..	..	..	..
4.17	Occupancy rate / bed-places		Percent	..	..	..	..	..
4.18	Average length of stay		Nights	8.00	..	..	..	..
4.19	Available capacity (bed-places per 1000 inhabitants)		Units	0.30	0.30	0.43	0.45	..
6.	**COMPLEMENTARY INDICATORS**							
	Demand							
6.1	Gross travel propensity		Units	..	..	..	..	..
6.2	(1.2 inbound tourists) / population		Units	0.01	0.02	0.02	0.02	0.02
	Macroeconomic indicators related to international tourism							
6.3	Inbound tourism expenditure over GDP		Percent	0.3	1.1	1.2	..	..
6.4	Outbound tourism expenditure over GDP		Percent	1.3	1.0	0.7	..	..
6.5	Tourism balance (inbound minus outbound tourism expenditure) over GDP		Percent	-1.0	0.1	0.5	..	..
6.6	Tourism openness (inbound plus outbound tourism expenditure) over GDP		Percent	1.6	2.1	1.9	..	..
6.7	Tourism coverage (inbound over outbound tourism expenditure)		Percent	19.1	110.4	168.0	220.3	486.7
6.8	Inbound tourism expenditure over exports of goods		Percent	1.8	19.0	16.1	21.7	29.9
6.9	Inbound tourism expenditure over exports of services		Percent	21.5	72.9	61.4	61.7	53.7
6.10	Inbound tourism expenditure over exports of goods and services		Percent	1.6	15.1	12.8	16.1	19.2
6.11	Inbound tourism expenditure over current account credits		Percent	1.4	11.6	9.4	12.0	14.7
6.12	Outbound tourism expenditure over imports of goods		Percent	11.5	8.6	5.3	5.4	2.3
6.13	Outbound tourism expenditure over imports of services		Percent	32.3	33.1	22.7	21.2	11.0
6.14	Outbound tourism expenditure over imports of goods and		Percent	8.5	6.8	4.3	4.3	1.9
6.15	Outbound tourism expenditure over current account debits		Percent	7.8	6.4	4.1	4.1	1.8

SURINAME

Cod.	Basic data and indicators	Notes	Units	2011	2012	2013	2014	2015
1.	**INBOUND TOURISM**							
	Data							
	Arrivals							
1.1	Total		('000)	221	240	250	253	229
1.2	♦ Overnight visitors (tourists)		('000)	220	240	249	252	228
1.3	♦ Same-day visitors (excursionists)		('000)	0.3	0.3	0.7	0.8	0.8
1.4	* of which, cruise passengers		('000)	..	..	..	..	..
	Arrivals by region							
1.5	Total		('000)	220	240	249	252	228
1.6	♦ Africa		('000)	0.3	0.5	0.3	0.3	0.6
1.7	♦ Americas		('000)	104	124	136	130	117
1.8	♦ East Asia and the Pacific		('000)	4	5	5	6	5
1.9	♦ Europe		('000)	108	108	105	113	100
1.10	♦ Middle East		('000)	..	..	..	..	..
1.11	♦ South Asia		('000)	0.8	0.7	0.8	1.0	0.7
1.12	♦ Other not classified		('000)	3	3	2	2	5
1.13	* of which, nationals residing abroad		('000)	..	..	..	..	..
	Arrivals by main purpose							
1.14	Total		('000)	220	240	249	252	228
1.15	♦ Personal		('000)	197	217	224	229	209
1.16	* holidays, leisure and recreation		('000)	105	117	119	129	126
1.17	* other personal purposes		('000)	92	100	105	100	83
1.18	♦ Business and professional		('000)	23	23	25	23	19
	Arrivals by mode of transport							
1.19	Total		('000)	220	240	249	252	228
1.20	♦ Air		('000)	150	155	149	154	140
1.21	♦ Water		('000)	70	85	100	98	87
1.22	♦ Land		('000)	..	..	..	..	..
1.23	* railway		('000)	..	..	..	..	..
1.24	* road		('000)	..	..	..	..	..
1.25	* others		('000)	..	..	..	..	..
	Accommodation							
	Hotels and similar establishments							
1.31	♦ Guests		('000)	88	106	113	99	83
1.32	♦ Overnights		('000)	..	..	..	..	..
	Expenditure							
1.33	Total		US$ Mn	69	79	92	103	99
1.34	♦ Travel		US$ Mn	61	71	84	95	88
1.35	♦ Passenger transport		US$ Mn	8	8	8	8	11
	Expenditure by main purpose of the trip							
1.36	Total		US$ Mn	61	71	84	95	88
1.37	♦ Personal		US$ Mn	55	63	76	86	80
1.38	♦ Business and professional		US$ Mn	6	8	8	9	8
3.	**OUTBOUND TOURISM**							
	Data							
	Expenditure							
3.4	Total		US$ Mn	49	58	75	90	128
3.5	♦ Travel		US$ Mn	42	51	70	87	116
3.6	♦ Passenger transport		US$ Mn	7	7	5	3	12
	Expenditure by main purpose of the trip							
3.7	Total		US$ Mn	42	51	70	87	116
3.8	♦ Personal		US$ Mn	37	38	55	71	102
3.9	♦ Business and professional		US$ Mn	5	13	15	16	14
4.	**TOURISM INDUSTRIES**							
	Data							
	Accommodation for visitors in hotels and similar establishments							
	Non-monetary data							
4.13	♦ Number of establishments		Units	79	..	..	..	..
4.14	♦ Number of rooms		Units	1,229	..	..	..	..
4.15	♦ Number of bed-places		Units	1,913	..	..	..	..
	Indicators							
4.16	Occupancy rate / rooms		Percent	..	..	..	..	..
4.17	Occupancy rate / bed-places		Percent	..	..	..	..	..
4.18	Average length of stay		Nights	21.00	21.75	..	..	..
4.19	Available capacity (bed-places per 1000 inhabitants)		Units	3.65	..	..	..	..

SURINAME

Cod.	Basic data and indicators	Notes	Units	2011	2012	2013	2014	2015
6.	**COMPLEMENTARY INDICATORS**							
	Demand							
6.1	Gross travel propensity		Units	..	..	..	..	..
6.2	(1.2 inbound tourists) / population		Units	0.42	0.45	0.47	0.47	0.42
	Macroeconomic indicators related to international tourism							
6.3	Inbound tourism expenditure over GDP		Percent	..	..	..	..	..
6.4	Outbound tourism expenditure over GDP		Percent	..	..	..	..	..
6.5	Tourism balance (inbound minus outbound tourism expenditure) over GDP		Percent	..	..	..	..	..
6.6	Tourism openness (inbound plus outbound tourism expenditure) over GDP		Percent	..	..	..	..	..
6.7	Tourism coverage (inbound over outbound tourism expenditure)		Percent	140.8	136.2	122.7	114.4	77.3
6.8	Inbound tourism expenditure over exports of goods		Percent	2.6	2.9	3.8	4.8	5.9
6.9	Inbound tourism expenditure over exports of services		Percent	34.4	46.1	53.4	50.8	55.8
6.10	Inbound tourism expenditure over exports of goods and services		Percent	2.4	2.8	3.6	4.4	5.4
6.11	Inbound tourism expenditure over current account credits		Percent	2.3	2.6	3.3	4.1	5.0
6.12	Outbound tourism expenditure over imports of goods		Percent	2.9	2.9	3.5	4.6	6.5
6.13	Outbound tourism expenditure over imports of services		Percent	8.7	9.4	12.6	11.2	17.9
6.14	Outbound tourism expenditure over imports of goods and		Percent	2.2	2.2	2.8	3.3	4.8
6.15	Outbound tourism expenditure over current account debits		Percent	2.1	2.2	2.6	3.1	4.6

SWAZILAND

Cod.	Basic data and indicators	Notes	Units	2011	2012	2013	2014	2015
1.	**INBOUND TOURISM**							
	Data							
	Arrivals							
1.1	Total		('000)	1,328	1,278	1,299	1,325	1,256
1.2	♦ Overnight visitors (tourists)		('000)	879	888	968	939	873
1.3	♦ Same-day visitors (excursionists)		('000)	449	390	331	386	383
1.4	* of which, cruise passengers		('000)	..	..	..	..	..
	Arrivals by region							
1.5	Total		('000)	1,328	1,279	1,299	1,325	1,256
1.6	♦ Africa		('000)	1,225	1,165	1,170	1,178	1,105
1.7	♦ Americas		('000)	19	20	21	23	23
1.8	♦ East Asia and the Pacific		('000)	10	11	12	13	13
1.9	♦ Europe		('000)	67	74	87	101	105
1.10	♦ Middle East		('000)	..	..	..	..	..
1.11	♦ South Asia		('000)	7	8	9	10	10
1.12	♦ Other not classified		('000)	..	..	..	..	..
1.13	* of which, nationals residing abroad		('000)	..	..	..	..	..
	Arrivals by main purpose							
1.14	Total		('000)	1,328	1,279	1,299	1,325	1,256
1.15	♦ Personal		('000)	1,193	1,151	1,169	1,170	1,047
1.16	* holidays, leisure and recreation		('000)	675	678	761	709	551
1.17	* other personal purposes		('000)	518	473	408	461	496
1.18	♦ Business and professional		('000)	135	128	130	155	209
	Arrivals by mode of transport							
1.19	Total		('000)	1,328	1,279	1,299	1,325	1,256
1.20	♦ Air		('000)	22	23	22	16	20
1.21	♦ Water		('000)	..	..	..	..	..
1.22	♦ Land		('000)	1,306	1,256	1,277	1,308	1,236
1.23	* railway		('000)	..	..	..	..	..
1.24	* road		('000)	1,306	1,256	1,277	1,308	1,236
1.25	* others		('000)	..	..	..	..	..
	Arrivals by form of organization of the trip							
1.26	Total		('000)	1,328	1,279	1,299	1,325	1,256
1.27	♦ Package tour		('000)	69	74	147	78	75
1.28	♦ Other forms		('000)	1,259	1,205	1,152	1,247	1,181
	Accommodation							
	Hotels and similar establishments							
1.31	♦ Guests		('000)	308	305	303	307	296
1.32	♦ Overnights		('000)	..	..	..	..	..
	Expenditure							
1.33	Total		US$ Mn	21.3	30.3	13.3	16.1	14.4
1.34	♦ Travel		US$ Mn	21.0	30.0	13.0	15.0	14.0
1.35	♦ Passenger transport		US$ Mn	0.3	0.3	0.3	1.1	0.4
	Expenditure by main purpose of the trip							
1.36	Total		US$ Mn	21	30	13	15	14
1.37	♦ Personal		US$ Mn	13	13	8	8	7
1.38	♦ Business and professional		US$ Mn	8	17	5	7	7
	Indicators							
1.39	Average size of travel party		Persons	..	..	..	..	..
	Average length of stay							
1.40	Total		Days	2.61	2.37	2.80	3.10	3.42
1.41	♦ For all commercial accommodation services		Nights	0.90	1.27	0.91	0.92	0.88
1.42	* of which, "hotels and similar establishments"		Nights	..	..	..	..	..
1.43	♦ For non commercial accommodation services		Days	..	..	..	..	..
1.44	Average expenditure per day		US$	36.0	33.2	70.4	63.4	54.0
2.	**DOMESTIC TOURISM**							
	Data							
	Trips							
2.1	Total		('000)	180	185	218	222	234
2.2	♦ Overnight visitors (tourists)		('000)	95	102	108	111	115
2.3	♦ Same-day visitors (excursionists)		('000)	85	83	110	111	119
	Accommodation							
	Hotels and similar establishments							
2.21	♦ Guests		('000)	95	102	108	110	115
2.22	♦ Overnights		('000)	..	..	..	..	..
	Indicators							
2.23	Average size of travel party		Persons	..	..	..	..	..
	Average length of stay							
2.24	Total		Days	..	..	..	..	..
2.25	♦ For all commercial accommodation services		Nights	1.00	1.27	0.91	0.92	0.88
2.26	* of which, "hotels and similar establishments"		Nights	..	..	..	..	..

SWAZILAND

Cod.	Basic data and indicators	Notes	Units	2011	2012	2013	2014	2015
2.27	♦ For non commercial accommodation services		Days	..	..	..	..	..
2.28	Average expenditure per day		US$	..	..	..	..	..
3.	**OUTBOUND TOURISM**							
	Data							
	Departures							
3.1	Total		('000)	..	..	..	..	..
3.2	♦ Overnight visitors (tourists)		('000)	1,264	1,403	1,573	1,657	1,713
3.3	♦ Same-day visitors (excursionists)		('000)	..	..	..	..	..
	Expenditure							
3.4	Total		US$ Mn	78	91	96	105	105
3.5	♦ Travel		US$ Mn	69	72	76	89	77
3.6	♦ Passenger transport		US$ Mn	9	19	20	16	28
	Expenditure by main purpose of the trip							
3.7	Total		US$ Mn	69	71	76	89	77
3.8	♦ Personal		US$ Mn	58	60	63	76	67
3.9	♦ Business and professional		US$ Mn	11	11	13	13	10
4.	**TOURISM INDUSTRIES**							
	Data							
	Number of establishments							
4.1	Total		Units	..	..	..	..	..
4.2	♦ Accommodation for visitors		Units	..	..	..	..	..
4.3	* of which, "hotels and similar establishments"		Units	141	139	138	137	138
4.4	♦ Food and beverage serving activities		Units	..	..	..	..	..
4.5	♦ Passenger transportation		Units	..	..	..	..	..
4.6	♦ Travel agencies and other reservation services activities		Units	..	..	..	..	..
4.7	♦ Other tourism industries		Units	..	..	..	..	..
	Accommodation for visitors in hotels and similar establishments							
	Monetary data							
4.8	♦ Output		US$ Mn	35.5	33.8	35.4	40.0	46.2
4.9	♦ Intermediate consumption		US$ Mn	19.3	19.4	20.9	24.2	24.1
4.10	♦ Gross value added		US$ Mn	16.2	14.4	14.4	15.8	22.1
4.11	♦ Compensation of employees		US$ Mn	7.5	7.1	7.5	8.5	9.8
4.12	♦ Gross fixed capital formation		US$ Mn	..	..	..	..	..
	Non-monetary data							
4.13	♦ Number of establishments		Units	141	139	138	137	138
4.14	♦ Number of rooms		Units	2,571	2,326	2,650	2,678	2,556
4.15	♦ Number of bed-places		Units	5,364	5,441	5,382	5,439	5,079
	Indicators							
4.16	Occupancy rate / rooms		Percent	45.34	54.27	46.77	44.69	43.41
4.17	Occupancy rate / bed-places		Percent	34.41	37.51	35.20	36.21	34.46
4.18	Average length of stay		Nights	0.90	1.27	0.91	0.92	0.88
4.19	Available capacity (bed-places per 1000 inhabitants)		Units	4.42	4.42	4.30	4.29	3.95
6.	**COMPLEMENTARY INDICATORS**							
	Demand							
6.1	Gross travel propensity		Units	..	..	..	..	..
6.2	(1.2 inbound tourists + 2.2 domestic tourists) / population		Units	0.80	0.80	0.86	0.83	0.77
	Macroeconomic indicators related to international tourism							
6.3	Inbound tourism expenditure over GDP		Percent	..	..	..	..	..
6.4	Outbound tourism expenditure over GDP		Percent	..	..	..	..	..
6.5	Tourism balance (inbound minus outbound tourism expenditure) over GDP		Percent	..	..	..	..	..
6.6	Tourism openness (inbound plus outbound tourism expenditure) over GDP		Percent	..	..	..	..	..
6.7	Tourism coverage (inbound over outbound tourism expenditure)		Percent	27.3	33.3	13.9	15.3	13.7
6.8	Inbound tourism expenditure over exports of goods		Percent	1.1	1.6	0.7	0.9	..
6.9	Inbound tourism expenditure over exports of services		Percent	7.1	12.5	5.7	5.5	..
6.10	Inbound tourism expenditure over exports of goods and services		Percent	1.0	1.4	0.6	0.8	..
6.11	Inbound tourism expenditure over current account credits		Percent	0.7	0.9	0.4	0.5	..
6.12	Outbound tourism expenditure over imports of goods		Percent	4.0	4.9	5.7	6.2	..
6.13	Outbound tourism expenditure over imports of services		Percent	8.9	11.0	13.7	16.2	..
6.14	Outbound tourism expenditure over imports of goods and		Percent	2.8	3.4	4.0	4.5	..
6.15	Outbound tourism expenditure over current account debits		Percent	2.5	3.1	3.5	3.9	..

SWEDEN

Cod.	Basic data and indicators	Notes	Units	2011	2012	2013	2014	2015
1.	**INBOUND TOURISM**							
	Data							
	Arrivals	(1)						
1.1	Total		('000)	19,405	20,011	18,803	19,945	..
1.2	♦ Overnight visitors (tourists)		('000)	11,567	12,372	10,980	10,522	..
1.3	♦ Same-day visitors (excursionists)		('000)	7,838	7,639	7,823	9,423	..
1.4	* of which, cruise passengers		('000)	223	335	443	467	..
	Arrivals by region	(1)						
1.5	Total		('000)	19,405	20,011	18,803	19,945	..
1.6	♦ Africa		('000)	41	35	70	33	..
1.7	♦ Americas		('000)	671	652	724	686	..
1.8	♦ East Asia and the Pacific		('000)	356	314	363	336	..
1.9	♦ Europe		('000)	18,249	18,922	17,531	18,789	..
1.10	♦ Middle East		('000)	33	44	39	33	..
1.11	♦ South Asia		('000)	56	45	77	68	..
1.12	♦ Other not classified		('000)	..	..	..	..	..
1.13	* of which, nationals residing abroad		('000)	..	..	..	..	..
	Arrivals by main purpose	(1)						
1.14	Total		('000)	19,405	20,011	18,803	19,945	..
1.15	♦ Personal		('000)	16,565	16,555	15,441	16,754	..
1.16	* holidays, leisure and recreation		('000)	15,009	14,811	13,614	15,158	..
1.17	* other personal purposes		('000)	1,556	1,744	1,827	1,596	..
1.18	♦ Business and professional		('000)	2,840	3,456	3,362	3,191	..
	Arrivals by mode of transport	(1)						
1.19	Total		('000)	19,404	20,011	18,804	19,945	..
1.20	♦ Air		('000)	3,689	4,662	4,509	4,503	..
1.21	♦ Water		('000)	7,019	7,630	7,036	7,032	..
1.22	♦ Land		('000)	8,696	7,719	7,259	8,410	..
1.23	* railway		('000)	1,704	1,096	1,198	1,345	..
1.24	* road		('000)	6,992	6,623	6,017	7,065	..
1.25	* others		('000)	..	..	44	..	..
	Arrivals by form of organization of the trip	(1)						
1.26	Total		('000)	19,404	20,011	18,803	19,945	..
1.27	♦ Package tour		('000)	5,938	4,910	3,453	3,812	..
1.28	♦ Other forms		('000)	13,466	15,101	15,350	16,133	..
	Accommodation							
	Total							
1.29	♦ Guests		('000)	5,222	5,146	5,229	5,660	6,482
1.30	♦ Overnights		('000)	12,881	12,775	12,890	13,748	15,175
	Hotels and similar establishments							
1.31	♦ Guests	(2)	('000)	3,367	3,358	3,469	3,768	4,240
1.32	♦ Overnights	(2)	('000)	6,532	6,650	6,875	7,421	8,401
	Expenditure							
1.33	Total		US$ Mn	..	..	..	..	..
1.34	♦ Travel		US$ Mn	10,581	10,608	11,535	12,858	12,232
1.35	♦ Passenger transport		US$ Mn	..	..	..	..	..
	Indicators	(1)						
1.39	Average size of travel party		Persons	2.8	2.7	3.0	3.0	..
	Average length of stay							
1.40	Total		Days	4.98	5.36	5.58	4.44	..
1.41	♦ For all commercial accommodation services		Nights	3.40	5.02	5.40	4.36	..
1.42	* of which, "hotels and similar establishments"		Nights	2.50	3.29	3.23	2.95	..
1.43	♦ For non commercial accommodation services		Days	9.55	9.36	10.39	8.65	..
1.44	Average expenditure per day		US$	109.0	128.0	140.0	159.0	..
2.	**DOMESTIC TOURISM**							
	Data							
	Trips							
2.1	Total		('000)	..	..	..	..	..
2.2	♦ Overnight visitors (tourists)	(3)	('000)	44,756	44,449	48,926	..	..
2.3	♦ Same-day visitors (excursionists)		('000)	..	..	..	..	..
	Trips by main purpose							
2.4	Total	(3)	('000)	44,756	44,449	48,926	..	..
2.5	♦ Personal		('000)	39,571	38,474	42,281	..	..
2.6	* holidays, leisure and recreation		('000)	39,571	38,474	42,281	..	..
2.7	* other personal purposes		('000)	..	..	..	..	..
2.8	♦ Business and professional		('000)	5,185	5,975	6,645	..	..

SWEDEN

Cod.	Basic data and indicators	Notes	Units	2011	2012	2013	2014	2015
	Trips by mode of transport							
2.9	Total	(3)	('000)	44,756	44,449	48,926	..	..
2.10	♦ Air		('000)	2,388	2,306	2,712	..	..
2.11	♦ Water		('000)	654	717	791	..	..
2.12	♦ Land		('000)	41,714	41,426	45,423	..	..
2.13	* railway		('000)	5,824	6,447	7,075	..	..
2.14	* road		('000)	35,853	34,867	38,225	..	..
2.15	* others		('000)	37	112	123	..	..
	Accommodation							
	Total							
2.19	♦ Guests		('000)	18,818	18,931	19,578	20,397	21,789
2.20	♦ Overnights		('000)	37,078	37,287	38,268	40,020	41,999
	Hotels and similar establishments							
2.21	♦ Guests	(2)	('000)	13,414	13,638	14,069	14,646	15,514
2.22	♦ Overnights	(2)	('000)	21,458	21,916	22,558	23,652	25,117
3.	**OUTBOUND TOURISM**							
	Data							
	Departures							
3.1	Total		('000)	..	..	..	..	..
3.2	♦ Overnight visitors (tourists)	(3)	('000)	14,651	15,548	15,917	..	..
3.3	♦ Same-day visitors (excursionists)		('000)	..	..	..	..	..
	Expenditure							
3.4	Total		US$ Mn	..	..	..	..	..
3.5	♦ Travel		US$ Mn	15,446	15,628	17,620	18,531	16,854
3.6	♦ Passenger transport		US$ Mn	..	..	..	..	..
4.	**TOURISM INDUSTRIES**							
	Data							
	Number of establishments							
4.1	Total		Units	..	..	..	..	..
4.2	♦ Accommodation for visitors		Units	4,143	4,142	4,261	4,272	4,184
4.3	* of which, "hotels and similar establishments"	(2)	Units	1,998	2,003	2,045	2,033	1,992
4.4	♦ Food and beverage serving activities		Units	..	..	..	..	..
4.5	♦ Passenger transportation		Units	..	..	..	..	..
4.6	♦ Travel agencies and other reservation services activities		Units	..	..	..	..	..
4.7	♦ Other tourism industries		Units	..	..	..	..	..
	Accommodation for visitors in hotels and similar establishments							
	Non-monetary data	(2)						
4.13	♦ Number of establishments		Units	1,998	2,003	2,045	2,033	1,992
4.14	♦ Number of rooms		Units	112,628	133,944	117,228	118,614	117,707
4.15	♦ Number of bed-places		Units	225,343	228,387	235,752	238,852	236,555
	Indicators							
4.16	Occupancy rate / rooms		Percent	50.80	50.10	50.30	51.70	55.30
4.17	Occupancy rate / bed-places		Percent	37.90	37.80	38.30	39.80	43.20
4.18	Average length of stay		Nights	..	..	..	..	..
4.19	Available capacity (bed-places per 1000 inhabitants)		Units	23.81	23.93	24.50	24.62	24.19
5.	**EMPLOYMENT**							
	Data							
	Number of employees by tourism industries	(4)						
5.1	Total		('000)	145.7	155.3	154.1	156.4	165.4
5.2	♦ Accommodation services for visitors (hotels and similar establishments)		('000)	29.1	29.9	31.0	31.6	33.7
5.3	♦ Other accommodation services		('000)	..	..	..	..	..
5.4	♦ Food and beverage serving activities		('000)	32.7	38.4	38.4	41.2	45.6
5.5	♦ Passenger transportation		('000)	20.5	20.8	21.2	19.4	18.7
5.6	♦ Travel agencies and other reservation services activities		('000)	12.1	12.3	12.4	11.9	13.0
5.7	♦ Other tourism industries		('000)	51.3	53.9	51.1	52.3	54.4
6.	**COMPLEMENTARY INDICATORS**							
	Demand							
6.1	Gross travel propensity		Units	..	..	..	..	..
6.2	(1.2 inbound tourists + 2.2 domestic tourists) / population		Units	5.95	5.95	6.22	..	..

SWEDEN

Cod.	Basic data and indicators	Notes	Units	2011	2012	2013	2014	2015
	Macroeconomic indicators related to international tourism							
6.3	Inbound tourism expenditure over GDP		Percent	1.9	2.0	2.0	2.3	2.5
6.4	Outbound tourism expenditure over GDP		Percent	2.7	2.9	3.0	3.2	3.4
6.5	Tourism balance (inbound minus outbound tourism expenditure) over GDP		Percent	-0.8	-0.9	-1.0	-0.9	-0.9
6.6	Tourism openness (inbound plus outbound tourism expenditure) over GDP		Percent	4.6	4.9	5.0	5.5	5.9
6.7	Tourism coverage (inbound over outbound tourism expenditure)		Percent	68.5	67.9	65.5	69.4	72.6
6.8	Inbound tourism expenditure over exports of goods		Percent	5.4	5.7	6.4	7.2	8.1
6.9	Inbound tourism expenditure over exports of services		Percent	16.2	16.4	15.8	16.8	17.0
6.10	Inbound tourism expenditure over exports of goods and services		Percent	4.0	4.3	4.5	5.0	5.5
6.11	Inbound tourism expenditure over current account credits		Percent	3.2	3.4	3.6	4.0	4.4
6.12	Outbound tourism expenditure over imports of goods		Percent	8.7	9.5	11.0	11.5	12.3
6.13	Outbound tourism expenditure over imports of services		Percent	28.2	28.5	29.0	28.2	28.5
6.14	Outbound tourism expenditure over imports of goods and		Percent	6.7	7.1	8.0	8.2	8.6
6.15	Outbound tourism expenditure over current account debits		Percent	5.0	5.3	5.9	6.1	6.5

SWITZERLAND

Cod.	Basic data and indicators	Notes	Units	2011	2012	2013	2014	2015
1.	**INBOUND TOURISM**							
	Data							
	Arrivals							
1.1	Total		('000)	..	..	..	..	..
1.2	♦ Overnight visitors (tourists)	(1)	('000)	8,534	8,566	8,967	9,158	9,305
1.3	♦ Same-day visitors (excursionists)		('000)	..	..	..	..	..
1.4	* of which, cruise passengers		('000)	..	..	..	..	..
	Arrivals by region	(1)						
1.5	Total		('000)	8,534	8,566	8,967	9,158	9,305
1.6	♦ Africa		('000)	74	82	79	75	79
1.7	♦ Americas		('000)	924	952	1,004	1,037	1,096
1.8	♦ East Asia and the Pacific		('000)	1,300	1,491	1,696	1,847	2,242
1.9	♦ Europe		('000)	5,868	5,612	5,720	5,676	5,250
1.10	♦ Middle East		('000)	167	211	256	307	372
1.11	♦ South Asia		('000)	201	218	213	217	266
1.12	♦ Other not classified		('000)	..	..	..	..	..
1.13	* of which, nationals residing abroad		('000)	..	..	..	..	..
	Accommodation							
	Hotels and similar establishments							
1.31	♦ Guests	(1)	('000)	8,534	8,566	8,967	9,158	9,305
1.32	♦ Overnights	(1)	('000)	19,734	19,076	19,735	19,907	19,576
	Expenditure							
1.33	Total		US$ Mn	20,644	19,613	20,329	21,006	19,521
1.34	♦ Travel		US$ Mn	17,196	16,088	16,767	17,475	16,214
1.35	♦ Passenger transport		US$ Mn	3,448	3,525	3,562	3,531	3,307
	Indicators							
1.39	Average size of travel party		Persons	..	..	..	..	..
	Average length of stay							
1.40	Total		Days	..	..	..	..	..
1.41	♦ For all commercial accommodation services		Nights	..	..	..	..	..
1.42	* of which, "hotels and similar establishments"	(1)	Nights	2.19	2.13	2.12	2.09	2.04
1.43	♦ For non commercial accommodation services		Days	..	..	..	..	..
1.44	Average expenditure per day		US$	..	..	..	..	..
2.	**DOMESTIC TOURISM**							
	Data							
	Trips							
2.1	Total		('000)	61,119	63,084	66,166	67,535	68,120
2.2	♦ Overnight visitors (tourists)		('000)	5,779	6,653	7,227	6,526	6,545
2.3	♦ Same-day visitors (excursionists)		('000)	55,340	56,430	58,939	61,010	61,575
	Trips by main purpose							
2.4	Total		('000)	61,119	63,083	66,166	67,536	68,119
2.5	♦ Personal		('000)	58,120	59,089	62,019	64,910	62,915
2.6	* holidays, leisure and recreation		('000)	36,902	30,714	32,200	32,162	30,352
2.7	* other personal purposes	(2)	('000)	21,218	28,375	29,819	32,748	32,563
2.8	♦ Business and professional		('000)	2,999	3,994	4,147	2,626	5,204
	Trips by mode of transport							
2.9	Total		('000)	61,119	63,084	66,167	67,536	68,120
2.10	♦ Air	(3)	('000)	..	16	61	75	42
2.11	♦ Water	(3)	('000)	238	468	583	736	496
2.12	♦ Land		('000)	60,881	62,600	65,523	66,725	67,582
2.13	* railway		('000)	17,041	17,046	17,503	17,909	18,289
2.14	* road		('000)	42,529	43,469	46,823	47,655	47,803
2.15	* others	(4)	('000)	1,311	2,085	1,197	1,161	1,490
	Accommodation							
	Hotels and similar establishments							
2.21	♦ Guests	(1)	('000)	7,695	7,732	7,864	8,004	8,125
2.22	♦ Overnights	(1)	('000)	15,752	15,690	15,889	16,026	16,052
	Indicators							
2.23	Average size of travel party		Persons	..	..	..	..	..
	Average length of stay							
2.24	Total		Days	..	..	..	..	..
2.25	♦ For all commercial accommodation services		Nights	..	..	..	..	..
2.26	* of which, "hotels and similar establishments"	(1)	Nights	2.05	2.03	2.02	2.00	1.98
2.27	♦ For non commercial accommodation services		Days	..	..	..	..	..
2.28	Average expenditure per day		US$	158.2	136.7	160.5	146.3	144.1

SWITZERLAND

Cod.	Basic data and indicators	Notes	Units	2011	2012	2013	2014	2015
3.	**OUTBOUND TOURISM**							
	Data							
	Departures							
3.1	Total		('000)	18,949	20,293	20,303	19,833	22,086
3.2	♦ Overnight visitors (tourists)		('000)	10,466	12,098	12,403	12,518	13,601
3.3	♦ Same-day visitors (excursionists)		('000)	8,483	8,194	7,900	7,316	8,486
	Expenditure							
3.4	Total		US$ Mn	16,472	17,985	19,088	20,241	18,541
3.5	♦ Travel		US$ Mn	13,753	15,183	16,147	17,128	15,968
3.6	♦ Passenger transport		US$ Mn	2,719	2,802	2,941	3,113	2,573
	Indicators							
3.10	Average length of stay		Days	8.59	7.86	7.89	7.97	8.10
3.11	Average expenditure per day		US$	203.8	211.7	217.5	200.6	184.8
4.	**TOURISM INDUSTRIES**							
	Data							
	Number of establishments							
4.1	Total		Units	..	..	..	..	..
4.2	♦ Accommodation for visitors		Units	..	..	..	..	..
4.3	* of which, "hotels and similar establishments"	(1)(5)	Units	5,396	5,257	5,191	5,129	5,055
4.4	♦ Food and beverage serving activities		Units	..	..	..	..	..
4.5	♦ Passenger transportation		Units	..	..	..	..	..
4.6	♦ Travel agencies and other reservation services activities		Units	..	..	..	..	..
4.7	♦ Other tourism industries		Units	..	..	..	..	..
	Accommodation for visitors in hotels and similar establishments							
	Monetary data							
4.8	♦ Output		US$ Mn	4,875.1	4,552.2	4,672.9	4,920.0	4,665.7
4.9	♦ Intermediate consumption		US$ Mn	2,454.8	2,293.7	2,354.8	2,481.8	2,353.6
4.10	♦ Gross value added		US$ Mn	2,420.2	2,258.5	2,318.2	2,438.2	2,312.1
4.11	♦ Compensation of employees		US$ Mn	..	..	..	..	..
4.12	♦ Gross fixed capital formation		US$ Mn	..	..	..	..	..
	Non-monetary data							
4.13	♦ Number of establishments	(1)(5)	Units	5,396	5,257	5,191	5,129	5,055
4.14	♦ Number of rooms	(1)(6)	Units	142,102	140,371	140,192	140,722	141,018
4.15	♦ Number of bed-places	(1)(7)	Units	273,969	271,168	271,298	272,636	273,507
	Indicators							
4.16	Occupancy rate / rooms	(1)(8)	Percent	51.64	50.50	51.63	52.00	51.53
4.17	Occupancy rate / bed-places	(1)(8)	Percent	41.94	40.81	41.90	42.16	41.65
4.18	Average length of stay	(1)	Nights	2.19	2.13	2.12	2.09	2.04
4.19	Available capacity (bed-places per 1000 inhabitants)	(1)(7)	Units	34.57	33.80	33.42	33.20	32.96
	Travel agencies and other reservation service activities							
	Monetary data							
4.20	♦ Output		US$ Mn	8,388.5	7,646.8	7,405.0	6,784.3	6,017.1
4.21	♦ Intermediate consumption		US$ Mn	7,391.5	6,738.0	6,525.1	5,977.8	5,302.0
4.22	♦ Gross value added		US$ Mn	996.9	908.8	879.8	806.6	715.1
4.23	♦ Compensation of employees		US$ Mn	..	..	..	..	..
4.24	♦ Gross fixed capital formation		US$ Mn	..	..	..	..	..
5.	**EMPLOYMENT**							
	Data							
	Number of employees by tourism industries	(9)						
5.1	Total		('000)	48.2	48.3	48.3	..	..
5.2	♦ Accommodation services for visitors (hotels and similar establishments)		('000)	36.2	36.3	36.0	..	..
5.3	♦ Other accommodation services		('000)	3.2	3.3	3.2	..	..
5.4	♦ Food and beverage serving activities		('000)	..	..	..	..	..
5.5	♦ Passenger transportation		('000)	..	..	..	..	..
5.6	♦ Travel agencies and other reservation services activities		('000)	8.8	8.7	9.1	..	..
5.7	♦ Other tourism industries		('000)	..	..	..	..	..
6.	**COMPLEMENTARY INDICATORS**							
	Demand							
6.1	Gross travel propensity		Units	..	..	..	..	..
6.2	(1.2 inbound tourists + 2.2 domestic tourists) / population		Units	1.81	1.90	1.99	1.91	1.91

SWITZERLAND

Cod.	Basic data and indicators	Notes	Units	2011	2012	2013	2014	2015
	Macroeconomic indicators related to international tourism							
6.3	Inbound tourism expenditure over GDP		Percent	3.0	3.0	3.0	3.0	2.9
6.4	Outbound tourism expenditure over GDP		Percent	2.4	2.7	2.8	2.9	2.8
6.5	Tourism balance (inbound minus outbound tourism expenditure) over GDP		Percent	0.6	0.3	0.2	0.1	0.1
6.6	Tourism openness (inbound plus outbound tourism expenditure) over GDP		Percent	5.4	5.7	5.8	5.9	5.7
6.7	Tourism coverage (inbound over outbound tourism expenditure)		Percent	125.3	109.1	106.5	103.8	105.3
6.8	Inbound tourism expenditure over exports of goods		Percent	6.0	5.9	5.4	6.4	6.4
6.9	Inbound tourism expenditure over exports of services		Percent	19.1	18.0	17.8	17.7	17.8
6.10	Inbound tourism expenditure over exports of goods and services		Percent	4.6	4.4	4.2	4.7	4.7
6.11	Inbound tourism expenditure over current account credits		Percent	3.5	3.3	3.2	3.3	3.4
6.12	Outbound tourism expenditure over imports of goods		Percent	5.2	6.2	6.0	7.4	7.5
6.13	Outbound tourism expenditure over imports of services		Percent	19.8	20.9	20.6	20.6	20.0
6.14	Outbound tourism expenditure over imports of goods and		Percent	4.1	4.8	4.6	5.4	5.4
6.15	Outbound tourism expenditure over current account debits		Percent	3.0	3.3	3.3	3.5	3.6

TAIWAN PROVINCE OF CHINA

Cod.	Basic data and indicators	Notes	Units	2011	2012	2013	2014	2015
1.	**INBOUND TOURISM**							
	Data							
	Arrivals							
1.1	Total	(1)	('000)	6,087	7,311	8,016	9,910	10,440
1.2	♦ Overnight visitors (tourists)		('000)	..	..	..	..	..
1.3	♦ Same-day visitors (excursionists)		('000)	..	..	..	..	..
1.4	* of which, cruise passengers		('000)	..	..	..	..	..
	Arrivals by region	(1)						
1.5	Total		('000)	6,087	7,311	8,016	9,910	10,440
1.6	♦ Africa		('000)	9	9	9	10	10
1.7	♦ Americas		('000)	495	497	502	565	588
1.8	♦ East Asia and the Pacific		('000)	5,297	6,513	7,179	9,016	9,509
1.9	♦ Europe		('000)	212	218	223	265	274
1.10	♦ Middle East		('000)	14	13	14	17	19
1.11	♦ South Asia		('000)	24	23	23	30	32
1.12	♦ Other not classified		('000)	36	38	65	7	7
1.13	* of which, nationals residing abroad		('000)	..	..	..	..	..
	Arrivals by main purpose	(1)						
1.14	Total		('000)	6,087	7,311	8,016	9,910	10,440
1.15	♦ Personal		('000)	4,958	6,276	6,935	9,007	9,547
1.16	* holidays, leisure and recreation		('000)	3,634	4,677	5,479	7,192	7,505
1.17	* other personal purposes		('000)	1,324	1,599	1,456	1,815	2,042
1.18	♦ Business and professional		('000)	1,129	1,035	1,081	903	893
	Arrivals by mode of transport	(1)						
1.19	Total		('000)	6,087	7,311	8,016	9,910	10,440
1.20	♦ Air		('000)	5,762	6,955	7,660	9,432	9,839
1.21	♦ Water		('000)	325	356	356	478	600
1.22	♦ Land		('000)	..	..	..	..	..
1.23	* railway		('000)	..	..	..	..	..
1.24	* road		('000)	..	..	..	..	..
1.25	* others		('000)	..	..	..	..	..
	Arrivals by form of organization of the trip							
1.26	Total		('000)	6,087	7,311	8,016	9,910	10,440
1.27	♦ Package tour		('000)	2,524	2,943	2,498	2,910	3,052
1.28	♦ Other forms		('000)	3,563	4,368	5,518	7,000	7,388
	Accommodation							
	Total							
1.29	♦ Guests		('000)	5,519	6,736	7,384	9,110	9,569
1.30	♦ Overnights		('000)	38,935	46,298	50,634	60,584	63,486
	Expenditure							
1.33	Total		US$ Mn	13,067	14,115	14,782	17,419	17,006
1.34	♦ Travel		US$ Mn	11,065	11,770	12,323	14,614	14,406
1.35	♦ Passenger transport		US$ Mn	2,002	2,345	2,459	2,805	2,600
	Expenditure by main purpose of the trip							
1.36	Total		US$ Mn	11,065	11,770	12,323	14,614	14,406
1.37	♦ Personal		US$ Mn	9,124	10,201	10,773	13,365	13,254
1.38	♦ Business and professional		US$ Mn	1,941	1,569	1,550	1,249	1,152
	Indicators							
1.39	Average size of travel party		Persons	..	..	..	..	..
	Average length of stay							
1.40	Total		Days	..	..	..	..	..
1.41	♦ For all commercial accommodation services		Nights	7.05	6.87	6.86	6.65	6.63
1.42	* of which, "hotels and similar establishments"		Nights	..	..	..	..	..
1.43	♦ For non commercial accommodation services		Days	..	..	..	..	..
1.44	Average expenditure per day		US$	257.8	234.3	224.1	221.8	207.9
2.	**DOMESTIC TOURISM**							
	Data							
	Trips							
2.1	Total		('000)	152,268	142,069	142,615	156,260	178,524
2.2	♦ Overnight visitors (tourists)		('000)	46,137	39,921	40,503	43,909	50,700
2.3	♦ Same-day visitors (excursionists)		('000)	106,130	102,148	102,113	112,350	127,823
	Trips by main purpose							
2.4	Total		('000)	152,268	142,069	142,615	156,260	178,524
2.5	♦ Personal		('000)	150,745	140,790	141,189	154,697	176,917
2.6	* holidays, leisure and recreation		('000)	150,593	140,506	141,046	154,697	176,917
2.7	* other personal purposes		('000)	152	284	143	..	..
2.8	♦ Business and professional		('000)	1,523	1,279	1,426	1,563	1,607

TAIWAN PROVINCE OF CHINA

Cod.	Basic data and indicators	Notes	Units	2011	2012	2013	2014	2015
	Trips by mode of transport							
.9	Total		('000)	152,268	142,069	142,615	156,260	178,524
.10	♦ Air		('000)	1,827	1,563	1,426	1,406	1,250
.11	♦ Water		('000)	2,893	2,415	2,424	2,500	2,856
.12	♦ Land		('000)	147,548	138,091	138,765	152,354	174,418
.13	* railway		('000)	..	..	..	..	..
.14	* road		('000)	147,548	138,091	138,765	152,354	174,418
.15	* others		('000)	..	..	..	..	..
	Trips by form of organization							
.16	Total		('000)	152,268	142,069	142,615	156,260	178,524
.17	♦ Package tour		('000)	17,815	18,327	18,255	20,470	21,601
.18	♦ Other forms		('000)	134,453	123,742	124,360	135,790	156,923
	Indicators							
.23	Average size of travel party		Persons	..	..	..	..	..
	Average length of stay							
.24	Total		Days	1.50	1.47	1.47	1.45	1.44
.25	♦ For all commercial accommodation services		Nights	..	..	..	..	..
.26	* of which, "hotels and similar establishments"		Nights	..	..	..	..	..
.27	♦ For non commercial accommodation services		Days	..	..	..	..	..
.28	Average expenditure per day		US$	46.1	43.7	43.7	45.0	44.1
3.	**OUTBOUND TOURISM**							
	Data							
	Departures							
3.1	Total		('000)	..	..	..	..	..
3.2	♦ Overnight visitors (tourists)		('000)	9,584	10,240	11,053	11,845	13,183
3.3	♦ Same-day visitors (excursionists)		('000)	..	..	..	..	..
	Expenditure							
3.4	Total		US$ Mn	11,701	12,444	14,152	15,954	17,428
3.5	♦ Travel		US$ Mn	10,112	10,630	12,304	13,998	15,492
3.6	♦ Passenger transport		US$ Mn	1,589	1,814	1,848	1,956	1,936
	Expenditure by main purpose of the trip							
3.7	Total		US$ Mn	10,112	10,630	12,304	13,998	15,492
3.8	♦ Personal		US$ Mn	7,900	8,403	10,112	11,695	13,007
3.9	♦ Business and professional		US$ Mn	2,212	2,227	2,192	2,303	2,485
	Indicators							
3.10	Average length of stay		Days	9.33	9.06	8.72	8.62	8.33
3.11	Average expenditure per day	(2)	US$	185.7	193.1	198.4	212.1	199.9
4.	**TOURISM INDUSTRIES**							
	Data							
	Number of establishments							
4.1	Total		Units	5,110	5,259	5,433	5,731	5,847
4.2	♦ Accommodation for visitors		Units	..	..	..	..	..
4.3	* of which, "hotels and similar establishments"		Units	2,798	2,854	2,921	3,014	3,068
4.4	♦ Food and beverage serving activities		Units	..	..	..	..	..
4.5	♦ Passenger transportation		Units	..	..	..	..	..
4.6	♦ Travel agencies and other reservation services activities		Units	2,312	2,405	2,512	2,717	2,779
4.7	♦ Other tourism industries		Units	..	..	..	..	..
	Accommodation for visitors in hotels and similar establishments							
	Non-monetary data							
4.13	♦ Number of establishments		Units	2,798	2,854	2,921	3,014	3,068
4.14	♦ Number of rooms		Units	136,105	139,846	146,987	155,591	166,650
4.15	♦ Number of bed-places		Units	..	..	..	..	..
	Indicators							
4.16	Occupancy rate / rooms		Percent	68.11	69.99	69.28	72.15	69.28
4.17	Occupancy rate / bed-places		Percent	..	..	..	..	..
4.18	Average length of stay		Nights	..	..	..	..	..
4.19	Available capacity (bed-places per 1000 inhabitants)		Units	..	..	..	..	..

TAIWAN PROVINCE OF CHINA

Cod. Basic data and indicators	Notes	Units	2011	2012	2013	2014	2015
5. **EMPLOYMENT**							
Data							
Number of employees by tourism industries							
5.1 Total		('000)	145.0	154.7	160.5	171.7	185.2
5.2 ♦ Accommodation services for visitors (hotels and similar establishments)		('000)	65.4	68.0	70.2	75.7	84.7
5.3 ♦ Other accommodation services		('000)	..	..	..	..	.
5.4 ♦ Food and beverage serving activities		('000)	..	..	..	..	.
5.5 ♦ Passenger transportation		('000)	..	..	..	..	.
5.6 ♦ Travel agencies and other reservation services activities		('000)	75.5	82.8	86.4	91.3	95.9
5.7 ♦ Other tourism industries		('000)	4.1	3.9	3.9	4.7	4.6
6. **COMPLEMENTARY INDICATORS**							
Demand							
6.1 Gross travel propensity		Units	..	..	..	..	
6.2 (1.1 inbound visitors + 2.1 domestic visitors) / population		Units	6.82	6.41	6.44	7.09	8.04
Macroeconomic indicators related to international tourism							
6.3 Inbound tourism expenditure over GDP		Percent	2.7	2.8	3.0	3.3	3.3
6.4 Outbound tourism expenditure over GDP		Percent	2.4	2.5	2.8	3.0	3.3
6.5 Tourism balance (inbound minus outbound tourism expenditure) over GDP		Percent	0.3	0.3	0.2	0.3	-0.1
6.6 Tourism openness (inbound plus outbound tourism expenditure) over GDP		Percent	5.1	5.3	5.8	6.3	6.6
6.7 Tourism coverage (inbound over outbound tourism expenditure)		Percent	111.7	113.4	104.5	109.2	97.6
6.8 Inbound tourism expenditure over exports of goods		Percent	4.3	4.7	4.9	5.6	5.1
6.9 Inbound tourism expenditure over exports of services		Percent	28.5	28.8	28.9	30.5	41.3
6.10 Inbound tourism expenditure over exports of goods and services		Percent	3.7	4.1	4.2	4.7	4.8
6.11 Inbound tourism expenditure over current account credits		Percent	3.4	3.7	3.8	4.3	4.1
6.12 Outbound tourism expenditure over imports of goods		Percent	4.2	4.6	5.3	5.9	6.6
6.13 Outbound tourism expenditure over imports of services		Percent	27.8	29.2	33.2	34.7	33.8
6.14 Outbound tourism expenditure over imports of goods and		Percent	3.6	4.0	4.6	5.1	5.5
6.15 Outbound tourism expenditure over current account debits		Percent	3.3	3.6	4.1	4.5	5.2

TAJIKISTAN

Cod.	Basic data and indicators	Notes	Units	2011	2012	2013	2014	2015
1.	**INBOUND TOURISM**							
	Data							
	Arrivals							
1.1	Total		('000)	183	244	208	213	414
1.2	♦ Overnight visitors (tourists)		('000)	..	..	..	..	..
1.3	♦ Same-day visitors (excursionists)		('000)	..	..	..	..	..
1.4	* of which, cruise passengers		('000)	..	..	..	..	..
	Arrivals by region							
1.5	Total		('000)	183	244	208	213	414
1.6	♦ Africa		('000)	..	..	..	..	0.7
1.7	♦ Americas		('000)	1.0	1.0	0.8	1.8	4.3
1.8	♦ East Asia and the Pacific		('000)	4	4	1	6	16
1.9	♦ Europe		('000)	167	223	199	192	344
1.10	♦ Middle East		('000)	..	1.0	0.3	0.2	0.7
1.11	♦ South Asia		('000)	11	15	7	13	48
1.12	♦ Other not classified		('000)	..	..	..	..	..
1.13	* of which, nationals residing abroad		('000)	..	..	..	..	..
	Arrivals by main purpose							
1.14	Total		('000)	..	244	208	213	414
1.15	♦ Personal		('000)	..	242	206	182	392
1.16	* holidays, leisure and recreation		('000)	..	28	12	..	26
1.17	* other personal purposes		('000)	..	214	194	182	366
1.18	♦ Business and professional		('000)	..	2	2	31	22
	Arrivals by mode of transport							
1.19	Total		('000)	..	244	208	213	414
1.20	♦ Air		('000)	..	94	78	170	391
1.21	♦ Water		('000)	..	..	..	..	..
1.22	♦ Land		('000)	..	150	130	43	23
1.23	* railway		('000)	..	..	..	..	..
1.24	* road		('000)	..	150	130	43	23
1.25	* others		('000)	..	..	..	..	..
	Arrivals by form of organization of the trip							
1.26	Total		('000)	..	244	208	..	414
1.27	♦ Package tour		('000)	..	3	3	..	4
1.28	♦ Other forms		('000)	..	241	205	..	410
	Expenditure							
1.33	Total		US$ Mn	40	60	49	220	146
1.34	♦ Travel		US$ Mn	3	3	3	1	1
1.35	♦ Passenger transport		US$ Mn	37	57	46	219	145
	Expenditure by main purpose of the trip							
1.36	Total		US$ Mn	3	3	3	..	..
1.37	♦ Personal		US$ Mn	2	2	2	..	..
1.38	♦ Business and professional		US$ Mn	1	1	1	..	..
	Indicators							
1.39	Average size of travel party		Persons	..	..	..	..	..
	Average length of stay							
1.40	Total		Days	..	..	..	..	..
1.41	♦ For all commercial accommodation services		Nights	..	7.00	7.00	..	7.00
1.42	* of which, "hotels and similar establishments"		Nights	..	8.00	8.00	..	8.00
1.43	♦ For non commercial accommodation services		Days	..	..	..	..	7.00
1.44	Average expenditure per day		US$	..	500.0	500.0	..	500.0
2.	**DOMESTIC TOURISM**							
	Data							
	Trips							
2.1	Total		('000)	..	30	38	36	54
2.2	♦ Overnight visitors (tourists)		('000)	..	24	28	24	40
2.3	♦ Same-day visitors (excursionists)		('000)	..	6	10	12	14
	Trips by main purpose							
2.4	Total		('000)	..	..	38	36	54
2.5	♦ Personal		('000)	..	..	35	34	52
2.6	* holidays, leisure and recreation		('000)	..	..	20	18	11
2.7	* other personal purposes		('000)	..	..	15	16	41
2.8	♦ Business and professional		('000)	..	..	3	2	2
	Trips by mode of transport							
2.9	Total		('000)	..	..	38.0	36.0	54.0
2.10	♦ Air		('000)	..	..	2.0	2.0	4.0
2.11	♦ Water		('000)	..	..	..	..	..
2.12	♦ Land		('000)	..	..	36.0	34.0	50.0
2.13	* railway		('000)	..	..	1.0	..	1.0
2.14	* road		('000)	..	..	35.0	34.0	49.0
2.15	* others		('000)	..	..	..	..	..

TAJIKISTAN

Cod.	Basic data and indicators	Notes	Units	2011	2012	2013	2014	2015
	Trips by form of organization							
2.16	Total		('000)	..	30.2	38.0	36.0	54.0
2.17	♦ Package tour		('000)	..	0.2	2.0	2.0	1.0
2.18	♦ Other forms		('000)	..	30.0	36.0	34.0	53.0
	Indicators							
2.23	Average size of travel party		Persons	..	..	..	..	..
	Average length of stay							
2.24	Total		Days	..	..	..	..	..
2.25	♦ For all commercial accommodation services		Nights	..	6.00	6.00	6.00	7.00
2.26	* of which, "hotels and similar establishments"		Nights	..	..	..	..	..
2.27	♦ For non commercial accommodation services		Days	..	..	..	..	..
2.28	Average expenditure per day		US$	..	20.0	30.0	30.0	20.0
3.	**OUTBOUND TOURISM**							
	Data							
	Departures							
3.1	Total		('000)	..	..	..	..	..
3.2	♦ Overnight visitors (tourists)		('000)	..	15	15	19	16
3.3	♦ Same-day visitors (excursionists)		('000)	..	..	..	..	..
	Expenditure							
3.4	Total		US$ Mn	13	14	73	35	25
3.5	♦ Travel		US$ Mn	8	7	65	..	..
3.6	♦ Passenger transport		US$ Mn	5	7	8	35	25
	Indicators							
3.10	Average length of stay		Days	..	7.00	7.00	7.00	7.00
3.11	Average expenditure per day		US$	..	10.0	20.0	..	80.0
4.	**TOURISM INDUSTRIES**							
	Data							
	Number of establishments							
4.1	Total		Units	..	1,700	1,782	1,790	1,850
4.2	♦ Accommodation for visitors		Units	..	1,500	1,558	1,566	1,521
4.3	* of which, "hotels and similar establishments"		Units	..	..	..	..	..
4.4	♦ Food and beverage serving activities		Units	..	100	120	124	205
4.5	♦ Passenger transportation		Units	..	..	..	..	..
4.6	♦ Travel agencies and other reservation services activities		Units	..	90	94	90	114
4.7	♦ Other tourism industries		Units	..	10	10	10	10
	Accommodation for visitors in hotels and similar establishments							
	Monetary data							
4.8	♦ Output		US$ Mn	..	4.9	5.0	5.2	5.4
4.9	♦ Intermediate consumption		US$ Mn	..	..	..	..	..
4.10	♦ Gross value added		US$ Mn	..	..	..	..	..
4.11	♦ Compensation of employees		US$ Mn	..	..	..	..	..
4.12	♦ Gross fixed capital formation		US$ Mn	..	..	..	..	..
	Travel agencies and other reservation service activities							
	Monetary data							
4.20	♦ Output		US$ Mn	..	0.1	0.1	..	0.1
4.21	♦ Intermediate consumption		US$ Mn	..	..	..	..	..
4.22	♦ Gross value added		US$ Mn	..	..	..	..	..
4.23	♦ Compensation of employees		US$ Mn	..	..	..	..	..
4.24	♦ Gross fixed capital formation		US$ Mn	..	..	..	..	..
	Non-monetary data							
	♦ Domestic trips							
4.25	* with package tour		Percent	..	..	..	..	..
4.26	* without package tour		Percent	..	100.0	100.0	100.0	100.0
	♦ Inbound trips							
4.27	* with package tour		Percent	..	10.0	8.0	7.0	6.0
4.28	* without package tour		Percent	..	90.0	92.0	93.0	94.0
	♦ Outbound trips							
4.29	* with package tour		Percent	..	95.0	96.0	95.0	94.0
4.30	* without package tour		Percent	..	5.0	4.0	5.0	6.0

TAJIKISTAN

Cod.	Basic data and indicators	Notes	Units	2011	2012	2013	2014	2015
5.	**EMPLOYMENT**							
	Data							
	Number of employees by tourism industries							
5.1	Total		('000)	..	18.6	19.4	..	20.8
5.2	♦ Accommodation services for visitors (hotels and similar establishments)		('000)	..	1.0	1.5	..	1.6
5.3	♦ Other accommodation services		('000)	..	2.0	0.3	..	1.0
5.4	♦ Food and beverage serving activities		('000)	..	15.0	16.5	..	16.7
5.5	♦ Passenger transportation		('000)	..	0.2	0.5	..	0.7
5.6	♦ Travel agencies and other reservation services activities		('000)	..	0.3	0.4	..	0.5
5.7	♦ Other tourism industries		('000)	..	0.1	0.2	..	0.3
	Indicators							
	Number of full-time equivalent jobs by status in employment							
5.11	Total		('000)	..	10.0	10.0	..	..
5.12	♦ Employees		('000)	..	10.0	10.0	..	..
5.13	* male		('000)	..	7.0	7.0	..	..
5.14	* female		('000)	..	3.0	3.0	..	..
5.15	♦ Self employed		('000)	..	..	..	..	..
5.16	* male		('000)	..	..	..	..	..
5.17	* female		('000)	..	..	..	..	..
6.	**COMPLEMENTARY INDICATORS**							
	Demand							
6.1	Gross travel propensity		Units	..	..	..	..	..
6.2	(1.1 inbound visitors + 2.1 domestic visitors) / population		Units	..	0.03	0.03	0.03	0.06
	Macroeconomic indicators related to international tourism							
6.3	Inbound tourism expenditure over GDP		Percent	0.6	0.8	0.6	2.4	2.6
6.4	Outbound tourism expenditure over GDP		Percent	0.2	0.2	0.9	0.4	0.7
6.5	Tourism balance (inbound minus outbound tourism expenditure) over GDP		Percent	0.4	0.6	-0.3	2.0	3.0
6.6	Tourism openness (inbound plus outbound tourism expenditure) over GDP		Percent	0.8	1.0	1.5	2.8	3.1
6.7	Tourism coverage (inbound over outbound tourism expenditure)		Percent	307.7	428.6	67.1	628.6	584.0
6.8	Inbound tourism expenditure over exports of goods		Percent	6.7	7.3	8.5	41.8	25.5
6.9	Inbound tourism expenditure over exports of services		Percent	7.1	7.3	8.3	71.1	57.8
6.10	Inbound tourism expenditure over exports of goods and services		Percent	3.5	3.6	4.2	26.3	17.7
6.11	Inbound tourism expenditure over current account credits		Percent	0.9	1.1	0.9	5.1	4.5
6.12	Outbound tourism expenditure over imports of goods		Percent	0.4	0.3	1.6	1.0	0.9
6.13	Outbound tourism expenditure over imports of services		Percent	1.9	1.6	8.5	5.7	5.1
6.14	Outbound tourism expenditure over imports of goods and		Percent	0.3	0.3	1.4	0.8	0.8
6.15	Outbound tourism expenditure over current account debits		Percent	0.3	0.3	1.3	0.5	0.5

TANZANIA, UNITED REPUBLIC OF

Cod.	Basic data and indicators	Notes	Units	2011	2012	2013	2014	2015
1.	**INBOUND TOURISM**							
	Data							
	Arrivals							
1.1	Total		('000)	868	1,077	1,096	1,140	1,137
1.2	♦ Overnight visitors (tourists)		('000)	843	1,043	1,063	1,113	1,104
1.3	♦ Same-day visitors (excursionists)	(1)	('000)	25	34	33	27	33
1.4	* of which, cruise passengers		('000)	..	..	..	..	..
	Arrivals by region							
1.5	Total		('000)	868	1,077	1,096	1,140	1,137
1.6	♦ Africa		('000)	446	489	522	526	531
1.7	♦ Americas		('000)	95	101	101	124	99
1.8	♦ East Asia and the Pacific		('000)	40	79	57	71	71
1.9	♦ Europe		('000)	250	330	362	362	368
1.10	♦ Middle East		('000)	15	21	18	22	28
1.11	♦ South Asia		('000)	22	57	36	35	41
1.12	♦ Other not classified		('000)	..	..	..	..	..
1.13	* of which, nationals residing abroad		('000)	..	..	..	..	..
	Arrivals by main purpose							
1.14	Total		('000)	868	1,077	1,096	1,140	1,137
1.15	♦ Personal		('000)	821	1,021	1,030	1,072	1,061
1.16	* holidays, leisure and recreation		('000)	694	843	891	920	873
1.17	* other personal purposes		('000)	127	178	139	152	188
1.18	♦ Business and professional		('000)	47	56	66	68	76
	Arrivals by mode of transport							
1.19	Total		('000)	868	1,076	1,096	1,140	1,137
1.20	♦ Air		('000)	476	604	563	636	652
1.21	♦ Water		('000)	3	3	59	60	63
1.22	♦ Land		('000)	389	469	474	444	423
1.23	* railway		('000)	4	7	6	5	6
1.24	* road		('000)	385	462	469	439	417
1.25	* others		('000)	..	..	..	..	..
	Arrivals by form of organization of the trip							
1.26	Total		('000)	868	1,077	1,096	1,140	1,137
1.27	♦ Package tour		('000)	417	555	630	638	604
1.28	♦ Other forms		('000)	451	522	466	502	533
	Expenditure							
1.33	Total		US$ Mn	1,383	1,754	1,939	2,047	2,253
1.34	♦ Travel		US$ Mn	1,353	1,713	1,880	2,010	2,231
1.35	♦ Passenger transport		US$ Mn	30	41	59	37	22
3.	**OUTBOUND TOURISM**							
	Data							
	Expenditure							
3.4	Total		US$ Mn	928	1,003	1,101	1,206	1,345
3.5	♦ Travel		US$ Mn	899	967	1,034	1,102	1,211
3.6	♦ Passenger transport		US$ Mn	29	36	67	104	134
6.	**COMPLEMENTARY INDICATORS**							
	Demand							
6.1	Gross travel propensity		Units	..	..	..	..	..
6.2	(1.2 inbound tourists) / population		Units	0.02	0.02	0.02	0.02	0.02
	Macroeconomic indicators related to international tourism							
6.3	Inbound tourism expenditure over GDP		Percent	..	..	..	..	..
6.4	Outbound tourism expenditure over GDP		Percent	..	..	..	..	..
6.5	Tourism balance (inbound minus outbound tourism expenditure) over GDP		Percent	..	..	..	..	..
6.6	Tourism openness (inbound plus outbound tourism expenditure) over GDP		Percent	..	..	..	..	..
6.7	Tourism coverage (inbound over outbound tourism expenditure)		Percent	149.0	174.9	176.1	169.7	167.5
6.8	Inbound tourism expenditure over exports of goods		Percent	27.1	29.8	36.9	38.5	39.5
6.9	Inbound tourism expenditure over exports of services		Percent	60.1	62.9	60.6	60.3	60.1
6.10	Inbound tourism expenditure over exports of goods and services		Percent	18.7	20.2	22.9	23.5	23.8
6.11	Inbound tourism expenditure over current account credits		Percent	16.1	18.0	20.6	21.8	22.2
6.12	Outbound tourism expenditure over imports of goods		Percent	9.4	9.7	10.0	11.0	13.7
6.13	Outbound tourism expenditure over imports of services		Percent	42.0	42.5	44.2	45.2	50.1
6.14	Outbound tourism expenditure over imports of goods and		Percent	7.7	7.9	8.1	8.9	10.7
6.15	Outbound tourism expenditure over current account debits		Percent	7.5	7.8	8.0	8.8	10.6

THAILAND

Cod.	Basic data and indicators	Notes	Units	2011	2012	2013	2014	2015
1.	**INBOUND TOURISM**							
	Data							
	Arrivals							
1.1	Total		('000)	..	..	..	..	..
1.2	♦ Overnight visitors (tourists)	(1)	('000)	19,230	22,354	26,547	24,810	29,923
1.3	♦ Same-day visitors (excursionists)		('000)	..	..	..	..	..
1.4	* of which, cruise passengers		('000)	..	..	..	..	..
	Arrivals by region	(1)						
1.5	Total		('000)	19,230	22,354	26,547	24,810	29,923
1.6	♦ Africa		('000)	141	157	163	163	165
1.7	♦ Americas		('000)	886	1,007	1,104	1,049	1,169
1.8	♦ East Asia and the Pacific		('000)	11,481	13,811	17,117	15,712	21,018
1.9	♦ Europe		('000)	5,059	5,580	6,289	6,166	5,615
1.10	♦ Middle East		('000)	379	538	548	507	582
1.11	♦ South Asia		('000)	1,285	1,260	1,327	1,214	1,374
1.12	♦ Other not classified		('000)	..	..	..	..	..
1.13	* of which, nationals residing abroad		('000)	..	..	..	..	..
	Arrivals by main purpose	(1)						
1.14	Total		('000)	19,230	22,354	26,547	..	..
1.15	♦ Personal		('000)	17,265	20,179	24,206	..	..
1.16	* holidays, leisure and recreation		('000)	15,990	19,215	23,240	..	..
1.17	* other personal purposes		('000)	1,275	964	965	..	..
1.18	♦ Business and professional		('000)	1,965	2,175	2,341	..	..
	Arrivals by mode of transport	(1)						
1.19	Total		('000)	19,230	22,354	26,547	..	..
1.20	♦ Air		('000)	14,929	17,803	21,501	..	..
1.21	♦ Water		('000)	552	563	705	..	..
1.22	♦ Land		('000)	3,749	3,988	4,341	..	..
1.23	* railway		('000)	..	..	..	..	..
1.24	* road	(2)	('000)	3,749	3,988	4,341	..	..
1.25	* others		('000)	..	..	..	..	..
	Arrivals by form of organization of the trip							
1.26	Total		('000)	19,230	22,354	26,547	24,810	29,923
1.27	♦ Package tour		('000)	4,899	6,193	7,795	6,877	8,553
1.28	♦ Other forms		('000)	14,331	16,161	18,752	17,933	21,370
	Accommodation							
	Hotels and similar establishments							
1.31	♦ Guests		('000)	34,131	37,385	45,659	45,303	50,498
1.32	♦ Overnights		('000)	..	..	..	..	..
	Expenditure							
1.33	Total		US$ Mn	30,926	37,769	45,740	42,063	48,124
1.34	♦ Travel		US$ Mn	27,186	33,856	41,780	38,433	44,521
1.35	♦ Passenger transport		US$ Mn	3,740	3,913	3,960	3,630	3,603
	Expenditure by main purpose of the trip							
1.36	Total		US$ Mn	27,185	33,856	41,780	38,432	44,521
1.37	♦ Personal		US$ Mn	24,824	29,991	37,246	34,779	40,278
1.38	♦ Business and professional		US$ Mn	2,361	3,865	4,534	3,653	4,243
	Indicators							
1.39	Average size of travel party		Persons	..	..	..	..	..
	Average length of stay							
1.40	Total		Days	..	..	..	..	..
1.41	♦ For all commercial accommodation services	(3)	Nights	9.64	10.02	9.85	9.83	9.47
1.42	* of which, "hotels and similar establishments"		Nights	..	..	..	..	..
1.43	♦ For non commercial accommodation services		Days	..	..	..	..	..
1.44	Average expenditure per day		US$	137.3	141.3	150.2	148.1	150.1
2.	**DOMESTIC TOURISM**							
	Data							
	Trips							
2.1	Total		('000)	109,360	118,187	126,059	..	..
2.2	♦ Overnight visitors (tourists)		('000)	..	..	..	..	..
2.3	♦ Same-day visitors (excursionists)		('000)	..	..	..	..	..
	Accommodation							
	Hotels and similar establishments							
2.21	♦ Guests		('000)	52,109	61,401	71,692	76,021	85,508
2.22	♦ Overnights		('000)	..	..	..	..	..

THAILAND

Cod.	Basic data and indicators	Notes	Units	2011	2012	2013	2014	2015
	Indicators							
2.23	Average size of travel party		Persons	..	..	..	..	..
	Average length of stay							
2.24	Total		Days	2.73	2.73	2.62	2.70	2.64
2.25	♦ For all commercial accommodation services		Nights	..	..	..	..	..
2.26	* of which, "hotels and similar establishments"		Nights	..	..	..	..	..
2.27	♦ For non commercial accommodation services		Days	..	..	..	..	..
2.28	Average expenditure per day		US$	67.0	63.1	60.6	..	..
3.	**OUTBOUND TOURISM**							
	Data							
	Departures							
3.1	Total		('000)	..	..	..	..	..
3.2	♦ Overnight visitors (tourists)		('000)	5,397	5,721	5,970	6,444	6,794
3.3	♦ Same-day visitors (excursionists)		('000)	..	..	..	..	..
	Expenditure							
3.4	Total		US$ Mn	7,320	7,887	8,230	8,822	9,315
3.5	♦ Travel		US$ Mn	5,716	6,242	6,475	7,070	7,588
3.6	♦ Passenger transport		US$ Mn	1,604	1,645	1,755	1,752	1,727
	Expenditure by main purpose of the trip							
3.7	Total		US$ Mn	5,716	6,242	6,475	7,070	7,588
3.8	♦ Personal		US$ Mn	5,149	5,995	6,138	6,621	7,100
3.9	♦ Business and professional		US$ Mn	567	247	337	449	488
	Indicators							
3.10	Average length of stay		Days	5.02	5.14	5.00	5.09	5.38
3.11	Average expenditure per day		US$	147.8	150.8	159.6	159.6	159.7
4.	**TOURISM INDUSTRIES**							
	Data							
	Number of establishments							
4.1	Total		Units	..	..	..	..	..
4.2	♦ Accommodation for visitors		Units	..	..	..	..	..
4.3	* of which, "hotels and similar establishments"		Units	..	..	12,398	12,879	15,469
4.4	♦ Food and beverage serving activities		Units	..	..	..	..	..
4.5	♦ Passenger transportation		Units	..	..	..	..	..
4.6	♦ Travel agencies and other reservation services activities		Units	..	..	..	..	..
4.7	♦ Other tourism industries		Units	..	..	..	..	..
	Accommodation for visitors in hotels and similar establishments							
	Non-monetary data							
4.13	♦ Number of establishments		Units	..	..	12,398	12,879	15,469
4.14	♦ Number of rooms		Units	530,623	528,128	540,088	550,269	650,643
4.15	♦ Number of bed-places		Units	..	..	..	..	..
	Indicators							
4.16	Occupancy rate / rooms		Percent	43.84	48.69	56.30	58.96	65.12
4.17	Occupancy rate / bed-places		Percent	..	..	..	..	..
4.18	Average length of stay	(3)	Nights	..	..	1.84	1.77	2.24
4.19	Available capacity (bed-places per 1000 inhabitants)		Units	..	..	..	..	..
6.	**COMPLEMENTARY INDICATORS**							
	Demand							
6.1	Gross travel propensity		Units	..	..	..	..	..
6.2	(1.2 inbound tourists + 2.1 domestic visitors) / population		Units	1.92	2.09	2.26	..	..
	Macroeconomic indicators related to international tourism							
6.3	Inbound tourism expenditure over GDP		Percent	8.9	9.5	10.9	10.4	12.2
6.4	Outbound tourism expenditure over GDP		Percent	2.1	2.0	2.0	2.2	2.4
6.5	Tourism balance (inbound minus outbound tourism expenditure) over GDP		Percent	6.8	7.5	8.9	8.2	9.8
6.6	Tourism openness (inbound plus outbound tourism expenditure) over GDP		Percent	11.0	11.5	12.9	12.6	14.6
6.7	Tourism coverage (inbound over outbound tourism expenditure)		Percent	422.5	478.9	555.8	476.8	516.6
6.8	Inbound tourism expenditure over exports of goods		Percent	14.1	16.7	20.3	18.7	22.7
6.9	Inbound tourism expenditure over exports of services		Percent	74.4	76.1	78.0	76.0	78.8
6.10	Inbound tourism expenditure over exports of goods and services		Percent	11.9	13.7	16.1	15.0	17.6
6.11	Inbound tourism expenditure over current account credits		Percent	11.0	12.7	15.1	14.1	16.7
6.12	Outbound tourism expenditure over imports of goods		Percent	3.6	3.6	3.8	4.4	5.2
6.13	Outbound tourism expenditure over imports of services		Percent	14.0	14.9	15.0	16.6	18.3
6.14	Outbound tourism expenditure over imports of goods and		Percent	2.9	2.9	3.0	3.5	4.1
6.15	Outbound tourism expenditure over current account debits		Percent	2.8	2.8	2.9	3.4	3.9

THE FORMER YUGOSLAV REPUBLIC OF MACEDONIA

Cod.	Basic data and indicators	Notes	Units	2011	2012	2013	2014	2015
1.	**INBOUND TOURISM**							
	Data							
	Arrivals							
1.1	Total		('000)	..	..	..	..	..
1.2	♦ Overnight visitors (tourists)	(1)	('000)	327	351	400	425	486
1.3	♦ Same-day visitors (excursionists)		('000)	..	..	..	..	..
1.4	* of which, cruise passengers		('000)	..	..	..	..	..
	Arrivals by region	(1)						
1.5	Total		('000)	327	351	400	425	486
1.6	♦ Africa		('000)	..	..	1	1	1
1.7	♦ Americas		('000)	11	11	13	13	15
1.8	♦ East Asia and the Pacific		('000)	12	16	18	23	30
1.9	♦ Europe		('000)	304	325	368	388	440
1.10	♦ Middle East		('000)	..	..	..	..	..
1.11	♦ South Asia		('000)	..	..	..	..	..
1.12	♦ Other not classified		('000)	..	..	..	..	..
1.13	* of which, nationals residing abroad		('000)	..	..	..	..	..
	Accommodation							
	Total							
1.29	♦ Guests		('000)	327	351	400	425	486
1.30	♦ Overnights		('000)	755	812	881	923	1,036
	Hotels and similar establishments							
1.31	♦ Guests		('000)	301	324	373	392	456
1.32	♦ Overnights		('000)	667	727	796	827	958
	Expenditure							
1.33	Total		US$ Mn	242	237	270	298	270
1.34	♦ Travel		US$ Mn	240	234	267	295	267
1.35	♦ Passenger transport		US$ Mn	2	3	3	3	3
	Indicators							
1.39	Average size of travel party		Persons	..	..	..	..	..
	Average length of stay							
1.40	Total		Days	..	..	..	..	..
1.41	♦ For all commercial accommodation services		Nights	2.31	2.31	2.20	2.17	2.13
1.42	* of which, "hotels and similar establishments"		Nights	2.22	2.24	2.13	2.11	2.10
1.43	♦ For non commercial accommodation services		Days	..	..	..	..	..
1.44	Average expenditure per day		US$	..	..	..	..	..
2.	**DOMESTIC TOURISM**							
	Data							
	Accommodation							
	Total							
2.19	♦ Guests		('000)	320	312	302	310	331
2.20	♦ Overnights		('000)	1,418	1,340	1,276	1,273	1,358
	Hotels and similar establishments							
2.21	♦ Guests		('000)	121	125	129	140	153
2.22	♦ Overnights		('000)	236	238	241	257	284
	Indicators							
2.23	Average size of travel party		Persons	..	..	..	..	..
	Average length of stay							
2.24	Total		Days	..	..	..	..	..
2.25	♦ For all commercial accommodation services		Nights	4.43	4.29	4.22	4.11	4.10
2.26	* of which, "hotels and similar establishments"		Nights	1.95	1.90	1.87	1.84	1.86
2.27	♦ For non commercial accommodation services		Days	..	..	..	..	..
2.28	Average expenditure per day		US$	..	..	..	..	..
3.	**OUTBOUND TOURISM**							
	Data							
	Expenditure							
3.4	Total		US$ Mn	159	153	168	186	189
3.5	♦ Travel		US$ Mn	113	111	131	149	159
3.6	♦ Passenger transport		US$ Mn	46	42	37	37	30
	Expenditure by main purpose of the trip							
3.7	Total		US$ Mn	113	111	131	149	159
3.8	♦ Personal		US$ Mn	92	91	109	127	138
3.9	♦ Business and professional		US$ Mn	21	20	22	21	21

THE FORMER YUGOSLAV REPUBLIC OF MACEDONIA

Cod.	Basic data and indicators	Notes	Units	2011	2012	2013	2014	2015
4.	**TOURISM INDUSTRIES**							
	Data							
	Number of establishments							
4.1	Total		Units	..	..	..	..	..
4.2	♦ Accommodation for visitors		Units	404	423	434	445	451
4.3	* of which, "hotels and similar establishments"		Units	186	209	225	233	249
4.4	♦ Food and beverage serving activities		Units	..	..	..	..	..
4.5	♦ Passenger transportation		Units	..	..	..	..	..
4.6	♦ Travel agencies and other reservation services activities		Units	..	..	..	..	..
4.7	♦ Other tourism industries		Units	..	..	..	..	..
	Accommodation for visitors in hotels and similar establishments							
	Monetary data							
4.8	♦ Output		US$ Mn	..	..	..	..	..
4.9	♦ Intermediate consumption		US$ Mn	..	..	..	..	..
4.10	♦ Gross value added		US$ Mn	..	..	..	..	..
4.11	♦ Compensation of employees		US$ Mn	..	..	..	..	..
4.12	♦ Gross fixed capital formation		US$ Mn	3.2	..	..	..	..
	Non-monetary data							
4.13	♦ Number of establishments		Units	186	209	225	233	249
4.14	♦ Number of rooms		Units	6,372	6,820	7,232	7,692	8,271
4.15	♦ Number of bed-places		Units	13,943	14,864	15,744	16,687	18,160
	Indicators							
4.16	Occupancy rate / rooms		Percent	..	..	34.26	36.14	37.18
4.17	Occupancy rate / bed-places		Percent	17.75	17.80	22.14	22.54	22.99
4.18	Average length of stay	(2)	Nights	3.36	3.24	3.07	2.98	2.93
4.19	Available capacity (bed-places per 1000 inhabitants)		Units	6.75	7.18	7.60	8.04	8.74
	Travel agencies and other reservation service activities							
	Monetary data							
4.20	♦ Output		US$ Mn	..	..	..	..	..
4.21	♦ Intermediate consumption		US$ Mn	..	..	..	..	..
4.22	♦ Gross value added		US$ Mn	..	..	..	..	..
4.23	♦ Compensation of employees		US$ Mn	..	..	..	..	..
4.24	♦ Gross fixed capital formation		US$ Mn	0.4	..	..	..	..
6.	**COMPLEMENTARY INDICATORS**							
	Demand							
6.1	Gross travel propensity		Units	..	..	..	..	..
6.2	(1.2 inbound tourists) / population		Units	0.16	0.17	0.19	0.20	0.23
	Macroeconomic indicators related to international tourism							
6.3	Inbound tourism expenditure over GDP		Percent	2.3	2.5	2.6	2.6	2.7
6.4	Outbound tourism expenditure over GDP		Percent	1.5	1.6	1.6	1.6	1.9
6.5	Tourism balance (inbound minus outbound tourism expenditure) over GDP		Percent	0.8	0.9	1.0	1.0	0.8
6.6	Tourism openness (inbound plus outbound tourism expenditure) over GDP		Percent	3.8	4.1	4.2	4.2	4.6
6.7	Tourism coverage (inbound over outbound tourism expenditure)		Percent	152.2	154.9	160.7	160.2	142.9
6.8	Inbound tourism expenditure over exports of goods		Percent	7.2	8.0	8.6	8.1	8.0
6.9	Inbound tourism expenditure over exports of services		Percent	16.6	17.3	17.6	17.6	17.8
6.10	Inbound tourism expenditure over exports of goods and services		Percent	5.0	5.5	5.8	5.5	5.5
6.11	Inbound tourism expenditure over current account credits		Percent	3.4	3.5	3.8	3.8	3.9
6.12	Outbound tourism expenditure over imports of goods		Percent	2.7	2.8	3.0	3.0	3.5
6.13	Outbound tourism expenditure over imports of services		Percent	16.7	15.7	16.2	15.2	16.6
6.14	Outbound tourism expenditure over imports of goods and		Percent	2.3	2.3	2.5	2.5	2.9
6.15	Outbound tourism expenditure over current account debits		Percent	2.2	2.2	2.4	2.4	2.8

TIMOR-LESTE

Cod.	Basic data and indicators	Notes	Units	2011	2012	2013	2014	2015
1.	**INBOUND TOURISM**							
	Data							
	Arrivals							
1.1	Total		('000)	..	..	..	..	..
1.2	♦ Overnight visitors (tourists)	(1)	('000)	51	58	79	60	62
1.3	♦ Same-day visitors (excursionists)		('000)	..	..	..	..	..
1.4	* of which, cruise passengers		('000)	..	..	..	..	..
	Arrivals by region	(1)						
1.5	Total		('000)	51	58	78	60	62
1.6	♦ Africa		('000)	..	..	..	..	..
1.7	♦ Americas		('000)	3	4	3	2	3
1.8	♦ East Asia and the Pacific		('000)	35	42	44	42	42
1.9	♦ Europe		('000)	7	7	6	7	6
1.10	♦ Middle East		('000)	..	..	..	..	..
1.11	♦ South Asia		('000)	1.9	1.2	0.8	1.0	0.9
1.12	♦ Other not classified		('000)	4	4	24	8	10
1.13	* of which, nationals residing abroad		('000)	..	..	..	..	..
	Accommodation							
	Hotels and similar establishments	(2)						
1.31	♦ Guests		('000)	17	20	24	15	..
1.32	♦ Overnights		('000)	102	106	94	73	..
	Expenditure							
1.33	Total		US$ Mn	..	..	..	..	..
1.34	♦ Travel		US$ Mn	18	21	29	35	51
1.35	♦ Passenger transport		US$ Mn	..	..	..	..	..
	Expenditure by main purpose of the trip							
1.36	Total		US$ Mn	..	21	29	35	51
1.37	♦ Personal		US$ Mn	..	16	24	25	34
1.38	♦ Business and professional		US$ Mn	..	6	5	11	17
2.	**DOMESTIC TOURISM**							
	Data							
	Accommodation							
	Hotels and similar establishments	(2)						
2.21	♦ Guests		('000)	0.2	..	3.3	1.5	..
2.22	♦ Overnights		('000)	0.2	..	6.7	4.6	..
3.	**OUTBOUND TOURISM**							
	Data							
	Expenditure							
3.4	Total		US$ Mn	62	92	57	84	100
3.5	♦ Travel		US$ Mn	49	73	40	66	83
3.6	♦ Passenger transport		US$ Mn	13	19	17	18	17
	Expenditure by main purpose of the trip							
3.7	Total		US$ Mn	49	73	40	66	83
3.8	♦ Personal		US$ Mn	48	60	33	57	75
3.9	♦ Business and professional		US$ Mn	1	12	8	8	8
4.	**TOURISM INDUSTRIES**							
	Data							
	Number of establishments							
4.1	Total		Units	..	..	..	..	..
4.2	♦ Accommodation for visitors		Units	..	..	..	..	..
4.3	* of which, "hotels and similar establishments"	(2)	Units	18	18	18	18	..
4.4	♦ Food and beverage serving activities		Units	..	..	..	..	..
4.5	♦ Passenger transportation		Units	..	..	..	..	..
4.6	♦ Travel agencies and other reservation services activities		Units	..	..	..	..	..
4.7	♦ Other tourism industries		Units	..	..	..	..	..
	Accommodation for visitors in hotels and similar establishments							
	Non-monetary data	(2)						
4.13	♦ Number of establishments		Units	18	18	18	18	..
4.14	♦ Number of rooms		Units	869	875	905	886	..
4.15	♦ Number of bed-places		Units	871	998	1,011	1,115	..
	Indicators							
4.16	Occupancy rate / rooms		Percent	..	..	..	..	..
4.17	Occupancy rate / bed-places		Percent	..	..	..	..	..
4.18	Average length of stay		Nights	..	..	..	..	..
4.19	Available capacity (bed-places per 1000 inhabitants)		Units	0.81	0.91	0.90	0.96	..

TIMOR-LESTE

Cod.	Basic data and indicators	Notes	Units	2011	2012	2013	2014	2015
6.	**COMPLEMENTARY INDICATORS**							
	Demand							
6.1	Gross travel propensity		Units	..	..	..	..	..
6.2	(1.2 inbound tourists) / population		Units	0.05	0.05	0.07	0.05	0.05
	Macroeconomic indicators related to international tourism							
6.3	Inbound tourism expenditure over GDP		Percent	0.3	0.4	..	..	..
6.4	Outbound tourism expenditure over GDP		Percent	1.1	1.6	..	..	..
6.5	Tourism balance (inbound minus outbound tourism expenditure) over GDP		Percent	-0.8	-1.2	..	..	..
6.6	Tourism openness (inbound plus outbound tourism expenditure) over GDP		Percent	1.4	2.0	..	..	..
6.7	Tourism coverage (inbound over outbound tourism expenditure)		Percent	29.0	22.8	50.9	41.7	51.0
6.8	Inbound tourism expenditure over exports of goods		Percent	62.8	63.1	164.1	226.1	282.5
6.9	Inbound tourism expenditure over exports of services		Percent	24.8	30.3	41.3	47.2	69.9
6.10	Inbound tourism expenditure over exports of goods and services		Percent	17.8	20.4	33.0	39.1	56.0
6.11	Inbound tourism expenditure over current account credits		Percent	0.4	0.5	0.8	1.5	3.0
6.12	Outbound tourism expenditure over imports of goods		Percent	15.4	13.7	8.2	11.0	15.3
6.13	Outbound tourism expenditure over imports of services		Percent	4.2	9.3	11.2	18.6	15.3
6.14	Outbound tourism expenditure over imports of goods and		Percent	3.3	5.5	4.7	6.9	7.7
6.15	Outbound tourism expenditure over current account debits		Percent	1.1	1.6	1.3	2.5	3.6

TOGO

Cod.	Basic data and indicators	Notes	Units	2011	2012	2013	2014	2015
1.	**INBOUND TOURISM**							
	Data							
	Arrivals							
1.1	Total		('000)	..	..	..	..	..
1.2	♦ Overnight visitors (tourists)	(1)(2)	('000)	300	235	327	282	273
1.3	♦ Same-day visitors (excursionists)		('000)	..	..	2	1	1
1.4	* of which, cruise passengers		('000)	..	..	..	..	..
	Arrivals by region	(1)(2)						
1.5	Total		('000)	300	235	327	282	273
1.6	♦ Africa		('000)	136	127	150	156	140
1.7	♦ Americas		('000)	8	8	8	8	6
1.8	♦ East Asia and the Pacific		('000)	11	11	11	12	13
1.9	♦ Europe		('000)	144	88	99	86	90
1.10	♦ Middle East		('000)	1	1	1	1	1
1.11	♦ South Asia		('000)	..	..	..	..	..
1.12	♦ Other not classified		('000)	..	..	58	20	24
1.13	* of which, nationals residing abroad		('000)	..	..	58	20	24
	Arrivals by main purpose	(3)						
1.14	Total		('000)	..	..	..	..	249
1.15	♦ Personal		('000)	..	..	..	..	126
1.16	* holidays, leisure and recreation		('000)	..	..	..	..	19
1.17	* other personal purposes		('000)	..	..	..	..	107
1.18	♦ Business and professional		('000)	..	..	..	..	123
	Arrivals by mode of transport	(3)						
1.19	Total		('000)	..	..	..	..	249
1.20	♦ Air		('000)	..	..	..	..	126
1.21	♦ Water		('000)	..	..	..	..	..
1.22	♦ Land		('000)	..	..	..	..	123
1.23	* railway		('000)	..	..	..	..	..
1.24	* road		('000)	..	..	..	..	123
1.25	* others		('000)	..	..	..	..	..
	Accommodation							
	Hotels and similar establishments							
1.31	♦ Guests	(2)	('000)	300	235	327	282	273
1.32	♦ Overnights	(2)	('000)	673	515	795	660	644
	Expenditure							
1.33	Total		US$ Mn	209	206	233	233	..
1.34	♦ Travel		US$ Mn	98	111	125	125	..
1.35	♦ Passenger transport		US$ Mn	111	95	108	108	..
	Expenditure by main purpose of the trip							
1.36	Total		US$ Mn	98	111	125	125	..
1.37	♦ Personal		US$ Mn	24	56	64	64	..
1.38	♦ Business and professional		US$ Mn	74	55	61	61	..
	Indicators							
1.39	Average size of travel party		Persons	..	..	..	..	..
	Average length of stay							
1.40	Total		Days	..	..	..	..	..
1.41	♦ For all commercial accommodation services		Nights	2.16	2.25	2.40	2.36	2.36
1.42	* of which, "hotels and similar establishments"		Nights	..	..	..	..	..
1.43	♦ For non commercial accommodation services		Days	..	..	..	..	..
1.44	Average expenditure per day		US$	..	..	..	..	..
2.	**DOMESTIC TOURISM**							
	Data							
	Accommodation							
	Hotels and similar establishments							
2.21	♦ Guests		('000)	80	24	18	50	54
2.22	♦ Overnights		('000)	184	46	32	150	133
	Indicators							
2.23	Average size of travel party		Persons	..	..	..	..	..
	Average length of stay							
2.24	Total		Days	..	..	..	..	..
2.25	♦ For all commercial accommodation services		Nights	1.23	2.25	2.40	2.50	2.56
2.26	* of which, "hotels and similar establishments"		Nights	..	..	..	..	..
2.27	♦ For non commercial accommodation services		Days	..	..	..	..	..
2.28	Average expenditure per day		US$	..	..	..	..	..

TOGO

Cod.	Basic data and indicators	Notes	Units	2011	2012	2013	2014	2015
3.	**OUTBOUND TOURISM**							
	Data							
	Expenditure							
3.4	Total		US$ Mn	81	46	58	60	..
3.5	♦ Travel		US$ Mn	57	34	45	41	..
3.6	♦ Passenger transport		US$ Mn	24	12	13	19	..
	Expenditure by main purpose of the trip							
3.7	Total		US$ Mn	57	34	45	41	..
3.8	♦ Personal		US$ Mn	11	26	33	31	..
3.9	♦ Business and professional		US$ Mn	46	8	12	10	..
4.	**TOURISM INDUSTRIES**							
	Data							
	Number of establishments							
4.1	Total		Units	..	..	..	..	
4.2	♦ Accommodation for visitors		Units	..	..	..	..	
4.3	* of which, "hotels and similar establishments"		Units	501	501	501	501	600
4.4	♦ Food and beverage serving activities		Units	..	..	..	..	
4.5	♦ Passenger transportation		Units	..	..	..	..	
4.6	♦ Travel agencies and other reservation services activities		Units	..	..	..	..	
4.7	♦ Other tourism industries		Units	..	..	..	..	
	Accommodation for visitors in hotels and similar establishments							
	Non-monetary data							
4.13	♦ Number of establishments		Units	501	501	501	501	600
4.14	♦ Number of rooms		Units	7,576	7,576	7,576	7,576	7,576
4.15	♦ Number of bed-places		Units	8,000	8,000	8,000	8,000	8,000
	Indicators							
4.16	Occupancy rate / rooms		Percent	14.60	18.67	29.66	25.58	26.25
4.17	Occupancy rate / bed-places		Percent	..	..	..	..	
4.18	Average length of stay		Nights	2.16	2.25	2.25	2.36	2.36
4.19	Available capacity (bed-places per 1000 inhabitants)		Units	1.22	1.19	1.15	1.12	1.10
5.	**EMPLOYMENT**							
	Data							
	Number of employees by tourism industries							
5.1	Total		('000)	..	..	..	..	..
5.2	♦ Accommodation services for visitors (hotels and similar establishments)		('000)	4.3	4.3	4.3	4.3	4.3
5.3	♦ Other accommodation services		('000)	..	..	..	..	..
5.4	♦ Food and beverage serving activities		('000)	..	..	..	..	..
5.5	♦ Passenger transportation		('000)	..	..	..	..	..
5.6	♦ Travel agencies and other reservation services activities		('000)	..	..	..	..	..
5.7	♦ Other tourism industries		('000)	..	..	..	..	..
6.	**COMPLEMENTARY INDICATORS**							
	Demand							
6.1	Gross travel propensity		Units	..	..	..	..	..
6.2	(1.2 inbound tourists) / population		Units	0.05	0.03	0.05	0.04	0.04
	Macroeconomic indicators related to international tourism							
6.3	Inbound tourism expenditure over GDP		Percent	5.6	5.3	5.6	5.1	..
6.4	Outbound tourism expenditure over GDP		Percent	2.2	1.2	1.4	1.3	..
6.5	Tourism balance (inbound minus outbound tourism expenditure) over GDP		Percent	3.4	4.1	4.2	3.8	
6.6	Tourism openness (inbound plus outbound tourism expenditure) over GDP		Percent	7.8	6.5	7.0	6.4	
6.7	Tourism coverage (inbound over outbound tourism expenditure)		Percent	258.0	447.8	401.7	388.3	..
6.8	Inbound tourism expenditure over exports of goods		Percent	17.7	15.9	15.3	17.6	..
6.9	Inbound tourism expenditure over exports of services		Percent	41.1	45.0	47.9	47.7	..
6.10	Inbound tourism expenditure over exports of goods and services		Percent	12.4	11.8	11.6	12.8	..
6.11	Inbound tourism expenditure over current account credits		Percent	8.6	8.5	8.3	8.7	..
6.12	Outbound tourism expenditure over imports of goods		Percent	4.0	2.5	2.4	2.7	..
6.13	Outbound tourism expenditure over imports of services		Percent	17.1	10.4	12.3	14.1	..
6.14	Outbound tourism expenditure over imports of goods and		Percent	3.2	2.0	2.0	2.3	..
6.15	Outbound tourism expenditure over current account debits		Percent	2.7	1.7	1.7	1.9	..

TONGA

Cod.	Basic data and indicators	Notes	Units	2011	2012	2013	2014	2015
1.	**INBOUND TOURISM**							
	Data							
	Arrivals							
1.1	Total		('000)	68	57	60	66	73
1.2	♦ Overnight visitors (tourists)	(1)	('000)	46	47	48	50	54
1.3	♦ Same-day visitors (excursionists)	(2)	('000)	22	10	12	15	19
1.4	* of which, cruise passengers		('000)	22	10	12	15	19
	Arrivals by region	(1)						
1.5	Total		('000)	46	47	48	50	54
1.6	♦ Africa		('000)	..	0.1	..	..	..
1.7	♦ Americas		('000)	6	6	6	7	7
1.8	♦ East Asia and the Pacific		('000)	37	38	39	41	43
1.9	♦ Europe		('000)	3	3	3	3	4
1.10	♦ Middle East		('000)	..	..	..	..	..
1.11	♦ South Asia		('000)	..	..	..	..	..
1.12	♦ Other not classified		('000)	..	..	0.1	..	0.1
1.13	* of which, nationals residing abroad		('000)	..	..	..	..	..
	Arrivals by main purpose	(1)						
1.14	Total		('000)	46	47	48	50	54
1.15	♦ Personal		('000)	41	43	43	45	50
1.16	* holidays, leisure and recreation		('000)	18	18	18	18	17
1.17	* other personal purposes		('000)	23	25	25	27	32
1.18	♦ Business and professional		('000)	5	5	5	6	4
	Arrivals by mode of transport							
1.19	Total		('000)	68	57	60	66	73
1.20	♦ Air		('000)	46	47	48	50	54
1.21	♦ Water	(2)	('000)	22	10	12	15	19
1.22	♦ Land		('000)	..	..	..	..	..
1.23	* railway		('000)	..	..	..	..	..
1.24	* road		('000)	..	..	..	..	..
1.25	* others		('000)	..	..	..	..	..
	Expenditure							
1.33	Total		US$ Mn	32	46	48	..	..
1.34	♦ Travel		US$ Mn	30	44	45	..	..
1.35	♦ Passenger transport		US$ Mn	2	2	3	..	..
	Expenditure by main purpose of the trip							
1.36	Total		US$ Mn	30	44	45	..	..
1.37	♦ Personal		US$ Mn	27	39	42	..	..
1.38	♦ Business and professional		US$ Mn	3	5	3	..	..
	Indicators							
1.39	Average size of travel party		Persons	2.0	2.0	..	..	..
	Average length of stay							
1.40	Total		Days	7.05	7.00	..	..	..
1.41	♦ For all commercial accommodation services		Nights	..	..	..	..	..
1.42	* of which, "hotels and similar establishments"		Nights	..	..	..	..	..
1.43	♦ For non commercial accommodation services		Days	..	..	..	..	..
1.44	Average expenditure per day		US$	..	..	..	..	..
3.	**OUTBOUND TOURISM**							
	Data							
	Expenditure							
3.4	Total		US$ Mn	27	29	31	..	..
3.5	♦ Travel		US$ Mn	14	16	20	..	..
3.6	♦ Passenger transport		US$ Mn	13	14	11	..	..
	Expenditure by main purpose of the trip							
3.7	Total		US$ Mn	14	16	20	..	..
3.8	♦ Personal		US$ Mn	2	7	12	..	..
3.9	♦ Business and professional		US$ Mn	12	9	9	..	..
4.	**TOURISM INDUSTRIES**							
	Indicators							
4.16	Occupancy rate / rooms		Percent	..	..	..	..	..
4.17	Occupancy rate / bed-places		Percent	..	..	..	..	..
4.18	Average length of stay		Nights	7.00	7.00	..	..	..
4.19	Available capacity (bed-places per 1000 inhabitants)		Units	..	..	..	..	..

TONGA

Cod.	Basic data and indicators	Notes	Units	2011	2012	2013	2014	2015
6.	**COMPLEMENTARY INDICATORS**							
	Demand							
6.1	Gross travel propensity		Units	..	..	..	..	..
6.2	(1.2 inbound tourists) / population		Units	0.44	0.45	0.46	0.48	0.51
	Macroeconomic indicators related to international tourism							
6.3	Inbound tourism expenditure over GDP		Percent	7.1	9.9	..	..	..
6.4	Outbound tourism expenditure over GDP		Percent	6.0	6.3	..	..	..
6.5	Tourism balance (inbound minus outbound tourism expenditure) over GDP		Percent	1.1	3.6	..	..	..
6.6	Tourism openness (inbound plus outbound tourism expenditure) over GDP		Percent	13.1	16.2	..	..	..
6.7	Tourism coverage (inbound over outbound tourism expenditure)		Percent	118.3	155.8	154.7	..	..
6.8	Inbound tourism expenditure over exports of goods		Percent	190.4	295.7	283.9	..	..
6.9	Inbound tourism expenditure over exports of services		Percent	56.7	61.5	67.0	..	..
6.10	Inbound tourism expenditure over exports of goods and services		Percent	43.7	50.9	54.2	..	..
6.11	Inbound tourism expenditure over current account credits		Percent	14.8	17.7	17.9	..	..
6.12	Outbound tourism expenditure over imports of goods		Percent	12.7	15.4	16.7	..	..
6.13	Outbound tourism expenditure over imports of services		Percent	37.9	36.3	33.7	..	..
6.14	Outbound tourism expenditure over imports of goods and		Percent	9.5	10.8	11.2	..	..
6.15	Outbound tourism expenditure over current account debits		Percent	8.5	9.6	10.0	..	..

TRINIDAD AND TOBAGO

Cod.	Basic data and indicators	Notes	Units	2011	2012	2013	2014	2015
1.	**INBOUND TOURISM**							
	Data							
	Arrivals							
1.1	Total		('000)	491	504	467	446	519
1.2	♦ Overnight visitors (tourists)	(1)	('000)	431	455	434	412	440
1.3	♦ Same-day visitors (excursionists)		('000)	60	49	33	34	79
1.4	* of which, cruise passengers		('000)	60	49	33	34	79
	Arrivals by region	(1)						
1.5	Total		('000)	431	455	434	412	440
1.6	♦ Africa		('000)	3	3	1	2	2
1.7	♦ Americas		('000)	339	333	338	328	359
1.8	♦ East Asia and the Pacific		('000)	9	11	8	9	7
1.9	♦ Europe		('000)	74	68	65	70	66
1.10	♦ Middle East		('000)	..	..	..	..	..
1.11	♦ South Asia		('000)	5	5	5	4	4
1.12	♦ Other not classified		('000)	..	35	18	..	1
1.13	* of which, nationals residing abroad		('000)	..	..	..	..	..
	Arrivals by main purpose	(1)						
1.14	Total		('000)	431	455	434	412	440
1.15	♦ Personal		('000)	328	350	369	320	347
1.16	* holidays, leisure and recreation		('000)	164	173	96	114	140
1.17	* other personal purposes		('000)	164	177	273	206	207
1.18	♦ Business and professional		('000)	103	105	65	93	93
	Arrivals by mode of transport							
1.19	Total		('000)	491	504	467	446	519
1.20	♦ Air		('000)	431	455	434	412	440
1.21	♦ Water		('000)	60	49	33	34	79
1.22	♦ Land		('000)	..	..	..	..	..
1.23	* railway		('000)	..	..	..	..	..
1.24	* road		('000)	..	..	..	..	..
1.25	* others		('000)	..	..	..	..	..
	Expenditure							
1.33	Total		US$ Mn	650	..	..	..	..
1.34	♦ Travel		US$ Mn	472	..	..	..	..
1.35	♦ Passenger transport		US$ Mn	178	..	..	..	..
	Expenditure by main purpose of the trip							
1.36	Total		US$ Mn	472	..	..	..	..
1.37	♦ Personal		US$ Mn	383	..	..	..	..
1.38	♦ Business and professional		US$ Mn	89	..	..	..	..
	Indicators							
1.39	Average size of travel party		Persons	..	..	..	..	..
	Average length of stay							
1.40	Total	(2)	Days	15.00	14.00	16.00	14.00	14.00
1.41	♦ For all commercial accommodation services		Nights	..	..	..	..	..
1.42	* of which, "hotels and similar establishments"		Nights	..	..	..	..	..
1.43	♦ For non commercial accommodation services		Days	..	..	..	..	..
1.44	Average expenditure per day	(2)	US$	76.5	88.0	97.1	107.9	..
2.	**DOMESTIC TOURISM**	(3)						
	Data							
	Trips							
2.1	Total		('000)	..	..	..	..	..
2.2	♦ Overnight visitors (tourists)		('000)	546	..	627	..	..
2.3	♦ Same-day visitors (excursionists)		('000)	..	..	..	..	..
	Indicators							
2.23	Average size of travel party		Persons	2.3	..	2.4	..	..
	Average length of stay							
2.24	Total		Days	4.53	..	4.63	..	..
2.25	♦ For all commercial accommodation services		Nights	..	..	..	..	..
2.26	* of which, "hotels and similar establishments"		Nights	..	..	..	..	..
2.27	♦ For non commercial accommodation services		Days	..	..	..	..	..
2.28	Average expenditure per day		US$	39.8	..	46.5	..	..
3.	**OUTBOUND TOURISM**							
	Data							
	Expenditure							
3.4	Total		US$ Mn	192	..	..	..	..
3.5	♦ Travel		US$ Mn	150	..	..	..	..
3.6	♦ Passenger transport		US$ Mn	42	..	..	..	..

TRINIDAD AND TOBAGO

Cod.	Basic data and indicators	Notes	Units	2011	2012	2013	2014	2015
4.	**TOURISM INDUSTRIES**							
	Data							
	Number of establishments							
4.1	Total		Units	..	..	..	..	..
4.2	♦ Accommodation for visitors		Units	..	..	..	..	
4.3	* of which, "hotels and similar establishments"		Units	..	..	507	591	
4.4	♦ Food and beverage serving activities		Units	..	..	..	..	..
4.5	♦ Passenger transportation		Units	..	..	..	..	..
4.6	♦ Travel agencies and other reservation services activities		Units	..	..	..	..	..
4.7	♦ Other tourism industries		Units	..	..	..	..	..
	Accommodation for visitors in hotels and similar establishments							
	Non-monetary data							
4.13	♦ Number of establishments		Units	..	..	507	591	..
4.14	♦ Number of rooms		Units	..	6,803	6,842	7,768	..
4.15	♦ Number of bed-places		Units	..	..	..	..	..
	Indicators							
4.16	Occupancy rate / rooms		Percent	45.10	46.50	52.65	64.74	66.01
4.17	Occupancy rate / bed-places		Percent	..	..	..	..	..
4.18	Average length of stay		Nights	..	..	..	..	..
4.19	Available capacity (bed-places per 1000 inhabitants)		Units	..	..	..	..	..
6.	**COMPLEMENTARY INDICATORS**							
	Demand							
6.1	Gross travel propensity		Units	..	..	..	..	..
6.2	(1.2 inbound tourists + 2.2 domestic tourists) / population		Units	0.73	..	0.79	..	..
	Macroeconomic indicators related to international tourism							
6.3	Inbound tourism expenditure over GDP		Percent	2.8	..	..	..	..
6.4	Outbound tourism expenditure over GDP		Percent	0.8	..	..	..	..
6.5	Tourism balance (inbound minus outbound tourism expenditure) over GDP		Percent	2.0	..	..	..	..
6.6	Tourism openness (inbound plus outbound tourism expenditure) over GDP		Percent	3.6	..	..	..	..
6.7	Tourism coverage (inbound over outbound tourism expenditure)		Percent	338.5	..	..	..	..
6.8	Inbound tourism expenditure over exports of goods		Percent	4.4	..	..	..	..
6.9	Inbound tourism expenditure over exports of services		Percent	11.2	..	..	..	..
6.10	Inbound tourism expenditure over exports of goods and services		Percent	3.1	..	..	..	..
6.11	Inbound tourism expenditure over current account credits		Percent	3.1	..	..	..	..
6.12	Outbound tourism expenditure over imports of goods		Percent	2.0	..	..	..	..
6.13	Outbound tourism expenditure over imports of services		Percent	3.6	..	..	..	..
6.14	Outbound tourism expenditure over imports of goods and		Percent	1.3	..	..	..	..
6.15	Outbound tourism expenditure over current account debits		Percent	1.3	..	..	..	..

TUNISIA

Cod.	Basic data and indicators	Notes	Units	2011	2012	2013	2014	2015
1.	**INBOUND TOURISM**							
	Data							
	Arrivals							
1.1	Total		('000)	6,038	..	..	..	..
1.2	♦ Overnight visitors (tourists)		('000)	5,746	6,999	7,352	7,163	5,359
1.3	♦ Same-day visitors (excursionists)		('000)	292	..	..	..	..
1.4	* of which, cruise passengers		('000)	292	..	..	..	..
	Arrivals by region							
1.5	Total		('000)	5,745	6,999	7,352	7,163	5,359
1.6	♦ Africa		('000)	829	996	1,043	1,385	1,586
1.7	♦ Americas		('000)	24	31	26	27	25
1.8	♦ East Asia and the Pacific		('000)	16	13	13	14	7
1.9	♦ Europe		('000)	2,134	2,965	2,897	2,810	1,304
1.10	♦ Middle East		('000)	1,731	1,926	2,271	1,809	1,264
1.11	♦ South Asia		('000)	..	..	..	..	..
1.12	♦ Other not classified		('000)	1,011	1,068	1,103	1,119	1,174
1.13	* of which, nationals residing abroad		('000)	960	1,049	1,083	1,095	1,157
	Arrivals by mode of transport	(1)						
1.19	Total		('000)	4,785	5,950	6,269	6,070	..
1.20	♦ Air		('000)	2,406	3,597	3,766	3,449	..
1.21	♦ Water		('000)	90	96	78	89	..
1.22	♦ Land		('000)	2,289	2,257	2,425	2,532	..
1.23	* railway		('000)	..	..	..	..	..
1.24	* road		('000)	2,289	2,257	2,425	2,532	..
1.25	* others		('000)	..	..	..	..	..
	Accommodation							
	Hotels and similar establishments							
1.31	♦ Guests		('000)	2,623	4,086	3,952	3,913	2,143
1.32	♦ Overnights		('000)	17,208	25,921	25,762	24,788	11,170
	Expenditure							
1.33	Total		US$ Mn	2,529	2,931	2,863	3,042	1,869
1.34	♦ Travel		US$ Mn	1,914	2,227	2,191	2,359	1,381
1.35	♦ Passenger transport		US$ Mn	615	704	672	683	488
	Expenditure by main purpose of the trip							
1.36	Total		US$ Mn	1,914	2,227	2,191	2,359	1,381
1.37	♦ Personal		US$ Mn	1,871	2,173	2,133	2,297	1,346
1.38	♦ Business and professional		US$ Mn	43	54	58	62	35
	Indicators							
1.39	Average size of travel party		Persons	..	..	..	..	..
	Average length of stay							
1.40	Total		Days	..	..	..	..	..
1.41	♦ For all commercial accommodation services		Nights	3.60	4.40	4.10	4.10	4.10
1.42	* of which, "hotels and similar establishments"		Nights	..	..	..	..	..
1.43	♦ For non commercial accommodation services		Days	..	..	..	..	..
1.44	Average expenditure per day		US$	..	..	..	..	..
2.	**DOMESTIC TOURISM**							
	Data							
	Accommodation							
	Hotels and similar establishments							
2.21	♦ Guests		('000)	1,525	1,903	1,949	1,996	2,241
2.22	♦ Overnights		('000)	3,429	4,115	4,240	4,319	5,007
	Indicators							
2.23	Average size of travel party		Persons	..	..	..	..	..
	Average length of stay							
2.24	Total		Days	..	..	..	..	..
2.25	♦ For all commercial accommodation services		Nights	2.16	2.16	2.18	2.16	2.23
2.26	* of which, "hotels and similar establishments"		Nights	2.20	2.16	2.18	2.16	2.23
2.27	♦ For non commercial accommodation services		Days	..	..	..	..	..
2.28	Average expenditure per day		US$	..	..	..	..	..
3.	**OUTBOUND TOURISM**							
	Data							
	Departures							
3.1	Total		('000)	..	..	..	..	..
3.2	♦ Overnight visitors (tourists)		('000)	2,303	2,897	2,873	2,637	..
3.3	♦ Same-day visitors (excursionists)		('000)	..	..	..	..	..

TUNISIA

Cod.	Basic data and indicators	Notes	Units	2011	2012	2013	2014	2015
	Expenditure							
3.4	Total		US$ Mn	678	673	768	770	767
3.5	♦ Travel		US$ Mn	607	593	675	681	696
3.6	♦ Passenger transport		US$ Mn	71	80	93	89	71
	Expenditure by main purpose of the trip							
3.7	Total		US$ Mn	606	593	675	681	696
3.8	♦ Personal		US$ Mn	557	529	605	589	611
3.9	♦ Business and professional		US$ Mn	49	64	70	92	85
4.	**TOURISM INDUSTRIES**							
	Data							
	Number of establishments							
4.1	Total		Units	..	..	..	..	..
4.2	♦ Accommodation for visitors		Units	..	..	..	..	..
4.3	* of which, "hotels and similar establishments"	(2)	Units	861	846	847	848	862
4.4	♦ Food and beverage serving activities		Units	..	..	..	..	..
4.5	♦ Passenger transportation		Units	..	..	..	..	..
4.6	♦ Travel agencies and other reservation services activities		Units	..	..	..	..	..
4.7	♦ Other tourism industries		Units	..	..	..	..	..
	Accommodation for visitors in hotels and similar establishments							
	Non-monetary data	(2)						
4.13	♦ Number of establishments		Units	861	846	847	848	862
4.14	♦ Number of rooms		Units	121,073	120,999	120,125	120,039	120,495
4.15	♦ Number of bed-places		Units	242,146	241,997	240,249	240,077	240,989
	Indicators							
4.16	Occupancy rate / rooms		Percent	..	..	..	..	..
4.17	Occupancy rate / bed-places		Percent	34.30	45.90	46.10	44.90	27.90
4.18	Average length of stay		Nights	6.60	6.30	6.50	6.30	5.20
4.19	Available capacity (bed-places per 1000 inhabitants)		Units	22.51	22.24	21.83	21.57	21.41
6.	**COMPLEMENTARY INDICATORS**							
	Demand							
6.1	Gross travel propensity		Units	..	..	..	..	..
6.2	(1.2 inbound tourists) / population		Units	0.53	0.64	0.67	0.64	0.48
	Macroeconomic indicators related to international tourism							
6.3	Inbound tourism expenditure over GDP		Percent	5.5	6.5	6.2	6.4	..
6.4	Outbound tourism expenditure over GDP		Percent	1.5	1.5	1.7	1.6	..
6.5	Tourism balance (inbound minus outbound tourism expenditure) over GDP		Percent	4.0	5.0	4.5	4.8	..
6.6	Tourism openness (inbound plus outbound tourism expenditure) over GDP		Percent	7.0	8.0	7.9	8.0	..
6.7	Tourism coverage (inbound over outbound tourism expenditure)		Percent	373.0	435.5	372.8	395.1	..
6.8	Inbound tourism expenditure over exports of goods		Percent	14.1	17.2	16.7	18.1	..
6.9	Inbound tourism expenditure over exports of services		Percent	54.8	57.7	59.3	64.3	..
6.10	Inbound tourism expenditure over exports of goods and services		Percent	11.2	13.2	13.0	14.1	..
6.11	Inbound tourism expenditure over current account credits		Percent	10.2	11.8	11.5	12.4	..
6.12	Outbound tourism expenditure over imports of goods		Percent	3.0	2.9	3.3	3.3	..
6.13	Outbound tourism expenditure over imports of services		Percent	21.3	21.1	23.2	22.6	..
6.14	Outbound tourism expenditure over imports of goods and		Percent	2.6	2.6	2.9	2.9	..
6.15	Outbound tourism expenditure over current account debits		Percent	2.6	2.5	2.9	2.8	..

TURKEY

Cod. Basic data and indicators	Notes	Units	2011	2012	2013	2014	2015
1. **INBOUND TOURISM**							
Data							
Arrivals	**(1)**						
1.1 Total		('000)	36,769	37,715	39,861	41,627	41,114
1.2 ♦ Overnight visitors (tourists)		('000)	34,654	35,698	37,795	39,811	39,478
1.3 ♦ Same-day visitors (excursionists)	**(2)**	('000)	2,115	2,017	2,066	1,816	1,636
1.4 * of which, cruise passengers		('000)	..	..	..	..	..
Arrivals by region	**(1)**						
1.5 Total		('000)	34,653	35,698	37,795	39,811	39,478
1.6 ♦ Africa		('000)	301	372	420	491	535
1.7 ♦ Americas		('000)	660	714	790	846	936
1.8 ♦ East Asia and the Pacific		('000)	721	784	848	1,032	1,074
1.9 ♦ Europe		('000)	23,501	24,167	26,157	27,263	26,411
1.10 ♦ Middle East		('000)	2,133	2,377	3,244	3,554	3,663
1.11 ♦ South Asia		('000)	1,992	1,319	1,348	1,787	1,931
1.12 ♦ Other not classified		('000)	5,345	5,965	4,989	4,838	4,929
1.13 * of which, nationals residing abroad		('000)	5,311	5,929	4,948	4,787	4,866
Arrivals by main purpose	**(1)(3)**						
1.14 Total		('000)	36,151	36,464	39,226	41,415	41,618
1.15 ♦ Personal		('000)	33,776	34,083	36,703	38,923	39,261
1.16 * holidays, leisure and recreation		('000)	25,461	27,369	29,428	31,346	31,138
1.17 * other personal purposes		('000)	8,315	6,714	7,275	7,577	8,123
1.18 ♦ Business and professional		('000)	2,375	2,381	2,523	2,492	2,356
Arrivals by mode of transport	**(1)**						
1.19 Total		('000)	36,769	37,716	39,861	41,627	41,114
1.20 ♦ Air		('000)	26,026	27,733	29,418	31,034	31,040
1.21 ♦ Water		('000)	2,709	2,528	2,616	2,493	2,371
1.22 ♦ Land		('000)	8,034	7,455	7,827	8,100	7,703
1.23 * railway		('000)	54	31	29	25	19
1.24 * road		('000)	7,980	7,424	7,798	8,075	7,683
1.25 * others		('000)	..	..	..	..	..
Arrivals by form of organization of the trip	**(1)(3)**						
1.26 Total		('000)	30,395	30,304	32,431	35,031	35,845
1.27 ♦ Package tour		('000)	13,700	14,689	15,044	16,085	14,934
1.28 ♦ Other forms		('000)	16,695	15,615	17,387	18,946	20,911
Accommodation							
Total							
1.29 ♦ Guests	**(4)(5)**	('000)	19,264	20,481	21,182	23,609	23,138
1.30 ♦ Overnights	**(4)(5)**	('000)	78,889	90,822	89,594	97,581	96,400
Hotels and similar establishments							
1.31 ♦ Guests		('000)	18,791	19,999	20,678	22,985	22,585
1.32 ♦ Overnights		('000)	78,257	90,100	88,862	96,501	95,552
Expenditure							
1.33 Total		US$ Mn	30,302	31,566	36,192	38,766	35,413
1.34 ♦ Travel	**(6)**	US$ Mn	25,054	25,345	27,997	29,552	26,616
1.35 ♦ Passenger transport		US$ Mn	5,248	6,221	8,195	9,214	8,797
Expenditure by main purpose of the trip							
1.36 Total		US$ Mn	25,054	25,345	27,997	29,552	26,616
1.37 ♦ Personal		US$ Mn	23,394	22,978	25,229	26,028	23,567
1.38 ♦ Business and professional		US$ Mn	1,660	2,367	2,768	3,524	3,049
Indicators	**(1)**						
1.39 Average size of travel party		Persons	2.7	2.6	2.7	2.7	2.7
Average length of stay							
1.40 Total		Days	..	..	..	..	..
1.41 ♦ For all commercial accommodation services		Nights	6.02	5.78	5.91	5.84	5.87
1.42 * of which, "hotels and similar establishments"		Nights	5.93	5.57	5.68	5.66	5.64
1.43 ♦ For non commercial accommodation services		Days	19.70	21.15	19.03	18.27	17.23
1.44 Average expenditure per day		US$	81.3	85.2	92.4	94.9	..
2. **DOMESTIC TOURISM**							
Data							
Trips	**(7)**						
2.1 Total		('000)	104,171	106,226	112,161	155,088	115,381
2.2 ♦ Overnight visitors (tourists)		('000)	65,854	64,922	68,452	70,894	71,251
2.3 ♦ Same-day visitors (excursionists)		('000)	38,317	41,304	43,709	44,194	44,130

TURKEY

Cod.	Basic data and indicators	Notes	Units	2011	2012	2013	2014	2015
	Trips by main purpose	(7)						
2.4	Total		('000)	65,854	64,922	68,452	70,894	71,251
2.5	♦ Personal		('000)	63,745	62,794	66,396	68,788	68,973
2.6	* holidays, leisure and recreation		('000)	13,675	13,437	14,738	14,401	14,405
2.7	* other personal purposes		('000)	50,070	49,357	51,658	54,387	54,568
2.8	♦ Business and professional		('000)	2,109	2,128	2,056	2,106	2,278
	Trips by mode of transport	(7)						
2.9	Total		('000)	65,854	64,922	68,452	70,894	71,251
2.10	♦ Air		('000)	3,738	4,404	4,524	5,794	6,678
2.11	♦ Water		('000)	628	400	624	533	496
2.12	♦ Land		('000)	61,488	60,118	63,304	64,567	64,077
2.13	* railway		('000)	1,231	895	1,021	1,031	946
2.14	* road		('000)	60,189	59,084	62,150	63,374	63,000
2.15	* others		('000)	68	139	133	162	131
	Trips by form of organization	(7)						
2.16	Total		('000)	65,854	64,922	68,452	70,895	71,251
2.17	♦ Package tour		('000)	1,739	1,927	2,384	1,986	1,233
2.18	♦ Other forms		('000)	64,115	62,995	66,068	68,909	70,018
	Accommodation							
	Total							
2.19	♦ Guests	(5)	('000)	14,350	15,702	17,101	17,292	20,222
2.20	♦ Overnights	(5)	('000)	27,617	30,332	33,091	32,449	37,481
	Hotels and similar establishments							
2.21	♦ Guests		('000)	13,700	14,906	16,194	16,264	19,056
2.22	♦ Overnights		('000)	26,280	28,663	31,270	30,406	35,225
	Indicators	(7)						
2.23	Average size of travel party		Persons	2.9	2.9	2.9	2.9	2.9
	Average length of stay							
2.24	Total		Days	8.48	8.58	8.14	8.12	8.26
2.25	♦ For all commercial accommodation services		Nights	4.70	4.73	4.99	4.69	4.26
2.26	* of which, "hotels and similar establishments"		Nights	4.08	3.98	4.32	4.02	3.67
2.27	♦ For non commercial accommodation services		Days	9.27	9.38	8.82	8.91	9.21
2.28	Average expenditure per day		US$	16.6	16.8	17.2	18.1	15.0
3.	**OUTBOUND TOURISM**							
	Data							
	Departures							
3.1	Total		('000)	..	..	..	..	..
3.2	♦ Overnight visitors (tourists)		('000)	6,282	5,803	7,526	7,982	8,751
3.3	♦ Same-day visitors (excursionists)		('000)	..	..	..	..	..
	Expenditure							
3.4	Total		US$ Mn	5,372	4,585	5,253	5,475	5,686
3.5	♦ Travel		US$ Mn	4,883	4,094	4,817	5,072	5,368
3.6	♦ Passenger transport		US$ Mn	489	491	436	403	318
	Expenditure by main purpose of the trip							
3.7	Total		US$ Mn	4,883	4,094	4,817	5,072	5,368
3.8	♦ Personal		US$ Mn	3,149	2,209	3,213	3,085	3,302
3.9	♦ Business and professional		US$ Mn	1,734	1,885	1,604	1,987	2,066
	Indicators							
3.10	Average length of stay		Days	15.16	12.53	13.09	12.90	11.94
3.11	Average expenditure per day		US$	58.1	63.2	53.3	53.1	..
4.	**TOURISM INDUSTRIES**							
	Data							
	Number of establishments							
4.1	Total		Units	..	..	..	..	..
4.2	♦ Accommodation for visitors		Units	2,783	2,870	2,982	3,131	3,309
4.3	* of which, "hotels and similar establishments"		Units	2,740	2,814	2,917	3,061	3,237
4.4	♦ Food and beverage serving activities		Units	..	..	..	..	..
4.5	♦ Passenger transportation		Units	..	..	..	..	..
4.6	♦ Travel agencies and other reservation services activities		Units	..	..	..	..	..
4.7	♦ Other tourism industries		Units	..	..	..	..	..
	Accommodation for visitors in hotels and similar establishments							
	Non-monetary data							
4.13	♦ Number of establishments		Units	2,740	2,814	2,917	3,061	3,237
4.14	♦ Number of rooms		Units	313,391	328,133	348,348	374,016	393,521
4.15	♦ Number of bed-places		Units	655,827	688,053	729,747	784,469	826,255

408

TURKEY

Cod.	Basic data and indicators	Notes	Units	2011	2012	2013	2014	2015
	Indicators							
4.16	Occupancy rate / rooms		Percent	..	..	..	..	..
4.17	Occupancy rate / bed-places	(8)	Percent	51.46	54.34	52.60	51.84	51.18
4.18	Average length of stay	(8)	Nights	3.20	3.35	3.20	3.18	3.09
4.19	Available capacity (bed-places per 1000 inhabitants)		Units	8.92	9.19	9.57	10.12	10.50
5.	**EMPLOYMENT**	**(9)**						
	Data							
	Number of employees by tourism industries							
5.1	Total		('000)	..	..	..	..	1,368.0
5.2	♦ Accommodation services for visitors (hotels and similar establishments)	(10)	('000)	..	..	..	..	287.0
5.3	♦ Other accommodation services		('000)	..	..	..	..	..
5.4	♦ Food and beverage serving activities	(11)	('000)	..	..	..	..	840.0
5.5	♦ Passenger transportation	(12)	('000)	..	..	..	..	204.0
5.6	♦ Travel agencies and other reservation services activities	(13)	('000)	..	..	..	..	37.0
5.7	♦ Other tourism industries		('000)	..	..	..	..	..
	Number of jobs by status in employment							
5.8	Total		('000)	..	..	..	..	1,742.0
5.9	♦ Employees		('000)	..	..	..	..	1,368.0
5.10	♦ Self employed		('000)	..	..	..	..	374.0
6.	**COMPLEMENTARY INDICATORS**							
	Demand							
6.1	Gross travel propensity		Units	..	..	..	..	..
6.2	(1.2 inbound tourists + 2.2 domestic tourists) / population		Units	1.37	1.34	1.39	1.43	1.41
	Macroeconomic indicators related to international tourism							
6.3	Inbound tourism expenditure over GDP		Percent	3.9	4.0	4.4	4.9	4.9
6.4	Outbound tourism expenditure over GDP		Percent	0.7	0.6	0.6	0.7	0.8
6.5	Tourism balance (inbound minus outbound tourism expenditure) over GDP		Percent	3.2	3.4	3.8	4.2	4.1
6.6	Tourism openness (inbound plus outbound tourism expenditure) over GDP		Percent	4.6	4.6	5.0	5.6	5.7
6.7	Tourism coverage (inbound over outbound tourism expenditure)		Percent	564.1	688.5	689.0	708.1	622.8
6.8	Inbound tourism expenditure over exports of goods		Percent	21.3	19.5	22.4	22.9	23.3
6.9	Inbound tourism expenditure over exports of services		Percent	73.4	72.5	75.1	74.8	75.9
6.10	Inbound tourism expenditure over exports of goods and services		Percent	16.5	15.4	17.2	17.6	17.8
6.11	Inbound tourism expenditure over current account credits		Percent	15.9	14.8	16.6	17.0	17.2
6.12	Outbound tourism expenditure over imports of goods		Percent	2.3	2.0	2.2	2.4	2.8
6.13	Outbound tourism expenditure over imports of services		Percent	25.6	21.9	21.4	21.8	25.2
6.14	Outbound tourism expenditure over imports of goods and		Percent	2.1	1.8	2.0	2.1	2.6
6.15	Outbound tourism expenditure over current account debits		Percent	2.1	1.8	1.9	2.1	2.5

TURKS AND CAICOS ISLANDS

Cod.	Basic data and indicators	Notes	Units	2011	2012	2013	2014	2015
1.	**INBOUND TOURISM**							
	Data							
	Arrivals							
1.1	Total		('000)	1,010	968	1,069	1,329	1,316
1.2	♦ Overnight visitors (tourists)		('000)	354	292	291	357	386
1.3	♦ Same-day visitors (excursionists)		('000)	656	677	779	972	930
1.4	* of which, cruise passengers		('000)	656	677	779	972	930
	Arrivals by region							
1.5	Total		('000)	354	292	291	357	386
1.6	♦ Africa		('000)	..	..	..	..	..
1.7	♦ Americas		('000)	344	282	281	345	370
1.8	♦ East Asia and the Pacific		('000)	..	..	..	..	..
1.9	♦ Europe		('000)	7	7	7	8	11
1.10	♦ Middle East		('000)	..	..	..	..	..
1.11	♦ South Asia		('000)	..	..	..	..	..
1.12	♦ Other not classified		('000)	3	3	3	4	5
1.13	* of which, nationals residing abroad		('000)	..	..	..	..	..
6.	**COMPLEMENTARY INDICATORS**							
	Demand							
6.1	Gross travel propensity		Units	..	..	..	..	..
6.2	(1.2 inbound tourists) / population		Units	11.16	9.00	8.78	10.58	11.35

TUVALU

Cod.	Basic data and indicators	Notes	Units	2011	2012	2013	2014	2015
1.	**INBOUND TOURISM**							
	Data							
	Arrivals							
1.1	Total	(1)	('000)	..	..	..	..	..
1.2	♦ Overnight visitors (tourists)	(1)	('000)	1.2	1.1	1.3	1.4	2.4
1.3	♦ Same-day visitors (excursionists)		('000)	..	..	..	..	..
1.4	* of which, cruise passengers		('000)	..	..	..	..	..
	Arrivals by region							
1.5	Total	(1)	('000)	1.2	1.1	1.3	1.4	2.4
1.6	♦ Africa		('000)	..	..	..	..	..
1.7	♦ Americas		('000)	0.1	0.1	0.1	0.1	0.1
1.8	♦ East Asia and the Pacific		('000)	0.9	0.8	1.0	1.1	2.0
1.9	♦ Europe		('000)	0.1	0.1	0.1	0.1	0.2
1.10	♦ Middle East		('000)	..	..	..	..	..
1.11	♦ South Asia		('000)	..	..	..	..	..
1.12	♦ Other not classified		('000)	0.1	0.1	0.1	0.1	0.1
1.13	* of which, nationals residing abroad		('000)	..	..	..	..	..
	Arrivals by main purpose							
1.14	Total	(1)	('000)	1.2	1.1	1.3	1.4	2.4
1.15	♦ Personal		('000)	0.9	0.8	0.7	0.8	1.2
1.16	* holidays, leisure and recreation		('000)	0.3	0.3	0.4	0.4	0.6
1.17	* other personal purposes		('000)	0.6	0.5	0.3	0.4	0.6
1.18	♦ Business and professional		('000)	0.3	0.3	0.6	0.6	1.2
	Arrivals by mode of transport							
1.19	Total		('000)	1.2	..	..	..	..
1.20	♦ Air		('000)	1.1	..	..	..	..
1.21	♦ Water		('000)	0.1	..	..	..	..
1.22	♦ Land		('000)	..	..	..	..	..
1.23	* railway		('000)	..	..	..	..	..
1.24	* road		('000)	..	..	..	..	..
1.25	* others		('000)	..	..	..	..	..
	Expenditure							
1.33	Total		US$ Mn	..	..	..	..	..
1.34	♦ Travel		US$ Mn	2.4	2.7	2.4	..	..
1.35	♦ Passenger transport		US$ Mn	..	..	..	..	..
	Expenditure by main purpose of the trip							
1.36	Total		US$ Mn	2.4	2.7	2.4	..	..
1.37	♦ Personal		US$ Mn	0.7	0.8	0.7	..	..
1.38	♦ Business and professional		US$ Mn	1.7	1.9	1.7	..	..
3.	**OUTBOUND TOURISM**							
	Data							
	Departures							
3.1	Total		('000)	..	..	..	..	..
3.2	♦ Overnight visitors (tourists)		('000)	2.1	..	..	..	..
3.3	♦ Same-day visitors (excursionists)		('000)	..	..	..	..	..
	Expenditure							
3.4	Total		US$ Mn	11.5	11.5	7.6	..	..
3.5	♦ Travel		US$ Mn	9.7	9.5	6.1	..	..
3.6	♦ Passenger transport		US$ Mn	1.8	2.0	1.5	..	..
	Expenditure by main purpose of the trip							
3.7	Total		US$ Mn	9.7	9.5	6.0	..	..
3.8	♦ Personal		US$ Mn	8.6	8.4	5.1	..	..
3.9	♦ Business and professional		US$ Mn	1.1	1.1	0.9	..	..
6.	**COMPLEMENTARY INDICATORS**							
	Demand							
6.1	Gross travel propensity		Units	..	..	..	..	..
6.2	(1.2 inbound tourists) / population		Units	0.12	0.11	0.13	0.14	0.24
	Macroeconomic indicators related to international tourism							
6.3	Inbound tourism expenditure over GDP		Percent	..	..	..	..	..
6.4	Outbound tourism expenditure over GDP		Percent	..	..	..	..	..
6.5	Tourism balance (inbound minus outbound tourism expenditure) over GDP		Percent	..	..	..	..	..
6.6	Tourism openness (inbound plus outbound tourism expenditure) over GDP		Percent	..	..	..	..	..

TUVALU

Cod.	Basic data and indicators	Notes	Units	2011	2012	2013	2014	2015
6.7	Tourism coverage (inbound over outbound tourism expenditure)		Percent	21.0	23.5	31.8	..	..
6.8	Inbound tourism expenditure over exports of goods		Percent	22.9	13.1	14.6	..	..
6.9	Inbound tourism expenditure over exports of services		Percent	55.2	60.1	58.0	..	..
6.10	Inbound tourism expenditure over exports of goods and services		Percent	16.2	10.8	11.7	..	..
6.11	Inbound tourism expenditure over current account credits		Percent	5.2	4.3	4.6	..	..
6.12	Outbound tourism expenditure over imports of goods		Percent	54.2	51.9	35.1	..	..
6.13	Outbound tourism expenditure over imports of services		Percent	26.0	41.7	41.9	..	..
6.14	Outbound tourism expenditure over imports of goods and		Percent	17.6	23.1	19.1	..	..
6.15	Outbound tourism expenditure over current account debits		Percent	13.9	17.4	11.5	..	..

UGANDA

Cod.	Basic data and indicators	Notes	Units	2011	2012	2013	2014	2015
1.	**INBOUND TOURISM**							
	Data							
	Arrivals							
1.1	Total		('000)	..	..	..	..	..
1.2	♦ Overnight visitors (tourists)		('000)	1,151	1,197	1,206	1,266	1,303
1.3	♦ Same-day visitors (excursionists)		('000)	..	..	..	..	..
1.4	* of which, cruise passengers		('000)	..	..	..	..	..
	Arrivals by region							
1.5	Total		('000)	1,151	1,197	1,206	1,266	1,303
1.6	♦ Africa		('000)	873	928	933	986	1,044
1.7	♦ Americas		('000)	63	70	73	77	62
1.8	♦ East Asia and the Pacific		('000)	22	29	32	33	32
1.9	♦ Europe		('000)	153	115	112	114	111
1.10	♦ Middle East		('000)	8	9	10	10	12
1.11	♦ South Asia		('000)	30	38	46	45	40
1.12	♦ Other not classified		('000)	3	8	1	1	2
1.13	* of which, nationals residing abroad		('000)	..	..	..	..	..
	Arrivals by main purpose							
1.14	Total		('000)	1,151	1,197	1,206	1,266	1,303
1.15	♦ Personal		('000)	991	987	910	995	981
1.16	* holidays, leisure and recreation		('000)	76	225	188	220	208
1.17	* other personal purposes		('000)	915	762	722	774	773
1.18	♦ Business and professional		('000)	160	210	296	272	322
	Arrivals by mode of transport							
1.19	Total		('000)	1,151	1,197	1,206	1,266	1,303
1.20	♦ Air		('000)	369	416	423	443	402
1.21	♦ Water		('000)	..	..	..	..	..
1.22	♦ Land		('000)	782	781	783	823	901
1.23	* railway		('000)	..	..	..	..	..
1.24	* road		('000)	782	781	783	823	901
1.25	* others		('000)	..	..	..	..	..
	Arrivals by form of organization of the trip							
1.26	Total		('000)	..	..	..	1,130	..
1.27	♦ Package tour		('000)	..	..	..	63	..
1.28	♦ Other forms		('000)	..	..	..	1,067	..
	Expenditure							
1.33	Total		US$ Mn	977	1,157	1,355	810	1,171
1.34	♦ Travel		US$ Mn	960	1,135	1,334	791	1,149
1.35	♦ Passenger transport		US$ Mn	17	22	21	19	22
	Expenditure by main purpose of the trip							
1.36	Total		US$ Mn	960	1,135	1,334	791	1,149
1.37	♦ Personal		US$ Mn	547	641	775	466	671
1.38	♦ Business and professional		US$ Mn	413	494	559	325	478
	Indicators							
1.39	Average size of travel party		Persons	..	..	..	2.0	..
	Average length of stay							
1.40	Total		Days	..	..	..	7.00	..
1.41	♦ For all commercial accommodation services		Nights	..	..	..	..	..
1.42	* of which, "hotels and similar establishments"		Nights	..	..	..	..	..
1.43	♦ For non commercial accommodation services		Days	..	..	..	..	..
1.44	Average expenditure per day		US$	..	..	..	..	..
3.	**OUTBOUND TOURISM**							
	Data							
	Departures							
3.1	Total		('000)	..	..	..	..	..
3.2	♦ Overnight visitors (tourists)		('000)	367	382	378	511	523
3.3	♦ Same-day visitors (excursionists)		('000)	..	..	..	..	..
	Expenditure							
3.4	Total		US$ Mn	540	642	696	375	573
3.5	♦ Travel		US$ Mn	405	484	555	222	433
3.6	♦ Passenger transport		US$ Mn	135	158	141	153	140
	Expenditure by main purpose of the trip							
3.7	Total		US$ Mn	405	484	555	222	432
3.8	♦ Personal		US$ Mn	177	196	243	114	199
3.9	♦ Business and professional		US$ Mn	228	288	312	107	233

UGANDA

Cod.	Basic data and indicators	Notes	Units	2011	2012	2013	2014	2015
4.	**TOURISM INDUSTRIES**							
	Data							
	Accommodation for visitors in hotels and similar establishments							
	Non-monetary data							
4.13	♦ Number of establishments		Units	..	..	..	..	..
4.14	♦ Number of rooms		Units	..	..	261,030	328,920	..
4.15	♦ Number of bed-places		Units	..	..	290,884	354,232	..
	Indicators							
4.16	Occupancy rate / rooms		Percent	..	..	52.00	48.20	47.60
4.17	Occupancy rate / bed-places		Percent	..	..	51.00	47.50	46.20
4.18	Average length of stay		Nights	..	6.00	6.00	7.00	7.00
4.19	Available capacity (bed-places per 1000 inhabitants)		Units	..	..	7.95	9.38	..
5.	**EMPLOYMENT**							
	Data							
	Number of employees by tourism industries							
5.1	Total		('000)	487.3	475.9	551.1	592.5	1,173.0
5.2	♦ Accommodation services for visitors (hotels and similar establishments)		('000)	..	..	..	..	..
5.3	♦ Other accommodation services		('000)	..	..	..	..	..
5.4	♦ Food and beverage serving activities		('000)	..	..	..	..	..
5.5	♦ Passenger transportation		('000)	..	..	..	..	..
5.6	♦ Travel agencies and other reservation services activities		('000)	..	..	..	..	..
5.7	♦ Other tourism industries		('000)	..	..	..	..	..
6.	**COMPLEMENTARY INDICATORS**							
	Demand							
6.1	Gross travel propensity		Units	..	..	..	..	..
6.2	(1.2 inbound tourists) / population		Units	0.03	0.03	0.03	0.03	0.03
	Macroeconomic indicators related to international tourism							
6.3	Inbound tourism expenditure over GDP		Percent	6.3	5.8	6.3	..	..
6.4	Outbound tourism expenditure over GDP		Percent	3.5	3.2	3.2	..	..
6.5	Tourism balance (inbound minus outbound tourism expenditure) over GDP		Percent	2.8	2.6	3.1	..	..
6.6	Tourism openness (inbound plus outbound tourism expenditure) over GDP		Percent	9.8	9.0	9.5	..	..
6.7	Tourism coverage (inbound over outbound tourism expenditure)		Percent	180.9	180.2	194.7	216.0	204.4
6.8	Inbound tourism expenditure over exports of goods		Percent	38.8	41.2	47.9	29.7	43.9
6.9	Inbound tourism expenditure over exports of services		Percent	54.9	54.6	54.2	40.4	53.7
6.10	Inbound tourism expenditure over exports of goods and services		Percent	22.7	23.5	25.4	17.1	24.2
6.11	Inbound tourism expenditure over current account credits		Percent	16.2	17.2	20.1	13.1	18.2
6.12	Outbound tourism expenditure over imports of goods		Percent	10.8	12.2	14.0	7.4	11.7
6.13	Outbound tourism expenditure over imports of services		Percent	22.2	25.8	25.1	13.9	21.0
6.14	Outbound tourism expenditure over imports of goods and		Percent	7.3	8.3	9.0	4.8	7.5
6.15	Outbound tourism expenditure over current account debits		Percent	7.0	8.1	8.8	4.7	7.3

UKRAINE

Cod.	Basic data and indicators	Notes	Units	2011	2012	2013	2014	2015
1.	**INBOUND TOURISM**							
	Data							
	Arrivals							
1.1	Total		('000)	24,535	25,061	26,025	13,227	13,025
1.2	♦ Overnight visitors (tourists)		('000)	21,415	23,013	24,671	12,712	12,428
1.3	♦ Same-day visitors (excursionists)		('000)	3,120	2,048	1,354	516	597
1.4	* of which, cruise passengers		('000)	..	..	..	..	..
	Arrivals by region							
1.5	Total		('000)	21,415	23,013	24,671	12,712	12,428
1.6	♦ Africa		('000)	15	15	17	15	16
1.7	♦ Americas		('000)	165	176	178	106	138
1.8	♦ East Asia and the Pacific		('000)	50	53	50	29	35
1.9	♦ Europe		('000)	21,118	22,706	24,368	12,516	12,186
1.10	♦ Middle East		('000)	28	29	29	24	30
1.11	♦ South Asia		('000)	22	20	18	15	18
1.12	♦ Other not classified		('000)	17	14	11	6	6
1.13	* of which, nationals residing abroad		('000)	..	..	..	..	..
	Arrivals by main purpose							
1.14	Total		('000)	21,415	23,013	24,671	12,712	12,428
1.15	♦ Personal		('000)	20,711	22,639	24,503	12,661	12,387
1.16	* holidays, leisure and recreation		('000)	1,226	940	488	147	138
1.17	* other personal purposes		('000)	19,485	21,699	24,015	12,514	12,249
1.18	♦ Business and professional		('000)	704	374	168	51	41
	Arrivals by mode of transport							
1.19	Total		('000)	24,535	25,061	26,025	13,227	13,025
1.20	♦ Air		('000)	2,004	2,298	2,497	1,193	1,319
1.21	♦ Water		('000)	255	240	263	148	127
1.22	♦ Land		('000)	22,276	22,523	23,265	11,886	11,579
1.23	* railway		('000)	..	..	..	..	..
1.24	* road		('000)	22,276	22,523	23,265	11,886	11,579
1.25	* others		('000)	..	..	..	..	..
	Arrivals by form of organization of the trip							
1.26	Total		('000)	21,415	23,013	24,671	12,712	12,428
1.27	♦ Package tour		('000)	234	270	154	48	41
1.28	♦ Other forms		('000)	21,181	22,743	24,517	12,664	12,387
	Accommodation							
	Total							
1.29	♦ Guests		('000)	1,428	1,555	1,665	552	666
1.30	♦ Overnights		('000)	7,099	7,762	7,863	1,483	1,731
	Hotels and similar establishments							
1.31	♦ Guests		('000)	1,059	1,165	1,278	527	628
1.32	♦ Overnights		('000)	2,599	3,208	3,249	1,135	1,289
	Expenditure							
1.33	Total		US$ Mn	5,406	5,988	5,931	2,264	1,656
1.34	♦ Travel		US$ Mn	4,294	4,842	5,083	1,612	1,082
1.35	♦ Passenger transport		US$ Mn	1,112	1,146	848	652	574
	Expenditure by main purpose of the trip							
1.36	Total		US$ Mn	4,294	4,842	5,083	1,612	1,082
1.37	♦ Personal		US$ Mn	4,069	4,561	4,799	1,491	996
1.38	♦ Business and professional		US$ Mn	225	281	284	121	86
	Indicators							
1.39	Average size of travel party		Persons	2.4	1.8	1.6	1.5	2.2
	Average length of stay							
1.40	Total		Days	..	..	..	..	..
1.41	♦ For all commercial accommodation services		Nights	4.97	4.99	4.72	2.69	2.60
1.42	* of which, "hotels and similar establishments"		Nights	2.45	2.75	2.55	2.15	2.05
1.43	♦ For non commercial accommodation services		Days	..	..	..	..	..
1.44	Average expenditure per day		US$	..	..	..	..	..
2.	**DOMESTIC TOURISM**							
	Data							
	Accommodation							
	Total							
2.19	♦ Guests		('000)	5,999	6,333	6,638	4,872	5,114
2.20	♦ Overnights		('000)	40,228	41,312	41,780	28,150	24,204
	Hotels and similar establishments							
2.21	♦ Guests		('000)	3,598	3,819	4,192	3,287	3,669
2.22	♦ Overnights		('000)	9,259	9,713	10,223	8,088	7,869

UKRAINE

Cod.	Basic data and indicators	Notes	Units	2011	2012	2013	2014	2015
	Indicators							
2.23	Average size of travel party		Persons	..	..	..	..	..
	Average length of stay							
2.24	Total		Days	..	..	..	..	..
2.25	♦ For all commercial accommodation services		Nights	6.71	6.52	6.29	5.78	4.73
2.26	* of which, "hotels and similar establishments"		Nights	2.57	2.54	2.44	2.46	2.14
2.27	♦ For non commercial accommodation services		Days	..	..	..	..	..
2.28	Average expenditure per day		US$	..	..	..	..	..
3.	**OUTBOUND TOURISM**							
	Data							
	Departures							
3.1	Total		('000)	20,335	21,755	23,988	22,637	23,336
3.2	♦ Overnight visitors (tourists)		('000)	19,773	21,433	23,761	22,438	23,142
3.3	♦ Same-day visitors (excursionists)		('000)	562	322	227	199	194
	Expenditure							
3.4	Total		US$ Mn	4,829	5,536	6,300	5,470	4,750
3.5	♦ Travel		US$ Mn	4,461	5,104	5,763	5,061	4,443
3.6	♦ Passenger transport		US$ Mn	368	432	537	409	307
	Expenditure by main purpose of the trip							
3.7	Total		US$ Mn	4,461	5,104	5,763	5,061	4,443
3.8	♦ Personal		US$ Mn	3,283	3,643	4,011	3,566	3,117
3.9	♦ Business and professional		US$ Mn	1,178	1,461	1,752	1,495	1,326
	Indicators							
3.10	Average length of stay		Days	4.88	5.36	4.46	3.87	4.19
3.11	Average expenditure per day		US$	..	..	..	..	..
4.	**TOURISM INDUSTRIES**							
	Data							
	Number of establishments							
4.1	Total		Units	10,925	10,499	10,558	8,312	7,730
4.2	♦ Accommodation for visitors		Units	6,174	6,041	6,411	4,572	4,341
4.3	* of which, "hotels and similar establishments"		Units	3,162	3,144	3,582	2,644	2,478
4.4	♦ Food and beverage serving activities		Units	4,751	4,458	4,147	3,740	3,389
4.5	♦ Passenger transportation		Units	..	..	..	..	..
4.6	♦ Travel agencies and other reservation services activities		Units	..	..	..	..	..
4.7	♦ Other tourism industries		Units	..	..	..	..	..
	Accommodation for visitors in hotels and similar establishments							
	Non-monetary data							
4.13	♦ Number of establishments		Units	3,162	3,144	3,582	2,644	2,478
4.14	♦ Number of rooms		Units	76,567	81,157	89,441	69,052	68,114
4.15	♦ Number of bed-places		Units	153,249	162,061	178,506	135,049	132,203
	Indicators							
4.16	Occupancy rate / rooms		Percent	..	..	..	..	..
4.17	Occupancy rate / bed-places		Percent	..	26.40	27.10	31.10	35.30
4.18	Average length of stay		Nights	2.54	2.59	2.46	2.42	2.13
4.19	Available capacity (bed-places per 1000 inhabitants)		Units	3.37	3.58	3.95	3.00	2.95
	Travel agencies and other reservation service activities							
	Non-monetary data							
	♦ Domestic trips							
4.25	* with package tour		Percent	..	..	..	..	..
4.26	* without package tour		Percent	..	..	..	..	..
	♦ Inbound trips							
4.27	* with package tour		Percent	1.1	1.2	1.0	0.1	0.1
4.28	* without package tour		Percent	98.9	98.8	99.0	99.9	99.9
	♦ Outbound trips							
4.29	* with package tour		Percent	5.7	9.0	10.6	9.3	7.1
4.30	* without package tour		Percent	94.3	91.0	89.4	90.7	92.9
6.	**COMPLEMENTARY INDICATORS**							
	Demand							
6.1	Gross travel propensity		Units	..	..	..	..	..
6.2	(1.2 inbound tourists) / population		Units	0.47	0.51	0.55	0.28	0.28

UKRAINE

Cod.	Basic data and indicators	Notes	Units	2011	2012	2013	2014	2015
	Macroeconomic indicators related to international tourism							
6.3	Inbound tourism expenditure over GDP		Percent	3.3	3.4	3.2	1.7	1.8
6.4	Outbound tourism expenditure over GDP		Percent	3.0	3.1	3.4	4.1	5.2
6.5	Tourism balance (inbound minus outbound tourism expenditure) over GDP		Percent	0.3	0.3	-0.2	-2.4	-3.4
6.6	Tourism openness (inbound plus outbound tourism expenditure) over GDP		Percent	6.3	6.5	6.6	5.8	7.0
6.7	Tourism coverage (inbound over outbound tourism expenditure)		Percent	111.9	108.2	94.1	41.4	34.9
6.8	Inbound tourism expenditure over exports of goods		Percent	8.7	9.3	10.0	4.5	4.7
6.9	Inbound tourism expenditure over exports of services		Percent	25.4	27.1	26.2	15.2	13.4
6.10	Inbound tourism expenditure over exports of goods and services		Percent	6.5	6.9	7.3	3.5	3.5
6.11	Inbound tourism expenditure over current account credits		Percent	5.8	6.1	6.3	3.0	3.0
6.12	Outbound tourism expenditure over imports of goods		Percent	6.0	6.4	7.8	9.5	12.3
6.13	Outbound tourism expenditure over imports of services		Percent	36.1	37.9	39.1	44.2	44.2
6.14	Outbound tourism expenditure over imports of goods and		Percent	5.1	5.5	6.5	7.8	9.6
6.15	Outbound tourism expenditure over current account debits		Percent	4.8	5.1	5.9	7.1	8.7

UNITED KINGDOM

Cod.	Basic data and indicators	Notes	Units	2011	2012	2013	2014	2015
1.	**INBOUND TOURISM**							
	Data							
	Arrivals							
1.1	Total		('000)	30,798	31,084	32,692	34,377	36,115
1.2	♦ Overnight visitors (tourists)		('000)	29,306	29,282	31,063	32,613	34,436
1.3	♦ Same-day visitors (excursionists)		('000)	1,492	1,802	1,629	1,764	1,679
1.4	* of which, cruise passengers		('000)	..	..	..	..	..
	Arrivals by region							
1.5	Total		('000)	30,797	31,083	32,692	34,377	36,113
1.6	♦ Africa		('000)	527	571	606	563	576
1.7	♦ Americas		('000)	4,177	4,134	4,218	4,341	4,730
1.8	♦ East Asia and the Pacific		('000)	2,433	2,339	2,589	2,639	2,809
1.9	♦ Europe		('000)	22,604	22,934	24,044	25,626	26,688
1.10	♦ Middle East		('000)	589	630	799	743	830
1.11	♦ South Asia		('000)	467	475	436	465	480
1.12	♦ Other not classified		('000)	..	..	..	..	..
1.13	* of which, nationals residing abroad		('000)	..	..	..	..	..
	Arrivals by main purpose							
1.14	Total		('000)	30,797	31,084	32,692	34,377	36,116
1.15	♦ Personal		('000)	23,072	23,153	24,274	25,456	26,689
1.16	* holidays, leisure and recreation		('000)	12,008	11,961	12,668	13,578	13,857
1.17	* other personal purposes		('000)	11,064	11,192	11,606	11,878	12,832
1.18	♦ Business and professional		('000)	7,725	7,931	8,419	8,921	9,427
	Arrivals by mode of transport							
1.19	Total		('000)	30,797	31,084	32,692	34,377	36,115
1.20	♦ Air		('000)	22,631	22,670	23,753	24,955	26,252
1.21	♦ Water		('000)	4,496	4,257	4,460	4,951	5,239
1.22	♦ Land		('000)	3,670	4,157	4,479	4,471	4,625
1.23	* railway	(1)	('000)	3,670	4,157	4,479	4,471	4,625
1.24	* road		('000)	..	..	..	..	..
1.25	* others		('000)	..	..	..	..	..
	Arrivals by form of organization of the trip							
1.26	Total		('000)	30,797	31,084	32,692	34,377	36,115
1.27	♦ Package tour		('000)	2,361	2,467	2,528	2,698	2,624
1.28	♦ Other forms		('000)	28,436	28,617	30,164	31,679	33,491
	Accommodation							
	Total							
1.29	♦ Guests		('000)	30,907	31,078	32,665	34,491	36,530
1.30	♦ Overnights		('000)	235,197	230,191	245,477	264,577	273,054
	Hotels and similar establishments							
1.31	♦ Guests	(2)	('000)	15,491	15,467	16,852	17,596	18,205
1.32	♦ Overnights	(2)	('000)	66,326	65,781	77,553	79,972	81,818
	Expenditure							
1.33	Total		US$ Mn	44,741	47,070	53,052	58,935	60,744
1.34	♦ Travel		US$ Mn	35,644	37,199	41,617	46,628	45,532
1.35	♦ Passenger transport		US$ Mn	9,097	9,871	11,435	12,307	15,212
	Expenditure by main purpose of the trip							
1.36	Total		US$ Mn	35,643	37,199	41,617	46,627	45,532
1.37	♦ Personal		US$ Mn	28,080	29,546	32,995	37,364	36,394
1.38	♦ Business and professional		US$ Mn	7,563	7,653	8,622	9,263	9,138
	Indicators							
1.39	Average size of travel party		Persons	..	..	..	..	..
	Average length of stay							
1.40	Total		Days	..	..	..	..	..
1.41	♦ For all commercial accommodation services	(3)	Nights	7.64	7.41	7.48	7.70	7.56
1.42	* of which, "hotels and similar establishments"		Nights	..	..	..	..	..
1.43	♦ For non commercial accommodation services		Days	..	..	..	..	..
1.44	Average expenditure per day		US$	..	..	..	..	..
2.	**DOMESTIC TOURISM**	(4)						
	Data							
	Trips							
2.1	Total		('000)	1,668,640	1,836,020	1,710,905	1,698,942	1,649,626
2.2	♦ Overnight visitors (tourists)		('000)	126,640	126,020	122,905	114,242	124,426
2.3	♦ Same-day visitors (excursionists)		('000)	1,542,000	1,710,000	1,588,000	1,584,700	1,525,200

UNITED KINGDOM

Cod.	Basic data and indicators	Notes	Units	2011	2012	2013	2014	2015
	Trips by main purpose							
2.4	Total		('000)	122,730	121,776	120,089	111,331	119,009
2.5	♦ Personal		('000)	104,158	102,832	101,169	95,436	102,514
2.6	* holidays, leisure and recreation		('000)	58,435	57,695	56,969	52,903	55,960
2.7	* other personal purposes		('000)	45,723	45,137	44,200	42,533	46,554
2.8	♦ Business and professional		('000)	18,572	18,944	18,920	15,895	16,495
	Trips by mode of transport							
2.9	Total		('000)	118,480	115,710	112,500	114,140	124,250
2.10	♦ Air		('000)	2,300	2,600	2,880	2,290	3,210
2.11	♦ Water		('000)	150	430	350	370	350
2.12	♦ Land		('000)	116,030	112,680	109,270	111,480	120,690
2.13	* railway		('000)	17,610	19,140	18,090	16,250	18,620
2.14	* road		('000)	98,300	92,070	89,970	94,340	101,120
2.15	* others		('000)	120	1,470	1,210	890	950
	Trips by form of organization							
2.16	Total		('000)	126,110	125,440	122,910	114,240	124,420
2.17	♦ Package tour		('000)	4,770	5,190	5,360	4,690	4,720
2.18	♦ Other forms		('000)	121,340	120,250	117,550	109,550	119,700
	Accommodation							
	Total							
2.19	♦ Guests		('000)	126,640	126,020	122,905	114,242	124,426
2.20	♦ Overnights		('000)	387,329	388,240	376,607	349,546	377,101
	Hotels and similar establishments							
2.21	♦ Guests		('000)	41,920	43,120	43,160	40,470	41,820
2.22	♦ Overnights		('000)	86,100	89,300	89,200	86,400	87,330
	**Indicators**							
2.23	Average size of travel party		Persons	2.6	2.6	2.6	2.6	2.3
	Average length of stay							
2.24	Total		Days	3.06	3.08	3.04	3.06	3.03
2.25	♦ For all commercial accommodation services		Nights	2.99	2.94	2.92	3.19	2.92
2.26	* of which, "hotels and similar establishments"		Nights	2.05	2.07	2.07	2.13	2.09
2.27	♦ For non commercial accommodation services		Days	2.92	3.02	3.22	2.90	3.04
2.28	Average expenditure per day		US$	95.5	100.5	95.0	98.7	85.8
3.	**OUTBOUND TOURISM**							
	**Data**							
	Departures							
3.1	Total		('000)	56,836	56,538	57,792	60,082	65,720
3.2	♦ Overnight visitors (tourists)		('000)	54,946	54,604	56,088	58,364	64,165
3.3	♦ Same-day visitors (excursionists)		('000)	1,890	1,934	1,704	1,718	1,555
	Expenditure							
3.4	Total		US$ Mn	69,251	70,569	72,379	77,429	79,602
3.5	♦ Travel		US$ Mn	55,718	56,061	57,333	62,794	63,426
3.6	♦ Passenger transport		US$ Mn	13,533	14,508	15,046	14,635	16,176
	Expenditure by main purpose of the trip							
3.7	Total		US$ Mn	55,718	56,061	57,333	62,794	63,426
3.8	♦ Personal		US$ Mn	47,797	48,015	49,723	55,062	53,693
3.9	♦ Business and professional		US$ Mn	7,921	8,046	7,610	7,732	9,733
4.	**TOURISM INDUSTRIES**							
	**Data**							
	Number of establishments	(5)						
4.1	Total		Units	254,668	261,261	263,610	270,239	..
4.2	♦ Accommodation for visitors		Units	19,255	19,595	19,660	20,890	..
4.3	* of which, "hotels and similar establishments"		Units	12,285	12,435	12,390	12,650	..
4.4	♦ Food and beverage serving activities		Units	143,805	148,285	147,260	154,320	..
4.5	♦ Passenger transportation		Units	17,330	17,209	19,300	16,690	..
4.6	♦ Travel agencies and other reservation services activities		Units	10,465	10,695	10,630	11,105	..
4.7	♦ Other tourism industries		Units	63,813	65,477	66,760	67,234	..
	Accommodation for visitors in hotels and similar establishments							
	Monetary data							
4.8	♦ Output		US$ Mn	..	..	..	..	..
4.9	♦ Intermediate consumption		US$ Mn	..	..	..	..	..
4.10	♦ Gross value added	(6)	US$ Mn	12,188.0	17,771.0	..	..	..
4.11	♦ Compensation of employees		US$ Mn	..	..	..	..	..
4.12	♦ Gross fixed capital formation		US$ Mn	..	..	..	..	..

UNITED KINGDOM

Cod.	Basic data and indicators	Notes	Units	2011	2012	2013	2014	2015
	Non-monetary data	(7)						
4.13	♦ Number of establishments		Units	38,939	38,996	..	33,499	..
4.14	♦ Number of rooms		Units	647,777	718,405	..	790,707	..
4.15	♦ Number of bed-places		Units	1,410,580	1,571,120	..	1,781,294	..
	Indicators							
4.16	Occupancy rate / rooms	(8)	Percent	64.00	64.00	66.00	68.00	69.00
4.17	Occupancy rate / bed-places	(8)	Percent	48.00	48.00	50.00	50.00	51.00
4.18	Average length of stay		Nights	..	..	..	..	..
4.19	Available capacity (bed-places per 1000 inhabitants)		Units	22.33	24.71	..	27.69	..
	Travel agencies and other reservation service activities							
	Monetary data							
4.20	♦ Output		US$ Mn	..	..	..	..	..
4.21	♦ Intermediate consumption		US$ Mn	..	..	..	..	..
4.22	♦ Gross value added	(6)	US$ Mn	8,815.0	12,065.0	..	..	..
4.23	♦ Compensation of employees		US$ Mn	..	..	..	..	..
4.24	♦ Gross fixed capital formation		US$ Mn	..	..	..	..	..
5.	**EMPLOYMENT**	(9)						
	Data							
	Number of employees by tourism industries							
5.1	Total		('000)	2,671.7	2,709.5	2,708.9	2,902.0	..
5.2	♦ Accommodation services for visitors (hotels and similar establishments)		('000)	343.2	339.1	346.5	351.5	..
5.3	♦ Other accommodation services		('000)	73.8	72.9	74.5	79.1	..
5.4	♦ Food and beverage serving activities		('000)	1,437.0	1,452.0	1,424.0	1,604.0	..
5.5	♦ Passenger transportation		('000)	218.9	220.9	223.5	226.0	..
5.6	♦ Travel agencies and other reservation services activities		('000)	94.0	99.0	95.0	93.0	..
5.7	♦ Other tourism industries		('000)	504.9	525.5	545.4	548.4	..
	Number of jobs by status in employment							
5.8	Total		('000)	3,179.1	3,264.1	3,251.5	3,458.7	..
5.9	♦ Employees		('000)	2,671.7	2,709.5	2,708.9	2,902.0	..
5.10	♦ Self employed		('000)	507.3	554.7	542.6	556.7	..
	Indicators							
	Number of full-time equivalent jobs by status in employment							
5.11	Total		('000)	2,621.1	2,727.9	2,716.7	2,822.5	..
5.12	♦ Employees		('000)	2,196.0	2,253.3	2,261.5	2,362.5	..
5.13	* male		('000)	1,118.8	1,184.8	1,194.3	1,241.2	..
5.14	* female		('000)	1,077.2	1,068.5	1,067.2	1,121.3	..
5.15	♦ Self employed		('000)	425.1	474.7	455.2	460.0	..
5.16	* male		('000)	304.4	338.6	307.7	311.1	..
5.17	* female		('000)	120.7	136.0	147.4	148.9	..
6.	**COMPLEMENTARY INDICATORS**							
	Demand							
6.1	Gross travel propensity		Units	..	..	..	..	..
6.2	(1.2 inbound tourists + 2.2 domestic tourists) / population		Units	2.47	2.44	2.41	2.28	2.45
	Macroeconomic indicators related to international tourism							
6.3	Inbound tourism expenditure over GDP		Percent	1.7	1.8	2.0	2.0	2.1
6.4	Outbound tourism expenditure over GDP		Percent	2.7	2.7	2.7	2.6	2.8
6.5	Tourism balance (inbound minus outbound tourism expenditure) over GDP		Percent	-1.0	-0.9	-0.7	-0.6	-0.7
6.6	Tourism openness (inbound plus outbound tourism expenditure) over GDP		Percent	4.4	4.5	4.7	4.6	4.9
6.7	Tourism coverage (inbound over outbound tourism expenditure)		Percent	64.6	66.7	73.3	76.1	76.3
6.8	Inbound tourism expenditure over exports of goods		Percent	9.1	9.9	11.2	12.2	14.0
6.9	Inbound tourism expenditure over exports of services		Percent	14.8	15.1	15.8	16.4	17.6
6.10	Inbound tourism expenditure over exports of goods and services		Percent	5.6	6.0	6.6	7.0	7.8
6.11	Inbound tourism expenditure over current account credits		Percent	3.9	4.3	4.9	5.3	5.9
6.12	Outbound tourism expenditure over imports of goods		Percent	10.7	10.8	10.9	11.3	12.7
6.13	Outbound tourism expenditure over imports of services		Percent	35.7	36.0	34.8	35.5	37.8
6.14	Outbound tourism expenditure over imports of goods and		Percent	8.2	8.3	8.3	8.6	9.5
6.15	Outbound tourism expenditure over current account debits		Percent	5.7	6.0	6.1	6.4	7.1

UNITED STATES OF AMERICA

Cod.	Basic data and indicators	Notes	Units	2011	2012	2013	2014	2015
1.	**INBOUND TOURISM**							
	Data							
	Arrivals							
1.1	Total		('000)	146,615	152,915	156,746	156,929	156,245
1.2	♦ Overnight visitors (tourists)	(1)	('000)	62,821	66,657	69,995	75,022	77,510
1.3	♦ Same-day visitors (excursionists)	(2)	('000)	83,794	86,258	86,751	81,907	78,735
1.4	* of which, cruise passengers		('000)	..	..	..	..	..
	Arrivals by region							
1.5	Total		('000)	62,821	66,657	69,995	75,022	77,510
1.6	♦ Africa		('000)	326	371	436	511	555
1.7	♦ Americas		('000)	40,532	43,247	45,086	47,837	47,329
1.8	♦ East Asia and the Pacific		('000)	7,728	8,797	9,519	10,149	11,252
1.9	♦ Europe		('000)	13,115	12,954	13,425	14,731	16,334
1.10	♦ Middle East		('000)	363	463	544	666	717
1.11	♦ South Asia		('000)	755	826	983	1,126	1,317
1.12	♦ Other not classified		('000)	1	..	2	3	7
1.13	* of which, nationals residing abroad		('000)	..	..	..	..	..
	Arrivals by main purpose	(3)(4)						
1.14	Total		('000)	27,883	29,761	32,038	34,419	38,393
1.15	♦ Personal		('000)	22,028	23,690	25,727	28,120	31,175
1.16	* holidays, leisure and recreation		('000)	14,806	16,874	18,230	20,032	22,191
1.17	* other personal purposes		('000)	7,222	6,815	7,497	8,088	8,984
1.18	♦ Business and professional		('000)	5,855	6,071	6,311	6,299	7,218
	Arrivals by mode of transport	(5)						
1.19	Total		('000)	62,821	66,657	69,995	75,022	77,510
1.20	♦ Air		('000)	35,608	37,590	40,329	43,657	47,416
1.21	♦ Water		('000)	407	449	525	582	555
1.22	♦ Land		('000)	26,805	28,618	29,141	30,783	29,539
1.23	* railway		('000)	46	44	43	43	37
1.24	* road		('000)	26,343	28,108	28,659	30,440	29,140
1.25	* others		('000)	417	466	440	300	362
	Arrivals by form of organization of the trip	(3)						
1.26	Total		('000)	27,883	29,761	32,038	34,419	38,392
1.27	♦ Package tour	(4)	('000)	4,489	5,655	5,799	5,886	6,181
1.28	♦ Other forms		('000)	23,394	24,106	26,239	28,533	32,211
	Accommodation							
	Hotels and similar establishments							
1.31	♦ Guests	(3)	('000)	22,111	23,422	25,118	26,537	29,024
1.32	♦ Overnights	(3)	('000)	194,579	217,824	243,643	257,409	287,341
	Expenditure							
1.33	Total		US$ Mn	187,629	200,997	218,496	235,396	246,229
1.34	♦ Travel	(6)	US$ Mn	150,866	161,633	177,483	191,325	204,525
1.35	♦ Passenger transport		US$ Mn	36,763	39,364	41,013	44,071	41,704
	Expenditure by main purpose of the trip							
1.36	Total		US$ Mn	150,866	161,633	177,483	191,325	204,525
1.37	♦ Personal		US$ Mn	110,585	122,103	132,607	147,817	161,770
1.38	♦ Business and professional		US$ Mn	40,281	39,530	44,876	43,508	42,755
	Indicators	(3)						
1.39	Average size of travel party		Persons	1.6	1.6	1.6	1.7	1.7
	Average length of stay							
1.40	Total		Days	18.10	17.00	17.50	18.40	17.80
1.41	♦ For all commercial accommodation services		Nights	..	..	..	..	..
1.42	* of which, "hotels and similar establishments"		Nights	8.80	9.30	9.70	9.70	9.90
1.43	♦ For non commercial accommodation services		Days	..	..	..	..	..
1.44	Average expenditure per day	(7)	US$	202.0	192.0	196.0	176.0	161.0
2.	**DOMESTIC TOURISM**	(8)						
	Data							
	Trips							
2.1	Total	(9)	('000)	1,998,500	2,030,300	2,059,600	2,109,300	2,178,200
2.2	♦ Overnight visitors (tourists)	(10)	('000)	..	..	..	..	..
2.3	♦ Same-day visitors (excursionists)	(10)	('000)	..	..	..	..	..
	Trips by main purpose							
2.4	Total		('000)	1,997,500	2,030,300	2,059,600	2,109,300	2,178,200
2.5	♦ Personal		('000)	1,556,800	1,590,900	1,614,700	1,658,300	1,718,800
2.6	* holidays, leisure and recreation		('000)	1,556,800	1,590,900	1,614,700	1,658,300	1,718,800
2.7	* other personal purposes		('000)	..	..	..	..	..
2.8	♦ Business and professional		('000)	440,700	439,400	444,900	451,000	459,400

421

UNITED STATES OF AMERICA

Cod.	Basic data and indicators	Notes	Units	2011	2012	2013	2014	2015
3.	**OUTBOUND TOURISM**							
	Data							
	Departures							
3.1	Total		('000)	114,089	116,329	118,968	121,699	130,364
3.2	♦ Overnight visitors (tourists)	(11)	('000)	59,209	60,697	61,874	68,176	73,453
3.3	♦ Same-day visitors (excursionists)	(2)	('000)	54,880	55,632	57,094	53,523	56,911
	Expenditure							
3.4	Total		US$ Mn	116,448	129,902	130,148	140,419	148,366
3.5	♦ Travel	(6)	US$ Mn	89,701	100,337	98,119	105,529	112,872
3.6	♦ Passenger transport		US$ Mn	26,747	29,565	32,029	34,890	35,494
	Expenditure by main purpose of the trip							
3.7	Total		US$ Mn	89,701	100,337	98,119	105,529	112,872
3.8	♦ Personal		US$ Mn	69,025	80,192	78,505	88,257	96,952
3.9	♦ Business and professional		US$ Mn	20,676	20,145	19,614	17,272	15,920
	Indicators							
3.10	Average length of stay	(3)	Days	19.60	18.30	18.10	17.70	17.20
3.11	Average expenditure per day	(3)(12)	US$	150.0	165.0	203.0	160.0	159.0
4.	**TOURISM INDUSTRIES**							
	Data							
	Number of establishments	(13)						
4.1	Total		Units	681,357	694,699	699,715	..	
4.2	♦ Accommodation for visitors	(14)	Units	54,126	54,559	55,159	..	.
4.3	* of which, "hotels and similar establishments"	(15)	Units	49,791	50,226	50,407	..	
4.4	♦ Food and beverage serving activities	(16)	Units	585,613	598,512	609,123	..	.
4.5	♦ Passenger transportation		Units	21,025	21,556	19,198	..	
4.6	♦ Travel agencies and other reservation services activities		Units	20,593	20,072	16,235	..	.
4.7	♦ Other tourism industries		Units			..	..	
	Accommodation for visitors in hotels and similar establishments							
	Monetary data							
4.8	♦ Output	(17)	US$ Mn	162,319.0	174,173.0	184,405.0	224,755.0	243,743.1
4.9	♦ Intermediate consumption		US$ Mn	..	..	..	..	
4.10	♦ Gross value added		US$ Mn	..	..	..	..	
4.11	♦ Compensation of employees		US$ Mn	..	..	..	..	
4.12	♦ Gross fixed capital formation		US$ Mn	..	..	..	..	
	Non-monetary data	(18)						
4.13	♦ Number of establishments		Units	52,214	52,529	52,887	53,432	54,020
4.14	♦ Number of rooms		Units	4,874,837	4,900,642	4,926,543	4,978,705	5,033,471
4.15	♦ Number of bed-places		Units	..	..	..	..	
	Indicators							
4.16	Occupancy rate / rooms		Percent	..	..	..	..	
4.17	Occupancy rate / bed-places	(19)	Percent	59.90	61.30	62.30	64.40	65.60
4.18	Average length of stay		Nights	..	..	..	..	
4.19	Available capacity (bed-places per 1000 inhabitants)		Units	..	..	..	..	
5.	**EMPLOYMENT**							
	Data							
	Number of employees by tourism industries	(17)(20)						
5.1	Total		('000)	5,107.1	5,175.7	5,375.8	5,374.1	5,352.0
5.2	♦ Accommodation services for visitors (hotels and similar establishments)	(21)	('000)	1,300.1	1,327.9	1,357.3	1,383.4	1,384.0
5.3	♦ Other accommodation services		('000)	..	..	..	..	
5.4	♦ Food and beverage serving activities	(22)	('000)	1,625.2	1,659.7	1,654.9	1,641.0	1,626.0
5.5	♦ Passenger transportation	(23)	('000)	1,020.1	1,030.4	1,178.1	1,186.7	1,188.0
5.6	♦ Travel agencies and other reservation services activities		('000)	..	..	..	..	
5.7	♦ Other tourism industries	(24)	('000)	1,161.7	1,157.7	1,185.5	1,163.0	1,154.0
6.	**COMPLEMENTARY INDICATORS**							
	Demand							
6.1	Gross travel propensity		Units	..	..	..	..	
6.2	(1.2 inbound tourists + 2.1 domestic visitors) / population		Units	6.60	6.66	6.72	6.84	7.01

UNITED STATES OF AMERICA

Cod.	Basic data and indicators	Notes	Units	2011	2012	2013	2014	2015
	Macroeconomic indicators related to international tourism							
.3	Inbound tourism expenditure over GDP		Percent	1.2	1.2	1.3	1.4	1.4
.4	Outbound tourism expenditure over GDP		Percent	0.8	0.8	0.8	0.8	0.8
.5	Tourism balance (inbound minus outbound tourism expenditure) over GDP		Percent	0.4	0.4	0.5	0.6	0.6
.6	Tourism openness (inbound plus outbound tourism expenditure) over GDP		Percent	2.0	2.0	2.1	2.2	2.2
.7	Tourism coverage (inbound over outbound tourism expenditure)		Percent	161.1	154.7	167.9	167.6	166.0
.8	Inbound tourism expenditure over exports of goods		Percent	12.5	12.9	13.7	14.4	16.3
.9	Inbound tourism expenditure over exports of services		Percent	29.9	30.6	31.1	31.7	32.8
.10	Inbound tourism expenditure over exports of goods and services		Percent	8.8	9.1	9.5	9.9	10.9
.11	Inbound tourism expenditure over current account credits		Percent	6.3	6.5	6.8	7.1	7.8
.12	Outbound tourism expenditure over imports of goods		Percent	5.2	5.6	5.7	5.9	6.5
.13	Outbound tourism expenditure over imports of services		Percent	26.7	28.7	28.2	29.2	30.4
.14	Outbound tourism expenditure over imports of goods and		Percent	4.4	4.7	4.7	4.9	5.4
.15	Outbound tourism expenditure over current account debits		Percent	3.2	3.5	3.4	3.6	3.9

UNITED STATES VIRGIN ISLANDS

Cod.	Basic data and indicators	Notes	Units	2011	2012	2013	2014	2015
1.	**INBOUND TOURISM**							
	Data							
	Arrivals							
1.1	Total		('000)	2,723	2,682	2,722	2,827	2,667
1.2	♦ Overnight visitors (tourists)		('000)	567	620	590	615	637
1.3	♦ Same-day visitors (excursionists)		('000)	2,156	2,062	2,132	2,212	2,030
1.4	* of which, cruise passengers		('000)	2,009	1,904	1,999	2,084	1,879
	Arrivals by region	(1)						
1.5	Total		('000)	680	681	756	799	844
1.6	♦ Africa		('000)	..	..	..	..	..
1.7	♦ Americas		('000)	653	634	718	772	812
1.8	♦ East Asia and the Pacific		('000)	..	0.5	1.0	0.6	0.4
1.9	♦ Europe		('000)	23	31	23	18	21
1.10	♦ Middle East		('000)	..	..	..	..	..
1.11	♦ South Asia		('000)	..	..	..	..	..
1.12	♦ Other not classified		('000)	4	16	14	8	12
1.13	* of which, nationals residing abroad		('000)	..	..	..	..	..
	Arrivals by mode of transport							
1.19	Total		('000)	2,686	2,642	2,702	2,814	2,643
1.20	♦ Air	(2)	('000)	677	738	703	730	764
1.21	♦ Water	(3)	('000)	2,009	1,904	1,999	2,084	1,879
1.22	♦ Land		('000)	..	..	..	..	..
1.23	* railway		('000)	..	..	..	..	..
1.24	* road		('000)	..	..	..	..	..
1.25	* others		('000)	..	..	..	..	..
	Accommodation							
	Total							
1.29	♦ Guests		('000)	..	..	..	..	..
1.30	♦ Overnights	(4)	('000)	920	930	966	945	989
	Hotels and similar establishments							
1.31	♦ Guests		('000)	680	681	756	799	844
1.32	♦ Overnights		('000)	..	..	..	..	..
	Expenditure							
1.33	Total	(5)	US$ Mn	1,122	1,210	1,168	1,319	1,324
1.34	♦ Travel		US$ Mn	..	..	..	..	..
1.35	♦ Passenger transport		US$ Mn	..	..	..	..	..
2.	**DOMESTIC TOURISM**							
	Data							
	Accommodation							
	Hotels and similar establishments							
2.21	♦ Guests		('000)	54	50	53	53	48
2.22	♦ Overnights		('000)	..	..	..	..	..
4.	**TOURISM INDUSTRIES**							
	Data							
	Number of establishments							
4.1	Total		Units	..	..	..	..	..
4.2	♦ Accommodation for visitors		Units	..	..	..	..	..
4.3	* of which, "hotels and similar establishments"		Units	47	46	44	44	41
4.4	♦ Food and beverage serving activities		Units	..	..	..	..	..
4.5	♦ Passenger transportation		Units	..	..	..	..	..
4.6	♦ Travel agencies and other reservation services activities		Units	..	..	..	..	..
4.7	♦ Other tourism industries		Units	..	..	..	..	..
	Accommodation for visitors in hotels and similar establishments							
	Non-monetary data							
4.13	♦ Number of establishments		Units	47	46	44	44	41
4.14	♦ Number of rooms	(6)	Units	4,889	5,030	5,016	4,975	5,060
4.15	♦ Number of bed-places		Units	..	..	..	..	..
	Indicators							
4.16	Occupancy rate / rooms	(6)	Percent	51.60	50.90	53.80	53.70	57.10
4.17	Occupancy rate / bed-places		Percent	..	..	..	..	..
4.18	Average length of stay		Nights	..	..	..	..	..
4.19	Available capacity (bed-places per 1000 inhabitants)		Units	..	..	..	..	..

UNITED STATES VIRGIN ISLANDS

Cod.	Basic data and indicators	Notes	Units	2011	2012	2013	2014	2015
5.	**EMPLOYMENT**							
	Data							
	Number of employees by tourism industries							
5.1	Total		('000)	8.5	8.3	8.2	8.2	8.2
5.2	♦ Accommodation services for visitors (hotels and similar establishments)		('000)	3.5	3.6	3.6	3.6	3.6
5.3	♦ Other accommodation services		('000)	..	..	..	..	..
5.4	♦ Food and beverage serving activities		('000)	3.0	2.8	2.8	2.8	2.8
5.5	♦ Passenger transportation		('000)	0.5	0.5	0.6	0.6	0.5
5.6	♦ Travel agencies and other reservation services activities		('000)	..	..	..	..	..
5.7	♦ Other tourism industries		('000)	1.5	1.4	1.3	1.2	1.2
6.	**COMPLEMENTARY INDICATORS**							
	Demand							
6.1	Gross travel propensity		Units	..	..	..	..	..
6.2	(1.2 inbound tourists) / population		Units	5.36	5.89	5.63	5.90	6.13

URUGUAY

Cod.	Basic data and indicators	Notes	Units	2011	2012	2013	2014	2015
1.	**INBOUND TOURISM**							
	Data							
	Arrivals							
1.1	Total		('000)	3,244	3,155	3,242	3,195	3,286
1.2	♦ Overnight visitors (tourists)		('000)	2,857	2,695	2,683	2,682	2,773
1.3	♦ Same-day visitors (excursionists)		('000)	387	460	559	513	513
1.4	* of which, cruise passengers		('000)	284	319	428	385	321
	Arrivals by region	(1)						
1.5	Total		('000)	2,960	2,846	2,815	2,811	3,353
1.6	♦ Africa		('000)	..	..	..	..	
1.7	♦ Americas		('000)	2,401	2,417	2,308	2,208	2,391
1.8	♦ East Asia and the Pacific		('000)	19	19	18	20	15
1.9	♦ Europe		('000)	151	130	139	151	160
1.10	♦ Middle East		('000)	..	..	..	1	1
1.11	♦ South Asia		('000)	..	..	..	..	398
1.12	♦ Other not classified		('000)	389	280	349	431	389
1.13	* of which, nationals residing abroad		('000)	338	278	315	429	..
	Arrivals by main purpose	(1)						
1.14	Total		('000)	2,960	2,846	2,815	2,811	2,965
1.15	♦ Personal		('000)	2,754	2,658	2,599	2,607	2,744
1.16	* holidays, leisure and recreation		('000)	1,928	1,906	1,782	1,698	1,829
1.17	* other personal purposes		('000)	826	752	817	909	915
1.18	♦ Business and professional		('000)	206	188	216	204	221
	Arrivals by mode of transport	(1)						
1.19	Total		('000)	2,960	2,846	2,815	2,811	2,965
1.20	♦ Air		('000)	628	568	503	565	531
1.21	♦ Water		('000)	984	909	910	814	1,026
1.22	♦ Land		('000)	1,348	1,369	1,402	1,432	1,408
1.23	* railway		('000)	..	..	..	..	
1.24	* road	(2)	('000)	1,227	1,273	1,275	1,291	1,299
1.25	* others		('000)	121	96	127	141	109
	Arrivals by form of organization of the trip							
1.26	Total		('000)	2,961	2,845	2,815	2,810	2,965
1.27	♦ Package tour		('000)	102	98	77	102	69
1.28	♦ Other forms		('000)	2,859	2,747	2,738	2,708	2,896
	Accommodation							
	Total							
1.29	♦ Guests		('000)	1,297	1,226	1,167	1,163	1,218
1.30	♦ Overnights		('000)	6,679	6,129	5,687	5,535	5,829
	Hotels and similar establishments							
1.31	♦ Guests		('000)	1,215	1,160	1,098	1,116	1,170
1.32	♦ Overnights		('000)	6,078	5,627	5,174	5,248	5,518
	Expenditure							
1.33	Total		US$ Mn	2,401	2,219	2,015	1,869	1,880
1.34	♦ Travel		US$ Mn	2,203	2,076	1,922	1,757	1,777
1.35	♦ Passenger transport		US$ Mn	198	143	93	112	103
	Expenditure by main purpose of the trip							
1.36	Total		US$ Mn	2,172	2,036	1,878	1,704	1,766
1.37	♦ Personal		US$ Mn	2,048	1,912	1,750	1,600	1,676
1.38	♦ Business and professional		US$ Mn	124	124	128	104	90
	Indicators							
1.39	Average size of travel party		Persons	3.0	3.0	2.9	2.9	2.9
	Average length of stay							
1.40	Total		Days	6.30	6.10	6.00	5.80	6.20
1.41	♦ For all commercial accommodation services	(3)	Nights	6.00	5.80	5.80	5.40	5.61
1.42	* of which, "hotels and similar establishments"		Nights	5.00	4.80	4.70	4.70	4.81
1.43	♦ For non commercial accommodation services		Days	7.20	7.30	7.00	7.00	6.28
1.44	Average expenditure per day		US$	116.6	117.0	112.0	104.8	95.6
2.	**DOMESTIC TOURISM**							
	Data							
	Trips							
2.1	Total		('000)	7,668	9,083	6,565	6,673	6,626
2.2	♦ Overnight visitors (tourists)		('000)	6,509	7,681	5,340	5,276	5,388
2.3	♦ Same-day visitors (excursionists)		('000)	1,159	1,402	1,225	1,397	1,238

URUGUAY

Cod.	Basic data and indicators	Notes	Units	2011	2012	2013	2014	2015
	Trips by main purpose	**(4)**						
2.4	Total		('000)	4,198	4,931	3,932	4,273	3,969
2.5	♦ Personal		('000)	4,049	4,780	3,830	4,178	3,893
2.6	* holidays, leisure and recreation		('000)	2,365	2,864	2,239	2,402	2,155
2.7	* other personal purposes		('000)	1,684	1,916	1,591	1,776	1,738
2.8	♦ Business and professional		('000)	149	151	102	95	76
	Trips by mode of transport	**(4)**						
2.9	Total		('000)	4,198	4,931	3,932	4,273	3,969
2.10	♦ Air		('000)	3	1	..	..	..
2.11	♦ Water		('000)	..	..	..	..	..
2.12	♦ Land		('000)	4,195	4,930	3,932	4,273	3,969
2.13	* railway		('000)	..	..	..	..	..
2.14	* road		('000)	4,195	4,930	3,932	4,273	3,969
2.15	* others		('000)	..	..	..	..	..
	Accommodation							
	Total							
2.19	♦ Guests		('000)	3,070	3,181	2,651	3,013	2,938
2.20	♦ Overnights		('000)	..	..	..	..	..
	Hotels and similar establishments							
2.21	♦ Guests		('000)	387	458	638	390	364
2.22	♦ Overnights		('000)	..	..	..	..	..
3.	**OUTBOUND TOURISM**							
	Data							
	Departures							
3.1	Total		('000)	..	..	..	..	..
3.2	♦ Overnight visitors (tourists)		('000)	1,534	1,816	2,281	2,396	2,217
3.3	♦ Same-day visitors (excursionists)		('000)	..	..	..	..	..
	Expenditure							
3.4	Total		US$ Mn	797	1,043	1,504	1,596	1,390
3.5	♦ Travel		US$ Mn	644	878	1,312	1,356	1,162
3.6	♦ Passenger transport		US$ Mn	153	165	192	240	228
	Expenditure by main purpose of the trip							
3.7	Total		US$ Mn	..	877	1,312	1,356	1,162
3.8	♦ Personal		US$ Mn	..	790	1,200	1,235	1,070
3.9	♦ Business and professional		US$ Mn	..	87	112	121	92
	Indicators							
3.10	Average length of stay		Days	6.40	6.70	6.80	6.90	6.90
3.11	Average expenditure per day		US$	65.6	73.0	84.6	81.8	76.4
4.	**TOURISM INDUSTRIES**							
	Data							
	Number of establishments							
4.1	Total	**(5)**	Units	6,417	6,679	7,368	7,464	..
4.2	♦ Accommodation for visitors		Units	1,083	1,150	1,271	1,273	..
4.3	* of which, "hotels and similar establishments"		Units	..	..	..	..	..
4.4	♦ Food and beverage serving activities		Units	5,024	5,185	5,730	5,808	..
4.5	♦ Passenger transportation		Units	..	..	..	..	..
4.6	♦ Travel agencies and other reservation services activities		Units	310	344	367	383	..
4.7	♦ Other tourism industries		Units	..	..	..	..	..
	Accommodation for visitors in hotels and similar establishments							
	Monetary data							
4.8	♦ Output		US$ Mn	287.8	..	..	..	..
4.9	♦ Intermediate consumption		US$ Mn	133.9	..	..	..	..
4.10	♦ Gross value added		US$ Mn	153.9	..	..	..	..
4.11	♦ Compensation of employees		US$ Mn	86.3	..	..	..	..
4.12	♦ Gross fixed capital formation		US$ Mn	..	..	..	..	..
	Non-monetary data	**(6)**						
4.13	♦ Number of establishments		Units	1,083	..	470	474	472
4.14	♦ Number of rooms		Units	18,773	13,980	14,923	14,946	15,775
4.15	♦ Number of bed-places		Units	44,189	30,481	33,200	34,618	36,354
	Indicators							
4.16	Occupancy rate / rooms		Percent	..	..	..	..	..
4.17	Occupancy rate / bed-places		Percent	..	..	..	..	..
4.18	Average length of stay		Nights	4.90	4.80	4.70	4.70	5.00
4.19	Available capacity (bed-places per 1000 inhabitants)		Units	13.05	8.97	9.74	10.12	10.59

URUGUAY

Cod.	Basic data and indicators	Notes	Units	2011	2012	2013	2014	2015
	Travel agencies and other reservation service activities							
	Monetary data							
4.20	♦ Output		US$ Mn	309.1	..	..	..	..
4.21	♦ Intermediate consumption		US$ Mn	270.9	..	..	..	..
4.22	♦ Gross value added		US$ Mn	38.3	..	..	..	..
4.23	♦ Compensation of employees		US$ Mn	21.1	..	..	..	..
4.24	♦ Gross fixed capital formation		US$ Mn	..	..	..	..	..
5.	**EMPLOYMENT**	**(6)**						
	Data							
	Number of employees by tourism industries							
5.1	Total		('000)	147.0	95.8	99.9	109.1	109.4
5.2	♦ Accommodation services for visitors (hotels and similar establishments)		('000)	11.9	9.8	13.1	11.9	11.9
5.3	♦ Other accommodation services	**(7)**	('000)	7.2	6.3	7.5	9.8	10.0
5.4	♦ Food and beverage serving activities		('000)	41.0	38.5	38.0	42.1	44.7
5.5	♦ Passenger transportation		('000)	38.5	23.2	23.7	19.3	19.4
5.6	♦ Travel agencies and other reservation services activities		('000)	2.7	3.8	3.4	3.5	3.0
5.7	♦ Other tourism industries		('000)	45.7	14.2	14.2	22.5	20.4
	Number of jobs by status in employment							
5.8	Total		('000)	..	96.9	100.8	110.1	110.8
5.9	♦ Employees		('000)	..	74.0	75.9	83.0	83.3
5.10	♦ Self employed		('000)	..	22.9	24.9	27.2	27.5
	Indicators	**(8)**						
	Number of full-time equivalent jobs by status in employment							
5.11	Total		('000)	..	64.1	85.8	92.0	92.7
5.12	♦ Employees		('000)	..	51.5	66.7	72.3	72.8
5.13	* male		('000)	..	32.4	38.9	43.6	44.3
5.14	* female		('000)	..	19.1	27.8	28.7	28.5
5.15	♦ Self employed		('000)	..	12.6	19.1	19.7	19.9
5.16	* male		('000)	..	7.6	11.1	11.5	10.9
5.17	* female		('000)	..	5.0	8.0	8.2	9.0
6.	**COMPLEMENTARY INDICATORS**							
	Demand							
6.1	Gross travel propensity		Units	..	..	..	..	..
6.2	(1.2 inbound tourists + 2.2 domestic tourists) / population		Units	2.77	3.05	2.35	2.33	2.38
	Macroeconomic indicators related to international tourism							
6.3	Inbound tourism expenditure over GDP		Percent	5.0	4.5	3.8	3.5	3.9
6.4	Outbound tourism expenditure over GDP		Percent	1.7	2.1	2.8	3.0	2.9
6.5	Tourism balance (inbound minus outbound tourism expenditure) over GDP		Percent	3.3	2.4	1.0	0.5	1.0
6.6	Tourism openness (inbound plus outbound tourism expenditure) over GDP		Percent	6.7	6.6	6.6	6.5	6.8
6.7	Tourism coverage (inbound over outbound tourism expenditure)		Percent	301.3	212.8	134.0	117.1	135.3
6.8	Inbound tourism expenditure over exports of goods		Percent	25.9	22.4	19.6	18.1	20.7
6.9	Inbound tourism expenditure over exports of services		Percent	65.9	61.6	57.9	55.9	62.6
6.10	Inbound tourism expenditure over exports of goods and services		Percent	18.6	16.4	14.7	13.7	15.6
6.11	Inbound tourism expenditure over current account credits		Percent	17.6	15.8	14.2	13.2	15.0
6.12	Outbound tourism expenditure over imports of goods		Percent	7.4	8.5	13.0	14.2	14.9
6.13	Outbound tourism expenditure over imports of services		Percent	38.9	43.3	46.4	49.8	52.1
6.14	Outbound tourism expenditure over imports of goods and		Percent	6.2	7.1	10.1	11.0	11.6
6.15	Outbound tourism expenditure over current account debits		Percent	6.0	6.9	9.9	10.8	11.3

VANUATU

Cod.	Basic data and indicators	Notes	Units	2011	2012	2013	2014	2015
1.	**INBOUND TOURISM**							
	Data							
	Arrivals							
1.1	Total		('000)	249	321	357	329	287
1.2	♦ Overnight visitors (tourists)		('000)	94	108	110	109	90
1.3	♦ Same-day visitors (excursionists)		('000)	155	213	247	220	197
1.4	* of which, cruise passengers		('000)	155	213	247	220	197
	Arrivals by region							
1.5	Total		('000)	94	108	110	109	90
1.6	♦ Africa		('000)	..	..	..	..	..
1.7	♦ Americas		('000)	2	2	3	2	3
1.8	♦ East Asia and the Pacific		('000)	85	99	100	99	79
1.9	♦ Europe		('000)	5	6	6	6	6
1.10	♦ Middle East		('000)	..	..	..	..	..
1.11	♦ South Asia		('000)	..	..	..	..	..
1.12	♦ Other not classified		('000)	2	2	2	2	2
1.13	* of which, nationals residing abroad		('000)	..	..	..	..	..
	Arrivals by main purpose							
1.14	Total		('000)	94	108	110	109	90
1.15	♦ Personal		('000)	84	97	101	101	81
1.16	* holidays, leisure and recreation		('000)	76	88	89	86	64
1.17	* other personal purposes		('000)	8	9	12	15	18
1.18	♦ Business and professional		('000)	10	11	9	8	9
	Arrivals by mode of transport							
1.19	Total		('000)	249	321	357	329	287
1.20	♦ Air		('000)	94	108	110	109	90
1.21	♦ Water	(1)	('000)	155	213	247	220	197
1.22	♦ Land		('000)	..	..	..	..	..
1.23	* railway		('000)	..	..	..	..	..
1.24	* road		('000)	..	..	..	..	..
1.25	* others		('000)	..	..	..	..	..
	Expenditure							
1.33	Total		US$ Mn	249	268	314	284	254
1.34	♦ Travel		US$ Mn	223	241	287	257	228
1.35	♦ Passenger transport		US$ Mn	26	27	27	27	26
	Expenditure by main purpose of the trip							
1.36	Total		US$ Mn	223	241	287	257	228
1.37	♦ Personal		US$ Mn	200	216	264	241	212
1.38	♦ Business and professional		US$ Mn	23	25	23	16	16
	Indicators							
1.39	Average size of travel party		Persons	..	..	..	..	..
	Average length of stay							
1.40	Total	(2)	Days	9.90	10.50	11.20	10.60	11.10
1.41	♦ For all commercial accommodation services		Nights	..	..	..	..	..
1.42	* of which, "hotels and similar establishments"		Nights	..	..	..	..	..
1.43	♦ For non commercial accommodation services		Days	..	..	..	..	..
1.44	Average expenditure per day		US$	..	..	..	..	..
3.	**OUTBOUND TOURISM**							
	Data							
	Departures							
3.1	Total		('000)	..	..	..	..	..
3.2	♦ Overnight visitors (tourists)		('000)	22	23	26	26	27
3.3	♦ Same-day visitors (excursionists)		('000)	..	..	..	..	..
	Expenditure							
3.4	Total		US$ Mn	39	43	46	41	34
3.5	♦ Travel		US$ Mn	35	37	41	37	30
3.6	♦ Passenger transport		US$ Mn	4	6	5	4	4
	Expenditure by main purpose of the trip							
3.7	Total		US$ Mn	35	37	41	37	30
3.8	♦ Personal		US$ Mn	25	27	31	27	21
3.9	♦ Business and professional		US$ Mn	10	10	10	10	9

VANUATU

Cod.	Basic data and indicators	Notes	Units	2011	2012	2013	2014	2015
6.	**COMPLEMENTARY INDICATORS**							
	Demand							
6.1	Gross travel propensity		Units	..	..	..	..	..
6.2	(1.2 inbound tourists) / population		Units	0.39	0.44	0.43	0.42	0.34
	Macroeconomic indicators related to international tourism							
6.3	Inbound tourism expenditure over GDP		Percent	31.4	34.3	39.2	..	..
6.4	Outbound tourism expenditure over GDP		Percent	4.9	5.5	5.7	..	..
6.5	Tourism balance (inbound minus outbound tourism expenditure) over GDP		Percent	26.5	28.8	33.5	..	..
6.6	Tourism openness (inbound plus outbound tourism expenditure) over GDP		Percent	36.3	39.8	44.9	..	..
6.7	Tourism coverage (inbound over outbound tourism expenditure)		Percent	638.5	623.3	682.6	692.7	747.1
6.8	Inbound tourism expenditure over exports of goods		Percent	369.9	489.8	814.9	448.1	..
6.9	Inbound tourism expenditure over exports of services		Percent	87.9	88.8	89.1	85.1	..
6.10	Inbound tourism expenditure over exports of goods and services		Percent	71.0	75.2	80.3	71.5	..
6.11	Inbound tourism expenditure over current account credits		Percent	61.1	64.8	69.8	60.3	..
6.12	Outbound tourism expenditure over imports of goods		Percent	15.0	17.0	17.2	15.2	..
6.13	Outbound tourism expenditure over imports of services		Percent	26.9	29.5	30.9	28.3	..
6.14	Outbound tourism expenditure over imports of goods and		Percent	9.6	10.8	11.0	9.9	..
6.15	Outbound tourism expenditure over current account debits		Percent	8.7	9.8	10.1	9.0	..

VENEZUELA, BOLIVARIAN REPUBLIC OF

Cod.	Basic data and indicators	Notes	Units	2011	2012	2013	2014	2015
1.	**INBOUND TOURISM**							
	Data							
	Arrivals							
1.1	Total		('000)	625	1,061	1,085	967	882
1.2	♦ Overnight visitors (tourists)		('000)	595	988	986	857	789
1.3	♦ Same-day visitors (excursionists)		('000)	30	73	99	110	93
1.4	* of which, cruise passengers		('000)	30	73	99	110	93
	Arrivals by region							
1.5	Total		('000)	595	988	986	857	789
1.6	♦ Africa		('000)	1	3	4	4	3
1.7	♦ Americas		('000)	373	688	676	605	537
1.8	♦ East Asia and the Pacific		('000)	13	32	44	41	38
1.9	♦ Europe		('000)	194	240	230	180	187
1.10	♦ Middle East		('000)	8	14	17	15	13
1.11	♦ South Asia		('000)	1	3	4	3	2
1.12	♦ Other not classified		('000)	5	8	11	9	9
1.13	* of which, nationals residing abroad		('000)	..	..	..	..	..
	Arrivals by main purpose							
1.14	Total		('000)	595	988	986	857	789
1.15	♦ Personal		('000)	448	766	727	667	532
1.16	* holidays, leisure and recreation		('000)	161	365	348	332	251
1.17	* other personal purposes		('000)	287	402	379	335	281
1.18	♦ Business and professional		('000)	147	222	259	190	257
	Arrivals by mode of transport							
1.19	Total		('000)	595	988	986	857	788
1.20	♦ Air		('000)	529	721	752	614	549
1.21	♦ Water		('000)	..	..	..	..	..
1.22	♦ Land		('000)	66	267	233	242	239
1.23	* railway		('000)	..	..	..	..	..
1.24	* road		('000)	66	267	233	242	239
1.25	* others		('000)	..	..	..	..	..
	Arrivals by form of organization of the trip							
1.26	Total		('000)	625	1,061	1,085	967	882
1.27	♦ Package tour		('000)	63	282	246	141	97
1.28	♦ Other forms		('000)	562	779	839	826	785
	Accommodation							
	Hotels and similar establishments							
1.31	♦ Guests		('000)	275	486	485	456	562
1.32	♦ Overnights		('000)	..	..	..	..	..
	Expenditure							
1.33	Total		US$ Mn	806	904	926	707	654
1.34	♦ Travel		US$ Mn	740	844	858	643	575
1.35	♦ Passenger transport		US$ Mn	66	60	68	64	79
	Expenditure by main purpose of the trip							
1.36	Total		US$ Mn	740	844	858	643	575
1.37	♦ Personal		US$ Mn	430	455	509	386	340
1.38	♦ Business and professional		US$ Mn	310	389	349	257	235
	Indicators							
1.39	Average size of travel party		Persons	..	..	..	..	..
	Average length of stay							
1.40	Total		Days	..	..	..	..	..
1.41	♦ For all commercial accommodation services		Nights	16.48	18.88	16.71	15.30	12.82
1.42	* of which, "hotels and similar establishments"		Nights	..	..	..	..	..
1.43	♦ For non commercial accommodation services		Days	..	..	..	..	..
1.44	Average expenditure per day		US$	65.1	93.4	109.5	121.4	143.8
2.	**DOMESTIC TOURISM**							
	Data							
	Trips							
2.1	Total		('000)	18,264	17,315	21,526	20,689	16,144
2.2	♦ Overnight visitors (tourists)		('000)	13,232	12,209	15,774	14,890	10,975
2.3	♦ Same-day visitors (excursionists)		('000)	5,032	5,106	5,752	5,799	5,169
	Trips by main purpose							
2.4	Total		('000)	18,264	17,315	21,526	20,689	16,144
2.5	♦ Personal		('000)	17,022	16,349	20,533	20,071	15,372
2.6	* holidays, leisure and recreation		('000)	7,598	7,484	10,103	8,961	7,448
2.7	* other personal purposes		('000)	9,424	8,865	10,430	11,110	7,924
2.8	♦ Business and professional		('000)	1,242	966	993	618	772

VENEZUELA, BOLIVARIAN REPUBLIC OF

Cod.	Basic data and indicators	Notes	Units	2011	2012	2013	2014	2015
	Trips by mode of transport							
2.9	Total		('000)	18,264	17,315	21,526	20,689	16,144
2.10	♦ Air		('000)	378	450	791	769	627
2.11	♦ Water		('000)	501	447	670	560	440
2.12	♦ Land		('000)	17,385	16,418	20,065	19,360	15,077
2.13	* railway		('000)	..	..	..	..	..
2.14	* road		('000)	16,507	16,033	19,652	18,970	14,770
2.15	* others		('000)	878	385	413	390	307
	Trips by form of organization							
2.16	Total		('000)	18,264	17,315	21,526	20,689	16,144
2.17	♦ Package tour		('000)	107	180	164	249	48
2.18	♦ Other forms		('000)	18,157	17,135	21,362	20,440	16,096
	Indicators							
2.23	Average size of travel party		Persons	..	..	..	..	..
	Average length of stay							
2.24	Total		Days	..	..	..	..	..
2.25	♦ For all commercial accommodation services		Nights	4.64	4.20	4.49	4.44	4.80
2.26	* of which, "hotels and similar establishments"		Nights	..	..	..	..	..
2.27	♦ For non commercial accommodation services		Days	..	..	..	..	..
2.28	Average expenditure per day		US$	33.2	50.6	52.2	79.6	133.6
3.	**OUTBOUND TOURISM**							
	Data							
	Departures							
3.1	Total		('000)	..	..	..	..	..
3.2	♦ Overnight visitors (tourists)		('000)	1,719	1,734	1,931	1,589	1,539
3.3	♦ Same-day visitors (excursionists)		('000)	..	..	..	..	..
	Expenditure							
3.4	Total		US$ Mn	3,994	4,592	5,417	4,014	3,272
3.5	♦ Travel		US$ Mn	2,584	2,637	3,230	2,324	2,124
3.6	♦ Passenger transport		US$ Mn	1,410	1,955	2,187	1,690	1,148
	Expenditure by main purpose of the trip							
3.7	Total		US$ Mn	2,584	2,637	3,230	2,324	2,124
3.8	♦ Personal		US$ Mn	2,117	2,142	2,668	1,845	1,678
3.9	♦ Business and professional		US$ Mn	467	495	562	479	446
	Indicators							
3.10	Average length of stay	(1)	Days	17.43	16.97	13.86	12.32	13.92
3.11	Average expenditure per day		US$	75.5	84.7	113.8	176.9	122.6
4.	**TOURISM INDUSTRIES**							
	Data							
	Number of establishments							
4.1	Total		Units	..	..	..	..	..
4.2	♦ Accommodation for visitors		Units	..	..	..	..	..
4.3	* of which, "hotels and similar establishments"	(2)	Units	3,422	3,474	3,633	4,003	4,171
4.4	♦ Food and beverage serving activities		Units	..	..	..	..	..
4.5	♦ Passenger transportation		Units	..	..	..	..	..
4.6	♦ Travel agencies and other reservation services activities		Units	..	..	..	..	..
4.7	♦ Other tourism industries		Units	..	..	..	..	..
	Accommodation for visitors in hotels and similar establishments							
	Non-monetary data	(2)						
4.13	♦ Number of establishments		Units	3,422	3,474	3,633	4,003	4,171
4.14	♦ Number of rooms		Units	121,659	122,912	126,317	138,783	143,581
4.15	♦ Number of bed-places		Units	279,233	281,628	286,312	318,975	329,027
	Indicators							
4.16	Occupancy rate / rooms		Percent	..	..	..	..	..
4.17	Occupancy rate / bed-places		Percent	54.75	59.51	57.65	57.92	61.65
4.18	Average length of stay		Nights	16.48	18.88	16.71	15.30	12.80
4.19	Available capacity (bed-places per 1000 inhabitants)		Units	9.49	9.43	9.46	10.39	10.58
6.	**COMPLEMENTARY INDICATORS**							
	Demand							
6.1	Gross travel propensity		Units	..	..	..	..	..
6.2	(1.2 inbound tourists + 2.2 domestic tourists) / population		Units	0.47	0.44	0.55	0.51	0.38

VENEZUELA, BOLIVARIAN REPUBLIC OF

Cod.	Basic data and indicators	Notes	Units	2011	2012	2013	2014	2015
	Macroeconomic indicators related to international tourism							
6.3	Inbound tourism expenditure over GDP		Percent	0.3	0.2	0.2	0.1	..
6.4	Outbound tourism expenditure over GDP		Percent	1.3	1.2	1.5	0.8	..
6.5	Tourism balance (inbound minus outbound tourism expenditure) over GDP		Percent	-1.0	-1.0	-1.3	-0.7	..
6.6	Tourism openness (inbound plus outbound tourism expenditure) over GDP		Percent	1.6	1.4	1.7	0.9	..
6.7	Tourism coverage (inbound over outbound tourism expenditure)		Percent	20.2	19.7	17.1	17.6	20.0
6.8	Inbound tourism expenditure over exports of goods		Percent	0.9	0.9	1.0	0.9	1.8
6.9	Inbound tourism expenditure over exports of services		Percent	42.2	41.9	41.8	37.7	41.1
6.10	Inbound tourism expenditure over exports of goods and services		Percent	0.8	0.9	1.0	0.9	1.7
6.11	Inbound tourism expenditure over current account credits		Percent	0.8	0.9	1.0	0.9	1.6
6.12	Outbound tourism expenditure over imports of goods		Percent	7.6	7.0	9.5	8.5	9.0
6.13	Outbound tourism expenditure over imports of services		Percent	23.6	23.6	28.1	23.7	22.9
6.14	Outbound tourism expenditure over imports of goods and		Percent	5.8	5.4	7.1	6.2	6.4
6.15	Outbound tourism expenditure over current account debits		Percent	5.5	5.2	6.7	6.0	6.2

433

VIET NAM

Cod.	Basic data and indicators	Notes	Units	2011	2012	2013	2014	2015
1.	**INBOUND TOURISM**							
	Data							
	Arrivals							
1.1	Total	(1)	('000)	6,014	6,848	7,572	7,874	7,944
1.2	♦ Overnight visitors (tourists)		('000)				..	..
1.3	♦ Same-day visitors (excursionists)		('000)	46	286	193	48	170
1.4	* of which, cruise passengers	(2)	('000)	46	286	193	48	170
	Arrivals by region	(1)						
1.5	Total		('000)	6,014	6,847	7,572	7,874	7,944
1.6	♦ Africa		('000)	..	..	..	..	..
1.7	♦ Americas		('000)	546	557	537	548	597
1.8	♦ East Asia and the Pacific		('000)	4,384	4,809	5,461	5,696	5,641
1.9	♦ Europe		('000)	812	927	1,046	1,198	1,199
1.10	♦ Middle East		('000)	..	..	..	..	..
1.11	♦ South Asia		('000)	..	..	..	..	..
1.12	♦ Other not classified		('000)	272	554	528	432	507
1.13	* of which, nationals residing abroad		('000)	..	..	..	..	..
	Arrivals by main purpose	(1)						
1.14	Total		('000)	6,014	6,848	7,572	7,874	..
1.15	♦ Personal		('000)	5,011	5,682	6,305	6,552	..
1.16	* holidays, leisure and recreation		('000)	3,651	4,171	4,641	4,762	..
1.17	* other personal purposes		('000)	1,360	1,511	1,664	1,790	..
1.18	♦ Business and professional		('000)	1,003	1,166	1,267	1,322	..
	Arrivals by mode of transport	(1)						
1.19	Total		('000)	6,014	6,848	7,572	7,874	7,944
1.20	♦ Air		('000)	5,032	5,576	5,980	6,220	6,271
1.21	♦ Water	(2)	('000)	46	286	193	48	170
1.22	♦ Land		('000)	936	986	1,399	1,606	1,503
1.23	* railway		('000)	..	..	..	..	..
1.24	* road		('000)	936	986	1,399	1,606	1,503
1.25	* others		('000)	..	..	..	..	..
	Expenditure	(3)						
1.33	Total		US$ Mn	5,710	6,850	7,250	7,410	7,350
1.34	♦ Travel		US$ Mn	..	..	..	..	..
1.35	♦ Passenger transport		US$ Mn	..	..	..	..	..
	Indicators							
1.39	Average size of travel party		Persons	..	..	..	..	..
	Average length of stay							
1.40	Total		Days	..	..	..	..	..
1.41	♦ For all commercial accommodation services		Nights	..	..	..	..	..
1.42	* of which, "hotels and similar establishments"		Nights	..	..	..	..	..
1.43	♦ For non commercial accommodation services		Days	..	..	..	..	..
1.44	Average expenditure per day		US$	105.7	..	95.8	..	..
2.	**DOMESTIC TOURISM**							
	Data							
	Trips							
2.1	Total		('000)	30,000	32,500	35,000	..	..
2.2	♦ Overnight visitors (tourists)		('000)	..	..	..	..	..
2.3	♦ Same-day visitors (excursionists)		('000)	..	..	..	..	..
3.	**OUTBOUND TOURISM**							
	Data							
	Expenditure	(3)						
3.4	Total		US$ Mn	1,710	1,856	2,050	2,650	3,500
3.5	♦ Travel		US$ Mn	..	..	..	..	..
3.6	♦ Passenger transport		US$ Mn	..	..	..	..	..
4.	**TOURISM INDUSTRIES**							
	Data							
	Number of establishments							
4.1	Total		Units	..	..	..	..	..
4.2	♦ Accommodation for visitors		Units	..	..	..	..	..
4.3	* of which, "hotels and similar establishments"		Units	13,756	15,381	15,120	..	..
4.4	♦ Food and beverage serving activities		Units	..	..	..	..	..
4.5	♦ Passenger transportation		Units	..	..	..	..	..
4.6	♦ Travel agencies and other reservation services activities		Units	..	..	..	..	..
4.7	♦ Other tourism industries		Units	..	..	..	..	..

VIET NAM

Cod.	Basic data and indicators	Notes	Units	2011	2012	2013	2014	2015
	Accommodation for visitors in hotels and similar establishments							
	Non-monetary data							
4.13	♦ Number of establishments		Units	13,756	15,381	15,120	..	..
4.14	♦ Number of rooms		Units	256,739	277,661	324,800	..	..
4.15	♦ Number of bed-places		Units	..	..	..	..	..
	Indicators							
4.16	Occupancy rate / rooms		Percent	59.70	58.80	..	..	..
4.17	Occupancy rate / bed-places		Percent	..	..	..	..	..
4.18	Average length of stay		Nights	..	..	..	..	..
4.19	Available capacity (bed-places per 1000 inhabitants)		Units	..	..	..	..	..
6.	**COMPLEMENTARY INDICATORS**							
	Demand							
6.1	Gross travel propensity		Units	..	..	..	..	..
6.2	(1.1 inbound visitors + 2.2 domestic tourists) / population		Units	0.40	0.44	0.47	..	..
	Macroeconomic indicators related to international tourism							
6.3	Inbound tourism expenditure over GDP		Percent	4.2	4.4	4.2	4.0	..
6.4	Outbound tourism expenditure over GDP		Percent	1.3	1.2	1.2	1.4	..
6.5	Tourism balance (inbound minus outbound tourism expenditure) over GDP		Percent	2.9	3.2	3.0	2.6	..
6.6	Tourism openness (inbound plus outbound tourism expenditure) over GDP		Percent	5.5	5.6	5.4	5.4	..
6.7	Tourism coverage (inbound over outbound tourism expenditure)		Percent	333.9	369.1	353.7	279.6	210.0
6.8	Inbound tourism expenditure over exports of goods		Percent	5.9	6.0	5.5	4.9	4.5
6.9	Inbound tourism expenditure over exports of services		Percent	64.3	71.2	67.7	67.5	65.6
6.10	Inbound tourism expenditure over exports of goods and services		Percent	5.4	5.5	5.1	4.6	4.2
6.11	Inbound tourism expenditure over current account credits		Percent	5.0	5.2	4.7	4.3	4.0
6.12	Outbound tourism expenditure over imports of goods		Percent	1.8	1.8	1.7	1.9	2.3
6.13	Outbound tourism expenditure over imports of services		Percent	14.4	15.4	14.8	18.3	22.6
6.14	Outbound tourism expenditure over imports of goods and		Percent	1.6	1.6	1.5	1.7	2.1
6.15	Outbound tourism expenditure over current account debits		Percent	1.6	1.6	1.5	1.7	2.0

YEMEN

Cod.	Basic data and indicators	Notes	Units	2011	2012	2013	2014	2015
1.	**INBOUND TOURISM**							
	Data							
	Arrivals							
1.1	Total		('000)	1,175	1,282	1,323	1,218	398
1.2	♦ Overnight visitors (tourists)	(1)	('000)	829	874	990	1,018	367
1.3	♦ Same-day visitors (excursionists)		('000)	346	408	333	200	32
1.4	* of which, cruise passengers		('000)	..	..	..	..	
	Arrivals by region	(1)						
1.5	Total		('000)	829	875	990	1,018	367
1.6	♦ Africa		('000)	28	33	37	15	6
1.7	♦ Americas		('000)	18	28	30	24	9
1.8	♦ East Asia and the Pacific		('000)	13	14	17	15	24
1.9	♦ Europe		('000)	19	22	24	22	9
1.10	♦ Middle East		('000)	289	336	354	356	137
1.11	♦ South Asia		('000)	20	27	32	30	10
1.12	♦ Other not classified		('000)	442	415	496	557	172
1.13	* of which, nationals residing abroad		('000)	442	415	496	557	172
	Arrivals by mode of transport	(1)						
1.19	Total		('000)	829	874	990	..	367
1.20	♦ Air		('000)	268	382	411	..	179
1.21	♦ Water		('000)	2	2	3	..	1
1.22	♦ Land		('000)	558	490	576	..	187
1.23	* railway		('000)	..	..	..	..	..
1.24	* road		('000)	558	490	576	..	187
1.25	* others		('000)	..	..	..	..	..
	Accommodation							
	Hotels and similar establishments							
1.31	♦ Guests		('000)	..	..	..	..	
1.32	♦ Overnights	(1)	('000)	9,284	9,486	10,891	..	4,140
	Expenditure							
1.33	Total		US$ Mn	910	1,005	1,097	1,199	116
1.34	♦ Travel		US$ Mn	780	848	940	1,026	100
1.35	♦ Passenger transport		US$ Mn	130	157	157	173	16
	Indicators							
1.39	Average size of travel party		Persons	..	..	..	..	..
	Average length of stay							
1.40	Total		Days	..	..	..	..	..
1.41	♦ For all commercial accommodation services		Nights	8.00	8.00	8.00	8.00	8.00
1.42	* of which, "hotels and similar establishments"		Nights	..	..	..	..	..
1.43	♦ For non commercial accommodation services		Days	..	..	..	..	..
1.44	Average expenditure per day		US$	..	..	..	..	..
3.	**OUTBOUND TOURISM**							
	Data							
	Expenditure							
3.4	Total		US$ Mn	258	148	161	158	79
3.5	♦ Travel		US$ Mn	182	73	86	77	72
3.6	♦ Passenger transport		US$ Mn	76	75	75	81	7
6.	**COMPLEMENTARY INDICATORS**							
	Demand							
6.1	Gross travel propensity		Units	..	..	..	..	..
6.2	(1.2 inbound tourists) / population		Units	0.03	0.04	0.04	0.04	0.01
	Macroeconomic indicators related to international tourism							
6.3	Inbound tourism expenditure over GDP		Percent	2.9	3.1	3.2	..	..
6.4	Outbound tourism expenditure over GDP		Percent	0.8	0.5	0.5	..	..
6.5	Tourism balance (inbound minus outbound tourism expenditure) over GDP		Percent	2.1	2.6	2.7	..	..
6.6	Tourism openness (inbound plus outbound tourism expenditure) over GDP		Percent	3.7	3.6	3.7	..	..
6.7	Tourism coverage (inbound over outbound tourism expenditure)		Percent	352.7	679.1	681.4	758.9	146.8
6.8	Inbound tourism expenditure over exports of goods		Percent	10.0	12.9	14.0	15.8	..
6.9	Inbound tourism expenditure over exports of services		Percent	71.8	63.7	63.6	70.3	..
6.10	Inbound tourism expenditure over exports of goods and services		Percent	8.8	10.7	11.5	12.9	..
6.11	Inbound tourism expenditure over current account credits		Percent	7.2	6.7	8.3	8.4	..
6.12	Outbound tourism expenditure over imports of goods		Percent	3.0	1.3	1.5	1.5	..
6.13	Outbound tourism expenditure over imports of services		Percent	11.9	6.3	7.1	6.2	..
6.14	Outbound tourism expenditure over imports of goods and		Percent	2.4	1.1	1.2	1.2	..
6.15	Outbound tourism expenditure over current account debits		Percent	2.4	1.1	1.2	1.2	..

ZAMBIA

Cod.	Basic data and indicators	Notes	Units	2011	2012	2013	2014	2015
1.	**INBOUND TOURISM**							
	Data							
	Arrivals							
1.1	Total		('000)	..	..	..	..	..
1.2	♦ Overnight visitors (tourists)		('000)	920	859	915	947	932
1.3	♦ Same-day visitors (excursionists)		('000)	..	..	..	..	..
1.4	* of which, cruise passengers		('000)	..	..	..	..	..
	Arrivals by region							
1.5	Total		('000)	920	859	915	947	932
1.6	♦ Africa		('000)	652	654	720	732	710
1.7	♦ Americas		('000)	52	32	41	45	49
1.8	♦ East Asia and the Pacific		('000)	80	92	57	72	59
1.9	♦ Europe		('000)	114	66	79	78	89
1.10	♦ Middle East		('000)	..	..	..	..	..
1.11	♦ South Asia		('000)	22	15	17	21	26
1.12	♦ Other not classified		('000)	..	..	..	..	..
1.13	* of which, nationals residing abroad		('000)	..	..	..	..	..
	Arrivals by main purpose							
1.14	Total		('000)	920	859	915	947	932
1.15	♦ Personal		('000)	350	385	379	513	350
1.16	* holidays, leisure and recreation		('000)	194	223	252	237	235
1.17	* other personal purposes		('000)	156	162	127	276	114
1.18	♦ Business and professional		('000)	571	474	535	434	582
	Arrivals by mode of transport							
1.19	Total		('000)	920	859	915	947	932
1.20	♦ Air		('000)	297	252	241	262	273
1.21	♦ Water		('000)	..	8	8	4	3
1.22	♦ Land		('000)	623	599	666	680	656
1.23	* railway		('000)	45	52	16	15	3
1.24	* road		('000)	578	547	650	665	653
1.25	* others		('000)	..	..	..	..	..
	Expenditure							
1.33	Total		US$ Mn	..	..	..	..	..
1.34	♦ Travel		US$ Mn	555	518	552	642	660
1.35	♦ Passenger transport		US$ Mn	..	..	..	..	..
	Expenditure by main purpose of the trip							
1.36	Total		US$ Mn	555	518	552	642	660
1.37	♦ Personal		US$ Mn	239	233	239	278	286
1.38	♦ Business and professional		US$ Mn	316	285	313	364	374
3.	**OUTBOUND TOURISM**							
	Data							
	Expenditure							
3.4	Total		US$ Mn	223	303	357	378	400
3.5	♦ Travel		US$ Mn	111	165	210	222	234
3.6	♦ Passenger transport		US$ Mn	112	138	147	156	166
	Expenditure by main purpose of the trip							
3.7	Total		US$ Mn	111	165	210	222	234
3.8	♦ Personal		US$ Mn	33	50	63	67	70
3.9	♦ Business and professional		US$ Mn	78	116	147	156	164
4.	**TOURISM INDUSTRIES**							
	Data							
	Number of establishments							
4.1	Total		Units	..	..	..	..	..
4.2	♦ Accommodation for visitors		Units	842	933	1,139	1,166	1,172
4.3	* of which, "hotels and similar establishments"		Units	812	897	1,092	1,115	1,117
4.4	♦ Food and beverage serving activities		Units	..	..	..	..	..
4.5	♦ Passenger transportation		Units	..	..	..	..	..
4.6	♦ Travel agencies and other reservation services activities		Units	..	..	..	..	..
4.7	♦ Other tourism industries		Units	..	..	..	..	..
	Accommodation for visitors in hotels and similar establishments							
	Non-monetary data							
4.13	♦ Number of establishments		Units	..	897	1,092	1,115	1,117
4.14	♦ Number of rooms		Units	..	35,337	42,141	42,647	42,843
4.15	♦ Number of bed-places		Units	..	51,288	73,579	74,433	74,854

ZAMBIA

Cod.	Basic data and indicators	Notes	Units	2011	2012	2013	2014	2015
	Indicators							
4.16	Occupancy rate / rooms		Percent	..	54.90	60.05	61.90	69.70
4.17	Occupancy rate / bed-places		Percent	..	..	..	..	..
4.18	Average length of stay		Nights	..	5.00	6.00	5.50	4.00
4.19	Available capacity (bed-places per 1000 inhabitants)		Units	..	3.47	4.83	4.73	4.62
5.	**EMPLOYMENT**							
	Data							
	Number of employees by tourism industries							
5.1	Total		('000)	..	44.3	57.3	57.0	57.4
5.2	♦ Accommodation services for visitors (hotels and similar establishments)		('000)	..	44.3	57.3	57.0	57.4
5.3	♦ Other accommodation services		('000)	..	..	..	..	..
5.4	♦ Food and beverage serving activities		('000)	..	..	..	..	..
5.5	♦ Passenger transportation		('000)	..	..	..	..	..
5.6	♦ Travel agencies and other reservation services activities		('000)	..	..	..	..	..
5.7	♦ Other tourism industries		('000)	..	..	..	..	..
	Number of jobs by status in employment							
5.8	Total		('000)	..	44.3	57.3	57.0	57.4
5.9	♦ Employees		('000)	..	44.3	57.3	57.0	57.4
5.10	♦ Self employed		('000)	..	..	..	..	..
	Indicators							
	Number of full-time equivalent jobs by status in employment							
5.11	Total		('000)	..	44.3	57.3	..	57.4
5.12	♦ Employees		('000)	..	44.3	57.3	..	57.4
5.13	* male		('000)	..	19.7	25.4	..	25.9
5.14	* female		('000)	..	24.6	32.0	..	31.5
5.15	♦ Self employed		('000)	..	..	..	..	..
5.16	* male		('000)	..	..	..	..	..
5.17	* female		('000)	..	..	..	..	..
6.	**COMPLEMENTARY INDICATORS**							
	Demand							
6.1	Gross travel propensity		Units	..	..	..	..	..
6.2	(1.2 inbound tourists) / population		Units	0.06	0.06	0.06	0.06	0.06
	Macroeconomic indicators related to international tourism							
6.3	Inbound tourism expenditure over GDP		Percent	2.7	2.3	2.1	2.4	..
6.4	Outbound tourism expenditure over GDP		Percent	1.1	1.3	1.3	1.4	..
6.5	Tourism balance (inbound minus outbound tourism expenditure) over GDP		Percent	1.6	1.0	0.8	1.0	..
6.6	Tourism openness (inbound plus outbound tourism expenditure) over GDP		Percent	3.8	3.6	3.4	3.8	..
6.7	Tourism coverage (inbound over outbound tourism expenditure)		Percent	248.9	171.0	154.6	169.8	165.0
6.8	Inbound tourism expenditure over exports of goods		Percent	6.3	5.4	5.1	6.3	..
6.9	Inbound tourism expenditure over exports of services		Percent	83.4	52.3	72.8	75.5	..
6.10	Inbound tourism expenditure over exports of goods and services		Percent	5.9	4.9	4.8	5.8	..
6.11	Inbound tourism expenditure over current account credits		Percent	5.6	4.7	4.6	5.6	..
6.12	Outbound tourism expenditure over imports of goods		Percent	3.5	3.8	3.9	4.4	..
6.13	Outbound tourism expenditure over imports of services		Percent	20.4	22.7	19.7	23.0	..
6.14	Outbound tourism expenditure over imports of goods and		Percent	3.0	3.3	3.2	3.7	..
6.15	Outbound tourism expenditure over current account debits		Percent	2.9	3.2	3.2	3.7	..

ZIMBABWE

Cod.	Basic data and indicators	Notes	Units	2011	2012	2013	2014	2015
1.	**INBOUND TOURISM**							
	Data							
	Arrivals							
1.1	Total		('000)	2,423	1,794	1,833	1,880	2,057
1.2	♦ Overnight visitors (tourists)		('000)	..	..	..	..	..
1.3	♦ Same-day visitors (excursionists)		('000)	..	..	..	..	..
1.4	* of which, cruise passengers		('000)	..	..	..	..	..
	Arrivals by region							
1.5	Total		('000)	2,423	1,794	1,833	1,880	2,057
1.6	♦ Africa		('000)	2,041	1,562	1,570	1,598	1,760
1.7	♦ Americas		('000)	90	59	54	67	77
1.8	♦ East Asia and the Pacific		('000)	125	56	73	67	59
1.9	♦ Europe		('000)	158	114	131	144	153
1.10	♦ Middle East		('000)	3	1	1	2	1
1.11	♦ South Asia		('000)	6	2	3	2	7
1.12	♦ Other not classified		('000)	..	..	..	..	..
1.13	* of which, nationals residing abroad		('000)	..	..	..	..	..
	Arrivals by main purpose							
1.14	Total		('000)	2,423	1,794	1,833	1,880	2,057
1.15	♦ Personal		('000)	2,006	1,425	1,595	1,696	1,897
1.16	* holidays, leisure and recreation		('000)	1,969	1,373	1,534	980	1,154
1.17	* other personal purposes	(1)	('000)	37	52	61	716	743
1.18	♦ Business and professional		('000)	417	369	237	184	160
	Arrivals by mode of transport							
1.19	Total		('000)	2,423	1,794	1,833	1,880	2,057
1.20	♦ Air		('000)	350	228	223	198	281
1.21	♦ Water		('000)	..	..	..	..	..
1.22	♦ Land		('000)	2,073	1,566	1,610	1,682	1,776
1.23	* railway		('000)	..	..	..	..	..
1.24	* road		('000)	2,073	1,566	1,610	1,682	1,776
1.25	* others		('000)	..	..	..	..	..
	Accommodation							
	Total							
1.29	♦ Guests		('000)	115	120	88	86	114
1.30	♦ Overnights		('000)	325	352	281	258	360
	Hotels and similar establishments							
1.31	♦ Guests		('000)	91	86	71	69	97
1.32	♦ Overnights		('000)	226	213	213	207	290
	Expenditure							
1.33	Total	(2)	US$ Mn	662	749	856	827	886
1.34	♦ Travel		US$ Mn	..	..	..	..	..
1.35	♦ Passenger transport		US$ Mn	..	..	..	..	..
	Indicators							
1.39	Average size of travel party		Persons	..	..	..	..	..
	Average length of stay							
1.40	Total		Days	..	..	..	..	..
1.41	♦ For all commercial accommodation services		Nights	3.00	3.00	3.00	3.00	3.00
1.42	* of which, "hotels and similar establishments"		Nights	..	..	..	..	..
1.43	♦ For non commercial accommodation services		Days	..	..	..	..	..
1.44	Average expenditure per day		US$	..	..	..	..	..
2.	**DOMESTIC TOURISM**	(3)						
	Data							
	Trips							
2.1	Total		('000)	1,105	995	980	1,020	915
2.2	♦ Overnight visitors (tourists)		('000)	778	726	704	691	573
2.3	♦ Same-day visitors (excursionists)	(4)	('000)	327	269	276	329	342
	Accommodation							
	Total							
2.19	♦ Guests		('000)	778	726	704	691	573
2.20	♦ Overnights		('000)	2,279	2,052	1,883	1,844	1,490
	Hotels and similar establishments							
2.21	♦ Guests		('000)	556	569	474	461	343
2.22	♦ Overnights		('000)	1,390	1,423	1,423	1,385	1,031
	Indicators							
2.23	Average size of travel party		Persons	..	..	..	..	..
	Average length of stay							
2.24	Total		Days	..	..	..	..	..
2.25	♦ For all commercial accommodation services		Nights	3.00	3.00	3.00	3.00	3.00
2.26	* of which, "hotels and similar establishments"		Nights	..	..	..	..	..
2.27	♦ For non commercial accommodation services		Days	..	..	..	..	..
2.28	Average expenditure per day		US$	..	..	..	..	..

ZIMBABWE

Cod.	Basic data and indicators	Notes	Units	2011	2012	2013	2014	2015
3.	**OUTBOUND TOURISM**	(3)						
	Data							
	Departures							
3.1	Total		('000)	..	..	..	..	..
3.2	♦ Overnight visitors (tourists)		('000)	693	720	757	792	824
3.3	♦ Same-day visitors (excursionists)		('000)	..	..	..	..	..
4.	**TOURISM INDUSTRIES**							
	Data							
	Number of establishments							
4.1	Total		Units	1,669	1,332	1,332	1,285	1,252
4.2	♦ Accommodation for visitors		Units	633	564	564	542	521
4.3	* of which, "hotels and similar establishments"		Units	116	116	99	99	96
4.4	♦ Food and beverage serving activities		Units	549	298	298	290	268
4.5	♦ Passenger transportation		Units	167	147	147	105	48
4.6	♦ Travel agencies and other reservation services activities		Units	116	129	129	132	227
4.7	♦ Other tourism industries		Units	204	194	194	216	188
	Accommodation for visitors in hotels and similar establishments							
	Non-monetary data							
4.13	♦ Number of establishments		Units	116	116	99	99	96
4.14	♦ Number of rooms	(5)	Units	6,360	6,427	6,427	6,427	6,188
4.15	♦ Number of bed-places	(5)	Units	11,935	12,081	12,081	12,081	11,658
	Indicators							
4.16	Occupancy rate / rooms		Percent	52.00	52.00	48.00	48.00	47.00
4.17	Occupancy rate / bed-places		Percent	37.00	37.00	37.00	36.00	31.00
4.18	Average length of stay		Nights	3.00	3.00	3.00	3.00	3.00
4.19	Available capacity (bed-places per 1000 inhabitants)		Units	0.84	0.83	0.81	0.79	0.75
6.	**COMPLEMENTARY INDICATORS**							
	Demand							
6.1	Gross travel propensity		Units	0.1	0.1	0.1	0.1	0.1
6.2	(1.1 inbound visitors + 2.1 domestic visitors) / population		Units	0.25	0.19	0.19	0.19	0.19

Index of indicators and basic data

Indice des indicateurs et données de base

Índice de indicadores y datos básicos

INDEX OF INDICATORS AND BASIC DATA

Basic data and indicators		Notes	Units
1.	**INBOUND TOURISM**		
	Data		
	Arrivals		
1.1	Total		('000)
1.2	♦ Overnight visitors (tourists)		('000)
1.3	♦ Same-day visitors (excursionists)		('000)
1.4	* of which, cruise passengers		('000)
	Arrivals by region		
1.5	Total		('000)
1.6	♦ Africa		('000)
1.7	♦ Americas		('000)
1.8	♦ East Asia and the Pacific		('000)
1.9	♦ Europe		('000)
1.10	♦ Middle East		('000)
1.11	♦ South Asia		('000)
1.12	♦ Other not classified		('000)
1.13	* of which, nationals residing abroad		('000)
	Arrivals by main purpose		
1.14	Total		('000)
1.15	♦ Personal		('000)
1.16	* holidays, leisure and recreation		('000)
1.17	* other personal purposes		('000)
1.18	♦ Business and professional		('000)
	Arrivals by mode of transport		
1.19	Total		('000)
1.20	♦ Air		('000)
1.21	♦ Water		('000)
1.22	♦ Land		('000)
1.23	* railway		('000)
1.24	* road		('000)
1.25	* others		('000)
	Arrivals by form of organization of the trip		
1.26	Total		('000)
1.27	♦ Package tour		('000)
1.28	♦ Other forms		('000)
	Accommodation		
	Total		
1.29	♦ Guests		('000)
1.30	♦ Overnights		('000)
	Hotels and similar establishments		
1.31	♦ Guests		('000)
1.32	♦ Overnights		('000)
	Expenditure		
1.33	Total		US$ Mn
1.34	♦ Travel		US$ Mn
1.35	♦ Passenger transport		US$ Mn
	Expenditure by main purpose of the trip		
1.36	Total		US$ Mn
1.37	♦ Personal		US$ Mn
1.38	♦ Business and professional		US$ Mn
	Indicators		
1.39	Average size of travel party		Persons
	Average length of stay		
1.40	Total		Days
1.41	♦ For all commercial accommodation services		Nights
1.42	* of which, "hotels and similar establishments"		Nights
1.43	♦ For non commercial accommodation services		Days
1.44	Average expenditure per day		US$

Basic data and indicators		Notes	Units
2.	**DOMESTIC TOURISM**		
	Data		
	Trips		
2.1	Total		('000)
2.2	♦ Overnight visitors (tourists)		('000)
2.3	♦ Same-day visitors (excursionists)		('000)
	Trips by main purpose		
2.4	Total		('000)
2.5	♦ Personal		('000)
2.6	* holidays, leisure and recreation		('000)
2.7	* other personal purposes		('000)
2.8	♦ Business and professional		('000)
	Trips by mode of transport		
2.9	Total		('000)
2.10	♦ Air		('000)
2.11	♦ Water		('000)
2.12	♦ Land		('000)
2.13	* railway		('000)
2.14	* road		('000)
2.15	* others		('000)
	Trips by form of organization		
2.16	Total		('000)
2.17	♦ Package tour		('000)
2.18	♦ Other forms		('000)
	Accommodation		
	Total		
2.19	♦ Guests		('000)
2.20	♦ Overnights		('000)
	Hotels and similar establishments		
2.21	♦ Guests		('000)
2.22	♦ Overnights		('000)
	Indicators		
2.23	Average size of travel party		Persons
	Average length of stay		
2.24	Total		Days
2.25	♦ For all commercial accommodation services		Nights
2.26	* of which, "hotels and similar establishments"		Nights
2.27	♦ For non commercial accommodation services		Days
2.28	Average expenditure per day		US$
3.	**OUTBOUND TOURISM**		
	Data		
	Departures		
3.1	Total		('000)
3.2	♦ Overnight visitors (tourists)		('000)
3.3	♦ Same-day visitors (excursionists)		('000)
	Expenditure		
3.4	Total		US$ Mn
3.5	♦ Travel		US$ Mn
3.6	♦ Passenger transport		US$ Mn
	Expenditure by main purpose of the trip		
3.7	Total		US$ Mn
3.8	♦ Personal		US$ Mn
3.9	♦ Business and professional		US$ Mn
	Indicators		
3.10	Average length of stay		Days
3.11	Average expenditure per day		US$

INDEX OF INDICATORS AND BASIC DATA

Basic data and indicators	Notes	Units
4. TOURISM INDUSTRIES		
Data		
Number of establishments		
4.1 Total		Units
4.2 ♦ Accommodation for visitors		Units
4.3 * of which, "hotels and similar establishments"		Units
4.4 ♦ Food and beverage serving activities		Units
4.5 ♦ Passenger transportation		Units
4.6 ♦ Travel agencies and other reservation services activities		Units
4.7 ♦ Other tourism industries		Units
Accommodation for visitors in hotels and similar establishments		
Monetary data		
4.8 ♦ Output		US$ Mn
4.9 ♦ Intermediate consumption		US$ Mn
4.10 ♦ Gross value added		US$ Mn
4.11 ♦ Compensation of employees		US$ Mn
4.12 ♦ Gross fixed capital formation		US$ Mn
Non-monetary data		
4.13 ♦ Number of establishments		Units
4.14 ♦ Number of rooms		Units
4.15 ♦ Number of bed-places		Units
Indicators		
4.16 Occupancy rate / rooms		Percent
4.17 Occupancy rate / bed-places		Percent
4.18 Average length of stay		Nights
4.19 Available capacity (bed-places per 1000 inhabitants)		Units
Travel agencies and other reservation service activities		
Monetary data		
4.20 ♦ Output		US$ Mn
4.21 ♦ Intermediate consumption		US$ Mn
4.22 ♦ Gross value added		US$ Mn
4.23 ♦ Compensation of employees		US$ Mn
4.24 ♦ Gross fixed capital formation		US$ Mn
Non-monetary data		
♦ Domestic trips		
4.25 * with package tour		Percent
4.26 * without package tour		Percent
♦ Inbound trips		
4.27 * with package tour		Percent
4.28 * without package tour		Percent
♦ Outbound trips		
4.29 * with package tour		Percent
4.30 * without package tour		Percent

INDEX OF INDICATORS AND BASIC DATA

Basic data and indicators	Notes	Units
5. **EMPLOYMENT**		
Data		
Number of employees by tourism industries		
5.1 Total		('000)
5.2 ♦ Accommodation services for visitors (hotels and similar establishments)		('000)
5.3 ♦ Other accommodation services		('000)
5.4 ♦ Food and beverage serving activities		('000)
5.5 ♦ Passenger transportation		('000)
5.6 ♦ Travel agencies and other reservation services activities		('000)
5.7 ♦ Other tourism industries		('000)
Number of jobs by status in employment		
5.8 Total		('000)
5.9 ♦ Employees		('000)
5.10 ♦ Self employed		('000)
Indicators		
Number of full-time equivalent jobs by status in employment		
5.11 Total		('000)
5.12 ♦ Employees		('000)
5.13 * male		('000)
5.14 * female		('000)
5.15 ♦ Self employed		('000)
5.16 * male		('000)
5.17 * female		('000)
6. **COMPLEMENTARY INDICATORS**		
Demand		
6.1 Gross travel propensity		Units
6.2 (inbound tourists + domestic tourists) / population		Units
Macroeconomic indicators related to international tourism		
6.3 Inbound tourism expenditure over GDP		Percent
6.4 Outbound tourism expenditure over GDP		Percent
6.5 Tourism balance (inbound minus outbound tourism expenditure) over GDP		Percent
6.6 Tourism openness (inbound plus outbound tourism expenditure) over GDP		Percent
6.7 Tourism coverage (inbound over outbound tourism expenditure)		Percent
6.8 Inbound tourism expenditure over exports of goods		Percent
6.9 Inbound tourism expenditure over exports of services		Percent
6.10 Inbound tourism expenditure over exports of goods and services		Percent
6.11 Inbound tourism expenditure over current account credits		Percent
6.12 Outbound tourism expenditure over imports of goods		Percent
6.13 Outbound tourism expenditure over imports of services		Percent
6.14 Outbound tourism expenditure over imports of goods and services		Percent
6.15 Outbound tourism expenditure over current account debits		Percent

INDICE DES INDICATEURS ET DONNÉES DE BASE

Données de base et indicateurs		Notes	Unités
1.	**TOURISME RÉCEPTEUR**		
	Données		
	Arrivées		
1.1	Total		('000)
1.2	♦ Visiteurs qui passent la nuit (touristes)		('000)
1.3	♦ Visiteurs de la journée (excursionnistes)		('000)
1.4	* dont croisiéristes		('000)
	Arrivées par région		
1.5	Total		('000)
1.6	♦ Afrique		('000)
1.7	♦ Amériques		('000)
1.8	♦ Asie de l'Est et Pacifique		('000)
1.9	♦ Europe		('000)
1.10	♦ Moyen-Orient		('000)
1.11	♦ Asie du Sud		('000)
1.12	♦ Autres, non classés		('000)
1.13	* dont nationaux résidant à l'étranger		('000)
	Arrivées, par motif principal		
1.14	Total		('000)
1.15	♦ Motifs personnels		('000)
1.16	* vacances, loisirs et détente		('000)
1.17	* autres motifs personnels		('000)
1.18	♦ Affaires et motifs professionnels		('000)
	Arrivées, par mode de transport		
1.19	Total		('000)
1.20	♦ Voie aérienne		('000)
1.21	♦ Voie fluviale		('000)
1.22	♦ Voie terrestre		('000)
1.23	* chemin de fer		('000)
1.24	* route		('000)
1.25	* autres		('000)
	Arrivées, par mode d'organisation du voyage		
1.26	Total		('000)
1.27	♦ Voyages à forfait		('000)
1.28	♦ Autres		('000)
	Hébergement		
	Total		
1.29	♦ Clients		('000)
1.30	♦ Nuitées		('000)
	Hôtels et établissements assimilés		
1.31	♦ Clients		('000)
1.32	♦ Nuitées		('000)
	Dépenses		
1.33	Total		Mn $E.U.
1.34	♦ Voyages		Mn $E.U.
1.35	♦ Transport de passagers		Mn $E.U.
	Dépenses, par motif principal du voyage		
1.36	Total		Mn $E.U.
1.37	♦ Motifs personnels		Mn $E.U.
1.38	♦ Affaires et motifs professionnels		Mn $E.U.
	Indicateurs		
1.39	Taille moyenne du groupe de voyageurs		Personnes
	Durée moyenne du séjour		
1.40	Total		Journées
1.41	♦ Pour tous les services d'hébergement commercial		Nuitées
1.42	* dont "hôtels et établissements assimilés"		Nuitées
1.43	♦ Pour les services d'hébergement non commercial		Journées
1.44	Dépenses moyennes par jour		$E.U.

Données de base et indicateurs	Notes	Unités
2. TOURISME INTERNE		
Données		
Voyages		
2.1 Total		('000)
2.2 ♦ Visiteurs qui passent la nuit (touristes)		('000)
2.3 ♦ Visiteurs à la journée (excursionnistes)		('000)
Voyages, par motif principal		
2.4 Total		('000)
2.5 ♦ Voyages personnels		('000)
2.6 * vacances, loisirs et détente		('000)
2.7 * autres motifs personnels		('000)
2.8 ♦ Affaires et motifs professionnels		('000)
Voyages, par mode de transport		
2.9 Total		('000)
2.10 ♦ Voie aérienne		('000)
2.11 ♦ Voie fluviale		('000)
2.12 ♦ Voie terrestre		('000)
2.13 * chemin de fer		('000)
2.14 * route		('000)
2.15 * autres		('000)
Voyages, par mode d'organisation		
2.16 Total		('000)
2.17 ♦ Voyages à forfait		('000)
2.18 ♦ Autres		('000)
Hébergement		
Total		
2.19 ♦ Clients		('000)
2.20 ♦ Nuitées		('000)
Hôtels et établissements assimilés		
2.21 ♦ Clients		('000)
2.22 ♦ Nuitées		('000)
Indicateurs		
2.23 Taille moyenne du groupe de voyageurs		Personnes
Durée moyenne du séjour		
2.24 Total		Journées
2.25 ♦ Pour tous les services d'hébergement commercial		Nuitées
2.26 * dont "hôtels et établissements assimilés"		Nuitées
2.27 ♦ Pour les services d'hébergement non commercial		Journées
2.28 Dépenses moyennes par jour		$E.U.
3. TOURISME ÉMETTEUR		
Données		
Départs		
3.1 Total		('000)
3.2 ♦ Visiteurs qui passent la nuit (touristes)		('000)
3.3 ♦ Visiteurs à la journée (excursionnistes)		('000)
Dépenses		
3.4 Total		Mn $E.U.
3.5 ♦ Voyages		Mn $E.U.
3.6 ♦ Transport de passagers		Mn $E.U.
Dépenses, par motif principal du voyage		
3.7 Total		Mn $E.U.
3.8 ♦ Motifs personnels		Mn $E.U.
3.9 ♦ Affaires et motifs professionnels		Mn $E.U.
Indicateurs		
3.10 Durée moyenne du séjour		Journées
3.11 Dépenses moyennes par jour		$E.U.

Données de base et indicateurs	Notes	Unités
4. INDUSTRIES TOURISTIQUES		
Données		
Nombre d'établissements		
4.1 Total		Unités
4.2 ♦ Hébergement des visiteurs		Unités
4.3 * dont "hôtels et établissements assimilés"		Unités
4.4 ♦ Restaurants et débits de boissons		Unités
4.5 ♦ Transport de passagers		Unités
4.6 ♦ Agences de voyage et autres activités de services de réservation		Unités
4.7 ♦ Autres sous-secteurs touristiques		Unités
Hébergement des visiteurs dans des hôtels et des établissements assimilés		
Données monétaires		
4.8 ♦ Données de sortie		Mn $E.U.
4.9 ♦ Consommation intermédiaire		Mn $E.U.
4.10 ♦ Valeur ajoutée brute		Mn $E.U.
4.11 ♦ Rémunération des salariés		Mn $E.U.
4.12 ♦ Formation brute de capital fixe		Mn $E.U.
Données non monétaires		
4.13 ♦ Nombre d'établissements		Unités
4.14 ♦ Nombre de chambres		Unités
4.15 ♦ Nombre de places-lit		Unités
Indicateurs		
4.16 Taux d'occupation / chambres		Pour cent
4.17 Taux d'occupation / places-lit		Pour cent
4.18 Durée moyenne du séjour		Nuitées
4.19 Capacité disponible (places-lit pour 1000 habitants)		Unités
Agences de voyage et autres activités de services de réservation		
Données monétaires		
4.20 ♦ Données de sortie		Mn $E.U.
4.21 ♦ Consommation intermédiaire		Mn $E.U.
4.22 ♦ Valeur ajoutée brute		Mn $E.U.
4.23 ♦ Rémunération des salariés		Mn $E.U.
4.24 ♦ Formation brute de capital fixe		Mn $E.U.
Données non monétaires		
♦ Voyages internes		
4.25 * avec forfait		Pour cent
4.26 * sans forfait		Pour cent
♦ Voyages récepteurs		
4.27 * avec forfait		Pour cent
4.28 * sans forfait		Pour cent
♦ Voyages émetteurs		
4.29 * avec forfait		Pour cent
4.30 * sans forfait		Pour cent

INDICE DES INDICATEURS ET DONNÉES DE BASE

Données de base et indicateurs		Notes	Unités
5.	**EMPLOI**		
	Données		
	Nombre d'employés par sous-secteur touristique		
5.1	Total		('000)
5.2	♦ Services d'hébergement pour les visiteurs (hôtels et établissements assimilés)		('000)
5.3	♦ Autres services d'hébergement		('000)
5.4	♦ Restaurants et débits de boissons		('000)
5.5	♦ Transport de passagers		('000)
5.6	♦ Agences de voyage et autres activités de services de réservation		('000)
5.7	♦ Autres industries touristiques		('000)
	Nombre d'emplois par statut		
5.8	Total		('000)
5.9	♦ Employés		('000)
5.10	♦ Travailleurs indépendants		('000)
	Indicateurs		
	Nombre d'emplois équivalents à temps plein par statut		
5.11	Total		('000)
5.12	♦ Employés		('000)
5.13	* hommes		('000)
5.14	* femmes		('000)
5.15	♦ Travailleurs indépendants		('000)
5.16	* hommes		('000)
5.17	* femmes		('000)
6.	**INDICATEURS COMPLÉMENTAIRES**		
	Demande		
6.1	Propension brute à voyager		Unités
6.2	(touristes d'entrée + touristes internes) / population		Unités
	Indicateurs macroéconomiques liés au tourisme international		
6.3	Rapport dépenses du tourisme récepteur / PIB		Pour cent
6.4	Rapport dépenses du tourisme émetteur / PIB		Pour cent
6.5	Rapport balance du tourisme (dépenses du tourisme récepteur moins dépenses du tourisme émetteur) / PIB		Pour cent
6.6	Ouverture touristique (dépenses du tourisme récepteur + dépenses du tourisme émetteur / PIB)		Pour cent
6.7	Couverture touristique (rapport dépenses du tourisme émetteur / dépenses du tourisme récepteur)		Pour cent
6.8	Rapport dépenses du tourisme récepteur / exportations de biens		Pour cent
6.9	Rapport dépenses du tourisme récepteur / exportations de services		Pour cent
6.10	Rapport dépenses du tourisme récepteur / exportations de biens et de services		Pour cent
6.11	Rapport dépenses du tourisme récepteur / crédits du compte courant		Pour cent
6.12	Rapport dépenses du tourisme émetteur / importations de biens		Pour cent
6.13	Rapport dépenses du tourisme émetteur / importations de services		Pour cent
6.14	Rapport dépenses du tourisme émetteur / importations de biens et de services		Pour cent
6.15	Rapport dépenses du tourisme émetteur / débits du compte courant		Pour cent

ÍNDICE DE INDICADORES Y DATOS BÁSICOS

Datos básicos e indicadores	Notas	Unidades
1. TURISMO RECEPTOR		
Datos		
Llegadas		
1.1 Total		('000)
1.2 ♦ Visitantes que pernoctan (turistas)		('000)
1.3 ♦ Visitantes del día (excursionistas)		('000)
1.4 * de los cuales, pasajeros en crucero		('000)
Llegadas por región		
1.5 Total		('000)
1.6 ♦ África		('000)
1.7 ♦ Américas		('000)
1.8 ♦ Asia Oriental y el Pacífico		('000)
1.9 ♦ Europa		('000)
1.10 ♦ Oriente Medio		('000)
1.11 ♦ Asia Meridional		('000)
1.12 ♦ Otros no clasificados		('000)
1.13 * de los cuales, nacionales residentes en el extranjero		('000)
Llegadas por motivo principal		
1.14 Total		('000)
1.15 ♦ Motivos personales		('000)
1.16 * vacaciones, recreo y ocio		('000)
1.17 * otros motivos personales		('000)
1.18 ♦ Negocios y motivos profesionales		('000)
Llegadas por medio de transporte		
1.19 Total		('000)
1.20 ♦ Aéreo		('000)
1.21 ♦ Acuático		('000)
1.22 ♦ Terrestre		('000)
1.23 * ferrocarril		('000)
1.24 * carretera		('000)
1.25 * otros		('000)
Llegadas por forma de organización del viaje		
1.26 Total		('000)
1.27 ♦ Paquete turístico		('000)
1.28 ♦ Otras formas		('000)
Alojamiento		
Total		
1.29 ♦ Huéspedes		('000)
1.30 ♦ Pernoctaciones		('000)
Hoteles y establecimientos asimilados		
1.31 ♦ Huéspedes		('000)
1.32 ♦ Pernoctaciones		('000)
Gastos		
1.33 Total		Mill. $EE.UU.
1.34 ♦ Viajes		Mill. $EE.UU.
1.35 ♦ Transporte de pasajeros		Mill. $EE.UU.
Gastos por motivo principal del viaje		
1.36 Total		Mill. $EE.UU.
1.37 ♦ Motivos personales		Mill. $EE.UU.
1.38 ♦ Negocios y motivos profesionales		Mill. $EE.UU.
Indicadores		
1.39 Tamaño medio de los grupos de viaje		Personas
Duración media de la estancia		
1.40 Total		Días
1.41 ♦ Para todos los servicios de alojamiento comercial		Noches
1.42 * de los cuales, "hoteles y establecimientos asimilados"		Noches
1.43 ♦ Para los servicios de alojamiento no comercial		Días
1.44 Gasto medio por día		$EE.UU.

451

ÍNDICE DE INDICADORES Y DATOS BÁSICOS

Datos básicos e indicadores	Notas	Unidades
2. TURISMO INTERNO		
Datos		
Viajes		
2.1 Total		('000)
2.2 ♦ Visitantes que pernoctan (turistas)		('000)
2.3 ♦ Visitantes del día (excursionistas)		('000)
Viajes por motivo principal		
2.4 Total		('000)
2.5 ♦ Motivos personales		('000)
2.6 * vacaciones, recreo y ocio		('000)
2.7 * otros motivos personales		('000)
2.8 ♦ Negocios y motivos profesionales		('000)
Viajes por medio de transporte		
2.9 Total		('000)
2.10 ♦ Aéreo		('000)
2.11 ♦ Acuático		('000)
2.12 ♦ Terrestre		('000)
2.13 * ferrocarril		('000)
2.14 * carretera		('000)
2.15 * otros		('000)
Viajes por forma de organización		
2.16 Total		('000)
2.17 ♦ Paquete turístico		('000)
2.18 ♦ Otras formas		('000)
Alojamiento		
Total		
2.19 ♦ Huéspedes		('000)
2.20 ♦ Pernoctaciones		('000)
Hoteles y establecimientos asimilados		
2.21 ♦ Huéspedes		('000)
2.22 ♦ Pernoctaciones		('000)
Indicadores		
2.23 Tamaño medio de los grupos de viaje		Personas
Duración media de la estancia		
2.24 Total		Días
2.25 ♦ Para todos los servicios de alojamiento comercial		Noches
2.26 * de los cuales, "hoteles y establecimientos asimilados"		Noches
2.27 ♦ Para los servicios de alojamiento no comercial		Días
2.28 Gasto medio por día		$EE.UU.
3. TURISMO EMISOR		
Datos		
Salidas		
3.1 Total		('000)
3.2 ♦ Visitantes que pernoctan (turistas)		('000)
3.3 ♦ Visitantes del día (excursionistas)		('000)
Gastos		
3.4 Total		Mill. $EE.UU.
3.5 ♦ Viajes		Mill. $EE.UU.
3.6 ♦ Transporte de pasajeros		Mill. $EE.UU.
Gastos por motivo principal del viaje		
3.7 Total		Mill. $EE.UU.
3.8 ♦ Motivos personales		Mill. $EE.UU.
3.9 ♦ Negocios y motivos profesionales		Mill. $EE.UU.
Indicadores		
3.10 Duración media de la estancia		Días
3.11 Gasto medio por día		$EE.UU.

452

ÍNDICE DE INDICADORES Y DATOS BÁSICOS

Datos básicos e indicadores	Notas	Unidades
4. INDUSTRIAS TURÍSTICAS		
Datos		
Número de establecimientos		
4.1 Total		Unidades
4.2 ♦ Alojamiento para visitantes		Unidades
4.3 * de los cuales, "hoteles y establecimientos asimilados"		Unidades
4.4 ♦ Actividades de provisión de alimentos y bebidas		Unidades
4.5 ♦ Transporte de pasajeros		Unidades
4.6 ♦ Actividades de agencias de viajes y de otros servicios de reservas		Unidades
4.7 ♦ Otras industrias turísticas		Unidades
Alojamiento para los visitantes en hoteles y establecimientos asimilados		
Datos monetarios		
4.8 ♦ Producción		Mill. $EE.UU.
4.9 ♦ Consumo intermedio		Mill. $EE.UU.
4.10 ♦ Valor añadido bruto		Mill. $EE.UU.
4.11 ♦ Remuneración de los trabajadores asalariados		Mill. $EE.UU.
4.12 ♦ Formación bruta de capital fijo		Mill. $EE.UU.
Datos no monetarios		
4.13 ♦ Número de establecimientos		Unidades
4.14 ♦ Número de habitaciones		Unidades
4.15 ♦ Número de plazas-cama		Unidades
Indicadores		
4.16 Tasa de ocupación / habitaciones		%
4.17 Tasa de ocupación / plazas-cama		%
4.18 Duración media de la estancia		Noches
4.19 Capacidad disponible (plazas-cama por 1000 habitantes)		Unidades
Actividades de agencias de viajes y de otros servicios de reserva		
Datos monetarios		
4.20 ♦ Producción		Mill. $EE.UU.
4.21 ♦ Consumo intermedio		Mill. $EE.UU.
4.22 ♦ Valor añadido bruto		Mill. $EE.UU.
4.23 ♦ Remuneración de los trabajadores asalariados		Mill. $EE.UU.
4.24 ♦ Formación bruta de capital fijo		Mill. $EE.UU.
Datos no monetarios		
♦ Viajes internos		
4.25 * con paquete turístico		%
4.26 * sin paquete turístico		%
♦ Viajes receptores		
4.27 * con paquete turístico		%
4.28 * sin paquete turístico		%
♦ Viajes emisores		
4.29 * con paquete turístico		%
4.30 * sin paquete turístico		%

Datos básicos e indicadores	Notas	Unidades
5. EMPLEO		
Datos		
Número de empleados por industria turística		
5.1 Total		('000)
5.2 ♦ Servicios de alojamiento para visitantes (hoteles y establecimientos asimilados)		('000)
5.3 ♦ Otros servicios de alojamiento		('000)
5.4 ♦ Actividades de provisión de alimentos y bebidas		('000)
5.5 ♦ Transporte de pasajeros		('000)
5.6 ♦ Actividades de agencias de viajes y de otros servicios de reservas		('000)
5.7 ♦ Otras industrias turísticas		('000)
Número de puestos de trabajo según la situación en el empleo		
5.8 Total		('000)
5.9 ♦ Asalariados		('000)
5.10 ♦ Trabajadores autónomos		('000)
Indicadores		
Número de puestos de trabajo equivalentes a tiempo completo según la situación en el empleo		
5.11 Total		('000)
5.12 ♦ Asalariados		('000)
5.13 * hombres		('000)
5.14 * mujeres		('000)
5.15 ♦ Trabajadores autónomos		('000)
5.16 * hombres		('000)
5.17 * mujeres		('000)
6. INDICADORES COMPLEMENTARIOS		
Demanda		
6.1 Propensión bruta a viajar		Unidades
6.2 (turistas receptores + turistas internos) / población		Unidades
Indicadores macroeconómicos relacionados con el turismo internacional		
6.3 Gasto turístico receptor sobre el PIB		%
6.4 Gasto turístico emisor sobre el PIB		%
6.5 Balanza turística (gasto turístico receptor menos gasto turístico emisor) sobre el PIB		%
6.6 Apertura turística (gasto turístico receptor más gasto turístico emisor) sobre el PIB		%
6.7 Cobertura turística (gasto turístico receptor sobre gasto turístico emisor)		%
6.8 Gasto turístico receptor sobre las exportaciones de bienes		%
6.9 Gasto turístico receptor sobre las exportaciones de servicios		%
6.10 Gasto turístico receptor sobre las exportaciones de bienes y de servicios		%
6.11 Gasto turístico receptor sobre los créditos de la cuenta corriente		%
6.12 Gasto turístico emisor sobre las importaciones de bienes		%
6.13 Gasto turístico emisor sobre las importaciones de servicios		%
6.14 Gasto turístico emisor sobre las importaciones de bienes y de servicios		%
6.15 Gasto turístico emisor sobre los débitos de la cuenta corriente		%

Country notes

Notes des pays

Notas de los países

Country notes

ALBANIA

(1)   Excluding nationals residing abroad;
(2)   Including transit visitors;
(3)   Source: Short Term Survey. Hotels only;
(4)   2011: the classification used is NACE Rev. 1.1 (Classification of economic activities). From 2012, the classification used for SBS is NACE Rev. 2;
(5)   Value added at Basic prices;
(6)   Total investments;
(7)   The figures are updated with the Structural Business Survey;
(8)   Includes all enterprises classified in NACE 55 and 56 of NACE Rev. 2;
(9)   Includes all enterprises classified in NACE 49, 50 or 51 of NACE Rev. 2;
(10) Includes all enterprises classified in NACE 79 of NACE Rev. 2.

Institute of Statistics – INSTAT
www.instat.gov.al/

ALGERIA

(1)   Including nationals residing abroad;
(2)   Excluding nationals residing abroad.

“Ministère de l'Aménagement du Territoire, du Tourisme et de l'Artisanat” and “Office National des Statistiques”

AMERICAN SAMOA

Department of Commerce – Statistics Division
www.spc.int/prism/americansamoa/

ANDORRA

(1)   In 2009 and 2011 there were changes in the methodology for calculating the number of visitors of the country. In this regard, it is not possible to have comparability for data obtained using different methodologies because the variations reflect not only the variation in the number of visitors but also variations caused by the methodological changes.

“Ministerio de Turismo y Medio Ambiente” and “Ministerio de Finanzas”
www.estadistica.ad/serveiestudis/web/index.asp?lang=2

ANGOLA

(1)   Hotels only.

“Ministério de Hotelaria e Turismo – Gabinete de Estudos, Planeamento e Estatística”

ANGUILLA

(1)   Excluding nationals residing abroad;
(2)   Including same-day visitors (excursionists);
(3)   Source: Visitor exit survey.

Anguilla Statistics Department – Ministry of Finance, Economic Development, Investment, Commerce and Tourism
www.gov.ai/statistics/cab_external.htm

ANTIGUA AND BARBUDA

(1)   Excluding yacht passenger arrivals;
(2)   Arrivals by air; excluding nationals residing abroad;
(3)   Cruise passengers only.

Ministry of Tourism
http://members.antiguahotels.org/tourism-statistics-for-antigua-and-barbuda/

ARGENTINA

(1)   Change of methodology from 2013. The data are not comparable with those of previous years;
(2)   Hotel Occupancy Survey (EOH);
(3)   Household Survey on Travel and Tourism (EVyTH);
(4)   It should be noted that a change was made in the methodology used in past years for the analysis of Employment in the tourism sector. The previous analysis was based on a single Survey covering 32 urban clusters. In the current analysis, however, the results are based on a synthesis that draws on the most substantive information for the sector; it includes various information sources that provide data on employment in the entire country and provides more accurate aggregates of tourism characteristic activities. This new methodology is available from 2010 onwards;
(5)   The classification includes state and private sector employees, whether or not they make Social Security contributions or deductions (formal or informal);
(6)   Consisting of the following occupational categories: owner, self-employed (formal) and self-employed (informal).

“Dirección de Estudios de Mercado y Estadística – Secretaría de Turismo de la Nación”
www.turismo.gov.ar/
http://desarrolloturistico.gob.ar/estadistica/ultimas-cifras

ARMENIA

Tourism Department – Ministry of Economy of the Republic of Armenia
www.armstat.am/en/

457

ARUBA

(1) Arrivals by air;
(2) Cruise passengers only.

Aruba Tourism Authority
www.cbs.aw/index.php/statistics/tables-statistics/68-tables/
tourism

AUSTRALIA

(1) Excluding nationals residing abroad and crew members;
(2) Source: Tourism Research Australia – National Visitor Survey (NVS);
(3) Hotels, motels, guests houses and serviced apartments with 15 rooms or more. As at June. Source: Cat 8635.0 Tourist Accommodation Australia, Table 1;
(4) Source: Cat. 5249.0 – Australian National Accounts: Tourism Satellite Account, Table 14 Direct Tourism Employment by Industry.

Australian Bureau of Statistics
www.abs.gov.au/

AUSTRIA

(1) Non-resident tourists staying in all types of accommodation establishments;
(2) Only paid accommodation; excluding stays at friends and relatives and second homes;
(3) Hotels only;
(4) Leisure and business trips abroad with at least one overnight stay, including stays at friends and relatives and second homes;
(5) Based on summer season (May-October);
(6) Tourism Satellite Account (TSA) data;
(7) Full-time equivalents.

Statistics Austria
www.statistik.at/web_en/statistics/tourism/accommodation/
index.html

AZERBAIJAN

Ministry of Culture and Tourism and Statistical Committee
www.stat.gov.az

BAHAMAS

(1) Arrivals in hotels only;
(2) Hotels, apartments, cottages and villas – Licensed properties only.

Bahamas Ministry of Tourism
www.tourismtoday.com/home/statistics/

BAHRAIN

(1) Excluding nationals residing abroad;
(2) Arrivals at Bahrain International Airport;
(3) Arrivals at Mina Salman Port;
(4) Arrivals through King Fahad Causeway;
(5) Classified hotels only.

Tourism Sector – Ministry of Culture and Information and Information and eGovernment Authority

BANGLADESH

Bangladesh Bureau of Statistics (BBS)

BARBADOS

(1) Hotels, apartment hotels, apartments and cottages, guest houses.

Barbados Tourism Marketing Inc
www.tourism.gov.bb/tourism-publications.html

BELARUS

(1) Non-resident tourists staying in all types of accommodation establishments;
(2) Package tour;
(3) Major groupings only;
(4) Data based on the state statistical observation of the number of employees in collective accommodation establishments and travel agencies.

State Border Committee and National Statistical Committee of the Republic of Belarus

BELGIUM

(1) Non-resident tourists staying in all types of accommodation establishments;
(2) Due to a change in the methodology, from 2015 the data are not comparable with those of previous years;
(3) Hotels only;
(4) Hotels and holiday villages. From 2012 including bed and breakfast.

"Institut National de Statistique"

BELIZE

Belize Tourist Board

BENIN

"Direction du développement et de promotion touristiques – Ministère de la culture, de l'alphabétisation, de l'artisanat et du tourisme"

BERMUDA

(1) Excluding nationals residing abroad;
(2) Arrivals by air;
(3) Cruise passengers;
(4) Including overnight stays at private houses.

Bermuda Department of Tourism
www.gov.bm/portal/
CommunityPage&control=SetCommunity&CommunityID=227

COUNTRY NOTES

BHUTAN

(1) Total arrivals 2011: 65,756; 2012: 105,407; 2013: 116,209; 2014: 134,254; 2015: 155,121. The huge margin of difference in 2011–2015 as compared to the previous years is because starting from 2010 the regional high end tourists are included in the total figures;
(2) Provisional data.

Department of Tourism – Royal Government of Bhutan
www.nsb.gov.bt/index.php?id=13
www.tourism.gov.bt/annual-reports/bhutan-tourism-monitor

BOLIVIA, PLURINATIONAL STATE OF

(1) Preliminary data;
(2) Information obtained through the specific percentage breakdown in the Survey "expenditure of inbound and outbound tourism";
(3) Arrivals by lake;
(4) The 7.6% of travellers corresponds to organized tourism;
(5) Source: Survey "expenditure of inbound and outbound tourism";
(6) Department capitals only;
(7) Average size of travel party for families: 2.8 persons.

Note:
The tourism indicators are obtained from the relationship of the results of the survey "expenditure of inbound and outbound tourism" between/among the statistics of Foreign Trade, Balance of Payments services, National Accounts (GDP), determining the participation of tourism in each of the sectors.

"Instituto Nacional de Estadística"
www.ine.gob.bo/default.aspx

BOSNIA AND HERZEGOVINA

(1) Non-resident tourists staying in all types of accommodation establishments;
(2) 2011, 2012: less than 500 arrivals;
(3) Data is taken from Cross-border traffic of passengers statistical report for 2015 and includes total arrivals of non-resident passengers at national borders. Passengers in transit are included;
(4) Data from monthly statistical survey RAD.

Agency for Statistics of Bosnia and Herzegovina
www.bhas.ba

BOTSWANA

(1) Including returning residents.

Department of Tourism – Ministry of Environment, Wildlife and Tourism

BRAZIL

(1) Including nationals residing abroad;
(2) Including arrivals by river;
(3) Data refer to "Encuesta Anual de Servicios (PAS) 2013, do Instituto Brasileiro de Estatísticas e Geografia – IBGE";

(4) 2011: data refer to "Pesquisa de Serviços de Hospedagem (PSH) do Instituto Brasileiro de Estatísticas e Geografia – IBGE". 2013–2015: data reflect the number of tourism services providers regularly registered in the System for Enterprises Register, Equipment and Professionals for Tourism (Cadastur) who reported exercising an activity of infrastructures services providers for events. Each service provider can register in more than one activity;
(5) Annual Directory of Corporate Information (RAIS) – 2014 – Ministério do Trabalho; Formal employees: registered and covered by social security – National Household Survey – 2014 – IBGE – Informal employees: not registered and not covered by social security.

"Ministério do Turismo"
www.dadosefatos.turismo.gov.br/dadosefatos/home.html

BRITISH VIRGIN ISLANDS

(1) Including cruise passengers;
(2) The expenditure figures are those provided by the country to UNWTO, which do not appear in the International Monetary Fund data used in the preparation of this edition of the Compendium.

Central Statistics Office

BRUNEI DARUSSALAM

(1) Arrivals by air.

Brunei Tourism – Ministry of Industry and Primary Resources

BULGARIA

(1) Transit visitors;
(2) Source: Eurostat;
(3) Hotels only.

National Statistical Institute, Bulgarian National Bank and Ministry of Tourism
www.nsi.bg

BURKINA FASO

(1) Non-resident tourists staying in hotels and similar establishments;
(2) Including domestic tourism.

"Service de l'analyse statistique et de la Coopération touristique – Ministère de la Culture, des Arts et du Tourisme"
www.insd.bf/

BURUNDI

(1) Including nationals residing abroad;
(2) Arrivals by lake.

"Office National du Tourisme"

CABO VERDE

(1) Non-resident tourists staying in hotels and similar establishments.

"Instituto Nacional de Estatística" and "Ministério da Economia, Crescimento e Competitividade"
www.ine.cv/dadostats/dados.aspx?d=2

CAMBODIA

(1) Arrivals by all mode of transport;
(2) Arrivals by boat;
(3) Days.

Ministry of Tourism
www.tourismcambodia.org/mot/index.php?view=statistic_report#comp

CAMEROON

(1) Non-resident tourists staying in hotels and similar establishments.

"Ministère du Tourisme"

CANADA

(1) Data based on customs counts and adjusted using questionnaire surveys;
(2) A redesigned domestic survey (Travel Survey of Residents of Canada) came into effect in 2011, resulting in a break in the time series. Consequently, 2011 data points are not comparable to previous years;
(3) Departures are estimated from arrivals of Canadian residents returning from abroad;
(4) 5.13 and 5.14 are calculated using average annual hours worked in full-time jobs by males and females respectively.

Canadian Tourism Commission and Statistics Canada
http://en-corporate.canada.travel/research/statistics-figures

CAYMAN ISLANDS

(1) Arrivals by air;
(2) Cruise passengers only;
(3) The expenditure figures are those provided by the country to UNWTO, which do not appear in the International Monetary Fund data used in the preparation of this edition of the Compendium;
(4) Including expenditure by cruise passengers;
(5) Hotels and apartments;
(6) Days.

Cayman Islands Department of Tourism
www.caymanislands.ky/statistics/
www.eso.ky

CENTRAL AFRICAN REPUBLIC

(1) Arrivals by air to Bangui only;
(2) Country data.

"Ministère des Arts, du Tourisme, de la Culture et de la Francophonie"

CHAD

"Ministère du Tourisme et de l'Artisanat – Direction de la Planification et des Études Prospectives"

CHILE

(1) Including nationals residing abroad;
(2) Cruise passengers plus Arica-Tacna agreement;
(3) Due to a change in the methodology, from 2014 the data are not comparable with those of previous years;
(4) Excluding camping sites;
(5) Starting in 2012, tourism packages are estimated only through airports;
(6) Source: "SII (Servicio de Impuestos Internos)";
(7) 2015: estimated data.

"Subsecretaría de Turismo – Ministerio de Economía, Fomento y Turismo"
www.sernatur.cl/estadisticas/

CHINA

(1) Including ethnic Chinese arriving from "Hong Kong, China", "Macao, China", "Taiwan, Province of China" and overseas Chinese, of which most same-day visitors are from "Hong Kong, China" and "Macao, China";
(2) Excluding ethnic Chinese arriving from "Hong Kong, China", "Macao, China", "Taiwan, Province of China" and overseas Chinese;
(3) On foot;
(4) Including air crew members and other servicemen;
(5) Only refer to the star-rated hotels;
(6) Inbound tourism only.

National Tourism Administration
http://en.cnta.gov.cn/

COLOMBIA

(1) Arrivals of non-resident travellers by immigration checkpoints;
(2) Including cross-border visitors ('000): 2011: 999; 2012: 1,063; 2013: 1,153; 2014: 1,313; 2015: 1,197;
(3) Including nationals residing abroad;
(4) Excluding cross-border visitors and cruise passengers;
(5) Excluding nationals residing abroad.
Note: provisional data.

"Migración Colombia / Sociedades portuarias / Dirección de Análisis Sectorial y Promoción – Ministerio de Comercio, Industria y Turismo (MINCIT)"
www.mincit.gov.co/publicaciones.php?id=16590

CONGO

(1) Surveys 2011 to 2015;
(2) Including nationals residing abroad. Total 2011: 45,800;
(3) Surveys 2011 to 2013;
(4) Source: "Banque des Etats d'Afrique Centrale (B.E.A.C)".
2012, 2013: estimates.
Note 2015: estimates.

"Direction Générale du Tourisme et de l'Hôtellerie – Ministère du tourisme et de l'environnement"

CONGO, DEMOCRATIC REPUBLIC OF THE

(1) The arrivals data relate only to three border posts (N'Djili airport in Kinshasa, the Luano airport in Lubumbashi, and the land border-crossing of Kasumbalesa in Katanga province).

"Office National du Tourisme"

COOK ISLANDS

(1) Arrivals by air and sea;
(2) The expenditure figures are those provided by the country to UNWTO, which do not appear in the International Monetary Fund data used in the preparation of this edition of the Compendium.

Cook Islands Tourism Corporation and Cook Islands Statistics Office
www.mfem.gov.ck/statistics

COSTA RICA

(1) Surveys of Non resident at international airports, "ICT";
(2) Accommodation survey, Department of Macroeconomic Statistics, "BCCR";
(3) Employent in the tourism industries, continuous survey on employment ("ECE"), "INEC".

"Banco Central de Costa Rica (BCCR)", "Instituto Costarricense de Turismo (ICT)" and "Instituto Nacional de Estadística y Censos (INEC)"
www.visitcostarica.com/ict/paginas/modEst/informes_estadisticos.asp

COTE D'IVOIRE

(1) 2011–2014: arrivals to Félix Houphouët Boigny Airport only. 2015: break in the series: figures include arrivals by land (road and railway).

"Ministère du Tourisme"

CROATIA

(1) Non-resident tourists staying in all types of accommodation establishments;
(2) Data on total number of establishments includes only collective tourist accommodation establishments. Since 2010, nautical ports have no longer been considered reporting units or types of accommodation facilities in the monthly survey on tourist arrivals and nights because of the implementation of the new legal basis of monitoring the tourists. Due to the mentioned change in the methodology, data from 2005 to 2009 were revised so they can be comparable to 2010 (nautical ports were excluded);
(3) Includes road passengers in transit;
(4) Data from survey on traffic in airports, all international arrivals;
(5) Data from survey on traffic in sea ports, all international arrivals. Includes passengers on cruise ships;
(6) Data from survey on rail transport of passengers, includes all international arrivals by rail;
(7) Data includes total arrivals of non-resident passengers at national borders by road. Passengers in transit are included;
(8) Data do not include number of households that rent tourist accommodation (rooms to let, apartments, studio-type suite and summer houses in households);
(9) Source: CBS, Survey on Tourist Activity of Croatian Population;
(10) 2015: provisional data;
(11) The application of the new Regulation caused changes in the methodology of the data collection method for the following types of accommodation facilities: rooms to let, apartments, studio-type apartments and summer houses. Since 2013, reporting units for these facilities have been tourist boards, irrespective of whether they are rented by legal entities, tradesmen or households. Data on accommodation facilities are considered provisional due to the fact that their registry is still not adequately organised in all tourist boards;
(12) Due to a constant process of categorisation, there are changes in types and categories of accommodation facilities;
(13) According to the Regulation on Classification, Minimum Standards and Categorization of Accommodation Facilities, data for hotels and similar establishments do not include Inns and Bed and Breakfast since 2006;
(14) Since 2013, the method of presenting the capacities have been changed (they are no longer monitored with the situation as on 31 August), which is in line with the Regulation No 692/2011 of the European Parliament and of the Council concerning European statistics on tourism. The application of the Regulation No 692/2011 of the European Parliament and of the Council of European tourism statistics, the capacity of an accommodation establishment presented is taken over from a month when it reached its maximum;
(15) Gross occupancy rate;
(16) The classification used is NACE Rev. 2.

Croatian Bureau of Statistics
www.dzs.hr/default_e.htm
www.mint.hr/default.aspx?id=363

CUBA

(1) Arrivals by air;
(2) Hotels, motels, apart-hotels, camping/caravaning and other;
(3) Hotels, motels and apart-hotels;
(4) The expenditure figures are those provided by the country to UNWTO, which do not appear in the International Monetary Fund data used in the preparation of this edition of the Compendium;

COUNTRY NOTES

(5) Including only tours authorized by the "Instituto de Turismo".

"Oficina Nacional de Estadística e Información"
www.one.cu/sitioone2006.asp

CURAÇAO

(1) Arrivals by air;
(2) Differences in overall totals due to incompletion of items on the E/D card by visitors;
(3) Cruise ship arrivals;
(4) Large and small hotels, guest houses, apartments and bungalows;
(5) Hotels, guest houses, apartments.

Curaçao Tourist Board
www.curacao.com/en/directory/corporate/statistics-and-downloads/

CYPRUS

(1) Source: Passenger Survey, conducted by the Statistical Service of Cyprus;
(2) Including transit and cruise passengers;
(3) Data for 2012 and 2013 refer only to eleven months since the data for March 2012 and January 2013 are not available;
(4) Including transit passengers;
(5) Accommodation data (arrivals, overnight stays and occupancy rates) is collected from the licensed tourist accommodation establishments on a monthly basis and produced by the Cyprus Tourism Organization (C.T.O.);
(6) Data concerning Hotels and Similar establishments from 2010 onwards has been revised to include tourist villas under "Similar establishments". Prior to this revision, tourist villas were included in "Other Collective Establishments" (under the "Holiday Dwellings" section);
(7) Average expenditure per day calculated by dividing the relevant total expenditure (item 1.33) with the total number of inbound overnight visitors (item 1.2) and their average length of stay (item 1.40);
(8) Average length of stay calculations are based on overnight stays and arrivals at licensed tourist accommodation establishments;
(9) Average expenditure per day calculated by dividing the relevant Total Expenditure (item 3.4) with the total number of outbound overnight visitors (tourists) (item 3.2) and their average length of stay (item 3.10);
(10) Data extracted from the Hotels and Restaurants Statistics which result from the Services Survey conducted by the Statistical Service of Cyprus. It refers to NACE Rev. 2 code 55;
(11) Data extracted from the Hotels and Restaurants Statistics which result from the Services Survey conducted by the Statistical Service of Cyprus. In items 4.3 and 5.2, data reported concerns tourist enterprises which fall under the NACE Rev.2 codes 55101 and 55102;
(12) Data extracted from the Hotels and Restaurants Statistics which result from the Services Survey conducted by the Statistical Service of Cyprus. It refers to NACE Rev. 2 code 56;
(13) Number of travel agencies (item 4.6) and monetary data (items 4.20-4.24): Data extracted from the Statistics on Business Services which result from the Services Survey conducted by the Statistical Service of Cyprus. It refers to NACE Rev. 2 code 79;

(14) Monetary data reported in items 4.8-4.12 is extracted from the Hotels and Restaurants Statistics which result from the Services Survey conducted by the Statistical Service of Cyprus and it pertains to Hotels and Similar tourist enterprises which fall under the NACE Rev.2 codes 55101 and 55102;
(15) Non-monetary data is compiled and produced by the C.T.O. and it concerns licensed hotels and similar tourist accommodation establishments. The data provided differs from the data shown in the items 4.2-4.3 and 4.8-4.12, which is extracted from the Hotels and Restaurants Statistics which result from the Services Survey conducted by the Statistical Service of Cyprus. The differences in the two sets of data, are due to reasons such as the fact that the Services Survey treats enterprises or persons owning/operating more than one tourist accommodation units (establishments) as one entity whereas the C.T.O. data counts individual tourist accommodation units regardless whether they belong to one owner or are managed by one operator;
(16) Average length of stay calculations are based on overnight stays and arrivals at hotels and similar licensed tourist accommodation establishments (C.T.O. data);
(17) Data extracted from the Hotels and Restaurants Statistics which result from the Services Survey conducted by the Statistical Service of Cyprus. It refers to NACE Rev. 2 codes 5520+, 5530+ and 5590).

Note for all the data supplied:
information on real estate activities with own or leased property and real estate activities on a fee or contract basis is not included.

Statistical Service of Cyprus, Cyprus Tourism Organization and Central Bank of Cyprus
www.mof.gov.cy/mof/cystat/statistics.nsf/index_en/index_en?OpenDocument

CZECH REPUBLIC

(1) TSA of the Czech Republic;
(2) 2015: preliminary data;
(3) Including transit visitors;
(4) Non-resident tourists staying in all collective accommodation establishments – Source: CZSO;
(5) Source: Domestic and Outbound Tourism Survey and TSA;
(6) Long trips + short trips;
(7) Business trips;
(8) Due to a change in the methodology of the survey, from 2011 the data are not comparable with those of previous years (Source: CZSO). Long trips + short trips;
(9) Source: Business Register of the Czech Republic;
(10) Hotels and restaurants;
(11) Source: National Accounts;
(12) Fixed capital consumption;
(13) Net use of beds;
(14) Supporting and auxiliary transport activities, activities of tour-operators and travel agencies;
(15) Tourism trips (1 overnight stay and more).

Czech Statistical Office, TSA and Ministry for Regional Development
www.czso.cz/eng/redakce.nsf/i/home

COUNTRY NOTES

DENMARK

(1) 2011, 2014 : change of methodology ;
(2) Non-resident tourists staying in all types of accommodation establishments ;
(3) Including non-commercial tourism ;
(4) Hotels only ;
(5) The expenditure figures are those provided by the country to UNWTO, which do not appear in the International Monetary Fund data used in the preparation of this edition of the Compendium. Source : VisitDenmark ;
(6) Source : Eurostat ;
(7) Only hotels and holiday dwellings with 40 beds or more.

VisitDenmark and Statistics Denmark
www.dst.dk/HomeUK.aspx

DJIBOUTI

(1) Non-resident tourists staying in hotels.

"Office national du tourisme"

DOMINICA

(1) Days.

Discover Dominica Authority
http://tourism.gov.dm/statistics

DOMINICAN REPUBLIC

(1) Including nationals residing abroad ;
(2) Arrivals by air only ;
(3) All arrivals by sea ;
(4) Hotels.

"Ministerio de Turismo"
www.bancentral.gov.do/estadisticas_economicas/turismo/

ECUADOR

(1) Excluding nationals residing abroad ;
(2) 2015 : provisional data.

"Ministerio de Turismo"
http://servicios.turismo.gob.ec/index.php/portfolio/turismo-cifras

EGYPT

Ministry of Tourism, CAPMAS and Central Bank of Egypt

EL SALVADOR

(1) Including private accommodation.

"Corporación Salvadoreña de Turismo (CORSATUR) – Ministerio de Turismo"

ESTONIA

(1) Based on mobile positioning data by the Bank of Estonia and Positium LBS ;
(2) Due to a change in the methodology, from 2015 data are not comparable with those of 2011–2014 ;
(3) Non-resident tourists staying in all types of accommodation establishments ;
(4) Due to a change in the methodology, from 2014 data are not comparable with those of 2011–2013 ;
(5) Source : household survey by "Statistics Estonia".

Estonian Tourist Board / Enterprise Estonia
http://pub.stat.ee/px-web.2001/I_Databas/Economy/databasetree.asp
http://visitestonia.com/en/additional-navigation/press-room/eas-views-on-tourism/estonian-tourism-statistics

ETHIOPIA

(1) Arrivals through all ports of entry ; including nationals residing abroad.

Ministry of Culture and Tourism

FIJI

(1) Excluding nationals residing abroad ;
(2) Days.

Fiji Islands Bureau of Statistics
www.statsfiji.gov.fj/

FINLAND

(1) Border Interview survey. Note : the survey was cancelled at the end of 2012 ;
(2) Accommodation survey ;
(3) Balance of Payments (BOP) ;
(4) Finnish Travel survey ;
(5) Including only domestic leisure trips at rented accommodation for visitors ;
(6) Overnight trips abroad, including cruises abroad with overnight on board only ;
(7) Tourism Satellite Account (TSA) data ;
(8) Domestic and outbound overnight trips including cruises abroad with overnight on board only.

Tourism Statistics – Statistics Finland
www.mek.fi/w5/mekfi/index.nsf/(pages)/Tutkimukset_ja_tilastot

FRANCE

(1) Source : DGE, Banque de France. Non resident visitor survey (EVE) – 2011 to 2014 back-extrapolated results, results 2015 provisional ;
(2) All personal purposes ;
(3) Transit and not stated ;
(4) Source : INSEE, DGE, regional partners. Hotel occupancy surveys (EFH), campgrounds (EFHPA) and, from 2011, other collective accommodation (EFAHCT) – holiday residences and serviced apartments, holiday villages and youth hostels –; break in series in 2011 ; individual

commercial accommodation (furnished and hotel rooms) excluded;

(5) Source: INSEE, DGE, regional partners. Hotel occupancy survey (EFH); stays for all purposes;

(6) Average length of stay in nights;

(7) Source: DGE. Survey Follow-up of tourism demand (SDT). Resident population aged 15 years and above; trips in Overseas Departments are counted together with those abroad;

(8) Personal trips;

(9) Total commercial group accommodation capacity (hotels, campsites, tourist residences, serviced apartments, holiday villages, family houses, hostels, sports centers, international accommodation centers); Source: INSEE, DGE, SNRT, UNAT, FUAJ;

(10) Number of hotels; Source: INSEE, DGE;

(11) Scope: private employment in France (incl. Overseas Departments) 31/12; Source: Acoss;

(12) Short-term rentals (cars, sports and leisure equipment), amusement and theme park activities and other recreational and leisure activities, management of museums, historic sites, tourist attractions, botanical and zoological gardens and nature reserves, organization of gambling and betting activities, cable cars and ski lifts;

(13) Net room occupancy rate;

(14) Scope: Mainland France, Source: INSEE, Population Census for 2010, demographic report for 2011–2014.

"DGE (Direction générale des entreprises)" and "INSEE (Institut national de la statistique et des études économiques)"
www.entreprises.gouv.fr/etudes-et-statistiques/statistiques-du-tourisme/accueil
www.insee.fr/fr/default.asp

FRENCH GUIANA

(1) Survey at Cayenne-Rochambeau airport on departure;

(2) France only;

(3) Hotels only.

"Comité du Tourisme de la Guyane"

FRENCH POLYNESIA

(1) Arrivals by air only; excluding nationals residing abroad;

(2) Days;

(3) Hotels and guest houses; at 31st December of each year;

(4) Rooms in hotels.

"Institut de la Statistique – ISPF"
www.ispf.pf/Home.aspx

GAMBIA

(1) Including nationals residing abroad;

(2) Charter tourists only.

Gambia Tourism Board

GEORGIA

(1) Arrivals in hotels only;

(2) Source: Survey of hotels and similar establishments;

(3) NACE Rev. 1.1.;

(4) Data refers only to investment in fixed capital.

Georgian National Tourism Agency – Ministry of Economy and Sustainable Development and National Statistics Office of Georgia
http://gnta.ge/statistics/

GERMANY

(1) Non-resident tourists staying in all types of accommodation establishments;

(2) Source: Eurostat;

(3) Inbound tourism in hotels and similar establishments.

"Statistiches Bundesamt"
www.destatis.de

GHANA

(1) Including nationals residing abroad;

(2) Estimates.

Ghana Tourist Board and Ministry of Tourism and Modernisation of the Capital City
www.statsghana.gov.gh

GREECE

(1) The information is based on the border survey conducted by the Bank of Greece;

(2) Number of trips with 4 or more overnights by visitors aged 15+;

(3) Source: Hellenic Chamber of Hotels.

Hellenic Statistical Authority (EL.STAT.)
www.statistics.gr/en/statistics/ind

GRENADA

(1) 2013–2015: arrivals by air only;

(2) Yacht and cruise ship arrivals;

(3) Hotels, cottages/apartments and guest houses.

Grenada Board of Tourism

GUADELOUPE

(1) Arrivals by air; excluding the north islands (Saint Martin and Saint Barthelemy);

(2) 2014, 2015: arrivals by air;

(3) The expenditure figures are those provided by the country to UNWTO, which do not appear in the International Monetary Fund data used in the preparation of this edition of the Compendium;

(4) Hotels.

"Comité du Tourisme des Îles de la Guadeloupe"

GUAM

(1) Arrivals by air and sea;
(2) Civilian arrivals by air only;
(3) Rooms available.

Guam Visitors Bureau
www.guamvisitorsbureau.com/research-and-reports/reports/annual-report

GUATEMALA

(1) Series updated since 2009 with a new methodology.
(2) All the accommodation establishments registered in INGUAT.

"Instituto Guatemalteco de Turismo – INGUAT"
www.inguat.gob.gt/estadisticas.php

GUINEA

(1) Arrivals by air at Conakry airport;
(2) Non-resident overnights in hotels, all categories included. Data come from length of stay in hotels that have been declared by visitors in the E/D cards at their airport arrival (non-declarations of length of stay are not included);
(3) Including private accommodation;
(4) Cross-checking of "arrivals" and "type of accommodation" declared in the E/D cards.

"Direction Observatoire du Tourisme – Ministère du Tourisme, de l'Hôtellerie et de l'Artisanat"

GUINEA-BISSAU

(1) Arrivals at "Osvaldo Vieira" Airport.

"Ministère du commerce, de l'industrie, du tourisme et de l'artisanat"

GUYANA

(1) Arrivals to Timehri airport only;
(2) Canada and United States only.

Guyana Tourism Authority

HAITI

(1) Arrivals by air;
(2) Including nationals residing abroad.

"Ministère du Tourisme"

HONDURAS

(1) Nights;
(2) 2015: preliminary data.

"Instituto Hondureño de Turismo"
www.iht.hn

HONG KONG, CHINA

(1) The expenditure figures used were the ones provided by the country to UNWTO, as this data series is more complete than that provided by the International Monetary Fund (IMF) for the preparation of this Compendium (Source: HKTB Visitors Survey);
(2) Source: Census and Statistics Department;
(3) Nights;
(4) Hotels (high/medium tariffs) and hostels/ guest houses;
(5) The figures cover the service activities for inbound tourism;
(6) The figures cover the service activities for outbound tourism;
(7) The figures cover retail trade, transport and personal services for inbound tourism as well as transport services for outbound tourism.

Hong Kong Tourism Board
http://partnernet.hktb.com/en/research_statistics/index.html
www.censtatd.gov.hk/hong_kong_statistics/index.jsp

HUNGARY

(1) The observation of the borders with the countries of the Schengen Area ceased from the year 2008. 2011: the air passenger traffic and road are estimates;
(2) Departures of non-resident visitors;
(3) By river;
(4) Excluding lorry drivers;
(5) Free accommodation;
(6) Nights;
(7) Based on new TSA classification (TSA:RMF 2008);
(8) Including the estimates of private accommodation;
(9) Including the following IRTS / TSA:RMF tourism characteristic activities: Transport equipment rental, Cultural activities, Sports and recreational activities, Spa services as country-specific tourism characteristic services, Transport support activities;
(10) July-June;
(11) 2011: TSA classification; 2012–2014: Labour Force Survey (LFS);
(12) NACE Rev. 2.

Hungarian Central Statistical Office
www.ksh.hu/tourism_catering

ICELAND

(1) Source: Icelandic Tourist Board;
(2) 2012–2015: arrivals at Keflavik airport only;
(3) Including cruise passengers;
(4) Scheduled air transport.

"Hagstofa Íslands Statistics Iceland"
www.statice.is/statistics/business-sectors/tourism/

INDIA

(1) Excluding nationals residing abroad;
(2) Including other purposes;
(3) Departures of nationals only, irrespective of purpose;
(4) In classified hotels.

Ministry of Tourism – Government of India
http://tourism.gov.in/

INDONESIA

(1) 2015: by nationality.
(2) Classified hotels only;
(3) 2015: estimates;
(4) All forms of commercial accommodation;
(5) Current prices.

Ministry of Tourism and Creative Economy and BPS Statistics
Indonesia
www.bps.go.id/Subjek/view/
id/16#subjekViewTab3|accordion-daftar-subjek2

IRAN, ISLAMIC REPUBLIC OF

(1) Source: Central Bank of Islamic Republic of Iran.

Iran Cultural Heritage and Tourism Organization (ICHTO)

IRAQ

Ministry of Tourism and Antiquities

IRELAND

(1) Including tourists from North Ireland;
(2) Including rail;
(3) Due to a change in methodology, data for 2011 were revised and is not comparable with earlier years;
(4) Due to a change in methodology, data for 2012–2014 were revised and is not comparable with previous years;
(5) Excluding hostels;
(6) Hotels only.

Fáilte Ireland
www.failteireland.ie/

ISRAEL

(1) Excluding nationals residing abroad;
(2) Including visit friends and relatives and pilgrimage;
(3) Including tourists' reentry after a visit of up to 7 days in Sinai;
(4) Tourist hotels and aparthotels;
(5) Including the expenditures of foreign workers in Israel;
(6) Bed-occupancy in hotels and similar establishments open;
(7) Inbound tourism in tourist hotels.

Ministry of Tourism
http://www1.cbs.gov.il/reader/?MIval=cw_usr_view_
SHTML&ID=432

ITALY

(1) Excluding seasonal and border workers;
(2) Border survey of the "Banca d'Italia";
(3) Including cruise passengers;
(4) Hotels only;
(5) 2014: break in the series due to the change data collection technique (survey: "Trips and Holidays"), from CATI to CAPI;
(6) Nights;

(7) "Non commercial accommodation services" consist of owned dwellings (including those ones in a time-sharing contract), accommodation provided by relatives / friends and others non-commercial private accommodation;
(8) Number of resident tourists (overnight visitors) abroad;
(9) Excluding the estimates of private accommodation.

"Banca d'Italia" and "Istituto Nazionale di Statistica (ISTAT)"
www.bancaditalia.it
www.istat.it

JAMAICA

(1) Arrivals of non-resident tourists by air; including nationals residing abroad; E/D cards;
(2) Cruise passengers only;
(3) Data is garnered from the distribution of overnight visitors (tourists) stating their organization of the trip in exit surveys conducted at international airports;
(4) New series; including nationals residing abroad;
(5) Nights;
(6) Intended length of stay;
(7) Average expenditure per person per night for overnight visitors (tourists);
(8) Excluding closed establishments;
(9) Hotel nights only.

Jamaica Tourist Board
www.jtbonline.org/statistics/Annual%20Travel/Forms/
AllItems.aspx

JAPAN

(1) Excluding nationals residing abroad;
(2) Arrivals of non-resident visitors at national borders; including foreign residents in Japan;
(3) Up to March 2010, accommodations which have less than 9 employees are excluded;
(4) Day use is excluded;
(5) Including overlapping;
(6) Government registered and unregistered hotels and "ryokans" (inns);
(7) Estimate from occupancy rate;
(8) Including passenger transport supporting services.

Source of data:
1.19-1.21: Ministry of Internal Affairs and Communications – Immigration Statistics; 1.30, 4.2, 4.3, 4.13-4.15, 4.16-4.18: Japan Tourism Agency – accommodation survey; 1.40-1.43, 2.1-2.18, 4.25-4.26, 4.29-4.30, 5.1-5.10, 6.1: Japan Tourism Agency – Japan national tourism survey; 2.24-2.27: Japan Tourism Agency – accommodation survey – Japan national tourism survey; 3.1, 3.10: Japan National Tourism Organization; 4.4, 4.7: Ministry of Internal Affairs and Communications – The economic census; 4.6: Japan travel and tourism association; 4.8-4.11: Japan Tourism Agency – Japan national tourism survey – Japanese Tourism Satellite Account – Table 5: Production accounts of tourism industries and other industries; 4.27-4.28: Japan Tourism Agency – Consumption Trend Survey for Foreigners Visiting Japan; 5.2: Japanese Tourism Satellite Account – Table 7: Employment in the tourism industries.

Japan Tourism Agency and Japan National Tourism Organization
www.mlit.go.jp/kankocho/en/siryou/toukei/index.html
www.tourism.jp/en/statistics/

COUNTRY NOTES

JORDAN

(1) Including nationals residing abroad;
(2) 2011–2014: arrivals of resident and non resident visitors;
(3) For organized tours only.

Ministry of Tourism and Antiquities
www.tourism.jo

KAZAKHSTAN

Agency of Statistics of the Republic of Kazakhstan

KENYA

(1) Arrivals of non-resident visitors from all border entry points; excluding nationals residing abroad;
(2) Days.

Kenya National Bureau of Statistics

KIRIBATI

(1) Arrivals by air.Tarawa and Christmas Island.

Kiribati National Tourism Office, Ministry of Communication, Transport and Tourism Development and PATA

KOREA, REPUBLIC OF

(1) Including nationals residing abroad and crew members;
(2) Including overseas Koreans and crew members;
(3) The country provides UNWTO with aggregate expenditure figures that differ significantly from the International Monetary Fund data used in the preparation of this edition of the Compendium (excluding expenses of students studying overseas). The country figures are as follows (US$ million): 2011: 15,544; 2012: 15,737.
(4) Hotels only.

Ministry of Culture, Sports and Tourism
http://kto.visitkorea.or.kr/eng/tourismStatics/keyFacts/visitorArrivals.kto

KUWAIT

(1) Non-resident tourists staying in hotels and similar establishments.

Central Statistical Bureau
www.csb.gov.kw/Socan_Statistic_EN.aspx?ID=19

KYRGYZSTAN

National Statistical Committee

LAO PEOPLE´S DEMOCRATIC REPUBLIC

Lao National Tourism Administration and Ministry of Information, Culture and Tourism – Tourism Development Department
www.tourismlaos.org/show.php?Cont_ID=43

LATVIA

(1) Arrivals of non-resident visitors at national border. Data by State Border Guard;
(2) Non-resident departures. Survey of persons crossing the state border;
(3) Including visit friends and relatives and health treatment;
(4) Since 2015 Hotels and similar establishments according to NACE REV.2 classification: Section I, Division 55, Class 55.1 – Hotels and similar accommodation (services include daily housekeeping);
(5) Overnight stays in all collective accommodation establishments;
(6) Source: Border survey;
(7) From 2012 source: Household survey;
(8) From 2012 data by State Border Guard.

Transport and Tourism Statistics Section – Central Statistical Bureau
www.csb.gov.lv/en/statistikas-temas/tourism-key-indicators-30715.html

LEBANON

(1) Excluding the Lebanon, Syria and Palestine nationalities;
(2) For the year 2015, the survey was conducted with 291 establishments;
(3) Data source, hotels and institutions authorized by the Ministry of Tourism;
(4) Source: Tourism workers' associations in Lebanon.

Ministère du Tourisme

LESOTHO

(1) Due to an improvement in the data collection with the help of "Statistics South Africa", from 2014 the data are not comparable with those of previous years.

Lesotho Tourism Development Corporation
www.ltdc.org.ls/researchArrivalStats.php

LIECHTENSTEIN

(1) Non-resident tourists staying in all types of accommodation establishments;
(2) Since 2012 excluding long term tourists on campgrounds and in holiday flats;
(3) 2011: non-resident tourists staying in hotels and similar establishments;
(4) Since 2012: non-resident tourists staying in all types of accommodation establishments;
(5) Since 2012 excluding campgrounds and holiday flats of long term;
(6) Annual average;
(7) Annual average of available rooms;
(8) Annual average of available bed-places.

Office of Statistics Liechtenstein. Tourism Statistics
www.llv.li/#/11961/tourismusstatistik

LITHUANIA

(1) Hotels and motels;
(2) Structural Business Survey;
(3) National Accounts data;
(4) Tourism Satellite Account (TSA) data.

Lithuanian State Department of Tourism
www.stat.gov.lt/

LUXEMBOURG

(1) Non-resident tourists staying in all types of accommodation establishments; including youth hostels, tourist private accommodation and others;
(2) Estimate for tourists who spent at least one night in a tourist accommodation establishment;
(3) NACE Rev2 55.100;
(4) The expenditure figures used were the ones provided by the country to UNWTO, as this data series is more complete than that provided by the International Monetary Fund (IMF);
(5) Resident tourists staying in all types of accommodation establishments; including youth hostels, tourist private accommodation and others;
(6) Net occupancy rate.

"STATEC"
www.statistiques.public.lu

MACAO, CHINA

(1) Before 2014, data included visitors on package tours and those joining local tours;
(2) Since 2011, data are obtained by the Public Security Police, while those of previous years are results of the samples;
(3) Hotels and guest houses;
(4) Restaurants and similar establishments;
(5) Establishments providing passenger transport services;
(6) Travel Agencies;
(7) Gaming enterprises;
(8) Excluding part-time employees.

Source of data:
1.1-1.13, 1.19-1.25, 1.26, 4.27-4.28, 6.2: Public Security Police; 1.27, 3.1, 4.27-4.30: Monthly Survey of Travel Agencies; 1.31-1.32, 1.41-1.42, 4.14-4.19: Monthly Survey of Hotels and Similar Establishments; 1.40, 1.44: Visitor Expenditure Survey; 4.2-4.3, 4.8-4.12, 4.13, 5.2: Hotels and Similar Establishments Survey; 4.4, 5.4: Restaurant and Similar Establishments Survey; 4.5, 5.5: Transport, Storage and Communications Survey; 4.6, 4.20-4.24, 5.6: Travel Agencies Survey; 4.7: Gaming Sector Survey; 4.19, 6.2: Population Estimate of Macao; 5.7: Survey on Manpower Needs and Wages – Gaming Industry.

Statistics and Census Service and Macau Government Tourist Office
www.dsec.gov.mo/Statistic/TourismAndServices/VisitorArrivals.aspx
http://industry.macautourism.gov.mo/en/index.php

MADAGASCAR

(1) Arrivals of non-resident tourists by air.

"Ministère du Tourisme, des Transports et de la Météorologie"

MALAWI

(1) Departures.

Ministry of Tourism, Wildlife and Culture

MALAYSIA

(1) Including Singapore residents crossing the frontier by road through Johore Causeway;
(2) Due to a change in the methodology, from 2013 the data are not comparable with those of previous years;
(3) Domestic tourism survey;
(4) Hotels with 10 rooms and above;
(5) Hotel survey.

Source of data:
1.2, 1.5-1.12, 1.19-1.24, 1.31, 1.4, 4.3, 4.13, 4.14, 4.16: Tourism Malaysia; 2.1-2.28: Department of Statistics Malaysia.

Department of Statistics Malaysia and Tourism Malaysia
www.tourism.gov.my/statistics

MALDIVES

(1) Arrivals by air;
(2) Days.

Ministry of Tourism
www.tourism.gov.mv

MALI

(1) 2012–2015: arrivals by air only (Bamako-Sénou airport);
(2) Arrivals by air only (Bamako-Sénou airport);
(3) 2015: partial data corresponding to Bih frontier, in the Mopti region.

"Direction Nationale du Tourisme et de l'Hotellerie (DNTH)"

MALTA

(1) Data based on departures by air and by sea;
(2) Source: Eurostat;
(3) Source: MTA Licensing Data.

Malta Tourism Authority and National Statistics Office
www.mta.com.mt/research
www.nso.gov.mt

MARSHALL ISLANDS

(1) Arrivals by air. 2014–2015 Source: South Pacific Tourism Organisation – Regional Tourism Resource Centre.

Marshall Islands Visitors Authority

COUNTRY NOTES

MARTINIQUE

(1) The expenditure figures are those provided by the country to UNWTO, which do not appear in the International Monetary Fund data used in the preparation of this edition of the Compendium.

"Comité Martiniquais du Tourisme"

MAURITIUS

(1) Estimated from Survey of Inbound Tourism;
(2) Large hotels;
(3) Hotels only;
(4) Data relate to large establishments (i.e employing 10 or more persons) of the tourism sector.

Note 2015: provisional data.

Ministry of Tourism and Leisure
http://statsmauritius.govmu.org/English/StatsbySubj/Pages/INTERNATIONAL-TRAVEL-and-TOURISM.aspx

MEXICO

(1) Including nationals residing abroad;
(2) Including visitors of the US border zone with a length of stay under 24 hours;
(3) By air only;
(4) Non-border tourists and border tourists;
(5) Including rail;
(6) Hotels only;
(7) Selected tourism resorts;
(8) Days;
(9) Foreign tourism only;
(10) The information does not correspond to employment, strictly speaking, but to equivalent remunerated jobs needed for the production of goods and services related with tourism activities. Source: "Cuenta Satélite de Turismo de México, cambio de año base a 2008".

"Secretaría de Turismo de México (SECTUR)", "Instituto Nacional de Estadística y Geografía (INEGI)" and "Unidad de Política Migratoria
Banco de México"
www.datatur.sectur.gob.mx/
www.inegi.org.mx

MICRONESIA, FEDERATED STATES OF

(1) Arrivals in the States of Kosrae, Chuuk, Pohnpei and Yap; excluding FSM citizens;
(2) Fiscal years (October 1 to September 30).

Office of Statistics, Budget and Economic Management, Overseas Development Assistance, and Compact Management
www.sboc.fm

MOLDOVA, REPUBLIC OF

(1) Non-resident tourists staying in all types of accommodation establishments;
(2) Visitors who have benefited from tourism services provided by the tourism agencies and tour operators (titulars of tourism licences).

Note:
Excluding the left side of the river Nistru and the municipality of Bender.

National Bureau of Statistics
www.statistica.md/category.php?l=en&idc=293&

MONACO

(1) Non-resident tourists staying in hotels and similar establishments.

"Direction du Tourisme et des Congrès"
www.imsee.mc

MONGOLIA

(1) Excluding diplomats and foreign residents in Mongolia.

National Tourism Center – Ministry of Nature, Environment and Tourism

MONTENEGRO

(1) Non-resident tourists staying in all types of accommodation establishments.

Ministry of Sustainable Development and Tourism
www.monstat.org/eng/page.php?id=43&pageid=43

MONTSERRAT

Statistics Department Montserrat

MOROCCO

(1) Including nationals residing abroad;
(2) Classified hotels, holiday villages, tourist residences and Riad;
(3) Foreign tourists.

"Ministère du tourisme"
www.tourisme.gov.ma/

MOZAMBIQUE

(1) Arrivals at all border posts of the country;
(2) The Domestic Tourism survey is a module of the Household Budget Survey which is conducted every 5 years and in 2008/2009 was the first time that the domestic tourism appeared in this survey. In 2012/2013 was held the Continuous Household Budget Survey.

"Ministry of Tourism" and "Instituto Nacional de Estatística"
www.ine.gov.mz

MYANMAR

(1) State-run hotels and similar establishments only. The increase in the total for the year 2014 is due to the sum of arrivals from China, India, Thailand and Myanmar Border Checkpoints with 7 days stay border pass and arrivals from International Entry Points;
(2) State-run hotels and private registered guest houses.

Ministry of Hotels and Tourism
www.myanmartourism.org/

NAMIBIA

Ministry of Environment and Tourism and Namibian Tourism Board

NEPAL

(1) Including arrivals from India;
(2) Days;
(3) Hotels in Kathmandu; excluding hotels under construction;
(4) Travel and trekking agencies.

Nepal Tourism Board and Ministry of Culture, Tourism and Civil Aviation
www.tourism.gov.np/np/category/tourism/tourism_statistics

NETHERLANDS

(1) Non-resident tourists staying in all types of accommodation establishments;
(2) 2013: break in the series because of methodological changes in determining the population;
(3) Hotels and boarding houses;
(4) 2013–2015: the expenditure figures used were the ones provided by the country to UNWTO, as this data series is more complete than that provided by the International Monetary Fund (IMF) for the preparation of this Compendium;
(5) Source: Eurostat;
(6) Holiday departures of nationals;
(7) Hotels;
(8) All types of accommodation establishments.

Statistics Netherlands
www.cbs.nl/en-GB/menu/themas/vrije-tijd-cultuur/nieuws/default.htm

NEW CALEDONIA

(1) Including nationals residing abroad;
(2) Hotels in Noumea only;
(3) Returning residents;
(4) Rooms in Noumea;
(5) Days, hotels in Noumea.

"Institut de la Statistique et des Études Économiques (ISEE)"
www.isee.nc/

NEW ZEALAND

(1) International Travel and Migration, SNZ;
(2) Total includes cruise visitors;
(3) Accommodation Survey, SNZ;
(4) Includes hotels, motels and backpackers but excludes holiday parks;
(5) Balance of payments, SNZ;
(6) Domestic Travel Survey, MBIE (discontinued in 2013);
(7) Data provided in this section is based on the type of transport used on multiple legs within each domestic tourism trip, not just the main transport of the trip. Hence, the total specified will not match the sum of 2.10, 2.11 and 2.12. The Domestic Travel Survey allows multiple responses to the "type of transport" question;
(8) Domestic Travel Survey – overnight visitors, MBIE;
(9) Overnight trips expenditure only;
(10) Business Demography Statistics, SNZ (data revised in 2011 to reflect the new industry classification, ANZSIC06) as at February 2011–2013;
(11) Provisional data.

Statistics New Zealand (SNZ) and Ministry of Business, Innovation & Employment (MBIE)
www.stats.govt.nz/

NICARAGUA

(1) Including nationals residing abroad;
(2) Total number of establishments in the country;
(3) Main accommodation establishments in the country;
(4) Hotels and similar establishments classified in higher categories;
(5) All types of accommodation establishments, inbound tourism.

"Instituto Nicaragüense de Turismo (INTUR)"
www.intur.gob.ni

NIGER

(1) Days.

"Ministère du Tourisme et de l'Artisanat" and "Institut National de la Statistique"
www.stat-niger.org/statistique/

NIGERIA

(1) In a bid to sanitize the tourism industry, the Nigerian Tourism Development Corporation set up a task force to enforce the hotel registration exercise. All hospitality establishments especially hotels were forced to register with the Corporation or be shut down, hence, this singular effort brought about the increase in number of hotels and similar establishment for year 2011.

Nigerian Tourism Development Corporation

COUNTRY NOTES

NIUE

(1)   Including Niuans residing usually in New Zealand.
        2014–2015 Source: South Pacific Tourism Organisation
        – Regional Tourism Resource Centre. 2015: estimates.

Statistics Niue

NORTHERN MARIANA ISLANDS

(1)   Arrivals by air;
(2)   Including Guam;
(3)   Covers 68 per cent of the total hotel room inventory.
        Source of the data for 2012–2015: PATA.

Marianas Visitors Authority

NORWAY

(1)   2011: figures are based on "The Guest survey" carried
        out by "Institute of Transport Economics". The survey
        has been discontinued since 2012;
(2)   2012–2015: non-resident tourists staying in all types of
        accommodation establishments;
(3)   2011: United States only;
(4)   2011: Japan only;
(5)   Overnights in registered establishments;
(6)   Figures for hotels and similar establishments relate to
        establishments with 20 or more beds the whole year;
(7)   2014: provisional data;
(8)   2011: data revised.

Statistics Norway and Institute of Transport Economics
www.ssb.no/english/subjects/

OMAN

(1)   Inbound Tourism Survey;
(2)   Including domestic tourism.

Ministry of Tourism, Ministry of National Economy and National
Centre for Statistics and Information
www.omantourism.gov.om

PALAU

(1)   Arrivals by air (Palau International Airport);
(2)   Fiscal years – September 30.

Office of Planning and Statistics, Bureau of Budget and
Planning – Ministry of Finance and Palau Visitors Authority
www.visit-palau.com/

PANAMA

(1)   Arrivals of non-resident visitors, Tocúmen International
        Airport (TIA), Paso Canoa frontier (PCF) and the ports of
        Cristóbal and Balboa (PCB);
(2)   Arrivals of non-resident visitors, TIA;
(3)   Arrivals of non-resident tourists, TIA;
(4)   Hotels in Panama City;
(5)   Rooms/bed-places recorded for international tourism.

"Autoridad de Turismo de Panamá"
www.atp.gob.pa/estadisticas-de-turismo-en-panama

PAPUA NEW GUINEA

(1)   Estimates.
(2)   Days.

Papua New Guinea Tourism Promotion Authority
www.tpa.papuanewguinea.travel/

PARAGUAY

(1)   E/D cards in the "Silvio Petirossi" airport and passenger
        counts at the national border crossings – National Police
        and SENATUR;
(2)   Excluding nationals residing abroad and crew members;
(3)   River.

"Secretaría Nacional de Turismo – SENATUR"
www.senatur.gov.py

PERU

(1)   Including nationals residing abroad;
(2)   Overnight cruise passengers;
(3)   Including arrivals by river and lake.

"Superintendencia Nacional de Migraciones", "Banco Central
de Reserva del Perú" and "Ministerio de Comercio Exterior y
Turismo"
http://ww2.mincetur.gob.pe/

PHILIPPINES

(1)   Including nationals residing abroad;
(2)   Arrivals by air;
(3)   Nights;
(4)   Metro Manila hotels only;
(5)   For 2013, data include accredited accommodation
        establishments with certificate of accreditation issued
        and those approved for accreditation although certificate
        of accreditation not yet issued. Previous to 2013, data
        only include accredited accommodation establishment
        with issued certificate of accreditation;
(6)   Classified hotels in Metro Manila;
(7)   Based on the Philippine Tourism Satellite Accounts
        (PTSA) – June 2016.

Department of Tourism
www.tourism.gov.ph/Pages/TourismResearch.aspx

POLAND

(1)   Since Poland joined the Schengen area, precise counting
        of incoming traffic is not possible. Only approximate
        results can be given this year;
(2)   Data 2011, 2012 are based on surveys by the Institute
        of Tourism; 2013: Activ Group; 2014, 2015: Central
        Statistical Office;
(3)   Data from Central Statistical Office;
(4)   Both   collective   and   private   accommodation
        establishments;

COUNTRY NOTES

(5) Trips for 4 nights and more;
(6) Establishments with 10 or more bed places. As of July 31.

Institute of Tourism
www.intur.com.pl/itenglish/institute_en.htm

PORTUGAL

(1) Arrivals of non-resident tourists in all types of accommodation establishments;
(2) Source: Eurostat;
(3) Statistics Portugal (INE), Structural Business Survey;
(4) Net occupancy rate;
(5) All types of accommodation establishments.

"Turismo de Portugal, I.P."
www.ine.pt/xportal/xmain?xpid=INE&xpgid=ine_main

PUERTO RICO

(1) Arrivals of non-resident tourists by air;
(2) United States Virgin Islands and the United States only;
(3) The expenditure figures are those provided by the country to UNWTO, which do not appear in the International Monetary Fund data used in the preparation of this edition of the Compendium;
(4) Including residents and non-residents;
(5) Rooms classified by the "Compañía de Turismo" of Puerto Rico;
(6) Including rooms occupied by residents of Puerto Rico. Data: Fiscal years (July-June).

"Junta de Planificación de Puerto Rico" and "Compañía de Turismo de Puerto Rico"
www.jp.gobierno.pr/

QATAR

(1) From 2015, including apartment-hotels data, not collected previously.

Qatar Statistics Authority

REUNION

(1) Arrivals by air only;
(2) Source: INSEE: Survey on Tourism Flows;
(3) Source: INSEE: Survey on Hotel Occupancy;
(4) This corresponds to the total number of overnights in classified hotels, from 2015 classified and unclassified hotels. Residents and non-residents;
(5) The expenditure figures are those provided by the country to UNWTO, which do not appear in the International Monetary Fund data used in the preparation of this edition of the Compendium;
(6) Source: INSEE Clap. This corresponds to all the establishments under the selected nomenclatures. Without certainty about the actual purpose of the activity (tourism-related or not);
(7) This corresponds to all the establishments/ rooms/ beds available per day in classified hotels, from 2015 classified and unclassified hotels;

(8) Source: INSEE Clap. This corresponds to all the jobs under the selected nomenclatures. Without certainty about the actual purpose of the activity (tourism-related or not).

"Institut National de la Statistique et des Études Économique – INSEE" and "Comité du Tourisme de la Réunion"
http://observatoire.reunion.fr/les-chiffres-cles.html

ROMANIA

(1) Only domestic trips for holidays (including visit friends and relatives VFR) and business purposes;
(2) The category "Other personal purposes" refers only to VFR trips;
(3) The categories "air" and "water" are included in the "others" category;
(4) Calculated by dividing number of overnights by number of trips. Source: ACTR, household survey;
(5) Only for holidays (including VFR) and business purposes – overnight trips. The figures are compiled by dividing the expenditure by the number of overnights;
(6) Number of departures of Romanians abroad registered at borders;
(7) At 31st of July, for licensed establishments only;
(8) The indicator is represented by the number of tourists purchasing packages/individual services. Please be aware that the values cumulate both tour-operators and classic travel agencies;
(9) The indicator is actually represented by the "average number of employees" and the source is represented by Structural Business Statistics which is carried out annually;
(10) Includes also freight transportation;
(11) This category is not fully in line with tourism industries categories due to high level of aggregation in the publication. It includes only the following activities: Creative arts and entertainment services, Libraries, archives, museums and other cultural services, Gambling and betting activities, Sports activities and amusements and recreational activities.

National Institute of Statistics
www.insse.ro/cms/en

RUSSIAN FEDERATION

(1) On foot;
(2) Accommodation in hotels and other tourist establishments.

Russian Federal Agency for Tourism

RWANDA

Rwanda Development Board
www.rdb.rw/welcome-to-rwanda/tourism-research-and-statistics.html

COUNTRY NOTES

SAINT KITTS AND NEVIS

(1) Arrivals of non-resident tourists by air;
(2) Yacht and cruise ship arrivals.

Ministry of Sustainable Development and Eastern Caribbean Central Bank
www.eccb-centralbank.org/Statistics/index.asp#tourismdata

SAINT LUCIA

(1) Excluding nationals residing abroad;
(2) Excluding yacht passenger arrivals.

Saint Lucia Tourist Board
http://investstlucia.com/sectors/view/tourism.html

SAINT VINCENT AND THE GRENADINES

(1) Arrivals of non-resident tourists by air;
(2) Including cruise ship and yacht passengers.

St. Vincent and the Grenadines Tourism Authority
www.discoversvg.com/index.php/es/about-svg/tourism-statistics

SAMOA

Samoa Tourism Authority and Statistical Services Division (Ministry of Finance)
www.sbs.gov.ws/index.php/sector-statistics/tourism-statistics
www.mof.gov.ws

SAN MARINO

(1) Including Italian visitors;
(2) Non-resident tourists staying in all types of accommodation establishments; including Italian tourists;
(3) Hotels only.

"Segreteria di Stato per il Turismo ed i Rapporti con l'AASS"
www.statistica.sm/on-line/home/dati-statistici/attivita-economiche-e-turismo.html

SAUDI ARABIA

(1) Source: (IVS), MAS Center;
(2) Nights;
(3) Recreation service;
(4) 2012, 2013: estimated by MAS Center.

The Saudi Commission for Tourism and Antiquities (SCTA)
www.mas.gov.sa/en/Pages/default.aspx

SENEGAL

(1) Estimated data;
(2) Arrivals by air at "Léopold Sédar Senghor (LSS)" only. Including the nationals residing abroad;
(3) Hotels and holiday villages.

"Ministère du Tourisme et des Transports Aériens"

SERBIA

(1) Tourists staying in visitor accommodation establishments;
(2) Total number of beds (permanent and extra) up to 2012. Since 2013, maximum capacity (number of permanent beds) over the year;
(3) Since 2012, net occupancy rate. Up to 2011, gross occupancy rate;
(4) Number of employed persons.

Statistical Office of the Republic of Serbia and National Bank of Serbia
http://webrzs.stat.gov.rs/WebSite/Public/PageView.aspx?pKey=181

SEYCHELLES

(1) Nights based on departures;
(2) 2012: January-October;
(3) Hotels and guest houses.

National Bureau of Statistics and Seychelles Tourism Board
www.nbs.gov.sc/

SIERRA LEONE

(1) Arrivals by air.

National Tourist Board and Statistics Sierra Leone
www.statistics.sl/

SINGAPORE

(1) Excluding arrivals of Malaysian citizens by land;
(2) Days;
(3) Hotels (gazetted and non-gazetted);
(4) Classified hotels only.

Singapore Tourism Board
www.singstat.gov.sg
www.stb.gov.sg

SINT MAARTEN (DUTCH PART)

(1) By air; including arrivals to Saint Maarten (the French side of the island);
(2) Arrivals at Juliana Airport (including visitors destined to Saint Maarten, French side).

St. Maarten Tourist Bureau and Department of Statistics Sint Maarten
http://stat.gov.sx/

SLOVAKIA

(1) The number of inbound arrivals is based on a combination of accommodation statistics and border survey statistics (as calculated within the Tourism Satellite Account);
(2) Non-resident tourists staying in commercial accommodation only (representing approximately 25% of all tourists (item 1.2));
(3) Source: Tourism Satellite Account (TSA) – methodology TSA: RMF 2008, number of establishments including number of self-employed in internationally comparable tourism industries;
(4) Culture, sport and recreational services;
(5) Tourism Satellite Account (TSA) – methodology TSA: RMF 2008, internationally comparable tourism industries;
(6) Household survey. Number of domestic and outbound tourism trips over 15 years / number of residents over 15 years.

Statistical Office of the Slovak Republic and National Bank of Slovakia
www.statistics.sk
www.nbs.sk/en/home
www.telecom.gov.sk/index/index.php?ids=103017&lang=en

SLOVENIA

(1) Source: accommodation survey;
(2) Including other countries of Asia;
(3) Aggregates from accommodation survey, shares from 3 yearly surveys on foreign tourists in Slovenia;
(4) Source: 3 yearly surveys on foreign tourists in Slovenia;
(5) Source: survey on travels of domestic population (due to different methodology differences between data on monthly accommodation statistics and data gathered with household survey may appear);
(6) Only private trips are taken into account;
(7) Nights are used for unit;
(8) Source: Structural Business Statistics;
(9) Private accommodations (rented rooms, dwellings), tourists farms with accommodation, mountain huts, company vacations facilities and facilities for youths are not included;
(10) Included only permanent beds;
(11) Source: Statistical Register of Employment;
(12) Information on number of full-time equivalent jobs is not available. Instead number of jobs is used in this indicator.

Statistical Office – Tourism Statistics, Structual Business Statistics, Statistical register of employment and Bank of Slovenia
www.stat.si

SOLOMON ISLANDS

Solomon Islands National Statistics Office

SOUTH AFRICA

(1) Since 2014 a new methodology has been applied and therefore, the information is not comparable to previous years. 2014, 2015: excluding transit;
(2) Source: Domestic Tourism Survey 2007–2011;
(3) The large difference between 2012 and 2013 in the number of nights spent in paid accommodation can

be explained by changes in the purpose of visit, i.e. a decrease in VFR trips in 2013 with an increase in holiday and business trips. Furthermore, there was a decrease in the average length of stay among all domestic tourists in 2013;
(4) (Total size of travel party) / (Total number of trips);
(5) Data concerns all paid accommodation;
(6) Including visit friends and relatives and Church Halls;
(7) Hotels;
(8) Tourism Satellite Account (TSA) data.

Statistics South Africa and South African Tourism
www.statssa.gov.za/

SPAIN

(1) Including nationals residing abroad;
(2) Hotels, "hostales", camping sites, tourism apartments and rural dwellings;
(3) Hotels and "hostales" (accommodation establishments providing limited services);
(4) Source: Annual survey on services.

Source of data:
Up to 2014 IET: FRONTUR – Survey on tourism movements at borders; EGATUR – Survey on tourism expenditure; FAMILITUR – Survey on tourism movements by Spaniards.
Since 2015 INE: ETR/Familitur – Tourism survey of residents; FRONTUR and EGATUR – 2015 provisional data, calculated by extrapolating the data of Turespaña until September to calculate the data for October, November and December. Since October 2015 this operation is carried out by the National Statistics Institute – INE. The break in the series will occur next year with 2016 data.
INE: Surveys on accommodation occupancy; DIRCE (Central Directory of Companies) – tourism supply – annual survey on services; Labour force survey.

"Instituto Nacional de Estadística y TURESPAÑA"
FRONTUR-INE: www.ine.es/jaxi/menu.o?type=pcaxis&path=%2Ft11%2Fp16028&file=inebase&L=0
EGATUR-INE: www.ine.es/jaxi/menu.o?type=pcaxis&path=%2Ft11%2Fp16029&file=inebase&L=0
ETR/Familitur: www.ine.es/jaxi/menu.o?type=pcaxis&path=%2Ft11%2Fp16023&file=inebase&L=0
Encuestas de Ocupación en Alojamientos Turísticos:
www.ine.es/inebmenu/mnu_hosteleria.htm
Datos hasta 2014 de TURESPAÑA:
www.iet.tourspain.es/paginas/home.aspx?idioma=es-ES

SRI LANKA

(1) Excluding nationals residing abroad;
(2) Hotels, motels, inns, guest houses and apart-hotels;
(3) Hotels and restaurants.

Sri Lanka Tourist Board
www.sltda.lk/statistics

STATE OF PALESTINE

(1) Non-resident tourists staying in hotels and similar establishments;
(2) West Bank and Gaza.

COUNTRY NOTES

Note:
the data on hotel activity for 2012–2015 represent the West Bank only.

Sources:
Palestinian Central Bureau of Statistics. Hotel Activity Survey. Tourism Activities. Palestine Monetary Authority.

Palestinian Central Bureau of Statistics
www.pcbs.gov.ps

SUDAN

(1)   Including nationals residing abroad.

Ministry of Tourism and Wildlife

SURINAME

Suriname Tourism Foundation
www.surinametourism.sr/#!en&events-more&statistics

SWAZILAND

Swaziland Tourism Authority and Ministry of Tourism and Environmental Affairs
www.thekingdomofswaziland.com/pages/content/index.asp?PageID=57

SWEDEN

(1)   Data for 2011–2014 according to new national border survey (IBIS, Incoming Visitors to Sweden). Source: Swedish Agency for Economic and Regional Growth. No data collected in 2015;
(2)   Hotels only;
(3)   Due to a change of supplier, domestic and outbound tourism statistics are not available for 2014–2015;
(4)   Number of full-time equivalent jobs.

Swedish Agency for Economic and Regional Growth – Tillväxtverket
www.tillvaxtverket.se/english
www.scb.se/en_/

SWITZERLAND

(1)   Hotels and similar establishments (including health establishments);
(2)   Including unknown purposes;
(3)   Unreliable data, not published;
(4)   Including unknown modes of transport;
(5)   Establishments surveyed;
(6)   Rooms surveyed;
(7)   Bed-places surveyed;
(8)   Net occupancy rate;
(9)   full-time equivalent jobs.

Swiss Federal Statistical Office
www.bfs.admin.ch/bfs/portal/fr/index/themen/10.html

TAIWAN PROVINCE OF CHINA

(1)   Including nationals residing abroad;
(2)   Including the flight tickets fee.

Planning Division Tourism Bureau – Ministry of Transportation and Communication
http://admin.taiwan.net.tw/statistics/release_en.aspx?no=7

TAJIKISTAN

Committee of Youth Affairs, Sports and Tourism under the Government of the Republic of Tajikistan

TANZANIA, UNITED REPUBLIC OF

(1)   In transit.

Tourism Division – Ministry of Natural Resources and Tourism and National Bureau of Statistics

THAILAND

(1)   Excluding arrivals of nationals residing abroad;
(2)   Including rail;
(3)   Days.

Ministry of Tourism and Sports
www.tourism.go.th/home

THE FORMER YUGOSLAV REPUBLIC OF MACEDONIA

(1)   Non-resident tourists staying in all types of accommodation establishments;
(2)   Average length of stay in all accommodation establishments.

State Statistical Office
www.stat.gov.mk/OblastOpsto_en.aspx?id=25

TIMOR-LESTE

(1)   Arrivals by air at Dili Airport;
(2)   Hotels survey (20 or more rooms).

Statistics Timor-Leste – General Directorate of Statistics
www.statistics.gov.tl/category/survey-indicators/quarterly-statistical-indicators/

TOGO

(1)   Non-resident tourists staying in hotels and similar establishments;
(2)   2013–2015: including nationals residing abroad;
(3)   Excluding nationals residing abroad.

"Ministère du Tourisme"

COUNTRY NOTES

TONGA

(1) Arrivals by air;
(2) Including cruise ship and yacht passengers and crew members.

Ministry of Commerce, Tourism and Labour
www.spc.int/prism/tonga/

TRINIDAD AND TOBAGO

(1) Arrivals by air;
(2) Departing visitors survey. Source: Central Statistical Office;
(3) Domestic tourism survey conducted every 2 years.

Tourism Development Company Limited
www.tdc.co.tt/index.php/research

TUNISIA

(1) Excluding nationals residing abroad;
(2) Classified and unclassified hotels, boarding houses and holiday villages.

"Ministère du Tourisme – Office National du Tourisme" and "Institut National de la Statistique "
www.ins.nat.tn/indexfr.php

TURKEY

(1) Including Turkish citizens resident abroad;
(2) Arrivals by sea;
(3) Departing visitors survey carrying out at departure gates;
(4) Survey in accommodation establishments licensed by Ministry of Tourism;
(5) Including camping sites;
(6) Including expenditure of the nationals residing abroad;
(7) Source: Turkstat Household Domestic Tourism Survey;
(8) Classified hotels; excluding camping sites.
(9) Source: Turkstat Labour Force Survey;
(10) NACE 55;
(11) NACE 56;
(12) NACE 491, 4932, 4939, 501, 503, 511;
(13) NACE 79.

Ministry of Culture and Tourism
http://sgb.kulturturizm.gov.tr/belge/1-90750/turizm-istatistikleri.html
www.turkstat.gov.tr/PreTablo.do?alt_id=1072

TURKS AND CAICOS ISLANDS

Turks and Caicos Tourist Board
http://turksandcaicostourism.com

TUVALU

(1) 2015 Source: South Pacific Tourism Organisation – Regional Tourism Resource Centre

Ministry of Foreign Affairs, Trade, Tourism, Environment and Labour. and 2015 Source: South Pacific Tourism Organisation – Regional Tourism Resource Centre

UGANDA

Ministry of Tourism, Trade and Industry and Uganda Bureau of Statistics
www.ubos.org/?st=pagerelations2&id=19&p=related%20pages%202:Migration%20and%20Tourism%20Statistics

UKRAINE

State Statistics Committee of Ukraine
www.ukrstat.gov.ua/operativ/operativ2007/tyr/tyr_e/arh_vig_e.html

UNITED KINGDOM

(1) Tunnel;
(2) International Passenger survey; Source: Office for National Statistics (ONS);
(3) Days;
(4) From 2013: Great Britain only (not including Northern Ireland) and Day Visit survey;
(5) Number of Local Units in VAT and/or PAYE based Enterprises, source: ONS Inter Departmental Business Register;
(6) Source: ONS Annual Business Survey;
(7) Source: ONS compilation for EUROSTAT;
(8) Source: UK Occupancy Survey (Annual Report);
(9) Source: ONS, based on Workforce Jobs, Business Register and Employment Survey, Labour Force Survey.

VisitBritain and Office for National Statistics
www.visitbritain.org/insightsandstatistics/
www.ons.gov.uk/ons/index.html

UNITED STATES OF AMERICA

(1) Beginning with 2014 data, automation changes in the methodology for tracking inbound visitors enabled the precise counting of one-night stays. This change likely added several percentage points to the 2014 performance, and therefore data from 2014 onwards is not comparable to previous years. 2015 changes (except Canada and Mexico) reflect a combination of additional records counted and market conditions;
(2) Includes Mexico and Canada same-day trips only;
(3) Overseas only; excluding Mexico and Canada (not available);
(4) Questionnaire wording changed beginning in 2012;
(5) Preliminary estimates;
(6) The Bureau of Economic Analysis of the U.S. Department of Commerce completed a major overhaul of the trade accounts system to bring it closer into line with International Monetary Fund guidelines. Among the key changes is the inclusion of education, health care, and migrant or seasonal workers in the travel export and import accounts. Figures were revised going back to 1999 and are not comparable to previous years' data;
(7) 2011–2015 represents mean average spending per overseas travel party divided by mean average stay length;
(8) Source: U.S. Travel Association;
(9) Includes all domestic trips of 50 or more miles from home one-way or any overnight trip;
(10) Approximately 50%;
(11) Source: NTTO, Statistics Canada, Banco de Mexico;
(12) 2011–2015 represents mean average spending per

COUNTRY NOTES

U.S. resident travel party divided by mean average stay length;

(13) Establishment data comes from U.S. Dept. of Commerce, Bureau of Census (County Business Patterns) and is not perfectly consistent with other output and employment data. It is the best source of establishment data;
(14) NAICS 7211, 7212;
(15) NAICS 72111, 72112;
(16) NAICS 722;
(17) U.S. Department of Commerce / Bureau of Economic Analysis;
(18) Source: American Hotel & Lodging Association (AHLA) (properties of 15+ rooms);
(19) Source: Smith Travel Research;
(20) Full-time equivalent jobs;
(21) Traveler accommodations;
(22) Food services and drinking places;
(23) Air transportation services and all other transportation related industries;
(24) Residual.

U.S. Department of Commerce – National Travel and Tourism Office
http://travel.trade.gov
www.ahla.com/content.aspx?id=3448

UNITED STATES VIRGIN ISLANDS

(1) Non-resident tourists staying in hotels and similar establishments;
(2) Visitor arrivals by air; excluding resident arrivals and inter-island traffic but including same-day visitors;
(3) Cruise passengers;
(4) Including domestic tourist overnights (about 40% of total);
(5) The expenditure figures are those provided by the country to UNWTO, which do not appear in the International Monetary Fund data used in the preparation of this edition of the Compendium;
(6) Hotel units and condominium or villa units.
2015: Provisional data.

Bureau of Economic Research
www.usviber.org/publications.htm

URUGUAY

(1) Excluding cruise passengers arrivals;
(2) Including rail;
(3) Days;
(4) Considering only the first trip;
(5) Source: "INE";
(6) Due to a change in the methodology, from 2012 the data are not comparable with those of previous years;
(7) Real state services;
(8) For methodological reasons, only the first occupation is considered. Full-time = 40 hours per week or more.

"Ministerio de Turismo y Deporte"
www.mintur.gub.uy/index.php/es/estadistica

VANUATU

(1) Cruise passengers only;
(2) Intended length of stay.

Vanuatu National Statistics Office
www.vnso.gov.vu/

VENEZUELA, BOLIVARIAN REPUBLIC OF

(1) Nights;
(2) Hotels only.

"Ministerio del Poder Popular para el Turismo"
www.mintur.gob.ve/mintur/turismo-en-cifras-2/

VIET NAM

(1) Including nationals residing abroad;
(2) Including cruise and sea passengers;
(3) The expenditure figures are those provided by the country to UNWTO, which do not appear in the International Monetary Fund data used in the preparation of this edition of the Compendium.

Viet Nam National Administration of Tourism and General Statistics Office
www.vietnamtourism.com/en/index.php/news
www.gso.gov.vn/default_en.aspx?tabid=491

YEMEN

(1) Including nationals residing abroad.

Ministry of Tourism and Central Statistical Organization
www.yementourism.com/statistics/
www.csoyemen.org/content.php?lng=english&pcat=11

ZAMBIA

Ministry of Tourism and Arts

ZIMBABWE

(1) 2014, 2015: including transit visitors that spend at least a night;
(2) The expenditure figures are those provided by the country to UNWTO, which do not appear in the International Monetary Fund data used in the preparation of this edition of the Compendium;
(3) The country is yet to conduct Domestic and Outbound Market Survey to obtain missing indicators on domestic and outbound Tourism;
(4) Based on arrivals at national parks and national museums;
(5) Graded hotels only.

Zimbabwe Tourism Authority – ZTA
www.zimbabwetourism.net/index.php/trends-statistics/

Notes des pays

AFRIQUE DU SUD

(1) À partir de 2014, une nouvelle méthodologie a été appliquée. L'information n'est donc pas comparable à celle des années précédentes. 2014, 2015 : à l'exclusion du transit ;
(2) Source : « Domestic Tourism Survey 2007–2011 » ;
(3) La grande différence entre 2012 et 2013 dans le nombre de nuitées passées en hébergement commercial s'explique par le fait qu'il y a eu des changements dans le motif principal des voyages, c'est-à-dire qu'il y a eu une diminution des visites à des parents et amis en 2013 avec une augmentation des voyages pour vacances et affaires. De plus, il y a eu une diminution de la durée moyenne du séjour parmi tous les touristes internes en 2013 ;
(4) (Taille totale du groupe de voyageurs) / (Nombre total de voyages) ;
(5) Les données se réfèrent à tous les hébergements marchands ;
(6) Y compris visites à des parents et amis et « Church Halls » ;
(7) Hôtels ;
(8) Données du Compte satellite du tourisme (CST).

« Statistics South Africa » et « South African Tourism »
www.statssa.gov.za/

ALBANIE

(1) Á l'exclusion des nationaux résidant à l'étranger ;
(2) Y compris les visiteurs en transit ;
(3) Source : Enquête à court terme. Hôtels uniquement ;
(4) 2011 : la classification utilisée est NACE Rév. 1.1 (Nomenclature des activités économiques). À partir de 2012, la classification utilisée pour SBS est NACE Rév. 2 ;
(5) Valeur ajoutée aux prix de base ;
(6) Total des investissements ;
(7) Les chiffres sont mis à jour avec l'enquête sur la structure des entreprises ;
(8) Y compris les entreprises classifiées par la NACE 55 et 56 de la NACE Rév. 2 ;
(9) Y compris les entreprises classifiées par la NACE 49, 50 ou 51 de la NACE Rév. 2 ;
(10) Y compris les entreprises classifiées par la NACE 79 de la NACE Rév. 2.

« Institute of Statistics – INSTAT »
www.instat.gov.al/

ALGÉRIE

(1) Y compris les nationaux résidant à l'étranger ;
(2) À l'exclusion des nationaux résidant à l'étranger.

Ministère de l'Aménagement du Territoire, du Tourisme et de l'Artisanat et Office National des Statistiques

ALLEMAGNE

(1) Touristes non résidents séjournant dans tous types d'établissements d'hébergement ;
(2) Source : Eurostat ;
(3) Tourisme récepteur, hôtels et établissements assimilés.

« Statistiches Bundesamt »
www.destatis.de

ANDORRE

(1) En 2009 et 2011, des changements ont été apportés à la méthodologie de calcul du nombre de visiteurs du pays. De ce fait, la comparabilité des données obtenues à l'aide des différentes méthodologies n'est pas possible, car les variations reflètent les variations du nombre de visiteurs mais également les variations induites par les changements méthodologiques.

« Ministerio de Turismo y Medio Ambiente » et « Ministerio de Finanzas »
www.estadistica.ad/serveiestudis/web/index.asp?lang=2

ANGOLA

(1) Hôtels uniquement.

« Ministério de Hotelaria e Turismo – Gabinete de Estudos, Planeamento e Estatística »

ANGUILLA

(1) À l'exclusion des nationaux résidant à l'étranger ;
(2) Y compris les visiteurs de la journée (excursionnistes) ;
(3) Source : « Visitor exit survey ».

« Anguilla Statistics Department – Ministry of Finance, Economic Development, Investment, Commerce and Tourism »
www.gov.ai/statistics/cab_external.htm

ANTIGUA-ET-BARBUDA

(1) À l'exclusion des arrivées de passagers en yacht ;
(2) Arrivées par voie aérienne ; à l'exclusion des nationaux résidant à l'étranger ;
(3) Croisiéristes uniquement.

« Ministry of Tourism »
http://members.antiguahotels.org/tourism-statistics-for-antigua-and-barbuda/

ARABIE SAOUDITE

(1) Source : (IVS), centre MAS ;
(2) Nuitées ;
(3) Services de loisirs ;
(4) 2012, 2013 : estimation par le centre MAS.

NOTES DES PAYS

«The Saudi Commission for Tourism and Antiquities (SCTA)»
www.mas.gov.sa/en/Pages/default.aspx

ARGENTINE

(1) Changement de méthodologie à partir de 2013. Les données ne sont pas comparables avec celles des années précédentes;
(2) Enquête sur l'occupation hôtelière (EOH);
(3) Encuesta de Viajes y Turismo de los Hogares (Enquête sur les voyages et le tourisme des ménages);
(4) Signalons un changement par rapport à la méthodologie employée les années précédentes pour analyser l'emploi dans le secteur du tourisme. L'analyse se fondait auparavant sur une seule enquête, qui couvrait 32 agglomérations urbaines. En revanche, dans l'analyse actuelle, les résultats sont le fruit d'un travail de synthèse à partir de l'information la plus substantielle pour le secteur; l'analyse s'appuie sur différentes sources d'information fournissant des données sur l'emploi dans le pays tout entier; et elle est plus précise sur les agrégats qui composent les branches caractéristiques du tourisme. Cette nouvelle méthodologie est disponible depuis l'année 2010;
(5) La classification comprend les employés de l'État et privés, qu'il y ait ou non des cotisations sociales (travail formel ou informel);
(6) Constitué des catégories professionnelles suivantes: patron, personne travaillant pour son propre compte à titre formel, personne travaillant pour son propre compte à titre informel.

«Dirección de Estudios de Mercado y Estadística – Secretaría de Turismo de la Nación»
www.turismo.gov.ar/
http://desarrolloturistico.gob.ar/estadistica/ultimas-cifras

ARMÉNIE

«Tourism Department – Ministry of Economy of the Republic of Armenia»
www.armstat.am/en/

ARUBA

(1) Arrivées par voie aérienne;
(2) Passagers en croisière uniquement.

«Aruba Tourism Authority»
www.cbs.aw/index.php/statistics/tables-statistics/68-tables/tourism

AUSTRALIE

(1) À l'exclusion des nationaux résidant à l'étranger et membres des équipages;
(2) Source: «Tourism Research Australia – National Visitor Survey (NVS)»;
(3) Hôtels, motels, pensions de famille et appartements avec services hôteliers avec 15 chambres ou plus. Au juin. Source: «Cat 8635.0 Tourist Accommodation Australia, Table 1»;
(4) Source: «Cat. 5249.0 – Australian National Accounts: Tourism Satellite Account, Table 14 Direct Tourism Employment by Industry».

«Australian Bureau of Statistics»
www.abs.gov.au/

AUTRICHE

(1) Touristes non résidents séjournant dans tous types d'établissements d'hébergement;
(2) Seulement logement commercial; sont exclus les séjours chez des parents et amis, et les résidences secondaires;
(3) Hôtels uniquement;
(4) Voyages à l'étranger pour vacances et affaires avec au moins une nuitée, y compris les séjours chez des parents et amis, et les résidences secondaires;
(5) Sur la base de la saison d'été (mai-octobre);
(6) Données du Compte satellite du tourisme (CST);
(7) Équivalents à temps plein.

«Statistics Austria»
www.statistik.at/web_en/statistics/tourism/accommodation/index.html

AZERBAÏDJAN

«Ministry of Culture and Tourism» et «Statistical Committee»
www.stat.gov.az

BAHAMAS

(1) Arrivées dans les hôtels uniquement;
(2) Hôtels, appartements, bungalows et villas – Établissements homologués uniquement.

«Bahamas Ministry of Tourism»
www.tourismtoday.com/home/statistics/

BAHREÏN

(1) À l'exclusion des nationaux résidant à l'étranger;
(2) Arrivées à l'aéroport international de Bahreïn;
(3) Arrivées au port Mina Salman;
(4) Arrivées à travers le «King Fahad Causeway»;
(5) Hôtels homologués uniquement.

«Tourism Sector – Ministry of Culture and Information» et «Information and eGovernment Authority»

BANGLADESH

«Bangladesh Bureau of Statistics (BBS)»

BARBADE

(1) Hôtels, aparthôtels, appartements et bungalows, pensions de famille.

«Barbados Tourism Marketing Inc»
www.tourism.gov.bb/tourism-publications.html

BÉLARUS

(1) Touristes non résidents séjournant dans tous types d›établissements d›hébergement;
(2) Voyages à forfait;
(3) Grands groupes uniquement;
(4) Les données se basent sur l'observation statistique que mène le pays concernant le nombre d'employés des établissements d'hébergement collectif et des agences de voyages.

«State Border Committee» et «National Statistical Committee of the Republic of Belarus»

BÉLGIQUE

(1) Touristes non résidents séjournant dans tous types d›établissements d›hébergement;
(2) La méthodologie a été modifiée et pour cela, à partir de 2015 les données ne sont pas comparable avec celles des années précédentes;
(3) Hôtels uniquement;
(4) Hôtels et villages de vacances. À partir de 2012 les chambres d'hôtes sont incluses.

Institut National de Statistique

BÉLIZE

«Belize Tourist Board»

BÉNIN

Direction du développement et de promotion touristiques – Ministère de la culture, de l'alphabétisation, de l'artisanat et du tourisme

BERMUDES

(1) À l'exclusion des nationaux résidant à l'étranger;
(2) Arrivées par voie aérienne;
(3) Croisiéristes;
(4) Y compris les nuitées dans les résidences privées.

«Bermuda Department of Tourism»
www.gov.bm/portal/server.

CommunityPage&control=SetCommunity&CommunityID=227

BHOUTAN

(1) Total des arrivées 2011: 65.756; 2012: 105.407; 2013: 116.209; 2014: 134.254; 2015: 155.121. L'écart important que l'on peut observer en 2011–2015 par rapport aux années précédentes tient au fait que l'on a inclus les touristes régionaux haut de gamme dans les totaux à partir de 2010;
(2) Données provisoires.

«Department of Tourism – Royal Government of Bhutan»
www.nsb.gov.bt/index.php?id=13
www.tourism.gov.bt/annual-reports/bhutan-tourism-monitor

BOLIVIE (ÉTAT PLURINATIONAL DE)

(1) Données préliminaires;
(2) Information obtenue à partir des valeurs en pourcentage de l'Enquête «dépenses du tourisme récepteur et émetteur»;
(3) Arrivées par voie lacustre;
(4) 7,6 % des voyageurs correspondant au tourisme organisé;
(5) Source: Enquête «dépenses du tourisme récepteur et émetteur»;
(6) Capitales de département seulement;
(7) Taille moyenne des groupes de touristes pour les familles: 2,8 personnes.

Note:
Les indicateurs du tourisme sont tirés de la relation des résultats de l'enquête «dépenses du tourisme récepteur et émetteur» entre les statistiques du commerce extérieur, services de la balance des paiements, la comptabilité nationale (PIB), ce qui détermine la part du tourisme dans chacun des secteurs.

«Instituto Nacional de Estadística»
www.ine.gob.bo/default.aspx

BOSNIE-HERZEGOVINE

(1) Touristes non résidents séjournant dans tous types d›établissements d›hébergement;
(2) 2011, 2012: Moins de 500 arrivées;
(3) Les données sont tirées du rapport statistique 2015 sur le trafic transfrontalier de passagers et incluent les arrivées totales des passagers non-résidents aux frontières nationales. Les passagers en transit y sont inclus;
(4) Données de l'enquête statistique mensuelle «RAD».

«Agency for Statistics of Bosnia and Herzegovina»
www.bhas.ba

BOTSWANA

(1) Y compris les retours des résidents.

«Department of Tourism – Ministry of Environment, Wildlife and Tourism»

BRÉSIL

(1) Y compris les nationaux résidant à l'étranger;
(2) Y compris les arrivées par voie fluviale;
(3) Les données se réfèrent à «Encuesta Anual de Servicios (PAS) 2013, do Instituto Brasileiro de Estatísticas e Geografia – IBGE»;
(4) 2011: les données se réfèrent à «Pesquisa de Serviços de Hospedagem (PSH) do Instituto Brasileiro de Estatísticas e Geografia – IBGE». 2013–2015: les données reflètent le nombre de fournisseurs de services du tourisme régulièrement inscrits dans le Système du Registre des entreprises, équipements et professionnels du tourisme (Cadastur) ayant déclarés exercer l'activité de prestataire de services d'infrastructures pour événements. Chaque fournisseur de services peut s'inscrire dans plus d'une activité;

NOTES DES PAYS

(5) Rapport annuel d'informations sociales (RAIS) – 2014 – Ministério do Trabalho ; Salariés formels : inscrits et couverts par la sécurité sociale – Enquête nationale auprès des ménages – 2014 – IBGE – Salariés informels : pas inscrits et pas couverts par la sécurité sociale.

« Ministério do Turismo »
www.dadosefatos.turismo.gov.br/dadosefatos/home.html

BRUNEI DARUSSALAM

(1) Arrivées par voie aérienne.

« Brunei Tourism – Ministry of Industry and Primary Resources »

BULGARIE

(1) Visiteurs en transit ;
(2) Source : « Eurostat » ;
(3) Hôtels uniquement.

« National Statistical Institute, Bulgarian National Bank and Ministry of Tourism »
www.nsi.bg

BURKINA FASO

(1) Touristes non résidents séjournant dans les hôtels et établissements assimilés ;
(2) Y compris le tourisme interne.

Service de l'analyse statistique et de la Coopération touristique – Ministère de la Culture, des Arts et du Tourisme
www.insd.bf/

BURUNDI

(1) Y compris les nationaux résidant à l'étranger ;
(2) Arrivées par voie lacustre.

Office National du Tourisme

CABO VERDE

(1) Touristes non résidents séjournant dans les hôtels et établissements assimilés.

« Instituto Nacional de Estatística » et « Ministério da Economia, Crescimento e Competitividade »
www.ine.cv/dadostats/dados.aspx?d=2

CAMBODGE

(1) Arrivées par tous modes de transport ;
(2) Arrivées par navire ;
(3) Jours.

« Ministry of Tourism »
www.tourismcambodia.org/mot/index.php?view=statistic_report#comp

CAMEROUN

(1) Touristes non résidents séjournant dans les hôtels et établissements assimilés.

Ministère du Tourisme

CANADA

(1) Données élaborées à partir des inventaires douaniers et ajustées en fonction des résultats d'enquêtes ;
(2) Une enquête remaniée sur les voyages internes (Enquête sur les voyages des résidents du Canada) est entrée en vigueur en 2011, ce qui a entraîné une rupture des séries chronologiques. En conséquence, les points de données de 2011 ne sont pas comparables aux années précédentes ;
(3) Les départs sont estimés sur la base des arrivées de résidents canadiens revenant de l'étranger ;
(4) 5.13 et 5.14 sont calculés à l'aide du nombre d'heures annuelles moyennes travaillées dans des emplois à temps complet par les hommes et les femmes respectivement.

« Canadian Tourism Commission » et « Statistics Canada »
http://en-corporate.canada.travel/research/statistics-figures

CHILI

(1) Y compris les nationaux résidant à l'étranger ;
(2) Croisiéristes plus accord Arica-Tacna ;
(3) La méthodologie a été modifiée et pour cela, à partir de 2014 les données ne sont pas comparable avec celles des années précédentes ;
(4) À l'exclusion des terrains de camping ;
(5) À compter de 2012, le forfait touristique est estimé uniquement via les aéroports ;
(6) Source : « SII (Servicio de Impuestos Internos) » ;
(7) 2015 : données estimées.

« Subsecretaría de Turismo – Ministerio de Economía, Fomento y Turismo »
www.sernatur.cl/estadisticas/

CHINE

(1) Y compris les arrivées de personnes d'origine ethnique chinoise en provenance de « Hong Kong (Chine) », « Macao (Chine) », « Taïwan (Province de Chine) » et chinois de l'étranger, la plupart visiteurs de la journée (excursionnistes) en provenance de « Hong Kong (Chine) » et de « Macao (Chine) » ;
(2) À l'exclusion des arrivées de personnes d'origine ethnique chinoise en provenance de « Hong Kong (Chine) », « Macao (Chine) », « Taïwan (Province de Chine) » et chinois de l'étranger ;
(3) À pied ;
(4) Y compris les membres des équipages et autres membres des forces armées ;
(5) Hôtels classés par étoiles uniquement ;
(6) Tourisme récepteur uniquement.

« National Tourism Administration »
http://en.cnta.gov.cn/

NOTES DES PAYS

CHYPRE

(1) Source : Enquête auprès des passagers, conduite par le Service statistique de Chypre « Statistical Service of Cyprus » ;

(2) Y compris les croisiéristes et les passagers en transit ;

(3) Les données de 2012 et 2013 font référence uniquement à onze mois car les données du mois de mars 2012 et janvier 2013 ne sont pas disponibles ;

(4) Y compris les passagers en transit ;

(5) Les données sur l'hébergement (arrivées, nuitées et taux d'occupation) ont été collectées tous les mois auprès des établissements hôteliers de tourisme agréés et fournies par la C.T.O ;

(6) Les données concernant les hôtels et établissements assimilés à partir de 2010 ont été révisées afin d'inclure les villas touristiques dans la catégorie « établissements assimilés ». Avant cette révision, les villas étaient incluses dans « autres établissements collectifs » (sous la section « logements pour vacances ») ;

(7) La dépense moyenne par jour est obtenue en divisant le total des dépenses concernées (élément 1.33) par le nombre de visiteurs d'entrée qui passent la nuit (élément 1.2) et la durée moyenne de leur séjour (élément 1.40) ;

(8) La durée moyenne d'un séjour est basée sur le nombre d'arrivées et de nuitées dans les établissements hôteliers de tourisme agréés ;

(9) La dépense moyenne par jour est calculée en divisant le total des dépenses concernées (élément 3.4) par le nombre total des visiteurs à l'étranger qui passent la nuit (élément 3.2) et la durée moyenne de leur séjour (élément 3.10) ;

(10) Données extraites des statistiques des hôtels et des restaurants provenant de l'enquête sur les services réalisée par le Service de statistique de Chypre. Référence : NACE Rev. 2 code 55 ;

(11) Données extraites des statistiques des hôtels et des restaurants provenant de l'enquête sur les services réalisée par le Service de statistique de Chypre. Aux postes 4.3 et 5.2, les données indiquées concernent les entreprises touristiques au sens de la NACE Rev.2 codes 55101 et 55102 ;

(12) Données extraites des statistiques des hôtels et des restaurants provenant de l'enquête sur les services réalisée par le Service de statistique de Chypre. Référence : NACE Rev. 2 code 56 ;

(13) Nombre d'agences de voyage (code 4.6) et données monétaires (postes 4.20-4.24) : données extraites des statistiques sur les services commerciaux provenant de l'enquête sur les services réalisée par le Service de statistique de Chypre. Référence : NACE Rev. 2 code 79 ;

(14) Les données monétaires indiquées aux postes 4.8-4.12 sont extraites des statistiques des hôtels et des restaurants provenant de l'enquête sur les services réalisée par le Service de statistique de Chypre. Elles se rapportent aux Hôtels et entreprises touristiques similaires au sens de la NACE Rev.2 codes 55101 and 55102 ;

(15) Les données non monétaires sont rassemblées et élaborées par l'Organisation du tourisme de Chypre (CTO). Elles concernent les hôtels titulaires d'une licence et autres établissements similaires d'hébergement touristique. Les données fournies diffèrent des données apparaissant aux postes 4.2-4.3 et 4.8-4.12, qui sont extraites des statistiques des hôtels et des restaurants provenant de l'enquête sur les services réalisée par le Service de statistique de Chypre. Les différences dans les deux ensembles de données tiennent, entre autres, au fait que l'enquête sur les services traite les entreprises ou les personnes qui sont propriétaires/ gérants de plus d'une unité d'hébergement touristique (établissement) comme une seule entité tandis que les données de la CTO comptent les unités individuelles d'hébergement touristique indépendamment de savoir si elles appartiennent à un seul propriétaire ou sont gérées par un seul gérant ;

(16) Les calculs de durée moyenne de séjour sont basés sur les nuitées et les arrivées dans les hôtels et autres établissements agréés similaires d'hébergement pour touristes (C.T.O.) ;

(17) Données extraites des statistiques des hôtels et des restaurants provenant de l'enquête sur les services réalisée par le Service de statistique de Chypre. Référence : NACE Rev. 2 codes 5520+, 5530+ et 5590. Remarque sur l'ensemble des données fournies : sont exclues les informations sur les activités immobilières en bien propre ou en location et les opérations immobilières basées sur une redevance ou un contrat.

« Statistical Service of Cyprus », « Cyprus Tourism Organization » et « Central Bank of Cyprus »
www.mof.gov.cy/mof/cystat/statistics.nsf/index_en/index_en?OpenDocument

COLOMBIE

(1) Arrivées de voyageurs non-résidents par des contrôles d'immigration ;

(2) Y compris les visiteurs transfrontaliers ('000) : 2011 : 999 ; 2012: 1.063 ; 2013: 1.153 ; 2014: 1.313 ; 2015 : 1.197 ;

(3) Y compris les nationaux résidant à l'étranger ;

(4) À l'exclusion des visiteurs transfrontaliers et des croisiéristes ;

(5) À l'exclusion des nationaux résidant à l'étranger.
Note : données provisoires.

« Migración Colombia / Sociedades portuarias / Dirección de Análisis Sectorial y Promoción – Ministerio de Comercio, Industria y Turismo (MINCIT) »
www.mincit.gov.co/publicaciones.php?id=16590

CONGO

(1) Enquêtes de 2011 à 2015 ;

(2) Y compris les nationaux résidant à l'étranger. Total 2011 : 45.800 ;

(3) Enquêtes 2011 à 2013 ;

(4) Source : Banque des Etats d'Afrique Centrale (B.E.A.C). 2012, 2013 : estimations.
Note 2015 : estimations.

Direction Générale du Tourisme et de l'Hôtellerie – Ministère du tourisme et de l'environnement

CONGO (RÉPUBLIQUE DÉMOCRATIQUE DU)

(1) les données des arrivées ne concernent que 3 postes frontaliers (aéroport de N'Djili à Kinshasa ; aéroport de la Luano à Lubumbashi et le poste terrestre de Kasumbalesa de la province du Katanga).

Office National du Tourisme

CORÉE (RÉPUBLIQUE DE)

(1) Y compris les nationaux résidant à l'étranger et membres des équipages;
(2) Y compris les nationaux résidant à l'étranger et membres des équipages;
(3) Pour la dépense, le pays fournit à l'OMT des niveaux d'agrégation qui diffèrent de façon significative des données du Fonds monétaire international utilisées pour la préparation de la présente édition du Compendium (à l'exclusion des dépenses des étudiants qui font des études à l'étranger). Les données du pays sont les suivantes (Mn $E.U.): 2011: 15.544; 2012: 15.737.
(4) Hôtels uniquement.

«Ministry of Culture, Sports and Tourism»
http://kto.visitkorea.or.kr/eng/tourismStatics/keyFacts/
visitorArrivals.kto

COSTA RICA

(1) Enquêtes des non-résidents menées dans les aéroports internationaux, «ICT»;
(2) Enquête sur l'hébergement, Département de la Statistique Macroéconomique, «BCCR»;
(3) Emploi dans les industries touristiques, Enquête continue sur l'emploi («ECE»), «INEC».

«Banco Central de Costa Rica (BCCR)», «Instituto Costarricense de Turismo (ICT)» et «Instituto Nacional de Estadística y Censos (INEC)»
www.visitcostarica.com/ict/paginas/modEst/informes_estadisticos.asp

CÔTE D'IVOIRE

(1) 2011–2014: arrivées à l'aéroport Félix Houphouët Boigny seulement. 2015: rupture de série: les chiffres incluent les arrivées par voie terrestre (route et chemin de fer).

Ministère du Tourisme

CROATIE

(1) Touristes non résidents séjournant dans tous types d'établissements d'hébergement;
(2) Le total des établissements inclut uniquement les établissements d'hébergements collectifs touristiques. Depuis 2010, les ports de plaisance ne sont plus considérés comme des unités déclarantes ni comme des types de mode d'hébergement dans les enquêtes mensuelles sur les arrivées de touristes et les nuitées, le suivi des touristes reposant désormais sur de nouveaux fondements juridiques. À cause de ce changement de méthodologie, les données de 2005 à 2009 ont été révisées afin d'être comparables avec celles de 2010 (les ports de plaisance ont été exclus);
(3) Inclut les voyageurs par route en transit;
(4) Données tirées de l'enquête sur la circulation dans les aéroports, toutes arrivées internationales;
(5) Données tirées de l'enquête sur la circulation dans les ports maritimes, toutes arrivées internationales. Inclut les passagers des navires de croisière;

(6) Données tirées de l'enquête sur le transport de voyageurs par chemin de fer, inclut toutes les arrivées internationales par chemin de fer;
(7) Données comprenant les arrivées totales de voyageurs non résidents aux frontières nationales par la route. Les passagers en transit sont inclus;
(8) Les données n'incluent pas le nombre de ménages louant un hébergement touristique (chambres à louer, appartements, studios et locations d'été de maisons d'hôtes);
(9) Source: «CBS, Survey on Tourist Activity of Croatian Population»;
(10) 2015: données provisoires;
(11) L'application du nouveau Règlement a induit des changements dans la méthodologie pour la collecte de données concernant les types suivants d'hébergements: chambres à louer, appartements, studios et maisons d'été. Depuis 2013, les unités déclarantes pour ces hébergements sont les bureaux de tourisme, que ces hébergements soient loués par des sociétés ayant la personnalité juridique, des commerçants ou des ménages. Les données relatives aux hébergements sont considérées comme des données provisoires car leur enregistrement n'est pas encore organisé convenablement dans tous les bureaux de tourisme;
(12) En raison du processus constant de catégorisation, des changements sont intervenus dans les types et les catégories d'hébergements;
(13) Conformément au Règlement sur la classification, les normes minimales et la catégorisation des structures d'hébergement, les données relatives aux hôtels et établissements assimilés ne comprennent pas les auberges et chambres d'hôtes depuis 2006;
(14) Depuis 2013, la méthode de présentation des capacités a changé (elles ne sont plus suivies par rapport à la situation au 31 août), ce qui est conforme au Règlement 692/2011 du Parlement européen et du Conseil concernant les statistiques européennes sur le tourisme. En application du Règlement 692/2011 du Parlement européen et du Conseil concernant les statistiques européennes sur le tourisme, la capacité d'un établissement d'hébergement est celle du mois où elle a atteint son maximum;
(15) Taux brut d'ocupation;
(16) La classification utilisée est NACE Rev. 2.

«Croatian Bureau of Statistics»
www.dzs.hr/default_e.htm
www.mint.hr/default.aspx?id=363"

CUBA

(1) Arrivées par voie aérienne;
(2) Hôtels, motels, apart-hôtels, terrains de camping/caravaning et autres;
(3) Hôtels, motels et apart-hôtels;
(4) Les chiffres de dépense sont ceux que le pays a fournis à l'OMT mais ils ne figurent pas dans les données du Fonds monétaire international qui ont servi à la préparation de la présente édition du Compendium;
(5) Comprend seulement les circuits contrôlés par «Instituto de Turismo».

«Oficina Nacional de Estadística e Información»
www.one.cu/sitioone2006.asp

NOTES DES PAYS

CURAÇAO

(1)   Arrivées par voie aérienne;
(2)   Les différences entre les totaux globaux sont dues au caractère incomplet des cartes d'embarquement et de débarquement remplies par les visiteurs;
(3)   Arrivées de croisiéristes;
(4)   Grands et petits hôtels, pensions de famille, appartements et bungalows;
(5)   Hôtels, pensions de famille, appartements.

« Curaçao Tourist Board »
www.curacao.com/en/directory/corporate/statistics-and-downloads/

DANEMARK

(1)   2011, 2014: changement de méthodologie;
(2)   Touristes non résidents séjournant dans tous types d'établissements d'hébergement;
(3)   Y compris le tourisme non commercial;
(4)   Hôtels uniquement;
(5)   Les chiffres de dépense sont ceux que le pays a fournis à l'OMT mais ils ne figurent pas dans les données du Fonds monétaire international qui ont servi à la préparation de la présente édition du Compendium. Source: « VisitDenmark »;
(6)   Source: Eurostat;
(7)   Uniquement hôtels et logements pour vacances avec 40 lits et plus.

« VisitDenmark » et « Statistics Denmark »
www.dst.dk/HomeUK.aspx

DJIBOUTI

(1)   Touristes non résidents séjournant dans les hôtels.

Office national du tourisme

DOMINIQUE

(1)   Jours.

« Discover Dominica Authority »
http://tourism.gov.dm/statistics

ÉGYPTE

« Ministry of Tourism », « CAPMAS » et « Central Bank of Egypt »

EL SALVADOR

(1)   Y compris l'hébergement privé.

« Corporación Salvadoreña de Turismo (CORSATUR) – Ministerio de Turismo »

ÉQUATEUR

(1)   À l'exclusion des nationaux résidant à l'étranger;
(2)   2015: données provisoires.

« Ministerio de Turismo »
http://servicios.turismo.gob.ec/index.php/portfolio/turismo-cifras

ESPAGNE

(1)   Y compris les nationaux résidant à l'étranger;
(2)   Hôtels, « hostales », terrains de camping, appartements touristiques et logements ruraux;
(3)   Hôtels et « hostales » (établissements d'hébergement offrant des services limités);
(4)   Source: « Encuesta Anual de Servicios ».

Source des données:
Jusqu'à 2014 IET: FRONTUR – Enquête sur les flux touristiques aux frontières; EGATUR – Enquête sur les dépenses touristiques; FAMILITUR – Enquête sur les flux touristiques des Espagnols.
À partir de 2015 INE: ETR/Familitur – Enquête du tourisme des résidents; FRONTUR et EGATUR – 2015 données provisoires calculées en extrapolant les données de Turespaña jusqu'à septembre pour calculer les données d'octobre, novembre et décembre. À partir de 2015, cette opération est menée par l'Institut national de la statistique – INE. La rupture de série aura lieu l'année prochaine avec les données de 2016.
INE: Enquêtes sur l'occupation dans l'hébergement; DIRCE (Annuaire central des entreprises) – offre touristique – enquête annuelle sur les services; Enquête sur la population active.

« Instituto Nacional de Estadística y TURESPAÑA »
FRONTUR-INE: www.ine.es/jaxi/menu.o?type=pcaxis&path=%2Ft11%2Fp16028&file=inebase&L=0
EGATUR-INE: www.ine.es/jaxi/menu.o?type=pcaxis&path=%2Ft11%2Fp16029&file=inebase&L=0
ETR/Familitur: www.ine.es/jaxi/menu.o?type=pcaxis&path=%2Ft11%2Fp16023&file=inebase&L=0
Encuestas de Ocupación en Alojamientos Turísticos:
www.ine.es/inebmenu/mnu_hosteleria.htm
Datos hasta 2014 de TURESPAÑA:
www.iet.tourspain.es/paginas/home.aspx?idioma=es-ES

ESTONIE

(1)   D'après les données de localisation mobile de la Banque d'Estonie et Positium LBS;
(2)   La méthodologie a été modifiée et pour cela, à partir de 2015 les données ne sont pas comparable avec celles des années 2011–2014;
(3)   Touristes non résidents séjournant dans tous types d'établissements d'hébergement;
(4)   La méthodologie a été modifiée et pour cela, à partir de 2014 les données ne sont pas comparable avec celles des années 2011–2013;
(5)   Source: enquête auprès des ménages par « Statistics Estonia ».

« Estonian Tourist Board / Enterprise Estonia »
http://pub.stat.ee/px-web.2001/I_Databas/Economy/databasetree.asp
http://visitestonia.com/en/additional-navigation/press-room/eas-views-on-tourism/estonian-tourism-statistics"

NOTES DES PAYS

ÉTAT DE PALESTINE

(1) Touristes non résidents séjournant dans les hôtels et établissements assimilés;
(2) Cisjordanie et Gaza.

Note:
les données sur l'activité hôtelière pour 2012–2015 répresentent la Cisjordanie seulement.

Sources:
«Palestinian Central Bureau of Statistics. Hotel Activity Survey. Tourism Activities. Palestine Monetary Authority".

«Palestinian Central Bureau of Statistics»
www.pcbs.gov.ps

ÉTATS-UNIS D'AMÉRIQUE

(1) À partir des données de 2014, l'automatisation introduite dans la méthodologie de suivi des visiteurs d'entrée a permis un comptage précis des séjours d'une nuit. Ce changement a vraisemblablement ajouté plusieurs points de pourcentage aux chiffres de 2014, de sorte que les données de 2014 et suivantes ne sont pas comparables avec celles des années précédentes. Les changements en 2015 (sauf Canada et Mexique) sont dus à la fois au comptage de registres supplémentaires et aux conditions du marché;
(2) Inclut uniquement les excursions d'une journée en provenance du Mexique et du Canada;
(3) Outre-mer uniquement; à l'exclusion du Mexique et du Canada (les données ne sont pas disponibles);
(4) La formulation du questionnaire a changé à compter de 2012;
(5) Estimations préliminaires;
(6) Le Bureau d'analyse économique du Ministère du commerce des États-Unis d'Amérique a procédé à une vaste refonte du système de comptabilité commerciale pour qu'il soit plus en adéquation avec les directives du Fonds monétaire international. Parmi les principaux changements figure l'inclusion de l'éducation, des soins de santé ainsi que des travailleurs migrants et saisonniers dans les comptes d'exportations et d'importations des voyages. Les chiffres ont été révisés en remontant jusqu'à 1999. Ils ne sont pas comparables avec les données des années précédentes;
(7) 2011–2015: correspond aux dépenses moyennes par groupe de voyageurs d'outre-mer, divisées par la durée moyenne du séjour;
(8) Source: «U.S. Travel Association»;
(9) Comprend tous les voyages internes de 50 miles (environ 80 kilomètres), ou plus, en aller simple depuis le domicile ou tout voyage avec nuitée;
(10) Environ 50 %;
(11) Source: «NTTO, Statistics Canada, Banco de Mexico";
(12) 2011–2015: correspond aux dépenses moyennes par groupe de voyageurs résidants aux États-Unis, divisées par la durée moyenne du séjour;
(13) Les données sur les établissements proviennent du Bureau of Census (County Business Patterns) du Ministère américain au commerce. Elles ne concordent pas totalement avec les autres données sur la production et l'emploi. C'est la meilleure source de données sur les établissements;
(14) NAICS 7211, 7212;
(15) NAICS 72111, 72112;

(16) NAICS 722;
(17) Ministère du commerce des États-Unis d'Amérique / Bureau d'analyse économique;
(18) Source «American Hotel & Lodging Association (AHLA)» (demeures comportant au moins 15 chambres);
(19) Source: «Smith Travel Research»;
(20) Emplois équivalents à temps plein;
(21) Hébergement des voyageurs;
(22) Services de restauration et débits de boisson;
(23) Services de transports aériens et toutes les autres industries liées au transport;
(24) Résiduel.

«U.S. Department of Commerce – National Travel and Tourism Office»
http://travel.trade.gov
www.ahla.com/content.aspx?id=3448

ÉTHIOPIE

(1) Arrivées à travers tous les ports d'entrée; y compris les nationaux résidant à l'étranger.

«Ministry of Culture and Tourism»

EX-RÉPUBLIQUE YOUGOSLAVE DE MACÉDOINE

(1) Touristes non résidents séjournant dans tous types d›établissements d›hébergement;
(2) Durée moyenne du séjour dans tous les établissements d'hébergement.

«State Statistical Office»
www.stat.gov.mk/OblastOpsto_en.aspx?id=25

FÉDÉRATION DE RUSSIE

(1) À pied;
(2) Hébergement dans les hôtels et autres établissements touristiques.

«Russian Federal Agency for Tourism»

FIDJI

(1) À l'exclusion des nationaux résidant à l'étranger;
(2) Jours.

«Fiji Islands Bureau of Statistics»
www.statsfiji.gov.fj/

FINLANDE

(1) Enquête basée sur des questionnaires à la frontière. Note: l'enquête a été annulée à la fin de 2012;
(2) Enquête sur l'hébergement;
(3) Balance des paiements (BdP);
(4) Enquête finlandaise sur les voyages;
(5) Ne comprend que les voyages internes de loisirs dans des locations pour les visiteurs;
(6) Voyages à l'étranger avec nuitée, y compris les croisières avec nuitée à bord uniquement;
(7) Données du Compte satellite du tourisme (CST);

NOTES DES PAYS

(8) Voyages internes et émetteurs avec nuitée, y compris les croisières avec nuitée à bord uniquement.

« Tourism Statistics – Statistics Finland »
www.mek.fi/w5/mekfi/index.nsf/(pages)/Tutkimukset_ja_
tilastot

FRANCE

(1) Source : Dge, Banque de France. Enquête auprès des visiteurs venant de l'étranger (EVE) – résultats 2011 à 2014 rétropolés, résultats 2015 provisoires ;
(2) Tous motifs personnels ;
(3) Transit et non spécifiés ;
(4) Source : Insee, Dge, partenaires territoriaux. Enquêtes de fréquentation hôtelière (EFH), campings (EFHPA) et, à partir de 2011, autres hébergements collectifs (EFAHCT) – résidences de tourisme et résidences hôtelières, villages de vacances et auberges de jeunesse - ; rupture de série en 2011 ; hébergements marchands individuels (meublés et chambres d'hôtel) exclus ;
(5) Source : Insee, Dge, partenaires territoriaux. Enquête de fréquentation hôtelière (EFH) ; séjours pour tous les motifs ;
(6) Durée moyenne du séjour en nuitées ;
(7) Source : Dge. Enquête Suivi de la demande touristique (SDT). Population résidente de 15 ans et plus ; les déplacements dans les DOM sont comptés avec l'étranger ;
(8) Voyages personnels ;
(9) Parc de l'hébergement collectif marchand (hôtels, campings, résidences de tourisme, résidences hôtelières, villages de vacances, maisons familiales, auberges de jeunesse, centres sportifs, centres internationaux de séjour) ; Source : Insee, Dge, SNRT, UNAT, FUAJ ;
(10) Parc hôtelier ; Source : Insee, Dge ;
(11) Champ : emploi salarié privé en France (y c. DOM) au 31/12 ; Source : Acoss ;
(12) Location de courte durée de matériel (voitures, articles de loisirs et de sport), activités des parcs d'attraction et parcs à thèmes et autres activités récréatives et de loisirs, gestion des musées, des sites historiques, des attractions touristiques, des jardins botaniques et zoologiques et des réserves naturelles, organisation de jeux de hasard et d'argent, téléphériques et remontées mécaniques ;
(13) Taux net des chambres ;
(14) Champ : France métropolitaine ; Source : Insee. Recensement de la population pour 2010, bilan démographique pour 2011–2014.

DGE (Direction générale des entreprises) et INSEE (Institut national de la statistique et des études économiques)
www.entreprises.gouv.fr/etudes-et-statistiques/statistiques-du-tourisme/accueil
www.insee.fr/fr/default.asp

GAMBIE

(1) Y compris les nationaux résidant à l'étranger ;
(2) Arrivées en vols à la demande seulement.

« Gambia Tourism Board »

GÉORGIE

(1) Arrivées dans les hôtels uniquement ;
(2) Source : Enquête sur les hôtels et établissements assimilés ;
(3) NACE Rév. 1.1. ;
(4) Les données se réfèrent uniquement à l'investissement en capital fixe.

« Georgian National Tourism Agency – Ministry of Economy and Sustainable Development » et « National Statistics Office of Georgia »
http://gnta.ge/statistics/

GHANA

(1) Y compris les nationaux résidant à l'étranger ;
(2) Estimations.

« Ghana Tourist Board and Ministry of Tourism and Modernisation of the Capital City »
www.statsghana.gov.gh

GRÈCE

(1) L'information est basée sur l'enquête aux frontières réalisée par la Banque de Grèce ;
(2) Nombre de voyages avec 4 nuitées ou plus des visiteurs âgés de 15 ans ou plus ;
(3) Source : « Hellenic Chamber of Hotels ».

« Hellenic Statistical Authority (EL.STAT.) »
www.statistics.gr/en/statistics/ind

GRENADE

(1) 2013–2015 : arrivées par voie aérienne uniquement ;
(2) Arrivées en yacht et en bateau de croisière ;
(3) Hôtels, bungalows/ appartements et pensions de famille.

« Grenada Board of Tourism »

GUADELOUPE

(1) Arrivées par voie aérienne ; À l'exclusion des îles du nord (Saint Martin et Saint Barthélemy) ;
(2) 2014, 2015 : arrivées par voie aérienne ;
(3) Les chiffres de dépense sont ceux que le pays a fournis à l'OMT mais ils ne figurent pas dans les données du Fonds monétaire international qui ont servi à la préparation de la présente édition du Compendium ;
(4) Hôtels.

Comité du Tourisme des Îles de la Guadeloupe

GUAM

(1) Arrivées par voies aérienne et maritime ;
(2) Uniquement arrivées de civils par voie aérienne ;
(3) Chambres disponibles.

« Guam Visitors Bureau »
www.guamvisitorsbureau.com/research-and-reports/reports/annual-report

NOTES DES PAYS

GUATEMALA

(1) Série mise à jour depuis 2009 avec une nouvelle méthodologie.
(2) Ensemble des établissements d'hébergement inscrits à l'INGUAT.

«Instituto Guatemalteco de Turismo – INGUAT»
www.inguat.gob.gt/estadisticas.php

GUINÉE

(1) Arrivées par voie aérienne à l'aéroport de Conakry;
(2) Il s'agit des nuitées réalisées par les non- résidents dans les hôtels toutes catégories confondues. Les données proviennent de la durée de séjour dans les hôtels déclarée (hormis les non-déclaration de durée de séjour) sur les talons des fiches embarquement/débarquement par les visiteurs à leur arrivée à l'aéroport;
(3) Y compris l'hébergement privé;
(4) Croisement du champ «arrivées» et «mode hébergement» déclarés sur les fiches embarquement/débarquement.

Direction Observatoire du Tourisme – Ministère du Tourisme, de l'Hôtellerie et de l'Artisanat

GUINÉE-BISSAU

(1) Arrivées à l'aéroport «Osvaldo Vieira».

Ministère du commerce, de l'industrie, du tourisme et de l'artisanat

GUYANE

(1) Arrivées à l'aéroport de Timehri seulement;
(2) Canada et État-Unis uniquement.

«Guyana Tourism Authority»

GUYANE FRANÇAISE

(1) Enquête au départ de l'aéroport de Cayenne-Rochambeau;
(2) France uniquement;
(3) Hôtels uniquement.

Comité du Tourisme de la Guyane

HAÏTI

(1) Arrivées par voie aérienne;
(2) Y compris les nationaux résidant à l'étranger.

Ministère du Tourisme

HONDURAS

(1) Nuitées;
(2) 2015: données préliminaires.

«Instituto Hondureño de Turismo»
www.iht.hn

HONG KONG (CHINE)

(1) Les données de dépense sont celles que le pays a fournies à l'OMT car il s'agit d'une série plus complète que celle obtenue du Fonds monétaire international (FMI) pour la préparation de la présente édition du Compendium. (Source: «HKTB Visitors Survey»);
(2) Source: «Census and Statistics Department»;
(3) Nuitées;
(4) Hôtels (tarifs élevés/moyens) et auberges/ pensions de famille;
(5) Les chiffres couvrent les activités de services pour le tourisme récepteur;
(6) Les chiffres couvrent les activités de services pour le tourisme émetteur;
(7) Les chiffres couvrent le commerce de détail, le transport et les services personnels pour le tourisme récepteur ainsi que les services de transport pour le tourisme émetteur.

«Hong Kong Tourism Board»
http://partnernet.hktb.com/en/research_statistics/index.html
www.censtatd.gov.hk/hong_kong_statistics/index.jsp

HONGRIE

(1) L'observation des frontières avec les pays de l'espace de Schengen a cessé à partir de l'année 2008. 2011: le trafic aérien de passagers et de la route sont des estimations;
(2) Départs de visiteurs non résidents;
(3) Voie fluviale;
(4) À l'exclusion des chauffeurs de camion;
(5) Hébergement gratuit;
(6) Nuitées;
(7) Basé sur la nouvelle classification contenue dans le Compte satellite du tourisme: recommandations concernant le cadre conceptuel 2008 (CST: RCC 2008);
(8) Y compris les estimations de logements privés;
(9) Incluant les activités caractéristiques du tourisme suivantes selon les RIST et TSA: RCC 2008: location de matériel de transport, activités culturelles, sports et activités récréatives, services de spa en tant qu'autre activité caractéristique du tourisme propre au pays;
(10) Juillet-juin;
(11) 2011: classification CST; 2012–2014 Enquête sur les forces de travail (EFT);
(12) NACE Rév. 2.

«Hungarian Central Statistical Office»
www.ksh.hu/tourism_catering

ILES CAÏMANES

(1) Arrivées par voie aérienne;
(2) Croisiéristes uniquement;
(3) Les chiffres de dépense sont ceux que le pays a fournis à l'OMT mais ils ne figurent pas dans les données du Fonds

monétaire international qui ont servi à la préparation de la présente édition du Compendium ;
(4)   Y compris les dépenses des croisiéristes ;
(5)   Hôtels et appartements ;
(6)   Jours.

« Cayman Islands Department of Tourism »
www.caymanislands.ky/statistics/
www.eso.ky

ILES COOK

(1)   Arrivées par voies aérienne et maritime ;
(2)   Les chiffres de dépense sont ceux que le pays a fournis à l'OMT mais ils ne figurent pas dans les données du Fonds monétaire international qui ont servi à la préparation de la présente édition du Compendium.

« Cook Islands Tourism Corporation » et « Cook Islands Statistics Office »
www.mfem.gov.ck/statistics

ILES MARIANNES DU NORD

(1)   Arrivées par voie aérienne ;
(2)   Y compris Guam ;
(3)   Couvre 68 pour cent du nombre total de chambres recensées.
Source des données pour la période 2012–2015 : PATA.

« Marianas Visitors Authority »

ILES MARSHALL

(1)   Arrivées par voie aérienne. 2014–2015 Source : « South Pacific Tourism Organisation – Regional Tourism Resource Centre".

« Marshall Islands Visitors Authority »

ILES SALOMON

« Solomon Islands National Statistics Office »

ILES TURQUES ET CAÏQUES

« Turks and Caicos Tourist Board »
http://turksandcaicostourism.com

ILES VIERGES AMÉRICAINES

(1)   Touristes non résidents séjournant dans les hôtels et établissements assimilés ;
(2)   Arrivées de visiteurs par voie aérienne ; à l'exclusion des arrivées de résidents et le trafic entre les îles, mais compris les visiteurs de la journée (excursionnistes) ;
(3)   Croisiéristes ;
(4)   Y compris celles des touristes internes (environ 40 pour cent de l'ensemble) ;
(5)   Les chiffres de dépense sont ceux que le pays a fournis à l'OMT mais ils ne figurent pas dans les données du Fonds

monétaire international qui ont servi à la préparation de la présente édition du Compendium ;
(6)   Hôtels et condominiums ou villas.
2015 : Données provisoires.

« Bureau of Economic Research »
www.usviber.org/publications.htm

ILES VIERGES BRITANNIQUES

(1)   Y compris les croisiéristes ;
(2)   Les chiffres de dépense sont ceux que le pays a fournis à l'OMT mais ils ne figurent pas dans les données du Fonds monétaire international qui ont servi à la préparation de la présente édition du Compendium.

« Central Statistics Office »

INDE

(1)   À l'exclusion des nationaux résidant à l'étranger ;
(2)   Y compris autres motifs ;
(3)   Départs de nationaux seulement, pour tous motifs de visite ;
(4)   Hôtels homologués.

« Ministry of Tourism – Government of India »
http://tourism.gov.in/

INDONÉSIE

(1)   2015 : par nationalité ;
(2)   Hôtels homologués uniquement ;
(3)   2015 : estimations ;
(4)   Toutes formes d'hébergement commercial.
(5)   Prix courants

« Ministry of Tourism and Creative Economy » et « BPS Statistics Indonesia »
www.bps.go.id/Subjek/view/
id/16#subjekViewTab3|accordion-daftar-subjek2

IRAN (RÉPUBLIQUE ISLAMIQUE D')

(1)   Source : « Central Bank of Islamic Republic of Iran ».

« Iran Cultural Heritage and Tourism Organization (ICHTO) »

IRAQ

« Ministry of Tourism and Antiquities »

IRLANDE

(1)   Y compris les touristes en provenance de l'Irlande du Nord ;
(2)   Y compris chemin de fer ;
(3)   À cause d'un changement de méthodologie, les données pour 2011 ont été révisées et ne sont pas comparables avec celles des années précédentes ;
(4)   À cause d'un changement de méthodologie, les

données pour 2012–2014 ont été révisées et ne sont pas comparables avec celles des années précédentes ;

(5) À l'exclusion des hôtelleries ;

(6) Hôtels seulement.

« Fáilte Ireland »
www.failteireland.ie/

ISLANDE

(1) Source : « Icelandic Tourist Board » ;
(2) 2012–2015 : arrivées à l'aéroport Keflavik uniquement ;
(3) Y compris les croisiéristes ;
(4) Transport aérien régulier.

« Hagstofa Íslands Statistics Iceland »
www.statice.is/statistics/business-sectors/tourism/

ISRAËL

(1) À l'exclusion des nationaux résidant à l'étranger ;
(2) Y compris visites à des parents et amis et pèlerinages ;
(3) Y compris nouvelles entrées de touristes après une visite au Sinaï d'un maximum de 7 jours ;
(4) Hôtels de touristes et aparthôtels ;
(5) Y compris les dépenses des travailleurs étrangers en Israël ;
(6) Taux d'occupation/lits dans hôtels et établissements assimilés ouverts ;
(7) Tourisme récepteur dans hôtels touristiques.

« Ministry of Tourism »
http://www1.cbs.gov.il/reader/?MIval=cw_usr_view_
SHTML&ID=432

ITALIE

(1) À l'exclusion des travailleurs saisonniers et frontaliers ;
(2) Enquête aux frontières de la ' »Banca d'Italia » ;
(3) Y compris les croisiéristes ;
(4) Hôtels uniquement ;
(5) 2014 : rupture de séries due à un changement de technique pour la collecte de données (survey : « Trips and Holidays »), du système CATI au CAPI ;
(6) Nuitées ;
(7) « Les services d'hébergement non commercial » sont composées des logements occupés par leurs propriétaires (y compris ceux qui ont un contrat en temps partagé), des hébergements cédés par des membres de la famille ou par des amis et d'autres hébergements privés non commerciaux ;
(8) Nombre de touristes résidents (visiteurs qui passent la nuit) voyageant à l'étranger ;
(9) À l'exclusion des estimations de logements privés.

« Banca d'Italia » et « Istituto Nazionale di Statistica (ISTAT) »
www.bancaditalia.it
www.istat.it

JAMAÏQUE

(1) Arrivées de touristes non résidents par voie aérienne ; y compris les nationaux résidant à l'étranger ; cartes E/D ;
(2) Croisiéristes uniquement ;

(3) Les données sont obtenues à travers les enquêtes menées auprès des visiteurs qui passent la nuit (touristes) déclarant le mode d'organisation de leur voyage à leur sortie des aéroports internationaux ;
(4) Nouvelle série ; y compris les nationaux résidant à l'étranger ;
(5) Nuitées ;
(6) Durée de séjour prévue ;
(7) Dépense moyenne des visiteurs qui passent la nuit (touristes) par jour et par personne ;
(8) À l'exclusion des établissements fermés ;
(9) Nuitées dans les hôtels seulement.

« Jamaica Tourist Board »
www.jtbonline.org/statistics/Annual%20Travel/Forms/
AllItems.aspx

JAPON

(1) À l'exclusion des nationaux résidant à l'étranger ;
(2) Arrivées de visiteurs non résidents aux frontières nationales ; y compris les résidents étrangers au Japon ;
(3) Jusqu'en mars 2010, les lieux d'hébergement comptant moins de 9 employés sont exclus ;
(4) L'utilisation diurne est exclue ;
(5) Y compris les chevauchements ;
(6) Hôtels homologués et non homologués, ainsi que « ryokans » (auberges) ;
(7) Estimation à partir du taux d'occupation ;
(8) Y compris les services d'appui au transport de voyageurs.

Source des données :
1.19-1.21 : Ministère de l'intérieur et des communications – statistiques de l'immigration ; 1.30, 4.2, 4.3, 4.13-4.15, 4.16-4.18 : Agence japonaise de tourisme – enquête sur l'hébergement ; 1.40-1.43, 2.1-2.18, 4.25-4.26, 4.29-4.30, 5.1-5.10, 6.1 : Agence japonaise de tourisme – enquête sur le tourisme national du Japon ; 2.24-2.27 : Agence japonaise de tourisme – enquête sur l'hébergement – enquête sur le tourisme national du Japon ; 3.1, 3.10 : Organisation nationale japonaise du tourisme ; 4.4, 4.7 : Ministère de l'intérieur et des communications – recensement économique ; 4.6 : Association japonaise du voyage et du tourisme ; 4.8-4.11 : Agence japonaise de tourisme – enquête sur le tourisme national du Japon – compte satellite du tourisme du Japon – Tableau 5 : comptes de production des industries du tourisme et des autres industries ; 4.27-4.28 : Agence japonaise de tourisme – enquête sur les tendances de consommation des étrangers visitant le Japon ; 5.2 : Compte satellite du tourisme du Japon – Tableau 7 : emploi dans les industries du tourisme.

« Japan Tourism Agency » et « Japan National Tourism Organization »
www.mlit.go.jp/kankocho/en/siryou/toukei/index.html
www.tourism.jp/en/statistics/

JORDANIE

(1) Y compris les nationaux résidant à l'étranger ;
(2) 2011–2014 : arrivées de visiteurs résidents et non résidents ;
(3) Circuits organisés seulement.

« Ministry of Tourism and Antiquities »
www.tourism.jo

NOTES DES PAYS

KAZAKHSTAN

« Agency of Statistics of the Republic of Kazakhstan »

KENYA

(1) Arrivées de visiteurs non résidents à travers tous les postes frontières ; à l'exclusion des nationaux résidant à l'étranger ;
(2) Jours.

« Kenya National Bureau of Statistics »

KIRGHIZISTAN

« National Statistical Committee »

KIRIBATI

(1) Arrivées par voie aérienne. Tarawa et Ile Christmas.

« Kiribati National Tourism Office », « Ministry of Communication, Transport and Tourism Development » et « PATA »

KOWEÏT

(1) Touristes non résidents séjournant dans les hôtels et établissements assimilés.

« Central Statistical Bureau »
www.csb.gov.kw/Socan_Statistic_EN.aspx?ID=19

LESOTHO

(1) Grâce à l'amélioration de la collecte des données faite avec l'aide de « Statistics South Africa", à partir de 2014 les données ne sont pas comparables avec celles des années précédentes.

« Lesotho Tourism Development Corporation »
www.ltdc.org.ls/researchArrivalStats.php

LETTONIE

(1) Arrivées de visiteurs non résidents aux frontières nationales. Données provenant de la Police d'Etat aux frontières ;
(2) Départs des non-résidents. Enquête auprès des personnes qui traversent les frontières du pays ;
(3) Y compris les visites à des parents et amis et traitement médical ;
(4) Depuis 2015 Hôtels et établissements assimilés selon la classification de la NACE Rév.2 : section I, division 55, classe 55.1 – hôtels et établissements assimilés (les services comprennent le nettoyage quiotidien) ;
(5) Nuitées dans tous les établissements d'hébergement collectif ;
(6) Source : enquête aux frontières ;
(7) À partir de 2012 source : enquête auprès des ménages ;
(8) À partir de 2012 données provenant de la Police d'Etat aux frontières.

« Transport and Tourism Statistics Section – Central Statistical Bureau »
www.csb.gov.lv/en/statistikas-temas/tourism-key-indicators-30715.html

LIBAN

(1) À l'exclusion des nationalités libanaise, syrienne et palestinienne ;
(2) Pour l'année 2015, l'enquête a été menée sur 291 établissements ;
(3) Source des données, hôtels et établissements autorisés par le Ministère du tourisme ;
(4) Source : syndicats touristiques au Liban.

« Ministère du Tourisme »

LIECHTENSTEIN

(1) Touristes non résidents séjournant dans tous types d›établissements d›hébergement ;
(2) Depuis 2012, à l'exclusion des touristes à long terme dans les campements et les appartements touristiques ;
(3) 2011 : touristes non résidents séjournant dans les hôtels et établissements assimilés ;
(4) Depuis 2012 : touristes non résidents séjournant dans tous types d›établissements d›hébergement ;
(5) Depuis 2012, à l'exclusion des campements et des appartements touristiques de long terme ;
(6) Moyenne annuelle ;
(7) Moyenne annuelle des chambres disponibles ;
(8) Moyenne annuelle des places-lits disponibles.

« Office of Statistics Liechtenstein. Tourism Statistics »
www.llv.li/#/11961/tourismusstatistik

LITUANIE

(1) Hôtels et motels ;
(2) Enquête sur la structure des entreprises ;
(3) Données des comptes nationaux ;
(4) Données du Compte satellite du tourisme (CST).

« Lithuanian State Department of Tourism »
www.stat.gov.lt/

LUXEMBOURG

(1) Touristes non résidents séjournant dans tous types d›établissements d›hébergement ; y compris auberges de jeunesse, hébergement touristique privé et autres ;
(2) Estimation pour les touristes ayant passé au moins une nuit dans un établissement d'hébergement touristique ;
(3) NACE Rev2 55.100 ;
(4) Les données de dépense sont celles que le pays a fournies à l'OMT car il s'agit d'une série plus complète que celle obtenue du Fonds monétaire international (FMI) ;
(5) Touristes résidents dans tous types d'établisuments d'hébergement ; y compris auberges de jeunesse, hébergement touristique privé et autres ;
(6) Taux d'occupation net.

STATEC
www.statistiques.public.lu

NOTES DES PAYS

MACAO (CHINE)

(1) Les données antérieures à 2014 incluent les visiteurs avec voyage à forfait et ceux contractant des excursions locales;
(2) Depuis 2011, les données sont obtenues par la police de sécurité publique tandis que celles des années antérieures viennent des échantillons;
(3) Hôtels et pensions de famille;
(4) Restaurants et établissements assimilés;
(5) Établissements qui offrent des services de transport de passagers;
(6) Agences de voyage;
(7) Entreprises de jeu;
(8) À l'exclusion des salariés à temps partiel.

Source des données: 1.1-1.13, 1.19-1.25, 1.26, 4.27-4.28, 6.2: Police de sécurité publique; 1.27, 3.1, 4.27-4.30: Enquête mensuelle auprès des agences de voyage; 1.31-1.32, 1.41-1.42, 4.14-4.19: Enquête mensuelle auprès des hôtels et établissements assimilés; 1.40, 1.44: Enquête sur les dépenses des visiteurs; 4.2-4.3, 4.8-4.12, 4.13, 5.2: Enquête sur les hôtels et établissements assimilés; 4.4, 5.4: Enquête sur les restaurants et établissements assimilés; 4.5, 5.5: Enquête sur le transport, l'entreposage et les communications; 4.6, 4.20-4.24, 5.6: Enquête auprès des agences de voyage; 4.7: enquête sur le secteur du jeu; 4.19, 6.2: Estimation démographique de Macao; 5.7: enquête sur les besoins de main-d'œuvre et les traitements – industrie du jeu.

«Statistics and Census Service» et «Macau Government Tourist Office»
www.dsec.gov.mo/Statistic/TourismAndServices/VisitorArrivals.aspx
http://industry.macautourism.gov.mo/en/index.php

MADAGASCAR

(1) Arrivées de touristes non résidents par voie aérienne.

Ministère du Tourisme, des Transports et de la Météorologie

MALAISIE

(1) Y compris les résidents de Singapour qui traversent la frontière par le Johore Causeway;
(2) La méthodologie a été modifiée et pour cela, à partir de 2013 les données ne sont pas comparables avec celles des années précédentes;
(3) Enquête sur le tourisme interne;
(4) Hôtels avec 10 chambres et plus;
(5) Enquête dans les hôtels.
Source des données: 1.2, 1.5-1.12, 1.19-1.24, 1.31, 1.4, 4.3, 4.13, 4.14, 4.16: «Tourism Malaysia»; 2.1-2.28: «Department of Statistics Malaysia».

«Department of Statistics Malaysia» et «Tourism Malaysia»
www.tourism.gov.my/statistics

MALAWI

(1) Départs.

«Ministry of Tourism, Wildlife and Culture»

MALDIVES

(1) Arrivées par voie aérienne;
(2) Jours.

«Ministry of Tourism»
www.tourism.gov.mv

MALI

(1) 2012–2015: arrivées par voie aérienne uniquement (aéroport de Bamako-Sénou);
(2) Arrivées par voie aérienne uniquement (aéroport de Bamako-Sénou);
(3) 2015: données partielles qui correspondent au poste frontalier de Bih, dans la région de Mopti.

Direction Nationale du Tourisme et de l'Hotellerie (DNTH)

MALTE

(1) Données tirées des départs par voies aérienne et maritime;
(2) Source: Eurostat;
(3) Source: «MTA Licensing Data».

«Malta Tourism Authority» et «National Statistics Office»
www.mta.com.mt/research
www.nso.gov.mt

MAROC

(1) Y compris les nationaux résidant à l'étranger;
(2) Hôtels homologués, villages de vacances, résidences touristiques et Riad;
(3) Touristes étrangers.

Ministère du tourisme
www.tourisme.gov.ma/

MARTINIQUE

(1) Les chiffres de dépense sont ceux que le pays a fournis à l'OMT mais ils ne figurent pas dans les données du Fonds monétaire international qui ont servi à la préparation de la présente édition du Compendium.

Comité Martiniquais du Tourisme

MAURICE

(1) Estimations à partir de l'enquête du tourisme récepteur, année 2013;
(2) Grands hôtels;
(3) Hôtels seulement;
(4) Les données concernent les établissements de grande taille (c'est-à-dire employant 10 personnes ou plus) du secteur touristique.
Note 2015: données provisoires.

«Ministry of Tourism and Leisure»
http://statsmauritius.govmu.org/English/StatsbySubj/Pages/INTERNATIONAL-TRAVEL-and-TOURISM.aspx

NOTES DES PAYS

MEXIQUE

(1) Y compris les nationaux résidant à l'étranger;
(2) Y compris les visiteurs de la frange frontalière avec les États-Unis avec séjour inférieur à 24h;
(3) Voie aérienne uniquement;
(4) Touristes dans les régions intérieures et touristes dans les régions frontalières;
(5) Y compris chemin de fer;
(6) Hôtels seulement;
(7) Sélection de centres touristiques;
(8) Jours;
(9) Tourisme étranger seulement;
(10) L'information ne se réfère pas exactement à l'emploi mais aux équivalents emplois rémunérés nécessaires pour produire les biens et les services liés aux activités touristiques. Source: «Cuenta Satélite de Turismo de México, cambio de año base a 2008».

«Secretaría de Turismo de México (SECTUR)», «Instituto Nacional de Estadística y Geografía (INEGI)» et «Unidad de Política Migratoria
Banco de México»
www.datatur.sectur.gob.mx/
www.inegi.org.mx

MICRONÉSIE (ÉTATS FÉDÉRÉS DE)

(1) Arrivées dans les États de Kosrae, Chuuk, Pohnpei et Yap; à l'exclusion des citoyens de EFM;
(2) Années fiscales (1 octobre – 30 septembre).

«Office of Statistics, Budget and Economic Management, Overseas Development Assistance, and Compact Management»
www.sboc.fm

MOLDOVA (RÉPUBLIQUE DE)

(1) Touristes non résidents séjournant dans tous types d'établissements d'hébergement;
(2) Visiteurs qui ont bénéficié des services touristiques des agences de tourisme et des voyagistes (titulaires d'une licence touristique).
Note: À l'exception de la rive gauche de la rivière Nistru et de la municipalité de Bender.

«National Bureau of Statistics»
www.statistica.md/category.php?l=en&idc=293&

MONACO

(1) Touristes non résidents séjournant dans les hôtels et établissements assimilés.

Direction du Tourisme et des Congrès
www.imsee.mc

MONGOLIE

(1) À l'exclusion des diplomates et des étrangers qui résident en Mongolie.

«National Tourism Center – Ministry of Nature, Environment and Tourism»

MONTÉNÉGRO

(1) Touristes non résidents séjournant dans tous types d'établissements d'hébergement.

«Ministry of Sustainable Development and Tourism»
www.monstat.org/eng/page.php?id=43&pageid=43

MONTSERRAT

«Statistics Department Montserrat»

MOZAMBIQUE

(1) Arrivées à tous les postes frontaliers du pays;
(2) L'enquête sur le tourisme interne est un module de l'enquête sur le budget des ménages, laquelle est conduite tous les 5 ans. C'est en 2008–2009 que le tourisme interne a figuré dans cette enquête pour la première fois. En 2012–2013 a eu lieu l'enquête continue sur le budget des ménages.

«Ministry of Tourism» et «Instituto Nacional de Estatística»
www.ine.gov.mz

MYANMAR

(1) Hôtels et établissements assimilés gérés par l'État uniquement. L'augmentation du total en 2014 provient de la somme des arrivées ayant un laissez-passer frontalier pour un séjour de 7 jours aux postes frontaliers de la Chine, l'Inde, la Thaïlande et le Myanmar, ainsi que les arrivées aux points d'entrée internationaux;
(2) Hôtels gérés par l'État et pensions de famille privées homologuées.

«Ministry of Hotels and Tourism»
www.myanmartourism.org/

NAMIBIE

«Ministry of Environment and Tourism» et «Namibian Tourism Board»

NÉPAL

(1) Y compris les arrivées en provenance de l'Inde;
(2) Jours;
(3) Hôtels à Katmandou; à l'exclusion des hôtels en cours de construction;
(4) Agences de voyage et de trekking.

«Nepal Tourism Board» et «Ministry of Culture, Tourism and Civil Aviation»
www.tourism.gov.np/np/category/tourism/tourism_statistics

NICARAGUA

(1) Y compris les nationaux résidant à l'étranger;
(2) Nombre total des établissements dans l'ensemble du pays;
(3) Principaux établissements d'hébergement dans l'ensemble du pays;

NOTES DES PAYS

(4) Hôtels et établissements assimilés classés en catégories supérieures ;

(5) Tous types d'établissements d'hébergement, tourisme récepteur.

« Instituto Nicaragüense de Turismo (INTUR) »
www.intur.gob.ni

NIGER

(1) Jours.

Ministère du Tourisme et de l'Artisanat et Institut National de la Statistique
www.stat-niger.org/statistique/

NIGÉRIA

(1) Dans une tentative d'assainir le secteur du tourisme, la Société de développement du tourisme du Nigeria a créé un groupe de travail pour mettre en œuvre le processus d'inscription des hôtels. Tous les établissements de l'hôtellerie, en particulier les hôtels, ont été obligés de s'inscrire auprès de la Société ou être fermé et donc cet effort singulier a provoqué l'augmentation du nombre d'hôtels et établissements assimilés en 2011.

« Nigerian Tourism Development Corporation »

NIOUÉ

(1) « Y compris les nationaux de Niue résidant habituellement en Nouvelle-Zélande ».
2014–2015 Source : « South Pacific Tourism Organisation – Regional Tourism Resource Centre ». 2015 : estimations. »

« Statistics Niue »

NORVÈGE

(1) 2011 : les chiffres se fondent sur l'enquête auprès de la clientèle de l'Institut d'économie des transports. À partir de 2012, l'enquête a été interrompue ;

(2) 2012–2015 : touristes non résidents séjournant dans tous types d'établissements d'hébergement ;

(3) 2011 : États-Unis seulement ;

(4) 2011 : Japon seulement ;

(5) Nuitées dans les établissements classés ;

(6) Les chiffres des hôtels et établissements assimilés se réfèrent aux établissements de 20 places-lit et plus tout au long de l'année ;

(7) 2014 : données provisoires ;

(8) 2011 : données révisées.

« Statistics Norway » et « Institute of Transport Economics »
www.ssb.no/english/subjects/

NOUVELLE-CALÉDONIE

(1) Y compris les nationaux résidant à l'étranger ;

(2) Hôtels de Nouméa uniquement ;

(3) Retours des résidents ;

(4) Chambres à Nouméa ;

(5) Jours, hôtels de Nouméa.

Institut de la Statistique et des Études Économiques (ISEE)
www.isee.nc/

NOUVELLE-ZÉLANDE

(1) Voyages internationaux et migration, SNZ ;

(2) Y compris les croisiéristes ;

(3) Enquête sur l'hébergement, SNZ ;

(4) Y compris les hôtels, motels et les auberges, mais exclut les parcs de vacances ;

(5) Balance des paiements, SNZ ;

(6) Enquête voyages internes, MBIE (interrompue en 2013) ;

(7) Les données fournies dans cette section se fondent sur le type de transport utilisé lors des divers trajets effectués dans le cadre de chaque voyage de tourisme interne et pas seulement le type de transport principal du voyage. En conséquence, le total indiqué ne correspond pas à la somme de 2.10, 2.11 et 2.12. L'enquête sur les voyages internes autorise des réponses multiples à la question du « type de transport » ;

(8) Enquête voyages internes – visiteurs qui passent la nuit, MBIE ;

(9) Dépenses des voyages avec nuitée uniquement ;

(10) Statistiques démographiques des entreprises, SNZ (données révisées en 2011 pour refléter la nouvelle classification du secteur, ANZSIC06) en février 2011–2013 ;

(11) Données provisoires.

« Statistics New Zealand (SNZ) » et « Ministry of Business, Innovation & Employment (MBIE) »
www.stats.govt.nz/

OMAN

(1) Enquête du tourisme récepteur ;

(2) Y compris le turisme interne.

« Ministry of Tourism », « Ministry of National Economy » et « National Centre for Statistics and Information »
www.omantourism.gov.om

OUGANDA

« Ministry of Tourism, Trade and Industry » et « Uganda Bureau of Statistics »
www.ubos.org/?st=pagerelations2&id=19&p=related%20
pages%202:Migration%20and%20Tourism%20Statistics

PALAOS

(1) Arrivées par voie aérienne (aéroport international de Palau) ;

(2) Années fiscales – 30 septembre.

« Office of Planning and Statistics, Bureau of Budget and Planning – Ministry of Finance » et « Palau Visitors Authority »
www.visit-palau.com/

NOTES DES PAYS

PANAMA

(1) Arrivées de visiteurs non résidents, aéroport international de Tocúmen (AIT), frontière de Paso Canoa (FPC) et ports de Cristóbal et Balboa (PCB);
(2) Arrivées de visiteurs non résidents, AIT;
(3) Arrivées de touristes non résidents, AIT;
(4) Hôtels de Panama-City;
(5) Chambres/places-lit recensées pour le tourisme international.

«Autoridad de Turismo de Panamá»
www.atp.gob.pa/estadisticas-de-turismo-en-panama

PAPOUASIE-NOUVELLE-GUINÉE

(1) Estimations.
(2) Jours.

«Papua New Guinea Tourism Promotion Authority»
www.tpa.papuanewguinea.travel/

PARAGUAY

(1) Cartes d'embarquement et de débarquement à l'aéroport Silvio Petirossi et comptages des passagers lors du franchissement des frontières nationales – Police nationale et SENATUR;
(2) À l'exclusion des nationaux résidant à l'étranger et membres des équipages;
(3) Voie fluviale.

«Secretaría Nacional de Turismo – SENATUR»
www.senatur.gov.py

PAYS-BAS

(1) Touristes non résidents séjournant dans tous types d'établissements d'hébergement;
(2) 2013: rupture de série due aux changements méthodologiques dans la détermination de la population;
(3) Hôtels et pensions;
(4) 2013–2015: les données de dépense sont celles que le pays a fournies à l'OMT car il s'agit d'une série plus complète que celle obtenue du Fonds monétaire international (FMI) pour la préparation de la présente édition du Compendium;
(5) Source: Eurostat;
(6) Départs en vacances des ressortissants nationaux;
(7) Hôtels;
(8) Tous types d'établissement d'hébergement.

«Statistics Netherlands»
www.cbs.nl/en-GB/menu/themas/vrije-tijd-cultuur/nieuws/default.htm

PÉROU

(1) Y compris les nationaux résidant à l'étranger;
(2) Croisiéristes qui passent la nuit;
(3) Y compris les arrivées par voie fluviale et lacustre.

«Superintendencia Nacional de Migraciones», «Banco Central de Reserva del Perú» et «Ministerio de Comercio Exterior y Turismo»
http://ww2.mincetur.gob.pe/

PHILIPPINES

(1) Y compris les nationaux résidant à l'étranger;
(2) Arrivées par voie aérienne;
(3) Nuitées;
(4) Hôtels dans la région de Manille seulement;
(5) Pour 2013, les données comprennent les établissements d'hébergement autorisés ayant une licence d'exploitation et ceux dont la licence d'exploitation a été approuvée, mais pas encore émise. Avant 2013, les données comprennent uniquement les hébergements ayant reçu leur licence d'exploitation;
(6) Hôtels homologués dans la région de Manille seulement;
(7) Basé sur les Comptes satellites du tourisme de Philippines (PTSA) – juin 2016.

«Department of Tourism»
www.tourism.gov.ph/Pages/TourismResearch.aspx

POLOGNE

(1) Depuis que la Pologne est entrée dans l'espace Schengen, le comptage précis du trafic entrant n'est pas possible. Seuls des résultats approximatifs peuvent être fournis cette année;
(2) Les données 2011, 2012 sont basées sur les enquêtes de l'Institut du Tourisme; 2013: «Activ Group»; 2014, 2015: Bureau central des statistiques;
(3) Données du Bureau central des statistiques;
(4) Établissements d'hébergement collectif et privé;
(5) Voyages de 4 nuits et plus;
(6) Établissements avec 10 ou places-lit. Au 31 juillet.

«Institute of Tourism»
www.intur.com.pl/itenglish/institute_en.htm

POLYNÉSIE FRANÇAISE

(1) Arrivées par voie aérienne uniquement; à l'exclusion des nationaux résidant à l'étranger;
(2) Jours;
(3) Hôtels et pensions de famille; au 31 décembre de chaque année;
(4) Chambres dans les hôtels.

Institut de la Statistique – ISPF
www.ispf.pf/Home.aspx

PORTO RICO

(1) Arrivées de touristes non résidents par voie aérienne;
(2) Îles Vierges Américaines et États-Unis seulement;
(3) Les chiffres de dépense sont ceux que le pays a fournis à l'OMT mais ils ne figurent pas dans les données du Fonds monétaire international qui ont servi à la préparation de la présente édition du Compendium;
(4) Y compris résidents et non résidents;
(5) Chambres classées par la «Compañía de Turismo» de Porto Rico;

NOTES DES PAYS

(6) Y compris les chambres occupées par des résidents de Porto Rico.
Données : Années fiscales (juillet-juin).

« Junta de Planificación de Puerto Rico » et « Compañía de Turismo de Puerto Rico »
www.jp.gobierno.pr/

PORTUGAL

(1) Arrivées de touristes non résidents dans tous les types d'établissements d'hébergement ;
(2) Source : Eurostat ;
(3) « Statistics Portugal (INE) », Enquête sur la structure des entreprises ;
(4) Taux d'occupation net ;
(5) Tous types d'établissements d'hébergement.

« Turismo de Portugal, I.P. »
www.ine.pt/xportal/xmain?xpid=INE&xpgid=ine_main

PROVINCE CHINOISE DE TAÏWAN

(1) Y compris les nationaux résidant à l'étranger ;
(2) Y compris le coût des billets d'avion.

« Planning Division Tourism Bureau – Ministry of Transportation and Communication »
http://admin.taiwan.net.tw/statistics/release_en.aspx?no=7

QATAR

(1) A partir de 2015, sont incluses les données des aparthôtels (qui n'étaient pas collectées auparavant).

« Qatar Statistics Authority »

RÉPUBLIQUE CENTRAFRICAINE

(1) Arrivées par voie aérienne à Bangui uniquement ;
(2) Données du pays.

Ministère des Arts, du Tourisme, de la Culture et de la Francophonie

RÉPUBLIQUE DÉMOCRATIQUE POPULAIRE LAO

« Lao National Tourism Administration » et « Ministry of Information, Culture and Tourism – Tourism Development Department »
www.tourismlaos.org/show.php?Cont_ID=43

RÉPUBLIQUE DOMINICAINE

(1) Y compris les nationaux résidant à l'étranger ;
(2) Arrivées par voie aérienne uniquement ;
(3) Toutes les arrivées par voie maritime ;
(4) Hôtels.

« Ministerio de Turismo »
www.bancentral.gov.do/estadisticas_economicas/turismo/

RÉPUBLIQUE TCHÈQUE

(1) CST de la République tchèque ;
(2) 2015 : données préliminaires ;
(3) Y compris les visiteurs en transit ;
(4) Touristes non-résidents séjournant dans tous les établissements d'hébergement collectif – Source : CZSO ;
(5) Source : Enquête sur le tourisme interne et le tourisme émetteur et CST ;
(6) Voyages longs + voyages courts ;
(7) Voyages d'affaires ;
(8) La méthodologie de l'enquête a été modifiée et pour cela, à partir de 2011 les données ne sont pas comparables avec celles des années précédentes (Source CZSO). Voyages longs + voyages courts ;
(9) Source : registre des entreprises de la République tchèque ;
(10) Hôtels et restaurants ;
(11) Source : Comptabilité nationale ;
(12) Consommation de capital fixe ;
(13) Utilisation nette de lits ;
(14) Les activités de soutien et de transport annexe, les activités des tours opérateurs et des agences de voyage ;
(15) Voyages touristiques (1 nuitée et plus).

« Czech Statistical Office, TSA » et « Ministry for Regional Development »
www.czso.cz/eng/redakce.nsf/i/home

RÉUNION

(1) Arrivés par voie aérienne uniquement ;
(2) Source : INSEE : Enquête flux touristiques ;
(3) Source : INSEE : Enquête de fréquentation hôtelière ;
(4) Il s'agit de l'ensemble des nuitées passées dans les hôtels classés, à partir de 2015 hôtels classés et non classés. Résidents et non résidents ;
(5) Les chiffres de dépense sont ceux que le pays a fournis à l'OMT mais ils ne figurent pas dans les données du Fonds monétaire international qui ont servi à la préparation de la présente édition du Compendium ;
(6) Source : INSEE Clap. Il s'agit de l'ensemble des établissements des nomenclatures sélectionnées. Sans certitude sur la destination réelle de l'activité (touristique ou non) ;
(7) Il s'agit de l'ensemble des établissements/chambres/lits disponibles par jour dans les hôtels classés, à partir de 2015 hôtels classés et non classés ;
(8) Source : INSEE Clap. Il s'agit de l'ensemble des emplois des nomenclatures sélectionnées. Sans certitude sur la destination réelle de l'activité (touristique ou non).

Institut National de la Statistique et des Études Économique – INSEE et Comité du Tourisme de la Réunion
http://observatoire.reunion.fr/les-chiffres-cles.html

ROUMANIE

(1) Seulement les voyages internes pour les vacances (y compris les visites à des parents ou amis VPA) et pour motifs professionnels ;
(2) La catégorie « Autres motifs personnels » ne fait référence qu'aux voyages VPA ;
(3) A partir de 2005, les catégories « voie aérienne » et « voie fluviale » sont incluses dans la catégorie « autres » ;

NOTES DES PAYS

(4) Calculé en divisant le nombre de nuitées par le nombre de voyages. Source : ACTR, Enquête sur les foyers ;

(5) Seulement pour les vacances (y compris les VPA) et pour motifs professionnels. Les chiffres sont obtenus en divisant la dépense par le nombre de nuitées ;

(6) Nombre de départs de Roumains à l'étranger enregistrés aux frontières ;

(7) Au 31 juillet, pour les établissements agréés seulement ;

(8) L'indicateur est représenté par le nombre de touristes qui achètent des services à forfait/individuels. Il est à noter que les chiffres cumulent les tours-opérateurs et les agences de voyage classiques ;

(9) L'indicateur est représenté réellement par « le nombre moyen d'employés » et la source est représentée par les statistiques structurelles sur les entreprises qui sont établies annuellement ;

(10) Inclus aussi le transport du fret ;

(11) Cette catégorie ne correspond pas parfaitement aux catégories de l'industrie du tourisme car elle est publiée avec un niveau de consolidation plus élevé. Y compris les activités suivantes : activités créatives, arts et spectacles, bibliothèques, archives, musées et autres services culturels, activités de jeux de hasard et de pari, activités sportives et activités récréatives et de loisir.

« National Institute of Statistics »
www.insse.ro/cms/en

ROYAUME-UNI

(1) Tunnel ;

(2) Enquête sur les passagers internationaux ; Source : « Office for National Statistics (ONS) » ;

(3) Jours ;

(4) À partir de 2013 : Grande Bretagne uniquement (hors Irlande du Nord) et « Day Visits survey » ;

(5) Nombre d'unités locales dans les entreprises assujetties à la TVA et/ou appliquant la retenue à la source, source : ONS Inter-Departmental Business Register (registre interdépartemental des entreprises du bureau des statistiques nationales) ;

(6) Source : enquête annuelle auprès des entreprises du Bureau national de statistique (ONS) ;

(7) Source : compilation de l'ONS pour EUROSTAT ;

(8) Source : enquête du Royaume-Uni sur l'occupation (rapport annuel) ;

(9) Source : ONS, sur la base de Workforce Jobs, Business Register Employment Survey et Labour Force Survey.

« VisitBritain » et « Office for National Statistics »
www.visitbritain.org/insightsandstatistics/
www.ons.gov.uk/ons/index.html »

RWANDA

« Rwanda Development Board »
www.rdb.rw/welcome-to-rwanda/tourism-research-and-statistics.html

SAINTE-LUCIE

(1) À l'exclusion des nationaux résidant à l'étranger ;

(2) À l'exclusion des arrivées de passagers en yacht.

« Saint Lucia Tourist Board »
http://investstlucia.com/sectors/view/tourism.html

SAINT-KITTS-ET-NEVIS

(1) Arrivées de touristes non résidents par voie aérienne ;

(2) Arrivées en yacht et en bateau de croisière.

« Ministry of Sustainable Development » et « Eastern Caribbean Central Bank »
www.eccb-centralbank.org/Statistics/index.asp#tourismdata

SAINT-MARIN

(1) Y compris les visiteurs Italiens ;

(2) Touristes non résidents séjournant dans tous types d'établissements d'hébergement ; y compris les touristes Italiens ;

(3) Hôtels uniquement.

« Segreteria di Stato per il Turismo ed i Rapporti con l'AASS »
www.statistica.sm/on-line/home/dati-statistici/attivita-economiche-e-turismo.html

SAINT-VINCENT-ET-LES-GRENADINES

(1) Arrivées de touristes non résidents par voie aérienne ;

(2) Y compris les croisièristes et passagers en yacht.

« St. Vincent and the Grenadines Tourism Authority »
www.discoversvg.com/index.php/es/about-svg/tourism-statistics

SAMOA

« Samoa Tourism Authority » et « Statistical Services Division (Ministry of Finance) »
www.sbs.gov.ws/index.php/sector-statistics/tourism-statistics
www.mof.gov.ws

SAMOA AMÉRICAINES

« Department of Commerce – Statistics Division »
www.spc.int/prism/americansamoa/

SÉNÉGAL

(1) Données estimées ;

(2) Arrivées par voie aérienne à l'aéroport Léopold Sédar Senghor (LSS) seulement. Y compris les nationaux résidant à l'étranger ;

(3) Hôtels et villages de vacances.

Ministère du Tourisme et des Transports Aériens

SERBIE

(1) Touristes séjournant dans les établissements d'hébergement pour les visiteurs ;

(2) Nombre total de lits (permanents et supplémentaires) jusqu'en 2012. Depuis 2013 : capacité maximale (nombre de lits permanents) sur l'année ;

(3) À partir de 2012, taux d'occupation net. Jusqu'à 2011, taux brut d'occupation ;

(4) Nombre de personnes employées.

NOTES DES PAYS

«Statistical Office of the Republic of Serbia» et «National Bank of Serbia»
http://webrzs.stat.gov.rs/WebSite/Public/PageView.aspx?pKey=181

SEYCHELLES

(1) Chiffres des nuitées élaborés à partir des départs;
(2) 2012 : janvier-octobre;
(3) Hôtels et pensions de famille.

«National Bureau of Statistics» et «Seychelles Tourism Board»
www.nbs.gov.sc/

SIERRA LEONE

(1) Arrivées par voie aérienne.

«National Tourist Board» et «Statistics Sierra Leone»
www.statistics.sl/

SINGAPOUR

(1) À l'exclusion des arrivées de Malaisiens par voie terrestre;
(2) Jours;
(3) Hôtels (homologués et non-homologués);
(4) Hôtels homologués seulement.

«Singapore Tourism Board»
www.singstat.gov.sg
www.stb.gov.sg

SINT MAARTEN (PARTIE NÉERLANDAISE)

(1) Par voie aérienne; y compris les arrivées à Saint-Martin (côté français de l'île);
(2) Arrivées à l'aéroport «Juliana» (y compris les visiteurs à destination de Saint-Martin (côté français).

«St. Maarten Tourist Bureau» et «Department of Statistics Sint Maarten»
http://stat.gov.sx/

SLOVAQUIE

(1) Le nombre d'arrivées du tourisme récepteur est basée sur une combinaison de statistiques du logement et statistiques de l'enquête aux frontières (tel que calculé par le Compte satellite du tourisme);
(2) Touristes non résidants séjournant dans des établissements commerciaux uniquement (représentant environ 25 % de l'ensemble des touristes (élément 1.2));
(3) Source: Compte satellite du tourisme (CST) – méthodologie CST: RCC 2008, nombre d'établissements y compris le nombre de personnes travaillant pour leur propre compte dans des industries touristiques comparables à l'échelon international;
(4) Services culturels, sportifs et de loisirs;
(5) Compte satellite du tourisme (CST) – méthodologie CST: RCC 2008, industries touristiques comparables à l'échelon international;

(6) Enquête sur les foyers. Nombre de voyages touristiques internes ou à l'étranger pendant une période de 15 ans / nombre de résidants pendant la période de 15 ans.

«Statistical Office of the Slovak Republic» et «National Bank of Slovakia»
www.statistics.sk
www.nbs.sk/en/home
www.telecom.gov.sk/index/index.php?ids=103017&lang=en

SLOVÉNIE

(1) Source: Enquête sur l'hébergement;
(2) Y compris autres pays d'Asie;
(3) Agrégats issus d'une enquête sur le logement, pourcentages issus de 3 enquêtes annuelles sur les touristes étrangers en Slovénie;
(4) Source: 3 enquêtes annuelles sur les touristes étrangers en Slovénie;
(5) Source: Enquête sur les voyages de la population nationale (comme les méthodologies sont différentes, des différences peuvent apparaître entre les statistiques sur les nuitées mensuelles et les données issues de l'enquête sur les ménages);
(6) Seuls les voyages d'ordre privé sont pris en compte;
(7) L'unité de mesure est la nuitée;
(8) Source: statistiques structurelles sur les entreprises;
(9) L'hébergement du secteur privé (chambres à louer, résidences), les fermes d'hôtes, les refuges de montagne, les centres de vacances d'entreprise et les centres pour la jeunesse sont exclus;
(10) Comprend uniquement les lits permanents;
(11) Source: Registre statistique de l'emploi;
(12) Les données sur le nombre de postes équivalents plein temps ne sont pas disponibles. En remplacement, l'indicateur est basé sur le nombre d'emplois.

«Statistical Office – Tourism Statistics, Structual Business Statistics, Statistical register of employment» et «Bank of Slovenia»
www.stat.si

SOUDAN

(1) Y compris les nationaux résidant à l'étranger.

«Ministry of Tourism and Wildlife»

SRI LANKA

(1) À l'exclusion des nationaux résidant à l'étranger;
(2) Hôtels, motels, auberges, pensions de famille et apart-hôtels;
(3) Hôtels et restaurants.

«Sri Lanka Tourist Board»
www.sltda.lk/statistics

SUÈDE

(1) Données pour 2011–2014 d'après la nouvelle enquête aux frontières nationales (IBIS, visiteurs entrant en Suède). Source: Agence suédoise pour la croissance économique et régionale. Pas de données recueillies en 2015;

NOTES DES PAYS

(2) Hôtels seulement;
(3) Dû à un changement de fournisseur de données, les statistiques du tourisme interne et émetteur ne sont pas disponibles pour 2014–2015;
(4) Nombre d'emplois équivalents à temps plein.

« Swedish Agency for Economic and Regional Growth – Tillväxtverket »
www.tillvaxtverket.se/english
www.scb.se/en_/

SUISSE

(1) Hôtels et établissements assimilés (y compris les établissements de cure);
(2) Y compris motifs inconnus;
(3) Données peu fiables, non publiées;
(4) Y compris modes de transports inconnus;
(5) Établissements enquêtés;
(6) Chambres enquêtées;
(7) Places-lit enquêtées;
(8) Taux d'occupation nets;
(9) Emplois équivalents à temps plein.

« Swiss Federal Statistical Office »
www.bfs.admin.ch/bfs/portal/fr/index/themen/10.html

SURINAME

« Suriname Tourism Foundation »
www.surinametourism.sr/#!en&events-more&statistics

SWAZILAND

« Swaziland Tourism Authority » et « Ministry of Tourism and Environmental Affairs »
www.thekingdomofswaziland.com/pages/content/index.asp?PageID=57

TADJIKISTAN

« Committee of Youth Affairs, Sports and Tourism under the Government of the Republic of Tajikistan »

TANZANIE (RÉPUBLIQUE UNIE DE)

(1) En transit.

« Tourism Division – Ministry of Natural Resources and Tourism » et « National Bureau of Statistics »

TCHAD

Ministère du Tourisme et de l'Artisanat – Direction de la Planification et des Études Prospectives

---

THAÏLANDE

(1) À l'exclusion des arrivées des nationaux résidant à l'étranger;
(2) Y compris chemin de fer;
(3) Jours.

« Ministry of Tourism and Sports »
www.tourism.go.th/home

TIMOR-LESTE

(1) Arrivées par voie aérienne à l'aéroport de Dili;
(2) Enquête dans les hôtels (20 chambres ou plus).

« Statistics Timor-Leste – General Directorate of Statistics »
www.statistics.gov.tl/category/survey-indicators/quarterly-statistical-indicators/

TOGO

(1) Touristes non résidents séjournant dans les hôtels et établissements assimilés;
(2) 2013–2015 : y compris les nationaux résidant à l'étranger;
(3) Á l'exclusion des nationaux résidant à l'étranger.

Ministère du Tourisme

TONGA

(1) Arrivées par voie aérienne;
(2) Y compris les croisièristes et passagers en yacht et membres des équipages.

« Ministry of Commerce, Tourism and Labour »
www.spc.int/prism/tonga/

TRINITÉ-ET-TOBAGO

(1) Arrivées par voie aérienne;
(2) Enquête faite au départ des visiteurs. Source : « Central Statistical Office »;
(3) Enquête sur le tourisme interne, laquelle est conduite tous les 2 ans.

« Tourism Development Company Limited »
www.tdc.co.tt/index.php/research

TUNISIE

(1) À l'exclusion des nationaux résidant à l'étranger;
(2) Hôtels homologués et non-homologués, pensions et villages de vacances.

Ministère du Tourisme – Office National du Tourisme et Institut National de la Statistique
www.ins.nat.tn/indexfr.php

TURQUIE

(1) Y compris les citoyens turcs résidant à l'étranger;
(2) Arrivées par mer;
(3) Enquête faite au départ des visiteurs effectué aux portes d'embarquement;
(4) Enquête auprès des établissements d'hébergement autorisés par le Ministère du Tourisme;
(5) Y compris les terrains de camping;
(6) Y compris les dépenses des nationaux résidant à l'étranger;

NOTES DES PAYS

(7)   Source: «Turkstat Household Domestic Tourism Survey»;
(8)   Hôtels homologués; à l'exclusion des terrains de camping.
(9)   Source: Turkstat Labour Force Survey;
(10) NACE 55;
(11) NACE 56;
(12) NACE 491, 4932, 4939, 501, 503, 511;
(13) NACE 79.

«Ministry of Culture and Tourism»
http://sgb.kulturturizm.gov.tr/belge/1-90750/turizm-istatistikleri.html
www.turkstat.gov.tr/PreTablo.do?alt_id=1072

TUVALU

(1)   2015 Source: «South Pacific Tourism Organisation – Regional Tourism Resource Centre»

«Ministry of Foreign Affairs, Trade, Tourism, Environment and Labour.» et «2015 Source: South Pacific Tourism Organisation – Regional Tourism Resource Centre»

UKRAINE

«State Statistics Committee of Ukraine»
www.ukrstat.gov.ua/operativ/operativ2007/tyr/tyr_e/arh_vig_e.html

URUGUAY

(1)   À l'exclusion des croisiéristes;
(2)   Y compris chemin de fer;
(3)   Jours;
(4)   Considérant le premier voyage uniquement;
(5)   Source: «INE»;
(6)   La méthodologie a été modifiée et pour cela, à partir de 2012 les données ne sont pas comparables avec celles des années précédentes;
(7)   Services immobiliers;
(8)   Pour des raisons méthodologiques, seul le premier emploi est pris en considération. Temps complet = 40 heures hebdomadaires ou plus.

«Ministerio de Turismo y Deporte»
www.mintur.gub.uy/index.php/es/estadistica

VANUATU

(1)   Croisiéristes uniquement;
(2)   Durée de séjour prévue.

«Vanuatu National Statistics Office»
www.vnso.gov.vu/

VENEZUELA (RÉPUBLIQUE BOLIVARIENNE DU)

(1)   Nuitées;
(2)   Hôtels uniquement.

«Ministerio del Poder Popular para el Turismo»
www.mintur.gob.ve/mintur/turismo-en-cifras-2/

VIET NAM

(1)   Y compris les nationaux résidant à l'étranger;
(2)   Y compris les arrivées de croisiéristes et par voie maritime;
(3)   Les chiffres de dépense sont ceux que le pays a fournis à l'OMT mais ils ne figurent pas dans les données du Fonds monétaire international qui ont servi à la préparation de la présente édition du Compendium.

«Viet Nam National Administration of Tourism» et «General Statistics Office»
www.vietnamtourism.com/en/index.php/news
www.gso.gov.vn/default_en.aspx?tabid=491

YEMEN

(1)   Y compris les nationaux résidant à l'étranger.

«Ministry of Tourism» et «Central Statistical Organization»
www.yementourism.com/statistics/
www.cso-yemen.org/content.php?lng=english&pcat=131

ZAMBIE

«Ministry of Tourism and Arts»

ZIMBABWE

(1)   2014, 2015: y compris les visiteurs en transit qui passent au moins une nuit;
(2)   Les chiffres de dépense sont ceux que le pays a fournis à l'OMT mais ils ne figurent pas dans les données du Fonds monétaire international qui ont servi à la préparation de la présente édition du Compendium;
(3)   Le pays n'a pas encore réalisé d'enquête sur le marché interne et émetteur pour obtenir les indicateurs qui lui manquent sur le tourisme interne et émetteur;
(4)   Sur la base des arrivées dans les parcs nationaux et les musées nationaux;
(5)   Hôtels classés uniquement.

«Zimbabwe Tourism Authority – ZTA»
www.zimbabwetourism.net/index.php/trends-statistics/

Notas de los países

ALBANIA

(1) Excluidos los nacionales residentes en el extranjero;
(2) Incluidos los visitantes en tránsito;
(3) Fuente: Encuesta a corto plazo. Hoteles únicamente;
(4) 2011: la clasificación utilizada es NACE Rev. 1.1 (Nomenclatura de actividades económicas). A partir de 2012, la clasificación utilizada para SBS es NACE Rev. 2;
(5) Valor añadido a precios básicos;
(6) Total de inversiones;
(7) Las cifras son actualizadas con la encuesta sobre la estructura de negocios;
(8) Incluye todas las empresas clasificadas en NACE 55 y 56 de NACE Rev. 2;
(9) Incluye todas las empresas clasificadas en NACE 46, 50 o 51 de NACE Rev. 2;
(10) Incluye todas las empresas clasificadas en NACE 79 de NACE Rev. 2.

«Institute of Statistics – INSTAT»
www.instat.gov.al/

ALEMANIA

(1) Turistas no residentes alojados en todo tipo de establecimientos de alojamiento;
(2) Fuente: Eurostat;
(3) Turismo receptor, hoteles y establecimientos asimilados.

«Statistiches Bundesamt»
www.destatis.de

ANDORRA

(1) En 2009 y 2011 se produjeron cambios en la metodología de cálculo del número de visitantes del país. En éste sentido, la comparabilidad de los datos obtenidos con diferentes metodologías no es posible porque las variaciones recogen la variación del número de visitantes, pero también las variaciones motivadas por los cambios metodológicos.

Ministerio de Turismo y Medio Ambiente y Ministerio de Finanzas
www.estadistica.ad/serveiestudis/web/index.asp?lang=2

ANGOLA

(1) Hoteles únicamente.

«Ministério de Hotelaria e Turismo – Gabinete de Estudos, Planeamento e Estatística»

ANGUILA

(1) Excluidos los nacionales residentes en el extranjero;
(2) Incluidos los visitantes del día (excursionistas);
(3) Fuente: «Visitor exit survey».

«Anguilla Statistics Department – Ministry of Finance, Economic Development, Investment, Commerce and Tourism»
www.gov.ai/statistics/cab_external.htm

ANTIGUA Y BARBUDA

(1) Excluidas las llegadas de pasajeros en yate;
(2) Llegadas por vía aérea; excluidos los nacionales residentes en el extranjero;
(3) Pasajeros en crucero únicamente.

«Ministry of Tourism»
http://members.antiguahotels.org/tourism-statistics-for-antigua-and-barbuda/

ARABIA SAUDITA

(1) Fuente: (IVS), MAS Center;
(2) Noches;
(3) Servicio de esparcimiento;
(4) 2012, 2013: estimado por el MAS Center.

«The Saudi Commission for Tourism and Antiquities (SCTA)»
www.mas.gov.sa/en/Pages/default.aspx

ARGELIA

(1) Incluidos los nacionales residentes en el extranjero;
(2) Excluidos los nacionales residentes en el extranjero.

«Ministère de l'Aménagement du Territoire, du Tourisme et de l'Artisanat» y «Office National des Statistiques»

ARGENTINA

(1) Cambio de metodología a partir de 2013. Los datos no son comparables con los de años anteriores;
(2) Encuesta de ocupación hotelera (EOH);
(3) Encuesta de Viajes y Turismo de los Hogares (EVyTH);
(4) Cabe mencionar que se realizó un cambio en la metodología empleada años anteriores en el análisis del Empleo en el sector turístico. El análisis antecedente se basaba en una sola Encuesta que abarcaba 32 aglomerados urbanos. En el análisis actual, en cambio, los resultados surgen de una síntesis que se nutre de la información más sustantiva para el sector, contiene distintas fuentes de información que proporcionan datos sobre empleo en el país en toda su extensión y presenta mayor precisión de los agregados que componen las ramas características del turismo. Esta nueva metodología está disponible a partir del año 2010;
(5) La clasificación incluye Empleados Estatales y Privados, realicen o no Descuentos y Aportes Previsionales (formales o informales);
(6) Constituido por las categorías ocupacionales: Patrón, Cuenta Propia Formal y Cuenta Propia Informal.

Dirección de Estudios de Mercado y Estadística – Secretaría de Turismo de la Nación
www.turismo.gov.ar/
http://desarrolloturistico.gob.ar/estadistica/ultimas-cifras

NOTAS DE LOS PAÍSES

ARMENIA

« Tourism Department – Ministry of Economy of the Republic of Armenia »
www.armstat.am/en/

ARUBA

(1)   Llegadas por vía aérea ;
(2)   Pasajeros en crucero únicamente.

« Aruba Tourism Authority »
www.cbs.aw/index.php/statistics/tables-statistics/68-tables/tourism

AUSTRALIA

(1)   Excluidos los nacionales residentes en el extranjero y miembros de tripulaciones ;
(2)   Fuente : « Tourism Research Australia – National Visitor Survey (NVS) » ;
(3)   Hoteles, moteles, casas de huéspedes y apartamentos de servicio hotelero con 15 habitaciones o más. A Junio. Fuente : « Cat 8635.0 Tourist Accommodation Australia, Table 1 » ;
(4)   Fuente : « Cat. 5249.0 – Australian National Accounts : Tourism Satellite Account, Table 14 Direct Tourism Employment by Industry ».

« Australian Bureau of Statistics »
www.abs.gov.au/

AUSTRIA

(1)   Turistas no residentes alojados en todo tipo de establecimientos de alojamiento ;
(2)   Únicamente alojamiento de pago ; excluidas las estancias con amigos y familiares y las viviendas secundarias ;
(3)   Hoteles únicamente ;
(4)   Viajes al extranjero por vacaciones y negocios con al menos una pernoctación, incluye estancias con amigos y familiares y viviendas secundarias ;
(5)   Basado en la temporada de verano (mayo-octubre) ;
(6)   Datos de la Cuenta Satélite de Turismo (CST) ;
(7)   Equivalentes a tiempo completo.

« Statistics Austria »
www.statistik.at/web_en/statistics/tourism/accommodation/index.html

AZERBAIYÁN

« Ministry of Culture and Tourism » y « Statistical Committee »
www.stat.gov.az

BAHAMAS

(1)   Llegadas en hoteles únicamente ;
(2)   Hoteles, apartamentos, bungalows y villas – Establecimientos clasificados únicamente.

« Bahamas Ministry of Tourism »
www.tourismtoday.com/home/statistics/

BAHREIN

(1)   Excluidos los nacionales residentes en el extranjero ;
(2)   Llegadas al aeropuerto internacional de Bahrein ;
(3)   Llegadas al puerto Mina Salman ;
(4)   Llegadas a través del « King Fahad Causeway » ;
(5)   Hoteles clasificados únicamente.

« Tourism Sector – Ministry of Culture and Information » y « Information and eGovernment Authority »

BANGLADESH

« Bangladesh Bureau of Statistics (BBS) »

BARBADOS

(1)   Hoteles, aparthoteles, apartamentos y bungalows, casas de huéspedes.

« Barbados Tourism Marketing Inc »
www.tourism.gov.bb/tourism-publications.html

BELARÚS

(1)   Turistas no residentes alojados en todo tipo de establecimientos de alojamiento ;
(2)   Paquete turístico ;
(3)   Únicamente grupos principales ;
(4)   Los datos se basan en la observación estadística que hace el estado sobre el número de empleados en establecimientos de alojamiento colectivo y agencias de viajes.

« State Border Committee » y « National Statistical Committee of the Republic of Belarus »

BÉLGICA

(1)   Turistas no residentes alojados en todo tipo de establecimientos de alojamiento ;
(2)   Debido a un cambio de metodología, a partir de 2015 los datos no son comparables con los de años anteriores ;
(3)   Hoteles únicamente ;
(4)   Hoteles y poblados de vacaciones. A partir de 2012 se incluye « bed and breakfast ».

« Institut National de Statistique »

BELICE

« Belize Tourist Board »

BENIN

« Direction du développement et de promotion touristiques – Ministère de la culture, de l'alphabétisation, de l'artisanat et du tourisme »

501

NOTAS DE LOS PAÍSES

BERMUDAS

(1) Excluidos los nacionales residentes en el extranjero;
(2) Llegadas por vía aérea;
(3) Pasajeros en crucero;
(4) Incluidas las pernoctaciones en casas particulares.

«Bermuda Department of Tourism»
www.gov.bm/portal/server.
CommunityPage&control=SetCommunity&CommunityID=227

BHUTÁN

(1) Total de llegadas 2011: 65.756; 2012: 105.407; 2013: 116.209; 2014: 134.254; 2015: 155.121. El gran margen de diferencia en 2011–2015 en comparación con los años anteriores se debe a que a partir de 2010 se incluyen en las cifras totales los turistas regionales de alto nivel de renta;
(2) Datos provisionales.

«Department of Tourism – Royal Government of Bhutan»
www.nsb.gov.bt/index.php?id=13
www.tourism.gov.bt/annual-reports/bhutan-tourism-monitor

BOLIVIA (ESTADO PLURINACIONAL DE)

(1) Datos preliminares;
(2) Información obtenida a través de la estructura porcentual determinada en la Encuesta «Gasto del Turismo Receptor y Emisor»;
(3) Llegadas por vía lacustre;
(4) El 7,6% de los viajeros corresponde a turismo organizado;
(5) Fuente: Encuesta «Gasto del Turismo Receptor y Emisor»;
(6) Capitales de departamento únicamente;
(7) Tamaño promedio grupos de viaje en familia: 2,8 personas.

Nota:
Los indicadores de turismo son obtenidos a partir de la relación de los resultados de la encuesta «Gasto del Turismo Receptor y Emisor» entre las estadísticas de Comercio Exterior, Servicios de la Balanza de Pagos, Cuentas Nacionales (PIB), determinando la participación del turismo en cada uno de los sectores.

Instituto Nacional de Estadística
www.ine.gob.bo/default.aspx

BOSNIA Y HERZEGOVINA

(1) Turistas no residentes alojados en todo tipo de establecimientos de alojamiento;
(2) 2011, 2012: menos de 500 llegadas;
(3) Los datos se obtienen del informe estadístico de 2015 sobre tráfico transfronterizo de pasajeros e incluye el total de llegadas de pasajeros no residentes en las fronteras nacionales. Los pasajeros en tránsito están incluidos;
(4) Datos de la encuesta estadística mensual RAD.

«Agency for Statistics of Bosnia and Herzegovina»
www.bhas.ba

BOTSWANA

(1) Incluye a los residentes que regresan.

«Department of Tourism – Ministry of Environment, Wildlife and Tourism»

BRASIL

(1) Incluidos los nacionales residentes en el extranjero;
(2) Incluidas las llegadas por vía fluvial;
(3) Los datos se refieren a «Encuesta Anual de Servicios (PAS) 2013, do Instituto Brasileiro de Estatísticas e Geografia – IBGE»;
(4) 2011: los datos se refieren a «Pesquisa de Serviços de Hospedagem (PSH) do Instituto Brasileiro de Estatísticas e Geografia – IBGE». 2013–2015: los datos reflejan el número de prestadores de servicios turísticos regularmente registrados en el Sistema de Registro de Empresas, equipamientos y profesionales del área de turismo (Cadastur), que informaron ejercer la actividad de proveedor de servicios de infraestructuras para eventos. Cada proveedor de servicios puede inscribirse en más de una actividad;
(5) Relación Anual de Informaciones Sociales (RAIS) – 2014 – Ministério do Trabalho; Asalariados formales: registrados y cubiertos por la seguridad social – Encuesta Nacional de Hogares – 2014 – IBGE – Asalariados informales: no registrados y no cubiertos por la seguridad social.

«Ministério do Turismo»
www.dadosefatos.turismo.gov.br/dadosefatos/home.html

BRUNEI DARUSSALAM

(1) Llegadas por vía aérea.

«Brunei Tourism – Ministry of Industry and Primary Resources»

BULGARIA

(1) Visitantes en tránsito;
(2) Fuente: «Eurostat»;
(3) Hoteles únicamente.

«National Statistical Institute, Bulgarian National Bank and Ministry of Tourism»
www.nsi.bg

BURKINA FASO

(1) Turistas no residentes alojados en hoteles y establecimientos asimilados;
(2) Incluido el turismo interno.

«Service de l'analyse statistique et de la Coopération touristique – Ministère de la Culture, des Arts et du Tourisme»
www.insd.bf/

NOTAS DE LOS PAÍSES

BURUNDI

(1) Incluidos los nacionales residentes en el extranjero;
(2) Llegadas por vía lacustre.

«Office National du Tourisme»

CABO VERDE

(1) Turistas no residentes alojados en hoteles y establecimientos asimilados.

«Instituto Nacional de Estatística» y «Ministério da Economia, Crescimento e Competitividade»
www.ine.cv/dadostats/dados.aspx?d=2

CAMBOYA

(1) Llegadas por todo el conjunto de medios de transporte;
(2) Llegadas por barco;
(3) Días.

«Ministry of Tourism»
www.tourismcambodia.org/mot/index.php?view=statistic_report#comp

---

CAMERÚN

(1) Turistas no residentes alojados en hoteles y establecimientos asimilados.

«Ministère du Tourisme»

CANADÁ

(1) Datos basados en la contabilidad aduanera, ajustándola en función de los resultados de las encuestas;
(2) En 2011, se llevó a cabo una encuesta nacional rediseñada (encuesta sobre viajes de los residentes de Canadá), causante de una ruptura en la serie cronológica. Por consiguiente, los puntos correspondientes a los datos de 2011 no son comparables con los de años anteriores;
(3) Las salidas se calculan a partir de las llegadas de residentes canadienses que vuelven desde el extranjero;
(4) Las rúbricas 5.13 y 5.14 se calculan utilizando la media de horas trabajadas en empleos de jornada completa por hombres y mujeres respectivamente.

«Canadian Tourism Commission» y «Statistics Canada»
http://en-corporate.canada.travel/research/statistics-figures

---

CHAD

«Ministère du Tourisme et de l'Artisanat – Direction de la Planification et des Études Prospectives»

CHILE

(1) Incluidos los nacionales residentes en el extranjero;
(2) Pasajeros en crucero mas convenio Arica-Tacna;
(3) Debido a un cambio de metodología, a partir de 2014 los datos no son comparables con los de años anteriores;

(4) Excluido camping;
(5) A partir de 2012 el paquete turístico es estimado sólo por vía aeropuertos;
(6) Fuente: SII (Servicio de Impuestos Internos);
(7) 2015: datos estimados.

Subsecretaría de Turismo – Ministerio de Economía, Fomento y Turismo
www.sernatur.cl/estadisticas/

CHINA

(1) Incluidas las llegadas de personas de origen étnico chino procedentes de «Hong Kong (China)», «Macao (China)», «Taiwán (Provincia de China)» y de ultramar, la mayor parte de excursionistas proceden de «Hong Kong (China)» y «Macao (China)»;
(2) Excluidas las llegadas de turistas de origen étnico chino procedentes de «Hong Kong (China)», «Macao (China)», «Taiwán (Provincia de China)» y de ultramar;
(3) A pie;
(4) Incluidos los miembros de las tripulaciones y otros miembros de las fuerzas armadas;
(5) Hoteles clasificados con estrellas únicamente;
(6) Turismo receptor únicamente.

«National Tourism Administration»
http://en.cnta.gov.cn/

CHIPRE

(1) Fuente: Encuesta de pasajeros, realizada por el Servicio estadístico de Chipre «Statistical Service of Cyprus»;
(2) Incluidos los pasajeros en crucero y en tránsito;
(3) Los datos de 2012 y 2013 se refieren únicamente a once meses ya que los datos de marzo 2012 y enero 2013 no están disponibles;
(4) Incluidos los pasajeros en tránsito;
(5) Los datos sobre alojamiento (llegadas, pernoctaciones y tasas de ocupación) los recopila mensualmente entre los establecimientos de alojamiento turístico autorizados y los produce la C.T.O.;
(6) Los datos relativos a los hoteles y establecimientos asimilados han sido revisados a partir de 2010 para incluir la categoría de villas turísticas bajo «establecimientos asimilados». Antes de esta revisión, las villas turísticas estaban incluidas en «otros establecimientos colectivos» (bajo la sección «alojamiento de vacaciones»);
(7) Gasto medio por día calculado dividiendo el gasto total (punto 1.33) por el número total de visitantes receptores que pernoctan (punto 1.2) y la duración media de su estancia (punto 1.40);
(8) Los cálculos de la duración media de la estancia se basan en las pernoctaciones y las llegadas registradas en establecimientos de alojamiento turístico autorizados;
(9) Gasto medio por día calculado dividiendo el gasto total (punto 3.4) por el número total de visitantes emisores que pernoctan (punto 3.2) y la duración media de su estancia (punto 3.10);
(10) Datos extraídos de las estadísticas de hoteles y restaurantes, derivadas de la encuesta sobre servicios llevada a cabo por el Servicio de Estadísticas de Chipre. Se refieren al código 55 de la NACE Rev. 2;
(11) Datos extraídos de las estadísticas de hoteles y restaurantes, derivadas de la encuesta sobre servicios llevada a cabo por el Servicio de Estadísticas de Chipre.

503

NOTAS DE LOS PAÍSES

En los puntos 4.3 y 5.2, los datos comunicados se refieren a empresas turísticas que se integran en los códigos 55101 y 55102 de la NACE Rev.2;

(12) Datos extraídos de las estadísticas de hoteles y restaurantes, derivadas de la encuesta sobre servicios llevada a cabo por el Servicio de Estadísticas de Chipre. Se refieren al código 56 de la NACE Rev. 2.;

(13) Número de agencias de viaje (código 4.6) y datos monetarios (puntos 4.20-4.24): datos extraídos de las estadísticas sobre servicios empresariales, derivadas de la encuesta sobre servicios llevada a cabo por el Servicio de Estadísticas de Chipre. Se refiere al código 79 de la NACE Rev. 2;

(14) Los datos monetarios comunicados para los puntos 4.8-4.12 proceden de las estadísticas de hoteles y restaurantes, derivadas de la encuesta sobre servicios que lleva a cabo el Servicio de Estadísticas de Chipre y corresponden a hoteles y empresas turísticas similares incluidas en los códigos 55101 y 55102 de la NACE Rev.2.;

(15) Los datos no monetarios los compila y produce la Organización de Turismo de Chipre (C.T.O.) y se refieren a hoteles con licencia y establecimientos similares de alojamiento turístico. Los datos suministrados difieren de los datos que se muestran en los puntos 4.2-4.3 y 4.8-4.12, que están extraídos de las estadísticas de hoteles y restaurantes, derivadas de la encuesta sobre servicios llevada a cabo por el Servicio de Estadísticas de Chipre. Las diferencias entre los dos conjuntos de datos obedecen a razones tales como el hecho de que la encuesta sobre servicios trata a las empresas o a las personas que poseen u operan más de una unidad de alojamiento turístico (establecimientos) como una entidad, mientras que los datos de la C.T.O. cuentan las unidades de alojamiento, independientemente de que pertenezcan a un propietario o estén dirigidas por un operador;

(16) Los cálculos de la duración media de la estancia se basan en las pernoctaciones y las llegadas registradas en hoteles y en establecimientos de alojamiento turístico similares autorizados (C.T.O.);

(17) Datos extraídos de las estadísticas de hoteles y restaurantes, derivadas de la encuesta sobre servicios llevada a cabo por el Servicio de Estadísticas de Chipre. Se refieren a los códigos 5520+, 5530+ y 5590 de la NACE Rev. 2.
Nota para todos los datos suministrados: No está incluida la información sobre las actividades inmobiliarias realizadas con bienes propios o arrendados y las actividades inmobiliarias realizadas a cambio de una retribución o por contrato.

«Statistical Service of Cyprus», «Cyprus Tourism Organization» y «Central Bank of Cyprus»
www.mof.gov.cy/mof/cystat/statistics.nsf/index_en/index_en?OpenDocument

COLOMBIA

(1) Llegadas de viajeros no residentes por puntos de control migratorio;

(2) Incluidos transfronterizos ('000): 2011: 999; 2012: 1.063; 2013: 1.153; 2014: 1.313; 2015: 1.197;

(3) Incluidos los nacionales residentes en el extranjero;

(4) Excluidos transfronterizos y pasajeros en crucero;

(5) Excluidos los nacionales residentes en el extranjero.
Nota: datos provisionales.

Migración Colombia / Sociedades portuarias / Dirección de Análisis Sectorial y Promoción – Ministerio de Comercio, Industria y Turismo (MINCIT)
www.mincit.gov.co/publicaciones.php?id=16590

CONGO

(1) Encuestas de 2011 a 2015;

(2) Incluidos los nacionales residentes en el extranjero. Total 2011: 45.800;

(3) Encuestas 2011 a 2013;

(4) Fuente: «Banque des Etats d'Afrique Centrale (B.E.A.C)». 2012, 2013: estimaciones.
Nota 2015: estimaciones.

«Direction Générale du Tourisme et de l'Hôtellerie – Ministère du tourisme et de l'environnement»

CONGO (REPÚBLICA DEMOCRÁTICA DEL)

(1) Los datos de llegadas se refieren sólo a 3 puestos fronterizos (aeropuerto de N'Djili, en Kinshasa; aeropuerto de Luano, en Lubumbashi, y puesto terrestre de Kasumbalesa, en la provincia de Katanga).

«Office National du Tourisme»

COREA (REPÚBLICA DE)

(1) Incluidos los nacionales residentes en el extranjero y miembros de las tripulaciones;

(2) Incluidos los nacionales residentes en el extranjero y los miembros de las tripulaciones;

(3) El país facilita a la OMT niveles agregados de gasto que son significativamente diferentes a los datos del Fondo Monetario Internacional utilizados para la preparación de esta edición del Compendio (excluidos los gastos de los estudiantes que realizan sus estudios fuera del país). Los datos del país son (Mill. $EE.UU.): 2011: 15.544; 2012: 15.737.

(4) Hoteles únicamente.

«Ministry of Culture, Sports and Tourism»
http://kto.visitkorea.or.kr/eng/tourismStatics/keyFacts/visitorArrivals.kto

COSTA RICA

(1) Encuestas de No Residentes en los Aeropuertos Internacionales, ICT;

(2) Encuesta de Hospedaje, Departamento de Estadística Macroeconómica, BCCR;

(3) Empleo en la industria turística, Encuesta Continua de Empleo (ECE), INEC.

Banco Central de Costa Rica (BCCR), Instituto Costarricense de Turismo (ICT) y Instituto Nacional de Estadística y Censos (INEC)
www.visitcostarica.com/ict/paginas/modEst/informes_estadisticos.asp

NOTAS DE LOS PAÍSES

CÔTE D´IVOIRE

(1) 2011–2014: llegadas al aeropuerto Félix Houphouët Boigny únicamente. 2015: ruptura de serie: las cifras incluyen las llegadas por vía terrestre (carretera y ferrocarril).

«Ministère du Tourisme»

CROACIA

(1) Turistas no residentes alojados en todo tipo de establecimientos de alojamiento;
(2) El total de establecimientos solo incluye los establecimientos de alojamiento colectivo turístico. Debido a la implantación del nuevo fundamento jurídico de la supervisión de los turistas, desde 2010, los puertos náuticos no se consideran como unidades informantes o tipos de instalación para alojamiento en la encuesta mensual sobre llegadas y pernoctaciones de turistas. En respuesta a este cambio en la metodología, se revisaron los datos correspondientes al periodo 2005–2009 para que pudieran compararse con los de 2010 (excluyéndose los puertos náuticos);
(3) Incluye pasajeros en tránsito que viajan por carretera;
(4) Datos de la encuesta sobre el tráfico en aeropuertos, todas las llegadas internacionales;
(5) Datos de la encuesta sobre tráfico en puertos de mar, todas las llegadas internacionales. Incluye pasajeros de cruceros;
(6) Datos de la encuesta sobre transporte ferroviario de pasajeros, incluye todas las llegadas internacionales por ferrocarril;
(7) Los datos incluyen el total de llegadas por carretera a las fronteras nacionales de pasajeros no residentes, incluidos los pasajeros en tránsito;
(8) Los datos no incluyen el número de hogares que alquilan un alojamiento turístico (habitaciones de alquiler, apartamentos, estudios y casas de vacaciones);
(9) Fuente: «CBS, Survey on Tourist Activity of Croatian Population»;
(10) 2015: datos provisionales;
(11) La aplicación del nuevo Reglamento obligó a introducir cambios en la metodología de recopilación de datos para los siguientes tipos de instalaciones de alojamiento: habitaciones en alquiler, apartamentos, estudios y casas de verano. Desde 2013, las unidades encargadas de presentar los datos han sido las oficinas de turismo, independientemente de si las instalaciones fueron alquiladas por entidades jurídicas, comerciantes o familias. Los datos sobre instalaciones de alojamiento se consideran provisionales por el hecho de que el registro no está aún debidamente organizado en todas las oficinas de turismo;
(12) Debido al constante proceso de categorización, hay cambios en los tipos y categorías de instalación de alojamiento;
(13) Según el Reglamento sobre clasificación, normas mínimas y categorización de las instalaciones de alojamiento, los datos para los hoteles y establecimientos asimilados no incluyen posadas ni «Bed and Breakfast» (habitación con desayuno) desde 2006;
(14) Desde 2013, el método para presentar la capacidad ha sido modificado (ya no se hace el seguimiento en relación con la situación al 31 de agosto), lo cual concuerda con el Reglamento Nº 692/2011 del Parlamento Europeo y del Consejo relativo a las estadísticas europeas sobre turismo. En virtud de la aplicación de dicho Reglamento,

la capacidad de un establecimiento de alojamiento se estima en el mes en que ha alcanzado su valor máximo;
(15) Tasa bruta de ocupación;
(16) La clasificación utilizada es NACE Rev. 2.

«Croatian Bureau of Statistics»
www.dzs.hr/default_e.htm
www.mint.hr/default.aspx?id=363»

CUBA

(1) Llegadas por vía aérea;
(2) Hoteles, moteles, aparthoteles, terrenos para camping/caravanas y otros;
(3) Hoteles, moteles y aparthoteles;
(4) Las cifras de gasto corresponden a las facilitadas por el país a la OMT y que, sin embargo, no figuran en los datos del Fondo Monetario Internacional utilizados para la preparación de esta edición del Compendio;
(5) Comprende sólo giras controladas por el Instituto del Turismo.

Oficina Nacional de Estadística e Información
www.one.cu/sitioone2006.asp

CURAÇAO

(1) Llegadas por vía aérea;
(2) Diferencias en los totales globales debido a la falta de datos completos en las tarjetas de embarque y desembarque de los visitantes;
(3) Llegadas de pasajeros en crucero;
(4) Grandes y pequeños hoteles, casas de huéspedes, apartamentos y bungalows;
(5) Hoteles, casas de huéspedes y apartamentos.

«Curaçao Tourist Board»
www.curacao.com/en/directory/corporate/statistics-and-downloads/

DINAMARCA

(1) 2011, 2014: cambio de metodología;
(2) Turistas no residentes alojados en todo tipo de establecimientos de alojamiento;
(3) Incluye el turismo no comercial;
(4) Hoteles únicamente;
(5) Las cifras de gasto corresponden a las facilitadas por el país a la OMT y que, sin embargo, no figuran en los datos del Fondo Monetario Internacional utilizados para la preparación de esta edición del Compendio. Fuente: «VisitDenmark»;
(6) Fuente: Eurostat;
(7) Únicamente hoteles y alojamientos de vacaciones con 40 camas o más.

«VisitDenmark» y «Statistics Denmark»
www.dst.dk/HomeUK.aspx

DJIBOUTI

(1) Turistas no residentes alojados en hoteles.

«Office national du tourisme»

NOTAS DE LOS PAÍSES

DOMINICA

(1)   Días.

«Discover Dominica Authority»
http://tourism.gov.dm/statistics

ECUADOR

(1)   Excluidos los nacionales residentes en el extranjero;
(2)   2015: datos provisionales.

Ministerio de Turismo
http://servicios.turismo.gob.ec/index.php/portfolio/turismo-cifras

EGIPTO

«Ministry of Tourism», «CAPMAS» y «Central Bank of Egypt»

EL SALVADOR

(1)   Incluido el alojamiento privado.

Corporación Salvadoreña de Turismo (CORSATUR) – Ministerio de Turismo

ESLOVAQUIA

(1)   El número de llegadas del turismo receptor se basa en una combinación de las estadísticas de alojamiento y las estadísticas de encuestas en fronteras (según los cálculos de la Cuenta satélite de turismo);
(2)   Sólo los turistas no residentes que se alojan en establecimientos comerciales (y que representan aproximadamente el 25% del total de turistas [punto 1.2]);
(3)   Fuente: Cuenta satélite de turismo (CST) – metodología CST: RMC 2008, número de establecimientos, incluido el número de trabajadores por cuenta propia en industrias turísticas comparables a nivel internacional;
(4)   Servicios culturales, deportivos y de ocio;
(5)   Cuenta satélite de turismo (CST) – metodología CST: RMC 2008, industrias turísticas comparables a nivel internacional;
(6)   Encuesta de hogares. Número de viajes de turismo interno y emisor durante 15 años / número de residentes durante 15 años.

«Statistical Office of the Slovak Republic» y «National Bank of Slovakia»
www.statistics.sk
www.nbs.sk/en/home
www.telecom.gov.sk/index/index.php?ids=103017&lang=en

ESLOVENIA

(1)   Fuente: encuesta de alojamiento;
(2)   Incluye otros países de Asia;
(3)   Agregados de la encuesta de alojamiento, parte de las encuestas trienales sobre turistas extranjeros en Eslovenia;

(4)   Fuente: encuestas trienales sobre turistas extranjeros en Eslovenia;
(5)   Fuente: encuesta sobre viajes de población nacional (debido a la aplicación de diferentes metodologías, pueden surgir diferencias entre los datos de las estadísticas mensuales de alojamiento y los datos extraídos de las encuestas de hogares);
(6)   Sólo se tienen en cuenta los viajes privados;
(7)   Las noches se utilizan como unidad;
(8)   Fuente: estadísticas estructurales de las empresas;
(9)   No se incluye el alojamiento privado (habitaciones alquiladas, viviendas), las casas de campo turísticas que ofrecen alojamiento, las cabañas de montaña, las instalaciones vacacionales de las empresas y las instalaciones para jóvenes;
(10) Incluye únicamente camas permanentes;
(11) Fuente: Registro estadístico de empleo;
(12) No se dispone de información sobre el número de puestos de trabajo equivalentes a puestos de jornada completa. En su lugar, en este indicador se usa el número de puestos de trabajo.

«Statistical Office – Tourism Statistics, Structual Business Statistics, Statistical register of employment» y «Bank of Slovenia»
www.stat.si

ESPAÑA

(1)   Incluidos los nacionales residentes en el extranjero;
(2)   Hoteles, hostales, terrenos de camping, apartamentos turísticos y alojamientos/casas rurales;
(3)   Hoteles y hostales;
(4)   Fuente: Encuesta Anual de Servicios.

Fuente de los datos:
Hasta 2014 IET: FRONTUR – Encuesta de movimientos turísticos en fronteras; EGATUR – Encuesta de gasto turístico; FAMILITUR – Encuesta de movimientos turísticos de los españoles.
A partir de 2015 INE: ETR/Familitur – Encuesta de turismo de residentes; FRONTUR y EGATUR – 2015: datos provisionales, calculados extrapolando los datos de Turespaña hasta septiembre para calcular los datos de octubre, noviembre y diciembre. Desde octubre de 2015 esta operación la lleva a cabo el INE. La ruptura de serie se producirá el próximo año con los datos de 2016.
INE: Encuestas de ocupación en alojamiento; DIRCE (Directorio central de empresas) – oferta turística – encuesta anual de servicios; Encuesta de población activa.

Instituto Nacional de Estadística y TURESPAÑA
FRONTUR-INE: www.ine.es/jaxi/menu.o?type=pcaxis&path=%2Ft11%2Fp16028&file=inebase&L=0
EGATUR-INE: www.ine.es/jaxi/menu.o?type=pcaxis&path=%2Ft11%2Fp16029&file=inebase&L=0
ETR/Familitur: www.ine.es/jaxi/menu.o?type=pcaxis&path=%2Ft11%2Fp16023&file=inebase&L=0
Encuestas de Ocupación en Alojamientos Turísticos:
www.ine.es/inebmenu/mnu_hosteleria.htm
Datos hasta 2014 de TURESPAÑA:
www.iet.tourspain.es/paginas/home.aspx?idioma=es-ES

NOTAS DE LOS PAÍSES

ESTADO DE PALESTINA

(1) Turistas no residentes alojados en hoteles y establecimientos asimilados;
(2) Cisjordania y Gaza.
Nota: los datos sobre la industria hotelera para 2012–2015 representan a Cisjordania únicamente.
Fuentes: «Palestinian Central Bureau of Statistics. Hotel Activity Survey. Tourism Activities. Palestine Monetary Authority».

«Palestinian Central Bureau of Statistics»
www.pcbs.gov.ps

ESTADOS UNIDOS DE AMÉRICA

(1) A partir de 2014, se han modificado algunos elementos automatizados en la metodología de seguimiento de los visitantes recibidos que han permitido contabilizar con precisión las estancias con una pernoctación. Este cambio ha añadido posiblemente varios puntos porcentuales a los resultados, por lo que los datos de 2014 no son comparables con los de los años previos. Los cambios en 2015 (excepto Canadá y México) reflejan una combinación de registros adicionales contados y condiciones de mercado;
(2) Incluye sólo los viajes del día procedentes de México y Canadá;
(3) Ultramar únicamente; excluido México y Canadá (no disponible);
(4) La redacción del cuestionario se modificó a principios de 2012;
(5) Estimaciones preliminares;
(6) La Oficina de Análisis Económico del Departamento de Comercio de los Estados Unidos llevó a cabo una revisión de gran alcance del sistema de cuentas comerciales en busca de una mayor confluencia con las directrices del Fondo Monetario Internacional. Entre los principales cambios figuran la inclusión de la educación, la atención médica y los trabajadores migrantes o estacionales en las cuentas de exportaciones e importaciones de viajes. Los datos se han ido revisando hasta 1999 y no son comparables con los datos de años anteriores;
(7) 2011–2015: representa el gasto medio por grupo de viaje de los turistas de ultramar, dividido por la duración media de la estancia;
(8) Fuente: «U.S. Travel Association»;
(9) Incluye todos los viajes internos de al menos 50 millas (aproximadamente 80 km) desde el lugar de residencia o cualquier viaje con pernoctación;
(10) Aproximadamente el 50%;
(11) Fuente: «NTTO, Statistics Canada, Banco de Mexico»;
(12) 2011–2015: representa el gasto medio por grupo de viaje de los residentes en EE.UU., dividido por la duración media de la estancia;
(13) Los datos sobre establecimientos proceden del Departamento de Comercio de los Estados Unidos, Oficina del Censo (datos sobre patrones empresariales de los condados [County Business Patterns]) y no son completamente coherentes con otros datos de producción y de empleo. Es la mejor fuente de datos sobre establecimientos;
(14) NAICS 7211, 7212;
(15) NAICS 72111, 72112;
(16) NAICS 722;
(17) Departamento de Comercio de los EE.UU. / Oficina de Análisis Económico;

(18) Fuente: «American Hotel & Lodging Association (AHLA)» (propiedades de más de 15 habitaciones);
(19) Fuente: «Smith Travel Research»;
(20) Puestos de trabajo equivalentes a tiempo completo;
(21) Alojamientos para viajeros;
(22) Servicios de alimentación y lugares donde se sirven bebidas;
(23) Servicios de transporte aéreo y todas las otras industrias relacionadas con el transporte;
(24) Residual.

«U.S. Department of Commerce – National Travel and Tourism Office»
http://travel.trade.gov
www.ahla.com/content.aspx?id=3448

ESTONIA

(1) Basado en los datos de posicionamiento móvil facilitados por el Banco de Estonia y Positium LBS;
(2) Debido a un cambio de metodología, a partir de 2015 los datos no son comparable con los años 2011–2014;
(3) Turistas no residentes alojados en todo tipo de establecimientos de alojamiento;
(4) Debido a un cambio de metodología, a partir de 2014 los datos no son comparable con los años 2011–2013;
(5) Fuente: encuesta de hogares por «Statistics Estonia».

«Estonian Tourist Board / Enterprise Estonia»
http://pub.stat.ee/px-web.2001/I_Databas/Economy/databasetree.asp
http://visitestonia.com/en/additional-navigation/press-room/eas-views-on-tourism/estonian-tourism-statistics

ETIOPÍA

(1) Llegadas a todos los puestos fronterizos; incluidos los nacionales residentes en el extranjero.

«Ministry of Culture and Tourism»

EX REPÚBLICA YUGOSLAVA DE MACEDONIA

(1) Turistas no residentes alojados en todo tipo de establecimientos de alojamiento;
(2) Duración media de la estancia en todos los establecimientos de alojamiento.

«State Statistical Office»
www.stat.gov.mk/OblastOpsto_en.aspx?id=25

FEDERACIÓN DE RUSIA

(1) A pie;
(2) Alojamiento en hoteles y en otros establecimientos turísticos.

«Russian Federal Agency for Tourism»

507

NOTAS DE LOS PAÍSES

FIJI

(1)   Excluidos los nacionales residentes en el extranjero;
(2)   Días.

«Fiji Islands Bureau of Statistics»
www.statsfiji.gov.fj/

FILIPINAS

(1)   Incluidos los nacionales residentes en el extranjero;
(2)   Llegadas por vía aérea;
(3)   Noches;
(4)   Únicamente hoteles en Metro Manila;
(5)   Para 2013, los datos incluyen los establecimientos de alojamiento cuya acreditación ha sido aprobada, tanto si se ha emitido ya el certificado de acreditación como si no se ha emitido aún. Antes de 2013, los datos solo incluían los establecimientos de alojamiento cuyo certificado de acreditación había sido emitido;
(6)   Hoteles clasificados en Metro Manila;
(7)   Sobre la base de las Cuentas satélite de turismo de Filipinas (PTSA) – junio de 2016.

«Department of Tourism»
www.tourism.gov.ph/Pages/TourismResearch.aspx

FINLANDIA

(1)   Encuesta de entrevistas de fronteras. Nota: la encuesta fue cancelada a finales de 2012;
(2)   Encuesta sobre alojamiento;
(3)   Balanza de pagos (BdP);
(4)   Encuesta de viajes finlandesa;
(5)   Incluidos únicamente los viajes internos de ocio en alojamientos para visitantes alquilados;
(6)   Viajes al extranjero con pernoctación, incluidos los cruceros con pernoctación a bordo únicamente;
(7)   Datos de la Cuenta Satélite de Turismo (CST);
(8)   Viajes internos y emisores con pernoctación, incluidos los cruceros con pernoctación a bordo únicamente.

«Tourism Statistics – Statistics Finland»
www.mek.fi/w5/mekfi/index.nsf/(pages)/Tutkimukset_ja_tilastot

FRANCIA

(1)   Fuente: DGE, Banque de France. Encuesta a los visitantes que vienen del extranjero (EVE) – resultados 2011 a 2014 extrapolados, resultados 2015 provisionales;
(2)   Todos los motivos personales;
(3)   Tránsito y sin especificar;
(4)   Fuente: INSEE, DGE, socios regionales. Encuestas de frecuentación hotelera (EFH por su sigla en francés), campings (EFHPA) y, a partir de 2011, otros alojamientos colectivos (EFAHCT) -residencias de turismo y residencias hoteleras, ciudades de vacaciones y albergues juveniles -; ruptura de la serie en 2011; excluidos los alojamientos comerciales individuales (apartamentos amueblados y habitaciones de hotel);
(5)   Fuente: INSEE, DGE, socios regionales. Encuesta de ocupación hotelera (EFH); estancias por todos los motivos;

(6)   Duración media de la estancia en noches;
(7)   Fuente: DGE. Encuesta Seguimiento de la demanda turística (SDT). Población residente de 15 años o más; los desplazamientos en los departamentos de ultramar se cuentan con el extranjero;
(8)   Viajes por motivos personales;
(9)   Parque de alojamiento colectivo de carácter comercial (hoteles, campings, complejos de apartamentos, residencias, parques de vacaciones, casas familiares, albergues juveniles, centros deportivos, centros internacionales de estancia); Fuente: INSEE, DGE, SNRT, UNAT, FUAJ;
(10) Parque hotelero; Fuente: INSEE, DGE;
(11) Campo: empleo asalariado privado en Francia (incluidos los departamentos de ultramar) a 31/12; Fuente: ACOSS;
(12) Alquiler de corta duración de material (automóviles, equipo recreativo y deportivo), actividades de parques de atracciones y parques temáticos y otras actividades de recreo y ocio, gestión de museos, sitios históricos, atractivos turísticos, jardines botánicos y zoológicos y reservas naturales, actividades de juegos de azar y apuestas, teleféricos y remontes mecánicos;
(13) Tasa neta de ocupación de las habitaciones;
(14) Campo: Francia metropolitana; Fuente: INSEE, censo de población para 2010, balance demográfico para 2011–2014.

«DGE (Direction générale des entreprises)» y «INSEE (Institut national de la statistique et des études économiques)»
www.entreprises.gouv.fr/etudes-et-statistiques/statistiques-du-tourisme/accueil
www.insee.fr/fr/default.asp

GAMBIA

(1)   Incluidos los nacionales residentes en el extranjero;
(2)   Llegadas en vuelos fletados únicamente.

«Gambia Tourism Board»

GEORGIA

(1)   Llegadas en hoteles únicamente;
(2)   Fuente: Encuesta de hoteles y establecimientos asimilados;
(3)   NACE Rev. 1.1.;
(4)   Los datos se refieren únicamente a la inversión en capital fijo.

«Georgian National Tourism Agency – Ministry of Economy and Sustainable Development» y «National Statistics Office of Georgia «
http://gnta.ge/statistics/

GHANA

(1)   Incluidos los nacionales residentes en el extranjero;
(2)   Estimaciones.

«Ghana Tourist Board and Ministry of Tourism and Modernisation of the Capital City»
www.statsghana.gov.gh

GRANADA

(1) 2013–2015: llegadas por vía aérea únicamente;
(2) Llegadas en yates y cruceros;
(3) Hoteles, bungalows/ apartamentos y casas de huéspedes.

«Grenada Board of Tourism»

GRECIA

(1) La información se basa en la encuesta en fronteras realizada por el Banco de Grecia;
(2) Número de viajes con 4 o más noches de visitantes de 15 años o más;
(3) Fuente: «Hellenic Chamber of Hotels».

«Hellenic Statistical Authority (EL.STAT.)»
www.statistics.gr/en/statistics/ind

GUADALUPE

(1) Llegadas por vía aérea; excluidas las islas del norte (San Martín y San Barthelemy);
(2) 2014, 2015: llegadas por vía aérea;
(3) Las cifras de gasto corresponden a las facilitadas por el país a la OMT y que, sin embargo, no figuran en los datos del Fondo Monetario Internacional utilizados para la preparación de esta edición del Compendio;
(4) Hoteles.

«Comité du Tourisme des Îles de la Guadeloupe»

GUAM

(1) Llegadas por vías aérea y marítima;
(2) Llegadas de civiles por vía aérea únicamente;
(3) Habitaciones disponibles.

«Guam Visitors Bureau»
www.guamvisitorsbureau.com/research-and-reports/reports/annual-report

GUATEMALA

(1) Serie actualizada desde 2009 con una nueva metodología.
(2) Todos los establecimientos de alojamiento inscritos en INGUAT.

Instituto Guatemalteco de Turismo – INGUAT
www.inguat.gob.gt/estadisticas.php

GUINEA

(1) Llegadas por vía aérea al aeropuerto de Conakry;
(2) Se trata de las pernoctaciones de los no residentes en hoteles, incluidas todas las categorías. Los datos proceden de la declaración de los visitantes en las tarjetas de embarque/desembarque sobre la duración de la estancia en hoteles a su llegada al aeropuerto (excluidas las no declaraciones de la duración de la estancia);
(3) Incluido el alojamiento privado;
(4) Cruce de los campos «llegadas» y «tipo de alojamiento» declarados en las tarjetas de embarque/desembarque.

«Direction Observatoire du Tourisme – Ministère du Tourisme, de l'Hôtellerie et de l'Artisanat»

GUINEA-BISSAU

(1) Llegadas al aeropuerto «Osvaldo Vieira».

«Ministère du commerce, de l'industrie, du tourisme et de l'artisanat»

GUYANA

(1) Llegadas al aeropuerto de Timehri únicamente;
(2) Canadá y Estados Unidos únicamente.

«Guyana Tourism Authority»

GUYANA FRANCESA

(1) Encuesta en el aeropuerto de Cayenne-Rochambeau a la salida;
(2) Francia únicamente;
(3) Hoteles únicamente.

«Comité du Tourisme de la Guyane»

HAITÍ

(1) Llegadas por vía aérea;
(2) Incluidos los nacionales residentes en el extranjero.

«Ministère du Tourisme»

HONDURAS

(1) Noches;
(2) 2015: datos preliminares.

Instituto Hondureño de Turismo
www.iht.hn

HONG KONG (CHINA)

(1) Los datos de gastos corresponden a los facilitados por el país a la OMT, por tratarse de una serie más completa que la facilitada por el Fondo Monetario Internacional (FMI) para la preparación de esta edición del Compendio. (Fuente: «HKTB Visitors Survey»);
(2) Fuente: «Census and Statistics Department»;
(3) Noches;
(4) Hoteles (tarifas altas/medias) y albergues/ casas huéspedes;
(5) Las cifras cubren las actividades de servicios para el turismo receptor;

(6) Las cifras cubren las actividades de servicios para el turismo emisor;
(7) Las cifras cubren el comercio minorista, los servicios personales y de transporte para el turismo receptor, y los servicios de transporte para el turismo emisor.

« Hong Kong Tourism Board »
http://partnernet.hktb.com/en/research_statistics/index.html
www.censtatd.gov.hk/hong_kong_statistics/index.jsp

HUNGRÍA

(1) La observación de las fronteras con los países del espacio de Schengen cesó a partir del año 2008. 2011: el tráfico aéreo de pasajeros y carretera son estimaciones;
(2) Salidas de visitantes no residentes;
(3) Por vía fluvial;
(4) Se excluyen los conductores de camiones;
(5) Alojamiento gratuito;
(6) Noches;
(7) Basado en la nueva clasificación de la Cuenta satélite de turismo: Recomendaciones sobre el marco conceptual, 2008 (CST: RMC 2008);
(8) Se incluyen las estimaciones sobre alojamiento privado;
(9) Incluidas las siguientes actividades características del turismo según las RIET y TSA: RMC 2008: alquiler de equipos de transporte, actividades culturales, actividades deportistas y recreativas, servicios de spa como otra actividad característica del turismo específica del país;
(10) Julio-junio;
(11) 2011: clasificación CST; 2012–2014: Encuesta de la fuerza de trabajo (EFT);
(12) NACE Rev. 2.

« Hungarian Central Statistical Office »
www.ksh.hu/tourism_catering

INDIA

(1) Excluidos los nacionales residentes en el extranjero;
(2) Incluye otros motivos;
(3) Salidas de nacionales del país únicamente, por cualquier motivo de visita;
(4) En hoteles homologados.

« Ministry of Tourism – Government of India »
http://tourism.gov.in/

INDONESIA

(1) 2015: por nacionalidad;
(2) Únicamente hoteles clasificados;
(3) 2015: estimaciones;
(4) Todo tipo de alojamiento comercial.
(5) Precios corrientes.

« Ministry of Tourism and Creative Economy » y « BPS Statistics Indonesia »
www.bps.go.id/Subjek/view/
id/16#subjekViewTab3|accordion-daftar-subjek2

IRÁN (REPÚBLICA ISLÁMICA DEL)

(1) Fuente « Central Bank of Islamic Republic of Iran ».

« Iran Cultural Heritage and Tourism Organization (ICHTO) »

IRAQ

« Ministry of Tourism and Antiquities »

IRLANDA

(1) Incluidos los turistas procedentes de Irlanda del Norte;
(2) Incluye ferrocarril;
(3) Debido a un cambio en la metodología, los datos para 2011 se revisaron y no son comparables con años anteriores;
(4) Debido a un cambio en la metodología, los datos para 2012–2014 se revisaron y no son comparables con años anteriores;
(5) Excluidos los hostales;
(6) Hoteles únicamente.

« Fáilte Ireland »
www.failteireland.ie/

ISLANDIA

(1) Fuente: « Icelandic Tourist Board »;
(2) 2012–2015: llegadas al aeropuerto Keflavik únicamente;
(3) Incluidos los pasajeros en crucero;
(4) Transporte aéreo regular.

« Hagstofa Íslands Statistics Iceland »
www.statice.is/statistics/business-sectors/tourism/

ISLAS CAIMÁN

(1) Llegadas por vía aérea;
(2) Pasajeros en crucero únicamente;
(3) Las cifras de gasto corresponden a las facilitadas por el país a la OMT y que, sin embargo, no figuran en los datos del Fondo Monetario Internacional utilizados para la preparación de esta edición del Compendio;
(4) Incluidos los gastos de los pasajeros en crucero;
(5) Hoteles y apartamentos;
(6) Días.

« Cayman Islands Department of Tourism »
www.caymanislands.ky/statistics/
www.eso.ky

ISLAS COOK

(1) Llegadas por vías aérea y marítima;
(2) Las cifras de gasto corresponden a las facilitadas por el país a la OMT y que, sin embargo, no figuran en los datos del Fondo Monetario Internacional utilizados para la preparación de esta edición del Compendio.

« Cook Islands Tourism Corporation » y « Cook Islands Statistics Office »
www.mfem.gov.ck/statistics

NOTAS DE LOS PAÍSES

ISLAS MARIANAS SEPTENTRIONALES

(1) Llegadas por vía aérea;
(2) Incluye Guam;
(3) Cubre el 68 por ciento del total de habitaciones censadas. Fuente de los datos para 2012–2015: PATA.

« Marianas Visitors Authority »

ISLAS MARSHALL

(1) Llegadas por vía aérea. 2014–2015 Fuente: «South Pacific Tourism Organisation – Regional Tourism Resource Centre».

« Marshall Islands Visitors Authority »

ISLAS SALOMÓN

« Solomon Islands National Statistics Office »

ISLAS TURCAS Y CAICOS

« Turks and Caicos Tourist Board »
http://turksandcaicostourism.com

ISLAS VÍRGENES AMERICANAS

(1) Turistas no residentes alojados en hoteles y establecimientos asimilados;
(2) Llegadas de visitantes por vía aérea; excluidas las llegadas de residentes y el tráfico entre las islas pero incluidos los excursionistas;
(3) Pasajeros en crucero;
(4) Incluido el turismo interno (cerca del 40% del total);
(5) Las cifras de gasto corresponden a las facilitadas por el país a la OMT y que, sin embargo, no figuran en los datos del Fondo Monetario Internacional utilizados para la preparación de esta edición del Compendio;
(6) Hoteles y condominios o villas.
2015: Datos provisionales.

« Bureau of Economic Research »
www.usviber.org/publications.htm

ISLAS VÍRGENES BRITÁNICAS

(1) Incluidos los pasajeros en crucero;
(2) Las cifras de gasto corresponden a las facilitadas por el país a la OMT y que, sin embargo, no figuran en los datos del Fondo Monetario Internacional utilizados para la preparación de esta edición del Compendio.

« Central Statistics Office »

ISRAEL

(1) Excluidos los nacionales residentes en el extranjero;
(2) Incluidas las visitas a familiares y amigos y peregrinaciones;
(3) Incluidas las nuevas entradas tras una visita de hasta 7 días en el Sinaí;

(4) Hoteles turísticos y apart-hoteles;
(5) Incluidos los gastos de los trabajadores extranjeros en Israel;
(6) Tasa de ocupación/camas en hoteles y establecimientos asimilados abiertos;
(7) Turismo receptor en hoteles turísticos.

« Ministry of Tourism »
http://www1.cbs.gov.il/reader/?MIval=cw_usr_view_SHTML&ID=432

ITALIA

(1) Excluidos los trabajadores estacionales o fronterizos;
(2) Encuesta en fronteras de la «Banca d'Italia»;
(3) Incluidos los pasajeros en crucero;
(4) Hoteles únicamente;
(5) 2014: ruptura de series debido a un cambio de técnica para colectar los datos (encuesta: «Trips and Holidays»), de CATI (entrevista telefónica asistida por ordenador) a CAPI (entrevista personal asistida por ordenador);
(6) Noches;
(7) «Los servicios de alojamiento no comercial» se componen de las viviendas en propiedad (incluyendo las que tienen un contrato de tiempo compartido), del alojamiento proporcionado por familiares o amigos y otros alojamientos privados no comerciales;
(8) Número de turistas residentes (visitantes que pernoctan) que viajan al extranjero;
(9) Excluidas las estimaciones sobre alojamiento privado.

« Banca d'Italia » y « Istituto Nazionale di Statistica (ISTAT) »
www.bancaditalia.it
www.istat.it

JAMAICA

(1) Llegadas por vía aérea de turistas no residentes; incluidos los nacionales residentes en el extranjero; tarjetas E/D;
(2) Pasajeros en crucero únicamente;
(3) Los datos son obtenidos a partir de la distribución de los visitantes que pernoctan (turistas) declarando su forma de organización del viaje en las encuestas realizadas a las salidas de los aeropuertos internacionales;
(4) Nueva serie; incluidos los nacionales residentes en el extranjero;
(5) Noches;
(6) Duración de estancia prevista;
(7) Gasto medio de los visitantes que pernoctan (turistas) por día y por persona;
(8) Excluidos los establecimientos cerrados;
(9) Pernoctaciones en los hoteles únicamente.

« Jamaica Tourist Board »
www.jtbonline.org/statistics/Annual%20Travel/Forms/AllItems.aspx

JAPÓN

(1) Excluidos los nacionales residentes en el extranjero;
(2) Llegadas de visitantes no residentes en las fronteras nacionales; incluídos los residentes extranjeros en Japón;
(3) Hasta marzo de 2010, se excluyen los alojamientos con menos de nueve empleados;

511

NOTAS DE LOS PAÍSES

(4) Se excluye el uso durante el día;
(5) Se incluye el solapamiento;
(6) Hoteles homologados y no homologados así como « ryokans » (posadas);
(7) Estimación derivada de la tasa de ocupación;
(8) Se incluyen los servicios de apoyo al transporte de pasajeros.

Fuente de los datos:
1.19-1.21: Ministerio de Asuntos Internos y Comunicación – Estadísticas de inmigración; 1.30, 4.2, 4.3, 4.13-4.15, 4.16-4.18: Agencia de Turismo de Japón – encuesta sobre alojamiento; 1.40-1.43, 2.1-2.18, 4.25-4.26, 4.29-4.30, 5.1-5.10, 6.1: Agencia de Turismo de Japón – encuesta nacional sobre turismo de Japón; 2.24-2.27: Agencia de Turismo de Japón – encuesta sobre alojamiento – encuesta nacional sobre turismo de Japón; 3.1, 3.10: Organización Nacional de Turismo de Japón; 4.4, 4.7: Ministerio de Asuntos Internos y Comunicación – Censo económico; 4.6: Asociación de Viajes y Turismo de Japón; 4.8-4.11: Agencia de Turismo de Japón – Encuesta nacional de turismo de Japón – Cuenta satélite de turismo de Japón – Cuadro 5: Cuentas de producción de industrias turísticas y otras industrias; 4.27-4.28: Agencia de Turismo de Japón – Encuesta sobre tendencias de consumo de los extranjeros que visitan Japón; 5.2: Cuenta satélite de turismo de Japón – Cuadro 7: Empleo en industrias turísticas.

« Japan Tourism Agency » y « Japan National Tourism Organization »
www.mlit.go.jp/kankocho/en/siryou/toukei/index.html
www.tourism.jp/en/statistics/ »

JORDANIA

(1) Incluidos los nacionales residentes en el extranjero;
(2) 2011–2014: llegadas de visitantes residentes y no residentes;
(3) Para visitas organizadas únicamente.

« Ministry of Tourism and Antiquities »
www.tourism.jo

KAZAJSTÁN

« Agency of Statistics of the Republic of Kazakhstan »

KENYA

(1) Llegadas de visitantes no residentes a través de todos los puestos fronterizos; excluidos los nacionales residentes en el extranjero;
(2) Días.

« Kenya National Bureau of Statistics »

KIRGUISTÁN

« National Statistical Committee »

KIRIBATI

(1) Llegadas por vía aérea. Tarawa e Isla Christmas.

« Kiribati National Tourism Office », « Ministry of Communication, Transport and Tourism Development » y « PATA »

KUWAIT

(1) Turistas no residentes alojados en hoteles y establecimientos asimilados.

« Central Statistical Bureau »
www.csb.gov.kw/Socan_Statistic_EN.aspx?ID=19

LESOTHO

(1) Debido a una mejora en la recopilación de datos con la ayuda de « Statistics South Africa », a partir de 2014 los datos no son comparables con los de años anteriores.

« Lesotho Tourism Development Corporation »
www.ltdc.org.ls/researchArrivalStats.php

LETONIA

(1) Llegadas de visitantes no residentes en las fronteras nacionales. Datos procedentes de la Policía Estatal de Fronteras;
(2) Salidas de no residentes. Encuesta realizada en los puestos fronterizos del país;
(3) Incluidas las visitas a familiares y amigos y tratamientos de salud;
(4) Desde 2015 Hoteles y establecimientos asimilados según la clasificación de la NACE Rev. 2: Sección I, División 55, Clase 55.1 – Hoteles y alojamientos asimilados (los servicios incluyen la limpieza diaria);
(5) Pernoctaciones en todos los establecimientos de alojamiento colectivo;
(6) Fuente: encuesta en las fronteras;
(7) A partir de 2012 fuente: encuesta de hogares;
(8) A partir de 2012 datos procedentes de la Policía Estatal de Fronteras.

« Transport and Tourism Statistics Section – Central Statistical Bureau »
www.csb.gov.lv/en/statistikas-temas/tourism-key-indicators-30715.html

LÍBANO

(1) Excluidas las nacionalidades libanesa, siria y palestina;
(2) Para el año 2014, la encuesta se llevó a cabo en 291 establecimientos;
(3) Fuente de los datos, hoteles y establecimientos autorizados por el Ministerio de Turismo;
(4) Fuente: sindicatos turísticos del Líbano.

« Ministère du Tourisme »

NOTAS DE LOS PAÍSES

LIECHTENSTEIN

(1) Turistas no residentes alojados en todo tipo de establecimientos de alojamiento;
(2) Desde 2012 se excluye a los turistas de larga duración en campamentos y en apartamentos turísticos;
(3) 2011: turistas no residentes alojados en hoteles y establecimientos asimilados;
(4) Desde 2012: turistas no residentes alojados en todo tipo de establecimientos de alojamiento;
(5) Desde 2012 se excluyen los campamentos y apartamentos turísticos de larga duración;
(6) Promedio anual;
(7) Promedio anual de las habitaciones disponibles;
(8) Promedio anual de las plazas-camas disponibles.

« Office of Statistics Liechtenstein. Tourism Statistics »
www.llv.li/#/11961/tourismusstatistik

LITUANIA

(1) Hoteles y moteles;
(2) Encuesta sobre la estructura de negocios;
(3) Datos de las cuentas nacionales;
(4) Datos de la Cuenta Satélite de Turismo (CST).

« Lithuanian State Department of Tourism »
www.stat.gov.lt/

LUXEMBURGO

(1) Turistas no residentes alojados en todo tipo de establecimientos de alojamiento; incluye albergues de juventud, alojamientos turísticos privados y otros;
(2) Estimación de los turistas que pasaron al menos una noche en un establecimiento de alojamiento turístico;
(3) NACE Rev2 55.100;
(4) Los datos de gastos corresponden a los facilitados por el país a la OMT, por tratarse de una serie más completa que la facilitada por el Fondo Monetario Internacional (FMI);
(5) Turistas residentes alojados en todo tipo de establecimientos de alojamiento; incluye albergues de juventud, alojamientos turísticos privados y otros;
(6) Tasa de ocupación neta.

« STATEC »
www.statistiques.public.lu

MACAO (CHINA)

(1) Los datos anteriores a 2014 incluyen a los visitantes con paquete turístico y a los que se unían a excursiones locales;
(2) Desde 2011, los datos se obtienen de la policía de seguridad pública, mientras que los de los años previos son resultado de las muestras;
(3) Hoteles y casas de huéspedes;
(4) Restaurantes y establecimientos asimilados;
(5) Establecimientos que prestan servicios de transporte de pasajeros;
(6) Agencias de viaje;
(7) Empresas del juego;
(8) Excluidos los asalariados a tiempo parcial.

Fuente de los datos:
1.1-1.13, 1.19-1.25, 1.26, 4.27-4.28, 6.2: Policía de seguridad pública; 1.27, 3.1, 4.27-4.30: Encuesta mensual de agencias de viajes; 1.31-1.32, 1.41-1.42, 4.14-4.19: Encuesta mensual de hoteles y establecimientos asimilados; 1.40, 1.44: Encuesta de gasto de visitantes; 4.2-4.3, 4.8-4.12, 4.13, 5.2: Encuesta de hoteles y establecimientos asimilados; 4.4, 5.4: Encuesta de restaurantes y establecimientos asimilados; 4.5, 5.5: Encuesta de transporte, almacenamiento y comunicación; 4.6, 4.20-4.24, 5.6: Encuesta de agencias de viaje; 4.7: Encuesta del sector del juego; 4.19, 6.2: Estimación de la población de Macao; 5.7: Encuesta sobre necesidades de mano de obra y sueldos: sector del juego.

« Statistics and Census Service » y « Macau Government Tourist Office »
www.dsec.gov.mo/Statistic/TourismAndServices/VisitorArrivals.aspx
http://industry.macautourism.gov.mo/en/index.php

MADAGASCAR

(1) Llegadas de turistas no residentes por vía aérea.

« Ministère du Tourisme, des Transports et de la Météorologie »

MALASIA

(1) Incluidos los residentes de Singapur que cruzan la frontera por la Johore Causeway;
(2) La méthodologie a été modifiée et pour cela, à partir de 2013 les données ne sont pas comparables avec celles des années précédentes;
(3) Encuesta de turismo interno;
(4) Hoteles con 10 habitaciones y más;
(5) Encuesta en hoteles.
Fuente de los datos: 1.2, 1.5-1.12, 1.19-1.24, 1.31, 1.4, 4.3, 4.13, 4.14, 4.16: « Tourism Malaysia »; 2.1-2.28: « Department of Statistics Malaysia ».

« Department of Statistics Malaysia » y « Tourism Malaysia »
www.tourism.gov.my/statistics

MALAWI

(1) Salidas.

« Ministry of Tourism, Wildlife and Culture »

MALDIVAS

(1) Llegadas por vía aérea;
(2) Días.

« Ministry of Tourism »
www.tourism.gov.mv

MALÍ

(1) 2012–2015: llegadas por vía aérea únicamente (aeropuerto de Bamako-Sénou);
(2) Llegadas por vía aérea únicamente (aeropuerto de Bamako-Sénou);

(3) 2015: datos parciales correspondientes a la frontera de Bih, en la región de Mopti.

«Direction Nationale du Tourisme et de l'Hotellerie (DNTH)»

MALTA

(1) Datos procedentes de las salidas por vías aérea y marítima;
(2) Fuente: Eurostat;
(3) Fuente: «MTA Licensing Data».

«Malta Tourism Authority» y «National Statistics Office»
www.mta.com.mt/research
www.nso.gov.mt

MARRUECOS

(1) Incluidos los nacionales residentes en el extranjero;
(2) Hoteles clasificados, ciudades de vacaciones, residencias turísticas y Riad;
(3) Turistas extranjeros.

«Ministère du tourisme»
www.tourisme.gov.ma/

MARTINICA

(1) Las cifras de gasto corresponden a las facilitadas por el país a la OMT y que, sin embargo, no figuran en los datos del Fondo Monetario Internacional utilizados para la preparación de esta edición del Compendio.

«Comité Martiniquais du Tourisme»

MAURICIO

(1) Estimaciones a partir de la encuesta de turismo receptor, año 2013;
(2) Grandes hoteles;
(3) Hoteles únicamente;
(4) Los datos se refieren a grandes establecimientos (es decir, que emplean a 10 o más personas) del sector turístico.
Nota 2015: datos provisionales.

«Ministry of Tourism and Leisure»
http://statsmauritius.govmu.org/English/StatsbySubj/Pages/INTERNATIONAL-TRAVEL-and-TOURISM.aspx

MÉXICO

(1) Incluidos los nacionales residentes en el extranjero;
(2) Incluidos los visitantes de la franja fronteriza con los Estados Unidos y estancia inferior a 24h;
(3) Vía aérea únicamente;
(4) Turistas al interior y turistas fronterizos;
(5) Incluye ferrocarril;
(6) Hoteles únicamente;
(7) Centros turísticos seleccionados;
(8) Días;
(9) Turismo extranjero únicamente;

(10) La información no corresponde propiamente a empleo sino a puestos de trabajo equivalentes remunerados necesarios para realizar la producción de los bienes y servicios relacionados con actividades turísticas.
Fuente: Cuenta Satélite de Turismo de México, cambio de año base a 2008.

«Secretaría de Turismo de México (SECTUR), Instituto Nacional de Estadística y Geografía (INEGI) y Unidad de Política Migratoria
Banco de México»
www.datatur.sectur.gob.mx/
www.inegi.org.mx

MICRONESIA (ESTADOS FEDERADOS DE)

(1) Llegadas en los Estados de Kosrae, Chuuk, Pohnpei y Yap; excluidos los ciudadanos de EFM;
(2) Años fiscales (1 octubre – 30 septiembre).

«Office of Statistics, Budget and Economic Management, Overseas Development Assistance, and Compact Management»
www.sboc.fm

MOLDOVA (REPÚBLICA DE)

(1) Turistas no residentes alojados en todo tipo de establecimientos de alojamiento;
(2) Visitantes que se beneficiaron de los servicios turísticos de las agencias de turismo y operadores turísticos (titulares de licencias turísticas).
Nota: Excluido el margen izquierdo del río Nistru y la municipalidad de Bender.

«National Bureau of Statistics»
www.statistica.md/category.php?l=en&idc=293&

MÓNACO

(1) Turistas no residentes alojados en hoteles y establecimientos asimilados.

«Direction du Tourisme et des Congrès»
www.imsee.mc

MONGOLIA

(1) Excluidos los diplomáticos y extranjeros residentes en Mongolia.

«National Tourism Center – Ministry of Nature, Environment and Tourism»

MONTENEGRO

(1) Turistas no residentes alojados en todo tipo de establecimientos de alojamiento.

«Ministry of Sustainable Development and Tourism»
www.monstat.org/eng/page.php?id=43&pageid=43

NOTAS DE LOS PAÍSES

MONTSERRAT

«Statistics Department Montserrat»

MOZAMBIQUE

(1) Llegadas a todos los puestos fronterizos del país;
(2) La encuesta sobre turismo interno es un módulo de la encuesta sobre los presupuestos de los hogares que se lleva a cabo cada cinco años, incluido por primera vez en 2008/2009. En 2012/2013 se efectuó la encuesta continua sobre los presupuestos de los hogares.

«Ministry of Tourism» y «Instituto Nacional de Estatística»
www.ine.gov.mz

MYANMAR

(1) Hoteles y establecimientos asimilados administrados por el Estado únicamente. El aumento en el total para el año 2014 se debe a la suma de las llegadas con pases para 7 días de estancia desde los puntos de control fronterizos de China, India, Tailandia y Myanmar así como las llegadas desde los puntos de entradas internacionales;
(2) Hoteles administrados por el Estado y casas de huéspedes privadas homologadas.

«Ministry of Hotels and Tourism»
www.myanmartourism.org/

NAMIBIA

«Ministry of Environment and Tourism» y «Namibian Tourism Board»

NEPAL

(1) Incluidas las llegadas procedentes de la India;
(2) Días;
(3) Hoteles en Katmandú; excluidos los hoteles en proceso de construcción;
(4) Agencias de viajes y de trekking.

«Nepal Tourism Board» y «Ministry of Culture, Tourism and Civil Aviation»
www.tourism.gov.np/np/category/tourism/tourism_statistics

NICARAGUA

(1) Incluidos los nacionales residentes en el extranjero;
(2) Total de establecimientos del país;
(3) Principales establecimientos de alojamiento del país;
(4) Hoteles y establecimientos asimilados ubicados en categorías superiores;
(5) Todo tipo de establecimientos de alojamiento, turismo receptor.

Instituto Nicaragüense de Turismo (INTUR)
www.intur.gob.ni

NÍGER

(1) Días.

«Ministère du Tourisme et de l'Artisanat» y «Institut National de la Statistique»
www.stat-niger.org/statistique/

NIGERIA

(1) En un intento de sanear la industria del turismo, la Corporación de Desarrollo de Turismo de Nigeria creó un grupo de trabajo para aplicar el proceso de registro de los hoteles. Todos los establecimientos de hostelería, en especial los hoteles, se vieron obligados a registrarse ante la Corporación o ser cerrados y por tanto, este esfuerzo singular provocó el aumento en el número de hoteles y establecimientos asimilados para el año 2011.

«Nigerian Tourism Development Corporation»

NIUE

(1) «Incluidos los nacionales de Niue que residen habitualmente en Nueva Zelandia.

2014–2015 Fuente: «South Pacific Tourism Organisation – Regional Tourism Resource Centre». 2015: estimaciones.
«Statistics Niue»

NORUEGA

(1) 2011: las cifras se basan en «The Guest Survey», un estudio realizado por el «Institute of Transport Economics». A partir de 2012 la encuesta ha sido suspendida;
(2) 2012–2015: turistas no residentes alojados en todo tipo de establecimientos de alojamiento;
(3) 2011: Estados Unidos únicamente;
(4) 2011: Japón únicamente;
(5) Pernoctaciones en establecimientos registrados;
(6) Las cifras para hoteles y establecimientos asimilados se refieren a establecimientos con 20 camas o más durante todo el año;
(7) 2014: datos provisionales;
(8) 2011: datos revisados.

«Statistics Norway» y «Institute of Transport Economics»
www.ssb.no/english/subjects/

NUEVA CALEDONIA

(1) Incluidos los nacionales residentes en el extranjero;
(2) Hoteles en Noumea únicamente;
(3) Residentes que regresan;
(4) Habitaciones en Noumea;
(5) Días, hoteles en Noumea.

«Institut de la Statistique et des Études Économiques (ISEE)»
www.isee.nc/

NUEVA ZELANDIA

(1) Viajes internacionales y Migración, SNZ;
(2) El total incluye a los visitantes en crucero;
(3) Encuesta de alojamiento, SNZ;
(4) Incluye hoteles, moteles y hostales, pero excluye los parques de vacaciones;
(5) Balanza de pagos, SNZ;
(6) Encuesta de viajes internos, MBIE (suspendida en 2013);
(7) Los datos facilitados en esta sección se basan en el tipo de transporte utilizado en los múltiples desplazamientos dentro de cada viaje de turismo interno, no sólo el principal transporte del viaje. Por lo tanto, el total especificado no será igual a la suma de los puntos 2.10, 2.11 y 2.12. La encuesta de viajes internos permite dar múltiples respuestas a la pregunta sobre «medio de transporte»;
(8) Encuesta de viajes internos – visitantes que pernoctan, MBIE;
(9) Sólo el gasto de los viajes con pernoctación;
(10) Estadísticas sobre demografía de las empresas, SNZ (datos revisados en 2011 para reflejar la nueva clasificación sectorial, ANZSIC06) a febrero de 2011–2013;
(11) Datos provisionales.

«Statistics New Zealand (SNZ)» y «Ministry of Business, Innovation & Employment (MBIE)»
www.stats.govt.nz/

OMÁN

(1) Encuesta de turismo receptor;
(2) Incluido el turismo interno.

«Ministry of Tourism», «Ministry of National Economy» y «National Centre for Statistics and Information»
www.omantourism.gov.om

PAÍSES BAJOS

(1) Turistas no residentes alojados en todo tipo de establecimientos de alojamiento;
(2) 2013: ruptura en la serie debido a los cambios metodológicos en la determinación de la población;
(3) Hoteles y pensiones;
(4) 2013–2015: los datos de gastos corresponden a los facilitados por el país a la OMT, por tratarse de una serie más completa que la facilitada por el Fondo Monetario Internacional (FMI) para la preparación de esta edición del Compendio;
(5) Source: Eurostat;
(6) Salidas de nacionales por vacaciones;
(7) Hoteles;
(8) Todo tipo de establecimientos de alojamiento.

«Statistics Netherlands»
www.cbs.nl/en-GB/menu/themes/vrije-tijd-cultuur/nieuws/default.htm

PALAU

(1) Llegadas por vía aérea (aeropuerto internacional de Palau);
(2) Años fiscales – 30 septiembre.

«Office of Planning and Statistics, Bureau of Budget and Planning – Ministry of Finance» y «Palau Visitors Authority»
www.visit-palau.com/

PANAMÁ

(1) Llegadas de visitantes no residentes: Aeropuerto Internacional Tocúmen (AIT), frontera de Paso Canoa (FPC) y puertos de Cristóbal y Balboa (PCB);
(2) Llegadas de visitantes no residentes, AIT;
(3) Llegadas de turistas no residentes, AIT;
(4) Hoteles de la Ciudad de Panamá;
(5) Habitaciones/ plazas cama inventariadas para turismo internacional.

Autoridad de Turismo de Panamá
www.atp.gob.pa/estadisticas-de-turismo-en-panama

PAPUA NUEVA GUINEA

(1) Estimaciones
(2) Días.

«Papua New Guinea Tourism Promotion Authority»
www.tpa.papuanewguinea.travel/

PARAGUAY

(1) Tarjetas E/D en el aeropuerto Silvio Petirossi y planillas de pasajeros en los puestos terrestres – Policía Nacional y SENATUR;
(2) Excluidos los nacionales residentes en el extranjero y miembros de tripulación;
(3) Vía fluvial.

Secretaría Nacional de Turismo – SENATUR
www.senatur.gov.py

PERÚ

(1) Incluidos los nacionales residentes en el extranjero;
(2) Pasajeros en crucero que pernoctan;
(3) Incluye las llegadas por vía fluvial y lacustre.

Superintendencia Nacional de Migraciones, Banco Central de Reserva del Perú y Ministerio de Comercio Exterior y Turismo
http://ww2.mincetur.gob.pe/

POLINESIA FRANCESA

(1) Llegadas por vía aérea únicamente; excluidos los nacionales residentes en el extranjero;
(2) Días;
(3) Hoteles y casas de huéspedes; al 31 de diciembre de cada año;
(4) Habitaciones en hoteles.

«Institut de la Statistique – ISPF»
www.ispf.pf/Home.aspx

NOTAS DE LOS PAÍSES

POLONIA

(1) Dado que Polonia se unió al espacio Schengen, el recuento preciso de tráfico entrante no es posible. Para este año únicamente se pueden dar resultados aproximados;
(2) Los datos 2011, 2012 se basan en encuestas realizadas por el Instituto de Turismo; 2013: «Activ Group»; 2014, 2015: Oficina central de estadística;
(3) Datos de la Oficina central de estadística;
(4) Establecimientos de alojamiento colectivo y privado;
(5) Viajes de 4 noches y más;
(6) Establecimientos con 10 o más plazas cama. A 31 de julio.

«Institute of Tourism»
www.intur.com.pl/itenglish/institute_en.htm

PORTUGAL

(1) Llegadas de turistas no residentes en todo tipo de establecimientos de alojamiento;
(2) Fuente: Eurostat;
(3) «Statistics Portugal (INE)», Encuesta sobre la estructura de negocios;
(4) Tasa de ocupación neta;
(5) Todo tipo de establecimientos de alojamiento.

«Turismo de Portugal, I.P.»
www.ine.pt/xportal/xmain?xpid=INE&xpgid=ine_main

PROVINCIA CHINA DE TAIWÁN

(1) Incluidos los nacionales residentes en el extranjero;
(2) incluye el coste de los pasajes aéreos.

«Planning Division Tourism Bureau – Ministry of Transportation and Communication»
http://admin.taiwan.net.tw/statistics/release_en.aspx?no=7

PUERTO RICO

(1) Llegadas de turistas no residentes por vía aérea;
(2) Únicamente Islas Vírgenes Americanas y Estados Unidos;
(3) Las cifras de gasto corresponden a las facilitadas por el país a la OMT y que, sin embargo, no figuran en los datos del Fondo Monetario Internacional utilizados para la preparación de esta edición del Compendio;
(4) Incluye residentes y no residentes;
(5) Habitaciones endosadas por la Compañía de Turismo de Puerto Rico;
(6) Incluidas las habitaciones ocupadas por residentes de Puerto Rico.
Datos: Años fiscales (julio-junio).

Junta de Planificación de Puerto Rico y Compañía de Turismo de Puerto Rico
www.jp.gobierno.pr/

QATAR

(1) A partir de 2015, se incluyen datos de aparthoteles, no recogidos anteriormente.

«Qatar Statistics Authority»

REINO UNIDO

(1) Túnel;
(2) Encuesta internacional de pasajeros; Fuente: «Office for National Statistics (ONS)»;
(3) Días;
(4) A partir de 2013: Gran Bretaña solamente (exluido Irlanda del Norte) y «Day Visits survey»;
(5) Número de unidades locales en empresas que aplican IVA o retenciones fiscales en origen Fuente: Oficina de Estadísticas Nacionales (ONS), Inter Departmental Business Register;
(6) Fuente: Encuesta anual de negocios de la Oficina de Estadísticas Nacionales (ONS por su sigla inglesa);
(7) Fuente: compilación de la ONS para EUROSTAT;
(8) Fuente: Encuesta de ocupación del Reino Unido (informe anual);
(9) Fuente: ONS, a partir de datos de empleo de población activa, encuesta sobre registro de empresas y empleo y encuesta sobre población activa.

«VisitBritain» y «Office for National Statistics»
www.visitbritain.org/insightsandstatistics/
www.ons.gov.uk/ons/index.html

REPÚBLICA CENTROAFRICANA

(1) Llegadas por vía aérea a Bangui únicamente;
(2) Datos del país.

«Ministère des Arts, du Tourisme, de la Culture et de la Francophonie»

REPÚBLICA CHECA

(1) CST de la República Checa;
(2) 2015: datos preliminares;
(3) Incluidos los visitantes en tránsito;
(4) Turistas no residentes alojados en todos los establecimientos de alojamiento colectivo – Fuente: CZSO;
(5) Fuente: Encuesta sobre turismo interno y turismo emisor y CST;
(6) Viajes largos + viajes cortos;
(7) Viajes de negocios;
(8) Debido a un cambio de metodología de la encuesta, a partir de 2011 los datos no son comparables con los de años anteriores (Fuente: CZSO). Viajes largos + viajes cortos;
(9) Fuente: Registro de empresas de la República Checa;
(10) Hoteles y restaurantes;
(11) Fuente: Cuentas Nacionales;
(12) Consumo de capital fijo;
(13) Utilización neta de camas;
(14) Actividades de apoyo y transporte auxiliar, actividades de agencias de viajes y operadores turísticos;
(15) Viajes turísticos (1 pernoctación y más).

517

NOTAS DE LOS PAÍSES

«Czech Statistical Office, TSA» y «Ministry for Regional Development»
www.czso.cz/eng/redakce.nsf/i/home

REPÚBLICA DEMOCRÁTICA POPULAR LAO

«Lao National Tourism Administration» y «Ministry of Information, Culture and Tourism – Tourism Development Department»
www.tourismlaos.org/show.php?Cont_ID=43

REPÚBLICA DOMINICANA

(1) Incluidos los nacionales residentes en el extranjero;
(2) Llegadas por vía aérea únicamente;
(3) Todas las llegadas por mar;
(4) Hoteles.

Ministerio de Turismo
www.bancentral.gov.do/estadisticas_economicas/turismo/

REUNIÓN

(1) Llegadas por vía aérea únicamente;
(2) Fuente: INSEE, encuesta de flujos turísticos;
(3) Fuente: INSEE, encuesta de ocupación hotelera;
(4) Se trata del conjunto de pernoctaciones en los hoteles clasificados, a partir de 2015 hoteles clasificados y no clasificados. Residentes y no residentes;
(5) Las cifras de gasto corresponden a las facilitadas por el país a la OMT y que, sin embargo, no figuran en los datos del Fondo Monetario Internacional utilizados para la preparación de esta edición del Compendio;
(6) Fuente: INSEE Clap. Se trata del conjunto de establecimientos de las nomenclaturas seleccionadas. No se conoce con certeza el destino real de la actividad (turístico o no);
(7) Se trata del conjunto de establecimientos/ habitaciones/ camas disponibles diariamente en los hoteles clasificados, a partir de 2015 hoteles clasificados y no clasificados;
(8) Fuente: INSEE Clap. Se trata del conjunto de empleos de las nomenclaturas seleccionadas. No se conoce con certeza el destino real de la actividad (turístico o no).

«Institut National de la Statistique et des Études Économique – INSEE» y «Comité du Tourisme de la Réunion»
http://observatoire.reunion.fr/les-chiffres-cles.html

RUMANIA

(1) Sólo los viajes internos por motivo de vacaciones (incluidas las visitas a familiares y a amigos) y de negocios;
(2) La categoría «otros motivos personales» se refiere sólo a los viajes para visitar a familiares y a amigos;
(3) Las categorías «aéreo» y «acuático» se incluyen en la categoría «otros»;
(4) Calculado dividiendo el número de pernoctaciones por el número de viajes. Fuente: ACTR, encuesta de hogares;
(5) Sólo por motivo de vacaciones (incluidas visitas a familiares y a amigos) y de negocios. Las cifras se compilan dividiendo el gasto por el número de pernoctaciones;

(6) Número de salidas al extranjero de rumanos registradas en las fronteras;
(7) A 31 de julio, sólo para establecimientos autorizados;
(8) El indicador consiste en el número de turistas que compran servicios combinados/ individuales. Debe tenerse en cuenta que los valores incluyen tanto a operadores turísticos como a las clásicas agencias de viajes;
(9) El indicador está representado en realidad por el «número medio de asalariados» y la fuente consiste en las estadísticas estructurales de las empresas que se compilan cada año;
(10) Incluye también el transporte de carga;
(11) Esta categoría no concuerda exactamente con las categorías de las industrias turísticas debido al alto nivel de agregación de la publicación. Incluye sólo las siguientes actividades: actividades creativas, artísticas y de entretenimiento, bibliotecas, archivos, museos y otras actividades culturales, actividades de juegos de azar y apuestas, actividades deportivas y actividades de esparcimiento y recreativas.

«National Institute of Statistics»
www.insse.ro/cms/en

RWANDA

«Rwanda Development Board»
www.rdb.rw/welcome-to-rwanda/tourism-research-and-statistics.html

SAINT KITTS Y NEVIS

(1) Llegadas de turistas no residentes por vía aérea;
(2) Llegadas en yates y cruceros.

«Ministry of Sustainable Development» y «Eastern Caribbean Central Bank»
www.eccb-centralbank.org/Statistics/index.asp#tourismdata

SAMOA

«Samoa Tourism Authority» y «Statistical Services Division (Ministry of Finance)»
www.sbs.gov.ws/index.php/sector-statistics/tourism-statistics
www.mof.gov.ws»

SAMOA AMERICANA

«Department of Commerce – Statistics Division»
www.spc.int/prism/americansamoa/

SAN MARINO

(1) Incluidos los visitantes italianos;
(2) Turistas no residentes alojados en todo tipo de establecimientos de alojamiento; incluidos los turistas italianos;
(3) Hoteles únicamente.

«Segreteria di Stato per il Turismo ed i Rapporti con l'AASS»
www.statistica.sm/on-line/home/dati-statistici/attivita-economiche-e-turismo.html

NOTAS DE LOS PAÍSES

SAN VICENTE Y LAS GRANADINAS

(1) Llegadas de turistas no residentes por vía aérea;
(2) Incluidos los pasajeros en crucero y en yate.

« St. Vincent and the Grenadines Tourism Authority »
www.discoversvg.com/index.php/es/about-svg/tourism-statistics

SANTA LUCÍA

(1) Excluidos los nacionales residentes en el extranjero;
(2) Excluidas las llegadas de pasajeros en yate.

« Saint Lucia Tourist Board »
http://investstlucia.com/sectors/view/tourism.html

SENEGAL

(1) Datos estimados;
(2) Llegadas por vía aérea al aeropuerto « Léopold Sédar Senghor (LSS) » únicamente. Incluidos los nacionales residentes en el extranjero;
(3) Hoteles y ciudades de vacaciones.

« Ministère du Tourisme et des Transports Aériens »

SERBIA

(1) Turistas alojados en establecimientos de alojamiento para visitantes;
(2) El número total de camas (fijas y supletorias) hasta 2012. A partir de 2013, la capacidad máxima (número de camas fijas) durante el año;
(3) A partir de 2012, tasa de ocupación neta. Hasta 2011, tasa bruta de ocupación;
(4) Número de personas empleadas.

« Statistical Office of the Republic of Serbia » y « National Bank of Serbia »
http://webrzs.stat.gov.rs/WebSite/Public/PageView.aspx?pKey=181

SEYCHELLES

(1) Pernoctaciones basadas en las salidas;
(2) 2012: enero-octubre;
(3) Hoteles y casas de huéspedes.

« National Bureau of Statistics » y « Seychelles Tourism Board »
www.nbs.gov.sc/

SIERRA LEONA

(1) Llegadas por vía aérea.

« National Tourist Board » y « Statistics Sierra Leone »
www.statistics.sl/

SINGAPUR

(1) Excluidas las llegadas de ciudadanos malasios por vía terrestre;
(2) Días;
(3) Hoteles (clasificados y no clasificados);
(4) Hoteles clasificados únicamente.

« Singapore Tourism Board »
www.singstat.gov.sg
www.stb.gov.sg »

SINT MAARTEN (PARTE DE LOS PAÍSES BAJOS)

(1) Por vía aérea; incluidas las llegadas a San Martín (parte francesa de la isla);
(2) Llegadas al aeropuerto « Juliana » (incluidos los visitantes con destino a San Martín (parte francesa).

« St. Maarten Tourist Bureau » y « Department of Statistics Sint Maarten »
http://stat.gov.sx/

SRI LANKA

(1) Excluidos los nacionales residentes en el extranjero;
(2) Hoteles, moteles, albergues, casas de huéspedes y aparthoteles;
(3) Hoteles y restaurantes.

« Sri Lanka Tourist Board »
www.sltda.lk/statistics

SUDÁFRICA

(1) A partir de 2014 se aplicó una nueva metodología y por lo tanto la información no es comparable con años anteriores. 2014, 2015: excluido tránsito;
(2) Fuente: « Domestic Tourism Survey 2007–2011 »;
(3) La gran diferencia entre 2012 y 2013 en el número de pernoctaciones en alojamiento de pago se explica por los cambios en el motivo de la visita, es decir, una disminución de los viajes para visitar a familiares y amigos en 2013 con un aumento de los viajes de vacaciones y negocios. Además, hubo una disminución en la duración media de la estancia entre todos los turistas nacionales en 2013;
(4) (Tamaño total de los grupos de viaje) / (Número total de viajes);
(5) Los datos se refieren a todos los alojamientos de pago;
(6) Incluidas las visitas a familiares y amigos y « Church Halls »;
(7) Hoteles;
(8) Datos de la Cuenta Satélite de Turismo (CST).

« Statistics South Africa » y « South African Tourism «
www.statssa.gov.za/

SUDÁN

(1) Incluidos los nacionales residentes en el extranjero.

« Ministry of Tourism and Wildlife »

NOTAS DE LOS PAÍSES

SUECIA

(1) Datos para 2011–2014 según una nueva encuesta nacional de fronteras (IBIS, visitantes que entran en Suecia). Fuente: Agencia Sueca de Crecimiento Económico y Regional. En 2015 no se recopilaron datos;
(2) Hoteles únicamente;
(3) Debido a un cambio de proveedor, las estadísticas de turismo interno y emisor no están disponibles para el 2014–2015;
(4) Número de puestos de trabajo equivalentes a tiempo completo.

«Swedish Agency for Economic and Regional Growth – Tillväxtverket»
www.tillvaxtverket.se/english
www.scb.se/en_/

SUIZA

(1) Hoteles y establecimientos asimilados (incluye los establecimientos de cura);
(2) Incluye motivos desconocidos;
(3) Datos poco fiables, no se publican;
(4) Incluye medios de transporte desconocidos;
(5) Establecimientos encuestados;
(6) Habitaciones encuestadas;
(7) Plazas-cama encuestadas;
(8) Tasa neta de ocupación;
(9) Puestos de trabajo equivalentes a tiempo completo.

«Swiss Federal Statistical Office»
www.bfs.admin.ch/bfs/portal/fr/index/themen/10.html

SURINAME

«Suriname Tourism Foundation»
www.surinametourism.sr/#!en&events-more&statistics

SWAZILANDIA

«Swaziland Tourism Authority» y «Ministry of Tourism and Environmental Affairs»
www.thekingdomofswaziland.com/pages/content/index.asp?PageID=57

TAILANDIA

(1) Excluidas las llegadas de nacionales residentes en el extranjero;
(2) Incluye ferrocarril;
(3) Días.

«Ministry of Tourism and Sports»
www.tourism.go.th/home

TANZANÍA (REPÚBLICA UNIDA DE)

(1) En tránsito.

«Tourism Division – Ministry of Natural Resources and Tourism» y «National Bureau of Statistics»

TAYIKISTÁN

«Committee of Youth Affairs, Sports and Tourism under the Government of the Republic of Tajikistan»

TIMOR-LESTE

(1) Llegadas por vía aérea al Aeropuerto de Dili;
(2) Encuesta en hoteles (20 habitaciones o más).

«Statistics Timor-Leste – General Directorate of Statistics»
www.statistics.gov.tl/category/survey-indicators/quarterly-statistical-indicators/

TOGO

(1) Turistas no residentes alojados en hoteles y establecimientos asimilados;
(2) 2013–2015: incluidos los nacionales residentes en el extranjero;
(3) Excluidos los nacionales residentes en el extranjero.

«Ministère du Tourisme»

TONGA

(1) Llegadas por vía aérea;
(2) Incluidos los pasajeros en crucero y en yate y miembros de tripulaciones.

«Ministry of Commerce, Tourism and Labour»
www.spc.int/prism/tonga/

TRINIDAD Y TABAGO

(1) Llegadas por vía aérea;
(2) Encuesta a la salida de los visitantes. Fuente: «Central Statistical Office»;
(3) Encuesta de turismo interno que se lleva a cabo cada 2 años.

«Tourism Development Company Limited»
www.tdc.co.tt/index.php/research

TÚNEZ

(1) Excluidos los nacionales residentes en el extranjero;
(2) Hoteles clasificados y no clasificados, pensiones y ciudades de vacaciones.

«Ministère du Tourisme – Office National du Tourisme» y «Institut National de la Statistique»
www.ins.nat.tn/indexfr.php

TURQUÍA

(1) Incluidos los ciudadanos turcos residentes en el extranjero;
(2) Llegadas por mar;
(3) Encuesta a la salida de los visitantes que se lleva a cabo en las puertas de embarque;
(4) Encuesta en establecimientos de alojamiento autorizados por el Ministerio de Turismo;

NOTAS DE LOS PAÍSES

(5) Incluidos los terrenos de camping;
(6) Incluidos los gastos de los nacionales residentes en el extranjero;
(7) Fuente: «Turkstat Household Domestic Tourism Survey»;
(8) Hoteles clasificados, excluidos los terrenos de camping.
(9) Fuente: Turkstat Labour Force Survey;
(10) NACE 55;
(11) NACE 56;
(12) NACE 491, 4932, 4939, 501, 503, 511;
(13) NACE 79.

«Ministry of Culture and Tourism»
http://sgb.kulturturizm.gov.tr/belge/1-90750/turizm-istatistikleri.html
www.turkstat.gov.tr/PreTablo.do?alt_id=1072

TUVALU

(1) 2015 Fuente: «South Pacific Tourism Organisation – Regional Tourism Resource Centre»

«Ministry of Foreign Affairs, Trade, Tourism, Environment and Labour.» y «2015 Source: South Pacific Tourism Organisation – Regional Tourism Resource Centre»

UCRANIA

«State Statistics Committee of Ukraine»
www.ukrstat.gov.ua/operativ/operativ2007/tyr/tyr_e/arh_vig_e.html

UGANDA

«Ministry of Tourism, Trade and Industry» y «Uganda Bureau of Statistics»
www.ubos.org/?st=pagerelations2&id=19&p=related%20 pages%202:Migration%20and%20Tourism%20Statistics

URUGUAY

(1) Excluidas las llegadas de pasajeros en crucero;
(2) Incluye ferrocarril;
(3) Días;
(4) Considerando solo el primer viaje;
(5) Fuente: INE;
(6) Debido a un cambio de metodología, a partir de 2012 los datos no son comparables con los años anteriores;
(7) Servicios inmobiliarios;
(8) Por razones metodológicas, se considera sólo la primera ocupación. Tiempo completo = 40 horas semanales o más.

Ministerio de Turismo y Deporte
www.mintur.gub.uy/index.php/es/estadistica

VANUATU

(1) Pasajeros en crucero únicamente;
(2) Duración de estancia prevista.

«Vanuatu National Statistics Office»
www.vnso.gov.vu/

VENEZUELA (REPÚBLICA BOLIVARIANA DE)

(1) Noches;
(2) Hoteles únicamente.

Ministerio del Poder Popular para el Turismo
www.mintur.gob.ve/mintur/turismo-en-cifras-2/

VIET NAM

(1) Incluidos los nacionales residentes en el extranjero;
(2) Incluidas las llegadas de pasajeros en crucero y por vía marítima;
(3) Las cifras de gasto corresponden a las facilitadas por el país a la OMT y que, sin embargo, no figuran en los datos del Fondo Monetario Internacional utilizados para la preparación de esta edición del Compendio.

«Viet Nam National Administration of Tourism» y «General Statistics Office»
www.vietnamtourism.com/en/index.php/news
www.gso.gov.vn/default_en.aspx?tabid=491

YEMEN

(1) Incluidos los nacionales residentes en el extranjero.

«Ministry of Tourism» y «Central Statistical Organization»
www.yementourism.com/statistics/
www.cso-yemen.org/content.php?lng=english&pcat=131

ZAMBIA

«Ministry of Tourism and Arts»

ZIMBABWE

(1) 2014, 2015: incluye a los visitantes en tránsito que pasan al menos una noche;
(2) Las cifras de gasto corresponden a las facilitadas por el país a la OMT y que, sin embargo, no figuran en los datos del Fondo Monetario Internacional utilizados para la preparación de esta edición del Compendio;
(3) El país tiene que realizar aún la encuesta sobre el mercado interno y el emisor para obtener los indicadores que faltan sobre turismo interno y emisor;
(4) Sobre la base de las llegadas en los parques nacionales y museos nacionales;
(5) Sólo hoteles clasificados.

«Zimbabwe Tourism Authority – ZTA»
www.zimbabwetourism.net/index.php/trends-statistics/

Conceptual references and technical notes

Références conceptuelles et notes techniques

Referencias conceptuales y notas técnicas

Conceptual references and technical notes

Note: This document also includes four annexes:
  Annex 1: National System of Tourism Statistics and international comparability
  Annex 2: Understanding tourism: basic glossary
  Annex 3: Finding tourism in International Standard Classifications
  Annex 4: List of tourism industries and grouping by main categories according to ISIC Rev. 4

For additional references, visit:

http://statistics.unwto.org/en

http://statistics.unwto.org/en/content/international-recommendations-tourism-statistics-2008-irts-2008

1. Inbound tourism

Inbound tourism comprises the activities of a non-resident visitor within the country of reference on an inbound tourism trip. The corresponding expenditure of such a visitor is identified as inbound tourism expenditure.

Data

Arrivals

Arrivals data measure the flows of international visitors to the country of reference: each arrival corresponds to one inbound tourism trip. If a person visits several countries during the course of a single trip, his/her arrival in each country is recorded separately. In an accounting period, arrivals are not necessarily equal to the number of persons travelling (when a person visits the same country several times a year, each trip by the same person is counted as a separate arrival).

Arrivals data should correspond to *inbound visitors* by including both tourists and same-day non-resident visitors. All other types of travellers (such as border, seasonal and other short-term workers, long-term students and others) should be excluded, as they do not qualify as visitors.

Data are obtained from different sources: administrative records (immigration, traffic counts, and other possible types of controls), border surveys or a mix of them. If data are obtained from accommodation surveys, the number of guests is used as estimate of arrival figures; consequently, in this case, breakdowns by regions, main purpose of the trip, modes of transport used or forms of organization of the trip are based on complementary visitor surveys.

Arrivals are broken down by five characteristics; two of them deserve some comments:
  – Type of visitors (**Compendium** items 1.1 to 1.4). If a country cannot distinguish between overnight visitors and same-day visitors, no breakdown is provided.
  – Regions (**Compendium** items 1.5 to 1.13). The basic concept behind is that the country associated to the arrival should be the country of residence. Some countries do not accept UNWTO recommendations and classify nationals residing abroad instead of as residents in such countries as a separate category (**Compendium** item 1.13).

The *main purpose* of a trip is defined as the purpose in the absence of which the trip would not have taken place. The following classification applies:
  1. Personal
    1.1. Holidays, leisure and recreation
    1.2. Visiting friends and relatives
    1.3. Education and training
    1.4. Health and medical care
    1.5. Religion/pilgrimages
    1.6. Shopping
    1.7. Transit
    1.8. Other
  2. Business and professional

Complementary information is provided in the UNWTO Yearbook of Tourism Statistics that contains arrivals with a breakdown by country of origin:
  – Table 1:
    Arrivals of non-resident overnight visitors (tourists) at national borders
  – Table 2:
    Arrivals of non-resident visitors (overnight visitors – tourists – and same-day visitors –excursionists–) at national borders

Accommodation

The term "accommodation" refers to services provided by commercial establishments to visitors. Of these, the most important post is usually "hotels and similar establishments", identified in ISIC, Rev.4 as 5510 "Short term accommodation activities".

Overnights (or "guest nights") refer to the number of nights spent by non-resident guests (inbound tourists).

Complementary information is provided in the UNWTO Yearbook of Tourism Statistics that contains data on guests with a breakdown by country of origin:
  – Table 3:
    Arrivals of non-resident overnight visitors (tourists) in "hotels and similar establishments"
  – Table 4:
    Arrivals of non-resident overnight visitors (tourists) in all types of establishments providing accommodation services for visitors

- Table 5:
  Overnight stays of non-resident overnight visitors (tourists) in "hotels and similar establishments"
- Table 6:
  Overnight stays of non-resident overnight visitors (tourists) in all types of establishments providing accommodation services for visitors

Expenditure

Expenditure associated with the activity of international visitors has been traditionally identified with the travel item of the Balance of Payments (BOP): in the case of inbound tourism, those expenditures associated with inbound visitors are registered as "credits" in the BOP and refers to "travel receipts".

The *2008 International Recommendations for Tourism Statistics* consider that "tourism industries and products" includes transport of passengers. Consequently, a better estimate of tourism-related expenditure by inbound and outbound visitors in an international scenario would be, in terms of the BOP, the value of the travel item plus that of the passenger transport item.

Nevertheless, users should be aware that BOP estimates include, in addition to expenditures associated to visitors, those related to other types of travellers (these might be substantial in some countries; for instance, long-term students or patients, border and seasonal workers, etc).

Also data on expenditure by *main purpose of the trip* are BOP data.

The data published correspond to those published by the International Monetary Fund (IMF) (and provided by the Central Banks). Expenditure data on inbound and outbound tourism is taken from the BOPS (Balance of Payments Statistics) CD-ROM of the IMF.

In the case of a significant difference with data provided to UNWTO by National Tourism Administrations (NTAs) for the preparation of this Compendium, the NTA data will be given separately in the "Country notes".

Indicators

Average size of travel party

A travel party is defined as visitors travelling together on a trip and whose expenditures are pooled. The average size of travel parties allows for an estimate of the total number of trips by international visitors, which is useful for marketing and policy design purposes.

Average length of stay

All these indicators refer to the duration of inbound tourism trips by international visitors (expressed as number of days or nights).

Total average length of stay refers to both commercial and non commercial accommodation services provided to visitors, as well as to other types of stays.

Since a non-resident visitor might use different accommodation facilities during his / her stay, such total figures can only be estimated using border survey information or by checking dates from official arrival/departure cards for a sample (or the totality) of visitors.

Average expenditure per day

This indicator refers to total expenditure of overall visitors divided by the total number of days spent, estimated using visitors' survey.

2. Domestic tourism

Domestic tourism comprises the activities of a resident visitor within the country of reference (either as part of a domestic tourism trip or part of an outbound tourism trip).

The corresponding expenditure in the economy of reference of such a visitor is identified as domestic tourism expenditure. Also, the expenditure of outbound visitors on products received from resident businesses is included in domestic expenditure.

Data

Trips taken by visitors are tourism trips. A domestic tourism trip refers to the travel of a visitor from the time of leaving his/her usual residence until he/she returns: it refers to a roundtrip.

The term "accommodation" refers to services provided by commercial establishments to visitors. Of these, the most important post is usually "hotels and similar establishments", identified in ISIC, Rev.4 as 5510 "Short term accommodation activities".

Overnights (or "guest nights") refer to the number of nights spent by resident guests (domestic tourists). Accommodation surveys (addressed to establishments) should be the preferred source of data.

Indicators

Average length of stay

Total average length of stay refers to both commercial and non commercial accommodation services provided to visitors, as well as to other types of stays.

Total data can only be estimated using household surveys.

Average expenditure per day

This indicator refers to total expenditure divided by the total number of days spent, estimated using visitors' survey.

3. Outbound tourism

Outbound tourism comprises the activities of a resident visitor outside the country of reference (either as part of an outbound tourism trip or as part of a domestic tourism trip). The corresponding expenditure of such a visitor is identified as outbound tourism expenditure.

Data

Departures data measure the flows of resident visitors leaving the country of reference. Departures are not necessarily equal to the number of arrivals reported by international destinations for the country of reference.

Expenditure associated with the activity of visitors has been traditionally identified with the travel item of the Balance of Payments (BOP): in the case of outbound tourism, those expenditures associated with resident visitors are registered as "debits" in the BOP and refers to "travel expenditure". As in the case of *inbound tourism*, BOP data are used.

The 2008 International Recommendations for Tourism Statistics consider that "tourism industries and products" includes transport of passengers. Consequently, a better estimate of tourism-related expenditures data by resident and non-resident visitors in an international scenario would be, in terms of the BOP, the value of the travel item plus that of the passenger transport item.

Nevertheless, users should be aware that BOP estimates include, in addition to expenditures associated with visitors, those related to other types of travellers.

Likewise, data on expenditure by *main purpose* of the trip are BOP data.
The data published correspond to those published by the International Monetary Fund (IMF) (and provided by the Central Banks); in the case of a significant difference with data provided to UNWTO by National Tourism Administrations (NTAs) for the preparation of this Compendium, the NTA data will be given separately in the "Country notes". Please, refer to the paragraph on inbound expenditure for more information on IMF country notes.

Complementary information on "trips abroad by resident visitors to countries of destination" can be obtained through the website www.e-unwto.org/home/main.mpx. It is important to point out that the information presented is obtained on the basis of data supplied by each of the destination countries and therefore corresponds to arrivals in these countries.

Indicators

Average length of stay

This indicator refers to the duration of trips abroad by outbound visitors (expressed as number of days) and reflects the total average using border surveys and/or household information.

Average expenditure per day

This indicator refers to total expenditure divided by total days spent using border surveys and/or household information.

4. Tourism industries

The term *tourism industries* includes those industries that typically produce tourism characteristic products; it is equivalent to the more colloquial term "tourism sector". The following list identifies such industries:

1. Accommodation for visitors
2. Food and beverage serving activities
3. Railway passenger transport
4. Road passenger transport
5. Water passenger transport
6. Air passenger transport
7. Transport equipment rental
8. Travel agencies and other reservation services activities
9. Cultural activities
10. Sports and recreational activities
11. Retail trade of country-specific tourism characteristic goods
12. Other country-specific tourism characteristic activities

The following explanatory notes refer to *Accommodation for visitors* and *Travel agencies and other reservation services activities* being the only two industries for which monetary and non-monetary data are published in this Compendium.

These notes can be consulted in Annex 4; they have been extracted from *International Standard Industrial Classification of All Economic Activities (ISIC), Rev. 4*. Statistical papers (Series M No. 4/Rev.4), United Nations. New York, 2008.

Accommodation for visitors

The number of establishments in the *Accommodation for visitors* industry (Compendium item 4.2) refers to all type of establishments providing accommodation services to visitors on a commercial (market) basis; that is, as a paid service. Consequently, data should include all the following ISIC classes:

5510   Short term accommodation activities

This class is labelled in the **Compendium** section 4 as *"Accommodation for visitors in hotels and similar establishments"* and includes the provision of accommodation, typically on a daily or weekly basis, principally for short stay by visitors. This includes the provision of furnished accommodation in guest rooms and suites or complete self-contained units with kitchens, with or without daily or other regular housekeeping services, and may often include a range of additional services such as food and beverage services, parking, laundry services, swimming pools and exercise rooms, recreational facilities and conference and convention facilities.

This class includes the provision of short-term accommodation provided by:
- hotels
- resort hotels
- suite / apartment hotels
- motels
- motor hotels
- guesthouses
- pensions
- bed and breakfast units
- visitor flats and bungalows

- time-share units
- holiday homes
- chalets, housekeeping cottages and cabins
- youth hostels and mountain refuges

This class excludes:
- provision of homes and furnished or unfurnished flats or apartments for more permanent use, typically on a monthly or annual basis, see division 68

5520 Camping grounds, recreational vehicle parks and trailer parks

This class includes:
- provision of accommodation in campgrounds, trailer parks, recreational camps and fishing and hunting camps for short stay visitors
- provision of space and facilities for recreational vehicles

This class also includes accommodation provided by:
- protective shelters or plain bivouac facilities for placing tents and/or sleeping bags

5590 Other accommodation

This class includes the provision of temporary or longer-term accommodation in single or shared rooms or dormitories for students, migrant (seasonal) workers and other individuals.

This class includes accommodation provided by:
- student residences
- school dormitories
- workers hostels
- rooming and boarding houses
- railway sleeping cars

6810 Real estate activities with own or leased property

This class includes:
- buying, selling, renting and operating of self-owned or leased real estate, such as:
  - apartment buildings and dwellings
  - non-residential buildings, including exhibition halls, self-storage facilities, malls and shopping centers
  - land
- provision of homes and furnished or unfurnished flats or apartments for more permanent
- use, typically on a monthly or annual basis

This class also includes:
- development of building projects for own operation, i.e. for renting of space in these buildings
- subdividing real estate into lots, without land improvement
- operation of residential mobile home sites

This class excludes:
- development of building projects for sale, see 4100
- subdividing and improving of land, see 4290
- operation of hotels, suite hotels and similar accommodation, see 5510
- operation of campgrounds, trailer parks and similar accommodation, see 5520

- operation of workers hostels, rooming houses and similar accommodation, see 5590

6820 Real estate activities on a fee or contract basis

This class includes the provision of real estate activities on a fee or contract basis including real estate related services.

This class includes:
- activities of real estate agents and brokers
- intermediation in buying, selling and renting of real estate on a fee or contract basis
- management of real estate on a fee or contract basis
- appraisal services for real estate
- activities of real estate escrow agents

This class excludes:
- legal activities, see 6910
- facilities support services, see 8110
- management of facilities, such as military bases, prisons and other facilities (except computer facilities management), see 8110

Travel agencies and other reservation service activities

7911 Travel agency activities

This class includes:
- activities of agencies primarily engaged in selling travel, tour, transportation and accommodation services to the general public and commercial clients

7912 Tour operator activities

This class includes:
- arranging and assembling tours that are sold through travel agencies or directly by tour operators. The tours may include any or all of the following:
  - transportation
  - accommodation
  - food
  - visits to museums, historical or cultural sites, theatrical, musical or sporting events

7990 Other reservation service and related activities

This class includes:
- provision of other travel-related reservation services:
  - reservations for transportation, hotels, restaurants, car rentals, entertainment and sport etc.
- provision of time-share exchange services
- ticket sales activities for theatrical, sports and other amusement and entertainment events
- provision of visitor assistance services:
  - provision of travel information to visitors
  - activities of tourist guides
- tourism promotion activities

This class excludes:
- activities of travel agencies and tour operators, see 7911, 7912
- organization and management of events such as meetings, conventions and conferences, see 8230

Data

Regarding the *number of establishments*, (Compendium item 4.3) includes establishments associated with classes 5520, 5590, 6810 and 6820 (see above explanatory notes for accommodation for visitors).

The number of *rooms* and *bed-places* refers to the capacity in "hotels and similar establishments" for providing temporary accommodation to visitors.

Indicators

All of the first three indicators are based on the overall number of overnights of both resident and non-residents tourists in hotels and similar establishments.

Occupancy rates refer to the relationship between existing capacity to provide accommodation services to visitors and the extent to which it is used. This rate may refer to the use of rooms or of bed-places.

Available capacity refers to the number of bed-places in hotels and similar establishments per 1000 inhabitants of the permanent resident population of the country of reference. Data are assigned by UNWTO if not provided by the country.

5. Employment

The category of persons employed in the tourism industries can be either *employees* (persons who work for an enterprise in return for remuneration in cash or in kind as agreed) or *self-employed* (own-account workers who hold the type of job defined as "self-employment job" and have not engaged on a continuous basis any "employees" during the reference period).

Some employed persons may have more than one job; consequently, the number of jobs (demand side) and the number of persons employed (supply side) are dissimilar categories and therefore usually do not match.

The intensity of work may vary from job to job, industry to industry and from period to period. Jobs may differ by working time of persons employed and therefore be expressed in terms of full- or part-time jobs. For this reason, it is not sufficient to have data on the number of jobs or persons employed in order to obtain information on the volume of labour performed during a specified period of time (for example, a month or a year). Data on the total number of working hours will be required. Finally, if all jobs are converted into full-time equivalent employment or annual total hours worked, the total volume of labour of a given tourism industry for a given period can be obtained.

Figures on "Number of jobs by status in employment" and "Number of full time equivalent jobs by status in employment" should refer to tourism industries.

6. Complementary indicators

These indicators are derived from the Balance of Payments, National Accounts and tourism statistics.

Demand

Gross travel propensity measures the number of outbound and domestic tourism trips in terms of total permanent resident population of the country of reference. Bigger values of the indicator mean greater frequency of such trips, indicating the present mobility of the population travelling.

The indicator "arrivals/population" provides an estimate of tourism intensity in the country of reference. This indicator is calculated by UNWTO based on the available basic data on inbound and domestic tourism, which can be either the number of visitors (code 1.1 for inbound tourism and 2.1 for domestic tourism) or the number of tourists (code 1.2 for inbound tourism and 2.2 for domestic tourism). The calculation is made according to the following formulas, listed in order of preference, and taking into account the basic data available for the country of reference:

(1.2 inbound tourists + 2.2 domestic tourists) / population
(1.2 inbound tourists + 2.1 domestic visitors) / population
(1.2 inbound tourists) / population
(1.1 inbound visitors + 2.1 domestic visitors) / population
(1.1 inbound visitors + 2.2 domestic tourists) / population
(1.1 inbound visitors) / population

The population data correspond to those published by the International Monetary Fund (IMF), the World Bank or, in their absence, to those published by the National Statistical Office of the country of reference.

In each new edition of the Compendium, the formula will be adapted according to the basic data available for the reference period (5 years).

Macroeconomic international tourism related indicators

The indicators are based on the International Monetary Fund's *Balance of Payments Statistics* and *International Financial Statistics*.

These and other complementary indicators represent a preliminary and very basic evaluation of tourism's economic contribution to the national economy, valuable because they are largely available for most countries, internationally comparable, and comparable to other economic indicators.

It must be noted that the term 'expenditure' is used similarly for inbound as well as for outbound tourism to indicate "the amount paid for the acquisition of consumption goods and services, as well as valuables, for own use or to give away, for and during tourism trips". Foreign visitors in the reference country generate inbound tourism expenditure (credits in the Balance of Payments), while resident visitors in foreign countries generate outbound tourism expenditure (debits in the Balance of Payments).

Inbound tourism expenditure over GDP

Reflects the weight of expenditure by inbound visitors as a part of the total value of economic activity in the economy of reference. From the perspective of international trade, this indicator captures the economic importance of foreign revenue inflow associated to expenditures by such visitors.

Outbound tourism expenditure over GDP

Reflects the importance of the spending abroad by outbound visitors, expressed in terms of the national economy. From the perspective of international trade, this indicator captures the economic importance of domestic revenue outflow by means of such visitors.

Tourism balance over GDP

Reflects the economic importance of net tourism (inbound minus outbound) expenditures relative to the economy of reference. A significant surplus or deficit affects the country's balance of trade, and thus its GDP.

Tourism openness

Reflects how important the sum of cross-border tourism expenditures (i.e. international tourism, the sum of inbound and outbound tourism expenditure) are relative to the economy of reference. It could be used as a measure of the free flow of tourism between the country of reference and the rest of the world.

Tourism coverage

Reflects the proportion between inbound tourism expenditure and outbound tourism expenditure to show in what degree foreign revenue inflow cover for domestic revenue outflow. A value higher than 100 % means that inbound tourism indirectly finances more than all the expenditure of outbound visitors; a value lower than 100 % means that inbound tourism does not cover the expenditure of such visitors abroad.

Inbound tourism expenditure over exports of goods,
Inbound tourism expenditure over exports of services,
and
Inbound tourism expenditure over exports of goods and services

These three measures reflect the importance of tourism as an internationally traded service relative to other categories of exports. At the same time, such measures reveal the degree of tourism specialization in a country's export structure and the relative capability of tourism in generating foreign revenues.

Inbound tourism expenditure over current account credits

The current account credits of the Balance of Payments refer to all inflow of goods, services, income and current transfers into an economy. The larger the share of tourism in this aggregate, the larger is the importance of tourism activity in generating foreign revenue inflows.

Outbound tourism expenditure over imports of goods,
Outbound tourism expenditure over imports of services,
and
Outbound tourism expenditure over imports of goods and services

These three measures reflect the importance of tourism as an internationally traded service relative to other categories of imports. At the same time, such measures reveal the predilection for tourism in a country's import structure and the relative degree of an economy's domestic revenue outflows due to international tourism.

Outbound tourism expenditure over current account debits

The current account debits of the Balance of Payments refer to all outflows of goods, services, income and current transfers from an economy to the rest of the world. The larger the share of tourism in this aggregate, the larger is the importance of tourism activity in the leakage of domestic revenue.

Annex 1
National System of Tourism Statistics and international comparability

The structure of the **Compendium of Tourism Statistics** is based on the following scheme referred to the basic information framework of national Systems of Tourism Statistics for international comparability purposes (http://statistics.unwto.org/sites/all/files/docpdf/ststext.pdf)

The conceptual background for such a basic core of data and indicators is the *International Recommendations for Tourism Statistics 2008* (IRTS 2008).

International comparability and tourism statistics: the basic information framework

I. Conceptual framework

Concepts	Observation units	Main related characteristics
Visitor	Visitor	Classes (Overnight visitor-tourist-/same-day visitor-excursionist)
		Country of residence / regions
	Travel party	Size
Trip	Tourism trip	Main purpose
		Duration
		Main destination
		Modes of transport
		Types of accommodation used
		Organization
		Expenditure
Tourism industries	Establishment	**Monetary**
		Output
		Intermediate consumption
		Gross value added
		Compensation of employees
		Gross Fixed Capital Formation
		Non-monetary
		Non-monetary characteristics specific to each tourism industry
Employment	Establishment (in the tourism industries)	Persons
		Size
		Status in employment
	Households	Jobs
		Duration of work
		Full-time equivalent jobs

II. Classifications

1. Forms of tourism
2. Classification of consumption products acquired by visitors
3. Classification of productive activities serving visitors
4. Other classifications

III. Tables of results

1. Inbound tourism
2. Domestic tourism
3. Outbound tourism
4. Tourism industries
5. Employment
6. Complementary indicators

531

Annex 2
Understanding tourim: basic glossary

This Annex includes some key concepts and the corresponding definitions as in the *IRTS 2008*. http://statistics.unwto.org/en/content/international-recommendations-tourism-statistics-2008-irts-2008

A complete and updated Glossary of Tourism Terms is available through: https://s3-eu-west-1.amazonaws.com/staticunwto/Statistics/Glossary+of+terms.pdf

Domestic tourism	Comprises the activities of a resident *visitor* within the country of reference, either as part of a *domestic tourism trip* or part of an *outbound tourism trip*.
Domestic visitor	As a *visitor travels* within his/her country of residence, he/she is a *domestic visitor* and his/her activities are part of *domestic tourism*.
Employment in tourism industries	*Employment in tourism industries* may be measured as a count of the persons employed in *tourism industries* in any of their jobs, as a count of the persons employed in *tourism industries* in their main job, or as a count of the jobs in *tourism industries*.
Inbound tourism	Comprises the *activities* of a non-resident *visitor* within the country of reference on an *inbound tourism trip*.
Outbound tourism	Comprises the *activities* of a resident *visitor* outside the country of reference, either as an *outbound tourism trip* or as part of a *domestic tourism trip*.
Place of usual residence	The *place of usual residence* is the geographical place where the visitor usually resides, and is defined by the location of his/her principal dwelling (Principles and recommendations for population and housing censuses of the United Nations).
Purpose of a tourism trip (main)	The *main purpose* of a *tourism trip* is defined as the purpose in the absence of which the *trip* would not have taken place. Classification of *tourism trips* according to the *main purpose* refers to nine categories: this typology allows the identification of different subsets of *visitors* (business visitors, transit visitors, etc).
Tourism characteristic activities / products	*Tourism characteristic activities* are the activities that typically produce *tourism characteristic products*. *Tourism characteristic products* are those that satisfy one or both of the following criteria: *Tourism expenditure* on the product (either good or service) should represent a significant share of total *tourism expenditure* (share-of-expenditure/demand condition); *Tourism expenditure* on the product should represent a significant share of the supply of the product in the economy (share-of-supply condition). This criterion implies that the supply of a *tourism characteristic product* would cease to exist in meaningful quantity in the absence of visitors.
Tourism expenditure	*Tourism expenditure refers to the amount paid for the acquisition of consumption goods and services, as well as valuables, for own use or to give away, for and during tourism trips.*
Tourism industries	*The tourism industries comprise all establishments for which the principal activity is a tourism characteristic activity.*
Tourist (or overnight visitor) and Excursionist (or day visitor)	*A visitor (domestic, inbound or outbound) is classified as a tourist (or overnight visitor) if his/her trip includes an overnight stay, or as a same-day visitor (or excursionist) otherwise.*

CONCEPTUAL REFERENCES and TECHNICAL NOTES

Travel / tourism

Travel refers to the activities of travellers. A traveller is someone who moves between different geographic locations, for any purpose and any duration. The visitor is a particular type of traveller and consequently tourism is a subset of travel

Travel party

A travel party is defined as visitors travelling together on a trip and whose expenditures are pooled.

Trip

A trip refers to the travel by a person from the time of departure from his/her usual residence until he/she returns: it thus refers to a round trip. Trips taken by visitors are tourism trips.

Usual environment

The usual environment of an individual, a key concept in tourism, is defined as the geographical area (though not necessarily a contiguous one) within which an individual conducts his/her regular life routines.

Vacation home

A vacation home (sometimes also designated as a holiday home) is a secondary dwelling that is visited by the members of the household mostly for purposes of recreation, vacation or any other form of leisure.

Visit

A trip is made up of visits to different places. The term "tourism visit" refers to a stay in a place visited during a tourism trip.

Visitor

A visitor is a traveller taking a trip to a destination outside his/her usual environment, for less than a year, for any purpose (business, leisure or other personal purpose) other than to be employed by a resident entity in the country or place visited.

Annex 3
Finding tourism in International Standard Classifications

The importance of Tourism and the need to define and measure its significance as a part of the UN System of Statistics was recognized by the United Nations Statistical Commission with the approval in 1993 of "Recommendations on Tourism Statistics". The revised version of these recommendations was approved by the UN Statistical Commission in 2008 as *International Recommendations for Tourism Statistics 2008* (IRTS 2008).

To study the economic contribution of Tourism to the national economy, there was a need to integrate the economic analysis of Tourism into the reference framework of the System of National Accounts (SNA '93), leading to the approval by the United Nations Statistical Commission in 2000 of the "Tourism Satellite Account: Recommended Methodological Framework". This framework has been updated as *Tourism Satellite Account: Recommended Methodological Framework 2008* (TSA:RMF 2008).

The concepts, definitions and classifications in IRTS 2008 have been made consistent with TSA:RMF 2008 which in turn has been harmonized with the 2008 System of National Accounts, Balance of Payments and International Trade in Services.

For Tourism, there is an interest in identifying the products purchased by visitors, directly and indirectly, and the activities that produce them. The classifications used for the detailed activities and products required in the study of Tourism are drawn directly from and related to the United Nations reference classifications, ISIC and the CPC.

The focus of interest for Tourism analysis is the visitor. Initially, it is of interest to measure visitor expenditure and to identify the products, both goods and services, purchased by visitors, as well as the activities that produce those products. In a macroeconomic framework, such as the TSA, the concept of Tourism comprises both a demand perspective consisting of visitor consumption, tourism collective consumption, and tourism gross fixed capital formation and a supply perspective of tourism activities (a special issue being the share of their production that is purchased by visitors). Tourism, as such, is not identified in SNA 93 or in ISIC. For purposes of Tourism, activities from across the spectrum of ISIC, that produce goods and services that satisfy tourism demand are brought together and grouped as tourism activities.

The approach being from the demand side, the visitor is the basic unit of observation and analysis, and visitor expenditure is observed in terms of products (primarily services). On the supply side, related as it is to the System of National Accounts, Tourism statistics uses the "establishment" as the basic statistical unit as defined in the SNA, and uses "industry" as the unit of presentation and analysis, industry being defined as "groups of establishments engaged in the same kind of productive activities".

In the first instance it is necessary to identify the products purchased by visitors. For purposes of data collection from a demand perspective, products are grouped into broad categories by purpose; however, Tourism requires the simultaneous analysis of consumption and production hence the classification used for defining products is the Central Product Classification (CPC v 2.). The products purchased by visitors can be classified within the detailed classes of the CPC and the activities that produce them can be identified in terms of the detailed classes of ISIC.

Tourism defines certain of those products purchased by visitors and the activities that produce them, as Tourism characteristic products (those that satisfy certain criteria) and Tourism characteristic activities (those that typically produce tourism characteristic products). The IRTS 2008 explains in great detail the underlying concepts, definitions and classifications to be used in compiling Tourism statistics and the identification of Tourism characteristic products and activities. To facilitate international comparison, lists of these characteristic products and activities have been compiled. Annex 3 of the document provides a List of Tourism characteristic activities (tourism industries) grouped into main categories according to ISIC rev 4. Annex 4 provides a list of Tourism characteristic products grouped by main categories according to CPC ver 2. Even though the actual product purchased by the visitor may constitute only a portion of the CPC class or the activity producing it may constitute only a portion of the 4 digit ISIC class, by being expressed in terms of CPC classes and aggregations of ISIC classes, the lists provide a defined class within which each product or activity can be placed. Countries are advised to create more detailed classes below the lowest level of the CPC and ISIC for their own analytical purposes, if required.

The scope for analysis of Tourism statistics is widened when they are placed within the framework of the Tourism Satellite Account. Again in the core accounting framework, products and activities are expressed in terms of CPC v 2 and ISIC rev 4, including the products and activities associated with Tourism. The international product and activity classifications used to compile data for the TSA:RMF 2008 which in turn, establishes structural links with the System of National Accounts, make possible a deeper appreciation of tourism's linkages to other economic areas.

Annex 4
List of tourism industries (characteristic activities) and grouping by main categories according to ISIC Rev. 4

Tourism industries	ISIC Rev. 4	Description
1. Accommodation for visitors	5510	Short term accommodation activities
	5520	Camping grounds, recreational vehicle parks and trailer parks
	5590	Other accommodation
	6810	Real estate activities with own or leased property*
	6820	Real estate activities on a fee or contract basis*
2. Food and beverage serving activities	5610	Restaurants and mobile food service activities
	5629	Other food service activities
	5630	Beverage serving activities
3. Railway passenger transport	4911	Passenger rail transport, interurban
4. Road passenger transport	4922	Other passenger land transport
5. Water passenger transport	5011	Sea and coastal passenger water transport
	5021	Inland passenger water transport
6. Air passenger transport	5110	Passenger air transport
7. Transport equipment rental	7710	Renting and leasing of motor vehicles
8. Travel agencies and other reservation service activities	7911	Travel agency activities
	7912	Tour operator activities
	7990	Other reservation service and related activities
9. Cultural activities	9000	Creative, arts and entertainment activities
	9102	Museums activities and operation of historical sites and buildings
	9103	Botanical and zoological gardens and nature reserves activities
10. Sports and Recreational activities	7721	Renting and leasing of recreational and sports goods
	9200	Gambling and betting activities
	9311	Operation of sports facilities
	9319	Other sports activities
	9321	Activities of amusement parks and theme parks
	9329	Other amusement and recreation activities n.e.c.
11. Retail trade of country-specific tourism characteristic goods		Duty free shops**
		Specialized retail trade of souvernirs**
		Specialized retail trade of handicrafts**
		Other specialized retail trade of tourism characteristic goods**
12. Other country-specific tourism characteristic activities		

* Part related to second homes and timeshare properties

** Not a 4 digit ISIC

Explanatory notes

These explanatory notes refer exclusively to internationally comparable tourism characteristic activities and follow the same order as in Annex 4 above.

They have been extracted from *International Standard Industrial Classification of All Economic Activities (ISIC), Rev. 4. Statistical papers (Series M No. 4/Rev.4)*, United Nations. New York, 2008.

The complete document can be consulted in http://unstats. un.org/unsd/cr/registry/regdntransfer.asp?f=135

Accommodation for visitors

5510   Short term accommodation activities

This class includes the provision of accommodation, typically on a daily or weekly basis, principally for short stay by visitors. This includes the provision of furnished accommodation in guest rooms and suites or complete self-contained units with kitchens, with or without daily or other regular housekeeping services, and may often include a range of additional services such as food and beverage services, parking, laundry services, swimming pools and exercise rooms, recreational facilities and conference and convention facilities.
- This class includes the provision of short-term accommodation provided by:
- hotels
- resort hotels
- suite / apartment hotels
- motels
- motor hotels
- guesthouses
- pensions
- bed and breakfast units
- visitor flats and bungalows
- time-share units
- holiday homes
- chalets, housekeeping cottages and cabins
- youth hostels and mountain refuges

This class excludes:
- provision of homes and furnished or unfurnished flats or apartments for more permanent use, typically on a monthly or annual basis, see division 68

5520   Camping grounds, recreational vehicle parks and trailer parks

This class includes:
- provision of accommodation in campgrounds, trailer parks, recreational camps and fishing and hunting camps for short stay visitors
- provision of space and facilities for recreational vehicles

This class also includes accommodation provided by:
- protective shelters or plain bivouac facilities for placing tents and/or sleeping bags

5590   Other accommodation

This class includes the provision of temporary or longer-term accommodation in single or shared rooms or dormitories for students, migrant (seasonal) workers and other individuals.

This class includes accommodation provided by:
- student residences
- school dormitories
- workers hostels
- rooming and boarding houses
- railway sleeping cars

6810   Real estate activities with own or leased property

This class includes:
- buying, selling, renting and operating of self-owned or leased real estate, such as:
  - apartment buildings and dwellings
  - non-residential buildings, including exhibition halls, self-storage facilities, malls and shopping centers
  - land
- provision of homes and furnished or unfurnished flats or apartments for more permanent
- use, typically on a monthly or annual basis

This class also includes:
- development of building projects for own operation, i.e. for renting of space in these buildings
- subdividing real estate into lots, without land improvement
- operation of residential mobile home sites

This class excludes:
- development of building projects for sale, see 4100
- subdividing and improving of land, see 4290
- operation of hotels, suite hotels and similar accommodation, see 5510
- operation of campgrounds, trailer parks and similar accommodation, see 5520
- operation of workers hostels, rooming houses and similar accommodation, see 5590

6820   Real estate activities on a fee or contract basis

This class includes the provision of real estate activities on a fee or contract basis including real estate related services.

This class includes:
- activities of real estate agents and brokers
- intermediation in buying, selling and renting of real estate on a fee or contract basis
- management of real estate on a fee or contract basis
- appraisal services for real estate
- activities of real estate escrow agents

This class excludes:
- legal activities, see 6910
- facilities support services, see 8110
- management of facilities, such as military bases, prisons and other facilities (except computer facilities management), see 8110

Food and beverage serving activities

5610 Restaurants and mobile food service activities

This class includes the provision of food services to customers, whether they are served while seated or serve themselves from a display of items, whether they eat the prepared meals on the premises, take them out or have them delivered. This includes the preparation and serving of meals for immediate consumption from motorized vehicles or nonmotorized carts.

This class includes activities of:
- restaurants
- cafeterias
- fast-food restaurants
- pizza delivery
- take-out eating places
- ice cream truck vendors
- mobile food carts
- food preparation in market stalls

This class also includes:
- restaurant and bar activities connected to transportation, when carried out by separate units

This class excludes:
- concession operation of eating facilities, see 5629

5629 Other food service activities

This class includes industrial catering, i.e. the provision of food services based on contractual arrangements with the customer, for a specific period of time.

Also included is the operation of food concessions at sports and similar facilities. The food is often prepared in a central unit.

This class includes:
- activities of food service contractors (e.g. for transportation companies)
- operation of food concessions at sports and similar facilities
- operation of canteens or cafeterias (e.g. for factories, offices, hospitals or schools) on a concession basis

This class excludes:
- manufacture of perishable food items for resale, see 1079
- retail sale of perishable food items, see division 47

5630 Beverage serving activities

This class includes the preparation and serving of beverages for immediate consumption on the premises.

This class includes activities of:
- bars
- taverns
- cocktail lounges
- discotheques (with beverage serving predominant)
- beer parlors and pubs
- coffee shops
- fruit juice bars
- mobile beverage vendors

This class excludes:
- reselling packaged/prepared beverages, see 4711, 4722, 4781, 4799
- operation of discotheques and dance floors without beverage serving, see 9329

Railway passenger transport

4911 Passenger rail transport, interurban

This class includes:
- passenger transport by inter-urban railways
- operation of sleeping cars or dining cars as an integrated operation of railway companies

This class excludes:
- passenger transport by urban and suburban transit systems, see 4921
- passenger terminal activities, see 5221
- operation of sleeping cars or dining cars when operated by separate units, see 5590, 5610

Road passenger transport

4922 Other passenger land transport

This class includes:
- other passenger road transport:
  - scheduled long-distance bus services
  - charters, excursions and other occasional coach services
  - taxi operation
  - airport shuttles
- operation of telfers (téléphériques), funiculars, ski and cable lifts if not part of urban or suburban transit systems

This class also includes:
- other renting of private cars with driver
- operation of school buses and buses for transport of employees
- passenger transport by man- or animal-drawn vehicles

This class excludes:
- ambulance transport, see 8690

Water passenger transport

5011 Sea and coastal passenger water transport

This class includes:
- transport of passengers over seas and coastal waters, whether scheduled or not:
  - operation of excursion, cruise or sightseeing boats
  - operation of ferries, water taxis etc.

This class also includes:
- renting of pleasure boats with crew for sea and coastal water transport (e.g. for fishing cruises)

This class excludes:
- restaurant and bar activities on board ships, when provided by separate units, see 5610, 5630
- operation of "floating casinos", see 9200

5021   Inland passenger water transport

This class includes:
- transport of passenger via rivers, canals, lakes and other inland waterways, including inside harbours and ports

This class also includes:
- renting of pleasure boats with crew for inland water transport

Air passenger transport

5110   Passenger air transport

This class includes:
- transport of passengers by air over regular routes and on regular schedules
- charter flights for passengers
- scenic and sightseeing flights

This class also includes:
- renting of air-transport equipment with operator for the purpose of passenger transportation
- general aviation activities, such as:
  - transport of passengers by aero clubs for instruction or pleasure

Transport equipment rental

7710   Renting and leasing of motor vehicles

This class includes:
- renting and operational leasing of the following types of vehicles:
  - passenger cars (without drivers)
  - trucks, utility trailers and recreational vehicles

This class excludes:
- renting or leasing of vehicles or trucks with driver, see 4922, 4923
- financial leasing, see 6491

Travel agencies and other reservation service activities

7911   Travel agency activities

This class includes:
- activities of agencies primarily engaged in selling travel, tour, transportation and accommodation services to the general public and commercial clients

7912   Tour operator activities

This class includes:
- arranging and assembling tours that are sold through travel agencies or directly by tour operators. The tours may include any or all of the following:
  - transportation
  - accommodation
  - food
  - visits to museums, historical or cultural sites, theatrical, musical or sporting events

7990   Other reservation service and related activities

This class includes:
- provision of other travel-related reservation services:
  - reservations for transportation, hotels, restaurants, car rentals, entertainment and sport etc.
- provision of time-share exchange services
- ticket sales activities for theatrical, sports and other amusement and entertainment events
- provision of visitor assistance services:
  - provision of travel information to visitors
  - activities of tourist guides
- tourism promotion activities

This class excludes:
- activities of travel agencies and tour operators, see 7911, 7912
- organization and management of events such as meetings, conventions and conferences, see 8230

Cultural activities

9000   Creative, arts and entertainment activities

This class includes the operation of facilities and provision of services to meet the cultural and entertainment interests of their customers. This includes the production and promotion of, and participation in, live performances, events or exhibits intended for public viewing; the provision of artistic, creative or technical skills for the production of artistic products and live performances.

This class includes:
- production of live theatrical presentations, concerts and opera or dance productions and other stage productions:
  - activities of groups, circuses or companies, orchestras or bands
  - activities of individual artists such as authors, actors, directors, musicians, lecturers or speakers, stage-set designers and builders etc.
- operation of concert and theatre halls and other arts facilities
- activities of sculptors, painters, cartoonists, engravers, etchers etc.
- activities of individual writers, for all subjects including fictional writing, technical writing etc.
- activities of independent journalists
- restoring of works of art such as paintings etc.

This class also includes:
- activities of producers or entrepreneurs of arts live events, with or without facilities

This class excludes:
- restoring of stained glass windows, see 2310
- manufacture of statues, other than artistic originals, see 2396
- restoring of organs and other historical musical instruments, see 3319
- restoring of historical sites and buildings, see 4100
- motion picture and video production, see 5911, 5912
- operation of cinemas, see 5914
- activities of personal theatrical or artistic agents or agencies, see 7490
- casting activities, see 7810
- activities of ticket agencies, see 7990
- operation of museums of all kinds, see 9102
- sports and amusement and recreation activities, see division 93
- restoring of furniture (except museum type restoration), see 9524

9102 Museums activities and operation of historical sites and buildings

This class includes:
- operation of museums of all kinds:
  - art museums, museums of jewellery, furniture, costumes, ceramics, silverware
  - natural history, science and technological museums, historical museums, including military museums
  - other specialized museums
  - open-air museums
- operation of historical sites and buildings

This class excludes:
- renovation and restoration of historical sites and buildings, see section F
- restoration of works of art and museum collection objects, see 9000
- activities of libraries and archives, see 9101

9103 Botanical and zoological gardens and nature reserves activities

This class includes:
- operation of botanical and zoological gardens, including children's zoos
- operation of nature reserves, including wildlife preservation, etc.

This class excludes:
- landscape and gardening services, see 8130
- operation of sport fishing and hunting preserves, see 9319

Sports and recreational activities

7721 Renting and leasing of recreational and sports goods

This class includes:
- renting of recreational and sports equipment:
- pleasure boats, canoes, sailboats,
- bicycles
- beach chairs and umbrellas
- other sports equipment
- skis

This class excludes:
- renting of video tapes and disks, see 7722
- renting of other personal and household goods n.e.c., see 7729
- renting of leisure and pleasure equipment as an integral part of recreational facilities, see 9329

9200 Gambling and betting activities

This class includes:
- bookmaking and other betting operations
- off-track betting
- operation of casinos, including "floating casinos"
- sale of lottery tickets
- operation (exploitation) of coin-operated gambling machines
- operation of virtual gambling web sites

This class excludes:
- operation (exploitation) of coin-operated games, see 9329

9311 Operation of sports facilities

This class includes:
- operation of facilities for indoor or outdoor sports events (open, closed or covered, with or without spectator seating):
  - football, hockey, cricket, baseball, jai-alai stadiums
  - racetracks for auto, dog, horse races
  - swimming pools and stadiums
  - track and field stadiums
  - winter sports arenas and stadiums
  - ice-hockey arenas
  - boxing arenas
  - golf courses
  - bowling lanes
  - fitness centers
- organization and operation of outdoor or indoor sports events for professionals or amateurs by organizations with own facilities

This class includes managing and providing the staff to operate these facilities.

This class excludes:
- renting of recreation and sports equipment, see 7721
- operation of ski hills, see 9329
- park and beach activities, see 9329

9319   Other sports activities

This class includes:
- activities of producers or promoters of sports events, with or without facilities
- activities of individual own-account sportsmen and athletes, referees, judges, timekeepers etc.
- activities of sports leagues and regulating bodies
- activities related to promotion of sporting events
- activities of racing stables, kennels and garages
- operation of sport fishing and hunting preserves
- activities of mountain guides
- support activities for sport or recreational hunting and fishing

This class excludes:
- breeding of racing horses, see 0142
- renting of sports equipment, see 7721
- activities of sport and game schools, see 8541
- activities of sports instructors, teachers, coaches, see 8541
- organization and operation of outdoor or indoor sports events for professionals or amateurs by sports clubs with/without own facilities, see 9311, 9312
- park and beach activities, see 9329

9321   Activities of amusement parks and theme parks

This class includes:
- activities of amusement parks or theme parks, including the operation of a variety of attractions, such as mechanical rides, water rides, games, shows, theme exhibits and picnic grounds

9329   Other amusement and recreation activities n.e.c.

This class includes:
- activities of recreation parks, beaches, including renting of facilities such as bathhouses, lockers, chairs etc.
- operation of recreational transport facilities, e.g. marinas
- operation of ski hills
- renting of leisure and pleasure equipment as an integral part of recreational facilities
- operation of fairs and shows of a recreational nature
- operation of discotheques and dance floors
- operation (exploitation) of coin-operated games
- other amusement and recreation activities (except amusement parks and theme parks) not elsewhere classified

This class also includes:
- activities of producers or entrepreneurs of live events other than arts or sports events, with or without facilities

This class excludes:
- fishing cruises, see 5011, 5021
- provision of space and facilities for short stay by visitors in recreational parks and forests and campgrounds, see 5520
- beverage serving activities of discotheques, see 5630
- trailer parks, campgrounds, recreational camps, hunting and fishing camps, campsites and campgrounds, see 5520

- separate renting of leisure and pleasure equipment, see 7721
- operation (exploitation) of coin-operated gambling machines, see 9200
- activities of amusement parks and theme parks, see 9321

Références conceptuelles et notes techniques

Le présent document comprend aussi quatre annexes :
    Annexe 1. Système national de statistiques du tourisme et comparabilité internationale
    Annexe 2. Comprendre le tourisme : glossaire de base
    Annexe 3. Trouver le tourisme dans les classifications internationales types
    Annexe 4. Liste des industries touristiques regroupées par principales catégories conformément à la CITI Rev. 4

Pour des références complémentaires, voir

http://statistics.unwto.org/en

http://statistics.unwto.org/en/content/international-recommendations-tourism-statistics-2008-irts-200

1.   Tourisme récepteur

Le tourisme récepteur comprend les activités d'un visiteur non résident dans les limites du pays de référence, dans le cadre d'un voyage de tourisme récepteur. Les dépenses correspondantes sont recensées comme dépenses du tourisme récepteur.

Données

Arrivées

Les données concernant les *arrivées* mesurent les flux de visiteurs internationaux dans le pays de référence : chaque arrivée correspond à un voyage du tourisme récepteur. Si une personne se rend dans plusieurs pays à l'occasion d'un seul voyage, chaque arrivée dans un pays est comptabilisée séparément. Sur une période comptable, le nombre d'arrivées n'est pas forcément égal au nombre de personnes qui voyagent (quand une personne se rend dans un même pays plusieurs fois par an, chacun de ses voyages est comptabilisé comme une arrivée).

Les données concernant les *arrivées* doivent correspondre aux *visiteurs du tourisme récepteur* et inclure aussi bien les touristes que les visiteurs de la journée non résidents. Tous les autres types de voyageurs (comme les travailleurs frontaliers, les saisonniers et les autres personnes ayant un contrat de travail à court terme, les étudiants à long terme, etc.) doivent être exclus étant donné qu'ils n'entrent pas dans la catégorie des visiteurs.

Les données proviennent de différentes sources : dossiers administratifs (immigration, comptage de la circulation et autres types de contrôles), enquêtes aux frontières, ou une combinaison de tout cela. Si l'on dispose de données provenant d'enquêtes sur l'hébergement, le nombre de clients est utilisé pour estimer le nombre d'arrivées ; dans ce cas, la ventilation par région, motif principal du voyage, moyens de transport utilisés ou modes d'organisation du voyage se base sur des enquêtes complémentaires auprès des visiteurs.

Les arrivées sont ventilées en fonction de cinq caractéristiques dont deux appellent des commentaires :

– Type de visiteurs (points 1.1 à 1.4 du **Compendium**). Les données ne sont pas ventilées lorsqu'un pays ne peut distinguer un touriste d'un excursionniste.
– Régions (points 1.5 à 1.13 du **Compendium**). Le concept sous-jacent de base est que le pays associé à l'arrivée doit être le pays de résidence. Certains pays n'acceptent pas les recommandations de l'OMT et classent leurs ressortissants qui résident à l'étranger dans une catégorie distincte au lieu de les considérer comme résidents des pays en question (point 1.13 du **Compendium**).

Le *motif principal* d'un voyage se définit comme le motif en l'absence duquel le voyage n'aurait pas eu lieu. On applique la classification suivante :
  1. Motifs personnels
    1.1. Vacances, loisirs et détente
    1.2. Visites aux amis et à la famille
    1.3. Éducation et formation
    1.4. Santé et soins médicaux
    1.5. Religion/pèlerinages
    1.6. Achats
    1.7. Transit
    1.8. Autres
  2. Affaires et motifs professionnels

L'Annuaire des statistiques du tourisme de l'OMT contient des informations complémentaires et précise la répartition des arrivées par pays d'origine :
– **Tableau 1 :**
  Arrivées aux frontières nationales de visiteurs non résidents qui passent la nuit (touristes)
– **Tableau 2 :**
  Arrivées aux frontières nationales de visiteurs non résidents (visiteurs qui passent la nuit [touristes] et visiteurs de la journée [excursionnistes])

Hébergement

Le terme « hébergement » renvoie à des services fournis aux visiteurs par des établissements commerciaux. La catégorie la plus importante est généralement celle des « hôtels et établissements assimilés » recensée dans les CITI, Rev. 4, à la classe 5510 : « Activités d'hébergement temporaire ».
Les nuitées renvoient au nombre de nuits passées par les visiteurs non résidents (voyageurs du tourisme récepteur).

L'Annuaire des statistiques du tourisme de l'OMT contient des informations complémentaires et précise la répartition des arrivées et des nuitées par pays d'origine:
- **Tableau 3:**
  Arrivées de visiteurs non résidents qui passent la nuit (touristes) dans des «hôtels et établissements assimilés»
- **Tableau 4:**
  Arrivées de visiteurs non résidents qui passent la nuit (touristes) dans tous les types d'établissements offrant des services d'hébergement pour les visiteurs
- **Tableau 5:**
  Nuitées de visiteurs non résidents (touristes) dans des «hôtels et établissements assimilés»
- **Tableau 6:**
  Nuitées de visiteurs non résidents (touristes) dans tous les types d'établissements offrant des services d'hébergement pour les visiteurs

Dépenses

Les dépenses associées à l'activité des visiteurs internationaux ont jusqu'à présent été tirées du poste voyages de la balance des paiements: pour le tourisme récepteur, les dépenses associées aux visiteurs du tourisme récepteur sont enregistrées comme «crédits» dans la balance des paiements et renvoient aux «recettes des voyages».

Selon les *Recommandations internationales 2008 sur les statistiques du tourisme*, les «industries et produits touristiques» incluent le transport de passagers. Dans la balance des paiements, il faudrait donc, pour obtenir une estimation plus exacte des dépenses touristiques faites par les visiteurs du tourisme récepteur et du tourisme émetteur au niveau international, ajouter à la valeur du poste voyages celle du poste transport de passagers.

Toutefois, les utilisateurs devraient savoir que les estimations de la balance des paiements incluent, outre les dépenses associées aux visiteurs, celles liées à d'autres types de voyageurs (qui peuvent être importantes dans certains pays, par exemple dans ceux accueillant de nombreux étudiants ou patients de longue durée, travailleurs frontaliers ou saisonniers, etc.).

Les données relatives aux dépenses selon le *motif principal du voyage* sont également des données de la balance des paiements.

Les données publiées correspondent à celles diffusées par le Fonds monétaire international (FMI) (et fournies par les banques centrales). Les données relatives aux dépenses pour le tourisme récepteur et le tourisme émetteur proviennent du CD-ROM de statistiques de la balance des paiements du Fonds monétaire international (FMI).

En cas de divergence importante avec les données fournies à l'OMT par les administrations nationales du tourisme (ANT) pour la préparation du présent Compendium, les données des ANT figurent séparément dans les «notes du pays».

Indicateurs

Taille moyenne du groupe de voyageurs

Un groupe de voyageurs se définit comme un ensemble de visiteurs qui réalisent ensemble un voyage et dont les dépenses sont mises en commun. La taille moyenne des groupes de voyageurs permet de procéder à une estimation du nombre total de voyages des visiteurs internationaux, estimation utile pour le marketing et la formulation de politiques.

Durée moyenne du séjour

Tous ces indicateurs renvoient à la durée des voyages à l'étranger des visiteurs internationaux (exprimés en nombre de jours ou de nuits).

La durée moyenne totale du séjour renvoie aux services d'hébergement commerciaux et non commerciaux fournis aux visiteurs, ainsi qu'à d'autres types de séjours.

Attendu qu'un visiteur non résident peut utiliser plusieurs installations d'hébergement pendant son séjour, le total ne peut être estimé qu'en utilisant les informations recueillies dans le cadre des enquêtes aux frontières ou en vérifiant les dates des cartes d'arrivée et de départ d'un échantillon (ou de l'ensemble) de visiteurs.

Dépenses moyennes par jour

Cet indicateur se réfère aux dépenses totales de l'ensemble des visiteurs divisées par le nombre total de jours passés, calculées sur la base d'enquêtes menées auprès des visiteurs.

2. Tourisme interne

Le tourisme interne comprend les activités d'un visiteur résident dans les limites du pays de référence (dans le cadre d'un voyage de tourisme interne ou d'un voyage de tourisme émetteur).

Les dépenses correspondantes de ce visiteur dans l'économie de référence sont recensées comme dépenses de tourisme interne. En outre, les dépenses des visiteurs du tourisme émetteur relatives aux produits fournis par des entreprises résidentes sont incluses dans les dépenses internes.

Données

Les voyages effectués par les visiteurs sont des voyages touristiques. Un voyage de tourisme interne désigne le voyage d'un visiteur à partir du moment où il quitte son lieu de résidence habituelle jusqu'à son retour: il s'agit d'un voyage aller-retour.

Le terme «hébergement» renvoie à des services fournis aux visiteurs par des établissements commerciaux. La catégorie la plus importante est généralement celle des «hôtels et établissements assimilés» recensée dans les CITI, Rev. 4, à la classe 5510: «Activités d'hébergement temporaire».

Les nuitées renvoient au nombre de nuits passées par les visiteurs résidents (voyageurs du tourisme interne). Il y a lieu de privilégier, comme source de données, les enquêtes sur l'hébergement (adressées aux établissements).

Indicateurs

Durée moyenne du séjour

La durée moyenne totale du séjour renvoie aux services d'hébergement commerciaux et non commerciaux fournis aux visiteurs, ainsi qu'à d'autres types de séjours.

Les données totales ne peuvent être estimées que grâce à des enquêtes menées auprès des ménages.

Dépenses moyennes par jour

Cet indicateur se réfère aux dépenses totales divisées par le nombre total de jours passés, calculées sur la base d'enquêtes menées auprès des visiteurs.

3. Tourisme émetteur

Le tourisme émetteur désigne les activités d'un visiteur résident hors du pays de référence (dans le cadre d'un voyage du tourisme émetteur ou d'un voyage de tourisme interne). Les dépenses correspondantes sont recensées comme dépenses du tourisme émetteur.

Données

Les données concernant les *départs* mesurent les flux de visiteurs résidents qui quittent le pays de référence. Le nombre de départs n'est pas forcément égal au nombre d'arrivées déclarées par les destinations internationales pour le pays de référence.

Les dépenses associées à l'activité des visiteurs ont jusqu'à présent été tirées du poste voyages de la balance des paiements : pour le tourisme émetteur, les dépenses associées aux visiteurs résidents sont enregistrées comme « débits » dans la balance des paiements et renvoient aux « dépenses de voyages ». Comme dans le cas du *tourisme récepteur*, on utilise les données de la balance des paiements.

Selon les *Recommandations internationales 2008 sur les statistiques du tourisme,* les « industries et produits touristiques » incluent le transport de passagers. Dans la balance des paiements, il faudrait donc, pour obtenir une estimation plus exacte des dépenses touristiques faites par les visiteurs résidents et non résidents au niveau international, ajouter à la valeur du poste voyages celle du poste transport de passagers.
Toutefois, les utilisateurs devraient savoir que les estimations de la balance des paiements incluent, outre les dépenses associées aux visiteurs, celles liées à d'autres types de voyageurs.

Les données relatives aux dépenses selon le *motif principal* du voyage sont également des données de la balance des paiements.

Les données publiées correspondent à celles diffusées par le Fonds monétaire international (FMI) (et fournies par les banques centrales) ; en cas de divergence importante avec les données fournies à l'OMT par les administrations nationales du tourisme (ANT) pour la préparation du présent Compendium, les données des ANT seront données séparément dans les « notes du pays ». Pour de plus amples informations sur les notes de pays du FMI, veuillez consulter le paragraphe concernant les dépenses pour le tourisme récepteur.

Des informations complémentaires sur « les voyages à l'étranger des visiteurs résidents vers les pays de destination » sont disponibles à l'adresse suivante : www.e-unwto.org/home/main.mpx. Il y a lieu de préciser que les informations données dans les tableaux sont basées sur les données fournies par chaque pays de destination et qu'elles correspondent donc aux arrivées dans ces pays.

Indicateurs

Durée moyenne du séjour

Cet indicateur renvoie à la durée des voyages à l'étranger des visiteurs du tourisme émetteur (exprimée en nombre de jours) et reflète la moyenne totale, établie sur la base d'enquêtes aux frontières et/ou d'informations fournies par les ménages.

Dépenses moyennes par jour

Cet indicateur se réfère aux dépenses totales divisées par le nombre total de jours passés, calculées sur la base d'enquêtes aux frontières et/ou d'informations fournies par les ménages.

4. Industries touristiques

L'expression *industries touristiques* désigne les industries qui produisent généralement des produits caractéristiques du tourisme ; elle équivaut à l'expression plus courante de « secteur touristique ». Ces industries sont recensées ci-dessous :

1. Hébergement des visiteurs
2. Activités de services de restauration et de consommation de boissons
3. Transport de voyageurs par chemin de fer
4. Transport routier de voyageurs
5. Transport de voyageurs par voies navigables
6. Transport de voyageurs par voie aérienne
7. Location de matériels de transport
8. Activités des agences de voyages et autres activités de services de réservation
9. Activités culturelles
10. Activités sportives et récréatives
11. Commerce de détail de biens caractéristiques du tourisme, propres à chaque pays
12. Autres activités caractéristiques du tourisme, propres à chaque pays

Les notes explicatives suivantes se réfèrent aux industries *Hébergement des visiteurs* et *Activités des agences de voyages et autres activités de services de réservation*, qui sont les deux seules industries pour lesquelles des données monétaires et non monétaires sont publiées dans le présent Compendium.

Ces notes, qui peuvent être consultées à l'annexe 4, sont tirées de la *Classification internationale type, par industrie, de toutes les branches d'activité économique (CITI), Rev. 4. Études statistiques (Série M, N° 4/Rev.4), Nations Unies. New York, 2008.*

Hébergement des visiteurs

Le nombre d'établissements de l'industrie d'*Hébergement des visiteurs* (point 4.2. du Compendium) renvoie à tous les types d'établissements qui offrent des services d'hébergement aux visiteurs sur une base commerciale (de marché), c'est-à-dire moyennant rémunération. Par conséquent, les données doivent comprendre toutes les classes suivantes de l'ISIC :

5510 Activités d'hébergement temporaire

Cette classe figure dans la section 4 du Compendium sous le titre « Hébergement des visiteurs dans des hôtels et des établissements assimilés » et couvre les activités d'hébergement, généralement assuré à la journée ou à la semaine, essentiellement à l'intention de visiteurs pour des séjours temporaires. Il s'agit d'hébergement dans des chambres d'hôtes meublées, ou de plusieurs pièces attenantes ou encore d'appartements avec cuisine, avec ou sans services quotidiens de ménage, et pouvant souvent comprendre une gamme de services complémentaires tels que des services de repas et de boissons, de garage, de lessive, de piscines et de gymnastique, ainsi que installations récréatives et des salles de réunions et de conférences.

Cette classe comprend la fourniture d'hébergement temporaire assuré par les établissements suivants :
- hôtels
- centres de villégiature
- hôtels offrant des suites/appartements
- motels
- hôtels pour automobilistes
- chambres d'hôtes
- pensions
- foyers assurant gîte et couvert
- appartements et bungalows
- établissements d'hébergement en multipropriété
- maisons de vacances
- chalets, cottages et maisonnettes
- auberges de jeunesse et refuges de montagne

Exclusions :
- fourniture de maisons ou d'appartements meublés ou non meublés pour de plus longues durées, généralement sur une base mensuelle ou annuelle, voir division 68

5520 Terrains de camping, parcs pour véhicules de loisirs et caravanes

Cette classe comprend les activités suivantes :
- fourniture d'installations d'hébergement telles que terrains de camping, terrains de caravanage, parcs de loisirs, d'espaces de chasse et de pêche à l'intention de visiteurs temporaires
- fourniture d'espaces et d'installations pour les véhicules de loisirs.

Cette classe couvre en outre des lieux d'hébergement tels que :
- abris protecteurs ou aires de campement pour dresser des tentes et/ou installer des sacs de couchage

5590 Autres activités d'hébergement

Cette classe comprend la fourniture d'hébergement temporaire ou à plus long terme dans une seule pièce ou en salles communes ou dortoirs pour étudiants, travailleurs migrants (saisonniers) et autres personnes.

Cette classe comprend la fourniture de logement assurée par les entités suivantes :
- résidences d'étudiants
- dortoirs de pensionnats
- foyers pour travailleurs
- pensions
- voitures-lits de chemins de fer

6810 Activités immobilières sur biens propres ou loués

Cette classe comprend les activités suivantes :
- achat, vente, location et exploitation de biens immobiliers propres ou loués :
  - immeubles résidentiels et habitations
  - bâtiments non résidentiels, y compris les halls d'exposition, les installations d'entreposage pour particuliers, les galeries marchandes et les centres commerciaux
  - terrains
- fourniture de maisons individuelles et d'appartements meublés et non meublés pour une utilisation plus permanente généralement sur une base mensuelle ou annuelle

Cette classe comprend en outre les activités suivantes :
- mise en œuvre de projets de construction immobilière pour compte propre en vue, par exemple, de locations dans ces immeubles
- subdivision de biens immobiliers en lotissements, sans viabilisation de terrains
- exploitation d'emplacements pour caravanes

Exclusions :
- mise en œuvre de projets de construction immobilière dans un but de vente, voir 4100
- subdivision et viabilisation de terrains, voir 4290
- exploitation d'hôtels, appartements en hôtel et lieux d'hébergement analogues, voir 5510
- exploitation de terrains de camping, de parcs pour caravanes et autres lieux d'hébergement, voir 5520
- exploitation de foyers de travailleurs, de maisons meublées et autres lieux d'hébergement, voir 5590

6820   Activités immobilières à forfait ou sous contrat

Cette classe couvre la prestation d'activités dans le domaine de l'immobilier, à forfait ou sous contrat, y compris les services connexes

Cette classe comprend les activités suivantes :
- activités des agents et courtiers immobiliers
- intermédiation en matière d'achat, vente et location immobilière à forfait ou sous contrat
- gestion de biens immobiliers à forfait ou sous contrat
- services d'évaluation pour l'immobilier
- activités des dépositaires légaux en matière immobilière

Exclusions :
- activités juridiques, voir 6910
- services d'appui aux installations, voir 8110
- gestion d'installations, par exemple les bases militaires, les prisons, etc. (sauf la gestion d'installations informatiques), voir 8110

Activités des agences de voyages et autres activités de services de réservation

7911   Activités des agences de voyages

Cette classe comprend les activités suivantes :
- activités d'agences dont le rôle principal est de vendre des voyages, des excursions, des services de transport et d'hébergement au grand public et à des clients commerciaux.

7912   Activités des voyagistes

Cette classe comprend les activités suivantes :
- organisation et groupement d'excursions vendues par l'intermédiaire d'agences de voyage ou directement par des voyagistes. Les excursions peuvent inclure toutes ou partie des activités suivantes :
  - transport
  - hébergement
  - restauration
  - visites de musées, de sites historiques ou culturels, théâtre, événements musicaux ou sportifs

7990   Autres activités de services de réservation et activités connexes

Cette classe comprend les activités suivantes :
- fourniture d'autres services de réservation relatifs aux voyages :
  - réservations dans les moyens de transport, les hôtels, les restaurants, location de voitures, spectacles et événements sportifs, etc.
- fourniture de services en multipropriété
- vente de billets pour le théâtre, les événements sportifs et spectacles divers
- fourniture de services d'assistance aux visiteurs :
  - fourniture de renseignements concernant les voyages
  - activités de guides touristiques
- activités de promotion du tourisme

Exclusions :
- activités d'agences de voyage et de voyagistes, voir 7911, 7912
- organisation et gestion d'événements tels que réunions, congrès et conférences, voir 8230

Données

Concernant le *nombre d'établissements*, le point 4.3 du Compendium inclut les établissements associés aux classes 5520, 5590, 6810 et 6820 (voir plus haut les notes explicatives pour l'hébergement des visiteurs).

Le nombre de *chambres* et de *places-lits* se réfère à la capacité des « hôtels et établissements assimilés » de fournir un hébergement temporaire aux visiteurs.

Indicateurs

Les trois premiers indicateurs se basent sur le nombre total de nuitées des touristes résidents et non résidents dans des hôtels et établissements assimilés.

Le *taux d'occupation* se réfère au rapport entre la capacité existante de fournir des services d'hébergement aux visiteurs et le degré d'utilisation de ces services. Ce taux peut se référer à l'utilisation soit des chambres soit des places-lits.

La *capacité disponible* renvoie au nombre de places-lits dans les hôtels et établissements similaires pour 1 000 habitants de la population résidente permanente du pays de référence. Les données sont attribuées par l'OMT lorsqu'elles ne sont pas fournies par le pays.

5. Emploi

Les personnes qui travaillent dans les industries touristiques peuvent être des *employés* (personnes qui travaillent pour une entreprise moyennant une rémunération en espèces ou en nature, selon ce qui a été convenu) ou des *travailleurs indépendants* (personnes qui travaillent à leur compte, ont un « travail indépendant » et n'ont engagé de manière continue aucun « employé » durant la période de référence).

Certains employés peuvent avoir plusieurs postes de travail ; par conséquent, le nombre de postes de travail (du côté de la demande) et le nombre de personnes employées (du côté de l'offre) ne sont pas des catégories similaires et en général elles ne coïncident pas.

L'intensité du travail peut varier selon le poste, l'industrie ou la période. Les postes de travail peuvent être différents selon le temps de travail des personnes employées et donc être exprimés en termes d'emplois à temps plein ou à temps partiel. C'est pourquoi il ne suffit pas de disposer de données sur le nombre de postes de travail ou de personnes employées pour avoir des informations sur le volume du travail accompli durant une période déterminée (par exemple, un mois ou un an). Des données sur le nombre total d'heures de travail seront nécessaires. Enfin, si l'on convertit tous les postes de travail en emploi à plein temps équivalent ou en nombre total d'heures travaillées par an, on pourra obtenir le volume total du travail d'une industrie touristique donnée pour une période donnée.

Les chiffres concernant le «Nombre d'emplois par situation dans la profession» et le «Nombre d'emplois équivalents plein temps par situation dans la profession» doivent renvoyer aux industries touristiques.

6. Indicateurs complémentaires

Ces indicateurs proviennent de la balance des paiements, des comptes nationaux et des statistiques du tourisme.

Demande

La propension brute à voyager mesure le nombre de voyages du tourisme émetteur et du tourisme interne au regard du total de la population résidente permanente du pays de référence. Des valeurs élevées de cet indicateur indiquent une grande fréquence des voyages et traduisent la mobilité actuelle de la population voyageant.

L'indicateur «arrivées/population» donne une estimation de l'intensité touristique dans le pays de référence. Cet indicateur est calculé par l'OMT d'après les données de base disponibles concernant le tourisme récepteur et le tourisme interne, pouvant être le nombre de visiteurs (code 1.1 pour le tourisme récepteur et 2.1 pour le tourisme interne) ou le nombre de touristes (code 1.2 pour le tourisme récepteur et 2.2 pour le tourisme interne). Le calcul est fait à l'aide des formules suivantes, indiquées par ordre de préférence, en tenant compte des données de base disponibles pour le pays de référence :

(1.2 touristes d'entrée + 2.2 touristes internes) / population
(1.2 touristes d'entrée + 2.1 visiteurs internes) / population
(1.2 touristes d'entrée) / population
(1.1 Visiteurs d'entrée + 2.1 Visiteurs internes) / population
(1.1 Visiteurs d'entrée + 2.2 touristes internes) / population
(1.1 Visiteurs d'entrée) / population

Les données relatives à la population correspondent à celles publiées par le Fonds monétaire international (FMI), la Banque mondiale ou, à défaut, par le bureau national de statistique du pays de référence.

À chaque nouvelle édition du Compendium, la formule sera adaptée en fonction des données de base disponibles pour la période de référence (5 ans).

Indicateurs macroéconomiques liés au tourisme international

Les indicateurs se fondent sur les *Statistiques de la balance des paiements* et les *Statistiques financières internationales* du Fonds monétaire international.

Ces indicateurs, et d'autres indicateurs complémentaires, constituent un système préliminaire très simple d'évaluation de la contribution économique du tourisme à l'économie nationale. Ils sont précieux du fait qu'ils sont généralement disponibles dans la plupart des pays, que l'on peut les comparer sur le plan international et les rapprocher d'autres indicateurs économiques.

Il y a lieu de remarquer que le terme «dépenses» est utilisé de la même manière dans le tourisme récepteur et le tourisme émetteur pour indiquer la somme payée pour l'acquisition de biens et de services de consommation, mais aussi de biens de valeur, en vue de leur usage personnel ou pour les offrir, pour et durant des voyages touristiques. Les visiteurs étrangers dans le pays de référence réalisent des dépenses de tourisme récepteur (crédits dans la balance des paiements), tandis que les visiteurs résidents présents dans des pays étrangers réalisent des dépenses du tourisme émetteur (débits dans la balance des paiements).

Dépenses du tourisme récepteur sur PIB

Elles reflètent le poids des dépenses des visiteurs du tourisme récepteur en tant qu'élément de la valeur totale de l'activité économique dans l'économie de référence. Du point de vue du commerce international, cet indicateur rend compte de l'importance économique des rentrées de devises associées aux dépenses de ces visiteurs.

Dépenses du tourisme émetteur sur PIB

Elles reflètent l'importance des dépenses à l'étranger des visiteurs du tourisme émetteur au regard de l'économie nationale. Du point de vue du commerce international, cet indicateur rend compte de l'importance économique des sorties de revenus nationaux attribuables à ces visiteurs.

Balance des paiements du tourisme sur PIB

Elle rend compte de l'importance économique des dépenses nettes du tourisme (récepteur moins émetteur) pour l'économie de référence. Un excédent ou un déficit important affecte la balance commerciale du pays, et par conséquent son PIB.

Ouverture touristique

Elle montre l'importance de la somme des dépenses touristiques transfrontalières (c'est-à-dire du tourisme international, la somme des dépenses du tourisme récepteur et émetteur) pour l'économie de référence. Cet indicateur pourrait également être utilisé pour mesurer le flux libre de tourisme entre le pays de référence et le reste du monde.

Couverture touristique

Elle rend compte de la proportion entre les dépenses du tourisme récepteur et les dépenses du tourisme émetteur pour montrer dans quelle mesure les influx de revenus étrangers couvrent les sorties de revenus nationaux. Une valeur supérieure à 100 signifie que le tourisme récepteur finance indirectement plus que toutes les dépenses des visiteurs du tourisme émetteur, tandis qu'une valeur inférieure à 100 signifie que le tourisme récepteur ne couvre pas les dépenses que font les visiteurs résidents à l'étranger.

Dépenses du tourisme récepteur sur exportations de biens
Dépenses du tourisme récepteur sur exportations de services
Dépenses du tourisme récepteur sur exportations de biens et de services

Ces trois indicateurs reflètent l'importance du tourisme en tant que service dont le commerce s'effectue à l'échelle internationale par rapport à d'autres catégories d'exportations. En même temps, ils révèlent le degré de spécialisation touristique de la structure des exportations d'un pays, et la capacité relative du tourisme de générer des devises.

Dépenses du tourisme récepteur sur crédits du compte courant

Les crédits du compte courant de la balance des paiements se réfèrent à tous les afflux de biens et de services, de revenus et de transferts courants dans une économie. Plus la part occupée par le tourisme dans cet ensemble est grande, plus l'activité touristique est importante en tant que génératrice d'afflux de devises.

Dépenses du tourisme émetteur sur importations de biens
Dépenses du tourisme émetteur sur importations de services
Dépenses du tourisme émetteur sur importations de biens et de services

Ces trois indicateurs reflètent l'importance du tourisme en tant que service dont le commerce s'effectue à l'échelle internationale par rapport à d'autres catégories d'importations. En même temps, ils montrent la prédilection pour le tourisme de la structure des importations d'un pays et le degré relatif de sorties de revenus nationaux d'une économie résultant du tourisme international.

Dépenses du tourisme émetteur sur débits des comptes courants

Les débits du compte courant de la balance des paiements se réfèrent à toutes les sorties de biens, de services, de revenus et de transferts courants d'un pays vers le reste du monde. Plus la part du tourisme dans cet ensemble est grande, plus l'activité touristique occupe une place importante dans la fuite de revenus nationaux.

Annexe 1
Système national de statistiques du tourisme et comparabilité internationale

La structure du **Compendium des statistiques du tourisme** se fonde sur le système suivant qui renvoie au cadre d'informations de base des systèmes nationaux de statistiques du tourisme à des fins de comparabilité internationale (http://statistics.unwto.org/sites/all/files/docpdf/ststext.pdf).

Les *Recommandations internationales 2008 sur les statistiques du tourisme* (RIST 2008) constituent le cadre conceptuel de ce noyau essentiel de données et d'indicateurs.

Comparabilité internationale et statistiques du tourisme : le cadre d'informations de base

I. Cadre conceptuel

Concepts	Unités d'observation	Principales caractéristiques connexes
Visiteur	Visiteur	Classes : Visiteur qui passe la nuit (touriste), visiteur de la journée (excursionniste)
		Pays de résidence/régions
	Groupe de voyageurs	Taille
Voyage	Voyage touristique	Motif principal
		Durée
		Destination principale
		Modes de transport
		Types d'hébergement utilisés
		Organisation
		Dépenses
Industries touristiques	Établissement	**Monétaires**
		Production
		Consommation intermédiaire
		Valeur ajoutée brute
		Rémunération des employés
		Formation brute de capital fixe
		Non monétaires
		Caractéristiques non monétaires propres à chaque industrie touristique
Emploi	Établissement (dans les industries touristiques)	Personnes
		Taille
		Statut
		Postes de travail
		Durée du travail
		Postes de travail équivalents à temps plein

II. Classifications

1. Formes de tourisme
2. Classification des produits de consommation achetés par les visiteurs
3. Classification des activités productives au service des visiteurs
4. Autres classifications

III. Tableaux de résultats

1. Tourisme récepteur
2. Tourisme interne
3. Tourisme émetteur
4. Industries touristiques
5. Emploi
6. Indicateurs complémentaires

Annexe 2
Comprendre le tourisme : glossaire de base

Cette annexe reprend certains concepts clés qu'elle définit conformément aux nouvelles *RIST 2008*.
http://statistics.unwto.org/en/content/international-recommendations-tourism-statistics-2008-irts-2008

Un glossaire plus complet et récemment actualisé des termes touristiques est disponible uniquement en anglais :
https://s3-eu-west-1.amazonaws.com/staticunwto/Statistics/Glossary+of+terms.pdf

Activités/produits caractéristiques du tourisme	*Les activités caractéristiques du tourisme désignent les activités productives dont la production principale est caractéristique du tourisme.* *Les produits caractéristiques du tourisme sont ceux qui remplissent au moins une des deux conditions suivantes :* *Les dépenses touristiques concernant le produit (bien ou service) doivent représenter une part importante des dépenses touristiques totales (condition relative à la part correspondant aux dépenses/demande) ;* *Les dépenses touristiques concernant le produit doivent représenter une part importante de l'offre du produit dans l'économie (condition relative à la part correspondant à l'offre). Cette condition suppose que la fourniture d'un produit caractéristique du tourisme serait susceptible de cesser d'exister en quantité significative en cas d'absence de visiteurs.*
Dépenses touristiques	*Les dépenses touristiques renvoient à la somme payée pour l'acquisition de biens et de services de consommation, mais aussi de biens de valeur, en vue de leur usage personnel ou pour les offrir, pour et durant des voyages touristiques.*
Emploi dans les industries touristiques	*L'emploi dans les industries touristiques peut être mesuré en effectuant le dénombrement des personnes employées dans les industries touristiques, quel que soit leur poste de travail, le dénombrement des personnes ayant leur emploi principal dans les industries touristiques, ou le dénombrement des postes de travail dans les industries touristiques.*
Environnement habituel	*L'environnement habituel d'une personne, concept clé du tourisme, se définit comme la zone géographique (pas forcément contiguë) à l'intérieur de laquelle une personne mène ses activités quotidiennes habituelles.*
Groupe de voyageurs	*Un groupe de voyageurs se définit comme un ensemble de visiteurs qui réalisent ensemble un voyage et dont les dépenses sont mises en commun.*
Industries touristiques	*Les industries touristiques désignent tous les établissements dont l'activité productive principale est une activité caractéristique du tourisme.*
Lieu de résidence habituelle	*Le lieu de résidence habituelle est le lieu géographique où le visiteur réside habituellement, et se définit par l'endroit de son lieu d'habitation principal (Principes et recommandations pour les recensements de la population et de l'habitation, Nations Unies).*
Maison de vacances	*Une maison de vacances est une habitation secondaire où se rendent les membres du ménage essentiellement à des fins récréatives, pour des vacances ou toute autre forme de loisir.*
Motif (principal) d'un voyage touristique	*Le motif principal d'un voyage touristique se définit comme le motif en l'absence duquel le voyage n'aurait pas eu lieu. La classification des voyages touristiques en fonction du motif principal du voyage se réfère à neuf catégories : cette typologie permet d'identifier différents sous-ensembles de visiteurs (visiteurs en voyages d'affaires, visiteurs en transit, etc.).*
Tourisme émetteur	*Comprend les activités d'un visiteur résident hors du pays de référence, dans le cadre d'un voyage du tourisme émetteur ou d'un voyage de tourisme interne.*

RÉFÉRENCES CONCEPTUELLES et NOTES TECHNIQUES

Tourisme interne	*Comprend les activités d'un visiteur résident dans les limites du pays de référence, dans le cadre d'un voyage de tourisme interne ou d'un voyage du tourisme émetteur.*
Tourisme récepteur	*Comprend les activités d'un visiteur non résident dans les limites du pays de référence, dans le cadre d'un voyage du tourisme récepteur.*
Touriste (ou visiteur qui passe la nuit) et excursionniste (visiteur de la journée)	*Un visiteur (du tourisme interne, récepteur ou émetteur) est qualifié de touriste (ou visiteur qui passe la nuit) s'il passe une nuit sur place, et de touriste de la journée (ou excursionniste) dans le cas contraire.*
Visite	*Un voyage se compose de visites effectuées à différents endroits. L'expression «visite touristique» fait référence à un séjour dans un endroit visité durant un voyage touristique.*
Visiteur	*Un visiteur est une personne qui se déplace vers une destination située en dehors de son environnement habituel, pour une durée inférieure à un an, et dont le motif de la visite (affaires, loisirs ou autre motif personnel) est autre que celui d'exercer une activité rémunérée dans le pays ou le lieu visité.*
Visiteur interne	*Une personne qui se rend dans un lieu situé dans son pays de résidence est un visiteur interne et ses activités s'inscrivent dans le cadre du tourisme interne.*
Voyage	*Un voyage désigne le déplacement d'une personne depuis le moment où elle quitte son lieu de résidence habituelle jusqu'à son retour : il s'agit donc d'un voyage aller-retour. Les voyages des visiteurs sont des voyages touristiques.*
Voyage/Tourisme	*Le terme «voyage» désigne les activités des voyageurs. Un voyageur est une personne qui se déplace entre différents lieux géographiques pour quelque motif et durée que ce soit. Le visiteur est un type particulier de voyageur, de sorte que le tourisme est un sous-ensemble des voyages.*

Annexe 3
Trouver le tourisme dans les classifications internationales types

L'importance du tourisme et la nécessité de définir et de mesurer son importance au sein du système de statistique des Nations Unies a été reconnue par la Commission de statistique de l'ONU avec l'approbation en 1993 des Recommandations sur les statistiques du tourisme. Ladite Commission a approuvé en 2008 la version révisée de ces recommandations, intitulée *Recommandations internationales 2008 sur les statistiques du tourisme* (RIST 2008).

Pour étudier la contribution économique du tourisme à l'économie nationale, il était nécessaire d'intégrer l'analyse économique du tourisme dans le cadre de référence du Système de comptabilité nationale (le SCN 1993). Cela a conduit à l'approbation, en 2000, par la Commission de statistique de l'ONU du «Compte satellite du tourisme: Recommandations concernant le cadre conceptuel», qui a été actualisé par la suite en tant que «Compte satellite du tourisme: Recommandations concernant le cadre conceptuel 2008» (CST: RCC 2008).

Les concepts, définitions et classifications contenus dans les RIST 2008 ont été harmonisés avec le CST: RCC 2008, lequel a été harmonisé à son tour avec le Système de comptabilité nationale de 2008, la balance des paiements et le commerce international de services.

Pour le tourisme, il est intéressant de recenser les produits achetés par les visiteurs, directement et indirectement, et les activités qui en sont à l'origine. Les classifications utilisées pour les activités et les produits détaillés requis dans l'étude du tourisme sont tirées directement des classifications de référence des Nations Unies, et y sont liées: CITI et CPC.

L'analyse du tourisme est axée sur le visiteur. Dans un premier temps, il est intéressant de mesurer les dépenses des visiteurs et de recenser les produits, tant les biens que les services, achetés par les visiteurs, ainsi que les activités qui sont à l'origine de ces produits. Dans un cadre macroéconomique, comme celui du CST, le concept de tourisme englobe aussi bien la perspective de la demande, qui consiste en la consommation du visiteur, la consommation touristique collective et la formation brute de capital fixe du tourisme, que la perspective de l'offre d'activités touristiques (en s'intéressant en particulier à la part de leur production achetée par les visiteurs). Le tourisme en tant que tel n'est pas mentionné dans le SCN 1993 ni dans la CITI. S'agissant du tourisme, les activités couvertes par la CITI qui produisent des biens et des services satisfaisant la demande touristique sont réunies et regroupées en tant qu'activités touristiques.

Si l'on se place du point de vue de la demande, le visiteur est l'unité basique d'observation et d'analyse, et les dépenses des visiteurs sont observées en termes de produits (essentiellement des services). Du point de vue de l'offre, vu leur relation avec le système de comptabilité nationale, les statistiques du tourisme utilisent «l'établissement» comme unité statistique de base, ainsi qu'il est défini dans le SCN, et «l'industrie» comme unité de présentation et d'analyse, l'industrie étant définie comme un «groupe d'établissements exerçant le même type d'activités de production».

Au premier chef, il y a lieu de recenser les produits achetés par les visiteurs. Pour la compilation des données du point de vue de la demande, les produits sont regroupés en grandes catégories en fonction du motif; cependant, le tourisme exige une analyse simultanée de la consommation et de la production, d'où la classification utilisée pour définir les produits dans la Classification centrale de produits (CPC ver. 2.). Les produits achetés par les visiteurs peuvent être regroupés dans les classes détaillées de la CPC et les activités qui en sont à l'origine recensées sur la base des classes détaillées de la CITI.

Le tourisme définit certains des produits achetés par les visiteurs et les activités qui en sont à l'origine comme des «produits caractéristiques du tourisme» (ceux qui réunissent certaines conditions) et des «activités caractéristiques du tourisme» (celles qui produisent normalement des produits caractéristiques du tourisme). Les RIST 2008 expliquent de manière détaillée les concepts sous-jacents, les définitions et les classifications qui doivent être utilisés pour compiler les statistiques du tourisme et recenser les produits et activités caractéristiques du tourisme. Pour faciliter la comparaison au niveau international, des listes de ces produits et activités caractéristiques ont été dressées. L'annexe 3 du présent document fournit une liste des activités caractéristiques du tourisme (industries touristiques) regroupées en grandes catégories d'après la CITI rev. 4. L'annexe 4 quant à elle fournit une liste des produits caractéristiques du tourisme regroupés par grandes catégories d'après la CPC ver. 2. Même dans le cas où le produit acheté par le visiteur ne constitue qu'une partie de la classe de la CPC ou lorsque l'activité qui en est à l'origine ne constitue qu'une partie d'une classe à quatre chiffres de la CITI, les listes étant exprimées en termes de classes de la CPC et d'agrégats des classes de la CITI, elles fournissent une classe définie dans laquelle chaque produit ou activité peut être placé. Il est recommandé aux pays qui en auraient besoin pour leur propre analyse de créer des classes plus détaillées en dessous du niveau le plus bas de la CPC et de la CITI.

La portée de l'analyse des statistiques du tourisme est plus large quand on place celles-ci dans le cadre du compte satellite du tourisme. Dans le cadre de la comptabilité, les produits et les activités sont exprimés au regard de la CPC ver. 2 et de la CITI rev. 4, notamment ceux et celles associés au tourisme. Les classifications internationales de produits et d'activités utilisées pour compiler les données pour le CST: RCC 2008, lequel établit des liens structurels avec le système de comptabilité nationale, permettent une meilleure appréciation des liens qui unissent le tourisme à d'autres secteurs économiques.

Annexe 4
Liste des industries touristiques (activités caractéristiques) regroupées par principales catégories conformément à la CITI Rev. 4

Industries touristiques	CITI Rev.4	Description
1. Hébergement des visiteurs	5510	Activités d'hébergement temporaire
	5520	Terrains de camping, parcs pour véhicules de loisirs et caravanes
	5590	Autres activités d'hébergement
	6810	Activités immobilières sur biens propres ou loués*
	6820	Activités immobilières à forfait ou sous contrat*
2. Activités de services de restauration et de consommation de boissons	5610	Activités de restaurants et de services de restauration mobiles
	5629	Autres activités de services de restauration
	5630	Activités de consommation de boissons
3. Transport de voyageurs par chemin de fer	4911	Transport de voyageurs par chemin de fer interurbain
4. Transport routier de voyageurs	4922	Autres transports terrestres de voyageurs
5. Transport de voyageurs par voies navigables	5011	Transports maritimes et côtiers de voyageurs
	5021	Transport de voyageurs par voies navigables intérieures
6. Transport de voyageurs par voie aérienne	5110	Transport aérien de voyageurs
7. Location de matériels de transport	7710	Location de véhicules automobiles
8. Activités des agences de voyages et autres activités de services de réservation	7911	Activités des agences de voyages
	7912	Activités des voyagistes
	7990	Autres activités de services de réservation et activités connexes
9. Activités culturelles	9000	Activités créatives, arts et spectacles
	9102	Activités des musées et exploitation des sites et monuments historiques
	9103	Activités des jardins botaniques et zoologiques et des réserves naturelles
10. Activités sportives et récréatives	7721	Location d'articles pour le sport et les loisirs
	9200	Activités de jeux de hasard et de pari
	9311	Exploitation d'installations sportives
	9319	Autres activités sportives
	9321	Activités des parcs d'attraction et à thèmes
	9329	Autres activités récréatives et de loisirs, n.c.a.
11. Commerce de détail de biens caractéristiques du tourisme, propres à chaque pays		Boutiques hors taxes**
		Commerce de détail de souvenirs dans des établissements spécialisés**
		Commerce de détail d'artisanat dans des établissements spécialisés**
		Autre commerce de détail de biens caractéristiques du tourisme dans des établissements spécialisés**
12. Autres activités caractéristiques du tourisme, propres à chaque pays		

* partie relative aux résidences secondaires et multipropriétés
** pas d'indice CITI à quatre chiffres

Notes explicatives

Ces notes explicatives font référence uniquement à des activités caractéristiques du tourisme comparables au plan international et suivent l'ordre donné ci-dessus à l'annexe 4.

Elles sont tirées de la *Classification internationale type, par industrie, de toutes les branches d'activité économique (CITI), Rev. 4. Études statistiques (Série M, N° 4/Rev.4), Nations Unies, New York, 2008.*

Le document complet est disponible à l'adresse suivante : http://unstats.un.org/unsd/cr/registry/regdntransfer. asp?f=135

Hébergement des visiteurs

5510   Activités d'hébergement temporaire

Cette classe couvre les activités d'hébergement, généralement assuré à la journée ou à la semaine, essentiellement à l'intention de visiteurs pour des séjours temporaires. Il s'agit d'hébergement dans des chambres d'hôtes meublées, ou de plusieurs pièces attenantes ou encore d'appartements avec cuisine, avec ou sans services quotidiens de ménage, et pouvant souvent comprendre une gamme de services complémentaires tels que des services de repas et de boissons, de garage, de lessive, de piscines et de gymnastique, ainsi que des salles de réunions et de conférences et des installations récréatives.
–   Cette classe comprend la fourniture d'hébergement temporaire assuré par les établissements suivants :
–   hôtels
–   centres de villégiature
–   hôtels offrant des suites/appartements
–   motels
–   hôtels pour automobilistes
–   chambres d'hôtes
–   pensions
–   foyers assurant gîte et couvert
–   appartements et bungalows
–   établissements d'hébergement en multipropriété
–   maisons de vacances
–   chalets, cottages et maisonnettes
–   auberges de jeunesse et refuges de montagne

Exclusions :
–   fourniture de maisons ou d'appartements meublés ou non meublés pour de plus longues durées, généralement sur une base mensuelle ou annuelle, voir division 68

5520   Terrains de camping, parcs pour véhicules de loisirs et caravanes

Cette classe comprend les activités suivantes :
–   fourniture d'installations d'hébergement telles que terrains de camping, terrains de caravanage, parcs de loisirs, d'espaces de chasse et de pêche à l'intention de visiteurs temporaires
–   fourniture d'espaces et d'installations pour les véhicules de loisirs.

Cette classe couvre en outre des lieux d'hébergement tels que :
–   abris protecteurs ou aires de campement pour dresser des tentes et/ou installer des sacs de couchage

5590   Autres activités d'hébergement

Cette classe comprend la fourniture d'hébergement temporaire ou à plus long terme dans une seule pièce ou en salles communes ou dortoirs pour étudiants, travailleurs migrants (saisonniers) et autres personnes.

Cette classe comprend la fourniture de logement assurée par les entités suivantes :
–   résidences d'étudiants
–   dortoirs de pensionnats
–   foyers pour travailleurs
–   pensions
–   voitures-lits de chemins de fer

6810   Activités immobilières sur biens propres ou loués

Cette classe comprend les activités suivantes :
–   achat, vente, location et exploitation de biens immobiliers propres ou loués :
–   immeubles résidentiels et habitations
–   bâtiments non résidentiels, y compris les halls d'exposition, les installations d'entreposage pour particuliers, les galeries marchandes et les centres commerciaux
–   terrains
–   fourniture de maisons individuelles et d'appartements meublés et non meublés pour une utilisation plus permanente généralement sur une base mensuelle ou annuelle

Cette classe comprend en outre les activités suivantes :
–   mise en œuvre de projets de construction immobilière pour compte propre en vue, par exemple, de locations dans ces immeubles
–   subdivision de biens immobiliers en lotissements, sans viabilisation de terrains
–   exploitation d'emplacements pour caravanes

Exclusions :
–   mise en œuvre de projets de construction immobilière dans un but de vente, voir 4100
–   subdivision et viabilisation de terrains, voir 4290
–   exploitation d'hôtels, appartements en hôtel et lieux d'hébergement analogues, voir 5510
–   exploitation de terrains de camping, de parcs pour caravanes et autres lieux d'hébergement, voir 5520
–   exploitation de foyers de travailleurs, de maisons meublées, etc., voir 5590

6820   Activités immobilières à forfait ou sous contrat

Cette classe couvre la prestation d'activités dans le domaine de l'immobilier, à forfait ou sous contrat, y compris les services connexes.

Cette classe comprend les activités suivantes :
–   activités des agents et courtiers immobiliers
–   intermédiation en matière d'achat, vente et location immobilière à forfait ou sous contrat

- gestion de biens immobiliers à forfait ou sous contrat
- services d'évaluation pour l'immobilier
- activités des dépositaires légaux en matière immobilière

Exclusions :
- activités juridiques, voir 6910
- services d'appui aux installations, voir 8110
- gestion d'installations, par exemple les bases militaires, les prisons, etc. (sauf la gestion d'installations informatiques), voir 8110

Activités de services de restauration et de consommation de boissons

5610 Activités de restaurants et de services de restauration mobiles

Cette classe couvre la fourniture de services de restauration à des clients, que ces derniers soient servis à table ou se servent eux-mêmes, choisissant parmi un assortiment de plats qu'ils peuvent manger sur place, ou emporter ou se faire livrer. Est également comprise dans cette classe la préparation et le service de repas destinés à une consommation immédiate, vendus à bord de véhicules automobiles ou non.

Cette classe comprend les activités des entités suivantes :
- restaurants
- cafétérias
- *établissements de restauration rapide*
- pizzerias
- restaurants servant des plats à emporter
- marchands ambulants (motorisés) de crème glacée
- marchands ambulants de produits alimentaires
- préparation d'aliments sur des éventaires de marché

Cette classe comprend également :
- les activités des restaurants et bars liés aux transports lorsqu'ils sont exploités par des unités distinctes

Exclusions :
- exploitation de concessions de restauration dans diverses installations, voir 5629

5629 Autres activités de services de restauration

Cette classe couvre les activités des restaurants d'entreprises, à savoir la fourniture de services de restauration sur la base d'arrangements contractuels passés avec le client pour une période déterminée.

Elle porte également sur les concessions de restauration dans les installations sportives ou installations similaires. Les plats sont souvent confectionnés dans une unité de préparation centrale.
Cette classe comprend les activités suivantes :
- activités de sous-traitants en restauration (par exemple pour les compagnies de transports)
- exploitation de concessions de restauration dans les installations sportives et installations similaires
- exploitation de cantines ou de cafétérias (par exemple dans les usines, bureaux, hôpitaux ou écoles) au titre d'une concession.

Exclusions :
- fabrication de produits alimentaires périssables destinés à la revente, voir 1079
- commerce de détail de denrées périssables, voir division 47

5630 Activités de consommation de boissons

Cette classe comprend la préparation et le service de boissons à consommer sur place immédiatement.

Cette classe comprend les activités des établissements suivants :
- bars
- cafés
- salons pour apéritifs
- discothèques (où prédomine le service de boissons)
- brasseries, bars à bière
- cafétérias
- bars à jus de fruits
- distributeurs mobiles de boissons

Exclusions :
- revente de boissons sous emballage/préparées, voir 4711, 4722, 4781, 4799
- exploitation de discothèques et de pistes de danse, sans service de boissons, voir 9329

Transport de voyageurs par chemin de fer

4911 Transport de voyageurs par chemin de fer interurbain

Cette classe comprend les activités suivantes :
- transport de voyageurs par chemin de fer interurbain
- exploitation de voitures-lits et de voitures-restaurants en tant qu'exploitation intégrée des compagnies de chemin de fer

Exclusions :
- transport de voyageurs par des réseaux de transport urbain et suburbain, voir 4921
- exploitation de gares de voyageurs, voir 5221
- exploitation de voitures-lits et de voitures-restaurants par des unités distinctes, voir 5590, 5610

Transport routier de voyageurs

4922 Autres transports terrestres de voyageurs

Cette classe comprend les activités suivantes :
- autres transports routiers de voyageurs :
  - services réguliers d'autocars sur de longues distances
  - transports à demande, excursions et autres services occasionnels de transports par autocar
  - exploitation de taxis
  - navettes desservant les aéroports
- exploitation de téléphériques, de funiculaires, de télésièges et remonte-pentes s'ils ne font pas partie des réseaux suburbains de transit

Cette classe comprend en outre les activités suivantes :
- autres locations de voitures particulières avec chauffeur
- exploitation d'autocars scolaires et d'autobus pour le transport d'employés
- transport de personnes par véhicules à traction humaine ou animale

Exclusions :
- transport par ambulance, voir 8690

Transport maritime de voyageurs

5011 Transports maritimes et côtiers de voyageurs

Cette classe comprend les activités suivantes :
- transports maritimes et côtiers de voyageurs, même réguliers :
    - exploitation de bateaux d'excursion, de croisière et de tourisme
    - exploitation de bacs, bateaux-taxis, etc.

Cette classe comporte aussi les activités suivantes :
- location de bateaux de plaisance avec équipage pour le transport maritime et côtier de voyageurs (par exemple : pour des croisières de pêche)

Exclusions :
- activités de restauration et de bar à bord de bateaux lorsqu'elles sont fournies par des unités séparées, voir 5610, 5630
- exploitation de « casinos flottants », voir 9200

5021 Transport de voyageurs par voies navigables intérieures

Cette classe comprend les activités suivantes :
- transport de voyageurs sur les cours d'eau, les canaux, lacs et autres voies d'eau intérieures, y compris les zones portuaires

Cette classe comporte en outre les activités suivantes :
- location de bateaux de plaisance avec équipage pour le transport sur les voies navigables intérieures

Transport aérien de voyageurs

5110 Transport aérien de voyageurs

Cette classe comprend les activités suivantes :
- transport aérien de voyageurs sur des lignes régulières avec des horaires réguliers
- vols affrétés pour voyageurs
- vols d'excursion

Cette classe comporte également les activités suivantes :
- location d'équipements de transport aérien avec pilote en vue de transporter des voyageurs
- activités générales d'aviation, par exemple :
    - transport de voyageurs par des aéroclubs pour apprendre à piloter ou pour le plaisir

Location de matériels de transport

7710 Location de véhicules automobiles

Cette classe comprend les activités suivantes :
- location et location-exploitation des types suivants de véhicules :
    - voitures particulières (sans chauffeur)
    - camions, remorques utilitaires et véhicules de loisirs

Exclusions :
- location de véhicules avec chauffeur, voir 4922, 4923
- crédit-bail, voir 6491

Activités des agences de voyages et autres activités de services de réservation

7911 Activités des agences de voyages

Cette classe comprend les activités suivantes :
- activités d'agences dont le rôle principal est de vendre des voyages, des excursions, des services de transport et d'hébergement au grand public et à des clients commerciaux.

7912 Activités des voyagistes

Cette classe comprend les activités suivantes :
- organisation et groupement d'excursions vendues par l'intermédiaire d'agences de voyage ou directement par des voyagistes. Les excursions peuvent inclure toutes ou partie des activités suivantes :
    - transport
    - hébergement
    - restauration
    - visites de musées, de sites historiques ou culturels, théâtre, événements musicaux ou sportifs

7990 Autres activités de services de réservation et activités connexes

Cette classe comprend les activités suivantes :
- fourniture d'autres services de réservation relatifs aux voyages :
    - réservations dans les moyens de transport, les hôtels, les restaurants ; location de voitures, spectacles et événements sportifs, etc.
- fourniture de services en multipropriété
- vente de billets pour le théâtre, les événements sportifs et spectacles divers
- fourniture de services d'assistance aux touristes :
    - fourniture de renseignements concernant les voyages
    - activités de guides touristiques
- activités de promotion du tourisme

Exclusions :
- activités d'agences de voyage et de voyagistes, voir 7911, 7912
- organisation et gestion d'événements tels que réunions, congrès et conférences, voir 8230

Activités culturelles

9000   Activités créatives, arts et spectacles

Cette classe couvre l'exploitation d'installations et la fourniture de services pour répondre aux besoins des clients dans les domaines de la culture et des spectacles. Ces activités comprennent la production et la promotion de spectacles en direct, d'événements et d'expositions pour le public, et la participation de celui-ci à ces activités ; la promotion de talents artistiques, de compétences créatrices ou techniques pour la production d'œuvres artistiques et de spectacles en direct.

Cette classe comprend les activités suivantes :
- production de représentations théâtrales, de concerts et d'opéras ou de ballets et autres productions de scène :
  - activités de groupes, de compagnies de cirque, d'orchestres symphoniques ou autres formations musicales
  - activités individuelles d'artistes, tels que les auteurs, acteurs, metteurs en scène, musiciens, conférenciers ou orateurs, décorateurs de théâtre, etc.
- exploitation de salle de théâtre et de concerts et d'autres installations pour la production de spectacles
- activités des sculpteurs, peintres, caricaturistes, graveurs d'art au burin et à l'eau forte, etc.
- activités d'écrivains sur tous les sujets, y compris les ouvrages de fiction, les ouvrages techniques, etc.
- activités de journalistes indépendants
- restauration d'œuvres d'art telles que les tableaux, etc.

Cette classe comporte aussi les activités suivantes :
- réalisations de producteurs ou d'organisateurs de manifestations artistiques en direct avec ou sans installations

Excusions :
- restauration de vitraux, voir 2310
- fabrication de statues autres que les originaux d'artistes, voir 2396
- restauration d'orgues et autres instruments de musiques historiques, voir 3319
- restauration de sites et monuments historiques, voir 4100
- production de films cinématographiques et vidéo, voir 5911, 5912
- exploitation de salles de cinéma, voir 5914
- activités des agences de professionnels du théâtre et d'artistes, voir 7490
- activités de distribution des rôles, voir 7810
- activités des billetteries, voir 7990
- exploitation de musées de types divers, voir 9102
- activités de sports et de loisirs et activités récréatives, voir division 93
- restauration de meubles (à l'exception des meubles de musées), voir 9524

9102   Activités des musées et exploitation des sites et monuments historiques

Cette classe comprend les activités suivantes :
- exploitation de tous types de musées :
  - musées d'art, d'orfèvrerie, de meubles, de costumes, de céramique, d'argenterie
  - musées d'histoire naturelle, des sciences et des techniques, musées d'histoire, y compris les musées militaires
  - autres musées spécialisés
  - musées en plein air
- gestion et préservation de sites et monuments historiques

Exclusions :
- rénovation et restauration de sites et monuments historiques, voir section F
- restauration d'œuvres d'art et d'objets appartenant à des collections de musées, voir 9000
- activités des bibliothèques et des archives, voir 9101

9103   Activités des jardins botaniques et zoologiques et des réserves naturelles

Cette classe couvre les activités suivantes :
- administration des jardins botaniques et zoologiques, y compris les zoos pour enfants
- administration de réserves naturelles, y compris la protection de la flore et de la faune sauvages, etc.

Exclusions :
- services d'entretien des espaces verts, voir 8130
- exploitation des réserves consacrées à la chasse et à la pêche sportives, voir 9319

Activités sportives et récréatives

7721   Location d'articles pour le sport et les loisirs

Cette classe couvre les activités suivantes :
- location d'articles pour le sport et les loisirs :
- bateaux de plaisance, canoës, bateaux à voile
- bicyclettes
- chaises de plage et parasols
- autres articles de sport
- skis

Exclusions :
- location de vidéocassettes et de vidéodisques, voir 7722
- location d'articles personnels et ménagers, n.c.a., voir 7729
- locations d'articles pour les activités récréatives et les loisirs en tant que parties intégrantes des installations récréatives, voir 9329

9200   Activités de jeux de hasard et de pari

Cette classe couvre les activités suivantes:
- activités de bookmakers et autres opérations de pari
- pari sur les courses de chevaux
- activités des casinos, y compris les casinos à bord de navires de croisière
- vente de billets de loterie
- exploitation de machines de jeu automatiques (à pièces de monnaie)
- exploitation de sites Web de jeux virtuels

Exclusions:
- exploitation de machines à sous, voir 9329

9311   Exploitation d'installations sportives

Cette classe comprend les activités suivantes:
- exploitation d'installations pour les activités sportives en plein air ou en salle (ouverte, fermée ou couverte avec ou sans places assises):
  - terrains de football, de hockey, de cricket, de baseball, de jai alai
  - champs de courses pour les courses d'automobiles, de chiens, de chevaux, etc.
  - piscines et stades
  - stades d'athlétisme
  - arènes et stades de sports d'hiver
  - arènes de hockey sur glace
  - arènes de boxe
  - terrains de golfe
  - pistes de quilles
  - centres de mise en forme physique
- Mise en place et exploitation de manifestations sportives en plein air ou en salle pour les sportifs professionnels ou amateurs par des organisations dotées de leurs propres installations.

Les activités rangées dans cette classe comprennent la gestion et la fourniture du personnel chargé du fonctionnement de ces installations.

Exclusions:
- location de matériel de sport et de loisirs, voir 7721
- exploitation de pistes de ski, voir 9329
- activités de parcs et de plages, voir 9329

9319   Autres activités sportives

Cette classe comprend les activités suivantes:
- activités des producteurs ou promoteurs de manifestations sportives même sans installations
- activités des sportifs individuels pour compte propre et des athlètes, arbitres, juges, chronométreurs, etc.
- activités des ligues sportives et d'organismes régulateurs
- activités relatives à la promotion de manifestations sportives
- activités des écuries de course, des chenils et des garages
- exploitation des réserves de pêche et de chasse sportives
- activités des guides de montagne
- activités d'appui à la chasse ou à la pêche sportive ou de loisir

Exclusions:
- élevage de chevaux de courses, voir 0142
- location de matériel de sport, voir 7721
- activités des écoles de sport ou de jeu, voir 8541
- activités des moniteurs, instructeurs, entraîneurs, voir 8541
- organisation et réalisation de manifestations sportives en plein air ou en salle pour professionnels ou amateurs par des clubs sportifs dotés ou non de leurs propres installations, voir 9311, 9312
- activités de parcs et de plages, voir 9329

9321   Activités des parcs d'attractions et à thèmes

Cette classe comprend les activités suivantes:
- activités de parcs d'attractions ou de parcs à thèmes, y compris l'exploitation d'attractions foraines, manèges, tours aquatiques, jeux, spectacles, expositions à thèmes et terrains de pique-nique.

9329   Autres activités récréatives et de loisirs, n.c.a.

Cette classe comprend:
- activités de parcs d'attraction et de plages, y compris la location d'installations telles que les cabines de bain, de vestiaires, de sièges, etc.
- exploitation d'installations de transport à des fins récréatives, par exemple les marinas
- exploitation des pistes de ski
- location de matériel pour l'amusement et le divertissement en tant que partie intégrante d'équipements récréatifs
- organisation de foires et expositions à des fins récréatives
- exploitation de discothèques et de salles de bal
- exploitation de jeux électroniques payants
- autres activités d'amusement et de divertissement (sauf les parcs d'attractions et les parcs à thèmes), n.c.a.

Cette classe comprend aussi:
- activités de producteurs et d'organisateurs de manifestations en direct autres que des manifestations relatives aux arts ou aux sports même sans installations.

Exclusions:
- croisières de pêche, voir 5011, 5021
- fourniture d'espace et d'installations pour de courts séjours de visiteurs dans des parcs et forêts de loisirs et les terrains de camping, voir 5520
- services de boissons dans les discothèques, voir 5630
- parcs de stationnement de caravanes, terrains de camping, camps de loisirs, réserves de chasse et de pêche, campings, campements, voir 5520
- location séparée de matériel pour les activités de divertissement et de loisirs, voir 7721
- exploitation de machines de jeu automatiques à pièces de monnaie, voir 9200
- activités des parcs d'attraction et à thèmes, voir 9321

Referencias conceptuales y notas técnicas

Este documento contiene además cuatro anexos:
Anexo 1. Sistema nacional de estadísticas de turismo y comparabilidad internacional
Anexo 2. Comprender el turismo: glosario básico
Anexo 3. Cómo encontrar el turismo en las clasificaciones internacionales uniformes.
Anexo 4. Lista de industrias turísticas y agrupadas por categorías principales según la CIIU, Rev. 4

Para consultar referencias adicionales, visite:

http://statistics.unwto.org/en

http://statistics.unwto.org/en/content/international-recommendations-tourism-statistics-2008-irts-2008

1. Turismo receptor

El turismo receptor comprende las actividades de un visitante no residente dentro del país de referencia en un viaje de turismo receptor. El gasto de ese visitante se identifica como gasto del turismo receptor.

Datos

Llegadas

Los datos de *llegadas* miden la afluencia de visitantes internacionales al país de referencia: cada llegada corresponde a un viaje de turismo receptor. Si una persona visita varios países en el transcurso de un solo viaje, cada llegada a un país se registra separadamente. En un ejercicio contable, la cifra de llegadas no es necesariamente igual a la del número de personas que viajan (cuando una persona visita el mismo país varias veces al año, cada viaje de esa misma persona se contabiliza como una llegada distinta).

Los datos de *llegadas* deben corresponder a los *visitantes recibidos* (no residentes en el país visitado) incluidos tanto los turistas como los visitantes del día no residentes. Deben excluirse todos los demás tipos de viajeros (trabajadores fronterizos, estacionales y con contratos de corta duración, estudiantes por periodos largos, etc.), ya que no pueden calificarse de visitantes.

Los datos se obtienen de diversas fuentes: registros administrativos (inmigración, censos de tránsito y otros posibles tipos de control), encuestas de fronteras o una combinación de todos ellos. Si se obtienen datos de encuestas sobre alojamiento, el número de huéspedes sirve para estimar las cifras de llegadas; por consiguiente, en este caso, los desgloses por regiones, motivo principal del viaje, medio de transporte utilizado o formas de organización del viaje se basan en encuestas de visitantes complementarias.

Las llegadas se dividen en función de cinco características, de las cuales dos merecen algunos comentarios:
- Tipo de visitantes (del punto 1.1 al 1.4 del **Compendio**). Por consiguiente, si un país no puede distinguir entre visitantes que pernoctan y visitantes del día, no se proporciona ningún desglose.

- Regiones (del punto 1.5 al 1.13 del **Compendio**). El concepto básico subyacente es que el país asociado a la llegada debe ser el país de residencia. Algunos países no aceptan las recomendaciones de la OMT y clasifican a los nacionales del país residentes en el extranjero en lugar de como residentes en esos países como una categoría separada (punto 1.13 del **Compendio**).

El *motivo principal* de un viaje se define como el motivo en ausencia del cual el viaje no habría tenido lugar. La clasificación aplicada es la siguiente:
1. Motivos personales
    1.1. Vacaciones, recreo y ocio
    1.2. Visitas a familiares y amigos
    1.3. Educación y formación
    1.4. Salud y atención médica
    1.5. Religión/peregrinaciones
    1.6. Compras
    1.7. Tránsito
    1.8. Otros motivos
2. Negocios y motivos profesionales

En el Anuario de estadísticas de turismo de la OMT se incluye información complementaria sobre llegadas, desglosadas por país de origen.
- **Cuadro 1:**
    Llegadas a las fronteras nacionales de visitantes no residentes que pernoctan (turistas).
- **Cuadro 2:**
    Llegadas a las fronteras nacionales de visitantes no residentes (que pernoctan –turistas– y visitantes del día –excursionistas–).

Alojamiento

El término «alojamiento» se refiere a los servicios prestados por establecimientos comerciales a los visitantes, siendo normalmente la categoría más importante la de «hoteles y establecimientos asimilados», identificada en la CIIU, Rev.4 como 5510 «Actividades de alojamiento para estancias cortas».

Las *pernoctaciones* (o «noches de huéspedes») se refieren al número de noches que pasan los huéspedes no residentes (turistas recibidos).

En el Anuario de estadísticas de turismo de la OMT se incluye información complementaria sobre los huéspedes, desglosada por país de origen.

- **Cuadro 3:**
  Llegadas de visitantes no residentes que pernoctan (turistas) a «hoteles y establecimientos asimilados»
- **Cuadro 4:**
  Llegadas de visitantes no residentes que pernoctan (turistas) a todo tipo de establecimientos que ofrezcan servicios de alojamiento para visitantes.
- **Cuadro 5:**
  Pernoctaciones de visitantes no residentes (turistas) a «hoteles y establecimientos asimilados»
- **Cuadro 6:**
  Pernoctaciones de visitantes no residentes (turistas) a todo tipo de establecimientos que ofrezcan servicios de alojamiento para visitantes.

Gasto

El *gasto* asociado con la actividad de los visitantes internacionales se ha identificado tradicionalmente con la partida de viajes en la balanza de pagos: en el caso del turismo receptor, estos gastos asociados con los visitantes recibidos se registran como «crédito» en la balanza de pagos y se denominan «ingresos por viajes».

Las *Recomendaciones internacionales para estadísticas de turismo de 2008* consideran que en las «industrias y productos turísticos» se incluye el transporte de pasajeros. Por lo tanto, en términos de balanza de pagos, sería mejor para la estimación de los datos de gastos relacionados con el turismo, efectuados por los visitantes recibidos y emitidos en un contexto internacional, contar el valor de la partida de viajes más el de la partida de transporte de pasajeros.

No obstante, los usuarios deberían ser conscientes de que las estimaciones de la balanza de pagos incluyen, además de los gastos asociados a los visitantes, los relativos a otros tipos de viajeros (que pueden ser sustanciales en algunos países, por ejemplo, estudiantes o pacientes por periodos largos, trabajadores fronterizos y estacionales, etc.).

También los datos de gastos por *motivo principal del viaje* son datos de la balanza de pagos.

Los datos publicados corresponden a los que publica el Fondo Monetario Internacional (FMI) (y que proporcionan los bancos centrales). Los datos de gasto del turismo receptor y emisor proceden del CD-ROM de estadísticas de balanza de pagos del Fondo Monetario Internacional (FMI).

En el caso de detectarse una diferencia significativa con los datos suministrados a la OMT por las administraciones nacionales de turismo (ANT) para la preparación del Compendio, los datos de las ANT se facilitarán separadamente en las «notas de los países».

Indicadores

Tamaño medio del grupo de viaje

Un grupo de viaje se define como un conjunto de visitantes que realizan juntos un viaje y comparten los gastos. El tamaño medio de los grupos de viaje permite la estimación del número total de viajes de visitantes internacionales, una estimación útil para labores de marketing y formulación de políticas.

Duración media de la estancia

Todos estos indicadores se refieren a la duración de los viajes de turismo receptor realizados por visitantes internacionales (expresados como número de días o de noches).

La duración media de la estancia se refiere a los servicios de alojamiento tanto comerciales como no comerciales suministrados a los visitantes, así como a otros tipos de estancias.

Puesto que un visitante no residente podría alojarse en diferentes instalaciones durante su estancia, esas cifras totales solo pueden estimarse utilizando la información de las encuestas de fronteras o comprobando las fechas en las tarjetas oficiales de llegada/partida para una muestra de visitantes (o para todos ellos).

Gasto medio por día

Este indicador se refiere al gasto total de los visitantes en general, dividido por el número total de días empleados, estimado mediante la encuesta de visitantes.

2. Turismo interno

El turismo interno comprende las actividades de un visitante residente dentro del país de referencia (como parte de un viaje de turismo interno o como parte de un viaje de turismo emisor).

El gasto correspondiente de ese visitante en la economía de referencia se identifica como gasto turístico interno. Además, el gasto de los visitantes emitidos en productos recibidos de empresas residentes se incluye en el gasto interno.

Datos

Los *viajes* de los visitantes son viajes turísticos. Un viaje de turismo interno se refiere al viaje de un visitante desde el momento de dejar su residencia habitual hasta que regresa; se refiere a un viaje de ida y vuelta.

El término «alojamiento» se refiere a los servicios prestados por establecimientos comerciales a los visitantes, siendo normalmente la categoría más importante la de «hoteles y establecimientos asimilados», identificada en la CIIU, Rev.4 como 5510 «Actividades de alojamiento para estancias cortas».

Las *pernoctaciones* (o «noches de huéspedes») se refieren al número de noches que pasan los huéspedes residentes (turistas internos). Las encuestas sobre alojamiento (dirigidas a los establecimientos) deberían ser la fuente de datos preferida.

Indicadores

Duración media de la estancia

La duración media de la estancia se refiere a los servicios de alojamiento tanto comerciales como no comerciales suministrados a los visitantes, así como a otros tipos de estancias.

Los datos totales solo pueden estimarse utilizando las encuestas de hogares.

Gasto medio por día

Este indicador se refiere al gasto total, dividido por el número total de días empleados, estimado mediante la encuesta de visitantes.

3. Turismo emisor

El turismo emisor comprende las actividades de un visitante residente fuera del país de referencia (como parte de un viaje de turismo emisor o como parte de un viaje de turismo interno). El gasto correspondiente de ese visitante se identifica como gasto del turismo emisor.

Datos

Los datos de *salidas* miden el flujo de visitantes residentes que salen del país de referencia. Las salidas no coinciden necesariamente con el número de llegadas notificadas por los destinos internacionales para el país de referencia.

El *gasto* asociado con la actividad de los visitantes se ha identificado tradicionalmente con la partida de viajes en la balanza de pagos: en el caso del turismo emisor, estos gastos asociados con los visitantes no residentes se registran como «débito» en la balanza de pagos y se denominan «gastos por viajes». Como en el caso del *turismo receptor*, se utilizan los datos de la balanza de pagos.

Las Recomendaciones internacionales para estadísticas de turismo de 2008 consideran que en las «industrias y productos turísticos» se incluye el transporte de pasajeros. Por lo tanto, en términos de balanza de pagos, sería mejor para la estimación de los datos de gastos relacionados con el turismo, efectuados por los visitantes residentes y no residentes en un contexto internacional, contar el valor de la partida de viajes más el de la partida de transporte de pasajeros.

No obstante, los usuarios deberían ser conscientes de que las estimaciones de la balanza de pagos incluyen, además de los gastos asociados a los visitantes, los relativos a otros tipos de viajeros.

De igual forma, los datos de gastos por *motivo principal* del viaje son datos de la balanza de pagos.

Los datos publicados corresponden a los que publica el Fondo Monetario Internacional (FMI) (y que proporcionan los bancos centrales); en el caso de detectarse una diferencia significativa con los datos suministrados a la OMT por las administraciones nacionales de turismo (ANT) para la preparación del Compendio, los datos de las ANT se facilitarán separadamente en las «notas de los países». Para más información sobre las notas de los países del FMI, refiéranse al párrafo sobre el gasto del turismo receptor.

Puede obtenerse información complementaria sobre «viajes al extranjero de visitantes residentes a países de destino» en la página web: www.e-unwto.org/home/main.mpx. Es importante indicar que la información presentada se basa en los datos suministrados por cada país de destino y corresponde por lo tanto a las llegadas a esos países.

Indicadores

Duración media de la estancia

Este indicador se refiere a la duración de los viajes de visitantes emitidos (expresada en número de días) y refleja la media total utilizando las encuestas de fronteras o la información de los hogares.

Gasto medio por día

Este indicador se refiere al gasto total dividido por el número total de días empleados, calculado a partir de las encuestas de fronteras o la información de los hogares.

4. Industrias turísticas

El término *industrias turísticas* incluye aquellas industrias que producen normalmente productos característicos del turismo; equivale al más coloquial de «sector turístico». En la siguiente lista se especifican esas industrias:
1. Alojamiento para visitantes
2. Actividades de provisión de alimentos y bebidas
3. Transporte de pasajeros por ferrocarril
4. Transporte de pasajeros por carretera
5. Transporte de pasajeros por agua
6. Transporte aéreo de pasajeros
7. Alquiler de equipos de transporte
8. Actividades de agencias de viajes y de otros servicios de reservas
9. Actividades culturales
10. Actividades deportivas y recreativas
11. Comercio al por menor de bienes característicos del turismo, específicos de cada país
12. Otras actividades características del turismo, específicas de cada país

Las siguientes notas explicativas se refieren al *alojamiento para visitantes* y a *agencias de viajes y otros servicios de reservas*, que son las dos únicas industrias para las que se publican datos monetarios y no monetarios en este **Compendio.**

Estas notas pueden consultarse en el Anexo 4: Se han extraído del documento *Clasificación Industrial Internacional Uniforme de todas las actividades económicas (CIIU), Rev.4.* Informes estadísticos (serie M, No. 4/Rev.4), Naciones Unidas. Nueva York, 2008.

Alojamiento para visitantes

El número de establecimientos en la industria de *Alojamiento para visitantes* (punto 4.2 del Compendio se refiere a todos los tipos de establecimientos que ofrecen servicios de alojamiento a los visitantes con carácter comercial (de mercado), es decir, mediante pago. Por consiguiente, los datos deberían incluir las siguientes clases de la CIIU:

5510 Actividades de alojamiento para estancias cortas

Esta clase figura en la sección 4 del Compendio como «*alojamiento para visitantes en hoteles y establecimientos asimilados*» e incluye el suministro de alojamiento, normalmente por días o semanas, sobre todo para estancias cortas de visitantes. Abarca el suministro de alojamiento amueblado en habitaciones y apartamentos o unidades totalmente independientes con cocina, con o sin servicio diario o regular de limpieza, y que incluyen a menudo diversos servicios adicionales, como los de comidas y bebidas, aparcamiento, lavandería, piscina y gimnasio, instalaciones de recreo e instalaciones para conferencias y convenciones.

Esta clase comprende el suministro de alojamiento por estancias cortas en:
– hoteles
– centros vacacionales
– hoteles de suites/apartamentos
– moteles
– hoteles para automovilistas
– casas de huéspedes
– pensiones
– unidades de alojamiento y desayuno
– pisos y bungalows
– unidades utilizadas en régimen de tiempo compartido
– casas de vacaciones
– chalets y cabañas con servicio de mantenimiento y limpieza
– albergues juveniles y refugios de montaña

No se incluyen las siguientes actividades:
– suministro de viviendas y de pisos o apartamentos amueblados o sin amueblar para períodos más largos, en general por meses o por años; véase la división 68

5520 Actividades de campamentos, parques de vehículos de recreo y parques de caravanas

Esta clase comprende las siguientes actividades:
– suministro de alojamiento en campamentos, parques para caravanas, campamentos recreativos y campamentos de caza y de pesca para estancias cortas
– suministro de espacio e instalaciones para vehículos de recreo

Se incluyen también los servicios de alojamiento de:
– refugios o simples instalaciones de acampada para plantar tiendas o pernoctar en sacos de dormir

5590 Otras actividades de alojamiento

Esta clase comprende el suministro de alojamiento temporal o a largo plazo en habitaciones individuales o compartidas o dormitorios para estudiantes, trabajadores migrantes (estacionales) y otras categorías de personas.

Se incluyen los servicios de alojamiento proporcionados por:
– residencias de estudiantes
– dormitorios escolares
– albergues para trabajadores
– casas de huéspedes e internados
– coches cama ferroviarios

6810 Actividades inmobiliarias realizadas con bienes propios o arrendados

Esta clase comprende las siguientes actividades:
– compra, venta, alquiler y explotación de bienes inmuebles propios o arrendados, como:
  – edificios de apartamentos y viviendas
  – edificios no residenciales, incluso salas de exposiciones, instalaciones de autoalmacenamiento y centros comerciales
  – terrenos
– alquiler de casas y pisos o apartamentos amueblados o sin amueblar por períodos largos, en general por meses o por años

Se incluyen también las siguientes actividades:
– promoción de proyectos de construcción para su posterior explotación, es decir, para alquilar espacio en esos edificios
– subdivisión de propiedades inmobiliarias en lotes, sin mejora de los terrenos
– explotación de campamentos residenciales para casas móviles

No se incluyen las siguientes actividades:
– promoción de proyectos de construcción para la venta; véase la clase 4100
– subdivisión y mejora de terrenos; véase la clase 4290
– explotación de hoteles, hoteles de apartamentos e instalaciones de alojamiento similares; véase la clase 5510
– explotación de campamentos, parques de caravanas e instalaciones de alojamiento similares; véase la clase 5520
– explotación de albergues para trabajadores, casas de huéspedes e instalaciones de alojamiento similares; véase la clase 5590

6820 Actividades inmobiliarias realizadas a cambio de una retribución o por contrata

Esta clase comprende las actividades inmobiliarias que se realizan a cambio de una retribución o por contrata, incluidos los servicios inmobiliarios.

Esta clase comprende las siguientes actividades:
– actividades de agentes y corredores inmobiliarios
– intermediación en la compra, la venta y el alquiler de bienes inmuebles a cambio de una retribución o por contrata
– administración de bienes inmuebles a cambio de una retribución o por contrata

- servicios de tasación inmobiliaria
- actividades de agentes depositarios de plicas inmobiliarias

No se incluyen las siguientes actividades:
- actividades jurídicas; véase la clase 6910
- servicios de apoyo a instalaciones; véase la clase 8110
- administración de instalaciones, como bases militares, prisiones y otras instalaciones (excepto administración de instalaciones informáticas); véase la clase 8110

Actividades de agencias de viajes y de otros servicios de reservas

7911 Actividades de agencias de viajes

Esta clase comprende las siguientes actividades:
- actividades de agencias dedicadas principalmente a vender servicios de viajes, de viajes organizados, de transporte y de alojamiento al público en general y a clientes comerciales

7912 Actividades de operadores turísticos

Esta clase comprende las siguientes actividades:
- organización de paquetes de servicios de viajes para su venta a través de agencias de viajes o por los propios operadores turísticos. Esos viajes organizados pueden incluir uno o varios de los elementos siguientes:
  - transporte
  - alojamiento
  - comidas
  - visitas a museos, lugares históricos o culturales y asistencia a espectáculos teatrales, musicales o deportivos

7990 Otros servicios de reservas y actividades conexas

Esta clase comprende las siguientes actividades:
- prestación de otros servicios de reservas relacionados con los viajes:
  - reservas de transporte, hoteles, restaurantes, alquiler de automóviles, entretenimiento y deporte, etcétera
- prestación de servicios de intercambio en régimen de tiempo compartido o multipropiedad
- actividades de venta de billetes para obras de teatro, competiciones deportivas y otras actividades de diversión y entretenimiento
- prestación de servicios de asistencia a los visitantes:
  - suministro a los clientes de información sobre los viajes
  - actividades de guías de turismo
- actividades de promoción turística

No se incluyen las siguientes actividades:
- actividades de agencias de viajes y operadores turísticos, véanse las clases 7911 y 7912
- organización y gestión de reuniones, convenciones, conferencias y acontecimientos similares; véase la clase 8230

Datos

Respecto al *número de establecimientos* (punto 4.3 del **Compendio**) incluye los establecimientos asimilados a las clases 5520, 5590, 6810 y 6820 (véanse las notas explicativas anteriores sobre alojamiento para visitantes).

El número de *habitaciones* y *plazas-cama* se refiere a la capacidad de «hoteles y establecimientos asimilados» de proporcionar alojamiento temporal a los visitantes.

Indicadores

Los tres primeros indicadores se basan en el número global de pernoctaciones de turistas residentes y no residentes en hoteles y establecimientos asimilados.

Las *tasas de ocupación* se refieren a la relación entre la capacidad existente de prestar servicios de alojamiento a los visitantes y la medida en que se utilizan. Esta tasa puede referirse al uso de habitaciones o de plazas-cama.

La *capacidad disponible* se refiere al número de plazas-cama en hoteles y establecimientos asimilados por cada 1000 habitantes de la población residente permanente del país de referencia. Cuando el país no aporta los datos, lo hace la OMT.

5. Empleo

La categoría de personas empleadas en las industrias turísticas puede ser de *asalariados* (personas que trabajan para una empresa a cambio de una remuneración en efectivo o en especie según lo convenido) o de *autoempleados* (trabajadores por cuenta propia que tienen el tipo de trabajo definido como «empleo independiente» y no han contratado de manera continua a ningún «asalariado» durante el periodo de referencia).

Algunas personas empleadas pueden tener más de un puesto de trabajo; por consiguiente el número de puestos de trabajo (por el lado de la demanda) y el número de personas empleadas (por el lado de la oferta) son categorías diferentes y por lo general no suelen coincidir.

La intensidad del trabajo puede variar de un puesto a otro, de una industria a otra y de un periodo a otro. Los puestos de trabajo pueden diferir en el horario laboral de las personas empleadas y, por lo tanto, pueden expresarse en términos de empleos a tiempo completo o a tiempo parcial. Por esta razón, no es suficiente con tener datos sobre el número de puestos de trabajo o personas empleadas para obtener información sobre el volumen del trabajo efectuado durante un determinado periodo de tiempo (por ejemplo, un mes o un año). Harán falta datos sobre el número total de horas de trabajo. Finalmente, si todos los puestos de trabajo se convierten en empleo equivalente a tiempo completo o total de horas trabajadas al año, podrá obtenerse el volumen total del trabajo de una determinada industria por un periodo determinado.

Las cifras sobre «número de puestos de trabajo por situación en el empleo» y «número de puestos de trabajo equivalentes a empleos de jornada completa por situación en el empleo» deben referirse a las industrias turísticas.

6. Indicadores complementarios

Estos indicadores se derivan de la balanza de pagos, las cuentas nacionales y las estadísticas de turismo.

Demanda

La *propensión bruta a viajar* mide el número de viajes de turismo emisor e interno en términos de población residente permanente total del país de referencia. Los valores más altos del indicador implican la mayor frecuencia de estos viajes e indican la movilidad presente de la población que viaja.

El indicador «llegadas/población» ofrece una estimación de la intensidad turística del país de referencia. La OMT calcula dicho indicador a partir de los datos básicos disponibles del turismo receptor y del turismo interno, pudiendo ser el número de visitantes (código 1.1 para el turismo receptor y 2.1 para el turismo interno) o el número de turistas (código 1.2 para el turismo receptor y 2.2 para el turismo interno). El cálculo se realiza según las fórmulas relacionadas a continuación, por orden de preferencia, y teniendo en cuenta los datos básicos disponibles para el país de referencia:

(1.2 turistas receptores + 2.2 turistas internos) / población
(1.2 turistas receptores + 2.1 visitantes internos) / población
(1.2 turistas receptores) / población
(1.1 visitantes receptores + 2.1 visitantes internos) / población
(1.1 visitantes receptores + 2.2 turistas internos) / población
(1.1 visitantes receptores) / población

Los datos de población proceden del Fondo Monetario Internacional (IMF), del Banco Mundial, o en su defecto de la oficina nacional de estadísticas del país de referencia.

Para cada nueva edición del Compendio, la fórmula se adaptará según los datos básicos disponibles para el periodo de referencia (5 años).

Indicadores macroeconómicos relacionados con el turismo internacional

Los indicadores se basan en las *estadísticas de balanza de pagos* y las *estadísticas financieras internacionales* del Fondo Monetario Internacional.

Estos y otros indicadores complementarios representan un sistema preliminar muy básico de evaluación de la contribución económica del turismo a la economía nacional, y son valiosos porque disponen de ellos la mayoría de los países, son comparables internacionalmente y pueden compararse también con otros indicadores económicos.

Cabe observar que el término «gasto» se utiliza del mismo modo para el turismo receptor que para el emisor a fin de indicar «el importe pagado para la adquisición de bienes de consumo y servicios, así como de objetos de valor, para uso propio o para regalo, para y durante los viajes turísticos». Los visitantes extranjeros en el país de referencia generan un gasto de turismo receptor (crédito en la balanza de pagos), mientras que los visitantes residentes que se encuentran en países extranjeros generan un gasto de turismo emisor (débito en la balanza de pagos).

Gasto turístico receptor sobre el PIB

Refleja el peso del gasto de los visitantes recibidos como parte del valor total de la actividad económica en la economía de referencia. Desde la perspectiva del comercio internacional, este indicador capta la importancia económica de la afluencia de ingresos procedentes del extranjero asociada al gasto de estos visitantes.

Gasto turístico emisor sobre el PIB

Refleja la importancia del gasto en el extranjero de los visitantes emitidos, expresada en términos de la economía nacional. Desde la perspectiva del comercio internacional, este indicador capta la importancia económica de la salida de ingresos nacionales a través de estos visitantes.

Balanza turística sobre el PIB

Refleja la importancia económica del gasto turístico neto (turismo receptor menos turismo emisor) en relación con la economía de referencia. Un superávit o un déficit significativo afecta a la balanza comercial del país y, por lo tanto, a su PIB.

Apertura turística

Refleja la importancia de la suma del gasto del turismo transfronterizo (es decir, el turismo internacional, la suma del gasto del turismo receptor y el emisor) en relación con la economía de referencia. También podría utilizarse como medida del flujo libre de turismo bilateral entre el país de referencia y el resto del mundo.

Cobertura turística

Refleja la proporción entre el gasto del turismo receptor y el gasto del turismo emisor para mostrar en qué grado la afluencia de ingresos procedentes del extranjero cubre la salida de ingresos nacionales. Un valor superior al 100% significa que el turismo receptor financia indirecta y sobradamente el gasto de los visitantes emitidos; un valor inferior al 100% significa que el turismo receptor no cubre el gasto de estos visitantes en el extranjero.

Gasto turístico receptor sobre las exportaciones de bienes
Gasto turístico receptor sobre las exportaciones de servicios
Gasto turístico receptor sobre las exportaciones de bienes y servicios

Estas tres medidas reflejan la importancia del turismo como servicio con el que se comercia internacionalmente en relación con otras categorías de exportaciones. Al mismo tiempo, estas medidas revelan el grado de especialización turística de la estructura exportadora de un país y la capacidad relativa del turismo de generar ingresos procedentes del extranjero.

Gasto turístico receptor sobre los créditos de la cuenta corriente

Los créditos de la cuenta corriente de la balanza de pagos se refieren a toda la afluencia de bienes, servicios, ingresos y transferencias corrientes a la economía. Cuanto mayor es la cuota del turismo en este agregado, mayor es la importancia de la actividad turística en la generación de una afluencia de ingresos procedentes del extranjero.

Gasto turístico emisor sobre las importaciones de bienes
Gasto turístico emisor sobre las importaciones de servicios
Gasto turístico emisor sobre las importaciones de bienes y servicios

Estas tres medidas reflejan la importancia del turismo como servicio con el que se comercia internacionalmente en relación con otras categorías de importaciones. Al mismo tiempo, estas medidas revelan la predilección por el turismo de la estructura importadora de un país y el grado relativo de salida de ingresos nacionales de una economía a causa del turismo internacional.

Gasto turístico emisor sobre los débitos de la cuenta corriente

Los débitos de la cuenta corriente de la balanza de pagos se refieren a toda la salida de bienes, servicios, ingresos y transferencias corrientes de una economía al resto del mundo. Cuanto mayor es la cuota del turismo en este agregado, mayor es la importancia de la actividad turística en la fuga de ingresos nacionales.

Anexo 1
Sistema nacional de estadísticas de turismo y comparabilidad internacional

La estructura del **Compendio de estadísticas de turismo** se basa en el siguiente esquema, referido al marco de información básico de los sistemas nacionales de estadísticas de turismo con fines de comparabilidad internacional (http://statistics.unwto.org/sites/all/files/docpdf/ststext.pdf).

El marco conceptual para este núcleo básico de datos e indicadores está constituido por las *Recomendaciones internacionales para estadísticas de turismo 2008* (RIET 2008).

Comparabilidad internacional y estadísticas de turismo: el marco de información básico

I. Marco conceptual

Conceptos	Unidades de observación	Principales características relacionadas
Visitante	Visitante	Clases: visitante que pernocta (turista), visitante del día (excursionista)
		País de residencia / regiones
	Grupo de viaje	Tamaño
Viaje	Viaje por turismo	Motivo principal
		Duración
		Destino principal
		Medio de transporte
		Tipos de alojamiento utilizado
		Organización
		Gasto
Industrias turísticas	Establecimiento	**Monetarios**
		Producción
		Consumo intermedio
		Valor añadido bruto
		Remuneración de los trabajadores asalariados
		Formación bruta de capital fijo
		No-monetarios
		Características específicas no monetarias para cada industria turística
Empleo	Establecimiento (en las industrias turísticas)	Personas
		Tamaño
		Situación en el empleo
		Puestos de trabajo
		Duración del trabajo
		Puestos de trabajo equivalentes a tiempo completo

II. Clasificaciones

1. Formas de turismo
2. Clasificación de los productos de consumo adquiridos por los visitantes
3. Clasificación de las actividades productivas que dan servicio a los visitantes
4. Otras clasificaciones

III. Tablas de resultados

1. Turismo receptor
2. Turismo interno
3. Turismo emisor
4. Industrias turísticas
5. Empleo
6. Indicadores complementarios

Anexo 2
Comprender el turismo : glosario básico

En este Anexo se incluyen algunos conceptos fundamentales y las definiciones correspondientes según las *RIET 2008*. http://statistics.unwto.org/en/content/international-recommendations-tourism-statistics-2008-irts-2008

Un glosario de términos turísticos más completo y recién actualizado está disponible en inglés únicamente : https ://s3-eu-west-1.amazonaws.com/staticunwto/Statistics/Glossary+of+terms.pdf

Actividades / productos característicos del turismo	Las *actividades características del turismo* son aquellas que generan principalmente *productos característicos del turismo*. Los *productos característicos del turismo* son aquellos que cumplen uno o ambos de los siguientes criterios : El *gasto turístico* en el producto debería representar una parte importante del *gasto total turístico* (condición de la proporción que corresponde al gasto/demanda). El *gasto turístico* en el producto debería representar una parte importante de la oferta del producto en la economía (condición de la proporción que corresponde a la oferta). Este criterio supone que la oferta de un *producto característico del turismo* se reduciría considerablemente si no hubiera visitantes.
Empleo en las industrias turísticas	El *empleo en las industrias turísticas* puede medirse como un recuento de las personas empleadas en las *industrias turísticas*, en cualquiera de sus empleos, como un recuento de las personas que desempeñan su empleo principal en las *industrias turísticas*, o como un recuento de los empleos en las *industrias turísticas*.
Entorno habitual	*El entorno habitual de una persona, concepto clave en turismo, se define como la zona geográfica (aunque no necesariamente contigua) en la que una persona realiza sus actividades cotidianas habituales.*
Gasto turístico	*El gasto turístico hace referencia a la suma pagada por la adquisición de bienes y servicios de consumo, y de objetos valiosos, para uso propio o para regalar, durante los viajes turísticos y para los mismos.*
Grupo de viaje	*Un grupo de viaje se define como visitantes que realizan juntos un viaje y comparten los gastos vinculados con el mismo.*
Industrias turísticas	*Las industrias turísticas incluyen todos los establecimientos en los cuales la actividad principal es una actividad característica del turismo.*
Lugar de residencia habitual	El *lugar de residencia habitual* es el lugar geográfico en que el visitante reside habitualmente, y se define por la ubicación de su vivienda principal (Principios y recomendaciones para los censos de población y habitación de las Naciones Unidas).
Motivo (principal) de un viaje turístico	El *motivo principal* de un *viaje turístico* se define como el motivo sin el cual el *viaje* no habría tenido lugar. La clasificación de los *viajes turísticos* con arreglo al *motivo principal* hace referencia a nueve categorías : esta tipología permite identificar diferentes subconjuntos de *visitantes* (visitantes de negocios, visitantes en tránsito, etc.).
Turismo emisor	El *turismo emisor* abarca las *actividades* realizadas por un *visitante* residente fuera del país de referencia, como parte de un *viaje turístico emisor* o de un *viaje turístico interno*.
Turismo interno	El *turismo interno* incluye las actividades realizadas por un *visitante residente* en el *país de referencia*, como parte de *un viaje turístico interno* o de un *viaje turístico emisor*.
Turismo receptor	Engloba las *actividades* realizadas por un *visitante* no residente en el *país de referencia*, como parte de un *viaje turístico receptor*.

Turista (o visitante que pernocta) y excursionista (o visitante del día)	*Un visitante (interno, receptor o emisor) se clasifica como turista (o visitante que pernocta), si su viaje incluye una pernoctación, o como visitante del día (o excursionista) en caso contrario.*
Viaje / turismo	*El termino viaje designa la actividad de los viajeros. Un viajero es toda persona que se desplaza entre dos lugares geográficos distintos por cualquier motivo y duración. El visitante es un tipo particular de viajero y, por lo tanto, el turismo es un subconjunto de viaje.*
Viaje turístico	*El término viaje turístico designa todo desplazamiento de una persona a un lugar fuera de su lugar de residencia habitual, desde el momento de su salida hasta su regreso. Por lo tanto, se refiere a un viaje de ida y vuelta. Los viajes de los visitantes son viajes turísticos.*
Visita	*Un viaje se compone de visitas a diferentes lugares. El término «visita turística» hace referencia a una estancia en un lugar visitado durante un viaje turístico.*
Visitante	*Un visitante es una persona que viaja a un destino principal distinto al de su entorno habitual, por una duración inferior a un año, con cualquier finalidad principal (ocio, negocios u otro motivo personal) que no sea la de ser empleado por una entidad residente en el país o lugar visitados.*
Visitante interno	*Cuando un visitante viaja dentro de su propio país de residencia, se trata de un visitante interno y sus actividades forman parte del turismo interno.*
Vivienda de vacaciones	*Una vivienda de vacaciones (también conocida como casa u hogar de vacaciones) es una vivienda secundaria visitada por los miembros del hogar, fundamentalmente con fines de ocio, vacaciones o cualquier otra forma de esparcimiento.*

Anexo 3
Cómo encontrar el turismo en las clasificaciones internacionales uniformes

La importancia del turismo y la necesidad de definir y medir su significación dentro del sistema de estadísticas de las Naciones Unidas fueron reconocidas por la Comisión de Estadística de las Naciones Unidas con la aprobación en 1993 de las *Recomendaciones sobre estadísticas del turismo*. La versión revisada de estas recomendaciones fue aprobada por la Comisión de Estadística de las Naciones Unidas en 2008 bajo el título de *Recomendaciones internacionales para estadísticas de turismo 2008* (RIET 2008).

Para estudiar la contribución del turismo a la economía nacional, era necesario integrar el análisis económico del turismo en el marco de referencia del Sistema de Cuentas Nacionales (SCN 93), lo cual condujo a la aprobación por parte de la Comisión de Estadística de las Naciones Unidas en 2000 de *Cuenta satélite de turismo: Recomendaciones sobre el marco conceptual*. Este marco se actualizó posteriormente como *Cuenta satélite de turismo: Recomendaciones sobre el marco conceptual 2008* (CST:RMC 2008).

Los conceptos, las definiciones y las clasificaciones de las RIET 2008 son coherentes con los de CST:RMC 2008, que a su vez se habían armonizado con el Sistema de Cuentas Nacionales de 2008, la balanza de pagos y el comercio internacional de servicios.

Para el turismo, es interesante identificar los productos que compran los visitantes, directa e indirectamente, y las actividades que los producen. Las clasificaciones utilizadas para las actividades y los productos detallados que se piden en el estudio del turismo se extraen directamente y se relacionan con las clasificaciones de referencia de las Naciones Unidas: la CIIU y la CCP.

El foco de interés para el análisis del turismo es el visitante. En un principio, resulta interesante medir el gasto de los visitantes y localizar los productos, tanto bienes como servicios, que compran los visitantes, así como las actividades que producen estos productos. En un marco macroeconómico, como el de la CST, el concepto de turismo engloba tanto la perspectiva de la demanda, consistente en el consumo de los visitantes, el consumo colectivo turístico y la formación bruta de capital fijo del turismo, como la perspectiva de la oferta de las actividades turísticas (siendo un punto especial la cuota de su producción que es adquirida por los visitantes). El turismo, como tal, no se identifica en la SCN 93 o en la CIIU. A efectos de turismo, las actividades de todo el espectro de la CIIU que producen bienes y servicios que satisfacen la demanda turística se reúnen y agrupan como actividades turísticas.

Si se adopta el enfoque de la demanda, el visitante es la unidad básica de observación y análisis y el gasto de los visitantes se estudia en términos de productos (primordialmente servicios). Desde el punto de vista de la oferta, teniendo en cuenta su relación con el Sistema de Cuentas Nacionales, las estadísticas de turismo utilizan el «establecimiento» como unidad estadística básica, tal como se define en el SCN y utilizan «industria» como la unidad de presentación y análisis, definida como «grupos de establecimientos dedicados a la misma clase de actividad productiva».

En primera instancia, es preciso reconocer qué productos compran los visitantes. A efectos de recopilación de datos desde la perspectiva de la demanda, los productos se agrupan en categorías amplias en función del motivo; no obstante, el turismo requiere el análisis simultáneo del consumo y de la producción y, por tanto, la clasificación utilizada para definir los productos es la Clasificación Central de Productos (CCP ver. 2.). Los productos adquiridos por los visitantes pueden agruparse en clases detalladas de la CCP y las actividades que los producen pueden identificarse en los términos de las clases detalladas en la CIIU.

El turismo define algunos de los productos que compran los visitantes y las actividades que los producen como «productos característicos del turismo» (los que satisfacen ciertos criterios) y «actividades características del turismo» (las que normalmente producen productos característicos del turismo). Las RIET 2008 explican en todo detalle los conceptos subyacentes, las definiciones y las clasificaciones que deben utilizarse para compilar estadísticas de turismo e identificar los productos y actividades característicos del turismo. A fin de facilitar la comparación internacional, se han preparado listas de estos productos y actividades característicos. En el anexo 3 de este documento figura la lista de las actividades características del turismo (industrias turísticas) agrupadas en categorías principales según la CIIU rev 4. El anexo 4 muestra una lista de productos característicos del turismo agrupados por categorías principales según la CCP ver 2. Aun cuando el verdadero producto adquirido por el visitante pueda constituir solo una porción de la clase de la CCP o la actividad productora pueda ser solo una parte de la clase de cuatro dígitos de la CIIU, al expresarse en términos de clases de la CCP y agregados de clases de la CIIU, las listas ofrecen una clase definida en la que es posible incluir cada uno de los productos o actividades. Se aconseja a los países que, en caso de que lo requieran para sus propios análisis, creen clases más detalladas por debajo del nivel inferior de la CCP y la CIIU.

El alcance del análisis de las estadísticas de turismo se amplía cuando se sitúan en el marco de la cuenta satélite de turismo. De nuevo, en el marco esencial de contabilidad, los productos y las actividades se expresan en los términos de la CCP ver. 2 y la CIIU ver. 4, incluyendo los productos y las actividades asociados con el turismo. Las clasificaciones internacionales de productos y actividades empleadas para compilar los datos para CST:RMC 2008 que, a su vez, establecen vínculos estructurales con el Sistema de Cuentas Nacionales, hacen posible una apreciación más profunda de los vínculos del turismo con otros ámbitos económicos.

Anexo 4
Lista de industrias turísticas (actividades características) y agrupadas por categorías principales según la CIIU, rev.4

Industrias turísticas	CIIU Rev. 4	Descripción
1. Alojamiento para visitantes	5510	Actividades de alojamiento para estancias cortas
	5520	Actividades de campamentos, parques de vehículos recreativos y parques de caravanas
	5590	Otras actividades de alojamiento
	6810	Actividades inmobiliarias realizadas con bienes propios o arrendados*
	6820	Actividades inmobiliarias realizadas a cambio de una retribución o por contrata*
2. Actividades de provisión de alimentos y bebidas	5610	Actividades de restaurantes y de servicio móvil de comidas
	5629	Otras actividades de servicio de comidas
	5630	Actividades de servicio de bebidas
3. Transporte de pasajeros por ferrocarril	4911	Transporte interurbano de pasajeros por ferrocarril
4. Transporte de pasajeros por carretera	4922	Otras actividades de transporte por vía terrestre
5. Transporte de pasajeros por agua	5011	Transporte de pasajeros marítimo y de cabotaje
	5021	Transporte de pasajeros por vías de navegación interiores
6. Transporte aéreo de pasajeros	5110	Transporte de pasajeros por vía aérea
7. Alquiler de equipos de transporte	7710	Alquiler y arrendamiento de vehículos automotores
8. Actividades de agencias de viajes y de otros servicios de reservas	7911	Actividades de agencias de viajes
	7912	Actividades de operadores turísticos
	7990	Otros servicios de reservas y actividades conexas
9. Actividades culturales	9000	Actividades creativas, artísticas y de entretenimiento
	9102	Actividades de museos y conservación de lugares y edificios históricos
	9103	Actividades de jardines botánicos y zoológicos y de reservas naturales
10. Actividades deportivas y recreativas	7721	Alquiler y arrendamiento de equipo recreativo y deportivo
	9200	Actividades de juegos de azar y apuestas
	9311	Gestión de instalaciones deportivas
	9319	Otras actividades deportivas
	9321	Actividades de parques de atracciones y parques temáticos
	9329	Otras actividades de esparcimiento y recreativas n.c.p.
11. Comercio al por menor de bienes característicos del turismo, específicos de cada país		Comercios libres de impuestos**
		Comercio al por menor de recuerdos en establecimientos especializados**
		Comercio al por menor de artesanía en establecimientos especializados**
		Otro comercio al por menor de bienes característicos del turismo en establecimientos especializados**
12. Otras actividades características del turismo, específicas de cada país		

* Parte relacionada con segundos hogares y multipropiedades
** No es una categoría de cuatro cifras de la CIIU

Notas explicativas

Estas notas explicativas hacen referencia exclusivamente a actividades características del turismo internacionalmente comparables, y siguen el mismo orden que en el anexo 4 que figura más arriba.

Se han extraído del documento *Clasificación Industrial Internacional Uniforme de todas las actividades económicas (CIIU), Rev.4.* Informes estadísticos (serie M, No. 4/Rev.4), Naciones Unidas. Nueva York, 2008.

El documento completo puede consultarse en el sitio Web: http://unstats.un.org/unsd/cr/registry/regdntransfer. asp?f=135

Alojamiento para visitantes

5510 Actividades de alojamiento para estancias cortas

Esta clase comprende el suministro de alojamiento, en general por días o por semanas, principalmente para estancias cortas de los visitantes. Abarca el suministro de alojamiento amueblado en habitaciones y apartamentos o unidades totalmente independientes con cocina, con o sin servicio diario o regular de limpieza, y que incluyen a menudo diversos servicios adicionales, como los de comidas y bebidas, aparcamiento, lavandería, piscina y gimnasio, instalaciones de recreo e instalaciones para conferencias y convenciones.
- Esta clase comprende el suministro de alojamiento por estancias cortas en:
- hoteles
- centros vacacionales
- hoteles de suites/apartamentos
- moteles
- hoteles para automovilistas
- casas de huéspedes
- pensiones
- unidades de alojamiento y desayuno
- pisos y bungalows
- unidades utilizadas en régimen de tiempo compartido
- casas de vacaciones
- chalets y cabañas con servicio de mantenimiento y limpieza
- albergues juveniles y refugios de montaña

No se incluyen las siguientes actividades:
- suministro de viviendas y de pisos o apartamentos amueblados o sin amueblar para períodos más largos, en general por meses o por años; véase la división 6868

5520 Actividades de campamentos, parques de vehículos de recreo y parques de caravanas

Esta clase comprende las siguientes actividades:
- suministro de alojamiento en campamentos, parques para caravanas, campamentos recreativos y campamentos de caza y de pesca para estancias cortas
- suministro de espacio e instalaciones para vehículos de recreo

Se incluyen también los servicios de alojamiento de:
- refugios o simples instalaciones de acampada para plantar tiendas o pernoctar en sacos de dormir

5590 Otras actividades de alojamiento

Esta clase comprende el suministro de alojamiento temporal o a largo plazo en habitaciones individuales o compartidas o dormitorios para estudiantes, trabajadores migrantes (estacionales) y otras categorías de personas.

Se incluyen los servicios de alojamiento proporcionados por:
- residencias de estudiantes
- dormitorios escolares
- albergues para trabajadores
- casas de huéspedes e internados
- coches cama ferroviarios

6810 Actividades inmobiliarias realizadas con bienes propios o arrendados

Esta clase comprende las siguientes actividades:
- compra, venta, alquiler y explotación de bienes inmuebles propios o arrendados, como:
- edificios de apartamentos y viviendas
- edificios no residenciales, incluso salas de exposiciones, instalaciones de autoalmacenamiento y centros comerciales
- terrenos
- alquiler de casas y pisos o apartamentos amueblados o sin amueblar por
- períodos largos, en general por meses o por años

Se incluyen también las siguientes actividades:
- promoción de proyectos de construcción para su posterior explotación, es decir, para alquilar espacio en esos edificios
- subdivisión de propiedades inmobiliarias en lotes, sin mejora de los terrenos
- explotación de campamentos residenciales para casas móviles

No se incluyen las siguientes actividades:
- promoción de proyectos de construcción para la venta; véase la clase 4100
- subdivisión y mejora de terrenos; véase la clase 4290
- explotación de hoteles, hoteles de apartamentos e instalaciones de alojamiento similares; véase la clase 5510
- explotación de campamentos, parques de caravanas e instalaciones de alojamiento similares; véase la clase 5520
- explotación de albergues para trabajadores, casas de huéspedes e instalaciones de alojamiento similares; véase la clase 5590

6820 Actividades inmobiliarias realizadas a cambio de una retribución o por contrata

Esta clase comprende las actividades inmobiliarias que se realizan a cambio de una retribución o por contrata, incluidos los servicios inmobiliarios.

Estaclase comprende las siguientes actividades:
- actividades de agentes y corredores inmobiliarios
- intermediación en la compra, la venta y el alquiler de bienes inmuebles a cambio de una retribución o por contrata
- administración de bienes inmuebles a cambio de una retribución o por contrata
- servicios de tasación inmobiliaria
- actividades de agentes depositarios de plicas inmobiliarias

No se incluyen las siguientes actividades:
- actividades jurídicas; véase la clase 6910
- servicios de apoyo a instalaciones; véase la clase 8110
- administración de instalaciones, como bases militares, prisiones y otras instalaciones (excepto administración de instalaciones informáticas); véase la clase 8110

Actividades de provisión de alimentos y bebidas

5610 Actividades de restaurantes y de servicio móvil de comidas

Esta clase comprende el servicio de comidas a los clientes, ya se les sirvan en mesas o se sirvan ellos mismos de un surtido de platos expuestos, y ya se trate de comida para consumir en el local, para llevar o para entrega a domicilio. Abarca la preparación y el servicio de comidas para su consumo inmediato desde vehículos, sean o no motorizados

Esta clase comprende las actividades de:
- restaurantes
- cafeterías
- restaurantes de comida rápida
- reparto de pizza a domicilio
- restaurantes de comida para llevar
- vendedores ambulantes de helados
- puestos ambulantes de comida
- preparación de alimentos en puestos de mercado

Se incluyen también las siguientes actividades:
- actividades de restaurantes y bares vinculadas a actividades de transporte, si las realizan unidades separadas

No se incluyen las siguientes actividades:
- explotación de instalaciones de comedor en régimen de concesión; véase la clase 56290

5629 Otras actividades de servicio de comidas

Esta clase comprende el suministro industrial de comidas por encargo, es decir, el suministro de comidas basado en acuerdos contractuales con los clientes, durante un período convenido.

Abarca también la explotación de concesiones de servicio de comida en instalaciones deportivas e instalaciones similares. La comida se prepara a menudo en una unidad central.

Esta clase comprende las siguientes actividades:
- actividades de contratistas de servicio de comidas (p. ej., para compañías de transporte)
- explotación de concesiones de servicio de comidas en instalaciones deportivas e instalaciones similares
- explotación de cantinas o cafeterías (p. ej., para fábricas, oficinas, hospitales o escuelas) en régimen de concesión

No se incluyen las siguientes actividades:
- elaboración de productos alimenticios perecederos para su reventa; véase la clase 1079
- venta al por menor de productos alimenticios perecederos; véase la división 47

5630 Actividades de servicio de bebidas

Esta clase comprende la preparación y el servicio de bebidas para su consumo inmediato en el local.

Esta clase comprende las actividades de:
- bares
- tabernas
- coctelerías
- discotecas (con predominio del servicio de bebidas)
- cervecerías y pubs
- cafeterías
- tiendas de jugos de frutas
- vendedores ambulantes de bebidas

No se incluyen las siguientes actividades:
- reventa de bebidas envasadas o preparadas; véanse las clases 4711, 4722, 4781 y 4799
- explotación de discotecas y salas de baile sin servicio de bebidas; véase la clase 9329

Transporte de pasajeros por ferrocarril

4911 Transporte interurbano de pasajeros por ferrocarril

Esta clase comprende las siguientes actividades:
- transporte de pasajeros por ferrocarriles interurbanos
- servicios de coches cama y coches restaurante integrados en los servicios de las compañías de ferrocarril

No se incluyen las siguientes actividades:
- transporte de pasajeros por los sistemas de transporte urbano y suburbano; véase la clase 4921
- actividades de terminales de pasajeros; véase la clase 5221
- servicios de coches cama y coches restaurante cuando los suministran unidades separadas, véanse las clases 5590 y 5610

Transporte de pasajeros por carretera

4922   Otras actividades de transporte de pasajeros por vía terrestre

Esta clase comprende las siguientes actividades:
- otras actividades de transporte de pasajeros por carretera:
  - servicios regulares de autobuses de larga distancia
  - servicios de viajes contratados, excursiones y otros servicios ocasionales de transporte en autobús
  - servicios de taxis
  - servicios de enlace con aeropuertos
- servicios de teleféricos, funiculares, telesillas y telecabinas, si no forman parte de sistemas de transporte urbano o suburbano

Se incluyen también las siguientes actividades:
- otras actividades de alquiler de automóviles privados con conductor
- servicios de autobuses escolares y autobuses para el transporte de empleados
- transporte de pasajeros en vehículos de tracción humana o animal

No se incluyen las siguientes actividades:
- transporte en ambulancia; véase la clase 8690

Transporte de pasajeros por agua

5011   Transporte de pasajeros marítimo y de cabotaje

Esta clase comprende las siguientes actividades:
- transporte marítimo y de cabotaje, regular y no regular, de pasajeros y carga:
  - explotación de embarcaciones de excursión, de crucero o de turismo
  - explotación de transbordadores, taxis acuáticos, etcétera

Se incluyen también las siguientes actividades:
- alquiler de embarcaciones de placer con tripulación para el transporte marítimo y de cabotaje (p. ej., cruceros de pesca)

No se incluyen las siguientes actividades:
- actividades de servicios de bar y de restaurante a bordo de embarcaciones, si las realizan unidades separadas; véanse las clases 5610 y 5630
- explotación de «casinos flotantes»; véase la clase 9200

5021   Transporte de pasajeros por vías de navegación interiores

Esta clase comprende las siguientes actividades:
- transporte de pasajeros por ríos, canales, lagos y otras vías de navegación interiores, incluidos puertos interiores

Se incluyen también las siguientes actividades:
- alquiler de embarcaciones de placer con tripulación para el transporte por vías de navegación interiores

Transporte aéreo de pasajeros

5110   Transporte de pasajeros por vía aérea

Esta clase comprende las siguientes actividades:
- transporte aéreo de pasajeros con itinerarios y horarios establecidos
- vuelos contratados (charter) para pasajeros
- vuelos panorámicos y turísticos

Se incluyen también las siguientes actividades:
- alquiler de equipo de transporte aéreo con operadores para el transporte de pasajeros
- actividades generales de aviación, como:
  - transporte de pasajeros por clubes aéreos con fines de instrucción o de recreo

Alquiler de equipos de transporte

7710   Alquiler y arrendamiento de vehículos automotores

Esta clase comprende las siguientes actividades:
- alquiler y arrendamiento con fines operativos de los siguientes tipos de vehículos:
- automóviles de pasajeros (sin conductor)
- camiones, remolques y vehículos de recreo

No se incluyen las siguientes actividades:
- alquiler o arrendamiento de vehículos o camiones con conductor; véanse las clases 4922 y 4923
- arrendamiento financiero; véase la clase 6491

Actividades de agencias de viajes y de otros servicios de reservas

7911   Actividades de agencias de viajes

Esta clase comprende las siguientes actividades:
- actividades de agencias dedicadas principalmente a vender servicios de viajes, de viajes organizados, de transporte y de alojamiento al público en general y a clientes comerciales

7912   Actividades de operadores turísticos

Esta clase comprende las siguientes actividades:
- organización de paquetes de servicios de viajes para su venta a través de agencias de viajes o por los propios operadores turísticos. Esos viajes organizados pueden incluir uno o varios de los elementos siguientes:
  - transporte
  - alojamiento
  - comidas
  - visitas a museos, lugares históricos o culturales y asistencia a espectáculos teatrales, musicales o deportivos

7990 Otros servicios de reservas y actividades conexas

Esta clase comprende las siguientes actividades:
- prestación de otros servicios de reservas relacionados con los viajes:
  - reservas de transporte, hoteles, restaurantes, alquiler de automóviles, entretenimiento y deporte, etcétera
- prestación de servicios de intercambio en régimen de tiempo compartido o multipropiedad
- actividades de venta de billetes para obras de teatro, competiciones deportivas y otras actividades de diversión y entretenimiento
- prestación de servicios de asistencia a los visitantes:
  - suministro a los clientes de información sobre los viajes
  - actividades de guías de turismo
- actividades de promoción turística

No se incluyen las siguientes actividades:
- actividades de agencias de viajes y operadores turísticos, véanse las clases 7911 y 7912
- organización y gestión de reuniones, convenciones, conferencias y acontecimientos similares; véase la clase 8230

Actividades culturales

9000 Actividades creativas, artísticas y de entretenimiento

Esta clase comprende la explotación de instalaciones y la prestación de servicios para atender a los intereses culturales y de entretenimiento de los clientes. Abarca la producción y promoción de espectáculos, actos o exposiciones destinados al público, y la participación en ellos; y la aportación de conocimientos y aptitudes artísticos, creativos o técnicos para la creación de productos artísticos y espectáculos.

Esta clase comprende las siguientes actividades:
- producción de obras de teatro, conciertos, espectáculos operísticos o de danza y otras producciones escénicas:
  - actividades de grupos, circos o compañías, orquestas o bandas
  - actividades de artistas individuales, como escritores, directores, músicos, conferenciantes, escenógrafos y constructores de decorados, etcétera
- gestión de salas de conciertos, teatros y otras instalaciones similares
- actividades de escultores, pintores, dibujantes, grabadores, etcétera
- actividades de escritores de todo tipo; por ejemplo, de obras de ficción, de obras técnicas, etcétera
- actividades de periodistas independientes
- restauración de obras de arte, como cuadros, etcétera

Se incluyen también las siguientes actividades:
- actividades de productores o empresarios de espectáculos artísticos en vivo, aporten o no ellos mismos las instalaciones correspondientes

No se incluyen las siguientes actividades:
- restauración de vidrieras de colores; véase la clase 2310
- fabricación de estatuas, excepto originales artísticos; véase la clase 2396
- restauración de órganos y otros instrumentos musicales históricos; véase la clase 3319
- restauración de lugares y edificios históricos; véase la clase 4100
- producción de películas cinematográficas y vídeos; véanse las clases 5911 y 5912
- explotación de cines; véase la clase 5914
- actividades de agentes o agencias de actores y artistas; véase la clase 7490
- actividades de selección de actores; véase la clase 7810
- actividades de venta de entradas; véase la clase 7990
- gestión de museos de todo tipo; véase la clase 9102
- actividades deportivas, de esparcimiento y recreativas; véase la división 93
- restauración de muebles (excepto la del tipo realizado en museos); véase la clase 9524

9102 Actividades de museos y gestión de lugares y edificios históricos

Esta clase comprende las siguientes actividades:
- actividades de todo tipo de museos:
  - museos de arte, orfebrería, muebles, trajes, cerámica, platería
  - museos de historia natural y de ciencias, museos tecnológicos y museos históricos, incluidos los museos militares
  - otros museos especializados
  - museos al aire libre
- gestión de lugares y edificios históricos

No se incluyen las siguientes actividades:
- renovación y restauración de lugares y edificios históricos; véase la sección F
- restauración de obras de arte y piezas de museo; véase la clase 9000
- actividades de bibliotecas y archivos; véase la clase 9101

9103 Actividades de jardines botánicos y zoológicos y reservas naturales

Esta clase comprende las siguientes actividades:
- gestión de jardines botánicos y zoológicos, incluidos zoológicos infantiles
- gestión de reservas naturales, incluidas las actividades de preservación de la flora y la fauna silvestres, etcétera

No se incluyen las siguientes actividades:
- servicios de paisajismo y jardinería; véase la clase 8130
- explotación de reservas de pesca y de caza deportivas; véase la clase 9319

Actividades deportivas y recreativas

7721 Alquiler y arrendamiento de equipo recreativo y deportivo

Esta clase comprende las siguientes actividades:
- alquiler de equipo recreativo y deportivo:
- embarcaciones de recreo, canoas, veleros
- bicicletas
- hamacas de playa y sombrillas
- otros tipos de equipo de deporte
- esquíes

No se incluyen las siguientes actividades:
- alquiler de cintas de vídeo y discos; véase la clase 7722
- alquiler de otros efectos personales y enseres domésticos n.c.p.; véase la clase 7729
- alquiler de equipo de esparcimiento y recreo como parte integral de servicios de esparcimiento; véase la clase 9329

9200 Actividades de juegos de azar y apuestas

Esta clase comprende las siguientes actividades:
- apuestas sobre carreras de caballos en el propio hipódromo y otros servicios de apuestas
- apuestas sobre carreras de caballos fuera del hipódromo
- explotación de casinos, incluidos «casinos flotantes»
- venta de boletos de lotería
- gestión (explotación) de máquinas de juegos de azar accionadas con monedas
- gestión de sitios web de juegos de azar virtuales

No se incluyen las siguientes actividades:
- gestión (explotación) de juegos accionados con monedas; véase la clase 9329

9311 Gestión de instalaciones deportivas

Esta clase comprende las siguientes actividades:
- gestión de instalaciones para actividades deportivas bajo techo o al aire libre (abiertas, cerradas o techadas, con o sin asientos para espectadores):
  - campos y estadios de fútbol, hockey, cricket, béisbol, canchas de frontón
  - circuitos de carreras de automóviles, canódromos, hipódromos
  - piscinas y estadios
  - estadios de atletismo
  - pistas y estadios para deportes de invierno
  - pistas de hockey sobre hielo
  - pabellones de boxeo
  - campos de golf
  - boleras
  - gimnasios
- organización y gestión de competiciones deportivas al aire libre o bajo techo, con participación de deportistas profesionales o aficionados, por parte de organizaciones con instalaciones propias

Se incluyen la gestión de esas instalaciones y la dotación del personal necesario para su funcionamiento.

No se incluyen las siguientes actividades:
- alquiler de equipo recreativo y deportivo; véase la clase 7721
- gestión de estaciones de esquí; véase la clase 9329
- actividades realizadas en parques y playas; véase la clase 9329

9319 Otras actividades deportivas

Esta clase comprende las siguientes actividades:
- actividades de productores o promotores de competiciones deportivas, con o sin instalaciones
- actividades por cuenta propia de deportistas y atletas, árbitros, jueces, cronometradores, etcétera
- actividades de ligas y órganos reguladores
- actividades relacionadas con la promoción de competiciones deportivas
- actividades relacionadas con carreras de caballos, galgos y automóviles
- gestión de reservas de pesca y caza deportivas
- actividades de guías de montaña
- actividades de apoyo para la caza y la pesca deportivas o recreativas
-

No se incluyen las siguientes actividades:
- cría de caballos de carreras; véase la clase 0142
- alquiler de equipo de deporte; véase la clase 7721
- actividades de escuelas de deportes y de juegos; véase la clase 8541
- actividades de instructores, profesores y entrenadores; véase la clase 8541
- organización y explotación de competiciones deportivas al aire libre o bajo techo, con participación de deportistas profesionales o aficionados, por parte de clubes deportivos con o sin instalaciones propias, véanse las clases 9311 y 9312
- actividades realizadas en parques y playas; véase la clase 9329

9321 Actividades de parques de atracciones y parques temáticos

Esta clase comprende las siguientes actividades:
- actividades de parques de atracciones y parques temáticos, incluida la explotación de diversas atracciones mecánicas y acuáticas, juegos, espectáculos, exposiciones temáticas y lugares para picnics

9329 Otras actividades de esparcimiento y recreativas n.c.p.

Esta clase comprende las siguientes actividades:
- actividades de parques recreativos y playas, incluido el alquiler de casetas, taquillas, hamacas, etcétera
- gestión de instalaciones de transporte recreativo;
- gestión de estaciones de esquí
- alquiler de equipo de esparcimiento y recreo como parte integral de servicios de esparcimiento
- explotación de ferias y exposiciones de carácter recreativo
- explotación de discotecas y pistas de baile
- operación (explotación) de juegos accionados por monedas

- otras actividades de esparcimiento y recreativas (excepto las de parques de atracciones y parques temáticos) no clasificadas en otra parte

Se incluyen también las siguientes actividades:
- actividades de productores o empresarios de espectáculos en vivo, que no sean ni artísticos ni deportivos, aporten o no ellos mismos las instalaciones correspondientes

No se incluyen las siguientes actividades:
- cruceros de pesca, véanse las clases 5011 y 5021
- suministro de espacio e instalaciones para estancias cortas en parques recreativos, parques forestales y campamentos; véase la clase 5520
- actividades de servicio de bebidas en discotecas; véase la clase 5630
- parques de caravanas, campamentos, campamentos recreativos, campamentos de caza y de pesca; véase la clase 5520
- alquiler por separado de equipo recreativo; véase la clase 7721
- gestión (explotación) de máquinas de juegos accionadas con monedas; véase la clase 9200
- actividades de parques de atracciones y parques temáticos; véase la clase 9321

Other UNWTO publications of interest!

**Yearbook
of Tourism Statistics
Data 2011 – 2015
2017 Edition**

trilingual version

**Measuring Employment in the
Tourism Industry –
Guide and Best Practices**

published in English

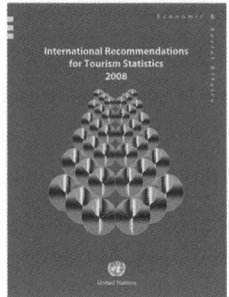

**International
Recommendations for
Tourism Statistics 2008**

published in
English, Spanish, French, Russian
Arabic and Chinese

**Tourism Satellite Account –
Recommended
Methodological Framework
2008**

published in
English, Spanish, French, Russian
Arabic and Chinese

**UNWTO
World Tourism Barometer**

Six numbers per year
published in English, Spanish,
French and Russian

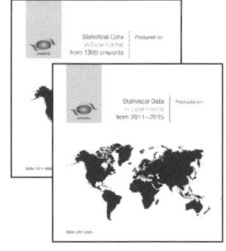

**Statistical Data in Excel™
Format**
  – **Data from 2011 – 2015**
  – **Data from 1995 onwards**

Seperate country tables
in Excel™ format,
updated three times per year

**Statistics and TSA
Issue Paper Series**

Latest issue:
– Tourism Statistics
  and TSA Compilation Methods
  in Asian Countries

**Sources and Methods: Labour
Statistics – Employment in the
Tourism Industries
(Special Edition)**

published in English

For UNWTO publications in printed version and for CD ROM data please contact pub @ unwto.org…
… and for the electronic versions visit the UNWTO Elibrary: www.e-unwto.org